THE
NEW ENCYCLOPEDIA
OF
CHRISTIAN QUOTATIONS

THE
NEW ENCYCLOPEDIA
OF
CHRISTIAN QUOTATIONS

COMPILED BY

MARK WATER

Baker Books

A Division of Baker Book House Co
Grand Rapids, Michigan 49516

ACKNOWLEDGEMENTS

Unless otherwise stated scripture quotations are taken from
The Holy Bible, New International Version/Æ.
Copyright © 1973, 1978, 1984 by the International Bible Society.

Scripture quotations are also taken from:
The New Living Translation (NLT):
Holy Bible, New Living Translation,
copyright © by Tyndale Charitable Trust.

New American Standard Bible (NASB):
New American Standard Bible.
Copyright © 1960, 1962, 1963, 1968, 1971, 1972, 1973, 1975, 1977, 1995
by The Lockman Foundation.

The Message: *THE MESSAGE:* New Testament. Copyright © 1993 by Eugene H. Peterson.

King James Version/Authorized Version (KJV, AV): Oxford University Presss.

New King James Version (NKJV): Copyright © 1979, 1980, 1982 by Thomas Nelson, Inc., Publishers.

Good News Bible (GNB): New Testament © American Bible Society, New York 1966, 1971, and 4th
edition 1976 Old Testament © American Bible Society, New York.

THE NEW ENCYCLOPEDIA OF CHRISTIAN QUOTATIONS

Copyright © 2000 John Hunt Publishing Ltd
Compiled by Mark Water

Published by Baker Books
A division of Baker Book House Company
P.O. Box 6287, Grand Rapids, MI 49516-6287.

Original edition published in English under the title
The New Encyclopedia of Christian Quotations by
John Hunt Publishing Ltd, New Alresford, Hants, UK.

Printed in Finland
Book design by Trinity Creations, UK

ISBN 0-8010-1206-6

Library of Congress Cataloging-in-Publication Data is on file at
the Library of Congress, Washington, D.C.

For current information about all releases from Baker Book House,
visit out web site: **http://www.bakerbooks.com**

Contents

INTRODUCTION

The New Encyclopedia of Christian Quotations encapsulates the rich heritage of Christian wisdom of the first 2,000 years of the Christian era.

The value and appeal of quotations are hard to overestimate.

"It is a good thing for an uneducated man to read books of quotations."
Winston Churchill

"The wisdom of the wise and the experience of the ages are perpetuated by quotations."
Benjamin Disraeli

"Instruct a wise man and he will be wiser still."
Proverbs 9:9

"I quote others only the better to express myself."
Montaigne

"To make good use of a thought found in a book requires almost as much cleverness as to originate it. Cardinal du Perron said that the apt quotation of a line of Virgil was worthy of the highest talent."
Stendhal

Finding your way around

- *List of Entries*
  The New Encyclopedia of Christian Quotations opens with an extensive *List of Entries*, giving an alphabetical bird's eye view of the topics found in subsequent pages. For example, under the head word "Bible" there are scores of sub-divisions listed to enable you to locate a particular topic under the general topic of the Bible.

- *Cross-references*
  The quotations are cross-referenced. The cross-reference system in the book suggests different headings under which you may find the quotations you are seeking. So when you look up the work "Grief" you are directed to "Bereavement; Death; Sorrow; Tears", in case such topics had slipped your mind. The sub-divisions of each topic listed in the *List of Entries* are not repeated here, so the best place to see an overall picture of the divisions of any large topic is the *List of Entries*.

- *Individual entries*
  The order of the entries under each head word is arranged in the same way.
  A. Any quotations from the Bible appear at the beginning of this list, and are in Bible order.
  B. These Bible quotes are followed by any quotations which are assigned to

"Author unknown".

C.   After that the entries are alphabetical according to the author/source of the quotations. So it is easy to spot if there are any quotations by Augustine about faith by glancing at the entries towards the end of the entries under the letter "A".

D.   Proverbs are listed under the letter "P". Anonymous inscriptions are listed under the letter "I".

- *Index of Sources*
  At the back of the book the *Index of Sources* lists the people, and other sources, from which the quotations were gleaned. This enables you to view and/or look up all the quotations of your favorite author. Authors, such as, Augustine of Hippo, John Calvin, Martin Luther, Blaise Pascal, C.H. Spurgeon, Thomas ‡ Kempis and John Wesley have all their quotations listed alphabetically under their names, even when this exceeds 100 entries.

Length of quotations

1. One-liners

Most of the quotations in *The New Encyclopedia of Christian Quotations* are one-liners. These include a number of well-known Latin, Greek, and English proverbs, as well as German, Spanish and Italian proverbs which are rarely found in books of quotations.

2. Paragraph-long quotations

Quotations up to the length of a paragraph are also sometimes included so that the context and full force of the quotation in hand can be appreciated.

3. Extended quotations

Scattered throughout *The New Encyclopedia of Christian Quotations* are extended quotations from leading Christian theologians over the centuries on basic teaching about the Christian faith. These are listed under *Feature Pages* and include important Christian documents such as *The Westminster Catechism* and Luther's *95 Theses*.

Categories of quotations

Any quotation which can be used to help communicate the truth was eligible for inclusion in *The New Encyclopedia of Christian Quotations*. That may appear to be an all-embracing criteria. This means that as well as "The great and the good", especially the Puritans, a minority of quotations from heretics and unorthodox theologians are included in this book. They are useful to know about, so that we can read what they actually said, and understand where they are coming from, even if this means that they may need to be refuted. But, sometimes, quotations from seemingly anti-Christian people prove to contain something we can benefit from.

"All truth, wherever it is found, belongs to us as Christians."
Justin Martyr

"Wherever Truth may be, were it in a Turk or Tarter, it must be cherished. Let us seek the honeycomb even within the lion's mouth."
Johan de Brune

"All truth is from God; and consequently, if wicked men have said anything that is true and just, we ought not to reject it; for it has come from God. Besides, all things are of God; and, therefore, why should it not be lawful to dedicate to his glory everything that can properly be employed for such a purpose?"
John Calvin

"A thing is not necessarily true because badly uttered, nor false because spoken magnificently."
Augustine of Canterbury

"Let us rejoice in the Truth, wherever we find its lamp burning."
Albert Schweitzer

"I believe that truths are truths, however questionable the voice which utters them."
Warren Kramer

It is possible to classify the quotations in *The New Encyclopedia of Christian Quotations* under three headings.

1. Biblical quotations

Quotations from the Bible are included as the first entries in the topics. They give snippets of God's teaching on the wide variety of subjects covered in this book. Verses from the Bible give the yardstick by which all the other quotations in the book are to be measured. It is a constant surprise to find just how relevant such quotations are on contemporary issues which face us today.

Most biblical quotations are taken from the *New International Bible,* but the *King James Version* is also extensively quoted from, as well as a number of other Bible versions.

2. Christian quotations

The great majority of the quotations in this book are Christian quotations. They have been culled from statements of faith, books, sermons, hymns, letters, diaries, journals, commentaries, and speeches.

3. Secular quotations

Some quotations in *The New Encyclopedia of Christian Quotations* come from the pens and personal computers of agnostics and atheists.

The apostle Paul was not adverse to using "secular" quotations. When he told Titus to take in hand some of the godless people who lived in Crete, he wrote, "rebuke them sharply, so that they will be sound in the faith and will pay no attention to Jewish myths or to the commands of those who reject the truth" (Titus 1:13, 14). Paul highlighted the need for this tough advice with an quotation from a poet whom Calvin identifies as Epimenides: "Even one of their own prophets has said, 'Cretans are always liars, evil brutes, lazy gluttons'" (Titus 1:12).

Jesus used quotations

In his teaching ministry Jesus often made use of quotations. Most of his quotations, but not all, were from the Old Testament. Jesus was fond of using a biblical quotation to clinch an argument.

Benefitting from these quotations

All Christians, whether or not they are preachers, teachers or leaders should be able to derive great spiritual benefit from the quotations in this encyclopedia. Good quotations instruct our minds, warm our hearts and strengthen our wills. They can be used in our own personal devotions, as they provide a rich source of inspirational teaching.

Mark Water

LIST OF FEATURES

LIST OF ENTRIES

A

A-Z of life

See also: Friendship, Value of

Avoid negative sources, people, places, things, and habits.

Believe in yourself.

Consider things from every angle.

Don't give up and don't give in.

Enjoy life today, yesterday is gone, tomorrow may never come.

Family and friends are hidden treasures, seek them and enjoy their riches.

Give more than you planned to.

Hang on to your dreams.

Ignore those who try to discourage you.

Just do it.

Keep trying no matter how hard it seems, it will get easier.

Love God first and most.

Make it happen.

Never lie, cheat or steal, always strike a fair deal.

Open your eyes and see things as they really are.

Practice makes perfect.

Quitters never win and winners never quit.

Read, study and learn about everything important in your life.

Stop procrastinating.

Take control of your destiny.

Understand yourself in order to better understand others.

Visualize it.

Want it more than anything.

Xcellerate your efforts.

You are unique of all God's creations, nothing can replace YOU.

Zero in on your target and go for it!

Author unknown

Our Spiritual ABC's

Ask the Father daily in prayer and He will answer.

BELIEVE!

Christ must be the center of your life.

Dare to be a Disciple of Jesus.

Even you can make a difference in the lives of others by acting out God's will in your daily life.

Friends are special gifts from God.

Give to others cheerfully.

Harmony is what you should strive for in your relationships with others.

Interest in others will make you a broader minded person.

Judge others with love and compassion.

Knowledge and wisdom come from the Lord.

Live in such a way that those who know you but don't know God will come to know God because they know you.

Make sure to always love others as Jesus does.

New life comes to you when you accept Christ.

Obedience of God's will leads to God's blessings.

Please God in all of your actions.

Question your priorities often. Make sure God always comes first.

Read God's word daily.

Shepherd's protect the sheep, and I am grateful that the Lord is my shepherd.

Talk with God often.

Use your heart to show concern for others.

Vent feelings, but always with the love of Christ.

eXault the Lord always!

Yesterday's sins are already paid for by the grace of Jesus Christ.

Zeal in living my spiritual ABCs will help me grow in the Lord

Author unknown

Abandon

… in later times some will abandon the faith …

The Bible, 1 Timothy 4:1

Abandoned/Abandonment

My God, my God, why have you forsaken me?
The Bible, Psalm 22:1

Though my father and mother forsake me, the Lord will receive me.
The Bible, Psalm 27:10

Every vice was re-awakened within me. I would have chosen rather to be roasted than to endure such pains.
Angela of Foligno

My heart I give you, Lord, eagerly and entirely.
John Calvin

When we have reached this total deprivation what shall we do? Abide in simplicity and peace, as Job on his ash heap, repeating, "Blessed are the poor in spirit; those who have nothing have all, since they have God."
Jean-Pierre de Caussade

God felt, God tasted and enjoyed is indeed God, but God with those gifts which flatter the soul. God in darkness, in privation, in forsakenness, in insensibility, is so much God, that He is so to speak God bare and alone. Shall we fear this death, which is to produce in us the true divine life of grace?
F. Fénelon

It is when God appears to have abandoned us that we must abandon ourselves most wholly to God.
F. Fénelon

After Thou hadst wounded me so deeply as I have described, Thou didst begin, oh my God, to withdraw Thyself from me: and the pain of Thy absence was the more bitter to me, because Thy presence had been so sweet to me, Thy love so strong in me. ... Thy way, oh my God, before Thou didst make me enter into the state of death, was the way of the dying life: sometimes to hide Thyself and leave me to myself in a hundred weaknesses,

sometimes to show Thyself with more sweetness and love. The nearer the soul drew to the state of death, the more her desolations were long and weary, her weaknesses increased, and also her joys became shorter, but purer and more intimate, until the time in which she fell into total privation.
Madame Guyon

That which this anguished soul feels most deeply is the conviction that God has abandoned it, of which it has no doubt; that He has cast it away into darkness as an abominable thing ... the shadow of death and the pains and torments of hell are most acutely felt, and this comes from the sense of being abandoned by God, being chastised and cast out by His wrath and heavy displeasure. All this and even more the soul feels now, for a terrible apprehension has come upon it that thus it will be with it for ever. It has also the same sense of abandonment with respect to all creatures, and that it is an object of contempt to all, especially to its friends.
John of the Cross

This [sense of spiritual abandonment] is one of the most bitter sufferings of this purgation. The soul is conscious of a profound emptiness in itself, a cruel destitution of the three kinds of goods, natural, temporal, and spiritual, which are ordained for its comfort. It sees itself in the midst of the opposite evils, miserable imperfections, dryness and emptiness of the understanding, and abandonment of the spirit in darkness.
John of the Cross

To reach satisfaction in all, desire its possession in nothing. To come to possess all, desire the possession of nothing. To arrive at being all, desire to be nothing. To come to the knowledge of all, desire the knowledge of nothing.
John of the Cross

Lord, since Thou hast taken from me all that I had of Thee, yet of Thy grace leave

me the gift which every dog has by nature:
that of being true to Thee in my distress;
when I am deprived of all consolation.
This I desire more fervently than thy
heavenly Kingdom!
Mechthild of Magdeburg

Prayer is continual abandonment to God.
Sadhu Sundar Singh

As long as this pain lasts we cannot even
remember our own existence; for in an
instant all the faculties of the soul are so
fettered as to lie incapable of any action save
that of increasing our torture. Do not think
I am exaggerating; on the contrary, that
which I say is less than the truth, for lack of
words in which it may be expressed. This is a
trance of the senses and the faculties, save as
regards all which helps to make the agony
more intense. The understanding realizes
acutely what cause there is for grief in
separation from God: and our Lord increases
this sorrow by a vivid manifestation of
Himself. The pain thus grows to such a
degree that in spite of herself the sufferer
gives vent to loud cries, which she cannot
stifle, however patient and accustomed to
pain she may be, because this is not a pain
which is felt in the body, but in the depths
of the soul. The person I speak of learned
from this how much more acutely the spirit
is capable of suffering than the body.
Teresa of Avila

Abba
See also: God, as Father
Because you are sons, God sent the Spirit
of his Son into our hearts, the Spirit who
calls out, *"Abba,* Father."
The Bible, Galatians 4:6

Christ asserted that he had a relationship
with God which no one ever claimed
before. It comes out in the Aramaic word
Abba which He was so fond of using,
especially in prayer. Nobody before Him in
all the history of Israel had addressed God
by this word. ... *Abba* is the familiar word
of closest intimacy.
Michael Green

"Abba" is only a little word, and yet
contains everything. It is not the mouth
but the heart's affection which speaks like
this. Even if I am oppressed with anguish
and terror on every side, and seem to be
forsaken and utterly cast away from your
presence, yet am I your child, and you are
my Father. For Christ's sake: I am loved
because of the Beloved. So this little word
"Abba", Father, deeply felt in the heart,
surpasses all the eloquence of
Demosthenes, Cicero, and the most
eloquent speakers that ever lived. This
matter is not expressed with words, but
with groanings, and these groanings
cannot be uttered with any words of
eloquence, for no tongue can express them.
Martin Luther

Abiding
See also: Fellowship with God
Abide with us, for it is toward evening, and
the day is far spent.
The Bible, Luke 24:29

I am the vine, you are the branches. Those
who abide in me and I in them bear much
fruit, because apart from me you can do
nothing.
The Bible, John 15:5 NRSV

No human tongue could describe the
passionate love with which Francis burned
for Christ, his spouse; he seemed to be
completely absorbed by the fire of divine
love like a glowing coal.
*Author unknown: An early biographer of
Francis of Assisi*

Every thing that a man leans upon but
God, will be a dart that will certainly
pierce his heart through and through. He
who leans only upon Christ, lives the
highest, choicest, safest, and sweetest life.
Thomas Brooks

It is not the mere touching of the flower by
the bee that gathers honey, but her abiding
for a time on the flower that draws out the
sweet.
Thomas Brooks

Oh! For a closer walk with God,
    A calm and heavenly frame;
A light to shine upon the road
    That leads me to the Lamb!
So shall my walk be close with God,
    Calm and serene my frame;
So purer light shall mark the road
    That leads me to the Lamb.
William Cowper

Our Savior Christ is both the first beginner of our spiritual life (who first begetteth us into God his Father), and also afterwards he is our lively food and spiritual life.
Thomas Cranmer

I had rather be in hell with Christ, than be in heaven without him.
Martin Luther

Hold thou thy cross
    before my closing eyes;
Shine through the gloom,
    and point me to the skies;
Heaven's morning breaks,
    and earth's vain shadows flee;
In life, in death, O Lord,
    abide with me.
Henry Francis Lyte

Watch against lip religion. Above all abide in Christ and he will abide in you.
Robert Murray M'Cheyne

Live near to God, and so all things will appear to you little in comparison with eternal realities.
Robert Murray M'Cheyne

You have nothing to do in life except to live in union with Christ.
Rufus Mosely

Abide in Jesus, the sinless one – which means, give up all of self and its life, and dwell in God's will and rest in his strength. This is what brings the power that does not commit sin.
Andrew Murray

All practical power over sin and over men depends on maintaining closet communion. Those who abide in the secret place with God show themselves mighty to conquer evil, and strong to work and to war for God. They are seers who read His secrets; they know His will; they are the meek whom He guides in judgment and teaches His way. They are His prophets who speak for Him to others, and even forecast things to come. They watch the signs of the times and discern His tokens and read His signals.
A.T. Pierson

Abide in me says Jesus. Cling to me. Stick fast to me. Live the life of close and intimate communion with me. Get nearer to me. Roll every burden on me. Cast your whole weight on me. Never let go your hold on me for a moment. Be, as it were, rooted and planted in me. Do this and I will never fail you. I will ever abide in you.
J.C. Ryle

I must take care above all that I cultivate communion with Christ, for though that can never be the basis of my peace – mark that – yet it will be the channel of it.
C.H. Spurgeon

Let your lives adorn your faith, let your example adorn your creed. Above all live in Christ Jesus, and walk in Him, giving credence to no teaching but that which is manifestly approved of Him, and owned by the Holy Spirit. Cleave fast to the Word of God.
C.H. Spurgeon

If in everything you seek Jesus, you will doubtless find him. But if you seek yourself, you will indeed find yourself, to your own ruin. For you do yourself more harm by not seeking Jesus than the whole world and all your enemies could do to you.
Thomas à Kempis

Ability
See also: Talents
It is not enough to be good if you have the ability to be better.
Alberta Lee Cox

The fox has many tricks. The hedgehog has but one. But that is the best of all.
Desiderius Erasmus

It's not your ability, it's God's ability flowing through you.
Benny Hinn

There is something rarer than ability. It is the ability to recognize ability.
Elbert Hubbard

There is great ability in knowing how to conceal ability.
La Rochefoucauld

Abortion

For you created my inmost being;
you knit me together in my mother's womb.
I praise you because I am fearfully and
  wonderfully made;
your works are wonderful,
I know that full well.
My frame was not hidden from you when I
    was made in the secret place.
When I was woven together in the depths of the earth,
  your eyes saw my unformed body.
All the days ordained for me
  were written in your book
  before one of them came to be.
How precious to me are your thoughts,
  O God!
  How vast is the sum of them!
The Bible, Psalm 139:13-17

The poor expose their children, the rich kill the fruit of their own bodies in the womb, lest their property be divided up, so they destroy their own children in the womb with murderous poisons, and before life has been passed on, it is annihilated.
Ambrose

Guilty? Yes, no matter what the motive, love of ease, or a desire to save from suffering the unborn innocent, the woman is awfully guilty who commits the deed. It will burden her conscience in life, it will burden her soul in death; but oh! thrice guilty is he who, for selfish gratification, heedless of her prayers, indifferent to her fate, drove her to the desperation which impels her to the crime.
Susan B. Anthony

[Christians] call women who take medications to induce an abortion murderers.
Athenagoras

Four situations
1. There's a preacher and wife who are very, very poor. They already have 14 children. Now she finds out she's pregnant with their 15th! They're living in tremendous poverty. Considering their poverty and the excessive world population, would you recommend that she should have an abortion?
2. The father is sick with sniffles, the mother has TB. They have four children. The first child is blind, the second is dead. The third child is deaf, the fourth has TB. She finds she's pregnant again. Given the extreme situation, would you consider recommending abortion?
3. A white man raped a 13 year old black girl and she became pregnant. If you were her parents, would you consider recommending abortion?
4. A teenage girl is pregnant. She's not married. Her fiancé is not the father of the baby, and he's very upset. Would you consider recommending abortion?
If you would have recommended abortion in any of these situations:
then, in the first case, you recommended killing John Wesley;
in the second case, you recommended killing Ludwig Von Beethoven;
in the third case, you recommended killing the famous gospel singer Ethel Waters;
in the fourth case, you have just recommended killing Jesus Christ.
Author unknown

You shall not kill either the fetus by abortion or the new born.
Letter of Barnabas

Abortion is "the great modern sin."
Karl Barth

A woman who intentionally destroys a fetus is guilty of murder. And we do not even talk about the fine distinction as to its being completely formed or unformed.
Basil the Great

Abortions will not let you forget. You remember the children you got that you did not get.
Gwendolyn Brooks

We are totally opposed to abortion under any circumstances. We are also opposed to abortifacient drugs and chemicals like the Pill and the IUD, and we are also opposed to all forms of birth control with the exception of natural family planning.
Judie Brown, President, American Life Lobby

For the fetus, though enclosed in the womb of its mother, is already a human being, and it is a monstrous crime to rob it of the life which it has not yet begun to enjoy. If it seems more horrible to kill a man in his own house than in a field, because a man's house is his place of most secure refuge, it ought surely to be deemed more atrocious to destroy a fetus in the womb before it has come to light.
John Calvin

Abortion leads to an appalling trivialization of the art of procreation.
Donald Coggan

Concerning abortion, the Didache refers to "child-murderers, who go the way of death, who slay God's image in the womb."
Didache

You shall not kill the embryo by abortion and shall not cause the newborn to perish.
Didache

Christians are differentiated from other people by country, language, or customs. They do not live in cities of their own or speak some strange dialect. They live in their own native lands, but as resident aliens. They marry and have children just like everyone else, but they do not kill unwanted babies.
Epistle to Diognetus

Some women take medicines to destroy the germ of future life in their own bodies. They commit infanticide before they have given birth to the infant.
Minicius Felix

The earliest Christian ethic, from Jesus to Constantine, can be described as a consistent pro-life ethic … It pleaded for the poor, the weak, women, children and the unborn. This pro-life ethic discarded hate in favor of love, war in favor of peace, oppression in favor of justice, bloodshed in favor of life.
Michael Gorman

The cemetery of the victims of human cruelty in our century is extended to include yet another vast cemetery, that of the unborn.
Pope John Paul II

How great, therefore, the wickedness of human nature is! How many girls there are who prevent conception and kill and expel tender fetuses, although procreation is the work of God.
Martin Luther

However we may pity the mother whose health and even life imperilled by the performance of her natural duty, there yet remains no sufficient reason for condoning the direct murder of the innocent.
Pope Pius XI

We have to assert as normative the general inviolability of the foetus. We shall be right to continue to see as one of Christianity's great gifts to the world the belief that the human foetus is to be reverenced as the embryo of a life capable of coming to reflect the glory of God.
Michael Ramsey

The cemetery of the victims of human cruelty in our century is extended to include yet another vast cemetery, that of the unborn.
Ronald Reagan

Abortion is advocated only by persons who have themselves been born.
Ronald Reagan

I will never forget that kindness of Martin and Coretta King. Whenever I hear their names it brings tears to my eyes.
Actress Julia Roberts
[Julia Roberts says that she owes her life to Martin Luther King. In 1967, Julia's mother was pregnant and without any money. Martin Luther King knew the family and when he heard about this he funded Julia's mother through her pregnancy. Julia was born six months after King's assassination.]

State officials must know that we are serious about stopping abortion, which is a matter of clear principle concerning the babies themselves and concerning a high view of human life.
Francis Schaeffer

We are fighting abortion by adoption. We have sent word to the clinics, to the hospitals, to the police stations. "Please do not destroy the child. We will take the child."
Mother Teresa

Human rights are not a privilege conferred by government. They are every human being's entitlement by virtue of his humanity. The right to life does not depend, and must not be declared to be contingent, on the pleasure of anyone else, not even a parent or a sovereign.
Mother Teresa

What is taking place in America is a war against the child. And if we accept that the mother can kill her own child, how can we tell other people not to kill one another.
Mother Teresa

Abortion is the greatest destroyer of peace because if a mother can kill her own child,

what is left for me to kill you, and you to kill me? There is nothing between.
Mother Teresa

Any country that accepts abortion is not teaching the people to love, but to use any violence to get what they want. That is why the greatest destroyer of love and peace is abortion.
Mother Teresa

I feel that the greatest destroyer of peace today is abortion, because it is a war against the child – a direct killing of the innocent child–murder by the mother herself.
Mother Teresa

It is not possible to speak of the right to choose when a clear moral evil is involved, when what is at stake is the commandment Do not kill!
Mother Teresa

Please don't kill the child. I want the child. Please give me the child. I am willing to accept any child who would be aborted, and to give that child to a married couple who will love the child, and be loved by the child. From our children's home in Calcutta alone, we have saved over 3,000 children from abortions. These children have brought such love and joy to their adopting parents, and have grown up so full of love and joy!
Mother Teresa

It is a poverty to decide that a child must die so that you may live as you wish.
Mother Teresa

We are not permitted, since murder has been prohibited to us once and for all, even to destroy the fetus in the womb. It makes no difference whether one destroys a life that has already been born or one that is in the process of birth.
Tertullian

About turn
See also: Repentance
We all want progress, but if you're on the

wrong road, progress means doing an about-turn and walking back to the right road; in that case, the man who turns back soonest is the most progressive.
C.S. Lewis

Absence
Absence from whom we love is worse than death, and frustrates hope severer than despair.
Author unknown

Absence diminishes small loves, and increases great ones, as the wind blows out the candle and fans the bonfire.
La Rochefoucauld

Absolutes
Without absolutes revealed from without by God Himself, we are left rudderless in a sea of conflicting ideas about manners, justice and right and wrong, issuing from a multitude of self-opinionated thinkers.
John Owen

The moral absolutes rest upon God's character. The moral commands He has given to men are an expression of His character. Men as created in His image are to live by choice on the basis of what God is. The standards of morality are determined by what conforms to His character, while those things which do not conform are immoral.
Francis Schaeffer

Abstinence
See also: Alcohol; Drink; Drunkenness
Touch not; taste not; handle not.
The Bible, Colossians 2:21 KJV

Dear friends, I urge you, as aliens and strangers in the world, to abstain from sinful desires, which war against your soul.
The Bible, 1 Peter 2:11

Total abstinence is easier than perfect moderation.
Augustine of Hippo

Abstainer: a weak person who yields to the temptation of denying himself a pleasure.
Ambrose Bierce

If you say, "Would there were no wine" because of the drunkards, then you must say, going on by degrees, "Would there were no steel," because of the murderers, "Would there were no night," because of the thieves, "Would there were no light," because of the informers, and "Would there were no women," because of adultery.
John Chrysostom

All philosophy lies in two words, sustain and abstain.
Epictetus

Abstinence without charity is useless.
Gildas

An individual Christian may see fit to give up all sorts of things for special reasons – marriage, or meat, or beer, or cinema; but the moment he starts saying the things are bad in themselves, or looking down his nose at other people who do use them, he has taken the wrong turning.
C.S. Lewis

Abstinence by itself is not holiness, but if it be discreet it helps us to be holy.
Richard Rolle

Absurd
One of the main reasons why the words of Moses and Paul are not taken in their plain sense is their `absurdity.' But against what article of faith does that `absurdity' transgress? And who is offended by it? It is human reason that is offended; which, though it is blind, deaf, senseless, godless, and sacrilegious, in its dealing with all God's words and works, is at this point brought in as judge of God's words and works! On these same grounds you will deny all the articles of the faith, for it is the highest absurdity by far that God should be man, a virgin's son, crucified, sitting at the Father's right hand. It is, I repeat, absurd to believe such things!
Martin Luther

Abundance
My cup runneth over.
The Bible, Psalm 23:1 KJV

Out of the abundance of the heart the
mouth speaketh.
The Bible, Matthew 12:34 KJV

Abundance, like want, ruins many.
Romanian proverb

Abuse
See also: Adversity
Iron, when heated in the flames and
pounded, becomes a fine sword. Wise men
and saints are tested by abuse.
Nichiren Daishonin

Acceptance
Be Yourself – Truthfully
Accept Yourself – Gracefully
Value Yourself – Joyfully
Forgive Yourself – Completely
Treat Yourself – Generously
Balance Yourself – Harmoniously
Bless Yourself – Abundantly
Trust Yourself – Confidently
Love Yourself – Wholeheartedly
Empower Yourself – Prayerfully
Give Yourself – Enthusiastically
Express Yourself – Radiantly
Author unknown

Blessed are those who can give without
remembering and take without forgetting.
Elizabeth Bibesco

The art of acceptance is the art of making
someone who has just done you a small
favor wish that he might have done you a
greater one.
Russell Lynes

Jesus accepts you the way you are, but
loves you too much to leave you that
way.
Lee Venden

Accepting God
See also: Consecration; Conversion
… Whoever is thirsty, let him come; and

whoever wishes, let him take the free gift
of the water of life.
The Bible, Revelation 22:17

Just as I am, thou wilt receive,
Wilt welcome, pardon, cleanse, relieve:
Because thy promise I believe,
O Lamb of God, I come.
Charlotte Elliott

I take God the Father to be my God;
I take God the Son to be my Savior;
I take the Holy Ghost to be my Sanctifier;
I take the Word of God to be my rule;
I take the people of God to be my people;
And I do hereby dedicate and yield my
whole self to the Lord:
And I do this deliberately, freely, and for ever.
Amen.
*Act of commitment taught to Matthew Henry
by his father*

Accidents
See also: Providence
Accidents will occur in the best-regulated
families.
Charles Dickens

The accidents that befall thee thou shalt
receive as good, knowing that nothing is
done without God.
Didache

The most important events are often the
results of accidents.
Polybius

Accusation, False
When a man is accused falsely, the
reproach does not go farther than his ears.
Æschines

Achievement
See also: Success
I have fought the good fight, I have
finished my course, I have kept the faith.
The Bible, 2 Timothy 4:7 KJV

Yard by yard, all tasks are hard.
Inch by inch, they're all a cinch.
Author unknown

To leave footprints on the sands of time, wear work shoes.
Author unknown

Life affords no greater pleasure than overcoming obstacles.
Author unknown

Veni, Vidi, Vici. I came. I saw. I conquered.
Julius Caesar

You can do what you have to do, and sometimes you can do it even better than you think you can.
Jimmy Carter

Nothing great was ever achieved without enthusiasm.
Ralph Waldo Emerson

Those who believe that they are exclusively in the right are generally those who achieve something.
Aldous Huxley

Said will be a little ahead, but done should follow at his heel.
C.H. Spurgeon

That man is a success who has lived well, laughed often and loved much; who has gained the respect of intelligent men and the love of children; who has filled his niche and accomplished his task; who leaves the world better than he found it, whether by an improved poppy, a perfect poem or a rescued soul; who never lacked appreciation of earth's beauty or failed to express it; who looked for the best in others and gave the best he had.
Robert Louis Stevenson

Thou shalt ever joy at eventide if you spend the day fruitfully.
Thomas à Kempis

The way to do is to be.
Lao Tzu

Four steps to achievement:
1. Plan purposefully.
2. Prepare prayerfully.
3. Proceed positively.
4. Pursue persistently.
William A. Ward

Acknowledging God
Religion holds the solution to all problems of human relationship, whether they are between parents and children or nation and nation. Sooner or later, man has always had to decide whether he worships his own power or the power of God.
A.J. Toynbee

Action
See also: Faith and action; Idleness; Starting
Cast thy bread upon the waters: for thou shalt find it after many days.
The Bible, Ecclesiastes 11:1 KJV

Do to others what you would have them do to you.
The Bible, Matthew 7:12

Go, and do thou likewise.
The Bible, Luke 10:37 KJV

Each one should use whatever gift he has received to serve others, faithfully administering God's grace in its various forms.
The Bible, 1 Peter 4:10

Know that it is not the knowing, nor the talking, nor the reading man, but the doing man that at last will be found the happiest man.
Author unknown

Action speaks louder than words but not nearly as often.
Author unknown

The smallest good deed is better than the greatest intention.
Author unknown

"I must do something" will always solve more problems than "Something must be done."
Author unknown

Lord grant that the FIRE of my heart may melt the lead in my feet.
Author unknown

It's no good to sit up and take notice if we just keep on sitting.
Author unknown

There is a time to let things happen, and a time to make things happen.
Author unknown

Ten armchair theoreticians cannot match one doer.
Author unknown

What saves a man is to take a step. Then another step.
Author unknown

After all is said and done, there is usually more said than done.
Author unknown

He who passively accepts evil is as much involved in it as he who helps to perpetuate it.
Author unknown

True glory lies in noble deeds.
Author unknown

For purposes of action nothing is more useful than narrowness of thought combined with energy of will.
H.F. Amiel

An evil action cannot be justified by reference to a good intention.
Thomas Aquinas

Procrastination and worry are the twin thieves that will try to rob you of your brilliance – but even the smallest action will drive them from your camp.
Gil Atkinson

No one doth well what he doth against his will.
Augustine of Hippo

No man has a right to lead such a life of contemplation as to forget in his own ease the service due to his neighbor; nor has any man a right to be so immersed in active life as to neglect the contemplation of God.
Augustine of Hippo

You will give yourself relief if you do every act of your life as if it were the last.
Marcus Aurelius

Action is the antidote for despair.
Joan Baez

There is no such thing as great talent without great will-power.
Honoré de Balzac

Unless we do his teachings, we do not demonstrate faith in him.
Ezra Taft Benson

He who desires but acts not breeds pestilence. He who would do good to another must do it in minute particulars.
William Blake

Action springs not from thought, but from a readiness for responsibility.
Dietrich Bonhoeffer

This is as true in everyday life as it is in battle: we are given one life and the decision is ours whether to wait for circumstances to make up our mind, or whether to act, and in acting, to live.
General Omar Bradley

We never become truly spiritual by sitting down and wishing to become so.
Phillips Brooks

If any man should ask me what is the first, second, and third part of being a Christian, I must answer "Action!"
Thomas Brooks

Nobody makes a greater mistake than he who does nothing because he could only do a little.
Edmund Burke

A dog barks when his master is attacked. I would be a coward if I saw that God's truth is attacked and yet would remain silent.
John Calvin

Whatever is worth doing at all is worth doing well.
Lord Chesterfield

A man's best friends are his ten fingers.
Robert Collyer

Deliberation is the work of many people. Action, of one alone.
De Gaulle, Charles

Action may not always bring happiness; but there is no happiness without action.
Benjamin Disraeli

This only is charity, to do all, all that we can.
John Donne

You can either take action, or you can hang back and hope for a miracle. Miracles are great, but they are so unpredictable.
Peter Drucker

The ancestor of every action is thought.
Ralph Waldo Emerson

Thought is the blossom; language the bud; action the fruit behind it.
Ralph Waldo Emerson

Love's secret is always to be doing things for God, and not to mind because they are such very little ones.
F.W. Faber

The smallest things become great when God requires them of us; they are small only in themselves; they are always great when they are done for God, and when they serve to unite us with Him eternally.
Francois Fenelon

Deeds, not words shall speak me.
John Fletcher

You can't build a reputation on what you are going to do.
Henry Ford

The sleeping fox catches no poultry.
Benjamin Franklin

Let not thy will roar, when thy power can but whisper.
Thomas Fuller

Give me the ready hand rather than the ready tongue.
Giuseppe Garibaldi

Knowing is not enough, we must apply. Willing is not enough, we must do.
Johann Wolfgang von Goethe

I find the great thing in this world is, not so much where we stand, as in what direction we are moving.
Johann Wolfgang von Goethe

I am only one,
But still I am one.
I cannot do everything,
But still I can do something;
And because I cannot do everything
I will not refuse to do the something that I can do.
Edward Everett Hale

The vision must be followed by the venture. It is not enough to stare up the steps – we must step up the stairs.
Vance Havner

The more we do, the more we can do.
William Hazlitt

The shortest answer is doing.
George Herbert

The great end of life is not knowledge but action.
Thomas H. Huxley

A thousand words will not leave so deep an impression as one deed.
Henrik Ibsen

The hands that help are better far than the lips that pray.
Robert G. Ingersoll

Act as if what you do makes a difference. It does.
William James

Nothing will ever be attempted, if all possible objections must be first overcome.
Samuel Johnson

It is what you do with your life that counts.
Martin Luther King, Jr.

Iron rusts from disuse; stagnant water loses its purity and in cold weather becomes frozen; even so does inaction sap the vigor of the mind.
Leonardo da Vinci

The probability that we may fail in the struggle ought not to deter us from the support of a cause we believe to be just.
Abraham Lincoln

God loves not the questioner, but the runner.
Martin Luther

Commitment without reflection is fanaticism in action, though reflection without commitment is the paralysis of all action.
John Mackay, former President of Princetown Theological Seminary

Often the difference between a successful person and a failure is not one's better abilities or ideas, but the courage that one has to bet on one's ideas, to take a calculated risk – and to act.
Maxwell Maltz

It is well to think well; it is Divine to act well.
Horace Mann

Let us not be content to wait and see what will happen, but give us the determination to make the right things happen.
Peter Marshall

We can't all, and some of us don't. That's all there is to it.
Eeyore (A.A. Milne)

One drop of water helps to swell the ocean; a spark of fire helps to give light to the world. None are too small, too feeble, too poor to be of service. Think of this and act.
Hannah More

Activity may lead to evil; but inactivity cannot be led to good.
Hannah More

Action, to be effective, must be directed to clearly conceived ends.
Jawaharlal Nehru

A man would do nothing, if he waited until he could do it so well that no one would find fault with what he has done.
J.H. Newman

The world is blessed by people who do things, and not by those who merely talk about them.
James Oliver

Our nature consists in motion; complete inaction is death.
Blaise Pascal

"He means well" is useless unless he does well.
Plautus

The best way to make your dreams come true is to wake up.
J.M. Power

Little strokes fell great oaks.
Proverb

We cannot direct the wind, but we can adjust the sails.
Proverb

Ideas without action are worthless.
Proverb

He does not believe, that does not live according to his belief.
Proverb

Talk doesn't cook rice.
Chinese proverb

To talk much and arrive nowhere is the same as climbing a tree to catch a fish.
Chinese proverb

He who deliberates fully before taking a step will spend his entire life on one leg.
Chinese proverb

Better to light a candle than to curse the darkness.
Chinese proverb

If there is no wind, row.
Latin proverb

I have so much to do that I am going to bed.
Savoyard proverb

Even if you're on the right track, you'll get run over if you just sit there.
Will Rogers

Whatever you do, do cautiously, and look to the end.
Gesta Romanorum

Stop worrying about whether or not you're effective. Worry about what is possible for you to do, which is always greater than you imagine.
Archbishop Oscar Romero

Take a method and try it. If it fails, admit it frankly, and try another. But by all means, try something.
Franklin Delano Roosevelt

It is not the critic who counts, not the man who points out how the strong man stumbled, or where the doers of deeds could have done better. The credit belongs to the man who is actually in the arena; whose face is marred by dust and sweat and blood; who strives valiantly; who errs and comes short again and again … who knows the great enthusiasms, the great devotions, and spends himself in a worthy cause; who at the least knows in the end the triumph of high achievement; and who, at the worst, if he fails, at least fails while daring greatly, so that his place shall never be with those cold and timid souls who know neither victory nor defeat.
Theodore Roosevelt

Things won are done, joy's soul lies in the doing.
William Shakespeare

The shortest way to do many things is to do one thing at once.
Samuel Smiles

If you don't place your foot on the rope, you'll never cross the chasm.
Liz Smith

Heaven never helps the men who will not act.
Sophocles

"Speech" any man may attain unto, but "act" is difficult.
C.H. Spurgeon

There is not a spider hanging on the wall that doesn't have an errand; there is not a weed growing in the corner of the church lot that doesn't have a purpose; there is not a single insect fluttering in the breeze that does not accomplish some divine decree. And I will never believe that God created any man, especially any Christian man, to be a blank, and to be a nothing.
C.H. Spurgeon

If you cannot feed a hundred people, then feed just one.
Mother Teresa

There should be less talk. What do you do then? Take a broom and clean someone's house. That says enough.
Mother Teresa

He does much who loves much
Thomas à Kempis

How vain it is to sit down and write when you have not stood up to live!
Henry David Thoreau

Be not simply good, but good for something.
Henry David Thoreau

Affection without action is like Rachel, beautiful but barren.
John Trapp

Sometimes you gotta create what you want to be a part of.
Geri Weitzman

I am never better than when I am on the full march for God.
George Whitefield

Ideas won't keep; something must be done about them.
Alfred North Whitehead

Do not let what you cannot do interfere with what you can do.
John Wooden

Many of us spend half our time wishing for things we could have if we didn't spend half our time wishing.
Alexander Woollcott

Action, Lack of
Anyone, then, who knows the good he ought to do and doesn't do it, sins.
The Bible, James 4:17

Action, Right
To do what is right and just is more acceptable to the LORD than sacrifice.
The Bible, Proverbs 21:3

Action, Useless
There is nothing so useless as doing efficiently that which should not be done at all.
Peter Drucker

Action and faith
We are not made righteous by doing righteous deeds; but when we have been made righteous we do righteous deeds.
Martin Luther

Action and love
Love doesn't just sit there like a stone, it has to be made, like bread; remade all the time, made new.
Ursula K. LeGuin

Even devotion must give way to a work of love to the spiritual and to the physical man. For even should one rise in prayer higher than Peter or Paul, and hear that a poor man needed a drink of water, he would have to cease from the devotional exercise, sweet though it were, and do the deed of love.
John of Ruysbroeck

Action and the present moment
Our grand business is not to see what lies dimly at a distance, but to do what lies clearly at hand.
Thomas Carlyle

No one notices what is at his feet; we all gaze at the stars.
Quintus Ennius

Act well at the moment, and you have performed a good action to all eternity.
Johann Kaspar Lavater

Love cannot be practiced right unless we first exercise it the moment God gives the opportunity.
John Wesley

Action and trust
Leave nothing to chance, and then leave everything to God.
Author unknown

Action and words
Men will not attend to what we say, but examine into what we do; and will say, "First obey your own words, and then exhort others." This is the great battle, this is the unanswerable

demonstration, which is made by our acts.
John Chrysostom

Well-done is better than well-said.
Benjamin Franklin

Actions speak louder than words.
Proverb

Deeds, and not fine speeches, are the proof of love.
Spanish proverb

Activity and prayer
No man has a right to lead such a life of contemplation as to forget in his own ease the service due to his neighbor; nor has any man a right to be so immersed in active life as to neglect the contemplation of God.
Augustine of Hippo

To give our Lord a perfect hospitality, Mary and Martha must combine.
Teresa of Avila

Acts of the Apostles
If you are feeling tired and therefore in need of a spiritual tonic, go to the book of Acts.
Martyn Lloyd-Jones

Adam
See also: Adam and Eve
For as in Adam all die, so in Christ all will be made alive.
The Bible, 1 Corinthians 15:22

Adam and Eve
See also: Genders, Complementarity of
The man said, "The woman you put here with me – she gave me some fruit from the tree, and I ate it."
The Bible, Genesis 3:12

Eve was not taken from the feet of Adam to be his slave, nor from his head to be his lord, but from his side to be his partner.
Peter Lombard

Admiration
No nobler feeling than this of admiration for one higher than himself dwells in the breast of man.
Thomas Carlyle

Adoption
Nothing has challenged our faith more than the grief of wanting children. And nothing has brought us more joy than the process of adoption.
Christine Wyrtzen

Adoration
See also: Worship
We cannot by searching find the bottom, we must sit down at the brink and adore the depths.
Matthew Arnold

We do better to adore the mysteries of deity than to investigate them.
Philip Melanchthon

Open wide the windows of our spirits and fill us full of light; open wide the door of our hearts, that we may receive and entertain Thee with all our powers of adoration.
Christina Rossetti

The most fundamental need, duty, honor and happiness of mankind is not petition, nor even contrition, nor again even thanksgiving – these three kinds of prayer which, indeed, must never disappear out of our spiritual lives – but adoration.
Von Hügel, Friedrich

It is a beauteous evening, calm and free;
The holy time is quiet as a nun
Breathless with adoration.
William Wordsworth

Adultery
For the lips of an adulteress drip honey, and her speech is smoother than oil, but in the end she is bitter as gall, sharp as a double-edged sword.
The Bible, Proverbs 5:3-4

… the prostitute reduces you to a loaf of bread,

and the adulteress preys upon your very life.
The Bible, Proverbs 6:26

The mouth of an adulteress is a deep pit.
The Bible, Proverbs 22:14

You have heard that it was said, "Do not commit adultery." But I tell you that anyone who looks at a woman lustfully has already committed adultery with her in his heart.
The Bible, Matthew 5:27-28

If a husband, separated from his wife, approaches another woman, he is an adulterer because he makes that woman commit adultery; and the woman who lives with him is an adulteress, because she has drawn another's husband to herself.
Basil the Great

Do not commit adultery. Adultery destroys a marriage and is a sin against God and against your mate.
Billy Graham

There are highly respectable men and women who would never dream of committing an act of adultery, but look at the way in which they enjoy sinning in the mind and in the imagination. We are dealing with practical matters, we are dealing with life as it is…How often do men sin by reading novels and biographies. You read the reviews of a book and find that it contains something about a man's misconduct or behavior, and you buy it. We pretend we have a general philosophical interest in life, and that we are sociologists reading out of pure interest. No, no; it is because we love the thing; we like it. It is sin in the heart; sin in the mind!
Martyn Lloyd-Jones

Every Jew must die before he will commit idolatry, murder or adultery.
Rabbinic saying

Adultery is a sin and is opposed to the will of God and to all that is pure in body, mind and heart.
W. H. Griffith Thomas

Adventure
Adventure is the champagne of life.
G.K. Chesterton

Do not follow where the path may lead. Go instead where there is no path and leave a trail.
Ralph Waldo Emerson

Adventure is not outside a man, it is within.
David Grayson

Adversity
See also: Affliction; Burdens; Difficulties; Hardships; Trials; Suffering
Those who sow in tears
will reap with songs of joy.
The Bible, Psalm 126:5

If thou faint in the day of adversity thy strength is small.
The Bible, Proverbs 24:10 KJV

Although the LORD gives you the bread of adversity and the water of affliction, your teachers will be hidden no more; with your own eyes you will see them. Whether you turn to the right or to the left, your ears will hear a voice behind you saying, "This is the way; walk in it."
The Bible, Isaiah 30:20-21

No man is more unhappy than the one who is never in adversity; the greatest affliction of life is never to be afflicted.
Author unknown

A smooth sea never made a skillful mariner, neither do uninterrupted prosperity and success qualify for usefulness and happiness. The storms of adversity, like those of the ocean, rouse the faculties, and excite the invention, prudence, skill and fortitude of the voyager. The martyrs of ancient times, in bracing their minds to outward calamities, acquired a loftiness of purpose and a moral heroism worth a lifetime of softness and security.
Author unknown

Adversity may be a blessing in disguise!
Author unknown

It is the crushed grape that yields the wine.
Author unknown

In all trouble you should seek God. You should not set him over against your troubles, but within them. God can only relieve your troubles if you in your anxiety cling to him. Trouble should not really be thought of as this thing or that in particular, for our whole life on earth involves trouble; and through the troubles of our earthly pilgrimage we find God.
Augustine of Hippo

Prosperity is not without many fears and distastes; and adversity is not without comforts and hopes. Prosperity is the blessing of the Old Testament; adversity is the blessing of the New.
Francis Bacon

Prosperity doth best discover vice;
but adversity doth best discover virtue.
Francis Bacon

Misfortune, no less than happiness, inspires us to dream.
Honoré de Balzac

He is not drowning His sheep when He washeth them, nor killing them when He is shearing them. But by this He showeth that they are His own; and the new shorn sheep do most visibly bear His name or mark, when it is almost worn out and scarce discernible on them that have the longest fleece.
Richard Baxter

We are always in the forge, or on the anvil; by trials God is shaping us for higher things.
H. W. Beecher

A prosperous state makes a secure Christian, but adversity makes him Consider.
Anne Bradstreet

Seeing that a Pilot steers the ship in which we sail, who will never allow us to perish even in the midst of shipwrecks, there is no reason why our minds should be overwhelmed with fear and overcome with weariness.
John Calvin

Whomever the Lord has adopted and deemed worthy of his fellowship ought to prepare themselves for a hard, toilsome, and unquiet life, crammed with very many and various kinds of evil. It is the Heavenly Father's will thus to exercise them so as to put his own children to a definite test. Beginning with Christ, his first-born, he follows this plan with all his children.
John Calvin

A man of character finds a special attractiveness in difficulty, since it is only by coming to grips with difficulty that he can realize his potentialities.
Charles de Gaulle

Adversity is the trial of principle. Without it a man hardly knows whether he is honest or not.
Henry Fielding

That which does not kill you makes you stronger.
Viktor Frankl

What thwarts us and demands of us the greatest effort is also what can teach us most.
André Gide

As aromatic plants bestow
No spicy fragrance while they grow;
But crushed or trodden to the ground,
Diffuse their balmy sweets around.
Oliver Goldsmith

God would not rub so hard if it were not to fetch out the dirt that is ingrained in our natures. God loves purity so well He had rather see a hole than a spot in His child's garments.
William Gurnall

Prosperity is a great teacher; adversity a greater.
William Hazlitt

Adversity reveals genius, prosperity conceals it.
Horace

Never forget that God tests his real friends more severely than the lukewarm ones.
Kathryn Hulme

See that you are not suddenly saddened by the adversities of this world, for you do not know the good they bring, being ordained in the judgments of God for the everlasting joy of the elect.
John of the Cross

We could never learn to be brave and patient, if there were only joy in the world.
Helen Keller

Only in winter can you tell which trees are truly green. Only when the winds of adversity blow can you tell whether an individual or a country has steadfastness.
John F. Kennedy

Adversity is the diamond dust heaven polishes its jewels with.
Robert Leighton

It has done me good to be somewhat parched by the heat and drenched by the rain of life.
Henry Wadsworth Longfellow

Mishaps are like knives, that either serve us or cut us, as we grasp them by the blade or the handle.
James Russell Lowell

They gave our Master a crown of thorns. Why do we hope for a crown of roses?
Martin Luther

Afflictions are but the shadow of God's wings.
George Macdonald

God's people have no assurances that the dark experiences of life will be held at bay, much less that God will provide some sort of running commentary on the meaning of each day's allotment of confusion, boredom, pain, or achievement. It is no great matter where we are, provided we see that the Lord has placed us there, and that He is with us.
John Newton

Prosperity is no just scale; adversity is the only balance to weigh friends.
Plutarch

Gold is tested by fire; man is tested by adversity.
Proverb

Smooth seas do not make skillful sailors.
African proverb

When the storm passes over, the grass will stand up again.
Kikuyu proverb

Adversity makes a man wise, not rich.
Romanian proverb

The good are better made by ill,
As odors crushed are sweeter still.
Samuel Rogers

Grace grows best in winter.
Samuel Rutherford

Whenever I find myself in the cellar of affliction, I always look about for the wine.
Samuel Rutherford

After winter comes the summer. After night comes the dawn. And after every storm, there come clear, open skies.
Samuel Rutherford

If it were no more than once to see the face of the Prince of this good land, and to be feasted for eternity with the fatness, sweetness, dainties of the rays and beams of matchless glory, and incomparable fountain-love, it were a well-spent

journey to creep hands and feet through seven deaths and seven hells, to enjoy Him up at the well-head. Only let us not weary: the miles to that land are fewer and shorter than when we first believed. Strangers are not wise to quarrel with their host, and complain of their lodging. It is a foul way, but a fair home. Oh that I had but such grapes and clusters out of the land as I have sometimes seen and tasted in the place whereof your Ladyship maketh mention! But the hope of it in the end is a heartsome convoy in the way. If I see little more of the gold till the race be ended, I dare not quarrel. It is the Lord!
Samuel Rutherford, Letter to Lady Kenmure

I assure you by the Lord, your adversaries shall get no advantage against you, except you sin, and offend your Lord, in your sufferings.
Samuel Rutherford

One who gains strength by overcoming obstacles possesses the only strength which can overcome adversity.
Albert Schweitzer

Adversity is like the period of the rain … cold, comfortless, unfriendly to man and to animal; yet from that season have their birth the flower, the fruit, the date, the rose and the pomegranate.
Sir Walter Scott

Fire is the test of gold; adversity, of strong men.
Seneca

Misfortune is the test of a man's merit.
Seneca

The good things which belong to prosperity are to be wished, but the good things that belong to adversity are to be admired.
Seneca

Sweet are the uses of adversity,
Which, like the toad, ugly and
  venomous,

Wears yet a precious jewel in his head;
And this our life, exempt in public
  haunt,
Finds tongues in trees, books in the
  running brooks,
Sermons in stones, and good in every
  thing.
I would not change it.
William Shakespeare

Bless you, prison, for having been in my life. The meaning of earthly existence lies, not as we have grown used to thinking, in prospering, but in the development of the soul.
Alexander Solzhenitsyn

Christian, remember the goodness of God in the frost of adversity.
C.H. Spurgeon

No faith is so precious as that which lives and triumphs in adversity.
C.H. Spurgeon

At the timberline where the storms strike with the most fury, the sturdiest trees are found.
Hudson Taylor

The measure of every man's virtue is best revealed in time of adversity – adversity that does not weaken a man but rather shows what he is.
Thomas à Kempis

Many love Jesus so long as no adversities happen to them. Many praise Him and bless Him, so long as they receive any comforts from Him. But if Jesus hide Himself and withdraw a little while, they fall either into complaining or into too great dejection of mind.
Thomas à Kempis

We must face today as children of tomorrow. We must meet the uncertainties of this world with the certainty of the world to come.
A.W. Tozer

The godly have some good in them, therefore the devil afflicts them; and some evil in them, therefore God afflicts them.
Thomas Watson

The person who bears and suffers evils with meekness and silence, is the sum of a Christian man.
John Wesley

Advice
See also: Criticism
My tongue is the pen of a ready writer.
The Bible, Psalm 45:1 KJV

Your statutes are my delight;
they are my counselors.
The Bible, Psalm 119:24

In the multitude of counsellors there is safety.
The Bible, Proverbs 11:14 KJV

The way of a fool seems right to him, but a wise man listens to advice.
The Bible, Proverbs 12:15

Plans fail for lack of counsel, but with many advisers they succeed.
The Bible, Proverbs 15:22

A man finds joy in giving an apt reply – and how good is a timely word!
The Bible, Proverbs 15:23

Advice is the only commodity on the market where the supply always exceeds the demand.
Author unknown

Never give advice…
A wise man won't need it
A fool won't heed it.
Author unknown

Advice is what we ask for when we already know the answer but wish we didn't.
Author unknown

A woman seldom asks advice before she has bought her wedding clothes.
Joseph Addison

It is easy when we are in prosperity to give advice to the afflicted.
Aeschylus

There is as much difference between the counsel that a friend giveth, and that a man giveth himself, as there is between the counsel of a friend and a flatterer.
Francis Bacon

He that gives good advice, builds with one hand; he that gives good counsel and example, builds with both; but he that gives good admonition and bad example, builds with one hand and pulls down with the other.
Francis Bacon

Advice is like castor oil … easy enough to give but dreadful uneasy to take.
Josh Billings

Good advice is always certain to be ignored, but that's no reason not to give it.
Agatha Christie

In those days he was wiser than he is now – he used frequently to take my advice.
Winston Churchill

Advice is like snow; the softer it falls, the longer it dwells upon, and the deeper it sinks into the mind.
Samuel Taylor Coleridge

No gift is more precious than good advice.
Erasmus

He that won't be counseled can't be helped.
Benjamin Franklin

The man who does not learn to wait upon the Lord and have his thoughts molded by Him will never possess that steady purpose and calm trust, which is essential to the exercise of wise influence upon others, in times of crisis and difficulty.
D.E. Hoste

No man is so foolish but he may sometimes give another good counsel, and

no man so wise that he may not easily err
if he takes no other counsel than his own.
He that is taught only by himself has a fool
for a master.
Ben Jonson

He who can take advice is sometimes
superior to him who can give it.
Karl von Knebel

Nothing is given so profusely as advice.
François de la Rochefoucauld

Men give away nothing so liberally as their
advice.
François de La Rochefoucauld

Write down the advice of him who loves
you, though you like it not at present.
Proverb

Let no man give advice to others that he
has not first given himself.
Seneca

If you ask enough people, you can usually
find someone who will advise you to do
what you were going to do anyway.
Weston Smith

Seek the advice of your betters in preference
to following your own inclinations.
Thomas à Kempis

Do not open your heart to every man, but
discuss your affairs with one who is wise
and who fears God.
Thomas à Kempis

Affection
Most people would rather get than give
affection.
Aristotle

Affection has no price.
Jerome

Affection is responsible for nine-tenths of
whatever solid and durable happiness there
is in our lives.
C.S. Lewis

Affection is the humblest love.
C.S. Lewis

Talk not of wasted affection; affection
never was wasted.
Henry Wadsworth Longfellow

Affection hides three times as many virtues
as charity does sins.
Horace Mann

Affections
See also: Emotions
True religious affections are distinguished
from false. Affections that are truly spiritual
and gracious, do arise from those influences
and operations on the heart, which are
spiritual, supernatural and divine.
Jonathan Edwards

Affliction
See also: Adversity; Burdens; Difficulties; Hardships; Suffering; Trials
A righteous man may have many troubles,
but the LORD delivers him from them all.
The Bible, Psalm 34:19

He was afflicted, yet he opened not his
mouth: he is brought as a lamb to the
slaughter, and as a sheep before her shearers
is dumb, so he openeth not his mouth.
The Bible, Isaiah 53:7 KJV

For our light affliction, which is but for a
moment, worketh for us a far more
exceeding and eternal weight of glory.
The Bible, 2 Corinthians 4:17 KJV

Be ... patient in affliction ...
The Bible, Romans 12:12

The labors of the farm do not seem
strange to the farmer; the storm at sea is
not unexpected by the sailor; sweat causes
no wonder to the hired laborer; and so to
those who have chosen to live the life of
piety the afflictions of this world are not
unforeseen. Nay, to each of the aforesaid
is joined a labor that is appropriate and
well known to those who share it – a
labor that is not chosen for its own sake,

but for the enjoyment of expected
blessings. For hopes, which hold and weld
together man's entire life, give consolation
for the hardships which fall to the lot of
each of these.
Basil the Great

Saints spring and thrive most internally,
when they are most externally afflicted.
Afflictions are the mother of virtue.
Thomas Brooks

In times of affliction we commonly meet with
the sweetest experiences of the love of God.
John Bunyan

Blessed is he who bears affliction with
thankfulness.
Abba Copres

Through Christ's satisfaction for sin, the
very nature of affliction is changed with
regard to believers. As death, which was, at
first, the wages of sin, is now become a bed
of rest (Is. 57:2); so afflictions are not the
rod of God's anger, but the gentle
medicine of a tender father.
Tobias Crisp

God does not lead His children around
hardship, but leads them straight
through hardship. But He leads! And
amidst the hardship, He is nearer to
them than ever before.
Otto Dibelius

If afflictions refine some, they consume
others.
Thomas Fuller

God's wounds cure, sin's kisses kill.
William Gurnall

Not to be afflicted is a sign of weakness;
for, therefore God imposeth no more on
me, because he sees I can bear no more.
Joseph Hall

Strength is born in the deep silence of
long-suffering hearts; not amid joy.
Felicia Hemans

Extraordinary afflictions are not always the
punishment of extraordinary sins, but
sometimes the trial of extraordinary graces.
Sanctified afflictions are spiritual
promotions.
Matthew Henry

The sorest afflictions never appear
intolerable, but when we see them in the
wrong light: when we see them in the hand
of God, Who dispenses them; when we
know that it is our loving Father who
abases and distresses us; our sufferings will
lose their bitterness and become even a
matter of consolation.
Brother Lawrence

No words can express how much the world
owes to sorrow. Most of the Psalms were
born in a wilderness. Most of the Epistles
were written in a prison. The greatest
thoughts of the greatest thinkers have all
passed through fire. The greatest poets
have "learned in suffering what they taught
in song." In bonds Bunyan lived the
allegory that he afterwards wrote, and we
may thank Bedford Jail for the *Pilgrim's
Progress*. Take comfort, afflicted Christian!
When God is about to make pre-eminent
use of a person, He puts them in the fire.
George MacDonald

There is more safety with Christ in the
tempest, than without Christ in the
calmest waters. The brook would lose its
song if you removed the stones. My soul,
alas, needs these uneasinesses in outward
things, to be driven to take refuge in God.
Henry Martyn

No affliction would trouble a child of
God, if they knew God's reasons for
sending it.
G. Campbell Morgan

A believer may pass through much
affliction, and yet secure very little blessing
from it all. Abiding in Christ is the secret
of securing all that the Father meant the
chastisement to bring us.
Andrew Murray

He knows our sorrows, not merely as He knows all things, but as one who has been in our situation, and who, though without sin Himself, endured when upon earth inexpressibly more for us than He will ever lay upon us.
John Newton

I asked the Lord that I might grow,
In faith and love and every grace,
Might more of His salvation know,
And seek more earnestly His face.
It was He who taught me thus to pray,
And He I trust has answered prayer.
But it has been in such a way,
As almost drove me to despair.
I hoped that in some favored hour,
At once He'd answer my request.
And by his love's constraining power,
Subdue my sins and give me rest.
Instead of this, He made me feel,
The hidden evils of my heart.
And let the angry powers of hell,
Assault my soul in every part.
Yes, more with His own hand, he seemed,
Intent to aggravate my woe.
Crossed all the fair designs I schemed,
Blasted my gourds, and laid me low.
"Lord, why is this?" I trembling cried.
"Will You pursue this worm to death?"
"This is the way," the Lord replied,
"I answer prayer for grace and strength."
John Newton

The gem cannot be polished without friction, nor man perfected without trials.
Chinese proverb

The hammer shatters glass but forges steel.
Russian proverb

I exhort you and beseech you in the compassion of Christ, faint not, weary not. There is a great necessity of heaven; you must have it. Think it not easy; for it is a steep ascent to eternal glory; many are lying dead by the way, that were slain with security.
Samuel Rutherford

A fact, which cannot be disputed is the weakening of human personality in the West while in the East it has become firmer and stronger…we have been through a spiritual training far in advance of Western experience. The complex and deadly crush of life has produced stronger, deeper and more interesting personalities than those generated by standardized Western well-being.
Alexander Solzhenitsyn

The furnace of affliction is a good place for you, Christian; it benefits you; it helps you to become more like Christ, and it is fitting you for heaven.
C.H. Spurgeon

The Lord gets His best soldiers out of the highlands of affliction.
C.H. Spurgeon

Many men owe the grandeur of their lives to their tremendous difficulties.
C.H. Spurgeon

Afflictions cannot sanctify us except as they are used by Christ as His mallet and His chisel.
C.H. Spurgeon

This will deliver you from clinging to the present world, and make you long for those eternal things which are so soon to be revealed to you.
C.H. Spurgeon

Eminent usefulness usually necessitates eminent affliction.
C.H. Spurgeon

As sure as God puts His children in the furnace of affliction, He will be with them in it.
C.H. Spurgeon

The jewels of a Christian are his afflictions.
C.H. Spurgeon

We must believe that the only reason why God afflicts his people must be this:
  "In love I correct you, your gold to refine

To make you at length in my likeness to shine."
C.H. Spurgeon

Most of the grand truths of God have to be learned by trouble; they must be burned into us with the hot iron of affliction, otherwise we shall not truly receive them.
C.H. Spurgeon

Affliction may be lasting, but it is not everlasting. Affliction was a sting, but withal a wing: sorrow shall soon fly away.
Thomas Watson

The godly have some good in them,
therefore the devil afflicts them;
and some evil in them,
therefore God afflicts them.
Thomas Watson

"Man is born to trouble" (Job); he is heir apparent to it; he comes into the world with a cry, and goes out with a groan.
Thomas Watson

Afflictions add to the saints' glory. The more the diamond is cut, the more it sparkles; the heavier the saints' cross is, the heavier will be their crown.
Thomas Watson

What if we have more of the rough file, if we have less rust! Afflictions carry away nothing but the dross of sin.
Thomas Watson

I am mended by my sickness, enriched by my poverty, and strengthened by my weakness. Thus was it with Manasseh, when he was in affliction, "He besought the Lord his God": even that king's iron was more precious to him than his gold, his jail a more happy lodging than his palace, Babylon a better school than Jerusalem. What fools are we, then, to frown upon our afflictions! These are our best friends. They are not, indeed, for our pleasure, but for our profit.
Abraham Wright

Affluence
See also: Wealth
We are stripped bare by the curse of plenty.
Winston Churchill

Afterlife
There the wicked cease from troubling;
and there the weary be at rest.
The Bible, Job 3:17 KJV

The land of darkness and the shadow of death.
The Bible, Job 10:21 KJV

Hark, how the birds do sing,
And woods do ring!
All creatures have their joy, and man hath his.
Yet if we rightly measure,
Man's joy and pleasure
Rather hereafter, than in present, is.
George Herbert

The humble, meek, merciful, just, pious and devout souls are everywhere of one religion; and when death has taken off the mask they will know one another, though the divers liveries they wear here makes them strangers.
William Penn

Age
See also: Ages of man; Old age
Therefore we do not lose heart. Though outwardly we are wasting away, yet inwardly we are being renewed day by day.
The Bible, 2 Corinthians 4:16

Alonso of Aragon was wont to say in commendation of age, that age appears to be best in four things – old wood best to burn, old wine to drink, old friends to trust, and old authors to read.
Francis Bacon

Age, health, and stage in life have nothing to do with serving or not serving. In each season of life there are attributes and qualities of life and experience that God values in service.
Bruce Kemper

It would be a good thing if young people were wise and old people were strong, but God has arranged things better.
Martin Luther

Ages of man
Youth is a blunder;
manhood a struggle;
old age a regret.
Benjamin Disraeli

Forty is the old age of youth;
fifty the youth of old age.
Victor Hugo

When, as a child, I laughed and wept,
Time crept.
When, as a youth, I dreamed and talked,
Time walked.
When I became a full-grown man,
Time ran.
And later, as I older grew,
Time flew.
Soon I shall find, while traveling on,
Time gone.
Will Christ have saved my soul by then?
Amen.
Inscription on clock in Chester Cathedral, England

Youth is made rich by its dreams of the future; age is made poor by its regrets for the past.
Rochepèdre

Aggression
What is the arms race and the cold war but the continuation of male competitiveness and aggression into the inhuman sphere of computer-run institutions? If women are to cease producing cannon fodder for the final holocaust they must rescue men from the perversities of their own polarization.
Germaine Greer

Agnosticism
See also: Belief; God, belief in; Unbelief
Agnosticism: the denial that it is possible to know the existence of god(s).
Author unknown

Those who deny Thee could not deny, if Thou didst not exist; and their denial is never complete, for if it were so, they would not exist.
T.S. Eliot

Agnosticism simply means that a man shall not say he knows or believes that for which he has no grounds for professing to believe.
Thomas Henry Huxley

Amiable agnostics will talk cheerfully about man's search for God. For me, they might as well talk about the mouse's search for a cat.
C.S. Lewis

The agnostic's prayer: "O God, if there is a god, save my soul, if I have a soul."
Ernest Renan

Agnosticism is epistemologically self-contradictory on its own assumptions because its claim to make no assertion about ultimate reality rests upon a most comprehensive assertion about ultimate reality
Cornelius Van Til

Agreement
When you say that you agree to a thing in principle you mean that you have not the slightest intention of carrying it out in practice.
Otto von Bismarck

He that complies against his will is of his own opinion still.
Samuel Butler

"My idea of an agreeable person," said Hugo Bohun, "is a person who agrees with me."
Benjamin Disraeli

Aid
See also: Caring; Charity; Giving
If you feed a man a meal, you only feed him for a day – but if you teach a man to grow food, you feed him for a lifetime.
Peace Pilgrim

The present social order is the most abject failure the world has ever seen. Governments have never learned how to legislate as to distribute the fruits of its industry of the people. The countries of the earth produce enough to support all, and if the earnings of each was fairly distributed it would make all men toil some, but no man toil too much.
C.I. Scofield

The race of mankind would perish did they cease to aid each other. We cannot exist without mutual help. All therefore that need aid have a right to ask it of their fellow-men; and no one who has the power of granting can refuse it without guilt.
Walter Scott

AIDS

AIDS is the wrath of a just God against homosexuals. To oppose it would be like an Israelite jumping in the Red Sea to save one of Pharaoh's charioteers.
Jerry Falwell

To say God has judged people with AIDS would be very wrong and very cruel.
Billy Graham

Men are not punished for their sins, but by them.
Elbert Hubbard

Alcohol
See also: Abstinence; Drink
Wine … gladdens the heart of man.
The Bible, Psalm 104:15

Wine is a mocker and beer a brawler.
The Bible, Proverbs 20:1

Stop drinking only water, and use a little wine because of your stomach and your frequent illnesses.
The Bible, 1 Timothy 5:23

The steps of a program of recovery of *Alcoholics Anonymous* (A.A.)
STEP 1
We admitted we were powerless over alcohol – that our lives had become unmanageable.
STEP 2
Came to believe that a Power greater than ourselves could restore us to sanity.
STEP 3
Made a decision to turn our will and our lives over to the care of God as we understood Him.
STEP 4
Made a searching and fearless moral inventory of ourselves.
STEP 5
Admitted to God, to ourselves, and to another human being the exact nature of our wrongs.
STEP 6
Were entirely ready to have God remove all these defects of character.
STEP 7
Humbly asked Him to remove our shortcomings.
STEP 8
Made a list of all persons we had harmed, and became willing to make amends to them all.
STEP 9
Made direct amends to such people wherever possible, except when to do so would injure them or others.
STEP 10
Continued to take personal inventory and when we were wrong promptly admitted it.
STEP 11
Sought through prayer and meditation to improve our conscious contact with God, as we understood Him, praying only for knowledge of His will for us and the power to carry that out.
STEP 12
Having had a spiritual awakening as the result of these steps, we tried to carry this message to alcoholics, and to practice these principles in all our affairs.
Alcoholics Anonymous

Twelve Traditions of Alcoholics *Anonymous* (A.A.)
TRADITION 1
Our common welfare should come first; personal recovery depends upon A.A. unity.

TRADITION 2
For our group purpose there is but one ultimate authority – a loving God as He may express Himself in our group conscience. Our leaders are but trusted servants; they do not govern.

TRADITION 3
The only requirement for A.A. membership is a desire to stop drinking.

Tradition 4
Each group should be autonomous except in matters affecting other groups or A.A. as a whole.

TRADITION 5
Each group has but one primary purpose – to carry its message to the alcoholic who still suffers.

TRADITION 6
An A.A. group ought never endorse, finance or lend the A.A. name to any related facility or outside enterprise, lest problems of money, property and prestige divert us from our primary purpose.

TRADITION 7
Every A.A. group ought to be fully self-supporting, declining outside contributions.

TRADITION 8
Alcoholics Anonymous should remain forever nonprofessional, but our service centers may employ special workers.

TRADITION 9
A.A., as such, ought never be organized; but we may create service boards or committees directly responsible to those they serve.

TRADITION 10
Alcoholics Anonymous has no opinion on outside issues; hence the A.A. name ought never be drawn into public controversy.

TRADITION 11
Our public relations policy is based on attraction rather than promotion; we need always maintain personal anonymity at the level of press, radio and films.

TRADITION 12
Anonymity is the spiritual foundation of all our traditions, ever reminding us to place principles before personalities.
Alcoholics Anonymous

The Promises of *Alcoholics Anonymous* (A.A.)
   1. If we are painstaking about this phase of our development, we will be amazed before we are half way through.
   2. We are going to know a new freedom and a new happiness.
   3. We will not regret the past nor wish to shut the door on it.
   4. We will comprehend the word serenity and we will know peace.
   5. No matter how far down the scale we have gone, we will see how our experience can benefit others.
   6. That feeling of uselessness and self-pity will disappear.
   7. We will lose interest in selfish things and gain interest in our fellows.
   8. Self-seeking will slip away. Our whole attitude and outlook upon life will change.
   9. Fear of people and of economic insecurity will leave us.
   10. We will intuitively know how to handle situations which used to baffle us.
   11. We will suddenly realize that God is doing for us what we could not do for ourselves.
Alcoholics Anonymous

Let those that merely talk and never think,
That live in the wild anarchy of drink.
Ben Jonson

I am a firm believer in the people. If given the truth, they can be depended upon to meet any national crisis. The great point is to bring them the real facts, and beer.
Abraham Lincoln

Alertness
Be on your guard…
The Bible, 1 Corinthians 16:13

Allegiance
I pledge allegiance to the Christian flag and to the Savior, for whose Kingdom it stands, one Savior, crucified, risen, and coming again, with life and liberty for all who believe.
Dan Quayle

Aloneness
The deepest need of man is the need to overcome his separateness, to leave the prison of his aloneness.
Erich Fromm

Ambassador
We are therefore Christ's ambassadors, as though God were making his appeal through us. We implore you on Christ's behalf: Be reconciled to God.
The Bible, 2 Corinthians 5:20

An ambassador is an honest man sent to lie abroad for the good of his country.
Henry Wootton

Ambition
See also: Ambition; Ambition, Warnings against; Aspirations; Goals
But seek first his kingdom and his righteousness, and all these things will be given to you as well.
The Bible, Matthew 6:33

Make it your ambition to lead a quiet life, to mind your own business and to work with your hands, just as we told you.
The Bible, 1 Thessalonians 4:11

Even the fool knows we can't reach out and touch the stars, but that doesn't keep the wise man from trying.
Author unknown

Only those who attempt the absurd achieve the impossible.
Author unknown

The person who really wants to do something finds a way; the other finds an excuse.
Author unknown

Failure to plan is knowingly planning to fail.
Author unknown

Winning is everything. The only ones who remember when you come second are your wife and your dog.
Author unknown

The world stands aside to let anyone pass who knows where he is going.
Author unknown

Be careful what you set your heart upon – for it will surely be yours.
James Baldwin

We need to learn to set our course by the stars, not by the lights of every passing ship.
Omar Bradley

The aim, if reached or not, makes great the life: try to be Shakespeare, leave the rest to fate.
Robert Browning

To reach the height of our ambition is like trying to reach the rainbow; as we advance it recedes.
Edmund Burke

The past should be a springboard, not a hammock.
Edmond Burke

The longer I live, the stronger becomes my conviction that the truest difference between the success and the failure, between the strong and the weak, between the big and the small man, that separates the boys and the men, is nothing but a powerful aim in life, a purpose once fixed and then death or victory. And no perfect speech or manners, no culture or education, no pull or influence, can make a two-legged creature a man without it.
Thomas Buxton

Attempt great things for God, expect great things from God.
William Carey

Every man is the architect of his own fortune.
Appius Claudius

Love's the frailty of the mind
When 'tis not with ambition join'd.
William Congreve

It's only those who do nothing that make no mistakes.
Joseph Conrad

If you risk nothing, then you risk everything.
Geena Davis

If you can DREAM it,
you can DO it.
Walt Disney

Try not to become a man of success but rather try to become a man of value.
Albert Einstein

Hitch your wagon to a star.
Ralph Waldo Emerson

Ambition is the germ from which all growth of nobleness proceeds.
Thomas Dunn English

You'll miss 100% of all the shots you don't take.
Wayne Gretzsky

I am only one, but still I am one. I cannot do everything, but still I can do something; I will not refuse to do the something I can do.
Helen Keller

Only those who dare to fail greatly can ever achieve greatly.
Robert F. Kennedy

Set yourself earnestly to discover what you are made to do, and then give yourself passionately to the doing of it.
Martin Luther King, Jr.

One desire has been the ruling passion of my life. One high motive has acted like a spur upon my mind and soul. And sooner than that I should seek escape from the sacred necessity that is laid upon me, let the breath of life fail me. It is this: That in spite of all worldly opposition, God's holy ordinances shall be established again in the home, in the school and in the State for the good of the people; to carve as it were into the conscience of the nation the ordinances of the Lord, to which Bible and Creation bear witness, until the nation pays homage again to God.
Abraham Kuyper

If you here stop and ask yourselves why you are not as pious as the early Christians were, your own heart will tell you that it is neither through ignorance nor through inability, but purely because you never thoroughly intended it.
William Law

As Christians, I challenge you. Have a great aim – have a high standard – make Jesus your ideal…make Him an ideal not merely to be admired but also to be followed.
Eric Liddell

If you would hit the mark, you must aim a little above it.
Henry Wadsworth Longfellow

Not failure, but low aim, is crime.
James Russell Lowell

It's a funny thing about life; if you refuse to accept anything but the best, you very often get it.
Somerset Maugham

Lord, grant that I may always desire more than I accomplish.
Michelangelo

Every French soldier carries in his cartridge-pouch the baton of a marshal of France.
Napoleon

It is not enough to aim, you must hit.
Italian proverb

The crowd, the world, and sometimes even the grave, step aside for the man who knows where he's going, but pushes the aimless drifter aside.
Latin proverb

May I know thee more clearly,
Love thee more dearly,

And follow thee more nearly,
Day by day.
Richard of Chichester

If you think you're too small to have an
impact, try going to bed with a mosquito
in the room.
Anita Roddick

You must do the thing you think you
cannot do.
Eleanor Roosevelt

I had rather attempt something great
and fail, than to attempt nothing at all
and succeed.
Dr Robert Schuller

Unless you know what you want, you can't
ask for it.
Jeanne Segal

I would rather be Head of the Ragged
Schools than have the command of armies.
Lord Shaftesbury

The best ambition is: Who shall be the
servant of all.
C.H. Spurgeon

Keep away from people who try to belittle
your ambitions. Small people always do
that, but the really great make you feel that
you, too, can become great.
Mark Twain

It's not the size of the dog in the fight, it's
the size of the fight in the dog.
Mark Twain

Opportunities multiply as they are seized.
Sun Tzu

Think like a queen. A queen is not afraid
to fail. Failure is another stepping-stone
to greatness.
Oprah Winfrey

Ambition, Warnings against
Do nothing out of selfish ambition.
The Bible, Philippians 2:3

Ambition can creep as well as soar.
Edmund Burke

Accursed ambition,
How dearly I have bought you.
John Dryden

There is no peace in ambition
Madame de Pompadour

Cromwell, I charge thee, fling away
ambition:
By that sin fell the angels. How can man
then,
The image of his maker, hope to win by it?
William Shakespeare, Henry VIII

Love and meekness, lord,
Become a churchman better than
ambition.
William Shakespeare, Henry VIII

Who soars too near the sun
    with golden wings,
Melts them; to ruin his own
    fortune brings.
William Shakespeare

Ambition is an enemy to peace in the
church. "Diotrephes loves to have the
pre-eminence," and that fellow has spoiled
many a happy church.
C.H. Spurgeon

Ambition often puts men upon doing the
meanest offices: so climbing is performed
in the same posture with creeping.
Jonathan Swift

Ambition destroys its possessor.
The Talmud

Oh, beware! Do not seek to be something!
Let me be nothing, and Christ be all in all.
John Wesley

America
The general principles on which the
fathers achieved independence were the
general principles of Christianity.
John Adams

The highest glory of the American Revolution was this: it connected, in one indissoluble bond the principles of civil government with the principles of Christianity.
John Adams

America's future will be determined by the home and the school. The child becomes largely what he is taught; hence we must watch what we teach, and how we live.
Jane Addams

Good Americans, when they die, go to Paris.
Thomas Gold Appleton

Americans are probably more interested in spiritual matters than they have been in any other time in the past forty years.
George Barna, president of the Barna Research Group

America is the country where you buy a lifetime supply of aspirin for one dollar and use it up in two weeks.
John Barrymore

Congress shall make no law respecting an establishment of religion, or prohibiting the free exercise thereof; or abridging the freedom of speech, or of the press; or the right of the people peaceably to assemble, and to petition the government for a redress of grievances.
Bill of Rights

I am willing to love all mankind, except an American.
James Boswell

American secular tradition sneers at Constantine, because he began the process of creating a Christian state. The American evangelical tradition disdains him, because he established Catholicism as the empire's official faith (a Catholicism not yet Roman, of course). Americans speak with relief rather than with regret of being Post-Constantinian.
Harold O.J. Brown

America is the only nation in the world that is founded on a creed. That creed is set forth with dogmatic and even theological lucidity in the Declaration of Independence.
G.K. Chesterton

Our Founding Fathers believed devoutly that there was a God and that the inalienable rights of man were rooted not in the state, nor the legislature, nor in any other human power – but in God alone.
Tom Clark, Associate Justice of the U.S. Supreme Court

There is nothing wrong with America that cannot be cured by what is right with America.
Bill Clinton

We the People of the United States, in Order to form a more perfect Union, establish Justice, insure domestic Tranquility, provide for the common defense, promote the general Welfare, and secure the Blessings of Liberty to ourselves and our Posterity, do ordain and establish this Constitution for the United States of America.
The Constitution of the United States of America, 1787

America seeks no earthly empire built on blood and force.
No ambition, no temptation, lures her to thought of foreign dominions.
The legions which she sends forth are armed, not with the sword, but with the cross.
The higher state to which she seeks the allegiance of all mankind is not of human, but of divine origin.
She cherishes no other purpose save to merit the favor of Almighty God.
Calvin Coolidge

We hold these truths to be self-evident, that all men are created equal; that they are endowed by their Creator with certain inalienable rights; that among these are life, liberty, and the pursuit of happiness...
For the support of this declaration, with a

firm reliance on the protection of the Divine Providence, we mutually pledge to each other, our lives, our fortunes, and our sacred honor.
The Declaration of Independence

When asked by an anthropologist what the Indians called America before the white man came, an Indian said simply, "Ours."
Vine Deloria, Jr.

Then join in hand, brave Americans all! By uniting we stand, by dividing we fall.
John Dickinson

Too many of us look upon Americans as dollar chasers. This is a cruel libel, even if it is reiterated thoughtlessly by the Americans themselves.
Albert Einstein

I have only one yardstick by which I test every major problem – and that yardstick is: Is it good for America?
Dwight D. Eisenhower

Our abundant plains and mountains would yield little if it were not for the applied skill and energy of Americans working together as fellow citizens bound up in common destiny.
The achievement of brotherhood is the crowning objective of our society.
Dwight D. Eisenhower

The Holy God having by a long and Continual Series of his Afflictive dispensations in and by the present War with the Heathen Natives of this land, written and brought to pass bitter things against his own Covenant people in this wilderness, yet so that we evidently discern that in the midst of his judgements he hath remembered mercy, having remembered his Footstool in the day of his sore displeasure against us for our sins, with many singular Intimations of his Fatherly Compassion, and regard; reserving many of our Towns from Desolation Threatened, and attempted by the Enemy, and giving us especially of late with many of our

Confederates many signal Advantages against them, without such Disadvantage to ourselves as formerly we have been sensible of, if it be the Lord's mercy that we are not consumed, It certainly bespeaks our positive Thankfulness, when our Enemies are in any measure disappointed or destroyed; and fearing the Lord should take notice under so many Intimations of his returning mercy, we should be found an Insensible people, as not standing before Him with Thanksgiving, as well as lading him with our Complaints in the time of pressing Afflictions:
The Council has thought meet to appoint and set apart the 29th day of this instant June, as a day of Solemn Thanksgiving and praise to God for such his Goodness and Favor, many Particulars of which mercy might be Instanced, but we doubt not those who are sensible of God's Afflictions, have been as diligent to espy him returning to us; and that the Lord may behold us as a People offering Praise and thereby glorifying Him; the Council doth commend it to the Respective Ministers, Elders and people of this Jurisdiction; Solemnly and seriously to keep the same Beseeching that being persuaded by the mercies of God we may all, even this whole people offer up our bodies and souls as a living and acceptable Service unto God by Jesus Christ.
The First Thanksgiving Day Proclamation, June 20, 1676

America is a willingness of the heart.
F. Scott Fitzgerald

The best kept secret in America today is that people would rather work hard for something they believe in than live a life of aimless diversion.
John Gardner

The organization of American society is an interlocking system of semi-monopolies notoriously venal, an electorate notoriously unenlightened, misled by a mass media notoriously phony.
Paul Goodman

It cannot be emphasized too strongly or too often that this great nation was founded, not by religionists, but by Christians; not on religions, but on the gospel of Jesus Christ!
Patrick Henry

The Bible is the rock on which our Republic rests.
Andrew Jackson

Indeed, I tremble for my country when I reflect that God is just.
Thomas Jefferson

Freedom of religion, freedom of the press, and freedom of person under the protection of the *habeus corpus*, these are the principles that guided our steps through an age of revolution and reformation.
Thomas Jefferson

The men who have guided the destiny of the United States have found the strength for their tasks by going to their knees. This private unity of public men and their God is an enduring source of reassurance for the people of America.
Lyndon Baines Johnson

If there is one word that describes our form of society in America, it may be the word – voluntary.
Lyndon Baines Johnson

For this is what America is all about. It is the uncrossed desert and the unclimbed ridge. It is the star that is not reached and the harvest that's sleeping in the unplowed ground.
Lyndon Baines Johnson

The cost of freedom is always high, but Americans have always paid it. And one path we shall never choose, and that is the path of surrender, or submission.
John Fitzgerald Kennedy

Now, I say to you today, my friends, even though we face the difficulties of today and tomorrow, I still have a dream. It is a dream deeply rooted in the American dream. I have a dream that one day this nation will rise up and live out the true meaning of its creed: "We hold these truths to be self-evident, that all men are created equal."
Martin Luther King, Jr.

Give me your tired, your poor,
Your huddled masses yearning to breathe
    free,
The wretched refuse of your teeming
    shore.
Send these, the homeless, tempest-tossed
    to me.
I lift my lamp beside the golden door.
Emma Lazarus

Four score and seven years ago our fathers brought forth on this continent, a new nation, conceived in liberty, and dedicated to the proposition that all men are created equal. ... That this nation, under God, shall have a new birth of freedom – and that government of the people, by the people, and for the people, shall not perish from the earth.
Abraham Lincoln

We have forgotten the gracious hand which has preserved us in peace and multiplied and enriched and strengthened us, and have vainly imagined in the deceitfulness of our hearts that all these blessings were produced by some superior wisdom and virtue of our own. Intoxicated with unbroken success, we have become too self sufficient to feel the necessity of redeeming and preserving Grace, too proud to pray to the God that made us.
Abraham Lincoln

Americans never quit.
Douglas MacArthur

In time, the rest of the world will appreciate the demonstration that the American way of life is best. They will then seek for themselves the good life of freedom and prosperity. This will be the greatest impetus toward an end of global conflict. The way to get along with people is to beware

of religious dictums and dogma. The ideal
is to be a nice person and to live by the
Creed of Tolerance. Thus we offend few
people. We live and let live. This is the
American Way.
Catherine Marshall

Unquestionably, there is progress. The
average American now pays out twice as
much in taxes as he formerly got in wages.
H.L. Mencken

The big majority of Americans, who are
comparatively well off, have developed an
ability to have enclaves of people living in
the greatest misery without almost
noticing them.
Gunnar Myrdal

The gospel cannot be preached with truth
and power if it does not challenge the
pretensions and pride, not only of
individuals, but of nations, cultures,
civilizations, economic and political
systems. The good fortune of America and
its power place it under the most grievous
temptations to self-adulation.
Reinhold Niebuhr

If you think the United States has stood
still, who built the largest shopping center
in the world?
Richard M. Nixon

This spot marks the final resting-place of
the Pilgrims of the Mayflower.
In weariness and hunger and in cold,
fighting the wilderness… they here laid the
foundations of a state in which all men for
countless ages should have liberty to
worship God in their own way.
All ye who pass by and see this stone
remember, and dedicate yourselves anew to
the resolution that you will not rest until
this lofty ideal shall have been realized
throughout the earth.
Plymouth Rock Inscription

Americans will put up with anything
provided it doesn't block traffic.
Dan Rather

America has begun a spiritual reawakening.
Faith and hope are being restored.
Americans are turning back to God.
Church attendance is up. Audiences for
religious books and broadcasts are growing.
And I do believe that he has begun to heal
our blessed land.
Ronald Reagan

Above all, we must realize that no arsenal,
or no weapon in the arsenals of the world,
is so formidable as the will and moral
courage of free men and women.
Ronald Reagan

The time has come to turn to God and
reassert our trust in Him for the healing of
America. Our country is in need of and
ready for a spiritual renewal.
Ronald Reagan

So we pray to Him now for the vision to
see our way clearly – to see the way that
leads to a better life for ourselves and for
all our fellow men – to the achievement of
His will to peace on earth.
Franklin D. Roosevelt

When an American says that he loves his
country, he means not only that he loves the
New England hills, the prairies glistening in
the sun, the wide and rising plains, the great
mountains, and the sea.
He means that he loves an inner air, an inner
light in which freedom lives and in which a
man can draw the breath of self-respect.
Adlai Stevenson

In America, anybody can be president.
That's one of the risks you take.
Adlai Stevenson

I sought for the greatness and genius of
America in her commodious harbors and in
her ample rivers, and it was not there.
I sought for the greatness and genius of
America in her fertile fields and boundless
forests, and it was not there.
I sought for the greatness and genius of
America in her rich mines and her vast
world commerce, and it was not there.

I sought for the greatness and genius of America in her public school system and her institutions of learning, and it was not there. I sought for the genius and greatness of America in her democratic congress and her matchless constitution, and it was not there. Not until I went into the churches of America and heard her pulpits flame with righteousness did I understand the secret of her genius and power.
America is great because America is good, and if America ever ceases to be good, America will cease to be great.
Alexis de Tocqueville

The fundamental basis of this nation's laws was given to Moses on the Mount. The fundamental basis of our Bill of Rights comes from the teachings we get from Exodus and St. Matthew, from Isaiah and St. Paul. I don't think we emphasize that enough these days. If we don't have a proper fundamental moral background, we will finally end up with a totalitarian government which does not believe in rights for anybody except the State!
Harry S. Truman

Our religious faith gives us the answer to the false beliefs of Communism ... I have the feeling that God has created us and brought us to our present position of power and strength for some great purpose.
Harry S. Truman

This is America. We can do anything here.
Ted Turner

It is by the fortune of God that, in this country, we have three benefits: freedom of speech, freedom of thought, and the wisdom never to use either.
Mark Twain

In America, we hurry – which is well; but when the day's work is done, we go on thinking of losses and gains, we plan for the morrow, we even carry our business cares to bed with us... we burn up our energies with these excitements, and either

die early or drop into a lean and mean old age at a time of life which they call a man's prime in Europe ... What a robust people, what a nation of thinkers we might be, if we would only lay ourselves on the shelf occasionally and renew our edges!
Mark Twain

America is a land where a citizen will cross the ocean to fight for democracy – and won't cross the street to vote in a national election.
Bill Vaughan

Do not ever let anyone claim to be a true American patriot if they ever attempt to separate Religion from politics.
George Washington

America has no north, no south, no east, no west. The sun rises over the hills and sets over the mountains, the compass just points up and down, and we can laugh now at the absurd notion of there being a north and a south. We are one and undivided.
Sam Watkins

If there is anything in my thoughts or style to commend, the credit is due to my parents for instilling in me an early love of the Scriptures. If we abide by the principles taught in the Bible, our country will go on prospering and to prosper; but if we and our posterity neglect its instructions and authority, no man can tell how sudden a catastrophe may overwhelm us and bury all our glory in profound obscurity.
Daniel Webster

America was born a Christian nation. America was born to exemplify that devotion to the elements of righteousness which are derived from the revelations of Holy Scriptures. Ladies and gentlemen, I have a very simple thing to ask of you. I ask of every man and woman in this audience that from this night on they will realize that part of the destiny of America lies in their daily perusal of this great book of revelations. That if they would see

America free and pure they will make their own spirits free and pure by this baptism of the Holy Scripture.
Woodrow Wilson

American Presidents, *Quotes of*

A

Abortion
The cemetery of the victims of human cruelty in our century is extended to include yet another vast cemetery, that of the unborn.
Ronald Reagan

Abortion is advocated only by persons who have themselves been born.
Ronald Reagan

Achievement
You can do what you have to do, and sometimes you can do it even better than you think you can.
Jimmy Carter

Action
The probability that we may fail in the struggle ought not to deter us from the support of a cause we believe to be just.
Abraham Lincoln

Take a method and try it. If it fails, admit it frankly, and try another. But by all means, try something.
Franklin Delano Roosevelt

Adversity
Only in winter can you tell which trees are truly green. Only when the winds of adversity blow can you tell whether an individual or a country has steadfastness.
John F. Kennedy

America
The highest glory of the American Revolution is this: it connected in one

indissoluble bond the principles of civil government with the principles of Christianity.
John Adams

The general principles on which the fathers achieved independence were the general principles of Christianity.
John Adams

There is nothing wrong with America that cannot be cured by what is right with America.
Bill Clinton

I have only one yardstick by which I test every major problem – and that yardstick is: Is it good for America?
Dwight D. Eisenhower

Our abundant plains and mountains would yield little if it were not for the applied skill and energy of Americans working together as fellow citizens bound up in common destiny.
The achievement of brotherhood is the crowning objective of our society.
Dwight D. Eisenhower

That book [the Bible], sir, is the rock on which our republic rests.
Andrew Jackson

Freedom of religion, freedom of the press, and freedom of person under the protection of the *habeus corpus*, these are the principles that guided our steps through an age of revolution and reformation.
Thomas Jefferson

Indeed, I tremble for my country when I reflect that God is just.
Thomas Jefferson

The men who have guided the destiny of the United States have found the strength for their tasks by going to their knees. This private unity of public men and their God is an enduring source of reassurance for the people of America.
Lyndon B. Johnson

If there is one word that describes our form of society in America, it may be the word – voluntary.
Lyndon B. Johnson

For this is what America is all about. It is the uncrossed desert and the unclimbed ridge. It is the star that is not reached and the harvest that's sleeping in the unplowed ground.
Lyndon B. Johnson

The cost of freedom is always high, but Americans have always paid it. And one path we shall never choose, and that is the path of surrender, or submission.
John Fitzgerald Kennedy

Let us at all times remember that all American citizens are brothers of a common country, and should dwell together in bonds of fraternal feeling.
Abraham Lincoln

Four score and seven years ago our fathers brought forth on this continent, a new nation, conceived in liberty, and dedicated to the proposition that all men are created equal. ... That this nation, under God, shall have a new birth of freedom – and that government of the people, by the people, and for the people, shall not perish from the earth.
Abraham Lincoln

We have forgotten the gracious hand which has preserved us in peace and multiplied and enriched and strengthened us, and have vainly imagined in the deceitfulness of our hearts that all these blessings were produced by some superior wisdom and virtue of our own. Intoxicated with unbroken success, we have become too self sufficient to feel the necessity of redeeming and preserving Grace, too proud to pray to the God that made us.
Abraham Lincoln

If you think the United States has stood still, who built the largest shopping center in the world?
Richard M. Nixon

America has begun a spiritual reawakening. Faith and hope are being restored. Americans are turning back to God. Church attendance is up. Audiences for religious books and broadcasts are growing. And I do believe that he has begun to heal our blessed land.
Ronald Reagan

The time has come to turn to God and reassert our trust in Him for the healing of America. Our country is in need of and ready for a spiritual renewal.
Ronald Reagan

Above all, we must realize that no arsenal, or no weapon in the arsenals of the world, is so formidable as the will and moral courage of free men and women.
Ronald Reagan

So we pray to Him now for the vision to see our way clearly – to see the way that leads to a better life for ourselves and for all our fellow men – to the achievement of His will to peace on earth.
Franklin D. Roosevelt

In America, anybody can be president. That's one of the risks you take.
Adlai Stevenson

When an American says that he loves his country, he means not only that he loves the New England hills, the prairies glistening in the sun, the wide and rising plains, the great mountains, and the sea.
He means that he loves an inner air, an inner light in which freedom lives and in which a man can draw the breath of self-respect.
Adlai Stevenson

The fundamental basis of this nation's laws was given to Moses on the Mount. The fundamental basis of our Bill of Rights comes from the teachings we get from Exodus and St. Matthew, from Isaiah and St. Paul. I don't think we emphasize that enough these days. If we don't have a proper fundamental moral background, we will finally end up with a totalitarian

government which does not believe in rights for anybody except the State!
Harry S. Truman

Our religious faith gives us the answer to the false beliefs of Communism … I have the feeling that God has created us and brought us to our present position of power and strength for some great purpose.
President Harry Truman

Do not ever let anyone claim to be a true American patriot if they ever attempt to separate Religion from politics.
George Washington

America was born a Christian nation. America was born to exemplify that devotion to the elements of righteousness which are derived from the revelations of Holy Scriptures. Ladies and gentlemen, I have a very simple thing to ask of you. I ask of every man and woman in this audience that from this night on they will realize that part of the destiny of America lies in their daily perusal of this great book of revelations. That if they would see America free and pure they will make their own spirits free and pure by this baptism of the Holy Scripture.
Woodrow Wilson

Art

We must never forget that art is not a form of propaganda, it is a form of truth.
John Fitzgerald Kennedy

Atheism

I can see how it might be possible for a man to look down upon the earth and be an atheist, but I cannot conceive how he could look up into the heavens and say there is no God.
Abraham Lincoln

B

Bereavement

Grief drives men into the habits of serious reflection, sharpens the understanding and softens the heart.
John Adams, letter to Thomas Jefferson, 6 May 1816

Being

Whatever you are, be a good one.
Abraham Lincoln

Belief

I can see how it might be possible for a man to look down upon the earth and be an atheist, but I cannot conceive how he could look up into the heavens and say there is no God.
Abraham Lincoln

Bible

The Bible is the authoritative Word of God and contains all truth.
Bill Clinton

I believe the Bible is the best gift God has given to man.
Abraham Lincoln

All the good from the Savior of the world is communicated through this book; but for the book we could not know right from wrong. All the things desirable to man are contained in it.
Abraham Lincoln

Bible, Bible study

Thorough knowledge of the Bible is worth more than a college education.
Theodore Roosevelt

Bible, Importance of

The first and almost the only book deserving of universal attention is the Bible. I speak as a man of the world.
Thomas Jefferson

Bible, Influence of

So great is my veneration for the Bible that the earlier my children begin to read it, the more confident my hope that they will prove useful citizens, and respectful members of society.
John Quincy Adams

Bible reading

When you have read the Bible, you will know it is the word of God, because you will have found it the key to your own

heart, your own happiness and your duty.
Woodrow Wilson

C

Change
Those who make peaceful revolution impossible will make violent revolution inevitable.
John F. Kennedy

Change is the law. And those who look only to the past or present are certain to miss the future.
John F. Kennedy

Character
Die when I may, I want it said by those who knew me best that I always plucked a thistle and planted a flower where I thought a flower would grow.
Abraham Lincoln

Alike for the nation and the individual, the one indispensable requisite is character.
Theodore Roosevelt

Character is a by-product; it is produced in the great manufacture of daily duty.
Woodrow Wilson

Christ, Words of
I hold the precepts of Jesus as delivered by Himself, to be the most pure, benevolent and sublime which have ever been preached to man…
Thomas Jefferson

Christianity
All the world would be Christian if they were taught the pure Gospel of Christ!
Thomas Jefferson

Comfort
To ease another's heartache is to forget one's own.
Abraham Lincoln

Conscience
Labor to keep alive in your breast that little spark of celestial fire, called conscience.
George Washington

Cover up
There will be no whitewash at the White House.
Richard Mulhoure Nixon

Crisis
When written in Chinese, the word "crisis" is composed of two characters – one represents danger and the other represents opportunity.
John F. Kennedy

D

Death, Facing
John Quincy Adams at the age of ninety-four when asked how he felt one morning, said, "Quite well. Quite well. But the house I live in is not so good."

Decisions
In any moment of decision the best thing you can do is the right thing, the next best thing is the wrong thing, and the worst thing you can do is nothing.
Theodore Roosevelt

Defeat
A man is not finished when he is defeated. He is finished when he quits.
Richard Mulhouse Nixon

Democracy
Democracy is, first and foremost, a spiritual force, it is built upon a spiritual basis – and on a belief in God and an observance of moral principle. And in the long run only the church can provide that basis. Our founder knew this truth – and we will neglect it at our peril.
Harry Truman

Discernment
A president's hardest task is not to do what is right, but to know what is right.
Lyndon B. Johnson

E

Empathy
To ease another's heartache is to forget one's own.
Abraham Lincoln

Enemies

The best way to destroy an enemy is to make him a friend.
Abraham Lincoln

Error

Error of opinion may be tolerated where reason is left free to combat it.
Thomas Jefferson

F

Failure

Success has many fathers, but failure is an orphan; no one wants to claim it.
John F. Kennedy

The probability that we may fail in the struggle ought not to deter us from the support of a cause we believe to be just.
Abraham Lincoln

It is not the critic who counts; not the man who points out how the strong man stumbles, or where the doer of deeds could have done them better. The credit belongs to the man who is actually in the arena, whose face is marred by dust and sweat and blood; who strives valiantly; who errs, and comes short again and again, because there is no effort without error and shortcoming; but who does actually strive to do the deeds; who knows the great enthusiasms, the great devotions; who spends himself in a worthy cause; who at the best knows in the end the triumph of high achievement, and who at the worst, if he fails, at least fails while daring greatly, so that his place shall never be with those cold and timid souls who know neither victory nor defeat.
Theodore Roosevelt

Failure, Attitude to

My great concern is not whether you have failed, but whether you are content with your failure.
Abraham Lincoln

Faith

Let us have faith that right makes might; and in that faith let us to the end dare to do our duty as we understand it.
Abraham Lincoln

Fear

The only thing we have to fear is fear itself – nameless, unreasoning, unjustified, terror which paralyzes needed efforts to convert retreat into advance.
Franklin D. Roosevelt

Fitness

Physical fitness is not only one of the most important keys to a healthy body, it is the basis of dynamic and creative intellectual activity. The relationship between the soundness of the body and the activities of the mind is subtle and complex. Much is not yet understood. But we do know what the Greeks knew: that intelligence and skill can only function at the peak of their capacity when the body is healthy and strong; that hardy spirits and tough minds usually inhabit sound bodies.
John F. Kennedy

Force

Force is all-conquering, but its victories are short-lived.
Abraham Lincoln

Forgiving

Forgive your enemies, but never forget their names.
John F. Kennedy

Freedom

Freedom is indivisible. When one man is enslaved, all are not free.
John Fitzgerald Kennedy

The unity of freedom has never relied on uniformity of opinion.
John Fitzgerald Kennedy

Those who deny freedom to others deserve it not for themselves.
Abraham Lincoln

Freedom prospers when religion is vibrant and the rule of law under God is acknowledged.
Ronald Reagan.

Friendship
True friendship is a plant of low growth, and must undergo and withstand the shocks of adversity before it is entitled to the appellation
George Washington

Friendship is the only cement that will ever hold the world together.
Woodrow Wilson

G
God, Fatherhood of
Our doctrine of equality and liberty and humanity comes from our belief in the brotherhood of man, through the fatherhood of God.
Calvin Coolidge

God's provision
Providence has at all times been my only dependence, for all other resources seem to have failed us.
George Washington

Good deeds
Good deeds are such things that no man is saved for them, nor without them.
Thomas Adams

Government
That government is best which governs the least, because its people discipline themselves.
Thomas Jefferson

Now the trumpet summons us again – not as a call to bear arms, though arms we need – not as a call to battle, though embattled we are – but a call to bear the burden of a long twilight struggle year in and year out, "rejoicing in hope, patient in tribulation" – a struggle against the common enemies of man: tyranny, poverty and war itself.
John F. Kennedy

It is impossible to rightly govern the world without God and the Bible.
George Washington

Graham, Billy
America's pastor.
George Bush

A counterfeit.
Harry Truman

H
Happiness
Happiness is the full use of your powers along lines of excellence.
John F. Kennedy

People are just about as happy as they make up their minds to be.
Abraham Lincoln

Hate
Always remember that others may hate you, but those who hate you don't win unless you hate them. And then you destroy yourself.
Richard M. Nixon

Honesty
Honesty is the first chapter of the book of wisdom.
Thomas Jefferson

Humanity, Nature of
Human action can be modified to some extent, but human nature cannot be changed.
Abraham Lincoln

J
Justice
I tremble for my country when I reflect that God is just.
Thomas Jefferson

K
Kindness
Human kindness has never weakened the stamina or softened the fiber of a free people. A nation does not have to be cruel to be tough.
Franklin D. Roosevelt

L
Laughter
With the fearful strain that is on me day and night, if I did not laugh, I should die.
Abraham Lincoln

Law

The propitious smiles of Heaven can never be expected on a nation that disregards the eternal rules of order and right which Heaven itself has ordained.

George Washington

Learning

You do well to learn above all the religion of Jesus Christ.

George Washington

Liberty

The God who gave us life, gave us liberty at the same time.

Thomas Jefferson

Lies

He who permits himself to tell a lie once, finds it much easier to do it a second and third time, till at length it becomes habitual; he tells lies without attending to it, and truth without the world's believing him. This falsehood of the tongue leads to that of the heart, and in time depraves all its good dispositions.

Thomas Jefferson

Living

You cannot bring about prosperity by discouraging thrift.
You cannot strengthen the weak by weakening the strong.
You cannot help the wage earner by pulling down the wage payer.
You cannot further brotherhood by encouraging class hatred.
You cannot help the poor by destroying the rich.
You cannot establish sound security on borrowed money.
You cannot keep out of trouble by spending more than you earn.
You cannot build character and courage by taking away man's initiative and independence.
You cannot help men permanently by doing for them what they could and should do for themselves.

Abraham Lincoln

M

Money

You can see what God thinks of money when you see the people he gives it to.

Abraham Lincoln

Morality

Give up money, give up fame, give up science, give up the earth itself and all it contains, rather than do an immoral act.

Thomas Jefferson

Lord, give us faith that right makes might.

Abraham Lincoln

P

Parenting

There is only one way to bring up a child in the way he should go and that is to travel that way yourself.

Abraham Lincoln

The tasks connected with the home are the fundamental tasks of humanity.

Theodore Roosevelt

Patience

Patience and perseverence have a magical effect before which difficulties disappear and obstacles vanish.

John Quincy Adams

Peace

But peace does not rest in the charters and covenants alone. It lies in the hearts and minds of all people. So let us not rest all our hopes on parchment and on paper, let us strive to build peace, a desire for peace, a willingness to work for peace in the hearts and minds of all of our people. I believe that we can. I believe the problems of human destiny are not beyond the reach of human beings.

John F. Kennedy

The real differences around the world today are not between Jews and Arabs; Protestants and Catholics; Muslims, Croats, and Serbs. The real differences are between those who embrace peace and those who would destroy it. Between those who look to the future and those who cling to the past. Between those

who open their arms and those who are determined to clench their fists.
Bill Clinton

Perseverence
Nothing in the world can take the place of persistence. Talent will not; nothing is more common than unsuccessful individuals with talent. Genius will not; unrewarded genius is almost a proverb. Education will not; the world is full of educated derelicts. Persistence and determination alone are omnipotent.
Calvin Coolidge

I am a slow walker, but I never walk backwards.
Abraham Lincoln

Perseverence to the end
With malice toward none; with charity for all; with firmness in the right, as God gives us to see the right – let us strive on to finish the work we are in.
Abraham Lincoln

Persistence
When you get to the end of your rope, tie a knot and hang on.
Franklin D. Roosevelt

Politics
You can't divorce religious belief and public service ... I've never detected any conflict between God's will and my political duty. If you violate one, you violate the other.
Jimmy Carter

When a man assumes a public trust, he should consider himself as public property.
Thomas Jefferson

You can fool all the people some of the time, and some of the people all the time, but you cannot fool all the people all the time.
Abraham Lincoln

Power
Nearly all men can stand adversity, but if you want to test a man's character, give

him power.
Abraham Lincoln

The essence of Government is power; and power, lodged as it must be in human hands, will ever be liable to abuse.
James Madison

Principles
We must adjust to changing times and still hold to unchanging principles.
Jimmy Carter, quoting his high school teacher Julia Coleman

Progress
You're not very smart if you're not a little kinder and wiser than yesterday.
Abraham Lincoln

Proverbs
Mankind would lose half its wisdom built up over the centuries if it lost its great sayings. They contain the best parts of the best books.
Thomas Jefferson

Any reading is better than none, but I prefer the book of the century rather than the book of the week or any cheap novel. Better still the book of four centuries – the book of proverbs.
Theodore Roosevelt

I use all the brains I have and borrow all I can from the classics and wise sayings.
Thomas Woodrow Wilson

S
Security
Those who desire to give up Freedom in order to gain Security, will not have, nor do they deserve, either one.
Thomas Jefferson

Selfishness
The things that will destroy America are peace at any price, prosperity at any cost, safety first instead of duty first, the love of soft living, and the getting-rich-quick theory of life.
Theodore Roosevelt

Service

No man was ever honored for what he received. Honor has been the reward for what he gave.
Calvin Coolidge

Do what you can, with what you have, where you are.
Theodore Roosevelt

The object of love is to serve, not to win.
Woodrow Wilson

Single-mindedness

You can have anything you want – if you want it badly enough. You can be anything you want to be, do anything you set out to accomplish if you hold to that desire with singleness of purpose.
Abraham Lincoln

Slavery

Whenever I hear anyone arguing for slavery, I feel a strong impulse to see it tried on him personally.
Abraham Lincoln

Sneer

It is as hard to do your duty when men are sneering at you as when they are shooting at you.
Woodrow Wilson

Spirituality

I doubt if there is any problem – political or economic – that will not melt before the fire of a spiritual awakening.
Franklin Roosevelt

T

Tact

Tact is the ability to describe others as they see themselves.
Abraham Lincoln

Ten Commandments

We have staked the whole of all our political institutions upon the capacity of mankind for self-government, upon the capacity of each and all of us to govern ourselves, to control ourselves, to sustain ourselves according to the Ten Commandments of God.
James Madison

Troubles

If you see ten troubles coming down the road, you can be sure that nine will run into the ditch before they reach you.
Calvin Coolidge

Truth

Nearly everyone will lie to you given the right circumstances.
Bill Clinton

There is no truth existing which I fear, or would wish unknown to the whole world.
Thomas Jefferson

Let us begin by committing ourselves to the truth – to see it like it is, and tell it like it is – to find the truth, to speak the truth, and to live the truth.
Richard M. Nixon

U

Understanding

If we could first know where we are and whither we are tending, we could then better judge what to do and how to do it.
Abraham Lincoln

W

Wisdom

I don't think much of a man who is not wiser today than he was yesterday.
Abraham Lincoln

Work

All growth depends upon activity. There is no development physically or intellectually without effort, and effort means work. Work is not a curse; it is the prerogative of intelligence, the only means to adulthood, and the measure of civilization.
Calvin Coolidge

I find that the harder I work, the more luck I seem to have.
Thomas Jefferson

They say hard work never killed anyone, but I figure: why take the chance?
Ronald Reagan

Worry
Worry, the interest paid by those who borrow trouble.
George Washington

Amusement
If those who are the enemies of innocent amusements had the direction of the world, they would take away the spring, and youth, the former from the year, the latter from human life.
Honoré de Balzac

Amusement to an observing mind is study.
Benjamin Disraeli
You can't live on amusement. It is the froth on water – an inch deep and then the mud.
George MacDonald

The mind ought sometimes to be diverted, that it may return the better to thinking.
Phaedrus

The real character of a man is found out by his amusements.
Joshua Reynolds

Life would be tolerable but for its amusements.
George Bernard Shaw

This is the age of excessive amusement. Everybody craves for it, like a baby for its rattle.
C.H. Spurgeon

Anabaptism
See Baptism, Infant

Analysis
He suffered from paralysis by analysis.
Author unknown

Anarchy
In those days there was no king in Israel:

every man did that which was right in his own eyes.
The Bible, Judges 21:25 KJV

Ancestry
It is of no consequence of what parents a man is born, so he be man of merit.
Horace

Birth is nothing where virtue is not.
Jean-Baptiste Molière

Whoever serves his country well has no need of ancestors.
François de Voltaire

Angels
See also: Angles
And the angels who did not keep their positions of authority but abandoned their own home – these he has kept in darkness, bound with everlasting chains for judgment on the great Day.
The Bible, Jude 6

But if these beings [angels] guard you, they do so because they have been summoned by your prayers.
Ambrose

An angel can illumine the thought and mind of man by strengthening the power of vision, and by bringing within his reach some truth which the angel himself contemplates.
Thomas Aquinas

Beside each believer stands an angel as protector and shepherd leading him to life.
Basil the Great

If we would be duly wise, we must renounce those vain babblings of idle men, concerning the nature, ranks, and number of angels, without any authority from the Word of God.
John Calvin

In Scripture we uniformly read that angels are heavenly spirits, whose obedience and ministry God employs to execute all the

purposes which he has decreed, and hence their name as being a kind of intermediate messengers to manifest his will to men.
John Calvin

Angels being the ministers appointed to execute the commands of God, must, of course, be admitted to be his creatures, but to stir up questions concerning the time or order in which they were created, bespeaks more perverseness than industry.
John Calvin

Whether or not each believer has a single angel assigned to him for his defense, I dare not positively affirm.
John Calvin

Angels can fly because they take themselves lightly.
G. K. Chesterton

They, above all, are pre-eminently worthy of the name Angel because they first receive the Divine Light, and through them are transmitted to us the revelations which are above us.
Dionysius the Areopagite

[Some of the "advanced" theologians in old Rowland Hill's day tried to shake the old man's faith by assuring him that there were really no such beings as angels, and that they were simply "Oriental metaphors." Hill replied:]
Very well, then it was a company of Oriental metaphors that sang at the birth of Christ; and it was an Oriental metaphor that slew 185,000 of Sennacherib's army in a single night; and it was an Oriental metaphor that appeared to Peter in prison and knocked the chains off his hand, and led him through the streets. Truly these Oriental metaphors are wonderful things.
Rowland Hill

In Scripture the visitation of an angel is always alarming; it has to begin by saying "Fear not." The Victorian angel looks as if it were going to say, "There, there."
C.S. Lewis

An angel is a spiritual creature created by God without a body for the service of Christendom and the church.
Martin Luther

Millions of spiritual creatures walk the earth Unseen, both when we wake and when we sleep.
John Milton.

The word "Angel" simply means "messenger." If angels are messengers, then someone, somewhere must be sending a message.
Dan Schaeffer

Angels are bright still, though the brightest fell.
William Shakespeare

I heard a soft melodious voice, more pure and harmonious than any I had heard with my ears before; I believed it was the voice of an angel who spake to the other angels.
John Woolman

Anger
See also: Anger, Positive views of;
Anger, Righteous
A quick-tempered man does foolish things.
The Bible, Proverbs 14:17

A patient man has great understanding, but a quick-tempered man displays folly.
The Bible, Proverbs 14:29

A gentle answer turns away wrath, but a harsh word stirs up anger.
The Bible, Proverbs 15:1

Better a patient man than a warrior, a man who controls his temper than one who takes a city.
The Bible, Proverbs 16:32

A fool gives full vent to his anger, but a wise man keeps himself under control.
The Bible, Proverbs 29:11

My dear brothers, take note of this: Everyone should be quick to listen, slow to

speak and slow to become angry, for man's anger does not bring about the righteous life that God desires.
The Bible, James 1:19-20

"In your anger do not sin": do not let the sun go down while you are still angry.
The Bible, Ephesians 4:26

For every minute of anger, you lose 60 seconds of happiness!
Author unknown

Never answer an angry word with an angry word. It's always the second remark that starts the trouble.
Author unknown

Keep cool; anger is not an argument.
Author unknown

Anger blows out the lamp of the mind. It's a child's reaction to an adult situation.
Author unknown

The two best times to keep your mouth shut are when you're swimming and when you're angry.
Author unknown

The trouble with letting off steam is that it only gets you into more hot water.
Author unknown

Anger is one letter short of danger.
Author unknown

The wind of anger blows out the lamp of intelligence.
Author unknown

To seek to extinguish anger utterly is but a bravery of the Stoics. We have better oracles: "Be angry, but sin not." "Let not the sun go down upon your wrath."
Francis Bacon

Never forget what a man says to you when he is angry.
Henry Ward Beecher

Life appears to me too short to be spent in nursing animosity or registering wrong.
Charlotte Brontë

Holding on to anger is like grasping a hot coal with the intent of throwing it at someone else; you are the one who gets burned.
Buddha

An angry man opens his mouth and shuts up his eyes.
Cato

No matter how just your words may be, you ruin everything when you speak with anger.
John Chrysostom

Just as the winds whip up the sea, so does anger stir confusion in the mind.
John Climacus

Love of humiliation is the cure for anger.
John Climacus

As long as anger lives, she continues to be the fruitful mother of many unhappy children.
John Climacus

There is no greater obstacle to the presence of the Spirit in us than anger.
John Climacus

An angry man is full of poison.
Confucius

Be not angry, for anger leadeth to murder, nor jealous nor contentious nor wrathful; for of all these things murders are engendered.
Didache

The sun must not set upon anger, much less will I let the sun set upon the anger of God towards me.
John Donne

No form of vice, not worldliness, not greed of gold, not drunkenness itself, does more to un-Christianize society than evil temper. For embittering life, for breaking up communities, for destroying the most

sacred relationships, for devastating homes, for withering up men and women, for taking the bloom off childhood; in short, for sheer gratuitous misery-producing power, this influence stands alone.
Henry Drummond

Beware the fury of a patient man.
John Dryden

We get angry with others in direct proportion that we are angry with ourselves.
Albert Ellis

Whenever you are angry, be assured that it is not only a present evil, but that you have increased a habit.
Epictetus

There was never an angry man that thought his anger unjust.
Francis de Sales

Whatever is begun in anger ends in shame.
Benjamin Franklin

Anger is never without a reason but seldom a good one.
Benjamin Franklin

Anger is the fever and frenzy of the soul.
Thomas Fuller

Anger is short-lived in a good man.
Thomas Fuller

Anger and intolerance are the twin enemies of correct understanding.
Mahatma Gandhi

You cannot acquire the gift of peace if by your anger you destroy the peace of the Lord.
Gregory the Great

Anger is seldom without argument but seldom with a good one.
Lord Halifax

Wise anger is like fire from a flint: there is great ado to get it out; and when it does

come, it is out again immediately.
Matthew Henry

Angry temper is in the first place foolish, fickle and senseless; then from foolishness is engendered bitterness, and from bitterness wrath, and from wrath anger, and from anger spite; then spite being composed of all these evil elements becometh a great sin and incurable.
Hermas

Anger is short madness.
Horace

My life is in the hands of any fool who makes me lose my temper.
Joseph Hunter

Anger blows out the lamp of the mind.
Robert Green Ingersoll

The best is not to be angry; the next is not to show in words or countenance your anger.
Thomas Lupset

I never work better than when I am inspired by anger; for when I am angry, I can write, pray, and preach well, for then my whole temperament is quickened, my understanding sharpened, and all mundane vexations and temptations depart.
Martin Luther

Everything that is in agreement with our personal desires seems true. Everything that is not puts us in a rage.
André Maurois

Everything a man does in anger will in the end be found to have been done wrong.
Meander

He who angers you, conquers you.
Proverb

If you are patient in one moment of anger, you will avoid one hundred days of sorrow.
Chinese proverb

The best answer to anger is silence.
German proverb

He that overcomes his anger conquers his greatest enemy.
Latin proverb

Anger is as a stone cast into a nest of wasps.
Malabar proverb

Little folk are soon angry.
Scottish proverb

Anger begins with folly, and ends with repentance.
Pythagoras

When anger spreads through the breast, guard thy tongue from barking idly.
Sappho

The best remedy for anger is a little time for thought.
Seneca

Anger, if not restrained, is frequently more hurtful to us than the injury that provokes it.
Seneca

Heat not a furnace for your foe so hot
That it do singe yourself.
William Shakespeare, Henry VIII

Be not angry that you cannot make others as you wish them to be, since you cannot make yourself as you wish to be.
Thomas à Kempis

Anger, Positive view of

Anybody can become angry – that is easy; but to be angry with the right person, and to the right degree, and at the right time, and for the right purpose, and in the right way – that is not within everybody's power and is not easy.
Aristotle

The dove loves when it quarrels;
the wolf hates when it flatters.
Augustine of Hippo

A man is as big as the things that make him angry.
Winston Churchill

Anger is one of the sinews of the soul. He who lacks it hath a maimed mind.
Thomas Fuller

Anger, Righteous

So he made a whip out of cords, and drove all from the temple area, both sheep and cattle; he scattered the coins of the money changers and overturned their tables. To those who sold doves he said, "Get these out of here! How dare you turn my Father's house into a market!"
The Bible, John 2:15-16

A man who does not know how to be angry does not know how to be good. And a man that does not know how to be shaken to his heart's core with indignation over things evil is either a fungus or a wicked man.
Henry Ward Beecher

Angles

Tradition says that Gregory the Great (c. 540-604), before he became pope, saw a group of young Anglo-Saxon slaves in the marketplace in Rome. When he enquired about them he was told that they were Angles. At once he wanted them converted and said, "non Angli, sed Angeli" – "not Angles but angels." When Gregory became pope he sent Augustine of Canterbury and 30 monks to evangelize England.

Anglican Church

The merit claimed for the Anglican Church is, that if you let it alone, it will let you alone.
Ralph Waldo Emerson

When an Anglican is asked, "Where was your Church before the Reformation?" his best answer is to put the counter-question, "Where was your face before you washed it?"
Michael Ramsay

Animals

See also: Animals, Care of

A righteous man cares for the needs of his animal,
but the kindest acts of the wicked are cruel.
The Bible, Proverbs 12:10

A man of kindness to his beast is kind,
But brutal actions show a brutal mind.
Remember, he who made thee made the brute;
Who gave thee speech and reason, formed him mute.
He can't complain, but God's all-seeing eye
Beholds thy cruelty – he hears his cry.
Author unknown

A Robin Redbreast in a cage
Puts all heaven in a rage.
William Blake

A dog starv'd at his master's gate
Predicts the ruin of the State,
A horse misus'd upon the road
Calls all Heaven for human blood
Each outcry of the hunted hare
A fibre from the brain does tare,
A skylark wounded in the wing,
A cherubim does cease to sing.
William Blake

He who shall hurt the little wren
Shall never be belov'd by men.
He who the ox to wrath hath mov'd
Shall never be by woman lov'd.
William Blake

The saints are exceedingly loving and gentle to mankind, and even to brute beasts … Surely we ought to show them [animals] great kindness and gentleness for many reasons, but, above all, because they are of the same origin as ourselves.
John Chrysostom

Animals are such agreeable friends – they ask no questions, they pass no criticisms.
George Eliot

Animals, Care of

Love animals: God has given them the rudiments of thought and joy untroubled. Do not trouble their joy, don't harass them, don't deprive them of their happiness, don't work against God's intent. Man, do not pride yourself on superiority to animals; they are without sin, and you, with your greatness, defile the earth by your appearance on it, and leave the traces of your foulness after you – alas, it is true of almost every one of us!
Fyodor Dostoevsky

I am to ask your Lordships, in the name of that God who gave to man his dominion over the lower world, to acknowledge and recognize that dominion to be a moral trust.
Thomas Erskine

If you have men who will exclude any of God's creatures from the shelter of compassion and pity, you will have men who deal likewise with their fellow men.
Francis of Assisi

Kindness to all God's creatures is an absolute rock-bottom necessity if peace and righteousness are to prevail.
Sir Wilfred Grenfell

Nobody is truly Christian unless his cat or dog is the better off for it.
Rowland Hill

Cruelty to animals is the degrading attitude of paganism.
Cardinal Hinsley

We have enslaved the rest of the animal creation, and have treated our distant cousins in fur and feather so badly that beyond doubt, if they were able to formulate a religion, they would depict the Devil in human form.
W.R. Inge

Be careful that the love of gain draw us not into any business which may weaken our love of our Heavenly Father, or bring unnecessary trouble to any of His creatures.
John Woolman

Annunciation

The feast we call the Annunciation of
the Virgin Mary, when the angel came to
Mary and brought her the message from
God, may be fitly called the Feast of
Christ's Humanity; for then began our
deliverance.
Martin Luther

Anointing

You were rubbed with oil like an athlete,
Christ's athlete, as though in preparation
for an earthly wrestling-match, and you
agreed to take on your opponent.
Ambrose of Milan

The anointing of the Holy Spirit is
unlimited. It is we that set the limits.
Benny Hinn

The anointing is not some mystical
something out there. The anointing is the
presence and power of God manifested.
Rodney Howard-Browne

Don't blame the anointing for the
imperfection of the vessel.
Rodney Howard-Browne

John's words "unction" or "anointing" are
just a very graphic way of describing the
influence and the effect of the Holy Spirit
upon the believer.
Martyn Lloyd-Jones

Your inner man needs to be as strong, if
not stronger than, the gift and anointing
God has given you to carry on His
ministry in the earth.
Smith Wigglesworth

Anti-Christ

There is going to be an ultimate anti-Christ,
one person, able to do such wonders that he
almost deceives the elect themselves.
Martyn Lloyd-Jones

Anti-intellectualism

Whenever evangelicals have an experience of
direct, personal access to God, we are
tempted to think or act as if we can dispense

with doctrine, sacraments, history, and all the
other "superfluous paraphernalia" of the
Church and make our experience the sum
and soul of our faith. We are still attracted to
movements that replace thinking and
theology by other emphases relational,
therapeutic, charismatic, and managerial (as
in church growth). Whatever the other
virtues of these movements and the
unquestionable importance of piety, we must
courageously repudiate anti-intellectualism
for the sin it is.
Os Guinness

Anxiety
See also: Dying; Providence; Worry
An anxious heart weighs a man down.
The Bible, Proverbs 12:25

Let not your heart be troubled.
The Bible, John 14:1 KJV

Do not be anxious about anything, but in
everything, by prayer and petition, with
thanksgiving, present your requests to
God.
The Bible, Philippians 4:6

Cast all your anxiety on him because he
cares for you.
The Bible, 1 Peter 5:7

Every tomorrow has two handles. We can
take hold of it by the handle of anxiety, or
by the handle of faith.
Author unknown

Many of us crucify ourselves between two
thieves – regret for the past and fear of the
future.
Author unknown

Anxiety is the rust of life, destroying its
brightness and weakening its power. A
childlike and abiding trust in Providence is
its best preventive and remedy.
Author unknown

Never trouble trouble till trouble troubles
you.
Author unknown

Worry is the interest you pay on borrowed trouble.
Author unknown

Today is the tomorrow you worried about yesterday.
Author unknown

You don't get to choose how you're going to die. Or when. You can only decide how you're going to live. Now.
Joan Baez

We have a lot of anxieties, and one cancels out another very often.
Winston Churchill

Anxiety is the greatest evil that can befall us except sin; for just as revolt and sedition in a country cause havoc and sap its resistance to a foreign invasion, so we, when troubled and worried, are unable to preserve the virtues we have already acquired, or resist the temptations of the devil, who then diligently fishes, as they say, in troubled waters.
Francis de Sales

Do not anticipate trouble, or worry about what may never happen. Keep in the sunlight.
Benjamin Franklin

An undivided heart, which worships God alone and trusts him as it should, is raised above all anxiety for earthly wants.
J.C. Geikie

If you spend your whole life waiting for the storm, you'll never enjoy the sunshine.
Horace

How much have cost us the evils that never happened!
Thomas Jefferson

The misfortunes hardest to bear are these which never came.
James Russell Lowell

Pray, and let God worry.
Martin Luther

The natural role of twentieth-century man is anxiety.
Norman Mailer

I compare the troubles which we have to undergo in the course of the year to a great bundle of faggots, far too large for us to lift. But God does not require us to carry the whole at once. He mercifully unties the bundle, and gives us first one stick, which we are to carry today, and then another, which we are to carry tomorrow, and so on. This we might easily manage, if we would only take the burden appointed for each day; but we choose to increase our troubles by carrying yesterday's stick over again today, and adding tomorrow's burden to the load, before we are required to bear it.
John Newton

Anxiety does not empty tomorrow of its sorrows, but only empties today of its strength.
C.H. Spurgeon

Oh, how great peace and quietness would he possess who should cut off all vain anxiety and place all his confidence in God.
Thomas à Kempis

I suggest that we distinguish three types of anxiety according to the three directions in which nonbeing threatens being. Nonbeing threatens man's ontic self-affirmation, relatively in terms of fate, absolutely in terms of death. It threatens man's spiritual self-affirmation, relatively in terms of emptiness, absolutely in terms of meaninglessness. It threatens man's moral self-affirmation, relatively in terms of guilt, absolutely in terms of condemnation. The awareness of this threefold threat is anxiety appearing in three forms, that of fate and death (briefly, the anxiety of death), that of emptiness and loss of meaning (briefly, the anxiety of meaninglessness), that of guilt and condemnation (briefly, the anxiety of condemnation). In all three forms anxiety

is existential in the sense that it belongs to existence as such and not to an abnormal state of mind as in neurotic (and psychotic) anxiety.
Paul Tillich

Our whole life is taken up with anxiety for personal security, with preparations for living, so that we really never live at all.
Leo Tolstoy

Apathy
Lost interest? It's so bad I've lost apathy.
Author unknown

Everyone talks about apathy, but no one does anything about it.
Author unknown

What is reprehensible is that while leading good lives themselves and abhorring those of wicked men, some, fearing to offend, shut their eyes to evil deeds instead of condemning them and pointing out their malice.
Augustine of Hippo

Nothing is so fatal to religion as indifference, which is, at least, half infidelity.
Edmund Burke

The only thing necessary for the triumph of evil is for good men to do nothing.
Edmund Burke

All heaven is interested in the cross of Christ, all hell terribly afraid of it, while men are the only beings who more or less ignore its meaning.
Oswald Chambers

The hottest places in Hell are reserved for those who, in times of moral crisis, preserved their neutrality.
Dante

Science may have found a cure for most evils; but it has found no remedy for the worst of them all – the apathy of human beings.
Helen Keller

Our lives begin to end the day we become silent about the things that matter.
Martin Luther King, Jr.

In the End, we will remember not the words of our enemies, but the silence of our friends.
Martin Luther King Jr.

Interest speaks all sorts of tongues, and plays all sorts of parts, even that of disinterestedness.
François de la Rochefoucauld

Ten people who speak make more noise than ten thousand who are silent.
Napoleon

When something important is going on, silence is a lie.
A.M. Rosenthal

The worst sin towards our fellow creatures is not to hate them, but to be indifferent to them: that's the essence of inhumanity.
George Bernard Shaw

A single death is a tragedy, a million deaths is a statistic.
Joseph Stalin

Apathy is the glove into which evil slips its hand.
Bodie Thoene

The greatest evil today is indifference. To know and not to act is a way of consenting to injustice. The planet has become a very small place. What happens in other countries affects us.
Eli Wiesel

Apologetics
But in your hearts set apart Christ as Lord. Always be prepared to give an answer to everyone who asks you to give the reason for the hope that you have. But do this with gentleness and respect.
The Bible, 1 Peter 3:15

Ever since I became a Christian, I have

thought that the best, perhaps the only service I could do for my unbelieving neighbors was to explain and defend the belief that has been common to nearly all Christians at all times.
C.S. Lewis

It is as absurd to argue men, as to torture them, into believing.
J.H. Newman

The task of commending Christianity to thinking people as needed truth.
J.I. Packer

Apology
A stiff apology is a second insult.
G.K. Chesterton

The self-righteous never apologize.
Leonard Ravenhill

Apostles
The things that mark an apostle – signs, wonders and miracles – were done among you with great perseverance.
The Bible, 2 Corinthians 12:12

I do not, as Peter and Paul, issue commandments to you. They were apostles; I am just a condemned man.
Ignatius of Antioch

Apostolic doctrine
We are in communion with the apostolic churches because there is no difference of doctrine. This is our guarantee of truth.
Tertullian

Apostolic succession
I must believe in the Apostolic Succession, there being no other way of accounting for the descent of the Bishop of Exeter from Judas Iscariot.
Sydney Smith

Appearances
But the LORD said to Samuel, "Do not consider his appearance or his height, for I have rejected him. The LORD does not look at the things man looks at. Man looks at the outward appearance, but the LORD looks at the heart."
The Bible, 1 Samuel 16:7

Stop judging by mere appearances, and make a right judgment.
The Bible, John 7:24

There are no greater wretches in the world than many of those whom people in general take to be happy.
Author unknown

Just because the river is quiet does not mean the crocodiles have left.
Malay proverb

Don't rely too much on labels,
Far too often they are fables.
C.H. Spurgeon

Appetite
Let the stoics say what they please, we do not eat for the good of living, but because the meat is savory and the appetite is keen.
Ralph Waldo Emerson

A well-governed appetite is a great part of liberty.
Seneca

Appreciation
The deepest principle in human nature is the craving to be appreciated and the desire to be important.
Dale Carnegie

Appreciation is a wonderful thing: it makes what is excellent in others belong to us as well.
François de Voltaire

Archaeology
The reader may rest assured that nothing has been found [by archaeologists] to disturb a reasonable faith, and nothing has been discovered which can disprove a single theological doctrine. We no longer trouble ourselves with attempts to "harmonize" religion and science, or to "prove" the Bible. The Bible can stand for itself.
William F. Albright

Through the wealth of data uncovered by historical and archaeological research, we are able to measure the Bible's historical accuracy. In every case where its claims can thus be tested, the Bible proves to be accurate and reliable.
Jack Cottrell

Archaeology has confirmed countless passages which have been rejected by critics as unhistorical or contradictory to known facts.
Dr Joseph Free

It may be stated categorically that no archaeological discovery has ever controverted a biblical reference. Scores of archaeological findings have been made which confirm in clear outline or exact detail historical statements in the Bible.
Nelson Glueck

The interval between the date of the original composition and the earliest extant evidence becomes so small as to be negligible, and the last foundation for any doubt that the Scriptures have come to us substantially as they were written has now been removed. Both the authenticity and the general integrity of the books of the New Testament may be regarded as finally established.
Kathleen Kenyon

I take the view that Luke's history is unsurpassed in regard to his trustworthiness.
Sir William M. Ramsay

Luke is a historian of the first rank; not merely are his statements of fact trustworthy; he is possessed of the true historic sense. He seizes the important and critical events and shows their true nature at greater length. In short, this author should be placed along with the very greatest of historians.
Sir William M. Ramsay

I set out to look for truth on the borderland where Greece and Asia meet, and found it there. You may press the words of Luke in a degree beyond any other historian's and they stand the keenest scrutiny and the hardest treatment.
Sir William M. Ramsay

Arguing
See also: Argument
Just as a blind person is no use as an archer, so a disciple with the mania of contradiction will end in perdition.
John Climacus

Argument
From the strife of tongues.
The Bible, Psalm 31:20 KJV

Starting a quarrel is like breaching a dam; so drop the matter before a dispute breaks out.
The Bible, Proverbs 17:14

I plead with Euodia and I plead with Syntyche to agree with each other in the Lord.
The Bible, Philippians 4:2

When you argue with a fool, chances are he is doing just the same.
Author unknown

Never argue with a fool – people might not know the difference.
Author unknown

Discussion is an exchange of intelligence; argument is an exchange of ignorance.
Author unknown

It is not necessary to understand things in order to argue about them.
Pierre de Beaumarchais

People generally quarrel because they cannot argue.
G.K. Chesterton

Silence is the unbearable repartee.
Charles Dickens

I never deny, I never contradict. I sometimes forget.
Benjamin Disraeli

Never contend with one that is foolish, proud, positive, testy, or with a superior, or a clown, in matter of argument.
Thomas Fuller

The best way I know of to win an argument is to start by being in the right.
Lord Hailsham

Flee from discussions of dogma as from an unruly lion; and never embark upon them yourself, either with those raised in the Church, or with strangers.
Isaac from Syria

All married couples should learn the art of battle as they should learn the art of making love. Good battle is objective and honest – never vicious or cruel. Good battle is healthy and constructive, and brings to a marriage the principle of equal partnership.
Ann Landers

Think of all the squabbles Adam and Eve must have had in the course of their nine hundred years. Eve would say, "You ate the apple," and Adam would retort, "You gave it to me!"
Martin Luther

Let go of your attachment to being right, and suddenly your mind is more open. You're able to benefit from the unique viewpoints of others, without being crippled by your own judgement.
Ralph Marston

It is impossible to defeat an ignorant man in argument.
William G. McAdoo

He who establishes his argument by noise and command shows that his reason is weak.
Michel de Montaigne

Half the controversies in the world are verbal ones; and could they be brought to a plain issue they would be brought to a prompt termination. Parties engaged in

them would then perceive either that in substance they agreed together, or that their difference was one of first principles. We need not dispute, we need not prove, we need but define. At all events, let us, if we can, do this first of all and then see who are left for us to dispute; what is left for us to prove.
John Newman

Truth often suffers more by the heat of its defenders, than from the arguments of its opposers.
William Penn

Discussion is an exchange of knowledge; argument is an exchange of ignorance.
Robert Quillen

Two educated doctors are angrily discussing the nature of food, and allowing their meal to lie untasted, while a simple countryman is eating as heartily as he can of that which is set before him. The religious world is full of faultfinders, critics, and skeptics, who, like the doctors, fight over Christianity without profit either to themselves or others; and those are far happier who imitate the farmer and feed upon the Word of God, which is the true food of the soul. Luther's prayer was, "From nice questions the Lord deliver us."
C.H. Spurgeon

It is useless for us to reason a man out of a thing he has never been reasoned into.
Jonathan Swift

Argument is the worst sort of conversation.
Jonathan Swift

Who is so wise as to have a perfect knowledge of all things? Therefore trust not too much to thine own opinion, but be ready also to hear the opinion of others. Though thine own opinion be good, yet if for the love of God thou foregoest it, and followest that of another, thou shalt the more profit thereby.
Thomas à Kempis

For thirty years I have tried to see the face of Christ in those with whom I differed.
Bishop Whipple

Aridity, Spiritual
See: Dark night of the soul; Dryness

Aristocracy
Democracy means government by the uneducated, while aristocracy means government by the badly educated.
G.K. Chesterton

There is a natural aristocracy among men. The grounds of this are virtue and talent.
Thomas Jefferson

Arminianism and Calvinism
See also: Calvinism versus Arminianism

The Canons of Dordt

Introduction
The Decision of the Synod of Dordt on the Five Main Points of Doctrine in Dispute in the Netherlands is popularly known as the Canons of Dordt. It consists of statements of doctrine adopted by the great Synod of Dordt which met in the city of Dordrecht in 1618-19. Although this was a national synod of the Reformed churches of the Netherlands, it had an international character, since it was composed not only of Dutch delegates but also of twenty-six delegates from eight countries.

The Synod of Dordt
The Synod of Dordt was held in order to settle a serious controversy in the Dutch churches initiated by the rise of Arminianism. Jacob Arminius, a theological professor at Leiden University, questioned the teaching of Calvin and his followers on a number of important points. After Arminius's death, his own followers presented their views on five of these points in the Remonstrance of 1610. In this document or in later more explicit writings, the Arminians taught election based on foreseen faith, universal atonement, partial depravity, resistible grace, and the possibility of a lapse from grace. In the Canons the Synod of Dordt rejected these views and set forth the Reformed doctrine on these points, namely, unconditional election, limited atonement, total depravity, irresistible grace, and the perseverance of saints.

The original preface called them a "judgment, in which both the true view, agreeing with God's Word, concerning the aforesaid five points of doctrine is explained, and the false view, disagreeing with God's Word, is rejected." Each of the main points consists of a positive and a negative part, the former being an exposition of the Reformed doctrine on the subject, the latter a repudiation of the corresponding errors.

The Canons of Dordt, formally Titled, The Decision of the Synod of Dordt on the Five Main Points of Doctrine in Dispute in the Netherlands

The First Main Point of Doctrine
1 Divine Election and Reprobation
The Judgment Concerning Divine Predestination Which the Synod Declares to Be in Agreement with the Word of God and Accepted Till Now in the Reformed Churches, Set Forth in Several Articles

ARTICLE 1 GOD'S RIGHT TO CONDEMN ALL PEOPLE
Since all people have sinned in Adam and have come under the sentence of the curse and eternal death, God would have done no one an injustice if it had been his will to leave the entire human race in sin and under the curse, and to condemn them on account of their sin. As the apostle says: The whole world is liable to the condemnation of God (Rom. 3:19), All have sinned and are deprived of the glory of God (Rom. 3:23), and The wages of sin is death (Rom. 6:23).

ARTICLE 2 THE MANIFESTATION OF GOD'S LOVE
But this is how God showed his love: he sent his only begotten Son into the world,

so that whoever believes in him should not perish but have eternal life.

ARTICLE 3: THE PREACHING OF THE GOSPEL

In order that people may be brought to faith, God mercifully sends proclaimers of this very joyful message to the people he wishes and at the time he wishes. By this ministry people are called to repentance and faith in Christ crucified. For how shall they believe in him of whom they have not heard? And how shall they hear without someone preaching? And how shall they preach unless they have been sent? (Rom. 10:14-15).

ARTICLE 4 A TWOFOLD RESPONSE TO THE GOSPEL

God's anger remains on those who do not believe this gospel. But those who do accept it and embrace Jesus the Savior with a true and living faith are delivered through him from God's anger and from destruction, and receive the gift of eternal life.

ARTICLE 5 THE SOURCES OF UNBELIEF AND OF FAITH

The cause or blame for this unbelief, as well as for all other sins, is not at all in God, but in man. Faith in Jesus Christ, however, and salvation through him is a free gift of God. As Scripture says, It is by grace you have been saved, through faith, and this not from yourselves; it is a gift of God (Eph. 2:8). Likewise: It has been freely given to you to believe in Christ (Phil. 1:29).

ARTICLE 6: GOD'S ETERNAL DECISION

The fact that some receive from God the gift of faith within time, and that others do not, stems from his eternal decision. For all his works are known to God from eternity (Acts 15:18; Eph. 1:11). In accordance with this decision he graciously softens the hearts, however hard, of his chosen ones and inclines them to believe, but by his just judgment he leaves in their wickedness and hardness of heart those who have not been chosen. And in this especially is disclosed to us his act—unfathomable, and as merciful as it is just—of distinguishing between people

equally lost. This is the well-known decision of election and reprobation revealed in God's Word. This decision the wicked, impure, and unstable distort to their own ruin, but it provides holy and godly souls with comfort beyond words.

ARTICLE 7: ELECTION

Election [or choosing] is God's unchangeable purpose by which he did the following:

Before the foundation of the world, by sheer grace, according to the free good pleasure of his will, he chose in Christ to salvation a definite number of particular people out of the entire human race, which had fallen by its own fault from its original innocence into sin and ruin. Those chosen were neither better nor more deserving than the others, but lay with them in the common misery. He did this in Christ, whom he also appointed from eternity to be the mediator, the head of all those chosen, and the foundation of their salvation. And so he decided to give the chosen ones to Christ to be saved, and to call and draw them effectively into Christ's fellowship through his Word and Spirit. In other words, he decided to grant them true faith in Christ, to justify them, to sanctify them, and finally, after powerfully preserving them in the fellowship of his Son, to glorify them.

God did all this in order to demonstrate his mercy, to the praise of the riches of his glorious grace.

As Scripture says, God chose us in Christ, before the foundation of the world, so that we should be holy and blameless before him with love; he predestined us whom he adopted as his children through Jesus Christ, in himself, according to the good pleasure of his will, to the praise of his glorious grace, by which he freely made us pleasing to himself in his beloved (Eph. 1:4-6). And elsewhere, Those whom he predestined, he also called; and those whom he called, he also justified; and those whom he justified, he also glorified (Rom. 8:30).

ARTICLE 8: A SINGLE DECISION OF ELECTION

This election is not of many kinds; it is one

and the same election for all who were to be saved in the Old and the New Testament. For Scripture declares that there is a single good pleasure, purpose, and plan of God's will, by which he chose us from eternity both to grace and to glory, both to salvation and to the way of salvation, which he prepared in advance for us to walk in.

ARTICLE 9: ELECTION NOT BASED ON FORESEEN FAITH

This same election took place, not on the basis of foreseen faith, of the obedience of faith, of holiness, or of any other good quality and disposition, as though it were based on a prerequisite cause or condition in the person to be chosen, but rather for the purpose of faith, of the obedience of faith, of holiness, and so on. Accordingly, election is the source of each of the benefits of salvation. Faith, holiness, and the other saving gifts, and at last eternal life itself, flow forth from election as its fruits and effects. As the apostle says, He chose us (not because we were, but) so that we should be holy and blameless before him in love (Eph. 1:4).

ARTICLE 10: ELECTION BASED ON GOD'S GOOD PLEASURE

But the cause of this undeserved election is exclusively the good pleasure of God. This does not involve his choosing certain human qualities or actions from among all those possible as a condition of salvation, but rather involves his adopting certain particular persons from among the common mass of sinners as his own possession. As Scripture says, When the children were not yet born, and had done nothing either good or bad..., she (Rebecca) was told, "The older will serve the younger." As it is written, "Jacob I loved, but Esau I hated" (Rom. 9:11-13). Also, All who were appointed for eternal life believed (Acts 13:48).

ARTICLE 11: ELECTION UNCHANGEABLE

Just as God himself is most wise, unchangeable, all-knowing, and almighty,

so the election made by him can neither be suspended nor altered, revoked, or annulled; neither can his chosen ones be cast off, nor their number reduced.

ARTICLE 12: THE ASSURANCE OF ELECTION

Assurance of this their eternal and unchangeable election to salvation is given to the chosen in due time, though by various stages and in differing measure. Such assurance comes not by inquisitive searching into the hidden and deep things of God, but by noticing within themselves, with spiritual joy and holy delight, the unmistakable fruits of election pointed out in God's Word– such as a true faith in Christ, a childlike fear of God, a godly sorrow for their sins, a hunger and thirst for righteousness, and so on.

ARTICLE 13: THE FRUIT OF THIS ASSURANCE

In their awareness and assurance of this election God's children daily find greater cause to humble themselves before God, to adore the fathomless depth of his mercies, to cleanse themselves, and to give fervent love in return to him who first so greatly loved them. This is far from saying that this teaching concerning election, and reflection upon it, make God's children lax in observing his commandments or carnally self-assured. By God's just judgment this does usually happen to those who casually take for granted the grace of election or engage in idle and brazen talk about it but are unwilling to walk in the ways of the chosen.

ARTICLE 14: TEACHING ELECTION PROPERLY

Just as, by God's wise plan, this teaching concerning divine election has been proclaimed through the prophets, Christ himself, and the apostles, in Old and New Testament times, and has subsequently been committed to writing in the Holy Scriptures, so also today in God's church, for which it was specifically intended, this teaching must be set forth–with a spirit of discretion, in a godly and holy manner, at the appropriate time and place, without inquisitive searching into the ways of the

Most High. This must be done for the glory of God's most holy name, and for the lively comfort of his people.

ARTICLE 15: REPROBATION

Moreover, Holy Scripture most especially highlights this eternal and undeserved grace of our election and brings it out more clearly for us, in that it further bears witness that not all people have been chosen but that some have not been chosen or have been passed by in God's eternal election—those, that is, concerning whom God, on the basis of his entirely free, most just, irreproachable, and unchangeable good pleasure, made the following decision: to leave them in the common misery into which, by their own fault, they have plunged themselves; not to grant them saving faith and the grace of conversion; but finally to condemn and eternally punish them (having been left in their own ways and under his just judgment), not only for their unbelief but also for all their other sins, in order to display his justice. And this is the decision of reprobation, which does not at all make God the author of sin (a blasphemous thought!) but rather its fearful, irreproachable, just judge and avenger.

ARTICLE 16: RESPONSES TO THE TEACHING OF REPROBATION

Those who do not yet actively experience within themselves a living faith in Christ or an assured confidence of heart, peace of conscience, a zeal for childlike obedience, and a glorying in God through Christ, but who nevertheless use the means by which God has promised to work these things in us—such people ought not to be alarmed at the mention of reprobation, nor to count themselves among the reprobate; rather they ought to continue diligently in the use of the means, to desire fervently a time of more abundant grace, and to wait for it in reverence and humility. On the other hand, those who seriously desire to turn to God, to be pleasing to him alone, and to be delivered from the body of death, but are not yet able to make such progress along the way of godliness and faith as they

would like—such people ought much less to stand in fear of the teaching concerning reprobation, since our merciful God has promised that he will not snuff out a smoldering wick and that he will not break a bruised reed. However, those who have forgotten God and their Savior Jesus Christ and have abandoned themselves wholly to the cares of the world and the pleasures of the flesh—such people have every reason to stand in fear of this teaching, as long as they do not seriously turn to God.

ARTICLE 17: THE SALVATION OF THE INFANTS OF BELIEVERS

Since we must make judgments about God's will from his Word, which testifies that the children of believers are holy, not by nature but by virtue of the gracious covenant in which they together with their parents are included, godly parents ought not to doubt the election and salvation of their children whom God calls out of this life in infancy.

ARTICLE 18: THE PROPER ATTITUDE TOWARD ELECTION AND REPROBATION

To those who complain about this grace of an undeserved election and about the severity of a just reprobation, we reply with the words of the apostle, Who are you, O man, to talk back to God? (Rom. 9:20), and with the words of our Savior, Have I no right to do what I want with my own? (Matt. 20:15). We, however, with reverent adoration of these secret things, cry out with the apostle: Oh, the depths of the riches both of the wisdom and the knowledge of God! How unsearchable are his judgments, and his ways beyond tracing out! For who has known the mind of the Lord? Or who has been his counselor? Or who has first given to God, that God should repay him? For from him and through him and to him are all things. To him be the glory forever! Amen (Rom. 11:33-36).

Rejection of the Errors
by Which the Dutch Churches Have for Some Time Been Disturbed

Having set forth the orthodox teaching

concerning election and reprobation, the Synod rejects the errors of those

I

Who teach that the will of God to save those who would believe and persevere in faith and in the obedience of faith is the whole and entire decision of election to salvation, and that nothing else concerning this decision has been revealed in God's Word.

For they deceive the simple and plainly contradict Holy Scripture in its testimony that God does not only wish to save those who would believe, but that he has also from eternity chosen certain particular people to whom, rather than to others, he would within time grant faith in Christ and perseverance. As Scripture says, I have revealed your name to those whom you gave me (John 17:6). Likewise, All who were appointed for eternal life believed (Acts 13:48), and He chose us before the foundation of the world so that we should be holy... (Eph. 1:4).

II

Who teach that God's election to eternal life is of many kinds: one general and indefinite, the other particular and definite; and the latter in turn either incomplete, revocable, nonperemptory (or conditional), or else complete, irrevocable, and peremptory (or absolute). Likewise, who teach that there is one election to faith and another to salvation, so that there can be an election to justifying faith apart from a peremptory election to salvation.

For this is an invention of the human brain, devised apart from the Scriptures, which distorts the teaching concerning election and breaks up this golden chain of salvation: Those whom he predestined, he also called; and those whom he called, he also justified; and those whom he justified, he also glorified (Rom. 8:30).

III

Who teach that God's good pleasure and purpose, which Scripture mentions in its teaching of election, does not involve God's choosing certain particular people rather than others, but involves God's choosing, out of all possible conditions (including the works of the law) or out of the whole order of things, the intrinsically unworthy act of faith, as well as the imperfect obedience of faith, to be a condition of salvation; and it involves his graciously wishing to count this as perfect obedience and to look upon it as worthy of the reward of eternal life.

For by this pernicious error the good pleasure of God and the merit of Christ are robbed of their effectiveness and people are drawn away, by unprofitable inquiries, from the truth of undeserved justification and from the simplicity of the Scriptures. It also gives the lie to these words of the apostle: God called us with a holy calling, not in virtue of works, but in virtue of his own purpose and the grace which was given to us in Christ Jesus before the beginning of time (2 Tim. 1:9).

IV

Who teach that in election to faith a prerequisite condition is that man should rightly use the light of nature, be upright, unassuming, humble, and disposed to eternal life, as though election depended to some extent on these factors.

For this smacks of Pelagius, and it clearly calls into question the words of the apostle: We lived at one time in the passions of our flesh, following the will of our flesh and thoughts, and we were by nature children of wrath, like everyone else. But God, who is rich in mercy, out of the great love with which he loved us, even when we were dead in transgressions, made us alive with Christ, by whose grace you have been saved. And God raised us up with him and seated us with him in heaven in Christ Jesus, in order that in the coming ages we might show the surpassing riches of his grace, according to his kindness toward us in Christ Jesus. For it is by grace you have been saved, through faith (and this not from yourselves; it is the gift of God) not by works, so that no one can boast (Eph. 2:3-9).

V

Who teach that the incomplete and non-peremptory election of particular persons to salvation occurred on the basis of a foreseen faith, repentance, holiness, and godliness, which has just begun or continued for some time; but that complete and peremptory election occurred on the basis of a foreseen perseverance to the end in faith, repentance, holiness, and godliness. And that this is the gracious and evangelical worthiness, on account of which the one who is chosen is more worthy than the one who is not chosen. And therefore that faith, the obedience of faith, holiness, godliness, and perseverance are not fruits or effects of an unchangeable election to glory, but indispensable conditions and causes, which are prerequisite in those who are to be chosen in the complete election, and which are foreseen as achieved in them. This runs counter to the entire Scripture, which throughout impresses upon our ears and hearts these sayings among others: Election is not by works, but by him who calls (Rom. 9:11-12); All who were appointed for eternal life believed (Acts 13:48); He chose us in himself so that we should be holy (Eph. 1:4); You did not choose me, but I chose you (John 15:16); If by grace, not by works (Rom. 11:6); In this is love, not that we loved God, but that he loved us and sent his Son (1 John 4:10).

VI

Who teach that not every election to salvation is unchangeable, but that some of the chosen can perish and do in fact perish eternally, with no decision of God to prevent it.

By this gross error they make God changeable, destroy the comfort of the godly concerning the steadfastness of their election, and contradict the Holy Scriptures, which teach that the elect cannot be led astray (Matt. 24:24), that Christ does not lose those given to him by the Father (John 6:39), and that those whom God predestined, called, and justified, he also glorifies (Rom. 8:30).

VII

Who teach that in this life there is no fruit, no awareness, and no assurance of one's unchangeable election to glory, except as conditional upon something changeable and contingent.

For not only is it absurd to speak of an uncertain assurance, but these things also militate against the experience of the saints, who with the apostle rejoice from an awareness of their election and sing the praises of this gift of God; who, as Christ urged, rejoice with his disciples that their names have been written in heaven (Luke 10:20); and finally who hold up against the flaming arrows of the devil's temptations the awareness of their election, with the question Who will bring any charge against those whom God has chosen? (Rom. 8:33).

VIII

Who teach that it was not on the basis of his just will alone that God decided to leave anyone in the fall of Adam and in the common state of sin and condemnation or to pass anyone by in the imparting of grace necessary for faith and conversion.

For these words stand fast: He has mercy on whom he wishes, and he hardens whom he wishes (Rom. 9:18). And also: To you it has been given to know the secrets of the kingdom of heaven, but to them it has not been given (Matt. 13:11). Likewise: I give glory to you, Father, Lord of heaven and earth, that you have hidden these things from the wise and understanding, and have revealed them to little children; yes, Father, because that was your pleasure (Matt. 11:25-26).

IX

Who teach that the cause for God's sending the gospel to one people rather than to another is not merely and solely God's good pleasure, but rather that one people is better and worthier than the other to whom the gospel is not communicated.

For Moses contradicts this when he addresses the people of Israel as follows: Behold, to Jehovah your God belong the heavens and the highest heavens, the earth and whatever is in it. But Jehovah was inclined in his affection to love your ancestors alone, and chose out their descendants after them, you above all peoples, as at this day (Deut. 10:14-15). And also Christ: Woe to you, Korazin! Woe to you, Bethsaida! for if those mighty works done in you had been done in Tyre and Sidon, they would have repented long ago in sackcloth and ashes (Matt. 11:21).

The Second Main Point of Doctrine
Christ's Death and Human Redemption Through It

ARTICLE 1: THE PUNISHMENT WHICH GOD'S JUSTICE REQUIRES
God is not only supremely merciful, but also supremely just. His justice requires (as he has revealed himself in the Word) that the sins we have committed against his infinite majesty be punished with both temporal and eternal punishments, of soul as well as body. We cannot escape these punishments unless satisfaction is given to God's justice.

ARTICLE 2: THE SATISFACTION MADE BY CHRIST
Since, however, we ourselves cannot give this satisfaction or deliver ourselves from God's anger, God in his boundless mercy has given us as a guarantee his only begotten Son, who was made to be sin and a curse for us, in our place, on the cross, in order that he might give satisfaction for us.

ARTICLE 3: THE INFINITE VALUE OF CHRIST'S DEATH
This death of God's Son is the only and entirely complete sacrifice and satisfaction for sins; it is of infinite value and worth, more than sufficient to atone for the sins of the whole world.

ARTICLE 4: REASONS FOR THIS INFINITE VALUE
This death is of such great value and worth for the reason that the person who suffered it is—as was necessary to be our Savior—not only a true and perfectly holy man, but also the only begotten Son of God, of the

same eternal and infinite essence with the Father and the Holy Spirit. Another reason is that this death was accompanied by the experience of God's anger and curse, which we by our sins had fully deserved.

ARTICLE 5: THE MANDATE TO PROCLAIM THE GOSPEL TO ALL
Moreover, it is the promise of the gospel that whoever believes in Christ crucified shall not perish but have eternal life. This promise, together with the command to repent and believe, ought to be announced and declared without differentiation or discrimination to all nations and people, to whom God in his good pleasure sends the gospel.

ARTICLE 6: UNBELIEF MAN'S RESPONSIBILITY
However, that many who have been called through the gospel do not repent or believe in Christ but perish in unbelief is not because the sacrifice of Christ offered on the cross is deficient or insufficient, but because they themselves are at fault.

ARTICLE 7: FAITH GOD'S GIFT
But all who genuinely believe and are delivered and saved by Christ's death from their sins and from destruction receive this favor solely from God's grace—which he owes to no one—given to them in Christ from eternity.

ARTICLE 8: THE SAVING EFFECTIVENESS OF CHRIST'S DEATH
For it was the entirely free plan and very gracious will and intention of God the Father that the enlivening and saving effectiveness of his Son's costly death should work itself out in all his chosen ones, in order that he might grant justifying faith to them only and thereby lead them without fail to salvation. In other words, it was God's will that Christ through the blood of the cross (by which he confirmed the new covenant) should effectively redeem from every people, tribe, nation, and language all those and only those who were chosen from eternity to salvation and given to him by the

Father; that he should grant them faith (which, like the Holy Spirit's other saving gifts, he acquired for them by his death); that he should cleanse them by his blood from all their sins, both original and actual, whether committed before or after their coming to faith; that he should faithfully preserve them to the very end; and that he should finally present them to himself, a glorious people, without spot or wrinkle.

ARTICLE 9: THE FULFILLMENT OF GOD'S PLAN
This plan, arising out of God's eternal love for his chosen ones, from the beginning of the world to the present time has been powerfully carried out and will also be carried out in the future, the gates of hell seeking vainly to prevail against it. As a result the chosen are gathered into one, all in their own time, and there is always a church of believers founded on Christ's blood, a church which steadfastly loves, persistently worships, and—here and in all eternity—praises him as her Savior who laid down his life for her on the cross, as a bridegroom for his bride.

Rejection of the Errors
Having set forth the orthodox teaching, the Synod rejects the errors of those

I
Who teach that God the Father appointed his Son to death on the cross without a fixed and definite plan to save anyone by name, so that the necessity, usefulness, and worth of what Christ's death obtained could have stood intact and altogether perfect, complete and whole, even if the redemption that was obtained had never in actual fact been applied to any individual.

For this assertion is an insult to the wisdom of God the Father and to the merit of Jesus Christ, and it is contrary to Scripture. For the Savior speaks as follows: I lay down my life for the sheep, and I know them (John 10:15, 27). And Isaiah the prophet says concerning the Savior: When he shall make himself an offering for sin, he shall see his offspring, he shall prolong his days, and the will of Jehovah shall prosper in his hand (Isa. 53:10). Finally, this undermines the article of the creed in which we confess what we believe concerning the Church.

II
Who teach that the purpose of Christ's death was not to establish in actual fact a new covenant of grace by his blood, but only to acquire for the Father the mere right to enter once more into a covenant with men, whether of grace or of works.

For this conflicts with Scripture, which teaches that Christ has become the guarantee and mediator of a better—that is, a new-covenant (Heb. 7:22; 9:15), and that a will is in force only when someone has died (Heb. 9:17).

III
Who teach that Christ, by the satisfaction which he gave, did not certainly merit for anyone salvation itself and the faith by which this satisfaction of Christ is effectively applied to salvation, but only acquired for the Father the authority or plenary will to relate in a new way with men and to impose such new conditions as he chose, and that the satisfying of these conditions depends on the free choice of man; consequently, that it was possible that either all or none would fulfill them.

For they have too low an opinion of the death of Christ, do not at all acknowledge the foremost fruit or benefit which it brings forth, and summon back from hell the Pelagian error.

IV
Who teach that what is involved in the new covenant of grace which God the Father made with men through the intervening of Christ's death is not that we are justified before God and saved through faith, insofar as it accepts Christ's merit, but rather that God, having withdrawn his demand for perfect obedience to the law, counts faith itself, and the imperfect obedience of faith, as perfect obedience to

the law, and graciously looks upon this as worthy of the reward of eternal life.

For they contradict Scripture: They are justified freely by his grace through the redemption that came by Jesus Christ, whom God presented as a sacrifice of atonement, through faith in his blood (Rom. 3:24-25). And along with the ungodly Socinus, they introduce a new and foreign justification of man before God, against the consensus of the whole church.

V

Who teach that all people have been received into the state of reconciliation and into the grace of the covenant, so that no one on account of original sin is liable to condemnation, or is to be condemned, but that all are free from the guilt of this sin.

For this opinion conflicts with Scripture which asserts that we are by nature children of wrath.

VI

Who make use of the distinction between obtaining and applying in order to instill in the unwary and inexperienced the opinion that God, as far as he is concerned, wished to bestow equally upon all people the benefits which are gained by Christ's death; but that the distinction by which some rather than others come to share in the forgiveness of sins and eternal life depends on their own free choice (which applies itself to the grace offered indiscriminately) but does not depend on the unique gift of mercy which effectively works in them, so that they, rather than others, apply that grace to themselves.

For, while pretending to set forth this distinction in an acceptable sense, they attempt to give the people the deadly poison of Pelagianism.

VII

Who teach that Christ neither could die, nor had to die, nor did die for those whom God so dearly loved and chose to eternal life, since such people do not need the death of Christ.

For they contradict the apostle, who says: Christ loved me and gave himself up for me (Gal. 2:20), and likewise: Who will bring any charge against those whom God has chosen? It is God who justifies. Who is he that condemns? It is Christ who died, that is, for them (Rom. 8:33-34). They also contradict the Savior, who asserts: I lay down my life for the sheep (John 10:15), and My command is this: Love one another as I have loved you. Greater love has no one than this, that one lay down his life for his friends (John 15:12-13).

The Third and Fourth Main Points of Doctrine
Human Corruption, Conversion to God, and the Way It Occurs

ARTICLE 1: THE EFFECT OF THE FALL ON HUMAN NATURE

Man was originally created in the image of God and was furnished in his mind with a true and salutary knowledge of his Creator and things spiritual, in his will and heart with righteousness, and in all his emotions with purity; indeed, the whole man was holy. However, rebelling against God at the devil's instigation and by his own free will, he deprived himself of these outstanding gifts. Rather, in their place he brought upon himself blindness, terrible darkness, futility, and distortion of judgment in his mind; perversity, defiance, and hardness in his heart and will; and finally impurity in all his emotions.

ARTICLE 2: THE SPREAD OF CORRUPTION

Man brought forth children of the same nature as himself after the fall. That is to say, being corrupt he brought forth corrupt children. The corruption spread, by God's just judgment, from Adam to all his descendants— except for Christ alone–not by way of imitation (as in former times the Pelagians would have it) but by way of the propagation of his perverted nature.

ARTICLE 3: TOTAL INABILITY

Therefore, all people are conceived in sin and are born children of wrath, unfit for any saving good, inclined to evil, dead in their sins, and slaves to sin; without the grace of the regenerating Holy Spirit they are neither willing nor able to return to God, to reform their distorted nature, or even to dispose themselves to such reform.

ARTICLE 4: THE INADEQUACY OF THE LIGHT OF NATURE

There is, to be sure, a certain light of nature remaining in man after the fall, by virtue of which he retains some notions about God, natural things, and the difference between what is moral and immoral, and demonstrates a certain eagerness for virtue and for good outward behavior. But this light of nature is far from enabling man to come to a saving knowledge of God and conversion to him—so far, in fact, that man does not use it rightly even in matters of nature and society. Instead, in various ways he completely distorts this light, whatever its precise character, and suppresses it in unrighteousness. In doing so he renders himself without excuse before God.

ARTICLE 5: THE INADEQUACY OF THE LAW

In this respect, what is true of the light of nature is true also of the Ten Commandments given by God through Moses specifically to the Jews. For man cannot obtain saving grace through the Decalogue, because, although it does expose the magnitude of his sin and increasingly convict him of his guilt, yet it does not offer a remedy or enable him to escape from his misery, and, indeed, weakened as it is by the flesh, leaves the offender under the curse.

ARTICLE 6: THE SAVING POWER OF THE GOSPEL

What, therefore, neither the light of nature nor the law can do, God accomplishes by the power of the Holy Spirit, through the Word or the ministry of reconciliation. This is the gospel about the Messiah, through which it has pleased God to save believers, in both the Old and the New Testament.

ARTICLE 7: GOD'S FREEDOM IN REVEALING THE GOSPEL

In the Old Testament, God revealed this secret of his will to a small number; in the New Testament (now without any distinction between peoples) he discloses it to a large number. The reason for this difference must not be ascribed to the greater worth of one nation over another, or to a better use of the light of nature, but to the free good pleasure and undeserved love of God. Therefore, those who receive so much grace, beyond and in spite of all they deserve, ought to acknowledge it with humble and thankful hearts; on the other hand, with the apostle they ought to adore (but certainly not inquisitively search into) the severity and justice of God's judgments on the others, who do not receive this grace.

ARTICLE 8: THE SERIOUS CALL OF THE GOSPEL

Nevertheless, all who are called through the gospel are called seriously. For seriously and most genuinely God makes known in his Word what is pleasing to him: that those who are called should come to him. Seriously he also promises rest for their souls and eternal life to all who come to him and believe.

ARTICLE 9: HUMAN RESPONSIBILITY FOR REJECTING THE GOSPEL

The fact that many who are called through the ministry of the gospel do not come and are not brought to conversion must not be blamed on the gospel, nor on Christ, who is offered through the gospel, nor on God, who calls them through the gospel and even bestows various gifts on them, but on the people themselves who are called. Some in self-assurance do not even entertain the Word of life; others do entertain it but do not take it to heart, and for that reason, after the fleeting joy of a temporary faith, they relapse; others choke the seed of the Word with the thorns of life's cares and with the pleasures of the world and bring forth no fruits. This our Savior teaches in the parable of the sower (Matt. 13).

ARTICLE 10: CONVERSION AS THE WORK OF GOD

The fact that others who are called through the ministry of the gospel do come and are brought to conversion must not be credited to man, as though one distinguishes himself by free choice from others who are furnished with equal or sufficient grace for faith and conversion (as the proud heresy of Pelagius maintains). No, it must be credited to God: just as from eternity he chose his own in Christ, so within time he effectively calls them, grants them faith and repentance, and, having rescued them from the dominion of darkness, brings them into the kingdom of his Son, in order that they may declare the wonderful deeds of him who called them out of darkness into this marvelous light, and may boast not in themselves, but in the Lord, as apostolic words frequently testify in Scripture.

ARTICLE 11: THE HOLY SPIRIT'S WORK IN CONVERSION

Moreover, when God carries out this good pleasure in his chosen ones, or works true conversion in them, he not only sees to it that the gospel is proclaimed to them outwardly, and enlightens their minds powerfully by the Holy Spirit so that they may rightly understand and discern the things of the Spirit of God, but, by the effective operation of the same regenerating Spirit, he also penetrates into the inmost being of man, opens the closed heart, softens the hard heart, and circumcises the heart that is uncircumcised. He infuses new qualities into the will, making the dead will alive, the evil one good, the unwilling one willing, and the stubborn one compliant; he activates and strengthens the will so that, like a good tree, it may be enabled to produce the fruits of good deeds.

ARTICLE 12: REGENERATION A SUPERNATURAL WORK

And this is the regeneration, the new creation, the raising from the dead, and the making alive so clearly proclaimed in the Scriptures, which God works in us without our help. But this certainly does not happen only by outward teaching, by moral persuasion, or by such a way of working that, after God has done his work, it remains in man's power whether or not to be reborn or converted. Rather, it is an entirely supernatural work, one that is at the same time most powerful and most pleasing, a marvelous, hidden, and inexpressible work, which is not lesser than or inferior in power to that of creation or of raising the dead, as Scripture (inspired by the author of this work) teaches. As a result, all those in whose hearts God works in this marvelous way are certainly, unfailingly, and effectively reborn and do actually believe. And then the will, now renewed, is not only activated and motivated by God but in being activated by God is also itself active. For this reason, man himself, by that grace which he has received, is also rightly said to believe and to repent.

ARTICLE 13: THE INCOMPREHENSIBLE WAY OF REGENERATION

In this life believers cannot fully understand the way this work occurs; meanwhile, they rest content with knowing and experiencing that by this grace of God they do believe with the heart and love their Savior.

ARTICLE 14: THE WAY GOD GIVES FAITH

In this way, therefore, faith is a gift of God, not in the sense that it is offered by God for man to choose, but that it is in actual fact bestowed on man, breathed and infused into him. Nor is it a gift in the sense that God bestows only the potential to believe, but then awaits assent—the act of believing—from man's choice; rather, it is a gift in the sense that he who works both willing and acting and, indeed, works all things in all people produces in man both the will to believe and the belief itself.

ARTICLE 15: RESPONSES TO GOD'S GRACE

God does not owe this grace to anyone. For what could God owe to one who has nothing to give that can be paid back? Indeed, what could God owe to one who has nothing of his own to give but sin and falsehood? Therefore the person who receives this grace owes and gives eternal thanks to God alone; the person who does not receive it either does not care at all about these spiritual things and is satisfied with himself in his condition, or else in self-assurance foolishly boasts about having something which he lacks. Furthermore, following the example of the apostles, we are to think and to speak in the most favorable way about those who outwardly profess their faith and better their lives, for the inner chambers of the heart are unknown to us. But for others who have not yet been called, we are to pray to the God who calls things that do not exist as though they did. In no way, however, are we to pride ourselves as better than they, as though we had distinguished ourselves from them.

ARTICLE 16: REGENERATION'S EFFECT

However, just as by the fall man did not cease to be man, endowed with intellect and will, and just as sin, which has spread through the whole human race, did not abolish the nature of the human race but distorted and spiritually killed it, so also this divine grace of regeneration does not act in people as if they were blocks and stones; nor does it abolish the will and its properties or coerce a reluctant will by force, but spiritually revives, heals, reforms, and–in a manner at once pleasing and powerful–bends it back. As a result, a ready and sincere obedience of the Spirit now begins to prevail where before the rebellion and resistance of the flesh were completely dominant. It is in this that the true and spiritual restoration and freedom of our will consists. Thus, if the marvelous Maker of every good thing were not dealing with us, man would have no hope of getting up from his fall by his free choice, by which he plunged himself into ruin when still standing upright.

ARTICLE 17: GOD'S USE OF MEANS IN REGENERATION

Just as the almighty work of God by which he brings forth and sustains our natural life does not rule out but requires the use of means, by which God, according to his infinite wisdom and goodness, has wished to exercise his power, so also the aforementioned supernatural work of God by which he regenerates us in no way rules out or cancels the use of the gospel, which God in his great wisdom has appointed to be the seed of regeneration and the food of the soul. For this reason, the apostles and the teachers who followed them taught the people in a godly manner about this grace of God, to give him the glory and to humble all pride, and yet did not neglect meanwhile to keep the people, by means of the holy admonitions of the gospel, under the administration of the Word, the sacraments, and discipline. So even today it is out of the question that the teachers or those taught in the church should presume to test God by separating what he in his good pleasure has wished to be closely joined together. For grace is bestowed through admonitions, and the more readily we perform our duty, the more lustrous the benefit of God working in us usually is and the better his work advances. To him alone, both for the means and for their saving fruit and effectiveness, all glory is owed forever. Amen.

Rejection of the Errors

Having set forth the orthodox teaching, the Synod rejects the errors of those

I

Who teach that, properly speaking, it cannot be said that original sin in itself is enough to condemn the whole human race or to warrant temporal and eternal punishments. For they contradict the apostle when he says: Sin entered the world through one man, and death through sin, and in this way death passed on to all men because all sinned (Rom. 5:12); also: The guilt followed one sin and brought condemnation (Rom. 5:16); likewise: The wages of sin is death (Rom. 6:23).

II

Who teach that the spiritual gifts or the

good dispositions and virtues such as goodness, holiness, and righteousness could not have resided in man's will when he was first created, and therefore could not have been separated from the will at the fall.

For this conflicts with the apostle's description of the image of God in Ephesians 4:24, where he portrays the image in terms of righteousness and holiness, which definitely reside in the will.

III

Who teach that in spiritual death the spiritual gifts have not been separated from man's will, since the will in itself has never been corrupted but only hindered by the darkness of the mind and the unruliness of the emotions, and since the will is able to exercise its innate free capacity once these hindrances are removed, which is to say, it is able of itself to will or choose whatever good is set before it—or else not to will or choose it.

This is a novel idea and an error and has the effect of elevating the power of free choice, contrary to the words of Jeremiah the prophet: The heart itself is deceitful above all things and wicked (Jer. 17:9); and of the words of the apostle: All of us also lived among them (the sons of disobedience) at one time in the passions of our flesh, following the will of our flesh and thoughts (Eph. 2:3).

IV

Who teach that unregenerate man is not strictly or totally dead in his sins or deprived of all capacity for spiritual good but is able to hunger and thirst for righteousness or life and to offer the sacrifice of a broken and contrite spirit which is pleasing to God.

For these views are opposed to the plain testimonies of Scripture: You were dead in your transgressions and sins (Eph. 2:1, 5); The imagination of the thoughts of man's heart is only evil all the time (Gen. 6:5; 8:21). Besides, to hunger and thirst for deliverance from misery and for life, and to offer God the sacrifice of a broken spirit is characteristic only of the regenerate and of those called blessed (Ps. 51:17; Matt. 5:6).

V

Who teach that corrupt and natural man can make such good use of common grace(by which they mean the light of nature)or of the gifts remaining after the fall that he is able thereby gradually to obtain a greater grace– evangelical or saving grace–as well as salvation itself; and that in this way God, for his part, shows himself ready to reveal Christ to all people, since he provides to all, to a sufficient extent and in an effective manner, the means necessary for the revealing of Christ, for faith, and for repentance.

For Scripture, not to mention the experience of all ages, testifies that this is false: He makes known his words to Jacob, his statutes and his laws to Israel; he has done this for no other nation, and they do not know his laws (Ps. 147:19-20); In the past God let all nations go their own way (Acts 14:16); They (Paul and his companions) were kept by the Holy Spirit from speaking God's word in Asia; and When they had come to Mysia, they tried to go to Bithynia, but the Spirit would not allow them to (Acts 16:6-7).

VI

Who teach that in the true conversion of man new qualities, dispositions, or gifts cannot be infused or poured into his will by God, and indeed that the faith [or believing] by which we first come to conversion and from which we receive the name "believers" is not a quality or gift infused by God, but only an act of man, and that it cannot be called a gift except in respect to the power of attaining faith.

For these views contradict the Holy Scriptures, which testify that God does infuse or pour into our hearts the new qualities of faith, obedience, and the experiencing of his love: I will put my law in their minds, and write it on their hearts (Jer. 31:33); I will pour water on the thirsty land, and streams on the dry ground; I will pour out my Spirit on your offspring (Isa.

44:3); The love of God has been poured out in our hearts by the Holy Spirit, who has been given to us (Rom. 5:5). They also conflict with the continuous practice of the Church, which prays with the prophet: Convert me, Lord, and I shall be converted (Jer. 31:18).

VII

Who teach that the grace by which we are converted to God is nothing but a gentle persuasion, or(as others explain it) that the way of God's acting in man's conversion that is most noble and suited to human nature is that which happens by persuasion, and that nothing prevents this grace of moral suasion even by itself from making natural men spiritual; indeed, that God does not produce the assent of the will except in this manner of moral suasion, and that the effectiveness of God's work by which it surpasses the work of Satan consists in the fact that God promises eternal benefits while Satan promises temporal ones.

For this teaching is entirely Pelagian and contrary to the whole of Scripture, which recognizes besides this persuasion also another, far more effective and divine way in which the Holy Spirit acts in man's conversion. As Ezekiel 36:26 puts it: I will give you a new heart and put a new spirit in you; and I will remove your heart of stone and give you a heart of flesh....

VIII

Who teach that God in regenerating man does not bring to bear that power of his omnipotence whereby he may powerfully and unfailingly bend man's will to faith and conversion, but that even when God has accomplished all the works of grace which he uses for man's conversion, man nevertheless can, and in actual fact often does, so resist God and the Spirit in their intent and will to regenerate him, that man completely thwarts his own rebirth; and, indeed, that it remains in his own power whether or not to be reborn.

For this does away with all effective functioning of God's grace in our conversion and subjects the activity of Almighty God to the will of man; it is contrary to the apostles, who teach that we believe by virtue of the effective working of God's mighty strength (Eph. 1:19), and that God fulfills the undeserved good will of his kindness and the work of faith in us with power (2 Thess. 1:11), and likewise that his divine power has given us everything we need for life and godliness (2 Pet. 1:3).

IX

Who teach that grace and free choice are concurrent partial causes which cooperate to initiate conversion, and that grace does not precede—in the order of causality—the effective influence of the will; that is to say, that God does not effectively help man's will to come to conversion before man's will itself motivates and determines itself.

For the early church already condemned this doctrine long ago in the Pelagians, on the basis of the words of the apostle: It does not depend on man's willing or running but on God's mercy (Rom. 9:16); also: Who makes you different from anyone else? and What do you have that you did not receive? (1 Cor. 4:7); likewise: It is God who works in you to will and act according to his good pleasure (Phil. 2:13).

The Fifth Main Point of Doctrine
The Perseverance of the Saints

ARTICLE 1: THE REGENERATE NOT ENTIRELY FREE FROM SIN

Those people whom God according to his purpose calls into fellowship with his Son Jesus Christ our Lord and regenerates by the Holy Spirit, he also sets free from the reign and slavery of sin, though in this life not entirely from the flesh and from the body of sin.

ARTICLE 2: THE BELIEVER'S REACTION TO SINS OF WEAKNESS

Hence daily sins of weakness arise, and blemishes cling to even the best works of

God's people, giving them continual cause to humble themselves before God, to flee for refuge to Christ crucified, to put the flesh to death more and more by the Spirit of supplication and by holy exercises of godliness, and to strain toward the goal of perfection, until they are freed from this body of death and reign with the Lamb of God in heaven.

ARTICLE 3: GOD'S PRESERVATION OF THE CONVERTED

Because of these remnants of sin dwelling in them and also because of the temptations of the world and Satan, those who have been converted could not remain standing in this grace if left to their own resources. But God is faithful, mercifully strengthening them in the grace once conferred on them and powerfully preserving them in it to the end.

ARTICLE 4: THE DANGER OF TRUE BELIEVERS' FALLING INTO SERIOUS SINS

Although that power of God strengthening and preserving true believers in grace is more than a match for the flesh, yet those converted are not always so activated and motivated by God that in certain specific actions they cannot by their own fault depart from the leading of grace, be led astray by the desires of the flesh, and give in to them. For this reason they must constantly watch and pray that they may not be led into temptations. When they fail to do this, not only can they be carried away by the flesh, the world, and Satan into sins, even serious and outrageous ones, but also by God's just permission they sometimes are so carried away–witness the sad cases, described in Scripture, of David, Peter, and other saints falling into sins.

ARTICLE 5: THE EFFECTS OF SUCH SERIOUS SINS

By such monstrous sins, however, they greatly offend God, deserve the sentence of death, grieve the Holy Spirit, suspend the exercise of faith, severely wound the conscience, and sometimes lose the awareness of grace for a time–until, after they have returned to the

way by genuine repentance, God's fatherly face again shines upon them.

ARTICLE 6: GOD'S SAVING INTERVENTION

For God, who is rich in mercy, according to his unchangeable purpose of election does not take his Holy Spirit from his own completely, even when they fall grievously. Neither does he let them fall down so far that they forfeit the grace of adoption and the state of justification, or commit the sin which leads to death (the sin against the Holy Spirit), and plunge themselves, entirely forsaken by him, into eternal ruin.

ARTICLE 7: RENEWAL TO REPENTANCE

For, in the first place, God preserves in those saints when they fall his imperishable seed from which they have been born again, lest it perish or be dislodged. Secondly, by his Word and Spirit he certainly and effectively renews them to repentance so that they have a heartfelt and godly sorrow for the sins they have committed; seek and obtain, through faith and with a contrite heart, forgiveness in the blood of the Mediator; experience again the grace of a reconciled God; through faith adore his mercies; and from then on more eagerly work out their own salvation with fear and trembling.

ARTICLE 8: THE CERTAINTY OF THIS PRESERVATION

So it is not by their own merits or strength but by God's undeserved mercy that they neither forfeit faith and grace totally nor remain in their downfalls to the end and are lost. With respect to themselves this not only easily could happen, but also undoubtedly would happen; but with respect to God it cannot possibly happen, since his plan cannot be changed, his promise cannot fail, the calling according to his purpose cannot be revoked, the merit of Christ as well as his interceding and preserving cannot be nullified, and the sealing of the Holy Spirit can neither be invalidated nor wiped out.

ARTICLE 9: THE ASSURANCE OF THIS PRESERVATION

Concerning this preservation of those

chosen to salvation and concerning the perseverance of true believers in faith, believers themselves can and do become assured in accordance with the measure of their faith, by which they firmly believe that they are and always will remain true and living members of the church, and that they have the forgiveness of sins and eternal life.

ARTICLE 10: THE GROUND OF THIS ASSURANCE

Accordingly, this assurance does not derive from some private revelation beyond or outside the Word, but from faith in the promises of God which he has very plentifully revealed in his Word for our comfort, from the testimony of the Holy Spirit testifying with our spirit that we are God's children and heirs (Rom. 8:16-17), and finally from a serious and holy pursuit of a clear conscience and of good works. And if God's chosen ones in this world did not have this well-founded comfort that the victory will be theirs and this reliable guarantee of eternal glory, they would be of all people most miserable.

ARTICLE 11: DOUBTS CONCERNING THIS ASSURANCE

Meanwhile, Scripture testifies that believers have to contend in this life with various doubts of the flesh and that under severe temptation they do not always experience this full assurance of faith and certainty of perseverance. But God, the Father of all comfort, does not let them be tempted beyond what they can bear, but with the temptation he also provides a way out (1 Cor. 10:13), and by the Holy Spirit revives in them the assurance of their perseverance.

ARTICLE 12: THIS ASSURANCE AS AN INCENTIVE TO GODLINESS

This assurance of perseverance, however, so far from making true believers proud and carnally self-assured, is rather the true root of humility, of childlike respect, of genuine godliness, of endurance in every conflict, of fervent prayers, of steadfastness in cross-

bearing and in confessing the truth, and of well-founded joy in God. Reflecting on this benefit provides an incentive to a serious and continual practice of thanksgiving and good works, as is evident from the testimonies of Scripture and the examples of the saints.

ARTICLE 13: ASSURANCE NO INDUCEMENT TO CARELESSNESS

Neither does the renewed confidence of perseverance produce immorality or lack of concern for godliness in those put back on their feet after a fall, but it produces a much greater concern to observe carefully the ways of the Lord which he prepared in advance. They observe these ways in order that by walking in them they may maintain the assurance of their perseverance, lest, by their abuse of his fatherly goodness, the face of the gracious God (for the godly, looking upon his face is sweeter than life, but its withdrawal is more bitter than death) turn away from them again, with the result that they fall into greater anguish of spirit.

ARTICLE 14: GOD'S USE OF MEANS IN PERSEVERANCE

And, just as it has pleased God to begin this work of grace in us by the proclamation of the gospel, so he preserves, continues, and completes his work by the hearing and reading of the gospel, by meditation on it, by its exhortations, threats, and promises, and also by the use of the sacraments.

ARTICLE 15: CONTRASTING REACTIONS TO THE TEACHING OF PERSEVERANCE

This teaching about the perseverance of true believers and saints, and about their assurance of it–a teaching which God has very richly revealed in his Word for the glory of his name and for the comfort of the godly and which he impresses on the hearts of believers–is something which the flesh does not understand, Satan hates, the world ridicules, the ignorant and the hypocrites abuse, and the spirits of error attack. The bride of Christ, on the other hand, has always loved this teaching very tenderly and defended it steadfastly as a priceless treasure; and God, against whom no plan can avail and no strength can prevail, will ensure that she will continue to do this. To this God alone, Father, Son, and Holy Spirit, be honor and glory forever. Amen.

Rejection of the Errors
Concerning the Teaching of the Perseverance of the Saints
Having set forth the orthodox teaching, the Synod rejects the errors of those

I

Who teach that the perseverance of true believers is not an effect of election or a gift of God produced by Christ's death, but a condition of the new covenant which man, before what they call his "peremptory" election and justification, must fulfill by his free will.

For Holy Scripture testifies that perseverance follows from election and is granted to the chosen by virtue of Christ's death, resurrection, and intercession: The chosen obtained it; the others were hardened (Rom. 11:7); likewise, He who did not spare his own son, but gave him up for us all—how will he not, along with him, grant us all things? Who will bring any charge against those whom God has chosen? It is God who justifies. Who is he that condemns? It is Christ Jesus who died—more than that, who was raised—who also sits at the right hand of God, and is also interceding for us. Who shall separate us from the love of Christ? (Rom. 8:32-35).

II

Who teach that God does provide the believer with sufficient strength to persevere and is ready to preserve this strength in him if he performs his duty, but that even with all those things in place which are necessary to persevere in faith and which God is pleased to use to preserve faith, it still always depends on the choice of man's will whether or not he perseveres.

For this view is obviously Pelagian; and though it intends to make men free it makes them sacrilegious. It is against the enduring consensus of evangelical teaching which takes from man all cause for boasting and ascribes the praise for this benefit only to God's grace. It is also against the testimony of the apostle: It is God who keeps us strong to the end, so that we will be blameless on the day of our Lord Jesus Christ (1 Cor. 1:8).

III

Who teach that those who truly believe and have been born again not only can forfeit justifying faith as well as grace and salvation totally and to the end, but also in actual fact do often forfeit them and are lost forever.

For this opinion nullifies the very grace of justification and regeneration as well as the continual preservation by Christ, contrary to the plain words of the apostle Paul: If Christ died for us while we were still sinners, we will therefore much more be saved from God's wrath through him, since we have now been justified by his blood (Rom. 5:8-9); and contrary to the apostle John: No one who is born of God is intent on sin, because God's seed remains in him, nor can he sin, because he has been born of God (1 John 3:9); also contrary to the words of Jesus Christ: I give eternal life to my sheep, and they shall never perish; no one can snatch them out of my hand. My Father, who has given them to me, is greater than all; no one can snatch them out of my Father's hand (John 10: 28-29).

IV

Who teach that those who truly believe and have been born again can commit the sin that leads to death (the sin against the Holy Spirit).

For the same apostle John, after making mention of those who commit the sin that leads to death and forbidding prayer for them (1 John 5: 16-17), immediately adds: We know that anyone born of God does not commit sin (that is, that kind of sin), but the one who was born of God keeps himself safe, and the evil one does not touch him (v. 18).

V

Who teach that apart from a special revelation no one can have the assurance of future perseverance in this life.

For by this teaching the well-founded consolation of true believers in this life is taken away and the doubting of the Romanists is reintroduced into the church. Holy Scripture, however, in many places derives the assurance not from a special and extraordinary revelation but from the marks peculiar to God's children and from God's completely reliable promises. So especially the apostle Paul: Nothing in all creation can separate us from the love of God that is in Christ Jesus our Lord (Rom. 8:39); and John: They who obey his commands remain in him and he in them. And this is how we know that he remains in us: by the Spirit he gave us (1 John 3:24).

VI

Who teach that the teaching of the assurance of perseverance and of salvation is by its very nature and character an opiate of the flesh and is harmful to godliness, good morals, prayer, and other holy exercises, but that, on the contrary, to have doubt about this is praiseworthy.

For these people show that they do not know the effective operation of God's grace and the work of the indwelling Holy Spirit, and they contradict the apostle John, who asserts the opposite in plain words: Dear friends, now we are children of God, but what we will be has not yet been made known. But we know that when he is made known, we shall be like him, for we shall see him as he is. Everyone who has this hope in him purifies himself, just as he is pure (1 John 3:2-3). Moreover, they are refuted by the examples of the saints in both the Old and the New Testament, who though assured of their perseverance and salvation yet were constant in prayer and other exercises of godliness.

VII

Who teach that the faith of those who believe only temporarily does not differ from justifying and saving faith except in duration alone.

For Christ himself in Matthew 13:20ff. and Luke 8:13ff. clearly defines these further differences between temporary and true believers: he says that the former receive the seed on rocky ground, and the latter receive it in good ground, or a good heart; the former have no root, and the latter are firmly rooted; the former have no fruit, and the latter produce fruit in varying measure, with steadfastness, or perseverance.

VIII

Who teach that it is not absurd that a person, after losing his former regeneration, should once again, indeed quite often, be reborn.

For by this teaching they deny the imperishable nature of God's seed by which we are born again, contrary to the testimony of the apostle Peter: Born again, not of perishable seed, but of imperishable (1 Pet. 1:23).

IX

Who teach that Christ nowhere prayed for an unfailing perseverance of believers in faith.

For they contradict Christ himself when he says: I have prayed for you, Peter, that your faith may not fail (Luke 22:32); and John the gospel writer when he testifies in John 17 that it was not only for the apostles, but also for all those who were to believe by their message that Christ prayed: Holy Father, preserve them in your name (v. 11); and My prayer is not that you take them out of the world, but that you preserve them from the evil one (v. 15).

Conclusion
Rejection of False Accusations
And so this is the clear, simple, and straightforward explanation of the orthodox teaching on the five articles in dispute in the Netherlands, as well as the

rejection of the errors by which the Dutch churches have for some time been disturbed. This explanation and rejection the Synod declares to be derived from God's Word and in agreement with the confessions of the Reformed churches. Hence it clearly appears that those of whom one could hardly expect it have shown no truth, equity, and charity at all in wishing to make the public believe:

1...that the teaching of the Reformed churches on predestination and on the points associated with it by its very nature and tendency draws the minds of people away from all godliness and religion, is an opiate of the flesh and the devil, and is a stronghold of Satan where he lies in wait for all people, wounds most of them, and fatally pierces many of them with the arrows of both despair and self-assurance;

2...that this teaching makes God the author of sin, unjust, a tyrant, and a hypocrite; and is nothing but a refurbished Stoicism, Manicheism, Libertinism, and Mohammedanism;

3...that this teaching makes people carnally self-assured, since it persuades them that nothing endangers the salvation of the chosen, no matter how they live, so that they may commit the most outrageous crimes with self-assurance; and that on the other hand nothing is of use to the reprobate for salvation even if they have truly performed all the works of the saints;

4...that this teaching means that God predestined and created, by the bare and unqualified choice of his will, without the least regard or consideration of any sin, the greatest part of the world to eternal condemnation; that in the same manner in which election is the source and cause of faith and good works, reprobation is the cause of unbelief and ungodliness; that many infant children of believers are snatched in their innocence from their mothers' breasts and cruelly cast into hell

so that neither the blood of Christ nor their baptism nor the prayers of the church at their baptism can be of any use to them; and very many other slanderous accusations of this kind which the Reformed churches not only disavow but even denounce with their whole heart.

Therefore this Synod of Dordt in the name of the Lord pleads with all who devoutly call on the name of our Savior Jesus Christ to form their judgment about the faith of the Reformed churches, not on the basis of false accusations gathered from here or there, or even on the basis of the personal statements of a number of ancient and modern authorities–statements which are also often either quoted out of context or misquoted and twisted to convey a different meaning–but on the basis of the churches' own official confessions and of the present explanation of the orthodox teaching which has been endorsed by the unanimous consent of the members of the whole Synod, one and all.

Moreover, the Synod earnestly warns the false accusers themselves to consider how heavy a judgment of God awaits those who give false testimony against so many churches and their confessions, trouble the consciences of the weak, and seek to prejudice the minds of many against the fellowship of true believers.

Finally, this Synod urges all fellow ministers in the gospel of Christ to deal with this teaching in a godly and reverent manner, in the academic institutions as well as in the churches; to do so, both in their speaking and writing, with a view to the glory of God's name, holiness of life, and the comfort of anxious souls; to think and also speak with Scripture according to the analogy of faith; and, finally, to refrain from all those ways of speaking which go beyond the bounds set for us by the genuine sense of the Holy Scriptures and which could give impertinent sophists a just occasion to scoff at the teaching of the Reformed churches or even to bring false accusations against it.

May God's Son Jesus Christ, who sits at the right hand of God and gives gifts to men, sanctify us in the truth, lead to the truth those who err, silence the mouths of those who lay false accusations against sound teaching, and equip faithful ministers of his Word with a spirit of wisdom and discretion, that all they say may be to the glory of God and the building up of their hearers. Amen.

When I come to a text which speaks of election, I delight myself in the doctrine of election. When the apostles exhort me to repentance and obedience, and indicate my freedom of choice and action, I give myself up to that side of the question.
Charles Simeon

When a Calvinist says that all things happen according to the predestination of God, he speaks the truth, and I am willing to be called a Calvinist. But when an Arminian says that when a man sins, the sin is his own, and that if he continues in sin, and perishes, his eternal damnation will lie entirely at his own door, I believe that he speaks the truth, though I am not willing to be called an Arminian. The fact is, there is some truth in both these systems of theology.
C.H. Spurgeon

A Man's free will cannot cure him even of the tooth ache, or a sore finger; and yet he madly thinks it is in its power to cure his soul. The greatest judgement which God Himself can, in the present life, inflict upon a man is, to leave him in the hand of his own boasted free will. Look where you will, and you will generally find that free-willers are very free livers. According to Arminianism, grace has the name, but free-will has the game.
Augustus Toplady

Arrogance
See also: Pride
The LORD detests all the proud of heart.
The Bible, Proverbs 16:5

Art
The artist doesn't see things as they are, but as he is.
Author unknown

Life beats down and crushes the soul and art reminds you that you have one.
Stella Adler

Art takes nature as its model.
Aristotle

Every artist dips his brush in his own soul, and paints his own nature into his pictures.
Henry Ward Beecher

It is my opinion that art lost its basic creative drive the moment it was separated from worship. In former days the artist remained unknown and his work was to the glory of God. Today the individual has become the highest form and the greatest bane of artistic creation.
Ingmar Bergman

Art is I; Science is We.
Claude Bernard

Art is frozen Zen.
R.H. Blyth

Has the Lord adorned flowers with all the beauty which spontaneously presents itself to the eye, and the sweet odor which delights the sense of smell, and shall it be unlawful for us to enjoy that beauty and this odor? What? Has He not so distinguished colors as to make some more agreeable than others? ... In short, has He not given many things a value without having any necessary use?
John Calvin

In my heterodox heart there is yearly growing up the strangest, crabbed, one-sided persuasion, that art is but a reminiscence now; that for us in these days prophecy (well understood), not poetry, is the thing wanted. How can we sing and paint when we do not yet believe and see?
Thomas Carlyle

Art is Nature speeded up and God slowed down.
Chazal

Art for art's sake.
Victor Cousin

If the artist sees nothing within him, then he should also refrain from painting what he sees before him.
Caspar David Friedrich

Art is a collaboration between God and the artist, and the less the artist does the better.
André Gide

A man should hear a little music, read a little poetry, and see a fine picture every day of his life, in order that worldly cares may not obliterate the sense of the beautiful which God has implanted in the human soul.
Johann Wolfgang von Goethe

Art is not a thing; it is a way.
Elbert Hubbard

We must never forget that art is not a form of propaganda, it is a form of truth.
John Fitzgerald Kennedy

If God is and remains Sovereign, then art can work no enchantment except in keeping with the ordinances which God ordained for the beautiful, when He, as the Supreme Artist, called this world into existence. And further, if God is and remains Sovereign, then He also imparts these artistic gifts to whom He will, first even to Cain's, and not to Abel's posterity; not as if art were Cainitic, but in order that he who has sinned away the highest gifts, should at least, as Calvin so beautifully says, in the lesser gifts of art have some testimony of the Divine bounty.
Abraham Kuyper

A man paints with his brains and not with his hands.
Michelangelo

The true work of art is but a shadow of the divine perfection.
Michelangelo

Pictures of Christ are in principle a violation of the second commandment. A picture of Christ, if it serves any useful purpose, must evoke some thought or feeling respecting him and, in view of what he is, this thought or feeling will be worshipful. We cannot avoid making the picture a medium of worship. But since the materials for this medium of worship are not derived from the only revelation we possess respecting Jesus, namely, Scripture, the worship is constrained by a creation of the human mind that has no revelatory warrant. This is will worship. For the principle of the second commandment is that we are to worship God only in ways prescribed and authorized by him. It is a grievous sin to have worship constrained by a human figment, and that is what a picture of the Savior involves.
John Murray

The art of a people is a true mirror to their minds.
Jawaharial Nehru

Every child is an artist. The problem is how to remain an artist once he grows up.
Pablo Picasso

Everyone wants to understand art. Why not try to understand the song of a bird? Why does one love the night, flowers, everything around one, without trying to understand them?
Pablo Picasso

If my husband would ever meet a woman on the street who looked like the women in his paintings, he would fall over in a dead faint.
Mrs Pablo Picasso

Art is not the bread, but the wine of life.
Jean Paul Richter

If I am walking in an art gallery and see a

beautiful painting, it may be good to praise the Lord, and to thank Him for that great gift. The thing is beautiful, and therefore a joy and spiritually rich … But more than likely it will not even occur to us, for we place the arts out of the context of life, making them something autonomous; or say that the gift is just "natural," so opposing nature to grace, forgetting that there is no "nature" that is out of God's creation. No: let us give praise to God for every manifestation of His gifts.

H.R. Rookmaaker

Life without industry is guilt, and industry without art is brutality.

John Ruskin

Art is not a study of positive reality, it is the seeking for ideal truth.

George Sand

All art is but imitation of nature.

Seneca

Art is not a handicraft, it is the transmission of feeling the artist has experienced.

Leo Tolstoy

All art is quite useless.

Oscar Wilde

Ascension

After he said this, he was taken up before their very eyes, and a cloud hid him from their sight.

The Bible, Acts 1:9

As sign and wonder this exaltation is a pointer to the revelation that occurred in His resurrection, of Jesus Christ as the heart of all powers in heaven and earth.

Karl Barth

When Christ returned to heaven, he withdrew his physical presence from our sight. He didn't stop being with the disciples but by the ascension fulfilled his promise to be with us to the end of the

world. As his body was raised to heaven, so his power and reign have spread to the uttermost parts.

John Calvin

In the Christian story God descends to re-ascend.

C.S. Lewis

Hail the day that sees him rise
To his throne above the skies;
Christ, a while to mortals given,
Re-ascends his native heaven.

Charles Wesley

Asceticism

However great your zeal and many the efforts of your asceticism, they are all in vain and without useful result unless they attain to love in a broken spirit (Ps. 51:17, Ps. 34:18).

Symeon the New Theologian

Ask

Ask and it will be given yo you;
seek and you will find;
knock and the door will be opened to you.
For everyone who asks receives;
he who seeks finds;
and to him who knocks, the door will be opened.

The Bible, Matthew 7:7-8

Many things are lost for want of asking.

English proverb

Aspirations
See also: Ambition; Ambition, Warnings against; Goals

If you have no aspirations, then your life will control you rather than you controlling your life.

Author unknown

Far away there in the sunshine are my highest aspirations. I may not reach them, but I can look up and see their beauty, believe in them, and try to follow where they lead.

Louisa May Alcott

Assassination

Assassination has never changed the history of the world.

Benjamin Disraeli

Assurance

See also: Means of grace

Let us draw near to God with a sincere heart in full assurance of faith.

The Bible, Hebrews 10:22

Assurance

Horatius Bonar

"We know that we are of God, and the whole world lieth in wickedness. And we know that the Son of God is come, and hath given us an understanding, that we may know Him that is true; and we are in Him that is true, even in His Son Jesus Christ. This is the true God, and eternal life" (1 John 5:19-20).

In the early Church there was nothing of the uncertainty which we find among Christians now. They knew what they were, and it was on the authenticated facts concerning Christ that they rested this certainty. No one then thought of saying, "I believe, but I am not sure whether I am born of God;" for they took for granted that "whosoever believeth that Jesus is the Christ is born of God." They did not analyze their own faith to ascertain how far it was of the right quantity and quality. They never thought of themselves at all, but only of Him who, though rich, for their sakes had become poor. All the epistles take for granted that they knew that they were Christians; nor is anything written there to encourage them to suspect themselves, or to teach them the art of doubting. Nothing is there addressed to them to lead them to make much of their doubts, or to believe in their own faith as the true way of deliverance from doubting. "We know," was the apostle's language; "We know," was the response which that language met with from all to whom he wrote.

The frequent use of this expression in the epistles lead us to make inquiry as to its actual import, and its bearings on ourselves. It is undoubtedly the language of certainty; and, as such, let us see in what connection it is used.

It is used respecting things past, things present, and things future, all of which are represented as being absolutely certain to the person knowing.

(1) The Past – 1 John 5:20, "We know that the Son of God is come"; 3:14, "We know that we have passed from death unto life." These two things, one relating to the Son of God, and the other to the Christian, are spoken of as equally past, and as equally certain objects of sure knowledge.

(2) The Present – 1 John 2:18, "We know that it is the last time" 2:3, "We know that we know Him"; 2:5, "We know that He abideth in us"; 5:19, "We know that we are of God." All these things are represented as ascertained and conscious certainties, regarding which there could be no doubt whatever. This was the true state of the early Church universally. We do not read of anything short of this – anything corresponding to the state of doubt, and gloom, and uncertainty, in which we find so many Christians now.

(3) The Future – 1 John 3:2, "We know that when He shall appear, we shall be like Him." The early Christians counted the one as sure as the other. Their future was not darkened with the clouds of uncertainty: clouds of tribulation might envelope them, but their future was glorious.

We find the expression "I know" used in a similar way in other parts of Scripture. 2 Tim. 1:12, "I know whom I have believed." We find the words, "Ye know that ye were not redeemed with corruptible things."

All these passages show us what the condition of personal certainty was which the early Church enjoyed, of which we ought to be in possession. A Christian is not one who "thinks;" or "hopes," or "trusts" that he is forgiven and accepted, but who knows it as certainly as he knows the facts regarding Jesus, His death and resurrection. How did they come by this certainty?

They got it out of the promise which the gospel embodies. That gospel consists of two parts or testimonies, or rather a testimony and a promise. The testimony relates to the Christ of God, His person and His work; and the promise is, that whosoever believes the testimony is not only entitled, but commanded to draw the conclusion that he has eternal life. A testimony without a promise would not have done it; it would have merely brought us into the position of men who see that their salvation is a possibility. They could not, from the testimony alone, draw the conclusion, "I have eternal life;" but the promise annexed to the testimony, declaring that every one who receives the testimony is saved, enables them at once to draw the personal conclusion. Thus we see that, while personal assurance is not the first thing in faith, it ought to follow immediately, and will do so where the gospel is rightly understood.

It is out of this annexed promise that our assurance comes, and not out of subsequent acts, or feelings, or experiences of our own. He who has not this assurance must not be believing the very gospel, but either more than it, or less than it. He who takes the whole gospel, both testimony and promise, knows that he has eternal life.

But, let us inquire a little further into this apostolic and primitive certainty. Both John and Paul use this word "We know," frequently. They use it not merely as apostles, but in the name of all believers. They do not merely say I, but we (1 John 3:14; 2 Tim. 1:12). It is the language of certainty, not of opinion or conjecture. Let us ask, (1) What is the certainty? (2) how they got it? (3) how they kept it? (4) how they used it?

I. What is the certainty? – We know that we are of God – that is, that we belong to God, that we are His children. This is –
(1) Very definite. There is no mistaking what it means. We have passed from death to life; no longer condemned children of wrath, but God's property – God's sons, God's heirs. Not generally "we are Christians," but "we are of God."

(2) Very decided. It is not "We hope we are of God, We think we are, We trust we are, We are inclined to believe we are, but "We are." There is no want of decision here, no vagueness, no ambiguity, no hesitation, no "if", no "perhaps", but "we know."
(3) Very personal. It was something regarding themselves individually, not merely as classed with a certain body generally, but a personal thing, of which they were as cognizant as of the family, or city, or nation to which they belonged. Paul knew, and John knew, and all the early Christians knew that they were of God.
Yes, this was the apostolic watchword; "We know that we are of God." It was the Reformation watchword; it must be ours.

II. How they got it. In believing. It was not that they first believed themselves to be of God, and so were of God. They believed what God has told them concerning His Son, that Jesus was the Christ. They believed the record, the true record, concerning the eternal life which was in Him. In believing that record they became sons of God and they knew this. The assurance of their own sonship was the necessary and inseparable consequence of believing the record, the gospel, the report. They got this certainty at once – not after passing through a long and mysterious process; not after summing up all their own goodnesses, and being satisfied with the quality and the quantity of their faith; not as a result of tedious metaphysical investigation into their spiritual state – but as the simple and inevitable inference from their believing the gospel.

III. How they kept it. They held the beginning of their confidence steadfast to the end. They continued to believe all that they did at first, and just in the same simple way. That which gave them peace and assurance at first, continued to do so to the last. Not as if it were a light matter whether they became holy or not. Far from this. That gospel which they believed taught them that they were to deny ungodliness and worldly lusts. The peace they got was a holy peace, and could not exist in conjunction with an unholy life. The love of God out of which that peace had come to them was a holy love, and the indulgence of sin was incompatible with the belief of it. That sin in a true saint does not alter his standing as a pardoned man in the sight of God, is true; but it comes between him and God, and shuts God out. It may not tell upon God's feelings toward men; but it must tell upon man's feelings towards God, and also upon his knowledge of God's feelings towards him. The assurance does not come out of our holiness; yet it cannot be maintained save in connection with a holy life.

IV. How they used it. Not for pride, self-seeking, or vain-glory. It did not destroy humility and meekness in them, nor did it lead to careless living. It brought with it no contempt of others, and no ostentation in their religious profession. They used it in none of these ways, nor for such purposes. It was to them:

(1) A humbling truth – That God should have given them sonship was humbling; that He should have given them the assurance of it was more humbling still; for it brought out more fully all their own unworthiness, in contrast with God's boundless love. Compassed about with such love, so free and great, how could they be proud? Where is presumption? It is excluded. By what law? of faith and certainty.

(2) A quickening truth – It had true life in it, true power. It stirred, it roused, it animated, it nerved. Uncertainty as to our relationship to God is one of the most enfeebling and dispiriting of things. It makes a man heartless. It takes the pith out of him. He cannot fight; he cannot run. He is easily dismayed, and gives way. He can do nothing for God. But when we know that we are of God, we are vigorous, brave, invincible. There is no more quickening truth than this of assurance.

(3) A gladdening truth – This needs no long proof or illustration. What gladness is contained in these simple words, "We know that we are of God!" Until we can say this, where is joy? When we can say this, where

is sorrow? It has fled away. What can cast us down?

(4) A sanctifying truth – Yes, it sanctified the early Christians; and this in two ways: (a) separating them from a world that knew nothing of his love; (b) making them inwardly holy, like Him to whom they knew that they belonged. "Now are we the sons of God...He that hath this hope in Him purifieth himself."

Are you sure? Can you say, I am of God? Has your gospel brought you certainty? or has it left you in non-assurance, a prey to doubt? Then what has it really done for you?

The Bible is the book of certainties. It gives not uncertain sound anywhere. It does not speak the language of doubt, or speculation, or conjecture, or opinion, but of certainty. Its object is to place us on the same footing of certainty, absolute certainty; enabling us to say not merely I think, or I judge, but I know; enabling us to say without faltering, yet without boasting, I possess the true, the real, the certain, the authentic. Our certainty from such a source is as sure as demonstration, because it rests on the authority of the God only wise.

John's first is written in the language of certainty. "We know" is its motto, its burden from first to last. "Ye have an unction from the Holy One, and ye know all things" (2:20). "We know that we have passed from death to life" (3:14). "We know that we are of God" (5:19). "We know that the Son of God is come" (5:20).

We now look at three certainties from John's epistle.

1. We know that the Son of God is come. This is the central point of earth's history, the most real, and certain, and productive of all its facts and events. On it everything turns, whether men see it or not.

(1) There is such a being as the Son of God. He is not merely a son, but the Son, the eternal Son, the only begotten Son, the well-beloved Son; one with the Father.

(2) He has come. Not merely He is, but He has come down to us in very deed. The

word implies, remaining as well as coming. It is not, He has visited us, He has come and gone; but, He has come to us, and is with us. He has arrived, not to depart, but to remain.

(3) He is Jesus of Nazareth. A very man is He. Born at Bethlehem, brought up at Nazareth, the son of Mary, Jesus, who went out and in amongst us. The Word was made flesh, and dwelt among us.

(4) We know this. It is the most certain of all certainties; an event beyond the shadow of a doubt; the surest of all sure facts in earthly history. We know it on God's authority and on man's. Divine and human testimony unite here. Word and deed make us sure of this.

Ah, this is knowledge! The like of it is not to be found elsewhere. This is the knowledge that satisfies, gladdens, and gives us a foundation to rest on – THE SON OF GOD HAS COME.

2. We know that He has given us an understanding that we may know Him that is true – for the meaning of "understanding" we refer to Eph. 1:18: "The eyes of your understanding darkened." Christ is the giver of the new mind, whereby we discern the truth. He is, (1) Renewer; (2) Teacher; (3) the Wisdom itself. He is the knowledge, and He gives the power of knowing. "Who teacheth like Him?" He is the opener of the eye and ear. He that is true is evidently the true One, or true God. "This is life eternal, that they might know Thee, the only true God," to give us a mind capable of knowing and comprehending this true God. It is not a God that we need to know, but the God, the one living and true God. There is no knowledge of God out of Christ, apart from Christ, or without Christ. Where the knowledge of Christ is not, there is utter ignorance of God – the worship of a false or an unknown god. False worship is a serious thing, a fearful sin, a hideous blasphemy. Falsehood touching God is infinite dishonour. Misapprehension of God is the root of all idolatry; and worship under such misapprehension is idolatry or superstition. It is the true God that is to be worshipped,

none else. He will not give His glory to another. Nor will the knowledge of any false god fill or pacify the soul. It is only that God whom Jesus of Nazareth revealed that will suffice for the human spirit.

3. We know that we are in Him that is true. To be in Him is to be out of the world, and out of self. We are to be in Him as the flower is in the garden, as the star is in the sky, as the graft is in the olive tree. We are to be rooted and built up in Him. Here it is not near Him, nor on Him, but in Him. We dwell in Him, and He in us. We are in Him as the true God; as such He is our God, our habitation. Thus we are compassed about with Him as the earth is by the air; He compasses us about. It is not merely that in Him we live, and move, and have our being; but much more than this, something of another kind; something that involves spiritual life, fellowship, love, and everlasting blessedness. But it is added, "in His Son Jesus Christ." We are not only in the Father, but in the Son, as we read (1 Thess. 1:1), "The Church of the Thessalonians which is IN God the Father, and IN the Lord Jesus Christ." It is this inbeing, this indwelling, this participation or fellowship, that is our true standing and privilege.

(1.) This knowledge saves. There is no salvation without it. It is saving knowledge. In knowing the true God we are saved.

(2) This knowledge gladdens. False knowledge of God, or the knowledge of a false god, imparts no joy; this does. It is joy to know the true One.

(3) This knowledge purifies. Error or falsehood cannot deliver from sin, cannot purify the soul. All error is impurity, unholiness. All truth is good, and all truth respecting God sanctifies, expands, elevates.

(4) This knowledge makes us useful. It is like a light or a fire within us that cannot be hidden. It is like a power within us which cannot but work. It is irrepressible.

Acquaint thyself with God, and be at peace; thereby good shall come unto thee. He has revealed Himself in Jesus Christ,

His Son. Blessed the man that knows Him. Unhappy he that knows Him not. Better that he had been a beast; better that he had never been born.
Horatius Bonar

A well-grounded assurance is always attended with three fair handmaids: love, humility and holy joy.
Thomas Brooks

Blessed assurance, Jesus is mine!
Oh what a foretaste of Glory Divine!
Heir of salvation, purchase of God,
Born of the Spirit, washed in His Blood.
Fanny Crosby

Speculations I have none. I'm resting on certainties. "For I know whom I have believed, and am persuaded that he is able to keep that which I have committed unto him against that day."
Michael Faraday, nearing death, quoting from the Bible, 2 Timothy 1:12 KJV

Repose in the blood of Christ; a firm confidence in God, and persuasion of his favor; the highest tranquillity, serenity, and peace of mind, with a deliverance from every fleshly desire, and a cessation of all, even inward sins.
Arvid Gradin, defining "full assurance of faith" (Hebrews 10:22), for John Wesley

What a wonderful thing it is to be sure of one's faith! How wonderful to be a member of the evangelical church, which preaches the free grace of God through Christ as the hope of sinners! If we were to rely on our works, what would become of us?
G.F. Handel

The Holy Spirit is no skeptic. He has written neither doubt nor mere opinion into our hearts, but rather solid assurances, which are more sure and solid than all experience and even life itself.
Martin Luther, to Erasmus

Assurance grows by repeated conflict, by our repeated experimental proof of the Lord's power and goodness to save; when we have been brought very low and helped, sorely wounded and healed, cast down and raised again, have given up all hope, and been suddenly snatched from danger, and placed in safety; and when these things have been repeated to us and in us a thousand times over, we begin to learn to trust simply to the word and power of God, beyond and against appearances: and this trust, when habitual and strong, bears the name of assurance; for even assurance has degrees.
John Newton

God sometimes marvelously raiseth the souls of his saints with some close and near approaches unto them – gives them a sense of His eternal love, a taste of the embraces of His Son and the inhabitation of the Spirit, without the least intervening disturbance; and then this is their assurance. But this life is not a season to be always taking wages in; our work is not yet done; we are not always to abide in this mount; we must down again into the battle – fight again, cry again, complain again. Shall the soul be thought now to have lost its assurance? Not at all. It had before assurance with joy, triumph, and exultation; it hath it now, or may have, with wrestling, cries, tears, and supplications. And a man's assurance may be as good, as true, when he lies on the earth with a sense of sin, as when he is carried up to the third heaven with a sense of love and foretaste of glory.
John Owen

The wise Christian will not let his assurance depend upon his powers of imagination.
A.W. Tozer

Assurance

A.A. Hodge

I think the first essential mark of the difference between true and false assurance is to be found in the fact that the true works humility. There is nothing in the world that works such satanic, profound, God-defiant pride as false assurance; nothing works such utter humility, or brings to such utter self-emptiness, as the child-like spirit of true assurance. Surely this can be known. If a person is self-confident, there is self-assurance; if there is any evidence of pride in connection with his claim, it is a most deadly mark – it is the plague-spot which marks death and corruption. But if there is utter humility, you have the sign of the true spirit.

This will manifest itself in connection with another mark. If one is really united to Christ in a union so established that Christ is indeed in possession of the soul, the whole consciousness will be taken up with what I would call Christ-consciousness, and there will be no self-consciousness. Little children are very prompt to show their character. There is a great difference in them. Bring a child into a room. She comes thinking about nothing in particular, looking at her mother, then looking at the guests or anything that objectively strikes her, not thinking of herself. That is pure, sweet, and lovely. She grows older, and she comes to think of herself and what people think of her, and her manner has lost its unconsciousness. A great deal of what you call bashfulness is rottenness at the heart; it is self-consciousness. Nothing in the world so tends to defile the imagination, to pervert the affections, and to corrupt the morals, as self-consciousness. You know it is connected with every diseased and morbid action of the body.

A young woman told me that she wanted the witness of the Spirit, and she talked about it everlastingly; she wanted to tell her own experience and feelings always. I told her she must forget herself, not think of her own feelings. The man who is talking about his love unceasingly has no love; the man who is talking about his faith unceasingly has no faith: the two things cannot go together. When you love, what are you thinking about? Are you not thinking about the object of your love? And when you

believe, what are you thinking about? Why, the object that you believe. Suppose you ask yourself, "Am I believing?" Why, of course you are not believing when you are thinking of believing. No human being believes except when he thinks about Christ. Am I loving? Of course I am not loving when I am thinking about loving. No human being loves except when he is thinking about Christ as the object of his love.

In Virginia I once saw one human being in whom there was the perfect work of grace, as far as I could see as her pastor, and I was intimate with her six years. Even on earth she was one of those who had made their garments white in the blood of the Lamb, and she seemed always to walk upon the verge of heaven. I never heard her speak of any one particular of her character or of her own graces. I have come out of the pulpit when the congregation had gone, and have found her upon her knees in her pew, absolutely unconscious of all external objects, so far was she absorbed in worship. When I roused her from her trance, she cried instantly, "Is He not holy? Is He not glorious? Is He not beautiful? Is He not infinite?" She did not speak of her own love or of her feelings.

A great deal of Perfectionism is rotten to the core. All self-consciousness is of the very essence and nature of sin. Then, again, true confidence leads necessarily to strong desires for more knowledge and more holiness, for unceasing advances of grace.

I was told once, in a congregation where I preached, that I need not tell a certain young man anything about religion; he had finished it – that is, that, having finished it, he found nothing else to do. That is what the word "perfect" means. Now, when a man has finished eternal life, when he has finished learning all the revelation of God, when he has experienced all the infinite benefits of Christ's redemption, when he has finished all the mysterious work of the Holy Ghost in his heart, he ought to be annihilated. There is no place in heaven or on earth for such a man.

But a man who really has the love of God in his heart is always reaching forward to the things which are before. The more he

loves, the more he wants to love; the more he is consecrated, the more consecration he longs for. He has grand ideas and grand aims, but they lie beyond him in heaven.
A.A. Hodge

Astrology

The good Christian should beware of astrologers, and all those who make empty prophecies. The danger already exists that the astrologers have made a covenant with the devil to darken the spirit and to confine man in the bonds of Hell.
Augustine of Hippo

Esau and Jacob were born of the same father and mother, at the same time, and under the same planets, but their nature was wholly different. You would persuade me that astrology is a true science!
Martin Luther

Atheism
See also: Atheism and deism; Atheist; God, Belief in God
The fool says in his heart, "There is no God."
The Bible, Psalm 14:1

Lord, grant me the serenity to accept the things I cannot change, the courage to change the things I can, and the wisdom not to strangle the stubborn atheists who can't see You when You're right under their noses!
Author unknown

Why is the Atheist's main target always Jesus of Nazareth, and never Buddha, Confucius, or Mohammed? Why is the aspiring athlete's target always the true champion and never the also-rans?
Author unknown

How to trap an atheist: Serve him a fine meal, then ask him if he believes there is a cook.
Author unknown

The atheist can't find God for the same reason that a thief can't find a police officer.
Author unknown

Atheism is the death of hope, the suicide of the soul.
Author unknown

I tried atheism for a while, but my faith just wasn't strong enough.
Author unknown

To be an atheist requires an infinitely greater measure of faith than to receive all the great truths which atheism would deny.
Joseph Addison

God never wrought a miracle to convince Atheism, because His ordinary works convince it.
Francis Bacon

I had rather believe all the fables in the Legend and the Talmud and the Alcoran, than that this universal frame is without a mind.
Francis Bacon

It is true, that a little philosophy inclineth man's mind to Atheism; but depth in philosophy bringeth men's minds about to religion.
Francis Bacon

They are ill discoverers that think there is no land, when they can see nothing but sea.
Francis Bacon

Atheism is rather in the lip than in the heart of man.
Francis Bacon

How am I, an a-temporal being imprisoned in time and space, to escape from my imprisonment, when I know that outside space and time lies nothing, and that I, in the ultimate depths of my reality, am nothing also.
Samuel Beckett

We find the most terrible form of atheism, not in the militant and passionate struggle against the idea of God himself, but in the practical atheism of everyday living, in indifference and torpor. We often

encounter these forms of atheism among those who are formally Christians.
Nicolai A. Berdyaev

I claim that the heavenly Father is a myth; that in the face of a knowledge of life and the world, we cannot reasonably believe in him. There is no heavenly Father watching tenderly over us, his children. He is the baseless shadow of a wistful human dream.
Robert Blatchford

The atheist staring from his attic window is often nearer to God than the believer caught up in his own false image of God.
Martin Buber

An atheist is a man who has no invisible means of support.
John Buchan

Theist and Atheist – the fight between them is as to whether God shall be called God or have some other name.
Samuel Butler

A creedless race will quickly become a corrupt race. Atheism in the mind breeds anarchy in the life as like begets like. Creed and conduct are inseparably united. A faithless world must be a foul world. Waves of crime rise from seas of doubt.
Warren Akin Candler

If I did not believe in God, I should still want my doctor, my lawyer and my banker to do so.
G.K. Chesterton

When a man ceases to believe in God he does not believe in nothing, he believes almost in anything.
G.K. Chesterton

If God does not exist, everything is permissible.
Fyodor Dostoevsky

The complete atheist stands on the penultimate step to most perfect faith (he may or may not take a further step), but the indifferent person has no faith whatever except a bad fear, and that but rarely, and only if he is sensitive.
Fyodor Dostoevsky

Here lies an Atheist
All dressed up
And no place to go.
Epitaph in a Thurmont cemetery, Maryland

The personality of God is nothing else than the projected personality of man.
Ludwig Feuerbach

He only is a true atheist to whom the predicates of the Divine Being – for example, love, wisdom and justice – are nothing.
Ludwig Feuerbach

If thou beest ever so exact in thy morals, and not a worshiper of God, then thou art an atheist.
William Gurnall

All thinking men are atheists.
Ernest Hemingway

Whoever considers the study of anatomy, I believe will never be an atheist; the frame of man's body, and coherence of his parts, being so strange and paradoxical, that I hold it to be the greatest miracle of nature.
Edward Herbert

Calling Atheism a religion is like calling bald a hair color.
Don Hirschberg

An atheist is one who hopes the Lord will do nothing to disturb his disbelief.
Franklin P. Jones

An atheist's creed
There is no God.
There is no objective Truth.
There is no ground for Reason.
There is no absolute Morals.
There is no ultimate Value.
There is no ultimate Meaning.

There is no eternal Hope.
Steve Kumar

[As an atheist] I never noticed that the very strength of the pessimists' case poses us a problem. If the universe is so bad, how on earth did human beings ever come to attribute it to the activity of a wise and good Creator?
C.S. Lewis

I was at this time living, like so many Atheists or Antitheists, in a whirl of contradictions. I maintained that God did not exist. I was also very angry with God for not existing. I was equally angry with Him for creating a world.
C.S. Lewis

Atheism turns out to be too simple. If the whole universe has no meaning, we should never have found out that it has no meaning: just as, if there were no light in the universe and therefore no creatures with eyes, we should never know it was dark.
C.S. Lewis

I can see how it might be possible for a man to look down upon the earth and be an atheist, but I cannot conceive how he could look up into the heavens and say there is no God.
Abraham Lincoln

In agony or danger, no nature is atheist. The mind that knows not what to fly to, flies to God.
Henry More

God is dead.
Friedrich Nietzsche

What was formerly contemplated and worshiped as God is now perceived to be something human.
Friedrich Nietzsche

What thinking man is there who still requires the hypothesis of a God?
Friedrich Nietzsche

But we do not all want to enter into the kingdom of heaven: we have become men, – *so we want the kingdom of earth.*
Friedrich Nietzsche

The current cultural trend toward spirituality affirms a truth echoed down through the centuries that we are somehow incomplete, somehow unfulfilled without God.
Luis Palau

Belief is a wise wager. Granted that faith cannot be proved, what harm will come to you if you gamble on its truth and it proves false? If you gain, you gain all; if you lose, you lose nothing. Wager, then, without hesitation, that God exists.
Blaise Pascal

What reason have atheists for saying that we cannot rise again? Which is more difficult: to be born, or to rise again? That what has never been should be, or that what has been should be again? Is it more difficult to come into being than to return to it?
Blaise Pascal

I am an atheist who has lost his faith.
Boris Pasternak

Atheism is a disease of the soul before it is an error of the mind.
Plato

Were there no God we would be in this glorious world with grateful hearts and no one to thank.
Christina Rossetti

The worst moment for an atheist is when he is really thankful and has nobody to thank.
D.G. Rossetti

When one admits that nothing is certain one must, I think, also add that some things are more nearly certain than others.
Bertrand Russell

That God does not exist, I cannot deny,
That my whole being cries out for God

I cannot forget.
Jean-Paul Sartre

During Russell's ninetieth birthday a London lady sat next to him at his party, and over the soup she suggested to him that he was not only the world's most famous atheist but, by this time, very probably the world's oldest atheist. "What will you do, Bertie, if it turns out you're wrong?" she asked. "I mean, what if – uh – when the time comes, you should meet Him? What will you say?" Russell was delighted with the question. His bright, bird-like eyes grew even brighter as he contemplated this possible future dialogue, and then he pointed a finger upward and cried, "Why, I should say, 'God, you gave us insufficient evidence.'"
Al Seckel

If I were asked today to formulate as concisely as possible the main cause of the ruinous revolution that swallowed up some 60 million of our people, I could not put it more accurately than to repeat: "Men had forgotten God; that is why all this has happened."
Alexander Solzhenitsyn

Atheism is a crutch for those who cannot bear the reality of God.
Tom Stoppard

The atheist who is moved by love is moved by the spirit of God; an atheist who lives by love is saved by his faith in the God whose existence (under that name) he denies.
William Temple

An atheist is a man who believes himself an accident.
Francis Thompson

Among the repulsions of atheism for me has been its drastic uninterestingness as an intellectual position. Where was the ingenuity, the ambiguity, the humanity (in the Harvard sense) of saying that the universe just happened to happen and that when we're dead we're dead?
John Updike

Most of the great men of this world live as if they were atheists. Every man who has lived with his eyes open, knows that the knowledge of a God, his presence, and his justice, has not the slightest influence over the wars, the treaties, the objects of ambition, interest, or pleasure, in the pursuit of which they are wholly occupied.
François de Voltaire

Now, now my good man, this is no time for making enemies.
Voltaire on his deathbed in response to a priest asking that he renounce Satan.

The world embarrasses me, and I cannot think this watch exists and has no Watchmaker.
François-Marie Voltaire

The religion of the atheist has a God-shaped blank at its heart.
H.G. Wells

Atheism and deism
See also: Atheism
All who seek God apart from Jesus Christ, and who rest in nature, either find no light to satisfy them, or form for themselves a means of knowing God and serving him without a Mediator. Thus they fall either into atheism or into deism, two things which the Christian religion almost equally abhors.
Blaise Pascal

Atheist
See also: Atheism; Atheism and deism
God is an imaginary being created by the mental instability of man, onto which he blames his iniquities, and from which expects reward for his accomplishments.
Andy Benas

Atonement
See also: Atonement, Limited; Christ, Death of; Cross; Salvation
All of us have strayed away like sheep. We have left God's paths to follow our own.

Yet the Lord laid on him the guilt and sins of us all.
The Bible, Isaiah 53:6, NLT

"Look, the Lamb of God, who takes away the sins of the world!"
The Bible, John 1:29

The blood of Jesus, his Son, purifies us from all sin.
The Bible, 1 John 1:7

On the mount of crucifixion,
Fountains opened deep and wide,
Through the floodgates of God's mercy,
Flowed a vast and gracious tide,
Grace and love like mighty rivers,
Flowed incessant from above,
Heaven's peace and perfect justice,
Kissed a guilty world in love.
Author unknown, Love Song of the Welsh Revival

At – one – ment
Author unknown

If the death of Christ on the cross is the true meaning of the Incarnation, then there is no gospel without the cross. Christmas by itself is no gospel. The life of Christ is no gospel. Even the resurrection, important as it is in the total scheme of things, is no gospel by itself. For the good news is not just that God became man, nor that God has spoken to reveal a proper way of life for us, or even that death, the great enemy, is conquered. Rather, the good news is that sin has been dealt with (of which the resurrection is a proof); that Jesus has suffered its penalty for us as our representative, so that we might never have to suffer it; and that therefore all who believe in him can look forward to heaven.
James Montgomery Boice

If he hides the sin, or lesseneth it, He is faulty; if He leaves it still upon us, we die. He must then take our iniquity to Himself, make it His own, and so deliver us; for thus having taken the sin upon Himself, as lawfully He may, and lovingly He doth, it

followeth that we live if He lives; and who can desire more?
John Bunyan

The Creed sets forth what Christ suffered in the sight of men, and then appositely speaks of that invisible and incomprehensible judgement which he underwent in the sight of God in order that we might know not only that Christ's body was given as the price of our redemption, but that he paid a greater and more excellent price in suffering in his soul the terrible torments of a condemned and forsaken man.
John Calvin

Dear dying Lamb, Thy precious blood shall never lose its power
Till all the ransomed church of God be saved, to sin no more.
William Cowper

An atonement that does not regenerate is not an atonement in which men can be asked to believe.
James Denney

We deny that any view of the Atonement that rejects the substitutionary satisfaction of divine justice, accomplished vicariously for believers, is compatible with the teaching of the gospel.
The gospel of Jesus Christ: An evangelical celebration

If there be no sin, the Son of God would not have had to become a lamb, nor would he have had to become incarnate and be put to death.
Origen

Calvary not merely made possible the salvation of those for whom Christ died; it ensured that they would be brought to faith and their salvation made actual.
J.I. Packer

Atonement, Limited
The Father imposed His wrath due unto, and the Son underwent punishment for, either:

1. All the sins of all men.
2. All the sins of some men.
3. Some of the sins of some men.
In which case it may be said:
a. That if the last be true, all men have some sins to answer for, and so none are saved.
b. That if the second be true, then Christ, in their stead suffered for all the sins of all the elect in the whole world, and this is the truth.
c. But if the first be the case, why are not all men free from the punishment due unto their sins?
You answer, Because of unbelief. I ask, Is this unbelief a sin, or is it not? If it be, then Christ suffered the punishment due unto it, or He did not. If He did, why must that hinder them more than their other sins for which He died? If He did not, He did not die for all their sins!
John Owen

If the death of Jesus is what the Bible says it is – a substitutionary sacrifice for sins, an actual and not a hypothetical redemption, whereby the sinner is really reconciled to God – then, obviously, it cannot be for every man in the world. For then everybody would be saved, and obviously they are not. One of two things is true: either the atonement is limited in its extent or it is limited in its nature or power. It cannot be unlimited in both.
Edwin Palmer

We are often told that we limit the atonement of Christ, because we say that Christ has not made satisfaction for all men, or all men would be saved. Now, our reply to this is, that, on the other hand, our opponents limit it: we do not. The Arminians say, Christ died for all men. Ask them what they mean by it. Did Christ die so as to secure the salvation of all men? They say, "No, certainly not." We ask them the next question: Did Christ die so as to secure the salvation of any man in particular? They answer "No." They are obliged to admit this, if they are consistent. They say, "No. Christ has died that any man may be saved if" – and then

follow certain conditions of salvation. Now, who is it that limits the death of Christ? Why, you. You say that Christ did not die so as infallibly to secure the salvation of anybody. We beg your pardon, when you say we limit Christ's death; we say, "No, my dear sir, it is you that do it." We say Christ so died that he infallibly secured the salvation of a multitude that no man can number, who through Christ's death not only may be saved, but are saved, must be saved and cannot by any possibility run the hazard of being anything but saved. You are welcome to your atonement; you may keep it. We will never renounce ours for the sake of it.
C.H. Spurgeon

I would rather believe a limited atonement that is efficacious for all men for whom it was intended, than a universal atonement that is not efficacious for anybody, except the will of men be added to it.
C.H. Spurgeon

Attitude
See also: Response
You were taught, with regard to your former way of life, to put off your old self, which is being corrupted by its deceitful desires; to be made new in the attitude of your minds …
The Bible, Ephesians 4:22,23

Start with what you can do; don't stop because of what you can't do.
Author unknown

Attitudes are contagious. Are yours worth catching?
Author unknown

Don't count the days, make the days count.
Author unknown

It's a beautiful world to see,
Or it's dismal in every zone,
The thing it must be in its gloom or its gleam
Depends on yourself alone.
Author unknown

Never waste a minute of your precious life by squandering it thinking about people you don't like.
Author unknown

Attitude is everything.
Author unknown

Two men looked out from prison bars,
One saw mud, the other stars.
Author unknown

The attitude within is more important than the circumstances without.
Author unknown

If you look for the good, you will find it; if you look for the bad, you will also find it.
Author unknown

To be upset over what you don't have is to waste what you do have.
Author unknown

Never look at what you have lost … look at what you have left.
Author unknown

Some people's glass is half full, others' half empty, it just depends on their outlook, positive or negative.
Author unknown

Today I can complain because the weather is rainy or I can be thankful that the grass is getting watered for free.
Today I can feel sad that I don't have more money or I can be glad that my finances encourage me to plan my purchases wisely and guide me away from waste.
Today I can grumble about my health or I can rejoice that I am alive.
Today I can lament over all that my parents didn't give me when I was growing up or I can feel grateful that they allowed me to be born.
Today I can cry because roses have thorns or I can celebrate that thorns have roses.
Today I can mourn my lack of friends or I can excitedly embark upon a quest to discover new relationships.

Today I can whine because I have to go to work or I can shout for joy because I have a job to do.
Today I can complain because I have to go to school or eagerly open my mind and fill it with rich new bits of knowledge.
Today I can murmur dejectedly because I have to do housework or I can feel honored because the Lord has provided shelter for my mind, body and soul.
Today stretches ahead of me, waiting to be shaped. And here I am, the sculptor who gets to do the shaping. What today will be like is up to me.
I get to choose what kind of day I will have!
Author unknown

Hardening of the heart ages people faster than hardening of the arteries.
Author unknown

To be pleased with one's limits is a wretched state.
Unknown author

Attitude is the mind's paintbrush, it can color any situation.
Author unknown

Don't worry about what you want, concentrate on what you already have.
Author unknown

The pleasure you get from life is equal to the attitude you put in it.
Author unknown

Our attitude to all men would be Christian if we regarded them as though they were dying, and determined our relation to them in the light of death, both of their death and of our own.
Nicolai A. Berdyaev

Nothing is miserable but what is thought so, and contrariwise, every estate is happy if he that bears it be content.
Boethius

It is not my aching back that prevents me from helping my neighbor any more

than my choleric temperament. It's my don't-wanna-do-it attitude that does it.
Emily Carder

If life gives you lemons, make lemonade.
Dale Carnegie

I have no secret. You haven't learned life's lesson very well if you haven't noticed that you can give the tone or color, or decide the reaction you want of people in advance. It's unbelievably simple. If you want them to smile, smile first. If you want them to take an interest in you, take an interest in them first. If you want to make them nervous, become nervous yourself. If you want them to shout and raise their voices, raise yours and shout. If you want them to strike you, strike first. It's as simple as that. People will treat you like you treat them. It's no secret. Look about you. You can prove it with the next person you meet.
Winston Churchill

There are two kinds of men who never amount to very much: Those who cannot do what they are told, and those who can do nothing else.
Cyrus H.K. Curtis

A happy person is not a person in a certain set of circumstances, but rather a person with a certain set of attitudes.
Hugh Downs

Weakness of attitude becomes weakness of character.
Albert Einstein

The creation of a thousand forests is in one acorn.
Ralph Waldo Emerson

Men are not moved by things but by the views which they take of them.
Epictetus

It would be much more valuable for people to change their actions less, and to change

more rather the disposition which makes them act.
F. Fénelon

The inner attitude of the heart is far more crucial than the mechanics for coming into the reality of the spiritual life.
Richard Foster

The last of the human freedoms is to choose one's attitude in any given set of circumstances.
Victor Frankle

To look up and not down,
To look forward and not back,
To look out and not in, and
To lend a hand.
Edward Everett Hale

The only disability in life is a bad attitude.
Scott Hamilton

Keep your face to the sunshine and you cannot see the shadows.
Helen Keller

We must combine the toughness of the serpent with the softness of the dove, a tough mind and a tender heart.
Martin Luther King, Jr.

I discovered I always have choices and sometimes it's only a choice of attitude.
Judith M. Knowlton

You may live in an imperfect world but the frontiers are not closed and the doors are not all shut.
Maxwell Maltz

Attitudes are more important than facts.
Karl Menninger

A strong positive attitude will create more miracles than any wonder drug.
Patricia Neal

Any fact facing us is not as important as our attitude toward it, for that determines

our success or failure.
Norman Vincent Peale

Man is only miserable in so far as he thinks himself so.
Jacopo Sannazaro

The longer I live the more I realize the impact of attitude on life. Attitude to me is more important than the past, than education, than money, than circumstances, than failures, than success, than what others think, or say, or do. I am convinced that life is 10% what happens to me and 90% how I react to it.
Chuck Swindoll

The most courageous decision you make each day is the decision to be in a good mood.
François de Voltaire

Don't let what you cannot do interfere with what you can do.
John Wooden

The way you see life will largely determine what you get out of it.
Zig Ziglar

Your attitude, not your aptitude, will determine your altitude.
Zig Ziglar

A positive attitude will have positive results because attitudes are contagious.
Zig Ziglar

Attributes of God
God is:
eternal (without beginning or end) Ps 90:2;
gracious (loving beyond measure) 1 Jn 4:8;
holy (sinless and opposed to sin) Lv 19:2;
immutable (unchanging) Mal 3:6;
just (fair and intent on making justice) Dt 32:4;
merciful (overflowing with compassion) Ps 145:9;
omnipotent (unlimited power) Gn 17:1
omnipresent (everywhere at the same time) Jer 23:24;

omniscient (knowing all) Jn 21:17.
Author unknown

Austerity
Austerities, however severe, will not conquer the senses. To destroy their power, the most effectual means is, in general, to deny them firmly what will please, and to persevere in this, until they are reduced to be without desire or repugnance.
Madame Guyon

Authority
… he [Jesus] taught as one who had authority, and not as their teachers of the law.
The Bible, Matthew 7:29

All authority in heaven and on earth has been given to me.
The Bible, Matthew 28:18

The people were all so amazed that they asked each other, "What is this? A new teaching – and with authority! He even gives orders to evil spirits and they obey him."
The Bible, Mark 1:27

Nothing is more gratifying to the mind of man than power or dominion.
Joseph Addison

Authority without wisdom is like a heavy axe without an edge, fitter to bruise than polish.
Anne Bradstreet

Many refuse to accept the reality of a personal God because they are unwilling to submit to His authority.
Kurt Bruner

The wisest have the most authority.
Plato

If you wish to know what a man is, place him in authority.
Yugoslav proverb

Authorized Version
See: King James Version

Automation

If it keeps up, man will atrophy all his limbs but the push-button finger.
Frank Lloyd Wright

Autumn

Season of mists and mellow fruitfulness, Close bosom-friend of the maturing sun.
John Keats

Avarice
See also: Greed

If you would abolish avarice, you must abolish its mother, luxury.
Cicero

Avarice in old age is foolish; for what can be more absurd than to increase our provisions for the road the nearer we approach to our journey's end.
Cicero

Nobody can fight properly and boldly for the faith if he clings to a fear of being stripped of earthly possessions.
Peter Damian

Avarice is always poor.
Samuel Johnson

Avarice increases with the increasing pile of gold.
Juvenal

Avarice is as destitute of what it has, as poverty of what it has not.
Publilius Syrus

Avoiding God

There is practically nothing that men do not prefer to God. A tiresome detail of business, an occupation utterly pernicious to health, the employment of time in ways one does not dare to mention. Anything rather than God.
F. Fénelon

Awareness

Let us not look back in anger or forward in fear, but around in awareness.
James Thurber

Awareness of God

It is beyond dispute that some awareness of God exists in the human mind by natural instinct, since God himself has given everyone some idea of him so that no one can plead ignorance.
John Calvin

It is so easy to deny the nobility of something just because it mingles with our earthly clay.
George Macdonald

B

Backsliding

Ye are fallen from grace.
The Bible, Galatians 5:4 AV

… holding on to faith and a good
conscience. Some have rejected these and
so have shipwrecked their faith.
The Bible, 1 Timothy 1:19

Those who fall away have never been
thoroughly imbued with the knowledge of
Christ but only had a slight and passing
taste of it.
John Calvin

If repentance is neglected for an instant,
one can lose the power of the Resurrection
as he lives with the weakness of tepidity
and the potential of his fall.
John Chrysostom

Life's greatest tragedy is to lose God and
not to miss Him.
F.W. Norwood

Backsliding, generally first begins with
neglect of private prayer.
J.C. Ryle

The Lord Jesus will not cast away His
believing people because of shortcomings
and infirmities.
The husband does not put away his wife
because he finds failings in her. The
mother does not forsake her infant
because it is weak, feeble and ignorant.
And the Lord Christ does not cast off poor
sinners who have committed their souls
into His hands, because He sees in them
blemishes and imperfections. Oh, no, it is
His glory to pass over the faults of His
people, and heal their backslidings, to
make much of their weak graces, and to

pardon their many faults.
J.C. Ryle

[Some people] harm their souls …
without being exposed to great
temptations. They simply let their souls
wither. They allow themselves to be
dulled by the joys and worries and
distractions of life, not realizing that
thoughts which earlier meant a great deal
in them in their youth turned into
meaningless sounds.
Albert Schweitzer

Though Christians be not kept altogether
from falling, yet they are kept from falling
altogether.
William Secker

However advanced a man may be in piety
or age, he is still in danger of falling.
Charles Simeon

You, who have the most familiarity with
Christ, and enjoy the most holy fellowship
with him, may soon become the very
leaders of the hosts of Satan
if your Lord withdraws His grace.
David's eyes go astray, and the sweet
psalmist of Israel becomes the shameless
adulterer, who robs Uriah of his wife.
Samson one day slays a thousand of his
enemies with the might of his arm and the
valor of his heart;
another day his honor is betrayed, his locks
are shorn, and his eyes are put out by a
strumpet's treacherous wiles.
How soon are the mighty fallen!
C.H. Spurgeon

Behold Solomon, the wisest of men,
yet the greatest fool who ever lived.
Even Job fails in patience,

and Abraham, staggers as to his faith.
C.H. Spurgeon

The thief was on the cross and he was
justified by a single word; and Judas who
was counted in the number of the apostles
lost all his labor in one single night and
descended from heaven to hell. Therefore,
let no-one boast of his good works, for all
those who trust in themselves fall.
Abba Xanthias

Banks
A bank is a place where they lend you an
umbrella in fair weather and ask for it back
when it begins to rain.
Robert Frost

Baptism
*See also: Baptism, Infant; Baptism and
salvation*
Baptism is an ordinance of the Lord Jesus,
obligatory upon every believer, wherein he
is immersed in water in the Name of the
Father, and of the Son, and of the Holy
Spirit, as a sign of his fellowship with the
death and resurrection of Christ, of
remission of sins, and of his giving himself
up to God, to live and walk in newness of
life. It is a prerequisite to church
Fellowship, and to participation in the
Lord's Supper.
James Boyce, Abstract of Principles, 1858

Those who see baptism only as confession
of our faith have missed the main point.
Baptism is tied to the promise of
forgiveness. "Whoever believes and is
baptized will be saved" (Mark 16:16).
John Calvin

True believers when troubled by sin can
always remember their baptism, and so be
assured of eternal washing in the blood of
Christ.
John Calvin

Baptism is the sign of initiation by which
we are admitted to the fellowship of the
church.
John Calvin

Lest through a confidence in the Gift of
the Font you should turn negligent of your
conversation after it, even supposing you
receive baptism, yet if you are not minded
to be led by the Spirit afterwards, you lose
the dignity bestowed upon you and the
pre-eminence of your adoption.
John Chrysostom

He [the devil] does not dare look at you
directly because he sees the light blazing
from your head and blinding his eyes.
John Chrysostom

Concerning baptism, thus shall ye baptize.
Having first recited all these things, baptize
in the name of the Father and of the Son
and of the Holy Spirit.
Didache

Christians are made, not born.
Jerome

Baptism signifies that the old Adam in us
is to be drowned by daily sorrow and
repentance, and perish with all sins and
evil lusts; and that the new man should
daily come forth again and rise, who shall
live before God in righteousness and purity
forever.
Martin Luther

This is how we dedicate ourselves to God
after being newly created through Christ.
We bring them to somewhere where there
is water, where they are regenerated as we
were, for they then wash themselves in the
water in the name of God the Father and
Lord of all, and of our Savior Jesus Christ
and of Holy Spirit.
Justin Martyr

We believe that as in baptism we have been
united with Christ in His death and
resurrection, so we have died to sin and
should walk in newness of life. (Romans
6:1-11)
Moravian Covenant for Christian living

Those who are going to be baptized must
pray repeatedly, fasting and kneeling and

in vigils, and confess all their past sins.
Tertullian

Baptism, Infant

The children of believers are baptized not in order that they who were previously strangers to the church may then for the first time become children of God, but rather that, because by the blessing of the promise they already belonged to the body of Christ, they are received into the church with this solemn sign.
John Calvin

These darts are aimed more at God than at us. For it is very clear from many testimonies of Scripture that circumcision was also a sign of repentance. Then Paul calls it the seal of the righteousness of faith … For although infants, at the very moment they were circumcised, did not comprehend with their understanding what that sign meant, they were truly circumcised to the mortification of their corrupt and defiled nature, a mortification that they would afterward practice in mature years. To sum up, this objection can be solved without difficulty: infants are "baptized into future repentance and faith, and even though these have not yet been formed in them, the seed of both lies hidden within them by the secret working of the Spirit.
John Calvin

I do believe that something happens at the baptism of an infant, particularly if the parents are Christians and teach their children Christian truths from childhood. We cannot fully understand the mysteries of God, but I believe a miracle can happen in these children so that they are regenerated, that is, made Christians through infant baptism. If you want to call that baptismal regeneration, that's all right with me.
Billy Graham

Some one sent to know whether it was permissible to use warm water in baptism? The Doctor replied: "Tell the blockhead

that water, warm or cold, is water.
Martin Luther

The Anabaptists pretend that children, not as yet having reason, ought not to receive baptism. I answer: That reason in no way contributes to faith. Nay, in that children are destitute of reason, they are all the more fit and proper recipients of baptism. For reason is the greatest enemy that faith has: it never comes to the aid of spiritual things, but – more frequently than not – struggles against the Divine Word, treating with contempt all that emanates from God. If God can communicate the Holy Ghost to grown persons, he can, a fortiori, communicate it to young children. Faith comes of the Word of God, when this is heard; little children hear that Word when they receive baptism, and therewith they receive also faith.
Martin Luther

The offspring of believers are born holy, because their children, while yet in the womb, before they breathe the vital air, have been adopted into the covenant of eternal life. Nor are they brought into the church by baptism on any other ground than because they belonged to the body of the Church before they were born.
The Presbyterian Doctrine of Children in the Covenant

We have not a single command in the Scriptures that infants are baptized, or that the apostles practiced it. Therefore we confess with good sense that infant baptism is nothing but human invention and notion.
Menno Simons

Baptism and salvation

Not everyone is washed to receive salvation. We who have received the grace of baptism in the name of Christ have been washed; but I do not know which of us has been washed to salvation.
Origen

Baptists

The only problem with Baptists is that they aren't held under the water long enough.
Author unknown

Baptists are only funny underwater.
Neil Simon

Battle

Christianity is a battle, not a dream.
Wendell Phillips

Battles

The most important of life's battles is the one we fight daily in the silent chambers of the soul.
David O. McKay

Beatitudes

Blessed are the poor in spirit, for theirs is the kingdom of heaven.
Blessed are those who mourn, for they will be comforted.
Blessed are the meek, for they will inherit the earth.
Blessed are those who hunger and thirst for righteousness, for they will be filled.
Blessed are the merciful, for they will be shown mercy.
Blessed are the pure in heart, for they will see God.
Blessed are the peacemakers, for they will be called sons of God.
Blessed are those who are persecuted because of righteousness, for theirs is the kingdom of heaven.
Blessed are you when people insult you, persecute you and falsely say all kinds of evil against you because of me.
Rejoice and be glad, because great is your reward in heaven, for in the same way they persecuted the prophets who were before you.
The Bible, Matthew 5:3-12

Beautiful attitudes.
Author unknown

The character which we find in the Beatitudes is, beyond all question, nothing less than our Lord's own character, put into words. It is the description set side by side with an example.
Billy Graham

Beauty

Beauty: See Wives
Like a gold ring in a pig's snout is a beautiful woman who shows no discretion.
The Bible, Proverbs 11:22

Beauty is but skin deep.
Author unknown

The being of all things is derived from the divine beauty.
Thomas Aquinas

Characteristics which define beauty are wholeness, harmony and radiance.
Thomas Aquinas

Beauty is the gift of God.
Aristotle

Too late I loved you, O Beauty so ancient yet ever new! Too late I loved you! And, behold, you were within me, and I out of myself, and there I searched for you.
Augustine of Hippo

Ask the earth and the sea, the plains and the mountains, the sky and the clouds, the stars and the sun, the fish and animals, and all of them will say, "We are beautiful because God made us." This beauty is their testimony to God.
Ask men and women, too, and they know that their beauty comes from God. Yet what is it that sees the beauty? What is it that can be enraptured by the loveliness of God's creation? It is the soul which appreciates beauty. Indeed, God made men's souls so that they could appreciate the beauty of his handiwork.
Augustine of Hippo

Beauty is indeed a good gift of God; but that the good may not think it a great good, God dispenses it even to the wicked.
Augustine of Hippo

Virtue is like a rich stone – best plain set.
Francis Bacon

Beauty is but the sensible image of the
Infinite. Like truth and justice it lives
within us; like virtue and the moral law it
is a companion of the soul.
Richard Bancroft

If you get simple beauty and nought else,
you get about the best thing God invents.
Robert Browning

However, you're my man, you've seen the
  world
The beauty and the wonder and the power,
The shapes of things, their colors, lights
  and shades,
Changes, surprises and God made it all!
For what? Do you feel thankful, ay or no?
Robert Browning

I know a man who, when he saw a woman
of striking beauty, praised the Creator for
her. The sight of her lit within him the
love of God.
John Climacus

The pursuit of truth and beauty is a sphere
of activity in which we are permitted to
remain children all our lives.
Albert Einstein

Though we travel the world over to find
the beautiful, we must carry it with us or
we find it not.
Ralph Waldo Emerson

Never lose an opportunity of seeing
anything that is beautiful, for beauty is
God's handwriting – a wayside sacrament.
Welcome it in every fair face, in every fair
sky, in every flower, and thank God for it
as a cup of blessing.
Ralph Waldo Emerson

Beauty is the product of honest attention
to the particular.
Richard Harries

Without an affirmation of beauty there can
in the end be no faith and no God worth
our love.
Richard Harries

Glory be to God for dappled things –
For skies of couple-color as a brinded cow;
For rose-moles all in stipple upon trout
  that swim;
Fresh-firecoal chestnut-falls; finches' wings;
Landscapes plotted and pieced – fold,
  fallow, and plough;
And all trades, their gear and tackle and
  trim.
All things counter, original, spare, strange;
Whatever is fickle, freckled (who knows
  how?)
With swift, slow; sweet, sour; adazzle, dim;
He fathers-forth whose beauty is past
  change:
Praise him.
Gerard Manley Hopkins

God passes through the thicket of the
world, and wherever his glance falls he
turns all things to beauty.
John of the Cross

Youth is happy because it has the ability to
see beauty. Anyone who keeps the ability
to see beauty never grows old.
Franz Kafka

A thing of beauty is a joy forever:
Its loveliness increases; it will never
Pass into nothingness; but still will keep
A bower quiet for us, and a sleep
Full of sweet dreams, and health, and quiet
  breathing.
John Keats

Beauty is shy. It is not like a man rushing
out in front of a crowd. Religion too, if it is
wise, models itself upon the ways of
Scripture, where the treasure of truth is
hidden from the idle and unready, to be
seen only when the eye of the mind is pure.
John Keble

Beauty is God's handwriting. Welcome it in
every fair face, every fair day, every fair flower.
Charles Kingsley

There's nothing fair nor beautiful, but takes
Something from thee, that makes it beautiful.
Henry Wadsworth Longfellow

Beauty is excrescence, superabundance, random ebullience, and sheer delightful waste to be enjoyed in its own right.
Donald Culross Peattie

Beauty of whatever kind, in its supreme development, invariably excites the sensitive soul to tears.
Edgar Allen Poe

There should be as little merit in loving a woman for her beauty, as a man for his prosperity, both being equally subject to change.
Alexander Pope

Beauty unadorned, adorned the most.
Proverb

Beauty is a flower, fame a breath.
Latin proverb

Truth exists for the wise, beauty for the feeling heart.
Friedrich Schiller

Beautiful is that which we see, more beautiful that which we know, but by far the most beautiful that which we do not comprehend.
Nicolaus Steno, a professor of anatomy who later developed principles for describing sedimentary rocks that are still in use today.

Beauty is the only thing that time cannot harm. Philosophies fall away like sand, and creeds follow one another like the withered leaves of Autumn; but what is beautiful is a joy for all seasons and a possession for all eternity.
Oscar Wilde

Beauty, Spiritual
The being of all things is derived from divine beauty.
Thomas Aquinas

God's fingers can touch nothing but to mold it into loveliness.
George Macdonald

Each conception of spiritual beauty is a glimpse of God.
Moses Mendelssohn

How goodness heightens beauty!
Hannah More

I pray, O God, that I may be beautiful within.
Socrates

Becoming a Christian
See also: Accepting God; Conversion
The entrance fee into the kingdom of heaven is nothing: the annual subscription is everything.
Henry Drummond

By a Carpenter mankind was made, and only by that Carpenter can mankind be remade.
Desiderius Erasmus

Someone once asked Billy Graham, "If Christianity is valid, why is there so much evil in the world?" To this the famous preacher replied, "With so much soap, why are there so many dirty people in the world? Christianity, like soap, must be personally applied if it is to make a difference in our lives."
Billy Graham

Neither is it a verbal acknowledgment, in owning that which Christ suffered at Jerusalem, which will free any from this charge and guilt. Unless the Lord Christ, that Christ which is God and man in one person, is owned, received, believed in, loved, trusted unto, and obeyed in all things, as he is proposed unto us in the Scripture, and with respect unto all the ends of righteousness, holiness, life, and salvation, for which he is so proposed, he is renounced and forsaken.
John Owen

The best way I know how is by praying a simple prayer of faith. The important thing isn't saying the right words but, perhaps for the first time in your life, talking heart to heart with the Lord and inviting him in.
Luis Palau

When it comes to responding to Jesus, I find it's important to distinguish between reverence, religion, and relationship.
Luis Palau

Going to church doesn't make you a Christian, any more than going to a garage makes you an automobile.
Billy Sunday

Beginning
See: Starting

Behavior
See also: Anger; Kindness; Mottoes; Relationships
Rudeness, yelling, anger, and swearing are a weak man's imitation of strength.
Author unknown

Behavior is the mirror in which everyone shows their image.
Author unknown

Anyone can carry his burden for one day. Anyone can be pleasant, courteous, and friendly for one day. And that continued is all there is to life.
Author unknown

The central issue about the Bible is whether we live it.
John Alexander

When in Rome, live as the Romans do; when elsewhere, live as they live elsewhere.
Ambrose, giving advice to Augustine

If a man be gracious and courteous to strangers, it shows he is a citizen of the world.
Francis Bacon

Bad beliefs make bad behavior.
Warren Akin Candler

The perfect person does not only try to avoid evil. Nor does he do good for fear of punishment, still less in order to qualify for the hope of a promised reward. The perfect person does good through love.
Clement of Alexandria

A man's ethical behavior should be based effectually on sympathy, education, and social ties; no religious basis is necessary. Man would indeed be in a poor way if he had to be restrained by fear of punishment and hope of reward after death.
Albert Einstein

It seems to me to be the best proof of an evangelical disposition, that persons are not angry when reproached, and have a Christian charity for those that ill deserve it.
Desiderius Erasmus

What you do speaks so loud that I cannot hear what you say.
Millard Fuller

If moral behavior were simply following rules, we could program a computer to be moral.
Samuel P. Ginder

The best evidence of our having the truth is our walking in the truth.
Matthew Henry

He who makes a beast of himself gets rid of the pain of being a man.
Samuel Johnson

So act that your principles of action might safely be made a law for the whole world.
Immanuel Kant

Above all things, dear brethren, study to practice in life that which the Lord commands, and then be you assured that you shall never hear nor read the same without fruit.
John Knox

Perhaps there cannot be a better way of judging of what manner of spirit we are of, than to see whether the actions of our life are such as we may safely commend them to God in our prayers.
William Law

I firmly believe people have hitherto been a great deal too much taken up about doctrine and far too little about practice. The word "doctrine," as used in the Bible, means teaching of duty, not theory.
George Macdonald

People's behavior makes sense if you think about it in terms of their goals, needs, and motives.
Thomas Mann

Our walk counts far more than our talk, always!
George Muller

If you want to be respected for your actions, then your behavior must be above reproach.
   If our lives demonstrate that we are peaceful, humble, and trusted, this is recognized by others.
Rosa Parks

What use is it to us to hear it said of a man that he has thrown off the yoke, that he does not believe there is a God to watch over his actions, that he reckons himself the sole master of his behavior, and that he does not intend to give an account of it to anyone but himself?
Blaise Pascal

Behave towards your inferiors as you would wish your betters to behave to you.
Seneca

Be dogmatically true,
obstinately holy,
immovably honest,
desperately kind,
fixedly upright.
C.H. Spurgeon

Learn to overrule minor interests in favor of great ones, and generously to do all the good the heart prompts; a man is never injured by acting virtuously.
Vauvenargues

Do all the good you can
By all the means you can
In all the ways you can
In all the places you can
To all the people you can
As long as ever you can.
John Wesley

Being

One must not always think so much about what one should do, but rather what one should be. Our works do not ennoble us; but we must ennoble our works.
Meister Eckhart

What you are thunders so loud that I cannot hear what you say.
Ralph Waldo Emerson

Whatever you are, be a good one.
Abraham Lincoln

It is not that doing is unimportant. It is rather that right doing springs from right being.
Robert Llewelyn

Simply the thing that I am shall make me live.
William Shakespeare

The way to do is to be.
Lao Tzu

Being a Christian

A Christ-centered life is like a good watch: open face, busy hands, pure gold, and full of good works.
Author unknown

I guess as you get older – I'm getting ever closer to that day when I'll meet the King – the more you begin to realize that the only thing in life that matters is a relationship with Christ.
Chuck Colson

Nobody enjoys being a Christian more than I do. I wouldn't exchange it for anything else I know anything about.
Kathryn Kuhlman

Belief
See also: Agnosticism; Faith; God, Belief in; Unbelief
Everything is possible for him who believes.
The Bible, Mark 9:23

Lord, I believe; help thou mine unbelief.
The Bible, Mark 9:24 KJV

"Because you have seen me, you have believed; blessed are those who have not seen and yet have believed."
The Bible, John 20:29

I believe in the sun even when it is not shining. I believe in love even when I am not feeling it. I believe in God even when He is silent.
Anonymous Jewish holocaust victim

We must dream in order to be. We must believe in order to become.
Author unknown

For I seek not to understand in order that I may believe; but I believe in order that I may understand, for I believe for this reason: that unless I believe, I cannot understand.
Anselm of Canterbury

What can be hoped for which is not believed?
Augustine of Hippo

If you don't believe it you won't understand it.
Augustine of Hippo

Faith, noun. Belief without evidence in what is told by one who speaks without knowledge, of things without parallel.
Ambrose Bierce

Believe your beliefs and doubt your doubts.
F.F. Bosworth

As the body lives by breathing, so the soul lives by believing.
Thomas Brooks

We are what we believe we are.
Benjamin Cardozo

"I can't believe that," said Alice. "Can't you?" said the Queen, in a pitying tone. "Try again; draw a long breath and shut your eyes." Alice laughed. "There's no use trying," she said. "One can't believe impossible things." "I dare say you have not had much practice," said the Queen. "When I was younger, I always did it for half an hour a day. Why, sometimes I have believed as many as six impossible things before breakfast."
Lewis Carroll

Man is what he believes.
Anton Chekhov

The point of having an open mind, like having an open mouth, is to close it on something solid.
G.K. Chesterton

There is nothing on earth that you can not have once you have mentally accepted the fact that you can have it.
Robert Collier

He that will believe only what he can fully comprehend must have a long head or a very short creed.
Charles Caleb Colton

Absence of proof is not proof of absence.
Michael Crichton

Nothing is easier than self-deceit. For what each man wishes, that he also believes to be true.
Demosthenes

They can conquer who believe.
J. Dryden

Human beliefs, like all other natural growths, elude the barrier of systems.
George Eliot

Belief consists in accepting the affirmations of the soul; unbelief, in denying them.
Ralph Waldo Emerson

The gospel is of no profit except it be believed.
E. Schuyler English

Looking for loopholes.
W.C. Fields, a lifelong atheist, on being asked on his deathbed why he was reading the Bible

If you think you can or you think you can't, you're right.
Henry Ford

If a million people believe a foolish thing, it is still a foolish thing.
Anatole France

Devout believers are safeguarded in a high degree against the risk of certain neurotic illnesses; their acceptance of the universal neurosis spares them the task of constructing a personal one.
Sigmund Freud

We have not received the Spirit of God because we believe, but that we may believe.
Fulgentius of Ruspe

He that knows nothing will believe anything.
Thomas Fuller

He does not believe that does not live according to his belief.
Thomas Fuller

He is dead in this world who has no belief in another.
Johann Wolfgang von Goethe

There is a vast difference between intellectual belief and the total conversion that saves the soul.
Billy Graham

Although a Christian should believe simply, he should not "simply believe."
Os Guinness

He that believes all misseth; he that believes nothing, hits not.
George Herbert

Those who believe that they are exclusively in the right are generally those who achieve something.
Aldous Huxley

As I get older I seem to believe less and less and yet to believe what I do believe more and more.
David Jenkins

I now believe that the balance of reasoned considerations tells heavily in favor of the religious, even of the Christian view of the world.
C.E.M. Joad

You must believe in God, in spite of what the clergy say.
Benjamin Jowett

I could not say I believe. I know! I have had the experience of being gripped by something that is stronger than myself, something that people call God.
Carl Jung

You never know how much you really believe anything until its truth or falsehood becomes a matter of life and death to you.
C.S. Lewis

The sciences bring to the "facts" the philosophy they claim to derive from them.
C.S. Lewis

I believe in Christianity as I believe that the sun has risen, not only because I see it but because, by it, I see everything else.
C.S. Lewis

I can see how it might be possible for a man to look down upon the earth and be an atheist, but I cannot conceive how he could look up into the heavens and say there is no God.
Abraham Lincoln

Luke: I don't believe it.
Yoda: That, is why you fail.
George W. Lucas, Star Wars,
The Empire Strikes Back

A man's real belief is that which he lives by.
What a man believes is the thing he does,
not the thing he thinks.
George Macdonald

One can believe in the divinity of Jesus
Christ and feel no personal loyalty to
Him at all – indeed, pay no attention
whatever to His commandments and His
will for one's life. One can believe
intellectually in the efficacy of prayer and
never do any praying.
Catherine Marshall

If easy belief is impossible, it is that we
may learn what belief is, and in whom it is
to be placed.
F.D. Maurice

Make sure the thing you're living for is
worth dying for.
Charles Mayes

The ox and the ass understood more of the
first Christmas than the high priests in
Jerusalem. And it is the same today.
Thomas Merton

One person with a belief is equal to a force
of ninety-nine who have only interests.
John Stuart Mill

If we let ourselves believe that man began
with divine grace, that he forfeited this by
sin, and that he can be redeemed only by
divine grace through the crucified Christ
then we shall find a peace of mind never
granted to philosophers. He who cannot
believe is cursed, for he reveals by his unbelief
that God has not chosen to give him grace.
Blaise Pascal

Belief is a wise wager. Granted that faith
cannot be proved, what harm will come to
you if you gamble on its truth and it
proves false? … If you gain, you gain all; if

you lose, you lose nothing. Wager, then,
without hesitation, that He exists.
Blaise Pascal

If you can only believe! If you will only
believe! Then nothing, nothing, will be
impossible for you! That is the truth and the
gospel, and it is wonderful. It's the good news.
Norman Vincent Peale

When you affirm big, believe big, and pray
big, big things happen.
Norman Vincent Peale

First thing every morning before you arise
say out loud, "I believe," three times.
Norman Vincent Peale

Now you just believe. That is all you have
to do, just believe.
Norman Vincent Peale

To learn to believe is of primary
importance. It is the basic factor of
succeeding in any undertaking.
Norman Vincent Peale

If you can't believe in God, chances are
your God is too small.
J.B. Phillips

The only Zen you find on the tops of
mountains is the Zen you bring up there.
Robert M. Pirsig

For those who believe, no proof is
necessary. For those who don't believe, no
proof is possible.
Proverb

It is one thing to believe in justification by
faith, it is another thing to be justified by
faith.
Adolph Saphir

Belief must be something very different from
a mixture of opinions about God and the
world and of precepts for one life or two.
Piety cannot be an indistinct craving for a
mass of metaphysical and moral crumbs.
Friedrich Schleiermacher

Belief triggers the power to do.
David J Schwartz

The mind is the limit. As long as the mind can envision the fact that you can do something, you can do it – as long as you really believe 100 percent.
Arnold Schwarzenegger

There is no higher religion than human service. To work for the common good is the greatest creed.
Albert Schweitzer

I believe that there is one only living and true God, existing in three persons, the Father, the Son, and the Holy Ghost, the same in substance, equal in power and glory. That the Scriptures of the Old and New Testaments are a revelation from God and a complete rule to direct us how we may glorify and enjoy Him.
Roger Sherman, Signer of both the Declaration and the Constitution Belief

Believing right doctrine will no more save you, than doing good works will save you.
C.H. Spurgeon

Believing does not come by trying. If a person were to make a statement of something that happened this day I should not tell him that I would try to believe him. If I believed in the truthfulness of the man who told the incident to me, and who said he saw it, I should accept the statement at once. If I did not think him a true man I should, of course, disbelieve him; but there would be no trying in the matter. Now, when God declares there is salvation in Christ Jesus I must either believe Him at once or make Him a liar.
C.H. Spurgeon

If to believe in Jesus was man's first duty, not to believe in him was his chief sin.
John Stott

What do I believe? As an American I believe in generosity, in liberty, in the rights of man. These are social and political faiths that are part of me, as they are, I suppose, part of all of us. Such beliefs are easy to express. But part of me too is my relation to all life, my religion. And this is not so easy to talk about. Religious experience is highly intimate and, for me, ready words are not at hand.
Adlai E. Stevenson

It is more reverent to believe in the works of the Deity than to comprehend them.
Colnelius Tacitus

Once we think we know "the truth" about something, we seal it in our subconscious as a belief and we start acting like it. We don't even know we're doing it. That's because our subconscious causes us to behave like the person we believe ourselves to be.
Louis E Tice

They can because they think they can.
Virgil

If God created us in His image we have certainly returned the compliment.
François de Voltaire

To believe in God is impossible – not to believe in him is absurd.
François de Voltaire

When we believe in nothing, we open the doors to believing anything.
David Wells

Never allow what you do know to be disturbed by what you do not know.
Richard Whateley

I am not moved by what I see. I am not moved by what I feel. I am moved only by what I believe.
Smith Wigglesworth

I can get more out of God by believing Him for one minute than by shouting at Him all night.
Smith Wigglesworth

My philosophy is that not only are you responsible for your life, but doing the best

at this moment puts you in the best place for the next moment.
Oprah Winfrey

Belief, Christian

The Christian believes, not in the Bible, but in Him whom it attests;
the Christian believes, not in tradition, but in Him whom it transmits;
the Christian believes, not in the Church, but in Him whom it proclaims.
Hans Küng

Belief and doubt

There are two ways to slide easily through life: to believe everything or to doubt everything. Both ways save us from thinking.
Alfred Korzybski

Belief and obedience

Only he who believes is obedient. Only he who is obedient, believes.
D. Bonhoeffer

Believe by compulsion

No iron chain, or outward force of any kind, can ever compel the soul of a person to believe or to disbelieve.
Thomas Carlyle

Belief in Christ

I told you that you would die in your sins; if you do not believe that I am the one I claim to be, you will indeed die in your sins.
The Bible, John 8:24

Belief in God

More consequences for thought and action follow the affirmation or denial of God than from answering any other basic question.
Mortimer Adler

[Look for evidence] from the order of the motion of the stars, and of all things under the dominion of the mind which ordered the universe.
Plato

In a quiet revolution in thought and argument that hardly anyone could have

foreseen only two decades ago, God is making a comeback.
Time Magazine

Beliefs

Religion says, "Be good, conform yourself."
Epicureanism says, "Be sensuous, satisfy yourself."
Education says, "Be resourceful, expand yourself."
Psychology says, "Be confident, assert yourself."
Materialism says, "Be possessive, please yourself."
Asceticism says, "Be lowly, suppress yourself."
Humanism says, "Be capable, believe in yourself."
Pride says, "Be superior, promote yourself."
CHRIST SAYS, "BE UNSELFISH, HUMBLE YOURSELF."
Author unknown

Belonging

The first and prime want in human nature is the desire to be important.
John Dewey

The strongest want in human nature is the desire to be great.
Sigmund Freud

The deepest principle in human nature is the craving to be appreciated.
William James

More than anything else, people want to be noticed, recognized.
John Wolfgang von Goethe

Belonging to God

I am His by purchase and I am His by conquest; I am His by donation and I am His by election; I am His by covenant and I am His by marriage; I am wholly His; I am peculiarly His; I am universally His; I am eternally His.
Thomas Brooks

Bereavement
See also: Death of a baby; Death of a child; Grief

Bereavement

Letter from Samuel Rutherford to Mrs Taylor, on her son's death

MISTRESS, Grace, mercy, and peace be to you – Though I have no relation worldly or acquaintance with you, yet (upon the testimony and importunity of your elder son now at London, where I am, but chiefly because I esteem Jesus Christ in you to be in place of all relations) I make bold, in Christ, to speak my poor thoughts to you concerning your son lately fallen asleep in the Lord. I know that grace rooteth not out the affections of a mother, but putteth them on His wheel who maketh all things new, that they may be refined: therefore, sorrow for a dead child is allowed to you, though by measure and ounce-weights. The redeemed of the Lord have not a dominion, or lordship, over their sorrow and other affections, to lavish out Christ's goods at their pleasure. "For ye are not your own, but bought with a price;" and your sorrow is not your own. Nor has He redeemed you by halves; and therefore, ye are not to make Christ's cross no cross. He commandeth you to weep: and that princely One, who took up to heaven with Him a man's heart to be a compassionate High Priest, became your fellow and companion on earth by weeping for the dead (John 11.35). And, therefore, ye are to love that cross, because it was once at Christ's shoulders before you: so that by His own practice He has over-gilded and covered your cross with the Mediator's luster. The cup ye drink was at the lip of sweet Jesus, and He drank of it. The kind and compassionate Jesus, at every sigh you give for the loss of your now glorified child (so I believe, as is meet), with a man's heart crieth, "Half Mine."

I was not a witness to his death, being called out of the kingdom; but, if you will credit those whom I do credit (and I dare not lie), he died comfortably. It is true, he died before he did so much service to Christ on earth, as I hope and heartily desire that your son Mr Hugh (very dear to me in Jesus Christ) will do. But that were a real matter of sorrow if this were not to counterbalance it, that he has changed service-houses, but has not changed services or Master. "And there shall be no more curse; but the throne of God and of the Lamb shall be in it; and His servants shall serve Him" (Rev. 22.3). What he could have done in this lower house, he is now upon that same service in the higher house; and it is all one: it is the same service and same Master, only there is a change of conditions. And ye are not to think it a bad bargain for your beloved son, where he has gold for copper and brass, eternity for time.

I believe that Christ has taught you (for I give credit to such a witness of you as your son Mr Hugh) not to sorrow because he died. All the knot must be, "He died too soon, he died too young, he died in the morning of his life." This is all; but sovereignty must silence your thoughts. I was in your condition: I had but two children, and both are dead since I came hither. The supreme and absolute Former of all things giveth not an account of any of His matters. The good Husbandman may pluck His roses, and gather in His lilies at mid-summer, and, for aught I dare say, in the beginning of the first summer month, and He may transplant young trees out of the lower ground to the higher, where they may have more of the sun, and a more free air, at any season of the year. What is that to you or me? The goods are His own. The Creator of time and winds did a merciful injury, if I dare borrow the word, to nature, in landing the passenger so early. They love the sea too well, who complain of a fair wind and a desirable tide, and a speedy coming ashore, especially a coming ashore in that land where all the inhabitants have everlasting joy upon their heads. He cannot be too early in heaven; his twelve hours were not short hours. And withal, if you consider this, had you been at his bed-side, and should have seen Christ coming to him, you could not have adjourned Christ's free love, who would wants him no longer. And dying in another land, where his mother could not close his eyes, is not much. The whole earth is his Father's; any corner of his Father's house is good enough to die in.

It may be, the living child (I speak not of Mr Hugh) is more grief to you than the dead. Ye are to wait on, if at any time God shall give him repentance. Christ waited as long possibly on you and me, certainly longer on me: and if He should deny repentance to him, I could say something to that: but I hope better things of him. And think this a favor, that He has bestowed upon you fine, free grace, that is, mercy without hire; ye paid nothing for it: and who can put a price upon any thing of royal and princely Jesus Christ? And God has given to you to suffer for Him the spoiling of your goods. Esteem it as an act of free grace also. Ye are no loser, having Himself; and I persuade myself, if you could prize Christ, nothing could be bitter to you. Grace, grace be with you.

Your brother and well-wisher.

London, 1645
Samuel Rutherford

Bereavement

Letter from Samuel Rutherford to a Christian brother on the death of his daughter

Reverend and beloved in the Lord, It may be that I have been too long silent, but I hope that ye will not impute it to forgetfulness of you.

As I have heard of the death of your daughter with heaviness of mind on your behalf, so am I much comforted that she has evidenced to yourself and other witnesses the hope of the resurrection of the dead. As sown corn is not lost (for there is more hope of that which is sown than of that which is eaten) (I Cor. 15.42, 43), so also is it in the resurrection of the dead: the body "is sown

in corruption, it is raised in incorruption; it is sown in dishonor, it is raised in glory." I hope that ye wait for the crop and harvest; "for if we believe that Jesus died and rose again, even so also them which sleep in Jesus, will God bring with him." Then they are not lost who are gathered into that congregation of the first-born, and the general assembly of the saints. Though we cannot outrun nor overtake them that are gone before, yet we shall quickly follow them: and the difference is, that she has the advantage of some months or years of the crown, before you and her mother. And we do not take it ill, if our children outrun us in the life of grace; why then are we sad, if they outstrip us in the attainment of the life of glory? It would seem, that there is more reason to grieve that children live behind us, than that they are glorified and die before. All the difference is in some poor hungry accidents of time, less or more, sooner or later. So the godly child, though young, died a hundred years old; and you could not now have bestowed her better, though the choice was Christ's, not yours.

The King and Prince of ages can keep them better than you can do. While she was alive, you could intrust her to Christ, and recommend her to His keeping: now, by an after-faith, you have resigned her unto Him, in whose bosom do sleep all that are dead in the Lord: you would have lent her to glorify the Lord upon earth, and He has borrowed her, with promise to restore her again, to be an organ of the immediate glorifying of himself in heaven. Sinless glorifying of God is better than sinful glorifying of Him. And sure your prayers concerning her are fulfilled.

If the fountain be the love of God, as I hope it is, ye are enriched with losses. You know all I can say better, before I was in Christ, than I can express it. Grace be with you.

London, Jan. 6, 1646
Samuel Rutherford

Bereavement drives men into the habits of serious reflection, sharpens the understanding and softens the heart.

John Adams, letter to Thomas Jefferson, 6 May 1816

Tears are sometimes an inappropriate response to death. When a life has been lived completely honestly, completely successfully, or just completely, the correct response to death's perfect punctuation mark is a smile.
Julie Burchill

Grief should be the instructor of the wise.
Sorrow is knowledge: they who know the most
Must mourn the deepest.
Lord Byron

Never does one feel oneself so utterly helpless as in trying to speak comfort for great bereavement. I will not try it. Time is the only comforter for the loss of a mother.
Jane Welsh Carlyle

Him who is dead and gone honor with remembrance, not with tears.
John Chrysostom

It is proper that the minds of Christians should be familiar with thoughts of death.
R.L. Dabney

Part of every misery is, so to speak, the misery's shadow or reflection: the fact that you don't merely suffer but have to keep on thinking about the fact that you suffer. I not only live each endless day in grief, but live each day thinking about living each day in grief.
C. S. Lewis

To lose a friend is the greatest of all losses.
Latin proverb

Guilt is perhaps the most painful companion of death.
Elisabeth Ross

We see his smile of love even when others see nothing but the black hand of Death smiting our best beloved.
C.H. Spurgeon

Bereavement, Individuals' reaction to
I subdue my grief as well as I can, but you know how tender, or rather soft, my mind is. Had not strong self-control been given me I could not have borne up so long.
John Calvin, after the death of his wife

My little daughter Elizabeth is dead. She has left me wonderfully sick at heart and almost womanish. I am so moved by pity for her. I could never have believed a father's heart could be so tender for his child. Pray to God for me.
Martin Luther

Betrayal
The wounds I was given in the house of my friends.
The Bible, Zechariah 13:6

Bible
See also: New Testament; Old Testament
But God's word is not chained.
The Bible, 2 Timothy 2:9

All men are like grass, and all their glory is like the flowers of the field; the grass withers and the flowers fall, but the word of the Lord stands for ever.
The Bible, 1 Peter 1:24-25

Christ is its grand subject, our good its design, and the glory of God its end.
Author unknown

Men do not reject the Bible because it contradicts itself but because it contradicts them.
Author unknown

The Word is like a mirror, it reflects the sin that is in our lives.
Author unknown

Give me a candle and a Bible, and shut me up in a dark dungeon, and I will tell you what the whole world is doing.
Author unknown

It should fill the memory, rule the heart, and guide the feet.
Author unknown

It contains light to direct you, food to support you, and comfort to cheer you. It is the traveler's guide, the pilgrim's staff, the pilot's compass, the soldier's sword, the Christian's character.
Author unknown

The Bible is not meant merely to inform, but to transform.
Author unknown

The Bible contains the mind of God, the state of man, the way of salvation, the doom of sinners, the happiness of believers.
Author unknown

The income of God's Word is the outcome of a changed life.
Author unknown

The Bible is God's window through which we look into His eternity.
Author unknown

B.I.B.L.E:
Basic Instruction Before Leaving Earth
Author unknown

My Bible and I
We've traveled together through life's
  rugged way,
O'er land and o'er water, by night and by
  day:
To travel without it I never would try;
We keep close together, my Bible and I.
In sorrow I've proved it my comfort and joy,
When weak my strong tower which
  nought can destroy;
When death comes so near me 'tis thought
  I would die,
We still are together, my Bible and I.
If powers of evil against me would come,
And threaten to rob me of heaven and home,
God's Word then directs me to Him in the
  sky;
And nothing can part us, my Bible and I.
When evil temptations are brought to my
  view,
And I in my weakness know not what to
  do,

On Christ as my strength I am taught to
  rely;
And so we keep company, my Bible and I.
When life's path is ended; if Jesus should
  come
And take all his blood-purchased brethren
  home;
Or if, in long suffering, He waits till I die,
We'll never be parted, my Bible and I.
And when in the glory my Lord I behold,
With all His redeemed gathered safe in the
  fold,
My Bible and I close companions will be,
FOR GOD'S WORD ABIDES FOR ALL
ETERNITY.
Author unknown

The Bible is to us what the star was to the wise men; but if we spend all our time in gazing upon it, observing its motions, and admiring its splendor, without being led to Christ by it, the use of it will be lost on us.
Thomas Adams

Vainly do they run about with the pretext that they have demanded councils for the faith's sake; for divine Scripture is sufficient above all things.
Athanasius

The Holy Scriptures are our letters from home.
Augustine of Hippo

Whether concerning Christ or concerning His Church, or any other matter whatsoever which is connected with your faith and life, to say nothing of ourselves, who are by no means to be compared with him who said, "Though we," at any rate, as he went on to say, "Though an angel from heaven preach any other gospel unto you than that which ye have received" in the lawful and evangelical Scriptures, "let him be accursed."
Augustine of Hippo

The reason people are down on the Bible is that they are not up on the Bible.
William Ward Ayer

What is the mark of a faithful soul? To be in the disposition of full acceptance on the authority of the words, not venturing to reject anything, nor making additions. For, if "all that is not of faith is sin," as the Apostle says, and "faith cometh by hearing and hearing by the word of God," everything outside of Holy Scripture, not being of faith, is sin.
Basil

Concerning the hearer: that the hearers who are instructed in the Scriptures should examine what is said by the teachers, receiving what is in conformity with Scripture and rejecting what is opposed to them.
Basil

It is not the work of the Spirit to tell you the meaning of Scripture, and give you the knowledge of divinity, without your own study and labor, but to bless that study, and give you knowledge thereby ... To reject study on pretense of the sufficiency of the Spirit, is to reject the Scripture itself.
Richard Baxter

The Bible has always been regarded as part of the Common Law of England.
Sir William Blackstone

I have sometimes seen more in a line of the Bible than I could well tell how to stand under, yet at another time the whole Bible hath been as dry as a stick.
John Bunyan

God's book of "grace" is just like his book of nature; it is his thoughts written out. This great book, the Bible, this most precious volume is the heart of God made legible; it is the gold of God's love, beaten out into gold leaf, so that therewith our thoughts might be plated, and we also might have golden, good, and holy thoughts concerning him.
John Bunyan

The Bible is not only a book which I can understand, it is a book which understands me.
Emile Caillet

The Bible and the Bible only is the religion of the Protestants.
William Chillingworth

I exhort and entreat you all, disregard what this man and that man thinks about such things, and inquire from the Holy Scriptures all these things.
John Chrysostom

The Bible is the authoritative Word of God and contains all truth.
Bill Clinton

I have found in the Bible words for my inmost thoughts, songs for my joy, utterance for my hidden griefs and pleadings for my shame and feebleness.
Samuel Taylor Coleridge

Who speaks for God? He does quite nicely for Himself. Through His holy and infallible Word – and the quiet obedience of His servants.
Charles Colson

This book outlives, outloves, outlifts, outlasts, outreaches, outruns, and outranks all books. This Book is faith producing. It is hope awakening. It is death destroying, and those who embrace it find forgiveness of sin.
A.Z. Conrad

For concerning the divine and holy mysteries of the Faith, not even a casual statement must be delivered without the Holy Scriptures.
Even to me, who tells thee these things, give not absolute credence, unless thou receive the proof of the thing which I announce from the Divine Scriptures. For this salvation which was before depends not on ingenious reasoning, but on the demonstration of the Holy Scripture.
Cyril of Jerusalem

The Bible is a window in this prison of hope, through which we look into eternity.
Timothy Dwight

The Scriptures teach us the best way of living, the noblest way of suffering, and the most comfortable way of dying.
Flavel

The Bible as a book stands alone. There never was, nor ever will be, another like it. As there is but one sun to enlighten the world naturally, so there is but one Book to enlighten the world spiritually May that Book become to each of us the man of our counsel, the guide of our journey, and our support and comfort in life and in death.
A. Galloway

Christianity finds all its doctrines stated in the Bible, and Christianity denies no part, nor attempts to add anything to the word of God.
Billy Graham

The Bible easily qualifies as the only Book in which is God's revelation.
Billy Graham

If our children have the background of a godly, happy home and this unshakable faith that the Bible is indeed the Word of God, they will have a foundation that the forces of hell cannot shake.
Ruth Graham

Hold fast to the Bible as the sheet-anchor of your liberties; write its precepts in your hearts, and practice them in your lives.
Ulysses S. Grant

The Bible is the only source of all Christian Truth; the only rule for the Christian life; the only Book that unfolds to us the realities of eternity. There is no Book like the Bible for excellent wisdom and use.
Sir Matthew Hale

The Bible is worth all other books which have ever been printed.
Patrick Henry

There is a book worth all other books in the world.
Patrick Henry

Bibles laid open, millions of surprises.
George Herbert.

There can be nothing either more necessary or profitable, than the knowledge of Holy Scripture. And there is no truth nor doctrine, necessary for our justification and everlasting salvation, but that is, or may be, drawn out of that fountain and well of truth.
Homilies, The Book of

All Sacred Scripture is but one book, and that one book is Christ, because all divine Scripture speaks of Christ, and all divine Scripture is fulfilled in Christ.
Hugh of St Victor

The apostles at that time first preached the Gospel but later, by the will of God, they delivered it to us in the Scriptures, that it might be the foundation and pillar of our faith.
Irenaeus

The Bible is the Rock on which this Republic rests.
Andrew Jackson

The first and almost the only book deserving of universal attention is the Bible. I speak as a man of the world.
Thomas Jefferson

Ignorance of the Scriptures is ignorance of Christ.
Jerome

The Bible is the most thought-suggesting book in the world. No other deals with such grand themes.
Herrick Johnson

The Bible is the light of my understanding, the joy of my heart, the fullness of my hope, the clarified of my affections, the mirror of my thoughts, the consoler of my sorrows, the guide of my soul through this gloomy labyrinth of time, the telescope went from heaven to reveal to the eye of man the amazing glories of the far distant world.
Sir William Jones

The Bible is the greatest benefit which the human race has ever experienced. A single line in the Bible has consoled me more than all the books I ever read besides.
Immanuel Kant

The existence of the Bible, as a book for the people, is the greatest benefit which the human race has ever experienced. Every attempt to belittle it is a crime against humanity.
Immanuel Kant

I believe the Bible is the best gift God has given to man.
Abraham Lincoln

All the good from the Savior of the world is communicated through this book; but for the book we could not know right from wrong. All the things desirable to man are contained in it.
Abraham Lincoln

If you want to understand Christianity, do not shut your Bible – open it, read it!
M. Lloyd-Jones

Unless I am convicted of error by the testimony of Scripture or by manifest reasoning I stand convicted by the Scriptures to which I have appealed, and my conscience is taken captive by God's word. I cannot or will not recant anything. For to act against our conscience is neither safe for us, nor open to us.
Martin Luther

I will not be convinced by popes and councils but by Scripture and plain reason.
Martin Luther

The Scriptures alone are the foundation of our beliefs as Christians. I stand on the Word of God as recorded in the Bible.
Martin Luther

The book to read is not the one which thinks for you, but the one which makes you think. No book in the world equals

the Bible for that.
James McCosh

The Bible leads us to Jesus, the inexhaustible, the ever-unfolding Revelation of God. It is Christ "in whom are hid all the treasures of wisdom and knowledge," not the Bible, save as leading to Him.
George Macdonald

One gem from that ocean is worth all the pebbles from earthly streams.
Robert M'Cheyne

As to the book called the Bible, it is blasphemy to call it the Word of God. It is a book of lies and contradictions, and a history of bad times and bad men. There are but a few good characters in the whole book.
Thomas Paine

Back to the Bible, or back to the jungle.
Luis Palau

We may compare the Bible to the Old Testament Tabernacle in the wilderness with its three courts. The outer court is the letter of the Scriptures; the inner court, or holy place, is the truth of the Scriptures; the holiest place of all is the person of Jesus Christ; and only when we pass the inmost veil do we come to Him.
A. T. Pierson

From all human oracles, however self-confident, we turn at last to the inspired Word, where instead of ambiguous and untrustworthy utterances, we find teachings distinct and definite, authoritative and infallible.
A. T. Pierson

The Bible is still loved by millions, read by millions, and studied by millions. It remains the most published and most read book in the world of literature.
Bernard Ramm

The holy scriptures are that divine instrument by which we are taught what to believe,

concerning God, ourselves, and all things, and how to please God unto eternal life.
John Robinson

The Bible is the one Book to which any thoughtful man may go with any honest question of life or destiny and find the answer of God by honest searching.
John Ruskin

The theories of men changed from day to day. Much that is taught new will tomorrow be in the discard, but the word of the Lord will endure forever.
Joseph Fielding Smith

Nobody ever outgrows Scripture; the book widens and deepens with our years.
C.H. Spurgeon

It is wonderful the effect of a single verse of Scripture when the Spirit of God applies it to the soul. What power would come upon the soul if we would grasp a single line of Scripture and suck the honey out of it till our soul is filled with sweetness.
C.H. Spurgeon

The Bible is the portrait of Jesus Christ.
John Stott

I revere the fulness of His Scripture, in which He manifests to me both the Creator and creation. In the gospel, moreover, I discover a Minister and Witness of the Creator, even His Word.
Tertullian

God is not silent. It is the nature of God to speak. The second person of the Holy Trinity is called "The Word." The Bible is the inevitable outcome of God's continuous speech. It is the infallible declaration of His mind.
A.W. Tozer

Most people are bothered by those passages of Scripture they do not understand, but the passages that bother me are those I do understand.
Mark Twain

The word "Bible" designates the Scriptures of the Old and New Testaments recognized and used by the Christian churches. Judaism recognizes only the Scriptures of the Old Testament.

There is only one Bible – incomparable, unique as far as all other "sacred" literature is concerned, because: (1) It is the revelation of God. (2) It is "God-breathed" (2 Tim 3:16) and inspired in a different sense from all other literature. (3) It discloses God's plans and purposes for the ages of time and eternity. (4) It centers in God incarnate in Jesus Christ, the Savior of humankind (Heb 1:1-2).
M.F. Unger

When the Bible speaks, God speaks.
B.B. Warfield

The Scripture is both the breeder and feeder of grace. How is the convert born, but by "the word of truth"? (James 1:18). How doth he grow, but by "the sincere milk of the Word"? (1 Peter 2:2)
Thomas Watson

The Bible is a book of faith, and a book of doctrine, and a book of morals, and a book of religion, of special revelation from God; but it is also a book which teaches man his own individual responsibility, his own dignity, and his equity with his fellow-man.
Daniel Webster

It is not the Word of God but rather modernity that stands in need of being demythologized.
David F. Wells

I want to know one thing, the way to heaven: how to land safe on that happy shore. God himself has condescended to teach the way; for this very end he came from heaven. He has written it down in a book! Oh, give me that book! At any price, give me the book of God! I have it: here is knowledge enough for me. Let me be *homo unius libri*: "A man of one book."
John Wesley

My ground is the Bible. Yea, I am a Bible-bigot. I follow it in all things, both great and small.
John Wesley

A man has deprived himself of the best there is in the world who has deprived himself of the Bible.
Woodrow Wilson

Bible, Accuracy of
In one verse Luke alludes to fifteen historical references which any classical historian can verify.

In the fifteen year (one) of the reign of Tiberius Caesar (two) when Pontius Pilate (three) was governor (four) of Judea (five), Herod (six) tetrarch (seven) of Galilee (eight), his brother Philip (nine) tetrarch (ten) of Iturea (eleven) and Traconitis, (twelve) and Lysanias (thirteen) tetrarch (fourteen) of Abilene (fifteen).
Luke 3:1
Author unknown

Bible, Authority of
God spoke ... through the prophets.
The Bible, Hebrews 1:1

For prophecy never had its origin in the will of man, but men spoke from God as they were carried along by the Holy Spirit.
The Bible, 2 Peter 1:21

Let us therefore yield ourselves and bow to the authority of the Holy Scriptures, which can neither err nor deceive.
Augustine of Hippo

I do not understand the Doctrine of Luther, or Calvin, or Melancthon, nor the Confession of Augusta, or Geneva, nor the Catechism of Heidelberg, nor the Articles of the Church of England, no nor the Harmony of Protestant Confessions, but that wherein they all agree, and which they all subscribe with a greater harmony, as a perfect rule of their faith and action; that, is, the BIBLE. The BIBLE, I say, the BIBLE only, is the Religion of Protestants.

I am fully assured that God does not and therefore that men ought not to require any more of any man than this, to believe the Scripture to be God's Word, to endeavor to find the true sense of it, and to live according to it.
William Chillingworth

The authority of Scripture must be followed in all things, for in it we have the truth as it were in its secret haunts.
John Scotus Erigena

Unless I am convicted of error by the testimony of Scripture or by manifest reasoning I stand convicted by the Scriptures to which I have appealed, and my conscience is taken captive by God's word. I cannot or will not recant anything. For to act against our conscience is neither safe for us, nor open to us.
Martin Luther

Let us receive nothing, believe nothing, follow nothing which is not in the Bible, nor can be proved by the Bible.
J.C. Ryle

Our claim is that God has revealed himself by speaking; that this divine (or God-breathed) speech has been written down and preserved in Scripture; and that Scripture is, in fact, God's word written, which therefore is true and reliable and has divine authority over men.
John Stott

Authority resides in God's inspired Word (the Bible) interpreted by God's Spirit operating through Spirit-taught human agents.
M.F. Unger

The authority of the holy Scripture, for which it ought to be believed, and obeyed, dependeth not upon the testimony of any man, or church; but wholly upon God (who is truth itself) the author thereof: and therefore it is to be received, because it is the Word of God.
Westminster Confession

Bible, Authorship of

Scripture is both the word of God and the word of men.
John Stott

The dual authorship of Scripture is an important truth to be carefully guarded. On the one hand, God spoke, revealing the truth and preserving the human authors from error, yet without violating their personality.

On the other hand, men spoke, using their own faculties freely, yet without distorting the divine message. Their words were truly their own words. But they were (and still are) also God's words, so that what Scripture says, God says.
John Stott

Bible, Belief in

We cannot rely on the doctrine of Scripture until we are absolutely convinced that God is its author.
John Calvin

In 1987 of 10,000 American clergy who were asked whether they believed that the Scriptures are the inspired and inerrant Word of God in faith, history, and secular matters:
95% of Episcopalians,
87% of Methodists,
82% of Presbyterians,
77% of American Lutherans,
and 67% of American Baptists said "No."
Jeffery Hadden

Bible, Chapter divisions of

I feel vexed with the fellow [Sir Robert Stephens in 1551] who chopped the Bible up into chapters. I have heard that he did the most of his carving of the New Testament, between London and Paris, and rough work he made of it. Surely he was chaptering the Gospel of Matthew while he was crossing the Channel, for he has divided it in such unusual places.
C.H. Spurgeon

Bible, Criticism of

A thousand times over, the death knell of the Bible has been sounded, a funeral procession formed, the inscription cut on the tombstone, and committal read. But somehow the corpse never stays put.
Author unknown

They amuse themselves by playing an irrelevant ecclesiastical game called "Let's Pretend." Let's pretend that we possess the objective truth of God in our inerrant Scriptures or in our infallible pronouncements or in our unbroken apostolic traditions.
Bishop John Shelby Spong

Isn't it amazing that almost everyone has an opinion to offer about the Bible, and yet so few have studied it?
R.C. Sproul

Bible, Detail in

There are no meaningless details in the word.
Benny Hinn

Bible, Exposition of

What more can I teach you, than what we read in the Apostle? For holy Scripture setteth a rule to our teaching, that we dare not "be wise more than it behoveth to be wise." Be it not therefore for me to teach you any other thing, save to expound to you the words of the Teacher, and to treat of them as the Lord shall have given to me.
Augustine of Hippo

Bible, Faith in

What the church lacks in our day is not a reliable text of the Bible, but the faith in the sufficiently reliable text.
John Piper

Bible, Family Bible

Old Brother Higgins built a shelf
for the family bible to rest itself
lest a sticky finger or grimy thumb
might injure the delicate pages some.
He cautioned his children to touch it not
and it rested there with never a blot
though the Higgins tribe were a
troublesome lot.
His neighbor, Miggins, built a shelf

"Come children," he said, "and help yourself."

His book is old and ragged and worn, with some of the choicest pages torn, where children have fingered and thumbed and read.

But of the Miggins tribe I've heard it said, each carries a bible in his head.

Author unknown

Bible, Ignorance of

The reason people are down on the Bible is that they are not up on the Bible.

William Ward Ayer

Bible, Inerrancy of

None of these [canonical] authors has erred in any respect of writing.

Augustine of Hippo

In this long journey of thought the concept of inerrancy was not rejected but was seriously modified to fit the evidence of biblical criticism which showed that the Bible was not inerrant in questions of science, of history, and even of time-conditioned religious beliefs.

R.E. Brown, referring to the Vatican II position on the inerrancy of the Bible

The holy Scriptures which are given through the Holy Spirit ... nothing iniquitous or falsified is written.

Clement of Rome

If the Bible is a mixture of truth and error, then it is like any other book and simply not deserving of any special attention.

Dave Miller

Only truth can be authoritative; only an inerrant Bible can be used ... in the way that God means Scripture to be used.

J.I. Packer

We both must affirm the inerrancy of Scripture and then live under it in our personal lives and in society.

Francis A. Schaeffer

Does inerrancy make a difference?

Overwhelmingly; the difference is that with the Bible being what it is, God's Word and so absolute, God's objective truth, we do not need to be, and we should not be, caught in the ever-changing fallen cultures which surround us.

Francis A. Schaeffer

Bible, Influence of

So great is my veneration for the Bible that the earlier my children begin to read it, the more confident my hope that they will prove useful citizens, and respectful members of society.

John Quincy Adams

To the influence of the Bible we are indebted for the progress made in civilization, and to this we must look as our guide in the future.

Ulysses S. Grant

There is no need for bloodshed. The world will be conquered by the Word of God, and by the Word the Church will be rebuilt and reformed.

Martin Luther

We must allow the Word of God to confront us, to disturb our security, to undermine our complacency and to overthrow our patterns of thought and behavior.

John Stott

God did not write a book and send it by messenger to be read at a distance by unaided minds. He spoke a Book and lives in His spoken words, constantly speaking His words and causing the power of them to persist across the years.

A. W. Tozer

Bible, Inspiration of

All Scripture is God-breathed and is useful for teaching, rebuking, correcting and training in righteousness, so that the man of God may be thoroughly equipped for every good work.

The Bible, 2 Timothy 3:16-17

Just as the Holy Spirit came upon the womb of Mary, so He came upon the brain of a Moses, a David, an Isaiah, a Paul, a John and the rest of the writers of the divine library. The power of the Highest overshadowed them, therefore that holy thing which was born of their minds is called the Holy Bible, the word of God. The writing of Luke will, of course, have the vocabulary of Luke and the work of Paul will bear the stamp of Paul's mind. However, this is only in the same manner that the Lord Jesus might have had eyes like his mother's or hair that was the same color and texture as hers. He did not inherit her sins because the Holy Spirit has come upon her. If we ask, how could this be, the answer is God says so. And the writings of men of the Book did not inherit the errors of their carnal minds because their writings were conceived by the Holy Spirit and born out of their personalities without partaking of their fallen nature. If we ask, how could this be, again the answer is God says so.
Donald Grey Barnhouse

My whole energy of interpreting has been expended in an endeavor to see through and beyond history into the spirit of the Bible, which is the Eternal Spirit.
Karl Barth

I know the Bible is inspired because it finds me at a greater depth of my being than any other book.
Samuel Taylor Coleridge

The whole of Scripture and all of its parts, down to the very words of the original, were given by divine inspiration. The written word in its entirety is revelation given by God. Confession of the full authority, infallibility, and inerrancy of Scripture is vital to a sound understanding of the whole of Christian faith.
Warren Doud

Since the writers of the Bible wrote the things which God showed and uttered to them, it cannot be pretended that He is not the writer; for his members executed what their head dictated.
Gregory the Great

We loyally believe the Holy Spirit to be the author of the book. He wrote it who dictated it for writing; He wrote it who inspired its execution.
Gregory the Great

We do not assert that the common text, but only the original autographic text, was inspired.
A.A. Hodge

The plenary inspiration of the sacred writers made them infallible in all they taught; but it did not make them omniscient. The time of the second coming was not revealed to them. They profess their ignorance on that point.
Charles Hodge

The Bible is the only book that has been written not just by human characters inside the story but also by the divine author of the story. Its perspective is double, that of the characters and that of the author, or that of the human authors and that of the divine author. Like Christ – the word of God in person – the Bible, the Word of God in writing, is the Word of God in words of men. It has both a human nature and a divine nature.
Peter Kreeft

For all the books which the Church receives as sacred and canonical are written wholly and entirely, with all their parts, at the dictation of the Holy Spirit; and so far is it from being possible that any error can coexist with inspiration, that inspiration not only is essentially incompatible with error, but excludes and rejects it as absolutely and necessarily as it is impossible that God Himself, the supreme Truth, can utter that which is not true. This is the ancient and unchanging faith of the Church.
Pope Leo XIII

[The Holy Spirit] assisted the authors of the books of the Bible so that they "expressed in apt words and with infallible truth." Otherwise, it could not be said that He was the Author of the entire Scripture. Such has always been the persuasion of the Fathers.
Pope Leo XIII

The sacred books are pervaded by the Spirit. There is nothing either in the prophets, on in the law, or in the Gospels, or in the epistles, which does not spring from the fulness of the divine majesty.
Origen

The greatest proof that the Bible is inspired is that it has stood so much bad preaching.
A. T. Robertson

The particularity of each New Testament author was in no way smothered by the unique process of inspiration. On the contrary, the Holy Spirit first prepared, and then used, their individuality of upbringing, experience, temperament and personality, in order to convey through each some distinctive and appropriate truth.
John Stott

Divine inspiration makes the Bible uniquely the Word of God and not merely a book containing the Word of God, and as such is different from any other book sacred or secular.
M.F. Unger

The books of the Old and New Testament, whole and entire, with all their parts, as enumerated in the decree of the same Council [Trent] and in the ancient Latin Vulgate, are to be received as sacred and canonical. And the Church holds them as sacred and canonical not because, having been composed by human industry, they were afterwards approved by her authority; nor only because they contain revelation without errors, but because, having been written under the inspiration of the Holy Spirit, they have God for their Author.
The Council of the Vatican, 1869-1870
[This differs from the commonly held view that inerrancy and inspiration only refer to the original Hebrew, Aramaic and Greek documents.]

If criticism has made such discoveries as to necessitate the abandonment of the doctrine of plenary inspiration, it is not enough to say that we are compelled to abandon only a "particular theory of inspiration ..." We must go on to say that that "particular theory of inspiration" is the theory of the apostles and of the Lord, and that in abandoning it we are abandoning them.
B.B. Warfield

Bible, Interpretation of

In 1728, potatoes were outlawed in Scotland because they were not mentioned in the Bible.
Author unknown

I have nothing whatever to say against historical criticism. I recognize it, and once more state quite definitely that it is both necessary and justified. My complaint is that recent commentators confine themselves to an interpretation of the text which seems to me to be no commentary at all, but merely a first step towards a commentary.
Karl Barth

The historical-critical method of Biblical investigation has its rightful place; it is concerned with the preparation of the intelligence – and this can never be superfluous.
Karl Barth

Is there any way of penetrating the heart of a document – of any document! – except on the assumption that its spirit will speak to our spirit through the actual written words?
Karl Barth

John Calvin was committed to the interpretation that every word of the Bible is divinely inspired.
Karl Barth

Any part of the human body can only be properly explained in reference to the whole body. And any part of the Bible can only be properly explained in reference to the whole Bible.
F.F. Bruce

Let us know, then, that the true meaning of Scripture is the natural and obvious meaning; and let us embrace and abide by it resolutely. Let us not only neglect as doubtful, but boldly set aside as deadly corruptions those pretended expositions which lead us away from the natural meaning.
John Calvin

No man has a right to say, as some are in the habit of saying, "The Spirit tells me that such or such is the meaning of a passage." How is he assured that it is the Holy Spirit, and not a spirit of delusion, except from the evidence that the interpretation is the legitimate meaning of the words?
Alexander Carson

Sacred Scripture, though, whenever it wants to teach us something like this, gives its own interpretation, and doesn't let the listener go astray. On the other hand, since the majority of listeners apply their ears to the narrative, not for the sake of gaining some profit but for enjoyment, they are at pains to take note of things able to bring enjoyment rather than those that bring profit. So, I beg you, block your ears against all distractions of that kind, and let us follow the norm of Sacred Scripture.
Chrysostom

Be on guard against any tampering with the Word, whether disguised as a search for truth, or a scholarly attempt at apparently hidden meanings.
Martin R. DeHaan

Although the whole of Scripture is centered around Jesus Christ, each of its parts does not tell us all about him; just like the whole of a parable is designed for a purpose, or main object, though not every detail is immediately relevant to the end. Not every part of a lute produces

harmonious sounds, but each of them is necessary for their production. According to Saint Augustine, it is the same for Scripture. The whole of it resounds with the name and mysteries of Jesus Christ, though not each individual part does. We cannot expect each part to resound, but they all play a part in the overall effect.
Attributed to Jacques-Joseph Duguet

Always begin by establishing the literal meaning.
Attributed to Jacques-Joseph Duguet

(After the literal, or, historical meaning, look for the Christological meaning.) Jesus Christ is the end of the law and we cannot understand Scripture unless we see him present in all of it.
Attributed to Jacques-Joseph Duguet

It is extremely important to declare what the Bible holds, and be silent where the Bible is silent.
Billy Graham

It's not what you think, it's what the Bible says.
Rodney Howard-Browne

Mary Queen of Scots asked, "Ye interpret the Scriptures in one manner, and they in another; whom shall I believe, and who shall judge?"
   John Knox replied? "Believe God, that plainly speaketh in his word: and further than the word teacheth you, ye shall neither believe the one nor the other. The word of God is plain in itself; and if there appear any obscurity in one place, the Holy Ghost, which is never contrarious to himself, explains the same more clearly in other places."
John Knox

I have been suspected of being what is called a Fundamentalist. That is because I never regard any narrative as unhistorical simply on the ground that it includes the miraculous.
C.S. Lewis

Only the cry of Jesus on the Cross admits of no allegory; the rest of the Bible and of authentic tradition is to be interpreted spiritually as the echo of that cry throughout the history of Revelation.
Max Huot de Longchamp

I have observed that all the heresies and errors have arisen not from Scripture's own plain statements, but when that plainness of statement is ignored, and men follow the Scholastic arguments of their own brains.
Martin Luther

If there be any difference among professed believers as to the sense of Scripture, it is their duty to tolerate such difference in each other, until God shall have revealed the truth to all.
John Milton

A basic principle in the interpretation of the Bible is that one must first ask what a given Scripture was intended to mean to the people for whom it was originally written; only then is the interpreter free to ask what meaning it has for Christians today. Failure to ask this primary question and to investigate the historical setting of Scripture has prevented many Christians from coming to a correct understanding of some parts of the Bible.
Sir William M. Ramsay

Because of lack of fortitude and faithfulness on the part of God's people, God's Word has many times been allowed to be bent, to conform to the surrounding, passing, changing culture of that moment rather than to stand as the inerrant Word of God judging the form of the world spirit and the surrounding culture of that moment.
Francis A. Schaeffer

No public man in these islands ever believes that the Bible means what it says; he is always convinced that it says what he means.
George Bernard Shaw

I would sooner a hundred times over be inconsistent with myself than be inconsistent with the Word of God.
C.H. Spurgeon

Based on the assumption that an author is an articulate communicator (as we believe God to be), the primary presupposition of hermeneutical theory must be that the meaning of a text is the author's intended meaning, rather than the meanings we may wish to ascribe to his words. If we abandon this principle, there remains no normative, compelling criterion for discriminating between valid and invalid interpretations.
Henry A. Verkler

The general rule of interpreting Scripture is this: the literal sense of every text is to be taken, if it be not contrary to some other texts. But in that case, the obscure text is to be interpreted by those which speak more plainly.
John Wesley

Try all things by the written word, and let all bow down before it. You are in danger of fanaticism every hour, if you depart ever so little from Scripture; yea, or from the plain, literal meaning of an text, taken in connection with the context.
John Wesley

Bible, Interpretation by Church Fathers

[In the Middle Ages the traditional doctrine of the Church Fathers had been set out in the theory of the four meanings]:
Littera gesta docet, quid credas allegoria, Moralis quid agas, quo tendas anagogia.
Give the literal meaning, believe the allegorical meaning, agree with the moral meaning, receive the analogical meaning. For the "moral meaning" the term used nowadays would be hermeneutics, or the meaning of the text as applied to us, in contrast to exegesis, which is concerned with the meaning of the text at the time of writing.
Author unknown

Bible, Knowledge of

A man who is well-grounded in the testimonies of the Scripture is the bulwark of the Church.
Jerome

Bible, Learning from

There is one God, whom we do not otherwise acknowledge, brethren, but out of the Holy Scriptures. For as he that would profess the wisdom of this world cannot otherwise attain hereunto, unless he read the doctrine of the philosophers, so whosoever of us will exercise piety toward God, cannot learn this elsewhere but out of the Holy Scriptures. Whatsoever, therefore, the Holy Scriptures do preach, that let us know; and whatsoever they teach, that let us understand.
Hippolytus

Bible, Message of

In the Old Testament, we have Jesus predicted. In the Gospels, we have Jesus revealed. In Acts, we have Jesus preached. In the Epistles, we have Jesus explained. In the Revelation we have Jesus expected.
Alistair Begg

Bible, Misuse of

The devil can cite Scripture for his purpose.
William Shakespeare, The Merchant of Venice

Bible, Obedience to

Question: How shall we know that we love the reproofs of the Word?
Answer 1:
When we desire to sit under a heart-searching ministry. Who cares for medicines that will not work? A godly man does not choose to sit under a ministry that will not work upon his conscience.
Answer 2:
When we pray that the Word may meet with our sins. If there is any traitorous lust in our heart, we would have it found out and executed. We do not want sin covered, but cured. We can open our breast to the "sword" of the Word and say, "Lord, smite this sin."
Thomas Watson

Bible, Opposition to

Skepticism toward the reliability of Scripture seems to survive in many academic circles despite the repeated collapse of critical theories. One still finds a disposition to trust secular writers whose credentials in providing historical testimony are often less adequate than those of the biblical writers. Not long ago many scholars rejected the historicity of the patriarchal accounts, denied that writing existed in Moses' day, and ascribed the Gospels and Epistles to second-century writers. But higher criticism has sustained some spectacular and even stunning reverses, mainly through the findings of archaeology. No longer is it held that the glories of King Solomon's era are literary fabrication, that "Yahweh," the redemptive God of the Hebrews, was unknown before the eighth-century prophets, or that Ezra's representations about the Babylonian captivity are fictional. Archaeologists have located the long-lost copper mines of Solomon's time. Tablets discovered at Ebla near Aleppo confirm that names similar to those of the patriarchs were common among people who lived in Ebla shortly before the events recorded in the later chapters of Genesis took place.
Carl Henry

Every type of destruction that human philosophy, human science, human reason, human art, human cunning, human force, and human brutality could bring to bear against a book has been brought to bear against this Book, and yet the Bible stands absolutely unshaken today. At times almost all the wise and great of the earth have been pitted against the Bible, and only an obscure few for it. Yet it has stood.
Dr R.A. Torrey

Bible, Origin of

The chief reason why the Christian believes in the divine origin of the Bible is that Jesus Christ himself taught it.
John Stott

Bible, Power of
A layman who has Scripture is more than Pope or council without it.
Martin Luther

The Scriptures and the words of Jesus possess a terrible power in themselves and a wonderful sweetness. Straightway a flame was kindled in my soul, and a love of the prophets and of those men who were friends of Christ possessed me.
Justin Martyr

Bible, Purpose of
The Word of God is contained exactly and most purely in the Originals, and in all translations, so far as they agree therewith. Now though some translations may exceed others in Propriety, and significant rendering of the Originals: yet they generally, (even the most imperfect that we know of) express and hold forth so much of the Mind, Will, and Counsel of God, as is sufficient, by the Blessing of God upon a conscientious Reading thereof, to acquaint a man with the mysteries of salvation, to work in him true faith, and bring him to live godly, righteously, and soberly in this world, and to salvation in the next.
The Baptist Catechism

The Bible was given to bear witness to one God, Creator and Sustainer of the universe, through Christ, Redeemer of sinful man. It presents one continuous story – that of human redemption.
M.F. Unger

Bible, Reliability of
The variant readings about which any doubt remains among textual critics of the New Testament affect no material question of historic fact or of Christian faith and practice.
F.F. Bruce

The Christian can take the whole Bible in his hand and say without fear or hesitation that he holds in it the true Word of God, handed down without essential loss from generation to generation throughout the centuries.
Sir Frederic G. Kenyon, former Director of the British Museum

Skepticism regarding the historical credentials of Christianity is based upon an irrational basis.
Dr Clark Pinnock, professor of Interpretation at McMasters University, Canada

Bible, Reliance upon
He that thinks himself to be too good to be ruled by the Word, will be found too bad to be owned by God; and if God do not or will not own him, Satan will by his stratagems overthrow him.
Thomas Brooks

Bible, Reverence for
"Has not my hand made all these things, and so they came into being?" declares the LORD. "This is the one I esteem: he who is humble and contrite in spirit, and trembles at my word."
The Bible, Isaiah 66:2

Bible, Scope of
The whole counsel of God concerning all things necessary for His own glory, man's salvation, faith, and life, is either expressly set down in Scripture, or by good and necessary consequence may be deduced from Scripture: unto which nothing at any time is to be added, whether by new revelations of the Spirit, or traditions of men.
The Confession of Faith of the Westminster Assembly of Divines, 1646

Bible, Sufficiency of
For among the things that are plainly laid down in Scripture are to be found all matters that concern faith and the manner of life.
Augustine of Hippo

Bible, Teaching of
Its doctrines are holy, its precepts are binding, its decisions are immutable.
Author unknown

"God is in heaven, and thou art on earth." The relation between such a God and such a man, and the relation between such a man and such a God, is for me the theme of the Bible and the essence of philosophy.
Karl Barth

What is it the Bible teaches us? Rapine, cruelty, and murder. What is it the New Testament teaches us? To believe that the Almighty committed debauchery with a woman engaged to be married, and the belief of this debauchery is called faith.
Thomas Paine

Defend the Bible? I would as soon defend a lion! Unchain it and it will defend itself.
C.H. Spurgeon

Bible, Translation of

We affirm and avow, that the very meanest [poorest or least esteemed] translation of the Bible in English, set forth by men of our profession ... contains the Word of God, nay, is the Word of God. Though it be not interpreted by every Translator with like grace, the King's speech is still the King's speech; no cause therefore why the word translated should be denied to be the word, or forbidden to be current [used], notwithstanding that some imperfections and blemishes may be noted in the setting forth [translating] of it. Variety of translations is profitable for finding out of the sense of the scriptures.
Translators to the Readers' Preface of the King James Version 1611

The Holy Spirit chose as the language of the New Testament revelation the colloquial language of everyday people, not an ancient classical idea. The modern insistence upon the supremacy of the King James Version of 1611 represents a reversal of the action of the Holy Spirit by insisting that for us the best idiom for the word of God is not the modern colloquial idiom, but the ancient classical language of Shakespeare.
G.E. Ladd

To claim inerrancy for the King James Version, or even for the Revised Version, is to claim inerrancy for men who never professed it for themselves; is to clothe with the claim of verbal inspiration a company of men who would almost quit their graves to repudiate such equality with Prophet and Apostle.
W.B. Riley

I do not say that those who wrote copies of the original Hebrew and Greek Scriptures were incapable of making mistakes, and never left out or added a word. I lay no claim to the inspiration of every word in the various versions and translations of God's Word. So far as these translations and versions are faithfully and correctly done so far they are practically, of equal authority with the original Hebrew and Greek.
J.C. Ryle

Do not needlessly amend our Authorized Version. It is faulty in many places, but still it is a grand work taking it for all in all, and it is unwise to be making every old lady distrust the only Bible she can get at, or what is more likely, mistrust you for falling out with her cherished treasure. Correct where correction must be for truth's sake, but never for the vainglorious display of your critical ability.
C.H. Spurgeon

I do not hesitate to say that I believe that there is no mistake whatever in the original Holy Scriptures from beginning to end. There may be, and there are MISTAKES of translation – for translators are NOT INSPIRED – but even the historical facts are correct ... there is not an error in the whole compass of them. These words come from him who can make no mistake, and who can have no wish to deceive his creatures.
C.H. Spurgeon

Bible, Trustworthiness of

On my own part I confess to your charity that it is only to those books of Scripture which are now called canonical that I have

learned to pay such honor and reverence as to believe most firmly that none of their writers has fallen into any error. And if in these books I meet anything which seems contrary to truth, I shall not hesitate to conclude either that the text is faulty, or that the translator has not expressed the meaning of the passage, or that I myself do not understand.
Augustine of Hippo

The earliest preachers of the gospel knew the value of ... first-hand testimony, and appealed to it time and again. "We are witnesses of these things," was their constant and confident assertion. And it can have been by no means so easy as some writers think to invent words and deeds of Jesus in those early years, when so many of His disciples were about, who could remember what had and had not happened.
F. F. Bruce

There is, I imagine, no body of literature in the world that has been exposed to the stringent analytical study that the four Gospels have sustained for the past 200 years. This is not something to be regretted: it is something to be accepted with satisfaction. Scholars today who treat the Gospels as credible historical documents do so in the full light of this analytical study, not by closing their minds to it.
F. F. Bruce

There is no body of ancient literature in the world which enjoys such a wealth of good textual attestation as the New Testament.
F. F. Bruce

And it was not only friendly eyewitnesses that the early preachers had to reckon with; there were others less well disposed who were also conversant with the main facts of the ministry and death of Jesus. The disciples could not afford to risk inaccuracies (not to speak of willful manipulation of the facts), which would at once be exposed by those who would be only too glad to do so. On the contrary, one of the strong points in the original apostolic preaching is the confident appeal to the knowledge of the hearers; they not only said, "We are witnesses of these things," but also, "As you yourselves also know" [Acts 2:22]. Had there been any tendency to depart from the facts in any material respect, the possible presence of hostile witnesses in the audience would have served as a further corrective.
F. F. Bruce

Christians hold the Bible to be the Word of God (and inerrant) because they are convinced that Jesus, the Lord of the Church, believed it and taught his disciples to believe in it.
Kenneth Kantzer

I have heard professing Christians of our own day speak as though the historicity of the Gospels does not matter – all that matters is the contemporary Spirit of Christ. I contend that the historicity does matter, and I do not see why we, who live nearly two thousand years later, should call into question an Event for which there were many eyewitnesses still living at the time when most of the New Testament was written. It was no "cunningly devised fable" but an historic irruption of God into human history which gave birth to a young church so sturdy that the pagan world could not stifle or destroy it.
J.B. Phillips

The church has always believed her Scriptures to be the book of God, of which God was in such a sense the author that every one of its affirmations of whatever kind is to be esteemed as the utterance of God, of infallible truth and authority.
B.B. Warfield

Bible, Understanding the
It be a certain truth, that none can understand the prophets' and apostles' writings aright, without the same Spirit by which they were written.
George Fox

In expounding the Bible if one were always to confine oneself to the unadorned grammatical meaning, one might fall into error. Not only contradictions and propositions far from true might thus be made to appear in the Bible, but even grave heresies and follies. Thus it would be necessary to assign to God feet, hands and eyes.
Balilei Galileo

When Christ said on the Cross, "All is accomplished," and died, all the modes [of Revelation of the Old Covenant] ceased to exist, and along with them the ceremonies and rites of the Old Law.
John of the Cross

No one understands Scripture unless it is brought home to them, that is, unless they experience it.
Martin Luther

Bible, Unity of
In the Old Testament the New is concealed. In the New Testament the Old is revealed.
Augustine of Hippo

Bible, Use of
Give heed unto reading, exhortation and doctrine. Think upon these things contained in this book, be diligent in them, that the increase coming thereby, may be manifest unto all men. Take heed unto thyself, and unto teaching, and be diligent in doing them, for by doing this thou shalt save thyself, and them that hear thee.
1549 Book of Common Prayer. In the first prayer book of Edward VI, at the consecration of a bishop, the Archbishop laid the Bible upon the neck of the newly-ordained bishop, saying the above words

Bible, Usefulness of
God's Emergency Numbers
When in sorrow – call John 14
When you are lonely or fearful – call
    Psalm 23
When you want to be fruitful – call John
    15
When you have sinned – call Psalm 51

When you grow bitter and critical – call 1
    Corinthians 13
When you worry – call Matthew 6:19-34
When you feel down and out – call
    Romans 8:31-39
When your prayers grow selfish – call
    Psalm 67
When you are in danger – call Psalm 91
When your faith needs stirring – call
    Hebrews 11
When God seems far away – call Psalm 139
When others fail you – call Psalm 27
When you leave home to labor or travel –
    call Psalm 121
When you want assurance – call Romans
    1:1-30
For Paul's secret of happiness – call
    Colossians 3:12-17
For Paul's idea of Christianity – call 2
    Corinthians 5:15-20
When the world seems bigger than God –
    call Psalm 70 and Jeremiah 33:3
If you believe in Jesus Christ call Him up
Author unknown

The Scripture is the library of the Holy Ghost; it is an exact model and platform of religion. The Scripture contains in it the credenda,"things which we are to believe," and the agenda, "the things which are to be done."
Thomas Watson

Bible and Christ
Whatever God says is true. Jesus who is God says the Bible is God's Word, therefore the Bible is God's Word.
Steve Kumar

Every word of the Bible rings with Christ.
Martin Luther

The Bible is the cradle wherein Christ is laid.
Martin Luther

Remove Christ from the Scriptures and there is nothing left.
Martin Luther

The Bible is not infallible because it says so – but because Christ says so. There is no more

reliable witness to the nature of Scripture than the one who died and rose to be our Savior.
Clark Pinnock

To Christ the Bible is true, authoritative, inspired, to him the God of the Bible is the living God, and the teaching of the Bible is the teaching of the living God. To him what Scripture says, God says.
John W. Wenham

Not only did Jesus Christ look upon the Old Testament as forming an organic whole but also he believed that both as a unity and in its several parts it was finally and absolutely authoritative.
Edward J. Young

Bible and education
I am much afraid that schools will prove to be the great gates of Hell unless they diligently labor in explaining the Holy Scriptures, engraving them in the hearts of youth. I advise no one to place his child where the Scriptures do not reign paramount. Every institution in which men are not increasingly occupied with the Word of God must become corrupt.
Martin Luther

Bible and God's will
This Holy Scripture, thus written in Hebrew and Greek, in those languages wherein it was written, containeth nothing but the will of God and the whole will of God; so that there is nothing necessary to be believed concerning God, nor done in obedience unto God by us, but what is here revealed to us; and therefore all traditions of men which are contrary to this word of God are necessarily to be abhorred, and all traditions of men not recorded in this word of God are not necessarily to be believed. What is here written we are bound to believe because it is written; and what is not here written we are not bound to believe because it is not written.
William Beveridge

Bible and salvation
… from infancy you have known the holy Scriptures, which are able to make you wise for salvation through faith in Christ Jesus.
The Bible, 2 Timothy 3:15

If the Scriptures do thoroughly direct men to know God in Christ, and save their own souls, why should we look any further?
Thomas Manton

Bible and sin
Either the Bible will keep you away from sin, or sin will keep you away from the Bible!
C.S. Lewis

Bible and source criticism
We must not fall into the error of thinking that when we have come to a conclusion about the sources of a literary work we have learned all that needs to be known about it. Source Criticism is merely a preliminary piece of spade-work. Whatever their sources were, the Gospels are there before our eyes, each an individual literary work with its own characteristic viewpoint, which has in large measure controlled the choice and presentation of the subject matter. In attempting to discover how they were composed, we must beware of regarding them as scissors-and-paste compilations.
F.F. Bruce

Bible and Spirit
If you only have the Word, you will dry up. If you only have the Spirit, you will blow up. But if you have the Word and the Spirit, you will go up and grow up.
Author unknown

The Bible applied to the heart by the Holy Spirit, is the chief means by which men are built up and established in the faith, after their conversion.
J.C. Ryle

Bible and success
The secret of my success? It is simple. It is found in the Bible, "In all thy ways acknowledge Him and He shall direct thy paths."
George Washington Carver

Bible and truth

The Holy Scriptures given by inspiration of God are of themselves sufficient to the discovery of the truth.
Athanasius

There is one sure and infallible guide to truth, and therefore, one, and only one corrective for error, and that is the Word of God.
G. Campbell Morgan

Bible in England

The Bible has always been regarded as part of the Common Law of England.
Sir William Blackstone, the great English jurist

Bible reading
See also: Bible reading, Obstacles to; Bible reading, Preparation for; Bible reading and prayer

Bible reading

Cardiphonia: Letter from John Newton
My dear Madam;

I am farther to thank you for your letter of the 23rd of last month. The subject of my former, to which it principally relates, needs no further prosecution, as you express yourself satisfied with what I offered in answer to your question. I would, therefore, now offer something a little different. But the points of experimental religion are so nearly related, and so readily run into each other, that I cannot promise, at this distance of time, to avoid all repetition. Indeed, the truths essential to the peace of our souls are so simple, and may be reduced to so few heads, that while each of them singly may furnish a volume drawn out at length, they may all be comprised in small compass. Books and letters written in a proper spirit, may, if the Lord is pleased to smile upon them, have their use; but an awakened mind that thirsts after the Savior, and seeks wisdom by reading and praying over the scripture, has little occasion for a library of human writings. The Bible is the fountain from whence every stream that deserves our notice is drawn; and, though we may occasionally pay some attention to the streams – we have personally an equal right with others to apply immediately to the fountain-head, and draw the water of life for ourselves. The purest streams are not wholly freed from the gout de terroir – a twang of the soil through which they run; a mixture of human infirmity is inseparable from the best human composition; but in the fountain the truth is unmixed.

Again, men teach us by many words; and if they would give us their full views of the subject, require us to read a whole volume, the life and substance of which is perhaps expressed with greater force and greater advantage in the scripture by a single sentence, which is rather diluted than explained by our feeble expositions. A volume may be easily written upon the grace of humility, and to show the evil and folly of a self-seeking spirit. But if the author should introduce this subject with our Savior's words, " Even the Son of Man came not into the world to be ministered unto, but to minister, and to give his life a ransom for many;" whoever was duly impressed with that short introduction, would have no great occasion to read the rest of the book.

The preaching of the gospel being an instituted means of grace, ought to be thankfully and frequently improved. And books that have a savor and unction may likewise be helpful, provided we read them with caution, compare them with the scripture, and do not give ourselves implicitly to the rules or decisions of any man or set of men, but remember that one is our Master and infallible Teacher, even Christ. But the chief and grand means of edification, without which all other helps will disappoint us, and prove like clouds without water, are the Bible and prayer, the word of grace aud the throne of grace. A frequent perusal of the Bible will give us an enlarged and comprehensive view of the whole of religion, its origin, nature, genius, and tendency, aud preserve us from an over-attachment to any system of man's compilation. The fault of the several systems, under which, as under so many banners, the different denominations of Christians are ranged, is, that there is usually something left out which ought to have been taken in, and something admitted, of supposed advantage, not authorized by the scriptural standard. A Bible Christian, therefore, will see much to approve In a variety of forms and parties; the providence of God may lead or fix him in a more immediate connection with some one of them, but his spirit and affection will not be confined within these narrow enclosures. He insensibly borrows aud unites that which is excellent in each, perhaps without knowing how far he agrees with them, because he finds all in the written word.

I know not a better rule of reading the Scripture, than to read it through from beginning to end and, when we have finished it once, to begin it again. We shall meet with many passages which we can make little improvement of, but not so many in the second reading as in the first, and fewer in the third than in the second : provided we pray to him who has the keys to open our understandings, and to anoint our eyes with his spiritual ointment. The course of reading today will prepare some lights for what we shall read tomorrow, and throw a farther light upon what we read yesterday. Experience only can prove the advantage of this method, if steadily persevered in. To make a few efforts and then give over, is like making a few steps and then standing still, which would do little towards completing a long journey. But, though a person walked slowly, and but a little way in a day, if he walked every day, and with his face always in the same direction, year after year, he might in time encompass the globe. By thus traveling patiently and steadily through the Scripture, and repeating our progress, we should increase in knowledge to the end of life. The Old and New Testament, the doctrines, precepts, and promises, the history, the examples, admonitions, and

warnings, etc. would mutually illustrate and strengthen each other, and nothing that is written for our instruction would be overlooked. Happy should I be, could I fully follow the advice I am now offering to you. I wish you may profit by my experience. Alas, how much time have I lost and wasted, which, had I been wise, I should have devoted to reading and studying the Bible! But my evil heart obstructs the dictates of my judgment, I often feel a reluctance to read this book of books, and a disposition to hew out broken cisterns which afford me no water, while the fountain of living waters are close within my reach.

I am, Madam, your's, &c.

John Newton

_____

Bible reading

Letter from Thomas Boston

1. Follow a regular plan in reading of them, that you may be acquainted with the whole; and make this reading a part of your private devotions. Not that you should confine yourselves only to a set plan, so as never to read by choice, but ordinarily this tends most to edification. Some parts of the Bible are more difficult, some may seem very barren for an ordinary reader; but if you would look on it all as God's word, not to be scorned, and read it with faith and reverence, no doubt you would find advantage.

2. Set a special mark, however you find convenient, on those passages you read, which you find most suitable to your case, condition, or temptations; or such as you have found to move your hearts more than other passages. And it will be profitable often to review these.

3. Compare one Scripture with another, the more obscure with that which is more plain, 2 Pet. 1:20. This is an excellent means to find out the sense of the Scriptures; and to this good use serve the marginal notes on

Bibles. And keep Christ in your eye, for to him the scriptures of the Old Testament look (in its genealogies, types, and sacrifices), as well as those of the New.

4. Read with a holy attention, arising from the consideration of the majesty of God, and the reverence due to him. This must be done with attention, first, to the words; second, to the sense; and, third, to the divine authority of the Scripture, and the obligation it lays on the conscience for obedience, 1 Thess. 2:13, "For this reason we also thank God without ceasing, because when you received the word of God which you heard from us, you welcomed it not as the word of men, but as it is in truth, the word of God, which also effectively works in you who believe."

5. Let your main purpose in reading the Scriptures be practice, and not bare knowledge, James 1:22, "But be doers of the word, and not hearers only, deceiving yourselves." Read that you may learn and do, and that without any limitation or distinction, but that whatever you see God requires, you may study to practice.

6. Beg of God and look to him for his Spirit. For it is the Spirit that inspired it, that it must be savingly understood by, 1 Cor 2:11, "For what man knows the things of a man except the spirit of the man which is in him? Even so no one knows the things of God except the Spirit of God." And therefore before you read, it is highly reasonable you beg a blessing on what you are to read.

7. Beware of a worldly, fleshly mind: for fleshly sins blind the mind from the things of God; and the worldly heart cannot favor them. In an eclipse of the moon, the earth comes between the sun and the moon, and so keeps the light of the sun from it. So the world, in the heart, coming between you and the light of the word, keeps its divine light from you.

8. Labor to be disciplined toward godliness, and to observe your spiritual circumstances. For a disciplined attitude helps mightily to understand the scriptures. Such a Christian will find his circumstances in the word, and the word will give light to his circumstances, and his circumstances light into the word.

9. Whatever you learn from the word, labor to put it into practice. For to him that has, shall be given. No wonder those people get little insight into the Bible, who make no effort to practice what they know. But while the stream runs into a holy life, the fountain will be the freer.

Thomas Boston

There are three stages in Bible reading:
(1) the cod liver stage, when you take it like medicine;
(2) the shredded wheat stage when it's nourishing but dry;
(3) the peaches and cream stage when it's consumed with passion and pleasure.

Author unknown

The Disciples were not losing time when they sat down beside their Master, and held quiet converse with Him under the olives of Bethany or by the shores of Galilee. Those were their school hours; those were their feeding times. The healthiest Christian, the one who is best fitted for godly living and godly labors, is the person who feeds most on Christ. Here lies the benefit of Bible reading.

Author unknown

The Bible does not have to be rewritten, but reread.

Author unknown

Avoid truth decay – read your Bible.

Author unknown

Take away, O Lord, the veil of my heart while I read the Scriptures.

Lancelot Andrewes

Apply yourself wholly to the Scriptures, and apply the Scriptures wholly to yourself.

Bengel

The deceit, the lie of the devil consists of this, that he wishes to make man believe that he can live without God's Word. Thus he dangles before man's fantasy a

kingdom of faith, of power, and of peace, into which only he can enter who consents to the temptations; and he conceals from men that he, as the devil, is the most unfortunate and unhappy of beings, since he is finally and eternally rejected by God.
Dietrich Bonhoeffer

Read, mark, learn, and inwardly digest.
Book of Common Prayer

Remember that it is not hasty reading, but serious meditation on holy and heavenly truths, that makes them prove sweet and profitable to the soul.

It is not the mere touching of the flower by the bee that gathers honey, but her abiding for a time on the flower that draws out the sweet.

It is not he that reads most, but he that meditates most, that will prove to be the choicest, sweetest, wisest, and strongest Christian.
Thomas Brooks

Read the Bible as though it were something entirely unfamiliar, as though it had not been set before you ready-made. Face the book with a new attitude as something new.
Martin Buber

Read and read again, and do not despair of help to understand the will and mind of God though you think they are fast locked up from you. Neither trouble your heads though you have not commentaries and exposition. Pray and read, read and pray; for a little from God is better than a great deal from men.
John Bunyan

I am convinced that a downgrading in priority of ... prayer and biblical meditation is a major cause of weakness in many Christian communities ... Bible study demands pondering deeply on a short passage, like a cow chewing her cud. It is better to read a little and ponder a lot than to read a lot and ponder a little.
Denis Parsons Burkitt

Never did there exist a full faith in the divine word which did not expand the intellect while it purified the heart; which did not multiply the aims and objects of the understanding, while it fixed and simplified those of the desires and passions.
Samuel Taylor Coleridge

Kierkegaard said that most of us read the Bible the way a mouse tries to remove the cheese from the trap without getting caught. Some of us have mastered that. We read the story as though it were about someone else a long time ago; that way we don't get caught.
Maxie Dunnam

Listen less to your own thoughts and more to God's thoughts.
F. Fénelon

These things I did not see by the help of man, nor by the letter, though they are written in the letter; but I saw them in the light of the Lord Jesus Christ, and by his immediate Spirit and power, as did the Holy men of God, by whom the Holy Scriptures were written. Yet I had no slight esteem of the Holy Scriptures; they were very precious to me, for I was in that spirit by which they were given forth; and what the Lord opened in me, I afterwards found was agreeable to them.
George Fox

A knowledge of the Bible is essential to a rich and meaningful life.
Billy Graham

Christ teaches by the Spirit of wisdom in the heart, opening the understanding to the Spirit of revelation in the word.
Matthew Henry

Read the Bible, first and foremost, always, every day, unremittingly and often with a concordance, until the history and prophecy and the wisdom literature of the Old Testament get into our very bones; and until the Gospels and Epistles of the

New Testament become the foundation blocks of our thinking and way of life.
John S. Higgins

Once we truly grasp the message of the New Testament, it is impossible to read the Old Testament again without seeing Christ on every page, in every story, foreshadowed or anticipated in every event and narrative. The Bible must be read as a whole, beginning with Genesis and ending with Revelation, letting promise and fulfillment guide our expectations for what we will find there.
Michael Horton

The evangelical wins hands down in the history of the church when it comes to nurturing a biblically literate laity.
Thomas Howard

If God is a reality, and the soul is a reality, and you are an immortal being, what are you doing with your Bible shut?
Herrik Johnson

When you read God's word, you must constantly be saying to yourself, "It is talking to me, and about me."
Søren Kierkegaard

The Gospels contain what the Apostles preached; the Epistles, what they wrote after the preaching. And until we understand the Gospel, the good news about our brother-king – until we understand Him, until we have His Spirit, promised so freely to them that ask it – all the Epistles, the words of men who were full of Him, and wrote out of that fullness, who loved Him so utterly that by that very love they were lifted into the air of pure reason and right, and would die for Him, without two thoughts about it, in the very simplicity of no choice – the Letters, I say, of such men are to us a sealed book. Until we love the Lord so as to do what He tells us, we have no right to an opinion about what one of those men meant; for all they wrote is about things beyond us.
George Macdonald

By reading the Scriptures I am so renewed that all nature seems renewed around me and with me. The sky seems to be a pure, a cooler blue, the trees a deeper green. ... The whole world is charged with the glory of God and I feel fire and music ... under my feet.
Thomas Merton

The vigor of our spiritual life will be in exact proportion to the place held by the Bible in our life and thoughts.
George Müller

The Spirit will teach us to love the Word, to meditate on it and to keep it.
Andrew Murray

Some read the Bible to learn and some read the Bible to hear from heaven.
Andrew Murray

I know not a better rule of reading the Scripture, than to read it through from beginning to end and, when we have finished it once, to begin it again. We shall meet with many passages which we can make little improvement of, but not so many in the second reading as in the first, and fewer in the third than in the second: provided we pray to him who has the keys to open our understandings, and to anoint our eyes with his spiritual ointment.
John Newton

One of the many divine qualities of the Bible is this: it does not yield its secrets to the irreverent and censorious.
J.I. Packer

The Scriptures that are never read will never help us.
L. Tom Perry

I would very earnestly ask you to check your conception of Christ, the image of Him which as a Christian you hold in your mind, with the actual revealed Person who can be seen and studied in action in the pages of the Gospels.
J.B. Phillips

The Christian who is careless in Bible reading will be careless in Christian living.
Max Reich

The holy Scriptures are that divine instrument by which we are taught what to believe, concerning God, ourselves, and all things, and how to please God unto eternal life.
John Robinson

Lectio divina: essentially reading in the Spirit.
Read Scripture peacefully for its own sake, making the necessary efforts to reflect on it, *meditatio,* and thus be led as if naturally to prayer, *oratio.*
Jacques Rousseau

The Bible applied to the heart by the Holy Spirit, is the chief means by which men are built up and established in the faith, after their conversion.
J.C. Ryle

There is dust enough on some of your Bibles to write "damnation" with your fingers.
C.H. Spurgeon

Hear the true Word of God; lay hold of it, and spend your days not in raising hard questions, but in feasting upon precious truth.
C.H. Spurgeon

The more you read the Bible, and the more you meditate upon it, the more you will be astonished with it.
C.H. Spurgeon

The Bible sanctifies and molds the mind into the image of Christ.
C.H. Spurgeon

I venture to say that the bulk of Christians spend more time in reading the newspaper than they do in reading the Word of God.
C.H. Spurgeon

You know more about your ledgers than your Bible; you know more about your

magazines and novels than what God has written; many of you will read a novel from the beginning to the end, and what have you got? A mouthful of foam when you are done. But you cannot read the Bible; that solid, lasting, substantial, and satisfying food goes uneaten, locked up in the cupboard of neglect; while anything that a man writes, a best seller of the day, is greedily devoured.
C.H. Spurgeon

We need to repent of the haughty way in which we sometimes stand in judgment upon Scripture and must learn to sit humbly under its judgment instead.
John Stott

We must allow the Word of God to confront us, to disturb our security, to undermine our complacency and to overthrow our patterns of thought and behavior.
John Stott

From somewhere I got this desire to read the Bible again. That's the most important part of my conversion. I started with the Acts of the Apostles and then moved to Paul, letters – Romans and Corinthians. And it was only after that I came to the Gospels. In the New Testament I suddenly discovered the way that life should be followed.
David Suchet

It is Truth which we must look for in Holy Writ, not cunning of words. All Scripture ought to be read in the spirit in which it was written. We must rather seek for what is profitable in Scripture, than for what ministereth to subtlety in discourse.
Thomas à Kempis

I have read through the entire Bible many times. I now make it my practice to go through it once a year. It is the book of all others for lawyers as well as ministers; and I pity the person that cannot find in it a rich supply of thought, and of rules for his or her conduct. It fits a person for life – it prepares them for death.
Daniel Webster

We acknowledge the inward illumination of the Spirit of God to be necessary for the saving understanding of such things as are revealed in the Word.

The Confession of Faith of the Westminster Assembly of Divines, 1646

I began to read the holy Scriptures upon my knees, laying aside all other books, and praying over, if possible, every line and word. This proved meat indeed and drink indeed to my soul. I daily received fresh life, light and power from above.

George Whitefield

No spiritual discipline is more important than the intake of God's Word.

Donald S. Whitney

Some people read their Bible in Hebrew, some in Greek; I like to read mine in the Holy Ghost.

Smith Wigglesworth

When you have read the Bible, you will know it is the word of God, because you will have found it the key to your own heart, your own happiness and your duty.

Woodrow Wilson

Bible reading, *Preparation for*

Thomas Watson

1. Remove hindrances. (a) remove the love of every sin (b) remove the distracting concerns of this world, especially covetousness [Matt. 13:22] (c) Don't make jokes with and out of Scripture.
2. Prepare your heart. [1 Sam. 7:3] Do this by: (a) collecting your thoughts (b) purging unclean affections and desires (c) not coming to it rashly or carelessly.
3. Read it with reverence, considering that each line is God speaking directly to you.
4. Read the books of the Bible in order.
5. Get a true understanding of Scripture.

[Ps. 119:73] This is best achieved by comparing relevant parts of Scripture with each other.
6. Read with seriousness. [Deut. 32:47] The Christian life is to be taken seriously since it requires striving [Luke 13:24] and not falling short [Heb. 4:1].
7. Persevere in remembering what you read. [Ps. 119:52] Don't let it be stolen from you [Matt. 13:4,19]. If it doesn't stay in your memory it is unlikely to be much benefit to you.
8. Meditate on what you read. [Ps. 119:15] The Hebrew word for meditate' means to be intense in the mind'. Meditation without reading is wrong and bound to err; reading without meditation is barren and fruitless. It means to stir the affections, to be warmed by the fire of meditation [Ps. 39:3].
9. Read with a humble heart. Acknowledge that you are unworthy that God should reveal himself to you [James 4:6]
10. Believe it all to be God's Holy Word. [2 Tim 3:16] We know that no sinner could have written it because of the way it describes sin. No saint could blaspheme God by pretending his own Word was God's. No angel could have written it for the same reason. [Heb 4:2]
11. Prize the Bible highly. [Ps. 119:72] It is your lifeline; you were born by it [James 1:18] you need to grow by it [1 Pet 2:2] [cf. Job 23:12].
12. Love the Bible ardently [Ps. 119:159].
13. Come to read it with an honest heart. [Luke 8:15] (a) Willing to know the entire and complete will of God (b) reading in order to be changed and made better by it [John 17:17].
14. Apply to yourself everything that you read, take every word as spoken to yourself. Its condemnation of sins as the condemnation of your own sin; the duty that it requires as the duty God would require from you [2 Kings 22:11].
15. Pay close attention to the commands of the Word as much as the promises. Think of how you need direction just as much as you need comfort.
16. Don't get carried away with the minor

details, rather make sure to pay closest attention to the great things [Hosea 8:12].

17. Compare yourself with the Word. How do you compare? Is your heart something of a transcript of it, or not?

18. Pay special attention to those passages that speak to your individual, particular and present situation. e.g. (a) Affliction – [Heb. 12:7, Isaiah 27:9, John 16:20, 2 Cor 4:17. (b) Sense of Christ's presence and smile withdrawn – [Isaiah 54:8, Isaiah 57:16, Ps. 97:11] (c) Sin – [Gal 5:24, James 1:15, 1 Peter 2:11, Prov 7:10&22-23, Prov 22:14] (d) Unbelief – [Isaiah 26:3, 2 Sam 22:31, John 3:15, 1 John 5:10, John 3:36]

19. Pay special attention to the examples and lives of people in the Bible as living sermons. (a) Punishments [Nebuchadnezzar, Herod, Num 25:3-4&9, 1 Kings 14:9-10, Acts 5:5,10, 1 Cor 10:11, Jude 7] (b) mercies and deliverances [Daniel, Jeremiah, the 3 youths in the fiery furnace]

20. Don't stop reading the Bible until you find your heart warmed. [Ps 119:93] Let it not only inform you but also inflame you [Jer 23:29, Luke 24:32].

21. Put into practice what you read [Ps 119:66, Ps 119:105, Deut 17:19].

22. Christ is for us Prophet, Priest and King. Make use of His office as a Prophet [Rev 5:5, John 8:12, Ps 119:102-103]. Get Christ not only to open the Scriptures up to you, but to open up your mind and understanding [Luke 24:45]

23. Make sure to put yourself under a true ministry of the Word, faithfully and thoroughly expounding the Word [Prov 8:34] be earnest and eager in waiting on it.

24. Pray that you will profit from reading [Isaiah 48:17, Ps 119:18, Nehemiah 9:20].
Thomas Watson

Bible reading and prayer

Begin with reading or hearing. Go on with meditation; end in prayer.

Reading without meditation is unfruitful; meditation without reading is hurtful; to meditate and to read without prayer upon both, is without blessing.
William Bridge

Do not have your concert first and tune your instruments afterwards. Begin the day with God.
James Hudson Taylor

Bible study
See also: Bible study and prayer; Bible study and the Holy Spirit
Study to shew thyself approved unto God, a workman that needeth not to be ashamed, rightly dividing the word of truth.
The Bible, 2 Timothy 2:15 KJV

The treasures of the Bible can be found only by those who dig for them.
Author unknown

There are only two ways you can study the Bible:
1. Studying it with your mind made up.
2. Studying it to let it make up your mind.
Author unknown

The study of God's Word, for the purpose of discovering God's will, is the secret discipline that has formed the greatest characters.
J. W. Alexander

The depth of the Christian Scriptures is boundless. Even if I were attempting to study them and nothing else, from boyhood to decrepit old age, with the utmost leisure, the most unwearied zeal, and with talents greater than I possess, I would still be making progress in discovering their treasures.
Augustine of Hippo

Compare Scripture with Scripture. False doctrines, like false witnesses, agree not among themselves.
William Gurnall

The word of God will stand a thousand readings; and he who has gone over it most frequently is the surest of finding new wonders there.
James Hamilton

The Holy Scriptures have not only an elementary use, but a use of perfection, neither can they ever be exhausted.
George Herbert

We ought not to criticize, explain, or judge the Scriptures by our mere reason, but diligently, with prayer, meditate thereon, and seek their meaning.
Martin Luther

A favorite way to study the Bible with me is, first, to take up one expression, and run through the different places where they are found. Take the "I am's" of John: "I am the bread of life"; "I am the water of life"; "I am the way, the truth and the life"; "I am the resurrection"; etc.
D.L. Moody

Some say pray and pray and don't lean on the unspiritual human work of study. Others say, study and study because God is not going to tell you the meaning of a word in prayer. But the Bible will not have anything to do with this dichotomy. We must study and accurately handle the Word of God, and we must pray or we will not see in the Word the one thing needful, the glory of God in the face of Christ.
John Piper

Thorough knowledge of the Bible is worth more than a college education.
Theodore Roosevelt

The most learned, acute and diligent student cannot, in the longest life, obtain an entire knowledge of this one volume. The more deeply he works the mine, the richer and more abundant he finds the ore; new light continually beams from this source of heavenly knowledge, to direct the conduct, and illustrate the work of God and the ways of men; and he will at last leave the world confessing that the more he studied the Scriptures, the fuller conviction he had of his own ignorance and of their inestimable value.
Sir Walter Scott

1. READ THE BIBLE WITH AN EARNEST DESIRE TO UNDERSTAND IT.
Do not be content to just read the words of Scripture. Seek to grasp the message they contain.
2. READ THE SCRIPTURES WITH A SIMPLE, CHILDLIKE FAITH AND HUMILITY.
Believe what God reveals. Reason must bow to God's revelation.
3. READ THE WORD WITH A SPIRIT OF OBEDIENCE AND SELF-APPLICATION.
Apply what God says to yourself and obey His will in all things.
4. READ THE HOLY SCRIPTURES EVERY DAY.
We quickly lose the nourishment and strength of yesterday's bread. We must feed our souls daily upon the manna God has given us.
5. READ THE WHOLE BIBLE AND READ IT IN AN ORDERLY WAY.
"All Scripture is given by inspiration of God and is profitable." I know of no better way to read the Bible than to start at the beginning and read straight through to the end, a portion every day, comparing Scripture with Scripture.
6. READ THE WORD OF GOD FAIRLY AND HONESTLY.
As a general rule, any passage of Scripture means what it appears to mean.
Interpret every passage in this simple manner, in its context.
7. READ THE BIBLE WITH CHRIST CONSTANTLY IN VIEW.
The whole Book is about Him. Look for Him on every page. He is there. If you fail to see Him there, you need to read that page again.
C.H. Spurgeon

He who is but a casual reader of the Bible, does not know the height, the depth, the length and breadth of the mighty meanings contained in its pages.
There are certain times when I discover a new vein of thought, and I put my hand to my head and say in astonishment, "Oh, it

is wonderful I never saw this before in the Scriptures."

You will find the Scriptures enlarge as you enter them; the more you study them the less you will appear to know of them, for they widen out as we approach them. Especially will you find this the case with the "typical" parts of God's Word. Most of the historical books were intended to be types either of dispensations, or experiences, or offices of Jesus Christ.

Study the Bible with this as a key. One of the most interesting points of the Scriptures is their constant tendency to display Christ.
C.H. Spurgeon

Draw the honey out of the comb of Scripture, and live on its sweetness.
C.H. Spurgeon

Cease to meddle with matters that are concealed, and be satisfied to know the things that are clearly revealed.
C.H. Spurgeon

When you read a verse in the Bible ask yourself, What does this verse mean? Then ask: What does it mean for me? When that is answered ask yourself again: Is that all it means? And do not leave it until you are quite sure that is all it means for the present.
R.A. Torrey

A verse must be read often, and re-read and read again before the wondrous message of love and power that God has put into it begins to appear. Words must be turned over and over in the mind before their full force and beauty takes possession of us. One must look a long time at the great masterpieces of art to appreciate their beauty and understand their meaning, and so one must look a long time at the great verses of the Bible to appreciate their beauty and understand their meaning.
R.A. Torrey

The Scripture is to be its own interpreter, or rather the Spirit speaking in it; nothing can cut the diamond but the diamond; nothing can interpret Scripture but Scripture.
Thomas Watson

If the Bible is, as we devoutly believe, the very source and measure of our religious faith, it seems impossible to insist too earnestly on the supreme importance of patience, candor and truthfulness in investigating every problem which it involves. And unless all past experience is worthless, the difficulties of the Bible are the most fruitful guides to its divine depths. It was said long since that "God was pleased to leave difficulties upon the surface of Scripture, that men might be forced to look below the surface."
Brooke Foss Westcott, 1864, written when the rise of biblical scholarship was leading to criticism of the Bible, and causing some people to discount the findings of scholarship.

Bible study and prayer

If you would understand the Word of God in its knotty points, if you would comprehend the mystery of the gospel of Christ, remember, Christ's scholars must study upon their knees.
C.H. Spurgeon

Is there anything like the Word of God when the open book finds open hearts? The prayerful study of the Word is an act of devotion wherein the transforming power of grace is often exercised, changing us into the image of Him of whom the Word is a mirror.
C.H. Spurgeon

Let me tell you a little secret – whenever you cannot understand a text, open your Bible, bend your knee, and pray over that text; and if it does not split into atoms and open itself, try again.

If prayer does not explain it, it is one of the things God did not intend you to know, and you may be content to be ignorant of it.

Prayer is the key that opens the cabinets of mystery.

Prayer and faith are sacred picklocks that can open secrets, and obtain great treasures. There is no college for holy education like that of the blessed Spirit, for he is an ever-present tutor, to whom we have only to bend the knee, and he is at our side, the

great expositor of truth.
C.H. Spurgeon

Bibles with misprints

"Aching" Bible
Oxford Press once paid two guineas for the loss of two letters.

Two readers independently found that Matthew 26:55 was printed, "Christ was aching in the Temple," and were given a guinea each for their discovery.

"Breeches" Bible
The Geneva Bible, first published in 1560, was called the "Breeches" Bible by booksellers because of the unusual way in which it translated Genesis 3:7, "They sewed fig leaves together and made themselves breeches."

"Bug" Bible
Coverdale translated Psalm 91:5, "Thou shalt not nede to be afrayed for eny bugges by night."

"Good luck" Bible
Coverdale translated Psalm 129:8, "We wish you good luck in the name of the Lord."

"He" Bible
The first edition of the King James Version, printed by Robert Barker, early in 1611, is sometimes referred to as the "He" Bible because of its incorrect translation of Ruth 3:15 as, "… He went into the city."

"Place-maker's" Bible
The Geneva Bible of 1562 misprinted Matthew 5:9 as, "Blessed are the place-makers."

"Printers'" Bible
The "Printers'" Bible in 1702 managed to replace the word "princes," with "printers." So Psalm 119:161 read, "printers have persecuted me."

"Snowshoes" Bible
In the translation for the Mumac Indians of Nova Scotia, Matthew 24:7, instead of reading, "Nation shall rise against nation," reads, "A pair of snowshoes shall rise against a pair of snowshoes." The difference was made by the misplacement of one letter: "Naooktukumiksijik," meaning nation, "Naooktakumiksijik," meaning snowshoe.

"Treacle" Bible
The Bishop's Bible of 1569 translated Jeremiah 8:22, and spelled the words as follows: "There is no treacle at Galaad." ("There is no balm in Gilead" NIV.)

"Unrighteous" Bible
The "Unrighteous" Bible in 1653 may have given hope to unrepentant sinners when "Know ye not that the unrighteous shall inherit the kingdom of God" was printed – instead of "not inherit" (1 Corinthians 6:9).

"Unrighteous" Bible
An edition of the Bible printed in Cambridge in 1653 contained the following error: "Know ye not that the unrighteous shall inherit the kingdom of God?" (1 Corinthians 6:9).

"Vinegar" Bible
A Bible printed in 1717 had the heading for Luke 20, "The parable of the Vinegar" instead of "Vineyard."

"Wicked" Bible
In 1631 an English Bible printer forgot the "not" in one of the Ten Commandments. His version of Exodus 20:14 read: "Thou shalt commit adultery." This edition of the Bible became known as The Wicked Bible, and the printer had to pay a large fine, £300.00. King Charles I commanded that all the copies of this Bible should be destroyed.

Bigotry
Bigotry tries to keep truth safe in its hand with the grip that kills it.
Rabindranath Tagore

Birth
Behold, I was shapen in iniquity; and in sin did my mother conceive me.
The Bible, Psalms 51:5 KJV

And cradles rock us nearer to the tomb. Our birth is nothing but our death begun.
Edward Young

Bishops
After churches were planted in all places, and officers ordained, matters were settled otherwise than they were in the beginning. And hence it is that the Apostles' writings do not, in all things, agree with the present constitution of the Church; because they were written under the first rise of the Church; for he called Timothy, who was created a Presbyter by him, a Bishop, for so, at first, the Presbyters were called.
Ambrose

With you I am a Christian, and *for you* I am a bishop.
Augustine of Hippo

Every minister of Jesus is a missionary. So are the bishops, as His chief ministers, eminently missionaries – sent out by Christ Himself to preach the gospel.
Bishop Washington Doane

The Pope alone can dispose or reinstate bishops.
Gregory the Great

Let all follow the bishop, as Jesus Christ follows his Father, and the college of presbyters as the apostles; respect the deacons as you do God's law. Let no one do anything concerning the Church in separation from the bishop.
Ignatius of Antioch

Among the ancients, Presbyters and Bishops were the same. But by little and little, all the seeds of dissension might be plucked up, the whole care was devolved on one. As therefore, Presbyters know, that by the custom of the Church, they are subject to him who is their president, so let Bishops know, that they are above Presbyters more by the custom of the Church, than by the true dispensation of Jesus Christ.
Jerome

Bitterness
Get rid of all bitterness, rage and anger, brawling and slander, along with every form of malice.
The Bible, Ephesians 4:31

See to it that no one misses the grace of God and that no bitter root grows up to cause trouble and defile many.
The Bible, Hebrews 12:15

Bitterness is like cancer. It eats upon the host.
Author unknown

Bitterness imprisons life; love releases it.
Bitterness paralyzes life; love empowers it.
Bitterness sickens life; love heals it.
Bitterness blinds life; love anoints its eyes.
Harry Emerson Fosdick

Blaming others
The reason people blame things on previous generations is that there's only one other choice.
Doug Larson

Blessings
What a world this would be if we could forget our troubles as easily as we forget our blessings.
Author unknown

May the road rise to meet you.
May the wind be always at your back
May the sun shine warm upon your face
And the rain fall soft upon your fields
And until we meet again
May God hold you in the palm of His hand.
Author unknown, Irish blessing

God is more anxious to bestow his blessings on us than we are to receive them.
Augustine of Hippo

Reflect upon your present blessings – of which every man has many – not on your past misfortunes, of which all men have some.
Charles Dickens

Temporal blessings are not definite marks of divine favor, since God gives them to the unworthy, and to the wicked, as well as to the righteous.
C.H. Spurgeon

Blindness
It gives me a deep comforting sense that "things seen are temporal and things unseen are eternal."
Helen Keller, who became blind and deaf, aged nineteen months, after scarlet fever.

Blindness, Spiritual
A man once stood on a soap-box at Hyde Park Corner, pouring scorn on Christianity.
  "People tell me that God exists; but I can't see him.
  "People tell me that there is a life after death; but I can't see it.
  "People tell me that there is a judgment to come; but I can't see it.
  "People tell me that there is a heaven and a hell; but I can't see them."
  He won cheap applause, and climbed down from his "pulpit."
  Another struggled on to the soap-box.
  "People tell me that there is green grass all around, but I can't see it.
  "People tell me that there is blue sky above, but I can't see it.
  "People tell me that there are trees nearby, but I can't see them.
  "You see, I'm blind."
Author unknown

The very limit of human blindness is to glory in being blind.
Augustine of Hippo

Boasting
Therefore, as it is written: "Let him who boasts boast in the Lord."
The Bible, 1 Corinthians 1:31

He loves but little who tells how much he loves.
John Boys

The one sole thing in myself in which I glory is that I see in myself nothing in which I can glory.
Catherine of Genoa

Grace puts its hand on the boasting mouth, and shuts it once for all.
C.H. Spurgeon

Body
See also: Body, Human
The body is just a shell for the real person.
Author unknown

Despise the flesh, for it passes away. See to the welfare of your soul, for it never dies.
Basil

Our own theological Church, as we know, has scorned and vilified the body till it has seemed almost a reproach and a shame to have one, yet at the same time has credited it with power to drag the soul to perdition.
Eliza Farnham

That monkish hatred of the body which figures so prominently in the works of certain early devotional writers is wholly without support in the Word of God.
A.W. Tozer

Body of Christ
Paul's vision of the body of Christ is of a unity which consists in diversity, that is, a unity which is not denied by diversity, but which would be denied by uniformity, a unity which depends on its diversity functioning as such – in a word, the unity of a body, the body of Christ.
James D.G. Dunn

Boldness
See also: Martyrs
Even God lends a hand to honest
boldness.
Menander

One of the special marks of the Holy
Ghost in the Apostolic Church was the
spirit of boldness.
A.B. Simpson

Book reviewer
Thank you for sending me a copy of your
book – I'll waste no time reading it.
Moses Hadas

Books
See also: Study
Books could not teach me charity.
Augustine of Hippo

The Scriptures are sufficient for their
proper use, which is to be a law of faith
and life, if they be understood. But, 1.
They are not sufficient for that which they
were never intended for: 2. And we may by
other books be greatly helped in
understanding them. 3. If other books
were not needful, teachers were not
needful; for writing is but the most
advantageous way of teaching by fixed
characters, which fly not from our memory
as transient words do. And who is it that
understandeth the Scriptures that never
had a teacher? And why said the eunuch,
"How should I (understand what I read)
unless some man guide me?" Acts 8:31.
And why did Christ set teachers in his
church to the end, till it be perfected, Eph.
4:11-13, if they must not teach the church
unto the end? Therefore they may write
unto the end.
Richard Baxter

A book continues working when the
meeting has ended. It accompanies the
audience back to their homes. It goes on
speaking to them. Literature is the second
leg of Christian proclamation.
Klaus Bockmühl

[Any new Christian book] has to be tested
against the great body of Christian thought
down the ages.
C.S. Lewis

A good book is the precious life-blood of a
master-spirit, embalmed and treasured up
on purpose to a life beyond life.
John Milton

These diabolical people, [the Reformers],
print their books at great expense,
notwithstanding the great danger; not
looking for any gain, they give them away
to everybody, and even scatter them abroad
by night.
Sir Thomas More

Everywhere I have sought rest and not
found it, except sitting in a corner by
myself with a little book.
Thomas à Kempis

Boredom
There is only one thing worse than
boredom, and that is the fear of boredom.
E.M. Cioran

Millions long for immortality who do not
know what to do with themselves on a
rainy Sunday afternoon.
Susan Ertz

Boredom is rage spread thin.
Paul Tillich

Born again
See also: Conversion; Regeneration
Let them pretend what they please, the
true reason why any despise the new birth
is because they hate a new life. He that
cannot endure to live to God will as little
endure to hear of being born of God.
John Owen

Breakdown
One of the symptoms of an approaching
nervous breakdown is the belief that one's
work is terribly important.
Bertrand Russell

Brevity

The Ten Commandments contain 297 words, the Bill of Rights 463 words, and Lincoln's Gettysburg Address 266 words. A recent federal directive regulating the price of cabbage contains 26,911 words.
New York Times

Brevity is the soul of wit.
William Shakespeare, Hamlet

Bribes

By justice a king gives a country stability, but one who is greedy for bribes tears it down.
The Bible, Proverbs 29:4

Broken heart

Scorn has broken my heart and has left me helpless; I looked for sympathy, but there was none, for comforters, but I found none.
The Bible, Psalm 69:20

God can do wonders with a broken heart; if we give him all of the pieces.
Author unknown

The poor broken-hearted sinner, going into his bedroom, bends his knee, but can only utter his mournful cry in the language of sighs and tears. Look! that groan has made all the harps of heaven thrill with music; that tear has been caught by God, and put into a vase made especially for tears, to be perpetually preserved.
C.H. Spurgeon

Faith lives in a broken heart. "He cried out with tears, Lord, I believe." True faith is always in a heart bruised for sin. Saving faith always grows in a heart humbled for sin, in a weeping eye and a tearful conscience.
Thomas Watson

How else but through a broken heart may Lord Christ enter in.
Oscar Wilde

Brotherhood

A mystic bond of brotherhood makes all men one.
Thomas Carlyle

Buddha

Buddha certainly didn't believe in God or heaven.
Luis Palau

Buddha rejected India's pack of gods and never claimed to be one himself.
Luis Palau

Buildings

Inspired architecture does not change lives; nor do big buildings impart spiritual power.
Charles Colson

Buildings, Church

I never weary of great churches. It is my favorite kind of mountain scenery. Mankind was never so happily inspired as when it made a cathedral.
Robert Louis Stevenson

It is not meeting in a good building that is wrong, but making such a building a priority and fooling ourselves into believing that we can't get on without it. It is building with unnecessary luxury at a time when iniquity abounds, thinking more of the building than of the church, more of a good organ than of praise, more of the communion table than the body and blood of Christ.
John White

We do not in fact build beautiful buildings from a spirit of worship but for prestige and pride.
John White

Burden-bearing

Carry each other's burdens.
The Bible, Galatians 6:2

Give me a stout heart to bear my own burdens. Give me a willing heart to bear the burdens of others. Give me a believing heart to cast all burdens upon Thee, O Lord.
John Baillie

It is the fellowship of the Cross to experience the burden of the other. If one does not experience it, the fellowship he belongs to is not Christian. If any member refuses to bear that burden, he denies the law of Christ.
Dietrich Bonhoeffer

Burdened

To every toiling, heavy-laden sinner, Jesus says, "Come to me and rest." But there are many toiling, heavy-laden believers, too. For them this same invitation is meant. Note well the words of Jesus, if you are heavy-laden with your service, and do not mistake it.
Hudson Taylor

Burdens

See also: Adversity; Affliction; Difficulties; Hardships; Suffering; Trials

Burdens

Cardiphonia: Letter from John Newton
Dear Madam,
What a poor, uncertain, dying world is this! What a wilderness in itself! How dark, how desolate, without the light of the Gospel and the knowledge of Jesus! It does not appear so to us in a state of nature, because we are then in a state of enchantment, the magical lantern blinding us with a splendid delusion.
Thus in the desert's dreary waste,
By magic power produced in haste, As old romances say,
Castles and groves, and music sweet,
The senses of the traveler cheat,
And stop him in his way.
But while he gazes with surprise,
The charm dissolves, the vision dies;
'Twas but enchanted ground
Thus, if the Lord our spirit touch,
The world, which promised us so much,
A wilderness is found.
It is a great mercy to be undeceived in time; and though our gay dreams are at an end, and we awake to everything that is disgustful and dismaying, yet we see a highway through the wilderness; a powerful guard, an infallible Guide at hand to conduct us through; and we can discern, beyond the limits of the wilderness, a better land, where we shall be at rest and at home. What will the difficulties we meet by the way then signify? The remembrance of them will only remain to heighten our sense of the love, care, and power of our Savior and Leader. O how shall we then admire, adore, and praise Him, when He shall condescend to unfold to us the beauty, propriety, and harmony of the whole train of His dispensations towards us, and give us a clear retrospect of all the way, and all the turns of our pilgrimage!
In the mean while, the best method of adorning our profession, and of enjoying peace in our souls, is simply to trust Him, and absolutely to commit ourselves and our all to His management. By casting our burdens upon Him, our spirits become light and cheerful; we are freed from a thousand anxieties and inquietudes, which are wearisome to our minds, and which, with respect to events, are needless for us, yea useless.
But though it may be easy to speak of this trust, and it appears to our judgment perfectly right and reasonable, the actual attainment is a great thing; and especially so, to trust the Lord, not by fits and starts, surrendering one day and retracting the next, but to abide by our surrender, and go habitually trusting through all the changes we meet, knowing that His love, purpose, and promise are unchangeable. Some little faintings, perhaps, none are freed from; but I believe a power of trusting the Lord in good measure at all times, and living quietly under the shadow of His wing, is what the promise warrants us to expect, if we seek it by diligent prayer; if not all at once, yet by a gradual increase. May it be your experience and mine!
I am, &c.
John Newton

Cast thy burden upon the Lord, and He shall sustain thee.
Psalm 55:22 KJV

It's not the load that breaks you down, it's the way you carry it.
Author unknown

I have read in Plato and Cicero sayings that are wise and very beautiful; but I have never read in either of them: Come unto me all ye that labor and are heavy laden.
Augustine of Hippo

It's not the load that breaks you down, it's the way you carry it.
Lena Horne

If He bids us carry a burden, He carries it also.
C.H. Spurgeon

If you have a burden on your back, remember prayer, for you shall carry it well if you can pray.
C.H. Spurgeon

Business
Cast thy bread upon the waters: for thou shalt find it after many days.
The Bible, Ecclesiastes 11:1 KJV

Business, Honesty in
Use honest scales and honest weights, an honest ephah and an honest hin.
The Bible, Leviticus 19:36

Busybody
Study to be quiet, and to do your own business.
The Bible, 1 Thessalonians 4:11 KJV

The idea of strictly minding our own business is moldy rubbish. Who could be so selfish?
Myrtie Barker

"If everybody minded their own business," the Duchess said in a hoarse growl, "the world would go round a deal faster than it does."
Lewis Carroll, Alice in Wonderland

Why must the phrase, "It's none of my business…" always be followed by the word "but"?
Milwaukee Journal

Busyness
Crowding a life does not always enrich it.
Author unknown

O Lord! thou knowest how busy I must be this day: if I forget thee, do not thou forget me.
Sir Jacob Astley

"Let thine occupations be few," says the sage, "if thou wouldst lead a tranquil life."
Marcus Aurelius

In contemporary society our Adversity majors in three things: noise, hurry and crowds. If he can keep us engaged in "muchness" and "manyness," he will rest satisfied.
Richard J. Foster

Never mistake motion for action.
Ernest Hemingway

Extreme busyness, whether at school or college, kirk or market, is a symptom of deficient vitality.
Robert Louis Stevenson

A pure, simple, and steadfast spirit is not distracted by the number of things to be done, because it performs them all to the honor of God, and endeavors to be at rest from self-seeking.
Thomas à Kempis

C

Call

Jesus calls us, o'er the tumult
Of our life's wild, restless sea.
Cecil Frances Alexander

The responsible person seeks to make his
or her whole life a response to the question
and call of God.
Dietrich Bonhoeffer

It is not what I do that matters, but what
a sovereign God chooses to do through
me. God does not want worldly
successes, He wants me. He wants my
heart in submission to Him. Life is not
just a few years to spend on self-
indulgence and career advancement. It is
a privilege, a responsibility, a stewardship
to be lived according to a much higher
calling, God's calling. This alone gives
true meaning to life.
Elizabeth Dole

If a man is called to be a street-sweeper,
he should sweep streets even as
Michelangelo painted, or Beethoven
played music, or Shakespeare wrote
poetry. He should sweep streets so well
that all the hosts of heaven and earth will
pause to say, here lived a great street-
sweeper who did his job well.
Martin Luther King, Jr.

God doesn't call people who are qualified.
He calls people who are willing, and then
He qualifies them.
Richard Parker

Calvary
See also: Cross, Death of Christ
No scene in sacred history ever gladdens
the soul like the scene on Calvary.
C.H. Spurgeon

Calvinism
See also: Chosen; Chosen by God

Calvinism

A Defense of Calvinism
Sermon preached by C.H. Spurgeon

The old truth that Calvin preached, that
Augustine preached, that Paul preached, is
the truth that I must preach to-day, or else
be false to my conscience and my God. I
cannot shape the truth; I know of no such
thing as paring off the rough edges of a
doctrine. John Knox's gospel is my gospel.
That which thundered through Scotland
must thunder through England again.

...IT IS A GREAT THING to begin the
Christian life by believing good solid
doctrine. Some people have received
twenty different "gospels" in as many years;
how many more they will accept before
they get to their journey's end, it would be
difficult to predict. I thank God that He
early taught me the gospel, and I have been
so perfectly satisfied with it, that I do not
want to know any other. Constant change
of creed is sure loss. If a tree has to be taken
up two or three times a year, you will not
need to build a very large loft in which to
store the apples. When people are always
shifting their doctrinal principles, they are
not likely to bring forth much fruit to the
glory of God. It is good for young believers
to begin with a firm hold upon those great
fundamental doctrines which the Lord has
taught in His Word. Why, if I believed
what some preach about the temporary,
trumpery salvation which only lasts for a

time, I would scarcely be at all grateful for it; but when I know that those whom God saves He saves with an everlasting salvation, when I know that He gives to them an everlasting righteousness, when I know that He settles them on an everlasting foundation of everlasting love, and that He will bring them to His everlasting kingdom, oh, then I do wonder, and I am astonished that such a blessing as this should ever have been given to me!

"Pause, my soul! adore, and wonder!
Ask, 'Oh, why such love to me?'
Grace hath put me in the number
Of the Savior's family:
Hallelujah!
Thanks, eternal thanks, to Thee!"

I suppose there are some persons whose minds naturally incline towards the doctrine of free-will. I can only say that mine inclines as naturally towards the doctrines of sovereign grace. Sometimes, when I see some of the worst characters in the street, I feel as if my heart must burst forth in tears of gratitude that God has never let me act as they have done! I have thought, if God had left me alone, and had not touched me by His grace, what a great sinner I should have been! I should have run to the utmost lengths of sin, dived into the very depths of evil, nor should I have stopped at any vice or folly, if God had not restrained me. I feel that I should have been a very king of sinners, if God had let me alone. I cannot understand the reason why I am saved, except upon the ground that God would have it so. I cannot, if I look ever so earnestly, discover any kind of reason in myself why I should be a partaker of Divine grace. If I am not at this moment without Christ, it is only because Christ Jesus would have His will with me, and that will was that I should be with Him where He is, and should share His glory. I can put the crown nowhere but upon the head of Him whose mighty grace has saved me from going down into the pit. Looking back on my past life, I can see that the dawning of it all was of God; of God effectively. I took no torch

with which to light the sun, but the sun enlightened me. I did not commence my spiritual life, no, I rather kicked, and struggled against the things of the Spirit: when He drew me, for a time I did not run after Him: there was a natural hatred in my soul of everything holy and good. Wooings were lost upon me, warnings were cast to the wind, thunders were despised; and as for the whispers of His love, they were rejected as being less than nothing and vanity. But, sure I am, I can say now, speaking on behalf of myself, "He only is my salvation." It was He who turned my heart, and brought me down on my knees before Him. I can in very deed, say with Doddridge and Toplady:

"Grace taught my soul to pray,
And made my eyes o'erflow;"
and coming to this moment, I can add

"'Tis grace has kept me to this day,
And will not let me go."

…Well can I remember the manner in which I learned the doctrines of grace in a single instant. Born, as all of us are by nature, an Arminian, I still believed the old things I had heard continually from the pulpit, and did not see the grace of God. When I was coming to Christ, I thought I was doing it all myself, and though I sought the Lord earnestly, I had no idea the Lord was seeking me. I do not think the young convert is at first aware of this. I can recall the very day and hour when first I received those truths in my own soul when they were, as John Bunyan says, burnt into my heart as with a hot iron, and I can recollect how I felt that I had grown on a sudden from a babe into a man that I had made progress in Scriptural knowledge, through having found, once for all, the clue to the truth of God. One week-night, when I was sitting in the house of God, I was not thinking much about the preacher's sermon, for I did not believe it. The thought struck me, How did you come to be a Christian? I sought the Lord. But how did you come to seek the Lord? The truth flashed across my mind in a moment— I should not have sought Him unless there had been some previous influence in my mind to make me seek Him. I prayed, thought I, but then I asked myself, How came I to pray? I was induced to pray by reading the Scriptures. How came I to read the Scriptures? I did read them, but what led me to do so? Then, in a moment, I saw that God was at the bottom of it all, and that He was the Author of my faith, and so the whole doctrine of grace opened up to me, and from that doctrine I have not departed to this day, and I desire to make this my constant confession, "I ascribe my change wholly to God."

…I once attended a service where the text happened to be, "He shall choose our inheritance for us;" and the good man who occupied the pulpit was more than a little of an Arminian. Therefore, when he commenced, he said, "This passage refers entirely to our temporal inheritance, it has nothing whatever to do with our everlasting destiny, for," said he, "we do not want Christ to choose for us in the matter of Heaven or hell. It is so plain and easy, that every man who has a grain of common sense will choose Heaven, and any person would know better than to choose hell. We have no need of any superior intelligence, or any greater Being, to choose Heaven or hell for us. It is left to our own free-will, and we have enough wisdom given us, sufficiently correct means to judge for ourselves," and therefore, as he very logically inferred, there was no necessity for Jesus Christ, or anyone, to make a choice for us. We could choose the inheritance for ourselves without any assistance. "Ah!" I thought, "but, my good brother, it may be very true that we could, but I think we should want something more than common sense before we should choose aright."

First, let me ask, must we not all of us admit an over-ruling Providence, and the appointment of Jehovah's hand, as to the means whereby we came into this world? Those men who think that, afterwards, we are left to our own free-will to choose this one or the other to direct our steps, must admit that our entrance into the world was not of our own will, but that God had then to choose for us. What circumstances were those in our power which led us to elect certain persons to be our parents? Had we anything to do with it? Did not God Himself appoint our parents, native place, and friends? Could He not have caused me to be born with the skin of the Hottentot, brought forth by a filthy mother who would nurse me in her "kraal," and teach me to bow down to Pagan gods, quite as easily as to have given me a pious mother, who would each morning and night bend her knee in prayer on my behalf? Or, might He not, if He had pleased, have given me some profligate to have been my parent, from whose lips I might have early heard fearful, filthy, and obscene language? Might He not have placed me where I should have had a drunken father, who would have immured me in a very dungeon of ignorance, and brought me up in the chains of crime? Was it not God's Providence that I had so happy a lot, that both my parents were His children, and endeavored to train me up in the fear of the Lord?

…John Newton used to tell a whimsical story, and laugh at it, too, of a good woman who said, in order to prove the doctrine of election, "Ah! sir, the Lord must have loved me before I was born, or else He would not have seen anything in me to love afterwards." I am sure it is true in my case; I believe the doctrine of election, because I am quite certain that, if God had not chosen me, I should never have chosen Him; and I am sure He chose me before I was born, or else He never would have chosen me afterwards; and He must have elected me for reasons unknown to me, for I never could find any reason in myself why He should have looked upon me with special love. So I am forced to accept that great Biblical doctrine. I recollect an Arminian brother telling me that he had read the Scriptures through a score or more times, and could never find the doctrine of election in them. He added that he was sure he would have done so if it had been there, for he read the Word on his knees. I said to him, "I think you read the Bible in a very uncomfortable posture, and if you had read it in your easy chair, you would have been more likely to understand it. Pray, by all means, and the more, the better, but it is a piece of superstition to think there is anything in the posture in which a man puts himself for reading: and as to reading through the Bible twenty times without having found anything about the doctrine of election, the wonder is that you found anything at all: you must have galloped through it at such a rate that you were not likely to have any intelligible idea of the meaning of the Scriptures."

...If it would be marvelous to see one river leap up from the earth full-grown, what would it be to gaze upon a vast spring from which all the rivers of the earth should at once come bubbling up, a million of them born at a birth? What a vision would it be! Who can conceive it. And yet the love of God is that fountain, from which all the rivers of mercy, which have ever gladdened our race– all the rivers of grace in time, and of glory hereafter– take their rise. My soul, stand thou at that sacred fountain-head, and adore and magnify, for ever and ever, God, even our Father, who hath loved us! In the very beginning, when this great universe lay in the mind of God, like unborn forests in the acorn cup; long ere the echoes awoke the solitudes; before the mountains were brought forth; and long ere the light flashed through the sky, God loved His chosen creatures. Before there was any created being– when the ether was not fanned by an angel's wing, when space itself had not an existence, when there was nothing save God alone– even then, in that loneliness of Deity, and in that deep quiet and profundity, His bowels moved with love for His chosen. Their names were written on His heart, and then were they dear to His soul. Jesus loved His people before the foundation of the world– even from eternity! and when He called me by His grace, He said to me, "I have loved thee with an everlasting love: therefore with loving-kindness have I drawn thee." Then, in the fulness of time, He purchased me with His blood; He let His heart run out in one deep gaping wound for me long ere I loved Him. Yea, when He first came to me, did I not spurn Him? When He knocked at the door, and asked for entrance, did I not drive Him away, and do despite to His grace? Ah, I can remember that I full often did so until, at last, by the power of His effectual grace, He said, "I must, I will come in;" and then He turned my heart, and made me love Him. But even till now I should have resisted Him, had it not been for His grace. Well, then since He purchased me when I was dead in sins, does it not follow, as a consequence necessary and logical, that He must have loved me first? Did my Savior die for me because I believed on Him? No; I was not then in existence; I had then no being. Could the Savior, therefore, have died because I had faith, when I myself was not yet born? Could that have been possible? Could that have been the origin of the Savior's love towards me? Oh! no; my Savior died for me long before I believed. "But," says someone, "He foresaw that you would have faith; and, therefore, He loved you." What did He foresee about my faith? Did He foresee that I should get that faith myself, and that I should believe on Him of myself? No; Christ could not foresee that, because no Christian man will ever say that faith came of itself without the gift and without the working of the Holy Spirit. I have met with a great many believers, and talked with them about this matter; but I never knew one who could put his hand on his heart, and say, "I believed in Jesus without the assistance of the Holy Spirit."

I am bound to the doctrine of the depravity of the human heart, because I find myself depraved in heart, and have daily proofs that in my flesh there dwelleth no good thing. If God enters into covenant with unfallen man, man is so insignificant a creature that it must be an act of gracious condescension on the Lord's part; but if God enters into covenant with sinful man, he is then so offensive a creature that it must be, on God's part, an act of pure, free, rich, sovereign grace. When the Lord entered into covenant with me, I am sure that it was all of grace, nothing else but grace. When I remember what a den of unclean beasts and birds my heart was, and how strong was my unrenewed will, how obstinate and rebellious against the sovereignty of the Divine rule, I always feel inclined to take the very lowest room in my Father's house, and when I enter Heaven, it will be to go among the less than the least of all saints, and with the chief of sinners.

…The late lamented Mr. Denham has put, at the foot of his portrait, a most admirable text, "Salvation is of the Lord." That is just an epitome of Calvinism; it is the sum and substance of it. If anyone should ask me what I mean by a Calvinist, I should reply, "He is one who says, Salvation is of the Lord." I cannot find in Scripture any other doctrine than this. It is the essence of the Bible. "He only is my rock and my salvation." Tell me anything contrary to this truth, and it will be a heresy; tell me a heresy, and I shall find its essence here, that it has departed from this great, this fundamental, this rock-truth, "God is my rock and my salvation." What is the heresy of Rome, but the addition of something to the perfect merits of Jesus Christ— the bringing in of the works of the flesh, to assist in our justification? And what is the heresy of Arminianism but the addition of something to the work of the Redeemer? Every heresy, if brought to the touchstone, will discover itself here. I have my own private opinion that there is no such thing as preaching Christ and Him crucified, unless we preach what nowadays is called Calvinism. It is a nickname to call it Calvinism; Calvinism is the gospel, and nothing else. I do not believe we can preach the gospel, if we do not preach justification by faith, without works; nor unless we preach the sovereignty of God in His dispensation of grace; nor unless we exalt the electing, unchangeable, eternal, immutable, conquering love of Jehovah; nor do I think we can preach the gospel, unless we base it upon the special and particular redemption of His elect and chosen people which Christ wrought out

upon the cross; nor can I comprehend a gospel which lets saints fall away after they are called, and suffers the children of God to be burned in the fires of damnation after having once believed in Jesus. Such a gospel I abhor.

"If ever it should come to pass,
That sheep of Christ might fall away,
My fickle, feeble soul, alas!
Would fall a thousand times a day."

If one dear saint of God had perished, so might all; if one of the covenant ones be lost, so may all be; and then there is no gospel promise true, but the Bible is a lie, and there is nothing in it worth my acceptance. I will be an infidel at once when I can believe that a saint of God can ever fall finally. If God hath loved me once, then He will love me for ever. God has a master-mind; He arranged everything in His gigantic intellect long before He did it; and once having settled it, He never alters it, "This shall be done," saith He, and the iron hand of destiny marks it down, and it is brought to pass. "This is My purpose," and it stands, nor can earth or hell alter it. "This is My decree," saith He, "promulgate it, ye holy angels; rend it down from the gate of Heaven, ye devils, if ye can; but ye cannot alter the decree, it shall stand for ever." God altereth not His plans; why should He? He is Almighty, and therefore can perform His pleasure. Why should He? He is the All-wise, and therefore cannot have planned wrongly. Why should He? He is the everlasting God, and therefore cannot die before His plan is accomplished. Why should He change? Ye worthless atoms of earth, ephemera of a day, ye creeping insects upon this bay-leaf of existence, ye may change your plans, but He shall never, never change His. Has He told me that His plan is to save me? If so, I am for ever safe.

"My name from the palms of His hands
Eternity will not erase;
Impress'd on His heart it remains,
In marks of indelible grace."

I do not know how some people, who believe that a Christian can fall from grace, manage to be happy. It must be a very commendable thing in them to be able to get through a day without despair. If I did not believe the doctrine of the final perseverance of the saints, I think I should be of all men the most miserable, because I should lack any ground of comfort. I could not say, whatever state of heart I came into, that I should be like a well-spring of water, whose stream fails not; I should rather have to take the comparison of an intermittent spring, that might stop on a sudden, or a reservoir, which I had no reason to expect would always be full. I believe that the happiest of Christians and the truest of Christians are those who never dare to doubt God, but who take His Word simply as it stands, and believe it, and ask no questions, just feeling assured that if God has said it, it will be so. I bear my willing testimony that I have no reason, nor even the shadow of a reason, to doubt my Lord, and I challenge Heaven, and earth, and hell, to bring any proof that God is untrue. From the depths of hell I call the fiends, and from this earth I call the tried and afflicted believers, and to Heaven I appeal, and challenge the long experience of the blood-washed host, and there is not to be found in the three realms a single person who can bear witness to one fact which can disprove the faithfulness of God, or weaken His claim to be trusted by His servants. There are many things that may or may not happen, but this I know shall happen—

"He shall present my soul,
Unblemish'd and complete,
Before the glory of His face,
With joys divinely great."

All the purposes of man have been defeated, but not the purposes of God. The promises of man may be broken— many of them are made to be broken— but the promises of God shall all be fulfilled. He is a promise-maker, but He never was a promise-breaker; He is a promise-keeping God, and every one of His people shall prove it to be so. This is my grateful, personal confidence, "The Lord will perfect that which concerneth me"– unworthy me, lost and ruined me. He will yet save me; and—

"I, among the blood-wash'd throng,
Shall wave the palm, and wear the crown,
And shout loud victory."

I go to a land which the plough of earth hath never upturned, where it is greener than earth's best pastures, and richer than her most abundant harvests ever saw. I go to a building of more gorgeous architecture than man hath ever builded; it is not of mortal design; it is "a building of God, a house not made with hands, eternal in the Heavens." All I shall know and enjoy in Heaven, will be given to me by the Lord, and I shall say, when at last I appear before Him—

"Grace all the work shall crown
Through everlasting days;
It lays in Heaven the topmost stone,
And well deserves the praise."

I know there are some who think it necessary to their system of theology to limit the merit of the blood of Jesus: if my theological system needed such a limitation, I would cast it to the winds. I cannot, I dare not allow the thought to find a lodging in my mind, it seems so near akin to blasphemy. In Christ's finished work I see an ocean of merit; my plummet finds no bottom, my eye discovers no shore. There must be sufficient efficacy in the blood of Christ, if God had so willed it, to have saved not only all in this world, but all in ten thousand worlds, had they transgressed their Maker's law. Once admit infinity into the matter, and limit is out of the question. Having a Divine Person for an offering, it is not consistent to conceive of limited value; bound and measure are terms inapplicable to the Divine sacrifice. The intent of the Divine purpose fixes the application of the infinite offering, but does not change it into a finite work. Think of the numbers upon whom God has bestowed His grace already. Think of the countless hosts in Heaven: if thou wert introduced there to-day, thou wouldst find it as easy to tell the stars, or the sands of the sea, as to count the multitudes that are before the throne even now. They have come from the East, and from the West, from the North, and from the South, and they are sitting down with Abraham, and with Isaac, and with Jacob in the Kingdom of God; and beside those in Heaven, think of the saved ones on earth. Blessed be God, His elect on earth are to be counted by millions, I believe, and the days are coming, brighter days than these, when there shall be multitudes upon multitudes brought to know the Savior, and to rejoice in Him. The Father's love is not for a few only, but for an exceeding great company. "A great multitude, which no man could number," will be found in Heaven. A man can reckon up to very high figures; set to work your Newtons, your mightiest calculators, and they can count great numbers, but God and God alone can tell the multitude of His redeemed. I believe there will be more in Heaven than in hell. If anyone asks me why I think so, I answer, because Christ, in everything, is to "have the pre-eminence," and I cannot conceive how He could have the pre-eminence if there are to be more in the dominions of Satan than in Paradise. Moreover, I have never read that there is to be in hell a great multitude, which no man could number. I rejoice to know that the souls of all infants, as soon as they die, speed their way to Paradise. Think what a multitude there is of them! Then there are already in Heaven unnumbered myriads of the spirits of just men made perfect– the redeemed of all nations, and kindreds, and people, and tongues up till now; and there are better times coming, when the religion of Christ shall be universal; when–

"He shall reign from pole to pole,
With illimitable sway;"

when whole kingdoms shall bow down before Him, and nations shall be born in a day, and in the thousand years of the great millennial state there will be enough saved to make up all the deficiencies of the thousands of years that have gone before. Christ shall be Master everywhere, and His praise shall be sounded in every land. Christ shall have the pre-eminence at last; His train shall be far larger than that which shall attend the chariot of the grim monarch of hell.

Some persons love the doctrine of universal atonement because they say, "It is so beautiful. It is a lovely idea that Christ should have died for all men; it commends itself," they say, "to the instincts of humanity; there is something in it full of joy and beauty." I admit there is, but beauty may be often associated with falsehood. There is much which I might admire in the theory of universal redemption, but I will just show what the supposition necessarily involves. If Christ on His cross intended to save every man, then He intended to save those who were lost before He died. If the doctrine be true, that He died for all men, then He died for some who were in hell before He came into this world, for doubtless there were even then myriads there who had been cast away because of their sins. Once again, if it was Christ's intention to save all men, how deplorably has He been disappointed, for we have His own testimony that there is a lake which burneth with fire and brimstone, and into that pit of woe have been cast some of the very persons who, according to the theory of universal redemption, were bought with His blood. That seems to me a conception a thousand times more repulsive than any of those consequences which are said to be associated with the Calvinistic and Christian doctrine of special and particular redemption. To think that my Savior died for men who were or are in hell, seems a supposition too horrible for me to entertain. To imagine for a moment that He was the Substitute for all the sons of men, and that God, having first punished the Substitute, afterwards punished the sinners themselves, seems to conflict with all my ideas of Divine justice. That Christ should offer an atonement and satisfaction for the sins of all men, and that afterwards some of those very men should be punished for the sins for which Christ had already atoned, appears to me to be the most monstrous iniquity that could ever have been imputed to Saturn, to Janus, to the goddess of the Thugs, or to the most diabolical heathen deities. God forbid that we should ever think thus of Jehovah, the just and wise and good!

There is no soul living who holds more firmly to the doctrines of grace than I do, and if any man asks me whether I am ashamed to be called a Calvinist, I answer—I wish to be called nothing but a Christian; but if you ask me, do I hold the doctrinal views which were held by John Calvin, I reply, I do in the main hold them, and rejoice to avow it. But far be it from me even to imagine that Zion contains none but Calvinistic Christians within her walls, or that there are none saved who do not hold our views. Most atrocious things have been spoken about the character and spiritual condition of John Wesley, the modern prince of Arminians. I can only say concerning him that, while I detest many of the doctrines which he preached, yet for the man himself I have a reverence second to no Wesleyan; and if there were wanted two apostles to be added to the number of the twelve, I do not believe that there could be found two men more fit to be so added than George Whitefield and John Wesley. The character of John Wesley stands beyond all imputation for self-sacrifice, zeal, holiness, and communion with God; he lived far above the ordinary level of common Christians, and was one "of whom the world was not worthy." I believe there are multitudes of men who cannot see these truths, or, at least, cannot see them in the way in which we put them, who nevertheless have received Christ as their Savior, and are as dear to the heart of the God of grace as the soundest Calvinist in or out of Heaven.

I do not think I differ from any of my Hyper-Calvinistic brethren in what I do believe, but I differ from them in what they do not believe. I do not hold any less than they do, but I hold a little more, and, I think, a little more of the truth revealed in the Scriptures. Not only are there a few cardinal doctrines, by which we can steer our ship North, South, East, or West, but as we study the Word, we shall begin to learn something about the North-west and North-east, and all else that lies between the four cardinal points. The system of truth revealed in the Scriptures is not simply one straight line, but two; and no man will ever get a right view of the gospel until he knows how to look at the two lines at once. For instance, I read in one Book of the Bible, "The Spirit and the bride say, Come. And let him that heareth say, Come. And let him that is athirst come. And whosoever will, let him take the water of life freely." Yet I am taught, in another part of the same inspired Word, that "it is not of him that willeth, nor of him that runneth, but of God that sheweth mercy." I see, in one place, God in providence presiding over all, and yet I see, and I cannot help seeing, that man acts as he pleases, and that God has left his actions, in a great measure, to his own free-will. Now, if I were to declare that man was so free to act that there was no control of God over his actions, I should be driven very near to atheism; and if, on the other hand, I should declare that God so over-rules all things that man is not free enough to be responsible, I should be driven at once into Antinomianism or fatalism. That God predestines, and yet that man is responsible, are two facts that few can see clearly. They are believed to be inconsistent and contradictory to each other. If, then, I find taught in one part of the Bible that everything is fore-ordained, that is true; and if I find, in another Scripture, that man is responsible for all his actions, that is true; and it is only my folly that leads me to imagine that these two truths can ever contradict each other. I do not believe they can ever be welded into one upon any earthly anvil, but they certainly shall be one in eternity. They are two lines that are so nearly parallel, that the human mind which pursues them farthest will never discover that they converge, but they do converge, and they will meet somewhere in eternity, close to the throne of God, whence all truth doth spring.

It is often said that the doctrines we believe have a tendency to lead us to sin. I have heard it asserted most positively, that those high doctrines which we love, and which we find in the Scriptures, are licentious ones. I do not know who will have the hardihood to make that assertion, when they consider that the holiest of men have been believers in them. I ask the man who dares to say that Calvinism is a licentious religion, what he thinks of the character of Augustine, or Calvin, or Whitefield, who in successive ages were the great exponents of the system of grace; or what will he say of the Puritans, whose works are full of them? Had a man been an Arminian in those days, he would have been accounted the vilest heretic breathing, but now we are looked upon as the heretics, and they as the orthodox. We have gone back to the old school; we can trace our descent from the apostles. It is that vein of free-grace, running through the sermonizing of Baptists, which has saved us as a denomination. Were it not for that, we should not stand where we are today. We can run a golden line up to Jesus Christ Himself, through a holy succession of mighty fathers, who all held these glorious truths; and we can ask concerning them, "Where will you find holier and better men in the world?" No doctrine is so calculated to preserve a man from sin as the doctrine of the grace of God. Those who have called it "a licentious doctrine" did not know anything at all about it. Poor ignorant things, they little knew that their own vile stuff was the most licentious doctrine under Heaven. If they knew the grace of God in truth, they would soon see that there was no preservative from lying like a knowledge that we are elect of God from the foundation of the world. There is nothing like a belief in my eternal perseverance, and the immutability of my Father's affection, which can keep me near to Him from a motive of simple gratitude. Nothing makes a man so virtuous as belief of the truth. A lying doctrine will soon beget a lying practice. A man cannot have an erroneous belief without by-and-by having an erroneous life. I believe the one thing naturally begets the other. Of all men, those have the most disinterested piety, the sublimest reverence, the most ardent devotion, who believe that they are saved by grace, without works, through faith, and that not of themselves, it is the gift of God. Christians should take heed, and see that it always is so, lest by any means Christ should be crucified afresh, and put to an open shame.
C.H. Spurgeon

We call this system of doctrine "Calvinism," and accept the term "Calvinist" as our badge of honor; yet names are mere conveniences. "We might," says Warburton, "quite as appropriately, and with equally as much reason, call gravitation "Newtonism."
Loraine Boettner

Salvation is of the Lord. That is just an epitome of Calvinism; it is the sum and substance of it. If anyone should ask me what I mean by a Calvinist, I should reply, "He is one who says, 'Salvation is of the Lord.'" I cannot find in Scripture any other doctrine than this. It is the essence of the Bible: "He only is my rock and my salvation." Tell me anything contrary to this truth, and it will be a heresy; tell me a heresy, and I shall find its essence here, that it has departed from this great, this fundamental, this rock-truth, "God is my rock and my salvation…" I have my own private opinion that there is no such thing as preaching Christ and Him crucified, unless we preach what nowadays is called Calvinism. It is a nickname to call it Calvinism; Calvinism is the gospel, and nothing else.
John Calvin

It is most misleading to call this soteriology "Calvinism" at all, for it is not a peculiarity of John Calvin and the divines of Dort, but a part of the revealed truth of God and the catholic [universal] Christian faith. "Calvinism" is one of the "odious names" by which down the centuries prejudice has been raised against it. But the thing itself is just the biblical gospel.
J.I. Packer

I am a five point Calvinist and all the points are sharp!
Ian Paisley

The strength of that heretic (John Calvin) consisted in this, that money never had the slightest charm for him. If I had such servants my dominion would extend from sea to sea.
Pope Pius IV

We believe in the five great points commonly known as Calvinistic.
C.H. Spurgeon

"And he said, 'Therefore said I unto you, that no man can come unto me, except it were given him of my Father.'" Here our Lord uttered a bit of old-fashioned free-grace doctrine, such as people nowadays do not like. They call it "Calvinism," and put it aside among the old exploded tenets which this enlightened age knows nothing of. What right they have to ascribe to the Genevan reformer a doctrine as old as the hills I do not know. But our Lord Jesus never hesitated to fling that truth into the face of His enemies. He told them, "Ye believe not because ye are not of my sheep, as I said unto you." "No man can come to me, except the Father which hath sent me draw him." Here He tells them plainly that they could not come unto Him unless the Father gave them the grace to come. This humbling doctrine they could not receive, and so they went aside.
C.H. Spurgeon

It is a nickname to call it Calvinism; Calvinism is the gospel, and nothing else.
C.H. Spurgeon

The doctrines of original sin, election, effectual calling, final perseverance, and all those great truths which are called Calvinism – though Calvin was not the author of them, but simply an able writer and preacher upon the subject – are, I believe, the essential doctrines of the gospel that is in Jesus Christ. Now, I do not ask you whether you believe all this – it is possible you may not; but I believe you will before you enter heaven.
C.H. Spurgeon

Calvinism, Hyper-Calvinists
Calvinists, such men may call themselves, but, unlike the Reformer, whose name they adopt, they bring a system of divinity to the Bible to interpret it, instead of making every system, be its merits what they may, yield, and give place to the pure and unadulterated Word of God.
John Calvin

Calvinism versus Arminianism
See also Arminianism and Calvinism
Where God has begun a real work of grace, incidental mistakes will be lessened by time and experience; where he has not, it is of little significance what sentiments people hold, or whether they call themselves Arminians or Calvinists.
John Newton

When I come to a text which speaks of election, I delight myself in the doctrine of election. When the apostles exhort me to repentance and obedience, and indicate my freedom of choice and action, I give myself up to that side of the question.
Charles Simeon

Calvinists
I am afraid there are Calvinists, who, while they account it a proof of their humility that they are willing in words to debase the creature, and to give all the glory of salvation to the Lord, yet know not what manner of spirit they are of. Whatever it be that makes us trust in ourselves that we are comparatively wise or good, so as to treat those with contempt who do not subscribe

to our doctrines, or follow our party, is a proof and fruit of a self-righteous spirit. Self-righteousness can feed upon doctrines, as well as upon works; and a man may have the heart of a Pharisee, while his head is stored with orthodox notions of the unworthiness of the creature and the riches of free grace.
John Newton

There is a certain breed of Calvinist, whom I do not envy ... I have seen their long faces; I have heard their whining periods, and read their dismal sentences, in which they say something to this effect – "Groan in the Lord always, and again I say, groan! He that mourneth and weepeth, he that doubteth and feareth, he that distrusteth and dishonoreth his God, shall be saved." That seems to be the sum and substance of their very ungospel-like gospel. But why is it they do this? I speak now honestly and fearlessly. It is because there is a pride within them – a conceit which is fed on rottenness, and sucks marrow and fatness out of putrid carcasses. And what, say you, is the object of their pride? Why, the pride of being able to boast of a deep experience – the pride of being a blacker, grosser, and more detestable sinner than other people. "Whose glory is in their shame," may well apply to them. A more dangerous, because a more deceitful pride than this is not to be found. It has all the elements of self-righteousness in it.
C.H. Spurgeon

Capital punishment
Does capital punishment tend to the security of the people? By no means. It hardens the hearts of men.
Elizabeth Fry

Why do we kill people who are killing people to show that killing people is wrong?
Holly Near

Careers
Jenny, God has made me for a purpose –

for China; but he has also made me fast, and when I run, I feel his pleasure.
Eric Liddell

To choose a career on selfish grounds is probably the greatest single sin that any young person can commit, for it is the deliberate withdrawal from allegiance to God of the greatest part of time and strength.
William Temple

Carelessness
Be not careless in deeds, nor confused in words, nor rambling in thought.
Marcus Aurelius Antoninus

Cares
Obedience is a freely chosen death, a life without cares, danger without fears, unshakable trust in God, no fear of death. It is a voyage without perils, a journey in your sleep.
John Climacus

Caring
See also: Aid; Charity; Giving; Service
Nobody should seek his own good, but the good of others.
The Bible, 1 Corinthians 10:24

A church is as large as the lives that are touched through the congregation, by the love of God. Caring is the ultimate measure of a congregation's size.
Carl S. Dudley

If you're going to care about the fall of the sparrow, you can't pick and choose who's going to be the sparrow. It's everybody.
Madeleine L'Engle

The world doesn't care what you know until they know that you care.
David Havard

It is a kingly task, believe me, to help the afflicted.
Ovid

Dearest Lord, may I see you today and everyday in the person of your sick and,

while nursing them, minister unto you.
Mother Teresa

Caring for yourself

Be Yourself – Truthfully
Accept Yourself – Gracefully
Value Yourself – Joyfully
Forgive Yourself – Completely
Treat Yourself – Generously
Balance Yourself – Harmoniously
Bless Yourself – Abundantly
Trust Yourself – Confidently
Love Yourself – Wholeheartedly
Empower Yourself – Prayerfully
Give Yourself – Enthusiastically
Express Yourself – Radiantly
Author unknown

It is the part of a Christian to take care
of his own body for the very purpose
that by its soundness and well-being he
may be enabled to labor for the aid of
those who are in want, that thus the
stronger member may serve the weaker
member.
Martin Luther

Catechism

Come, my children, listen to me; I will
teach you the fear of the Lord.
The Bible, Psalm 34:11

Being a form of instruction for children in
the doctrine of Christ
  In this confused and divided state of
Christendom, I judge it useful that there
should be public testimonies, whereby
churches which, though widely separated
by space, agree in the doctrine of Christ,
may mutually recognize each other.
John Calvin

Q. What is your only comfort in life and
death?
A. That I am not my own, but belong
with body and soul, both in life and in
death, to my faithful Savior Jesus Christ.
He has fully paid for all my sins with His
precious blood, and has set me free from
all the power of the devil. He also
preserves me in such a way that without

the will of my heavenly Father not a hair
can fall from my head; indeed, all things
must work together for my salvation.
Because I belong to Him, Christ, His
Holy Spirit assures me of eternal life and
makes me heartily willing and ready from
now on to live for Him.
Heidelberg Catechism

I am persuaded that the use of a good
Catechism in all our families will be a
great safeguard against the increasing
errors of the times. Those who use
[them] in their families or classes must
labor to explain the sense; but the words
should be carefully learned by heart, for
they will be understood better as years
pass.
C.H. Spurgeon

Cathedrals
See also: Buildings, Church

I have been into many of the ancient
cathedrals – grand, wonderful, mysterious.
But I always leave them with the feeling of
indignation because of the generations of
human beings who have struggled in
poverty to build these altars to the
unknown god.
Elizabeth Cady Stanton

Caution

He that observeth the wind shall not sow;
and he that regardeth the clouds shall not
reap.
The Bible, Ecclesiastes 11:4 KJV

The desire for safety stands against every
great and noble enterprise.
Tacitus

Cautious

If one is forever cautious, can one remain a
human being?
Alexander Solzhenitsyn

Challenge

I have nothing to offer but blood, toil,
tears, and sweat.
Winston Churchill

The ultimate measure of a man is not where he stands in moments of comfort and convenience, but where he stands at times of challenge and controversy.
Martin Luther King Jr.

Chance
See also: Universe, Origin of; Providence
There may be some theoretical chance that wind and rain erosion could produce the face of four presidents on the side of a mountain, but it is still far more reasonable to assume that an intelligent sculptor created Mount Rushmore.
Norman Geisler

Chance favors only the prepared mind.
Louis Pasteur

I am glad there is no such thing as "chance," that nothing is left to itself, but that Christ everywhere has sway.
C.H. Spurgeon

Change
See also: Tradition
Little men with little minds and little imaginations go through life in little ruts, smugly resisting all changes which would jar their little worlds.
Author unknown

The only thing constant is change.
Author unknown

A bend in the road is not the end of the road, unless you fail to make the turn.
Author unknown

Everybody is in favor of progress. It's the change they don't like.
Author unknown

Courage is the strength or choice to begin a change. Determination is the persistence to continue in that change.
Author unknown

People avoid change until the pain of remaining the same is greater than the pain of changing.
Author unknown

Remember change and change for the better are often two different things.
Author unknown

[Christ] was primarily concerned to change men as men rather than the political regime under which they lived; to transform their attitude rather than their circumstances; to treat the sickness of their hearts rather than the problems of their environment. But he laid down in a single pregnant sentence man's duty both to God and to the State when he said: "Render to Caesar the things that are Caesar's and to God the things that are God's;" and it is certainly not his fault that the Christian church has been so slow, down the centuries, in applying to one after another of the world's social evils the principle he emphasized so strong that we must love our neighbors as ourselves.
J.N.D. Anderson

What single ability do we all have? The ability to change.
Leonard Andrews

Everything is in a state of metamorphosis. Thou thyself art in everlasting change and in corruption to correspond; so is the whole universe.
Marcus Aurelius Antoninus

The world is always changing, let's change it for the better through understanding and laughter.
Breyd

Only the wisest and the stupidest of men never change.
Confucius

Don't fear change, embrace it.
Anthony J. D'Angelo

Change is inevitable in a progressive country. Change is constant.
Benjamin Disraeli

Taking a new step, uttering a new word, is what people fear most.
F. Dostoevsky

Faced with the choice between changing one's mind and proving there is no need to do so, almost everyone gets busy on the proof.
John Kenneth Galbraith

Be the change you want to see in the world.
Mahatma Gandhi

We must always change, renew, rejuvenate ourselves; otherwise we harden.
Johann Wolfang von Goethe

Nothing endures but change.
Heraclitus

Change is not made without inconvenience, even from worse to better.
Richard Hooker

To change one's life: 1. Start immediately, 2. Do it flamboyantly, 3. No exceptions.
William James

Those who never retract their opinions love themselves more than they love truth.
Joseph Joubert

Those who make peaceful revolution impossible will make violent revolution inevitable.
John F. Kennedy

Change is the law. And those who look only to the past or present are certain to miss the future.
John F. Kennedy

There is a spirit and a need and a man at the beginning of every great human advance. Each of these must be right for that particular moment of history, or nothing happens.
Coretta Scott King

There is nothing more difficult to take in hand, more perilous to conduct or more uncertain in its success than to take the lead in the introduction of a new order of things.
Niccolo Machiavelli

Lord, when we are wrong, make us willing to change. And when we are right, make us easy to live with.
Peter Marshall

The philosophers have only interpreted the world, in various ways; the point, however, is to change it.
Karl Marx

Never doubt that a small group of thoughtful, committed people can change the world. Indeed, it is the only thing that ever has.
Margaret Mead

In a higher world it is otherwise, but here below to live is to change, and to be perfect is to have changed often.
John Henry Newman

Nothing is stronger than custom.
Ovid

The only difference between a rut and a grave is the depth.
Proverb

If we don't change, we don't grow. If we don't grow, we are not really living.
Gail Sheehy

It is not well to make great changes in old age.
C.H. Spurgeon

Change is inevitable. Change for the better is a full-time job.
Adlai Stevenson

Change itself comes to be seen as anarchic, even lunatic.
Alvin Toffler

Everyone thinks of changing the world, but no one thinks of changing himself.
Leo Tolstoy

He who rejects change is the architect of decay. The only human institution which rejects progress is the cemetery.
Harold Wilson

Change is "rut prevention."
Peg Wood

Character
Do not be misled: "Bad company corrupts good character."
The Bible, 1 Corinthians 15:33

Character is made by many acts; it may be lost by a single one.
Author unknown

A person's character and their garden both reflect the amount of weeding that was done in the growing season.
Author unknown

Certainly it is a world of scarcity. But the scarcity is not confined to iron ore and arable land. The most constricting scarcities are those of character and personality.
William R. Allen

It is not what he has, nor even what he does, which directly expresses the worth of a man, but what he is.
Henri-Frederic Amiel

A man should be upright, not be kept upright.
Marcus Aurelius Antoninus

Character is better than ancestry, and personal conduct is more important than the highest parentage.
Thomas Barnardo

We never know how much one loves till we know how much he is willing to endure and suffer for us; and it is the suffering element that measures love. The characters that are great must, of necessity, be characters that shall be willing, patient and strong to endure for others. To hold our nature in the willing service of another is the divine idea of manhood, of the human character.
Henry Ward Beecher

He is rich or poor according to what he is, not according to what he has.
Henry Ward Beecher

Happiness is not the end of life; character is.
Henry Ward Beecher

Character may be manifested in the great moments, but it is made in the small ones.
Phillip Brooks

The purpose of Christianity is not to avoid difficulty, but to produce a character adequate to meet it when it comes. It does not make life easy; rather it tries to make us great enough for life.
James L. Christensen

Of all the properties which belong to honorable men, not one is so highly prized as that of character.
Henry Clay

No change of circumstances can repair a defect of character.
Ralph Waldo Emerson

What lies beyond us and what lies before us are tiny matters compared to what lies within us.
Ralph Waldo Emerson.

The force of character is cumulative.
Ralph Waldo Emerson

It seems to me to be the best proof of an evangelical disposition, that persons are not angry when reproached, and have a Christian charity for those that ill deserve it.
Erasmus

Parents can only give good advice or put them on the right paths, but the final forming of a person's character lies in their own hands.
Anne Frank

Our character is but the stamp on our souls of the free choices of good and evil

we have made through life.
John Cunningham Geikie

Out of our beliefs are born deeds; out of our deeds we form habits; out of our habits grows our character; and on our character we build our destiny.
Henry Hancock

Many a man's reputation would not know his character if they met on the street.
Elbert Hubbard

He who makes a beast of himself gets rid of the pain of being a man.
Samuel Johnson

Character cannot be developed in ease and quiet. Only through experiences of trial and suffering can the soul be strengthened, vision cleared, ambition inspired and success achieved.
Helen Keller

Small kindnesses, small courtesies, small considerations, habitually practiced in our social intercourse, give a greater charm to the character than the display of great talents and accomplishments.
Mary Ann Kelty

Character is not made on the mountain tops of life; it is made in the valleys.
Kathryn Kuhlman

The true measure of a man is how he treats someone who can do him absolutely no good.
Ann Landers

Die when I may, I want it said by those who knew me best that I always plucked a thistle and planted a flower where I thought a flower would grow.
Abraham Lincoln

The quality of a person's life is in direct proportion to their commitment to excellence, regardless of their chosen field of endeavor.
Vince Lombardi

Character is what you are in the dark.
Dwight L. Moody

In war, three-quarters turn on personal character and relations; the balance of manpower and materials counts only for the remaining quarter.
Napoleon

Only when you can be extremely pliable and soft can you be extremely hard and strong.
Zen proverb

Perhaps there is no more important component of character than steadfast resolution. The boys and girls who are going to make great men and women, or are going to count in any way in after life, must make up their minds not merely to overcome a thousand obstacles, but to win in spite of a thousand repulses and defeats.
Theodore Roosevelt

Alike for the nation and the individual, the one indispensable requisite is character.
Theodore Roosevelt

The highest reward for a person's toil is not what they get for it, but what they become by it.
John Ruskin

Fame is a vapor, popularity is an accident, and money takes wings. The only thing that endures is character.
O.J. Simpson

Let him that would move the world, first move himself.
Socrates

What we are governs how we think, and how we think determines how we act.
John R. W. Stott

The study of God's word for the purpose of discovering God's will is the secret discipline which has formed the greatest characters.
Henry David Thoreau

Few things are harder to put up with than a good example.
Mark Twain

Character is a by-product; it is produced in the great manufacture of daily duty.
Woodrow Wilson

Be more concerned with your character than with your reputation, because your character is what you really are, while your reputation is merely what others think you are.
John Wooden

Charismatic

The fanaticism which discards the Scripture, under the pretense of resorting to immediate revelations is subversive of every principle of Christianity. For when they boast extravagantly of the Spirit, the tendency is always to bury the Word of God so they may make room for their own falsehoods.
John Calvin

As long as a person has a notion that he is guided by immediate direction from heaven, it makes him incorrigible and impregnable in all his misconduct.
Jonathan Edwards

Charismania is pietism gone to seed.
Dick Lucas

He who is not a charismatic when he is young has no heart. He who is still a charismatic when he is old has no brain.
Chris Stamper

Charismatic leaders

If charismatic leaders were as interested as being men of love as they have sometimes been in being men of power then the charismatic renewal would be a more wholesome thing than it has so often been.
Tom Smail

Charity

See also: Aid; Caring; Giving

Charity is twice blessed – it blesses the one who gives and the one who receives.
Author unknown

In faith and hope the world will disagree,
But all mankind's concern is charity.
Alexander the Great

No, Sir; to act from pure benevolence is not possible for finite beings. Human benevolence is mingled with vanity, interest, or some other motive.
James Boswell

Charity should begin at home, but should not stay there.
Philip Brooks

The highest exercise of charity is charity towards the uncharitable.
J.S. Buckminster

Charity is, indeed, a great thing, and a gift of God, and when it is rightly ordered likens us unto God himself, as far as that is possible; for it is charity which makes the man.
John Chrysostom

Loving one another with the charity of Christ, let the love you have in your hearts be shown outwardly in your deeds so that compelled by such an example, the sisters may also grow in the love of God and charity for one another.
Clare of Assisi

This only is charity, to do all, all that we can.
John Donne

In faith and hope the world will disagree,
But all mankind's concern is charity.
Charles H. Duell, Commissioner, U.S. Office of Patents, 1899

First the lover must learn charity and keep God's law. Then he shall be blessed a hundredfold, and he shall do great things without great effort, and bear all pain without suffering. And so his life will surpass human reason indeed.
Hadewijch

Charity says, "I desire nothing but Jesus."
Walter Hilton

If you haven't any charity in your heart, then you have the worst kind of heart trouble.
Bob Hope

He that has no charity deserves no mercy.
English proverb

Charity sees the need, not the cause.
German proverb

Charity is injurious unless it helps the recipient to become independent of it.
John D. Rockefeller

Charity degrades those who receive it and hardens those who dispense it.
George Sand

If we fail to feed the needy, we do not have God's love, no matter what we say.
Ronald Sider

Charm

There is no personal charm so great as the charm of a cheerful temperament.
Henry Van Dyke

Chastity

Indeed it is through chastity that we are gathered together and led back to the unity from which we were fragmented into multiplicity.
Augustine of Hippo

Seeing women when you go out is not forbidden, but it is sinful to desire them or to wish them to desire you, for it is not by tough or passionate feeling alone but by one's gaze also that lustful desires mutually arise. And do not say that your hearts are pure if there is immodesty of the eye, because the unchaste eye carries the message of an impure heart. And when such hearts disclose their unchaste desires in a mutual gaze, even without saying a word, then it is that chastity suddenly goes out of their life, even though their bodies remain unsullied by unchaste acts.
Augustine of Hippo, The Rule of St Augustine

The essence of chastity is not the suppression of lust, but the total orientation of one's life towards a goal.
Dietrich Bonhoeffer

There is no sin so gross as that of unchastity, which is so nearly tolerated in males, by public opinion, partly because so seldom discussed – teachers being deterred by a theory of delicacy. Hence the necessity that all the sins be rebuked.
R.L. Dabney

Chastity is the most unpopular of our Christian virtues.
C.S. Lewis

By our vow of chastity we are married to Jesus.
Mother Teresa

Cheerfulness

A merry heart maketh a cheerful countenance.
The Bible, Proverbs 15:13 KJV

A cheerful look brings joy to the heart, and good news gives health to the bones.
The Bible, Proverbs 15:30

Wondrous is the strength of cheerfulness, and its power of endurance – the cheerful man will do more in the same time, will do it better, will preserve it longer, than the sad or sullen.
Thomas Carlyle

I feel an earnest and humble desire, and shall till I die, to increase the stock of harmless cheerfulness.
Charles Dickens

So of cheerfulness, or a good temper, the more it is spent, the more it remains.
Ralph Waldo Emerson

Health is the condition of wisdom, and the sign is cheerfulness – an open and noble temper.
Ralph Waldo Emerson

It is not fitting, when one is in God's service, to have a gloomy face or a

chilling look.
Francis of Assisi

The true source of cheerfulness is
benevolence.
P. Godwin

Let us be of good cheer, remembering that
the misfortunes hardest to bear are those
which never happen.
James Russell Lowell

The best way to cheer yourself up is to try
to cheer somebody else up.
Mark Twain

Cheerfulness in most cheerful people, is
the rich and satisfying result of strenuous
discipline.
Edwin Percy Whipple

Children
***See also: Fathers; Mothers; Parenting;
Parents***
Happy is the man that hath his quiver full
of them.
The Bible, Psalm 127:5 KJV

Train a child in the way he should go, and
when he is old he will not turn from it.
The Bible, Proverbs 22:6 NLT

People were bringing little children to him
[Jesus] in order that he might touch them;
and the disciples spoke sternly to them. But
when Jesus saw this, he was indignant and
said to them, "Let the children come to me;
do not stop them; for it is to such as these
that the kingdom of God belongs. Truly I
tell you, whoever does not receive the
kingdom of God as a little child will never
enter it." And he took them up in his arms,
laid his hands on them, and blessed them.
Mark 10.13-16 NRSV

When you thought I wasn't looking, I saw
you hang my first painting on the
refrigerator, and I wanted to paint another
one. When you thought I wasn't looking, I
saw you feed a stray cat, and I thought it
was good to be kind to animals. When you
thought I wasn't looking, I saw you make
my favorite cake for me, and I knew that
little things are special things. When you
thought I wasn't looking, I heard you pray,
and I believed there is a God I could always
talk to. When you thought I wasn't looking,
I felt you kiss me good night, and I felt
loved. When you thought I wasn't looking, I
saw tears come from your eyes, and I
learned that sometimes things hurt, but it's
all right to cry. When you thought I wasn't
looking, I saw you give to someone needy
and I learned the joy of giving. When you
thought I wasn't looking, I saw you always
did your best and it made me want to be all
that I could be. When you thought I wasn't
looking, I heard you say "thank you" and I
wanted to say thanks for all the things I saw
when you thought I wasn't looking.
Author unknown

Times change. Not too many years ago
minding one's children didn't mean
obeying them.
Author unknown

If a child lives with criticism,
  he learns to condemn.
If a child lives with hostility,
  he learns to fight.
If a child lives with fear,
  he learns to be apprehensive.
If a child lives with pity,
  he learns to feel sorry for himself.
If a child lives with jealousy,
  he learns to feel guilty.
If a child lives with encouragement,
  he learns to be self-confident.
If a child lives with tolerance,
  he learns to be patient.
If a child lives with praise,
  he learns to be appreciative.
If a child lives with acceptance,
  he learns to love.
If a child lives with approval,
  he learns to like himself.
If a child lives with recognition,
  he learns to have a goal.
If a child lives with fairness,
  he learns what justice is.
If a child lives with honesty,

he learns what truth is.
If a child lives with sincerity,
  he learns to have faith in himself and
  those around him.
If a child lives with love,
  he learns that the world is
  a wonderful place to live in.
Author unknown

He has achieved success who has loved
much, laughed often and been an
inspiration to little children.
Author unknown

Invest in the future; have a child and teach
her well.
Author unknown

It is better to build strong children than to
try to repair adults.
Author unknown

He who helps a child helps humanity with
an immediateness which no other help
given to human creatures in any other
stage of human life can possibly give
again.
Phillips Brooks

Children, obey. Why does the apostle use
the word obey instead of honor, which has
a greater extent of meaning? It is because
obedience is the evidence of that honor
which children owe to their parents, and is
therefore more earnestly enforced. It is
likewise more difficult; for the human
mind recoils from the idea of subjection,
and with difficulty allows itself to be
placed under the control of another.
John Calvin

The best compliment to a child or a friend is
the feeling you give him that he has been set
free to make his own inquiries, to come to
conclusions that are right for him, whether
or not they coincide with your own.
Alistair Cooke

The first half of our lives is ruined by our
parents, and the second half by our children.
Clarence Darrow

I love little children, and it is not a slight
thing when they who are fresh from God,
love us.
Charles Dickens

The soul is healed by being with children.
Fyodor Dostoevsky

We can't form our children on our own
concepts; we must take them and love
them as God gives them to us.
Johann Wolfgang von Goethe

Children are our most valuable natural
resource.
Herbert Hoover

Kids today learn a lot about getting to the
moon, but very little about getting to
heaven.
David Jeremiah

We began by imagining that we are giving
to them; we end by realizing that they have
enriched us.
Pope John Paul II

Children are likely to live up to what their
fathers believe of them.
Lady Bird Johnson

You can learn many things from children.
How much patience you have, for instance.
Franklin P. Jones

Children need models more than they
need critics.
Joseph Joubert

Children are a great comfort in your old
age. And they help you reach it sooner, too.
Lionel M. Kauffman

What it is children become, that will the
community become.
Suzanne LaFollette

The traditional greeting of the Mesai tribe
in Africa is consistently, "How are the
children?"
Martin Marty

The hearts of small children are delicate organs. A cruel beginning in this world can twist them into curious shapes. The heart of a hurt child can shrink so that forever afterward it is hard and pitted as the seed of a peach. Or, again, the heart of such a child may fester and swell until it is misery to carry within the body, easily chafed and hurt by the most ordinary things.
Carson McCullers

A great man is one who has not lost the child's heart.
Mencius

Oh, what a tangled web do parents weave when they think that their children are naive.
Ogden Nash

To become mature is to recover that sense of seriousness which one had as a child at play.
Friedrich Nietzsche

Children are one-third of our population and all of our future.
Select Panel for the Promotion of Child Health, 1981

Remember children are born with a decided bias toward evil, and therefore if you let them choose for themselves, they are certain to choose wrong. The mother cannot tell what her tender infant may grow up to be – tall or short, weak or strong, wise or foolish; he may or may not be any of these it is all uncertain. But one thing the mother can say with certainty: he will have a corrupt and sinful heart. It is natural for us to do wrong…Our hearts are like the earth on which we tread; let it alone, and it is sure to bear weeds.
J.C. Ryle

A baby is God's opinion that life should go on.
Carl Sandburg

Children today are tyrants. They contradict their parents, gobble their food, and tyrannize their teachers.
Socrates

Could I climb to the highest place in Athens, I would lift up my voice and proclaim: Fellow citizens! Why do ye turn and scrape every stone to gather wealth, and take so little care of your children, to whom one day you must relinquish it all?
Socrates

Jesus loved everyone, but he loved children most of all. Today we know that unborn children are the targets of destruction. We must thank our parents for wanting us, for loving us and for taking such good care of us.
Mother Teresa

Our religion is one which challenges the ordinary human standards by holding that the ideal of life is the spirit of a little child. We tend to glorify adulthood and wisdom and worldly prudence, but the gospel reverses all this. The gospel says that the inescapable condition of entrance into the divine fellowship is that we turn and become as a little child. As against our natural judgment we must become tender and full of wonder and unspoiled by the hard skepticism on which we so often pride ourselves. But when we really look into the heart of a child, willful as he may be, we are often ashamed. God has sent children into the world, not only to replenish it, but to serve as sacred reminders of something ineffably precious which we are always in danger of losing. The sacrament of childhood is thus a continuing revelation.
Elton Trueblood

The heart of a child is the most precious of God's creation. Never break it. At all costs, never break it.
Joseph L. Whitten

The potential possibilities of any child are the most intriguing and stimulating in all creation.
Ray L. Wilbur

Before I got married I had six theories about bringing up children; now I have six

children and no theories.
John Wilmot, Earl of Rochester

The child is father of the man.
William Wordsworth

Give us the child, and we will give you the man.
Francis Xavier

Children and evangelism

Those children who are of sufficient years to sin and be saved by faith have to listen to the gospel and receive it by faith. And they can do this, God the Holy Spirit helping them. There is no doubt about it, because great numbers have done it. I will not say at what age children are first capable of receiving the knowledge of Christ, but it is much earlier than some fancy.
C.H. Spurgeon

Children and imagination

I doubt that the imagination can be suppressed. If you truly eradicated it in a child, he would grow up to be an eggplant.
Ursula Le Guin

Choices
See also: Decisions

Every moment you have a choice, regardless of what has happened before. Choose right now to move forward, positively and confidently into your incredible future.
Author unknown

Destiny is not a matter of chance, it is a matter of choice; it is not a thing to be waited for, it is a thing to be achieved.
William J. Bryan

One's philosophy is not best expressed in words; it is expressed in the choices one makes. In the long run, we shape our lives and we shape ourselves. The process never ends until we die. And the choices we make are ultimately our responsibility.
Eleanor Roosevelt

Chosen by God

It's a good thing God chose me before I was born, because he surely would not have afterwards.
C.H. Spurgeon

Christ
See also: Atonement; Cross, Incarnation; Lordship of Christ; Name of Jesus; Resurrection; Savior; Second Coming; Testimonies to Christ; Virgin Birth

He is the image of the invisible God, the firstborn over all creation.
The Bible, Colossians 1:15

The Son is the radiance of God's glory and the exact representation of his being, sustaining all things by his powerful word. After he had provided purification for sins, he sat down at the right hand of the Majesty in heaven.
The Bible, Hebrews 1:3

You have loved righteousness and hated wickedness; therefore God, your God, has set you above your companions by anointing you with the oil of joy.
The Bible, Hebrews 1:9

Jesus Christ is the same yesterday and today and forever.
The Bible, Hebrews 13:8

The soul stands at salute when he passes by.
Author unknown

Come, my Way, my Truth, my Life :
Such a Way, as gives us breath :
Such a Truth, as ends all strife :
And such a Life as killeth death.
Author unknown

In the Scriptures there is a portrait of God, but in Christ there is God himself. A coin bears the image of Caesar, but Caesar's son is his own lively resemblance. Christ is the living Bible.
Author unknown

All that I am I owe to Jesus Christ,

revealed to me in His divine Book.
Author unknown

No Jesus, No Peace. Know Jesus, Know Peace!
Author unknown

Our mind is where our pleasure is, our heart is where our treasure is, our love is where our life is, but all these, our pleasure, treasure, and life, are reposed in Jesus Christ.
Thomas Adams

When we speak about wisdom, we are speaking about Christ. When we speak about virtue, we are speaking about Christ. When we speak about justice, we are speaking about Christ. When we speak about peace, we are speaking about Christ. When we speak about truth and life and redemption, we are speaking about Christ.
Ambrose

Jesus Christ is the outstanding personality of our time. Every act and word of Jesus has value for us. He became the Light of the world. Why shouldn't I, a Jew, be proud of that?
Sholem Asch, Jewish novelist

What is offered to man's apprehension in any specific revelation of Christ is the living God himself.
Karl Barth

Christ as attested to us in Holy Scripture is the one Word of God whom we must hear and whom we must trust and obey in life and in death.
Karl Barth

Christ's statements are either cosmic or comic.
John Blanchard

Nothing is more clear than that Christ cannot be explained by any humanistic system. He does not fit into any theory of natural evolution, for in that case the perfect flower of humanity should have appeared at the end of human history and not in the middle of it.
Loraine Boettner

Christ is a jewel more worth than a thousand worlds, as all know who have him. Get him, and get all; miss him and miss all.
Thomas Brooks

He is a portion that exactly, and directly suits –
the condition of the soul,
the desires of the soul,
the necessities of the soul,
the wants of the soul,
the longings of the soul,
and the prayers of the soul.
The soul can crave nothing, nor wish for nothing, but what is to be found in Christ.
He is light to enlighten the soul,
wisdom to counsel the soul,
power to support the soul,
goodness to supply the soul,
mercy to pardon the soul,
beauty to delight the soul,
glory to ravish the soul,
and fullness to fill the soul.
Thomas Brooks

The rattle without the breast will not satisfy the child; the house without the husband will not satisfy the wife; the cabinet without the jewel will not satisfy the virgin; the world without Christ will not satisfy the soul.
Thomas Brooks

Jesus Christ is not revelation if he is recognized by nobody as the Christ, any more than he is redeemer if there is nobody whom he redeems.
E. Brunner

If ever man was God or God man, Jesus Christ was both.
Lord Byron

If we seek salvation, we are taught by the very name of Jesus that it is "of him" [1 Corinthians 1:30]. If we seek any other gifts of the Spirit, they will be found in his anointing. If we seek strength, it lies in his dominion; if purity, in his conception; if gentleness, it appears in his birth. For by his birth he was made like us in all respects [Hebrews 2:17] that he might learn to feel our pain [cf. Hebrews 5:2]. If we seek redemption, it lies in his passion; if acquittal, in his condemnation; if remission of the curse, in his cross [Galatians 3:13]; if satisfaction, in his sacrifice; if purification, in his blood; if reconciliation, in his descent into hell; if mortification of the flesh, in his tomb; if newness of life, in his resurrection; if immortality, in the same; if inheritance of the Heavenly Kingdom, in his entrance into heaven; if protection, if security, if abundant supply of all blessings, in his Kingdom; if untroubled expectation of judgment, in the power given to him to judge. In short, since rich store of every kind of good abounds in him, let us drink our fill from this fountain, and from no other.

John Calvin

[Jesus is] our divinest symbol. Higher has the human thought not yet reached. A symbol of quite perennial, infinite character; whose significance will ever demand to be anew inquired into, and anew made manifest.

Thomas Carlyle

I've always considered Christ to be one of the greatest revolutionaries in the history of humanity.

F. Castro

Today Jesus Christ is being dispatched as the Figurehead of a Religion, a mere example. He is that, but he is infinitely more; He is salvation itself, He is the Gospel of God.

Oswald Chambers

Christ has transformed all our sunsets into dawn.

Clement of Alexandria

The soul is exceedingly ravished when it first looks on the beauty of Christ. It is

never weary of Him.

Jonathan Edwards

Christ is like a river. A river is continually flowing, there are fresh supplies of water coming from the fountain-head continually, so that a man may live by it, and be supplied with water all his life. So Christ is an ever-flowing fountain; he is continually supplying his people, and the fountain is not spent. They who live upon Christ, may have fresh supplies from him to all eternity; they may have an increase of blessedness that is new, and new still, and which never will come to an end.

Jonathan Edwards

The determining factor of my existence is no longer my past. It is Christ's past.

Sinclair Ferguson

Christ is the very essence of all delights and pleasures, the very soul and substance of them. As all the rivers are gathered into the ocean, which is the meeting-place of all the waters in the world, so Christ is that ocean in which all true delights and pleasures meet.

John Flavel

The lines of all have, in some degree, been changed by his [Christ's] presence, his actions and the word spoken by his divine voice. I believe that he belongs not solely to Christianity, but to the entire world.

Gandhi

We must either worship Christ as God or despise or pity him as man.

John H. Gerstner

To the artist he is the one altogether lovely. To the educator he is the master teacher. To the philosopher he is the wisdom of God. To the lonely he is a brother; to the sorrowful, a comforter; to the bereaved, the resurrection and the life. And to the sinner he is the Lamb of God who takes away the sin of the world.

John H. Gerstner

Jesus was God spelling himself out in language humanity could understand.
S.D. Gordon

Christ is the pure Seal of the Father and His most unerring Impress.
Gregory the Theologian

Jesus Christ turns life right-side-up, and heaven outside-in.
Carl F. H. Henry

Christ is our temple, in whom by faith all believers meet.
Matthew Henry

Come, my Way, my Truth, my Life!
Such a Way as gives us breath,
Such a Truth as ends all strife,
Such a Life as killeth Death.
George Herbert

Christ is a substitute for everything, but nothing is a substitute for Christ.
H.A. Ironside

I hold the precepts of Jesus as delivered by Himself, to be the most pure, benevolent and sublime which have ever been preached to man...
Thomas Jefferson

The whole of Christ's life was a continual teaching: his silences, his miracles, his gestures, his prayer, his love for people, his special affection for the little and the poor, his acceptance of the total sacrifice on the cross for the redemption of the world, and his Resurrection are the actualization of the word and the fulfilment of Revelation.
John Paul II

As the centuries pass the evidence is accumulating that, measured by His effect on history, Jesus is the most influential life ever lived on this planet.
Kenneth Scott Latourette

Look for yourself and you will find in the long run only hatred, loneliness, despair, rage, ruin and decay. But look for Christ

and you will find Him, and with Him everything else thrown in.
C.S. Lewis

He came in complete human form to meet a universal need in a way that is adequate for all times and places and is without parallel or substitute.
H.D. Lewis

When Jesus Christ utters a word, He opens His mouth so wide that it embraces all heaven and earth, even though that word be but in a whisper.
Martin Luther

Either sin is with you, lying on your shoulders, or it is lying on Christ, the Lamb of God. Now if it is lying on your back, you are lost; but if it is resting on Christ, you are free, and you will be saved. Now choose what you want.
Martin Luther

In his life Christ is an example, showing us how to live;
In his death he is a sacrifice, satisfying for our sins;
In his resurrection, a conqueror;
In his ascension, a king;
In his intercession, a high priest.
Martin Luther

Christ alone has succeeded in so raising the mind of man towards the unseen that it become insensible to the barriers of time and space.
Napoleon

The Son is a concise demonstration and easy setting forth of the Father's Nature.
Gregory of Nazianzus

The Word is stronger that all the evils in the soul. The Word is the healing power who dwells in him.
Origen

The most excellent study of expanding the soul, is the science of Christ, and him crucified, and the knowledge of the

Godhead in the glorious Trinity.
J.I. Packer

I reject the misconception popular in certain pseudo-religious circles that Jesus was passionless, mild, weak. How pathetic and how utterly unsupported by the earliest historical records, which paint vivid pictures of Jesus' emotions.
Luis Palau

Of all the great sages and prophets throughout world history, Jesus alone claimed to be God-become-man.
Luis Palau

Only a Christ could have conceived a Christ.
Joseph Parker

After reading the doctrines of Plato, Socrates or Aristotle, we feel the specific difference between their words and Christ's is the difference between an inquiry and a revelation.
Joseph Parker

Not only do we not know God except through Jesus Christ; We do not even know ourselves except through Jesus Christ.
Blaise Pascal

Jesus Christ is a God whom we approach without pride, and before whom we humble ourselves without despair.
Blaise Pascal

Since He looked upon me my heart is not my own. He hath run away to heaven with it.
Samuel Rutherford.

Don't be fearful about the journey ahead; don't worry about where you are going or how you are going to get there. If you believe in the first person of the Trinity, God the Father, also believe in the Second Person of the Trinity, the One who came as the Light of the World, not only to die for people, but to light the way… This One, Jesus Christ, is Himself the Light and will guide your footsteps along the way.
Edith Schaeffer

The search for the historical Jesus has been the greatest achievement of German theology and one of the most significant events in the whole mental and spiritual life of humanity.
Albert Schweitzer

It is not Jesus as historically known, but Jesus as spiritually risen within men, who is significant for our time and can help it. Not the historical Jesus, but the spirit which goes forth from Him and in the spirits of men strives for new influence and rule, is that which overcomes the world.
Albert Schweitzer

Jesus means something to our world because a mighty spiritual force streams forth from him and flows through our being also. This fact can neither be shaken nor confirmed by any historical discovery. It is the solid foundation of Christianity.
Albert Schweitzer

The whole Christ seeks after each sinner, and when the Lord finds it, he gives himself to that one soul as if he had but that one soul to bless. How my heart admires the concentration of all the Godhead and humanity of Christ in his search after each sheep of his flock.
C.H. Spurgeon

Remember, sinner, it is not *your hold* of Christ that saves you – it is Christ.
C.H. Spurgeon

The Son of God alone is both God and man.
Symeon the New Theologian

He is life (Jn. 11:25) and lifegiver, truth (Jn. 14:6), righteousness, and sanctification (1 Cor. 1:30), simple, not compounded, good, all goodness, and above all goodness.
Symeon the New Theologian

Christus, from whom they got their name, had been executed by sentence of the procurator Pontius Pilate, when Tiberius

was emperor.
Cornelius Tacitus

He understands everything.
Helmut Thielicke

He is the greatest influence in the world today. There is ... a fifth Gospel being written – the work of Jesus Christ in the hearts and lives of men and nations.
W.H. Griffith Thomas

Christ's words are of permanent value because of His person; they endure because He endures.
W.H. Griffith Thomas

Jesus Christ will still be important for mankind two or three thousand years hence.
Arnold Toynbee

Is it any wonder that to this day this Galilean is too much for our small hearts?
H.G. Wells

I know Thee, Savior, Who Thou art:
Jesus, the feeble sinner's friend!
Nor wilt Thou with the night depart,
But stay and love me to the end.
Thy mercies never shall remove;
Thy nature and Thy name is Love.
Charles Wesley

Jesus was God and man in one person, that God and man might be happy together again.
George Whitefield

Christ, Claims of
He said that he was in existence before Abraham and that he was "lord" of the Sabbath; he claimed to forgive sins; he continually identified himself, in his work, his person and his glory, with the one he termed his heavenly Father; he accepted men's worship; and he said that he was to be the judge of men at the last day, and that their eternal destiny would depend on their attitude to him.
J.N.D. Anderson

No founder of any religion has dared to claim for himself one fraction of the assertions made by the Lord Jesus Christ about himself.
Henry J. Heydt

Christ, death of
But now in Christ Jesus you who once were far away have been brought near through the blood of Christ.
The Bible, Ephesians 2:13

To put the matter at its simplest, Jesus Christ came to make bad men good.
James Denney

We are told that Christ was killed for us, that His death has washed out our sins, and that by dying He disabled death itself. That is the formula. That is Christianity. That is what has to be believed.
C.S. Lewis

One drop of Christ's blood is worth more than heaven and earth.
Martin Luther

Take this to heart and doubt not that you are the one who killed Christ. Your sins certainly did, and when you see the nails driven through his hands, be sure that you are pondering, and when the thorns pierce his brow, know that they are your evil thoughts.
Martin Luther

If Socrates died like a philosopher, Jesus Christ died like a God.
Jean Jacques Rousseau

Christ, having sacrificed himself once, is to eternity a certain and valid sacrifice for the sins of all faithful.
Zwingli, Huldrych

Christ, Divinity
But Jesus remained silent and gave no answer. Again the high priest asked him, "Are you the Christ, the Son of the Blessed One?"
"I am," said Jesus. "And you will see the Son of Man sitting at the right hand of the

Mighty One and coming on the clouds of heaven."
The Bible, Mark 14:61-62

I and the Father are one.
The Bible, John 10:30

He [Jesus] is the image of the invisible God, the firstborn over all creation. For by him all things were created: things in heaven and on earth, visible and invisible, whether thrones or powers or rulers or authorities; all things were created by him and for him. He is before all things, and in him all things hold together. And he is the head of the body, the church; he is the beginning and the firstborn from among the dead, so that in everything he might have the supremacy. For God was pleased to have all his fullness dwell in him, and through him to reconcile to himself all things, whether things on earth or things in heaven, by making peace through his blood, shed on the cross.
The Bible, Colossians 1:15-20

For in Christ all the fullness of the Deity lives in bodily form ...
The Bible, Colossians 2:9

Behold, I am coming soon! My reward is with me, and I will give to everyone according to what he has done. I am the Alpha and the Omega, the First and the Last, the Beginning and the End.
The Bible, Revelation 22:12-13

God is best known in Christ; the sun is not seen but by the light of the sun.
William Bridge

[In the person of Christ] a man has not become God; God has become man.
Cyril of Alexandria

It pleases the Father that all fullness should be in Christ; therefore there is nothing but emptiness anywhere else.
W. Gadsby

If ever the Divine appeared on earth, it was in the person of Christ.
Johann Wolfgang von Goethe

For I have shown from the Scriptures, that no one of the sons of Adam is as to everything, and absolutely, called God, or named Lord. But that He is Himself in His own right, beyond all men who ever lived, God, and Lord, and King Eternal, and the Incarnate Word, proclaimed by all the prophets, the apostles, and by the Spirit Himself, may be seen by all who have attained to even a small portion of the truth. Now, the Scriptures would not have testified these things of Him, if, like others, He had been a mere man.
Irenaeus

Christians believe that Jesus Christ is the Son of God because He said so.
C.S. Lewis

Anything that one imagines of God apart from Christ is only useless thinking and vain idolatry.
Martin Luther

We may not like the Jesus of the historical documents; but like him or not, we meet him there as a divine being on whom our personal destiny depends.
John Warwick Montgomery

Although Christ was God, he took flesh; and having been made man, he remained what he was, God.
Origen

Jesus Christ's claim of divinity is the most serious claim anyone ever made. Everything about Christianity hinges on His incarnation, crucifixion, and resurrection. That's what Christmas, Good Friday, and Easter are all about.
Luis Palau

The divinity of Jesus is not a dispensable extra that has no significance for our salvation. On the contrary, our salvation depends on it. We can be saved only by

God Himself.
K. Runia

So close was Christ's connection with God
that he equated a man's attitude to himself
with the man's attitude to God.
John Stott

Christ, Early witnesses to

At this time there was a wise man who was
called Jesus. And his conduct was good
and he was known to be virtuous. And
many people from among the Jews and
other nations became his disciples. Pilate
condemned him to be crucified and to die.
And those who had become his disciples
did not abandon his discipleship. They
reported that he had appeared to them
three days after his crucifixion and that he
was alive. Accordingly he was perhaps the
Messiah concerning whom the prophets
have recounted wonders.
*Flavius Josephus, Epitome from the Universal
History of Agapius*

He [Annas the Younger] convened a
judicial session of the Sanhedrin and
brought before it the brother of Jesus the
so-called Christ – James by name – and
some others, whom he charged with
breaking the law and handed over to be
stoned to death.
Flavius Josephus, Antiquities

It is my rule, Sire, to refer to you in
matters where I am uncertain. For who can
better direct my hesitation or instruct my
ignorance? I was never present at any trial
of Christians; therefore I do not know
what are the customary penalties or
investigations, and what limits are
observed. I have hesitated a great deal on
the question whether there should be any
distinction of ages; whether the weak
should have the same treatment as the
most robust; whether those who recant
should be pardoned, or whether a man
who has ever been a Christian should gain
nothing by ceasing to be such; whether the
name itself, even if innocent of crime,
should be punished, or only the crimes

attaching to that name. Meanwhile, this is
the course that I have adopted in the case
of those brought before me as Christians. I
ask them if they are Christians. If they
admit it I repeat the question a second and
a third time, threatening capital
punishment; if they persist I sentence them
to death ... All who denied that they were
or had been Christians I considered should
be discharged, because they called upon
the gods at my dictation and did reverence,
with incense and wine, to your image ...
and especially because they cursed Christ, a
thing which, it is said, genuine Christians
cannot be induced to do. Others named by
the informer first said they were Christians
and then denied it, declaring that they had
been but were no longer, some having
recanted three years or more before and
one or two as long ago as twenty years.
They all worshiped your image and the
statues of the gods and cursed Christ. But
they declared that the sum of their guilt or
error had amounted only to this, that on
an appointed day they had been
accustomed to meet before daybreak, and
to recite a hymn antiphonally to Christ, as
to a god, and to bind themselves by an
oath, not for the commission of any crime
but to abstain from theft, robbery, adultery
and breach of faith and not to deny a
deposit when it was claimed. After the
conclusion of this ceremony it was their
custom to depart and meet again to take
food; but it was ordinary and harmless
food, and they had ceased this practice
after my edict in which, in accordance
with your orders, I had forbidden secret
societies. I thought it the more necessary,
therefore, to find out what truth there was
in this by applying torture to two
maidservants, who were called deaconesses.
But I found nothing but a depraved and
extravagant superstition, and I therefore
postponed my examination and had
recourse to you for consultation.
Pliny the Younger, c. 62–c. 114, Letters: to Trajan

What advantage did the Athenians gain
from putting Socrates to death? Famine and
plague came upon them as a judgment for

their crime. What advantage did the men of Samos gain from burning Pythagoras? In a moment their land was covered with sand. What advantage did the Jews gain from executing their wise king? It was just after that that their kingdom was abolished. God justly avenged these three wise men: the Athenians died of hunger; the Samians were overwhelmed by the sea; the Jews, ruined and driven from their land, live in complete dispersion. But Socrates did not die for good; he lived on in the teaching of Plato. Pythagoras did not die for good; he lived on in the statue of Hera. Nor did the wise king die for good; he lived on in the teaching which he had given.
Mara bar Serapion, Letter to His Son Serapion

Punishment was inflicted on the Christians, a body of people addicted to a novel and mischievous superstition.
Gaius Suetonius, Lives of the Twelve Caesars

He expelled the Jews from Rome, on account of riots in which they were constantly indulging, at the instigation of Chrestus.
Gaius Suetonius, Lives of the Twelve Caesars

But neither the aid of men, nor the emperor's bounty, nor propitiatory offerings to the gods, could remove the grim suspicion that the fire had been started by Nero's order. To put an end to this rumor, he shifted the charge on to others, and inflicted the most cruel tortures upon a group of people detested for their abominations, and popularly known as "Christians." Their name came from one Christus, who was put to death in the principate of Tiberius by the Procurator Pontius Pilate. Though checked for a time, the destructive superstition broke out again, not in Judaea only, where its mischief began, but even in Rome, where every abominable and shameful iniquity, from all the world, pours in and finds a welcome.
Cornelius Tacitus, c. 55–120, Annals

On the eve of Passover Yeshua was hanged. For forty days before the execution a herald went forth and cried, "He is going to be stoned because he has practiced sorcery and enticed Israel to apostasy. Anyone who can say anything in his favor, let him come forward and plead on his behalf." But since nothing was brought forward in his favor he was hanged on the eve of Passover
Babylonian Talmud

The method you have pursued, my dear Pliny, in sifting the cases of those denounced to you as Christians is extremely proper. It is not possible to lay down any general rule which can be applied as the fixed standard in all cases of this nature. No search should be made for these people; when they are denounced and found guilty they must be punished; with the restriction, however, that when the party denies himself to be a Christian, and shall give proof that he is not, that is by adoring our gods, he shall be pardoned on the ground of repentance, even though he may have formerly incurred suspicion. Information without the accuser's name subscribed must not be admitted in evidence against anyone, as it is introducing a very dangerous precedent, and by no means agreeable to the spirit of the age.
Trajan's Reply to letter of Pliny the Younger

Christ, Glorification of

For God to adorn His Son with all this glory in His ascension, thus to make Him ride conqueror up into the clouds, thus to go up with sound of trumpet, with shout of angels and with songs of praises, and let me add, to be accompanied also with those that rose from the dead after His resurrection, who were the very price of His blood – this does greatly demonstrate that Jesus Christ, by what he has done, has paid a full price to God for the souls of sinners, and obtained eternal redemption for them:
HE HAD NOT ELSE RODE THUS TRIUMPH TO HEAVEN.
John Bunyan

Christ, Glorying in

Let us serve Him faithfully as our Master. Let us obey Him loyally as our King. Let us study His teachings as our Prophet. Let us walk diligently after Him as our Example. Let us look anxiously for Him as our coming Redeemer of body as well as soul. But above all let us prize Him as our Sacrifice, and rest our whole weight on His death as atonement for sin. Let His blood be more precious in our eyes every year we live. Whatever else we glory in about Christ, let us glory above all things in His cross.
J.C. Ryle

Christ, Existence of

No serious scholar has ventured to postulate the non-historicity of Jesus.
Otto Betz

Whatever else may be thought of the evidence from early Jewish and Gentile writers it does at least establish, for those who refuse the witness of Christian writings, the historical character of Jesus himself.
F.F. Bruce

Some writers may toy with the fancy of a "Christ-myth," but they do not do so on the ground of historical evidence. The historicity of Christ is as axiomatic for an unbiased historian as the historicity of Julius Caesar. It is not historians who propagate the "Christ-myth" theories.
F.F. Bruce

It would be a dangerous error to imagine that the characteristics of an historical religion would be maintained if the Christ of the theologians were divorced from the Jesus of history.
Herbert Butterfield

That a few simple men should in one generation have invented so powerful and appealing a personality, so lofty an ethic, and so inspiring a vision of human brotherhood, would be a miracle far more incredible than any recorded in the Gospels.
Will Durant

The origin of a great religious and moral reform is inexplicable without the personal existence of a great reformer.
James Frazer, non-Christian writer

The doubts which have been cast on the historical reality of Jesus are, in my judgment, unworthy of serious attention.
James Frazer, non-Christian writer

Once disprove the historicity of Jesus Christ, and Christianity will collapse like a pack of cards.
Michael Green

It takes a Newton to forge a Newton. What man could have fabricated a Jesus? None but a Jesus.
Theodore Parker

The reason why I take my stand within the Christian community lies in certain events which took place in Palestine nearly two thousand years ago.
Dr John Polkinghorne, theoretical physicist

The person of Christ is to me the greatest and surest of all facts.
Philip Schaff

Christ, Honoring

Moreover, the Father judges no one, but has entrusted all judgment to the Son, that all may honor the Son just as they honor the Father. He who does not honor the Son does not honor the Father, who sent him.
The Bible, John 5:22-23

Christ, Humanity and divinity of

Christ was a complete man.
Augustine of Hippo

Jesus Christ is God in the form of man; as completely God as if he were not man; as completely man as if he were not God.
A.J.F. Behrends

Jesus Christ, the condescension of divinity, and the exaltation of humanity.
Phillips Brooks

Christ was wearied (Jn 4:6), hungry (Mt 4:2) and required sleep (Mt 8:24). Just as we say that the flesh, assumed in the incarnation, became his very own, in the same way the weakness of the flesh became his very own in an economic appropriation to the terms of the unification. So he is "made like his brethren in all things except sin alone" (Heb. 2:17).
Cyril of Alexandria

Christ's humanity is the great hem of the garment, through which we can touch his Godhead.
Richard Glover

We affirm that faith in the true humanity of Christ is essential to faith in the Gospel.
The gospel of Jesus Christ: An evangelical celebration

We affirm that Jesus Christ is God incarnate (John 1:14). The virgin-born descendant of David (Rom. 1:3), he had a true human nature, was subject to the Law of God (Gal. 4:5), and was like us at all points, except without sin (Heb. 2:17, 7:26–28).
The gospel of Jesus Christ: An evangelical celebration

He has himself gone through the whole of human experience from trivial irritations of family life and the cramping restrictions of hard work and lack of money to the worst horrors of pain and humiliation, defeat, despair and death. When he was a man, he played the man. He was born in poverty and died in disgrace and thought it well worthwhile.
Dorothy Sayers

Remember, Christ was not a deified man, neither was he a humanized God. He was perfectly God and at the same time perfectly man.
C.H. Spurgeon

Christ was not half a God and half a man; he was perfectly God and perfectly man.
James Stalker

Christ, In

Therefore, if anyone is in Christ, he is a new creation; the old has gone, the new has come!
The Bible, 2 Corinthians 5:17

To be in Christ is redemption, but for Christ to be in you is sanctification.
To be in Christ is to be fit for heaven, but for Christ to be in you is to be fit for earth.
Author unknown

When Christ reveals Himself there is satisfaction in the slenderest portion, and without Christ there is emptiness in the greatest fulness.
Alexander Grosse

All God's love and the fruits of it come to us as we are in Christ, and are one with him. Then in our passage to God again we must return all, and do all, to God in Christ.
Richard Sibbes

Christ, Influence of
One Solitary Life
He was born in an obscure village, the child of a peasant woman. He worked in a carpentry shop until he was thirty, and then for three years he was an itinerant preacher. When the tide of popular opinion turned against him, his friends ran away. He was turned over to his enemies. He was tried and convicted. He was nailed upon a cross between two thieves. When he was dead, he was laid in a borrowed grave. He never wrote a book. He never held an office. He never owned a home. He never went to college. He never traveled more than two hundred miles from the place where he was born. He never did one of the things that usually accompanies greatness. Yet all the armies that ever marched, and all the governments that ever sat, and all the kings that ever reigned, have not affected life upon this earth as powerfully as has that One Solitary Life.
Author unknown

Christ came when all things were growing old. He made them new.
Augustine of Hippo

After 1900 years, Jesus Christ still counts for more in human life than any other man that ever lived.
Dean Inge

The simple record of three short years of active life has done more to regenerate and to soften mankind, than all the disquisitions of philosophers and than all the exhortations of moralists.
W.E.H. Lecky

Jesus of Nazareth, without money and arms, conquered more millions than Alexander, Caesar, Mahomet, and Napoleon.
Philip Schaff

Christ, Kingship of

Latimer! Latimer! Latimer! Be careful what you say. Henry the king is here. [Pause] Latimer! Latimer! Latimer! Be careful what you say. The King of kings is here.
Hugh Latimer, preaching before Henry VIII

Christ, Knowing

I have known him all my life, and one day I learned his name.
Young Chinese girl

Christ, Lordship of

Christ is not valued at all, unless he is valued above all.
Augustine of Hippo

There is not an inch of any sphere of life over which Jesus Christ does not say, "Mine."
Abraham Kuyper

For every look at self take ten looks at Christ.
Robert Murray M'Cheyne

The seed is choked in our souls whenever Christ is not our all in all.
C.H. Spurgeon

Many are willing that Christ should be something, but few will consent that Christ should be everything.
Alexander Moody Stuart

Christ, Love of

I am nothing, I have nothing. I desire nothing but the love of Jesus in Jerusalem.
Walter Hilton

He loved us not because were lovable, but because He is Love.
C.S. Lewis

The love of Christ is like the blue sky, into which you may see clearly, but the real vastness of which you cannot measure.
Robert Murray McCheyne

Live on Christ's love while ye are here, and all the way.
Samuel Rutherford

Christ loved you before you loved him. He loved you when there was nothing good in you.
  He loved you though you insulted him, though you despised him and rebelled against him.
  He has loved you right on, and never ceased to love you.
  He has loved you in your backslidings and loved you out of them.
  He has loved you in your sins, in your wickedness and folly.
  His loving heart was still eternally the same, and he shed his heart's blood to prove his love for you.
  He has given you what you need on earth, and provided for you an habitation in heaven.
  Now, Christian, your religion claims from you, that you should love others, as your Master loved you. How can you imitate him, unless you love too?
  With you "un"kindness should be a strange anomaly. It is a gross contradiction to the spirit of your religion, and if you do not love your neighbor, I cannot see how you can be a true follower of the Lord Jesus.
C.H. Spurgeon

I believe that saying which is written – "As the Father has loved me, even so have I

loved you," and a higher degree of love we cannot imagine.
C.H. Spurgeon

Behold, what manner of love is this, that Christ should be arraigned and we adorned, that the curse should be laid on His head and the crown set on ours.
Thomas Watson

Christ, Need for
Miss Christ and you miss all.
Thomas Brooks

To the hurting, he is the great Physician.
To the confused, he is the Light.
To the lost, he is the Way.
To the hungry, he is the Bread of Life.
To the thirsty, he is the Water of Life.
To the broken, he is the Balm in Gilead.
Calvin Miller

I have a great need for Christ; I have a great Christ for my need.
C.H. Spurgeon

Christ, Person of
They replied, "You are the eschatological manifestation of the ground of our being, the kerygma of which we find the ultimate meaning in our inter-personal relationships."
Author unknown

Jesus is either God, or he is not good.
Anselm

He became what we are that he might make us what he is.
Athanasius of Alexandria

Brethren, we ought so to think of Jesus Christ as of God.
2 Clement, the oldest known sermon after the New Testament sermons.

We believe that Christ is God not because he mysteriously possessed a divine nature united to a human, but because as he is as man we find God in him, and God finds us through him.
A.E. Garvie

Pythagoras, Epicurus, Socrates, Plato, these are the torches of the world; Christ is the light of day.
Victor Hugo

In Christ Jesus heaven meets earth and earth ascends to heaven.
Henry Law

The only Christ for whom there is a shred of evidence is a miraculous figure making stupendous claims.
C.S. Lewis

Take hold of Jesus as a man and you will discover that he is God.
Martin Luther

Is it not a shame that we are always afraid of Christ, whereas there was never in heaven or earth a more loving, familiar, or milder man, in words, works and demeanor, especially towards the poor, sorrowful and tormented consciences?
Martin Luther

Jesus was man in guise, not in disguise.
Handley C.G. Moule

I know men; and I tell you that Jesus Christ is not a man.
Napoleon Bonaparte

The impression of Jesus which the Gospels give is not so much one of deity reduced as of divine capacities restrained.
J.I. Packer

Christ's character was more wonderful than the greatest miracle.
Alfred Tennyson

Christ, Reactions to
By a man's reaction to Jesus Christ, that man stands revealed.
William Barclay

It is not that Christians are narrow-minded or uncharitable about other faiths. But if Jesus is indeed, as the resurrection asserts, God himself come to our rescue, then to

reject him, or even to neglect him, is ultimate folly.
Michael Green

You can shut Him up for a fool, you can spit at Him and kill Him as a demon, or you can fall at his feet and call Him Lord and God.
C.S. Lewis

Christ, Second coming of
We must never speak to simple, excitable people about "the Day" without emphasizing again and again the utter impossibility of prediction.
C. S. Lewis

Christ, Testimony to
I confess Jesus Christ, the Son of God, with my whole being. Those whom you call gods are idols; they are made by hands.
Alban, first British martyr, when asked to offer sacrifices to the gods Jupiter and Apollo.

I believe there is nothing lovelier, deeper, more sympathetic and more perfect than the Savior; I say to myself with jealous love that not only is there no one else like him, but that there could be no one.
Fyodor Dostoevsky

I tell the Hindus that their lives will be imperfect if they do not also study reverently the teaching of Jesus.
Gandhi

I have found happiness and the fulfilment of all I have desired in Jesus Christ.
J.C. Martin, baseball player

Jesus was the greatest religious genius that ever lived. His beauty is eternal and his reign will never end. He is in every respect unique and nothing can be compared with him.
Ernest Renan

Christ is my Savior. He is my life. He is everything to me in heaven and earth.
Sadhu Sundar Singh

Christ and salvation
Christ had neither money, nor riches, nor earthly kingdom, for he gave the same to kings and princes. But he reserved one thing peculiarly to himself, which no human creature or angel could do – namely, to conquer sin and death, the devil and hell, and in the midst of death to deliver and save those that through his Word believe in him.
Martin Luther

Christ is the only way to salvation.
Zwingli, Huldrych

Christ and society
Jesus has also been accused of being ineffective, in a political sense, and of having done little to right social injustices. But it is clear from the Sermon on the Mount that he was deeply concerned that his disciples should be both the "salt" and the "light" of secular society; he endorsed the authority of those Old Testament prophets who vehemently rebuked social injustice; and he consistently identified himself with the poor and weak, with social outcasts and those who were regarded as morally disreputable … It is true that he did not lead a rebellion against Rome, seek to free slaves, or introduce a social revolution. He had come for a particular purpose, which was far more important than any of these things – and from that purpose nothing could or did deflect him.
J.N.D. Anderson

Christ and wisdom
My purpose is that they may be encouraged in heart and united in love, so that they may have the full riches of complete understanding, in order that they may know the mystery of God, namely, Christ, in whom are hidden all the treasures of wisdom and knowledge.
The Bible, Colossians 2:2-3

Christ as craftsman
Jesus himself did not come from the proletariat of day-laborers and landless tenants, but from the middle class of Galilee, the skilled workers. Like his [foster] father, he was an artisan, a *tekton*, a Greek

word which means mason, carpenter, cartwright and joiner all rolled into one.
Professor Martin Hengel

Christ as High Priest

Therefore, since we have a great high priest who has gone through the heavens, Jesus the Son of God, let us hold firmly to the faith we profess. For we do not have a high priest who is unable to sympathize with our weaknesses, but we have one who has been tempted in every way, just as we are – yet was without sin. Let us then approach the throne of grace with confidence, so that we may receive mercy and find grace to help us in our time of need.
The Bible, Hebrews 4:14-16

If I could hear Christ praying for me in the next room, I would not fear a million enemies. Yet distance makes no difference. He is praying for me.
Robert Murray M'Cheyne

Christ as Morning Star

Christ is the Morning Star who, when the night of this world is past brings to his saints the promise of the light of life and opens everlasting day.
Venerable Beds

Christ as Sin-bearer

Let the fact of what our Lord suffered for you grip you, and you will never again be the same.
Oliver B. Greene

He [Christ, our Sin-bearer] is not like Moses who only shows sin, but rather like Aaron who bears sin.
Martin Luther

Jesus became the greatest liar, perjurer, thief, adulterer and murderer that mankind has ever known – not because he committed these sins but because he was actually made sin for us.
Martin Luther

Christ as Substitute

The good news is that sin has been dealt with; that Jesus has suffered its penalty for us as our representative, so that we might never have to suffer it; and that therefore all who believe in him can look forward to heaven. The only true gospel is of the one mediator (1 Tim. 2:5-6), who gave himself for us.
J.M. Boice

If Christ is not the Substitute, He is nothing to the sinner. If He did not die as the Sin-bearer, He has died in vain. Let us not be deceived on this point nor misled by those who, when they announce Christ as the Deliverer, think they have preached the gospel. If I throw a rope to a drowning man, I am a deliverer. But is Christ no more than that? If I cast myself into the sea and risk myself to save another, I am a deliverer. But is Christ no more? Did He risk His life? The very essence of Christ's deliverance is THE SUBSTITUTION OF HIMSELF FOR US – HIS LIFE FOR OURS! He did not come to risk His life; He came to die! He did not redeem us by a little loss, a little sacrifice, a little labor, a little suffering; "He redeemed us to God by His blood" (1 Peter 1:18,19). He gave all He had, even His life, for us. This is the kind of deliverance that awakens the happy song, "To Him that loved us, and washed us from our sins in his own blood" (Rev. 1:5).
Horatius Bonar

Christ is a substitute for everything, but nothing is a substitute for Christ.
H.A. Ironside

Christ as the way to God

Jesus is not a good way to heaven, He's the only way.
Author unknown

Jesus does not give recipes that show the way to God as other teachers of religion do. He is himself the way.
Karl Barth

The way to Jesus is not by Cambridge and Oxford, Glasgow, Edinburgh, London, Princeton, Harvard, Yale, Socrates, Plato,

Shakespeare or the poets. It is over an old-fashioned hill called Calvary.
Gipsy Smith

Christ in the Bible

Concerning this salvation, the prophets, who spoke of the grace that was to come to you, searched intently and with the greatest care, trying to find out the time and circumstances to which the Spirit of Christ in them was pointing when he predicted the sufferings of Christ and the glories that would follow.
The Bible, 1 Peter 1:10-11

[Jesus said,] "Did not the Christ have to suffer these things and then enter his glory?" And beginning with Moses and all the Prophets, he explained to them what was said in all the Scriptures concerning himself.
The Bible, Luke 24:26-27

Old Testament
IN Genesis He is the Seed of the woman
IN Exodus the Lamb for sinners slain
IN Leviticus our High Priest
IN Numbers the Star of Jacob
IN Deuteronomy the Prophet like unto Moses and the Great Rock
IN Joshua the Captain of the Lord of Hosts
IN Judges the Messenger of Jehovah
IN Ruth our Kinsman Redeemer and Faithful Bridegroom
IN 1 Samuel He is seen as the Great Judge
IN 2 Samuel He is the Princely King
IN 1 Kings as David's choice
IN 2 Kings as the Holiest of all
IN 1 Chronicles as the King by birth
IN 2 Chronicles as King by judgment
IN Ezra He is seen as Lord of heaven and earth
IN Nehemiah as the Builder
IN Esther our Mordecai
IN Job our Daysman and our risen returning Redeemer
IN Psalms the Son of God and the Good Shepherd
IN Proverbs our Wisdom
IN Ecclesiastes as the One Above the Sun
IN the Song of Solomon the Great Church

Lover, the One Altogether Lovely and the Chiefest among Ten Thousand
IN Isaiah He is the Suffering and Glorified Servant
IN Jeremiah the Lord Our Righteousness
IN Lamentations the Man of Sorrows
IN Ezekiel the Glorious God
IN Daniel the Smithing Stone and the Messiah
IN Hosea He is the Risen Son of God
IN Joel the Out-Pourer of the Spirit
IN Amos the Eternal Christ
IN Obadiah the Forgiving Christ
IN Jonah the Risen Prophet
IN Micah the Bethlehemite
IN Nahum He is the Bringer of Good Tidings
IN Habakkuk the Lord in His Holy Temple
IN Zephaniah the Merciful Christ
IN Haggai the Desire of All Nations
IN Zechariah the Branch
IN Malachi the Son of Righteousness with Healing in His Wings
New Testament
IN Matthew He is the King of the Jews
IN Mark the Servant
IN Luke the Perfect Son of Man
IN John the Son of God
IN Acts He is the Ascended Lord
IN Romans the Lord Our Righteousness
IN 1 Corinthians Our Resurrection
IN 2 Corinthians Our Comforter
IN Galatians the End of the Law
IN Ephesians the Head of the Church
IN Philippians the Supplier of Every Need
IN Colossians the Fullness of the Godhead
IN 1 Thessalonians He comes for His Church
IN 2 Thessalonians He comes with His Church
IN 1 Timothy He is the Mediator
IN 2 Timothy the Bestower of Crowns
IN Titus our Great God and Savior
IN Philemon the Prayer of Crowns
IN Hebrews the Rest of the Faith and Fulfiller of Types
IN James the Lord Drawing Nigh
IN 1 Peter the Vicarious Sufferer
IN 2 Peter the Lord of Glory
IN 1 John the Way

IN 2 John the Truth
IN 3 John the Life
IN Jude He is our Security
IN Revelation the Lion of the Tribe of Judah, the Lamb of God, the Bright and Morning Star, the King of Kings and Lord of Lords.
James Hayes

Christadelphians
Their official teaching

Baptism
A believing, repentant person receives forgiveness of sins by being baptized.
Frank G. Jannaway

True baptism removes past sins.
Frank G. Jannaway

The wonderful work of baptism is essential to salvation.
Frank G. Jannaway

Christ
There is no hint in the Old Testament that the Son of God was already existent or in any way active at that time.
Frank G. Jannaway

Jesus Christ, the Son of God, was first promised, and came into being only when he was born of the virgin Mary.
Frank G. Jannaway

And it was for that very reason – being a member of a sinful race – that the Lord Jesus himself needed salvation.
Frank G. Jannaway

Cross
The cross is the source of the forgiveness of sins. It is not a debt settled by due payment. It is not a substitutionary offering whereby someone is paid a price so that others might then go free.
Frank G. Jannaway

Immortality
It will surprise some readers to know that nowhere in Scripture are the words "immortal" and "soul" brought together. Immortality is God's own inherent nature, and His alone.
Frank G. Jannaway

Satan
The terms Satan and Devil are simply expressive of "sin in the flesh" in individual, social, and political manifestations.
Frank G. Jannaway

Christian
The disciples were called Christians first at Antioch.
The Bible, Acts 11:26

Definition of a Christian – Under New Management
Author unknown

What is the mark of a Christian? Faith working by charity.
Basil

Christian: one who believes that the New Testament is a divinely inspired book admirably suited to the spiritual needs of his neighbors.
Ambrose Bierce

Christian, n. One who follows the teachings of Christ insofar as they are not inconsistent with a life of sin.
Ambrose Bierce

He alone is a true Christian, whose soul and Mind has entered again into its original matrix, out of which the life of man has taken its origin, that is to say: The Eternal Word.
Jacob Boehme

Once I was a slave but now I am a son; once I was dead but now I am alive; once I was darkness but now I am light in the Lord; once I was a child of wrath, an

heir of hell, but now I am an heir of heaven; once I was Satan's bond-servant but now I am God's freeman; once I was under the spirit of bondage but now I am under the Spirit of adoption that seals up to me the remission of my sins, the justification of my person and the salvation of my soul.
Thomas Brooks

If a person is what the world calls an honest moral man, if he deals justly, and is now and then good-natured, and gives to the poor, and receives the sacrament once or twice a year, and is outwardly sober and honest – the world looks upon such a man as a true Christian.

There are many like this who go on in a round of duties and performances, who think they shall go to heaven. But if you examine them, you will find that though they have a "Christ in their heads," they have no "Christ in their hearts."
Jonathan Edwards

Even the sinning of the regenerate man differs essentially from that of the unregenerate man.
R.B. Kuiper

By following Jesus Christ, man in the world of today can truly humanly live, act, suffer, and die: in happiness and unhappiness, life and death, sustained by God and helpful to men.
Hans Küng

God looks at you as if you were a little Christ: Christ stands beside you to turn you into one.
C.S. Lewis

The Christian is a man who can be certain about the ultimate even when he is most uncertain about the immediate.
D. Martyn Lloyd-Jones

One characteristic of the Christian is always this: a profound distrust of self and a realization of the power of God.
M. Lloyd-Jones

I am persuaded, a broken and a contrite spirit, a conviction of our vileness and nothingness, connected with a cordial acceptance of Jesus as revealed in the Gospel, is the highest attainment we can reach in this life.
John Newton

I am not what I ought to be. I am not what I wish to be. I am not even what I hope to be. But by the cross of Christ, I am not what I was.
John Newton

Converted, renewed, and sanctified though he be, he is still compassed with infirmity!
J.C. Ryle

We care little for those who are orthodox Christians in creed, if it is clear they are heterodox in life.
C.H. Spurgeon

The distinguishing mark of a Christian is his confidence in the love of Christ, and the yielding of his affections to Christ in return.
C.H. Spurgeon

Though we as Christians are like Christ, having the first fruits of the Spirit, yet we are unlike Him, having the remainders of the flesh.
Thomas Watson

There are many who go on in a round of duties, a model of performances, that think they shall go to heaven; but if you examine them, though they have a Christ in their heads, they have no Christ in their hearts.
George Whitefield

That man is out of reach of harm in this life, who is sure of possessing heaven in the next. This is the portion of every believer.
Samuel Willard

No man is a true Christian who does not think constantly of how he can lift his brother, how he can assist his friend, how he can enlighten mankind, how he can

make virtue the rule of conduct in the circle in which he lives.
Woodrow Wilson

A Christian is a man who feels repentance on Sunday for what he did on Saturday and is going to do on Monday.
Thomas Ybarra

Christian life
See also: Christian, Christian living

Christian life

Martin Luther
1. *Prayer.* For this reason you should despair of your wisdom and reason; for with these you will acquire nothing, but by your arrogance cast yourself and others into the pit of hell as did Lucifer. Kneel down in your chamber and ask God in true humility and seriousness to grant you true wisdom.
2. *Meditation.* In the second place, you should meditate, and not only in your heart, but also outwardly, the oral Word and the expressed words that are written in the Book, which you must always consider and reconsider, and read and read over with diligent attention and reflection to see what the Holy Spirit means thereby. And take care that you do not become weary of it, thinking that you have read it sufficiently if you have read, heard, or said it once or twice and understand it perfectly. For in this way no great theologian is made, but they (who do not study) are like immature fruit, which falls down before it is half ripe. For this reason you see in this Psalm 119 that David is always boasting that he would speak, meditate, declare, sing, hear, read, day and night forever nothing else than the Word of God alone and the commandments of God. For God does not purpose to give you His Spirit without the external Word. Be guided by that. For He did not command in vain to write, preach, read, hear, sing, and declare His external Word.

3. *Temptation.* In the third place, there is *tentatio*, that is, trial. That is the true touchstone which teaches you not only to know and understand, but also to experience how true, sincere, sweet, lovely, powerful, comforting the Word of God is, so that it is the wisdom above all wisdom. Thus you see how David in the Psalm just mentioned complains about all manner of enemies, wicked princes and tyrants, false prophets and factions, which he must endure because he always meditates, that is, deals with God's Word in every possible way, as stated. For as soon as the Word of God bears fruit through you, the devil will trouble you, make you a real teacher, and teach you through tribulation to seek and to love the Word of God. For I myself – if I am permitted to voice my humble opinion – must thank my papists very much for so buffeting, distressing, and terrifying me by the devil's fury that they made me a fairly good theologian, which otherwise I should never have become.
4. *Humility.* Then (namely, if you follow the rule of David exhibited in Psalm 119) you will find how shallow and unworthy will appear to you the writings of the Fathers, and you will condemn not only the books of the opponents, but also be ever less pleased with your own writing and preaching. If you have arrived at this stage, you may surely hope that you have just begun to be a real theologian, one who is able to teach not only the young and unlearned, but also the advanced and well-instructed Christians. For Christ's Church includes all manner of Christians – young, old, weak, sick, healthy, strong, aggressive, indolent, simple, wise, etc. But if you consider yourself learned and imagine that you have attained the goal and feel proud of your booklets, teaching and writing, as though you had done marvelously and preached wondrously, and if you are much pleased because people praise you before others and you must be praised or otherwise you are disappointed and feel like giving up – if you are minded like that, my friend, just grab yourself by the ears, and if you grab rightly, you will find a fine pair of big, long, rough, donkey ears.

Then go to a little more expense and adorn yourself with golden bells, so that wherever you go people can hear you, admiringly point at you with their fingers and say, "Lo and behold, there is that wonderful man who can write such excellent books and preach so remarkably!" Then certainly you will be blessed, yes, more than blessed, in the kingdom of heaven; indeed, in that kingdom in which the fire of hell has been prepared for the devil and his angels! . . In this Book, God's glory alone is set forth, and it says: *Deus superbis resistit, humilibus autem dat gratium. Cui est gloria in secula seculerum* [God resists the proud, but gives grace to the humble. To Whom be glory forever and ever]. Amen.
Martin Luther

Since we live by the Spirit, let us keep in step with the Spirit.
The Bible, Galatians 5:25

So then, just as you received Christ Jesus as Lord, continue to live in him, rooted and built up in him, strengthened in the faith as you were taught, and overflowing with thankfulness.
The Bible, Colossians 2:6,7

It is much better to be drawn by the joys of heaven, than driven by the sorrows of earth.
Author unknown

Grace experienced makes people gracious. Mercy enjoyed makes them merciful. Forgiveness received makes them forgiving. And faith bestowed makes them faithful.
Author unknown

To live well is nothing other than to love God with all one's heart, with all one's soul and with all one's efforts; from this it comes about that love is kept whole and uncorrupted. No misfortune can disturb it. It obeys only [God] and is careful in discerning things, so as not to be surprised by deceit or trickery.
Augustine of Hippo

We must always be on our guard lest, under the pretext of keeping one commandment, we be found breaking another.
Basil the Great

How blessed and amazing are God's gifts, dear friends! Life with immortality, splendor with righteousness, truth with confidence, faith with assurance, self-control with holiness! And all these things are within our comprehension.
Clement of Rome

People should think less about what they ought to do and more about what they ought to be. If only their being were good, their works would shine forth brightly. Do not imagine that you can ground your salvation upon actions; it must rest on what you are.
Meister Eckhart

For Paul the Spirit was the absolutely crucial matter for Christian life from beginning to end.
H. Gunkel

To be in Christ is the source of the Christian's life; to be like Christ is the sum of his excellence; to be with Christ is the fulness of his joy.
Charles Hodge

Wherever man may stand, whatever he may do, to whatever he may apply his hand, in agriculture, in commerce, and in industry, or his mind, in the world of art, and science he is, in whatsoever it may be, constantly standing before the face of God, he is employed in the service of his God, he has strictly to obey his God, and above all, he has to aim at the glory of his God.
Abraham Kuyper

The young Christian must realize that the test of his religious life is what he is and what he does when he is not on his knees in prayer, not reading his Bible, not listening to great preachers and not participating in religious meetings.
Dr John Meigs

If we get our information from the biblical material there is no doubt that the Christian life is a dancing, leaping, daring life.
Eugene Peterson

As followers of Christ, we must remember always to build our defense of the Christian faith on the sure foundation of the Bible. If we do so, there will be no weight too great to be supported; no wind too strong to be resisted.
Richard Pratt, Jr.

We do not segment our lives, giving some time to God, some to our business or schooling, while keeping parts to ourselves. The idea is to live all of our lives in the presence of God, under the authority of God, and for the honor and glory of God. That is what the Christian life is all about.
R.C. Sproul

The Christian's battle is first of all with sin.
C.H. Spurgeon

I bid you, Christian –
beware of your graces;
beware of your virtues;
beware of your experience;
beware of your prayers;
beware of your hope;
beware of your humility.
C.H. Spurgeon

Realize that you must lead a dying life; the more a man dies to himself, the more he begins to live unto God.
Thomas à Kempis

What can the world offer you without Jesus? To be without Jesus is hell most grievous, to be with Jesus is to know the sweetness of heaven. If Jesus is with you, no enemy can harm you. Whoever finds Jesus, finds a rich treasure, and a good above every good. He who loses Jesus loses much indeed, and more than the whole world. Poorest of all is he who lives without Jesus, and richest of all is he who stands in favor with Jesus.
Thomas à Kempis

Let us think of a Christian believer in whose life the twin wonders of repentance and the new birth have been wrought. Of such a one it may be said that every act of his life is or can be as truly sacred as prayer or baptism or the Lord's Supper. To say this is not to bring all acts down to one dead level; it is rather to lift every act up into a living kingdom and turn the whole life into a sacrament.
A.W. Tozer

Christian living

Richard Baxter

1. How contrary a voluptuous life is to the blessed example of our Lord, and of his servant Paul, and all the apostles! Paul tamed his body and brought it into subjection, lest, having preached to others, himself should be a castaway, 1 Cor. ix. 27. And all that are Christ's have crucified the flesh, with the affections and lusts thereof, Gal. v. 24. This was signified in the ancient manner of baptizing (and so is still by baptism itself) when they went over head in the water and then rose out of it, to signify that they were dead and buried with Christ, Rom. vi. 3, 4, and rose with him to newness of life. This is called our being "baptized into his death;" and seems the plain sense of I Cor. xv. 29, of being "baptized for the dead;" that is, "for dead" to show that we are dead to the world, and must die in the world, but shall rise again to the kingdom of Christ, both of grace and glory.

2. Sensuality showeth that there is no true belief of the life to come and proveth, so far as it prevaileth, the absence of all grace.

3. It is a homebred, continual traitor to the soul; a continual tempter, and nurse of all sin; the great withdrawer of the heart from God; and the common cause of apostasy itself: it still fighteth against the Spirit, Gal. v. 17; and is seeking advantage from all our liberties, Gal. v. 13; 2 Pet. ii. 10.

4. It turneth all our outward mercies into sin, and strengtheneth itself against God by his own benefits.

5. It is the great cause of our afflictions; for God will not spare that idol which is set up against him: flesh rebelleth, and flesh shall suffer.

6. And when it hath brought affliction, it is most impatient under it, and maketh it seem intolerable. A flesh-pleaser thinks he is undone, when affliction depriveth him of his pleasure.

7. Lastly, it exceedingly unfitteth men for death; for then flesh must be cast into the dust, and all its pleasure be at an end. Oh doleful day to those that had their good things here, and their portion in this life! when all is gone that ever they valued and sought; and all the true felicity lost, which they brutishly condemned ! If you would joyfully then bear the dissolution and ruin of your flesh, oh master it, and mortify it now. Seek not the ease and pleasure of a little walking, breathing clay, when you should be seeking and foretasting the everlasting pleasure. Here lieth your danger and your work. Strive more against your own flesh, than against all your enemies in earth and hell: if you be saved from this, you are saved from them all. Christ suffered in the flesh, to tell you that it is not pampering, but suffering, that your flesh must expect, if you will reign with him.

Richard Baxter

Be completely humble and gentle; be patient, bearing with one another in love.
The Bible, Ephesians 4:2

It is God's will that you should be sanctified: that you should avoid sexual immorality; that each of you should learn to control his own body in a way that is holy and honorable, not in passionate lust like the heathen, who do not know God
The Bible, 1 Thessalonians 4:3-5

Therefore, rid yourselves of all malice and all deceit, hypocrisy, envy, and slander of every kind.
The Bible, 1 Peter 2:1

For this very reason, make every effort to add to your faith goodness; and to goodness, knowledge; and to knowledge, self-control; and to self-control, perseverance; and to perseverance, godliness; and to godliness, brotherly kindness; and to brotherly kindness, love.
The Bible, 2 Peter 1:5-7

When you feel unlovable, unworthy and unclean, when you think that no one can heal you:
Remember, Friend,
God Can.
When you think that you are unforgivable for your guilt and your shame:
Remember, Friend,
God Can.
When you think that all is hidden and no one can see within:
Remember, Friend,
God Can.
And when you have reached the bottom and you think that no one can hear:
Remember, my dear Friend,
God Can.
And when you think that no one can love the real person deep inside of you:
Remember, my dear Friend,
God Does.
Author unknown

If you would have a clear evidence that that little love, that little faith, that little zeal, you have is true, then live up to that love, live up to that faith, live up to that zeal that you have; and this will be evidence beyond all contradiction.
Thomas Brooks

We have been adopted as sons by the Lord with this one condition: that our life express Christ, the bond of our adoption. Accordingly, unless we give and devote ourselves to righteousness, we not only revolt from our Creator with wicked perfidy, but we also abjure our Savior Himself.
John Calvin

Conduct as well as charism needs to be a

manifestation of the Spirit.
James Dunn

I resolve to endeavor to my utmost to act and think as if I had already seen the happiness of heaven and the torments of hell.
Jonathan Edwards

Think big, talk big, act big. Because we have a big God.
Kathryn Kuhlman

If our life is not a course of humility, self-denial, renunciation of the world, poverty of spirit, and heavenly affection, we do not live the lives of Christians.
William Law

If we do not die to ourselves, we cannot live to God, and he that does not live to God, is dead.
George MacDonald

Living the Christian life depends not only on our own effort but upon God our Father, who in Jesus Christ accepts us as heirs of God (Gal. 4:4-7) and strengthens and sustains us (Phil. 4:13).
Moravian Covenant for Christian living

A wise man has said that your Christian life is like a three-legged stool. The legs are doctrine, experience and practice (that is obedience), and you will not stay upright unless all three are there. In recent years many Christians have not kept these three together.
J.I. Packer

We are to order our lives by the light of His law, not our guesses about His plan.
J.I. Packer

The key to Christian living is a thirst and hunger for God. And one of the main reasons people do not understand or experience the sovereignty of grace and the way it works through the awakening of sovereign joy is that their hunger and thirst for God is so small.
John Piper

Contend to the death for the truth that no man is a true Christian who is not converted and is not a holy man.
But allow that a man be converted, have a new heart, and be a holy man, and yet be liable to infirmity, doubts, and fears.
J.C. Ryle

This is not an age in which to be a soft Christian.
Francis Schaeffer

Christianity is a warfare, and Christians are spiritual soldiers.
Robert Southwell

We are called to live in the presence of God, under the authority of God and to the glory of God.
R.C. Sproul

Learn to say no. It will be of more use to you than to be able to read Latin.
C.H. Spurgeon

Some Christians nowadays have a "butterfly Christianity." When time, and strength, and thought, and talent are all spent upon mere amusement, what else are men and women but mere butterflies?
C.H. Spurgeon

The course of thy life will speak more for thee than the discourse of thy lips.
George Swinnock

We are called to an everlasting preoccupation with God.
A.W. Tozer

The Methodists must take heed to their doctrine, their experience, their practice, and their discipline. If they attend to their doctrines only, they will make the people antinomians; if to the experimental part of religion only, they will make them enthusiasts; if to the practical part only, they will make them Pharisees; and if they do not attend to their discipline, they will be like persons who bestow much pain in cultivating their garden, and put no fence

round it, to save it from the wild boar of the forest.
John Wesley

Christian Science

Mary Baker Eddy
Christ
Jesus Christ is not God, as Jesus himself declared, but is the Son of God.
Mary Baker Eddy

If there had never existed such a person as the Galilean Prophet, it would make no difference to me.
Mary Baker Eddy

The word Christ is not properly a synonym for Jesus, thought it is commonly so used.
Mary Baker Eddy

God's wrath
One sacrifice, however great, is insufficient to pay the debt of sin. The atonement requires constant self-immolation on the sinner's part. That God's wrath should be vented upon His beloved Son, is divinely unnatural. Such a theory is man-made.
Mary Baker Eddy

Jesus' blood
The material blood of Jesus was no more efficacious to cleanse from sin when it was shed upon "the accursed tree," than when it was flowing in his veins as he went daily about his Father's business.
Mary Baker Eddy

Life
It is contrary to Christian Science to suppose that life is either material or organically spiritual.
Mary Baker Eddy

Pentecost
His students then received the Holy Ghost. By this is meant, that by all they had witnessed and suffered, they were roused to

an enlarged understanding of divine Science.
Mary Baker Eddy

Resurrection of Jesus
His disciples believed Jesus to be dead while he was hidden in the sepulcher, whereas he was alive.
Mary Baker Eddy

Trinity
The theory of three person in one God (that is, a personal Trinity or Tri-unity) suggest polytheism.
Mary Baker Eddy

Christianity
… strait is the gate, and narrow is the way, which leadeth unto life, and few there be that find it.
The Bible, Matthew 7:14 KJV

This is what Christianity is for – to teach men the art of Life. And its whole curriculum lies in three words, "Learn of me."
Author unknown

True Christianity is not a spasmodic religion of convenience. It is life in Christ.
Author unknown

Christianity is Christ!
Author unknown

It is the business of all false religion to patch up a righteousness in which the sinner is to stand before God. But it is the business of the glorious gospel to bring near to us, by the hand of the Holy Spirit, a righteousness ready wrought, a robe of perfection ready made, wherein God's people, to all the purposes of justification and happiness, stand perfect and without fault before the throne.
Author unknown

The Christian is not one who has gone all the way with Christ. None of us has. The Christian is one who has found the

right road.
Charles L. Allen

There never was found in any age of the world, either philosopher or sect, or law or discipline which did so highly exalt the public good as the Christian faith.
Francis Bacon

It is fatally easy to think of Christianity as something to be discussed and not as something to be experienced.
William Barclay

The essence of the Christian religion consists therein: that the creation of the Father, destroyed by sin, is again restored in the death of the Son of God and recreated by the grace of the Holy Spirit to a Kingdom of God.
Herman Bavinck

I like to hear a man dwell much on the same essentials of Christianity. For we have but one God, and one Christ, and one faith to preach; and I will not preach another Gospel to please men with variety, as if our Savior and our Gospel were grown stale.
Richard Baxter

Every time in history that man has tried to turn crucified truth into coercive truth he has betrayed the fundamental principle of Christianity.
Nicolas Berdyaev

Authentic Christianity never destroys what is good. It makes it grow, transfigures it, and enriches itself from it.
Claire Huchet Bishop

The glory of Christianity is to conquer by forgiveness.
William Blake

The thing that keeps coming back to me is, what is Christianity, and, indeed, what is Christ, for us today?
Dietrich Bonhoeffer

Christianity helps us face the music even when we don't like the tune.
Phillips Brooks

Christianity knows no truth which is not the child of love and the parent of duty.
Phillips Brooks

It is only Christianity, the great bond of love and duty to God, that makes any existence valuable or even tolerable.
Horace Bushnell

At least five times, with the Arian and the Albigensian, with the Humanist skeptic, after Voltaire and after Darwin, the [Christian] Faith has to all appearance gone to the dogs. In each of these five cases it was the dog that died.
G.K. Chesterton

Christianity has died many times and risen again; for it has a God who knew his way out of the grave.
G.K. Chesterton

Christianity is not a theory or speculation, but a life; not a philosophy of life, but a living presence.
Samuel Taylor Coleridge

Christianity isn't all that complicated … it's Jesus.
Joni Eareckson Tada

Christ does not save us by acting a parable of divine love; He acts the parable of divine love by saving us. That is the Christian faith.
Austin Farrer

True Christianity is an all-out commitment to Jesus Christ.
John Flavel

Christianity finds all its doctrines stated in the Bible, and Christianity denies no part, nor attempts to add anything to the word of God.
Billy Graham

The Christian life is not a way "out," but a way "through" life.
Billy Graham

For centuries, Christians have been the primary agents of charity and compassion in Western culture. From the first century forward to the founding of the American colonies, Christians took the lead in caring for the hungry, the dispossessed, and the afflicted. This was, in fact, the hallmark of authentic Christianity.
George Grant

The only reason any one should believe Christianity is that it is true. Its truth rests on historical facts which do not change, truths which are open to tests normally applied to other events or claims. It is not a matter of whether it sells or whether it works or whether it feels good or provides meaningful experiences. What Christianity teaches is the correct explanation of reality.
Dick Halverson

We are so steeped in the anti Christ philosophy … that we little sense how much of what passes for practical Christianity is really an apostate compromise with the spirit of the age.
Carl F. H. Henry

The Christian religion not only was at first attended with miracles, but even at this day cannot be believed by any reasonable person without one.
David Hume

Christianity is Christ!
H.A. Ironside

All the world would be Christian if they were taught the pure Gospel of Christ!
Thomas Jefferson

Christianity is the highest perfection of humanity.
Samuel Johnson

Christianity does not consist in any partial amendment of our lives, any particular moral virtues, but in an entire change of our natural temper, a life wholly devoted to God.
William Law

Christianity is a matter of willing God's will and through Christ become one with it.
John Leax

Christianity, if false, is of no importance, and if true, of infinite importance. The only thing it cannot be is moderately important.
C.S. Lewis

Any notion that Christianity is mainly the result of something that we do is always completely, fatally wrong. We must cast off any idea that the Christian church is the result of our action and that we are perpetuating some tradition. If that is our view of Christianity, it is false.
M. Lloyd-Jones

Christianity taught men that love is worth more than intelligence.
Jaques Maritain

We who formerly delighted in fornication, but now embrace chastity alone; we who formerly used magical arts, dedicated ourselves to the good and unbegotten God, who valued above all things the acquisition of wealth and possessions, now bring what we have into common stock, and communicate to everyone in need; we who hated and destroyed one another, and on account of their different tribe, now since the coming of Christ, live familiarly with them, and pray for our enemies, and endeavor to persuade those who hate us unjustly, to the end that they may become partakers of the same joyful hope of a reward from God the ruler of all.
Justin Martyr

The gospel of Jesus Christ can make bad men good and good men better, can alter human nature, can change human lives.
David O. McKay

Christianity is different from all other religions. They are the story of man's search for God. The gospel is the story of God's search for man.
Dewi Morgan

Marx and Freud are the two great destroyers of Christian civilization, the first replacing the gospel of love by the gospel of hate, the other undermining the essential concept of human responsibility.
Malcolm Muggeridge

Christianity is a missionary religion, converting, advancing, aggressive, encompassing the world; a non-missionary church is in the bands of death.
Friedrich Max Müller

People may say what they like about the decay of Christianity; the religious system that produced green Chartreuse can never totally die.
H.H. Munro

No sciences are better attested than the religion of the Bible.
Sir Isaac Newton

I call Christianity the one great curse, the one enormous and innermost perversion, the one great instinct for revenge, for which no means are too venomous, too underhand, too underground, and too petty – I call it the one immortal blemish of mankind.
Friedrich Nietzsche

In Christianity neither morality nor religion come into contact with reality at any point.
Friedrich Nietzsche

Christianity, sprung from Jewish roots and comprehensible only as a growth on this soil, represents the counter-movement to any morality of breeding, of race, of privilege: it is the anti-Aryan religion par excellence.
Friedrich Nietzsche

Christianity is one beggar telling another beggar where he found bread.
D.T. Niles

Christianity is God reaching down to humanity. Other religions are a matter of men and women seeking and struggling toward God.
Luis Palau

Christianity isn't just a message it's centered in a person. You can have Confucianism without Confucius, Buddhism without Buddha, and Judaism without Abraham or Moses. You can even have Islam without Muhammad.
Luis Palau

Christianity is different from all other world religions. Relationship with Jesus Christ is the origin, motivation, and goal of the Christian faith. This requires belief that Jesus Christ is alive, that he is divine, and that he is still inviting us to fellowship with him.
Luis Palau

Christianity is a battle, not a dream.
Wendell Phillips

I believe I am not mistaken in saying that Christianity is a demanding and serious religion. When it is delivered as easy and amusing, it is another kind of religion altogether.
Neil Postman

First, I believe it to be a grave mistake to present Christianity as something charming and popular with no offense in it.
Dorothy Sayers

The Christian faith is the most exciting drama that ever staggered the imagination of man …The plot pivots upon a single character, and the whole action is the answer to a single central problem: What think ye of Christ?
Dorothy Sayers

The gospel is not presented to mankind as an argument about religious principles. Nor is it offered as a philosophy of life. Christianity is a witness to certain facts – to events that have happened, to hopes that have been fulfilled, to realities that have been experienced, to a Person who has lived and died and been raised from the dead to reign for ever.
Massey H. Shepherd

While sitting on the bank of a river one day, I picked up a solid round stone from the water and broke it open. It was perfectly dry in spite of the fact that it had been immersed in water for centuries. The same is true of many people in the western world. For centuries they have been surrounded by Christianity; they live immersed in the waters of its benefits. And yet it has not penetrated their hearts; they do not love it. The fault is not in Christianity, but in men's hearts, which have been hardened by materialism and intellectualism.
Sadhu Sundar Singh

If you take Christ out of Christianity, Christianity is dead.
   If you remove grace out of the gospel, the gospel is gone.
   If the people do not like the doctrine of grace, give them all the more of it.
C.H. Spurgeon

Christianity is a rescue religion.
John Stott

Christ cannot live his life today in this world without our mouth, without our eyes, without our going and coming, without our heart. When we love, it is Christ loving through us.
Cardinal Suenens

Christianity does not remove you from the world and its problems; it makes you fit to live in it, triumphantly and usefully.
Charles Templeton

Christianity is not a system of philosophy, nor a ritual, nor a code of laws; it is the impartation of a divine vitality. Without the way there is no going, without the truth there is no knowing, without life there is no living.
Merrill Tenney

I think back to many discussions in my early life when we all agreed that if you try to take the fruits of Christianity without its roots, the fruits will wither. And they will not come again unless you nurture the roots. But we must not profess the Christian faith and go to church simply because we want social reforms and benefits or a better standard of behavior – but because we accept the sanctity of life, the responsibility that comes with freedom and the supreme sacrifice of Christ expressed so well in the hymn:
"When I survey the wondrous cross
On which the Prince of Glory died
My richest gain I count but loss
and pour contempt on all my pride."
Margaret Thatcher

Where the cross has been planted only superstitions have grown.
Lemuel K. Washburn

The trouble with some of us is that we have been inoculated with small doses of Christianity which keep us from catching the real thing.
Leslie Dixon Weatherhead

Christianity is not a religion but a relationship of love expressed toward God and men.
Sherwood Eliot Wirt

Christianity, Destruction of

It is at least possible that we are the generation of believers who will destroy much of historic Christianity from within – not, in the first instance, by rancid unbelief, but by raising relatively peripheral questions to the place where, functionally, they displace what is central.
D.A. Carson.

The greatest threat to the cause of Jesus always arises from those who lay claim to being his children.
Martin Luther

Christianity, New Testament

The Christianity of the New Testament simply does not exist. Millions of people through the centuries have little by little cheated God out of Christianity, and have succeeded in making Christianity exactly the opposite of what it is in the New Testament.
Søren Kierkegaard

Christianity, Spread of

The gospel will be spread abroad over the seas and the islands in the ocean, and among the people dwelling therein, who are called "the fulness thereof." And that word has been made good. For churches of Christ fill all the islands, and are being multiplied every day, and the teaching of the Word of salvation is gaining accessions.
Hippolytus

The Scriptures, both of the Old and New Testament, clearly reveal that the gospel is to exercise an influence over all branches of the human family, immeasurably more extensive and more thoroughly transforming than any it has ever realized in time past. This end is to be gradually attained through the spiritual presence of Christ in the ordinary dispensation of Providence and the ministrations of His church.
A.A. Hodge

There have been great and glorious days of the gospel in this land; but they have been small in comparison of what shall be.
James Renwick

Christianity, Uniqueness of

This is the unique element in the gospel, which tells us that what we could never do, God has done. We cannot climb up to heaven to discover God, but God has come down to earth, in the person of his Son, to reveal himself to us in the only way we

could really understand: in terms of a human life.
J.N.D. Anderson

The distinction between Christianity and all other systems of religion consists largely in this, that in these others men are found seeking after God, while Christianity is God seeking after men.
Thomas Arnold

Every religion except one puts upon you doing something in order to recommend yourself to God. It is only the religion of Christ which was not sold out to us on certain conditions to be fulfilled by ourselves.
Augustus Toplady

Christianity and world religions

The founders of the world's religions say, "Do! Do! Do!" but Christ says, "Done! It is finished!"
Steve Kumar

Christianity for everyone

Because Christianity became predominantly Gentile, it seemed as though God had abandoned Israel, and as though Gentiles had simply taken the place of Jews in God's plan. But that was certainly not how Paul saw it! Of course he himself contrasted the old and the new ... But he maintained to the end that God had been at work in the past; that the Law itself had been given by God, and that God had not abandoned his people. He saw continuity between his past beliefs and his present faith, as well as discontinuity. In stressing the new at the expense of the old, later Christians lost sight of something that our New Testament authors were maintaining.
Morna Hooker

Christians

The Christians do not commit adultery. They do not bear false witness. They do not covet their neighbor's goods. They honor father and mother. They love their neighbors. They judge justly. They avoid doing to others what they do not wish

done to them. They do good to their enemies. They are kind.
Aristides

The Christian may be a very ordinary person, but he acquires a new value and dignity and greatness because he belongs to God. The greatness of the Christian lies in the fact that he is God's.
William Barclay

This is a cheerful world as I see it from my garden under the shadows of my vines. But if I were to ascend some high mountain and look out over the wide lands, you know very well what I would see: brigands on the highways, pirates on the sea, armies fighting, cities burning; in the amphitheaters men murdered to please applauding crowds; selfishness and cruelty and misery and despair under all roofs. It is a bad world, Donatus, an incredibly bad world. But I have discovered in the midst of it a quiet and holy people who have learned a great secret. They have found a joy which is a thousand times better than any pleasure of our sinful life. They are despised and persecuted, but they care not. They are masters of their souls. They have overcome the world. These people, Donatus, are the Christians – and I am one of them.
Cyprian

They dwell in their own countries but simply as sojourners. As citizens, they share in all things with others, and yet endure all things as if foreigners. Every foreign land is to them as their native country, and every land of their birth as a land of strangers. They marry, as do others; they beget children; but they do not destroy their offspring. They have a common table but not a common bed. They are in the flesh, but they do not live after the flesh. They pass their days on earth, but are citizens of heaven. They obey the prescribed laws, and at the same time surpass the laws in their lives. They love all, and are persecuted by all. They are poor, yet they make many

rich; they are completely destitute, and yet they enjoy complete abundance. They are reviled, and yet they bless. When they do good they are punished as evildoers; undergoing punishment, they rejoice because they are brought to life.
Epistle to Diognetus, author unknown, written about AD 130. This is one of the earliest descriptions of Christians.

Because we are governed by new principles, we should be viewing events in a different way – our whole attitude towards everything is essentially different from the non-Christian attitude. Our view of death should be different, and our view of all other people should be different as well.
Martyn Lloyd-Jones

Although they do not inquire into the future, and either forget or do not know the past, yet defame present times as most unusually beset, as it were, by evils because there is belief in Christ and worship of God, and increasingly less worship of idols.
Paulus Orosius

They were in the habit of meeting on a certain fixed day before it was light, when they sang an anthem to Christ as God, and bound themselves by a solemn oath not to commit any wicked deed.
Pliny

Christians, False

A large part of the professing church is nothing better than the world, wrongfully named with Christ's name.
C.H. Spurgeon

The generality of nominal Christians are almost entirely taken up with the concerns of the present world. They know indeed that they are mortal, but they do not feel it. The truth rests in their understandings, and cannot gain admission into their hearts. This speculative persuasion is altogether different from that strong practical impression of the infinite importance of eternal things, which,

attended with a proportionate sense of the shortness and uncertainty of all below, while it prompts to activity from a conviction that the night cometh when no man can work, produces a certain firmness of texture, which hardens us against the buffetings of fortune, and prevents our being very deeply penetrated by the cares and interests, the good or evil, of this transitory state.
William Wilberforce

Christians and the Holy Spirit
We affirm that, while all believers are indwelt by the Holy Spirit and are in the process of being made holy and conformed to the image of Christ, those consequences of justification are not its ground.
The gospel of Jesus Christ: An evangelical celebration

Christians in heaven
A cloud of witnesses.
The Bible, Hebrews 12:1

Christlikeness
You will not stroll into Christlikeness with your hands in your pockets, shoving the door open with a careless shoulder. This is no hobby for one's leisure moments, taken up at intervals when we have nothing much to do, and put down and forgotten when our life grows full and interesting. It takes all one's strength, and all one's heart, and all one's mind, and all one's soul, given freely and recklessly and without restraint. This is a business for adventurous spirits; others would shrink out of it.
A.J. Gossip

This is our great need, to be more like Christ, that His likeness may be seen in our lives; and this is just what is promised to us as we yield ourselves in full surrender to the working of His Spirit.
G.T. Manley

It's not great talents that God blesses, but great likeness to Jesus.
Robert Murray M'Cheyne

You are saved – seek to be like your Savior.
C.H. Spurgeon

Be much with the solid teachings of God's word, and you will become solid and substantial men and women: drink them in, and feed upon them, and they shall produce in you a Christ-likeness, at which the world shall stand astonished.
C.H. Spurgeon

A Christian should be a striking likeness of Jesus Christ.
C.H. Spurgeon

Christmas
See also: Incarnation
Glory to God in the highest, and on earth peace, good will toward men.
The Bible, Luke 2:14

My husband likes those nativity cards, but I prefer something more Christmassy.
Conversation overheard in a charity shop.
Author unknown

Selfishness makes Christmas a burden; love makes it a delight.
Author unknown

Bethlehem and Golgotha, the Manger and the Cross, the birth and the death, must always be seen together.
J. Sidlow Baxter

It is good to be children sometimes, and never better than at Christmas, when its mighty Founder was a child Himself.
Charles Dickens

The shepherds sing; and shall I silent be?
My God, no hymn for Thee?
My soul's a shepherd too: a flock it feeds
Of thoughts, and words, and deeds.
The pasture is Thy Word, the streams, Thy
  Grace
Enriching all the place.
Shepherd and flock shall sing, and all my
  powers
Out-sing the daylight hours.
George Herbert

When we celebrate Christmas we are celebrating that amazing time when the Word that shouted all the galaxies into being, limited all power, and for love of us came to us in the powerless body of a human baby.
Madeline L'Engle

Ah, we poor people, to be so cold and sluggish in the face of the great joy that has clearly been prepared for us! This great benefaction exceeds by far all the other works of creation; and yet our faith in it is found to be so weak, although it is preached and sung to us by angels, who are heavenly theologians and who were so glad for our sake! Their song is very, very beautiful and describes the entire Christian religion. For giving glory to God in the highest heaven is the supreme worship. This they wish and bring to us in the Christ.
Martin Luther

The Christmas message is that there is hope for a ruined humanity – hope of pardon, hope of peace with God, hope of glory – because at the Father's will Jesus Christ became poor, and was born in a stable so that thirty years later He might hang on a cross.
J.I. Packer

What can I give him,
Poor as I am?
If I were a shepherd,
I would bring a lamb,
If I were a Wise Man,
I would do my part –
Yet what can I give Him?
Give my heart.
Christina Rossetti

Where is this stupendous stranger?
Prophets, shepherds, kings, advise;
Lead me to my Master's manger,
Show me where my Savior lies.
O most mighty, O most holy,
Far beyond the seraph's thought,
Art thou then so mean and lowly
As unheeded prophets taught?
O the magnitude of meekness,
Worth from worth immortal sprang,

O the strength of infant weakness,
If eternal is so young.
God all-bounteous, all creative,
Whom no ills from good dissuade,
Is incarnate, and a native
Of the very world he made.
Christopher Smart

The birth of Jesus is the sunrise in the Bible.
Henry Van Dyke

The King of glory sends his Son,
To make his entrance on this earth;
Behold the midnight bright as noon,
And heav'nly hosts declare his birth!
About the young Redeemer's head,
What wonders, and what glories meet!
An unknown star arose, and led
The eastern sages to his feet.
Simeon and Anna both conspire
The infant Savior to proclaim
Inward they felt the sacred fire,
And bless'd the babe, and own'd his name.
Let pagan hordes blaspheme aloud,
And treat the holy child with scorn;
Our souls adore th' eternal God
Who condescended to be born.
Isaac Watts

To perceive Christmas through its wrapping becomes more difficult every year.
E.B. White

Christmas, Observance of

The Church does not superstitiously observe days, merely as days, but as memorials of important facts. Christmas might be kept as well upon one day of the year as another; but there should be a stated day for commemorating the birth of our Savior, because there is danger that what may be done on any day, will be neglected.
Samuel Johnson

Christmas is coming! Quite so; but what is "Christmas"? Does not the very term itself denote its source – "Christ-mass." Thus it is of Romish origin, brought over from Paganism. But, says someone, Christmas is the time when we commemorate the Savior's

birth. It is? And who authorized such commemoration? Certainly God did not. The Redeemer bade His disciples "remember" Him in His death, but there is not a word in Scripture, from Genesis to Revelation, which tells us to celebrate His birth.
Arthur Pink

We have no superstitious regard for times and seasons. Certainly we do not believe in the present ecclesiastical arrangement called Christmas.

First, because we do not believe in the mass at all, but abhor it, whether it be sung in Latin or in English.

Secondly, because we find no scriptural warrant whatever for observing any day as the birthday of the Savior; and consequently, its observance is a superstition, because not of divine authority. "Superstition" has fixed most positively the day of our Savior's birth, although there is no possibility of discovering when it occurred … It was not till the middle of the third century that any part of the Church celebrated the nativity of our Lord; and it was not till very long after the Western Church had set the example, that the Eastern adopted it.

… Probably the fact is that the "holy" days were arranged to fit in with the heathen festivals. We venture to assert, that if there be any day in the year, of which we may be pretty sure that it was not the day on which the Savior was born, it is the 25th of December … Regarding not the day, let us, nevertheless, give God thanks for the gift of His dear Son.
C.H. Spurgeon

When it can be proved that the observance of Christmas, Whitsuntide, and other Popish festivals was ever instituted by a divine statute, we also will attend to them, but not till then.
C.H. Spurgeon

Church
His intent was that now, through the church, the manifold wisdom of God should be made known to the rulers and authorities in the heavenly realms.
The Bible, Ephesians 3:10

A black man was asked to leave an old white church. As he walked away, he expressed his frustration to the Lord. Suddenly God spoke, and told him, "I understand your frustration. I've been trying to get into that church for 200 years!"
Author unknown

For all in common she prays, for all in common she works, in the temptations of all she is tried.
Ambrose of Milan

Upon this rock which you have confessed – upon myself, the Son of the living God – I will build my church. I will build you on myself, and not myself on you.
Augustine of Hippo

He who does not have the church as his mother does not have God as his Father.
Augustine of Hippo

There is no salvation outside the church.
Augustine of Hippo

The crisis of the church is not at its deepest level a crisis of authority or a crisis of dogmatic theology. It is a crisis of powerlessness in which our sole recourse is to call on the help and inward power of the Holy Spirit.
James K. Baxter

We believe and confess one single catholic or universal church – a holy congregation and gathering of true Christian believers, awaiting their entire salvation in Jesus Christ being washed by his blood, and sanctified and sealed by the Holy Spirit. This church has existed from the beginning of the world and will last until the end, as appears from the fact that Christ is eternal King who cannot be without subjects.
Belgic Confession

The Church is a perpetually defeated thing that always survives her conquerors.
Hilaire Belloc

The Church is her true self only when she exists for humanity.
Dietrich Bonhoeffer

The visible Church of Christ is a congregation of faithful men, in the which the pure Word of God is preached, and the Sacraments are duly ministered.
Book of Common Prayer

What the church needs today is not more or better machinery, not new organizations, or more novel methods; but men whom the Holy Spirit can use – men of prayer, men mighty in prayer.
E.M. Bounds

The Lord Jesus is the Head of the Church, which is composed of all his true disciples, and in Him is invested supremely all power for its government. According to his commandment, Christians are to associate themselves into particular societies or churches; and to each of these churches he hath given needful authority for administering that order, discipline and worship which he hath appointed. The regular officers of a Church are Bishops, or Elders, and Deacons.
James Boyce

If ever a man could have felt the church to be unnecessary, he was Jesus. Yet he did not stay away from the "church" of his day. It was his custom to go to the synagogue on the Sabbath, and he made many trips to the temple.
R. Brokhoff

The church [is] the gathering of God's children, where they can be helped and fed like babies and then, guided by her motherly care, grow up to manhood in maturity of faith.
John Calvin

Wherever we see the Word of God purely preached and heard, there a church of God exists, even if it swarms with many faults.
John Calvin

The doors of Christ's churches on earth do not stand so wide open that all sorts of people, good or bad, may freely enter as they desire. Those who are admitted to church membership must first be examined and tested as to whether they are ready to be received into church fellowship or not. These things are required of all church members: repentance from sin and faith in Jesus Christ. Therefore repentance and faith are the things about which individuals must be examined before they are granted membership in a church, and they must profess and demonstrate these in such a way as to satisfy rational charity that they are genuinely present.
Cambridge Declaration, 1649

The Church of God is in the world to bring men to submit to the authority of the King of kings and Lord of lords; the message of the Church, therefore, must be spoken with authority and not uttered with the obsequiousness of one who begs for some petty food from those whom he approaches.
Warren Akin Candler

In the book of Revelation Christ desires a militant church that will absorb suffering rather than accommodate the powers that be.
Ellen T. Charry

You cannot pray at home as at church, where there is a great multitude, where exclamations are cried out to God as from one great heart, and where there is something more: the union of minds, the accord of souls, the bond of charity, the prayers of priests.
John Chrysostom

Just as God's will is creation and is called "the world," so his intention is the salvation of men, and it is called "the Church."
Clement of Alexandria

Christians in community must again show the world, not merely family values, but the bond of the love of Christ.
Edmund Clowney

The church is the only institution supernaturally endowed by God. It is the one institution of which Jesus promised that the gates of hell will not prevail against it.
Chuck Colson

The church an organism, not an organization; a movement, not a monument.
Charles Colson

The church is catholic, universal, so are all her actions; all that she does belongs to all. When she baptizes a child, that action concerns me, for that child is thereby connected to that body which is my head too, and ingrafted into that body whereof I am a member. And when she buries a man, that action concerns me: all mankind is of one author.
John Donne

Worship is half of the purpose of the church: the other half is mission, in its broadest sense.
Michael Green

According to the New Testament, God wills that the church be a people who show what God is like.
Stanley Grenz

When the world asks, "What is God like?" we should be able to say, "Look at the church." As the body of Christ, we are to be like Jesus so that we too reveal God to the world.
William R.L. Haley

What a wonderful thing it is to be sure of one's faith! How wonderful to be a member of the evangelical church, which preaches the free grace of God through Christ as the hope of sinners! If we were to rely on our works – my God, what would become of us?
G.F. Handel

The chief trouble with the church is that you and I are in it.
Charles H. Heimsath

It is common for those that are farthest from God, to boast themselves most of their being near to the Church.
Matthew Henry

Nothing lasts but the Church.
George Herbert

In biblical days prophets were astir while the world was asleep; today the world is astir while church and synagogue are busy with trivialities
Abraham Joshua Heschel

A church has no right to make anything a condition of membership which Christ has not made a condition of salvation.
A.A. Hodge

The church is in Christ as Eve was in Adam.
Richard Hooker

Where there is Christ Jesus, there is the Catholic Church.
Ignatius of Antioch

The Church which is married to the Spirit of the Age will be a widow in the next.
Dean Inge

This gift of God was entrusted to the Church that all the members might receive of him and be made alive; and none are partakers of him who do not assemble with the Church but defraud themselves of life.
Irenaeus

For where the Church is there is the Spirit of God, and where the Spirit of God, there is the Church and all grace.
Irenaeus

If I look at myself I am nothing. But if I look at us all I am hopeful.
Julian of Norwich, speaking of the Church

The church must be reminded that it is not the master or the servant of the state, but rather the conscience of the state.
Martin Luther King, Jr.

The church is: a conspiracy of love for a dying world, a spy mission into enemy occupied territory ruled by the powers of evil; a prophet from God with the greatest news the world has ever heard, the most life changing and most revolutionary institution that has existed on earth.
Peter Kreeft

One of our great allies at present is the Church itself. Do not misunderstand me. I do not mean the Church as we see her spread out through all time and space and rooted in eternity, terrible as an army with banners. That, I confess, is a spectacle which makes our boldest tempters uneasy. But fortunately it is quite invisible to these humans.
C.S. Lewis, Screwtape Letters

I believe that there are too many practitioners in the church who are not believers.
C.S. Lewis

All belong to the visible church, but all do not belong to the invisible church.
M. Lloyd-Jones

We must cease to think of the Church as a gathering of institutions and organizations, and we must get back the notion that we are the people of God.
M. Lloyd-Jones

The church is so constituted that every member matters, and matters in a very vital sense.
M. Lloyd-Jones

Let him who wants a true church cling to the Word by which everything is upheld.
Martin Luther

Anyone who is to find Christ must first find the church. How could anyone know where Christ is and what faith in him is unless he knew where his believers are?
Martin Luther

Now the church is not wood and stone, but the company of people who believe in Christ.
Martin Luther

It is absolutely essential that a church perceive itself as an institution established for the glory of God. I fear that the church in America has descended from that lofty purpose and focused instead on humanity.
John F. MacArthur

The Christian faith is made available to us through a historical tradition, transmitted and propagated through a community of faith, and shaped by the manner in which that community worships and prays.
Alister McGrath

The Church is a society of sinners – the only society in the world in which membership is based upon the single qualification that the candidate shall be unworthy of membership.
Charles C. Morrison

Theologically, we have been discovering anew that the Church is not an appendage to the gospel: it is itself a part of the gospel. The gospel cannot be separated from that new people of God in which its nature is to be made manifest.
Stephen Neill

Congregational life wherein each member has his opportunity to contribute to the life of the whole body those gifts with which the Spirit endows him, is as much of the esse of the Church as are ministry and sacraments.
Lesslie Newbigin

It is not the business of the church to adapt Christ to men, but men to Christ.
Dorothy Sayers

The church is the great lost and found department.
Robert Short

It can be exalting to belong to a church that is 550 years behind the times and sublimely indifferent to fashion; it is mortifying to belong to a church that is five minutes behind the times, huffing and puffing to catch up.
Joseph Sobran

The true Church is not an organization, nor does one join it through the noisy mechanics of denominational machinery. Rather it is a living organism, a body, and believers are joined to it by the quiet working of the Holy Spirit.
Cornelius Stam

The Christian church is not a congregation of righteous people. It is a society of those who know they are not good.
Dwight E. Stevenson

Consequently there emerges the new community of Christ's Church which begins in Christ risen from the dead. When he arose from the dead it was as the beginning of the Church.
Alan Stibbs

Nobody worries about Christ as long as he can be kept shut up in churches. He is quite safe inside. But there is always trouble if you try and let him out.
G.A. Studdert Kennedy

The Church is the only society on earth that exists for the benefit of non-members.
William Temple

I believe in the Church, one Holy Catholic and Apostolic Church; and nowhere does it exist.
William Temple

We are called to see that the Church does not adapt its thinking to the horizons that modernity prescribes for it but rather that it brings to those horizons the powerful antidote of God's truth.
David Wells

The fundamental problem in the evangelical world today is that God rests too inconsequentially upon the church. His truth is too distant, his grace is too ordinary, his judgment is too benign, his gospel is too easy, and his Christ is too common.
David Wells

The purest churches under heaven are subject both to mixture and error; and some have so degenerated, as to become no churches of Christ, but synagogues of Satan. Nevertheless, there shall be always a church on earth, to worship God according to his will.
Westminster Confession of Faith

The word "church" in Scripture has always one meaning, and one only: an assembly of the people of God, a society of Christians.
Thomas Witherow

The Church is an organism that grows best in an alien society.
C. Stacey Woods

Until we start thinking in terms of revolution instead of compromise the Church will continue to pat itself on the back with token steps of renewal.
Mike Yaconelli

The nature of the Church

J.C. Ryle

I want you to belong to the one true Church: to the Church outside of which there is no salvation. I do not ask where you go on a Sunday; I only ask, "Do you belong to the one true Church?"

Where is this one true Church? What is this one true Church like? What are the marks by which this one true Church may be known? You may well ask such questions. Give me your attention, and I will provide you with some answers.

1. The one true Church IS COMPOSED OF ALL BELIEVERS IN THE LORD JESUS. It is made up of all God's elect – of all converted men and women – of all true Christians. In whomsoever we can discern the election of God the Father, the sprinkling of the blood of God the Son, the sanctifying work of God the Spirit, in that person we see a member of Christ's true Church.

2. It is a Church OF WHICH ALL THE MEMBERS HAVE THE SAME MARKS. They are all born again of the Spirit; they all possess "repentance towards God, faith towards our Lord Jesus Christ," and holiness of life and conversation. They all hate sin, and they all love Christ. (They worship differently, and after various fashions; some worship with a form of prayer, and some with none; some worship kneeling, and some standing; but they all worship with one heart.) They are all led by one Spirit; they all build upon one foundation; they all draw their religion from one single book – that is the Bible. They are all joined to one great center – that is Jesus Christ. They all even now can say with one heart, "Hallelujah;" and they can all respond with one heart and voice, Amen and Amen.

3. It is a Church WHICH IS DEPENDENT UPON NO MINISTERS UPON EARTH, however much it values those who preach the gospel to its members. The life of its members does not hang upon Church-membership, or baptism, or the Lord's Supper – although they highly value these things when they are to be had. But it has only one great Head – one Shepherd, one chief Bishop – and that is Jesus Christ. He alone, by His Spirit, admits the members of this Church, though ministers may show the door. Till He opens the door no man on earth can open it – neither bishops, nor presbyters, nor convocations, nor synods. Once let a man repent and believe the gospel, and that moment he becomes a member of this Church. Like the penitent thief, he may have no opportunity of being baptized; but he has that which is far better

than any water-baptism – the baptism of the Spirit. He may not be able to receive the bread and wine in the Lord's Supper; but he eats Christ's body and drinks Christ's blood by faith every day he lives, and no minister on earth can prevent him. He may be ex-communicated by ordained men, and cut off from the outward ordinances of the professing Church; but all the ordained men in the world cannot shut him out of the true Church.

It is a Church whose existence does not depend on forms, ceremonies, cathedrals, churches, chapels, pulpits, fonts, vestments, organs, endowments, money, kings, governments, magistrates or any act of favor whatsoever from the hand of man. It has often lived on and continued when all these things have been taken from it. It has often been driven into the wilderness, or into dens and caves of the earth, by those who ought to have been its friends. Its existence depends on nothing but the presence of Christ and His Spirit; and they being ever with it, the Church cannot die.

4. This is the Church TO WHICH THE SCRIPTURAL TITLES OF PRESENT HONOR AND PRIVILEGE, AND THE PROMISES OF FUTURE GLORY ESPECIALLY BELONG; this is the Body of Christ; this is the flock of Christ; this is the household of faith and the family of God; this is God's building, God's foundation, and the temple of the Holy Ghost. This is the Church of the first-born, whose names are written in heaven; this is the royal priesthood, the chosen generation, the peculiar people, the purchased possession, the habitation of God, the light of the world, the salt and the wheat of the earth; this is the "Holy Catholic Church" of the Apostles' Creed; this is the "One Catholic and Apostolic Church" of the Nicene Creed; this is that Church to which the Lord Jesus promises "the gates of hell shall not prevail against it," and to which He says, "I am with you always, even unto the end of the world"(Matt.16:18; 28:2).

5. This is the only Church WHICH POSSESSES TRUE UNITY. Its members are entirely agreed on all the weightier matters of religion, for they are all taught by one Spirit. About God, and Christ, and the Spirit, and sin, and their own hearts, and faith, and repentance, and necessity of holiness, and the value of the Bible, and the importance of prayer, and the resurrection, and judgment to come – about all these points they are of one mind. Take three or four of them, strangers to one another, from the remotest corners of the earth; examine them separately on these points: you will find them all one judgment.

6. This is the only Church WHICH POSSESSES TRUE SANCTITY. Its members are all holy. They are not merely holy by profession, holy in name, and holy in the judgment of charity; they are all holy in act, and deed, and reality, and life, and truth. They are all more or less conformed to the image of Jesus Christ. No unholy man belongs to this Church.

7. This is the only Church WHICH IS TRULY CATHOLIC. It is not the Church of any one nation or people; its members are to be found in every part of the world where the gospel is received and believed. It is not confined within the limits of any one country, or pent up within the pale of any particular forms of outward government. In it there is no difference between Jew and Greek, black man and white, Episcopalian and Presbyterian – but faith in Christ is all. Its members will be gathered from north, and south, and east, and west, and will be of every name and tongue – but all one in Jesus Christ.

8. This is the only Church WHICH IS TRULY APOSTOLIC. It is built on the foundation laid by the Apostles, and holds the doctrines which they preached. The two grand objects at which its members aim are apostolic faith and apostolic practice; and they consider the man who talks of following the Apostles without

possessing these two things to be no better than sounding brass and tinkling cymbal.

9. This is the only Church WHICH IS CERTAIN TO ENDURE UNTO THE END. Nothing can altogether overthrow and destroy it. Its members may be persecuted, oppressed, imprisoned, beaten, beheaded, burned; but the true Church is never altogether extinguished; it rises again from its afflictions; it lives on through fire and water. When crushed in one land it springs up in another. The Pharaohs, the Herods, the Neros, have labored in vain to put down this Church; they slay their thousands, and then pass away and go to their own place. The true Church outlives them all, and sees them buried each in his turn. It is an anvil that has broken many a hammer in this world, and will break many a hammer still; it is a bush which is often burning, and yet is not consumed.

10. This is the only Church OF WHICH NO ONE MEMBER CAN PERISH. Once enrolled in the lists of this Church, sinners are safe for eternity; they are never cast away. The election of God the Father, the continual intercession of God the Son, the daily renewing and sanctifying power of God the Holy Ghost, surround and fence them in like a garden enclosed. Not one bone of Christ's mystical Body shall ever be broken; not one lamb of Christ's flock shall ever be plucked out of His hand.

11. This is the Church WHICH DOES THE WORK OF CHRIST UPON EARTH. Its members are a little flock, and few in numbers, compared with the children of the world; one or two here, and two or three there – a few in this place and a few in that. But these are they who shake the universe; these are they who change the fortunes of kingdoms by their prayers; these are they who are the active workers for spreading the knowledge of pure religion and undefiled; these are the life-blood of a country, the shield, the defense, the stay, and the support of any nation to which they belong.

12. This is the Church WHICH SHALL BE TRULY GLORIOUS AT THE END. When all earthly glory is passed away then shall this Church be presented without spot before God the Father's throne. Thrones, principalities, and powers upon earth shall come to nothing; dignities, and offices, and endowments shall all pass away; but the Church of the first-born shall shine as the stars at the last, and be presented with joy before the Father's throne, in the day of Christ's appearing. When the Lord's jewels are made up, and manifestation of the sons of God takes place, Episcopacy, and Presbyterianism, and Congregationalism will not be mentioned; one Church only will be named, and that is the Church of the elect.

13. Reader, THIS IS THE TRUE CHURCH TO WHICH A MAN MUST BELONG, IF HE WOULD BE SAVED. Till you belong to this, you are nothing better than a lost soul. You may have the form, the husk, the skin, and the shell of religion, but you have not got the substance and the life. Yes, you may have countless outward privileges; you may enjoy great light, and knowledge – but if you do not belong to the Body of Christ, your light and knowledge and privileges will not save your soul. Alas, for the ignorance that prevails on this point! Men fancy if they join this church or that church, and become communicants, and go through certain forms, that all must be right in their souls. It is an utter delusion, it is a gross mistake. All were not Israel who were called Israel, and all are not members of Christ's Body who profess themselves Christian. TAKE NOTICE; you may be a staunch Episcopalian, or Presbyterian, or Independent, or Baptist, or Wesleyan, or Plymouth Brother – and yet not belong to the true Church. And if you do not, it will be better at last if you had never been born.
J.C. Ryle

Church, Catholic

The church is called "catholic" or "universal" because it has spread throughout the entire world, from one end of the earth to the other. It is also called catholic because it teaches fully and unfailingly all the doctrines which men should know about, both visible things and invisible things, the realities of heaven and earthly things. The church is also called catholic because it brings under religious obedience all classes of men, subjects and rulers, uneducated and learned. The last reason the church deserves to be called catholic is because it cures and heals without restriction every type of sin that the soul or body can commit, and because it possesses within itself every type of virtue that can be named, whether exercised in words, actions or other types of spiritual charism.
Cyril of Jerusalem

Church, Duty of the

The duty of the church is to comfort the disturbed and to disturb the comfortable.
Michael Ramsey

Church, Mixed nature of

There are many sheep without, many wolves within.
Augustine of Hippo

Before Christ comes it is useless to expect to see the perfect church.
J.C. Ryle

The day we find the perfect church, it becomes imperfect the moment we join it.
C.H. Spurgeon

Church, Out of date

Tell me what the world is saying today, and I'll tell you what the church will be saying in seven years.
Francis Schaeffer

Church, True

The church of Christ is the multitude of all those who believe in Christ for the remission of sins, and who are thankful for that mercy and who love the law of God

purely, and who hate the sin in this world and long for the life to come. This is the church that cannot err damnably, nor for any length of time, nor all of them. But as soon as any question arises, the truth of God's promise stirs someone up to teach them the truth about everything that is necessary for salvation, from God's word. This enlightens the hearts of the other genuine members, to see the same, and to agree with it.
William Tyndale

Church, Withdrawing from

Although tares, or impure vessels, are found in the church, yet this is not a reason why we should withdraw from it. It only behoves us to labor that we may be vessels of gold or of silver. But to break in pieces the vessels of earth belongs to the Lord alone, to whom a rod of iron is also given. Nor let any one arrogate to himself what is exclusively the province of the Son of God, by pretending to fan the floor, clear away the chaff, and separate all the tares by the judgment of man. This is proud obstinacy and sacrilegious presumption, originating in a corrupt frenzy.
St Cyprian

Church and evangelism

Churching the unchurched is an absolute fallacy – it is like purposing to let the tares in. It is absolutely bizarre to want to make unsaved people feel comfortable in a church. The church is not a building – the church is a group of worshiping, redeemed, and sanctified people among whom an unbeliever should feel either miserable, convicted and drawn to Christ, or else alienated and isolated. Only if the church hides its message and ceases to be what God designed the church to be, can it make an unbeliever comfortable.
John MacArthur

Church and Holy Spirit

If you do not join in what the church is doing, you have no share in this Spirit. For where the church is, there is the Spirit of God; and where the Spirit of God is, there is the church and every kind of grace.
Irenaeus

The form of the church in any age is prescribed by the Holy Spirit.
A. Skevington Wood

Church and prayer

When a church is truly convinced that prayer is where the action is, that church will so construct its corporate activities that the prayer program will have the highest priority.
Paul E. Billheimer

The effectiveness of the prayer program of a church will be in direct proportion to the depth of the individual prayer life of its members. Without a deep devotional life on the part of the participants, the group cannot muster great prayer power.
Paul E. Billheimer

Why is there so much running to and fro to meetings, conventions, fellowship gatherings and yet so little time for prayer?
Andrew Bonar

Why need a church languish and die and have no one converted the year round? Somebody neglects to pray.
C.E. Cornell

The church that is not jealously protected by mighty intercession and sacrificial labors will before long become the abode of every evil bird and the hiding place for unsuspected corruption. The creeping wilderness will soon take over that church that trusts in its own strength and forgets to watch and pray.
A. W. Tozer

Church and state

The coziness between church and state is good for the state and bad for the church.
G.K. Chesterton

The church must be the critic and guide of the state, and never its tool.
Martin Luther King, Jr.

Church and the Bible

The church is the daughter of the Word, not the Word's mother.

Martin Luther

Church as mother

The title, Mother, underlines how essential it is to know about the visible church. There is no other way of entering into life unless we are conceived in her womb, brought to birth and then given her milk.

John Calvin

He cannot have God for his Father who has not the church for his mother.

Cyprian

Church Fathers

The Fathers are primarily to be considered as witnesses, not as authorities.

John Henry Newman

Church growth

One church growth marketer claims that the difference between "growth" and "evangelism" and "marketing" is only semantics. He is absolutely wrong. As historian David Potter pointed out in his penetrating analysis of advertising: "Once marketing becomes dominant, the concern is not with finding an audience to hear their message, but rather with finding a message to hold their audience."

Os Guinness

God never intended His Church to be a refrigerator in which to preserve perishable piety. He intended it to be an incubator in which to hatch out converts.

F. Lincicome

Church history

As we advance through the centuries, light and life begin to decrease in the church. Why? Because the torch of the Scripture begins to grow dim and because the deceitful light of human authorities begins to replace it.

Merle d'Aubigne

Church membership

There are four kinds of church members:

the tired, tireless, tiresome and retired.

Author unknown

There is no way of belonging to Jesus Christ except by belonging gladly and irrevocably to the glorious ragbag of saints and fat-heads who make up the One, Holy and Catholic [Universal] Church!

Bishop Geoffrey Paul

Church visible and invisible

Of course we believe in the invisible Church, evident to God's eye alone, but we are told to accept the visible Church and remain in communion with it.

John Calvin

Church wealth

As a fresh start, the church should give away all her endowments to the poor and needy.

Dietrich Bonhoeffer

Church-going

Morbus sabbaticus is a peculiar disease. The symptoms vary, but never interfere with the appetite. It never lasts more than 24 hours. No physician is ever called. It is contagious. The attack comes on suddenly on Sundays. The patient awakens as usual, feeling fine, and eats a hearty breakfast. About 9 a.m. the attack comes on and lasts until about noon. In the afternoon the patient is much improved and is able to take a ride, visit friends, watch TV, work in the garden, mow the lawn, or read the Sunday paper. The patient usually eats a hearty supper, and is able to go to work on Monday. This ailment is often FATAL in the end – to the soul!

Author unknown

WARNING: Do not attend a church which prefers science to Scripture, reason to revelation, theories to Truth, culture to conversion, benevolence to Blood, goodness to grace, sociability to spirituality, play to praise, programs to power, reformation to regeneration, speculation to salvation, jubilation to justification, feelings to faith, politics to precepts.

Author unknown

The British churchman goes to church as he goes to the bathroom, with the minimum of fuss and no explanation if he can help it.
Ronald Blythe

For a man to argue, "I do not go to church; I pray alone," is no wiser than if he should say, "I have no use for symphonies; I believe only in solo music."
George A. Buttrick

Do not ride in cars: they are responsible for 20% of all fatal accidents.
Do not stay at home: 17% of all accidents occur in the home.
Do not walk on the streets or pavements: 14% of all accidents occur to pedestrians.
Do not travel by air, rail, or water: 16% of all accidents happen on these.
Only .001% of all deaths occur in worship services in church, and these are usually related to previous physical disorders.
Hence the safest place for you to be at any time is at church!
Mark Leslie

Remembering that worship is one of our proper responses to Almighty God, an experience designed for our benefit, and a part of our Christian witness, we and our children will faithfully attend the worship services of the Church.
Moravian Covenant for Christian living

I believe a very large majority of church-goers are merely unthinking, slumbering worshipers of an unknown God.
C.H. Spurgeon

I know there are some who say, "Well, I have given myself to the Lord, but I do not intend to give myself to any church."
  Now why not?
  "Because I can be a Christian without it."
  Are you quite clear about that? You can be as good a Christian by disobedience to your Lord's commands as by being obedient? There is a brick. What is it made for? To help build a house. It is of no use for that brick to tell you that it is just as good a brick while it is kicking about on the ground as it would be in the house. It is a good-for-nothing brick. So you rolling-stone Christians, I do not believe you are answering your purpose. You are living contrary to the life which Christ would have you live, and you are much to blame for the injury you do.
C.H. Spurgeon

Going to church doesn't make you a Christian, any more than going to a garage makes you an automobile.
Billy Sunday

If absence makes the heart grow fonder, how some folks must love the Church!
Gerald I. Teague

Every one that hangs about the court does not speak with the king.
Thomas Watson

Circumstances

Man is not the creature of circumstances. Circumstances are the creatures of men.
Benjamin Disraeli

Circumstances are constantly affecting us and their purpose is to produce our sanctification. Pleasant circumstances and unpleasant circumstances. We should therefore be observant and always watching for lessons, seeking and asking questions.
D. Martyn Lloyd-Jones

People are always blaming their circumstances for what they are. The people who get on in this world are they who get up and look for the circumstances they want, and, if they can't find them, make them.
George Bernard Shaw

Grace is a plant which derives the whole of its support from God the Holy Spirit, and is therefore entirely independent of the circumstances of the man.
C.H. Spurgeon

Citizenship

Socrates, being asked what countryman he

was, answered, "I am a citizen of the whole world." But ask a Christian what countryman he is, and he will answer, "A citizen of heaven."
William Secker

Civility
Civility costs nothing.
Author unknown

Civilization
Culture of intellect, without religion in the heart, is only civilized barbarism and disguised animalism.
Christian Karl von Bunsen

You can't say civilization isn't advancing; in every way they kill you in a new way.
Will Rogers

Clairvoyant
A person, commonly a woman, who has the power of seeing that which is invisible to her patron, namely, that he is a blockhead.
Ambrose Bierce

Cleanliness
Cleanliness is indeed next to godliness.
John Wesley

Clothed
The poor one who is naked will be clothed; and the soul that is naked of desires and whims, God will clothe with his purity, pleasure, and will.
John of the Cross

Coincidences
A coincidence is a small miracle in which God chooses to remain anonymous.
Author unknown

Coincidences are spiritual puns.
G.K. Chesterton

Colors
RED is for the blood He gave.
GREEN is for the grass He made,
YELLOW is for the sun so bright.
ORANGE is for the edge of night.
BLACK is for the sins we made.
WHITE is for the grace He gave.
PURPLE is for His hour of sorrow.
PINK is for our new tomorrow.
A bag full of jelly beans colorful and sweet,
Is a prayer, Is a promise, Is a special treat.
The Jelly Bean prayer
Author unknown

Comfort
When anxiety was great within me, your consolation brought joy to my soul.
The Bible, Psalm 94:19

Is there no balm in Gilead? Is there no physician there?
The Bible, Jeremiah 8:22

Praise be to the God and Father of our Lord Jesus Christ, the Father of compassion and the God of all comfort, who comforts us in all our troubles, so that we can comfort those in any trouble with the comfort we ourselves have received from God.
The Bible, 2 Corinthians 1:3,4

But God, who comforts the downcast, comforted us by the coming of Titus.
The Bible, 2 Corinthians 7:6

If we have not quiet in our minds, outward comfort will do no more for us than a golden slipper on a gouty foot.
John Bunyan

The lust for comfort murders the passions of the soul.
Kahlil Gibran

God does not comfort us to make us comfortable, but to make us comforters.
J.H. Jowett

To ease another's heartache is to forget one's own.
Abraham Lincoln

Human comfort and divine comfort are of different natures: human comfort consists in external, visible help, which a man may

see, hold, and feel; divine comfort only in words and promises, where there is neither seeing, hearing, nor feeling.
Martin Luther

To comfort a sorrowful conscience is much better than to posses many kingdoms.
Martin Luther

In Christ the heart of the Father is revealed, and higher comfort there cannot be than to rest in the Father's heart.
Andrew Murray

Little things console us because little things afflict us.
Blaise Pascal

No affliction nor temptation, no guilt nor power of sin, no wounded spirit nor terrified conscience, should induce us to despair of help and comfort from God!
Thomas Scott

We ourselves know by experience that there is no place for comfort like the cross. It is a tree stripped of all foliage, and apparently dead; yet we sit under its shadow with great delight, and its fruit is sweet unto our taste.
C.H. Spurgeon

It will greatly comfort you if you can see God's hand in both your losses and your crosses.
C.H. Spurgeon

When spiritual comfort is sent to you by God, take it humbly and give thanks meekly for it. But know for certain that it is the great goodness of God that sends it to you, and not because you deserve it.
Thomas à Kempis

When comfort is withdrawn, do not be cast down, but humbly and patiently await the visitation of God. He is able and powerful to give you more grace and more spiritual comfort than you first had.
Thomas à Kempis

If I alone might have all the solace and comfort of this world, and might use the delights of this world according to my own desire and without sin, it is certain that they would not long endure. And so, my soul cannot be fully comforted or perfectly refreshed, except in God alone, who is the Comforter of the poor in spirit and the Embracer of the humble and low in heart.
Thomas à Kempis

Comfort

Letter from Samuel Rutherford
To Lady Kenmure (on the death of her husband),
My Very Noble And Worthy Lady,
I often call to mind the comforts that I, a poor friendless stranger, received from your ladyship here in a strange part of the country, when my Lord took from me the delight of mine eyes (Ezek. 24:16). Although my wound is not yet fully healed and cured, I trust that your Lord, remembering what He did for me, will give you comfort now that He has made you a widow. This has happened in order that you may be a free woman for Christ, who is now seeking the love of your true heart. Therefore, when you lie alone in your bed, let Christ be as a bundle of myrrh, to sleep and lie all the night between your breasts (Cant. 1:13).
Christian Character Proven in Suffering
Consider, that of all the crosses spoken of in our Lord's Word, this one gives you a special right to make God your Husband (which was not so yours while your husband was alive). Therefore try to read God's mercy out of this visitation; however I must say from the depths of my own suffering that the mourning for the husband of your youth is, as God' says Himself, the heaviest worldly sorrow (Joel 1:8). But though this be the heaviest burden that ever lay upon your back, yet you know that if we will wait upon Him who hides His face for a while, it lies upon

God's honor and truth to be a Husband to the widow. See and consider then what you have lost, in proportion to eternity. Madam, let me implore you, in the bowels of Christ Jesus, and by the comforts of His Spirit, and because you know that in the future you will appear before him: let God, and men, and angels now see what is in you. The Lord has pierced the vessel; it will be known whether there be in it wine or water. Let your faith and patience be seen, that it may be known your only beloved first and last has been Christ.

The Suitable Object of Your Love

Therefore, now cast your whole love upon Jesus Christ; He alone is a suitable object for your love and all the affections of your soul. God has dried up one channel of your love by the removal of your husband. Let now that river run upon Christ. I dare say that God's hammering of you from your youth is only to make you a fair carved stone in the high upper temple of the New Jerusalem. Your Lord never thought this world's worthless, imitation glory a gift worthy of you, and therefore would not bestow it on you, because he is offering you a better portion. Let the small change go; the great inheritance is yours. You are a child of the house, and joy is laid up for you; it is long in coming, but none the worse for that. I am now expecting to see, and that with joy and comfort, that which I hoped of you: that you have laid such strength upon the Holy One of Israel, that you defy troubles, and that your soul is a castle that may be besieged, but cannot be taken.

Fire and Ice

After all, why do you think this world is so important? This world has never treated you like a friend. You owe it little love. Why you should you go courting after it? The world will never be a faithful partner to you. Never seek warm fire under cold ice. This is not a field where your happiness grows; it is up above, where there are a great multitude, which no man can number, of all nations, and kindreds, and people, and tongues, standing before the throne and before the Lamb, clothed with white robes, and palms in their hands (Rev. 7:9). What

you could never get here you shall find there. Consider how in all these trials (and truly they have been many) your Lord has been loosening you at the root from perishing things, and hunting after you to grip your soul. Madam, for the Son of God's sake, do not weaken His grip on you, but stay and abide in the love of God, as Jude says (Jude 21).

Lift Up Your Head – Farewell

Now, Madam, I hope your Ladyship will not be offended by anything I have said. If I have failed your Ladyship, it is because I did not live up to your generous love and respect, and I beg a full pardon for it. Again, my dear and noble lady, let me beseech you to lift up your head, for the day of your redemption draws near. Remember, that star that shined in Galloway is now shining in another world. Now I pray that God may answer, in His own way, to your soul, and that He may be to you the God of all consolations.

Thus I remain,

Your Ladyship's at all dutiful obedience in the Lord,

Samuel Rutherford

Comforters

Miserable comforters are ye all.

Job 16:2 KJV

Job's friends chose the right time to visit him, but took not the right course of improving their visit; had they spent the time in praying for him which they did in hot disputes with him, they would have profited him, and pleased God more.

William Gurnall

Comforting

We have all sufficient strength to endure the misfortunes of others.

Francis, Duc de La Rochefoucauld

Comforts

Comforts corrode our consciences.

Steve Constable

Commandments

"Honor your father and mother" – which is the first commandment with a promise.
Ephesians 6:2

Jesus said, "Love the Lord our God with all your passion and prayer and intelligence." This is the most important [of God's commands], the first on any list.
The Bible, Matthew 22:37-38 THE MESSAGE

But there is a second [command of God] to set alongside it: "Love others as well as you love yourself."
The Bible, Matthew 22:39 THE MESSAGE

One of the scribes came and heard them arguing and recognizing that He had answered them well, asked Him, "What commandment is the foremost [or 'first'] of all?" Jesus answered, "The foremost is, 'HEAR, O ISRAEL; THE LORD OUR GOD IS ONE LORD; [Deuteronomy 6:4] AND YOU SHALL LOVE THE LORD YOUR GOD WITH ALL YOUR HEART, AND WITH ALL YOUR SOUL, AND WITH ALL YOUR MIND, AND WITH ALL YOUR STRENGTH.' [Deuteronomy 6:5] The second is this, 'YOU SHALL LOVE YOUR NEIGHBOR AS YOURSELF.' [Leviticus 19:18] There is no other commandment greater than these."
The Bible, Mark 12:28-31 NASB

The world invents its own good works and persuades itself that they are good. But Paul declares that good and right according to the world are to be judged by the commandments of God.
John Calvin

Commitment

Give your all to Christ, who gave His all for you.
Author unknown

The difference between involvement and commitment is like an eggs-and-ham breakfast: the chicken was involved – the pig was committed.
Author unknown

The dearest idol I have known,
Whate'er that idol be,
Help me to tear it from its throne,
And worship only thee.
William Cowper

Unless commitment is made, there are only promises and hopes ... but no plans.
Peter Drucker

The resolved mind hath no cares.
George Herbert

There are very few who in their hearts do not believe in God, but what they will not do is give Him exclusive right of way. They are not ready to promise full allegiance to God alone.
D.L. Moody

I feel that, if I could live a thousand lives, I would like to live them all for Christ, and even then, I would feel that they were all too little a return for His great love to me.
C.H. Spurgeon

Committee

To get something done, a committee should consist of three men, two of whom are absent.
Author unknown

A committee is a thing which takes a week to do what one good man can do in an hour.
Elbert Hubbard

Common grace
See: Grace, Common

Common sense

There is nothing more uncommon than common sense.
Frank Lloyd Wright

Communal living

Call nothing your own, but let everything be yours in common.
Augustine, The Rule of St Augustine

Communication

Incomprehensible jargon is the hallmark of a profession.
Kingman Brewster, Jr.

I guess I should warn you, if I turn out to be particularly clear, you've probably misunderstood what I've said.
Alan Greenspan, as Chairman of the Federal Reserve Board

When God wants to speak and deal with us, he does not avail himself of an angel but of parents, or the pastor, or of our neighbor.
Martin Luther

The Church faces the same problem today as it has faced in every era – the problem of communicating to our culture while not identifying with its values.
George M. Marsden

God has communicated to man, the infinite to the finite. The One who made man capable of language in the first place has communicated to man in language about both spiritual reality and physical reality, about the nature of God and the nature of man.
Francis Schaeffer

Every generation of Christians has this problem of learning how to speak meaningfully to its own age. It cannot be solved without an understanding of the changing existential situation which it faces. If we are to communicate the Christian faith effectively, therefore, we must know and understand the thought forms of our own generation.
Francis Schaeffer

Communication in silence

The Father has uttered only one word, and this word was his Son; he still utters it in eternal silence, and it is in silence that the soul should listen to it.
John of the Cross

Communism

From each according to his abilities, to each according to his needs.
Karl Marx

Community

My duty towards my neighbor is to love him as myself, and to do unto all men as I would they should do unto me.
Book of Common Prayer

No man is an island entire of itself. Every man is a piece of the continent, a part of the main. If a clod be washed away by the sea, Europe is the less, as well as if a promontory were, as well as if a manor of thy friends or of thine own were. Any man's death diminishes me, because I am involved in mankind. Therefore never send to know for whom the bell tolls. It tolls for thee.
John Donne

The individual's prerogative (inspiration or status) is always subordinate to the good of the whole.
James D.G. Dunn

Not until the creation and maintenance of decent conditions of life for all men are recognized and accepted as a common obligation of all men... shall we... be able to speak of mankind as civilized.
Albert Einstein

We must learn to live together as brothers or perish together as fools.
Martin Luther King, Jr.

Make it a rule, and pray to God to help you to keep it, never, if possible, to lie down at night without being able to say: "I have made one human being at least a little wiser, or a little happier, or at least a little better this day."
Charles Kingsley

If God is thy father, man is thy brother.
Alphonse de Lamartine

Man does not live for himself alone in this mortal body, in order to work on its account, but also for all men on earth; nay,

he lives only for others, and not for himself.
Martin Luther

No one may forsake his neighbor when he is in trouble. Everybody is under obligation to help and support his neighbor as he would himself like to be helped.
Martin Luther

If civilization is to survive, we must cultivate the science of human relationships – the ability of all peoples, of all kinds, to live together, in the same world at peace.
Franklin D. Roosevelt

You don't live in a world all alone. Your brothers are here, too.
Albert Schweitzer

The race of mankind would perish did they cease to aid each other. We cannot exist without mutual help. All therefore that need aid have a right to ask it from their fellow man; and no one who has the power of granting can refuse it without guilt.
Sir Walter Scott

During the New Testament period no universal economic practice was adopted by Christians.
John White

Compassion

Be kind and compassionate to one another, forgiving each other, just as in Christ God forgave you.
The Bible, Ephesians 4:32

Therefore, as God's chosen people, holy and dearly loved, clothe yourselves with compassion, kindness, humility, gentleness and patience. Bear with each other and forgive whatever grievances you have against one another. Forgive as the Lord forgave you. And over all these virtues put on love, which binds them all together in perfect unity.
The Bible, Colossians 3:12-14

… be sympathetic, love as brothers, be compassionate and humble.
The Bible, 1 Peter 3:8

Honesty without Compassion is Brutality.
Author unknown

Compassion will cure more sins than condemnation.
Henry Ward Beecher

The best exercise for strengthening the heart is reaching down and lifting people up.
Ernest Blevins

The dew of compassion is a tear.
Lord Byron

Man may dismiss compassion from his heart, but God never will.
William Cowper

For pity melts the mind to love.
John Dryden

If you want others to be happy, practice compassion. If you want to be happy, practice compassion.
Tenzin Gyatso, the 14th Dalai Lama of Tibet

Let all find compassion in you.
John of the Cross

Compassion means that if I see my friend and my enemy in equal need, I shall help both equally. Justice demands that we seek and find the stranger, the broken, the prisoner and comfort them and offer them our help. Here lies the holy compassion of God.
Mechtild of Magdeburg

When you make that one effort to feel compassion instead of blame or self-blame, the heart opens again and continues opening.
Sara Paddison

Until he extends his circle of compassion to include all living things, man will not himself find peace.
Albert Schweitzer

Until he extends the circle of his compassion to all living things, man will not himself find peace.
Albert Schweitzer

The value of compassion cannot be over-emphasized. Anyone can criticize. It takes a true believer to be compassionate. No greater burden can be borne by an individual than to know no one cares or understands.
Arthur H. Stainback

Compassion, God's
The Lord is full of compassion and mercy.
The Bible, James 5:11

Complacency
For the waywardness of the simple will kill them, and the complacency of fools will destroy them.
The Bible, Proverbs 1:32

Complacency is a deadly foe of all spiritual growth.
A. W. Tozer

Compliance
A "No" uttered from deepest conviction is better and greater than a "Yes" merely uttered to please, or what is worse, to avoid trouble.
Mohandis K. Gandhi

Compliments
Pleasant words are as an honeycomb, sweet to the soul, and health to the bones.
Author unknown

Some people pay a compliment as if they expected a receipt.
Elbert Hubbard

Compromise
Compromise is always wrong when it means sacrificing principle.
Drake Raft

Computer
The Internet is so big, so powerful and pointless that for some people it is a complete substitute for life.
Andrew Brown

Computer: a million morons working at the speed of light.
David Ferrier

Conceit
Do not be conceited.
The Bible, Romans 12:16

Let us not become conceited, provoking and envying each other.
The Bible, Galatians 5:26

A conceited person never gets anywhere because he thinks he is already there.
Author unknown

Conceit is self-given; be careful.
John Wooden

Condemnation
There is therefore now no condemnation to them which are in Christ Jesus.
The Bible, Romans 8:1 KJV

Confession of faith
See also: Creeds

Confession of sin
If we confess our sins, he [God] is faithful and just and will forgive us our sins and purify us from all unrighteousness.
The Bible, 1 John 1:9

Admission of wrongdoing is not an admission of weakness, but a sign of strength.
Author unknown

Confess your sins, not your neighbors'.
Author unknown

While anyone can admit to themselves they were wrong, the true test is admission to someone else.
Author unknown

The confession of evil works is the first beginning of good works.
Augustine of Hippo

At the earlier Methodist class meetings, members were expected every week to answer some extremely personal questions, such as the following: Have you experienced any particular temptations during the past week? How did you react or respond to those temptations? Is there anything you are trying to keep secret, and, if so, what? At this point, the modern Christian swallows hard! We are often coated with a thick layer of reserve and modesty which covers "a multitude of sins" – usually our own. Significantly, James 5:16-20, the original context of that phrase, is the passage which urges, "Confess your sins to one another, and pray for one another, that you may be healed."
Michael Griffiths

We must lay before Him what is in us, not what ought to be in us.
C.S. Lewis

The final contribution of religious faith to freedom is the freedom to confess our sins; the freedom to admit that we sit under the ultimate judgment of God.
Ursula W. Niebuhr

In case our sins have been public and scandalous, both reason and the practice of the Christian Church do require that when men have publicly offended they should give public satisfaction and open testimony of their repentance.
John Tillotson

The best of what we do and are, Just God, forgive!
William Wordsworth

Confidence
Religion is the possibility of the removal of every ground of confidence except confidence in God alone.
Karl Barth

Confidence is that feeling by which the mind embarks on great and honorable courses with a sure hope and trust in itself.
Cicero

Only the person who has faith in himself is able to be faithful to others.
Erich Fromm

Skill and confidence are an unconquered army.
George Herbert

Our belief at the beginning of a doubtful undertaking is the one thing that insures the successful outcome of our venture.
William James

Optimism is the faith that leads to achievement. Nothing can be done without hope and confidence.
Helen Keller

Faith is a living, daring confidence in God's grace, so sure and certain that a man would stake his life on it a thousand times. This confidence in God's grace and knowledge of it makes men glad and bold and happy in dealing with God and with all his creatures; and this is the work of the Holy Ghost in faith. Hence a man is ready and glad, without compulsion, to do good to everyone, to serve everyone, to suffer everything, in love and praise of God, who has shown him this grace.
Martin Luther

A widespread lack of confidence in Christ's sufficiency is threatening the contemporary church.
John MacArthur

Confidence thrives on honesty, on honor, on the sacredness of obligations, on faithful protection and on unselfish performance. Without them it cannot live.
Franklin D. Roosevelt

Experience tells you what to do; confidence allows you to do it.
Stan Smith

Nobody holds a good opinion of a man who has a low opinion of himself.
Anthony Trollope

They are able because they think they are able.
Virgil

Conflict

Never wrestle with a pig. You both get all dirty, and the pig likes it.
Author unknown

The conflict between good and evil is drama, but the conflict between good and good is tragedy.
Author unknown

In conflict, be fair and generous.
Tao Te Ching

When principles that run against your deepest convictions begin to win the day, then battle is your calling and peace has become sin. You must at the price of dearest peace lay your convictions bare before friend and enemy with all the fire of your faith.
Abraham Kuyper

The war existing between the senses and reason.
Blaise Pascal

To observe people in conflict is a necessary part of a child's education. It helps him to understand and accept his own occasional hostilities and to realize that differing opinions need not imply an absence of love.
Milton R. Sapirstein

Conformity

Why can't you be a nonconformist like everyone else?
Author unknown

Be different: conform.
Author unknown

The opposite of bravery is not cowardice, but conformity.
Robert Anthony

To get nowhere, follow the crowd.
Frank Baer

It is no measure of health to be well adjusted to a profoundly sick society.
Krishnamurti

Confrontation

Truth carries with it confrontation. Truth demands confrontation; loving confrontation, but confrontation nevertheless. If our reflex action is always accommodation regardless of the centrality of the truth involved, there is something wrong.
Francis Schaeffer

Confucius

Confucius wasn't even sure there was a God or heaven.
Luis Palau

Confucius never claimed he could knock on the door of someone's heart.
Luis Palau

Conscience

My conscience is clear, but that does not make me innocent. It is the Lord who judges me.
The Bible, 1 Corinthians 4:4
… keeping a clear conscience …
The Bible, 1 Peter 3:16

A bad conscience has a very good memory.
Author unknown

A bad conscience embitters the sweetest comforts; a good one sweetens the bitterest crosses.
Author unknown

Conscience is what hurts when everything else feels so good.
Author unknown

Cowardice asks the question, "Is it safe?" Expedience asks the question, "Is it political?" Vanity asks, "Is it popular?" But conscience asks the question, "Is it right?"
Author unknown

Conscience is condensed character.
Author unknown

Conscious is when you are aware of something, and conscience is when you wish you weren't.
Author unknown

A good conscience is the palace of Christ; the temple of the Holy Ghost; the paradise of delight, the standing Sabbath of the saints.
Augustine of Hippo

Conscience is the perfect interpreter of life.
Karl Barth

God alone is Lord of the conscience; and he hath left it free from the doctrines and commandments of men, which are in anything contrary to His word, or not contained in it. Civil magistrates being ordained of God, subjection in all lawful things commanded by them ought to be yielded by us in the Lord, not only for wrath, but also for conscience sake.
James Boyce

The world has achieved brilliance without wisdom, power without conscience.
Omar Bradley

A good conscience and a good confidence go together.
Thomas Brooks

Conscience is thoroughly well-bred and soon leaves off talking to those who do not wish to hear it.
Samuel Butler

The torture of a bad conscience is the hell of a living soul.
John Calvin

A sleeping pill will never take the place of a clear conscience.
Edie Cantor

Thy miseries are not hid from thee now, for the worm of conscience sleeps on longer.
Catherine of Siena

To endeavor to domineer over conscience is to invade the citadel of heaven.
Charles V, Emperor

Nothing is sweeter than a good conscience.
Columbanus

Never do anything against conscience even if the state demands it.
Albert Einstein

Conscience tells us in our innermost being of the presence of God and of the moral difference between good and evil.
Billy Graham

Most of us follow our conscience as we follow a wheelbarrow. We push it in front of us in the direction we want to go.
Billy Graham

Peace of conscience is nothing but the echo of pardoning mercy.
William Gurnall

Be the master of your will and the slave of your conscience.
Hasidic saying

There is a conscience in man; therefore there is a God in heaven.
Ezekiel Hopkins

There is a spectacle more grand than the sea; it is heaven; there is a spectacle more grand than heaven; it is the conscience.
Victor Hugo

There comes a time when one must take a position that's neither safe, nor political, nor popular, but he must take it because his conscience tells him that it's right.
Martin Luther King, Jr.

A lot of people mistake a short memory for a clear conscience.
Doug Larson

It is neither safe nor prudent to do anything against conscience.
Martin Luther

Conscience is the inner voice that warns us that someone might be looking.
H.L. Mencken

Christian joy is a gift of God flowing from a good conscience.
Philip Neri

Conscience is a law to the mind; yet [Christians] would not grant that it is nothing more; I mean that it was not a dictate, nor conveyed the notion of responsibility, of duty, or a threat and a promise.
J.H. Newman

Keep your conscience sensitive and alert.
John Owen

A bad conscience embitters the sweetest comforts; a good conscience sweetens the bitterest crosses.
Wendell Phillips

Do not lay open your conscience to anyone whom you do not trust in your heart.
Poemen, Abba

Strive greatly to have and to exercise a good conscience towards God, and men; to commit thy soul, life, and cause to the Lord; and then expect the worst of men, and the best of Christ.
Vavasor Powell

There is no pillow so soft as a clear conscience.
French proverb

At times, although one is perfectly in the right, one's legs tremble; at other times, although one is completely in the wrong, birds sing in one's soul.
Vasily V. Rozanov

Better I be a traitor to my country than a traitor to my conscience.
Lt. Colonel Claus Phillip Maria Schenk Graf von Stauffenberg (1907-1944), who attempted to assassinate Adolf Hitler

When a man won't listen to his conscience, it's usually because he doesn't want advice from a total stranger.
Lindsey Stewart

Do not be satisfied with as much Christianity as will only ease your conscience.
J.B. Stoney

Sweet shall be your rest if your heart does not reproach you.
Thomas à Kempis

Labor to keep alive in your breast that little spark of celestial fire, called conscience.
George Washington

No flattery can heal a bad conscience, so no slander can hurt a good one.
Thomas Watson

Consecration

Batter my heart, three-person'd God; for, you
As yet but knock, breathe, shine, and seek
 to mend;
That I may rise, and stand, o'erthrow me,
 and bend
Your force, to break, blow, burn and make
 me new.
I, like an usurp'd town, to another due,
Labor to admit you, but Oh, to no end,
Reason your viceroy in me, me should
 defend,
But is captiv'd, and proves weak or untrue.
Yet dearly I love you, and would be loved fain,
But am betroth'd unto your enemy:
Divorce me, untie, or break that knot again,
Take me to you, imprison me, for I
Except you enthral me, never shall be free,
Nor ever chaste, except you ravish me.
John Donne

The mark of a saint is not perfection, but consecration. A saint is not a man without faults, but a man who has given himself without reserve to God.
W. T. Richardson

The theory of a sudden, mysterious transition of a believer into a state of

blessedness and entire consecration, at one mighty bound, I cannot receive. It appears to me to be a man-made invention; and I do not see a single plain text to prove it in Scripture.
J.C. Ryle

Consecrate yourself anew this day wholly to your Master's service. You are not your own, but bought with a price, and if you would not be like these thorn-choked seeds, live while you live, with all-consuming zeal.
C.H. Spurgeon

By one act of consecration of our total selves to God, we can make every subsequent act express that consecration.
A.W. Tozer

Conservatism
A religious conservative is a fanatic about a dead radical.
Author unknown

Consideration
A little Consideration, a little Thought for Others, makes all the difference.
A.A. Milne

Consistency
We need to learn to set our course by the stars and not by the lights of every passing ship.
Omar Bradley

Consolation
See: Comfort

Constancy
Constancy is the foundation of virtue.
Francis Bacon

Constancy is the complement of all other human virtues.
Giuseppe Mazzini

Contemplation
Contemplation strengthens.
Bernard of Clairvaux

Place your mind before the mirrors of eternity!

Place your soul in the brilliance of glory.
Place your heart in the figure of the divine substance,
And transform your whole being into the magic of the Godhead itself through contemplation.
Clare of Assisi

In order to attain the citadel of contemplation you must begin by exercising yourself in the field of labor.
Gregory the Great

By the grace of contemplation the Voice of the Supernatural Intelligence occurs in the mind ... The words of God are perceived in the ear of the heart ... and by supernal grace, we are led to understand higher things.
Gregory the Great

The grace of contemplation is granted only in response to a longing and importunate desire.
Gregory the Great

He that contemplates hath a day without a night.
George Herbert

The fly that clings to honey hinders its flight, and the soul that allows itself attachment to spiritual sweetness hinders its own liberty and contemplation.
John of the Cross

I have often told thee, daughter, that thinking, weeping, and high contemplation is the best life on earth, and thou shalt have more merit in heaven for one year of thinking in thy mind than for a hundred years of praying with thy mouth.
Margery Kempe

Let us yoke contemplation to action.
The Lenten Triodion

Since contemplation cannot be had by our own efforts, we must humble ourselves.
Teresa of Avila

If Jesus crucified were often in our hearts
and in our memory, we should soon be
learned in all things that are necessary for us.
Thomas à Kempis

To think well is to serve God in the
interior court: To have a mind composed
of divine thoughts, and set frame, to be
like Him within.
Thomas Traherne

Contemplation, Four kinds of
The first and the greatest is to wonder at
majesty. This demands a heart made pure,
so that freed from vices and released from
sin, it can ascend easily to heavenly things.
Sometimes this contemplation holds the
watcher rapt in amazement and ecstasy, if
only for a moment.

A second kind of contemplation is
necessary for this man. He needs to look on
the judgments of God. While this
contemplation strikes fear into the onlooker
because it is indeed frightening, it drives out
vices, strengthens virtues, initiates into
wisdom, protects humility. Humility is the
true and solid foundation of virtues. For if
humility were to collapse, the building-up
of the virtues will fall down.

The third kind of contemplation is
occupied (or rather at leisure) in
remembering kindnesses and, so as to avoid
ingratitude, it urges him who remembers to
love his Benefactor. Of such says the
prophet, speaking to the Lord, "They shall
declare the memory of the abundance of
your sweetness" (Ps 14:7).

The fourth contemplation, which forgets
what is past, rests wholly in the expectation
of what is promised (Phil 3:13), which
nourishes patience and nerves the arm of
perseverance, for what is promised is eternal.
Bernard of Clairvaux

Contemporary
To be "contemporary" is to live in the
present. To be a "contemporary Christian,"
however, is to ensure that our present is
enriched both by our knowledge of the
past and by our expectation of the future.
John Stott

Contempt for self
No one has the right to look with
contempt on himself when God has shown
such an interest in him.
Author unknown

Contentment
See also: Covetousness
Give me neither poverty nor riches.
The Bible, Proverbs 30:8

I have learned, in whatsoever state I am,
therewith to be content.
The Bible, Philippians 4:11 KJV

The secret of contentment is the
realization that life is a gift, not a right.
Author unknown

If you cannot get what you like, why not
try to like what you get?
Author unknown

He who is not contented with what he has
would not be contented with what he
would like to have.
Author unknown

The Lord is my shepherd, that's all I want.
*Author unknown, young child misquoting the
23rd Psalm*

The utmost we can hope for in this life is
contentment.
Joseph Addison

Be content with your lot; one cannot be
first in everything.
Aesop

To be satisfied with a little, is the greatest
wisdom; and he that increaseth his riches,
increaseth his cares; but a contented mind is
a hidden treasure, and trouble findeth it not.
Akhenaton

Contentment is a pearl of great price, and
whoever procures it at the expense of ten
thousand desires makes a wise and happy
choice.
John Balguy

But if I'm content with a little,
Enough is as good as a feast.
Isaac Bickerstaffe

A little is as much as a lot, if it is enough.
Steve Brown

He that is down needs fear no fall,
He that is low no pride;
He that is humble ever shall
Have God to be his guide.
I am content with what I have,
Little be it or much;
And, Lord, contentment still I crave,
Because thou savest such.
Fulness to such a burden is
That go on pilgrimage:
Here little, and hereafter bliss,
Is best from age to age.
John Bunyan

If we have not quiet in our minds, outward
comfort will do no more for us than a
golden slipper on a gouty foot.
John Bunyan

Restlessness and discontent are the first
necessities of progress.
Thomas A. Edison

He is a wise man who does not grieve for
the things which he has not, but rejoices
for those which he has.
Epictetus

It is better for you to be free of fear lying
upon a pallet, than to have a golden
couch and a rich table and be full of
trouble.
Epicurus

He who doesn't find a little enough, will
find nothing enough.
Epicurus

To the discontented man no chair is easy.
Benjamin Franklin

Who is rich? He that is content. Who is
that? Nobody.
Benjamin Franklin

Content makes poor men rich; discontent
makes rich men poor.
Benjamin Franklin

There are times when a man should be
content with what he has, but never with
what he is.
William George Jordan

To be upset over what you don't have is to
waste what you do have.
Ken Keyes, Jr

Next to faith this is the highest art – to
be content with the calling in which
God has placed you. I have not learned
it yet.
Martin Luther

It's not very pleasant in my corner of the
world at three o'clock in the morning. But
for people who like cold, wet, ugly bits it is
something rather special.
Eeyore, A.A. Milne

The only ultimate disaster that can befall
us, I have come to realize, is to feel
ourselves at home here on earth.
Malcolm Muggeridge

Contentment: The smother of invention.
Ethel Mumford

Number one, God brought me here. It is
by His will that I am in this place. In that
fact I will rest.
   Number two, He will keep me here in
His love and give me grace to behave as
His child.
   Number three, He will make the trial a
blessing, teaching me the lessons He
intends for me to learn and working in
me the grace He means to bestow.
   Number four, in His good time He can
bring me out again. How and when, He
knows. So let me say I am here.
Andrew Murray

Great wealth and contentment seldom live
together.
Bob Phillips

God is most glorified in us when we are most satisfied in him.
John Piper

It is so important not to waste what is precious by spending all one's time and emotion on fretting or complaining over what one does not have.
Edith Schaeffer

Poor and content is rich and rich enough.
William Shakespeare, Othello

Being happy with God now means:
Loving as he loves,
Helping as he helps,
Giving as he gives,
Serving as he serves,
Rescuing as he rescues,
Being with him twenty-four hours,
Touching him in his distressing disguise.
Mother Teresa

When a man has arrived so far, that he seeks his consolation from no created thing, then at this point he begins truly to taste what God is; then, too, will he be well content with everything that happens.
Thomas à Kempis

Contradiction
Faith embraces many truths which seem to contradict each other.
Blaise Pascal

Control
Conquest is easy. Control is not.
Author unknown

Knowing that I am not the one in control gives great encouragement. Knowing the One who is in control is everything.
Alexander Michael

Controversy
... nor to devote themselves to myths and endless genealogies. These promote controversies rather than God's work – which is by faith.
The Bible, 1 Timothy 1:4

But avoid foolish controversies and genealogies and arguments and quarrels about the law, because these are unprofitable and useless.
The Bible, Titus 3:9

In a controversy the instant we feel anger we have already ceased striving for the truth, and have begun striving for ourselves.
Thomas Carlyle

Many controversies of these times grow up about religion, as suckers from the root and limbs of a fruit tree, which spend the vital sap that should make fruit.
John Flavel

Of all people who engage in controversy, we, who are called Calvinists, are most expressly bound by our own principles to the exercise of gentleness and moderation.
John Newton

Controversy is only dreaded by the advocates of error.
Benjamin Rush

Conversation
In conversation, humor is worth more than wit and easiness more than knowledge.
George Herbert

The character of a man is known from his conversation.
Menander

Devout conversation on spiritual things helpeth not a little to spiritual progress, most of all where those of kindred mind and spirit find their ground of fellowship in God.
Thomas à Kempis

Conversion
See also: Accepting God; Becoming a Christian; Regeneration
You can't tell the exact moment when night becomes day, but you know when it is daytime.
Author unknown

When you remember how hard it is to change yourself, you begin to understand what little chance we have of changing others.
Author unknown

Conversion is committing all of me to all I know of Christ.
Author unknown

It is spiritually dead until that day; but it then begins to live! A saved man may reckon his age from the time in which he first knew the Lord.
Joseph Alleine

For a soul to come to Jesus, is the grandest event in its history.
Joseph Alleine

It is one thing to have sin alarmed only by convictions, and another to have it crucified by converting grace. Many, because they have been troubled in conscience for their sins, think well of their case, miserably mistaking conviction for conversion.
Joseph Alleine

Before conversion man seeks to cover himself with his own fig-leaves, and to make himself whole by his duties. He is apt to trust in himself, and set up his own righteousness, and to reckon his counters for gold, and not to submit to the righteousness of God.

But conversion changes his mind; now he counts his own righteousness as filthy rags. He casts it off, as a man would the venomous tatters of a nasty beggar. Now he is brought to poverty of spirit, complains of and condemns himself, and all his inventory is "poor, and miserable, and wretched, and blind, and naked."
Joseph Alleine

I was brought to Christ in the year 1862. A Dr Hunt, of Harcourt Street, Dublin, had been the means in God's hands of awakening inquiry in the mind of my brother George. I actually found Christ without any human intervention when alone, some days after a special service with my brother Fred and Dr Hunt.
Thomas Barnardo

I had always thought much of how I might inherit the kingdom of heaven; but finding in myself a powerful opposition, in the desires that belong to the flesh and blood, I began a battle against my corrupted nature; and with the aid of God, I made up my mind to overcome the inherited evil will ... break it, and enter wholly into the love of God in Christ Jesus ... I sought the heart of Jesus Christ, the center of all truth; and I resolved to regard myself as dead in my inherited form, until the Spirit of God would take form in me, so that in and through him, I might conduct my life. I stood in this resolution, fighting a battle with myself, until the light of the Spirit, a light entirely foreign to my unruly nature, began to break through the clouds. Then, after some further hard fights with the powers of darkness, my spirit broke through the doors of hell, and penetrated even unto the innermost essence of its newly born divinity where it was received with great love, as a bridegroom welcomes his beloved bride.

No word can express the great joy and triumph I experienced, as of a life out of death, as of a resurrection from the dead! ... While in this state, as I was walking through a field of flowers, in fifteen minutes, I saw through the mystery of creation, the original of this world and of all creatures... . Then for seven days I was in a continual state of ecstasy, surrounded by the light of the Spirit, which immersed me in contemplation and happiness. I learned what God is, and what is his will ... I knew not how this happened to me, but my heart admired and praised the Lord for it!
Jacob Boehme

I remember as if it were but yesterday ... the rolling away from my heart of the guilty burden ... and the going forth to serve my God and my generation from that hour.
William Booth

But upon a day the good providence of God did cast me to Bedford to work on my calling, and in one of the streets of that town I came where there were three or four poor women sitting at a door in the sun and talking about the things of God; and being now willing to hear them discourse, I drew near to hear what they said, for I was now a brisk talker also myself in the matters of religion. But now I may say I heard, but I understood not; for they were far above, out of my reach; for their talk was about a new birth – the work of God on their hearts. And methought they spake as if Joy did make them speak; they spake with such pleasantness of scripture language and with such appearance of grace in all they said, that they were to me as if they had found a new world.
John Bunyan

Take the best-natured man in the world, plant him in the best soil, in the best ground, in church ground; plant him in the house of God, and there let him be watered by the rain of holy doctrine, and let him be dressed and cultivated every day, yet he will bring forth nothing but crabs, nothing but unsavory fruit, till he himself is changed. It is only by our implantation into Jesus Christ that we become fit to do good, so as to be acceptable unto God. It is this that makes the change.
Joseph Caryl

The reception of the Spirit was the decisive and determinative element in the crucial transaction of conversion.
James D.J. Dunn

Allowances must be made for our natural temperaments, for conversion does not entirely rule out our natural dispositions; for those sins towards which a man is naturally inclined before his conversion will still be the ones that he is apt to fall into.
Jonathan Edwards

On January 12th 1723, I made a solemn dedication of myself to God and wrote it down; giving up myself and all that I had to God; to be for the future in no respect my own.
Jonathan Edwards

God enters by a private door into every individual.
Ralph Waldo Emerson

Nothing less than unconditional surrender could ever be a fitting response to Calvary.
John Flavel

True conversion will involve the mind, the affection, and the will.
Billy Graham

Conversion can take many different forms.
Billy Graham

Just because you go to church it doesn't mean to say that you are a born again Christian.
Billy Graham

The devil will do everything in his power to sow seeds of doubt in your mind as to whether your conversion is a reality or not.
Billy Graham

Christ is the only way to God, but there are as many ways to Christ as there are people who come to him.
Os Guinness

Satan will ask the Christian the time of his conversion. Art thou a Christian, will he say, and dost thou not know when thou commencedst? Now content thyself with this, that thou seest the streams of grace. You may know the sun is up, though you did not observe when it rose.
William Gurnall

The first degree is the return of the Soul to God, when, being truly converted, it begins to subsist by means of his grace.
Madame Guyon

The hearts of the great can be changed.
Homer

In the Trinity Term of 1929, I gave in and admitted that God was God and knelt and prayed.
C.S. Lewis

I felt myself absolutely born again. The gates of paradise had been flung open and I had entered. There and then the whole of scripture took on another look to me.
Martin Luther

People who think that once they are converted all will be happy, have forgotten Satan.
M. Lloyd-Jones

The old sun shone a good deal brighter than it ever had before. I thought that it was just smiling upon me; and as I walked out upon Boston Common and heard the birds singing in the trees, I thought they were all singing a song to me … I had not a bitter feeling against any man, and I was ready to take all men to my heart.
Dwight L. Moody

You have not converted a man because you have silenced him.
John Morley

When the Jews, upon the conviction of their sin, were cut to the heart, Acts ii.37, and cried out, "What shall we do?" what doth Peter direct them to do? Does he bid them go and mortify their pride, wrath, malice, cruelty and the like? No; he knew that was not their present work, but he calls them to conversion and faith in Christ in general.
John Owen

I was like a stone lying in deep mud but he that is mighty lifted me up and placed me on top of the wall.
Patrick

This coming to know Christ is what makes Christian truth redemptive truth, the truth that transforms, not just informs.
Harold Cooke Phillips

Faith is the evidence of new birth, not the cause of it.
John Piper

I thoroughly dislike the notion of a second conversion.
J.C. Ryle

You will never be happy till you are converted.
J.C. Ryle

It is evident that our conversion is sound when we loathe and hate sin from the heart.
Richard Sibbes

We know people who have been "converted" many times. Every time there is a church revival they go to the altar and get "saved." One minister told of a man in his congregation who had been "saved" seventeen times. During a revival meeting the evangelist made an altar call for all who wanted to be filled with the Spirit. The man who had been converted so often made his way toward the altar again. A woman from the congregation shouted, "Don't fill him, Lord. He leaks!"…Those who become "unconverted" were never converted in the first place.
C. Sproul

Prayer in the heart proves the reality of conversion.
C.H. Spurgeon

Get men converted, and a thousand foolish ideas are destroyed.
C.H. Spurgeon

This change is radical –
it gives us new natures,
it makes us love what we hated and hate what we loved,
it sets us in a new road;
it makes our habits different,
it makes our thoughts different,
it makes us different in private,
and different in public.
C.H. Spurgeon

God does not violate the human will when he saves men. They are not converted against their will, but their will itself is converted.
C.H. Spurgeon

Suddenly I heard the words of Christ and understood them, and life and death ceased to seem to be evil, and instead of despair I experienced happiness and the joy of life undisturbed by death.
Leo Tolstoy

Self is the opaque veil that hides the Face of God from us. It can be removed only in spiritual experience, never by mere instruction.
A. W. Tozer

The doctrine of justification by faith (a biblical truth, and a blessed relief from sterile legalism and unavailing self-effort) has in our times fallen into evil company and has been interpreted by many in such a manner as actually to bar men from the knowledge of God. The whole transaction of religious conversion has been made mechanical and spiritless. Faith may now be exercised without a jar to the moral life and without embarrassment to the Adamic ego. Christ may be "received" without creating any special love for Him in the soul of the receiver. The man is "saved," but he is not hungry or thirsty after God. In fact, he is specifically taught to be satisfied and encouraged to be content with little. The modern scientist has lost God amid the wonders of His world; we Christians are in real danger of losing God amid the wonders of His Word.
A. W. Tozer

Entrance into heaven is not at the hour of death, but at the moment of conversion.
Benjamin Whichcote

Four principles of producing a human conversion: make people anxious, induce guilt, destroy their judgment, repeat the same cliché over and over, encourage exhaustion.
John White

I was delivered from the burden that had so heavily suppressed me. The spirit of mourning was taken from em, and I knew what it was to truly rejoice in God my savior.
George Whitefield

Conversion, Death-bed
Betwixt the stirrup and the ground,
Mercy I ask'd; mercy I found.
William Camden

Conversion, Holy Spirit's work in
We are so dead, so blind, so perverse, that neither can we feel when we are pricked, see the light when it shines, nor assent to the will of God when it is revealed, except the Spirit of the Lord Jesus quicken that which is dead, remove the darkness from our minds, and bow our stubborn wills to the obedience of the blessed gospel.
Scottish Confession

Conversions, Preachers' work for
He was infinitely and insatiably greedy of the conversion of souls.
Said of Joseph Alleine, by a friend

When he landed, in 1848, there were no Christians. When he left, in 1872, there were no heathen.
Memorial to John Geddie in Aneityum

Conversion of children
The following Christian leaders gave their lives to Christ Jesus in childhood: Polycarp was converted at 9 years; Matthew Henry, at 11 years; President Edwards, at 7 years; Isaac Watts, at 9 years.
Author unknown

Conviction of sin
Lord, when we are wrong, make us willing to change. And when we are right, make us easy to live with.
Peter Marshall

It was like a pent-up flood breaking forth; tears were streaming from the eyes of many, and some fell on the ground groaning and weeping and crying for mercy.
Robert Murray M'Cheyne

Before God saves a man, He convicts him of his "sinnership".
A.W. Pink

Those who have never felt anxiety on account of their sins are in the most dangerous condition of all.
John Tauler

Did the Spirit of God ever convince you of sin? Do you see yourself liable to the curse of the law, and the just vengeance of God, for the innate depravity of your nature, and the transgressions of your life? Do you come to Christ humbled and self-condemned: sensible that unless you are clothed with the merits of Him, our Elder Brother, you are ruined and undone, and can never stand with joy or safety before the holy Lord God? If so, lift up thy head; redemption is thine; thou art in a state of grace; thou art translated from death to life; thou art an heir of God, and a joint-heir with Christ. But if you never felt, nor desire to feel this work of the Holy Ghost upon thy heart, this conviction of sin, this penitential faith, all the supposed righteousness of thine own, wherein thou trusted, is but a broken reed; a painted sepulcher; and the trappings of a Pharisee.
Augustus Toplady

Co-operation with God
Without God we cannot; without us God will not.
Author unknown

A man's readiness and commitment are not enough if he does not enjoy help from above as well; equally help from above is no benefit to us unless there is also commitment and readiness on our part.
John Chrysostom

'Tis God gives skill, But not without men's hands: He could not make Antonio Stradivari's violins without Antonio.
George Eliot

Corinthians, First and second letters
The letters to the Corinthians reveal to us more of the personal character of the apostle than any of his other letters. They show him to us as a man, as a pastor, as a counselor, as in conflict not only with heretics, but with personal enemies. They reveal his wisdom, his zeal, his forbearance, his liberality of principle and practice in all matters not affecting salvation, his strictness in all matters of right and wrong, his humility, and perhaps above all, his unwearied activity and wonderful endurance.
Charles Hodge

Correction
He who heeds discipline shows the way to life, but whoever ignores correction leads others astray.
The Bible, Proverbs 10:17

Whoever loves discipline loves knowledge, but he who hates correction is stupid.
The Bible, Proverbs 12:1

He who ignores discipline despises himself, but whoever heeds correction gains understanding.
The Bible, Proverbs 15:32

Corruption
There is no such thing as a free lunch.
J.I. Friedman

Cost of following Christ
Christ had no interest in gathering vast crowds of professed adherents who would melt away as soon as they found out what following Him actually demanded of them. In our own presentation of Christ's gospel, therefore, we need to lay a similar stress on the cost of following Christ, and make sinners face it soberly before we urge them to respond to the message of free forgiveness. In common honesty, we must not conceal the fact that free forgiveness in one sense will cost everything.
J.I. Packer

Counsel
Who is this that darkeneth counsel by words without knowledge?
Job 38:2 KJV

Beware lest clamor be taken for counsel.
Desiderius Erasmus

Counseling
Listen long enough and the person will
generally come up with an adequate
solution.
Mary Kay Ash

When we are weighed down by poverty,
and grief makes us sad; when bodily pain
makes us restless, and exile despondent; or
when any other grievance afflicts us, if
there be good people at hand who
understand the art of rejoicing with the
joyful and weeping with the sorrowful,
who know how to speak a cheerful word
and uplift us, then bitterness is mitigated,
worries are alleviated and our troubles are
overcome.
Augustine of Hippo

Be aware of God's compassion, that it heals
with oil and wine. Do not lose hope of
salvation. Remember what is written – the
one who falls shall rise again, and the one
who turns away shall turn again; the
wounded is healed; the one caught by wild
beasts escapes; the one who confesses is not
rejected. For the Lord does not want the
sinner to die, but to return and live. There
is still time for endurance, time for
patience, time for healing, time for change.
Have you fallen? Rise up, Have you
sinned? Cease. Do not stand among
sinners, but keep away from them. For
when you turn back and weep, then you
will be saved.
*Basil the Great, Letter to a monk who had
sinned*

A minister is not only for public preaching,
but to be a known counselor for their
souls.
Richard Baxter

Just as a tempered metal can sharpen soft
or rusty metal, so can a zealous brother set
a tepid one on the right track.
John Climacus

There is a medicine in the Bible for every
sin-sick soul, but every soul does not need
the same medicine.
R.A. Torrey

Counterfeits
That there are some counterfeits is no
argument that nothing is true; such things
are always expected in a time of
reformation. If we look into church
history, we shall find no instance of any
great revival of religion but what has been
attended with many such things.
Jonathan Edwards

Courage
… be men of courage …
The Bible, 1 Corinthians 16:13

Courage is not the absence of fear, but the
mastery of fear.
Author unknown

Courage is what it takes to stand up and
speak; courage is also what it takes to sit
down and listen.
Author unknown

Courage is the strength or choice to begin
a change. Determination is the persistence
to continue in that change.
Author unknown

He who is not courageous enough to take
risks will accomplish nothing in life.
Muhammad Ali

You will never do anything in this world
without courage.
James Lane Allen

Courage is reckoned the greatest of all
virtues; because, unless a man has that
virtue, he has no security for preserving
any other.
James Boswell

Courage is the first of human qualities
because it is the quality which guarantees
all the others.
Winston Churchill

All our dreams can come true, if we have the courage to pursue them.
Walt Disney

It was a high counsel that I once heard given to a young person, "Always do what you are afraid to do."
Ralph Waldo Emerson

A hero is no braver than any other man, but he is braver for five minutes longer.
Ralph Waldo Emerson

Whatever you do, you need courage. Whatever course you decide upon, there is always someone to tell you that you are wrong. There are always difficulties arising that tempt you to believe your critics are right. To map out a course of action and follow it to an end requires some of the same courage that a soldier needs. Peace has its victories, but it takes brave men and women to win them.
Ralph Waldo Emerson

Without courage, wisdom bears no fruit.
Baltasar Gracian

Courage is grace under pressure.
Ernest Hemingway

It is courage, courage, courage, that raises the blood of life to crimson splendor. Live bravely and present a brave front to adversity!
Horace

The greatest test of courage on earth is to bear defeat without losing heart.
Robert G. Ingersoll

One man with courage makes a majority.
Andrew Jackson

Courage is an inner resolution to go forward in spite of obstacles and frightening situations; cowardice is a submissive surrender to circumstance. Courage breeds creative self-affirmation; cowardice produces destructive self-abnegation.

Courage faces fear and thereby masters it; cowardice represses fear and is thereby mastered by it.
Courageous men never lose the zest for living even though their life situation is zestless; cowardly men, overwhelmed by the uncertainties of life, lose the will to live.
We must constantly build dikes of courage to hold back the flood of fear.
Martin Luther King, Jr

Perfect courage is to do unwitnessed what we should be capable of doing before all the world.
La Rochefoucauld

God grant me the courage not to give up what I think is right, even though I think it is hopeless.
Admiral Chester W. Nimitz

Courage is the best gift of all; courage stands before everything. It is what preserves our liberty, safety, life, and our homes and parents, our country and our children. Courage comprises all things: a man with courage has every blessing.
Plautus

Great things are done more through courage than through wisdom.
German proverb

Courage is not the absence of fear, but the judgment that something else is more important than fear.
Ambrose Redmoon

Courage consists, not in blindly overlooking danger, but in seeing and conquering it!
Jean Paul Richter

Courage is doing what you're afraid to do. There can be no courage unless you're scared.
Eddie Rickenbacher

The world has no room for cowards. We must all be ready somehow to toil, to suffer,

to die. And yours is not the less noble because no drum beats before you when you go out to your daily battlefields, and no crowds shout your coming when you return from your daily victory and defeat.
Robert Louis Stevenson

It is curious that physical courage should be so common in the world and moral courage so rare.
Mark Twain

Courage is being scared to death – and saddling up anyway.
John Wayne

Courage and fear
Courage faces fear and thereby masters it. Cowardice represses fear and is thereby mastered by it.
Martin Luther King

As I stood at the table, and just before I opened my mouth, the words of God came forcibly to my mind, "Only be strong and of good courage."
Lord Shaftesbury, remembering the moment he introduced a Bill in the House of Commons to control child labor.

Courtesy
He who sows courtesy reaps friendship.
St Basil

Courtship
Keep from me thy loveliest Creature,
Till I prove
Jesus' Love
Infinitely sweeter.
Charles Wesley, written during his courtship

Covenant
Lord, I am no longer my own, but Yours. Put me to what You will, rank me with whom You will. Let be employed by You or laid aside for You, exalted for You or brought low by You. Let me have all things, let me have nothing, I freely and heartily yield all things to Your pleasure and disposal. And now, O glorious and blessed God, Father, Son, and Holy Spirit, You are mine and I am Yours. So be it. Amen.
John Wesley

Covenant theology
It is a new heart-righteousness which the prophets foresaw as one of the blessings of the Messianic age. "I will put my law within them, and I will write it upon their hearts," God promised through Jeremiah (31:33). How would He do it? He told Ezekiel: "I will put My Spirit within you, and cause you to walk in My statutes" (36:27).
John Stott

Cover up
There will be no whitewash at the White House.
Richard M. Nixon

Covetousness
See also: Contentment; Wealth

Covetousness

Covetousness, William Gouge
1. Observe the inward wishes of thine heart. If they be especially for the things of this world, they argue a covetous disposition. Covetousness is styled "the lust of the eye," 1 John ii. 16; that is, an inward inordinate desire arising from the sight of such and such a thing, Josh. vii. 21. Many things may be seen which are not desired, but if desired, and that inordinately, there is covetousness.
2. In things which differ, mark what is preferred. If earthly things be preferred before heavenly, temporal before spiritual, that disposition is covetous. Such was the disposition of those who were invited to the king's supper, and refused to go, Luke xiv. 18, etc.; and the disposition of the Gadarenes, Mark v. 17.
3. In the means of getting, consider whether they be just and right, or no; for all unjust and undue ways of getting, arise from covetousness. A mind free from it will

rest content with that portion which by the divine providence shall be allotted, Jer. xxii. 17, Micah ii. 12.

4. Compare with the stint which thou first settest to thyself, the issue that followeth. If, upon the obtaining of the first desire, a man remain unsatisfied, and his desire be more and more enlarged, he hath a covetous heart. For example, a poor man thinks if he could get ten shillings a week, it would serve his turn; he hath it, but then he desireth ten shillings a day; he hath that also, yet is not satisfied; from shillings his desire ariseth to pounds, and yet is not satisfied. These are such of whom the prophet thus speaketh, "Woe unto them that join house to house, that lay field to field, till there be no place, that they may be placed alone in the midst of the earth," Isa. v. 8. Such a one is said to "enlarge his desire as hell," Hab. ii. 5.

5. Well weigh the effects of thy desire of riches. If thoughts thereupon break thy sleep, and care thereabouts consume thy flesh, and labor and toil therein take up all thy time, and impair health and strength, that desire is immoderate – it is plain covetousness, Eccles. ii. 23, and v. 12. This argueth a greediness after "filthy lucre," as the apostle terms it, 1 Tim. iii. 3.

6. Take notice of thy disposition in hoarding up and keeping wealth, and sparing to spend it; for covetousness consisteth as much (if not more) in keeping as in getting. The rich man in the parable herein especially manifested his covetousness, Luke xii. 19. The Lord, therefore, for avoiding covetousness, forbids from laying up treasures on earth, Mat. vi. 19.

7. Observe thy manner of spending. If it be too sparingly, niggardly, and basely, if under thy degree and means, if against health and strength in general, not affording what is needful thereunto; or against special occasions, not affording physic or other requisites in sickness, or help of surgery in case of wounds, sores, or other maladies; or against the charge that belongs unto thee, as wife, children, servants, kindred, and neighbors; or against the duty and due which thou owest to the poor, state, and church; or in what thou doest in any of the foresaid kinds, thou doest perforce so as otherwise thou wouldst not of it, surely this kind of spending savoreth rank of covetousness, Eccles. 4:18.

William Gouge

———

Take heed, and beware of covetousness.
The Bible, Luke 12:15 KJV

Be content with what you have.
The Bible, Hebrews 13:5

Covetousness puts money above manhood.
Billy Graham

The soul of the covetous is far removed from God, as far as his memory, understanding and will are concerned. He forgets God as though He were not his God, owing to the fact that he has fashioned for himself a god of Mammon and of temporal possessions.
John of the Cross

"Take heed and beware of covetousness." …
"Take heed and beware of covetousness." …
"Take heed and beware of covetousness." …
What if I should say nothing else these three or four hours?
Hugh Latimer, preaching before King Edward VI

Charity gives itself rich; covetousness hoards itself poor.
German proverb

We are most of us far too ready to "seek great things" in this world: let us "seek them not" (Jeremiah 45:5).
J.C. Ryle

Greatness and riches are a perilous possession for the soul.
J.C. Ryle

Covetousness is perhaps the most serious sin in the West (or North) today, and no

covetous person will inherit the kingdom of God.
Ron Sider

Covetousness is a self-destructive passion, a craving which is never satisfied, even when what has been craved is now possessed.
John Stott

Covetousness is dry drunkenness.
Thomas Watson

Creation
See also: God as Creator; Nature
In the beginning God created the heavens and the earth.
The Bible, Genesis 1:1

Through him all things were made; without him nothing was made that has been made.
The Bible, John 1:3

To see a World in a grain of sand,
And a Heaven in a wild flower,
Hold Infinity in the palm of your hand,
And Eternity in an hour.
William Blake

The created world is but a small parenthesis in eternity.
Thomas Browne

When considering the creation, the how and the when does not matter so much as the why and the wherefore.
R. de Campoamor

We must constantly remind ourselves of William Temple's great statement that "Christianity is the most materialistic of the world's great religions."
Leighton Ford

The doctrine of creation and incarnation drive home the truth that God is down to earth. He made our bodies, He saw that they were good. Christ came in the flesh.
Leighton Ford

The Christian doctrine as to Creation involves the following points: first, "In the beginning," at some unknown point of definite commencement in time. Second, God called all things (that is, the original principles and causes of all things) into being out of nothing. Thus every thing which has or will or can exist, exterior to the Godhead, owes its being and substance as well as its form to God. Third, This creative act is an act of free self-determined will ... Fourth, It was not necessary to complete the divine excellence or blessedness ... But it was done in the exercise of absolute discretion for infinitely good reasons.
   This doctrine is essential to Theism. All opposing theories of the origin of the world are essentially Pantheistic or Atheistic.
Charles and A.A. Hodge

Also in this He shewed me a little thing, the quantity of an hazel-nut, in the palm of my hand; and it was as round as a ball. I looked thereupon with the eye of my understanding, and thought: What may this be? And it was answered generally thus: It is all that is made. I marveled how it might last, for methought it might suddenly have fallen to naught for little[ness]. And I was answered in my understanding: It lasteth, and ever shall [last] for that God loveth it. And so All-thing hath their Being by the love of God.
Julian of Norwich

Two things fill me with constantly increasing admiration and awe, the longer and more earnestly I reflect on them: the starry heavens without and the moral law within.
Immanuel Kant

No philosophical theory which I have yet come across is a radical improvement on the words of Genesis, that "in the beginning God made Heaven and Earth."
C.S. Lewis

God loves material things. He made them!
C.S. Lewis

Heaven and earth were created all together in the same instant, on October 23, 4004, BC at none in the morning.
Dr John Lightfoot, vice-chancellor of Cambridge University. He said this just before Darwin published his Origin of the Species.

God creates out of nothing. Therefore, until a man is nothing God can make nothing out of him.
Martin Luther

There is about us, if only we have eyes to see, a creation of such spectacular profusion, spendthrift richness, and absurd detail, as to make us catch our breath in astonished wonder.
Michael Mayne

The only way we can determine the true age of the earth is for God to tell us what it is. And since He has told us, very plainly, in the Holy Scriptures, that it is several thousand years in age, and no more, that ought to settle all basic questions of terrestrial chronology.
Henry Morris, ICR President, 1974

The higher the mountains, the more understandable is the glory of Him who made them and who holds them in His hand.
Francis Schaeffer

That the universe was formed by a fortuitous concourse of atoms, I will no more believe than that the accidental jumbling of the alphabet would fall into a most ingenious treatise of philosophy.
Jonathan Swift

Which beginning of time according to our Chronologie, fell upon the entrance of the night preceding the twenty-third day of October in the year of the Julian Calendar, 710 [4004] BC.
James Ussher

Creation, The first "day" of
God called the light "day", and the darkness he called "night". And there was evening, and there was morning—the first day.
The Bible, Genesis 1:5

Creation and Genesis
The six days of creation in Genesis 1 can represent (1) literal 24-hour days of creation, (2) literal 24-hour days of divine revelation of creation, (3) extended geological ages or epochs preparatory for the eventual occupancy of humankind, or (4) a revelatory framework to summarize God's creative activity (Col 1:16).
M.F. Unger

Creativity
A hunch is creativity trying to tell you something.
Author unknown

If you would create something, you must be something.
Johann Wolfgang von Goethe

An essential aspect of creativity is not being afraid to fail.
Dr Edwin Land, founder of Polaroid

There is a fountain of youth. It is your mind, your talents, the creativity you bring in your life and the lives of people you love.
Sophia Loren

We need to make the world safe for creativity and intuition, for it is creativity and intuition that will make the world safe for us.
Edgar Mitchell, Apollo astronaut

Credulity
The credulity of dupes is as inexhaustible as the invention of knaves.
Edmund Burke

The characteristic of the present age is craving credulity.
Benjamin Disraeli

Credulity is the man's weakness, but the child's strength.
Charles Lamb

Creeds

See also: Confession of Faith

[The basic creed of Reformed churches, as most familiarly known, is called the Apostles' Creed. It has received this title because of its great antiquity; it dates from the second century AD.]

I believe in God, the Father Almighty,
the Creator of heaven and earth, and in
Jesus Christ, His only Son, our Lord:
Who was conceived of the Holy Spirit,
born of the Virgin Mary,
suffered under Pontius Pilate,
was crucified, died, and was buried.
He descended into hell.
The third day He arose again from the dead.
He ascended into heaven and sits at the
right hand of God the Father Almighty,
whence He shall come to judge the living
and the dead.
I believe in the Holy Spirit, the holy
†catholic church,
the communion of saints,
the forgiveness of sins,
the resurrection of the body,
and life everlasting.
Amen.

*The word "catholic" refers not to the Roman Catholic Church, but to the universal church of the Lord Jesus Christ.

I believe in God the Father Almighty. And in Jesus Christ, his only Son, our Lord; who was born by the Holy Ghost of the virgin Mary; was crucified under Pontius Pilate and was buried; the third day He rose from the dead; He ascended into heaven; and sitteth on the right hand of the Father; from thence He shall come to judge the quick and the dead. And in the Holy Ghost; the holy Church; the forgiveness of sins; the resurrection of the body.

Apostles' Creed, Old Roman Form

[The faithful must believe the articles of the Creed] so that believing they may obey God, by obeying may live well, by living well may purify their hearts, and with pure hearts may understand what they believe.

Augustine of Hippo

We believe in one God, the Father, all sovereign, the Maker of things visible and invisible; and in one Lord Jesus Christ, the Word of God, God of God, Light of Light, Son only-begotten, Firstborn of all Creation, begotten of the Father before all ages, through whom also all things were made; who was made flesh for our salvation and lived among men, and suffered, and rose again on the third day, and ascended to the Father, who shall come again in glory to judge the living and the dead.

Eusebius of Caesarea, Council of Nicea, 325

So assent to certain propositions about God is not all of faith in God, but it is necessary to faith in God; and Christian faith, in particular, though it is more than assent to a creed, is impossible without assent to a creed.

J. Gresham Machen

Creeds, Early

Baptism service

When the person being baptized goes down into the water, he who baptizes him, putting his hand on him, shall say: "Do you believe in God, the Father Almighty?"

And the person being baptized shall say: "I believe."

Then holding his hand on his head, he shall baptize him once.

And then he shall say: "Do you believe in Christ Jesus, the Son of God, who was born of the Virgin Mary, and was crucified under Pontius Pilate, and was dead and buried, and rose again the third day, alive from the dead, and ascended into heaven, and sat at the right hand of the Father, and will come to judge the living and the dead?"

And when he says: "I believe," he is baptized again.

And again he shall say: "Do you believe in the Holy Spirit, in the holy church, and the resurrection of the body?"

The person being baptized shall say: "I believe," and then he is baptized a third time.

Hippolytus, account of a baptismal service

Rule of Faith
This faith: in one God, the Father Almighty,
who made the heaven and the earth and the seas and all the things that are in them;
and in one Christ Jesus, the Son of God, who was made flesh for our salvation;
and in the Holy Spirit, who made known through the prophets the plan of salvation, and the coming, and the birth from a virgin, and the passion, and the resurrection from the dead, and the bodily ascension into heaven of the beloved Christ Jesus, our Lord, and his future appearing from heaven in the glory of the Father to sum up all things and to raise anew all flesh of the whole human race.
Recorded by Irenaeus

Crises
Crises bring out the best in the best of us, and the worst in the worst of us.
Author unknown

Character is not made in a crisis – it is only exhibited.
Author unknown

When written in Chinese, the word "crisis" is composed of two characters – one represents danger and the other represents opportunity.
John F. Kennedy

There cannot be a crisis next week. My schedule is already full.
Henry Kissinger

Our extremities are the Lord's opportunities.
C.H. Spurgeon

Criticism
See also: Advice; Judging others; Rebuke
Criticizing anther's garden doesn't keep the weeds out of your own.

Author unknown
Criticism is easy; achievement is more difficult.
Winston Churchill

I criticize by creation – not by finding fault.
Cicero

Criticism, like rain, should be gentle enough to nourish a man's growth without destroying his roots.
Frank A. Clark

Any fool can criticize, condemn, and complain, and most fools do.
Benjamin Franklin

If a donkey bray at you, don't bray at him.
George Herbert

Our enemies come nearer the truth in the opinions they form of us than we do in our opinion of ourselves.
La Rochefoucauld

Censure from men afflicts the heart; but if patiently accepted it generates purity.
Mark the Ascetic

If it's painful for you to criticize your friends, you're safe in doing it; if you take the slightest pleasure in it, that's the time to hold your tongue.
Alice Duer Miller

It is much easier to fix blame than to fix problems.
Kathleen Parker

The trouble with most of us is that we would rather be ruined by praise than saved by criticism.
Norman Vincent Peale

If one man calls you a horse, ignore him;
If two men call you a horse, consider it;
If three men call you a horse, buy a saddle.
Persian proverb

Our souls may lose their peace and even disturb other people's, if we are always criticizing trivial actions – which often are not real defects at all, but we construe them wrongly through our ignorance of their motives.
Teresa of Avila

Be not angry that you cannot make others as you wish them to be, since you cannot make yourself as you wish to be.
Thomas à Kempis

Gladly we desire to make other men perfect, but we will not amend our own fault.
Thomas à Kempis

Humble yourself, and cease to care what men think.
A. W. Tozer

The labor of self-love is a heavy one indeed. Think whether much of your sorrow has not arisen from someone speaking slightingly of you. As long as you set yourself up as a little god to which you must be loyal, how can you hope to find inward peace?
A. W. Tozer

The longer I live, the larger allowances I make for human infirmities. I exact more from myself and less from others.
John Wesley

Criticism comes easier than craftsmanship.
Zeuxis

Critics
Pay no attention to what the critics say; no statue has ever been erected to a critic.
Jean Sibelius

Cross
See also: Atonement; Christ, Death of; Crucifixion; Salvation; Substitution; Thief on the cross
But he was pierced for our transgressions, he was crushed for our iniquities; the punishment that brought us peace was upon him, and by his wounds we are healed.
The Bible, Isaiah 53:5

For the message of the cross is foolishness to those who are perishing, but to us who are being saved it is the power of God.
The Bible, 1 Corinthians 1:18

… we preach Christ crucified: a stumbling block to Jews and foolishness to Gentiles.
The Bible, 1 Corinthians 1:23

Christ redeemed us from the curse of the law by becoming a curse for us, for it is written: "Cursed is everyone who is hung on a tree."
The Bible, Galatians 3:13

May I never boast except in the cross of our Lord Jesus Christ, through which the world has been crucified to me, and I to the world.
The Bible, Galatians 6:14

He [Jesus] himself bore our sins in his body on the tree [the cross], so that we might die to sins and live for righteousness.
The Bible, 1 Peter 2:24

For Christ died for sins once for all, the righteous for the unrighteous, to bring you to God. He was put to death in the body but made alive by the Spirit.
The Bible, 1 Peter 3:18

God proved his love on the cross. When Christ hung, and bled, and died it was God saying to the world – I love you.
Author unknown

Nails could not have kept Jesus on the cross had love not held Him there.
Author unknown

The cross is "I" crossed out.
Author unknown

He came to pay a debt he did not owe, because we owed a debt we could not pay.
Author unknown

But more than pains wracked Him there
Was the deep longing thirst divine
That thirsted for the souls of men,
Dear Lord – and one was mine!
Author unknown

There is a green hill far away,
Without a city wall,

Where the dear Lord was crucified,
Who died to save us all.
C.F. Alexander

What shall I say to the commendation of
Christ and His Cross? I bless the Lord He
has made my prison a palace to me. And
what am I that He should have dealt thus
with me? I have looked greedy-like to
such a lot as this, but still thought it was
too high for me when I saw how vile I
was.
Isabel Alison executed 26 January 1681

Jesus has been – declared to be the Son of
God with power, according to the Holy
Spirit, through his resurrection from the
dead. In this declaration and appointment
– which are beyond historical definition –
lies the true significance of Jesus. Jesus as
the Christ, as the Messiah, is the End of
History; and He can be comprehended
only as Paradox ... as Victor ... a Primal
History. As Christ, Jesus is the plane which
lies beyond our comprehension.
Karl Barth

The Cross is thus the Gate of Heaven, as
proclaimed by the Gospel of John
(Chapter One). It is formed by the
intersection of Time and Eternity (Space).
It is here that the vertical plane of
Eternity (Space) touches the horizontal
plane of Time. To stand here is to stand
truly at the foot of the cross. The true
crisis is present. Does one experience the
Resurrection or not?
Karl Barth

O sacred Head, once wounded,
With grief and pain weighed down,
How scornfully surrounded
With thorns, Thine only crown;
How pale art Thou with anguish,
With sore abuse and scorn!
How does that visage languish,
Which once was bright as morn!
Bernard of Clairvaux

Man of Sorrows! what a name
For the Son of God, who came

Ruined sinners to reclaim!
Hallelujah, what a Savior!
Philip Paul Bliss

The cross means this: Jesus taking our
place to satisfy the demands of God's
justice and turning aside God's wrath.
James M. Boice

'Twas I that shed the sacred blood;
I nailed him to the tree;
I crucified the Christ of God;
I joined the mockery.
Of all that shouting multitude
I feel that I am one;
And in that din of voices rude
I recognize my own.
Around the cross the throng I see,
Mocking the Sufferer's groan;
Yet still my voice it seems to be,
As if I mocked alone.
Horatius Bonar

The memory of Christ Jesus crucified was
ever present in the depths of his heart like
a bundle of myrrh.
Bonaventure

The cross is God's truth about us, and
therefore it is the only power which can
make us truthful. When we know the cross
we are no longer afraid of the truth.
Dietrich Bonhoeffer

Christ's blood is heaven's key.
Thomas Brooks

All the kings throughout history sent their
people out to die for them Only one person
ever died for their people willingly and lovingly.
Dave Brown

In the cross of Christ God says to man,
"That is where you ought to be. Jesus my
Son hangs there in your stead. His tragedy
is the tragedy of your life. You are the rebel
who should be hanged on the gallows. But
lo, I suffer instead of you and because of
you, because I love you in spite of what
you are. My love for you is so great that I
meet you there, there on the cross. I

cannot meet you anywhere else. You must meet me there by identifying yourself with the one on the cross. It is by this identification that I, God, can meet you in him, saying to you as I say to him, My beloved Son."
Emil Brunner

Now I saw in my dream, that the highway up which Christian was to go, was fenced on either side with a wall, and that wall was called Salvation. Isaiah 26:1. Up this way, therefore, did burdened Christian run, but not without great difficulty, because of the load on his back. He ran thus till he came at a place somewhat ascending; and upon that place stood a cross, and a little below, in the bottom, a sepulcher. So I saw in my dream, that just as Christian came up with the cross, his burden loosed from off his shoulders, and fell from off his back, and began to tumble, and so continued to do till it came to the mouth of the sepulcher, where it fell in, and I saw it no more. Then was Christian glad and lightsome, and said with a merry heart, "He hath given me rest by his sorrow, and life by his death." Then he stood still a while, to look and wonder; for it was very surprising to him that the sight of the cross should thus ease him of his burden. He looked, therefore, and looked again, even till the springs that were in his head sent the waters down his cheeks. Zech. 12:10. Now as he stood looking and weeping, behold, three Shining Ones came to him, and saluted him with, "Peace be to thee." So the first said to him, "Thy sins be forgiven thee," Mark 2:5; the second stripped him of his rags, and clothed him with change of raiment, Zech. 3:4; the third also set a mark on his forehead, Eph. 1:13, and gave him a roll with a seal upon it, which he bid him look on as he ran, and that he should give it in at the celestial gate: so they went their way. Then Christian gave three leaps for joy, and went on singing,
"Thus far did I come laden with my sin,
Nor could aught ease the grief that I was in,
Till I came hither. What a place is this!

Must here be the beginning of my bliss?
Must here the burden fall from off my back?
Must here the strings that bound it to me crack?
Blest cross! blest sepulcher! blest rather be
The Man that there was put to shame for me!"
John Bunyan

His death was sufficient for all: it was efficient in the case of many.
John Calvin

The Creed sets forth what Christ suffered in the sight of men, and then appositely speaks of that invisible and incomprehensible judgment which he underwent in the sight of God in order that we might know not only that Christ's body was given as the price of our redemption, but that he paid a greater and more excellent price in suffering in his soul the terrible torments of a condemned and forsaken man.
John Calvin

Many evangelical leaders simply assume the message of the cross, but no longer lay much emphasis on it.
D.A. Carson

By the cross we know the gravity of sin and the greatness of God's love towards us.
John Chrysostom

Lovely was the death
Of him whose life was love.
Samuel Taylor Coleridge

When Jesus bowed his head,
And dying took our place,
The veil was rent, a way was found
To that pure home of grace.
John Elias

If Christ, by dying, has made full satisfaction, then God can consistently pardon the greatest of sinners that believe in Jesus.
John Flavel

In the cross holiness and love, wrath and pity, justice and mercy, meet together, and kiss one another.
W.H.T. Gairdner

O sacred head, sore wounded,
Defiled and put to scorn;
O kingly head, surrounded
With mocking crown of thorn:

What sorrow mars thy grandeur?
Can death thy bloom deflower?
O countenance whose splendor
The hosts of heaven adore!

In thy most bitter passion
My heart to share doth cry,
With thee for my salvation
Upon the cross to die.

Ah, keep my heart thus movèd
To stand thy cross beneath,
To mourn thee, well-belovèd,
Yet thank thee for thy death.
P. Gerhardt

The poets themselves said, that *amor Deum gubernat*, that "love governed God." And, as Nazianzen well speaks, this love of God, this *dulcis tyrannus*, this "sweet tyrant," did overcome him when he was upon the cross. There were no cords could have held him to the whipping-post but those of love; no nails have fastened him to the cross but those of love.
Thomas Goodwin

In the cross of Christ I see three things: First, a description of the depth of man's sin. Second, the overwhelming love of God. Third, the only way of salvation.
Billy Graham

God is not only holy, but the source and pattern of holiness: He is the origin and the upholder of the moral order of the universe. He must be just. The Judge of all the earth must do right. Therefore it was impossible by the necessities of his own being that he should deal lightly with sin, and compromise the claims of holiness. If sin could be forgiven at all, it must be on the same basis which would vindicate the holy law of God, which is not a mere code, but the moral order of the whole creation.

But such vindication must be supremely costly. Costly to whom? Not to the forgiven sinner, for there could be no price asked from him for his forgiveness; both because the cost is far beyond his reach, and because God loves to give and not to sell.

Therefore God himself undertook to pay a cost, to offer a sacrifice, so tremendous that the gravity of his condemnation of sin should be absolutely beyond question even as he forgave it, while at the same the Love which impelled to pay the price would be the wonder of angels, and would call forth the worshiping gratitude of the redeemed sinner.

On Calvary this price was paid by God: the Son giving himself, bearing our sin and its curse; the Father giving the Son, his only Son whom he loved. But it was paid by God become man, who not only took the place of the guilty man, but also was his representative ...

The divine Son, one of the three persons of the one God, he through whom, from the beginning of the creation, the Father has revealed himself to man (Jn 1:18), took man's nature upon him, and so became our representative. He offered himself as a sacrifice in our stead, bearing our sin in his own body on the tree. He suffered, not only awful physical anguish, but also the unthinkable spiritual horror of becoming identified with the sin to which he was infinitely opposed. He thereby came under the curse of sin, so that for a time even his perfect fellowship with his Father was broken.

Thus God proclaimed his infinite abhorrence of sin by being willing himself to suffer all that, in place of the guilty ones, in order that he might justly forgive. Thus the love of God found its perfect fulfillment, because he did not hold back from even that uttermost sacrifice, in order that we might be saved from eternal death through what he endured. Thus it was

possible for him to be just, and to justify the believer, because as Lawgiver and as Substitute for the rebel race of man, he himself had suffered the penalty of the broken law.
H.E. Guillebaud

The cross is God's centerpiece on the table of time.
Paul Guttke

God gives the cross, and the cross gives us God.
Madame Guyon

The attributes of God were visible in their fullness on the day Jesus died. God's nature poured out on Golgotha in a cosmic flood of revelation, and the world quaked. Justice was done, mercy was granted, redemption was accomplished, power was displayed, holiness was vindicated, community was reestablished, perfect wisdom was demonstrated, and love ran wild.
William R.L. Haley

The cross is not an isolated individual aspect of theology, but is itself the foundation of that theology. The cross both dominates and permeates all true Christian theology, with its thread being woven throughout the entirety of its fabric.
Gerald Hawthorne

Though God loved Christ as a Son he frowned upon him as a Surety.
Matthew Henry

Come, and see the victories of the cross. Christ's wounds are thy healings, His agonies thy repose, His conflicts thy conquests, His groans thy songs, His pains thine ease, His shame thy glory, His death thy life, His sufferings, thy salvation.
Matthew Henry

Through a tree we were made debtors to God; so through a tree we have our debt canceled.
Irenaeus

He who seeks not the cross of Christ seeks not the glory of Christ.
John of the Cross

The cross is the key. If I lose this key I fumble. The universe will not open to me. But with the key in my hand I know I hold his secret.
E. Stanley Jones

As I looked I saw the body bleeding heavily, apparently from the flogging. The smooth skin was gashed and all over his body I saw deep weals in the tender flesh caused by many sharp blows. The blood flowed so hot and thick that neither the wounds nor the skin could be seen: it was all covered in blood. The blood flowed all down his body, but at the point of falling to the ground, it disappeared. The bleeding continued for a while, giving me time to see it and think about it. It was so heavy that I thought that if it had been real the whole bed and everything around would have been soaked in blood.
The beloved blood of our Lord Jesus Christ is truly as plentiful as it is precious. Look and see for yourself. It flows over the whole world ready to wash every human being from all sin, present, past and future, if they are willing.
Julian of Norwich

The more we meditate on the cross, the deeper our companionship and knowledge gets of Christ the Lord.
Kamel, Pishoy

The whole world in comparison with the cross of Christ is one grand impertinence.
Robert Leighton

At Calvary we see what sin deserves and what God requires. Calvary was too terrible to be optional, the suffering involved too enormous to be unnecessary, and the Sufferer too precious to his Father to have been given over needlessly to such pain.
Peter Lewis

In Christ crucified is the true theology and the knowledge of God. "No man comes to

the Father except through me." "I am the door." While a man does not know Christ, he does not know God hidden in sufferings. Such a man prefers works to sufferings, and glory to a cross.
Martin Luther

No man understands the Scriptures, unless he be acquainted with the cross.
Martin Luther

The cross alone is our theology.
Martin Luther

It pleased God to make Christ the perfect author of salvation and he used suffering as a way to fulfil this work.
Martin Luther

Jesus became the greatest liar, perjurer, thief, adulterer and murderer that mankind has ever known – not because he committed these sins but because he was actually made sin for us.
Martin Luther

The cross is proof of both the immense love of God and the profound wickedness of sin.
John MacArthur

Christ endured every kind of suffering in all those who foreshadowed him. In Abel he was slain, in Isaac bound, in Jacob exiled, in Joseph sold, in Moses exposed to die. He was sacrificed in the passover lamb, persecuted in David, dishonored in the prophets.
Melito of Sardis

The cross is seen as the saving act of Christ, but even more than this, it is seen as the final place of reconciliation between God and humanity.
Calvin Miller

Jesus surely died on the cross, for Roman crucifixion teams knew their business (they had enough practice). He could not possibly have rolled the heavy boulder from the door of the tomb after the crucifixion experience.
John W. Montgomery

The cross symbolizes a cosmic as well as historic truth. Love conquers the world, but its victory is not an easy one.
Reinhold Niebuhr

I saw One hanging on a tree!
In evil long I took delight,
Unawed by shame or fear,
Till a new object struck my sight,
And stopped my wild career.
I saw One hanging on a tree,
In agonies and blood;
He fixed His languid eyes on me,
As near His cross I stood.
Sure never till my latest breath,
Shall I forget that look!
It seemed to charge me with His death,
Though not a word He spoke.
A second look He gave, which said,
"I freely all forgive;
This blood is for thy ransom paid;
I die that thou mayest live."
Thus while His death my sin displays
In all its blackest hue,
Such is the mystery of grace,
It seals my pardon too!
John Newton

The Father imposed His wrath due unto, and the Son underwent punishment for, either:
1. All the sins of all men.
2. All the sins of some men, or
3. Some of the sins of all men. In which case it may be said:
a. That if the last be true, all men have some sins to answer for, and so, none are saved.
b. That if the second be true, then Christ, in their stead suffered for all the sins of all the elect in the whole world, and this is the truth.
c. But if the first be the case, why are not all men free from the punishment due unto their sins? You answer, "Because of unbelief." I ask, Is this unbelief a sin, or is it not? If it be, then Christ suffered the punishment due unto it, or He did not. If He did, why must that hinder them more than their other sins for which He died? If He did not, He did not die for all their sins!
John Owen

There is no death of sin without the death of Christ.
John Owen

He suffered not as God, but he who suffered was God.
John Owen

The cross saves.
J.I. Packer

We never move on from the cross of Christ, only into a more profound understanding of the cross.
David Prior

The way of the cross is the way of light.
Medieval proverb

Apart from the cross there is no other ladder by which we may get to heaven.
Rose of Lima

Christ triumphs in me, blessed be His name. I have all things. I burden no man. I see that this earth and the fulness thereof is my Father's. Sweet, sweet is the cross of my Lord. The blessing of God upon the cross of my Lord Jesus!
Samuel Rutherford

Christ's cross is the sweetest burden that ever I bore: it is such a burden as wings are to a bird, or sails are to a ship.
Samuel Rutherford

Christ would have lived, and taught, and preached, and prophesied, and wrought miracles in vain, if he had not crowned all by dying for our sins as our substitute! His death was our life. His death was the payment of our dept to God. Without his death we should have been of all creatures most miserable.
J.C. Ryle

A sight of His death – if it is a true sight – is the death of all love of sin.
C.H. Spurgeon

There are some sciences that may be learned by the head, but the science of Christ crucified can only be learned by the heart.
C.H. Spurgeon

Eternal Wisdom: The more mangled, the more deathly I am for love, the more lovely am I to a well-regulated mind. My unfathomable love shows itself in the great bitterness of My passion, like the sun in its brightness, like the fair rose in its perfume, like the strong fire in its glowing heat. Therefore, hear with devotion how cruelly I suffered for thee.
Henry Sumo

Carry the cross patiently, and with perfect submission; and in the end it shall carry you.
Thomas à Kempis

There is no health of soul, nor hope of eternal life, except in the cross.
Thomas à Kempis

Nothing in my hands I bring,
Simply to thy cross I cling;
Naked, come to thee for dress.
Helpless, look to thee for grace:
Foul, I to the fountain fly;
Wash me Savior, or I die.
Rock of Ages, cleft for me,
Let me hide myself in thee.

Could my tears forever flow
Could my zeal no languor know
These for sin could not atone
Thou must save, and Thou alone
In my hand no price I bring
Simply to Thy cross I cling
Augustus Toplady

The cross is the abyss of the wonders, the center of desires, the school of virtues, the house of wisdom, the throne of love, the theater of joys, and the place of sorrows; It is the root of happiness and the gate of heaven.
Thomas Traherne

The cross of Christ is Jacob's ladder by which we ascend into the Highest Heaven.
Thomas Traherne

When I survey the wondrous cross,
On which the Prince of Glory died,
My richest gain I count but loss,
And pour contempt on all my pride.
I. Watts

Your healing flows from his wounds,
your joy from his sorrow,
your glory from his abasement,
your riches from his poverty,
your hope beams through the darkness
which enshrouds his holy soul.
Octavius Winslow

Christ took your cup of grief, your cup of
the curse, pressed it to his lips, drank it to
its dregs, then filled it with his sweet,
pardoning, sympathizing love, and gave it
back for you to drink, and to drink for ever!
Octavius Winslow

If you look critically at the wondrous cross
you will see in it nothing but common
wood. The cross is best discerned through
penitential tears.
Dinsdale Young

Cross, Centrality of the
The preaching of the cross of Christ was
the very center and heart of the message of
the apostles, and there is nothing I know
of that is more important than that every
one of us should realize that this is still the
heart and the center of the Christian
message.
M. Lloyd-Jones

Cross, Christian's
Believer, Christ Jesus presents you with
your crosses, and they are no trivial gifts.
C.H. Spurgeon

Cross and the devil
The death of Christ was the most dreadful
blow ever given to the empire of darkness.
William S. Plumer

Cross and wisdom
In all truth, wisdom is the cross and the
cross is wisdom.
Louis de Montfort

The soul really desirous of wisdom should
first of all desire to enter more deeply into
the mystery of the cross, which is the way
to life.
Louis de Montfort

Crucified with Christ
Crucified inwardly and outwardly with
Christ, you will live in this life with fulness
and satisfaction of soul, and possess your
soul in patience.
John of the Cross

Crucifixion
See also: Cross
A crucified slave beside the Roman road
screamed until his voice died and then
hung, a filthy, festering clot of flies,
sometimes for days – a living man whose
hands and feet were swollen masses of
gangrenous meat. That is what our Lord
took upon himself.
Joy Davidman

First the upright wood was planted in the
ground. It was not high, and probably the
feet of the sufferer were not above one or
two feet from the ground. Thus could the
communication described in the Gospels
take place between him and others; thus
also might his sacred lips be moistened
with the sponge attached to a short stalk of
hyssop. Next the transverse wood
(*antenna*) was placed on the ground and
the sufferer laid upon it, when his arms
were extended, drawn up and bound to it.
Then (this not in Egypt, but in Carthage
and in Rome) a strong sharp nail was
driven first into the right, then into the left
hand (the *clavi trabales*).
Next the sufferer was drawn up by means
of ropes, perhaps ladders; the transverse
either bound or nailed to the upright and a
rest or support for the body (the *cornu* or
sedile) fastened on it. Lastly, the feet were
extended and either one nail hammered into
each or a larger piece of iron through the
two. And so might the crucified hang for
hours, even days, in the unutterable anguish
of suffering till consciousness at last failed.
Alfred Edersheim

Nor did demons crucify him; it is you who have crucified him and crucify him still, when you delight in your vices and sins.
Francis of Assisi

It is curious that people who are filled with horrified indignation whenever a cat kills a sparrow can hear the story of the killing of God told Sunday after Sunday and not experience any shock at all.
Dorothy Sayers

Cruelty
All cruelty springs from weakness.
Seneca

Culture
See also: Society
For the first time in our history the weird and the stupid and the coarse are becoming our cultural norm, even our cultural ideal.
Carl Bernstein

Because man is God's creature, some of his culture is rich in beauty and goodness. Because he is fallen, all of it is tainted with sin and some of it is demonic.
The Lausanne Covenant

Most men's conscience, habits, and opinions are borrowed from convention and gather continually comforting assurances from the same social consensus that originally suggested them.
George Santayana

Curiosity
Curiosity is the first step of pride.
Bernard of Clairvaux

Curiosity is the wick in the candle of learning.
William A. Ward

Customs
When I go to Rome, I also fast on Saturday: when here, I do not. If you go to any church, observe the local custom.
Ambrose

Conventionality is not morality. Self-righteousness is not religion. To attack the first is not to assail the last. To pluck the mask from the face of the Pharisee is not to lift an impious hand to the Crown of Thorns.
Charlotte Brontë

Custom reconciles us to everything.
Edmund Burke

Custom without reason is but ancient error.
Thomas Fuller

It is superstitious to put one's faith in conventions; but it is arrogance not to submit to them.
Blaise Pascal

Cynic
A cynic is a man who knows the price of everything, and the value of nothing.
Oscar Wilde

Cynicism
A thankful heart cannot be cynical.
A. W. Tozer

D

Daily

How often do we need to see God's face, hear His voice, feel His touch, know His power? The answer to all these questions is the same: Every day!
John Blanchard

We turn, not older with years, but newer every day.
Emily Dickinson

He who gives you the day will also give you the things necessary for the day.
Gregory of Nyssa

The path of God is a daily cross. No one has ascended into heaven by means of ease, for we know where the way of ease leads and how it ends.
Isaac from Syria

Receive every day as a resurrection from death, as a new enjoyment of life.
William Law

I do not ask to see
The distant scene – one step enough for me.
J.H. Newman

Unless we are daily cleansed from our sin by the blood of Jesus, and daily filled with the Spirit, we shall never overcome the evil one.
David Watson

Dancing

Dancing is the loftiest, the most moving, the most beautiful of the arts, because it is no mere translation or abstraction from life; it is life itself.
Havelock Ellis

Danger
See also: Church, Warnings to

Let me not pray to be sheltered from dangers, but to be fearless in facing them.
Author unknown

Danger, the spur of all great minds.
George Chapman

Dark Ages

There once was a time when all people believed in God and the church ruled. This time was called the Dark Ages.
Richard Lederer

Dark experiences

God's people have no assurances that the dark experiences of life will be held at bay, much less that God will provide some sort of running commentary on the meaning of each day's allotment of confusion, boredom, pain, or achievement.
David Wells

Dark night of the soul
See also: Darkness

The soul sees nothing but clouds and darkness. She seeks God, and cannot find the least marks or footsteps of His Presence
Augustine Baker

For first He not only withdraws all comfortable observable infusions of light and grace, but also deprives her [the soul] of a power to exercise any perceptible operations of her superior spirit, and of all comfortable reflections upon His love, plunging her into the depth of her inferior powers.
Augustine Baker

In order to raise the soul from imperfection I withdraw Myself from her sentiment, depriving her of former consolations which I do in order to humiliate her, and cause her to seek Me in

truth, and to prove her in the light of faith, so that she come to prudence. Then, if she love Me without thought of self, and with lively faith and with hatred of her own sensuality, she rejoices in the time of trouble, deeming herself unworthy of peace and quietness of mind.
Voice of God to Catherine of Genoa

When we have reached this total deprivation [when the spiritual world seems to disappear] what shall we do? Abide in simplicity and peace, as Job on his ash heap, repeating, "Blessed are the poor in spirit."
de Caussade

I endured long periods of privation, towards the end almost continual: but still I had from time to time inflowings of Thy Divinity so deep and intimate, so vivid and so penetrating, that it was easy for me to judge that Thou wast but hidden from me and not lost.
Madame Guyon

The presence of God never left me for an instant. But how dear I paid for this time of happiness! For this possession, which seemed to me entire and perfect – and the more perfect the more it was secret, and foreign to the senses, steadfast and exempt from change – was but the preparation for a total deprivation, lasting many years, without any support or hope of its return.
Madame Guyon

The less the soul thinketh that it loveth or seeth God, the nearer it nigheth for to perceive the gift of the blessed love. For then is love master, and worketh in the soul, and maketh it for to forget itself, and for to see and behold only how love doth. And then is the soul more suffering than doing, and that is clean love.
Walter Hilton

Thou hast been a child at the breast, a spoiled child. Now I will withdraw all this.
Suso

Then first do we attain to the fulness of God's love as His children, when it is no longer happiness or misery, prosperity or adversity, that draws us to Him or keeps us back from Him. What we should then experience none can utter; but it would be something far better than when we were burning with the first flame of love, and had great emotion, but less true submission.
John Tauler

In all those dark moments, O God, grant that I may understand that it is you who is painfully parting the fibers of my being in order to penetrate to the very marrow of my substance.
Teilhard de Chardin

I have never met a man so religious and devout that he has not experienced at some time a withdrawal of grace and felt a lessening of fervor.
Thomas à Kempis

Darkness
See also: Affliction; Dark night of the soul; Difficulties; Trials
Who among you fears the LORD and obeys the word of his servant? Let him who walks in the dark, who has no light, trust in the name of the LORD and rely on his God.
The Bible, Isaiah 50:10

You can't appreciate the miracle of the sunrise unless you've waited in the darkness.
Author unknown

Lord, it belongs not to my care
Whether I die or live;
To love and serve Thee is my share,
And this Thy grace must give.
If life be long I will be glad,
That I may long obey;
If short – yet why should I be sad
To soar to endless day?
Christ leads me through no darker rooms
Than He went through before;
He that unto God's kingdom comes,
Must enter by this door.
Come, Lord, when grace has made me meet

Thy blessed face to see;
Or if Thy work on earth be sweet,
What will Thy glory be!
Then shall I end my sad complaints,
And weary, sinful days;
And join with the triumphant saints,
To sing Jehovah's praise.
My knowledge of that life is small,
The eye of faith is dim;
But 'tis enough that Christ knows all,
And I shall be with him.
Richard Baxter

I would rather walk with God in the dark
than go alone in the light.
Mary Gardiner Brainard

If I stoop
Into a dark tremendous sea of cloud,
It is but for a time; I press God's lamp
Close to my breast; its splendor, soon or late,
Will pierce the gloom: I shall emerge one day.
Robert Browning

Reconcile yourself to wait in this darkness
as long as is necessary, but still go on
longing after him whom you love. For if
you are to feel him in this life, it must
always be in this cloud of darkness.
Cloud of Unknowing, The

Post tenebras lux. (After darkness, light.)
Latin saying

Christ chargeth me to believe His daylight
at midnight.
Samuel Rutherford

Some of us think at times that we could
cry, "My God, my God, why hast Thou
forsaken me?" There are seasons when the
brightness of our Father's smile is eclipsed
by clouds and darkness; but let us
remember that God never does really
forsake us. It is only a seeming forsaking
with us, but in Christ's case it was a real
forsaking. We grieve at a little withdrawal
of our Father's love; but the real turning
away of God's face from His Son, who
shall calculate how deep the agony which it
caused Him? In our case, our cry is often

dictated by unbelief: in His case, it was the
utterance of a dreadful fact, for God had
really turned away from Him for a season.
  O thou poor, distressed soul, who once
lived in the sunshine of God's face, but art
now in darkness, remember that He has not
really forsaken thee. God in the clouds is as
much our God as when He shines forth in
all the luster of His grace; but since even the
thought that He has forsaken us gives us
agony, what must the woe of the Savior
have been when He exclaimed, "My God,
my God, why hast Thou forsaken me?"
C.H. Spurgeon

Our longest sorrows have an ending, and
there is a bottom to the profoundest
depths of our misery. Our winters shall not
frown forever; summer shall soon smile.
The tide shall not eternally ebb out; the
floods must retrace their march. The night
shall not hang its darkness forever over our
souls; the sun shall yet arise with healing
beneath its wings.
C.H. Spurgeon

Deacons
Deacons should be blameless in the
presence of His righteousness, as deacons
of God and Christ and not of men; not
double-tongued, not lovers of money,
temperate in all things, compassionate,
diligent, walking according to the truth of
the Lord who became a minister (deacon)
of all.
Polycarp

Death
See also: Bereavement; Dying; Grief;
Life after death
For dust thou art, and unto dust shalt thou
return.
The Bible, Genesis 3:19 KJV

I am going the way of all the earth.
The Bible, Joshua 23:14 KJV

Thou shalt come to thy grave in a full age,
like as a shock of corn cometh in in his
season.
The Bible, Job 5:26 KJV

I would not live alway.
The Bible, Job 7:16 KJV

The sorrows of death compassed me.
The Bible, Psalm 18:4 KJV

Precious in the sight of the LORD is the death of his saints.
The Bible, Psalm 116:15

The righteous hath hope in his death.
The Bible, Proverbs 14:32 KJV

Then shall the dust return to the earth as it was: and the spirit shall return unto God who gave it.
The Bible, Ecclesiastes 12:7 KJV

The last enemy to be destroyed is death.
The Bible, 1 Corinthians 15:26

O death, where is thy sting? O grave, where is thy victory?
The Bible, 1 Corinthians 15:55 KJV

To live is Christ, and to die is gain.
The Bible, Philippians 1:21 KJV

For we brought nothing into this world, and it is certain we can carry nothing out.
The Bible, 1 Timothy 6:7 KJV

… it has now been revealed through the appearing of our Savior, Christ Jesus, who has destroyed death and has brought life and immortality to light through the gospel.
The Bible, 2 Timothy 1:10

God buries His workmen but carries on His work.
Author unknown

Many who plan to seek God at the eleventh hour die at 10:30.
Author unknown

I have sent for you that you may see how a Christian can die.
Joseph Addison, on his deathbed to his stepson.

God who redeemed me by Himself, who by His grace bound me to Himself in this life of the cloister without my merit. To Him I go.
St Aelred of Rievaulx, his farewell words to his monks, as he was dying, in 1167

I don't want to achieve immortality through my work; I want to achieve immortality through not dying.
Woody Allen

There are three kinds of death in this world. There's heart death, there's brain death, and there's being off the network.
Guy Almes

To the good man to die is gain. The foolish fear death as the greatest of evils, the wise desire it as a rest after labors and the end of ills.
Ambrose

It is necessary to die, but nobody wants to; you don't want to, but you are going to, willy-nilly. A hard necessity that is, not to want something which can not be avoided. If it could be managed, we would much rather not die; we would like to become like the angels by some other means than death. We want to reach the kingdom of God, but we don't want to travel by way of death. And yet there stands Necessity saying: "This way, please." Do you hesitate, man, to go this way, when this is the way that God came to you?
Augustine of Hippo

Of this I am certain, that no one has ever died who was not destined to die some time. Now the end of life puts the longest life on a par with the shortest … And of what consequence is it what kind of death puts an end to life, since he who has died once is not forced to go through the same ordeal a second time? They, then, who are destined to die, need not be careful to inquire what death they are to die, but into what place death will usher them.
Augustine of Hippo

Men fear death as children fear to go in the dark.
Francis Bacon

On this side of the grave we are exiles, on that, citizens; on this side, orphans; on that, children; on this side, captives; on that, freemen.
Henry Ward Beecher

Ignorance of death is destroying us. Death is the dark backing a mirror needs if we are to see anything.
Saul Bellow

Day by day remind yourself that you are going to die.
Rule of St Benedict

Die: To stop sinning suddenly.
A. Bierce

They shall not grow old, as we that are left
  grow old:
Age shall not weary them, nor the years
  condemn.
At the going down of the sun and in the
  morning
We will remember them.
Lawrence Binyon

Through the half-open door in one room of the huts I saw Pastor Bonhoeffer, before taking off his prison garb, kneeling on the floor praying fervently to his God. I was most deeply moved by the way this lovable man prayed, so devout and so certain that God heard his prayer. At the place of execution, he again said a short prayer and then climbed the steps to the gallows, brave and composed. His death ensued after a few seconds. In almost fifty years that I worked as a doctor, I have hardly ever seen a man die so entirely submissive to the will of God.
Prison doctor describing Dietrich Bonhoeffer's death

In the midst of life we are in death.
Book of Common Prayer

The waters are rising, but so am I. I am not going under but over. Do not be concerned about dying; go on living well, the dying will be right.
Last words of Catherine Booth, wife of Salvation Army founder William Booth

I do not dare read the New Testament for fear of awakening a storm of anxiety and doubt and dread, of having taken the wrong path, of having been a traitor to the plain and simple God.
Gamaliel Bradford, famous biographer, as he neared the end of his life

Lord, if any have to die this day, let it be me, for I am ready.
Billy Bray

To go back is nothing but death: to go forward is fear of death, and life everlasting beyond it. I will yet go forward.
John Bunyan

I John Calvin, servant of the Word of God in the church of Geneva, weakened by many illnesses ... thank God that he has not only shown mercy to me, his poor creature ... and suffered me in all sins and weaknesses, but what is more than that, he has made me a partaker of his grace to serve him through my work ...   I confess to live and die in this faith which he has given me, inasmuch as I have no other hope or refuge than his predestination upon which my entire salvation is grounded. I embrace the grace which he has offered me in our Lord Jesus Christ, and accept the merits of his suffering and dying that through him all my sins are buried; and I humbly beg him to wash me and cleanse me with the blood of our great Redeemer, as it was shed for all poor sinners so that I, when I appear before his face, may bear his likeness.
Calvin's will

We don't know life: how can we know death?
Confucius

Come Love, come Lord, and that long day
For which I languish, come away.

When this dry soul those eyes shall see
And drink the unseal'd source of Thee,
When glory's sun faith's shades shall chase,
Then for Thy veil give me Thy face.
Richard Crashaw

One short sleep past, we wake eternally,
And Death shall be no more: Death, thou
   shalt die!
John Donne

Death be not proud, though some have
   called thee
Mighty and dreadful, for thou art not so,
For those whom thou think'st thou dost
   overthrow,
Die not, poor death, nor yet canst thou kill
   me.
John Donne

Death comes equally to us all, and makes
us all equal when it comes.
John Donne

Death in itself is nothing; but we fear
To be we know not what, we know not
where.
John Dryden

So softly death succeeded life in her,
She did but dream of heaven, and she was
there.
John Dryden

I must not think it strange if God takes in
youth those whom I would have kept on
earth until they were older. God is peopling
eternity, and I must not restrict him to old
men and women.
Jim Elliot

"Who gathered this flower?" The gardener
answered, "The Master." And his fellow-
servant held his peace.
Epitaph

A Christian in this world is but gold in
the ore; at death the pure gold is melted
out and separated and the dross cast away
and consumed.
Flavel

No man should be afraid to die, who hath
understood what it is to live.
Thomas Fuller

The boast of heraldry, the pomp of power,
And all that beauty, all that wealth e'er gave,
Awaits alike the inevitable hour.
The paths of glory lead but to the grave.
Gray's Elegy Written in a Country Churchyard

This machine will take off a head in a
twinkling, and the victim will feel
nothing but a sense of refreshing coolness.
We cannot make too much haste,
gentlemen, to allow the nation to enjoy
this advantage.
J.I. Guillotin

Death borders upon our birth, and our
cradle stands in the grave.
Bishop Hall

He whose head is in heaven need not fear
to put his feet into the grave.
Matthew Henry

Death is as the foreshadowing of life. We
die that we may die no more!
Herman Hooker

God hath my daily petitions, for I am at
peace with all men, and He is at peace
with me, and this witness makes the
thoughts of death joyful.
Richard Hooker, his last words

The approach of death is very dreadful. I
am afraid to think on that which I know I
cannot avoid. It is vain to look round and
round for that help which cannot be had.
Yet we hope and hope, and fancy that he
who has lived today my live tomorrow.
Samuel Johnson,
who however found when his death actually
approached that his fears "were calmed and
absorbed by the prevalence of his faith, and his
trust in the merits and propitiation of Jesus Christ."

Teach me to live that I may dread,
the grave as little as my bed.
Thomas Ken

In the long run we are all dead.
John Maynard Keynes

It is not darkness you are going to, for God is Light. It is not lonely, for Christ is with you. It is not unknown country, for Christ is there.
Charles Kingsley

Neither the sun nor death can be looked at with a steady eye.
Francis, Duc de La Rochefoucauld

While I thought I was learning how to live, I have been learning how to die.
Leonardo da Vinci

There are better things ahead than any we leave behind.
C.S. Lewis

It is hard to have patience with people who say, "There is no death," or, "Death doesn't matter." There is death. And whatever is matters. And whatever happens has consequences, and it and they are irrevocable and irreversible. You might as well say that birth doesn't matter.
C.S. Lewis

All the first Christians could face death with a smile.
M. Lloyd-Jones

Oh, not in cruelty, not in wrath,
The Reaper came that day;
'T was an angel visited the green earth,
And took the flowers away.
Henry Wadsworth Longfellow

Everybody wants to go to heaven, but nobody wants to die.
Joe Louis

Every man must do two things alone; he must do his own believing and his own dying.
Martin Luther

How strange this fear of death is! We are never frightened at a sunset.
George Macdonald

I came from God, and I'm going back to God, and I won't have any gaps of death in the middle of my life.
George Macdonald

Now I leave off to speak any more to creatures, and turn my speech to Thee, O Lord. Now I begin my intercourse with God which shall never be broken off. Farewell, father and mother, friends and relations.
Farewell, meat and drink.
Farewell, the world and all delights.
Farewell, sun, moon, and stars.
Welcome, God and Father.
Welcome, sweet Lord Jesus, Mediator of the New Covenant.
Welcome, Blessed Spirit of Grace, God of all Consolation.
Welcome, Glory.
Welcome, Eternal Life.
Welcome, death.
The martyrdom of Hugh MacKail
And to the faithful, death the gate of life.
John Milton

Death is the golden key that opens the palace of eternity.
John Milton

The valley of the shadow of death holds no darkness for the child of God. There must be light, else there could be no shadow. Jesus is the light. He has overcome death.
D.L. Moody

Some day you will read in the papers that D.L. Moody of East Northfield, is dead. Don't you believe a word of it! At that moment I shall be more alive than I am now; I shall have gone up higher, that is all, out of this old clay tenement into a house that is immortal – a body that death cannot touch, that sin cannot taint; a body fashioned like unto His glorious body.
D.L. Moody

There is one single fact which we may oppose to all the wit and argument of

infidelity, namely, that no man ever repented of being a Christian on his death bed.
Hannah More

So that he seemed not to relinquish life, but to leave one home for another.
Cornelius Nepos

After the fever of life; after weariness, sicknesses, fightings and despondings, languor and fretfulness, struggling and failing, struggling and succeeding; after all the changes and chances of this troubled and unhealthy state, at length comes death; at length the white throne of God; at length the beatific vision.
J.H. Newman

Death stung himself to death when he stung Christ.
William Romaine

Death – the last sleep? No, it is the final awakening.
Walter Scott

Remember death and the attractions of life will fade away before you.
Shenouda III

To die well is the action of the whole life.
Richard Sibbes

Death is only a grim porter to let us into a stately palace.
Richard Sibbes

A single death is a tragedy; a million deaths is a statistic.
Josef Stalin

He is not dead, this friend; not dead,
Gone some few, trifling steps ahead,
And nearer to the end;
So that you, too, once past the bend,
Shall meet again, as face to face, this friend
You fancy dead.
Robert Louis Stevenson

God's finger touched him, and he slept.
Alfred Lord Tennyson

Until our Master summons us, not a hair on our head can perish, not a moment of our life be snatched from us. When He sends for us, it should seem but the message that the child is wanted at home.
Anthony Thorold

The reports of my death have been greatly exaggerated.
Mark Twain

Let us endeavor so to live that when we come to die even the undertaker will be sorry.
Mark Twain

The faith that looks through death.
William Wordsworth

Death, Non-Christian view of

Once a man dies there is no resurrection.
Aeschylus

When once our brief light sets, there is one perpetual night through which we must sleep.
Catullus

There is hope for those who are alive, but those who have died are without hope.
Theocritus

As Adam's spiritual life would have consisted in remaining united and bound to his Maker, so estrangement from him was the death of his soul.
John Calvin

Death of a baby

I everywhere teach that no one can be justly condemned and perish except on account of actual sin; and to say that the countless mortals taken from life while yet infants are precipitated from their mother's arms into eternal death is a blasphemy to be universally detested.
John Calvin

Death of a child

I'm so glad Elisabeth is with the Lord, and

not in that box.
Mrs R.A. Torrey, at the funeral of her twelve-year-old daughter.

Dead! dead! the Child I lov'd so well!
Transported to the world above!
I need no more my heart conceal.
I never dar'd indulge my love;
But may I not indulge my grief,
And seek in tears a sad relief?
Charles Wesley, on the death of his son

Death, *Directions For a Peaceful*

Richard Baxter

Comfort is not desirable only as it pleases us, but also as it strengthens us, and helps us in our greatest duties. And when is it more needful than in sickness, and the approach of death? I shall therefore add such directions as are necessary to make our departure comfortable or peaceful at the least, as well as safe.

Misunderstand not sickness, as if it were a greater evil than it is; but observe how great a mercy it is I know to those that have walked very close with God, and are always ready, a sudden death may be a mercy; as we have lately known divers holy ministers and others, that have died either after a sacrament, or in the evening of the Lord's day, or in the midst of some holy exercise, with so little pain, that none about them perceived when they died. But ordinarily it is a mercy to have the flesh brought down and weakened by painful sickness, to help to conquer our natural unwillingness to die.

Remember whose messenger sickness is, and who it is that calls you to die. It is He, that is the Lord of all the world, and gave us the lives which he takes from us; and it is He, that must dispose of angels and men, of princes and kingdoms, of heaven and earth; and therefore there is no reason that such worms as we should desire to be excepted. You cannot deny him to be the disposer of all things, without denying him to be God: it is He that loves us, and never meant us any harm in any thing that He has done to us; that gave the life of his Son to redeem us; and therefore thinks not life too good for us. Our sickness and death are sent by the same love that sent us a Savior, and sent us the powerful preachers of His word, and sent us His Spirit, and secretly and sweetly changed our hearts, and knit them to Himself in love; which gave us a life of precious mercies for our souls and bodies, and has promised to give us life eternal; and shall we think, that He now intends us any harm? Cannot He turn this also to our good, as He has done many an affliction which we have complained about?

Look by faith to your dying, buried, risen, ascended, glorified Lord. Nothing will more powerfully overcome both the poison and the fears of death, than the believing thoughts of Him that has triumphed over it. Is it terrible as it separates the soul from the body? So it did by our Lord, who yet overcame it. Is it terrible as it lays the body in the grave? So it did by our Savior; though He saw not corruption, but quickly rose by the power of his Godhead. He died to teach us believingly and boldly to submit to death. He was buried, to teach us not overmuch to fear a grave. He rose again to conquer death for us, and to assure those who rise to newness of life, that they shall be raised at last by His power unto glory; and being made partakers of the first resurrection, the second death shall have no power over them. He lives as our head, that we might live by him; and that He might assure all those that are here risen with Him, and seek first the things that are above, that though in themselves they are dead, "yet their life is hid with Christ in God; and when Christ who is our life shall appear, then shall we also appear with him in glory," (Col. 3:1,2,4,5). What a comfortable word is that, "Because I live, you shall live also," (John 14:19). Death could not hold the Lord of life; nor can it hold us against His will, who has the "keys of death and hell," (Rev. 1:18). He loves every one of his sanctified ones much better than you love an eye, or a hand, or any other member of your body, which you are not willing to lose if you are able to save it. When He ascended, He left us that message full of comfort for His followers, "Go to my brethren, and say unto them, I ascend unto my Father, and your Father; to my God, and your God," (John 20:17). Which, with these two following, I would have written before me on my sick bed. "If any man serve me, let him follow me; and where I am, there also shall my servant be," (John 12:26). And, "Verily, I say unto you, today shall you be with me in paradise," (Luke 23:43). Oh what a joyful thought should it be to a believer, to think when he is dying, that he is going to his Savior, and that our Lord is risen and gone before us, to prepare a place for us, and take us in season to Himself, John 14:2-4.

Choose out some promises most suitable to your condition, and roll them over and over in your mind, and feed and live on them by faith. A sick man is not (usually) fit to think of very many things; and therefore two or three comfortable promises, to be still before his eyes, may be the most profitable matter of his thoughts ... If he be most troubled with the greatness of his sin, let it be such as these. "God so loved the world, that he gave his only begotten Son, that whosoever believes in him should not perish, but have everlasting life," (John 3:16). "And by him all that believe are justified from all things, from which you could not be justified by the law of Moses," (Acts 13:39). "For I will be merciful unto their unrighteousness, and their sins and iniquities will I remember no more," (Heb. 8:12). If it be the weakness of his grace that troubles him, let him choose such passages as these: "He shall gather the lambs with his arm, and carry them in his bosom, and shall gently lead those that are with young," (Isa. 40:11). "The spirit is willing, but the flesh is weak," (Matt. 26:41). "All that the

Father gives me, shall come to me and him that comes to me, I will in no wise cast out," (John 6:37). If it be the fear of death, and strangeness to the other world, that troubles you, remember the words of Christ before cited, and 2 Cor. 5:1-6,8, "For we know, that if our earthly house of this tabernacle were dissolved, we have a building of God, an house not made with hands, eternal in the heavens. For in this we groan, earnestly desiring to be clothed upon with our house which is from heaven. For we that are in this tabernacle do groan being burdened, not for that we would be unclothed, but clothed upon, that mortality might be swallowed up of life. We are confident, and willing rather to be absent from the body, and present with the Lord." "O death, where is your sting? O grave, where is your victory?" 1 Cor. 15:55. Fix upon some such word or promise, which may support you in your extremity.

Look up to God, who is the glory of heaven, and the light, and life, and joy of souls, and believe that you are going to see His face, and to live in the perfect, everlasting fruition of His fullest love among the glorified. If it be delectable [enjoyable] here to know His works, what will it be to see the cause of all? All creatures in heaven and earth conjoined, can never afford such content and joy to holy souls, as God alone! Oh if we knew him whom we must there behold, how weary should we be of this dungeon of mortality and how fervently should we long to see his face! The chicken that comes out of the shell, or the infant that newly comes out of the womb, into this illuminated world of human converse, receives not such a joyful change, as the soul that is newly loosed from the flesh, and passes from this mortal life to God. One sight of God by a blessed soul, is worth more than all the kingdoms of the earth. "And there shall be no more curse: but the throne of God and of the Lamb shall be in it, and his servants shall serve him: and they shall see his face, and his name shall be in their foreheads: and there shall be no night there: and they need no candle, nor light of the sun; for the Lord God gives them light, and they shall reign for ever and ever," Rev. 22:3-5. When our perfected bodies shall have the perfect glorious body of Christ to see, and our perfected souls shall have the God of truth, the most perfect uncreated light to know, what more is a created understanding capable of? And yet this is not the top of our felicity; for the understanding is but the passage to the heart or will, and truth is but subservient to goodness: and therefore though the understanding be capable of no more than the beatific vision, yet the man is capable of more; even of receiving the fullest communications of God's love, and feeling it poured out upon the heart, and living in the returns of perfect love; and in this intercourse of love will be our highest joys, and this is the top of our heavenly felicity. Oh that God would make us foreknow by a lively faith, what it is to behold him in His glory, and to dwell in perfect love and joy, and then death would no more be able to dismay us, nor should we be unwilling of such a blessed change!

Look up to the blessed society of angels and saints with Christ, and remember their blessedness and joy, and that you also belong to the same society, and are going to be numbered with them. It will greatly overcome the fears of death, to see by faith the joys of them that have gone before us; and withal to think of their relation to us; as it will encourage a man that is to go beyond sea, if the far greatest part of his dearest friends be gone before him, and he hears of their safe arrival, and of their joy and happiness. Those angels that now see the face of God are our special friends and guardians, and entirely love us, better than any of our friends on earth do! They rejoiced at our conversion, and will rejoice at our glorification; and as they are better, and love us better, so therefore our love should be greater to them, than to any upon earth, and we should more desire to be with them. Those blessed souls that are now with Christ, were once as we are here on earth; they were compassed with temptations, and clogged with flesh, and

burdened with sin, and persecuted by the world, and they went out of the world by sickness and death, as we must do; and yet now their tears are wiped away, their pains, and groans, and fears are turned into inexpressible blessedness and joy: and would we not be with them? Is not their company desirable? And their felicity [joy] more desirable? The glory of the New Jerusalem is not described to us in vain, (Rev. 21 and 22). God will be all in all there to us, as the only sun and glory of that world; and yet we shall have pleasure, not only to see our glorified Redeemer, but also to converse with the heavenly society, and to sit down with Abraham, Isaac, and Jacob in the kingdom of God, and to love and praise Him in consort and harmony with all those holy, blessed spirits. And shall we be afraid to follow, where the saints of all generations have gone before us? And shall the company of our best, and most, and happiest friends, be no inducement to us? Though it must be our highest joy to think that we shall dwell with God, and next that we shall see the glory of Christ, yet is it no small part of my comfort to consider, that I shall follow all those holy persons, whom I once conversed with, that are gone before me. How few are all the saints on earth, in comparison of those that are now with Christ! And, alas, how weak, and ignorant, and corrupt, how selfish, and contentious, and troublesome, are God's poor infants here in flesh, when above there is nothing but holiness and perfection! If knowledge, or goodness, or any excellency do make the creatures truly amiable, all this is there in the highest degree; but here, alas, how little have we! Oh then what a place is the New Jerusalem; and how pleasant will it be with saints and angels to see and love and praise the Lord.

That sickness and death may be comfortable to you, as your passage to eternity, take notice of the seal and earnest of God, even the Spirit of grace which He has put into your heart. For this is God's mark upon his chosen and justified ones, by which they are "sealed up to the day of their redemption," (Eph. 4:33). And what a comfort should it be to us, when we look towards heaven, to find such a pledge of God within us! If you say, I fear I have not this earnest of the Spirit; whence then did your desires of holiness arise? What weaned you from the world, and made you place your hopes and happiness above? Whence came your enmity to sin, and opposition to it, and your earnest desires after the glory of God, the prosperity of the gospel, and the good of souls? The very love of holiness and holy persons, and your desires to know God and perfectly love Him, do show that heavenly nature or spirit within you, which is your surest evidence for eternal life: for that spirit was sent from heaven, to draw up your hearts, and fit you for it; and God does not give you such natures, and desires, and preparations in vain. This also is called, "The witness of the Spirit with (or to) our spirit, that we are the children of God; and if children then heirs, heirs of God, and joint heirs with Christ," (Rom. 8:15-17). God would not have given us a heavenly nature or desire, if he had not intended us for heaven.

Look also to the testimony of a holy life, since grace has employed you in seeking after the heavenly inheritance. Seeing therefore the Spirit has given you these evidences, to difference you from the wretched world, and prove your title to eternal life, if you overlook these, you resist your Comforter, and can see no other ground of comfort, than every graceless hypocrite may see. Imitate holy Paul: "For our rejoicing is this, the testimony of our conscience, that in simplicity and godly sincerity, not in fleshly wisdom, but by the grace of God, we have had our conversation in the world," (2 Cor. 1:12, 2). "I have fought a good fight; I have finished my course, I have kept the faith; henceforth there is laid up for me a crown of righteousness, which the Lord the righteous Judge shall give me at that day: and not to me only, but to all them also that love his appearing," (Tim. 4:7, 8). To look back and see that in sincerity you have gone the way to heaven, is a just and necessary ground of assurance, that you

shall attain it. If you say, But I have been a grievous sinner! I answer, so was Paul that yet rejoiced after in this evidence! Are not those sins repented of and pardoned? If you say, But I cannot look back upon a holy life with comfort, it has been so blotted and uneven! I answer, has it not been sincere, though it was imperfect? Did you not "first seek the kingdom of God and his righteousness?" (Matt. 6:33). If you say, My whole life has been ungodly, till now at last that God has humbled me; I answer, it is not the length of time, but the sincerity of your hearts and service, that is your evidence. If you came in it the last hour, if now you are faithfully devoted to God, you may look with comfort on this change at last, though you must look with repentance on your sinful lives.

When you see any of this evidence of your interest in Christ appeal to him to acquit you from all the sin that can be charged on you; for all that believe in him are justified from all things, from which they could not be justified by the law of Moses. "There is no condemnation to them that are in Christ Jesus, that walk not after the flesh, but after the Spirit," (Rom. 8:1). Whatever sin a penitent believer has committed, he is not chargeable with it; Christ has undertaken to answer for it, and justify him from it; and therefore look not on it with terror, but with penitent shame, and believing thankfulness, as that which shall tend to the honor of the Redeemer, and not to the condemnation of the sinner. He has borne our transgressions and we are healed by his stripes.

Look back upon all the mercies of your lives, and think whence they came and what they signify. Love tokens are to draw your hearts to him that sent them; these are dropped from heaven, to entice you thither! If God has been so good to you on earth, what will he be in glory! If He so blessed you in this wilderness, what will He do in the land of promise! It greatly emboldens my soul to go to that God, that has so tenderly loved me, and so graciously preserved me, and so much abounded in all sorts of mercies to me through all my life. Surely He is good that so delights to do good! And His presence must be sweet, when His distant mercies have been so sweet! What love shall I enjoy when perfection has fitted me for His love, who has tasted of so much in this state of sin and imperfection! The sense of mercy will banish the fears and misgivings of the heart.

Remember (if you have attained to a declining age) what a competent time you have had already in the world. When I think how many years of mercy I have had, since I was near to death, and since many younger than I are gone, and when I think what abundance of mercy I have had in all that time, candor forbids me to grudge at the season of my death, and makes me almost ashamed to ask for longer life. How long would you stay, before you would be willing to come to God? If He desired our company no more than we do His, and desired our happiness in heaven no more than we desire it ourselves, we should linger here as Lot in Sodom! Must we be snatched away against our wills, and carried by force to our Father's presence?

Remember that all mankind are mortal, and you are to go no other way than all that ever came into the world have gone before you (except Enoch and Elias). Yea, the poor brute creatures must die at your pleasure, to satisfy your hunger or delight. Beasts, and birds, and fishes, even many to make one meal, must die for you. And why then should you shrink at the entrance of such a trodden path, which leads you not to hell, as it does the wicked, nor merely to corruption, as it does the brutes: but to live in joy with Christ and his church triumphant?

Remember both how vile your body is, and how great an enemy it has proved to your soul; and then you will the more patiently bear its dissolution. It is not your dwelling-house, but your tent or prison, that God is pulling down. And yet even this vile body, when it is corrupted, shall at last be changed "into the likeness of Christ's glorious body, by the working of his irresistible power," (Phil. 3:20,21). And it is a flesh that has so rebelled against the

spirit, and made your way to heaven so difficult, and put the soul to so many conflicts, that we should more easily submit it to the will of justice, and let it perish for a time, when we are assured that mercy will at last recover it.

Remember what a world it is that you are to leave, and compare it with that which you are going to; and compare the life which is near an end, with that which you are next to enter upon. Was it not Enoch's reward when he had walked with God, to be taken to Him from a polluted world?

1. While you are here, you are yourselves defiled; sin is in your natures, and your graces are all imperfect; sin is in your lives, and your duties are all imperfect; you cannot be free from it one day or hour. And is it not a mercy to be delivered from it? Is it not desirable to you to sin no more? And to be perfect in holiness? To know God and love him as much and more than you can now desire? How oft have you prayed for a cure of all this! And now would you not have it, when God would give it you?

2. It is a life of grief as well as sin; and a life of cares, and doubts, and fears! When you are at the worst, you are fearing worse! If it were nothing but the fears of death itself, it should make you the more willing to submit to it, that you might be past those fears.

3. You are daily afflicted with the infirmities of that flesh, which are so unwilling to be dissolved. To satisfy its hunger and thirst, to cover its nakedness, to provide it a habitation, and supply all its wants, what care and labor does it cost you! Its infirmities, sicknesses, and pains, do make you oft weary of yourselves so that you "groan, being burdened," as Paul speaks, (2 Cor. 5:3,4,6). And yet is it not desirable to be with Christ?

4. You are compassed with temptations, and are in continual danger through your weakness: and yet would you not be past the danger? Would you have more of those horrid and odious temptations?

5. You are purposely turned here into a wilderness, among wild beasts; you are as lambs among wolves, and through many tribulations you must enter into heaven.

You must deny yourselves, and take up your cross, and forsake all that you have; and all that will live godly in Christ Jesus, must suffer persecution. In the world you must have trouble: the seed of the serpent must bruise your heel, before God bruises Satan under your feet! And is such a life as this more desirable than to be with Christ? Is a wicked world, a malicious world, a cruel world, an implacable world, more pleasing to us, than the joy of angels, and the sight of Christ, and God himself in the majesty of his glory? Has God on purpose made the world so bitter to us, and permitted it to use us unjustly and cruelly, and all to make us love it less, and to drive home our hearts unto himself? And yet are we so unwilling to be gone?

Settle your estates early, that worldly matters may not distract or discompose you. And if God has endowed you with riches, dispose of a due proportion to such pious or charitable uses, in which they may be most serviceable to Him that gave them to you. Though we should give what we can in the time of life and health, yet many that have but so much as will serve to their necessary maintenance, may well part with that to good uses at their death, which they could not spare in the time of their health: especially they that have no children, or such wicked children, as are like to do hurt with all that is given them above their daily bread.

If it may be, get some able, faithful guide and comforter to be with you in your sickness, to counsel you, and resolve your doubts, and pray with you, and discourse of heavenly things, when you are disabled by weakness for such exercises yourselves. Let not carnal persons disturb you with their vain babblings. Though the difference between good company and bad, be very great in the time of health, yet now in sickness it will be more discernible. And though a faithful friend and spiritual pastor be always a great mercy, yet now especially in your last necessity. Therefore make use of them as far as your pain and weakness will permit.

Be fortified against all the temptations of Satan by which he uses to assault men in their extremity: stand it out in the last conflict, and the crown is yours.
Richard Baxter

Death of Christ
See: Cross

Death-bed
It is grace at the beginning, and grace at the end. So that when you and I come to lie upon our death beds, the one thing that should comfort and help and strengthen us there is the thing that helped us in the beginning. Not what we have been, not what we have done, but the grace of God in Jesus Christ our Lord. The Christian life starts with grace, it must continue with grace, it ends with grace. Grace, wondrous grace. By the grace of God I am what I am. Yet not I, but the grace of God which was with me.
D. Martyn Lloyd-Jones

Debate
When you have no basis for an argument, abuse the plaintiff.
Cicero

An honest man speaks the truth, though it may give offence; a vain man, in order that it may.
William Hazlitt

Debt
The borrower is servant to the lender.
The Bible, Proverbs 22:7

He that goes a borrowing goes a sorrowing.
Benjamin Franklin

Neither a borrower nor a lender be;
For loan oft loses both itself and friend,
And borrowing dulls the edge of husbandry.
William Shakespeare, Hamlet

Debt to God
While a man lives, there is not a single

hour, day or night, when he is not a debtor.
Origen

Decay
When Catholicism goes bad it becomes
the religio [religion] of amulets and holy
places and priest craft: Protestantism, in
its corresponding decay, becomes a vague
mist of ethical platitudes.
C.S. Lewis

There is an element of decay in everything
that characterizes modern man.
Nietzsche

Deception
Do not deceive one another.
The Bible, Leviticus 19:11

Nothing is so easy as to deceive oneself; for
what we wish, we readily believe.
Demosthenes

No man was ever so much deceived by
another as by himself.
Fulke Greville

We like to be deceived.
Blaise Pascal

Deciding for God
Wilt thou leave thy sins and go to heaven,
or wilt thou have thy sins and go to hell?
The voice John Bunyan heard

It might be the Devil or it might be the
Lord, but you've got to serve somebody.
Bob Dylan

Our capacity to choose changes
constantly with our practice of life. The
longer we continue to make the wrong
decisions, the more our heart hardens; the
more often we make the right decisions,
the more our heart softens or better,
perhaps, comes alive.
Erich Fromm

The decision we all face is this: whether to
consciously lock God out of our lives or
open the door of our heart and invite Jesus

Christ to come in.
Luis Palau

Decisions
See also: Indecision
How long halt ye between two opinions?
The Bible, 1 Kings 18:21 KJV

Every accomplishment starts with the
decision to try.
Author unknown

Yes and No are the two most important
words that you will ever say. These are the
two words that determine your destiny in
life.
Author unknown

Those who insist upon seeing with
perfect clearness before they decide, never
decide.
Henri-Frederic Amiel

Thus we see that the all important thing is
not killing or giving life, drinking or not
drinking, living in the town or the country,
being unlucky or lucky, winning or losing.
It is how we win, how we lose, how we live
or die, finally, how we choose.
R.H. Blyth

Life often presents us with a choice of evils
rather than of goods.
Charles Caleb Colton

Between two evils, choose neither; between
two goods, choose both.
T. Edwards

We who lived in concentration camps can
remember the men who walked through
the huts comforting others, giving away
their last piece of bread. They may have
been few in number, but they offer
sufficient proof that everything can be
taken away from a man but one thing: the
last of the human freedoms – to choose
one's attitude in any given set of
circumstances, to choose one's own way.
Viktor Frankl

An entrepreneur is a person who makes decisions and is sometimes right.
William Heinecke

When you have to make a choice and don't make it, that in itself is a choice.
William James

Good and evil both increase at compound interest. That is why the little decisions you and I make every day are of such infinite importance.
C.S. Lewis

Every time you make a choice you are turning the central part of you, the part that chooses, into something a little different from what it was before.
C.S. Lewis

I determined never to stop until I had come to the end and achieved my purpose.
David Livingstone

The difficulty in life is the choice.
George Moore

Be willing to make decisions. That's the most important quality in a good leader. Don't fall victim to what I call the Ready-Aim-Aim-Aim Syndrome. You must be willing to fire.
T. Boone Pickens

In any moment of decision the best thing you can do is the right thing, the next best thing is the wrong thing, and the worst thing you can do is nothing.
Theodore Roosevelt

Never cut a tree down in the wintertime. Never make a negative decision in the low time.
Robert H. Schuller

Nature gives man corn but he must grind it; God gives man a will but he must make the right choices.
Fulton J. Sheen

Of two evils, the lesser is always to be chosen.
Thomas à Kempis

Decline
See: Backsliding

Dedication
See also: Consecration
Therefore, I urge you, brothers, in view of God's mercy, to offer your bodies as living sacrifices, holy and pleasing to God – this is your spiritual act of worship.
The Bible, Romans, 12:1

Let no one imagine he will lose anything of human dignity by this voluntary sell-out of his all to God.
Author unknown

Walk so close to God that nothing can come between you.
Author unknown

It took computers 800,000 hours to render the final animation of the film *Toy Shop*. Woody's mouth has 58 variables on the computer.
Author unknown

A state of temperance, sobriety and justice without devotion is a cold, lifeless, insipid condition of virtue, and is rather to be styled philosophy than religion.
Joseph Addison

We are consecrated and dedicated to God; therefore, we may not hereafter think, speak, meditate or do anything but with a view to his glory. We are God's; to him, therefore, let us live and die.
John Calvin

To get there is a question of will, not of debate nor of reasoning, but a surrender of will, an absolute and irrevocable surrender on that point. Shut out every other consideration and keep yourself before God for this one thing only.
Oswald Chambers

Anything that dims my vision for Christ, or takes away my taste for Bible study, or cramps me in my prayer life, or makes Christian work difficult, is wrong for me;

and I must, as a Christian, turn away from it.
J. Wilbur Chapman

To gain that which is worth having, it may be necessary to lose everything else.
Bernadette Devlin

I am resolved never to do anything which I should be afraid to do if it were the last hour of my life.
Jonathan Edwards

Sever me from myself
that I may be grateful to you;
may I perish to myself
that I may be safe in you;
may I die to myself
that I may live in you;
may I wither to myself
that I may blossom in you;
may I be emptied of myself
that I may abound in you;
may I be nothing to myself
that I may be all in you.
Desiderius Erasmus

Those who are wholly God's are always happy.
Francois Fénelon

Quit all, strip yourself of all and you will have all in God.
Gerson

Those who desire to live in love alone with all their might and heart shall so dispose all things that they shall soon possess her all.
Hadewijch

Beyond all reason they [who love God] will give their all and go through all.
Hadewijch

I take God the Father to be my God;
I take God the Son to be my Savior;
I take the Holy Ghost to be my Sanctifier;
I take the Word of God to be my rule;
I take the people of God to be my people;
And I do hereby dedicate and yield my whole self to the Lord:

And I do this deliberately, freely, and forever. Amen.
Matthew Henry's father

Since you have forsaken the world and turned wholly to God, you are symbolically dead in the eyes of men; therefore, let your heart be dead to all earthly affections and concerns, and wholly devoted to our Lord Jesus Christ. For you must be well aware that if we make an outward show of conversion to God without giving Him our hearts, it is only a shadow and pretense of virtue, and no true conversion. Any man or woman who neglects to maintain inward vigilance, and only makes an outward show of holiness in dress, speech, and behavior, is a wretched creature.
Walter Hilton

No one who really wants to count for God can afford to play at Christianity.
H.A. Ironside

In the total expanse of human life there is not a single square inch of which the Christ, who alone is sovereign, does not declare, "That is mine!"
Abraham Kuyper

Devotion signifies a life given, or devoted, to God. He therefore is the devout man, who lives no longer to his own will, or the way and spirit of the world, but to the sole will of God, who considers God in everything, who serves God in everything, who makes all the parts of his common life, parts of piety, by doing everything in the name of God, and under such rules as are conformable to His glory.
William Law

My Jesus, my King, my Life, my All; I again dedicate my whole self to Thee.
David Livingstone, written on his 59th birthday

All for God and nothing for self.
Mary Magdelene Dei Pazzi

We can have no power from Christ unless we live in a persuasion that we have none of our own.
John Owen

Every day seek to lose yourself more in Christ, to live more completely in him, by him, for him, with him.
C.H. Spurgeon

Many are willing that Christ should be something, but few will consent that Christ should be everything.
Alexander Moody Stuart

In short: in all his ways and walks, whether as touching his own business, or his dealings with other men, he must keep his heart with all diligence, lest he do aught, or turn aside to aught, or suffer aught to spring up or dwell within him or about him, or let anything be done in him or through him, otherwise than were meet for God, and would be possible and seemly if God Himself were verily made Man.
Theologia Germanica

Defeat
A man is not finished when he is defeated. He is finished when he quits.
Richard Mulhouse Nixon

Never talk defeat. Use words like hope, belief, faith, victory.
Norman Vincent Peal

Delay
Never think that God's delays are God's denials. Hold on; hold fast; hold out. Patience is genius.
George-Louis Leclerc de Buffon

Delight in God
All earthly delights are but "streams". But God is the ocean.
Jonathan Edwards

Our only business is to love and delight ourselves in God.
Brother Lawrence

Our continual apprehension of God may produce our continual satisfaction in God, under all His dispensations. Whatever enjoyments are by God conferred upon us, where lies the relish, where the sweetness of them? Truly, we may come to relish our enjoyments, only so far as we have something of God in them. It was required in Psal. xxxvii. 4, "Delight thyself in the Lord." Yea, and what if we should have no delight but the Lord? Let us ponder with ourselves over our enjoyments: "In these enjoyments I see God, and by these enjoyments, I serve God!"

And now, let all our delight in, and all our value and fondness for our enjoyments, be only, or mainly, upon such a divine score as this. As far as any of our enjoyments lead us unto God, so far let us relish it, affect it, embrace it, and rejoice in it: "O taste, and feed upon God in all;" and ask for nothing, no, not for life itself, any further than as it may help us, in our seeing and our serving of our God.

And then, whatever afflictions do lay fetters upon us, let us not only remember that we are concerned with God therein, but let our concernment with God procure a very profound submission in our souls. Be able to say with him in Psal. xxxix. 9, "I open not my mouth, because thou didst it." In all our afflictions, let us remark the justice of that God, before whom, "why should a living man complain for the punishment of his sin?" The wisdom of that God, "whose judgments are right." The goodness of that God, who "punishes us less than our iniquities do deserve." Let us behave ourselves, as having to do with none but God in our afflictions. And let our afflictions make us more conformable unto God: which conformity being effected, let us then say, "'Tis good for me that I have been afflicted."

Sirs, what were this, but a pitch of holiness, almost angelical! Oh! Mount up, as with the wings of eagles, of angels: be not a sorry, puny, mechanick sort of Christian any longer; but reach forth unto these things that are thus before you.
Cotton Mather

Deliverance

The Lord will rescue me from every evil attack and will bring me safely to his heavenly kingdom. To him be glory for ever and ever. Amen.
The Bible, 2 Timothy 4:18

Democracy

The best argument against democracy is a five minute conversation with the average voter.
Winston Churchill

A democracy – that is a government of all the people, by all the people, for all the people, of course, a government of the principles of eternal justice, the unchanging law of God, for shortness sake I will call it the idea of freedom.
Theodore Parker

Democracy is, first and foremost, a spiritual force, it is built upon a spiritual basis – and on a belief in God and an observance of moral principle. And in the long run only the church can provide that basis. Our founder knew this truth – and we will neglect it at our peril.
Harry Truman

Denominations

For one sect then to say, Ours is the true Church, and another to say, Nay, but ours is the true Church, is as mad as to dispute whether your hall, or kitchen, or parlor, or coal-house is your house; and for one to say, This is the house, and another, Nay, but it is that; when a child can tell them, that the best is but a part, and the house containeth them all.
Richard Baxter

Someone has said, "If we could get religion like a Baptist, experience it like a Methodist, be positive about it like a Disciple, be proud of it like an Episcopalian, pay for it like a Presbyterian, propagate it like an Adventist, and enjoy it like an Afro-American – that would be some religion!"
Harry Emerson Fosdick

Do not call yourselves Lutherans, call yourselves Christians. Has Luther been crucified to the world?
Martin Luther

A plague upon denominationalism! There should be but one denomination. We should be denominated by the name of Christ, as the wife is named by her husband's name. As long as the church of Christ has to say, "My right arm is Episcopalian, my left arm is Wesleyan, my right foot is Baptist, and my left foot is Presbyterian," she is not ready for the marriage. She will be ready when she has washed out these stains, when all her members have "one Lord, one faith, one baptism."
C.H. Spurgeon

If I see a man who loves the Lord Jesus in sincerity, I am not very solicitous to what communion he belongs. The kingdom of God, I think, does not consist in any such thing.
George Whitefield

Dependence on God
See: Trust

Depravity

There never was a man yet who was in a state of grace who did not know himself, in himself, to be in a state of ruin, a state of depravity and condemnation.
C.H. Spurgeon

The human race has improved everything except the human race.
Adlai Stevenson

Depression
See also: Sorrow

No matter how low you feel, if you count your blessings, you'll always show a profit.
Author unknown

It is an amazing thing for a soul that believed herself to be advanced in the way of perfection, when she sees herself thus go to pieces all at once.
Madame Guyon

Knowing your own darkness is the best method for dealing with the darknesses of other people.
Carl Jung

If you gaze long into an abyss, the abyss will gaze back into you.
Friedrich Nietzsche

O weary days, O evenings that never end! For how many long years I have watched that drawing-room clock and thought it would never reach the ten! ... In my thirty-first year I see nothing desirable but death.
Florence Nightingale, four years before going to the Crimea

There's nothing so blocks the spirit as gloom and despondency and downheartedness.
Seraphim

Before any great achievement, some measure of depression is very usual.
C.H. Spurgeon

All mental work tends to weary and depress, for much study is a weariness of the flesh. But ours [the work of pastors] is more than mental work; it is *heart* work – the labor of the inmost soul. How often on Lord's Day evenings do we feel as if life were completely washed out of us!
C.H. Spurgeon

When you come to the bottom, you find God.
Neville Talbot

Desertion
... for Demas, because he loved this world, has deserted me and has gone to Thessalonica. Crescens has gone to Galatia, and Titus to Dalmatia.
The Bible, 2 Timothy 4:10

Desire/Desires
The desire accomplished is sweet to the soul.
The Bible, Proverbs 13:19 KJV

As obedient children, do not conform to the evil desires you had when you lived in ignorance.
The Bible, 1 Peter 1:14

Dear friends, I urge you, as aliens and strangers in the world, to abstain from sinful desires, which war against your soul.
The Bible, 1 Peter 2:11

D etermination
E ffort
S acrifice
I nitiative
R esponsibility
E nthusiasm
Author unknown

Desire is half of life. Indifference is half of death.
Author unknown

Some people want it to happen, some wish it would happen, others make it happen.
Author unknown

Beware lest you lose the substance by grasping at the shadow.
Aesop

Remove every evil desire and clothe yourself with good and holy desire. For if you are clothed with good desire, you will hate evil desire and bridle it as you please.
Shepherd of Hermas

To have more, desire less.
Martin Luther

Man finds it hard to get what he wants, because he does not want the best; God finds it hard to give, because He would give the best, and man will not take it.
George Macdonald

After a time, you may find that "having" is not so pleasing a thing, after all, as "wanting." It is not logical, but it is often true.
Spock, "Amok Time," stardate 3372.7

We desire most what we ought not to have.
Publilius Syrus

When a man desires anything inordinately,
he is at once unquiet in himself.
Thomas à Kempis

Despair

In idleness there is a perpetual despair.
Thomas Carlyle

Despair is the conclusion of fools.
Benjamin Disraeli

To live without hope is to cease to live.
Fyodor Dostoevsky

Despair is suffering without meaning.
Viktor Frankl

Eternal Wisdom: Thou must not despair.
Did I not come into the world for the sake
of thee and all sinners, that I might lead
thee back to My Father in such beauty,
brightness, and purity, as otherwise thou
never couldst have acquired?
Henry Suso

It is impossible for that man to despair who
remembers that his Helper is omnipotent.
Jeremy Taylor

Never despair, but if you do, work on in
despair.
Terence

The mass of men lead lives of quiet
desperation.
Henry David Thoreau

Despising
For who hath despised the day of small
things?
The Bible, Zechariah 4:10 KJV

Blessed are those who heal us of our self-
despisings.
Mark Rutherford

Destination
A religious man is guided in his activity
not by the consequences of his action, but
by the consciousness of the destination of
his life.
Leo Tolstoy

Destiny
Don't let your past determine your
destiny.
Author unknown

Heaven is one's destiny. Becoming like
Jesus is one's goal.
Author unknown

Destiny is not a matter of chance, it is a
matter of choice. It is not a thing to be
waited for, it is a thing to be achieved.
William Jennings Bryan

Be inspired with the belief that life is a
great and noble calling; not a mean and
groveling thing that we are to shuffle
through as we can, but an elevated and
lofty destiny.
William E. Gladstone

Sow a thought, reap an act.
Sow an act, reap a habit.
Sow a habit, reap a character.
Sow a character, reap a destiny.
Samuel Smiles

Detachment
There is but one thing to do to purify our
hearts, to detach ourselves from creatures,
and abandon ourselves entirely to God.
Jean Pierre de Caussade

Keep yourself detached from all mankind;
keep yourself devoid of all incoming
images; emancipate yourself from
everything which entails addition,
attachment or encumbrance, and focus
your mind at all times on the saving
contemplation of God. Carry him within
your heart as the fixed object from which
your eyes never waver.
Meister Eckhart

The poor in spirit (Matthew 5:3) have no
attachment to the things that are present,
nor are they even in thought passionately

involved with them, not even to the extent of simple enjoyment.
Symeon the New Theologian

Details
Pay attention to minute particulars. Take care of the little ones. Generalization and abstraction are the plea of the hypocrite, scoundrel, and knave.
William Blake

Those who bestow too much application on trifling things become generally incapable of great ones.
La Rochefoucauld

Determination
Only dead fish go with the current.
Author unknown

Most men succeed because they are determined to.
George Allen

What this power is I cannot say; all I know is that it exists and it becomes available only when a man is in that state of mind in which he knows exactly what he wants and is fully determined not to quit until he finds it.
Alexander Graham Bell

Most of the important things in the world have been accomplished by people who have kept on trying when there seemed to be no hope at all.
Dale Carnegie

Each day you must say to yourself, "Today I am going to begin."
Jean-Pierre de Caussade

Firmness of purpose is one of the most necessary sinews of character, and one of the best instruments for success. Without it, genius wastes its efforts in a maze of inconsistencies.
Lord Chesterfield

Never give in, never give in, never, never, never, never – in nothing, great or small,

large or petty – never give in except to convictions of honor and good sense.
Winston Churchill

It does not matter how slowly you go, so long as you do not stop.
Confucius

We haven't failed. We now know a thousand things that won't work, so we're that much closer to finding what will.
Thomas Edison, after many abortive experiments trying to produce a light bulb.

Don't let life discourage you; everyone who got where he is had to begin where he was.
Richard L. Evans

Our future and our fate lie in our wills more than in our hands, for our hands are but the instruments of our wills.
B.C. Forbes

There are but two roads that lead to an important goal and to the doing of great things: strength and perseverance. Strength is the lot of but a few privileged men; but austere perseverance, harsh and continuous, may be employed by the smallest of us and rarely fails of its purpose, for its silent power grows irresistibly greater with time.
Johann Wolfgang von Goethe

It is still one of the tragedies of human history that the "children of darkness" are frequently more determined and zealous than the "children of light."
Martin Luther King

O Lord, you give us everything, at the price of an effort.
Leonardo Da Vinci

My thoughts before a big race are usually pretty simple. I tell myself: "Get out of the blocks, run your race, stay relaxed. If you run your race, you'll win … Channel your energy. Focus.
Carl Lewis

Tell your master that if there were as many devils at Worms as tiles on its roofs, I would enter.
Martin Luther

I've always made a total effort, even when the odds seemed entirely against me. I never quit trying; I never felt that I didn't have a chance to win.
Arnold Palmer

To become what we are capable of becoming is the only end in life.
Robert Louis Stevenson

Devil

So that by his death he might destroy him who holds the power of death – that is, the devil – and free those who all their lives were held in slavery by their fear of death.
The Bible, Hebrews 2:14-15

Resist the devil, and he will flee from you.
The Bible, James 4:7

Be self-controlled and alert. Your enemy the devil prowls around like a roaring lion looking for someone to devour. Resist him.
The Bible, 1 Peter 5:8,9

The devil has knowledge, but no wisdom.
Author unknown

The greatest trick the devil ever played was convincing the world he didn't exist.
Author unknown

The devil often transforms himself into an angel to tempt men, some for their instruction, some for their ruin.
Augustine of Hippo

The devil may also make use of morality.
Karl Barth

The existence of the devil is so clearly taught in the Bible that to doubt it is to doubt the Bible itself.
Archibald G. Brown

The devil has his elect.
Thomas Carlyle

The devil is kind to his own.
John Day

Every devil has not a cloven hoof.
Daniel Defoe

The devil's laws are easy, and his gentle sway, Makes it exceeding pleasant to obey.
Daniel Defoe

The devil can counterfeit all the saving operations and graces of the Spirit of God.
Jonathan Edwards

'Tis an easier matter to raise the devil than to lay him.
Desiderius Erasmus

The devil divides the world between atheism and superstition.
George Herbert

When the devil reminds you of your problems, you remind him of his defeat.
Gabriel Heymans

The world is all the richer for having a devil in it, so long as we keep our foot upon his neck.
William James

The devil fears a soul united to God as he does God himself.
John of the Cross

The devil is overcome by the precious Passion of Christ.
Julian of Norwich

It is so stupid of modern civilization to have given up believing in the devil when he is the only explanation of it.
Ronald Knox

When you close your eyes to the devil, make sure that it is not a wink.
John C. Kulp

Who is the most diligent bishop and prelate in England? I will tell you. It is the devil. He is never out of his diocese. The devil is diligent at his plough.
Hugh Latimer

The enemy will not see you vanish into God's company without an effort to reclaim you.
C.S. Lewis

For where God built a church, there the devil would also build a chapel.
Martin Luther

The best way to drive out the devil, if he will not yield to texts of scripture, is to jeer and flout him, for he cannot bear scorn.
Martin Luther

The devil seduces us at first by all the allurements of sin in order thereafter to plunge us into despair. He pampers up the flesh that he may by and by prostrate the spirit.
Martin Luther

Our bodies are always exposed to Satan. The maladies I suffer are not natural, but devil's spells.
Martin Luther

That there is a devil is a thing doubted by none but such as are under the influences of the devil.
Cotton Mather

Consider that the devil does not sleep, but seeks our ruin in a thousand ways.
Angela Merici

The devil, the proud spirit, cannot endure to be mocked.
Thomas More

One of the greatest artifices the devil uses to engage men in vice and debauchery, is to fasten names of contempt on certain virtues, and thus fill weak souls with a foolish fear of passing for scrupulous, should they desire to put them in practice.
Blaise Pascal

Satan is wiser now than before, and tempts by making rich instead of poor.
Alexander Pope

When the devil starts messing, God starts blessing.
R. W. Schambach

The devil can site Scripture for his purpose.
William Shakespeare, The Merchant of Venice

The devil comes where money is; where it is not he comes twice.
Swedish proverb

If you want to drive the devil out of the world, hit him with a cradle instead of a crutch.
Billy Sunday

The devil is a better theologian than any of us and is a devil still.
A. W. Tozer

The devil does not tempt unbelievers and sinners who are already his own.
Thomas à Kempis

The devil loves to fish in troubled waters.
John Trapp

Whenever science makes a discovery, the devil grabs it while the angels are debating the best way to use it.
Alan Valentine

There is nothing that Satan more desires than that we should believe that he does not exist.
Bishop Wordsworth

Devil and the Bible
The deceit, the lie of the devil consists of this, that he wishes to make man believe that he can live without God's Word.
Dietrich Bonhoeffer

Devotion
I need nothing but God, and to lose myself in the heart of Jesus.
Margaret Mary Alacoque

Open my eyes that I may see,
Incline my heart that I may desire,
Order my steps that I may follow
The way of your commandments.
Lancelot Andrewes

Prayer is the acid test of devotion.
Samuel Chadwick

That perfect devoting ourselves to God, from which devotion has its name, requires that we should not only do the will of God, but also that we should do it with love. "He loveth a cheerful giver," and without the heart no obedience is acceptable to Him.
François Fénelon

True and living devotion presupposes the love of God
Francis of Sales

Fidelity in trifles, and in earnest seeking to please God in little matters, is a test of real devotion and love.
Jean Nicholas Grou

No one ever lost out by excessive devotion to Christ.
H.A. Ironside

Lord, make me according to thy heart.
Brother Lawrence

Not everyone can have the same devotion.
Thomas à Kempis

Devout

A Serious Call to a Devout and Holy Life

William Law
Adapted to the State and Condition of All Orders of Christians
   He that hath ears to hear, let him hear
Luke 8:8.

And behold, I come quickly, and my reward is with me
Revelation 22:12.

Chapter 1
Concerning the nature and extent of Christian devotion.
DEVOTION is neither private nor public prayer; but prayers, whether private or public, are particular parts or instances of devotion. Devotion signifies a life given, or devoted, to God.

   He, therefore, is the devout man, who lives no longer to his own will, or the way and spirit of the world, but to the sole will of God, who considers God in everything, who serves God in everything, who makes all the parts of his common life parts of piety, by doing everything in the Name of God, and under such rules as are conformable to His glory.

   We readily acknowledge, that God alone is to be the rule and measure of our prayers; that in them we are to look wholly unto Him, and act wholly for Him; that we are only to pray in such a manner, for such things, and such ends, as are suitable to His glory.

   Now let any one but find out the reason why he is to be thus strictly pious in his prayers, and he will find the same as strong a reason to be as strictly pious in all the other parts of his life. For there is not the least shadow of a reason why we should make God the rule and measure of our prayers; why we should then look wholly unto Him, and pray according to His will; but what equally proves it necessary for us to look wholly unto God, and make Him the rule and measure of all the other actions of our life. For any ways of life, any employment of our talents, whether of our parts, our time, or money, that is not strictly according to the will of God, that is not for such ends as are suitable to His glory, are as great absurdities and failings, as prayers that are not according to the will of God. For there is no other reason why our prayers should be according to the will of God, why they should have nothing in them but what is wise, and holy, and heavenly; there is no other reason for this, but that our lives may be of the same nature, full of the same wisdom, holiness, and heavenly tempers, that we may live unto God in the same spirit that we pray unto Him. Were it not our strict duty to live by reason, to devote all the actions of our lives to God, were it not absolutely necessary to walk before Him in wisdom and holiness and all heavenly conversation, doing everything in His Name, and for His glory, there would be no excellency or wisdom in the most heavenly prayers. Nay, such prayers would be absurdities; they would be like prayers for wings, when it was no part of our duty to fly.

As sure, therefore, as there is any wisdom in praying for the Spirit of God, so sure is it, that we are to make that Spirit the rule of all our actions; as sure as it is our duty to look wholly unto God in our prayers, so sure is it that it is our duty to live wholly unto God in our lives. But we can no more be said to live unto God, unless we live unto Him in all the ordinary actions of our life, unless He be the rule and measure of all our ways, than we can be said to pray unto God, unless our prayers look wholly unto Him. So that unreasonable and absurd ways of life, whether in labor or diversion, whether they consume our time, or our money, are like unreasonable and absurd prayers, and are as truly an offence unto God.

It is for want of knowing, or at least considering this, that we see such a mixture of ridicule in the lives of many people. You see them strict as to some times and places of devotion, but when the service of the Church is over, they are but like those that seldom or never come there. In their way of life, their manner of spending their time and money, in their cares and fears, in their pleasures and indulgences, in their labor and diversions, they are like the rest of the world. This makes the loose part of the world generally make a jest of those that are devout, because they see their devotion goes no farther than their prayers, and that when they are over, they live no more unto God, till the time of prayer returns again;

but live by the same humor and fancy, and in as full an enjoyment of all the follies of life as other people. This is the reason why they are the jest and scorn of careless and worldly people; not because they are really devoted to God, but because they appear to have no other devotion but that of occasional prayers.

Julius is very fearful of missing prayers; all the parish supposes Julius to be sick, if he is not at Church. But if you were to ask him why he spends the rest of his time by humor or chance? why he is a companion of the silliest people in their most silly pleasures? why he is ready for every impertinent entertainment and diversion? If you were to ask him why there is no amusement too trifling to please him? why he is busy at all balls and assemblies? why he gives himself up to an idle, gossiping conversation? why he lives in foolish friendships and fondness for particular persons, that neither want nor deserve any particular kindness? why he allows himself in foolish hatreds and resentments against particular persons without considering that he is to love everybody as himself? If you ask him why he never puts his conversation, his time, and fortune, under the rules of religion? Julius has no more to say for himself than the most disorderly person. For the whole tenor of Scripture lies as directly against such a life, as against debauchery and intemperance: he that lives such a course of idleness and folly, lives no more according to the religion of Jesus Christ, than he that lives in gluttony and intemperance.

If a man was to tell Julius that there was no occasion for so much constancy at prayers, and that he might, without any harm to himself, neglect the service of the Church, as the generality of people do, Julius would think such a one to be no Christian, and that he ought to avoid his company. But if a person only tells him, that he may live as the generality of the world does, that he may enjoy himself as others do, that he may spend his time and money as people of fashion do, that he may conform to the follies and frailties of the generality, and gratify his tempers and passions as most people do, Julius never suspects that man to want a Christian spirit, or that he is doing the devil's work. And if Julius was to read all the New Testament from the beginning to the end, he would find his course of life condemned in every page of it.

And indeed there cannot anything be imagined more absurd in itself, than wise, and sublime, and heavenly prayers, added to a life of vanity and folly, where neither labor nor diversions, neither time nor money, are under the direction of the wisdom and heavenly tempers of our prayers. If we were to see a man pretending to act wholly with regard to God in everything that he did, that would neither spend time nor money, nor take any labor or diversion, but so far as he could act according to strict principles of reason and piety, and yet at the same time neglect all prayer, whether public or private, should we not be amazed at such a man, and wonder how he could have so much folly along with so much religion?

Yet this is as reasonable as for any person to pretend to strictness in devotion, to be careful of observing times and places of prayer, and yet letting the rest of his life, his time and labor, his talents and money, be disposed of without any regard to strict rules of piety and devotion. For it is as great an absurdity to suppose holy prayers, and Divine petitions, without a holiness of life suitable to them, as to suppose a holy and Divine life without prayers.

Let any one therefore think how easily he could confute a man that pretended to great strictness of life without prayer, and the same arguments will as plainly confute another, that pretends to strictness of prayer, without carrying the same strictness into every other part of life. For to be weak and foolish in spending our time and fortune, is no greater a mistake, than to be weak and foolish in relation to our prayers. And to allow ourselves in any ways of life that neither are, nor can be offered to God, is the same irreligion, as to neglect our prayers, or use them in such a manner as make them an offering unworthy of God.

The short of the matter is this; either reason and religion prescribe rules and ends to all the ordinary actions of our life, or they do not: if they do, then it is as necessary to govern all our actions by those rules, as it is necessary to worship God. For if religion teaches us anything concerning eating and drinking, or spending our time and money; if it teaches us how we are to use and contemn the world; if it tells us what tempers we are to have in common life, how we are to be disposed towards all people; how we are to behave towards the sick, the poor, the old, the destitute; if it tells us whom we are to treat with a particular love, whom we are to regard with a particular esteem; if it tells us how we are to treat our enemies, and how we are to mortify and deny ourselves; he must be very weak that can think these parts of religion are not to be observed with as much exactness, as any doctrines that relate to prayers.

It is very observable, that there is not one command in all the Gospel for public worship; and perhaps it is a duty that is least insisted upon in Scripture of any other. The frequent attendance at it is never so much as mentioned in all the New Testament. Whereas that religion or devotion which is to govern the ordinary actions of our life is to be found in almost every verse of Scripture. Our blessed Savior and His Apostles are wholly taken up in doctrines that relate to common life. They call us to renounce the world, and differ in every temper and way of life, from the spirit and the way of the world: to renounce all its goods, to fear none of its evils, to reject its joys, and have no value for its happiness: to be as new-born babes, that are born into a new state of things: to live as pilgrims in spiritual watching, in holy fear, and heavenly aspiring after another life: to take up our daily cross, to deny ourselves, to profess the blessedness of mourning, to seek the blessedness of poverty of spirit: to forsake the pride and vanity of riches, to take no thought for the morrow, to live in the profoundest state of humility, to rejoice in worldly sufferings: to reject the lust of the flesh, the lust of the eyes, and the pride of life: to bear injuries, to forgive and bless our enemies, and to love mankind as God loveth them: to give up our whole hearts and affections to God, and strive to enter through the strait gate into a life of eternal glory.

This is the common devotion which our blessed Savior taught, in order to make it the common life of all Christians. Is it not therefore exceeding strange that people should place so much piety in the attendance upon public worship, concerning which there is not one precept of our Lord's to be found, and yet neglect these common duties of our ordinary life, which are commanded in every page of the Gospel? I call these duties the devotion of our common life, because if they are to be practiced, they must be made parts of our common life; they can have no place anywhere else.

If contempt of the world and heavenly affection is a necessary temper of Christians, it is necessary that this temper appear in the whole course of their lives, in their manner of using the world, because it can have no place anywhere else. If self-denial be a condition of salvation, all that would be saved must make it a part of their ordinary life. If humility be a Christian duty, then the common life of a Christian is to be a constant course of humility in all its kinds. If poverty of spirit be necessary, it must be the spirit and temper of every day of our lives. If we are to relieve the naked, the sick, and the prisoner, it must be the common charity of our lives, as far as we can render ourselves able to perform it. If we are to love our enemies, we must make our common life a visible exercise and demonstration of that love. If content and thankfulness, if the patient bearing of evil be duties to God, they are the duties of every day, and in every circumstance of our life. If we are to be wise and holy as the new-born sons of God, we can no otherwise be so, but by renouncing everything that is foolish and vain in every part of our common life. If we are to be in Christ new creatures, we must show that we

are so, by having new ways of living in the world. If we are to follow Christ, it must be in our common way of spending every day.

Thus it is in all the virtues and holy tempers of Christianity; they are not ours unless they be the virtues and tempers of our ordinary life. So that Christianity is so far from leaving us to live in the common ways of life, conforming to the folly of customs, and gratifying the passions and tempers which the spirit of the world delights in, it is so far from indulging us in any of these things, that all its virtues which it makes necessary to salvation are only so many ways of living above and contrary to the world, in all the common actions of our life. If our common life is not a common course of humility, self-denial, renunciation of the world, poverty of spirit, and heavenly affection, we do not live the lives of Christians.

But yet though it is thus plain that this, and this alone, is Christianity, a uniform, open, and visible practice of all these virtues, yet it is as plain, that there is little or nothing of this to be found, even amongst the better sort of people. You see them often at Church, and pleased with fine preachers: but look into their lives, and you see them just the same sort of people as others are, that make no pretenses to devotion. The difference that you find betwixt them, is only the difference of their natural tempers. They have the same taste of the world, the same worldly cares, and fears, and joys; they have the same turn of mind, equally vain in their desires. You see the same fondness for state and equipage, the same pride and vanity of dress, the same self-love and indulgence, the same foolish friendships, and groundless hatreds, the same levity of mind, and trifling spirit, the same fondness for diversions, the same idle dispositions, and vain ways of spending their time in visiting and conversation, as the rest of the world, that make no pretenses to devotion.

I do not mean this comparison, betwixt people seemingly good and professed rakes, but betwixt people of sober lives. Let us take an instance in two modest women: let it be supposed that one of them is careful of times of devotion, and observes them through a sense of duty, and that the other has no hearty concern about it, but is at Church seldom or often, just as it happens. Now it is a very easy thing to see this difference betwixt these persons. But when you have seen this, can you find any farther difference betwixt them? Can you find that their common life is of a different kind? Are not the tempers, and customs, and manners of the one, of the same kind as of the other? Do they live as if they belonged to different worlds, had different views in their heads, and different rules and measures of all their actions? Have they not the same goods and evils? Are they not pleased and displeased in the same manner, and for the same things? Do they not live in the same course of life? does one seem to be of this world, looking at the things that are temporal, and the other to be of another world, looking wholly at the things that are eternal? Does the one live in pleasure, delighting herself in show or dress, and the other live in self-denial and mortification, renouncing everything that looks like vanity, either of person, dress, or carriage? Does the one follow public diversions, and trifle away her time in idle visits, and corrupt conversation, and does the other study all the arts of improving her time, living in prayer and watching, and such good works as may make all her time turn to her advantage, and be placed to her account at the last day? Is the one careless of expense, and glad to be able to adorn herself with every costly ornament of dress, and does the other consider her fortune as a talent given her by God, which is to be improved religiously, and no more to be spent on vain and needless ornaments than it is to be buried in the earth? Where must you look, to find one person of religion differing in this manner, from another that has none? And yet if they do not differ in these things which are here related, can it with any sense be said, the one is a good Christian, and the other not?

Take another instance amongst the men? Leo has a great deal of good nature, has kept what they call good company, hates everything that is false and base, is very generous and brave to his friends; but has concerned himself so little with religion that he hardly knows the difference betwixt a Jew and a Christian.

Eusebius, on the other hand, has had early impressions of religion, and buys books of devotion. He can talk of all the feasts and fasts of the Church, and knows the names of most men that have been eminent for piety. You never hear him swear, or make a loose jest; and when he talks of religion, he talks of it as of a matter of the last concern.

Here you see, that one person has religion enough, according to the way of the world, to be reckoned a pious Christian, and the other is so far from all appearance of religion, that he may fairly be reckoned a Heathen; and yet if you look into their common life; if you examine their chief and ruling tempers in the greatest articles of life, or the greatest doctrines of Christianity, you will not find the least difference imaginable.

Consider them with regard to the use of the world, because that is what everybody can see.

Now to have right notions and tempers with relation to this world, is as essential to religion as it have right notions of God. And it is as possible for a man to worship a crocodile, and yet be a pious man, as to have his affections set upon this world, and yet be a good Christian.

But now if you consider Leo and Eusebius in this respect, you will find them exactly alike, seeking, using, and enjoying, all that can be got in this world in the same manner, and for the same ends. You will find that riches, prosperity, pleasures, indulgences, state equipages, and honor, are just as much the happiness of Eusebius as they are of Leo. And yet if Christianity has not changed a man's mind and temper with relation to these things, what can we say that it has done for him? For if the doctrines of Christianity were practiced, they would make a man as different from other people, as to all worldly tempers, sensual pleasures,

and the pride of life, as a wise man is different from a natural; it would be as easy a thing to know a Christian by his outward course of life, as it is now difficult to find anybody that lives it. For it is notorious that Christians are now not only like other men in their frailties and infirmities, this might be in some degree excusable, but the complaint is, they are like Heathens in all the main and chief articles of their lives. They enjoy the world, and live every day in the same tempers, and the same designs, and the same indulgences, as they did who knew not God, nor of any happiness in another life. Everybody that is capable of any reflection, must have observed, that this is generally the state even of devout people, whether men or women. You may see them different from other people, so far as to times and places of prayer, but generally like the rest of the world in all the other parts of their lives: that is, adding Christian devotion to a Heathen life. I have the authority of our blessed Savior for this remark, where He says, "Take no thought, saying, What shall we eat? or, What shall we drink? or, Wherewithal shall we be clothed? For after all these things do the Gentiles seek." [Matt. vi. 31, 32] But if to be thus affected even with the necessary things of this life, shows that we are not yet of a Christian spirit, but are like the Heathens, surely to enjoy the vanity and folly of the world as they did, to be like them in the main chief tempers of our lives, in self-love and indulgence, in sensual pleasures and diversions, in the vanity of dress, the love of show and greatness, or any other gaudy distinctions of fortune, is a much greater sign of an Heathen temper. And, consequently, they who add devotion to such a life, must be said to pray as Christians, but live as Heathens.
William Law

Dialogue

Doctrinal disagreements call for debate. Dialogue for mutual understanding and, if possible, narrowing of the differences is valuable, doubly so when the avowed goal is unity in primary things, with liberty in secondary things, and charity in all things.
The gospel of Jesus Christ: An evangelical celebration

The Church needs to recapture the meaning of dialogue as used by Luke in the Acts of the Apostles, namely the method of discussing the merits of a particular set of convictions with a view to persuading others to commit themselves in a similar way.
J. Andrew Kirk

Many consider me as if I were an opponent of this Pope in everything. This is false. I am happy to learn that the Pope speaks in favor of dialogues with other religions and that he commits himself to favoring these in his voyages.
Hans Küng

Dieting

My doctor told me to stop having intimate dinners for four. Unless there are three other people.
Orson Welles

Difficulties

See also: Adversity; Affliction; Burdens; Hardships; Suffering; Trials

Difficulties are meant to rouse, not discourage. The human spirit is to grow strong by conflict.
William Ellery Channing

Never let life's hardships disturb you. After all, no one can avoid problems, not even saints or sages.
Nichiren Daishonin

There never yet was any great manifestation that God made of himself to the world, without many difficulties attending it.
Jonathan Edwards

Take courage, and turn your troubles, which are without remedy, into material for spiritual progress. Often turn to our Lord,

who is watching you, poor frail little being as you are, amid your labors and distractions.
Francis de Sales

Diligence overcomes difficulties, sloth makes them.
Benjamin Franklin

Life affords no higher pleasure than that of surmounting difficulties, passing from one step of success to another, forming new wishes and seeing them gratified.
Samuel Johnson

The difficulties, hardships, and trials of life, the obstacles one encounters on the road to fortune, are positive blessings. They knit the muscles more firmly, and teach self-reliance. Peril is the element in which power is developed.
William Matthews

God delights to increase the faith of his children. We ought, instead of wanting no trials before victory, no exercise for patience, to be willing to take them from God's hand as a means. Trials, obstacles, difficulties, and sometimes defeats, are the very food of faith.
George Müller

Out of every difficulty Omnipotence can bring us, only let us in childlike confidence cast our burden upon the Lord.
C.H. Spurgeon

There are three stages in the work of God: Impossible; Difficult; Done.
Hudson Taylor

All our difficulties are only platforms for the manifestation of His grace, power and love.
Hudson Taylor

From heaven even the most miserable life will look like one bad night at an inconvenient hotel.
Teresa of Avila

What then are we to do about our problems? We must learn to live with them until such time as God delivers us from them. We must pray for grace to endure them without murmuring. Problems patiently endured will work for our spiritual perfecting. They harm us only when we resist them or endure them unwillingly.
A. W. Tozer

Diffidence
Now Giant Despair had a wife, and her name was Diffidence.
John Bunyan

Dignity
True dignity is never gained by place, and never lost when honors are withdrawn.
Phillip Massinger

Diligence
See also: Idleness
He who labors diligently need never despair; for all things are accomplished by diligence and labor.
Menander of Athens

Follow the tasks of your calling carefully and diligently.
Thus:
(a) You will show that you are not sluggish and servants to your flesh (as those that cannot deny it ease), and you will further the putting to death of all the fleshly lusts and desires that are fed by ease and idleness.
(b) You will keep out idle thoughts from your mind, that swarm in the minds of idle persons.
(c) You will not lose precious time, something that idle persons are daily guilty of.
(d) You will be in a way of obedience to God when the slothful are in constant sins of omission.
(e) You may have more time to spend in holy duties if you follow your occupation diligently. Idle persons have no time for praying and reading because they lose time by loitering at their work.
(f) You may expect God's blessing and

comfortable provision for both yourself and your families.

(g) It may also encourage the health of your body which will increase its competence for the service of your soul.
Richard Baxter

Diplomacy

A diplomat is a man who always remembers a woman's birthday but never remembers her age.
Robert Frost

Disability

Blessed are you who take time to listen to difficult speech, for you help us to know that if we persevere we can be understood.

Blessed are you who walk with us in public places, and ignore the stares of strangers, for in your friendship we feel good to be ourselves.

Blessed are you who never bid us to "hurry up" and, more blessed, you who do not snatch our tasks from our hands to do them for us, for often we need time rather than help.

Blessed are you who stand beside us as we enter new and untried ventures, for our unsureness will be outweighed by the times when we surprise ourselves and you.

Blessed are you who ask for our help and realize our giftedness, for our greatest need is to be needed.

Blessed are you who help us with the graciousness of Christ, for often we need the help we cannot ask for.

Blessed are you when, by all things, you assure us that what makes us individuals is not our particular disability or difficulty but our beautiful God-given personhood which no handicapping condition can confine.

Rejoice and be exceedingly glad for your understanding and love have opened doors for us to enjoy life to its full and you have helped us believe in ourselves as valued and gifted people.
Author unknown

Let there be a law that no deformed child shall be reared.
Aristotle

I thank God for my handicaps for, through them, I have found myself, my work, and my God.
Helen Keller

When a retarded child is born, the religious question we often ask is, "Why does God let this happen?" The better question to pose is to ask, "What kind of community should we be so that mental retardation isn't a barrier to the enjoyment of one's full humanity?"
Rabbi Harold Kushner

Mad dogs we knock on the head; the fierce and savage ox we slay; sickly sheep we put to the knife and keep them from infecting the flock; unnatural progeny we destroy; we drown even children who at birth are weakly and abnormal.
Seneca

Disagreements

We find comfort among those who agree with us – growth among those who don't.
Frank A. Clark

We need not all agree, but if we disagree, let us not be disagreeable in our disagreements.
Martin R. DeHaan

In fundamentals unity,
in non-fundamentals liberty,
in all things charity.
Rupert Meldenius

We decline to determine as binding what the Scriptures have left undetermined, or to argue about mysteries impenetrable to human reason. In this regard, we hold to the principle, "In essentials, unity; in non-essentials, liberty; and in all things, charity."
Moravian Covenant for Christian living

Disappointment

YEAR: A period of three hundred and sixty-five disappointments.
Ambrose Bierce

Faith is often strengthened right at the place of disappointment.
Rodney McBride

I'm very grateful that I was too poor to get to art school until I was 21 ... I was old enough when I got there to know how to get something out of it.
Henry Moore

Disappointment

Letter from John Newton
August 17, 1767

It is indeed natural to us to wish and to plan, and it is merciful in the Lord to disappoint our plans, and to cross our wishes. For we cannot be safe, much less happy, but in proportion as we are weaned from our own wills, and made simply desirous of being directed by His guidance. This truth (when we are enlightened by His Word) is sufficiently familiar to the judgment; but we seldom learn to reduce it to practice, without being trained awhile in the school of disappointment. The schemes we form look so plausible and convenient, that when they are broken, we are ready to say, What a pity! We try again, and with no better success; we are grieved, and perhaps angry, and plan out another, and so on; at length, in a course of time, experience and observation begin to convince us, that we are not more able than we are worthy to choose aright for ourselves. Then the Lord's invitation to cast our cares upon Him, and His promise to take care of us, appear valuable; and when we have done planning, His plan in our favor gradually opens, and he does more and better for us than we either ask or think.

I can hardly recollect a single plan of mine, of which I have not since seen reason to be satisfied, that had it taken place in season and circumstance just as I proposed, it would, humanly speaking, have proved my ruin; or at least it would have deprived me of the greater good the Lord had designed for me. We judge of things by their present appearances, but the Lord sees them in their consequences, if we could do so likewise we should be perfectly of His mind; but as we cannot, it is an unspeakable mercy that He will manage for us, whether we are pleased with His management or not; and it is spoken of as one of his heaviest judgments, when He gives any person or people up to the way of their own hearts, and to walk after their own counsels.

Indeed we may admire His patience towards us. If we were blind, and reduced to desire a person to lead us, and should yet pretend to dispute with him, and direct him at every step, we should probably soon weary him, and provoke him to leave us to find the way by ourselves if we could. But our gracious Lord is long-suffering and full of compassion; He bears with our forwardness, yet He will take methods to both shame and to humble us, and to bring us to a confession that He is wiser than we. The great and unexpected benefits He intends us, by all the discipline we meet with, is to tread down our wills, and bring them into subjection to His. So far as we attain to this, we are out of the reach of disappointment; for when the will of God can please us, we shall be pleased every day, and from morning to night; I mean with respect to His dispensations. O the happiness of such a life! I have an idea of it; I hope I am aiming at it, but surely I have not attained it. Self is active in my heart, if it does not absolutely reign there. I profess to believe that one thing is needful and sufficient and yet my thoughts are prone to wander after a hundred more. If it be true that the light of His countenance is better than life, why am I solicitous about anything else? If He be all-sufficient, and gives me liberty to call Him mine, why do I go a-begging to creatures for help? If He be about my path and bed; if the smallest, as well as the greatest events in which I am concerned, are under His immediate direction; if the very hairs of my head are numbered then my care (any farther than a care to walk in the paths of His precepts, and to follow the openings of His providence) must be useless and needless, yea, indeed, sinful and heathenish, burdensome to myself, and dishonorable to my profession. Let us cast down the load we are unable to carry, and if the Lord be our Shepherd, refer all and trust all to Him. Let us endeavor to live to Him and for Him to-day, and be glad that to-morrow, with all that is behind it, is in His hands.

It is storied of Pompey, that when his friends would have dissuaded him from putting to sea in a storm, he answered, It is necessary for me to sail, but it is not necessary for me to live. A pompous speech, in Pompey's sense! He was full of the idea of his own importance, and would rather have died than have taken a step beneath his supposed dignity. But it may be accommodated with propriety to a believer's case. It becomes us to say, It is not necessary for me to be rich, or what the world accounts wise; to be healthy, or admired by my fellow-worms; to pass through life in a state of prosperity and outward comfort – these things may be, or they may be otherwise, as the Lord in His wisdom shall appoint – but it is necessary for me to be humble and spiritual, to seek communion with God, to adorn my profession of the gospel, and to yield submissively to His disposal, in whatever way, whether of service or suffering, He shall be pleased to call me to glorify Him in the world. It is not necessary for me to live long, but highly expedient that whilst I do live I should live to Him. Here, then, I would bound my desires; and here, having His word both for my rule and my warrant, I am secured from asking amiss. Let me have His presence and His Spirit, wisdom to know my calling, and opportunities and faithfulness to improve them; and as to the rest, Lord, help me to say, "What Thou wilt, when Thou wilt, and how Thou wilt."
I am, &c.
John Newton

Discernment

The discerning heart seeks knowledge, but the mouth of a fool feeds on folly.
The Bible, Proverbs 15:14

Prove all things; hold fast that which is good.
The Bible, 1 Thessalonians 5:21 KJV

Men of sound judgment will always be sure that a sense of divinity which can never be erased is engraved upon men's minds.
John Calvin

You cannot imagine how great is people's foolishness. They have no sense or discernment, having lost it by hoping in themselves and putting their trust in their own knowledge.
St Catherine, God speaking to St Catherine in a vision

God never gives us discernment in order that we may criticize, but that we may intercede.
Oswald Chambers

The greatest lesson in life is to know that even fools are right sometimes.
Winston Churchill

A president's hardest task is not to do what is right, but to know what is right.
Lyndon B. Johnson

The supreme end of education is expert discernment in all things – the power to tell the good from the bad, the genuine from the counterfeit, and to prefer the good and the genuine to the bad and the counterfeit.
Samuel Johnson

If you believe everything you read, you better not read.
Japanese proverb

Inability to distinguish differences in doctrine is spreading far and wide, and so long as the preacher is "clever" and "earnest," hundreds seem to think it must be all right, and call you dreadfully "narrow and uncharitable" if you hint that

he is unsound!
J.C. Ryle

The gift of discernment has been somewhat neglected in some contemporary charismatic circles, but it is perhaps the gift that most of all needs to be sought and cultivated, because its exercise is the key to the right use of all the rest.
Tom Smail

Discipleship

You must be willing to follow if you want God to lead.
Author unknown

The strength and happiness of a man consists in finding out the way in which God is going, and going that way too.
Henry Ward Beecher

The cross is laid on every Christian. It begins with the call to abandon the attachments of this world. It is that dying of the old man which is the result of his encounter with Christ.
Dietrich Bonhoeffer

When Christ calls a man, He bids him come and die. It may be a death like that of the first disciples who had to leave home and work to follow Him, or it may be a death like Luther's, who had to leave the monastery and go out into the world. But it is the same death every time – death in Jesus Christ, the death of the old man at His call.
Dietrich Bonhoeffer

The church is the God-ordained means for evangelism, for discipleship, and for witnessing of the kingdom.
Chuck Colson

We pray that if any, anywhere, are fearing that the cost of discipleship is too great, that they may be given to glimpse that treasure in heaven promised to all who forsake.
Elisabeth Elliot, on behalf of the five widows of slain missionaries to Ecuador one year after their deaths

No path of flowers leads to glory.
J. de La Fontaine

The resurrection is the faith requirement through which seekers become followers.
Calvin Miller

There are no crown wearers in heaven, who were not cross bearers on earth.
C.H. Spurgeon

Jesus hath many lovers of His heavenly kingdom, but few bearers of His cross.
Thomas à Kempis

Men expect that religion should cost them no pains, that happiness should drop into their laps without any design and endeavor on their part, and that, after they have done what they please while they live, God should snatch them up to heaven when they die. But though "the commandments of God be not grievous," yet it is fit to let men know that they are not thus easy.
John Tillotson

Discipleship, cost of

You must never doubt that I'm traveling with gratitude and cheerfulness along the road where I'm being led. My past life is brim full of God's goodness, and my sins are covered by the forgiving love of Christ crucified.
Dietrich Bonhoeffer, on learning that he was to be executed for plotting to kill Hitler

Discipline

Discipline your son, for in that there is hope; do not be a willing party to his death.
The Bible, Proverbs 19:18

No, I beat my body and make it my slave so that after I have preached to others, I myself will not be disqualified for the prize.
The Bible, 1 Corinthians 9:27

Whom the Lord loveth he chasteneth.
The Bible, Hebrews 12:6 KJV

Endure hardship as discipline; God is treating you as sons. For what son is not disciplined by his father? If you are not

disciplined (and everyone undergoes discipline), then you are illegitimate children and not true sons.
The Bible, Hebrews 12:7,8

No discipline seems pleasant at the time, but painful. Later on, however, it produces a harvest of righteousness and peace for those who have been trained by it.
The Bible, Hebrews 12:11

The goal of God's discipline is restoration – never condemnation.
Author unknown

Discipline is the secret of godliness. You must learn to discipline yourself for the purpose of godliness.
Jay Adams

I think I've always had the shots. But in the past, I've suffered too many mental lapses. Now, I'm starting to get away from that and my mental discipline and commitment to the game are much better. I think I'm really taking a good look at the big picture. That's the difference between being around for the final or watching the final from my sofa at home.
Andre Agassi

I will be a Pastor to none that will not be under Discipline: That were to be half Pastor, and indulge Men in an unruliness and contempt of the ordinance of Christ.
Richard Baxter

You will never be the person you can be if pressure, tension, and discipline are taken out of your life.
James G. Bilkey

If anything characterizes modern Protestantism, it is the absence of spiritual disciplines or spiritual exercises. Yet such disciplines form the core of the life of devotion. It is not an exaggeration to state that this is the lost dimension in modern Protestantism.
Donald Bloesch

Whomever the Lord has adopted and deemed worthy of his fellowship ought to prepare themselves for a hard, toilsome, and unquiet life, crammed with very many and various kinds of evil. It is the Heavenly Father's will thus to exercise them so as to put his own children to a definite test. Beginning with Christ, his first-born, he follows this plan with all his children.
John Calvin

Strong people always have strong weaknesses too.
Peter Drucker

Without discipline, there's no life at all.
Katharine Hepburn

A small but always persistent discipline is a great force; for a soft drop falling persistently hollows out hard rock.
Isaac from Syria

Conquering the tongue is better than fasting on bread and water.
John of the Cross

The best discipline, maybe the only discipline that really works, is self-discipline.
Walter Kiechel III

How often do we hear about the discipline of the Christian life these days? There was a time in the Christian church when this was at the very center, and it is, I profoundly believe, because of our neglect of this discipline that the church is in her present position. Indeed, I see no hope whatsoever of any true revival and reawakening until we return to it.
D. Martyn Lloyd-Jones

God has no pleasure in afflicting us, but He will not keep back even the most painful chastisement if He can but thereby guide His beloved child to come home and abide in the beloved Son.
Andrew Murray

When God chastises his children, he does not punish as a judge does; but he chastens

as a father.
C.H. Spurgeon

It hurts when God has to PRY things out of our hand!
Corrie Ten Boom

Discipline, Church
When you are assembled in the name of our Lord Jesus and I am with you in spirit, and the power of our Lord Jesus is present, hand this man over to Satan, so that the sinful nature may be destroyed and his spirit saved on the day of the Lord.
The Bible, 1 Corinthians 5:4,5

God will judge those outside. "Expel the wicked man from among you."
The Bible, 1 Corinthians 5:13

When ordained clergymen openly deny the divinity of Christ or reject the bodily resurrection of Christ, clear discipline needs to be taken.
David Watson

Discontent
If necessity is the mother of invention, discontent is the father of progress.
David Rockefeller

Discouragement
See: Adversity; Depression; Difficulties

Discoveries
If I have ever made any valuable discoveries, it has been owing more to patient attention, than to any other talent.
Isaac Newton

All great discoveries are made by men whose feelings run ahead of their thinking.
Charles Parkhurst

Discovery
I had an immense advantage over many others dealing with the problem inasmuch as I had no fixed ideas derived from long-established practice to control and bias my mind, and did not suffer from the general belief that whatever is, is right.
Sir Henry Bessemer (on his discovery of a new method of producing steel)

All truths are easy to understand once they are discovered; the point is to discover them.
Galileo Galilei

Discovery consists of seeing what everybody has seen and thinking what nobody has thought.
Albert von Szent-Gyorgy

The greatest discovery I ever made was that I was a great sinner and Jesus Christ a wonderful Savior.
Sir James Young, the discoverer of chloroform

Discretion
The better part of valor is discretion.
William Shakespeare, King Henry IV, Part 1

Disputes
We stand at better advantage to find truth, and keep it also, when devoutly praying for it, than fiercely wrangling and contending about it. Disputes roil the soul, and raise the dust of passion; prayer sweetly composes the mind, and lays the passions which disputes draw forth; for I am sure a man may see further in a still clear day, than in a windy and cloudy.
William Gurnall

The itch of disputing is the scab of the church.
George Herbert

No kingdom has ever had as many civil wars as the kingdom of Christ.
Charles, Baron de Montesquieu

Distractions
I neglect God and his angels for the noise of a fly, for the rattling of a coach, for the whining of a door.
John Donne

Divisions
See also: Unity
If a house be divided against itself, that

house cannot stand.
The Bible, Mark 3:25

I urge you, brothers, to watch out for those who cause divisions and put obstacles in your way that are contrary to the teaching you have learned. Keep away from them.
The Bible, Romans 16:17

He that is not a son of Peace is not a son of God. All other sins destroy the Church consequently; but Division and Separation demolish it directly ... Many doctrinal differences must be tolerated in a Church: And why? But for Unitie and Peace? Therefore Disunion and Separation is utterly intolerable.
Richard Baxter

Discord and division become no Christian. For wolves to worry the lambs is no wonder, but for one lamb to worry another, this is unnatural and monstrous.
Thomas Brooks

We fight one another, and envy arms against one another ... If everyone strives to unsettle the body of Christ, where shall we end up? We are engaged in making Christ's body a corpse ... We declare ourselves members of one and the same organism, yet we devour one another like beasts.
John Chrysostom

Be deeply affected with the mischievous effects and consequences of schisms and divisions in the societies of the saints, and let nothing beneath a plain necessity divide you from communion with one another; hold it fast till you can hold it no longer without sin. At the fire of your contentions your enemies warm their hands, and say, Aha, so would we have it.
John Flavel

If the gospel will not allow us to pay our enemies in their own coin, and give them wrath for wrath, much less will it suffer brethren to spit fire at one another's face
William Gurnall

To maintain pure truth in the church, we should be ready to make any sacrifice, to hazard peace, to risk dissension and run the chance of division.
J.C. Ryle

Divisive people
Warn a divisive person once, and then warn him a second time. After that, have nothing to do with him.
The Bible, Titus 3:10

Divorce
See also: Remarriage
What therefore God hath joined together, let not man put asunder.
The Bible, Matthew 19:6 KJV

Divorce lingers forever with children.
Gary Chapman

According to Jesus only illicit sex relations (*porneia*: adultery) provide reason to terminate a marriage.
James B. Hurley

It is the one exception that gives prominence to the illegitimacy of every other reason. Preoccupation with the one exception should never be permitted to obscure the force of the negation of all others.
John Murray, commenting on Matthew 5:32 and 19:9 ". . . anyone who divorces his wife except for marital unfaithfulness . . ."

Nothing less than a violation (by sexual infidelity) of this fundamental relationship can break the marriage covenant.
John Stott

Here is an unabashed quotation from John H. Adam and Nancy Williamson Adam: "Letting go of your marriage – if it is no longer a good one – can be the most successful thing you have ever done. Getting a divorce can be a positive, problem-solving, growth-orientated step. It can be a personal triumph." Here is the secular mind in all its shameless perversity. It celebrates failure as success, disintegration

as growth, and disaster as triumph.
John Stott

Doctrine
See also: Heresy
You must teach what is in accord with
sound doctrine.
The Bible, Titus 2:1

Doctrine is necessary to inform us how we
may be saved by Christ, but it is Christ
who saves.
*The gospel of Jesus Christ: An evangelical
celebration*

The question is not whether a doctrine is
beautiful but whether it is true. When we
wish to go to a place, we do not ask
whether the road leads through a pretty
country, but whether it is the right road.
Augustus William and Julius Charles Hare

Doctrine is the foundation for the
Christian life (Titus 2:12). Everything
about the execution of living a life pleasing
to the Lord is built upon it. We can't have
right living without right doctrine.
S. Lee Homoki

Start with the Scriptures. Then go to those
books that will help you. And above all,
read both – or all – sides of the matter, for
there are many sides. Do not be content
with reading one side only. I find it tragic
that people should read one side only.
Often they have never heard of another
side, or if they have, they are not prepared
to even consider it.
Martyn Lloyd-Jones

I will begin with this matter of the
inevitability of dogma, if Christianity is to
be anything more than a little mild wishful
thinking about ethical behavior.
Dorothy Sayers

It is an undoubted truth that every
doctrine that comes from God, leads to
God; and that which doth not tend to
promote holiness is not of God.
George Whitefield

Doctrine, False
We should no more tolerate false doctrine
than we would tolerate sin.
J.C. Ryle

Dogmatism
Dogmatism does not mean the absence of
thought, but the end of thought.
G.K. Chesterton

Doubt
See also: Belief and doubt; Fears
Doubt sees the obstacles,
Faith sees the way;
Doubt sees the blackest night,
Faith sees the day;
Doubt dreads to take a step,
Faith soars on high;
Doubt questions, "Who believes?"
Faith answers, "I!"
Author unknown

The art of doubting is easy, for it is an
ability that is born with us.
Author unknown

If a man will begin with certainties, he
shall end in doubts; but if he will be
content to begin with doubts, he shall end
in certainties.
Francis Bacon

A man was meant to be doubtful about
himself but undoubting about the truth.
This has been exactly reversed.
G.K. Chesterton

Doubt is the vestibule which all must pass,
before they can enter into the temple of
truth.
C.C. Colton

Every step toward Christ kills a doubt.
Every thought, word, and deed for Him
carries you away from discouragement.
Theodore L. Cuyler

I gradually came to disbelieve in
Christianity as a divine revelation. …
Disbelief crept over me at a very slow rate,
but was at last complete. The rate was so

slow that I felt no distress.
Charles Darwin

If you would be a real seeker after truth, it is necessary that at least once in your life you doubt, as far as possible, all things.
René Descartes

A closed mind is a sign of hidden doubt.
Harold deWold

Whenever I doubted something about God, I felt guilty and wondered whether I was really a Christian or not. This only led me to try harder at being a "super Christian." Finally, I was worn out, fed up and didn't know what to do. If this depresses you, stay tuned because it was at this point that I learnt the most important lesson of my Christian life. It's taken me about two hours to think how to summarize this lesson into one sentence, but here it is: God is happy with his children.
John Dickson

It is not as a child that I believe and confess Christ. My hosanna has passed through the furnace of doubt.
Fyodor Dostoevsky

Never doubt in the dark what God told you in the light.
V. Raymond Edman

Too often we forget that the great men of faith reached the heights they did only by going through the depths.
Os Guinness

Doubt is not the opposite of faith, nor is it the same as unbelief. Doubt is a state of mind in suspension between faith and unbelief so that it is neither of them wholly and it is each only partly.
Os Guinness

Doubt does not necessarily or automatically mean the end of faith, for doubt is faith in two minds. What destroys faith is that disobedience that

hardens into unbelief.
Os Guinness

Our English word doubt comes from the Latin *dubitare* which is rooted in an Aryan word meaning "two" ... to believe is to be "in one mind" about accepting something as true; to disbelieve is to be "in one mind" about rejecting it. To doubt is to waver between the two, to believe and disbelieve at once and so to be "in two minds".
Os Guinness

I doubt, therefore truth is.
Os Guinness

Most doubts have far more to do with wrong thinking or no thinking at all than with too much thinking.
Os Guinness

Don't give us your doubts, gives us your certainties, for we have doubts enough of our own.
Goethe

Why didn't someone tell me that I can become a Christian and settle the doubts afterward?
William Rainey Harper

Doubt indulged soon becomes doubt realized.
Frances Ridley Havergal

To doubt is not sin, but to be contented to remain in doubt when God has provided "many infallible proofs" to cure it, is.
Irwin H. Linton

A man may be haunted with doubts, and only grow thereby in faith. Doubts are the messengers of the Living One to the honest. They are the first knock at our door of things that are not yet, but have to be, understood. Doubt must precede every deeper assurance; for uncertainties are what we first see when we look into a region hitherto unknown, unexplored, unannexed.
George Macdonald

Those who insist on being sure about everything must be content to creep along the ground and never soar.
J.H. Newman

With great doubts come great understanding; with little doubts come little understanding.
Chinese proverb

Who knows nothing doubts nothing.
French proverb

The wise are prone to doubt.
Greek proverb

O Lord, if there is a Lord, save my soul, if I have a soul.
Ernest Renan, Prayer of a skeptic

The whole problem with the world is that fools and fanatics are always so certain of themselves, but wiser people so full of doubts.
Bertrand Russell

It is common for men to make doubts when they have the mind to desert the truth.
Samuel Rutherford

Our doubts are traitors and make us lose the good we oft might win by fearing to attempt.
William Shakespeare

The best way to get your faith strengthened is to have communion with Christ.
C.H. Spurgeon

It is never worth while to make rents in a garment for the sake of mending them. Nor to create doubts in order to show how cleverly we can quiet them.
C.H. Spurgeon

Where do you live? Many a believer lives in the "cottage of doubt," when he might live in the "mansion of faith."
C.H. Spurgeon

Faith lives in honest doubt.
Alfred Tennyson

He fought his doubts and gather'd strength,

He would not make his judgment blind, He faced the specters of the mind And laid them: thus he came at length To find a stronger faith his own.
Alfred Tennyson

Doubt isn't the opposite of faith; it is an element of faith.
Paul Tillich

Doubt

Letter from John Newton June 20, 1776.
Madam,

It would be both unkind and ungrateful in me to avail myself of any plea of business, for delaying the acknowledgment I owe you for your acceptable favor from – which, though dated the 6th instant, I did not receive till the 10th ...

Could I have known in time that you were at Mr. – 's I should have endeavored to have called upon you while there; and very glad should I have been to have seen you with us. But they who fear the Lord may be sure, that whatever is not practicable is not necessary. He could have overruled every difficulty in your way, had He seen it expedient; but He is pleased to show you that you depend not upon them, but upon Himself; and that, notwithstanding your connections may exclude you from some advantages in point of outward means, He who has begun a good work in you, is able to carry it on, in defiance of all seeming hindrances, and make all things (even those which have the most unfavorable appearances) work together for your good ...

A sure effect of His grace is a desire and longing for gospel ordinances; and when they are afforded, they cannot be neglected without loss. But the Lord sees many souls who are dear to Him, and whom He is training up in a growing meetness for His kingdom, who are, by His providence, so situated, that it is not in their power to attend upon gospel preaching; and, perhaps, they have seldom either Christian minister or Christian friend to assist or comfort them. Such a situation is a state of trial; but Jesus is all-sufficient, and He is always near. They cannot be debarred from His word of grace, which is everywhere at hand, nor from His throne of grace; for they who feel their need of Him, and whose hearts are drawn towards Him, are always at the foot of it. Every room in the house, yea, every spot they stand on, fields, lanes, and hedge-rows, all is holy ground to them; for the Lord is there. The chief difference between us and the disciples, when our Savior was upon earth, is in this: they then walked by sight, and we are called to walk by faith. They could see Him with their bodily eyes, we cannot; but He said, before He left them, "It is expedient for you that I go away." How could this be, unless that spiritual communion, which He promised to maintain with His people after his ascension, were preferable to that intercourse He allowed them whilst He was visibly with them? But we are sure it is preferable, and they who had tried both were well satisfied He had made good His promise; so that though they had known Him after the flesh, they were content not to know Him so any more.

Yes, Madam, though we cannot see Him, he sees us; He is nearer to us than we are to ourselves. In a natural state, we have very dark, and indeed, dishonorable thoughts of God; we conceive of Him as at a distance. But when the heart is awakened, we begin to make Jacob's reflection, "Surely the Lord is in this place, and I knew it not." And when we receive faith, we begin to know that this ever-present God is in Christ; that the government of heaven and earth, the dispensations of the kingdom of nature, providence, and grace, are in the hands of Jesus: that it is He with whom we have to do, who once suffered agony and death for our redemption, and whose compassion and tenderness are the same, now He reigns over all blessed for ever, as when He conversed amongst men in the days of His humiliation. Thus God is made known to us by the gospel, in the endearing views of a Savior, a Shepherd, a Husband, a Friend;

and a way of access is opened for us through the vail, that is, the human nature of our Redeemer, to enter, with humble confidence, into the holiest of all, and to repose all our cares and concerns upon the strength of that everlasting arm which upholds heaven and earth, and upon that infinite love which submitted to the shame, pain, and death of the cross, to redeem sinners from wrath and misery.

Though there is a height, a breadth, a length, and a depth, in this mystery of redeeming love, exceeding the comprehension of all finite minds; yet the great and leading principles which are necessary for the support and comfort of our souls may be summed up in a very few words. Such a summary we are favored with in Titus ii. 11-14, where the whole of salvation, all that is needful to be known, experienced, practiced, and hoped for, is comprised within the compass of four verses. If many books, much study, and great discernment, were necessary, in order to be happy, what must the poor and simple do? Yet for them especially is the gospel designed; and few but such as these attain the knowledge and comfort of it. The Bible is a sealed book till the heart be awakened; and then he that runs may read. The propositions are few. I am a sinner, therefore, I need a Savior, one who is able and willing to save to the uttermost; such a one is Jesus; He is all that I want – wisdom, righteousness, sanctification, and redemption.

But will He receive me? Can I answer a previous question? Am I willing to receive Him? If so, and if His word may be taken, if He meant what He said, and promised no more than He can perform, I may be sure of a welcome: He knew, long before, the doubts, fears, and suspicions, which would arise in my mind when I should come to know what I am, what I have done, and what I have deserved; and, therefore, He declared, before He left the earth, "Him that cometh to Me, I will in no wise cast out." I have no money or price in my hand, no worthiness to recommend me and I need none, for He saveth freely for His own name's sake. I have only to be thankful for what He has already shown me, and to wait upon Him for more. It is my part to commit myself to Him as the physician of sin-sick souls, not to prescribe to Him how He shall treat me. To begin, carry on, and perfect the cure, is His part.

The doubts and fears you speak of are, in a greater or lesser degree, the common experience of all the Lord's people, at least for a time: whilst any unbelief remains in the heart, and Satan is permitted to tempt, we shall feel these things. In themselves they are groundless and evil; yet the Lord permits and overrules them for good. They tend to make us know more of the plague of our own hearts, and feel more sensibly the need of a Savior, and make His rest (when we attain it) doubly sweet and sure. And they likewise qualify us for pitying and comforting others. Fear not; only believe, wait, and pray. Expect not all at once. A Christian is not of hasty growth, like a mushroom, but rather like the oak, the progress of which is hardly perceptible, but, in time, becomes a great deep-rooted tree.

If my writings have been useful to you, may the Lord have the praise. To administer any comfort to His children is the greatest honor and pleasure I can receive in this life. I cannot promise to be a very punctual correspondent, having many engagements; but I hope to do all in my power to show myself, Madam,
Yours, &c.
John Newton

Doubters
Doubters invert the metaphor and insist that they need faith as big as a mountain in order to move a mustard seed.
Author unknown

Dream
No dreamer is ever too small;
no dream is ever too big.
Author unknown

If your dreams turn to dust ... vacuum.
Author unknown

In dreams and in love there are no impossibilities.
Janos Arany

Dreams do come true, if we only wish hard enough. You can have anything in life if you will sacrifice everything else for it. "What will you have?" says God. "Pray for it and take it."
James M. Barrie

There were many ways of breaking a heart. Stories were full of hearts being broken by love, but what really broke a heart was taking away its dream whatever that dream might be.
Pearl Buck

When your heart is in your dream, no request is too extreme.
Jiminy Cricket

Dream as if you'll live forever.
Live as if you'll die today.
James Dean

If you can dream it, you can do it.
Walt Disney

To accomplish great things, we must not only act, but also dream; not only plan, but also believe.
Anatole France

Every challenge we face can be solved by a dream.
David Schwartz

A dream is an answer to a question we haven't quite yet learned how to ask.
Scully, the X-Files

The interpretation of dreams is the royal road to a knowledge of the unconscious activities of the mind.
Freud

Hold fast to dreams , for if dreams die, life is like a broken winged bird that cannot fly.
Robert Frost

It is not the duty and part of any Christian, under the pretense of the Holy Ghost, to bring in his own dreams and fantasies into the church; but he must diligently provide that his doctrine and decrees be agreeable to Christ's Holy Testament; otherwise, in making the Holy Ghost the Author thereof, he doth blaspheme and belie the Holy Ghost to his own condemnation.
Book of Homilies [A book of prescribed homilies, first published on 31st July 1547, which disaffected and unlearned clergy were obliged to read out to their congregations.]

Most people never run far enough on their first wind to find out they've got a second. Give your dreams all you've got and you'll be amazed at the energy that comes out of you.
William James

Those who dream by day are cognizant of many things which escape those who dream only by night.
Edgar Allen Poe

The best way to make your dreams come true is to wake up.
J.M. Power

Dreams grow holy put in action.
Adelaide Proctor

The future belongs to those who believe in the beauty of their dreams.
Eleanor Roosevelt

Nothing happens unless first a dream.
Carl Sandburg

Reach high, for stars lie hidden in your soul. Dream deep, for every dream precedes the goal.
Pamela Starr

I have learned at least this by my experiments: that if one advances confidently in the direction of his dreams and endeavors to live the life which he has imagined, he will meet with a success unexpected in common hours.
Henry David Thoreau

Never part with your illusions. Without dreams you may continue to exist, but you have ceased to live.
Mark Twain

Drinking
See also: Drunkenness
There is no medicinal cup to the body, that is poisonous to the conscience.
Thomas Adams

He that will never drink less than he may, sometimes will drink more than he should.
Thomas Fuller

We must picture these Puritans as the very opposite of those who bear that name today: as young, fierce, progressive intellectuals, very fashionable and up-to-date. They were not teetotalers; bishops, not beer, were their special aversion.
C.S. Lewis

Now al is done; bring home the bride againe,
Bring home the triumph of our victory,
Bring home with you the glory of her gaine…
Make feast therefore now all this line long day,
This day for euer to me holy is,
Poure out the wine without restraint or stay…
Edmund Spenser

Drugs
I don't think a person has to use drugs [to excel in athletics]. There is no substitute for hard work.
Florence Griffith-Joyner

Drunkenness
Wine is a mocker, strong drink is raging.
The Bible, Proverbs 20:1 KJV

Do not gaze at wine when it is red, when it

sparkles in the cup, when it goes down smoothly! In the end it bites like a snake and poisons like a viper.
The Bible, Proverbs 23:31,32

Do not get drunk on wine, which leads to debauchery. Instead, be filled with the Spirit.
The Bible, Ephesians 5:18

Drunkenness is nothing but voluntary madness.
Author unknown

God made wine for great and small.
Small fools drink too much.
Great fools drink none at all!
Author unknown

While the wine is in thy hand, thou art a man; when it is in thine head, thou art become a beast.
Thomas Adams

Abstainer: A weak person who yields to the temptation of denying himself a pleasure.
A. Bierce

Drunkenness is temporary suicide: the happiness that it brings is merely negative, a momentary cessation of unhappiness.
Bertrand Russell

My soul might be perpetually dropping showers of tears, if it might know the doom and destruction brought on by that one demon, and by that one demon only! Though I am no total abstainer, I hate drunkenness as much as any man breathing, and have been the means of bringing many poor creatures to relinquish this bestial indulgence. We believe drunkenness to be an awful crime and a horrid sin. We stand prepared to go to war with it. How many thousands are murdered every year by that accursed devil of drunkenness!
C.H. Spurgeon

Dryness
They discover that in the midst of their aridity, and without any distinct illumination, they are not the less enlightened; for this state is luminous in itself, though dark to the Soul that dwells in it.
Madame Guyon

God values in you the inclination to dryness and suffering for love of him more than all the consolations, spiritual visions, and meditations you could possibly have.
John of the Cross

My spirit has become dry because it forgets to feed on you.
John of the Cross

Duty
Fear God, and keep his commandments, for this is the whole duty of man.
The Bible, Ecclesiastes 12:13

It is good to follow the path of duty, though in the midst of darkness and discouragement.
David Brainerd

"Do the duty which lies nearest thee," which thou knowest to be a duty. The second duty will already have become clearer.
T. Carlyle

Duty is ours; consequences are God's.
General Stonewall Jackson

Do your duty, that is best;
leave unto the Lord the rest.
David O. McKay

England expects every man will do his duty.
Horotio Nelson of the Battle of Trafalgar

Duty is a very personal thing. It is what comes from knowing the need to take action and not just a need to urge others to do something.
Mother Teresa

Activate yourself to duty by remembering your position, who you are, and what you have obliged yourself to be.
Thomas à Kempis

Do something every day that you don't want to do; this is the golden rule for acquiring the habit of doing your duty without pain.
Mark Twain

Dying
See also: Death

Dying

Letter from Samuel Rutherford
To a Christian gentlewoman on her death-bed

Mistress – Grace, mercy, and peace be to you. If death, which is before you and us all, were any other thing than a friendly dissolution, and a change, not a destruction of life, it would seem a hard voyage to go through such a sad and dark trance, so thorny a valley, as is the wages of sin. But I am confident the way ye know, though your foot never trod in that black shadow. The loss of life is gain to you. If Christ Jesus be the period, the end, and lodging home, at the end of your journey, there is no fear; ye go to a friend. And since ye have had communion with Him in this life, and He has a pawn or pledge of yours, even the largest share of your love and heart, ye may look death in the face with joy.

But though He be the same Christ in the other life that ye found Him to be here, yet He is so far in His excellency, beauty, sweetness, irradiations, and beams of majesty, above what He appeared here, when He is seen as He is, that ye shall misken Him, and He shall appear a new Christ: as water at the fountain, apples in the orchard and beside the tree, have more of their native sweetness, taste, and beauty, than when transported to us some hundred miles.

I mean not that Christ can lose any of His sweetness in the carrying, or that He, in His Godhead and loveliness of presence, can be changed to the worse, betwixt the little spot of the earth that ye are in, and the right hand of the Father far above all heavens. But the change will be in you, when ye shall have new senses, and the soul shall be a more deep and more capacious vessel, to take in more of Christ; and when means (the chariot, the gospel, that He is now carried in, and ordinances that convey Him) shall be removed. Sure ye cannot now be said to see Him face to face; or to drink of the wine of the highest fountain, or to take in seas and tides of fresh love immediately, without vessels or messengers, at the Fountain itself, as ye will do a few days hence, when ye shall be so near as to be with Christ.

Death is but an awesome step, over time and sin, to sweet Jesus Christ, who knew and felt the worst of death, for death's teeth hurt Him. We know death has no teeth now, no jaws, for they are broken. It is a free prison; citizens pay nothing for the grave. The jailer who had the power of death is destroyed: praise and glory be to the First-begotten of the dead.

The worst possible that may be is, that ye leave behind you children, husband and the church of God in miseries. But ye cannot get them to heaven with you for the present. Ye shall not miss them, and Christ cannot miscount one of the poorest of His lambs. No lad, no girl, no poor one shall be a-missing in the day that the Son shall render up the kingdom to His Father.

As for the church which ye leave behind you, the government is upon Christ's shoulders, and He will plead for the blood of His saints. The Bush has been burning above five thousand years, and we never yet saw the ashes of this fire. Yet a little while, and the vision shall not tarry: it will speak, and not lie. I am more afraid of my duty, than of the Head Christ's government. He cannot fail to bring judgment to victory.

Now, if I have found favor with you, and if ye judge me faithful, my last suit to you is that ye would leave me a legacy; and that is, that my name may be, at the very last, in your prayers: as I desire also, it may be in the prayers of those of your Christian acquaintance with whom ye have been intimate.

London, Jan 9, 1646
Samuel Rutherford

See in what peace a Christian can die.
Joseph Addison

Life is pleasant. Death is peaceful. It's the
transition that's troublesome.
Isaac Asimov

It is time that I return to Him who
formed me out of nothing: I have lived
long; my merciful Judge well foresaw my
life for me; the time of my dissolution
draws nigh; for I desire to die and to be
with Christ.
Bede

Most men need patience to die, but a
saint who understands what death admits
him to should rather need patience to
live. I think he should often look out and
listen on a deathbed for his Lord's
coming; and when he receives the news of
his approaching change he should say,
"The voice of my beloved! behold, He
cometh leaping over the mountains,
skipping upon the hills" (Song of
Solomon 2:8).
John Flavel

I have a better Caretaker than you and all
the angels. He it is who lies in a manger.
But at the same time sits at the right hand
of God, the almighty Father. Therefore be
at rest.
*Martin Luther, letter to his wife Kate, 1546,
eleven days before his death.*

All of my life I have been learning to live
in Christ. Now I am learning how to die
in Christ.
*Dr Wesley Olsen, former President of
Southwestern Bible College, just prior to his
death*

Never fear dying, beloved. Dying is the
last, but the least matter that a Christian
has to be anxious about.
C.H. Spurgeon

I can only lie still in God's arms
I am so weak that I can hardly write, I
cannot read my Bible, I cannot even pray.

I can only lie still in God's arms like a little
child, and trust.
Hudson Taylor, during his final days

Whatever else is happening to me
physically, God is working deeply in my
life. In that position of security I have
experienced once again his perfect love, a
love that casts out fear.
*David Watson, written in the epilogue of his
last book, as he lay dying of cancer.*

Dying words
I cannot be sorry to go to Him. But it
does grieve me to leave you alone at such a
time. Yet he will be with you and meet all
your needs.
Maria Taylor, wife of Hudson Taylor

E

Ease

Worldly ease is a great foe to faith; it loosens the joints of holy valor, and snaps the sinews of sacred courage.
C.H. Spurgeon

Easter

Men and women disbelieve the Easter story not because of the evidence but in spite of it.
J.N.D. Anderson

Easter Wings

Lord, who createdst man in wealth and
  store,
Though foolishly he lost the same,
Decaying more and more,
Till he became
Most poor:
With thee
Oh let me rise
As larks, harmoniously,
And sing this day thy victories:
Then shall the fall farther the flight in me.
My tender age in sorrow did begin:
And still with sicknesses and shame
Thou did'st so punish sin,
That I became
Most thin
With thee
Let me combine,
And feel this day thy victory,
For, if I imp my wing on thine,
Affliction shall advance the flight in me.
George Herbert, The Temple

Spring bursts today,
For Christ is risen and all the earth's at play.
Christina Rossetti

Easter says to us that despite everything to the contrary, his will for us will prevail, love will prevail over hate, justice over injustice and oppression, peace over exploitation and bitterness.
Desmond Tutu

Eating

So whether you eat or drink or whatever you do, do it all for the glory of God.
The Bible, 1 Corinthians 10:31

Eating and drinking

Eat and drink with moderation and thankfulness for health, not for unprofitable pleasure. Never please your appetite in food or drink when it is prone to be detrimental to your health.
Remember the sin of Sodom: "Look, this was the iniquity of your sister Sodom: She and her daughter had pride, fullness of food and abundance of idleness" – Ezekiel 16:49. The apostle Paul wept when he mentioned those "whose end is destruction, whose god is their belly, and whose glory is in their shame – who set their minds on earthly things, being enemies to the cross of Christ" – Philippians 3:18-19. O then do not live according to the flesh lest you die (Romans 8:13).
Richard Baxter

Economist

An economist is an expert who will know tomorrow why the things he predicted yesterday didn't happen today.
Laurence J. Peter

Ecstasy

Ecstasy is a departure of the mind, which sometimes happens by fright, but sometimes by some revelation, through an alienation of the mind from the senses of the body, in order that that to the spirit may be shown what is to be shown.
Augustine of Hippo

The outflowing of a soul into her God is a true ecstasy, by which the soul quite transcends the limits of her natural way of existence, being wholly mingled with, absorbed and engulfed in, her God.
Francis of Sales

Education
Train up a child in the way he should go: and when he is old, he will not depart from it.
The Bible, Proverbs 22:6 KJV

Never discourage anyone who continually makes progress, no matter how slow.
Author unknown

An educational system isn't worth a great deal if it teaches young people how to make a living but doesn't teach them how to make a life.
Author unknown

Teaching children to count is not as important as teaching them what counts.
Author unknown

True education doesn't merely bring us learning, but love of learning; not merely work but love of work.
Author unknown

They know enough who know how to learn.
Henry Adams

All who have meditated on the art of governing mankind have been convinced that the fate of empires depends on the education of youth.
Aristotle

Find time still to be learning somewhat good, and give up being desultory.
Marcus Aurelius

Education: That which discloses to the wise and disguises from the foolish their lack of understanding.
Ambrose Bierce

You can do anything with children if you only play with them.
Bismarck

If you think education is expensive, try ignorance.
Derek Bok

It is possible to store the mind with a million facts and still be entirely uneducated.
Alec Bourne

There is work that is work and there is play that is play; there is play that is work and work that is play. And in only one of these lies happiness.
Gelett Burgess

There is little hope for children who are educated wickedly. If the dye have been in the wool, it is hard to get it out of the cloth.
Jeremiah Burroughs

The work will wait while you show the child the rainbow, but the rainbow won't wait while you do the work.
Patricia Clafford

Our educational establishment seeks to instill a passion for intellectual curiosity and openness, but allows for the existence of no truth worth pursuing.
Charles Colson

Better build schoolrooms for "the boy," than cells and gibbets for "the man."
Eliza Cook

Seeing the parental relation is what the Scripture describes it, and seeing Satan has perverted it since the fall for the diffusion and multiplication of depravity and eternal death, the education of children for God is the most important business done on earth.
R.L. Dabney

Education is not a preparation for life; education is life itself.
John Dewey

Education is a progressive discovery of our own ignorance.
Will Durant

The secret of education is respecting the pupil.
Ralph Waldo Emerson

To accuse others for one's own misfortunes is a sign of want of education. To accuse oneself shows that one's education has begun. To accuse neither oneself nor others shows that one's education is complete.
Epictetus

I hear and I forget. I see and I remember. I do and I understand.
Epictetus

I hope I live to see the day, when, as in the early days of our country, we won't have any public schools. The churches will have taken them over again and Christians will be running them. What a happy day that will be!
Jerry Falwell

Nations have recently been led to borrow billions for war; no nation has ever borrowed largely for education. Probably, no nation is rich enough to pay for both war and civilization. We must make our choice; we cannot have both.
Abraham Flexner

Only the educated are free.
Malcolm S. Forbes

Education's purpose is to replace an empty mind with an open one.
Malcolm S. Forbes

Spoon feeding in the long run teaches us nothing but the shape of the spoon.
E. M. Forster

The only thing more expensive than education is ignorance.
Benjamin Franklin

All I really need to know … I learned in kindergarten.
Robert Fulghum

Treat people as if they were what they ought to be and you help them to become what they are capable of being.
Goethe

Secular schools can never be tolerated because such schools have no religious instruction, and a general moral instruction without a religious foundation is built on air; consequently, all character training and religion must be derived from faith … we need believing people.
Adolf Hitler, April 26, 1933, from a speech made during negotiations leading to the Nazi-Vatican Concordant of 1933

Genius may have its limitations, but stupidity is not thus handicapped.
Elbert Hubbard

A school should not be a preparation for life. A school should be life.
Elbert Hubbard

The aim of education is the knowledge not of fact, but of values.
Dean William R. Inge

To neglect the wise sayings of great thinkers is to deny ourselves our truest education.
William James

The best-educated human being is the one who understands most about the life in which he is placed.
Helen Keller

College isn't the place to go for ideas.
Hellen Keller

The education of a man is never completed until he dies.
Robert E. Lee

Too often we give our children answers to remember rather than problems to solve.
Roger Lewin

The task of the modern educator is not to cut down jungles, but to irrigate deserts.
C.S. Lewis

Education without values, as useful as it is, seems rather to make man a more clever devil.
C.S. Lewis

Those who can, do. Those who can't, teach. Those who can't teach teach education.
Nicolas Martin

Children's games are hardly games. Children are never more serious than when they play.
Montaigne

Religious education must, I think, become the watchword of our church before we can expect abiding fruit on our labors. God forbid that I should limit the Holy One of Israel, but still I think that in the ordinary course of things education is our only hope.
Andrew Murray

Let me teach for a generation, and I will become ruler of the state.
Napoleon

Education is a method whereby one acquires a higher grade of prejudices.
Laurance Peter

It takes a village to raise a child.
African proverb

All the flowers of all the tomorrows are in the seeds of today.
Chinese proverb

A man who has never gone to school may steal from a freight car; but if he has a university education, he may steal the whole railroad.
Theodore Roosevelt

A good education is the next best thing to a pushy mother.
C. Schulz

Education is what survives when what has been learned has been forgotten.
B.F. Skinner

The illiterate of the 21st century will not be those who cannot read and write, but those who cannot learn, unlearn, and relearn.
Alvin Toffler

The man who does not read good books has no advantage over the man who cannot read them.
Mark Twain

I have never let my schooling interfere with my education.
Mark Twain

If you want children to keep their feet on the ground, put some responsibility on their shoulders.
Abigail Van Buren

As the twig is bent the tree inclines.
Virgil

Educate men without religion and you make them but clever devils.
Duke of Wellington

Give me the children until they are seven and anyone may have them afterward.
Francis Xavier

Education is not the filling of a pail, but the lighting of a fire.
William Butler Yeats

Effort

T. True
R. Righteous
Y. Yearnings
Thomas Hansen

I firmly believe that any man's finest hour is that moment when he has worked his heart out in a good cause and lies exhausted on the field of battle, victorious.
Vince Lombardi

If a man does his best, what else is there?
General George S. Patton (1885-1945)

Ego
Big egos are big shields for lots of empty space.
Diana Black

Egotist
An egotist is a person of low taste – more interested in himself than in me.
Ambrose Bierce

Elderly
"... show respect for the elderly ... "
The Bible, Leviticus 19:32

Elders
The elders who direct the affairs of the church well are worthy of double honor, especially those whose work is preaching and teaching.
The Bible, 1 Timothy 5:17

An elder must be blameless, the husband of but one wife, a man whose children believe and are not open to the charge of being wild and disobedient.
The Bible, Titus 1:6

Christians must remember, imitate, obey, and submit to:
Those elders who have spoken the word of God to them.
Those elders who have been close enough to consider their Christian lives, and the outcome of their conduct.
Those elders who rule, i.e. who require obedience of them.
Those elders who must give an account to God for them.
Douglas Wilson

Election
See also: Predestination
For many are called, but few are chosen.
The Bible, Matthew 22:14 KJV

God hath chosen the foolish things of the world to confound the wise; and God hath chosen the weak things of the world to confound the things that are mighty.
The Bible, 1 Corinthians 1:27

God ... set me apart from birth and called me by his grace ...
The Bible, Galatians 1:15

Therefore, as God's chosen people, holy and dearly loved, clothe yourselves with compassion, kindness, humility, gentleness and patience.
The Bible, Colossians 3:12

Peter, an apostle of Jesus Christ, To God's elect, strangers in the world, scattered throughout Pontus, Galatia, Cappadocia, Asia and Bithynia, who have been chosen according to the foreknowledge of God the Father, through the sanctifying work of the Spirit, for obedience to Jesus Christ and sprinkling by his blood: Grace and peace be yours in abundance.
The Bible, 1 Peter 1:1,2

Therefore, my brothers, be all the more eager to make your calling and election sure. For if you do these things, you will never fall.
The Bible, 2 Peter 1:10

Election

John Calvin, The Institutes of Christian Religion
CHAPTER 24.
ELECTION CONFIRMED BY THE CALLING OF GOD. THE REPROBATE BRING UPON THEMSELVES THE RIGHTEOUS DESTRUCTION TO WHICH THEY ARE DOOMED.
4. Therefore as those are in error who make the power of election dependent on the faith by which we perceive that we are elected, so we shall follow the best order, if, in seeking the certainty of our election, we cleave to those posterior signs which are sure attestations to it. Among the

temptations with which Satan assaults believers, none is greater or more perilous, than when disquieting them with doubts as to their election, he at the same time stimulates them with a depraved desire of inquiring after it out of the proper way.

By inquiring out of the proper way, I mean when puny man endeavors to penetrate to the hidden recesses of the divine wisdom, and goes back even to the remotest eternity, in order that he may understand what final determination God has made with regard to him. In this way he plunges headlong into an immense abyss, involves himself in numberless inextricable snares, and buries himself in the thickest darkness. For it is right that the stupidity of the human mind should be punished with fearful destruction, whenever it attempts to rise in its own strength to the height of divine wisdom. And this temptation is the more fatal, that it is the temptation to which of all others almost all of us are most prone. For there is scarcely a mind in which the thought does not sometimes rise, Whence your salvation but from the election of God? But what proof have you of your election? When once this thought has taken possession of any individual, it keeps him perpetually miserable, subjects him to dire torment, or throws him into a state of complete stupor. I cannot wish a stronger proof of the depraved ideas, which men of this description form of predestination, than experience itself furnishes, since the mind cannot be infected by a more pestilential error than that which disturbs the conscience, and deprives it of peace and tranquillity in regard to God. Therefore, as we dread shipwreck, we must avoid this rock, which is fatal to every one who strikes upon it. And though the discussion of predestination is regarded as a perilous sea, yet in sailing over it the navigation is calm and safe, nay pleasant, provided we do not voluntarily court danger. For as a fatal abyss engulfs those who, to be assured of their election, pry into the eternal counsel of God without the word, yet those who investigate it rightly, and in the order in which it is exhibited in the word, reap from it rich fruits of consolation.

Let our method of inquiry then be, to begin with the calling of God and to end with it. Although there is nothing in this to prevent believers from feeling that the blessings which they daily receive from the hand of God originate in that secret adoption, as they themselves express it in Isaiah, "Thou hast done wonderful things; thy counsels of old are faithfulness and truth," (Isa. 25:1). For with this as a pledge, God is pleased to assure us of as much of his counsel as can be lawfully known. But lest any should think that testimony weak, let us consider what clearness and certainty it gives us. On this subject there is an apposite passage in Bernard. After speaking of the reprobate, he says, "The purpose of God stands, the sentence of peace on those that fear him also stands, a sentence concealing their bad and recompensing their good qualities; so that, in a wondrous manner, not only their good but their bad qualities work together for good. Who will lay any thing to the charge of God's elect? It is completely sufficient for my justification to have him propitious against whom only I have sinned. Every thing which he has decreed not to impute to me, is as if it had never been." A little after he says, "O the place of true rest, a place which I consider not unworthy of the name of inner-chamber, where God is seen, not as if disturbed with anger, or distracted by care, but where his will is proved to be good, and acceptable, and perfect. That vision does not terrify but soothe, does not excite restless curiosity but calms it, does not fatigue but tranquillizes the senses. Here is true rest. A tranquil God tranquillizes all things; and to see him at rest, is to be at rest." (Bernard, super Cantic. Serm. 14).

5. First, if we seek for the paternal mercy and favor of God, we must turn our eyes to Christ, in whom alone the Father is well pleased (Mt. 3:17). When we seek for salvation, life, and a blessed immortality, to him also must we retake ourselves, since he

alone is the fountain of life and the anchor of salvation, and the heir of the kingdom of heaven. Then what is the end of election, but just that, being adopted as sons by the heavenly Father, we may by his favor obtain salvation and immortality? How much soever you may speculate and discuss you will perceive that in its ultimate object it goes no farther. Hence, those whom God has adopted as sons, he is said to have elected, not in themselves, but in Christ Jesus (Eph. 1:4); because he could love them only in him, and only as being previously made partakers with him, honor them with the inheritance of his kingdom. But if we are elected in him, we cannot find the certainty of our election in ourselves; and not even in God the Father, if we look at him apart from the Son.

Christ, then, is the mirror in which we ought, and in which, without deception, we may contemplate our election. For since it is into his body that the Father has decreed to ingraft those whom from eternity he wished to be his, that he may regard as sons all whom he acknowledges to be his members, if we are in communion with Christ, we have proof sufficiently clear and strong that we are written in the Book of Life. Moreover, he admitted us to sure communion with himself, when, by the preaching of the gospel, he declared that he was given us by the Father, to be ours with all his blessings (Rom. 8:32). We are said to be clothed with him, to be one with him, that we may live, because he himself lives. The doctrine is often repeated, "God so loved the world, that he gave his only begotten Son, that whosoever believeth in him should not perish, but have everlasting life," (John 3:16). He who believes in him is said to have passed from death unto life (John 5:24). In this sense he calls himself the *bread of life*, of which if a man eat, he shall never die (John 6:35). He, I say, was our witness, that all by whom he is received in faith will be regarded by our heavenly Father as sons. If we long for more than to be regarded as sons of God and heirs, we must ascend above Christ. But if this is our final goal, how infatuated is it to seek out of

him what we have already obtained in him, and can only find in him? Besides, as he is the Eternal Wisdom, the Immutable Truth, the Determinate Counsel of the Father, there is no room for fear that any thing which he tells us will vary in the minutest degree from that will of the Father after which we inquire. Nay, rather he faithfully discloses it to us as it was from the beginning, and always will be. The practical influence of this doctrine ought also to be exhibited in our prayers. For though a belief of our election animates us to involve God, yet when we frame our prayers, it were preposterous to obtrude it upon God, or to stipulate in this way, "O Lord, if I am elected, hear me." He would have us to rest satisfied with his promises, and not to inquire elsewhere whether or not he is disposed to hear us. We shall thus be disentangled from many snares, if we know how to make a right use of what is rightly written; but let us not inconsiderately wrest it to purposes different from that to which it ought to be confined.

6. Another confirmation tending to establish our confidence is, that our election is connected with our calling. For those whom Christ enlightens with the knowledge of his name, and admits into the bosom of his Church, he is said to take under his guardianship and protection. All whom he thus receives are said to be committed and entrusted to him by the Father, that they may be kept unto life eternal. What would we have? Christ proclaims aloud that all whom the Father is pleased to save he has delivered into his protection (John 6:37-39, 17:6, 12). Therefore, if we would know whether God cares for our salvation, let us ask whether he has committed us to Christ, whom he has appointed to be the only Savior of all his people. Then, if we doubt whether we are received into the protection of Christ, he obviates the doubt when he spontaneously offers himself as our Shepherd, and declares that we are of the number of his sheep if we hear his voice (John 10:3, 16). Let us, therefore, embrace Christ, who is kindly

offered to us, and comes forth to meet us: he will number us among his flock, and keep us within his fold.

But anxiety arises as to our future state. For as Paul teaches, that those are called who were previously elected, so our Savior shows that many are called, but few chosen (Mt. 22:14). Nay, even Paul himself dissuades us from security, when he says, "Let him that thinketh he standeth take heed lest he fall" (1 Cor. 10:12). And again, "Well, because of unbelief they were broken off, and thou standest by faith. Be not high-minded, but fear: for if God spared not the natural branches, take heed lest he also spare not thee" (Rom. 11:20, 21). In fine, we are sufficiently taught by experience itself, that calling and faith are of little value without perseverance, which, however, is not the gift of all. But Christ has freed us from anxiety on this head; for the following promises undoubtedly have respect to the future: "All that the Father giveth me shall come to me, and him that comes to me I will in no wise cast out." Again, "This is the will of him that sent me, that of all which he has given me I should lose nothing; but should raise it up at the last day" (John 6:37, 39). Again, "My sheep hear my voice, and I know them, and they follow me: and I give unto them eternal life, and they shall never perish, neither shall any man pluck them out of my hand. My Father which gave them me is greater than all: and no man is able to pluck them out of my Father's hand" (John 10:27, 28). Again, when he declares, "Every plant which my heavenly Father has not planted shall be rooted up" (Mt. 15:13), he intimates conversely that those who have their root in God can never be deprived of their salvation. Agreeable to this are the words of John, "If they had been of us, they would no doubt have continued with us" (1 John 2:19). Hence, also, the magnificent triumph of Paul over life and death, things present, and things to come (Rom. 8:38). This must be founded on the gift of perseverance. There is no doubt that he employs the sentiment as applicable to all the elect. Paul elsewhere says, "Being confident of this very thing, that he who has begun a good work in you will perform it until the day of Jesus Christ" (Phil. 1:6). David, also, when his faith threatened to fail, leant on this support, "Forsake not the works of thy hands." Moreover, it cannot be doubted, that since Christ prays for all the elect, he asks the same thing for them as he asked for Peter – viz. that their faith fail not (Luke 22:32). Hence we infer, that there is no danger of their falling away, since the Son of God, who asks that their piety may prove constant, never meets with a refusal. What then did our Savior intend to teach us by this prayer, but just to confide, that whenever we are his our eternal salvation is secure?

7. But it daily happens that those who seemed to belong to Christ revolt from him and fall away: Nay, in the very passage where he declares that none of those whom the Father has given to him have perished, he excepts the son of perdition. This, indeed, is true; but it is equally true that such persons never adhered to Christ with that heartfelt confidence by which I say that the certainty of our election is established: "They went out from us," says John, "but they were not of us; for if they had been of us, they would, no doubt, have continued with us" (1 John 2:19). I deny not that they have signs of calling similar to those given to the elect; but I do not at all admit that they have that sure confirmation of election which I desire believers to seek from the word of the gospel. Wherefore, let not examples of this kind move us away from tranquil confidence in the promise of the Lord, when he declares that all by whom he is received in true faith have been given him by the Father, and that none of them, while he is their Guardian and Shepherd, will perish (John 3:16; 6:39). Of Judas we shall shortly speak (sec. 9). Paul does not dissuade Christians from security simply, but from careless, carnal security, which is accompanied with pride, arrogance, and contempt of others, which extinguishes humility and reverence for God, and

produces a forgetfulness of grace received (Rom. 11:20). For he is addressing the Gentiles, and showing them that they ought not to exult proudly and cruelly over the Jews, in consequence of whose rejection they had been substituted in their stead. He also enjoins fear, not a fear under which they may waver in alarm, but a fear which, teaching us to receive the grace of God in humility, does not impair our confidence in it, as has elsewhere been said. We may add, that he is not speaking to individuals, but to sects in general (see 1 Cor. 10:12). The Church having been divided into two parties, and rivalship producing dissension, Paul reminds the Gentiles that their having been substituted in the place of a peculiar and holy people was a reason for modesty and fear. For there were many vain-glorious persons among them, whose empty boasting it was expedient to repress. But we have elsewhere seen, that our hope extends into the future, even beyond death, and that nothing is more contrary to its nature than to be in doubt as to our future destiny.

John Calvin

There are many reasons why God shouldn't have called you. But don't worry. You're in good company. Moses stuttered. John Mark was rejected by Paul. Timothy had ulcers. Hosea's wife was a prostitute. Amos' only training was in the school of fig-tree pruning. Jacob was a liar. David had an affair. Solomon was too rich. Abraham was too old. Peter was afraid of death. Lazarus was dead. Naomi was a widow. Paul was a murderer. So was Moses. Jonah ran from God. Miriam was a gossip. Gideon and Thomas both doubted. Jeremiah was depressed and suicidal. Elijah was burned out. John the Baptist was a loudmouth. Martha was a worrywart. Mary was lazy. Samson had long hair. Noah got drunk. Did I mention that Moses had a short fuse? So did Peter, Paul – well, lots of folks did.

Author unknown

We know there is a sun in heaven, yet we cannot see what matter it is made of, but perceive it only by the beams, light and heat. Election is a sun, the eyes of eagles cannot see it; yet we may find it in the heat of vocation, in the light of illumination, in the beams of good works.

Thomas Adams

Election having once pitched upon a man, it will find him out and call him home, wherever he be. It called Zaccheus out of accursed Jericho; Abraham out of idolatrous Ur of the Chaldees; Nicodemus and Paul, from the College of the Pharisees, Christ's sworn enemies; Dionysius and Damaris, out of superstitious Athens. In whatsoever dunghills God's elect are hid, election will find them out and bring them home.

John Arrowsmith

God chooses us, not because we believe, but that we may believe.

Augustine of Hippo

For it is utterly impossible that any finite cause, created power, or anything out of God himself, should primarily move and incline the eternal, immutable, uncreated, omnipotent will of God. The true original and prime motive of all gracious, bountiful expressions and effusions of love upon his elect, is the good pleasure of his will. And therefore to hold that election to life is made upon foresight of faith, good works, the right use of free will, or any created motive, is not only false and wicked, but also on ignorant and absurd tenet. To say no more at this time, it robs God of his all-sufficiency, making him go out of himself, looking to this or that in the creature, upon which his will may be determined to elect.

Robert Bolton

Election is God's eternal choice of some persons unto everlasting life – not because of foreseen merit in them, but of his mere mercy in Christ – in consequence of which choice they are

called, justified, and glorified.
James Boyce

We are searching for God's election
My Lord, I did not choose You,
For that could never be;
My heart would still refuse You,
Had You not chosen me.
You took the sin that stained me,
You cleansed me, made me new;
Of old you have ordained me,
That I should live in You.
Unless Your grace had called me
And taught my op'ning mind,
The world would have enthralled me,
To heav'nly glories blind.
My heart knows none above You;
For Your rich grace I thirst.
I know that if I love You,
You must have loved me first.
Josiah Conder

As God did not at first choose you because
you were high, so he will not forsake you
because you are low.
John Flavel

None can know their election but by their
conformity to Christ; for all who are
chosen are chosen to sanctification.
Matthew Henry

Holiness is the only evidence of election.
Charles Hodge

I knew nothing; I was nothing. For this
reason God picked me out.
Catherine Laboure

Wherever the missionary character of the
doctrine of election is forgotten; wherever
it is forgotten that we are chosen in order
to be sent; wherever the minds of believers
are concerned more to probe backwards
from their election into the reasons for it
in the secret counsel of God, than to press
forward from their election to the purpose
of it … that they should be Christ's
ambassadors and witnesses to the ends of
the earth, wherever men think that the
purpose of election is their own salvation

rather than the salvation of the world: then
God's people have betrayed their trust.
Leslie Newbigin

Christ did not die for any upon condition,
if they do believe; but He died for all God's
elect, that they should believe.
John Owen

The things that God is pleased to keep to
Himself (the number and identity of the
elect, for instance, and when and how He
purposes to convert whom) have no
bearing on any man's duty.
J.I. Packer

Like the doctrine of the Holy Trinity and
the miraculous birth of our Savior, the
truth of election must be received with
simple, unquestioning faith.
Arthur Pink

The names and number of the elect are a
secret thing, no doubt … But if there is
one thing clearly and plainly laid down
about election, it is this – that elect men
and women may be known and
distinguished by holy lives.
J.C. Ryle

The only reason why anyone believes in
election is because he finds it clearly taught
in God's Word. No man, or number of
men, ever originated this doctrine.
C.H. Spurgeon

None can guess the reasons of divine
election.
C.H. Spurgeon

There are two great truths which from this
platform I have proclaimed for many years.
The first is that salvation is free to every
man who will have it; the second is that
God gives salvation to a people whom He
has chosen; and these truths are not in
conflict with each other in the least degree.
C.H. Spurgeon

Election and predestination are but the
exercise of God's sovereignty in the affairs

of salvation, and all that we know about them is what has been revealed to us in the Scriptures of Truth.
C.H. Spurgeon

If God would have painted a yellow stripe on the backs of the elect I would go around lifting shirts. But since He didn't I must preach "whosoever will" and when "whosoever" believes I know he is one of the elect.
C.H. Spurgeon

Now if it be the Father's will that Christ should lose none of his elect; if Christ himself, in consequence of their covenant-donation to him, does actually give them eternal life, and solemnly avers that they shall never perish; if God be so for them that none can hinder their salvation; if nothing can be laid to their charge; if they cannot be condemned and nought shall separate them from the love of Christ; it clearly and inevitably follows that none of the elect can perish, but they must all necessarily be saved. Which salvation consists as much in the recovery of moral rectitude below, as in the enjoyment of eternal blessedness above.
Augustus Toplady

The marvel of marvels is not that God, in his infinite love, has not elected all this guilty race to be saved, but that he has elected any.
B.B. Warfield

We can never know that we are elected of God to eternal life except by manifesting in our lives the fruits of election.
B.B. Warfield

Election is the foundation-cause of our vocation. Before effectual calling, we were not only without strength, but enemies. So that the foundation of vocation is election.
Thomas Watson

Why was I made to hear thy voice,
And enter while there's room;

When thousands make a wretched choice,
And rather starve than come?
'Twas the same love that spread the feast,
That sweetly forced us in,
Else we had still refused to taste,
And perished in our sin.
Issaac Watts

Emotion
Don't come to me with your rubbish that there is no emotion in religion. You cannot have real religion without emotion.
Donald Gee

I use emotion for the many and reserve reason for the few.
Adolph Hitler

An ounce of emotion is equal to a ton of facts.
John Junor

I read of George Whitefield, preaching, and as he was preaching about the glories of grace and of salvation, the tears were pouring down his cheeks, and those who listened to him were weeping too. It is true of all these men, yet we may be so hard and so intellectual and so controlled. This is not a plea for emotionalism, which I have denounced, it is a plea for emotion.
M. Lloyd-Jones

A really intelligent man feels what other men only know.
Charles Montesquieu

Emotionalism
The man who screams at a football or baseball game but is distressed when he hears of a sinner weeping at the cross and murmurs something about the dangers of emotionalism hardly merits intelligent respect.
Dr W.E. Sangster

People don't ask for facts in making up their minds. They would rather have one good, soul-satisfying emotion than a dozen facts.
Robert Keith Leavitt

God has not created man to be a stock or stone but has given him five senses and a

heart of flesh, so that he loves his friends, is angry with his enemies, and commiserates with his dear friends in adversity.
Martin Luther

Crowds, and crying, and hot rooms, and high-flown singing, and an incessant rousing of the emotions, are the only things which many care for.
J.C. Ryle

Empathy
Rejoice with those who rejoice; mourn with those who mourn.
The Bible, Romans 12:15

Until you walk a mile in another man's moccasins, you can't imagine the smell.
Author unknown

To bear with patience wrongs done to oneself is a mark of perfection, but to bear with patience wrongs done to someone else is a mark of imperfection and even of actual sin.
Thomas Aquinas

To ease another's heartache is to forget one's own.
Abraham Lincoln

Shared joy is double joy and shared sorrow is half-sorrow.
Swedish proverb

The great gift of human beings is that we have the power of empathy.
Meryl Streep

Emptiness
There remains deep in the soul (if I dare use that word) a persistent and unconscious anxiety that something is missing – some ingredient that makes life worth living.
Prince Charles

The more a man has, the more he wants. Instead of its filling a vacuum, it makes one.
Benjamin Franklin

[The world is suffering] a neurosis of emptiness.
Carl Jung

Encouragement
Encouragement is oxygen of the soul.
Author unknown

Patting a fellow on the back is the best way to get a chip off his shoulder.
Author unknown

It is easier to point the finger than to offer a helping hand.
Author unknown

Encouragement costs you nothing to give, but it is priceless to receive.
Author unknown

"What do you give a man who has everything?" the pretty teenager asked her mother. "Encouragement, dear," she replied.
Author unknown

Expect people to be better than they are; it helps them to become better. But don't be disappointed when they are not; it helps them to keep trying.
Merry Browne

I praise loudly, I blame softly.
Catherine II of Russia

The really great man is the man who makes every man feel great.
G.K. Chesterton

Encouragement after censure is as the sun after a shower.
Goethe

I will not wish thee riches, nor the glow of
   greatness,
but that wherever thou go some weary
heart shall gladden at thy smile,
or shadowed life know sunshine for a while.
And so thy path shall be a track of light, like
angels' footsteps passing through the night.
Inscription, words on a church wall in Upwaltham, England

Keep your fears to yourself; share your courage with others.
Robert Louis Stevenson

End of the world
And at the end of the world, when the church of Christ shall be settled in its last, and most complete, and its eternal state, and all common gifts, such as convictions and illuminations, and all miraculous gifts, shall be eternally at an end, yet then divine love shall not fail, but shall be brought to its most glorious perfection in every individual member of the ransomed church above. Then, in every heart, that love which now seems as but a spark, shall be kindled to a bright and glowing flame, and every ransomed soul shall be as it were in a blaze of divine and holy love, and shall remain and grow in this glorious perfection and blessedness through all eternity!
Jonathan Edwards

Beloved men, realize what is true: this world is in haste and the end approaches: and therefore in the world things go from bad to worse, and so it must of necessity deteriorate greatly on account of the people's sins before the coming of Antichrist, and indeed it will then be dreadful and terrible far and of throughout the world.
Gregory the Great

Endurance
See also: Perseverence
Therefore I endure everything for the sake of the elect, that they too may obtain the salvation that is in Christ Jesus, with eternal glory.
The Bible, 2 Timothy 2:10

Who would wish for hardship and difficulty? You command us to endure these troubles, not to love them. No one loves what he endures even though he may be glad to endure it.
Augustine of Hippo

Endurance is not just the ability to bear a hard thing, but to turn it into glory.
William Barclay

Nothing great was ever done without much enduring.
Catherine of Siena

To endure is the first thing that a child ought to learn, and that which he will have the most need to know.
Jean Jacques Rousseau

Enemies
That you do it willingly pray for your enemy, that you are glad to do it, that you are delighted according to the inner man to obey your Lord and pray for your enemy – this shows you are gold. But that as soon as you begin to pray your fleshly weakness starts opposing you – that's the dross from which God wishes to purify you in the furnace.
Augustine of Hippo

Ye have enemies; for who can live on this earth without them? Take heed to yourselves: love them. In no way can thy enemy so hurt thee by his violence, as thou dost hurt thyself if thou love him not.
Augustine of Hippo

One should forgive one's enemies, but not before they're hanged.
Heinrich Heine

The best way to destroy an enemy is to make him a friend.
Abraham Lincoln

If you want to make peace with your enemy, you have to work with your enemy. Then he becomes your partner.
Nelson Mandela

In Jesus and for Him, enemies and friends alike are to be loved.
Thomas à Kempis

Engineers' Creed
I take the vision which comes from dreams and apply the magic of science and mathematics, adding the heritage of my profession and my knowledge of nature's materials to create a design.
  I organize the efforts and skills of my

fellow workers employing the capital of the thrifty and the products of many industries, and together we work toward our goal undaunted by hazards and obstacles.

And when we have completed our task all can see that the dreams and plans have materialized for the comfort and welfare of all.

I am an Engineer. I serve mankind by making dreams come true.
Author unknown (supposedly found pinned to a site hut during the construction of the Konkan railway)

Enjoyment

There is nothing better for a man, than that he should eat and drink, and that he should make his soul enjoy good in his labor.
The Bible, Ecclesiastes 2:24 KJV

Command those who are rich in this present world not to be arrogant nor to put their hope in wealth, which is so uncertain, but to put their hope in God, who richly provides us with everything for our enjoyment.
The Bible, 1 Timothy 6:17

All animals except man know that the ultimate of life is to enjoy it.
Samuel Butler

Let's get rid of the inhuman philosophy which only allows necessities. Not only does it wrongly deprive us of legitimate enjoyment of God's generosity, but it cannot be effected without depriving man of all his senses, reducing him to a block.
John Calvin

Anything good in life is either illegal, immoral, or fattening.
Pardo

Be absolutely determined to enjoy what you do.
Gerry Sikorski

Enlightenment

He who knows others is wise;

He who knows himself is enlightened.
Tao Te Ching

Entertaining
See: Hospitality

Enthusiasm

Man never rises to great truths without enthusiasm.
Author unknown

Truth without enthusiasm, morality without emotion, ritual without soul, are things Christ unsparingly condemned. Destitute of fire, they are nothing more than a godless philosophy, an ethical system, and a superstition.
Samuel Chadwick

Every great and commanding movement in the annals of the world is the triumph of enthusiasm. Nothing great was ever achieved without it.
Ralph Waldo Emerson

We act as though comfort and luxury were the chief requirements in life, when all we need to make us really happy is something to be enthusiastic about.
Charles Kingsley

The world belongs to the enthusiast who keeps cool.
William McFee

If you aren't enthusiastic about it (teaching the faith), it is obvious you don't really care. You're just a travel agent selling tickets to a place you've never been.
Brennon Manning

There is a real magic in enthusiasm. It spells the difference between mediocrity and accomplishment.
Norman Vincent Peale

Enthusiasm is as good a thing in the Church as fire is in a cook stove.
Billy Sunday

Years may wrinkle the skin, but to give up

enthusiasm wrinkles the soul.
Samuel Ullman

"Put down enthusiasm." The Church of
England in a nutshell.
Mary Augusta Ward

Catch on fire with enthusiasm and
people will come for miles to watch you
burn.
John Wesley

Environment
We should be pioneers in the care of
mankind.
Klaus Bockmühl

The destruction of the world around us is
a reflection of not being "God centered" as
human beings. Christ, as both God and
man, is our center, our truth and our life.
The pollution and defilement we
encounter exists through ignorance or
rejection of God.
Tod Connor

We are children of our landscape.
Lawrence Durrell

It is forbidden to live in a city that does
not have greenery.
Jerusalem Talmud, Kiddushin 12:12

What we call the environmental crisis is
not merely a crisis in the natural
environment of human beings. It is
nothing less than a crisis in human beings
themselves.
Jürgen Moltmann

Only after the last tree has been cut down,
Only after the last river has been poisoned,
Only after the last fish has been caught,
Only then will you find that money cannot
be eaten.
Cree Indian proverb

Loving the Lover who has made the world,
I should have respect for the thing He has
made.
Francis Schaeffer

If we squander our fossil fuels, we threaten
civilization, but if we squander the capital
represented by living nature around us, we
threaten life itself.
E.F. Schumacher

Our intermediate position [is] between God
and nature, between the Creator and the rest
of his creation. We combine dependence on
God with dominion over the earth.
John Stott

Envy
See also: Humanity
They that envy others are their inferiors.
Author unknown

[Envy is] *the* diabolical sin.
Augustine of Hippo

Congratulations: the civility of envy.
Ambrose Bierce

Love looks through a telescope; envy,
through a microscope.
Josh Billings

Envy is like a fly that passes all the body's
sounder parts, and dwells upon the sores.
Arthur Chapman

From envy are born hatred, detraction,
calumny, joy caused by the misfortune of a
neighbor, and displeasure caused by his
prosperity.
Gregory the Great

It is never wise to seek or wish for another's
misfortune. If malice or envy were tangible
and had a shape, it would be the shape of a
boomerang.
Charley Reese

There is not a passion so strongly rooted in
the human heart as envy.
R.B. Sheridan

A little grit in the eye destroyeth the sight
of the very Heavens; and a little Malice or
Envy, a World of Joy.
Thomas Traherne

Ephesians, Book of
The divinest composition of man.
Samuel Taylor Coleridge, commenting on Paul's letter to the Ephesians

Episcopacy
Having heard the bishop I am now convinced of the apostolic succession from Judas Iscariot.
Sydney Smith

Epitaph
Go my friends and shed no tears,
I must lie here till Christ appears
Anonymous epitaph

Here Lie
The earthly remains of
JOHN BERRIDGE,
Late vicar of Everton,
And an itinerant servant of Jesus Christ,
Who loved His Master and His work,
And after running on His errands many
  years
Was called to wait on Him above.
READER,
No Salvation without new birth!
I was born in sin, February 1716.
Remained ignorant of my fallen state till
  1730.
Lived proudly on faith and works for
salvation till 1754.
Was admitted to Everton Vicarage, 1755.
Fled to Jesus alone for refuge, 1756.
Fell asleep in Christ, January 22, 1793.
Rebellion to tyrants is obedience to God.
John Bradshaw (1602-59), English lawyer, regicide. Inscription at Bradshaw's final burial place near Martha Bay. He presided at the trial of Charles I. Buried in Westminster Abbey, his body was exhumed at the Restoration and hanged in public, like that of Cromwell.

Morning breaks upon the tomb,
Jesus scatters all its gloom.
Day of triumph through the skies –
See the glorious Savior rise.
Christians! Dry your flowing tears,
Chase those unbelieving fears;
Look on his deserted grave,
Doubt no more his power to save.

Ye who are of death afraid,
Triumph in the scattered shade:
Drive your anxious cares away,
See the place where Jesus lay.
Collyer

O Lord, the faith thou didst give to St Paul, I cannot ask; the mercy thou didst show to St Peter; I dare not ask; but Lord, the grace thou didst show unto the dying robber, that, Lord, show to me.
Copernicus, epitaph of his own composition

"Called Back"
West Cemetery; Amherst, Massachusetts, self-written, Emily Dickinson

The body of Benjamin Franklin, Printer (like the cover of an old book, its contents torn out and stripped of its lettering and gilding), lies here, food for worms; but the work shall not be lost, for it will (as he believed) appear once more in a new and more elegant edition, revised and corrected by the Author.
Self-written, Epitaph on Benjamin Franklin's grave

FREE AT LAST,
FREE AT LAST
THANK GOD ALMIGHTY
I'M FREE AT LAST.
Martin Luther King's tombstone

Man must endure his going hence.
Headington Quarry Churchyard; Oxfordshire, England, C.S. Lewis

For thirty years his life was spent in an unwearied effort to evangelize.
The inscription over David Livingstone's burial place in Westminster Abbey

"John Newton, Clerk,
Once an infidel and libertine,
A servant of slaves in Africa:
Was by the rich mercy of our Lord and
  Savior,
Jesus Christ,
Preserved, restored, pardoned,
And appointed to preach the Faith

He had long labored to destroy.
Near sixteen years at Olney in Bucks:
And twenty-seven years in this Church."
John Newton, self-written

"I look upon all the world as my parish."
"God buries his workmen but carries on
his work."
*On the monument to John and Charles Wesley
in Westminster Abbey*

Equality before God

Kneeling ne'er spoiled silk stocking:
quit thy state.
All equal are within the church's gate.
George Herbert

As regards our standing before God,
because we are "in Christ" and enjoy a
common relationship to him, racial,
national, social and sexual distinctions are
irrelevant.
John Stott

Error
See also: Mistakes; Truth

There is no error so monstrous that it fails
to find defenders among the ablest men.
John Dalberg Acton

The best may err.
Joseph Addison

It is human to err; it is devilish to remain
willfully in error.
Augustine of Hippo

Error never has true method. Confusion is
its characteristic.
R.L. Dabney

An error gracefully acknowledged is a
victory won.
Caroline Gascoigne

Error of opinion may be tolerated where
reason is left free to combat it.
Thomas Jefferson

He that sees another in error, and
endeavors not to correct it, testifies himself

to be in error.
Pope Leo I

If we escape one error, we usually glide
into its opposite.
C.H. Spurgeon

Error is dangerous; a man may as well go
to hell by error as by moral vice; gross
sins stab to the heart, error poisons; there
is less hope of an erroneous person than a
profane; the profane person sins, and
doth not repent; the erroneous sins, and
holds it a sin to repent; the one is
without tears, the other cries down tears.
The upright Christian is not tainted with
this leprosy; he hath rectitude in his mind.
Thomas Watson

Eternal

For our light and momentary troubles are
achieving for us an eternal glory that far
outweighs them all. So we fix our eyes not
on what is seen, but on what is unseen. For
what is seen is temporary, but what is
unseen is eternal.
The Bible, 2 Corinthians 4:17,18

Eternal life

Take hold of the eternal life to which you
were called when you made your good
profession in the presence of many
witnesses.
The Bible, 1 Timothy 6:12

For my Father's will is that everyone who
looks to the Son and believes in him shall
have eternal life, and I will raise him up at
the last day.
The Bible, John 6:40

… so that, having been justified by his
grace, we might become heirs having the
hope of eternal life.
The Bible, Titus 3:7

The truest end of life, is to find the life
that doesn't end.
Author unknown

I want to live for immortality, and I will

accept no compromise.
Alyosha, in Fyodor Dostoyevsky's, The Brothers Karamazov

People who dwell in God dwell in the Eternal Now.
Meister Eckhart

Where, except in the present, can the Eternal be met?
C.S. Lewis

Once a man is united to God, how could he not live for ever?
C.S. Lewis

Live near to God, and so all things will appear to you little in comparison with eternal realities.
Robert Murray M'Cheyne

Over the triple doorways of Milan Cathedral are three inscriptions spanning the magnificent arches.
Above one is carved a wreath of roses, with the words, "All that pleases is but for a moment."
Over the second is a cross, with the words, "All that troubles is but for a moment."
Underneath the great central entrance to the main aisle is inscribed: "That only is important which is eternal."
Inscription, Milan Cathedral

I was born of the flesh in 1837. I was born of the Spirit in 1856. That which is born of the flesh may die. That which is born of the Spirit will live forever.
D.L. Moody

Fear not that your life shall come to an end, but rather that it shall never have a beginning.
John Henry Newman

"Eternal life" is the sole sanction for the values of this life.
Dorothy L. Sayers

For a small reward, a man will hurry away on a long journey; while for eternal life,

many will hardly take a single step.
Thomas à Kempis

Seems it strange that thou shouldst live forever? Is it any less strange that thou shouldst live at all? This is a miracle; and that no more.
Edward Young

Eternity

If you live a Christian life and there is no heaven or hell, what have you lost? Nothing! If you live a sinner's life and there is a heaven and hell you've lost eternity.
Author unknown

Eternity is not something that begins after you are dead. It is going on all the time. We are in it now.
Charlotte Perkins Gilman

A man's greatest care should be for that place where he dwelleth longest; therefore eternity should be his scope.
Thomas Manton

Or sells eternity to get a toy.
William Shakespeare, King Henry VIII

Remember your eternity and always work towards it.
Shenouda III

Where there is no vision, the people perish (Proverbs 29:18). Where there is no vision of eternity, there is no prayer for the perishing.
David Smithers

Time is short. Eternity is long. It is only reasonable that this short life be lived in the light of eternity.
C.H. Spurgeon

He who provides for this life, but takes no care for eternity, is wise for a moment, but a fool for ever.
John Tillotson

Eternity to the godly is a day that has no

sunset; eternity to the wicked is a night that has no sunrise.
Thomas Watson

Eternity is the place where questions and answers become one.
Eli Wiessel

Ethics
See: Relativity
The real problem is in the hearts and minds of men. It is not a problem of physics but of ethics.
Albert Einstein

The ethic of the Bible reflects the character of the God of the Bible. Remove from Scripture the transcendent holiness, righteousness and truth of God and its ethic disappears.
John Murray

Good conduct arises out of good doctrine.
John R. W. Stott

Two things, belief and conduct, are indissolubly bound together; they are part of one whole, as roots and fruit are both alike parts of one tree, organically connected.
L. S. Thornton

Europe
If God had wanted us to use the metric system, Jesus would have had 10 apostles.
Author unknown

Euthanasia
Nuclear war threatens life on a previously unimaginable scale; abortion takes life daily on a horrendous scale; public executions are fast becoming weekly events in the most advanced technological society in history. Euthanasia is now openly discussed and even advocated ... The case for a consistent ethic of life ... joins the humanity of the unborn infant and the humanity of the hungry; it calls for positive legal action to prevent the killing of the unborn or the aged and positive societal action to provide shelter for the homeless and education for the illiterate.
Joseph Bernardin

Deception is not as creative as truth. We do best in life if we look at it with clear eyes, and I think that applies to coming up to death as well.
Cicely Saunders, founder of the modern hospice movement

Only God can decide life and death.
Mother Teresa

In time, they will start killing grown-up people, disabled people and so on.
Mother Teresa

Evangelical belief
The fundamental doctrines of our evangelical belief are the full inspiration and ruling authority of Holy Scripture, with its consequences, the divinity of Christ, the finality of His atonement, and salvation through faith alone.
G. T. Manley

A confident intellectualism expressive of robust faith in God, whose Word is truth, is part of the historic evangelical tradition.
J.I. Packer

Evangelicalism
Evangelicalism is like a swimming bath. Most noise at the shallow end.
J. Blanchard

Evangelicalism is not consistently evangelical unless there is a line drawn between those who take a full view of Scripture and those who do not.
Francis A. Schaeffer

If the spirit of Puritanism was best represented graphically by a preacher in an elevated pulpit, the arm raised in vigorous punctuation upon the truth of God, that of modern evangelicalism is probably best represented today by the ubiquitous happy face, a bright smile beckoning smiles in return.
David Wells

Evangelicals
As evangelicals united in the gospel, we promise to watch over and care for one

another, to pray for and forgive one another, and to reach out in love and truth to God's people everywhere, for we are one family, one in the Holy Spirit, and one in Christ.

The gospel of Jesus Christ: An evangelical celebration

Evangelism
See also: Church growth; Church and evangelism

So neither he who plants nor he who waters is anything, but only God, who makes things grow.

The Bible, 1 Corinthians 3:7

To the weak I became weak, to win the weak. I have become all things to all men so that by all possible means I might save some.

The Bible, 1 Corinthians 9:22

Since, then, we know what it is to fear the Lord, we try to persuade men. What we are is plain to God, and I hope it is also plain to your conscience.

The Bible, 2 Corinthians 5:11

There is a trend today that would put a new robe on the prodigal son while he is still feeding hogs. Some would put the ring on his finger while he is still in the pigsty. Others would paint the pigsty and advocate bigger and better hog pens.

Author unknown

To teach in order to lead others to faith is the task of every preacher and of each believer.

Thomas Aquinas

There is no joy in all the world like the joy of bringing one soul to Christ.

William Barclay

Methinks if by faith we did indeed look upon them as within a step of hell, it would more effectually untie our tongues, than Coresus' danger, as they tell us, did his son's.

Richard Baxter

Satan does not care what we do so long as we do not alert people to their sin. We may sing songs about the sweet by and by, preach sermons and say prayers until doomsday, and he will never concern himself about us, if we don't wake anybody up. But if we awake the sleeping sinner he will gnash on us with his teeth. This is our work – to wake people up.

Catherine Booth

"Young man, if I thought I could win one more soul for Christ by standing on my head and beating a tambourine with my feet I would learn how to do it."

William Booth, to Rudyard Kipling, after the latter had said how much he disliked tambourines.

Go for souls.
Go for souls, and go for the worst.

William Booth, his motto

How is it that the soul being of such value, and God so great, eternity so near and yet we are so little moved?

William Bramwell

One who receives this Word, and by it salvation, receives along with it the duty of passing this Word on … Where there is no mission, there is no Church, and where there is neither Church nor mission, there is no faith.

Emil Brunner

The Great Commission is far more than evangelism. I think many evangelicals have a very simplistic view of what it is that God is calling us to do. The Great Commission is to make disciples, "teaching them all I have taught you" (Matthew 28:20).

Chuck Colson

Christ beats his drum, but he does not press men; Christ is served with volunteers.

John Donne

We are the Bibles the world is reading;
We are the creeds the world is needing;

We are the sermons the world is heeding.
Billy Graham

Mass evangelism undoubtedly has its place; parochial missions can make their contribution; a specially gifted evangelist can proclaim his message; the specialist Christian can make his contribution in factory, in politics and in teaching; all these are genuine contributions to the evangelistic activity of the Christian Church: but in the last analysis it is the worshiping community, that part of the body of Christ that worships, lives and proclaims the gospel in all its activities in any given neighborhood, which is the real evangelizing agent used by the Spirit of God.
Bryan Green

There are a lot of Christians who are halfway fellows. They stand in the door, holding on to the Church with one hand while they play with the toys of the world with the other. They are in the doorway and we can't bring sinners in. And, until we get some of God's people right, we cannot hope to get sinners regenerated. Now they always accuse me of carrying around a sledge hammer with which to pound the church members. Yes sir, I do pound them, every time I come down, I knock one of the halfway fellows out of the doorway, and every time I knock one out I get a sinner in.
Mordecai Ham

Unless it shares the apostles' underlying assumptions about evangelism, it is difficult to see how the Church of today can be considered authentically "apostolic."
J. Andrew Kirk

Jesus Christ did not say, "Go into the world and tell the world that it is quite right."
C.S. Lewis

The devil studied the nature of each man, seized upon the traits of his soul, adjusted himself to them and insinuated himself gradually into his victims's confidence – suggesting splendors to the ambitious, gain to the covetous, delight to the sensuous,

and a false appearance of piety to the pious – and a winner of souls ought to act in the same cautious and skillful way.
Ignatius Loyola

The problem is not only to win souls, but to save minds.
Charles Malik

There is no better evangelist in the world than the Holy Spirit.
D.L. Moody

Once, when walking down a certain street in Chicago, D.L. Moody stepped up to a man, a perfect stranger to him, and said, "Sir, are you a Christian?" "You mind your own business," was the reply. Moody replied, "This is my business."

Our Lamb has conquered, let us follow Him.
Motto of Moravian Brotherhood

To call a man evangelical who is not evangelistic is an utter contradiction.
G. Campbell Morgan

The greatest hindrances to the evangelization of the world are those within the Church.
John R. Mott

The greatest mission field we face is not in some faraway land. It's barely across the street. The culture most lost to the gospel is our own – our children and neighbors.
Dwight Ozard

The command to evangelize is a part of God's law. It belongs to God's revealed will for His people. It could not, then, in principle be affected in the slightest degree by anything that we might believe about God's sovereignty in election and calling.
J.I. Packer

The task of the evangelist in communicating the gospel is not to make it easier, so that people will respond positively, but to make it clear. Neither Jesus nor his apostles ever reduced the

demands of the gospel in order to make converts. No cheap grace, but God's kindness which is meant to lead to repentance, provides the only solid basis for discipleship.
Rene Padilla

There is no true evangelization if the name, the teaching, the promises, the life, the death, the resurrection, the kingdom, and the mystery of Jesus Christ the Son of God are not proclaimed.
Pope Paul VI

I exhort you, press on in your course, and exhort all men that they may be saved.
Polycarp

If we spread the gospel, Jesus will spread the salvation.
Juha Räihä

Could a mariner sit idle if he heard the drowning cry?
Could a doctor sit in comfort and just let his patients die?
Could a fireman sit idle, let men burn and give no hand?
Can you sit at ease in Zion with the world around you damned?
Leonard Ravenhill

It will not do for us to go to heaven by ourselves. We must be on fire, friends, for saving others. To be workers will draw heaven down and will draw others to heaven.
Evan Roberts

God is in the people-saving business, and His method is to use His people.
David Siegmann

Christ sent me to preach the gospel and he will look after the results.
Mary Slessor

I'm God's messenger from the gypsy tent. And it's the message that's important, not the messenger.
Gipsy Smith

I would sooner pluck one single brand from the burning than explain all mysteries.
C.H. Spurgeon

It is pure irresponsibility to leave the evangelization of the lost to the "experts," as many are doing today.
Cornelius Stam

Don't judge each day by the harvest you reap, but by the seeds you plant.
Robert Louis Stevenson

Ultimately, evangelism is not a technique. It is the Lord of the Church who reserves to Himself His sovereign right to add to His Church.
John Stott

To evangelize is so to present Jesus Christ in the power of the Holy Spirit, that men shall come to put their trust in God through him, to accept him as their Savior, and serve him as their King in the fellowship of his church.
William Temple

It is certainly no part of religion to compel religion.
Tertullian

If you were an outstandingly gifted evangelist with an international reputation, and if, under God, you could win 1,000 persons for Christ every night of every year, how long would it take you to win the whole world for Christ? Answer, ignoring the population explosion, over 10,000 years. But if you are a true disciple for Christ, and if you are able under God to win just one person to Christ each year; and if you could then train that person to win one other person for Christ each year, how long would it take to win the whole world for Christ? Answer, just 32 years!
David Watson, speaking of James Kennedy's illustration

A charge to keep I have,
A God to glorify;
A never dying soul to save,

And fit it for the sky.
Charles Wesley

You have nothing to do but to save souls;
therefore spend and be spent in this
work.
John Wesley

The uncanny resemblance between
evangelistic campaigns and sales campaigns
undermined my confidence in what the
evangelists said.
John White

It is the temptation of this pragmatic age
to presume that technique is the secret of
evangelism.
A. Skevington Wood

Evangelism is not simply a matter of
bringing individuals to personal faith,
though of course that remains central to
the whole enterprise. It is a matter of
confronting the world with the good, but
deeply disturbing, news of a different way
of living … the way of love.
N.T. Wright

Our method of proclaiming salvation is
this: to point out to every heart the loving
Lamb, who died for us, and although He
was the Son of God, offered Himself for
our sins.
Count Zinzendorf

Evangelism and revival
Revival and evangelism, although closely
linked, are not to be confused. Revival is
an experience in the Church; evangelism is
an expression of the Church.
Paul S. Rees

Evangelist
… do the work of an evangelist …
The Bible, 2 Timothy 4:5

Evangelist: A bearer of good tidings,
particularly (in a religious sense) such as
assure us of our own salvation and the
damnation of our neighbors.
Ambrose Bierce

[Mr Gifford] made it much his business to
deliver the people of God from all those false
and unsound rests that by nature we are
prone to take and make to our souls. He
pressed us to take special heed that we took
not up any truth upon trust – as from this or
that, or any other man or men – but to cry
mightily to God that He would convince us
of the reality thereof, and set us down
therein by his own Spirit in the holy word.
John Bunyan

Evangelization
See: Evangelism

Eve
The mother of all living.
The Bible, Genesis 3:20

Evening
Before returning to sleep, it is wise and
necessary to review the actions and mercies
of the day past, so that you may be
thankful for all the special mercies and
humbled for all your sins.
  This is necessary in order that you might
renew your repentance as well as your
resolve for obedience, and in order that
you may examine yourself to see whether
your soul grew better or worse, whether sin
goes down and grace goes up and whether
you are better prepared for suffering, death
and eternity.
Richard Baxter

Abide with me from morn till eve,
For without Thee I cannot live;
Abide with me when night is nigh,
For without Thee I dare not die.
John Keble

Evil
The Lord saw how great man's wickedness
on the earth had become, and that every
inclination of the thoughts of his heart was
only evil all the time.
The Bible, Genesis 6:5

Do not fret because of evil men or be
envious of those who do wrong; for like
the grass they will soon wither, like green

plants they will soon die away.
The Bible, Psalm 37:1,2

If a man pays back evil for good, evil will never leave his house.
The Bible, Proverbs 17:13

Woe unto them that call evil good, and good evil.
The Bible, Isaiah 5:20 KJV

Be of good cheer; I have overcome the world.
The Bible, John 16:33 KJV

Hate what is evil; cling to what is good.
The Bible, Romans 12:9

Avoid every kind of evil.
The Bible, 1 Thessalonians 5:22

Let no man be called good who mixes good with evil.
Author unknown

For, were it not good that evil things should also exist, the omnipotent God would almost certainly not allow evil to be, since beyond doubt it is just as easy for Him not to allow what He does not will, as for Him to do what He will.
Augustine of Hippo

God judged it better to bring good out of evil than to suffer no evil to exist.
Augustine of Hippo

Sin is not confined to the evil things we do. It is the evil within us, the evil which we are.
Karl Barth

The truth of Christ's supremacy over all the powers in the universe is one which modern man sorely needs to learn ... To be united to Christ by faith is to throw off the thraldom of hostile powers, to enjoy perfect freedom, to gain the mastery over the dominion of evil – because Christ's victory is ours.
F.F. Bruce

Let a man avoid evil deeds as a man who

loves life avoids poison.
Buddha

One that confounds good and evil is an enemy to good.
Edmund Burke

If you cannot hate evil, you cannot love good.
Struthers Burt

There is no permanent place in [this universe] for evil ... Evil may hide behind this fallacy and that, but it will be hunted from fallacy to fallacy until there is no more fallacy for it to hide behind.
Thomas Carlyle

God is the author of the author of sin, but he cannot be the author of sin itself, for sin is the result of a rebellion against God. Can God rebel against himself?
E.J. Carnell

The cross of Christ is God's final answer to the problem of evil because the problem of evil is in the cross itself.
E.J. Carnell

Only if man can do evil is there any meaning to doing good.
Cherbonnier

It is hard for the good to suspect evil as it is hard for the bad to suspect good.
Cicero

They do more harm by their evil example than by their actual sin.
Cicero

We cannot do evil to others without doing it to ourselves.
Joseph Francois Eduard Desmahis

My child, flee from every evil and everything that resembleth it.
Didache

It is a Christian conviction that evil is permitted by a sovereign God in some way

that is ultimately compatible with his goodness.
William Dyrness

Evil is but an illusion, and it has no real basis. Evil is a false belief.
Mary Baker Eddy

The real problem is in the hearts and minds of men. It is not a problem of physics but of ethics. It is easier to denature plutonium than to denature the evil from the spirit of man.
Albert Einstein

Against the dark background of man's failure and sin, the cross shows us the measure of God's passion against evil and the measure of God's passion to redeem his sinful children.
W. H. T. Gairdner

Darkness is not nothing; it is the absence of light. Likewise, sickness is the absence of health, and death is the absence of life which belongs to a being. All these are real lacks. Similarly, evil is just as real, although it has no more being of its own than does darkness or sickness.
Norman L. Geisler

While we do not believe that personal freedom is the ultimate explanation of the origin of evil, we do believe that freedom was the means by which sin did come into the world.
John Gerstner

Man does not rule over evil except when he refuses to do it. When he has truly done evil, he is its servant.
Hildegard of Bingen

Today, I believe that I am acting in accordance with the will of the Almighty Creator: by defending myself against the Jew, I am fighting for the work of the Lord.
Adolf Hitler

If our hearing were sufficiently acute to catch every note of pain, we would be deafened by one continuous scream.
Thomas Huxley

To me, at any rate, the view of evil implied by Marxism, expressed by Shaw and maintained by modern psychotherapy, a view which regards evil as the by-product of circumstances which circumstances can, therefore, alter and even eliminate, has come to seem intolerably shallow.
C.E.M. Joad

No man ever became extremely wicked all at once.
Juvenal

We believe no evil till the evil's done.
La Fontaine

Philosophy triumphs easily over past evils and future evils; but present evils triumph over it.
Francis, Duc de La Rochefoucauld

Goodness is, so to speak, itself: badness is only spoiled goodness. And there must be something good first before it can be spoiled.
C.S. Lewis

Evil is a parasite, not an original thing.
C.S. Lewis

It is men, not God, who have produced racks, whips, prisons, slavery, guns, bayonets, and bombs; it is by human avarice or human stupidity, not by the churlishness of nature, that we have poverty and overwork.
C.S. Lewis

The descent to hell is easy, and those who begin by worshiping power soon worship evil.
C.S. Lewis

The teaching of the New Testament is that the whole time the world has been "lying in the wicked one."
M. Lloyd-Jones

Evil is only good perverted.
Henry Wadsworth Longfellow

Why is it any easier to account for goodness without God than it is to account for evil with him? That the problem of evil generates more fury than the problem of goodness may be more a matter of psychology than philosophy.
Ed. L. Miller

To create only those who "must" (in any sense) choose good is to create automata; and to whisk away evil effects as they are produced is to whisk away evil itself, for an act and its consequences are bound together.
John W. Montgomery

Good had but one enemy, the evil; but the evil has two enemies, the good and itself.
Johannes von Muller

Many have puzzled themselves about the origin of evil. I am content to observe that there is evil, and that there is a way to escape from it, and with this I begin and end.
John Newton

Whoever fights monsters should see to it that in the process he doesn't become a monster.
Frederick Nietzsche

A wayfarer takes shelter under a rock which, loosened by rain, comes tumbling down, killing him. That is natural evil. A wayfarer takes shelter in a little hut, but a wicked robber stabs him to death. That is moral evil.
J. Edwin Orr

Why suppose that if God does have a good reason for permitting evil, the theist would be the first to know? Perhaps God has a good reason, but that reason is too complicated for us to understand.
Alvin Plantinga

Two wrongs do not make a right.
English proverb

Every evil comes to us on wings and goes away limping.
French proverb

Avoid the evil, and it will avoid thee.
Gaelic proverb

One does evil enough when one does nothing good.
German proverb

No man is justified in doing evil on the ground of expedience.
Theodore Roosevelt

Evil often triumphs, but never conquers.
Joseph Roux

It is in our hearts that evil lies, and it is from our hearts that it must be plucked out.
Bertrand Russell

He [Christ] did not stop the crucifixion; He rose from the dead.
Dorothy Sayers

There is no evil that does not promise inducements. Avarice promises money; luxury, a varied assortment of pleasures; ambition, a purple robe and applause. Vices tempt you by the rewards they offer.
Seneca

There is nothing either good or bad, but thinking makes it so.
William Shakespeare, Hamlet

Of two evils choose neither.
C.H. Spurgeon

Often in this present world, the most wicked men are the most prosperous, while the most holy are the most afflicted.
C.H. Spurgeon

Every renewed heart is anxious to be free from even a speck of evil.
C.H. Spurgeon

There is no evil in the atom – only in men's souls.
Adlai Stevenson

The blessed person is not him who simply declines the evil, but he who does what is good.
Symeon the New Theologian

Never do evil for anything in the world, or for the love of any man.
Thomas à Kempis

The Christian has abundant reason to believe in God in the full theistic sense. If, then, he runs into some difficulty, even a difficulty as great as the problem of evil, he does not, for that reason, give up his faith. The reasons for his faith are so great that they can weather a few storms.
David Elton Trueblood

If all evil, whether moral, natural or intellectual, is truly illusory, we are foolish indeed to fight it; it would be far preferable to forget it.
David Elton Trueblood

He who does not punish evil commands it to be done.
Leonardo da Vinci

There is more evil in a drop of sin, than in a sea of affliction.
Thomas Watson

All the miseries and evils which men suffer from – vice, crime, ambition, injustice, oppression, slavery, and war, proceed from their despising or neglecting the precepts contained in the Bible.
Noah Webster

At the heart of the story stands the cross of Christ where evil did its worst and met its match.
John W. Wenham

When choosing between two evils, I always like to try the one I've never tried before.
Mae West

Evil indulged in eventually becomes evil that controls us.
John White

Evil, Fighting

Do not be overcome by evil, but overcome evil with good.
The Bible, Romans 12:21

For our struggle is not against flesh and blood, but against the rulers, against the authorities, against the powers of this dark world and against the spiritual forces of evil in the heavenly realms.
The Bible, Ephesians 6:12

There are a thousand hacking at the branches of evil to one who is striking at the root.
Henry David Thoreau

The problem of evil is one of the most crucial protests raised by unbelievers against the fact of God.
James Orr

Evil constitutes the biggest single argument against the existence of an almighty, loving God.
John W. Wenham

All simplifications of religious dogma are shipwrecked upon the rock of the problem of evil.
A.N. Whitehead

Evolution
See also creation

Intermediate links? Geology assuredly does not reveal any such finely graduated organic change, and this is perhaps the most obvious and serious objection which can be urged against the theory of evolution.
Charles Darwin

The more statistically improbable a thing is, the less we can believe that it just happened by blind chance. Superficially the obvious alternative to chance is an intelligent Designer.
R. Dawkins

To get a cell by chance would require at least one hundred functional proteins to appear simultaneously in one place. That is one hundred simultaneous events each of an independent probability which could hardly be more than 10-20 giving maximum combined probability of 10(-2000.)
Michael Denten

Darwinian Man, though well-behaved,
At best is only a monkey shaved.
W.S. Gilbert

The absence of fossil evidence for intermediary stages between major transitions in organic design, indeed our inability, even in our imagination, to construct functional intermediates in many cases, has been a persistent and nagging problem for gradualistic accounts of evolution.
Stephen Jay Gould, Professor of Geology and Paleontology, Harvard University

The probability of life having originated through random choice is about 10-255. The smallness of this number means that it is virtually impossible that life has originated by a random association of molecules. The proposition that a living structure could have arisen in a single event through random association of molecules must be rejected.
Henry Quastler

It may happen that in a little time the doctrine of evolution will be the standing jest of schoolboys.
C.H. Spurgeon

Scripture reveals religious truths about God, that he created all things by his word, that his creation was "good," and that his creative program culminated in man; science suggests that "evolution" may have been the mode which God employed in creating.
John Stott

Evolution is a bankrupt speculative philosophy, not a scientific fact. Only a spiritually bankrupt society could ever believe it. Only atheists could accept this satanic theory.
Jimmy Swaggart

Evolutionists

It must be significant that nearly all the evolutionary stories I learned as a student … have now been debunked.
Dr. Derek V. Ager, Department of Geology, Imperial College, London

I shall discuss the broad patterns of hominoid evolution, an exercise made enjoyable by the need to integrate diverse kinds of information, and use that as a vehicle to speculate about hominoid origins, an event for which there is no recognized fossil record. Hence, an opportunity to exercise some imagination.
David Pilbeam

One must conclude that, contrary to the established and current wisdom, a scenario describing the genesis of life on earth by chance and natural causes which can be accepted on the basis of fact and not faith has not yet been written.
Dr Hubert P. Yockey

Example
Therefore I urge you to imitate me.
The Bible, 1 Corinthians 4:16

Follow my example, as I follow the example of Christ.
The Bible, 1 Corinthians 11:1

In everything set them an example by doing what is good.
The Bible, Titus 2:7

A pint of example is worth a gallon of advice.
Author unknown

The greatest power for good is the power of example.
Author unknown

A good example is the best sermon.
Author unknown

Example sheds a genial ray which men are apt to borrow, so first improve yourself today, and then your friends tomorrow.
Author unknown

If you are looking for an example of humility, look at the cross.
Thomas Aquinas

Example is the school of mankind, and they will learn at no other.
Edmund Burke

They do more harm by their evil example than by their actual sin.
Cicero

Setting an example is not the main means of influencing others, it is the only means.
Albert Einstein

And as we let our light shine, we unconsciously give other people permission to do the same.
Nelson Mandela

The first great gift we can bestow on others is a good example.
Thomas Morell

It is not fair to ask of others what you are unwilling to do yourself.
Eleanor Roosevelt

We are not only to renounce evil, but to manifest the truth. We tell people the world is vain; let our lives manifest that it is so. We tell them that our home is above and that all these things are transitory. Does our dwelling look like it? O to live consistent lives!
James Hudson Taylor

Let us preach you, Dear Jesus, without preaching ... not by words but by our example ... by the casting force, the sympathetic influence of what we do, the evident fullness of the love our hearts bear to you. Amen.
Mother Teresa

Our models are successful businessmen, celebrated athletes and theatrical personalities.
A. W. Tozer

If doing a good act in public will excite others to do more good, then ... "Let your Light shine to all ..." Miss no opportunity to do good.
John Wesley

Exasperation
Exasperation is the mind's way of spinning its wheels until patience restores traction.
George L. Griggs

Excellence
Every job is a self-portrait of the person who did it. Autograph your work with excellence.
Author unknown

Excellence is best described as doing the right things right – selecting the most important things to be done and then accomplishing them 100 per cent correctly.
Author unknown

Excellence is an art won by training and habituation. We do not act rightly because we have virtue or excellence, but we rather have those because we have acted rightly. We are what we repeatedly do. Excellence, then, is not an act but a habit.
Aristotle

The quality of a person's life is in direct proportion to their commitment to excellence, regardless of their chosen field of endeavor.
Vincent T. Lombardi

Great men are little men expanded; great lives are ordinary lives intensified.
Wilferd A. Peterson

Excess
Too much of a good thing is WONDERFUL.
Mae West

Excommunication

The Church authorities have excommunicated me for heresy, I excommunicate them in the name of the sacred truth of God. Christ will judge whose excommunication will stand.
Martin Luther

Excuses

Whoever wants to be a judge of human nature should study people's excuses.
Hebbel

Excuses are the nails used to build a house of failure.
Don Wilder

Exercise

Too many people confine their exercise to jumping to conclusions, running up bills, stretching the truth, bending over backward, lying down on the job, side stepping responsibility and pushing their luck.
Author unknown

Whenever I feel like exercise I lie down until the feeling passes.
Robert Maynard Hutchins

Exertion

Energy is the power that drives every human being. It is not lost by exertion but maintained by it.
Germaine Greer

Existence of God

The Bible does not argue for the existence of God. It reveals him.
Roy E. Swim

Expansion

To the church "that plans to build a 'more adequate facility'… my advice is don't."
John White

Expectation

We block Christ's advance in our lives by failure of expectation. Of course this is just one form of lack of faith. But it is so purely negative that it escapes detection.
William Temple

Experience

Learn from the mistakes of others. You can't live long enough to make them all yourself.
Author unknown

The trouble with learning from experience is that you never graduate.
Author unknown

A man who views the world the same at fifty as he did at twenty has wasted thirty years of his life.
Muhammad Ali

Too many of us have a Christian vocabulary rather than a Christian experience.
Charles F. Banning

Each problem that I solved became a rule which served afterwards to solve other problems.
Rene Descartes

Experience is not what happens to a man; it is what a man does with what happens to him.
Aldous Huxley

The value of experience is not in seeing much, but in seeing wisely.
Sir William Osler

Nothing is a waste of time if you use the experience wisely.
Rodin

Time is a great teacher.
Carl Sandburg

Experiences of God
See also: Conversion

I am so washed in the tide of His measureless love that I seem to be below the surface of the sea and cannot touch or see or feel anything around me except its water.
Catherine of Genoa

A calm, sweet Abstraction of the Soul from all concerns of this world; and a kind of vision, or fix'd ideas and imaginations, of being alone in the mountains, or some solitary wilderness, far from all mankind; sweetly conversing with Christ, and wrapt and swallowed up in God. The sense I had of divine things would often of a sudden as it were, kindle up a sweet burning in my heart; an ardor of my soul, that I know not how to express.

[At about this time Edwards read 1 Timothy 1:17, "Now to the King eternal, immortal, invisible, the only God, be honor and glory for ever and ever. Amen." After he had read this scripture he had another experience of Christ:]

There came into my soul, and was as it were diffused through it, a sense of the glory of the divine being; a new sense, quite different from anything I had experienced before. From about that time I began to have a new kind of apprehension and idea of Christ, and the work of redemption, and the glorious way of salvation by him.

Jonathan Edwards

In a mournful melancholy state, on July 12, 1739, I [David Brainerd] was attempting to pray; but found no heart to engage in that or any other duty; my former concern, exercise, and religious affections were now gone. I thought that the Spirit of God had quite left me; but still was not distressed; yet disconsolate, as if there was nothing in heaven or earth could make me happy. Having been thus endeavoring to pray – though, as I thought, very stupid and senseless – for near half an hour; then, as I was walking in a thick grove, unspeakable glory seemed to open to the apprehension of my soul. I do not mean any external brightness, nor any imagination of a body of light, but it was a new inward apprehension or view that I had of God, such as I never had before, nor anything which had the least resemblance to it. I had no particular apprehension of any one person in the Trinity, either the Father, the Son, or the Holy Spirit; but it appeared to be Divine glory.

My soul rejoiced with joy unspeakable, to see such a God, such a glorious Divine Being; and I was inwardly pleased and satisfied that he should be God over all for ever and ever. My soul was so captivated and delighted with the excellency of God that I was even swallowed up in him; at least to that degree that I had no thought about my own salvation, and scarce reflected that there was such a creature as myself. I continued in this state of inward joy, peace, and astonishing, till near dark without any abatement; and then began to think and examine what I had seen; and felt sweetly composed in my mind all the evening following. I felt myself in a new world, and everything about me appeared with a different aspect from what it was wont to do.

Jonathan Edwards and S. E. Dwight, Life of Brainerd

Last night was the sweetest night I ever had in my life. I never before, for so long a time together, enjoyed so much of the light and rest and sweetness of heaven in my soul, but without the least agitation of body during the whole time. Part of the night I lay awake, sometimes asleep, and sometimes between sleeping and waking. But all night I continued in a constant, clear, and lively sense of the heavenly sweetness of Christ's excellent love, of his nearness to me, and of my dearness to him; with an inexpressibly sweet calmness of soul in an entire rest in him. I seemed to myself to perceive a glow of divine love come down from the heart of Christ in heaven into my heart in a constant stream, like a stream or pencil of sweet light. At the same time my heart and soul all flowed out in love to Christ, so that there seemed to be a constant flowing and reflowing of heavenly love, and I appeared to myself to float or swim, in these bright, sweet beams, like the motes swimming in the beams of the sun, or the streams of his light which come in at the window. I think that what I felt each minute was worth more than all the outward comfort and pleasure which I had enjoyed in my whole life put together. It was pleasure, without the least sting, or any interruption. It was a sweetness, which my soul was lost in; it seemed to be all that my feeble frame could sustain. There was but little difference, the sweetness was greatest while I was asleep. As I awoke early the next morning, it seemed to me that I had no more to do with any outward interest of my own than with that of a person whom I never saw. The glory of God seemed to swallow up every wish and desire of my heart.

And it seemed to me that I found a perfect willingness, quietness, and alacrity of soul in consenting that it should be so, if it were most for the glory of God, so that there was no hesitation, doubt, or darkness in my mind. The glory of God seemed to overcome me and swallow me up, and every conceivable suffering, and everything that was terrible to my nature, seemed to shrink to nothing before it. This resignation continued in its clearness and brightness the rest of the night, and all the next day and the night following, and on Monday in the forenoon, without interruption or abatement.
Mrs Edwards (Jonathan Edwards' wife)

This God that hath kept me ever since I was born, ever since I came out of your womb, my most dear mother, will preserve me to the end, I know, and give me grace that I shall live in his faith and die in his fear and favor, and rest in his peace, and rise in his power and reign in his glory.
Nicholas Ferrar

My greatest desire is that I may perceive the God whom I find everywhere in the external world, in like manner also within and inside myself.
Johannes Kepler

My experience of God is of being transcendent and immanent all at once.
Sister Madonna Kolbenschlag

I make it my business only to persevere in His holy presence, wherein I keep myself by a simple attention, and a general fond regard to God, which I may call an actual presence of God; or, to speak better, an habitual, silent, and secret conversation of the soul with God, which often causes me joys and raptures inwardly, and sometimes also outwardly, so great that I am forced to use means to moderate them and prevent their appearance to others.
Brother Lawrence

As we begin to focus upon God the things of the spirit will take shape before our inner eyes. Obedience to the word of Christ will bring an inward revelation of the Godhead (John 14:21-23). It will give acute perception enabling us to see God even as is promised to the pure in heart. A new God-consciousness will seize upon us and we shall begin to taste and hear and inwardly feel the God who is our life and our all. There will be seen the constant shining of the light that lighteth every man that cometh into the world. (John 1:9)
A. W. Tozer

Expert

Consult a real expert – call your mother!
Author unknown

An expert is a man who has made all the mistakes which can be made, in a narrow field.
Niels Bohr

An expert is one who knows more and more about less and less.
Nicholas Murray Butler

Expression

Of all the things you wear, your expression is the most important.
Author unknown

F

Facts
See also: Feelings
It is a capital mistake to theorize before one has data. Insensibly one begins to twist facts to suit theories instead of theories to suit facts.
Sir Arthur Conan Doyle, Sherlock Holmes to Dr Watson

Facts are stubborn things.
Ebenezeer Elliott

Faith does not feed on thin air but on facts.
Os Guinness

People don't ask for facts in making up their minds. They would rather have one good soul-satisfying emotion than a dozen facts.
Robert Keith Leavitt

Comment is free but facts are sacred.
C.P. Scott

Failure
See also: Denial; God's will; Persistence
Sometimes a noble failure serves the world as faithfully as a distinguished success.
Author unknown

A man can fail many times, but he isn't a failure until he begins to blame others.
Author unknown

The sin is not falling down, but staying down.
Author unknown

Excuses are the nails used to build a house of failure.
Author unknown

It is nobler to try something and fail than to try nothing and succeed. The result may be the same, but you won't be. We always grow more through defeats than victories.
Author unknown

Failure is more frequently from want of energy than want of capital.
Author unknown

Failure doesn't mean that you are a failure;
it *does* mean you haven't yet succeeded.
Failure doesn't mean that you have accomplished nothing;
it *does* mean you have learned something.
Failure doesn't mean that you have been a fool;
it *does* mean you have a lot of faith.
Failure doesn't mean that you have been disgraced;
it *does* mean you were willing to try.
Failure doesn't mean you don't have it;
it *does* mean you have to do something in a different way.
Failure doesn't mean you are inferior;
it *does* mean you are not perfect.
Failure doesn't mean you've wasted your life;
it *does* mean you have a reason to start afresh.
Failure doesn't mean you should give up;
it *does* mean you must try harder.
Failure doesn't mean you will never make it;
it *does* mean it will take a little longer.
Failure doesn't mean God has abandoned you;
it *does* mean God has a better way.
Author unknown

Most failures are caused by not realizing the power of momentum – getting started.
Author unknown

Failure is the line of least persistence.
Author unknown

Life's real failure is when you do not realize

how close you were to success when you gave up.
Author unknown

Past failures are guideposts to future successes.
Author unknown

Nothing is ever a complete failure; it can always serve as a bad example.
Author unknown

No one ever fails. They just quit trying. Many of our greatest men tried and failed so often they decided to quit – but tried once more – and won.
Author unknown

The last time you failed, did you stop trying because you failed – or did you fail because you stopped trying?
Author unknown

If you don't fail now and again, it's a sign you're playing it safe.
Woody Allen

Keep in mind that neither success nor failure is ever final.
Roger Babson

Men's best successes come after their disappointments.
Henry Ward Beecher

In great attempts it is glorious even to fail.
Cassius

The only people who never fail are those who never try.
Ilka Chase

You don't drown by falling in the water; you drown by staying there.
Edwin Louis Cole

I don't know the key to success, but the key to failure is trying to please everybody.
Bill Cosby

When you subsidize poverty and failure, you get more of both.
James Dale Davidson

Show me a thoroughly satisfied man, and I will show you a failure.
Thomas A. Edison

Never confuse a single defeat with a final defeat.
F. Scott Fitzgerald

Failure is the opportunity to begin again more intelligently.
Henry Ford

I haven't failed, I've found 10,000 ways that don't work.
Benjamin Franklin

He's no failure. He's not dead yet.
William Lloyd George

A failure is a man who has blundered but is not able to cash in the experience.
Elbert Hubbard

There is no failure except in no longer trying.
Elbert Hubbard

Success has many fathers, but failure is an orphan; no one wants to claim it.
John F. Kennedy

Only those who dare to fail greatly can ever achieve greatly.
Robert F. Kennedy

The probability that we may fail in the struggle ought not to deter us from the support of a cause we believe to be just.
Abraham Lincoln

There are some defeats more triumphant than victories.
Montaigne

Absorb the principle that failure is never final, so if you do not succeed the first time, keep on trying.
Daisy Osborn

I don't measure a man's success by how high he climbs but how high he bounces when he hits bottom.
General Patton

If you have made mistakes ... there is always another chance for you ... you may have a fresh start any moment you chose, for this thing we call "failure" is not the falling down, but the staying down.
Mary Pickford

Learn by failure.
Proverb

Fall seven times, stand up eight.
Japanese proverb

We pay just as dearly for our triumphs as we do for our defeats. Go ahead and fail. But fail with wit, fail with grace, fail with style. A mediocre failure is as insufferable as a mediocre success. Embrace failure! Seek it out. Learn to love it. That may be the only way any of us will ever be free.
Tom Robbins

I have no use for men who fail. The cause of their failure is no business of mine, but I want successful men as my associates.
John D. Rockefeller

It is not the critic who counts; not the man who points out how the strong man stumbles, or where the doer of deeds could have done them better. The credit belongs to the man who is actually in the arena, whose face is marred by dust and sweat and blood; who strives valiantly; who errs, and comes short again and again, because there is no effort without error and shortcoming; but who does actually strive to do the deeds; who knows the great enthusiasms, the great devotions; who spends himself in a worthy cause; who at the best knows in the end the triumph of high achievement, and who at the worst, if he fails, at least fails while daring greatly, so that his place shall never be with those cold and timid souls who know neither victory nor defeat.
Theodore Roosevelt

It is hard to fail, but it is worse never to have tried to succeed.
Theodore Roosevelt

Failures are divided into two classes – those who thought and never did, and those who did and never thought.
John Charles Salak

Failure, Spiritual
... for though a righteous man falls seven times, he rises again ...
The Bible, Proverbs 24:16

Do not make light of your habitual failures, but confess them and daily strive against them, taking care not to aggravate them by unrepentance and contempt.
Richard Baxter

We are told by all spiritual writers that one important point to bear in mind, as we seek to attain humility, is not to be surprised by our own faults and failures.
François Fénelon

There is a deep peace that grows out of illness and loneliness and a sense of failure. God cannot get close when everything is delightful. He seems to need these darker hours, these empty-hearted hours, to mean the most to people.
Frank C. Laubach

When you fail do not let Satan tempt you to discouragement, but come and cast yourself on Christ. Faith and repentance are not one-time acts; you must live your life believing and repenting.
Richard Sibbes

Faith
See also: Assurance; Belief; Confession of faith; Faith, Definitions of: Doubt; Impossible; Maturity
If you do not stand firm in your faith, you will not stand at all.
The Bible, Isaiah 7:9

... the righteous will live by his faith ...
The Bible, Habakkuk 2:4

"For nothing is impossible with God."
The Bible, Luke 1:37

... stand firm in the faith ...
The Bible, 1 Corinthians 16:13

We live by faith, not by sight.
The Bible, 2 Corinthians 5:7

... not everyone has faith.
The Bible, 2 Thessalonians 3:2

Fight the good fight of faith.
The Bible, 1 Timothy 6:12

And without faith it is impossible to please God, because anyone who comes to him must believe that he exists and that he rewards those who earnestly seek him.
The Bible, Hebrews 11:6

Faith does not ask for any other evidence than for the written Word of God.
Author unknown

It is never a question with any of us of faith or no faith; the question is always in what or whom do we put our faith.
Author unknown

Faith isn't faith until it's all you're holding on to.
Author unknown

All I have seen teaches me to trust the Creator for all that I have not seen.
Author unknown

Pure and simple, faith not lived every day is not faith, it is façade.
Author unknown

Amid trials hard, temptations strong, and troubles constant, true faith is persevering faith.
Author unknown

Every tomorrow has two handles. We can take hold of it by the handle of anxiety, or by the handle of faith.
Author unknown

I seek not for a faith that will move a mountain, but for faith that will some how move me.
Author unknown

Naked faith is no faith.
Thomas Adams

Faith is kept alive in us, and gathers strength, more from practice than from speculations.
Joseph Addison

It's lack of faith that makes people afraid of meeting challenges, and I believed in myself.
Muhammad Ali

Faith is a foretaste of the knowledge that will make us blessed in this life to come.
Thomas Aquinas

Faith acquires what the Law requires; nay, the Law requires, in order that faith may acquire what is thus required; nay, more, God demands of us faith itself, and finds not what he thus demands, until by giving he makes it possible to find it.
Augustine of Hippo

God orders what we cannot do, that we may know what we ought to ask of him.
Augustine of Hippo

Trust the past to God's mercy, the present to God's love and the future to God's providence.
Augustine of Hippo

There is no love without hope,
no hope without love,
and neither hope nor love without faith.
Augustine of Hippo

Faith is never identical with piety.
Karl Barth

We are not to look for manifestations of divine power to make natural faith easier.
Richard M. Benson

The fruit of our faith is the fulfilment of our hope.
Diane Benze

Faith knows nothing of external guarantees. – that is, of course, faith as an original experience of the life of the Spirit. It is only in the secondary esoteric sphere of the religious life that we find guarantees and a general attempt to compel faith. To demand guarantees and proofs of faith is to fail to understand its very nature by denying the free, heroic act which it inspires. In really authentic and original religious experience, to the existence of which the history of the human spirit bears abundant witness, faith springs up without the aid of guarantees and compelling proofs, without any external coercion or the use of authority.
Nicholas Berdyeev

Live by faith until you have faith.
Josh Billings

I see heaven's glories shine and faith shines equal.
Emily Brontë

He who lives up to a little faith shall have more faith.
Thomas Brooks

The only sufficient ground of faith is the authority of God Himself as he addresses me in His Word.
Emil Brunner

Strike from mankind the principles of faith, and man would have no more history than a flock of sheep.
John Bulwer

There is no other method of living piously and justly, than that of depending upon God.
John Calvin

When we have an atom of faith in our hearts, we can see God's face, gentle, serene and approving.
John Calvin

To us also, through every star, through every blade of grass, is not God made visible if we will open our minds and our eyes.
Thomas Carlyle

Man is what he believes.
Anton Chekhov

God has made for us two kinds of eyes: those of flesh and those of faith.
John Chrysostom

You honor Jesus when you act in faith on His word.
Ed Cole

We begin to think of our faith as a sparkling magic wand: we wave it, and presto, our problems are gone in a puff of smoke. But this is, bluntly put, heresy. It not only makes Christians incredibly naive in approaching complex problems, but it can shatter the fragile faith of the believer who expects the magic wand to work every time.
Charles Colson

Prayer does not cause faith to work, faith causes prayer to work.
Gloria Copeland

Faith needs her daily bread.
Dinah M Craik

To my Creator I resign myself, humbly confiding in His goodness and in His mercy through Jesus Christ for the events of eternity.
John Dickinson, Signer of The Constitution Faith

The disease with which the human mind now labors is want of faith.
Ralph Waldo Emerson

All I have seen teaches me to trust the Creator for all I have not seen.
Ralph Waldo Emerson

Our faith comes in moments. Yet there is a depth in those brief moments which

constrains us to ascribe more reality to them than to all other experiences.
Ralph Waldo Emerson

Believe that you have it [faith], and you have it.
Desiderius Erasmus

It is faith among men that holds the moral elements of society together, as it is faith in God that binds the world to his throne.
William Maxwell Evarts

Speculations I have none. I'm resting on certainties. "For I know whom I have believed, and am persuaded that he is able to keep that which I have committed unto him against that day." 2 Timothy 1:12 (KJV)
Michael Faraday

It is because of faith that we exchange the present for the future.
Fidelis of Sigmaringen

It is well to get rid of the idea that faith is a matter of spiritual heroism only for a few select spirits. It is a matter of spiritual manhood. It is a matter of maturity.
P.F. Forsyth

It is cynicism and fear that freeze life; it is faith that thaws it out, releases it, sets it free.
Harry Emerson Fosdick

The man of faith may face death as Columbus faced his first voyage from the shores of Spain. What lies beyond the sea he cannot tell; all his special expectation may be mistaken, but his insight into the clear meaning of present facts may persuade him beyond the doubt that the sea has another shore.
Harry Emerson Fosdick

Faith fills a man with love for the beauty of its truth, with faith in the truth of its beauty.
Francis de Sales

Faith is like breath in an infant's lungs. Breath is not the cause of life; but where there is no breath, there is no life. Even so, faith is not the cause of life, but where there is no faith, there is no spiritual life.
John Gill

Faith is blind – except upward. It is blind to impossibilities, and deaf to doubt. It listens only to God and sees only his power and acts accordingly.
S.D. Gordon

Sometimes people use the word faith to mean pretend, like saying, "I'm set free by faith," and then pretending you're free when you're not. That isn't faith. That's a sad joke.
Keith Green

Four levels must be built consciously or unconsciously into a healthy faith.
1. Being aware of one's dilemma without God
2. Being aware that if Christianity is true it provides the necessary answer to this dilemma
3. Being aware that Christianity is indeed true
4. Being prepared to choose Christianity and commit oneself to the consequences of that choice.
Os Guinness

One can believe in God with a very complete set of arguments, yet not have any faith that makes a difference in living.
Georgia Harkness

It's fundamental to my belief in God that he or she discloses him- or herself to all people in all cultures at all times, because all human beings are capable of having an apprehension of God.
Richard Harries

Christian faith is a grand cathedral, with divinely pictured windows. Standing without, you can see no glory, nor can imagine any, but standing within, every ray of light reveals a harmony of unspeakable splendors.
Nathaniel Hawthorne

Say to yourself, "I am loved by God more than I can either conceive or understand." Let this fill all your soul and never leave you. You will see that this is the way to find God.
Henri de Tourville

We are too apt to rest in a bare profession of faith, and to think that this will save us; it is a cheap and easy religion to say, "We believe the articles of the Christian faith;" but it is a great delusion to imagine that this is enough to bring us to heaven.
Matthew Henry

When I cannot enjoy the faith of assurance, I live by the faith of adherence.
Matthew Henry

We need humble faith.
History of Tablets

The ultimate ground of faith and knowledge is confidence in God.
Charles Hodge

If you accept that Jesus is the revelation and manifestation of the Father, then you are a follower of Christ and so a Christian.
Basil Hume

Christianity has stayed faithful, with no pope – who is only a man, because it has Jesus Christ at its head. Christ is its guide. The life of grace is its heartbeat, from which flow the seven gifts of the Holy Spirit. It is to Christ, wretched though I am, that I flee, in the sure hope that he will guide me with his life and help. I trust that he will deliver me from my sins and from my existing wretched life and will give me the reward of infinite joy.
John Huss, Letter from prison to two of his friends

Our faith was also prefigured in Abraham, and that he was the patriarch of our faith, and, as it were, the prophet of it, the apostle very fully taught, when he says in the epistle to the galatians: "Even as Abraham believed God, and it was accounted unto him for righteousness. Know ye therefore, that they which are of faith, the same are the children of Abraham." [Abraham's] faith and ours are one and the same.
Irenaeus

It is wrong always, everywhere, and for everyone, to believe anything upon insufficient evidence.
William James

All things are inconstant except the faith in the soul, which changes all things and fills their inconstancy with light, but though I seem to be driven out of my country as a misbeliever I have found no man yet with a faith like mine.
James Joyce

O man, believe in God with all your might, for hope rests on faith, love on hope, and victory on love.
Julian of Norwich

Our life is grounded in faith, with hope and love besides.
Julian of Norwich

God does not keep an extra supply of goodness that is higher than faith, and there is no help at all in anything that is below it. *Within* faith is where the Lord wants us to stay.
Julian of Norwich

O Lord, how happy should we be,
If we could cast our care on Thee,
If we from self could rest;
And feel at heart that One above
In perfect wisdom, perfect love,
Is working for the best.
How far from this our daily life
How oft disturb'd by anxious strife,
By sudden wild alarms;
Oh, could we but relinquish all
Our earthly props, and simply fall
On Thine Almighty arms!
John Keble.

If the blind put their hand in God's, they find their way more surely than those who see but have not faith or purpose.
Helen Keller

A simple, childlike faith in a Divine Friend solves all the problems that come to us by land or sea.
Helen Keller

Faith is the highest passion in a human being. Many in every generation may not come that far, but none comes further.
Søren Kierkegaard

Take the first step in faith. You don't have to see the whole staircase, just take the first step.
Martin Luther King, Jr

I do not want merely to possess a faith, I want a faith that possesses me.
Charles Kingsley

The history of modern epistemology from Descartes, Hume, and Kant to Popper and Lorenz has – it seems to me – made clear that the fact of any reality at all independent of our consciousness can be accepted only in an act of trust.
Hans Küng

Sight, or objective proof, is not the proper ground of faith.
Geoffrey W.H. Lampe

Never, never pin your whole faith on any human being: not if he is the best and wisest in the whole world. There are lots of nice things you can do with sand; but do not try building a house on it.
C.S. Lewis

With most people unbelief in one thing is founded upon blind belief in another.
G.C. Lichtenberg

Let us have faith that right makes might; and in that faith let us to the end dare to do our duty as we understand it.
Abraham Lincoln

All the works mentioned throughout the Bible are written up as works of faith.
Martin Luther

One article, the only solid rock, rules in my heart, namely faith in Christ; out of which, and to which all my theological opinions ebb and flow, day and night.
Martin Luther

Faith is from God, not from man. Man can do nothing to earn or receive it. We are right with God by faith alone.
Martin Luther

Ask a Christian by what work he is made worthy of the name of Christian and he can give no answer but hearing the word of God, which is faith. So the ears alone are the organs of a Christian man, because he is justified and judged as a Christian not by the works of any other part but by faith.
Martin Luther

Faith unites the soul with Christ as a bride is united with her bridegroom. Everything that they have is held in common, whether good or evil. So the believer can boast of and glory in whatever Christ possesses, as though it were his or her own; and whatever the believer has, Christ claims as his own. Christ is full of grace, life and salvation. The human soul is full of sins, death and damnation. Now let faith come between them. Sins, death and damnation will be Christ's. And grace, life and salvation will be the believer's.
Martin Luther

If God promises something, then faith must fight a long and bitter fight, for reason or the flesh judges that God's promises are impossible. Therefore faith must battle against reason and its doubts.
Martin Luther

Faith is a living, busy, active, powerful thing; it is impossible for it not to do us good continually.
Martin Luther

Ask God to work faith in you, or you will remain forever without faith, no matter what you wish, say or can do.
Martin Luther

Faith cannot be inherited or gained by being baptized into a Church. Faith is a matter between the individual and God.
Martin Luther

Faith is God's work in us, that changes us and gives new birth from God.
Martin Luther

Regret looks back.
Worry looks around.
Faith looks up.
John Mason

We can never have more of true faith than we have of true humility.
Andrew Murray

Let us step into the darkness and reach out for the hand of God. The path of faith and darkness is so much safer than the one we would choose by sight.
George Macdonald

This is a sane, wholesome, practical working faith: That it is a man's business to do the will of God; second, that God himself takes on the care of that man; and third, that therefore that man ought never to be afraid of anything.
George MacDonald

The source and foundation of goodness and nobility of character is faith in Jesus the Lord.
Alexander Maclaren

Removing all risks from your life renders faith unnecessary. Faith requires risks!
Ken Mahaynes

My faith is the grand drama of my life. I'm a believer, so I sing words of God to those who have no faith. I give bird songs to those who dwell in cities and have never heard them, make rhythms for those who know only military marches or jazz, and paint colors for those who see none.
Olivier Messiaen

Faith takes God without any ifs. If God says anything, faith says, "I believe it;" faith says, "Amen" to it.
D.L. Moody

I prayed for faith and thought it would strike me like a bolt of lightning, but faith did not come. One day I read, "Now faith comes by hearing and hearing by the word of God." I had closed my Bible and prayed for faith. I now began to study my Bible and faith has been growing ever since.
D.L. Moody

The only way to learn strong faith is to endure great trials. I have learned my faith by standing firm amid severe testings.
George Müller

Faith expects from God what is beyond all expectation.
Andrew Murray

All the scholastic scaffolding falls, as a ruined edifice, before one single word – faith.
Napoleon Bonaparte

Faith does not force obedience, though it increases responsibility; it heightens guilt, but it does not prevent sin.
John Henry Newman

Faith makes it possible, not easy.
Sally Nguyen

Nothing true or beautiful or good makes complete sense in any immediate context of history; therefore we must be saved by faith.
Reinhold Niebuhr

A living faith is not something you have to carry, but something that carries you.
J.H. Oldham

Men love to trust God (as they profess) for what they have in their hands, in possession, or what lies in an easy view; place their desires afar off, carry their accomplishment behind the clouds out of their sight, interpose difficulties and perplexities – their hearts are instantly sick. They cannot wait for God; they do not trust Him, nor ever did. Would you have the presence of God with you? Learn to wait quietly for the salvation you expect from Him.
John Owen

No man shall ever behold the glory of Christ by sight hereafter, who does not in some measure behold it by faith here in this world.
John Owen

Console yourself, you would not seek me if you had not already found me.
Blaise Pascal

The God of the infinite is the God of the infinitesimal.
Blaise Pascal

That which you confess today, you will perceive tomorrow.
Coventry Patmore

Weave in faith and God will find the thread.
Proverb

A person consists of his faith. Whatever is his faith, even so is he.
Indian proverb

Do not worry or fret that God has given more faith to others than He has given to you. Rest assured in the fact that God has imparted enough faith to you to make sure you are covered from head to toe!
Rick Renner

The errors of faith are better than the best thoughts of unbelief.
Thomas Russell

In actual life every great enterprise begins with and takes its first forward step in faith.
August Wilhelm von Schlegel

We have not lost faith, but we have transferred it from God to the medical profession.
George Bernard Shaw

One of the most essential qualities of a faith that is to attempt great things for God and expect great things from God, is holy audacity.
A.B. Simpson

The issue of faith is not so much whether we believe in God, but whether we believe the God we believe in.
R.C. Sproul

It is not faith in Christ that saves you (though faith is the instrument) — it is Christ's blood and merits.
C.H. Spurgeon

Faith goes up the stairs that love has made and looks out the window which hope has opened.
C.H. Spurgeon

Little faith is always lame.
C.H. Spurgeon

Faith gives to men on earth the protection of the God of heaven.
C.H. Spurgeon

As well could you expect a plant to grow without air and water as to expect your heart to grow without prayer and faith.
C.H. Spurgeon

The secret behind getting more faith, is to get to know God more.
Lester Sumrall

When you get to the end of all the light you know and it's time to step into the darkness of the unknown, faith is knowing that one of two things shall

happen: either you will be given something solid to stand on, or you will be taught how to fly.
Edward Teller

Strong Son of God, immortal Love, whom we, that have not seen thy face, by faith, and faith alone, embrace, believing where we cannot prove.
Alfred Tennyson

It's not dying for faith that's so hard, but living up to it.
William Makepeace Thackery

Faith is required of you, and a sincere life, not a lofty intellect nor a delving into the mysteries of God.
Thomas à Kempis

The words which express our faith and piety are not definite; yet they are significant and fragrant like frankincense to superior natures.
Henry David Thoreau

The smallest seed of faith is better than the largest fruit of happiness.
Henry David Thoreau

True faith rests upon the character of God and asks no further proof than the moral perfections of the One who cannot lie. It is enough that God has said it.
A. W. Tozer

Faith never means gullibility. Credulity never honors God.
A. W. Tozer

I learned really to practice mustard seed faith, and positive thinking, and remarkable things happened.
Sir John Walton

God does not choose us for faith but to faith.
Thomas Watson

Immediately it stuck into my mind, "Leave off preaching. How can you preach to others, who have not faith yourself?" I asked Boehler, whether he thought I should leave it off or not. He answered, "By no means." I asked, "But what can I preach?" He said, "Preach faith till you have it; and then, because you have it, you will preach faith."
John Wesley

By faith we are convinced that fellowship is possible with our fellow man and with God.
B. F. Westcott

It was a Person that God gave, it is a Person that we need, and it is a Person that we accept by faith.
Walter Lewis Wilson

Faith

The Westminster Confession
Part Four: The Evidences of True Faith
A. The Evidences of True Faith, Part (1 of 4)
For evidencing of true faith by fruits, these four things are requisite:

1) That the believer be soundly convinced, in his judgment, of his obligation to keep the whole moral law, all the days of his life; and that not the less, but so much the more, as he is delivered by Christ from the covenant of works, and curse of the law.

2) That he endeavor to grow in the exercise and daily practice of godliness and righteousness.

3) That the course of his new obedience run in the right channel, that is through faith in Christ, and through a good conscience, to all the duties of love towards God and man.

4) That he keep strait communion with the fountain Christ Jesus, from whom grace must run along, for furnishing of good fruits.
For the first, that is, to convince the believer, in his judgment, of his obligation

to keep the moral law, among many passages:

"Let your light so shine before men, that they may see your good works, and glorify your Father which is in heaven. Think not that I am come to destroy the law, or the prophets: I am not come to destroy, but to fulfil. For verily I say unto you, Till heaven and earth pass, one jot or one tittle shall in no wise pass from the law, till all be fulfilled. Whosoever therefore shall break one of these least commandments, and shall teach men so, he shall be called the least in the kingdom of heaven: but whosoever shall do and teach [them], the same shall be called great in the kingdom of heaven. For I say unto you, That except your righteousness shall exceed [the righteousness] of the scribes and Pharisees, ye shall in no case enter into the kingdom of heaven." Matthew 5.16-20

Wherein our Lord,

1. Gives commandment to believers, justified by faith, to give evidence of the grace of God in them before men, by doing good works: "Let your light so shine before men that they may see your good works."

2. He induces them so to do, by showing, that albeit they be not justified by works, yet spectators of their good works may be converted or edified; and so glory may redound to God by their good works, when its witnesses "shall glorify your Father which is in heaven."

3. He gives them no other rule for their new obedience than the moral law, set down and explicated by Moses and the prophets: "Think not that I am come to destroy the law or the prophets."

4. He gives them to understand, that the doctrine of grace, and freedom from the curse of the law by faith in him, is readily mistaken by men's corrupt judgments, as if it did loose or slacken the obligation of believers to obey the commands, and to be subject to the authority of the law; and that this error is indeed a destroying of the law and of the prophets, which he will in no case ever endure in any of his disciples, it is so contrary to the end of his coming, which is first to sanctify, and then to save believers: "Think not that I am come to destroy the law or the prophets."

5. He teaches, that the end of the gospel and covenant of grace is to procure men's obedience to the moral law: "I am come to fulfil the law and the prophets."

6. That the obligation of the moral law, in all points, to all holy duties, is perpetual, and shall stand to the world's end, that is, "till heaven and earth pass away."

7. That as God has had a care of the Scripture from the beginning, so shall he have a care of them still to the world's end, that there shall not one jot or one tittle of its substance be taken away; so says the text, verse 18.

8. That as the breaking of the moral law, and defending its transgressions to be no sin, does exclude men both from heaven, and justly also from the fellowship of the true church; so the obedience of the law, and teaching others to do the same, by example, counsel, and doctrine, according to every man's calling, proves a man to be a true believer, and in great estimation with God, and worthy to be much esteemed of by the true church, verse 19.

9. That the righteousness of every true Christian must be more than the righteousness of the scribes and Pharisees; for the scribes and Pharisees, albeit they took great pains to discharge various duties of the law, yet they cut short its exposition, that it might the less condemn their practice; they studied the outward part of the duty, but neglected the inward and spiritual part; they discharged some lesser duties carefully, but neglected judgment, mercy, and the love of God: in a word, they went about to establish their own righteousness, and rejected the righteousness of God by faith in Jesus. But a true Christian must

have more than all this; he must acknowledge the full extent of the spiritual meaning of the law, and have a respect to all the commandments, and labor to cleanse himself from all filthiness of flesh and spirit, and "not lay weight upon what service he has done, or shall do," but clothe himself with the imputed righteousness of Christ, which only can hide his nakedness, or else he cannot be saved; so says the text, "Except your righteousness ..."

B. The Evidences of True Faith, Part (2 of 4)
The second thing requisite to evidence of true faith is, that the believer endeavor to put the rules of godliness and righteousness in practice, and to grow in its daily exercise; as held forth:
"And beside this, giving all diligence, add to your faith virtue; and to virtue knowledge, and to knowledge temperance; and to temperance patience; and to patience godliness; and to godliness brotherly kindness; and to brotherly kindness charity. For if these things be in you, and abound, they make [you that ye shall] neither [be] barren nor unfruitful in the knowledge of our Lord Jesus Christ." 2 Pe. 1:5-8 Wherein,

1. The apostle teaches believers, for evidencing of precious faith in themselves, to endeavor to add to their faith seven other sister graces.

1a) The first is Virtue, or the active exercise and practice of all moral duties, that so faith is not idle, but puts forth itself in work.

1b) The second is Knowledge, which serves to furnish faith with information of the truth to be believed, and to furnish virtue with direction what duties are to be done, and how to go about them prudently.

1c) The third is Temperance, which serves to moderate the use of all pleasant things, that a man be not clogged therewith, nor made unfit for any duty to which he is called.

1d) The fourth is Patience, which serves to moderate a man's affections, when he meets with any difficulty or unpleasant thing; that he neither weary for pains required in well-doing, nor faint when the Lord chastises him, nor murmur when he crosses him.

1e) The fifth is Godliness, which may keep him up in all the exercises of religion, inward and outward; whereby he may be furnished from God for all other duties which he has to do.

1f) The sixth is Brotherly-kindness, which keeps estimation of, and affection to, all the household of faith, and to the image of God in every one where ever it is seen.

1g) The seventh is Love, which keeps the heart in readiness to do good to all men, whatever they be, upon all occasions which God shall offer.

2. Albeit it be true, that this is much corruption and infirmity in the godly; yet the apostle will have men mightily endeavoring, and doing their best, as they are able, to join all these graces one to another, and to grow in the measure of exercising them: "Giving all diligence, add to your faith ..."

3. He assures all professed believers, that as they shall profit in the obedience of this direction, so they shall profitably prove the soundness of their own faith; and if they not have these graces, that they shall be found blind deceivers of themselves, verse 9.

C. The Evidences of True Faith, Part (3 of 4)
The third thing requisite to evidence true faith is, that obedience to the law run in the right channel, that is, through faith in Christ, etc. as held forth:
"Now the end of the commandment is charity out of a pure heart, and [of] a good conscience, and [of] faith unfeigned:" 1 Ti. 1:5 Wherein the apostle teaches these seven doctrines:

1. That the obedience of the law must flow from love, and love from a pure heart, and a pure heart from a good conscience, and a good conscience from faith unfeigned: this he makes the only right channel of good works: "The end of the law is love …"

2. That the end of law is not, that men may be justified by their obedience of it, as the Jewish doctors did falsely teach; for it is impossible that sinners can be justified by the law, who, for every transgression, are condemned by the law: "For the end of the law is (not such as the Jewish doctors taught, but) love, out of a pure heart …"

3. That the true end of the law, preached to the people, is, that they, by the law, being made to see their deserved condemnation, should flee to Christ unfeignedly, to be justified by faith in him; so says the text, while it makes love to flow through faith in Christ.

4. That no man can set himself in love to obey the law, excepting as far as his conscience is quieted by faith, or is seeking to be quieted in Christ; for "the end of the law is love, out of good conscience, and faith unfeigned."

5. That feigned faith goes to Christ without reckoning with the law, and so wants an errand; but unfeigned faith reckons with the law, and is forced to flee for refuge to Christ, as the end of the law for righteousness, so often as it finds itself guilty for breaking of the law: "For the end of the law is faith unfeigned."

6. That the fruits of love may come forth in act particularly, it is necessary that the heart be brought to the hatred of all sin and uncleanness, and to a steadfast purpose to follow all holiness universally: "For the end of the law is love, out of a pure heart."

7. That unfeigned faith is able to make the conscience good, and the heart pure, and the man lovingly obedient to the law; for when Christ's blood is seen by faith to quiet justice, then the conscience becomes quiet also, and will not suffer the heart to entertain the love of sin, but set the man on work to fear God for his mercy, and to obey all his commandments, out of love to God, for his free gift of justification, by grace bestowed on him: "For this is the end of the law indeed," whereby it obtains of a man more obedience than any other way.

D. The Evidences of True Faith, Part (4 of 4)
The fourth thing requisite to evidence true faith is, the "keeping strait communion with Christ," the fountain of all graces, and of all good works; as held forth:
"I am the vine, ye [are] the branches: He that abideth in me, and I in him, the same bringeth forth much fruit: for without me ye can do nothing." John 15:5

Wherein Christ, in a similitude from a vine-tree, teaches us,
1. That by nature we are wild barren briers, till we be changed by coming to Christ; and that Christ is that noble vine-tree, having all life and sap of grace in himself, and able to change the nature of every one that comes to him, and to communicate spirit and life to as many as shall believe in him: "I am the vine, and ye are the branches."

2. That Christ loves to have believers so united to him, as that they be not separated at any time by unbelief: and that there may be a mutual inhabitation of them in him, by faith and love; and of him in them, by his word and Spirit; for he joins these together, "If ye abide in me, and I in you," as things inseparable.

3. That except a man be ingrafted into Christ, and united to him by faith, he cannot do any the least good works of his own strength; yes, except in as far as a man does draw spirit and life from Christ by faith, the work which he does is naughty and null in point of goodness in God's estimation: "For without me ye can do nothing."

4. That this mutual inhabitation is the fountain and infallible cause of constant continuing and abounding in well-doing: For: "he that abideth in me, and I in him, the same beareth much fruit." Now, as our abiding in Christ presupposes three things;
4a) That we have heard the joyful sound of the gospel, making offer of Christ to us, who are lost sinners by the law;

4b) That we have heartily embraced the gracious offer of Christ;

4c) That by receiving of him we are become the sons of God, John 1:12, and are incorporated into his mystical body, that he may dwell in us, as his temple, and we dwell in him, as in the residence of righteousness and life:

So our abiding in Christ imports other three things,
4d) An employing of Christ in all our addresses to God, and in all our undertakings of whatever piece of service to him.

4e) A contentedness with this sufficiency, without going out from him to seek righteousness, or life, or help in any case, in our own or any of the creature's worthiness.

4f) A fixedness in our believing in him, a fixedness in our employing and making use of him, and a fixedness in our contentment in him, and adhering to him, so that no allurement, not temptation of Satan or the world, no terror nor trouble, may be able to drive our spirits from firm adherence to him, or from the constant avowing of his truth, and obeying his commands, who has loved us, and given himself for us; and in whom not only our life is laid up, but also the fulness of the Godhead dwells bodily, by reason of the substantial and personal union of the divine and human nature in him. Hence let every watchful believer, for strengthening himself in faith and obedience, reason after this manner:

"Whoever does daily employ Christ Jesus for cleansing his conscience and affections from the guiltiness and filthiness of sins against the law, and for enabling him to give obedience to the law in love, he has the evidence of true faith in himself:" "But I (may every watchful believer say) do daily employ Jesus Christ for cleansing my conscience and affections from the guiltiness and filthiness of sins against the law, and for enabling of me to give obedience to the law in love:" "Therefore I have the evidence of true faith in myself."

And hence also let the sleepy and sluggish believer reason, for his own upstirring, thus:

"Whatever is necessary for giving evidence of true faith, I study to do it, except I would deceive myself and perish:" "But to employ Christ Jesus daily for cleansing of my conscience and affections from the guiltiness and filthiness of sins against the law, and for enabling me to give obedience to the law in love, is necessary for evidencing of true faith in me:" "Therefore this I must study to do, except I would deceive myself and perish."

And, lastly, seeing Christ himself has pointed this forth, as an undoubted evidence of a man elected of God to life, and given to Jesus Christ to be redeemed, "if he come unto him," that is, close covenant, and keep communion with him, as he teaches in John 6.37, saying:

"All that the Father giveth me shall come to me; and him that cometh to me I will in no wise cast out;" let every person, who does not in earnest make use of Christ for remission of sin, and amendment of life, reason hence, and from the whole premises, after this manner, that his conscience may be awakened:

"Whoever is neither by the law, nor by the gospel, so convinced of sin, righteousness, and judgment, as to make him come to Christ, and employ him daily for remission of sin, and amendment of life; he wants not only all evidence of saving faith, but also all appearance of his election, so long as he remains in this condition:"

"But I (may every impenitent person say) am neither by the law nor gospel so convinced of sin, righteousness, and judgment, as to make me come to Christ, and employ him daily for remission of sin, and amendment of life:"

"Therefore I lack not only all evidence of saving faith, but also all appearance of my election, so long as I remain in this condition."

Faith, Acrostics of

F-eeling
A-fraid
I
T-rust
H-im
Author unknown

F-aith
A-sks
I-mpossible
T-hings
H-umbly
Author unknown

F-loutng
A-ppearances
I
T-rust
Him
Author unknown

Forsaking
All
I
Take
Him
Author unknown

Faith, Definition of
See also: Faith
Now faith is being sure of what we hope for and certain of what we do not see.
The Bible, Hebrews 11:1

Faith is not believing that God can, but that God will!
Author unknown

Faith is not knowing what the future holds, but knowing who holds the future.
Author unknown

Faith is like electricity. You can't see it, but you can see the light.
Author unknown

Faith is not a sword just to grab; faith is a way of life.
Author unknown

Faith is not without worry or care, but faith is fear that has said a prayer.
Author unknown

Faith is the effect of God illuminating the mind and sealing the heart, and it is His mere gift.
James Arminius

Now we shall possess a right definition of faith if we call it a firm and certain knowledge of God's benevolence toward us, founded upon the truth of the freely given promise in Christ, both revealed to our minds and sealed upon our hearts through the Holy Spirit.
John Calvin

Faith is deliberate confidence in the character of God whose ways you may not understand at the time.
Oswald Chambers

Faith is just that total reliance of human weakness on divine grace which allows the Spirit to operate most effectively within the human condition.
James D.G. Dunn

Faith is an act of self-consecration, in which the will, the intellect, and the affections all have their place.
William R. Inge

Faith is the power that moves our ship

through the raging sea of this world.
Pishoy Kamel

Faith means just that blessed unrest, deep and strong, which so urges the believer onward that he cannot settle at ease in the world and anyone who was quite at ease would cease to be a believer.
Søren Kierkegaard

Faith is the refusal to panic.
Martyn Lloyd-Jones

Faith is the assent of any proposition not made out by the deduction of reason but upon the credit of the proposer.
John Locke

Faith is not the belief that God will do what you want. Faith is the belief that God will do what is right.
Max Lucado

Faith is the bird that sings while it is yet dark.
Max Lucado

Faith is something that is busy, powerful and creative, though properly speaking, it is essentially an enduring than a doing. It changes the mind and heart.
Martin Luther

Faith is something that effects in us.
Martin Luther

Faith is nothing but believing what God promises or says. Whatever remarkable thing we read of happening in the Old or New Testament, we read that it was done by faith – not by works, not by a general faith, but by faith directed to the matter in hand.
Martin Luther

Faith is a living, bold trust in God's grace, so certain of God's favor that it would risk death a thousand times trusting in it.
Martin Luther

Faith is not something we can achieve; it is something achieved within us by God.
Alister McGrath

Faith is the beginning of that which is eternal, the operation of the indwelling Power which acts from within outwards and round about … pours itself out into our whole mind, runs over into our thoughts, desires, feelings, purposes, attempts, and works, combines them all together into one, makes the whole man its one instrument … one embodied act of faith.
J.H. Newman

This is faith: a renouncing of everything we are apt to call our own and relying wholly upon the blood, righteousness and intercession of Jesus.
John Newton

Faith is extending an empty hand to God to receive His gift of grace.
A.W. Pink

The essence of faith is being satisfied with all God is for us in Jesus.
John Piper

As the essence of courage is to stake one's life on a possibility, so the essence of faith is to believe that the possibility exists.
William Salter

Faith is the subtle chain
Which binds us to the infinite.
Elizabeth Oakes Smith

Faith is nothing at all tangible. Faith is simply believing God; and, like sight, it is nothing apart from its object. You might as well shut your eyes and look inside to see whether you have sight, as to look inside to discover if you have faith.
Hannah Whitall Smith

Faith is the bird that feels the light and sings when the dawn is still dark.
Rabindranath Tagore

Faith is not the holding of correct doctrines, but personal fellowship with the Living God.
William Temple

Faith is the sense of life, that sense by virtue of which man does not destroy himself, but continues to live on. It is the force whereby we live.
Leo Tolstoy

Faith, as Paul saw it, was a living, flaming thing leading to surrender and obedience to the commandments of Christ.
A. W. Tozer

Faith is the gaze of a soul upon a saving God, a continuous gaze of the heart at the Triune God.
A. W. Tozer

Faith is not a once-done act, but a continuous gaze of the heart at the Triune God.
A. W. Tozer

Faith is not belief without proof, but trust without reservations.
Elton Trueblood

Faith is believing what you know ain't so.
Mark Twain

Faith is, then, a lively and steadfast trust in the favor of God, wherewith we commit ourselves altogether unto God. And that trust is so surely grounded and sticks so fast in our hearts, that a man would not once doubt of it, although he should die a thousand times thereof.
William Tyndale

Faith is not a refuge from reality. It is a demand that we face reality, with all its difficulties, opportunities, and implications.
Evelyn Underhill

Faith, *Definition of*

Martin Luther

Faith is not what some people think it is.

Their human dream is a delusion. Because they observe that faith is not followed by good works or a better life, they fall into error, even though they speak and hear much about faith. "Faith is not enough," they say, "you must do good works, you must be pious to be saved." They think that, when you hear the gospel, you start working, creating by your own strength a thankful heart which says, "I believe." That is what they think true faith is. But, because this is a human idea, a dream, the heart never learns anything from it, so it does nothing and reform doesn't come from this "faith," either.

Instead, faith is God's work in us, that changes us and gives new birth from God. (John 1:13). It kills the Old Adam and makes us completely different people. It changes our hearts, our spirits, our thoughts and all our powers. It brings the Holy Spirit with it. Yes, it is a living, creative, active and powerful thing, this faith. Faith cannot help doing good works constantly. It doesn't stop to ask if good works ought to be done, but before anyone asks, it already has done them and continues to do them without ceasing. Anyone who does not do good works in this manner is an unbeliever. He stumbles around and looks for faith and good works, even though he does not know what faith or good works are. Yet he gossips and chatters about faith and good works with many words.

Faith is a living, bold trust in God's grace, so certain of God's favor that it would risk death a thousand times trusting in it. Such confidence and knowledge of God's grace makes you happy, joyful and bold in your relationship to God and all creatures. The Holy Spirit makes this happen through faith. Because of it, you freely, willingly and joyfully do good to everyone, serve everyone, suffer all kinds of things, love and praise the God who has shown you such grace. Thus, it is just as impossible to separate faith and works as it is to separate heat and light from fire! Therefore, watch out for your own false ideas and guard

against good-for-nothing gossips, who think they're smart enough to define faith and works, but really are the greatest of fools. Ask God to work faith in you, or you will remain forever without faith, no matter what you wish, say or can do.
Martin Luther, An Introduction to St Paul's Letter to the Romans, Luther's German Bible of 1522

Faith, False

A false faith may be greatly enlightened and knowledgeable in gospel truth (Heb. 6:4).
A false faith excites the affections (Stony Ground Hearers).
A false faith reforms the outward life (The Pharisees).
A false faith may speak very well of Christ (The Jews).
A false faith confesses sin (Saul).
A false faith may humble itself in sackcloth and ashes (Ahab).
A false faith may repent (Esau, – Judas).
A false faith may diligently perform religious works (The Pharisees).
A false faith may be very charitable and generous (Ananias).
A false faith may tremble at the Word of God (Felix).
A false faith may experience much in religion (Heb. 6:1-4).
A false faith may enjoy great religious privileges (Lot's wife).
A false faith may preach, perform miracles, and cast out demons (Matt. 7:23).
A false faith may attain high office in the church (Diotrephes).
A false faith may walk with great preachers (Demas was Paul's companion).
A false faith may be peaceful and carnally secure (The Five Foolish Virgins).
A false faith may even persevere and hold out until the day of judgment (Matt. 7:22-23).
Don Fortner

Faith, Life of

... who through faith conquered kingdoms ...
The Bible, Hebrews 11:33

Those who pursue the way of faith and absolute abandonment have neither relish nor liberty for any other path; all else constrains and embarrasses them.
Madame Guyon

The life of faith is continually renewed victory over doubt, a continually renewed grasp of meaning in the midst of meaninglessness.
L. Newbigin

Let this be well weighed and considered, that the justified person lives and performs every act of spiritual life by faith. Everything is promised to, and is received by faith.
William Romaine

We seldom lose our faith by a blow out, usually it is just a slow leak.
Author unknown

You must not lose confidence in God because you lost confidence in your pastor. If our confidence in God had to depend upon our confidence in any human person, we would be on shifting sand.
Francis Schaeffer

When faith is lost, when honor dies, the man is dead.
John Greenleaf Whittier

Faith, Power of

... if you have faith as small as a mustard seed, you can say to this mountain, "Move from here to there" and it will move. Nothing will be impossible for you.
The Bible, Matthew 17:21

Everything is possible for him who believes.
The Bible, Mark 9:23

The world was never conquered by intrigue; it was conquered by faith.
Benjamin Disraeli

A little faith will bring your soul to heaven, but a lot of faith will bring heaven to your soul.
Dwight L. Moody

Faith, mighty faith, the promise sees
And looks to that alone,
Laughs at impossibilities
And cries: It shall be done.
Charles Wesley

Faith, Saving

For it is by grace you have been saved,
through faith ...
The Bible, Ephesians 2:8

Saving faith is the belief, on God's authority,
of whatsoever is revealed in His Word
concerning Christ; accepting and resting
upon Him alone for justification and eternal
life. It is wrought in the heart by the Holy
Spirit, and is accompanied by all other
saving graces, and leads to a life of holiness.
James Boyce, Abstract of Principles, 1858

Jesus proclaimed to sinners, to human
beings doomed to death, that they could
be saved only by a radical faith, a
wholehearted conversion and new
obedience to the one God.
Hans Küng

The only saving faith is that which casts
itself on God for life or death.
Martin Luther

It is never on account of its formal nature
as a psychic act that faith is conceived in
Scripture to be saving. It is not, strictly
speaking, even faith in Christ that saves,
but Christ that saves through faith. The
saving power resides exclusively, not in the
act of faith or the attitude of faith or
nature of faith, but in the object of faith.
B.B. Warfield

Faith and action
*See also: Achievement; Idleness;
Starting; Success*
... faith by itself, if it is not accompanied
by action, is dead.
The Bible, James 2:17

God gives every bird its food, but He
doesn't throw it into the nest!
Author unknown

Deeds, not creeds, are the true measure of
a man.
Author unknown

Faith must always have an accompanying
action.
Diane Benze

Expect great things from God,
Attempt great things for God.
William Carey

I began revolution with 82 men. If I had
[to] do it again, I'd do it with 10 or 15
and absolute faith. It does not matter
how small you are if you have faith and
plan of action.
Fidel Castro

Put your trust in God – but keep your
powder dry.
Oliver Cromwell

Faith is an active creative force.
J.H. Oldham

Faith and doubt
Faith lives in honest doubt.
Author unknown

Doubt sees the obstacles
Faith sees the way.
Doubt sees the darkest night
Faith sees the day.
Doubt dreads to take a step
Faith soars on high.
Doubt questions, "Who believes?"
Faith answer, "I."
Author unknown

Faith given back to us after a night of
doubt is a stronger thing, and far more
valuable to us than faith that has never
been tested.
Elizabeth Goudge

If faith does not resolve doubt doubt will
dissolve faith.
Os Guinness

Faith, like a jackal, feeds among the tombs,

and even from these dead doubts she
gathers her most vital hope.
Herman Melville

Feed your faith and starve your doubts to
death!
Andrew Murray

Talk faith.
The world is better off without,
Your uttered ignorance and morbid doubt.
Ella Wheeler Wilcox

Faith and fear

Faith attracts the positive. Fear attracts the
negative.
Author unknown

Fear imprisons, faith liberates;
fear paralyzes, faith empowers;
fear disheartens, faith encourages;
fear sickens, faith heals;
fear makes useless, faith makes serviceable;
most of all, fear puts hopelessness at the
  heart of life,
while faith rejoices in its God.
H.E. Fosdick

Fear forces, love leads, faith follows.
Keith Moore

Lead, kindly light, amid the encircling
gloom;
Lead thou me on;
The night is dark, and I am far from home;
Lead thou me on.
Keep thou my feet; I do not ask to see
The distant scene; one step enough for me.
J.H. Newman

The right fear comes from faith, false fear
from doubt.
Some fear to lose him, others to find him.
Blaise Pascal

Fear looks; faith jumps!
Smith Wigglesworth

Faith and good deeds

… faith without deeds is dead.
The Bible, James 2:26

Faith and works should travel side by side,
step answering to step, like the legs of men
walking. First faith, and then works; and
then faith again, and then works again –
until you can scarcely distinguish which is
the one and which is the other.
William Booth

The saints of God are sealed inwardly with
faith, but outwardly with good works.
John Boys

While it is faith alone that justifies, the
faith that justifies is never alone.
John Calvin

As the apple is not the cause of the apple
tree, but a fruit of it: even so good works
are not the cause of our salvation, but a
sign and a fruit of the same.
Daniel Cawdray

Faith justifies the person, and works justify
his faith.
Elisha Coles

The works of faith involve doing all that
is commanded in Scripture. That is why
the Mosaic law is a "law of faith" (Rom.
3:27; cf. 9:31f.) … Every command in
the Bible should be understood as
specifying an obedience which is inspired
from knowing that God has promised to
be one's God.
Daniel Fuller

We must take care lest, by exalting the
merit of faith, without adding any
distinction or explanation, we furnish
people with a pretext for relaxing in the
practice of good works.
Ignatius of Loyola

When we have taught faith in Christ, then
do we teach also good works. Because thou
hast laid hold upon Christ by faith,
through whom thou art made righteous,
begin now to work well. Love God and thy
neighbor, call upon God, give thanks unto
him, praise him, confess him. Do good to
thy neighbor and serve him; fulfill thine

office. These are good works indeed, which flow out of this faith.
Martin Luther

If faith produce no works, I see
That faith is not a living tree.
Thus faith and works together grow,
No separate life they never can know.
They're soul and body, hand and heart,
What God hath joined, let no man part.
Hannah More

We admit no faith to be justifying, which is not itself and in its own nature a spiritually vital principle of obedience and good works.
John Owen

No amount of good deeds can make us good persons. We must be good before we can do good.
Chester A. Pennington

We have to beware of magnifying faith and knowledge at the expense of love. For saving faith and serving love belong together. Whenever one is absent, so is the other.
John R.W. Stott

Faith is full of good works. It believes as if it did not work, and it works as if it did not believe.
Thomas Watson

As the flower is before the fruit, so is faith before good works.
Richard Whatley

Faith is the root of works. A root that produces nothing is dead.
Thomas Wilson

Faith and justification
… we have been justified through faith …
The Bible, Romans 5:1

It is through faith that Almighty God has justified all that have been from the beginning of time.
Clement of Rome

For if there was no justification before faith, there can be none by it, without making faith the cause or condition of it.
John Gill

Judas knew the Scriptures, and without doubt did assent to the truth of them, when he was so zealous a preacher of the gospel; but he never had so much as one drachma of justifying faith in his soul … Yea, Judas' master, the devil himself, one far enough (I suppose) from justifying faith, yet he assents to the truth of the Word. He goes against his conscience when he denies them; when he tempted Christ he did not dispute against the Scripture, drawing his arrows out of this quiver . . . Assent to the truth of the Word is but an act of the understanding, which reprobates and devils may exercise. But justifying faith is a compounded habit, and hath its seat both in the understanding and will: and, therefore, called a "believing with the heart" (Romans 10:10) yea, a "believing with all the heart" (Acts 8:37).
William Gurnall

1. Faith without works is sufficient for salvation, and alone justifies.
2. Justifying faith is a sure trust, by which one believes that his sins are remitted for Christ's sake; and they that are justified are to believe certainly that their sins are remitted.
3. By faith only we are able to appear before God, who neither regards nor has need of our works; faith only purifying us.
4. No previous disposition is necessary to justification; neither does faith justify because it disposes us, but because it is a means or instrument by which the promise and grace of God are laid hold on and received.
5. All the works of men, even the most sanctified, are sin.
6. Though the just ought to believe that his works are sins, yet he ought to be assured that they are not imputed.
7. Our righteousness is nothing but the imputation of the righteousness of Christ; and the just have need of a continual

justification and imputation of the
righteousness of Christ.
8. All the justified are received into equal
grace and glory; and all Christians are
equally great with the virgin Mary, and as
much saints as she is.
*Martin Luther, Eight statements on justifying
faith*

Faith alone justifies us ... because faith brings
us the spirit gained by the means of Christ.
Martin Luther

Faith, thus receiving and resting on Christ
and his righteousness, is the alone
instrument of justification; yet is it not
alone in the person justified, but is ever
accompanied with all the saving graces,
and is no dead faith, but worketh by love.
Westminster Confession

Faith and love
The only thing that counts is faith
expressing itself through love.
The Bible, Galatians 5:6

While faith makes all things possible, it is
love that makes all things easy.
Evan H. Hopkins

The whole being of any Christian is faith
and love. Faith brings the man to God,
love brings him to men.
Martin Luther

God shows Himself not to reason, but to
faith and love. Faith is an organ of knowledge,
and love is an organ of experience. To know
God is not through reason, nor is it through
emotions, but by faith and love.
A. W. Tozer

Faith and obedience
Only he who believes is obedient, and only
he who is obedient believes.
D. Bonhoeffer

See that your faith bringeth forth
obedience, and God in due time will cause
it to bring forth peace.
John Owen

Obedience is the fruit of faith; patience,
the bloom on the fruit.
Christina Rossetti

Faith and obedience are bound up in the
same bundle; he that obeys God trusts
God; and he that trusts God obeys God.
He that is without faith is without works,
and he that is without works is without
faith.
C.H. Spurgeon

Faith and prayer
Faith dies through lack of prayer.
Author unknown

Praying without faith is like trying to cut
with a blunt knife – much labor expended
to little purpose.
James O. Fraser

Faith is to prayer what the feather is to the
arrow; without faith it will not hit the mark.
J.C. Ryle

Men of prayer are men of faith; closet
supplicants make faith's heroes.
The War Cry, 1895

Bear up the hands that hang down, by
faith and prayer; support the tottering
knees.
John Wesley

There are many things that are essential to
arriving at true peace of mind, and one of
the most important is faith, which cannot
be acquired without prayer.
John Wooden

Faith and reason
Nothing is more reasonable than faith in
God; nothing is more unreasonable than a
blind leap of faith in reason.
Author unknown

Faith is a continuation of reason.
William Adams

Understanding is the reward of faith.
Therefore seek not to understand that thou

mayest believe, but believe that thou
mayest understand.
Augustine of Hippo

Faith is the first step in understanding;
understanding is the reward of faith.
Augustine of Hippo

Do not seek to understand in order that
you may believe, but believe so that you
may understand.
Augustine of Hippo

Faith is a higher faculty than reason.
Henry Christopher Bailey

If faith did not exist apart from intellect,
clever people would have a better hope of
salvation than stupid people.
R.H. Benson

I believe though I do not comprehend, and
I hold by faith what I cannot grasp with
the mind.
St Bernard

Reason is our soul's left hand,
Faith her right,
By these we reach divinity.
John Donne

Reason saw not, till faith sprung the
light.
John Dryden

Faith is not contrary to reason.
Sherwood Eddy

The way to see by faith is to shut the eye of
reason.
Benjamin Franklin

The seat of faith is not in the brain, but in
the heart, and the head is not the place to
keep the promises of God, but the heart is
the chest to lay them up in.
Richard Greenham

If the work of God could be
comprehended by reason, it would be no
longer wonderful, and faith would have no

merit if reason provided proof.
Gregory the Great

Some people think that having reasons
for faith is an insult to God. But
verification itself depends on the
unchanging authority and stability of
the Word of God. We are not insulting
God but bringing glory to him by
taking his Word as the stable,
authoritative truth it is.
Os Guinness

God does not require you to follow His
leadings on blind trust. Behold the
evidence of an invisible intelligence
pervading everything, even your own mind
and body.
Raymond Holliwell

The more you understand, the better you
can believe.
Raymond Lull

Faith is the master, and reason the
maid-servant.
Martin Luther

Faith must trample under foot all reason,
sense, and understanding.
Martin Luther

Reason is the enemy of faith.
Martin Luther

While reason holds to what is present,
faith apprehends the things that are not
seen. Contrary to reason, faith regards
the invisible things as already
materialized.
Martin Luther

All the scholastic scaffolding falls, as a
ruined edifice, before one single word –
faith.
Napoleon Bonaparte

That's the thing about faith. If you don't
have it you can't understand it. And if you
do, no explanation is necessary
Kira Nerys

Life is a battle between faith and reason in which each feeds upon the other, drawing sustenance from it and destroying it.
Reinhold Niebuhr

It is the heart which is conscious of God, not the reason. This then is faith: God is sensible to the heart, not to the reason.
Blaise Pascal

Faith embraces many truths which seem to contradict each other.
Blaise Pascal

Faith affirms what the senses do not affirm, but not the contrary of what they perceive. It is above and not contrary to.
Blaise Pascal

Reason is an action of the mind; knowledge is a possession of the mind; but faith is an attitude of the person. It means you are prepared to stake yourself on something being so.
Michael Ramsey

Christian faith lives on the discovery that not only is there such a thing as objective meaning, but this meaning knows me and loves me. I can entrust myself to it like the child that knows all its questions [are] answered in the "You" of its mother.
Joseph Ratzinger

Faithfulness
See also: Little things
Whither thou goest, I will go; and where thou lodgest, I will lodge: thy people shall be my people, and thy God my God.
The Bible, Ruth 1:16 KJV

He whose walk is blameless … keeps his oath even when it hurts.
The Bible, Psalm 15:1,4

I will speak of your faithfulness and salvation.
The Bible, Psalm 40:10

Only Luke is with me.
The Bible, 2 Timothy 4:11

Be faithful, even to the point of death.
The Bible, Revelation 2:10

O Lord my God,
give me understanding to know you,
diligence to seek you,
wisdom to find you,
and a faithfulness that may finally embrace you.
Thomas Aquinas

He is invited to do great things who receives small things greatly.
Cassiodorus

Nothing is more noble, nothing more venerable than fidelity. Faithfulness and truth are the most sacred excellencies and endowments of the human mind.
Cicero

The faithful person lives constantly with God.
Clement of Alexandria

Faithfulness in carrying out present duties is the best preparation for the future.
François Fénelon

Be content with doing with calmness the little which depends on yourself and let all else be to you as if it were not.
François Fénelon

It is only by fidelity in little things that a true and constant love of God can be distinguished from a passing fervor of spirit.
François Fénelon

When men cease to be faithful to their God, he who expects to find them faithful to each other will be much disappointed.
George Horne

He does most in God's great world who does his best in his own little world.
Thomas Jefferson

I long to accomplish a great and noble task, but it is my chief duty to accomplish

small tasks as if they were great and noble.
Helen Keller

Here I stand; I can do no otherwise. God
help me. Amen!
Martin Luther, Speech at the Diet of Worms.
[On the 16th April, 1521, Luther entered the
imperial city of Worms ... On his approach ... the
Elector's chancellor entreated him, in the name of
his Master, not to enter a town where his death was
decided. Luther gave him the above answer.]

Among the faithless, faithful only he;
Among innumerable false, unmoved,
Unshaken, unseduced, unterrified,
His loyalty he kept, his love, his zeal;
Nor number, nor example, with him
  wrought
To swerve from truth, or change his
constant mind
Though single.
John Milton

To take up the cross of Christ is no great
action done once for all; it consists in the
continual practice of small duties which
are distasteful to us.
John Henry Newman

Fidelity is seven-tenths of business success.
James Parton

The Lord rewards faithfulness above
fruitfulness, which puts us all on the same
footing, whether famous for our
effectiveness or unknown in our faithfulness.
John Piper

It is better to be faithful than famous.
Theodore Roosevelt

God did not call us to be successful, but to
be faithful.
Mother Theresa

I do not pray for success, I ask for
faithfulness.
Mother Teresa

Fall, The
When the woman [Eve] saw that the fruit

of the tree was good for food and pleasing
to the eye, and also desirable for gaining
wisdom, she took some and ate it. She also
gave some to her husband, who was with
her, and he ate it.
The Bible, Genesis 3:6

... in Adam all die ...
The Bible, 1 Corinthians 15:22

... Eve was deceived by the serpent's
cunning ...
The Bible, 2 Corinthians 11:3

God originally created man in His own
image, and free from sin; but, through the
temptation of Satan, he transgressed the
command of God, and fell from his
original holiness and righteousness;
whereby his posterity inherit a nature
corrupt and wholly opposed to God and
His Law, are under condemnation, and as
soon as they are capable of moral action,
become actual transgressors.
James Boyce, 1858

To the question, "What is meant by the
fall?" I could answer with complete
sincerity, "That whatever I am, I am not
myself."
G.K. Chesterton

What died in Adam and Eve when they ate
the apple was that intimate, unspoiled
relationship they'd had with God.
Michael Green

Satan lied;
Adam and Eve complied;
and we all died.
Douglas Groothuis

The first chapters of the Bible tell us of the
sin of man. The guilt of that sin had rested
upon every single one of us, its guilt and
its terrible results, but, it also tells us of
something greater still; it tells us of the
grace of the offended God.
J. Gresham Machen

[Adam wanted to] be like God [but]

without God, before God, and not in accordance with God.
Maximus the Confessor

In Adam's fall
We sinned all.
New England Primer

Falling away

So, if you think you are standing firm, be careful that you don't fall.
The Bible, 1 Corinthians 10:12

I am astonished that you are so quickly deserting the one who called you by the grace of Christ and are turning to a different gospel—which is really no gospel at all.
The Bible, Galatians 1:6

… you have fallen away from grace.
The Bible, Galatians 5:4

See to it, brothers, that none of you has a sinful, unbelieving heart that turns away from the living God.
The Bible, Hebrews 3:12

To him who is able to keep you from falling.
The Bible, Jude 24

… I hold this against you: You have forsaken your first love.
The Bible, Revelation 2:4

We will often fall; but the Lord will raise us up.
Author unknown

Those who fall away have never been thoroughly imbued with the knowledge of Christ but only had a slight and passing taste of it.
John Calvin

How ready are we to go astray! How easily are we drawn aside into innumerable snares, while in the mean time we are bold and confident, and doubt not but we are right and safe! How much do we stand in need of the wisdom, the power, the condescension,

patience, forgiveness, and gentleness of our good Shepherd!
Jonathan Edwards

I cannot comprehend a gospel which lets saints fall away after they are called.
C.H. Spurgeon

False

The righteous hate what is false, but the wicked bring shame and disgrace.
The Bible, Proverbs 13:5

Falsehood
Falsehood: See Violence

False teachers
See also: False teaching

See to it that no one takes you captive through hollow and deceptive philosophy, which depends on human tradition and the basic principles of this world rather than on Christ.
The Bible, Colossians 2:8

False teaching

Such teachings come through hypocritical liars, whose consciences have been seared as with a hot iron. They forbid people to marry and order them to abstain from certain foods, which God created to be received with thanksgiving by those who believe and who know the truth.
The Bible, 1 Timothy 4:2,3

… he is conceited and understands nothing. He has an unhealthy interest in controversies and quarrels about words that result in envy, strife, malicious talk, evil suspicions …
The Bible, 1 Timothy 6:4

Avoid godless chatter, because those who indulge in it will become more and more ungodly. Their teaching will spread like gangrene. Among them are Hymenaeus and Philetus, who have wandered away from the truth. They say that the resurrection has already taken place, and they destroy the faith of some.
The Bible, 2 Timothy 2:16-18

For the time will come when men will not put up with sound doctrine. Instead, to suit their own desires, they will gather around them a great number of teachers to say what their itching ears want to hear.
The Bible, 2 Timothy 4:3

Do not be carried away by all kinds of strange teachings. It is good for our hearts to be strengthened by grace, not by ceremonial foods, which are of no value to those who eat them.
The Bible, Hebrews 13:9

But there were also false prophets among the people, just as there will be false teachers among you. They will secretly introduce destructive heresies, even denying the sovereign Lord who bought them—bringing swift destruction on themselves. Many will follow their shameful ways and will bring the way of truth into disrepute.
The Bible, 2 Peter 2:1,2

With eyes full of adultery, they never stop sinning; they seduce the unstable; they are experts in greed—an accursed brood!
The Bible, 2 Peter 2:14

By entertaining of strange persons, men sometimes entertain angels unawares: but by entertaining of strange doctrines, many have entertained devils unawares.
John Flavel

Others tear it to pieces, scourge and crucify it, and subject it to all manner of torture until they stretch it sufficiently to apply to their heresy, meaning, and whim.
Martin Luther, about the false teachers' use of the Bible

Why is it more ridiculous to arraign ecclesiastics for their false teaching and acts of injustice to women, than members of Congress and the House of Commons?
Elizabeth Cady Stanton

Fame

Know the difference between success and fame. Success is Mother Teresa. Fame is Madonna.
Author unknown

All is ephemeral, fame and the famous as well.
Marcus Aurelius Antoninus

Fame is vapor, popularity an accident, riches take wings. Only one thing endures and that is character.
Horace Greeley

The fame of great men ought to be judged always by the means they used to acquire it.
François de La Rochefoucauld

Lives of great men all remind us
We can make our lives sublime,
And departing, leave behind us
Footprints on the sands of time.
H. W. Longfellow

For what is fame in itself but the blast of another man's mouth as soon passed as spoken?
Thomas More

Glory is fleeting, but obscurity is forever.
Napoleon Bonaparte

The charm of fame is so great that we like every object to which it is attached, even death.
Blaise Pascal

The highest form of vanity is love of fame.
George Santayana

The desire for fame is the last infirmity cast off even by the wise.
Cornelius Tacitus

Fame is man-given; be grateful.
John Wooden

Families
See also: Children; Church; Fathers; Husbands; Mothers; Parenting; Wives
God sets the lonely in families …
The Bible, Psalm 68:6

Do not suppose that I have come to bring peace to the earth. I did not come to bring peace, but a sword. For I have come to turn a man against his father, a daughter against her mother, a daughter-in-law against her mother-in-law – a man's enemies will be the members of his own household.
Anyone who loves his father or mother more than me is not worthy of me; anyone who loves his son or daughter more than me is not worthy of me ...
The Bible, Matthew 10:34-37

If anyone does not provide for his relatives, and especially for his immediate family, he has denied the faith and is worse than an unbeliever.
The Bible, 1 Timothy 5:8

I have been reminded of your sincere faith, which first lived in your grandmother Lois and in your mother Eunice and, I am persuaded, now lives in you also.
The Bible, 2 Timothy 1:5

A healthy family is sacred territory.
Author unknown

It is clear that a family without love is godless, but a family ruled by the clouded emotion of blood-ties will have no love to God and Christ.
J. Heinrich Arnold

Family is certainly not dead in America, but it looks and behaves very differently than it used to.
George Barna

It is an evident truth, that most of the mischiefs that now infest or seize upon mankind throughout the earth, consist in, or are caused by the disorders and ill-governedness of families.
Richard Baxter

If you desire the reformation and welfare of your people, do all you can to promote family religion.
Richard Baxter

The union of the family lies in love; and love is the only reconciliation of authority and liberty.
Robert Hugh Benson

A happy family is but an earlier heaven.
John Bowring

A saint abroad, and a devil at home.
John Bunyan

In family life, be completely present.
Tao Te Ching

The strength of a nation derives from the integrity of the home.
Confucius

It is my view that our society can be no more stable than the foundation of individual family units upon which it rests. Our government, our institutions, our schools, indeed, our way of life are dependent on healthy marriages and loyalty to the vulnerable little children around our feet.
James C. Dobson

The mind of Christ is to be learned in the family. Strength of character may be acquired at work, but beauty of character is learned at home. There the affections are trained.
Henry Drummond

Earthly fathers and mothers, husbands, wives, children and earthly friends, are all "shadows." But God is the "substance."
Jonathan Edwards

Men are what their mothers made them.
Ralph Waldo Emerson

The family was ordained by God before he established any other institution, even before he established the church.
Billy Graham

The foundations of civilization are no stronger and no more enduring than the corporate integrity of the homes on which

they rest. If the home deteriorates, civilization will crumble and fall.
Billy Graham

Unless [our love and care for our family] is a high priority, we may find that we may gain the whole world and lose our own children.
Michael Green

The most important thing a father can do for his children is to love their mother.
Theodore Hesburgh

The great high of winning Wimbledon lasts for about a week. You go down in the record book, but you don't have anything tangible to hold on to. But having a baby – there isn't any comparison.
Chris Evert Lloyd

They offer their children to God in baptism, and there they promise to teach them the doctrine of the gospel, and bring them up in the nurture of the Lord; but they easily promise, and easily break it; and educate their children for the world and the flesh, although they have renounced these, and dedicated them to God. This covenant-breaking with God, and betraying the souls of their children to the devil, must lie heavy on them here or hereafter. They beget children, and keep families, merely for the world and the flesh: but little consider what a charge is committed to them, and what it is to bring up a child for God, and govern a family as a sanctified society.
Thomas Manton

All the wealth in the world cannot be compared with the happiness of living together happily united.
Margaret of Youville

Well-ordered families naturally produce a good order in other societies. When families are under an ill discipline, all other societies [will be] ill disciplined.
Cotton Mather

No matter how many communes anybody invents, the family always creeps back.
Margaret Mead

A godly parentage is a costly boon. Its blessing not only rests upon the children of the first family, but has often been traced in many successive generations.
Andrew Murray

Family life is too intimate to be preserved by the spirit of justice. It can be sustained by a spirit of love which goes beyond justice.
Reinhold Niebuhr

To the Puritans, family life was enormously important, for they maintained, "a family is the seminary of church and state and if children be not well principled there, all miscarrieth." So "keep up the government of God in your families: holy families must be the chief preservers of the interest of religion in the world."
J.I. Packer

Every effort to make society sensitive to the importance of the family is a great service to humanity.
Pope John Paul II

As the family goes, so goes the nation and so goes the whole world in which we live.
Pope John Paul II

The family is one of nature's masterpieces.
George Santayana

The family should be a place where each new human being can have an early atmosphere conducive to the development of constructive creativity.
Edith Schaeffer

Perhaps the greatest social service that can be rendered by anybody to the country and to mankind is to bring up a family.
George Bernard Shaw

Some parents, like Eli, bring up their children to bring down their house.
George Swinnock

He who loves not his wife and children feeds a lioness at home and broods a nest of sorrows.
Jeremy Taylor

All happy families are like one another; each unhappy family is unhappy in its own way.
Leo Tolstoy

God is the first object of our love: Its next office is to bear the defects of others. And we should begin the practice of this amid our own household.
John Wesley

If you wish your children to be Christians you must really take the trouble to be Christian yourselves. Those are the only terms upon which the home will work the gracious miracle.
Woodrow Wilson

"The family that prays together, stays together" is much more than a cliché! And when the family adds the dimension of praying together in church, the truth becomes even stronger.
Zig Ziglar

Families worship
Let family worship be performed consistently and at a time when it is most likely for the family to be free of interruptions.
Richard Baxter

Pray together and read the Bible together. Nothing strengthens a marriage and family more. Nothing is a better defense against Satan.
Billy Graham

We realize that our Christian faith must continually be nourished if it is to remain living and vital. Therefore, we desire to grow in our Christian lives through family devotions, personal prayer and study, and the opportunities for spiritual development offered by the Church.
Moravian Covenant for Christian living

Read the Bible together as a family every day.
Kenneth Taylor

Family life
See: Families

Famine
There is a famine in America. Not a famine of food, but of love, of truth, of life.
Mother Teresa

Fanatic
It is part of the nature of fanaticism that it loses sight of the totality of evil and rushes like a bull at the red cloth instead of at the man who holds it.
Dietrich Bonhoeffer

Earth's fanatics make too frequently heaven's saints.
Elizabeth Barrett Browning

A fanatic is one who can't change his mind and won't change the subject.
Winston Churchill

Fanaticism, the false fire of an over-heated mind.
William Cowper

Fanaticism consists of redoubling your efforts when you have forgotten your aim.
George Santayana

Fashion
Your beauty should not come from outward adornment, such as braided hair and the wearing of gold jewelry and fine clothes.
The Bible, 1 Peter 3:3

Fashion: A despot whom the wise ridicule and obey.
Ambrose Bierce

Every generation laughs at the old fashions, but follows religiously the new.
Henry Thoreau

Fashion is a form of ugliness so intolerable that we have to alter it every six months.
Oscar Wilde

Fasting

I proclaimed a fast there, so that we might humble ourselves before our God.
The Bible, Ezra 8:21

Declare a holy fast …
The Bible, Joel 1:14

When you fast, do not look somber as the hypocrites do …
The Bible, Matthew 6:16

Do not limit the benefit of fasting merely to abstinence from food, for a true fast means refraining from evil. Do not let your fasting lead to wrangling and strife. You do not eat meat, but you devour your brother; you abstain from wine, but not from insults. So all the labor of your fast is useless.
Ambrose

If there is a man among them who is poor and in need, and they have not an abundance of what is needed, they fast for two or three days so that they may supply the needy with their necessary food.
Aristides of Athens

Christ saith that when the bridegroom was taken from them, his disciples should "fast" (Mk. 2:19,20). And even painful Paul was "in fasting often" (2 Cor. 6:5; 11:27), and, "I discipline my body and bring it into subjection" (1 Cor. 9:27). And I am sure that the ancient Christians (Acts 5:30; 14:23; Lk. 2:37), that lived in solitude, and ate many of them nothing, … did not find this cure [fasting] too dear.
Richard Baxter

If the appetite alone hath sinned, let it alone fast, and it sufficeth.
But if the other members also have sinned, why should they not fast, too?
Let the eye fast from strange sights and from every wantonness, so that which roamed in freedom in fault-doing may, abundantly humbled, be checked by penitence.
Let the ear, blameably eager to listen, fast from tales and rumors, and from whatsoever is of idle import, and tendeth least to salvation.
Let the tongue fast from slanders and murmurings, and from useless, vain, and scurrilous words, and sometimes also, in the seriousness of silence, even from things which may seem of essential import.
Let the hand abstain from all toils which are not imperatively necessary.
But also let the soul herself abstain from all evils and from acting out her own will. For without such abstinence the other things find no favor with the Lord.
Bernard of Clairvaux

Fasting is not approved by God, except for its end; it must be connected with something else, otherwise it is a vain thing. Men by private fastings, prepare themselves for the exercise of prayer, or they mortify their own flesh, or seek a remedy for some hidden vices.
John Calvin

What we gain from fasting does not compensate for what we lose in anger.
John Cassian

Do you fast? Give me proof of it by your works.
If you see a poor man, take pity on him.
If you see a friend being honored, do not envy him.
Do not let only your mouth fast, but also the eye and the ear and the feet and the hands and all the members of our bodies.
Let the hands fast, by being free of avarice.
Let the feet fast, by ceasing to run after sin.
Let the eyes fast, by disciplining them not to glare at that which is sinful.
Let the ear fast, by not listening to evil talk and gossip.
Let the mouth fast from foul words and unjust criticism.
For what good is it if we abstain from birds and fishes, but bite and devour our brothers? May HE who came to the world to save sinners strengthen us to complete the fast with humility, have mercy on us and save us.
John Chrysostom

To fast is to learn to love and appreciate food, and one's own good fortune in having it.
Monica Furlong

Abstinence is the mother of health. A few ounces of privation is an excellent recipe for any ailment.
Anthony Grassi

It is impossible to engage in spiritual conflict unless the appetite for food has first been subdued.
Gregory the Great

Do you not know that fasting can overcome concupiscence, lift up the soul, confirm it in the way of virtue and prepare a great reward for the Christian?
Hedwig of Silesia

There is no great excellency in watching and fasting till thy head aches, nor in running to Rome or Jerusalem with bare feet, nor in building churches and hospitals.
Walter Hilton

I find it a good thing to fast. I do not lay down rules for anyone in this matter, but I know it has been a good thing for me to go without meals to get time for prayer. So many say they have not sufficient time to pray. We think nothing of spending an hour or two in taking our meals.
D.E. Hoste

If you fast regularly, do not be inflated with pride, but if you think highly of yourself because of it, then you had better eat meat. It is better for a man to eat meat than to be inflated with pride and to glorify himself.
Abba Isidore

When the stomach is full, it is easy to talk of fasting.
St Jerome

The honor of fasting consists not in abstinence from food, but in withdrawing from sinful practices, since he who limits his fasting only to abstinence from meats is one who especially disparages fasting.
Abba John

If a king wishes to subdue a city belonging to enemies, he first of all keeps them without bread and water, and the enemy being in this wise, harassed by hunger, become subject unto him; and thus it is in respect of the hostile passions, for if a man endures fasting and hunger regularly, his enemies become stricken with weakness in the soul.
Abba John

Fasting is a medicine. But like all medicines, though it be very profitable to the person who knows how to use it, it frequently becomes useless (and even harmful) in the hands of him who is unskillful in its use.
Abba John

I speak not of such a fast as most persons keep, but of real fasting; not merely abstinence from meats, but from sins as well.
Abba John

The Publican did not fast, and yet he was accepted in preference to him who had fasted in order that you may learn that fasting is unprofitable unless all other duties accompany it.
Abba John

Leanness of body and soul may go together.
John Owen

Quit feasting, start fasting.
Leonard Ravenhill

Some are deceived by too much abstinence from meat and drink and sleep. That is a temptation of the devil, to make them all down in the middle of their work.
Richard Rolle

Fasting is a divine corrective to the pride of the human heart. It is a discipline of body with a tendency to humble the soul.
Arthur Wallis

If humility is the basic ingredient of true holiness, the soil in which the graces flourish, is it not needful that from time to time we should, like David, humble our souls with fasting? Behind many of our besetting sins and personal failures, behind the many ills that infect our church fellowships and clog the channels of Christian service – the clash of personalities and temperaments, the strife, the division – lies that insidious pride of the human heart.
Arthur Wallis

First, let fasting be done unto the Lord with our eye singly fixed on Him. Let our intention herein be this, and this alone, to glorify our Father which is in heaven.
John Wesley

Feast, and your halls are crowded; fast, and the world goes by.
Ella Wheeler Wilcox

Fasting and prayer
Fasting without prayer is starvation.
Author unknown

God will not let me get the blessing without asking. Today I am setting my face to fast and pray for enlightenment and refreshing. Until I can get up to the measure of at least two hours in pure prayer every day, I shall not be contented. Meditation and reading besides.
Andrew Bonar

I set apart this day for secret fasting and prayer, to entreat God to direct and bless me with regard to the great work I have in view, of preaching the gospel.
David Brainerd

Prayers belong strictly to the worship of God. Fasting is a subordinate aid, which is pleasing to God no farther than as it aids the earnestness and fervency of prayer.
John Calvin

Whoso will pray, he must fast and be clean, And fat his soul and make his body lean.
Geoffrey Chaucer

Prayer is reaching out after the unseen; fasting is letting go of all that is seen and temporal. Fasting helps express, deepen, confirm the resolution that we are ready to sacrifice anything, even ourselves to attain what we seek for the kingdom of God.
Andrew Murray

We have found no means so much blessed to keep religion alive as fasting and prayer.
Edward Parson

In Shansi I found Chinese Christians who were accustomed to spend time in fasting and prayer. They recognized that this fasting, which so many dislike, which requires faith in God, since it makes one feel weak and poorly, is really a divinely appointed means of grace. Perhaps the greatest hindrance to our work is our own imagined strength; and in fasting we learn what poor, weak creatures we are – dependent on a meal of meat for the little strength which we are so apt to lean upon.
J. Hudson Taylor

Have you any days of fasting and prayer?
John Wesley

Fate
See also: Fortune
Fate! There is no fate. Between the thought and the success God is the only agent.
Edward George Bulwer-Lytton

Fate does not jest and events are not a matter of chance. There is no existence out of nothing.
Gamal Abdel Nasser

I do not believe in that word fate. It is the refuge of every self-confessed failure.
Andrew Soutar

Fathers
See also: Children; Families; Mothers; Parenting; Wives
"Honor your father and your mother ..."
The Bible, Exodus 20:12

Fathers, do not exasperate your children; instead, bring them up in the training and instruction of the Lord.
The Bible, Ephesians 6:4

Father, do not embitter your children …
The Bible, Colossians 3:21

I wish I were half as great as my infant thinks I am, and only half as stupid as my teenager thinks I am.
Author unknown

By the time a son realizes his father is usually right, he has a son who thinks his father is usually wrong.
Author unknown

When a father, absent during the day, returns home at six, his children receive only his temperament, not his teaching.
Robert Bly

We need to restore fatherhood to its rightful place of honor.
James Dobson and Gary L. Bauer

It may be hard on some fathers not to have a son, but it is much harder on a boy not to have a father.
Sara D. Gilbert

It is easier for a father to have children than for children to have a real father.
Pope John XXIII

He that will have his son have respect for him and his orders, must himself have a great reverence for his son.
John Locke

The more a child becomes aware of a father's willingness to listen, the more a father will begin to hear.
Gordon MacDonald

One father is more than a hundred schoolmasters.
Proverb

What a father says to his children is not heard by the world, but it will be heard by posterity.
Jean Paul Richter

Most American children suffer too much mother and too little father.
Gloria Steinem

An angry father is most cruel towards himself.
P. Syrus

A child tells in the street what its father says at home.
The Talmud

My father gave me the greatest gift anyone could give another person, he believed in me.
Jim Valvano

Fathers and Scripture
The Fathers have handed on to us the books of Scripture as well as their true interpretation. They did not abandon the headspring to follow the course of the streams; they drew on Scripture for their devastating arguments that destroyed the heresies, and for the heavenly food that they gave to the Church for her nourishment.
Bernard Lamy of the Oratory

Fathers in Christ
Even though you have ten thousand guardians in Christ, you do not have many fathers, for in Christ Jesus I became your father through the gospel.
The Bible, 1 Corinthians 4:15

Faults
See also Confession of sin; Fault-finding; Mistakes; Perfection
A fault confessed is half redressed.
Author unknown

The greatest of all faults is to be conscious of none.
Thomas Carlyle

Do not be discouraged at your faults; bear with yourself in correcting them, as you would with your neighbor. Lay aside this ardor of mind, which exhausts your body,

and leads you to commit errors. Accustom yourself gradually to carry prayer into all your daily occupations. Speak, move, work, in peace, as if you were in prayer, as indeed you ought to be.
François Fénelon

We ought to hate our faults, but with a quiet, calm hatred; not pettishly and anxiously.
Francis de Sales

A fault, once denied, is twice committed.
Thomas Fuller

He is lifeless that is faultless.
J. Heywood

Not in committing, but in prolonging acts of folly is the shame.
Horace

It is right that someone who asks pardon for his own faults should be willing to pardon others.
Horace

Only great men have great defects.
La Rochefoucauld

Who never admits wrong loves pride more than facts.
Proverb

If we plant a flower or a shrub and water it daily it will grow so tall that in time we need a spade and a hoe to uproot it. It is just so, I think, when we commit a fault, however small, each day, and do not cure ourselves of it.
Teresa of Avila

Fault-finding
See also: Faults; Gossip
Every person should have a special cemetery lot in which to bury the faults of friends and loved ones.
Author unknown

When looking at faults, use a mirror, not a telescope.
Yazid Ibrahim

Gladly we desire to make other men perfect, but we will not amend our own fault.
Thomas à Kempis

Favoritism
For God does not show favoritism.
The Bible, Romans 2:11

But if you show favoritism, you sin and are convicted by the law as law-breakers.
The Bible, James 2:9

Fear
See also: Faith
Be strong, do not fear …
The Bible, Isaiah 35:4

Take courage! It is I. Don't be afraid.
The Bible, Matthew 14:27

There is no fear in love. But perfect love drives out fear, because fear has to do with punishment. The one who fears is not made perfect in love.
The Bible, 1 John 4:18

Fear knocked at the door. Faith answered and no one was there.
Author unknown

A coward gets scared and quits. A hero gets scared, but still goes on.
Author unknown

F.E.A.R – False Evidence Appearing Real.
Author unknown

Jesus came treading the waves; and so he puts all the swelling tumults of life under his feet. Christians – why afraid?
Augustine of Hippo

Nothing is terrible except fear itself.
Francis Bacon

Fear is never a good counselor and victory over fear is the first spiritual duty of man.
Nicolas Berdyaev

No passion so effectively robs the mind of

all its powers of acting and reasoning as fear.
Edmund Burke

The death of fear is in doing what you fear to do.
Sequichie Comingdeer

Nothing in life is to be feared. It is only to be understood.
Marie Curie

Always do what you are afraid to do.
Ralph Waldo Emerson

He has not learned a lesson of life, who does not every day surmount a fear.
Ralph Waldo Emerson

The wise man in a storm prays to God,
Not for safety from danger,
But for deliverance from fear.
Ralph Waldo Emerson

Fear always springs from ignorance.
Ralph Waldo Emerson

One of the greatest discoveries a man makes, one of his great surprises, is to find he can do what he was afraid he couldn't do.
Henry Ford

One of the things which danger does to you after a time is, well, to kill emotion. I don't think I shall ever feel anything again except fear. None of us can hate anymore – or love.
Graham Greene

A good scare is worth more to a man than good advice.
Edgar Watson Howe

Courage faces fear and thereby masters it. Cowardice represses fear and is thereby mastered by it.
Martin Luther King

The oldest and strongest emotion of mankind is fear.
H.P. Lovecraft

It is better to be feared than loved, if you cannot be both.
Niccolo Machiavelli

Fear not; the things you are afraid of are quite likely to happen to you, but they are nothing to be afraid of.
John Macmurray

As we are liberated from our fears, our presence automatically liberates others.
Nelson Mandela

We gain strength, and courage, and confidence by each experience in which we really stop to look fear in the face … we must do that which we think we cannot.
Eleanor Roosevelt

The only thing we have to fear is fear itself.
Franklin D. Roosevelt

Fear closes the ears of the mind.
Sallust

Whenever I hear about Christ as Savior it appears that he saves us from sin – and I don't wish to deny that – but in my experience he does more than that: he releases us from fear, and I think fear is the great killer.
Ivor Smith-Cameron

What we fear comes to pass more speedily than what we hope.
Publilius Syrus

A great fear, when it is ill-managed, is the parent of superstition; but a discreet and well-guided fear produces religion.
Jeremy Taylor

To the pure in heart nothing really bad can happen. Not death but sin should be our great fear.
A.W. Tozer

Fear is a tyrant and a despot, more terrible than the rack, more potent than the snake.
Edgar Wallace

The only thing I am afraid of is fear.
Duke of Wellington

What are fears but voices airy?
Whispering harm where harm is not.
And deluding the unwary
Till the fatal bolt is shot!
William Wordsworth

Fear

Letter from John Newton

Dear N.

Though I have the pleasure of hearing of you, and sending a remembrance from time to time, I am willing, by this opportunity, to direct a few lines to you, as a more express testimony of my sincere regard.

I think your experience is generally of the fearful doubting cast. Such souls, however, the Lord has given particular charge to his ministers to comfort. He knows our infirmities and what temptations mean, and as a good Shepherd He expresses a peculiar care and tenderness for the weak of the flock (Isa. 40: 1).

But how must I attempt your comfort? Surely not by strengthening a mistake to which we are all too liable, by leading you to look into your own heart for (what you will never find there) something in yourself whereon to ground your hopes, if not wholly, yet at least in part. Rather let me endeavor to lead you out of yourself; let me invite you to look unto Jesus. Should we look for light in our own eyes, or in the sun? Is it indwelling sin distresses you? Then I can tell you (though you know it) that Jesus died for sin and sinners. I can tell you that His blood and righteousness are of infinite value; that His arm is almighty and His compassions infinite; yea, you yourself read His promises every day, and why should you doubt their being fulfilled? If you say you do not question their truth, or that they are accomplished to many, but that you can hardly believe they belong to you, I would ask, what evidence you would

require? A voice or an angel from heaven you do not expect.

Consider, if many of the promises are not expressly directed to those to whom they belong. When you read your name on the superscription of this letter you make no scruple to open it: why, then, do you hesitate at embracing the promises of the gospel, where you read that they are addressed to those who mourn, who hunger and thirst after righteousness, who are poor in spirit, etc., and cannot but be sensible that a gracious God has begun to work these dispositions in your heart? If you say that though you do at times mourn, hunger, etc., you are afraid you do it not enough, or not aright, consider that this sort of reasoning is very far from the spirit and language of the gospel; for it is grounded on a secret supposition, that in the forgiveness of sin God has a respect to something more than the atonement and mediation of Jesus; namely, to some previous good qualifications in a sinner's heart, which are to share with the blood of Christ in the honor of salvation. The enemy deceives us in this matter the more easily, because a propensity to the covenant of works is a part of our natural depravity. Depend upon it you will never have a suitable and sufficient sense of the evil of sin, and of your share in it, so long as you have any sin remaining in you.

We must see Jesus as He is before our apprehension of any spiritual truth will be complete. But if we know that we must perish without Christ, and that He is able to save to the uttermost, we know enough to warrant us to cast our souls upon Him, and we dishonor Him by fearing that when we do so He will disappoint our hope. But if you are still perplexed about the high points of election, etc., I would advise you to leave the disposal of others to the great Judge; and as to yourself, I think I need not say much to persuade you, that if ever you are saved at all, it must be in a way of free and absolute grace.

Leave disputes to others; wait upon the Lord, and He will teach you all things in such degree and time as He sees best. Perhaps

you have suffered for taking things too much upon trust from men. Cease from man, whose breath is in his nostrils. One is your master, even Christ. Study and pray over the Bible; and you may take it as a sure rule, that whatever sentiment makes any part of the Word of God unwelcome to you is justly to be suspected. Aim at a cheerful spirit. The more you trust God, the better you will serve Him. While you indulge unbelief and suspicion, you weaken your own hands, and discourage others. Be thankful for what He has shown you, and wait upon Him for more: you shall find He has not said, "Seek ye My face" in vain. I heartily commend you to His grace and care, And am, &c.
John Newton

Fear of death
See also: Death
Yea, though I walk through the valley of the shadow of death, I will fear no evil.
The Bible, Psalm 23:4 KJV

Fear of God
Serve the LORD with fear …
The Bible, Psalm 2:11

The fear of the LORD is the beginning of knowledge …
The Bible, Proverbs 1:7

Fear God and give him glory …
The Bible, Revelation 14:7

"The fear of the Lord is the beginning of wisdom" (Prov. 1:7). Happy the soul that has been awed by a view of God's majesty, that has had a vision of God's awful greatness, His ineffable holiness, His perfect righteousness, His irresistible power, His sovereign grace.
Author unknown

John Knox feared God so much that he never feared the face of any man.
Author unknown

We will always live less than a responsible

life if we fear anything other than God.
Neil Anderson

The fear of God kills all other fears.
Hugh Black

I fear God, yet I am not afraid of him.
Thomas Browne

A hard heart is impenitent, and impenitence also makes the heart harder and harder. If you would be rid of a hard heart, that great enemy to the growth of the grace of fear, be much with Christ upon the cross in thy meditations, for that is an excellent remedy against the hardness of heart; a right sight of him, as he hanged there for thy sins, will dissolve thy heart into tears, and make it soft and tender. "They shall look upon me whom they have pierced, and they shall mourn." Now, a soft, a tender, and broken heart is a fit place for the grace of fear to thrive in.
John Bunyan

The remarkable thing about fearing God is that when you fear God, you fear nothing else, whereas if you do not fear God, you fear everything else.
Oswald Chambers

The remarkable thing about fearing God is that when you fear God you fear nothing else, whereas if you do not fear God you fear everything else.
Oswald Chambers

The fear of God furthers every enterprise that governments undertake.
Machiavelli

There is a virtuous fear which is the effect of faith, and a vicious fear which is the product of doubt and distrust. Persons of the one character fear to lose God; those of the other character fear to find Him.
Blaise Pascal

He that leaves off prayer leaves off the fear of God.
Thomas Watson

Feelings
See also: Facts

Mankind are governed more by their feelings than by reason.
Samuel Adams

The happiness and unhappiness of the rational, social animal depends not on what he feels but on what he does; just as his virtue and vice consist not in feeling but in doing.
Marcus Aurelius Antoninus

Never apologize for showing feeling. When you do so, you apologize for the truth.
Benjamin Disraeli

The best and most beautiful things in the world cannot be seen or even touched. They must be felt with the heart.
Helen Keller

The great thing to remember is that, though our feelings come and go, God's love for us does not.
C.S. Lewis

The value given to the testimony of any feeling must depend on our whole philosophy, not our whole philosophy on a feeling.
C.S. Lewis

You should not believe your conscience and your feelings more than the word which the Lord who receives sinners preaches to you.
Martin Luther

Luther was once asked, "Do you feel that you are a child of God this morning?" and he answered, "I cannot say that I do, but I know that I am."
Martin Luther

Savanarola appealed to feelings and transformed Florence into a model of righteousness. But Robespierre appealed to feelings and turned Paris into a pandemonium of immorality. Feelings cannot be made moral absolutes.
Henrietta Mears

Feeling always seeks something in itself; faith keeps itself occupied with who Jesus is. Do not forget that the faith of which God's Word speaks so much stands not only in opposition to works but also in opposition to feelings, and therefore for a pure life of faith you must cease to seek your salvation not only in works but also in feelings. Let faith always speak against feeling. When feeling says, "In myself I am sinful, I am dark, I am weak, I am poor, I am sad," let faith say, "In Christ I am holy, I am light, I am strong, I am rich, I am joyful."
Andrew Murray

It is as necessary for the heart to feel as for the body to be fed.
Napoleon

God often takes a course for accomplishing His purposes directly contrary to what our narrow views would prescribe. He brings a death upon our feelings, wishes and prospects when He is about to give us the desire of our hearts.
John Newton

Measure not God's love and favor by your own feelings. The sun shines as clearly in the darkest day as it does in the brightest. The difference is not in the sun, but in some clouds which hinder the manifestation of the light thereof.
Richard Sibbes

It is not prayer, it is not faith, it is not our doings, it is not our feelings upon which we must rest, but upon Christ and ON CHRIST ALONE!
C.H. Spurgeon

Faith is not a feeling. It is not even the feeling that something is going to happen in answer to our prayers. Faith may be easier to exercise when such feelings are present. Nevertheless, feelings of that sort never constitute faith. Faith is a response on our part, the obedient response of our wills to who God is and what He says.
John White

Feelings

Letter from John Newton
Rev Mr P.
January 11, 1777
Dear Sir,

We all need, and at the seasons the Lord sees best, we all receive chastisement. I hope you likewise have reason to praise Him, for supporting, sanctifying, and delivering mercy. The cowardly flesh presently sinks under the rod, but faith need not fear it, for it is in the hand of One who loves us better than we do ourselves, and who knows our frame, that we are but dust, and therefore will not suffer us to be overdone and overwhelmed.

I feel as a friend should feel for Mr. B---; were I able, I would soon send him health. If the Lord, who is able to remove his illness in a minute, permits it to continue, we may be sure, upon the whole, it will be better for him. It is, however, very lawful to pray that his health may be restored, and his usefulness prolonged. I beg you to give my love to him, and tell him that my heart bears him an affectionate remembrance; and I know the God whom he serves will make every dispensation supportable and profitable to him.

If, as you observe, the Song of Solomon describes the experience of his church, it shows the dark as well as the bright side. No one part of it is the experience of every individual at any particular time. Some are in his banqueting-house, others upon their beds. Some sit under His banner, supported by His arm; while others have a faint perception of Him at a distance, with many a hill and mountain between. In one thing, however, they all agree, that He is the leading object of their desires, and that they have had such a discovery of His person, work, and love, as makes Him precious to their hearts. Their judgment of Him is always the same, but their sensibility varies. The love they bear Him, though rooted and grounded in their hearts, is not always equally in exercise, nor can it be so. We are like trees, which, though alive, cannot put forth their leaves and fruit without the influence of the sun. They are alive in winter as well as in summer; but how different is their appearance in these different seasons! Were we always alike, could we always believe, love, and rejoice, we should think the power inherent and our own; but it is more for the Lord's glory, and more suited to form us to a temper becoming the gospel, that we should be made deeply sensible of our own inability and dependence, than that we should be always in a lively frame.

I am persuaded, a broken and a contrite spirit, a conviction of our vileness and nothingness, connected with a cordial acceptance of Jesus as revealed in the gospel, is the highest attainment we can reach in this life. Sensible comforts are desirable, and we must be sadly declined when they do not appear to us; but I believe there may be a real exercise of faith and growth in grace when our sensible feelings are faint and low. A soul may be in as thriving a state when thirsting, seeking, and mourning after the Lord, as when actually rejoicing in Him; as much in earnest when fighting in the valley, as when singing upon the mount; nay, dark seasons afford the surest and strongest manifestations of the power of faith. To hold fast the word of promise, to maintain a hatred of sin, to go on steadfastly in the path of duty, in defiance both of the frowns and the smiles of the world, when we have but little comfort, is a more certain evidence of grace, than a thousand things which we may do or forbear when our spirits are warm and lively.

I have seen many who have been upon the whole but uneven walkers, though at times they have seemed to enjoy, at least have talked of, great comforts. I have seen others, for the most part, complain of much darkness and coldness, who have been remarkably humble, tender, and exemplary in their spirit and conduct. Surely were I to choose my lot, it should be with the latter.
I am, &c.
John Newton

Fellow-workers

For we are God's fellow-workers ...
The Bible, 1 Corinthians 3:9

Fellowship with Christians

The right hand of fellowship.
The Bible, Galatians 2:9

Christians are not lone rangers.
Chuck Colson

And ye shall gather yourselves together
frequently, seeking what is fitting for your
souls.
Didache

Behind every saint stands another saint.
Friedrich von Hügel

Be eager for more frequent gatherings for
thanksgiving [eucharist] to God and for his
glory. For when you meet frequently the
forces of Satan are annulled and his
destructive power is canceled in the
concord of our faith.
Ignatius of Antioch

The virtuous soul that is alone and
without a master is like a lone burning
coal; it will grow colder rather than
hotter.
John of the Cross

Friendship between the friends of Jesus of
Nazareth is unlike any other friendship.
Stephen Neill

Satan watches for those vessels that sail
without convoy.
George Swinnock

Help us to help each other, Lord,
Each other's cross to bear,
Let each his friendly aid afford,
And feel his brother's care.
Charles Wesley

The Bible knows nothing of solitary religion.
John Wesley

Fellowship with God
See also: Abiding; Holiness

I would rather be a doorkeeper in the
house of my God than dwell in the tents of
the wicked.
The Bible, Psalm 84:10

May the grace of the Lord Jesus Christ,
and the love of God, and the fellowship of
the Holy Spirit be with you all.
The Bible, 2 Corinthians 13:14

Come near to God and he will come near
to you.
The Bible, James 4:8

We do not walk to God with the feet of
our body, nor would wings, if we had
them, carry us to Him, but we go to Him,
by the affections of our soul.
Augustine of Hippo

The Holy Spirit makes a man a Christian,
and if he is a Christian through the work
of the Holy Spirit, that same Spirit draws
him to other Christians in the church. An
individual Christian is no Christian at all.
R. Brokhoff

Having ingrafted us into his body, Christ
makes us partakers, not only of all his
benefits, but also himself. Christ is not
received merely in the understanding and
imagination. For the promises offer him,
not so that we end up with the mere sight
and knowledge of him, but that we enjoy
true fellowship with him.
John Calvin

Oh! for a closer walk with God,
A calm and heav'nly frame;
A light to shine upon the road
That leads me to the Lamb!

Where is the blessedness I knew
When first I saw the Lord?
Where is the soul-refreshing view
Of Jesus, and his word?
What peaceful hours I once enjoy'd
How sweet their mem'ry still!
But they have left an aching void,

The world can never fill.

Return, O holy Dove, return,
Sweet messenger of rest;
I hate the sins that made thee mourn,
And drove thee from my breast.

The dearest idol I have known,
Whate'er that idol be;
Help me to tear it from thy throne,
And worship only thee.

So shall my walk be close with God,
Calm and serene my frame;
So purer light shall mark the road
That leads me to the Lamb
William Cowper

The enjoyment of God is the only happiness
with which our souls can be satisfied.
Jonathan Edwards

The steady discipline of intimate friendship
with Jesus results in men becoming like Him.
H.E. Fosdick

Take God for your bridegroom and friend,
and walk with him continually; and you
will not sin and will learn to love, and the
things you must do will work out
prosperously for you.
John of the Cross

The relationship between God and a man is
more private and intimate than any possible
relation between two fellow creatures.
C.S. Lewis

All the doors that lead inward, to the
sacred place of the Most High, are doors
outward – out of self, out of smallness, out
of wrong.
George Macdonald

Some people become tired at the end of
ten minutes or half an hour of prayer.
What will they do when they have to
spend Eternity in the presence of God? We
must begin the habit here and become
used to being with God.
Sadhu Sundar Singh

Knowledge of God can be fully given to
man only in a Person, never in a doctrine.
Faith is not the holding of correct doctrine,
but personal fellowship with the living
God.
William Temple

To desire nothing outwardly brings peace
to a man's soul, so a man, by an inward
forsaking of himself, joins himself to God.
Thomas à Kempis

God desires and is pleased to communicate
with us through the avenues of our minds,
our wills, and our emotions. The
continuous and unembarrassed
interchange of love and thought between
God and the souls of the redeemed men
and women is the throbbing heart of the
New Testament.
A. W. Tozer

Feminism

There is neither ... male nor female, for
you are all one in Christ Jesus.
The Bible, Galatians 3:28

Women's Liberation is just a lot of
foolishness.
Golda Meir

I resolved to claim for my sex all that an
impartial Creator had bestowed, which, by
custom and a perverted application of the
Scriptures, had been wrested from woman.
Lucretia Mott

I am a feminist because I feel endangered,
psychically and physically, by this society
and because I believe that the women's
movement is saying that we have come to
an edge of history when men – insofar as
they are embodiments of the patriarchal
idea – have become dangerous to children
and other living things, themselves
included.
Adrienne Rich

... a movement for the elimination of sex-
based injustice.
Janet Radcliffe Richards

A Christian feminist program would include a critique of the contemporary humanism in which men define the norms.
Elaine Storkey

I owe nothing to Women's Lib.
Margaret Thatcher

It is the right of every woman in America to become all she is capable of becoming on her own, or in partnership with a man.
M.C. Thomas

Festivals
See also: Sunday
The life without festival is a long road without an inn.
Democritus of Abdera

Finding God
See: Searching for God

Fitness
Physical training is of some value ...
The Bible, 1 Timothy 4:8

Physical fitness is not only one of the most important keys to a healthy body, it is the basis of dynamic and creative intellectual activity. The relationship between the soundness of the body and the activities of the mind is subtle and complex. Much is not yet understood. But we do know what the Greeks knew: that intelligence and skill can only function at the peak of their capacity when the body is healthy and strong; that hardy spirits and tough minds usually inhabit sound bodies.
J.F. Kennedy

Flattery
... nor will I flatter any man ...
The Bible, Job 32:21

... we never used flattery ...
The Bible, 1 Thessalonians 2:5

A man's body is remarkably sensitive. Pat him on the back and his head swells.
Author unknown

Take heed of the flatteries of false brethren.
John Bunyan

Flattery corrupts both the receiver and giver.
Edmund Burke

I can't be your friend, and your flatterer too.
Thomas Fuller

Flattery is a false coinage, which our vanity puts into circulation.
La Rouchefoucauld

There is no other way of guarding oneself against flattery than by letting men understand that they will not offend you by speaking the truth; but when everyone can tell you the truth, you lose their respect.
Niccolo Machiavelli

We do not hate flattery, any one of us – we all like it.
C.H. Spurgeon

Among all the diseases of the mind there is not one more pernicious than the love of flattery.
Richard Steel

Following God
See: Christian life

Follow-up
See also: Conversion; Evangelism; Fellowship with Christians
If everyone who worked for the conversion of others was to introduce them immediately to prayer and to the interior life and made it their main aim to win over their hearts, innumerable, permanent conversions would definitely take place.
Madame Guyon

I determined by the grace of God not to strike one blow in any place where I cannot follow the blow.
John Wesley

My brother Wesley acted more wisely than I. The souls that were awakened under his ministry he joined together in classes, and

so preserved the fruit of his labors. I failed to do this, and as a result my people are a rope of sand.
George Whitefield

Food
See also: Fasting; Gluttony
So whether you eat or drink or whatever you do, do it all for the glory of God.
The Bible, 1 Corinthians 10:31

For a long life,
breakfast like a king;
lunch moderately
and dine like a pauper.
Author unknown

One eats in holiness and the table become an altar.
Martin Buber

A full belly makes a dull brain
Benjamin Franklin

Three good meals a day is bad living.
Benjamin Franklin

Man is what he eats.
German proverb

A fat paunch breeds no fine thoughts.
Greek proverb

Tell me what you eat, and I will tell you what manner of man you are.
Brillat Savarin

Fools
The fool says in his heart, "There is no God."
The Bible, Psalm 14:1

Answer a fool according to his folly.
The Bible, Proverbs 26:5

As the crackling of thorns under a pot, so is the laughter of a fool.
The Bible, Ecclesiastes 7:6 KJV

I'd rather be a fool in the eyes of men, than a fool in the eyes of God.
Author unknown

No one is a fool always, everyone sometimes.
Author unknown

A fool always finds a bigger fool to admire him.
Boileau

Wise men learn more from fools than fools from wise men.
Cato

Fools and wise folk are alike harmless. It is the half-wise, and the half-foolish, who are most dangerous.
Goethe

Fools rush in where angels fear to tread.
Alexander Pope

Force
Force is not a remedy.
John Bright

Right reason is stronger than force.
James A. Garfield

Force is all-conquering, but its victories are short-lived.
Abraham Lincoln

Force rules the world, and not opinion; but opinion is that which makes use of force.
Blaise Pascal

Foreigners
"When an alien lives with you in your land, do not ill-treat him ... Love him as yourself ..."
The Bible, Leviticus 19:33-34

Modern man is educated to understand foreign languages and misunderstand foreigners.
G.K. Chesterton

Foreknowledge
See: Election; Free will; Predestination

Forgiveness
See also: Forgiving
... as far as the east is from the west, so far

has he removed our transgressions from us.
The Bible, Psalm 103:12

Though your sins be as scarlet, they shall
be as white as snow.
The Bible, Isaiah 1:18 KJV

… God … forgave us all our sins.
The Bible, Colossians 2:13

Forgiveness does not mean the cancellation
of all consequences of wrongdoing. It
means the refusal on God's part to let our
guilty past affect His relationship with us.
Author unknown

Forgive or relive.
Author unknown

Do come in – Trespassers will be forgiven.
*Author unknown. Posted on a church bulletin
board*

There is only one person God cannot
forgive. The person who refuses to come to
him for forgiveness.
Author unknown

1 TREE + 3 NAILS = 4 GIVEN
Author unknown

Forgiveness is the key to happiness.
Author unknown

First of all, I … rely upon the merits of
Jesus Christ for a pardon of all my sins.
*Samuel Adams, Signer of the Declaration of
Independence*

Do not trust in your own righteousness; do
not grieve about a sin that is past and gone.
Antony of Egypt

I will love you, O Lord, and thank you,
and confess to your name, because you
have forgiven me my evil and nefarious
deeds.
Augustine of Hippo

Two works of mercy set a man free: forgive
and you will be forgiven, and give and you

will receive.
Augustine of Hippo

Thou must be emptied of that wherewith
thou art full, that thou mayest be filled
with that whereof thou art empty.
Augustine of Hippo

It is always the case that when the
Christian looks back, he is looking at the
forgiveness of sins.
Karl Barth

Look once again to Jesus Christ in his
death upon the cross. Look and try to
understand that what he did and suffered,
he did and suffered for you, for me, for us
all. He carried our sin, our captivity and
our suffering, and did not carry it in vain.
He carried it away.
Karl Barth

When Christ's hands were nailed to the
cross, he also nailed your sins to the cross.
Bernard of Clairvaux

Life has taught me to forgive much, but to
seek forgiveness still more.
Otto von Bismarck

There is a fountain filled with blood
Drawn from Immanuel's veins,
And sinners plunged beneath that flood
Lose all their guilty stains.
William Cowper

The sinner of today is the saint of
tomorrow. Wherefore, unmindful of the
sins and shortcomings of our neighbors,
let us look to our own imperfections,
surely forgetting what God has forgotten:
sins truly repented, which God has
forgotten, we have no business to
remember.
Meister Eckhart

Forgiveness is the answer to the child's
dream of a miracle by which what is
broken is made whole again, what is soiled
is again made clean.
Dag Hammarskjold

For Christ is the God over all, who has arranged to wash away sin from mankind, rendering the old man new.
Hippolytus

Jesus ventured – as no prophet had ever ventured – to proclaim God's forgiveness, completely gratis, instead of legal penalties, and also to grant it in a personal way in order by this very encouragement to make possible repentance and forgiveness towards our fellow-men.
Hans Küng

Only a Person can forgive.
C.S. Lewis

I think that if God forgives us we must forgive ourselves.
C.S. Lewis

In a dream Martin Luther once had he saw a book where all his sins were written. In the dream, the devil spoke to Luther, "Martin, here is one of your sins, here is another," pointing to the writing in the book. Then Luther said to the devil, "Take a pen and write, 'The blood of Jesus Christ, God's Son, cleanses us from all sin.'"
Martin Luther

Forgiveness of sins is the very heart of Christianity, and yet it is a very dangerous thing to preach.
Martin Luther

Forgiveness is God's command.
Martin Luther

God has cast our confessed sins into the depths of the sea, and He's even put a "No Fishing" sign over the spot.
D.L. Moody

All we like sheep have gone astray; we have turned every one to his own way; and the Lord hath laid on him the iniquity of us all. Go in at the first "all" and come out at the last "all".
D.L. Moody

No virtuous act is quite as virtuous from the standpoint of our friend or foe as from our own standpoint; therefore we must be saved by the final form of love, which is forgiveness.
Reinhold Niebuhr

Forgiveness is all-powerful.
Forgiveness heals all ills.
Catherine Ponder

Suicide is the only reasonable alternative unless there is real forgiveness. There is no way any of us can live with ourselves, or with others as bad as ourselves, unless the blood of Jesus Christ cleanses us from our guilt and shame. I work daily with those whose crimes are nauseating to any reasonable person. The stink of sin would be unbearable but for the historical reality, the moral reality, of the cross which reduces us all to the common ground of sinners who are equally deserving of hell and equally needing the mercy of God.
Prison Fellowship volunteer

If God were not willing to forgive sin, heaven would be empty.
German proverb

We are certain that there is forgiveness, because there is a gospel, and the very essence of the gospel lies in the proclamation of the pardon of sin.
C.H. Spurgeon

God will spare the sinner because he did not spare his Son. God can pass by your transgressions because he laid them upon his only begotten Son nearly two thousand years ago.
C.H Spurgeon

Once God preached to me by a similitude in the depth of winter. The earth was black, and there was scarcely a green thing or a flower to be seen. As I looked across the fields, there was nothing but barrenness – bare hedges and leafless trees, and black earth, wherever I gazed. All of a sudden God spoke, and unlocked the

treasures of the snow, and the white flakes descended until there was no blackness to be seen, and all was one sheet of dazzling whiteness. At the time I was seeking the Savior, and not long before I found Him, and I remember well that sermon which I saw before me in the snow: "Come now, and let us reason together, saith the Lord: though your sins be as scarlet, they shall be as white as snow; though they be red like crimson, they shall be as wool."
C.H. Spurgeon

God forgives not capriciously, but with wise, definite, Divine pre-arrangement; forgives universally, on the grounds of an atonement and on the condition of repentance and faith.
Richard Salter Storrs

The symbol of the religion of Jesus is the cross, not the scales.
John Stott

Only one petition in the Lord's Prayer has any condition attached to it: it is the petition for forgiveness.
William Temple

Dear Lord and Father of mankind,
Forgive our foolish ways!
Reclothe us in our rightful mind,
In purer lives thy service find,
In deeper reverence, praise.
John Greenleaf Whittier

Forgiving
See also: Forgiveness
He who covers over an offence promotes love ...
The Bible, Proverbs 17:9

"Lord, how many times shall I forgive my brother when he sins against me? Up to seven times?"
Jesus answered, "I tell you, not seven times, but seventy-seven times."
The Bible, Matthew 18:21,22

Forgive, and you will be forgiven.
The Bible, Luke 6:37

Bear with each other and forgive whatever grievances you may have against one another. Forgive as the Lord forgave you.
The Bible, Colossians 3:13

The glory of Christianity is to conquer by forgiveness.
Author unknown

When someone hurts me, forgiveness is cheaper than a lawsuit. But not nearly as gratifying.
Author unknown

A person's ability to forgive is in proportion to the greatness of his soul.
Author unknown

To forgive is to set a prisoner free and discover the prisoner was you.
Author unknown

Every person should have a special cemetery lot in which to bury the faults of friends and loved ones.
Author unknown

We are most like beasts when we kill, most like men when we judge; most like God when we forgive.
Author unknown

Little men cannot forgive.
Author unknown

He who forgives ends the quarrel.
Author unknown

"I can forgive but I cannot forget," is only another way of saying, "I cannot forgive."
Henry Ward Beecher

It is easier to forgive an enemy than to forgive a friend.
William Blake

We all like to forgive, and love best not those who offend us least, nor who have done most for us, but those who make it most easy for us to forgive them.
Samuel Butler

The more a man knows, the more he forgives.
Catherine the Great

I can pardon everyone's mistakes but my own.
Cato

Dost thou wish to receive mercy? Show mercy to thy neighbor.
John Chrysostom

Once a woman has forgiven her man, she must not reheat his sins for breakfast.
Marlene Dietrich

Forgotten is forgiven.
F. Scott Fitzgerald

Doing an injury puts you below your enemy; Revenging one makes you but even with him; Forgiving it sets you above him.
Benjamin Franklin

The weak can never forgive. Forgiveness is the attribute of the strong.
Mahatma Gandhi

Forgiveness breaks the chain of causality because he who "forgives" you – out of love – takes upon himself the consequences of what you have done.
Dag Hammarskjold

There's no point in burying the hatchet if you're going to put up a marker on the site.
Sydney J. Harris

The offender never pardons.
George Herbert

He that cannot forgive others, breaks the bridge over which he himself must pass if he would ever reach heaven; for everyone has need to be forgiven.
George Herbert

I can have peace of mind only when I forgive rather than judge.
Gerald Jampolsky

A wise man will make haste to forgive, because he knows the true value of time, and will not suffer it to pass away in unnecessary pain.
Samuel Johnson

The moment an individual can accept and forgive himself, even a little, is the moment in which he becomes to some degree lovable.
Eugene Kennedy

Forgiveness is not an occasional act: it is an attitude.
Martin Luther King, Jr

We pardon in the degree that we love.
La Rochefoucauld

To understand is not only to pardon, but in the end to love.
Walter Lippmann

It is idle for us to say that we know that God has forgiven us if we are not loving and forgiving ourselves.
Martyn Lloyd-Jones

The man who is truly forgiven and knows it, is a man who forgives.
Martyn Lloyd-Jones

If we keep remembering the wrongs which men have done us, we destroy the power of the remembrance of God.
Abba Macarius the Great

Forgiveness proceeds from a generous soul.
Machiavelli

God forgives talents; we cannot forgive pence. God forgives a hundred thousand; we cannot forgive a hundred (Matthew 18). We look that God should forgive us, and we will not forgive others.
Thomas Manton

When you forgive, you in no way change the past – but you sure do change the future.
Bernard Meltzer.

When a deep injury is done us, we never

recover until we forgive.
Alan Paton

If then we entreat the Lord that He would forgive us, we also ought to forgive: for we are before the eyes of our Lord and God, and we must all stand at the judgment-seat of Christ, and each man must give an account of himself.
Polycarp

To err is human, to forgive, divine.
Alexander Pope

He who forgives ends a quarrel.
African proverb

He never pardons those he injures.
Italian proverb

The noblest vengeance is to forgive.
Proverb

Humanity is never so beautiful as when praying for forgiveness or else forgiving another.
Jean Paul Richter

The quality of mercy is not strain'd,
It droppeth as the gentle rain from heaven
Upon the place beneath: it is twice blest;
It blesseth him that gives, and him that
  takes.
William Shakespeare, The Merchant of Venice

As we forgive, we achieve the right to be forgiven.
As we forgive, we increase our capacity for light and understanding.
As we forgive, we live beyond the power of the adversary.
Robert L. Simpson

The stupid neither forgive nor forget; the naïve forgive and forget; the wise forgive but do not forget.
Thomas Szasz

Without forgiveness, there's no future.
Desmond Tutu

Forgiveness is the fragrance the violet sheds

on the heel that has crushed it.
Mark Twain

Love truth, but pardon error.
Voltaire

To carry a grudge is like being stung to death by one bee.
William H. Walton

Forgiving those who hurt us is the key to personal peace.
G. Weatherly

General Oglethorpe: "I never forgive."
John Wesley: "Then, sir, I hope that you never sin."

It's very easy to forgive others their mistakes, it takes more guts and gumption to forgive them for having witnessed your own.
Jessamyn West

The practice of forgiveness is our most important contribution to the healing of the world.
Marianne Williamson

Lo, here is a token that I forgive thee.
George Wishart, as he kissed his hesitant executioner

Formalism
Formality, formality, formality is the great sin of England at this day, under which she groans. There is more light than there was, but less life; more shadow, but less substance; more profession, but less sanctification.
Thomas Hall, 1658

He that hath but a form is a hypocrite; but he that hath not a form is an atheist.
Joseph Hall

There are no formalities between the closest of friends.
Japanese proverb

There is no devil so dangerous as

evangelical formalism.
J.C. Ryle

Fortune
See also Fate
There is a tide in the affairs of men.
Which, taken at the flood, leads on to
fortune.
William Shakespeare, Julius Caesar

Fraud
The first and worst of all frauds is to cheat
oneself.
Gamaliel Bailey

The more gross the fraud the more glibly
will it go down, and the more greedily be
swallowed, since folly will always find
faith where impostors will find
imprudence.
Charles Caleb Colton

For the most part fraud in the end
secures for its companions repentance
and shame.
Charles Simmons

It is fraud to accept what you cannot repay.
Publilius Syrus

All frauds, like the wall daubed with
untempered mortar always tend to the
decay of what they are devised to support.
Richard Whately

Free will
See also: Election; Predestination
Without free will, how shall God judge the
world?
Without grace, how shall God save the
world?
Author unknown

Concerning free will it is taught that to
some extent man has freedom of will to lead
a just and honorable life, to choose between
things which reason comprehends; but
without grace, assistance, and the operation
of the Holy Spirit he is unable to become
pleasing to God, or to fear God in heart, or
to believe in him, or to cast out of his heart

that innate evil propensity; but these things
are effected through the Holy Spirit, which
is given through the word of God.
Augsburg Confession

He who created us without our help will
not save us without our consent.
Augustine of Hippo

Free-will, without God's grace and the
Holy Ghost, can do nothing but sin.
Augustine of Hippo

Few have defined what free will is, although
it repeatedly occurs in the writings of all.
Origen seems to have put forward a
definition generally agreed upon among
ecclesiastical writers when he said that it is
a faculty of the reason to distinguish
between good and evil, a faculty of the will
to choose one or the other. Augustine does
not disagree with this when he teaches that
it is a faculty of the reason and the will to
choose good with the assistance of grace;
evil, when grace is absent.
John Calvin

God, having placed good and evil in our
power, has given us full freedom of choice;
he does not keep back the unwilling, but
embraces the willing.
John Chrysostom

Reformed definition of free will: "The
power to choose according to one's
strongest motive, nature and character." In
the unregenerate, to freely choose evil. In
the regenerate, to freely choose God and
the good.
Byron Curtis

I have a great liking for many of Wesley's
hymns; but when I read some of them, I
ask, "What's become of your free will now,
friend?"
George Duncan

You will notice that Scripture just sails
over the problem [of the whole puzzle
about grace and free will]. "Work out
your own salvation in fear and

trembling" – pure Pelagianism. But why?
"For it is God who worketh in you" –
pure Augustinianism. It is presumably
only our presuppositions that make this
appear nonsensical.
C.S. Lewis

Why did God give them free will? Because
free will, though it makes evil possible, is
also the only thing that makes possible any
love or goodness or joy worth having.
C.S. Lewis

In divine and spiritual things we have no
free will, but only in name.
Martin Luther

If any man doth ascribe aught of salvation,
even the very least, to the free will of man,
he knoweth nothing of grace, and he hath
not learnt Jesus Christ aright.
Martin Luther

Man was predestined to have free will.
Hal Lee Luyah

The two ideas of free will and divine
sovereignty can not be reconciled in our
own minds, but that does not prevent
them from being reconciled in God's
mind. We measure Him by our own
intellectual standard if we think
otherwise. And so our solution of the
problem of free will and of the problems
of history and of individual salvation
must finally lie in the full acceptance
and realization of what is implied by the
infinity and the omniscience of God.
William Sanday and Arthur C. Headlam

We have to believe in free will. We've got
no choice.
Isaac Bashevis Singer

I do not come into this pulpit hoping that
perhaps somebody will of his own free will
return to Christ. My hope lies in another
quarter. I hope that my Master will lay
hold of some of them and say, "You are
mine, and you shall be mine. I claim you
for myself." My hope arises from the
freeness of grace, and not from the
freedom of the will.
C.H. Spurgeon

God wants only one thing in the whole
world – to find the innermost part of the
spirit of man clean and ready for him to
accomplish the divine purpose therein. He
has all power in heaven and earth, but the
power to do his work in man against man's
will he has not got.
John Tauler

The greatest judgment which God Himself
can, in this present life, inflict upon a man
is to leave him in the hand of his own
boasted free will.
Augustus Toplady

I infer that God's decrees, and the necessity
of events flowing thence, neither destroy
the true free agency of men, nor render the
commission of sin a jot less heinous. They
neither force the human will, nor extenuate
the evil of human actions. Predestination,
foreknowledge, and providence, only secure
the event, and render it certainly future, in
a way and manner (incomprehensibly
indeed by us; but) perfectly consistent with
the nature of second causes.
Augustus Toplady

The friends of free will are the enemies of
free grace.
John Trapp

Man, by his fall into a state of sin, hath
wholly lost all ability of will to any
spiritual good accompanying salvation; so
as a natural man, being altogether averse
from that good, and dead in sin, is not
able, by his own strength, to convert
himself, or to prepare himself thereunto.
Westminster Confession

Freedom
See also: Freedom of speech
Remember that to change thy mind and to
follow him that sets thee right, is to be none
the less the free agent that thou wast before.
Marcus Aurelius Antoninus

Experience should teach us to be most on our guard to protect liberty when the government's purposes are beneficent. Men born to freedom are naturally alert to repel invasion of their liberty by evil-minded rulers. The greatest dangers to liberty lurk in insidious encroachment by men of zeal, well-meaning but without understanding.
Louis D. Brandeis, US Supreme Court Justice

Men are qualified for civil liberties in exact proportion to their disposition to put moral chains upon their appetites: in proportion as their love of justice is above their rapacity.
Edmund Burke

This world has no importance. Once a man realizes that, he wins freedom.
Camus

The Battle of Britain is about to begin. Upon this battle depends the survival of Christian civilization. Upon it depends our own British life ... Hitler knows that he will have to break us in this Island or lose the war. If we can stand up to him, all Europe may be free and the life of the world may move forward into broad, sunlit uplands. But if we fail, then the whole world, including the United States, including all that we have known and cared for, will sink into the abyss of a new Dark Age made more sinister, and perhaps more protracted, by the light of perverted science. Let us therefore brace ourselves to our duties, and so bear ourselves that, if the British Empire and Commonwealth last for a thousand years, men will still say, "This was their finest hour."
Winston Churchill

Freedom is participation in power.
Cicero

The instinct of nearly all societies is to lock up anybody who is truly free.
First, society begins by trying to beat you up. If this fails, they try to poison you.
If this fails too, they finish by loading honors on your head.
Jean Cocteau

But what is freedom? Rightly understood, A universal license to be good.
Hartley Coleridge

If liberty is to be saved, it will not be by the doubters, the men of science or the materialists; it will be by religious conviction, by the faith of individuals, who believe that God wills man to be free but also pure.
Samuel Taylor Coleridge

They that can give up essential liberty to obtain a little temporary safety deserve neither liberty nor safety.
Benjamin Franklin

The moment the slave resolves that he will no longer be a slave, his fetters fall. He frees himself and shows the way to others. Freedom and slavery are mental states.
Gandhi

Enslave the liberty of one human being and the liberties of the world are put in peril.
William Lloyd Garrison

None are more hopelessly enslaved than those who falsely believe they are free.
Goethe

Liberty is the power that we have over ourselves.
Hugho Grotius

The greatest glory of a free born people, Is to transmit that freedom to their children.
William Havard

Our professed love of freedom is increasingly shown to be a sophistry that replaces wisdom and righteousness with self-gratification.
Carl Henry

There is a road to freedom. Its milestones are Obedience, Endeavor, Honesty, Order, Cleanliness, Sobriety, Truthfulness, Sacrifice, and love of the Fatherland.
Adolf Hitler

The basic test of freedom is perhaps less in

what we are free to do than in what we are free not to do.
Eric Hoffer

When people are free to do as they please, they usually imitate each other.
Eric Hoffer

When we lose the right to be different, we lose the privilege to be free.
Charles Evans Hughes

A man's worst difficulties begin when he is able to do as he likes.
Thomas Huxley

Freedom is that faculty which enlarges the usefulness of all other faculties.
Immanuel Kant

Freedom is indivisible. When one man is enslaved, all are not free.
John Fitzgerald Kennedy

The unity of freedom has never relied on uniformity of opinion.
John Fitzgerald Kennedy

When we let freedom ring … when we let it ring from every village and every hamlet, from every state and every city, we will be able to speed up that day when all of God's children: black men and white men, Jews and Gentiles, Protestants and Catholics will be able to join hands and sing in the words of the old Negro spiritual, Free at last, free at last. Thank God almighty, we are free at last.
Martin Luther King, Jr

There are two freedoms: the false where a man is free to do what he likes; and the true where a man is free to do what he ought.
Charles Kingsley

Respect for individual rights is the essential precondition for a free and prosperous world … and that only through freedom can peace and prosperity be realized.
Preamble to the Libertarian Platform

Those who deny freedom to others deserve it not for themselves.
Abraham Lincoln

No man is entitled to the blessings of freedom unless he be vigilant in its preservation.
Douglas MacArthur

O Lord my God, I have hoped in thee,
O dear Jesus, set me free.
Though hard the chains that fasten me,
And sore my lot, yet I long for thee
I languish and groaning bend my knee,
Adoring, imploring, O set me free.
Mary Queen of Scots

If liberty means anything at all, it means the right to tell people what they do not want to hear.
George Orwell

Those who expect to reap the blessings of freedom, must, like men, undergo the fatigues of supporting it.
Thomas Paine

It is not good to be too free. It is not good to have everything one wants.
Blaise Pascal

To give up the task of reforming society is to give up one's responsibility as a free man.
Alan Paton

If the sea were ink, and the earth parchment, it would never serve to describe the praises of liberty.
Rabbinical saying

Freedom prospers when religion is vibrant and the rule of law under God is acknowledged.
Ronald Reagan.

If negro freedom is taken away, or that of any minority group, the freedom of all the people is taken away.
Paul Robson

Man is born free, but everywhere he is in chains.
Jean-Jacques Rousseau

Liberty without virtue would be no blessing to us.
Benjamin Rush

Liberty means responsibility. That's why most men dread it.
G.B. Shaw

If vice and corruption prevail, liberty cannot subsist; but if virtue have the advantage, arbitrary power cannot be established.
Algernon Sidney

Freedom is like a coin. It has the word privilege on one side and responsibility on the other. It does not have privilege on both sides. There are too many today who want everything involved in privilege but refuse to accept anything that approaches the sense of responsibility.
Joseph Sizoo

When you have robbed a man of everything, he's no longer in your power. He is free again.
Alexander Solzhenitsyn

A free society is one where it is safe to be unpopular.
Adlai Stevenson

Liberty cannot be established without morality, nor morality without faith.
Alexis de Tocqueville

Loyalty to petrified opinion never yet broke a chain or freed a human soul.
Mark Twain, inscription beneath his bust in the Hall of Fame

Work like you don't need the money.
Dance like no one is watching.
And love like you've never been hurt.
Mark Twain

God grants liberty only to those who love it, and are always ready to guard and defend it.
Daniel Webster.

We are free when our lives are uncommitted, but not to be what we were intended to be. Real freedom is not freedom From, but freedom For.
Robert W. Young

Freedom, Christian

Be careful, however, that the exercise of your freedom does not become a stumbling-block to the weak.
The Bible, 1 Corinthians 8:9

"Everything is permissible" – but not everything is beneficial. "Everything is permissible" – but not everything is constructive.
The Bible, 1 Corinthians 10:23

It is for freedom that Christ has set us free. Stand firm, then, and do not let yourselves be burdened again by a yoke of slavery.
The Bible, Galatians 5:1

Live as free men, but do not use your freedom as a cover-up for evil …
The Bible, 1 Peter 2:16

The human image needs the support of a higher nature, and human freedom reaches its definitive expression in a higher freedom, freedom in truth.
Berdyaev on Dostoevsky

I have freed my soul.
Bernard of Clairvaux

Christian freedom, in my opinion, consists of three parts. The first: that the consciences of believers, in seeking assurance of their justification before God, should rise above and advance beyond the law, forgetting all law righteousness.
The second part, dependent upon the first, is that consciences observe the law, not as if constrained by the necessity of the law, but that freed from the law's yoke they willingly obey God's will.
The third part of Christian freedom lies

in this: regarding outward things that are of themselves "indifferent," we are not bound before God by any religious obligation preventing us from sometimes using them and other times not using them, indifferently.

Accordingly, it is perversely interpreted both by those who allege it as an excuse for their desires that they may abuse God's good gifts to their own lust and by those who think that freedom does not exist unless it is used before men, and consequently, in using it have no regard for weaker brethren. Nothing is plainer than this rule: that we should use our freedom if it results in the edification of our neighbor, but if it does not help our neighbor, then we should forego it.
John Calvin

A Christian is a perfectly free lord of all, subject to none. A Christian is a perfectly dutiful servant of all, subject of all, subject to all.
Martin Luther King

We find freedom when we find God; we lose it when we lose Him.
Paul E. Scherer

Set me free from evil passions, and heal my heart of all inordinate affections; that being inwardly cured and thoroughly cleansed, I may be made fit to love, courageous to suffer, steady to persevere.
Thomas à Kempis

Long my imprisoned spirit lay
Fast bound in sin and nature's night,
Thine eye diffused a quickening ray
I woke, the dungeon flamed with light.
My chains fell off, my heart was free
I rose, went forth, and followed Thee.
Charles Wesley

O Thou, to whose all-searching sight
The darkness shineth as the light,
Search, prove my heart; it pants for Thee;
O burst these bonds, and set it free!
Nicolaus Ludwig von Zinzendorf

Freedom of speech
See also Freedom
Every man has a right to utter what he thinks as truth, and every other man has a right to knock him down for it.
Samuel Johnson

I disapprove of what you say, but will defend to the death your right to say it.
Voltaire

Freemasonry
To fight against papacy is a social necessity and constitutes the constant duty of freemasonry.
Masonic international congress, 1904

Fretting
See also: Anxiety
I feel and grieve, but, by the grace of God, I fret at nothing.
John Wesley

Friars
Live in obedience, in chastity, and without property, following the teaching and footsteps of our Lord Jesus Christ.
Franciscan Rule of 1221

Friends of God
The Lord would speak to Moses face to face, as a man speaks with his friend.
The Bible, Exodus 33:11

"You are my friends ..."
The Bible, John 15:14

... he [Abraham] was called God's friend.
The Bible, James 2:23

Friendship
See also: Fellowship with Christians;
Fellowship with God
A friend loves at all times ...
The Bible, Proverbs 17:17

Into a box of friendship
To insure that it is strong
First a layer of respect
On the bottom does belong.

Then to the sides attach
In the corners where they meet
Several anchors full of trust
Devoid of all deceit.
The height of friendship can be measured
By the sides of four
So make them all a larger cut
And the box will hold much more.
Now fill it up with courtesy,
Honor and esteem,
Understanding, sympathy
And passion for a dream.
Add to that your honesty,
Emotions joy and love
And since they're so important
Place them up above.
But leave the box wide open
So all can see inside
To learn what makes a friendship work
From the box you built with pride.
Author unknown

True friendship is seen through the heart
not through the eyes.
Author unknown

It is better to have one true friend than all
the acquaintances in the world.
Author unknown

To have a good friend is one of the highest
delights of life; to be a good friend is one
of the noblest and most difficult
undertakings.
Author unknown

Friendship is like a bank account. You can't
continue to draw on it without making
deposits.
Author unknown

Love is blind, but friendship closes its eyes.
Author unknown

Remember, no man is a failure who has
friends.
Author unknown

One friend in a lifetime is much; two are
many; three are hardly possible.
Henry B. Adams.

Without friends no one would choose to
live, though he had all other goods.
Aristotle

What is a friend? A single soul dwelling in
two bodies.
Aristotle

Bad company is like a nail driven into a
post, which, after the first or second blow,
may be drawn out with little difficulty; but
being once driven up to the head, the
pincers cannot take hold to draw it out,
but which can only be done by the
destruction of the wood.
Augustine of Hippo

Do not keep the alabaster boxes of your
love and tenderness sealed up until your
friends are dead. Fill their lives with
sweetness. Speak approving cheering words
while their ears can hear them and while
their hearts can be thrilled by them.
Henry Ward Beecher

Two souls with but a single thought,
Two hearts that beat as one.
Von Munch Bellinghausen

The bird a nest
the spider a web
the human friendship.
W. Blake

Sometimes being a friend means mastering
the art of timing. There is a time for
silence. A time to let go and allow people
to hurl themselves into their own destiny.
And a time to prepare to pick up the pieces
when it's all over.
Octavia Butler

Friendship is like money, easier made than
kept.
Samuel Butler

Don't walk behind me,
I may not lead.
Don't walk in front of me,
I may not follow.
Just walk beside me

and be my friend.
Albert Camus

Tell me what company you keep, and I'll
tell you what you are.
Cervantes

Meeting Franklin Roosevelt was like
opening your first bottle of champagne;
knowing him was like drinking it.
Winston Churchill

Friendship, of itself a holy tie, is made
more sacred by adversity.
Charles Caleb Colton

Fate chooses our relatives, we choose our
friends.
Jacques Delille

Life is not worth living for a man who has
not even one good friend.
Democritus of Abdera

Blessed is the influence of one true, loving
soul on another.
George Eliot

A friend might well be reckoned the
masterpiece of nature.
Ralph Waldo Emerson

Life goes headlong. But if suddenly we
encounter a friend, we pause.
Ralph Waldo Emerson

Of all the things which wisdom provides to
make us entirely happy, much the greatest
is the possession of friendship.
Epicurus

Let me live in a house by the side of the
road and be a friend to man.
Sam Walter Foss

You cannot shake hands with a clenched fist.
Indira Gandhi

Friendship is always a sweet responsibility,
never an opportunity.
Kahlil Gibran

I love everything that's old, old friends, old
times, old manners, old books, old wine.
Oliver Goldsmith

Friends are the sunshine of life.
John Hay

Your friend is the man who knows all
about you and still likes you.
Elbert Hubbard

From acquaintances, we conceal our real
selves. To our friends we reveal our
weaknesses.
Basil Hume

The friendship that can cease has never
been real.
Jerome

I had a friend.
*Charles Kingsley, referring to his friendship with
F.D. Maurice, when asked about the secret of his
life.*

A true friend is the most precious of all
possessions and the one we take the least
thought about acquiring.
La Rochefoucauld

It is more shameful to mistrust one's
friends than to be deceived by them.
La Rochefoucauld

Friendship is only a reciprocal conciliation
of interests, and an exchange of good
offices; it is a species of commerce out of
which self-love always expects to gain
something.
La Rochefoucauld

Remember, the greatest gift is not found in
a store nor under a tree, but in the hearts
of true friends.
Cindy Lew

True friends don't spend time gazing into
each other's eyes. They may show great
tenderness towards each other, but they
face in the same direction – toward
common projects, goals – above all,

towards a common Lord.
C.S. Lewis

Is any pleasure on earth as great as a circle of Christian friends by a fire?
C.S. Lewis

Friendship is born at that moment when one person says to another: "What? You, too? I thought I was the only one."
C.S. Lewis

If you want to win a man to your cause, first convince him that you are his sincere friend.
Abraham Lincoln

Ships that pass in the night, and speak to each other in passing,
Only a signal shown and a distant voice in the darkness;
So on the ocean of life we pass and speak to one another,
Only a look and a voice, then darkness again and a silence.
Henry Wadsworth Longfellow

As gold is tried in the furnace, so friends are tried in adversity.
Menander

One can't complain. I have my friends. Someone spoke to me only yesterday.
A.A. Milne, Eeyore

It's so much more friendly with two.
A.A. Milne, Piglet

Love is rarer than genius itself.
And friendship is rarer than love.
Charels Péguy

Prosperity is no just scale; adversity is the only balance to weigh friends.
Plutarch

Friendly is as friendly does.
Proverb

Do not use a hatchet to remove a fly from your friend's forehead.
Chinese proverb

A faithful friend is an image of God.
French proverb

One who looks for a friend without faults will have none.
Hasidic proverb

A friend is a second self.
Latin proverb

Friends are lost by calling often and calling seldom.
Scottish proverb

Neither armies, nor treasures, but friends, are the surest protection of a king.
Sallust

The loneliest woman in the world is a woman without a close woman friend.
George Santayana

Sometimes our light goes out but is blown into flame by another human being. Each of us owes deepest thanks to those who have rekindled this light.
Albert Schweitzer

Old friends are best. King James used to call for his old shoes; they were easiest for his feet.
Selden

This belonged to the best friend I ever had.
Lord Shaftesbury, as he showed people the gold watch given to him by his family housekeeper, who had taught him about Jesus.

A friend should bear his friend's infirmities.
Shakespeare, Julius Caesar

Life is to be fortified by many friendships. To love and to be loved is the greatest happiness of existence.
Sydney Smith

The more we love, the better we are, and the greater our friendships are, the dearer we are to God.
Jeremy Taylor

By friendship you mean the greatest love, the greatest usefulness, the most open communication, the noblest sufferings, the severest truth, the heartiest counsel, and the greatest union of minds of which brave men and women are capable.
Jeremy Taylor

The language of friendship is not words but meanings.
Henry David Thoreau

A true friend is one who knows all about you and likes you anyway.
Christi Mary Warner

True friendship is a plant of low growth, and must undergo and withstand the shocks of adversity before it is entitled to the appellation
George Washington

Bad company is a disease;
Who lies with dogs, shall rise with fleas.
Rowland Watkyns

A true friend is someone who is there for you when he'd rather be anywhere else.
Len Wein

A true friend stabs you in the front.
Oscar Wilde

Friendship is the only cement that will ever hold the world together.
Woodrow Wilson

Friendship, Acquiring
A man that hath friends must show himself friendly: and there is a friend that sticketh closer than a brother.
Proverbs 18:24 KJV

Friendship is built on caring, sharing, and trust.
Author unknown

You can make more friends in two months by becoming interested in other people than you can in two years by trying to get other people interested in you.
Dale Carnegie

The only way to have a friend is to be one.
Ralph Waldo Emerson

Many a friendship – long, loyal, and self-sacrificing – rested at first upon no thicker a foundation than a kind word.
Frederick W. Faber

I look upon every day to be lost, in which I do not make a new acquaintance.
Samuel Johnson

If a man does not make new acquaintances as he advances through life, he will soon find himself left alone. A man, Sir, should keep his friendship in constant repair.
Samuel Johnson

Friendship, In times of need
A friend loves at all times, and a brother is born for adversity.
The Bible, Proverbs 17:17

A friend ought to be like the blood, which runs quickly to the wound without waiting to be called.
A. Perez

There is nothing more friendly than a friend in need.
Plautus

A friend in need is a friend indeed.
English proverb

Friends are needed both for joy and for sorrow.
Yiddish proverb

Rare is the faithful friend who is constant in all his friends' disgresses.
Thomas à Kempis

Friendship, Value of
He who walks with the wise grows wise, but a companion of fools suffers harm.
The Bible, Proverbs 13:20

Faithful are the wounds of a friend.
The Bible, Proverbs 27:6 KJV

Iron sharpeneth iron; so a man sharpeneth the countenance of his friend.
The Bible, Proverbs 27:17 KJV

Two are better than one, because they have a good return for their work: If one falls down, his friend can help him up. But pity the man who falls and has no one to help him up!
The Bible, Ecclesiastes 4: 9-10

The A – Z of Friendship
A Friend:
(A)ccepts you as you are
(B)elieves in you
(C)alls you just to say "Hi"
(D)oesn't give up on you
(E)nvisions the whole of you (even the unfinished parts)
(F)orgives your mistakes
(G)ives unconditionally
(H)elps you
(I)nvites you over
(J)ust "be" with you
(K)eeps you close at heart
(L)oves you for who you are
(M)akes a difference in your life
(N)ever judges
(O)ffers support
(P)icks you up
(Q)uiets your fears
(R)aises your spirits
(S)ays nice things about you
(T)ells you the truth when you need to hear it
(U)nderstands you
(V)alues you
(W)alks beside you
(X)-plain things you don't understand
(Y)ells when you won't listen and
(Z)aps you back to reality
Author unknown

Insomuch as any one pushes you nearer to God, he or she is your friend.
Author unknown

No medicine is more valuable, none more efficacious, none better suited to the cure

of all our temporal ills than a friend to whom we may turn for consolation in time of trouble – and with whom we may share our happiness in time of joy.
Aelred of Rievaulx

It [friendship] redoubleth joy, and cutteth griefs in halves.
Francis Bacon

The glory of friendship is not the outstretched hand, nor the kindly smile, nor the joy of companionship; it is the spiritual inspiration that comes to one when he discovers that someone else believes in him and is willing to trust him with his friendship.
Ralph Waldo Emerson

My best friend is the one who brings out the best in me.
Henry Ford

God send me a friend that will tell me of my faults.
Thomas Fuller

A true friend never gets in your way unless you happen to be going down.
Arnold H. Glasow

There is no wilderness like a life without friends; friendship multiplies blessings and minimizes misfortunes; it is a unique remedy against adversity, and it soothes the soul.
Baltasar Gracian

The best mirror is an old friend.
George Herbert

The greatest blessing is a pleasant friend.
Horace

Life has no pleasure higher or nobler than that of friendship.
Samuel Johnson

My friends have made the story of my life. In a thousand ways they have turned my limitations into beautiful privileges, and enabled me to walk serene and happy in

the shadow cast by my deprivation.
Hellen Keller

By associating with wise people you will
become wise yourself.
Menander

Those who possess good friends are truly
rich.
Spanish proverb

So long as we love, we serve; so long as we
are loved by others I would almost say that
we are indispensable; and no man is useless
while he has a friend.
Robert Louis Stevenson

A judicious friend, into whose heart we
may pour out our souls, and tell our
corruptions as well as our comforts, is a
very great privilege.
George Whitefield

A real friend is one who walks in when the
rest of the world walks out.
Walter Winchell

Friendship and sincerity
A friend is a person with whom I may be
sincere. Before him, I may think aloud.
Ralph Waldo Emerson

True friendship ought never to conceal
what it thinks.
Jerome

Fruitfulness
… by their fruit you will recognize them.
The Bible, Matthew 7:20

But the fruit of the Spirit is love, joy,
peace, patience, kindness, goodness,
faithfulness, gentleness and self-control.
The Bible, Galatians 5:22,23

It is the laden bough that hangs low, and
the most fruitful Christian who is the most
humble.
Author unknown

It is said that in some countries trees will

grow, but will bear no fruit because there is
no winter there.
John Bunyan

It is no use to anybody for a tree to bud
and blossom if the blossom does not
develop into fruit. Many are the fold who
perish in blossom.
Martin Luther

I would put it to you, my dear hearer, have
you been fruitful?
Have you been fruitful with your wealth?
Have you been fruitful with your talent?
Have you been fruitful with your time?
What are you doing for Jesus now?
C.H. Spurgeon

Untilled soil, however fertile it may be, will
bear thistles and thorns; but so it is with
man's mind.
Teresa of Avila

Our actions disclose what goes on within
us, just as its fruit makes known a tree
otherwise unknown to us.
Thalassios the Liban

Fulfillment
See also: Meaninglessness
Go to the garden of pleasure, and gather all
the fragrant flowers there, would these
satisfy you?
Go to the treasures of mammon – suppose
you may carry away as much as you
desire.
Go to the towers, to the trophies of honor.
What do you think of being a man of
renown, and having a name like the name
of the great men of the earth?
Alleine

Desire only God, and your heart will be
satisfied.
Augustine of Hippo

Find satisfaction in him who made you,
and only then find satisfaction in yourself
as part of his creation.
Augustine of Hippo

One who finds no satisfaction in himself seeks for it in vain elsewhere.
La Rochefoucauld

If I find in myself a desire which no experience in this world can satisfy, the most probable explanation is that I was made for another world.
C.S. Lewis

If a man is not made for God, why is he happy only in God? If man is made for God, why is he opposed to God?
Blaise Pascal

The desire of man is like a sieve or pierced vessel which he ever tries to, and can never, fill.
Plato

It is better to be Socrates dissatisfied than a pig satisfied.
John Stuart Mill

Fulfillment of your destiny does not come in a moment, a month, or a year, but over a lifetime.
Casey Treat

Fun
See also: Humor; Pleasure
Seek the kind of fun that doesn't make you ashamed the next day.
Author unknown

Whence comes this idea that if what we are doing is fun, it can't be God's will? The God who made giraffes, a baby's fingernails, a puppy's tail, a crook necked squash, the bobwhite's call, and a young girl's giggle, has a sense of humor. Make no mistake about that.
Catherine Marshall

A good and wholesome thing is a little harmless fun in this world; it tones a body up and keeps him human and prevents him from souring.
Mark Twain

Fund-raising
See also: Stewardship

Depend on it! God's work done in God's way will never lack God's supply.
Hudson Taylor

Funerals
See also: Bereavement
The care of the funeral, the manner of burial, the pomp of obsequies, are rather a consolation to the living than of any service to the dead.
Augustine of Hippo

"Here lies he who neither feared nor flattered any flesh."
Spoken at the burial of John Knox, 1572

Ah, why should we wear black for the guests of God?
John Ruskin

Funeral oration for Martin Luther

Since Luther is no more, his cherished name shall from our hearts, a deathless tribute claim. We hailed him minister of Christ, the Lord, Jesus he preached, with faith, and taught his word.
Luther is dead, and now the church in tears
A mourner clothed in saddest garb appears.
She weeps her loved preceptor now no more,
Honored and dear, a father's name he bore.
Fallen on the field the mighty chieftain lies,
And Israel's voice proclaims his obsequies.
Then let us bathe In tears the muse's lay
And publish forth our sorrows to the day
It thus becomes us well-to weep and mourn
Whilst, orphans in our grief, we dress
    affection's urn.
Philip Melancthon

A funeral oration on the Rev. Dr. Martin Luther, pronounced at Wittenberg, by Philip Melancthon
Although amid this universal grief, my voice is impeded by sorrow and by tears, yet since in so large an assembly, we are

called upon for some expression of our feelings; let it not be after the manner of the heathen, a declamation in praise of the departed one, but rather a commemoration in the audience of those now present of the wonderful pilotage of the church in all her perils; that we may call to mind on what account it behoves us to mourn, what purposes we should ourselves most diligently pursue, and in what manner we should order our lives. For although irreligious men conceive that the interests of this world are borne along in a giddy tide of confusion and uncertainty, yet, reassured as we are by the many indubitable testimonies of God, we make a wide distinction between the church and the profane multitude, and we believe that she is indeed governed and upheld by the power of God: we clearly discern his polity – we acknowledge the true helmsmen, and we watch their course, – we choose also for ourselves, befitting leaders and teachers whom we devotedly follow and revere.

On these so weighty matters, it is necessary both to think and to speak, as often as mention is made of that revered man Dr. Martin Luther, our beloved father and teacher; and whilst he has been the object of most cruel hatred to many, let us who know that he was a divinely inspired minister of the gospel, regard his memory with love and esteem, and let us gather such testimonies as prove that his teaching was by no means a blind dissemination of seditious opinions, as the Epicureans give out, but a demonstration of the will and of the true worship of God, an unfolding of the sacred records and a declaration of the word of God, that is of the gospel of Jesus Christ. In orations such as the present, much is usually said of the individual excellencies of those whom we wish to commend; passing however, in silence over this part of my theme, it is my design to dwell principally on that main point, the call to gospel ministry; and here we may unite in opinion with all just thinkers, that if Luther has illustrated a wholesome and necessary doctrine in the church, we ought to return thanks unto God, that He has

been pleased to raise him up to this work, whilst his personal labors, his faith, his constancy, and his other virtues are to be commended, and his memory to be held most dear by all good men. Let this therefore be the beginning, of our oration.

The Son of God, as Paul says, sits on the right hand of the Eternal Father, and gives gifts unto men; these gifts are the voice of the Gospel and of the Holy Spirit, with which, as He imparts them, He inspires Prophets, Apostles, Pastors and Teachers, and selects them from this our assembly, that is to say, from those who are yet in the rudiments of divine knowledge, who read, who hear, and who love the prophetic and apostolic writings; nor does he often call to this warfare those who are in the exercise of established power, but it even pleases him to wage war on these very men through leaders chosen from other ranks. It is cheering and instructive to take a retrospect of the church throughout all past ages, and to contemplate the goodness of God who has sent out from its bosom gifted ministers in so unbroken a series, that as the first of these have passed away, others have pressed closely in their footsteps. The line of the first fathers is well worthy of our consideration. Adam, Seth, Enoch, Methuselah, Noah, and Abraham, who was raised up to be a fellow-helper of Sem and his associate in the all-important work of spreading true religion; and although at this time Sem was still dwelling in the neighborhood of Sodom, the people had lost the recollection both of his precepts and those of Noah, and were altogether abandoned to the worship of idols. To Abraham succeeded law and Jacob; next Joseph – who kindled the light of truth throughout all Egypt, at that time the most flourishing kingdom in the world. After these, we read of Moses, Joshua, Samuel, and David; then Elisha, of whose ministry the prophet Isaiah was a partaker; then … John the Baptist: and lastly, Christ and His Apostles.

It is delightful to behold this unbroken chain, which is a clear testimony to the presence of God in his church. After the Apostles followed a band, which although somewhat weaker, was nevertheless honored with the blessing of God. Polycarp, Irenaeus, Gregory the Niocaesarien, Basilius, Augustinus, Prosper, Maximus, Hugo, Bernardus, Taulerus, and others; and although this later age has become more corrupt, yet God has always preserved a remnant of the faithful, whilst it is evident that the light of the gospel has now been peculiarly manifested through the preaching of Luther. He is therefore to be numbered with that blessed company, the excellent of the earth, whom God has sent forth for the gathering together and the building up of his church, and whom we truly recognize as ornaments of the human race. Solon, Themistocles, Scipio, Augustus, and others were indeed great men, who founded, states, or ruled over vast empires; yet do they rank far below our spiritual leaders, Isaiah, John the Baptist, Paul and Luther. It is also well that we should regard the grand disputations which have existed in the church, and in connection with this subject let us look at those themes of deep and high import which have been brought to light by Luther, and which evince that the tenor of his life was worthy of our highest approbation. It is true that many exclaim "the church is in confusion," saying that inextricable controversies are engendered in it; to these I answer, such is the mode of divine Government, for when the Holy Spirit convicts the world, dissensions arise through the pertinacity of the wicked; and the guilt is on those who refuse to listen to the Son of God, and of whom our Heavenly Father says, "Hear Him."

That Luther illustrated the essential truths of the Gospel is manifest, as the deepest shades had previously veiled its doctrines, in dispersing these he clearly proved to us the nature of sincere repentance, he showed us in whom we must seek refuge, and what is the sure consolation of the mind that trembles under a sense of the wrath of God. He elucidated the doctrine of Paul which says,

that man is justified by faith; he showed the difference between the Law and the Gospel, between Spiritual righteousness and the Moral law; he pointed out the nature of true prayer, and he called back the church universal from that heathen madness which teaches that God, is to be invoked even when the mind, oppressed with metaphysical doubts, is flying far from Him: he enforced on us the conviction that prayer is to be made in faith, and in a good conscience, and he led us to the one Mediator, the Son of God sitting at the right hand of the Eternal Father, and interceding for us; not to those images and departed mortals, to whom the ungodly world, with awful infatuation, is wont to perform its devotions. He also pointed out other sacred duties which are acceptable to God, whilst he was himself careful to adorn and to preserve inviolate the institutions of civil life as no preceding writers had done; he also drew a line of distinction between works necessary to be performed, and the puerile observances of human ceremonies, including there rights and established laws which impede the offering of the heart to God. In order that this heavenly teaching might be transmitted unimpaired to posterity, lie translated the prophetic and apostolic writings into German, which work he executed with such perspicuity, that this version alone imparts more light to the mind of the reader, than the perusal of many commentaries would do.

To this he added various expositions which, as Erasmus was accustomed to say, were far superior to any others then extant; and as it is related of the builders of Jerusalem, that they wrought with one hand and held the sword in the other, so was he at the same time contending with the enemies of truth, and composing expositions fraught with divine philosophy; whilst by his pious counsels he strengthened the minds of many. Since the mystery of godliness lies far beyond the reach of human vision, as for instance, the doctrines of Faith, and of the Remission of Sins, we are constrained to acknowledge that Luther was taught of God; and how many of us have witnessed there wrestlings in which be was himself instructed, and by which we must be convinced that through faith alone we also can be heard and accepted of God. Therefore shall His people to all eternity celebrate the blessings which He has conferred on the church by this His servant: first they will offer up thanksgivings to God, then they will acknowledge that they owe much to the labors of this our friend and brother; although the irreligious who deride the church in general, say that these good deeds are but idle pastime or intoxicating madness. Let it not be said that endless disputations have been raised, or that the apple of discord has been thrown by the church, as some falsely assert; nor have the enigmas of the Sphynx been propounded by her, for to men of sense and piety who can give a candid judgment, it is by no means difficult on comparing opinions, to distinguish those which accord from those which do not accord with heavenly doctrine; and indeed there is no doubt that in these controversies we discover the revelation of Himself. For since it has pleased God to manifest Himself and His holy will in prophetic and apostolic writ, in which he has revealed himself, we cannot suppose that His word is ambiguous like the leaves of the Sybil, "Which flit abroad, the sport of playful winds."

Others however, without any evil design, have complained that Luther was unduly severe; I do not myself offer an opinion on this subject, but answer I them in the words of Erasmus: "God has administered to us of the present age, a bitter draught, on account of our abounding infirmities." But when he is pleased to raise up such an instrument against the shameless and insolent enemies of truth, as when the Lord said to Jeremiah, "Behold I have given my words into thy mouth, that thou shouldest destroy and build up," and when it is His pleasure to set as it were, His Gorgons in array against them, then it is a vain thing that they should expostulate with Him; for He governs His church not by human counsels, neither truly are His ways our ways. It is however, no uncommon thing for minds of limited scope to undervalue the more powerful energies with which others may be endowed, whether directed to good or evil purposes; thus it was with emotion that Aristides beheld Themistocles undertaking and bringing to a happy issue, vast enterprises; and although he rejoiced in the felicity of the state, he was earnest to arrest that ardent spirit in its career. Nor do I deny that strong and lively impulse often leads astray, since none who are subject to the infirmities of our nature, are without fault. If however, there be any living of whom we may say as the ancients did of Hercules, Cimon and others, "Unadorned indeed, but in all important points a good man," then was Luther a just man, and his name of good report; for in the church, if, as the apostle Paul says, "he war a good warfare, holding faith and a good conscience," then he pleases God and is to be revered by us. And such we know Luther to have been, for whilst he steadfastly maintained sound doctrine he preserved the integrity of his own conscience: and who that has known him can be ignorant with what large benevolence he was endowed, or forget his suavity in the intercourse of private life, and how far removed he was from contention and strife, whilst to all his actions lie imparted the gravity that became his character, as is depicted in the following passage; "His manner was dignified, and his discourse familiar;" or rather, all with him was in accordance with the language of Paul, "Whatsoever things are true, whatsoever things are honest, whatsoever things are just, whatsoever things are of good report;" so that the asperity of which we have spoken, appears to have arisen from the love of truth, not from a factious spirit, or from bitterness of feeling: of these things both we and many others have been witnesses.

But if I were to undertake an eulogium on the remaining points of Luther's life, a life which until the age of 63 was absorbed in subjects of the highest interest, and was passed in the pursuit of piety and of all that is noble and good, in what lofty strains of eloquence might I not indulge. His was a mind in which we never traced the inroads of wandering lusts; no seditious counsels held their seat there, on the contrary he rather advocated the laying down of arms, as he was unwilling to mingle with the interests of the church, schemes for the aggrandizement either of himself or his friends. Indeed, I esteem his wisdom and his virtue at so high a price as to feel assured that human efforts alone could never have attained to them. Thus it is essential that spirits bold, lofty, and ardent, such as every thing proves Luther's to have been, should be restrained by a power from on high. And now what shall I say of his other virtues? I have myself often surprised him, when with weeping he has been engaged in offering up prayers for the whole church. He devoted almost daily, a portion of time to the repetition of certain psalms with which amid his sighs and tears, he mingled his prayers; and be often said that he felt indignant against those who through slothfulness of spirit, or on account of worldly occupations, say that the prayer of a single sigh is enough. He considered therefore, that forms of prayer are prescribed to us by divine counsel, and that a perusal of them animates our minds even as our voices acknowledge the God whom we worship. And often when weighty deliberations have arisen on the danger of the state, we have seen him endowed with a mighty potency of soul, unmoved by fear and unsubdued by terror, for lie leaned on that sacred anchor which is the power of God; nor did he allow his faith therein to be shaken.

He was also distinguished for the acuteness of his perceptions, as by his own independent judgment lie could readily perceive the course to be pursued in cases of difficulty. Nor was he as many think, negligent of the public weal, or inadvertent to the interests of others; on the contrary he could fully appreciate the welfare of the community, whilst he most sagaciously perceived the sentiments and wishes of those with whom he mingled in social life. And although the genius of his mind was of a lively order, he read with avidity ecclesiastical writings as well as history in general, from which, with a peculiar dexterity, he derived precedents adapted to the present occasion.

Of his eloquence we possess enduring monuments, for in this science he undoubtedly equaled those to whom the highest palm in oratory has been conceded. We do then for our own sakes, justly mourn that such a man, endowed with the loftiest grade of intellect, instructed in wisdom, matured by long experience, adorned with many excellent and heroic virtues, and chosen by God for the building up of his church; that he who has embraced us all with a father's love, should have been thus called away from our earthly fellowship. For we are like orphans deprived of an excellent and faithful parent; but whilst we bow to the will of God, let us not in the memory of our friend allow his virtues, and the benefits which we have derived from his society to perish from amongst us. Let us rather bid him joy that he is now participating in sweet and unrestrained communion with God, and with his Son our Lord Jesus Christ, and with the Prophets and Apostles; which fellowship he ever sought and waited for through faith in the Son of God. In that blessed state he now receives the approval of God on the labors which he here sustained in the propagation of the gospel, with the testimony also of the Church universal in heaven; there, set free from the shackles of mortality as from a prison, and having joined that company which is perfected in wisdom, he now sees, not as in a glass darkly, the essential character of God, the union of the two natures in His Son, and the whole assembly of the gathered and redeemed church; whilst those divine real ties which he here knew but in part, which he briefly demonstrated, and which in faith he contemplated, he now beholds with open face, and moved with ecstatic joy, in all the ardor of his soul he gives God thanks for his unspeakable gift. He learns why the Son of God is called the Word, and the likeness of the Eternal Father; and in what way Holy Spirit is the bond of mutual love, no only between the Eternal Father and the Son, but also between them and the Church. He had learned whilst here on earth which be the first principles of the oracles of God and often did he most wisely and weightily descant on these highest themes; on the distinction between true and false prayer, and on the knowledge of God and of divine manifestations; also on distinguishing the true God from false deities. There are many in this assembly, who in times past, have heard him thus express himself, "You shall see the heavens opened, and the angels of God ascending and descending upon the Son of Man." Thus he delighted first to instill into the minds of his hearers this most full consolation, which declares that heaven is opened, that is to say, that there is a way made for us to God, that the barrier of divine wrath is removed as we flee for refuge to his Son; that God holds near communion with us, and that those who seek him in prayer are received, governed and kept by him. Luther admonished us that this divine promise, which infidels declare to be fabulous, is and must be opposed to human doubts, and to those fears which deter diffident minds from venturing to call upon God, or to put their trust in him; for he said that the angels ascending and descending on the body of Christ, are the ministers of the gospel who with Christ for their leader, first ascend to God and receive from him the gifts of the Gospel, and of the Holy Spirit, and afterwards descend, that is to fulfill their duty of teaching amongst men. He also added this interpretation, that those heavenly spirits themselves, whom we usually call angels, beholding the Son are enabled to comprehend and to rejoice in the mysterious union of the two natures, and as they are soldiers of their Lord in defense of His Church, so are they guided and governed as by the signal of His hand.

Now is our departed friend himself a spectator of these most sublime visions, and as he once among the ministers of the Gospel, ascended and descended with Christ for his leader, so now be descries angels sent on embassies by their Lord, and enjoys in common with them, the absorbing contemplation of divine wisdom and of the works of God. Let us call to mind with what delight he has recited to us the polity, the purposes, the dangers, and the deliverances of the prophets, and with what erudition he was wont to trace the history of the church in all ages; thus it is evident that his heart glowed with no common emotion when speaking of those favored servants of the Lord. The spirits of these he now embraces, with delight he listens to their living words, and with them he speaks face to face, whilst they with transport bail him as their fellow, and with one heart and one voice give thanks unto God for having thus gathered and preserved his church. Therefore we doubt. not that Luther is happy: we do indeed, mourn our bereavement, and whilst we bow to the fiat which has called him hence, we know it to be the will of God that we retain in our memories the virtues and the benefactions of this his servant.

Let us now be faithful to our trust. We must acknowledge that he was a hallowed instrument of God. Let us then devotedly embrace his doctrines, and strive to resemble him in those graces which are essential to our more humble walk, the fear of God, faith and fervency in prayer, soundness in ministry, purity, vigilance in avoiding seditious counsels, and an ardent thirst for knowledge. And as we are called upon to turn our thoughts with intentness and frequency towards those leaders in the church whose histories have been transmitted to us, as Jeremiah, John the Baptist, and Paul, so let us often dwell on the doctrine and experience of Luther. Let us now add the tribute of thanksgiving and prayers which are due from this assembly, and let us all unite in this devotion. "We give thanks unto Thee, oh omnipotent God! the eternal Father of our Lord Jesus

Christ and Founder of Thy church, with Thy co-eternal Son our Lord Jesus Christ and the Holy Spirit, wise, good, merciful, a true Judge, powerful and uncontrolled; in that Thou art by Thy dear Son, gathering unto Thyself an inheritance from amongst the human race, and art preserving the ministry of Thy gospel, for which Thou hast at this time raised up Luther. We beseech Thee that thou wilt henceforth sustain and govern thy church, and that thou wilt seal in us the true doctrine, as Isaiah prayed for his disciples. Deign Thou to quicken our hearts by Thy Holy Spirit, that we may offer prayer acceptably unto Thee, and that we may order our lives in Thy fear." In conclusion, as we are aware that the loss from amongst us of those who have directed us in our earthly course, often proves to survivors, the watchword of impending calamities; I would myself, with all to whom is committed the gift of teaching, implore you to consider to what the world now stands exposed. On the one hand the Turks are ravaging, on the other contending parties threaten us with a civil war; every where indeed, we trace the empire of misrule; and now that the enemies of the church no longer fear the power of Luther, they will doubtless with the greater daring, lay waste the doctrine which has been delivered to us by divine authority. That God may avert these evils, let us be more diligent in regulating our lives and directing our pursuits, and let us ever hold this sentiment fixed in our minds, so that whilst we retain, hear, learn, and love the pure truths of the Gospel, we may ourselves constitute the house and church of God: as the Son of God himself says, "If any man love me, he will keep my word, and my Father will love him, and we will come unto him and make our abode with him." Encouraged by this cheering promise of our blessed Lord, let us incite one another to the acquiring of heavenly wisdom, and let us not forget that human interests and human institutions are to be respected for the sake of his church. Let us realize to our minds, that future eternity to which God has called us, who indeed has

not in vain revealed Himself to us by such illustrious testimonies, neither has He sent His Son in vain, but He truly loves and preserves those who magnify His grace. Amen.

Future, The
See also: Christ, Second coming
Do not boast about tomorrow, for you do not know what a day may bring forth.
The Bible, Proverbs 27:1

The wolf will live with the lamb, the leopard will lie down with the goat, the calf and the lion and the yearling together; and a little child will lead them.
The Bible, Isaiah 11:6

... do not worry about tomorrow, for tomorrow will worry about itself.
The Bible, Matthew 6:34

I don't know what tomorrow holds, but I know who holds tomorrow.
Author unknown

Prediction is very difficult, especially about the future.
Neils Bohr

I never think of the future – it comes soon enough.
Albert Einstein

The future is as bright as the promises of God.
Adoniram Judson

The next moment is as much beyond our grasp, and as much in God's care, as that a hundred years away. Care for the next minute is just as foolish as care for a day in the next thousand years. In neither can we do anything, in both God is doing everything.
C.S. Lewis

The great thing is to be found at one's post as a child of God, living each day as though it were our last, but planning as though our

world might last a hundred years.
C.S. Lewis

Even if I knew that tomorrow the world
would go to pieces, I would still plant my
apple tree.
Martin Luther

The present is never our goal: the past and
present are our means: the future alone is
our goal. Thus, we never live but we hope
to live; and always hoping to be happy, it is
inevitable that we will never be so.
Blaise Pascal

The future belongs to those who believe in
the beauty of their dreams.
Eleanor Roosevelt

The wise man must remember that while
he is a descendant of the past, he is a
parent of the future.
Herbert Spencer

When people say: She's got everything. I've
only one answer: I haven't had tomorrow.
Elizabeth Taylor

Never be afraid to trust an unknown future
to a known God.
Corrie Ten Boom

I know not what the future hath
Of marvel or surprise;
Assured of this, that life and earth
His mercy underlies.
John Greenleaf Whittier

G

Gaining Christ

Do we give sufficient attention to the theme of gaining Christ? It is our joy and privilege to know Him as God's unspeakable gift. None knew this more fully than the apostle Paul.
Hudson Taylor

Gambling

Gambling: The sure way of getting nothing for something.
Wilson Mizner

Gambling challenges the view of life which the Christian Church exists to uphold and extend. Its glorification of mere chance is a denial of the divine order of nature. To risk money haphazard is to disregard the insistence of the Church in every age of living faith that possessions are a trust, and that men must account to God for their use. The persistent appeal to covetousness is fundamentally opposed to the unselfishness which was taught by Jesus Christ and by the New Testament as a whole. The attempt (which is inseparable from gambling) to make a profit out of the inevitable loss and possible suffering of others is the antithesis of that love of one's neighbor on which our Lord insisted.
William Temple

Garden

Jesus was in a garden, not of delights as the first Adam, in which he destroyed himself and the whole human race, but in one of agony, in which he saved the whole human race.
Blaise Pascal

For best results, this garden should be planted every day:
Five rows of "P"eas:
Preparedness,
Promptness,
Perseverance,
Politeness,
Prayer.
Three rows of squash:
Squash gossip,
Squash criticism,
Squash indifference.
Five rows of lettuce:
Let us love one another,
Let us be faithful,
Let us be loyal,
Let us be unselfish,
Let us be truthful.
Three rows of turnips:
Turn up for church,
Turn up with a new idea,
Turn up with the determination to do a better job tomorrow than you did today
Eugenie Prime

Garrulousness

Garrulousness is the platform from which vainglory preaches itself.
Author unknown

Garrulousness is a proof of ignorance, the door to scandal-mongering, the handmaid of trifling scurrilities and the helpmate of falsehood.
John Climacus

There are few wild beasts more to be dreaded than a talking man having nothing to say.
Jonathan Swift

Genders, Complementarity of

[Eve was] not made out of his [Adam's] head to top him, nor out of his feet to be trampled upon by him, but out of his side to be equal with him, under his arm to be protected, and his heart to be loved.
Matthew Henry

Eve was not taken from the feet of Adam to be his slave, nor from his head to be his lord, but from his side, to be his partner.
Peter Lombard

God made male and female *equal,* he also made them *different.*
John R.W. Stott

[Although men and women are equal before God] equality of *worth* is not identity of *role.*
J.H. Yoder

Generation gap
Be aware that young people have to be able to make their own mistakes and that times change.
Gina Shapira

Generosity
See also: Giving
Life begets life. Energy begets energy. It is by spending oneself that one becomes rich.
Sarah Bernhardt

Too many have dispensed with generosity in order to practice charity.
Albert Camus

Not he who has much is rich, but he who gives much.
Erich Fromm

The truly generous is the truly wise, and he who loves not others, lives unblest.
Henry Home

What I kept, I lost;
What I spent, I had;
What I gave, I have.
Persian proverb

If you give money, spend yourself with it.
Henry David Thoreau

Genesis
The only Bible-honoring conclusion is, of course, that Genesis 1-11 is actual historical truth, regardless of any scientific

or chronological problems thereby entailed.
Dr Henry Morris, President ICR, 1972

Genius
Genius usually starts great things; only labor and drudgery finish them.
Author unknown

Talent does what it can; genius does what it must.
Edward George Bulwer-Lytton

Mediocrity knows nothing higher than itself; but talent instantly recognizes genius.
Arthur Conan Doyle

Any intelligent fool can make things bigger, more complex, and more violent. It takes a touch of genius – and a lot of courage – to move in the opposite direction.
Albert Einstein

Intellectuals solve problems, geniuses prevent them.
Albert Einstein

I can make nobles and great lords when I please, but God alone can make such a man as this whom we are about to lose.
François I
(Said to have been his comment at Leonardo da Vinci's death-bed, when some courtiers thought the king honored the great artist too highly.)

Genius will live and thrive without training, but it does not the less reward the watering pot and the pruning knife.
Margaret Fuller

It is the great triumph of genius to make the common appear novel.
Johann Wolfgang von Goethe

Genius develops in quiet places, character out in the full current of human life.
Johann Wolfgang von Goethe

The first and last thing required of genius is the love of truth.
Johann Wolfgang von Goethe

The essence of genius is knowing what to overlook.
William James

There is no genius in life like the genius of energy and industry.
Donald Grant Mitchell

Neither a lofty degree of intelligence nor imagination nor both together go to the making of genius. Love, love, love, that is the soul of genius.
Mozart

Gentleness

A soft answer turneth away wrath.
The Bible, Proverbs 15:1 KJV

A bruised reed shall he not break, and the smoking flax shall he not quench.
The Bible, Isaiah 42:3

He who is gentle remembers good rather than evil, the good one has received rather than the good one has done.
Aristotle

Let your dealing with those you begin with be so gentle, convincing, and winning, that the report of it may be an encouragement to others to come.
Richard Baxter

The more vigor you need, the more gentleness and kindness you must combine with it. All stiff, harsh goodness is contrary to Jesus.
François Fénelon

Nothing is so strong as gentleness, nothing so gentle as real strength.
Francis de Sales

Be mild at their anger, humble at their boastings, to their blasphemies return your prayers, to their error your firmness in the faith; when they are cruel, be gentle; not endeavoring to imitate their ways, let us be their brethren in all kindness and moderation: but let us be followers of the Lord; for who was ever more unjustly used, more destitute, more despised?
Ignatius of Antioch

Gentleness does more than violence.
La Fontaine

It's so easy to laugh, it's so easy to hate. It takes strength to be gentle and kind.
Stephen Morrissey

Be gentle to all and stern with yourself.
Teresa of Avila

Gifts

How blessed and wonderful, beloved, are the gifts of God. Life in immortality, splendor in righteousness, truth in perfect confidence, faith in assurance, self-control in holiness! And all these fall under the cognizance of our understandings now; what then shall those things be which are prepared for such as wait for Him? The Creator and Father of all worlds, the Most Holy, alone knows their amount and their beauty. Let us therefore earnestly strive to be found in the number of those that wait for Him, in order that we may share in His promised gifts.
First Epistle of Clement

For every created being whatsoever that is endowed with power, whether of healing, or the like, possesses it not of itself, but as a thing given it by God. For to the creature all things are given, and wrought in it, and of itself it can do nothing (cf. Jn. 15:5; 1 Cor. 4:7).
Cyril of Alexandria

God's gifts now take the place of God, and the whole course of nature is upset by the monstrous substitution.
Meister Eckhart

Nothing is small if God accepts it.
Teresa of Avila

Gifts of the Holy Spirit

These gifts were not the possession of the

primitive Christian as such; nor for that matter of the Apostolic Church or the Apostolic age for themselves; they were distinctively the authentication of the Apostles. They were part of the credentials of the Apostles as the authoritative agents of God in founding the church. Their function thus confined them to distinctively the Apostolic Church, and they necessarily passed away with it. Of this we may make sure on the ground both of principle and of fact; that is to say both under the guidance of the New Testament teaching as to their origin and nature, and on the credit of the testimony of later ages as to their cessation.

B.B. Warfield

Giving
See also: Aid; Caring; Charity; Generosity

One man gives freely, yet gains ever more; another withholds unduly, but comes to poverty.

The Bible, Proverbs 11:24

Take heed that ye do not your alms before men, to be seen of them.

The Bible, Matthew 6:1 KJV

When thou doest alms, let not thy left hand know what thy right hand doeth.

The Bible, Matthew 6:3 KJV

It is more blessed to give than to receive.

The Bible, Acts 20:35

Share with God's people who are in need.

The Bible, Romans 12:13

On the first day of every week, each one of you should set aside a sum of money in keeping with his income, saving it up, so that when I come no collections will have to be made.

The Bible, 1 Corinthians 16:2

Remember this: Whoever sows sparingly will also reap sparingly, and whoever sows generously will also reap generously. Each man should give what he has decided in

his heart to give, not reluctantly or under compulsion, for God loves a cheerful giver.

The Bible, 2 Corinthians 9:6,7

Give strength, give thought, give deeds, give wealth;
Give love, give tears, and give thyself.
Give, give, be always giving.
Who gives not is not living;
The more you give, the more you live.

Author unknown

Am I giving God what is right or what is left?

Author unknown

It's not how much you've given, but how much you've kept, that really matters.

Author unknown

More blessings come from giving than from receiving.

Author unknown

Givers can be divided into three types: the flint, the sponge and the honeycomb.
Some givers are like a piece of flint – to get anything out of it you must hammer it, and even then you only get chips and sparks.
Others are like a sponge – to get anything out of a sponge you must squeeze it and squeeze it hard, because the more you squeeze a sponge, the more you get.
But others are like a honeycomb – which just overflows with its own sweetness. That is how God gives to us, and it is how we should give in turn.

Author unknown

You are never more like God, than when you give.

Author unknown

He who gives when he is asked has waited too long.

Author unknown

Give according to your income, lest God make your income according to your giving.

Author unknown

We're richer when we give and poorer when we keep.
Author unknown

When it comes to giving, some people stop at nothing.
Author unknown

Find out how much God has given you and take from it what you need; the remainder is needed by others.
Augustine of Hippo

Do not give, as many rich men do, like a hen that lays an egg, and then cackles.
Henry Ward Beecher

Blessed are those who can give without remembering and take without forgetting.
Elizabeth Bibesco

The world says, The more you take, the more you have. Christ says, the more you give, the more you are.
Frederick Buechner

A man there was, though some did count him mad,
The more he cast away the more he had.
John Bunyan

He who bestows his goods upon the poor shall have as much again, and ten times more.
John Bunyan

You can give without loving, but you cannot love without giving.
Amy Carmichael

We make a living by what we get. We make a life by what we give.
Winston Churchill

We receive but what we give.
Coleridge

One must be poor to know the luxury of giving.
George Eliot

The gospel is free, but it costs money to provide the pails in which to carry the water of salvation.
Dr Louis Evans

Time and money spent in helping men to do more for themselves is far better than mere giving.
Henry Ford

For it is in giving that we receive.
Francis of Assisi

Complete possession is proved only by giving. All you are unable to give possesses you.
Andre Gide

What we frankly give for ever is our own.
G. Granville

Who shuts his hand has lost his gold
Who opens it hath it twice told.
George Herbert

As the purse is emptied, the heart is filled.
Victor Hugo

A cheerful giver does not count the cost of what he gives. His heart is set on pleasing and cheering him to whom the gift is given.
Julian of Norwich

Nothing is really ours until we share it.
C.S. Lewis

If our expenditure on comforts, luxuries, amusements, etc., is up to the standard common among those with the same income as our own, we are probably giving away too little. If our charities do not at all pinch or hamper us, I should say they are too small. There ought to be things we should like to do and cannot because our charitable expenditure excludes them.
C.S. Lewis

When we eat out, most of us expect to tip the waiter or waitress 15 per cent. When we suggest 10 per cent as a minimum

church offering, some folks are aghast.
Felix A. Lorenz

When you give, see that you give that
which multiplies in giving.
Raymond Lull

I have held many things in my hands,
and I have lost them all; but whatever I
have placed in God's hands, that I still
possess.
Martin Luther

If you had a little money to spare, would
you not lend it to me, if I assured you it
should be repaid when you wanted? I can
point out to you better interest and better
security than I could possibly give you:
Prov. xix. 17: "He that hath pity upon the
poor, lendeth unto the Lord: and that
which he hath given, will he pay him
again." What think you of this text? Is it
the word of God or not?
John Newton

Spend and God will send.
Proverb

The hand that gives, gathers.
Proverb

He who takes but never gives,
may last for years but never lives.
Proverb

No purchase is as good as a gift.
French proverb

He gives twice who gives quickly.
Latin proverb

Giving is the secret of a healthy life. Not
necessarily money, but whatever a man has
of encouragement and sympathy and
understanding.
John D. Rockefeller, Jr

When a man dies he clutches in his hands
only that which he has given away during
his lifetime.
Jean-Jacques Rousseau

But what parent can tell when some ...
fragmentary gift of knowledge or wisdom
will enrich her children's lives? Or how a
small seed of information passed from one
generation to another may generate a new
science, a new industry – a seed which
neither the giver nor the receiver can truly
evaluate at the time.
Helena Rubinstein

We should give as we would receive,
cheerfully, quickly, and without hesitation;
for there is no grace in a benefit that sticks
to the fingers.
Seneca

If there be any truer measure of a man than
by what he does, it must be by what he gives.
Robert South

Feel for others – in your pocket.
C.H. Spurgeon

The seed that is sown is scattered with an
open hand. The sower in order to have a
harvest has to turn loose the seed. He can't
grip it in his fist; he can't hesitate to let it
go; he can't just sprinkle a little bit here
and there – he's got to generously sow it,
he's got to let it go and let it go liberally, if
he expects to have a great harvest. If he
sows sparingly, that's the way he's going to
reap; if he sows liberally and bountifully,
that's the way his harvest is going to be.
C.H. Spurgeon

Simple rules for saving money: To save
half, when you are fired by an eager
impulse to contribute to a charity, wait and
count to forty. To save three quarters,
count sixty. To save all, count sixty-five.
Mark Twain

If I leave behind me £10, you and all
mankind bear witness against me that I
lived and died a thief and a robber.
John Wesley

Any Christian who takes for himself
anything more than the plain necessaries of
life lives in an open, habitual denial of the

Lord. He has gained riches and hell-fire!
John Wesley

Glory

And the glory which thou gavest me I have given them; that they may be one, even as we are one: I in them, and thou in me, that they may be made perfect in one; and that the world may know that thou hast sent me, and hast loved them, as thou hast loved me.
The Bible, John 17:22-23 KJV

The great end of God's work which is variously expressed in Scripture, is indeed but one; and this one end is most properly and comprehensively called, "the glory of God."
Jonathan Edwards

Numerous passages of Scripture assert that the manifestation of the glory of God is the great end of creation, that he has himself chiefly in view in all his works and dispensations, and that it is a purpose in which he requires that all his intelligent creatures should acquiesce, and seek and promote it as their first and paramount duty.
Robert Haldane

The glory of God, and, as our only means to glorifying Him, the salvation of human souls, is the real business of life.
C.S. Lewis

Anxiety, sickness, suffering, or danger, now and then, with a foregoing of the common conveniences and charities of this life, may make us pause, and cause the spirit to waver, and the soul to sink; but let this be only for a moment. All these are nothing when compared with the glory which shall hereafter be revealed in, and for, us.
David Livingstone

Look at everything as though you were seeing it for the first time or the last time. Then your time on earth will be filled with glory.
Betty Smith

Gluttony

There are more gluttons than drunkards in hell.
Author unknown

We ought to eat in order to live, not live in order to eat.
Cicero

In general, mankind, since the improvement of cookery, eats twice as much as nature requires.
Benjamin Franklin

Gluttony kills more than the sword.
16th century proverb

Goals
See also: Ambition; Ambition, Warnings against; Aspirations
Be sure that you put your feet in the right place, and then stand firm.
Author unknown

A written down goal, in some way no one yet understands, tends to attract every ingredient it needs to realize it.
Author unknown

Goals that are not written down are just wishes.
Author unknown

The rational questions:
1. Where am I?
2. Where do I want to be?
3. How do I know I am getting there?
Author unknown

If you aim at nothing, you hit it.
Author unknown

No goals …
No glory!
Author unknown

DO IT NOW!
Author unknown

You become successful the moment you

start moving toward a worthwhile goal.
Author unknown

A team which has become a winner has done so by individuals setting and reaching goals for themselves.
Author unknown

People are like buttons, unattached, useless. Attached, indispensable. People, unattached to a goal, useless. Attached, men with missions.
Author unknown

The poorest of all men is not the one without gold, but without a goal. Life for him has no meaning – no reason for living.
Author unknown

Before you score, you must have a goal.
Author unknown

If you chase two rabbits, both will escape.
Author unknown

To see God is the promised goal of all our actions and the promised height of all our joys.
Augustine of Hippo

It's kind of fun to do the impossible.
Walt Disney

No one can be making much of his life who has not a very definite conception of what he is living for.
Henry Drummond

Accurst ambition,
How dearly I have bought you.
John Dryden

The fool wanders: the wise man travels.
Thomas Fuller

First build a proper goal. That proper goal will make it easy, almost automatic, to build a proper you.
Goethe

The goal of a virtuous life is to become like God.
Gregory of Nyssa

Ninety-five per cent of working American males have no goals in their life.
Owen Hendrix

Great minds have purposes, others have wishes. Little minds are tamed and subdued by misfortune; but great minds rise above them.
Washington Irving

When goal goes, meaning goes;
when meaning goes, purpose goes;
when purpose goes, life goes dead on our hands.
Carl Jung

If a man hasn't discovered something he will die for, he isn't fit to live.
Martin Luther King, Jr

If you don't know where you are going, every road will get you nowhere.
Henry Kissinger

Setting a goal is not the main thing. It is deciding how you will go about achieving it and staying with that plan.
Tom Landry

Aim at heaven and you will get earth thrown in. Aim at earth and you will get neither.
C.S. Lewis

Never undertake anything for which you would not have the courage to ask the blessing of heaven.
George Christopher Lichtenberg

Becoming a star may not be your destiny, but being the best that you can be is a goal that you can set for yourself.
Bryan Lindsay

Many are stubborn in pursuit of the path they have chosen, few in pursuit of the goal.
Friedrich Nietzsche

If we are facing in the right direction,
all we have to do is keep on walking.
Ancient Buddhist proverb

Unless we change direction, we are likely
to end up where we are going.
Chinese proverb

Question: What is the chief and highest
end of man? Answer: Man's chief and
highest end is to glorify God and to fully
enjoy Him forever.
Westminster Larger Catechism

Sometimes it is more important to discover
what one cannot do, than what one can do.
Lin Yutang

Goals, Examples of

I have found my destiny. I must take the
gospel to the people of the East End [of
London].
William Booth

If I had a thousand lives, I would give
them all for the women of China.
Lottie Moon

Give me grace always to desire and to will
what is most acceptable to you and most
pleasing in your sight.
Thomas à Kempis

God

God is great, and therefore He will be sought;
God is good, and therefore He will be found.
Author unknown

God: a perfect, omnipotent, omniscient,
immortal, omnipresent being that is thought
to have created the universe and now rules it.
Author unknown

If God was small enough for us to
understand, He wouldn't be big enough for
us to worship.
Author unknown

Essence beyond essence, Nature increate,
Framer of the world, I set thee, Lord,
before my face. I lift up my soul to thee, I

worship thee on my knees, and humble
myself under thy mighty hand.
Lancelot Andrewes

God alone satisfies.
Thomas Aquinas

God is not a deceiver, that he should
offer to support us, and then, when we
lean upon Him, should slip away from
us.
Augustine of Hippo

[God is] higher than my highest and more
inward than my innermost self.
Augustine of Hippo

He truly Is, because He is unchangeable.
Augustine of Hippo

I found thee not, O Lord, without,
because I erred in seeking thee without
that wert within.
Augustine of Hippo

God has been replaced, as he has all over
the West, with respectability and air
conditioning.
Imamu Amiri Baraka

The statement that "God is dead" comes
from Nietzsche and has recently been
trumpeted abroad by some German and
American theologians. But the good Lord
has not died of this; He who dwells in the
heaven laughs at them.
Karl Barth

God does not give us everything we want,
but He does fulfil all His promises …
leading us along the best and straightest
paths to Himself.
Dietrich Bonhoeffer

There is but one God, the Maker,
Preserver and Ruler of all things, having in
and of himself, all perfections, and being
infinite in them all; and to Him all
creatures owe the highest love, reverence
and obedience.
James Boyce

O God within my breast,
Almighty! ever-present Deity!
Emily Brontë

The most perfect way of seeking God, and
the most suitable order, is not for us to
attempt with bold curiosity to penetrate to
the investigation of His essence, which we
ought more to adore than meticulously to
search out, but for us to contemplate Him
in His works, whereby He renders Himself
near and familiar to us, and in some
manner communicates Himself .
John Calvin

Nobody seriously believes the universe was
made by God without being persuaded
that He takes care of His works.
John Calvin

God is the Best and Most Orderly
Workman of all.
Copernicus

God never built a Christian strong enough
to carry today's duties and tomorrow's
anxieties piled on top of them.
Theodore Ledyard Cuyler

Wherever the Father is (and he is
everywhere) there the Son is, and wherever
the Son is, there the Father is too.
Cyril of Alexandria

The enjoyment of God is the only happiness
with which our souls can be satisfied. To go
to heaven, fully to enjoy God, is infinitely
better than the most pleasant
accommodations here. Fathers and mothers,
husbands, wives, or children, or the
company of earthly friends, are but shadows;
but God is the substance. These are but
scattered beams, but God is the sun. These
are but streams. But God is the ocean.
Jonathan Edwards

True saints have their minds, in the first
place, inexpressibly pleased and delighted
with the sweet ideas of the glorious and
amiable nature of the things of God. And
this is the spring of all their delights, and

the cream of all their pleasures.
Jonathan Edwards

Either he is not good, or else he is not
almighty.
Epicurus

I believe God is managing affairs and that
He doesn't need any advice from me. With
God in charge, I believe everything will
work out for the best in the end. So what
is there to worry about.
Henry Ford

God loves us the way we are, but too much
to leave us that way.
Leighton Ford

Oh Thou who art! Ecclesiastes names thee
the Almighty. Maccabees names thee
Creator; the epistle to the Ephesians names
thee Liberty… the Psalms name thee
Wisdom and Truth; John names thee
Light; the Book of Kings names thee Lord;
Exodus calls thee Providence; Leviticus,
Holiness; Esdras, Justice; Creation calls
thee God; Man names thee Father; but
Solomon names thee Compassion, and
that is the most beautiful of all thy names.
Victor Hugo

God is the God of truth; and every spiritual
quality must live with that holy attribute.
Edwin Holt Hughes

Is he [God] willing to prevent evil, but not
able? Then he is impotent.
Is he able, but not willing? Then he is
malevolent.
Is he both able and willing? Whence then
is evil?
David Hume

God is a sea of infinite substance.
John of Damascus

Your Highness, I have no need of this
hypothesis.
*Pierre Laplace (1749-1827), to Napoleon on
why his works on celestial mechanics make no
mention of God.*

Can a mortal ask questions which God finds unanswerable? Quite easily, I should think. All nonsense questions are unanswerable.
C. S. Lewis

It is the most ungodly and dangerous business to abandon the certain and revealed will of God in order to search into the hidden mysteries of God.
Martin Luther

The ethic of the Bible reflects the character of the God of the Bible. Remove from Scripture the transcendent holiness, righteousness and truth of God and its ethic disappears.
John Murray

Faith keeps the soul at a holy distance from these infinite depths of divine wisdom, where it profits more by reverence and holy fear than any can do by their utmost attempt to draw nigh to that inaccessible light wherein these glories of the divine nature do dwell.
John Owen

There is a God shaped vacuum in the heart of every man which cannot be filled by any created thing, but only by God, the Creator, made known through Jesus.
Blaise Pascal

The God of the Christians is a God of love and consolation, a God who fills the soul and hearts of his own.
Blaise Pascal

The abstract metaphysical monotheism, the constant emphasis laid on God's unity and infinite and incomprehensible essence, could not give light to the mind or peace to the heart ... How human is the God of the Old Testament – the God who appears, speaks, guides, who loves and is loved, even as the Man of the New Testament, Christ Jesus, is divine! This difference between the idea of an absolute and infinite God and the God of Scripture is, after all, that which separates the true believer and Christian from the natural man.
Adolph Saphir

As God is simple goodness, inner knowledge and light, he is at the same time also our will, love, righteousness and truth, the innermost of all virtues.
Theologica Germanica

Don't think so much about who is for or against you, rather give all your care that God be with you in everything you do.
Thomas à Kempis

"Personal God" does not mean that God is "a" person. It means that God is the ground of everything personal and that he carries within him the ontological power of personality. He is not a person, but he is not less than personal.
Paul Tillich

He who knows about depth knows about God.
Paul Tillich

Without doubt, the mightiest thought the mind can entertain is the thought of God, and the weightiest word in any language is its word for God.
A. W. Tozer.

The one God, hidden in all things, All-pervading, the Inner Soul of all things.
Upanishad

If God created us in His image we have certainly returned the compliment.
Voltaire

A God all mercy is a God unjust.
Edward Young

God, Belief in
See also: Agnosticism; Belief; Unbelief
I had rather believe all the fables in the legends and the Talmud and the Alcoran, than that this universe is without a mind.
Francis Bacon

A little philosophy inclineth man's mind to atheism; but depth in philosophy bringeth men's minds about to religion.
Francis Bacon

I have never been able to conceive mankind without him [God].
Fyodor Dostoevsky

Denial of the infinite leads straight to nihilism: all creation becomes merely "a conception of the mind."
Victor Hugo

There is but one God the Father of whom are all things and we in him and one Lord Jesus Christ by whom are all things and we by him.
Sir Isaac Newton

To believe in God for me is to feel that there is a God, not a dead one, or a stuffed one, but a living one, who with irresistible force urges us towards more loving.
Vincent Van Gogh

God, Existence of

Since what may be known about God is plain to them [those who are evil], because God has made it plain to them. For since the creation of the world God's invisible qualities – his eternal power and divine nature – have been clearly seen, being understood from what has been made, so that men are without excuse. For although they knew God, they neither glorified him as God nor gave thanks to him, but their thinking became futile and their foolish hearts were darkened.
The Bible, Romans 1:19-21

God is that, nothing greater than which can be conceived.
Anselm

That there is a God my Reason would soon tell me by the wondrous works that I see, the vast frame of the Heaven and Earth, the order of all things, night and day, summer and winter, spring and autumn, the daily providing for this great household upon the Earth, the preserving and directing of All to its proper end.
Anne Bradstreet

If God does not exist, then everything is permitted.
Fyodor Dostoevsky

A purpose, an intention, or design strikes everywhere the most careless, the most stupid thinker; and no man can be so hardened in absurd systems, as at all times to reject it.
David Hume

The question whether there is or is not a God can and should be rewarding, in that it can yield definite results.
J.L. Mackie

If there is no God, then there is no problem of reconciling the existence of pain and sin with his love and power.
Eric Mascall

The evidence of God's existence and his gift is more than compelling, but those who insist that they have no need of him or it will always find ways to discount the offer.
B. Pascal

If God does not exist, we find no values or commands to turn to which legitimize our conduct. So, in the bright realm of values, we have no excuse behind us, nor justification before us. We are alone, with no excuses.
Jean-Paul Sartre

The conclusion we reach in our reflection on this question [of the existence of God] has the most momentous consequences in the orientation of our thinking and our daily living.
Edward Sillem

If we refuse to discuss the existence of God we are simply avoiding the central issue, which is the issue of delusion.
Elton Trueblood

If God did not exist, it would be necessary to invent him.
Voltaire

God, Fatherhood of

Our doctrine of equality and liberty and humanity comes from our belief in the

brotherhood of man, through the
fatherhood of God.
Calvin Coolidge

Trying to build the brotherhood of man
without the fatherhood of God is like
trying to make a wheel without a hub.
Irene Dunne

God, Knowing
God is above the sphere of our esteem,
And is best known, not defining him.
Robert Herrick

The Lord has taught us that nobody can
know God unless God teaches him.
Irenaeus

God, Motherhood of
You deserted the Rock, who fathered you;
your forgot the God who gave you birth.
Deuteronomy 32.18

As a mother comforts her child, so will I
comfort you.
Isaiah 66:13

Mother is the name of God in the hearts
and minds of children.
Author unknown

God is as truly our Mother as he is our
Father.
Julian of Norwich

God almighty is our loving Father, and
God all wisdom is our loving Mother, with
the love and the goodness of the Holy
Spirit, which is all one God, one Lord.
Julian of Norwich

Trust in God: She will provide.
Emmeline Pankhurst

In the Song of Moses, Yahweh is not only
"the Rock who fathered you" but also
"the God who gave you birth". It is a
remarkable statement that he is
simultaneously Israel's Father and
Mother.
John Stott

God, Rejection of
We can only reach with determination for
the warm hand of God, which we have so
rashly and self-confidently pushed away.
Alexander Solzhenitsyn

God, Understanding
A comprehended God is no God.
John Chrysostom

God, Unity of
No mortal creature can comprehend God
in his majesty, and therefore did he come
before us in the simplest manner, and was
made man, with, sin, death, and
weakness.
Martin Luther

If God is a living God, we should not
therefore be surprised to find a complexity
within his unity.
Robert Brow

God, the cause of all, is One.
Symeon the New Theologian

God and creation
God dwells in His creation and is
everywhere indivisibly present in all His
works. He is transcendent above all His
works even while He is immanent within
them.
A. W. Tozer

God and humankind
Without God, we cannot. Without us,
God will not.
Augustine of Hippo

Where there is no God, there is no man.
Nicholas Berdayev

The Ground of God and the ground of the
soul are one and the same.
Meister Eckhart

The relationship between God and a man
is more private and intimate than any
possible relation between two fellow
creatures.
C.S. Lewis

God, as Creator

"What is the object of my love?" I asked the earth and it said: "It is not I." I asked all that is in it; they made the same confession ... I asked the sea, the deeps, the living creatures that creep, and they responded: "We are not your God, look beyond us." I asked the breezes which blow and the entire air with its inhabitants ... heaven, sun, moon, and stars; they said: "Nor are we the God whom you seek." And I said to all these things in my external environment: "Tell me of my God who you are not, tell me something about him." And with a great voice they cried out: "He made us ... We are not God."
Augustine of Hippo

The world forgets you, its creator, and falls in love with what you have created instead of with you.
Augustine of Hippo

It is necessary to apply to Scripture in order to learn the sure marks which distinguish God, as the Creator of the world, from the whole herd of fictitious gods.
John Calvin

The difference between Creator and created is incomparable.
Cyril of Alexandria

The end of God's creating the world was to prepare a kingdom for his Son.
Jonathan Edwards

The almighty and everywhere present power of God; whereby, as it were by his hand, he upholds and governs heaven, earth, and all creatures; so that herbs and grass, rain and drought, fruitful and barren years, meat and drink, health and sickness, riches and poverty, yea, and all things come, not by chance, but by his fatherly hand.
Heidelberg Catechism

This is the creator:
by his love, our Father;
by his power, our Lord;
by his wisdom, our maker and designer.
Irenaeus

Out of him we have all come, in him we are all enfolded and towards him we are all journeying.
Julian of Norwich

I cannot forgive Descartes; in all his philosophy he did his best to dispense with God. But he could not avoid making him set the world in motion with a flip of his thumb; after that he had no more use for God.
Blaise Pascal

No rain, no mushrooms. No God, no world.
African proverb

Everything is good when it leaves the Creator's hands; everything degenerates in the hands of man.
Jean-Jacques Rousseau

We often praise the evening clouds,
And tints so gay and bold;
But seldom think upon our God,
Who tinged those clouds with gold.
Sir Walter Scott

God-centeredness

1. If you seek first to please God and are satisfied therein, you have but one to please instead of multitudes; and a multitude of masters are hardlier pleased than one.
2. And it is one that putteth upon you nothing that is unreasonable, for quantity or quality.
3. And one that is perfectly wise and good, not liable to misunderstand your case and actions.
4. And one that is most holy, and is not pleased in iniquity or dishonesty.
5. And he is one that is impartial and most just, and is no respecter of persons, Acts x. 34.
6. And he is one that is a competent judge, that hath fitness and authority, and is acquainted with your hearts, and every circumstance and reason of your actions.
7. And he is one that perfectly agreeth with himself, and putteth you not upon

contradictions or impossibilities.

8. And he is one that is constant and unchangeable; and is not pleased with one thing to-day, and another contrary to-morrow; nor with one person this year, whom he will be weary of the next.

9. And he is one that is merciful, and requireth you not to hurt yourselves to please him: nay, he is pleased with nothing of thine but that which tendeth to thy happiness, and displeased with nothing but that which hurts thyself or others, as a father that is displeased with his children when they defile or hurt themselves.

10. He is gentle, though just, in his censures of thee; judging truly, but not with unjust rigor, nor making your actions worse than they are.

11. He is one that is not subject to the passions of men, which blind their minds, and carry them to injustice.

12. He is one that will not be moved by tale-bearers, whisperers, or false accusers, nor can be perverted by any misinformation.
Richard Baxter

God was so precious to my soul that the world with all its enjoyments appeared vile. I had no more value for the favor of men than for pebbles.
David Brainerd

He loseth nothing that loseth not God.
George Herbert

Godless

A man without God is not like a cake without raisins; he is like a cake without the flour and milk; he lacks the essential ingredients.
Bishop Fulton J. Sheen

Godlessness

A world without God must soon be a world without goodness.
Warren Akin Candler

There is practically nothing that men do not prefer to God. A tiresome detail of business, an occupation utterly pernicious to health, the employment of time in ways one does not dare to mention. Anything rather than God.
Francois Fénelon

Godliness

A man after his own heart.
The Bible, 1 Samuel 13:14

One that feared God and eschewed evil.
The Bible, Job 1:1 KJV

But godliness with contentment is great gain.
The Bible, 1 Timothy 6:6

Godliness

Thomas Brookes

I shall proceed, as I said, and leave some legacies with you, which may, by the finger of the Spirit, be made advantageous to you, to whom am not advantaged to speak in person.

LEGACY 1.

The first legacy I would leave with you, shall be this: Secure your interest in Christ; make it your great business, your work, your heaven, to secure your interest in Christ. This is not an age, an hour, for a man to be between fears and hopes, between doubting and believing.

Take not up in a name to live, when you are dead God-ward and Christ-ward; take not up in an outward form, and outward privilege. They cried out, "The temple of the Lord, the temple of the Lord," that had no interest in, or love for, the Lord of the temple. Follow God leave no means unattempted whereby your blessed interest may be cleared up.

LEGACY 2.

Make Christ and Scripture the only foundation for your souls and faith to build on: as the apostle saith, 1 Cor. iii. 11,

"Other foundations can no man lay than that which is laid, even Jesus Christ." Isa. xxviii. 6, "Behold, I lay in Zion for a foundation, a stone, a tried stone, a corner stone, a precious stone, a sure foundation," Eph. ii. 10. Since it is a very dangerous thing, as much as your souls and eternity is worth, for you to build on anything beside Jesus Christ, many will say, Come, build on this authority and that, on this saying and that; but take heed.

LEGACY 3.

In all places and company, be sure to carry your soul preservative with you: go into no place or company, except you carry your soul preservatives with you, that is, a holy care and wisdom. You know, in infectious times, men will carry outward preservatives with them; you had need to carry your preservatives about you, else you will be in danger of being infected with the ill customs and vanities of the times wherein you live, and that is a third. [In the 17th C it was thought that bad air caused many diseases. People would therefore carry bags of herbs about with them to "preserve" the air.]

LEGACY 4.

I would leave this with you: Look that all within you rises higher and higher, by oppositions, threatenings and sufferings, that is, that your faith, your love, your courage, your zeal, your resolutions, and magnanimity rises higher by opposition and a spirit of prayer. Thus it did, Acts iv. 18-21, 29-31 compared; all their sufferings did but raise up a more noble spirit in them, they did but raise up their faith and courage. So Acts v. 40-42, they looked on it as a grace to be disgraced for Christ, and as an honor to be dishonored for him. They say, as David, "If this be to be vile, I will be more vile." If to be found in the way of my God, to act for my God, to be vile, I will be more vile.

LEGACY 5.

Take more pains, and make more conscience of keeping yourselves from sin than suffering; from the pollutions and defilements of the day, than from the sufferings of the day. This legacy I would beg that you would consider; take more pains, and make more conscience of keeping yourselves from the evil of sin than the evil of punishment, from the pollutions and corruptions of the times than the sufferings of the times: Acts ii. 40, "Save yourselves from this untoward generation." Philip. ii. 15, "The children of God must be harmless and blameless, without rebuke in the midst of a crooked and perverse generation." Heb. xi. speaks full to the point in hand. Rev. iii. 4, "Thou hast a few names even in Sardis that have not defiled their garments; and they shall walk with me in white: for they are worthy." White was the habit of nobles, which imports the honor that God will put on those that keep their garments pure in a defiling day. Rev. xviii. 4, "And I heard another voice from heaven, saying, Come out of her, my people, that ye be not partakers of her sins, and that ye receive not of her plagues." If you will be tasting and sipping at Babylon's cup, you must resolve to receive more or less of Babylon's plagues.

LEGACY 6.

I would leave this with you: Be always doing or receiving good. Our Lord and Master went up and down in this world doing good; he was still doing good to body and soul; he was motivated by an untired power. Be still doing or receiving good. This will make your lives comfortable, your deaths happy, and your account glorious, in the great day of our Lord. Oh! how useless are many men in their generation! Oh! that our lips might be as so many honey-combs, that we might scatter knowledge!

LEGACY 7.

I would leave this with you: Set the highest examples and patterns before your face of grace and godliness for your imitation. In the business of faith, set an Abraham before your eyes; in the business of courage, set a Joshua; in the business of uprightness, set a Job; of meekness, a Moses &c. Christians disadvantage themselves by looking more backwards than forwards. Men look on whom they excel, not on those they fall short of. Of all examples, set them before you that are most eminent for grace and holiness, for communion with God, and acting for God. Next to Christ, set the pattern of the choicest saints before you.

LEGACY 8.

Hold fast your integrity, and rather let all go than let that go. A man had better let liberty, estate, relations, and life go, than let his integrity go. Yea, let ordinances themselves go, when they cannot be held with the hand of integrity: Job xxvii. 5, 6, "God forbid that I should justify you till I die. I will not remove my integrity from me; my righteousness I will hold fast, and I will not let it go: my heart shall not reproach me so long as I live." Look, as the drowning man holds fast that which is cast forth for to save him, as the soldier holds fast his sword and buckler on which his life depends, so, saith Job, "I will hold fast my integrity; my heart shall not reproach me. I had rather all the world should reproach me, and my heart justify me, than that my heart should reproach me, and all the world justify me." That man will make but a sad exchange that shall exchange his integrity for any worldly concernment. Integrity maintained in the soul will be a feast of fat things in the worst of days; but let a man lose his integrity. and it is not in the power of all the world to make a feast of fat things in that soul.

LEGACY 9.

That I would leave this with you: Let not a day pass over your head without calling the whole man to an exact account. Well, where have you been acting to-day? Hands, what have you done for God to-day? Tongue, what have you spoken for God to-day? This will be an advantage many ways unto you, but I can only touch on these legacies.

LEGACY 10.

Labor mightily for a healing spirit. This legacy I would leave with you as a matter of great concernment. To repeat: Labor mightily for a healing spirit. Away with all discriminating names whatever that may hinder the applying of balm to heal your wounds. Labor for a healing spirit. Discord and division become no Christian. For wolves to worry the lambs, is no wonder; but for one lamb to worry another, this is unnatural and monstrous. God hath made his wrath to smoke against us for the divisions and heart-burnings that have been amongst us. Labor for a oneness in love and affection with every one that is one with Christ. Let their forms be what they will, that which wins most upon Christ's heart, should win most upon ours, and that is his own grace and holiness. The question should be, What of the Father, what of the Son, what of the Spirit shines in this or that person? and accordingly let your love and your affections run out. That is the tenth legacy.

LEGACY 11.

Be most in the spiritual exercises of religion. Improve this legacy, for much of the life and comfort, joy and peace of your souls is wrapped up in it. I say, be most in the spiritual exercises of religion. There are external exercises, as hearing, preaching, praying, and conference; and there are the more spiritual exercises of religion, exercise of grace, meditation, self-judging, self-trial, and examination. Bodily exercise will profit nothing if abstracted from those more spiritual. The glory that God hath, and the comfort and advantage that will accrue to your souls is mostly from the spiritual exercises of religion. How rare is it to find men in the work of meditation, of trial and examination, and of bringing home of truths to their own souls?

LEGACY 12.

Take no truths upon trust, but all upon trial, 1 Thes. v. 21, also 1 John iv. 1, Acts xvii. 11. It was the glory of that church, that they would not trust Paul himself; Paul, that had the advantage above all for external qualifications; no, not Paul himself. Take no truth upon trust; bring them to the balance of the sanctuary. If they will not hold weight there, reject them.

LEGACY 13.

The lesser and fewer opportunities and advantages you have in public to better and enrich your souls, the more abundantly address your souls to God in private: Mal. iii. 16, 17, "Then they that feared the Lord, spake often one to another, &c.

LEGACY 14.

Walk in those ways that are directly cross and contrary to the vain, sinful, and superstitious ways that men of a formal, carnal, lukewarm spirit walk in; this is the great concernment of Christians. But more of that by and by.

LEGACY 15.

Look upon all the things of this world as you will look upon them when you come to die. At what a poor rate do men look on the things of this world when they come to die! What a low value do men set upon the pomp and glory of it, when there is but a step between them and eternity! Men may now put a mask upon them, but then they will appear in their own colors. Men would not venture the loss of such great things for them did they but look on them now, as they will do at the last day.

LEGACY 16.

Never put off your conscience with any plea or with any argument that you dare not stand by in the great day of your account. It is dreadful to consider how many in these days put off their consciences. We did this and that for our families, else they would have perished. I have complied thus, and wronged my conscience thus, for this and that concernment. Will a man stand by this argument when he comes before Jesus Christ at the last day? Because of the souls of men, many plead this or that. Christ doth not stand in need of indirect ways to save souls; he hath ways enough to bring in souls to himself.

LEGACY 17.

Eye more, mind more, and lay to heart more, the spiritual and eternal workings of God in your souls, than the external providences of God in the world. Beloved, God looks that we should consider the operations of his hand; and despising the works of his hands is so provoking to him that he threatens to lead them into captivity for not considering them. But above all look to the work that God is carrying on in your souls. Not a soul but he is carrying on some work or other in it, either blinding or enlightening, bettering or worsening; therefore look to what God is doing in thy soul. All the motions of God within you are steps to eternity, and every soul shall be blessed or cursed, saved or lost to all eternity, not according to outward dispensations, but according to the inward operations of God in your souls. Observe what humbling work, reforming work, sanctifying work, he is about in thy spirit; what he is doing in that little world within thee. If God should carry on never so glorious a work in the world, as a conquest of the nations to Christ, what would it advantage thee if sin, Satan, and the world should triumph in thy soul, and carry the day there?

LEGACY 18.

Look as well on the bright side as on the dark side of the cloud; on the bright side of providence as well as on the dark side of providence. Beloved, there is a great weakness amongst Christians; they do so dwell on the dark side of the providence that they have no heart to consider the bright side. If you look on the dark side of the providence of God to Joseph, how terrible and amazing was it! But if you look on the bright side, his fourscore years' reign, how glorious was it! If you look on the dark side of the providence of God to David in his five years' banishment, much will arise to startle you; but if you turn to the bright side, his forty years' reign in glory, how amiable was it! Look on the dark side of the providence of God to Job, oh, how terrible was it in the first of Job!

but compare this with the last of Job, where you have the bright side of the cloud, and there God doubles all his mercies to him. Consider the patience of Job, and the end that the Lord made with him. Do not remember the beginning only, for that was the dark side; but turn to the end of him, and there was his bright side. Many sins, many temptations, and much affliction would be prevented by Christians looking on the bright side of providence as well as on the dark.

LEGACY 19.

Keep up precious thoughts of God under the sourest, sharpest, and severest dispensations of God to you: Ps. xxii. 1-3, "My God, my God, why hast thou forsaken me? Why art thou so far from helping me, and from the words of my roaring? O my God, I cry in the daytime but thou hearest not; and in the night season, and am not silent." There was the psalmist under smart dispensations, but what precious thoughts had he of God after all: "But thou art holy, O thou that inhabitest the praises of Israel: though I am thus and thus afflicted, yet thou art holy;" Ps. lxv. 5, "By terrible things in righteousness wilt thou answer us, O God of our salvation.

LEGACY 20.

Hold on and hold out in the ways of well-doing, in the want of out outward encouragements, and in the face of all outward discouragements. It is nothing to hold out when we meet with nothing but encouragements; but to hold out in the face of all discouragements is a Christian duty: Ps. xliv., "Though thou hast sore broken us in the place of dragons, and covered us with the shadow of death, yet have we not dealt falsely in thy covenant: our heart is not turned back, neither have we declined from thy way." It is perseverance that crowns all; "Be thou faithful to the death, and I will give thee a crown of life," Rev. ii. 10; "And he that endureth to the end shall be saved," Mat. xxiv. It is perseverance in well-doing that crowns all our actions. If you have begun

in the Spirit, don't end in the flesh; do not go away from the Captain of your salvation; follow the Lamb, though others follow the beast and the false prophets.

LEGACY 21.

In all your natural, civil, and religious actions, let divine glory still rest on your souls, Rom. xiv. 7, 8, 1 Cor. x. 31. In all your bearings, in all your prayers, let the glory of Christ carry it; in all your closet duties, let the glory of Christ lie nearest your hearts.

LEGACY 22.

Record all special favors, mercies, providences, and experiences. It is true, a man should do nothing else, should he record all the favors and experiences of God towards him; and therefore my legacy is, record all special favors, peculiar experiences. Little do you know the advantage that will increase to your soul upon this account by recording all the experiences of the shinings of his face, of the leadings of his Spirit. Many a Christian loseth much by neglecting this duty.

LEGACY 23.

Never enter upon the trial of your estate, but when your hearts are at the best, and in the fittest temper. It is a great design of Satan, when the soul is deserted and strangely afflicted, to put the soul on trying work. Come, see what thou art worth for another world, what thou hast to shew for a better state, for an interest in Christ, a title for heaven. This is not a time to be about this work. Thy work is now to get off from this temptation, and therefore to pray and believe, and wait upon God, and to be found in all those ways whereby you may get off the temptation.

LEGACY 24.

Always make the Scripture, and not yourselves, nor your carnal reason, nor your bare opinion, the judges of your spiritual state and condition. I cannot see my condition to be good. I cannot perceive it. What! must your sense and your carnal reason be the judge of your spiritual state? Isa. viii. 20, "To the law and to the testimony, if they speak not according to this rule, it is because there is no light, no morning in them," John xii. 48, "The word that I have spoken, the same shall judge you in the last day." The Scripture is that which must determine the case in the great day, whether you have grace or no, or whether it be true or no.

LEGACY 25.

Make much conscience of making good the terms on which you closed with Christ. You know the terms, how that you would deny yourselves, take up his cross, and follow the Lamb wheresoever he should go. Now you are put to take up the cross, to deny yourselves, to follow the Lamb over hedge and ditch, through thick and thin. Do not turn your backs on Christ; the worst of Christ is better than the best of the world. Make conscience of making good your terms, to deny yourself, your natural self, your sinful self, your religious self, to follow him; and if you do so, oh! what an honor will it be to Christ, and advantage to your souls, and a joy to the upright!

LEGACY 26.

Walk by no rule but such as you dare die by and stand by in the great day of Jesus Christ. You may have many ways prescribed to worship by; but walk by none but such as you dare die by, and stand by, before Jesus Christ. Walk not by a multitude, for who dares stand by that rule when he comes to die?

Make not the example of great men a rule to go by, for who dares die by and stand by this in the great day of account? Do not make any authority that stands in opposition to the authority of Christ a rule to walk by, for who dares stand by this before Jesus Christ? Ah! sirs, walk by no rule but what you dare die by, and stand by at the great day.

LEGACY 27.

And lastly, sit down and rejoice with fear: Ps. ii., "Let the righteous rejoice, but let them rejoice with fear." Rejoice, that God hath done your souls good by the everlasting gospel; that he did not leave you till he brought you to an acceptance of, to a closing with, and a resignation of, your souls to Christ, and the clearing up of your interest in him. Rejoice, that you have had the everlasting gospel! in so much light, purity, power, and glory, as you have had for many years together. Rejoice in the riches of grace that hath carried it in such a way towards you. And weep, that you have provoked God to take away the gospel, that you have no more improved it; that you have so neglected the seasons and opportunities of enriching your souls. When you should have come to church-fellowship, anything would turn you out of the way. Oh! sit down and tremble under your barrenness, under all your leanness. Notwithstanding all the cost and charge that God hath been at, that you have grown no more into communion with God, and conformity to God, and into the lively hope of the everlasting fruition of God. Here are your legacies, and the Lord make them to work in your souls, and then they will be of singular use to you, to preserve you so that you may give up your account before the great and glorious God with joy. Labor to make conscience of putting these legacies into practice, of sucking at these breasts, which will be of use to us, till we shall be gathered up into the fruition of God, where we shall need no more ordinances, no more preaching or praying.

Thomas Brookes

[His Farewell Sermon at the Great Ejection. Apparently he was not allowed to preach the sermon, so he prepared it in written form.]

We cannot learn fear of God and the basic principles of godliness, unless we are pierced by the sword of the Spirit and destroyed. It is as if God were saying that to rank among his sons our ordinary natures must be wiped out.

John Calvin

A baptism of holiness, a demonstration of godly living is the crying need of our day.
Duncan Campbell

Prayer – secret, fervent, believing prayer – lies at the root of all personal godliness.
Carey's Brotherhood

When God and his glory are made our end, we shall find a silent likeness pass in upon us; the beauty of God will, by degrees, enter upon our soul.
Stephen Charnock

Godliness is glory in the seed, and glory is godliness in the flower.
William Gurnall

You who never know what a groan is, or a falling tear, are destitute of vital godliness.
C.H. Spurgeon

A godly man is a praying man.
Thomas Watson

God's blessing
He shall come down like rain upon the mown grass.
The Bible, Psalm 72:6 KJV

It is seriously wrong to have more regard for God's blessings than for God himself: prayer and detachment.
John of the Cross

God's care
The very hairs of your head are all numbered.
The Bible, Matthew 10:30 KJV

You will support us both when little and even to grey hairs.
Augustine of Hippo

The heart of the Christian gospel is precisely that God is the all holy One; the all powerful One is also the One full of mercy and compassion.
  He is not a neutral God inhabiting some inaccessible Mount Olympus. He is a God who cares about His children and cares enormously for the weak, the poor, the naked, the downtrodden, the despised. He takes their side not because they are good, since many of them are demonstrably not so. He takes their side because He is that kind of God, and they have no one else to champion them.
Desmond Tutu

God's Faithfulness

Robert Murray M'Cheyne
"God is faithful, by whom ye were called unto the fellowship of his Son Jesus Christ our Lord." 1 Corinthians 1:9
The anxieties of a faithful pastor never end in this world. First he is anxious that his people be brought to Christ, and then he is anxious that they be kept abiding in Him to the end. What a fountain of consolation is this text while he looks upon those, of whom in his heart he has the sweet persuasion that they are "sanctified in Christ Jesus, and called to be saints", and repeats these words in his heart, "God is faithful, by whom ye were called unto the fellowship of his Son Jesus Christ". It is this sweet truth, the faithfulness of our covenant God, that is a rock to the pastor's soul, and makes him feel that those who are now "dearly beloved, and longed for", will soon be "his joy and crown". But not only to the pastor, to the flock also, especially in time of temptation, affliction, and desertion, these words are like "the snow of Lebanon, or the cold flowing waters from another place". Sometimes it pleases God to withdraw His comfortable presence from the soul, chiefly to humble us in the dust, to discover some unmortified corruption, or to lead us to hunger more vehemently after Him. Such was David's state when he said in his heart, "I shall now perish one day by the hand of Saul" (1 Samuel 27: 1). And again, when he wrote the 42nd Psalm. Such was the feeling of Job when he said, "the arrows of the Almighty are within me"; and again,

"Oh that it were with me as in months past, as in the days when God preserved me; when his candle shined upon my head, and when by his light I walked through darkness" (Job 29:2-3). In such an hour as this, when the feeling of distance from God is almost insupportable, ah! how cheering, how full of nourishment, what a heavenly cordial may this word in the hand of the Spirit be: "God is faithful, by whom ye were called unto the fellowship of his Son Jesus Christ our Lord."

1. Believers are called to share with Christ. To have fellowship with another, is to have things in common with him. Thus in Acts 4:32, it is said of the first Christians, that they were "of one heart and of one soul, neither said any that ought of the things which he possessed were his own, but they had all things in common " ' They had all their goods in common, they shared all they had with one another. This is what John desired to see amongst Christians in spiritual things, "That which we have seen and heard declare we unto you, that ye also may have fellowship with us" (I John 1:3). The same expressions is used here, "Ye are called unto the fellowship of his Son". How strange, that a creature of sin and shame should be called to share with God's dear Son. Yet so it is; He shared our flesh and blood with us, that we might share His throne with Him.

(i) We share with the Son in His justification. Once Jesus was unjustified. Once there were millions of sins laid to His charge. Men, devils, nay, even His holy Father, hurled their fierce accusations at Him. He stood silent. He could not answer a word. Although "he did no sin, neither was guile found his mouth"; yet He had agreed to bear the sins of many, and therefore, He was dumb under every accusation. "It was exacted, and he was made answerable". This was His chief agony in the garden, and on the cross, that at the bar of God He was unjustified; "He was numbered with the transgressors". His only comfort was, "He is near that justifieth me" (Isaiah 50:8). He knew that His trial would be short and that He

would overcome. The hour of darkness is now past. The wrath of God has all fallen upon Him. The thunder clouds have spent their lightnings on His head. The vials of God's anger have emptied their last drops upon Him. He is now justified from all the sins that were laid upon Him. He will bear the scars to all eternity, Revelation 5:6; but not another drop of agony shall ever fall upon His soul When He comes a second time it is "without sin" (Hebrews 9:28). Have you the Son? Do you believe the record that God has given concerning His Son? Do you with purpose of heart cleave to the Lord Jesus? then you share with Him in His justification. You suffered in His suffering, you obeyed in His obedience, you died in His death. You are as much justified as Christ is. You have as little to do with the guilt of your past sins as Christ has. There is as little guilt lying upon you as upon God's dear Son. The vials of wrath have not another drop for Christ, and not another drop for you. "By Jesus all that believe are justified from all things" (Acts 13:39).

(ii) We share with the Son in His Father's love. When Jesus was about to leave this world, He said to His disciples, "I leave the world and go to the Father". When He died He cried, "Father into thy hands I commend my spirit". When He entered into heaven and passed up the opening ranks of the adoring angels, the Father said, "Thou art my Son, this day have I begotten thee"; as if He had said, Never till this time did I see thee so worthy to be called my Son. Ah! it was a blessed exchange when He left the frowns and curses of the world for the embrace of His Father's arms; when He came from under the outpoured wrath of God into His full eternal love and smile; when He left the crown of thorns for the crown of glory. Such is the change of every poor sinner in the moment that he is persuaded and enabled to embrace Christ. Dost thou believe with all thine heart that Jesus is the Son of God? Can you say you have fled for refuge to Christ? Then you share with Christ in His Father's love. Christ says, "I ascend unto my Father and your Father, and to my God and your God" (John 20:17). God is as much your Father as He is Christ's Father. Your God as Christ's God. The Father loves you with the same full, unchanging, soul-satisfying love, with which He loves Jesus (see that never to be forgotten prayer, John 17:26). Oh! what a blessed change for an heir of hell to become an "heir of God, and a joint heir with Christ" (Romans 8:17). For one who deserved, and still deserves, to share with the devil and his angels, to share with Christ that sits at the right hand of God. Oh! to inherit God, to have a son's interest in God! Eternity alone can reveal the full meaning of that word, "Heir of God, and joint heir with Christ".

2. God is faithful to souls in Christ. "God is faithful, by whom ye are called unto the fellowship of his Son." When a soul is in affliction, temptation, or desertion, his cry is, "The Lord hath forsaken me, and my God hath forgotten me". Sometimes this feeling approaches to actual despair. Here is a rock for the soul to lean upon, "Christ is the same yesterday, to-day, and for ever", and "God is faithful" who called us to share with Christ. Hearken to the voice of the great Shepherd, "My sheep hear my voice, and they follow me, and I give unto them eternal life, and they shall never perish, neither shall any pluck them out of my hand. My Father which gave them me is greater than all, and none is able to pluck them out of my Father's hand." Satan desires to have you. The world are laying snares for you. Your own wicked heart would sometimes be for leaving the hand that has saved you. But "none is able to pluck you out of the Father's hand". Hearken to the Father's own word, "Thou art my servant, I have chosen the and not cast thee away" (Isaiah 41:9). The soul united to Jesus is not like the grass, but like the palm tree. Even in old age he shall bear fruit, he shall be full of sap and flourishing. "To show that the Lord is upright: he is my rock, and there is no unrighteousness in him" (Psalm 92:15). At the very time when Zion was saying, "My God hath

forgotten me", God had her walls engraven on His hands, Isaiah 49:16. Look still to Jesus, oh! deserted soul. The love of God shines unchangeably on Him. Abide in Him and you will abide in the Father's love. Your afflictions may only prove that you are more immediately under the Father's hand. There is no time that the patient is such an object of tender interest to the surgeon, as when he is bleeding beneath his knife. So you may be sure if you are suffering from the hand of a reconciled God, that His eye is all the more bent on you. "The eternal God is thy refuge, and underneath are the everlasting arms."

Robert Murray M'Cheyne

God's gifts

God's gifts put man's best dreams to shame.
Elizabeth Barrett Browning

I have experienced that the habit of taking out of the hand of our Lord every little blessing and brightness on our path, confirms us, in an especial manner, in communion with his love.
M.A. Schimmeleninck

God often gives in one brief moment that which he has for a long time denied.
Thomas à Kempis

God's glory

For though we very truly hear that the kingdom of God will be filled with splendor, joy, happiness and glory, yet when these things are spoken of, they remain utterly remote from our perception, and as it were, wrapped in obscurities, until that day when he will reveal to us his glory, that we may behold it face to face.
John Calvin

A man can no more diminish God's glory by refusing to worship him than a lunatic can put out the sun by scribbling the word darkness on the walls of his cell.
C.S. Lewis

I ask you neither for health nor for sickness, for life nor for death; but that you may dispose of my health and my sickness, my life and my death, for your glory … You alone know what is expedient for me; you are the sovereign master, do with me according to your will. Give to me, or take away from me, only conform my will to yours. I know but one thing, Lord, that it is good to follow you, and bad to offend you. Apart from that, I know not what is good or bad in anything. I know not which is most profitable to me, health or sickness, wealth or poverty, nor anything else in the world. That discernment is beyond the power of men or angels, and is hidden among the secrets of your providence, which I adore, but do not seek to fathom.
Blaise Pascal

The radiance of the divine beauty is wholly inexpressible: words cannot describe it, nor the ear grasp it.
Philimon

God's goodness
Or what man is there of you, whom if his son ask bread, will he give him a stone?
The Bible, Matthew 7:9 KJV

I am convinced that He [God] does not play dice.
Albert Einstein

Just as the body wears clothes and the flesh skin, and the bones flesh, and the heart the chest, so we, soul and body are clothed and enfolded in the goodness of God.
Julian of Norwich

Our heavenly Father never takes anything from his children unless he means to give them something better.
George Müller

God often takes a course for accomplishing His purposes directly contrary to what our narrow views would prescribe. He brings a death upon our feelings, wishes, and prospects when He is about to give us the desire of our hearts.
John Newton

Doth God give us a Christ, and will he deny us a crust? If God doth not give us what we crave, He will give us what we need.
Thomas Watson

God's grace
God's gifts put man's best dreams to shame.
Elizabeth Barrett Browning

Nor can a man with grace his soul inspire,
More than the candles set themselves on fire.
John Bunyan

And when the grand twelve million jury
Of our sins, with direful fury,
Against our souls black verdicts give,
Christ pleads His death, and then we live.
Sir Walter Raleigh, written in the Tower of London, as he awaited his execution.

God's holiness
A true love for God must begin with a delight in his holiness, and not with a delight in any other attribute; for no other attribute is truly lovely without this.
Jonathan Edwards

Before I begin to think and consider the love of God and the mercy and compassion of God, I must start with the holiness of God.
M. Lloyd-Jones

An ineffably holy God, who has the utmost abhorrence of all sin, was never invented by any of Adam's fallen descendants.
A. W. Pink

We cannot grasp the true meaning of the divine holiness by thinking of someone or something very pure and then raising the concept to the highest degree we are capable of. God's holiness is not simply the best we know infinitely bettered. We know nothing like the divine holiness. It stands apart, unique, unapproachable, incomprehensible and unattainable. The natural man is blind to it. He may fear God's power and admire His wisdom, but His holiness he cannot even imagine.
A. W. Tozer

God's image

The man who was made in God's image is
the inner man, the incorporeal,
incorruptible immortal one.
Origen

God's initiative

But I have raised you up for this very
purpose, that I might show you my power
and that my name might be proclaimed in
all the earth.
Exodus 9:16

No man ever believes with a true and
saving faith unless God inclines his heart;
and no man when God does incline his
heart can refrain from believing.
Blaise Pascal

God's knowledge

"My thoughts are not your thoughts, neither
are your ways my ways," declares the LORD.
The Bible, Isaiah 55:8

There are three things that only God
knows: the beginning of things, the cause
of things and the end of things.
Welsh proverb

God's love

For God so loved the world that he gave
his one and only Son, that whoever
believes in him shall not perish but have
eternal life.
The Bible, John 3:16

But God demonstrates his own love for us
in this: While we were still sinners, Christ
died for us.
The Bible, Romans 5:8

The love of God is like the Amazon River
flowing down to water one daisy.
Author unknown

God's love is persistent but never pushy.
Author unknown

Jesus did not come to make God's love
possible, but to make God's love visible.
Author unknow

God loves us not because of who we are,
but because of who He is.
Author unknown

Incomprehensible and immutable is the
love of God. For it was not after we were
reconciled to him by the blood of his Son
that he began to love us, but he loved us
before the foundation of the world, that
with his only begotten Son we too might be
sons of God before we were any thing at all.
Augustine of Hippo

O Love ever burning and never extinguished
caritas, my God, set me on fire.
Augustine of Hippo

God loves each one of us as if there were
only one of us to love.
Augustine of Hippo

Christianity does not think of a man
finally submitting to the power of God, it
thinks of him as finally surrendering to the
love of God. It is not that man's will is
crushed, but that man's heart is broken.
William Barclay

Is it a small thing in your eyes to be loved
by God – to be the son, the spouse, the
love, the delight of the King of glory?
Christian, believe this, and think about it:
you will be eternally embraced in the arms
of the love which was from everlasting, and
will extend to everlasting – of the love
which brought the Son of God's love from
heaven to earth, from earth to the cross,
from the cross to the grave, from the grave
to glory – that love which was weary,
hungry, tempted, scorned, scourged,
buffeted, spat upon, crucified, pierced –
which fasted, prayed, taught, healed, wept,
sweated, bled, died. That love will eternally
embrace you.
Richard Baxter

The true original and prime motive of all
gracious, bountiful expressions and
effusions of love upon his elect, is the good
pleasure of his will.
Robert Bolton

It is not after we were reconciled by the blood of his Son that God began to love us, but before the foundation of the world.
John Calvin

I am so washed in the tide of His measureless love that I seem to be below the surface of a sea and cannot touch or see or feel anything around me except its water.
Catherine of Genoa

Everything comes from love, all is ordained for the salvation of man, God does nothing without this goal in mind.
Catherine of Siena

Charity [love] means nothing else than to love God for himself above all creatures, and to love one's fellow men for God's sake as one loves oneself.
The Cloud of Unknowing

To stop God loving me would be to rob him of his Godhead, for God is love no less than he is truth.
Meister Eckhart

For however devoted you are to God, you may be sure that he is immeasurably more devoted to you.
Meister Eckhart

For the love of God is broader
Than the measures of man's mind;
And the heart of the Eternal
Is most wonderfully kind.
F. W. Faber

God's love to His elect is not of yesterday; it does not begin with their love to Him, We love Him, because He first loved us. It was bore in His heart towards them long before they were delivered from the power of darkness, and translated into the kingdom of His dear Son. It does not commence in time, but bears date from eternity, and is the ground and foundation of the elect's being called in time out of darkness into marvelous light: I have loved thee, says the Lord to the church, with an everlasting love; therefore with loving-kindness have I have drawn thee. that is in effectual vocation. Many are the instances which might be given in proof of the antiquity of God's love to His elect, and as it is antecedent to their being brought out of a state of nature. God's choosing them in Christ before the foundation of the world, was an act of His love towards them, the fruit and effect of it; for election presupposes love. His making an everlasting covenant with His Son, ordered in all things, and sure, on account of those He chose in Him; His setting Him up as the Mediator of the covenant from everlasting; His donation of grace to them in Him before the world began; his putting their persons into His hands, and so making them His care and charge, are so many demonstrative proofs of His early love to them; for can it ever be imagined that there should be a choice of persons made, a covenant of grace so well formed and stored, a promise of life granted, and a security made, both of persons and grace, and yet no love all this while?
John Gill

God proved his love on the cross. When Christ hung, and bled, and died it was God saying to the world – I love you.
Billy Graham

Love refuseth nothing that love sends.
William Gurnall

For love dwells so deep in the womb of the Father that her power will unfold only to those who serve her with utter devotion.
Hadewijch

Love bade me welcome: yet my soul drew
  back,
    Guilty of dust and sin.
But quick-ey'd Love, observing me grow
  slack
    From my first entrance in,
Drew nearer to me, sweetly questioning,
    If I lack'd any thing.
A guest, I answer'd, worthy to be here:
    Love said, You shall be he.

I the unkind, ungrateful? Ah my dear,
   I cannot look on thee.
Love took my hand, and smiling did reply,
   Who made the eyes but I?
Truth Lord, but I have marr'd them: let my
  shame
   Go where it doth deserve.
And know you not, says Love, who bore
  the blame?
   My dear, then I will serve.
You must sit down, says Love, and taste my
  meat:
   So I did sit and eat.
George Herbert

When a soul is purified by the love of
God, illumined by wisdom, stabled by the
might of God, then is the eye of the soul
opened to view spiritual things, such as
angels and heavenly beings. Then the
purified soul is able to feel the touch and
hear the voice of good angels. This feeling
and hearing is not bodily but spiritual.
For when the soul is lifted up and
ravished out of sensuality, and away from
all earthly things, then in great fervor and
light (if our Lord wills) the soul may hear
and feel heavenly sound, made by the
presence of angels as they love God. This
is the song of the angels.
Walter Hilton

We can love him because he loved us. It
produces gratitude, delight, zeal, filial
reverence, obedience. It elevates the soul
above the creature. It purifies all the
affections. This is its legitimate effect.
Where God is understood, and where his
love is really enjoyed, these effects follow.
Charles Hodge

The very fire of love which afterwards is
united with the soul, glorifying it, is that
which previously assails it by purging it,
just as the fire that penetrates a log of wood
is the same that first makes an assault on it,
wounding it with its flame, drying it out,
and stripping it of its unsightly qualities
until it is so disposed that it can be
penetrated and transformed into the fire.
John of the Cross

Painting and sculpture will lose their appeal
for the soul turned to that divine love which
opened its arms upon the cross to welcome us.
Michelangelo

Do you want to know what our Lord
meant in all this? Learn it well: love was
what he meant.
Who showed it to you? Love.
Why did he show it? Out of love.
So I was taught that love was what our
Lord meant.
Julian of Norwich

In his love he clothes us, enfolds us and
embraces us; that tender love completely
surrounds us, never to leave us.
Julian of Norwich

Thus I was taught that love is our Lord's
meaning, and I saw most certainly in this
and in all things that before God made us
He loved us; this love was never diminished
nor shall it ever be. And in His love He has
accomplished in all His works; and in this
love He has made all things profitable to us;
and in this love our life is everlasting. In our
creation, we had a beginning, but the love
out of which He made us was always within
Him. In this love we have our beginning
and in all this we shall see God eternally.
Julian of Norwich

Some of us believe that God is almighty and
may do everything, and that he is all-wisdom
and can do everything; but that he is all-love
and wishes to do everything – there we stop
short. It is this ignorance, it seems to me, that
hinders most of God's lovers.
Julian of Norwich

Daughter, I have suffered many pains for
thy love; therefore thou hast great cause to
love Me right well, for I have bought thy
love full dear.
Margery Kempe

God, who needs nothing, loves into
existence wholly superfluous creatures in
order that he may love and perfect them.
C.S. Lewis

God's love never imposes itself. It has to be discovered and welcomed.
Brother Roger

All God can give us is his love; and this love becomes tangible – a burning of the soul – it sets us on fire to the point of forgetting ourselves.
Brother Roger

Human love is capable of great things. What then must be the depth and height and intensity of divine love. Know nothing, think of nothing but Jesus Christ and him crucified.
Lord Shaftesbury, to his schoolboy son who had a terminal illness

He who counts the stars and calls them by their names, is in no danger of forgetting His own children. He knows your case as thoroughly as if you were the only creature He ever made, or the only saint He ever loved.
C.H. Spurgeon

Divine love can rake a dunghill, and find a diamond!
C.H. Spurgeon

Nothing binds me to my Lord like a strong belief in his changeless love.
C.H. Spurgeon

None of us ever desired anything more ardently than God desires to bring men to a knowledge of himself.
John Tauler

Love is the greatest thing that God can give us; for Himself is love; and it is the greatest thing we can give to God; for it will also give ourselves, and carry with it all that is ours.
Jeremy Taylor

Keep us little and unknown, prized and loved by God alone.
Charles Wesley

Love Divine, all loves excelling,

Joy of heaven, to earth come down,
Fix in us thy humble dwelling,
And thy faithful mercies crown.
Charles Wesley

God's love, Adversity and
His love in times past
Forbids me to think
He'll leave me at last
In trouble to sink;
Each sweet Ebenezer
I have in review,
Confirms his good pleasure
To help me quite through.
John Newton

God's love, Response to
A man receives God in the soul as often as for love of God he abstains from a fault, be it only a word or an idle glance.
Albert I

O Love that will not let me go,
I rest my weary soul in thee,
I give thee back the life I owe,
That in thine ocean depths its flow
May richer, fuller, be.
George Matheson

Jesu, lover of my soul,
Let me to thy bosom fly,
While the nearer waters roll,
While the tempest still is high;
Hide me, O my Savior, hide,
Till the storm of life is past;
Safe into the haven glide
O receive my soul at last.
Charles Wesley

God's majesty
Hence that dread and amazement with which as Scripture uniformly relates holy men were struck and overwhelmed whenever they beheld the presence of God men are never duly touched and impressed with a conviction of their insignificance until they have contrasted themselves with the majesty of God.
John Calvin

In the church we seem to have lost the

vision of the majesty of God.
John Stott

God's mercy

God's mercy may be found between bridge and stream.
Augustine of Hippo

The only haven of safety is in the mercy of God, as manifested in Christ, in whom every part of our salvation is complete.
John Calvin

Among the attributes of God, although they are all equal, mercy shines with even more brilliance than justice.
Miguel de Cervantes

There's a wideness in God's mercy,
Like the wideness of the sea;
There's a kindness in his justice,
Which is more than liberty.
F.W. Faber

His father saw him – there were eyes of
  mercy;
he ran to meet him – there were legs of
  mercy;
he put his arms round his neck – there
  were arms of mercy;
he kissed him – there were kisses of mercy;
he said to him – there were words of mercy;
Bring here the best robe – there were deeds
  of mercy;
Wonders of mercy – all mercy!
Oh, what a God of mercy he is!
Matthew Henry

God's mercy was not increased when Jesus came to earth, it was illustrated! Illustrated in a way we can understand.
Eugenia Price

God's name

The name of God is anything whereby God maketh himself known.
Westminster Shorter Catechism

God's nature

I am Alpha and Omega, the beginning and the end, the first and the last.
The Bible, Revelation 22:13 KJV

God is not in need of anything, but all things are in need of him.
Arcus Aristides

God is always active, always quiet.
Augustine of Hippo

God, to keep us sober, speaks sparingly of his essence.
John Calvin

The God of the universe has need of nothing.
Clement of Rome

God is neither soul nor angel ... nor can He be described or understood ... He neither stands still nor moves
The Cloud of Unknowing

God is incorporeal, immaterial, impalpable, beyond quantity and circumscription, beyond form and figure.
Cyril of Alexandria

God is the denial of denials.
Meister Eckhart

The more God is in all things, the more he is outside them. The more he is within, the more without.
Meister Eckhart

God is subtle but he is not malicious.
Albert Einstein

God is not a theorem; he is a person. As such, he is only known and encountered in a total relationship which involves and affects not only our mind but the life and character as well. To know God's dossier is nothing; to know him is everything.
R.T. France

The Father of all ... is all understanding, all spirit, all thought, all hearing, all seeing, all light, and the whole source of

everything good.
Irenaeus

The hardness of God is kinder than the
softness of men.
C.S. Lewis

God is not something ... God is beyond
nothing and beyond something ... God
cannot be called "this" rather than "that"...
Nicholas of Cusa

That One is not such as are visible
things. Rather, He transcends
incomparably and inalterably all the
visible world, at once all-good and
transcending all that is good.
Symeon the New Theologian

God's patience
Our ground of hope is that God does not
weary of mankind.
Ralph W. Sockman

God's power
He rode upon a cherub, and did fly: yea,
he did fly upon the wings of the wind.
The Bible, Psalm 18:10 KJV

The LORD reigneth; let the earth rejoice.
The Bible, Psalm 97:1 KJV

Before God there remains nothing of
which we can glory save only his mercy,
by which, without any merit of our own,
we are admitted to the hope of eternal
salvation: and before men not even this
much remains, since we can glory only in
our infirmity, a thing which, in
estimation of men, it is the greatest
ignominy even tacitly to confess.
But our doctrine must stand sublime
above all the glory of the world, and
invincible by all its power, because it is not
ours, but that of the living God and His
Anointed, whom the Father has appointed
King, that He may rule from sea to sea,
and from the rivers to the ends of the
earth; and so rule as to smite the whole
earth and its strength of iron and brass, its
splendor of gold and silver, with the mere

rod of his mouth, and break them in
pieces like a potter's vessel; according to
the magnificent predictions of the
prophets respecting His kingdom.
John Calvin

All the resources of the Godhead are at our
disposal!
Jonathan Goforth

One man with God is always in the
majority.
*Inscription on the Reformation Monument in
Geneva*

[God's power] means power to do all that
is intrinsically possible, not to do the
intrinsically impossible. You may attribute
miracles to him, but not nonsense. This is
no limit to his power ... It remains true
that all things are possible with God: the
intrinsic impossibilities are not things but
nonentities.
C.S. Lewis

The God of the Bible is the God who
reveals himself in all the glory and the
wonder of his miraculous, eternal power.
M. Lloyd-Jones

He can give only according to His might;
therefore He always gives more than we ask
for.
Martin Luther

A mighty fortress is our God,
A bulwark never failing;
Our helper He amid the flood
Of mortal ills prevailing.
Martin Luther

The greatest single distinguishing feature
of the omnipotence of God is that our
imagination gets lost thinking about it.
Blaise Pascal

The work done by human effort cannot be
compared to the divine work done by God
in the creature by His goodness for the
sake of the creature.
Marguerite Porete

God's presence

A still, small voice.
The Bible, 1 Kings 19:12 KJV

A day in thy courts is better than a
thousand. I had rather be a doorkeeper in
the house of my God than to dwell in the
tents of wickedness.
The Bible, Psalm 84:10

God has two thrones: one in the highest
heaven; the other is in the lowliest heart.
Author unknown

Many who do come into the secret place,
and who are God's children, enter it and
leave it just as they entered, without ever
so much as realizing the presence of God.
And there are some believers who, even
when they do obtain a blessing, and get a
little quickening of soul, leave the secret
place without seeking more.
William C. Burns

Hence that dread and amazement with
which, as Scripture uniformly relates, holy
men were struck and overwhelmed when
they beheld the presence of God. When we
see those who previously stood firm and
secure so quaking with terror, that the fear
of death takes hold of them, nay, they are,
in a manner, swallowed up and
annihilated, the inference to be drawn is,
that men are never duly touched and
impressed with a conviction of their
insignificance, until they have contrasted
themselves with the majesty of God.
John Calvin

Be thou a bright flame before me,
Be thou a guiding star above me,
Be thou a smooth path below me,
Be thou a kindly shepherd behind me,
Today – tonight – and for ever.
Columba of Iona

The seed of God is in us. Given an
intelligent and hard-working farmer, it will
thrive and grow up to God, whose seed it is;
and accordingly its fruits will be God-nature.
Pear seeds grow into pear trees, nut into nut

trees, and God seed into God.
Meister Eckhart

What our Lord did was done with this
intent, and this alone, that he might be
with us and we with him.
Meister Eckhart

A man may go into the field and say his
prayer and be aware of God, or he may be
in Church and be aware of God; but if he
is more aware of Him because he is in a
quiet place, that is his own deficiency and
not due to God, who is alike present in all
things and places, and is willing to give
Himself everywhere so far as lies in Him
… He knows God rightly who knows Him
everywhere.
Meister Eckhart

Oh, the fullness, pleasure, sheer excitement
of knowing God on Earth! I care not if I
never raise my voice again for Him, if only
I may love Him, please Him. Maybe in His
mercy He shall give me a host of children
that I may lead them through the vast star
fields to explore His delicacies whose finger
ends set them to burning. But if not, if
only I may see Him, touch His garments,
smile into His eyes – ah then, not stars nor
children shall matter, only Himself.
Jim Elliot

Just as a lamp lights up a dark room, so the
fear of God, when it penetrates the heart of
a man illuminates him, teaching him all
the virtues and commandments of God.
Abba James

I no longer believe that God is up there,
and I do not believe that God is only
within me, and I do not believe that God
is merely out there in history. I think we
are actually in God at all times.
Sister Madonna Kolbenschlag

I consider myself as the most wretched of
men, full of sores and corruption, and who
has committed all sorts of crimes against his
King. Touched with a sensible regret, I
confess to Him all my wickedness, I ask His

forgiveness, I abandon myself in His hands that He may do what He pleases with me. The King, full of mercy and goodness, very far from chastising me, embraces me with love, makes me eat at His table, serves me with His own hands, gives me the key of His treasures; He converses and delights Himself with me incessantly, in a thousand and a thousand ways, and treats me in all respects as His favorite. It is thus I consider myself from time to time in His holy presence.
Brother Lawrence

[Brother Lawrence said] that it was a great delusion to think that the times of prayer ought to differ from other times; that we are as strictly obliged to adhere to God by action in the time of action as by prayer in the season of prayer. That his view of prayer was nothing else but a sense of the Presence of God, his soul being at that time insensible to everything but Divine Love; and that when the appointed times of prayer were past, he found no difference, because he still continued with God, praising and blessing Him with all his might, so that he passed his life in continual Joy; yet hoped that God would give him somewhat to suffer when he should have grown stronger.
Brother Lawrence

I know that for the right practice of the presence of God, the heart must be empty of all other things, because God will possess the heart alone; and as He cannot possess it alone without emptying it of all besides, so neither can He act there, and do in it what He pleases, unless it be left vacant to Him.
Brother Lawrence

I continued some years, applying my mind carefully, and even in the midst of my business, to the presence of God, whom I considered always with me, often in me.
Brother Lawrence

God is always near you and with you; leave Him not alone.
Brother Lawrence

Packed in my skin from head to toe
Is one I know and do not know.
Edwin Muir

One of the most powerful concepts, one which is a sure cure for lack of confidence, is the thought that God is with you and helping you. This is one of the simplest teachings in religion, namely, that Almighty God will be your companion, will stand by you, help you, and see you through. No other idea is so powerful in developing self-confidence as this simple belief when practiced. To practice it simply affirm "God is with me; God is helping me; God is guiding me." Spend several minutes each day visualizing his presence. Then practice believing that affirmation.
Norman Vincent Peale

Salt, when dissolved in water, may disappear, but it does not cease to exist. We can be sure of its presence by tasting the water. Likewise, the indwelling Christ, though unseen, will be made evident to others from the love which he imparts to us.
Sadhu Sundar Singh

[God] is not far away from us. Rather he awaits us every instant in our action, in the work of the moment. There is a sense in which he is at the tip of my pen, my spake, my brush, my needle.
Pierre Teilhard de Chardin

When the Lord so wills, it may happen that the soul will be at prayer, and in possession of all its senses, and that then there will suddenly come to it a suspension in which the Lord communicates most secret things to it, which it seems to see within God Himself. These are not visions of the most sacred Humanity; although I say that the soul "sees" Him, it really sees nothing, for this is not an imaginary, but a notably intellectual vision, in which is revealed to the soul how all things are seen in God, and how within Himself He contains them all.
Teresa of Avila

God walks among the pots and pipkins.
Teresa of Avila

When Jesus is present, all is well, and
nothing seems difficult.
Thomas à Kempis

We should always honor and reverence
Him as if we were always in His bodily
presence.
Thomas à Kempis

When we sing, "Draw me nearer, nearer,
blessed Lord," we are not thinking of the
nearness of place, but of the nearness of
relationship. It is for increasing degrees of
awareness that we pray, for a more perfect
consciousness of the divine Presence. We
need never shout across the spaces to an
absent God. He is nearer than our own
soul, closer than our most secret thoughts.
A. W. Tozer

Best of all is, God is with us.
John Wesley

God's presence, practicing
Christ has been too long locked up in the
mass or in the Book: let him be your
prophet, priest and king. Obey him.
George Fox

In order to form a habit of conversing with
God continually, and referring all we do to
Him, we must at first apply to Him with
some diligence; but after a little care we
should find His love inwardly excite us to
it without any difficulty.
Brother Lawrence

God's presence when there is no other help
Would you like me to tell you what
supported me through all the years of exile
among a people whose language I could
not understand, and whose attitude to me
was always uncertain and often hostile? It
was this, "Lo, I am with you alway, even
unto the end of the world." On these words
I staked everything, and they never failed.
David Livingstone

Abide with me, fast falls the eventide;
The darkness deepens; Lord, with me abide:
When other helpers fail, and comforts flee,
Help of the helpless, oh abide with me.
Henry Francis Lyte

God's promises
See Promises of God

God's providence
It wasn't luck or influence. It was just hard
work – and God's providence.
Kathryn Kuhlman

Man proposes, but God disposes.
Thomas à Kempis

Providence has at all times been my only
dependence, for all other resources seem to
have failed us.
George Washington

God's provision
He maketh me to lie down in green pastures:
he leadeth me beside the still waters.
The Bible, Psalm 23:2 KJV

My cup runneth over.
The Bible, Psalm 23:5 KJV

What a wonderful experience mine has
been during these thirty-nine years! What
inexhaustible supplies have been
vouchsafed to the work in my hands. How
amazing to mere unaided human reason
have been the answers to prayer, even when
faith has almost failed and our timidity has
begotten distrust instead of love and hope!
And God has not failed us once!
Thomas Barnardo

If God sends us on stony paths, He will
provide us with strong shoes.
Alexander Maclaren

God's seeking
Whosoever walks toward God one cubit,
God runs toward him twain.
Author unknown

God often visits us, but most of the time

we are not at home.
Joseph Roux

God's sovereignty
Our God is in heaven; he does whatever pleases him.
The Bible, Psalm 115:3

Either God is totally sovereign, ordaining, ruling, and disposing of all things as he will, or he has no control over anything and faith in him is an utter absurdity.
Author unknown

To say that God is sovereign is to say that His power is superior to every other form or expression of power; it is to say that God is completely free of external influences so that He does what He chooses, as He chooses, when He chooses.
James Bordwine

Absolute sovereignty is what I love to ascribe to God. God's sovereignty has ever appeared to me, a great part of his glory. It has often been my delight to approach God, and adore him as a sovereign God.
Jonathan Edwards

Being born again (regenerated), not of corruptible seed, but of incorruptible seed, by the Word of God, which liveth and abideth forever" (1 Pet. 1:23). The new birth is "by the Word of God." That it is a sovereign act of God, by His Spirit, none can question. But this verse forbids us to separate, as has sometimes been done, new birth from faith in the gospel.
Samuel Ridout

Of all the doctrines of the Bible, none is so offensive to human nature as the doctrine of God's sovereignty
J.C. Ryle

Oh! for a spirit that bows always before the sovereignty of God!
C.H. Spurgeon

Here is divine sovereignty –

"I will be gracious to whom I will be gracious."
C.H. Spurgeon

God's thoughts
I want to know God's thoughts; the rest are details.
Albert Einstein

God's will
The will of God will never take you where the grace of God cannot keep you.
Author unknown

A man's heart is right when he wills what God wills.
Thomas Aquinas

When I vacillated about my decision to serve the Lord my God, it was I who willed, and I who willed not, and nobody else. I was fighting against myself. All you asked was that I cease to want what I willed, and begin to want what you willed.
Augustine of Hippo

Though the sky fall, let Thy will be done.
Thomas Browne

The ground of discrimination that exists among men is the sovereign will of God and that alone; but the ground of damnation to which the reprobate are consigned is sin and sin alone.
John Calvin

In doing [God's] will we find our peace.
Dante

The end of life is not to deny self, nor to be true, nor to keep the Ten Commandments – it is simply to do God's will.
Henry Drummond

Inside the will of God there is no failure. Outside the will of God there is no success.
Benard Edinger

If I want only pure water, what does it matter to me whether it be brought in a vase of gold or of glass? What is it to me whether the will of God be presented to

me in tribulation or consolation, since I desire and seek only the Divine will?
Francis de Sales

The whole science of the saints consists in finding out and following God's will.
Isidore of Seville

You are to think of yourself as only existing in this world to do God's will. To think that you are your own is as absurd as to think you are self-created. It as an obvious first principle that you belong completely to God.
William Law

There are two kinds of people: those who say to God, "Thy will be done," and those to whom God says, "All right, then, have it your way."
C.S. Lewis

Rule. Hold this as a fixed verity, that that is best which God wills.
Joseph Symonds

The center of God's will is our only safety.
Betsie ten Boom

God's word
I simply taught, preached, wrote God's word: otherwise I did nothing.
Martin Luther

God's word in creation
No creature has meaning without the word of God.
God's word is in all creation, visible and invisible.
The word is living, being, spirit, all verdant greening, all creativity.
This word flashes out in every creature.
This is how the spirit is in the flesh – the Word is indivisible from God.
Hildegard of Bingen

God's work
God buries his workmen, but carries on his work.
Proverb quoted by Charles Wesley in one of his letters

God's work in you
"It is God which worketh in you both to will and to do of his good pleasure."
Philippians 2:13 KJV

Have you not found it hard to be good? hard to keep from saying something naughty that you wanted to say? Very hard to keep down the angry feeling, even if you did not say the angry word? Hard to do a right thing, because you did not at all like doing it, and quite impossible to make yourself wish to do it? You asked God to help you to do it, and He did help you; but did you ever think of asking Him to make you like to do it?

Now, this is just what is meant by God's "working in you to will." It means that He can and will undertake the very thing which you can not manage. He can and will "take your will, and work it for you;" making you want to do just what He wants you to do; making you like the very things that He likes, and hate just what He hates. It is always easy to do what we like doing; so, when we have given up our will to Him, and asked Him to work it for us, it makes every thing easy. For then we shall want to "do according to his good pleasure," and we shall be very happy in it; because trying to please Him will not be fighting against our own wills, when God has taken them and is working them for us.

Do you not see what happy days are before you if you will only take God at His word about this? Only try Him, and you will see! Tell Him that you have found you can not manage your will yourself, and that now you will give it up to Him, and trust Him, from now, not only to work in you to do, but to work in you to will also, "according to his good pleasure."
Take my will, and make it Thine;
It shall be no longer mine.
Take my heart, it is Thine own;
It shall be Thy royal throne.
Frances Ridley Havergal

God's wrath
The wrath of God is being revealed from

heaven against all the godlessness and wickedness of men who suppress the truth by their wickedness …
The Bible, Romans 1:18

[God's wrath is] identical with the consuming fire of inexorable divine love in relation to our sins.
D.M. Baillie

God's wrath is God's punishment of sin and evil. It is a mighty declaration that God has done what he has always said he would do, namely, that he would punish sin, and the wages of sin is death.
M. Lloyd-Jones

Love can forbear, and Love can forgive but Love can never be reconciled to an unlovely object. He can never therefore be reconciled to your sin, because sin itself is incapable of being altered; but he may be reconciled to your person, because that may be restored.
Thomas Traherne

Good and evil
Every prudent man tolerates a lesser evil for fear of preventing a greater good.
Thomas Aquinas

Human beings know neither how to rejoice properly nor how to grieve properly, for they do not understand the distance between good and evil.
John of the Cross

The line separating good and evil passes not through states, nor between classes, nor between parties either – but right through every human heart – through all human hearts.
A. Solzhenitsyn

Good deeds
See also: Faith and good deeds
Rich in good works.
The Bible, 1 Timothy 6:18 KJV

And do not forget to do good and to share with others, for with such sacrifices

God is pleased.
The Bible, Hebrews 13:16

Faith without works is not faith at all.
Author unknown

Good works will never produce salvation, but salvation should produce good works.
Author unknown

Measure your day, not by what you harvest, but by what you plant.
Author unknown

People are unreasonable, illogical, and self-centered. Love them anyway.
If you do good, people may accuse you of selfish motives.
Do good anyway.
If you are successful, you may win false friends and true enemies.
Succeed anyway.
The good you do today may be forgotten tomorrow.
Do good anyway.
Honesty and transparency make you vulnerable.
Be honest and transparent anyway.
What you spend years building may be destroyed overnight.
Build anyway.
People who really want help may attack you if you help them.
Help them anyway.
Give the world the best you have and you may get hurt.
Give the world your best anyway.
Author unknown

We are not saved by good works, but for good works.
Author unknown

Good deeds are such things that no man is saved for them, nor without them.
Thomas Adams

We can do noble acts without ruling earth and sea.
Aristotle

We ought to do good to others as simply and as naturally as a horse runs, or a bee makes honey, or a vine bears grapes season after season without thinking of the grapes it has borne.
Marcus Aurelius

Since you cannot do good to all, you are to pay special regard to those who, by the accidents of time, or place, or circumstances, are brought into closer connection with you.
Augustine of Hippo

We do the good deeds, but God works in us the doing of them.
Augustine of Hippo

Every good work in us is performed only by grace.
Augustine of Hippo

Cato said the best way to keep good acts in memory was to refresh them with new.
Francis Bacon

A tree is known by its fruit; a man by his deeds. A good deed is never lost.
St Basil

Every charitable act is a stepping stone towards heaven.
Henry Ward Beecher

Till men have faith in Christ, their best services are but glorious sins.
Thomas Brooks

Though language forms the preacher, 'Tis "good works" make the man.
Eliza Cook

I have gotten more hurt by my *good* works than my bad ones. My bad works always drove me to the Savior for mercy; my good works often kept me from him, and I began to trust in myself.
Ralph Erskine

The more vigor you need, the more

gentleness and kindness you must combine with it. All stiff, harsh goodness is contrary to Jesus.
François Fénelon

Well done is better than well said.
Benjamin Franklin

Blessed is he who does good to others and desires not that others should do him good.
Giles of Assisi

We deny that any works we perform at any stage of our existence add to the merit of Christ or earn for us any merit that contributes in any way to the ground of our justification (Gal. 2:16; Eph. 2:8–9; Titus 3:5).
The gospel of Jesus Christ: An evangelical celebration

To fear God is never to pass over any good thing that ought to be done.
Gregory the Great

I do benefits for all religions – I'd hate to blow the hereafter on a technicality.
Bob Hope

Good actions are the invisible hinges on the doors of heaven.
Victor Hugo

The charity that hastens to proclaim its good deeds, ceases to be charity, and is only pride and ostentation.
William Hutton

He stands erect by bending over the fallen. He rises by lifting others.
Robert Green Ingersoll

God is more pleased by one work, however small, done secretly, without desire that it be known, than a thousand done with the desire that people know of them.
John of the Cross

He who waits to do a great deal of good at once, will never do anything.
Samuel Johnson

No, Sir; to act from pure benevolence is not possible for finite beings. Human benevolence is mingled with vanity, interest, or some other motive.
Samuel Johnson

I read somewhere that this young man, Jesus Christ, went about doing good. But I just go about.
Toyohiko Kagawa

The greatest pleasure I know is to do a good action by stealth, and to have it found out by accident.
Charles Lamb

By the work one knows the workman.
J. de La Fontaine

The merit of persons is to be no rule of our charity; but we are to do acts of kindness to those that least of all deserve it.
William Law

Brother Lawrence said: That we ought not to be weary of doing little things for the love of God, who regards not the greatness of the work, but the love with which it is performed.
Brother Lawrence

Faith never asks whether good works are to be done, but has done them before there is time to ask the question, and it is always doing them.
Martin Luther

A man cannot do good before he is made good.
Martin Luther

To preach faith (It has been said) is to prevent good works; but if a man should possess the strength of all men united, or even of all creatures this sole obligation of living in faith would be a task too great for him ever to accomplish. If I say to a sick man: "Be well, and thou shalt have the use of thy limbs," will anyone say that I forbid him to use his limbs? Must not health precede labor? It is the same when we preach faith: it should go before works, in order that the works themselves should exist.
Martin Luther

It is impossible for a person not to be puffed up by his good works unless he has first been deflated and destroyed by suffering and evil to the point that he knows that he is worthless and that his works are not his but God's.
Martin Luther

He who does something good and expects a reward is serving not God but his own will.
Mark the Ascetic

Each of us was put here to help dilute the misery of the world.
Dr Karl Menninger

One secret act of self-denial, one sacrifice of inclination to duty, is worth all the mere good thoughts, warm feelings, passionate prayers, in which idle people indulge themselves.
John Henry Newman

Q: "What good work is there that I could do?"
A: "Are not all actions equal? Scripture says that Abraham was hospitable and God was with him. David was humble, and God was with him. Elias loved interior peace and God was with him. So, do whatever you see your soul desires according to God and guard your heart."
Abba Nisterus

Do good with what thou hast; or it will do thee no good.
William Penn

We have a call to do good, as often as we have the power and the occasion.
William Penn

When ye are able to do good, defer it not.
Polycarp

How far that little candle throws his beams! So shines a good deed in a weary world.
William Shakespeare, The Merchant of Venice

You will as surely be lost if you trust to your good works, as if you had trusted to your sins.
C.H. Spurgeon

Says one, "Do you find fault with good works?" Not at all. Suppose I see a man building a house, and he were fool enough to lay the foundation with chimney pots. If I should say, "I do not like these chimney pots to be put into the foundation," you would not say I found fault with the chimney pots, but with the man for putting them in the wrong place. So with good works and ceremonies. They will not do for a foundation.
C.H. Spurgeon

Love to Jesus is the basis of all true piety, and the intensity of this love will ever be the measure of our zeal for His glory. Let us love Him with all our hearts, and then diligent labor, and consistent living will be sure to follow.
C.H. Spurgeon

Our best performances are so stained with sin, that it is hard to know whether they are good works or bad works.
C.H. Spurgeon

Whoever loves much, does much.
Thomas à Kempis

When the day of judgment comes, we shall not be asked what we have read, but what we have done.
Thomas à Kempis

Consider your sins with great displeasure and sorrow, and never think yourself to be someone because of your good works.
Thomas à Kempis

You shall in all your works take good heed what you do and say, and you shall set your whole intention to please Me, and you shall desire and seek nothing without Me.
Thomas à Kempis

Let us practice the fine art of making every work a priestly ministration. Let us believe that God is in all our simple deeds and learn to find Him there.
A.W. Tozer

My whole day is a feast of doing good!
Rachel Levin Varnhagen

Every man is guilty of all the good he didn't do.
Voltaire

Works? Works? A man get to heaven by works? I would as soon think of climbing to the moon on a rope of sand!
George Whitefield

Good deeds, Motive of
Good deeds that are done silently and for a good motive, are the dead that live even in the grave; they are flowers that withstand the storm; they are stars that know no setting.
Claudius

Do what good you can, and do it solely for God's glory, as free from it yourself as though you did not exist. Ask nothing whatever in return. Done in this way, your works are spiritual and godly.
Meister Eckhart

A Christian should always remember that the value of his good works is not based on their number and excellence, but on the love of God which prompts him to do these things.
John of the Cross

Our Lord does not care so much for the importance of our works as for the love with which they are done.
Teresa of Avila

The love of God is the principle and end of all our good works.
John Wesley

Goodness
Be not overcome of evil, but overcome evil

with good.
The Bible, Romans 12:21 KJV

Goodness is easier to recognize than to define.
W.H. Auden

Waste no more time arguing what a good man should be. Be one.
Marcus Aurelius

You've got to actively seek good. There's no such thing as a passive journey to heaven.
Halcyon Backhouse

When bad men combine, the good must associate, else they will fall one by one, an unpitied sacrifice in a contemptible struggle.
Edmund Burke

It is hard for the good to suspect evil as it is hard for the bad to suspect good.
Cicero

Did it ever strike you that goodness is not merely a beautiful thing, but by far the most beautiful thing in the whole world? So that nothing is to be compared for value with goodness; that riches, honor, power, pleasure, learning, the whole world and all in it, are not worth having in comparison with being good; and the utterly best thing for a man or woman is to be good, even though they were never rewarded for it.
Charles Kingsley

We need greater virtues to sustain good than evil fortune.
Francis, Duc de La Rochefoucauld

That which is striking and beautiful is not always good; but that which is good is always beautiful.
Ninon de Lenclos

Good, the more
Communicated, more abundant grows.
John Milton

To make the improving of our own

character our central aim is hardly the highest kind of goodness. True goodness forgets itself and goes out to do the right thing for no other reason than that it is right.
Lesslie Newbigin

All that is good, all that is true, all that is beautiful, all that is beneficent, be it great or small, be it perfect or fragmentary, natural as well as supernatural, moral as well as material, comes from God.
John Henry Newman

Conquer a man who never gives by gifts;
Subdue untruthful men by truthfulness;
Vanquish an angry man by gentleness;
And overcome the evil man by goodness.
Indian proverb

Good news
As cold waters to a thirsty soul, so is good news from a far country.
The Bible, Proverbs 25:25 KJV

And even if our gospel is veiled, it is veiled to those who are perishing.
The Bible, 2 Corinthians 4:3

The Christian message is for those who have done their best and failed!
Author unknown

The Gospel is:
G-ood news of
G-od's grace to
G-uilty men.
O-ffered to all and
O-beyed by faith.
S-alvation by a
S-ubstitionary Sacrifice
P-eace and pardon proclaimed through
P-ropitiation
E-ternal life given to
E-veryone that believeth, with
L-ight,
L-iberty and
L-ove.
Author unknown

If you believe what you like in the gospel,

and reject what you don't like, it is not the gospel you believe, but yourself.
Augustine of Hippo

The gospel has lost none of its ancient power. No human device need be tried to prepare the sinner to receive it, for if God has sent it no power can hinder it; and if He has not sent it, no power can make it effectual.
Dr Bullinger

Christ's riches are unsearchable, and this doctrine of the gospel is the field this treasure is hidden in.
Thomas Goodwin

The gospel of Jesus Christ is news, good news: the best and most important news that any human being ever hears.
The gospel of Jesus Christ: an evangelical celebration

The gospel is so simple that small children can understand it, and it is so profound that studies by the wisest theologians will never exhaust its riches.
Charles Hodge

The gospel is open to all; the most respectable sinner has no more claim on it than the worst.
D. Martyn Lloyd-Jones

The core of the gospel in one sentence. ["We are punished justly, for we are getting what our deeds deserve. But this man has done nothing wrong" Luke 24:42.] The essence of eternity through the mouth of a crook:
I am wrong; Jesus is right.
I have failed: Jesus has not.
I deserve to die; Jesus deserves to live.
Max Lucado

The gospel is a doctrine that teaches a far higher matter than the wisdom, righteousness, and religion of the world; it teaches free forgiveness of sins through Christ.
Martin Luther

Evangel is a Greek word, meaning glad tidings, good news, welcome information, a shout, or something that makes us sing, talk or rejoice. When David defeated the giant Goliath, there was a great shout, and an encouraging message was passed round among the Jews to say that their terrible enemy had been killed, and that they were free to enjoy liberty and peace; thereupon, they sang and danced, and made merry. Similarly, God's evangel, the New Testament, is a good piece of news, a war-cry. It was echoed throughout the world by the apostles. They proclaimed a true David, who had done combat with, and gained the victory over, sin, death, and the devil. In so doing, he had taken those who were enchained by sin, threatened by death, and overpowered by the devil; though they had merited no rewards he redeemed them, justified them, gave them life and salvation, and so brought them peace, and led them back to God.
Martin Luther

So tenaciously should we cling to the world revealed by the gospel, that were I to see all the angels of heaven coming down to me to tell me something different, not only would I not be tempted to doubt a single syllable, but I would shut my eyes and stop my ears, for they would not deserve to be either seen or heard.
Martin Luther

The gospel is not speculation but fact. It is truth, because it is the record of a person who is the Truth.
Alexander Maclaren

The gospel of Jesus Christ can make bad men good and good men better, can alter human nature, can change human lives.
David O. McKay

The beginning of the gospel is nothing but the whole Old Testament.
Origen

The gospel is not presented to mankind as an

argument about religious principles. Nor is it offered as a philosophy of life. Christianity is a witness to certain facts – to events that have happened, to hopes that have been fulfilled, to realities that have been experienced, to a Person who has lived and died and been raised from the dead to reign for ever.
Massey H. Shepherd

I do not believe that we can preach the gospel if we do not preach justification by faith, without works. Nor unless we preach the sovereignty of God in the dispensation of grace.
Nor unless we exalt the electing, unchangeable, eternal, immutable, conquering love of Jehovah.
Nor do I think we can preach the gospel, unless we base it upon the peculiar redemption which Christ made for his elect and chosen people. Nor can I comprehend a gospel which lets saints fall away after they are called.
C.H. Spurgeon

The gospel, like its blessed Master, is always crucified between two thieves – legalists of all sorts on the one hand and Antinomians on the other; the former robbing the Savior of the glory of his work for us, and the other robbing him of the glory of his work within us.
James Henley Thornwell

Euagelio (that we call gospel) is a Greek worde, and signyfyth good, mery, glad and joyfull tydings, and maketh a mannes hert glad, and makcth hym synge, daunce and leepe for joye.
William Tyndale

There are two things to do about the gospel – believe it and behave it.
Susanna Wesley

Gospel, Authority of
We deny that the truth or authority of the Gospel rests on the authority of any particular church or human institution.
The gospel of Jesus Christ: An evangelical celebration

Gospel, Luke's
Many have undertaken to draw up an account of the things that have been fulfilled among us, just as they were handed down to us by those who from the first were eyewitnesses and servants of the word. Therefore, since I myself have carefully investigated everything from the beginning, it seemed good also to me to write an orderly account for you, most excellent Theophilus, so that you may know the certainty of the things you have been taught.
The Bible, Luke 1:1-4

Gospel and the law
The law gives menaces. The gospel gives promises.
Thomas Adams

Gospel songs
Blues are the songs of despair, but gospel songs are the songs of hope.
Mahalia Jackson

Gospel versus world
I believe that there are too many accommodating preachers ... Jesus Christ did not say, "Go into the world and tell the world that it is quite right." The gospel is something completely different. In fact, it is directly opposed to the world.
C.S. Lewis

Gospels
The four Gospels all had the same purpose: to point out Christ.
The first three Gospels show his body, so to speak, but John shows his soul.
For this reason I usually say that this Gospel is a key to understanding the rest; for whoever understands the power of Christ strikingly pictured here will then profit by reading what the others tell about the Redeemer who appeared.
John Calvin

They record many incidents that mere inventors would have concealed – the competition of the apostles for high places in the kingdom, their flight after Jesus' arrest, Peter's denial, the failure of

Christ to work miracles in Galilee, the references of some auditors to his possible insanity. No one reading these scenes can doubt the reality of the figure behind them.
Will Durant

I esteem the Gospels to be thoroughly genuine, for there shines forth from them the reflected splendor of a sublimity, proceeding from the person of Jesus Christ, and of as Divine a king as was ever manifested upon earth.
Johann Wolfgang Goethe

If Mark's is the Gospel of Christ the suffering Servant, and Luke's the Gospel of Christ the universal Savior, Matthew's is the Gospel of Christ the ruling King.
John Stott

Almost our only sources of information about the personality of Jesus are derived from the four Gospels, all of which were certainly in existence a few decades after his death. Here is a man. This part of the tale could not have been invented.
H.G. Wells

Gossip

A gossip betrays a confidence, but a trustworthy man keeps a secret.
The Bible, Proverbs 11:13

A perverse man stirs up dissension, and a gossip separates close friends.
The Bible, Proverbs 16:28

The words of a gossip are like choice morsels; they go down to a man's inmost parts.
The Bible, Proverbs 18:8

A gossip betrays a confidence; so avoid a man who talks too much.
The Bible, Proverbs 20:19

Without wood a fire goes out; without gossip a quarrel dies down.
The Bible, Proverbs 26:20

For I am afraid that when I come I may not find you as I want you to be, and you may not find me as you want me to be. I fear that there may be quarreling, jealousy, outbursts of anger, factions, slander, gossip, arrogance and disorder.
The Bible, 2 Corinthians 12:20

Something that goes in one ear, out the other, and over the back fence.
Author unknown

Those who talk about others to us will talk about us to others.
Author unknown

Few Manage to Stem the Gossiping Tongue.
Author unknown

The three essential rules when speaking of others are: Is it true? Is it kind? Is it necessary?
Author unknown

Why do dogs have so many friends? Because they wag their tails and not their tongues!
Author unknown

"Let him who takes pleasure in mauling the lives of the absent know that his own is not such as to fit him to sit at this table."
Augustine had this notice displayed at his dinner table.

Confidant, confidante: One entrusted by A with the secrets of B confided to himself by C.
Ambrose Bierce

There's so much good in the worst of us, and so much bad in the best of us, that it little behoves any of us to talk about the rest of us.
John Brantingham.

Few are they who manage to dam the rush of water. Sill fewer are they who are able to stem the gossiping tongue.
John Climacus

It isn't what they say about you, it's what they whisper.
Errol Flynn

The nice thing about egotists is that they don't talk about other people.
Lucille S. Harper

And there 's a lust in man no charm can tame
Of loudly publishing our neighbor's shame;
On eagles' wings immortal scandals fly,
While virtuous actions are but born and die.
Stephen Harvey

Gossips are like frogs, they drink and talk.
George Herbert

Gossip is mischievous, light and easy to raise, but grievous to bear and hard to get rid of. No gossip ever dies away entirely, if many people voice it: it too is a kind of divinity.
Hesiod

Gossip is vice enjoyed vicariously.
Elbert Hubbard.

Never listen to talk about the weaknesses of others, and if someone complains of another, you can tell him humbly to say nothing of it to you
John of the Cross

If you haven't got anything nice to say about anybody, come sit next to me.
Alice Roosevelt Longworth

Do not listen gleefully to gossip at your neighbor's expense or chatter to anyone who likes finding fault.
Maximus the Confessor

I lay it down as a fact of life that if all men knew what others say of them, there would not be four friends in the world.
Blaise Pascal

At every word a reputation dies.
Alexander Pope

Thou wilt never be spiritually minded and godly unless thou art silent concerning other men's matters and take full heed to thyself.
Thomas à Kempis

Why do we talk and gossip so continually, seeing that we so rarely resume our silence without some hurt done to our conscience?
Thomas à Kempis

Shun the gossip of men as much as possible.
Thomas à Kempis

Government
See also: Politics
Everyone must submit himself to the governing authorities, for there is no authority except that which God has established. The authorities that exist have been established by God.
The Bible, Romans 13:1

Their office [civil government] is not only to have regard unto and watch for the welfare of the civil state, but also that they protect the sacred ministry, and thus may remove and prevent all idolatry and false worship, that the kingdom of anti-Christ may be thus destroyed and the kingdom of Christ promoted.
Belgic Confession

Too bad all the people who know how to run this country are busy running taxicabs or cutting hair.
George Burns

In governing, don't try to control.
Tao Te Ching

The foundations of our society and our government rest so much on the teachings of the Bible that it would be difficult to support them if faith in these teachings would cease to be practically universal in our country.
Calvin Coolidge

I have lived, sir, a long time, and the longer I live, the more convincing proofs I see of this truth – God governs in the affairs of men, and if a sparrow cannot fall to the ground without His notice, is it possible that an empire can rise without His aid?
Benjamin Franklin

He who shall introduce into public affairs the principles of a primitive Christianity, will change the face of the world.
Benjamin Franklin

Can the liberties of a nation be thought secure when we have removed their only firm basis, a conviction in the minds of the people that these liberties are the gift of God? That they are not to be violated but with His wrath? Indeed, I tremble for my country when I reflect that God is just; that His justice cannot sleep forever.
Thomas Jefferson

The reason that Christianity is the best friend of government is because Christianity is the only religion that changes the heart.
Thomas Jefferson

That government is best which governs the least, because its people discipline themselves.
Thomas Jefferson

Equal and exact justice to all men, of whatever state or persuasion, religious or political; peace, commerce, and honest friendship with all nations – entangling alliances with none; the support of the state governments in all their rights, as the most competent administrations for our domestic concerns, and the surest bulwarks against anti-republican tendencies; the preservation of the general government in its whole constitutional vigor, as the sheet anchor of our peace at home and safety abroad … freedom of religion; freedom of the press; freedom of person under the protection of the habeas corpus; and trial by juries impartially selected – these principles form the bright constellation which has gone before us, and guided our steps through an age of revolution and reformation.
Thomas Jefferson

Now the trumpet summons us again – not as a call to bear arms, though arms we need – not as a call to battle, though embattled we are – but a call to bear the burden of a long twilight struggle year in and year out, "rejoicing in hope, patient in tribulation" – a struggle against the common enemies of man: tyranny, poverty and war itself.
John Fitzgerald Kennedy

You can fool some of the people all the time and all of the people some of the time; but you can't fool all of the people all of the time.
Abraham Lincoln

I believe this government cannot endure permanently half slave and half free.
Abraham Lincoln

With malice towards none, with charity for all, with firmness in the right, as God gives us to see the right.
Abraham Lincoln

We here resolve that the dead shall not have died in vain, that this nation, under God, shall have a new birth of freedom; and that government of the people, by the people, and for the people, shall not perish from the earth.
Abraham Lincoln

Man's capacity for justice makes democracy possible, but man's inclination to injustice makes democracy necessary.
Reinhold Niebuhr

Government, even in its best state, is but a necessary evil; in its worst state, an intolerable one.
Thomas Paine

Those who will not be governed by God, will be ruled by tyrants.
William Penn

The government can not create a rugged individual. God alone can do that. The government can only destroy one.
Drake Raft

The United States was founded upon a Christian consensus. We today should

bring Judeo-Christian principles into play in regard to government.
Francis A. Schaeffer

There are no internal affairs left on this globe of ours. Mankind can be saved only if everybody takes an interest in everybody else's affairs.
A. Solzhenitsyn.

Despotism may govern without faith, but liberty cannot. How is it possible that society should escape destruction if the moral tie is not strengthened in proportion as the political tie is relaxed? And what can be done with a people who are their own masters if they are not submissive to the Deity?
Alexis De Tocqueville

Of all the dispositions and habits which lead to political prosperity, religion and morality are indispensable supports. It is impossible to rightly govern the world without God and the Bible.
George Washingtion

The moral principles and precepts contained in the Scriptures ought to form the basis of all our civil constitutions and laws.
Noah Webster

The religion which has introduced civil liberty is the religion of Christ and His Apostles … This is genuine Christianity and to this we owe our free constitutions of government.
Noah Webster

You can build a throne with bayonets, but you can't sit on it for long.
Boris Yeltsin

Governments

No one need think that the world can be ruled without blood. The civil sword shall and must be red and bloody.
Martin Luther

Grace

See also: Calvinism; Paul
But to each one of us grace has been given

as Christ apportioned it.
The Bible, Ephesians 4:7

Let your conversation be always full of grace, seasoned with salt, so that you may know how to answer everyone.
The Bible, Colossians 4:6

Grace be with you.
The Bible, 2 Timothy 4:22

Where the will of God leads you, the grace of God will keep you.
Author unknown

Grace is what God gives us when we don't deserve and mercy is when God doesn't give us what we do deserve.
Author unknown

Amid the darkness of sin, the light of God's grace shines in.
Author unknown

G-od's
R-iches
A-t
C-hrist's
E-xpense
Author unknown

I deserve to be damned, I deserve to be in hell; but God interfered!
Dying remark of John Allen of the Salvation Army

If you are to receive your due, you must be punished. What then is done? God has not rendered you due punishment, but bestows upon you unmerited grace. If you wish to be an alien from grace, boast your merits
Augustine of Hippo

What God promises, we ourselves do not through choice or nature, but he himself does by grace.
Augustine of Hippo

Nothing whatever pertaining to godliness and real holiness can be accomplished

without grace.
Augustine of Hippo

Let us hear what the Bible says and what we as Christians are called to hear together: By grace you have been saved!
Karl Barth

Grace is the gift of Christ, who exposes the gulf which separates God and man, and, by exposing it, bridges it.
Karl Barth

I take the love of God and self-denial to be the sum of all saving grace and religion.
Richard Baxter

The sinner, apart from grace, is unable to be willing and unwilling to be able.
W.E. Best

Cheap grace is grace without discipleship, grace without the cross, grace without Jesus Christ, living and incarnate. Costly grace is the treasure hidden in the field; for the sake of it a man will gladly go and sell all that he has.
Dietrich Bonhoeffer

For Paul teaches and proves, that our election to eternal glory must be either entirely of grace, or entirely of works; grace and works being directly opposite. They cannot, therefore, unite in producing the same effect, or in promoting the same end.
Abraham Booth

There, but for the grace of God, goes John Bradford.
John Bradford, as he saw criminals being taken off to be executed.

Your worst days are never so bad that you are beyond the reach of God's grace. And your best days are never so good that you are beyond the need of God's grace.
Jerry Bridges

Man's like a candle in a candlestick, Made up of tallow and a little wick; And as the candle is before 'tis lighted,

Just such be they who are in sin benighted. Nor can a man his soul with grace inspire, More than can candles set themselves on fire. Candles receive their light from what they are not; Men, grace from Him, for whom at first they care not.
John Bunyan

Thou Son of the Blessed, what grace was manifest in thy condescension! Grace brought thee down from heaven; Grace stripped thee of thy glory; Grace made thee poor and despicable; Grace made thee bear such burdens of sin, such burdens of sorrow, such burdens of God's curse as are unspeakable.
John Bunyan

I clearly recognize that all good is in God alone, and that in me, without Divine Grace, there is nothing but deficiency … The one sole thing in myself in which I glory, is that I see in myself nothing in which I can glory.
Catherine of Genoa

No one is safe by his own strength, but he is safe by the grace and mercy of God.
Cyprian

Don't be troubled when you meditate on the greatness of your former sins, but rather know that God's grace is so much greater in magnitude that it justifies the sinner and absolves the wicked.
Cyril of Alexandria

Thus all below is strength, and all above is grace.
John Dryden

God doesn't just give us grace, He gives us Jesus, the Lord of grace.
Joni Eareckson Tada

A state of mind that sees God in everything is evidence of growth in grace and a thankful heart.
Charles Finney

God does not basically give grace because

there is a need, but God gives grace because He is a gracious God.
Johnny Foglander

We have not received the Spirit of God because we believe, but that we may believe.
Fulgentius

Not only does understanding the gospel of the grace of God provide a proper motive for us to share our faith, it also gives us the proper motive and means to live the Christian life effectively.
David Havard

Grace is the free, undeserved goodness and favor of God to mankind.
Matthew Henry

If I am not [in a state of grace], God bring me there; if I am, God keep me there!
Joan of Arc

The greater perfection a soul aspires after, the more dependent it is upon divine grace.
Brother Lawrence

Blind as we are, we hinder God and stop the current of His graces. But when He finds a soul penetrated with a lively faith, He pours into it His graces and favors plentifully; there they flow like a torrent which, after being forcibly stopped against its ordinary course, when it has found a passage, spreads itself with impetuosity and abundance.
Brother Lawrence

We have forgotten the gracious hand which has preserved us in peace and multiplied and enriched and strengthened us, and have vainly imagined in the deceitfulness of our hearts that all these blessings were produced by some superior wisdom and virtue of our own. Intoxicated with unbroken success, we have become too self sufficient to feel the necessity of redeeming and preserving grace, too proud to pray to the God that made us.
Abraham Lincoln

It is grace at the beginning, and grace at the end. So that when you and I come to lie upon our death beds, the one thing that should comfort and help and strengthen us there is the thing that helped us in the beginning. Not what we have been, not what we have done, but the grace of God in Jesus Christ our Lord. The Christian life starts with grace, it must continue with grace, it ends with grace. Grace wondrous grace. By the grace of God I am what I am. Yet not I, but the grace of God which was with me.
D. Martyn Lloyd-Jones

Grace not to be abused

God forgives sins merely out of grace for Christ's sake; but we must not abuse the grace of God. God has given signs and tokens enough, that our sins shall be forgiven; namely, the preaching of the gospel, baptism, the Lord's Supper, and the Holy Ghost in our hearts.
Martin Luther

If any man ascribes anything of salvation, even the very least thing, to the free will of man, he knows nothing of grace, and he has not learned Jesus Christ rightly.
Martin Luther

Grace is given to heal the spiritually sick, not to decorate spiritual heroes.
Martin Luther

The law works fear and wrath; grace works hope and mercy.
Martin Luther

Grace keeps us from worrying because worry deals with the past, while grace deals with the present and future.
Joyce Meyer

Grace was in all her steps, heaven in her eye, In every gesture dignity and love.
John Milton

I am not what I ought to be; I am not what I wish to be; I am not what I hope to be; but by the grace of God I am what

I am.
John Newton

"Where is boasting then? It is excluded."
As the Apostle speaks in another place,
"If Abraham was justified by works, he
hath whereof to glory:" so if men were
saved either in whole or in part, by their
own wisdom and prudence, they might,
in the same degree, ascribe the glory and
praise to themselves. They might say, My
own power and wisdom gave me this;
and thus God would be robbed of the
honor due to his name. But now this is
prevented.
John Newton

If grace doth not change human nature, I
do not know what grace doth.
John Owen

Grace is young glory.
Alexander Peden

None but the Lord himself can afford us
any help from the awful workings of
unbelief, doubtings, carnal fears,
murmurings. Thank God one day we will
be done forever with unbelief.
Arthur W. Pink

Grace is not simply leniency when we
have sinned. Grace is the enabling gift of
God not to sin. Grace is power, not just
pardon. Therefore the effort we make to
obey God is not an effort done in our
own strength, but in the strength which
God supplies.
John Piper

Grace tried is better than grace, and more
than grace; it is glory in its infancy.
S. Rutherford

Well can I remember the manner in which
I learned the doctrines of grace in a single
instant.
Born, as all of us are by nature, an
Arminian, I still believed the old things I
had heard continually from the pulpit, and
did not see the grace of God.

I remember sitting one day in the house
of God and hearing a sermon as dry as
possible, and as worthless as all such
sermons are, when a thought struck my
mind – how did I come to be converted? I
prayed, thought I. Then I thought how did
I come to pray? I was induced to pray by
reading the Scriptures. How did I come to
read the Scriptures? Why, I did read them,
and what led me to that?
And then, in a moment, I saw that God
was at the bottom of all, and that he was
the author of faith; and then the whole
doctrine opened up to me, from which I
have not departed.
C.H. Spurgeon

Grace sends all its roots upwards, none
downwards; it draws no support from
poverty, and none from riches.
C.H. Spurgeon

If grace does not make us differ from other
men, it is not the grace which God gives
his elect.
C.H. Spurgeon

If the people do not like the doctrine of
grace, give them all the more of it.
C.H. Spurgeon

Should any here, supposing themselves to
be the children of God, imagine that there
is some reason in them why they should
have been chosen, let them know that as
yet they are in the dark concerning the
first principles of grace, and have not yet
learned the gospel.
C.H. Spurgeon

Ah! the bridge of grace will bear your
weight, brother. Thousands of big sinners
have gone across that bridge, yea, tens of
thousands have gone over it. I can hear
their trampings now as they traverse the
great arches of the bridge of salvation.
They come by their thousands, by their
myriads; e'er since the day when Christ
first entered into His glory, they come,
and yet never a stone has sprung in that
mighty bridge. Some have been the chief

of sinners, and some have come at the very last of their days, but the arch has never yielded beneath their weight. I will go with them trusting to the same support; it will bear me over as it has borne them.
C.H. Spurgeon

Free grace can go into the gutter, and bring up a jewel!
C.H. Spurgeon

It is not true gold if it will not stand the fire, and it is not true grace if it will not bear affliction.
C.H. Spurgeon

Between here and heaven, every minute that the Christian lives will be a minute of grace.
C.H. Spurgeon

There is nothing but God's grace. We walk upon it; we breathe it; we live and die by it; it makes the nails and axles of the universe.
Robert Louis Stevenson

Grace is love that cares and stoops and rescues.
John Stott

Grace will teach a Christian contentedly to take those potions that are wholesome, though they are not toothsome.
George Swinnock

The way that a man shall walk in this world is found not in himself, but in the grace of God.
Thomas à Kempis

Grace is always given to those ready to give thanks for it, and therefore it is wont to be given to the humble man, and to be taken from the proud man.
Thomas à Kempis

He rides pleasantly enough whom the grace of God carries.
Thomas à Kempis

Heaven goes by favor. If it went by merit, you would stay out and your dog would go in.
Mark Twain

None so empty of grace as he that thinks he is full.
Thomas Watson

I take it for granted you believe religion to be an inward thing; you believe it to be a work in the heart, a work wrought in the soul by the power of the Spirit of God. If you do not believe this, you do not believe your Bibles. If you do not believe this, though you have got your Bibles in your hand, you hate the Lord Jesus Christ in your heart; for religion is everywhere represented in Scripture as the work of God in the heart ... If any of you place religion in outward things, I shall not perhaps please you this morning; you will understand me no more when I speak of the work of God upon a poor sinner's heart, than if I were talking in an unknown tongue.
George Whitefield

Grace, Common

Every man is someone because he is a child of god.
Martin Luther King, Jr

If we discard common grace, we are driven inevitably to one of two conclusions; either man is not totally depraved. He can do good of himself; or the good which he does is not really good at all. His virtues, his patriotism, marital fidelity, filial piety, love of his children, common honesty are all of them glittering sins. In the doctrine of man the denial of common grace leads to rankest Modernism or darkest misanthropy.
R.B. Kuiper

Grace, Irresistible

We believe, that the work of regeneration, conversion, sanctification and faith, is not an act of man's free will and power, but of the mighty, efficacious and irresistible grace of God.
C.H. Spurgeon

Grace and good deeds

And God is able to make all grace abound to you, so that in all things at all times, having all that you need, you will abound in every good work.
The Bible, 2 Corinthians 9:8

Grace and human will
See also: Freewill

It is certain that we will when we will, but he causes us to will who works in us to will.
Augustine of Hippo

I reject and condemn as erroneous every doctrine which extols our free will, and fights against the assistance of our Savior Jesus Christ; because without Christ death and sin rule over us, and the devil is the god and prince of the unconverted world.
Martin Luther

Grace and nature

Grace does not abolish nature but perfects it.
Thomas Aquinas

Simply to will comes from man's nature; to will wickedly comes from corrupt nature; to will well, from supernatural grace.
Bernard of Clairvaux

Grace is sometimes so weak and feeble that it looks like nature. Nature is sometimes so plausible and well-dressed, that it looks like grace.
J.C. Ryle

Grace and salvation

For the grace of God that brings salvation has appeared to all men.
The Bible, Titus 2:11

Graces

Praise God from whom all blessings flow,
Praise him, all creatures here below,
Praise him above, angelic host,
Praise Father, Son and Holy Ghost.
Thomas Ke

Come Lord Jesus, be our guest,
And may our meal by you be blessed.
Martin Luther

Grandmothers

The two options taken by that old woman have marked my whole life. My grandmother took risks for those who were being badly treated at that time. And ... within herself she reconciled the current of faith of her Protestant background with the faith of the Catholic Church.
Brother Roger

The founder of the Taizé community, recalling how he was greatly influenced by his grandmother who, as a widow in France during the First World War, courageously welcomed refugees into her home. At the end of the war she was determined to do all she could to stop such horror re-occurring. Believing that reconciliation between Christians would help to create peace, she began by creating reconciliation within herself, and, though she came from old Protestant stock, she started going to the Catholic church.

Gratitude

A joyful and pleasant thing it is to be thankful.
The Bible, Psalm 147:16 (Coverdale)

Our favorite attitude should be gratitude.
Author unknown

The art of thanksgiving is thanksliving.
Author unknown

One act of thanksgiving made when things go wrong is worth a thousand when things go well.
Author unknown

Be on the lookout for mercies. The more we look for them, the more of them we will see ... Better to lose count while naming your blessings than to lose your blessings to counting your troubles.
Author unknown

He who can give thanks for little will always find he has enough.
Author unknown

Two of the most important phrases in the world are, "Thank you," and "Forgive me." Say the second often in your lifetime

and you will only need the first on your deathbed.
Author unknown

Gratitude is the praise we offer God: for teachers kind, benefactors never to be forgotten, for all who have advantaged me, by writings, sermons, converse, prayers, examples, for all these and all others which I know, which I know not, open, hidden, remembered, and forgotten.
Lancelot Andrewes

This day and your life are God's gift to you: so give thanks and be joyful always!
Jim Beggs

Gratitude is heaven itself.
William Blake

In ordinary life we hardly realize that we receive a great deal more than we give, and that it is only with gratitude that life becomes rich. It is very easy to overestimate the importance of our own achievements in comparison with what we owe others.
Dietrich Bonhoeffer

Gratitude changes the pangs of memory into a tranquil joy.
Dietrich Bonhoeffer

Some people always sigh in thanking God.
Elizabeth Barrett Browning

It is the highest and holiest of the paradoxes that the man who really knows he cannot pay his debt will be forever paying it.
G.K. Chesterton

A thankful heart is not only the greatest virtue, but the parent of all other virtues.
Cicero

Reflect upon your present blessings – of which every man has many – not on your past misfortunes, of which all men have some.
Charles Dickens

There is always one thing to be grateful for –

that one is one's self and not somebody else.
Emily Dickinson

I feel a very unusual sensation – if it is not indigestion, I think it must be gratitude.
Benjamin Disraeli

A hundred times every day I remind myself that my inner and outer life depend on the labors of other men, living and dead, and that I must exert myself in order to give in the same measure as I have received and am still receiving.
Albert Einstein

As to the kindness you mention, I wish I could have been of more service to you than I have been, but if I had, the only thanks that I should desire are that you would always be ready to serve any other person that may need your assistance, and so let good offices go around, for mankind are all of a family. As for my own part, when I am employed in serving others I do not look upon myself as conferring favors but paying debts.
Benjamin Franklin

Let me be thankful, first, because he never robbed me before; second, because although he took my purse, he did not take my life; third, because although he took all I possessed, it was not much; and fourth, because it was I who was robbed, not I who robbed.
Matthew Henry, meditating on the theft of his wallet.

Thou that has given so much to me,
Give one thing more – a grateful heart;
Not thankful when it pleaseth me,
As if thy blessings had spare days;
But such a heart, whose pulse may be
Thy praise.
George Herbert

The hardest arithmetic to master is that which enables us to count our blessings.
Eric Hoffer

The children of Israel did not find in the manna all the sweetness and strength they

might have found in it – not because the
manna did not contain them, but because
they longed for other food.
John of the Cross

Gratitude is from the same root word as
grace – the boundless mercy of God.
Thanksgiving is from the same root word
as think, so to think is to thank.
Willis P. King

Would you know who is the greatest saint
in the world? It is not he who prays most
or fasts most, it is not he who lives most,
but it is he who is always thankful to God,
who receives everything as an instance of
God's goodness and has a heart always
ready to praise God for it.
William Law

A single grateful thought raised to heaven
is the most perfect prayer.
Gotthold Ephraim Lessing

We ought to give thanks for all fortune: if
it is good, because it is good, if bad,
because it works in us patience, humility
and the contempt of this world and the
hope of our eternal country.
C.S. Lewis

Men are slower to recognize blessings than
evils.
Livy

See that you do not forget what you
were before, lest you take for granted
the grace and mercy you received from
God and forget to express your gratitude
each day.
Martin Luther

One of life's gifts is that each of us, no
matter how tired and downtrodden, finds
reasons for thankfulness.
J. Robert Maskin

Gratitude is the heart's memory.
Massieu

Both gratitude for God's past and current

mercies, as well as hope-filled expectation
of His future mercy are the strongest
motives to live for His glory.
Scott Meadows

When thou has truly thanked the Lord for
   every blessing sent,
But little time will then remain for
   murmur or lament.
Hannah More

When everything we receive from him is
received and prized as fruit and pledge of
his covenant love, then his bounties,
instead of being set up as rivals and idols to
draw our heart from him, awaken us to
fresh exercises of gratitude and furnish us
with fresh motives of cheerful obedience
every hour.
John Newton

Letter to church member
October 10, 1777
I am just come from seeing A–N–. The
people told me she is much better than
she was, but she is far from being well. She
was brought to me into a parlor, which
saved me the painful task of going to
inquire and seek for her among the
patients. My spirits always sink when I am
within these mournful walls, and I think
no money could prevail on me to spend
an hour there every day. Yet surely no
sight upon earth is more suited to teach
one thankfulness and resignation. Surely I
have reason, in my worst times, to be
thankful that I am out of hell, out of
Bedlam, out of Newgate. If my eyes were
as bad as yours, and my back worse, still I
hope I should set a great value upon this
mercy, that my senses are preserved. I
hope you will think so too. The Lord
afflicts us at times; but it is always a
thousand times less than we deserve, and
much less than many of our
fellow-creatures are suffering around us.
Let us therefore pray for grace to be
humble, thankful, and patient.
This day twelvemonth I was under Mr W.'s
knife; there is another cause for
thankfulness, that the Lord inclined me to

submit to the operation, and brought me happily through it. In short, I have so many reasons for thankfulness, that I cannot count them. I may truly say, they are more in number than the hairs of my head. And, yet, alas! how cold, insensible, and ungrateful! I could make as many complaints as you; but I find no good by complaining, except to Him who is able to help me. It is better for you and me to be admiring the compassion and fulness of grace that is in our Savior, than to dwell and pore too much upon our own poverty and vileness. He is able to help and save to the uttermost; there I desire to cast anchor, and wish you to do so likewise. Hope in God, for you shall yet praise Him.
I am, &c.
John Newton

Gratitude is the most fruitful way of deepening your consciousness that you are not an "accident," but a divine choice.
Henri J. Nouwen

A man receiving charity always hates his benefactor – it is a fixed characteristic of human nature.
George Orwell

Have you ever stopped to be thankful just for yourself?
Bill Pearce

Let us be grateful to people who make us happy – they are the charming gardeners who make our souls blossom.
Marcel Proust

We never know the worth of water till the well is dry.
French proverb

In gratitude for your own good fortune you must render in return some sacrifice of your life for other life.
Albert Schweitzer

The person who has stopped being thankful has fallen asleep in life.
Robert Louis Stevenson

A life in thankfulness releases the glory of God.
Bengt Sundberg

I realized I had never really thanked God for all the work he had done in my creation. I was overcome as I thought of how God had made plans for my life long before I was born.
Ingrid Trobisch

Gratitude and friendship
Gratitude preserves old friendship, and procures new.
Thomas Fuller

Gratitude and ingratitude
I believe the best definition of man is the ungrateful biped.
Fyodor Dostoevsky

Gratitude is the least of the virtues, but ingratitude is the worst of vices.
Thomas Fuller

The earth produces nothing viler than an ungrateful man.
Horace

Ingratitude is the sepulcher of love.
Portuguese proverb

Blow, blow, thou winter wind,
Thou art not so unkind
As man's ingratitude.
William Shakespeare, As You Like It

Ingratitude sickens the heart, chills and thickens goodwill's lifeblood.
William Wilberforce

Gratitude and trust
Let gratitude for the past inspire us with trust for the future.
François Fénelon

Greatness
When God measures the greatness of an individual, He puts the tape measure around the heart not the head.
Author unknown

Greatness lies not in being strong but in the right use of strength.
Henry Ward Beecher

The greatness of a man's power is the measure of his surrender.
William Booth

They're only great who are truly good.
George Chapman

There is a great man who makes every man feel small. But the real great man is the man who makes every man feel great.
G.K. Chesterton

The price of greatness is responsibility.
Winston Churchill

To be great is to be misunderstood.
Ralph Waldo Emerson

The most radical social teaching of Jesus was his total reversal of the contemporary notion of greatness.
Richard Foster

There would be no great men if there were no little ones.
George Herbert

It is true greatness to have in one the frailty of a man and the security of a god.
Seneca

Be not afraid of greatness: some are born great, some achieve greatness, and some have greatness thrust upon them.
William Shakespeare, Twelfth Night

He is truly great who is little in his own eyes and makes nothing of the highest honor.
Thomas à Kempis

There is not greatness where there is not simplicity, goodness and truth.
Leo Tolstoy

Greatest, in God's kingdom
"I tell you the truth: Among those born of women there has not risen anyone greater than John the Baptist; yet he who is least in the kingdom of heaven is greater than he."
The Bible, Matthew 11:11

Greed
See also: Contentment; Covetousness
A greedy man brings trouble to his family.
The Bible, Proverbs 15:27

Not greedy of filthy lucre.
The Bible, 1 Timothy 3:3 KJV

Greed, wealth, fame, and sex.
Leonard Capsman
The writer and producer of Dallas, the world's most popular TV soap, said that these were the four ingredients that went into making Dallas which accounted for its great success. Capsman said he deliberately placed greed at the top of his list.

He is not poor that hath not much, but he that craves much.
Thomas Fuller

The covetous man is ever in want.
Horace

Avarice is generally the last passion of those lives of which the first part has been squandered in pleasure, and the second devoted to ambition.
Samuel Johnson

The most grievous kind of destitution is to want [need] money in the midst of wealth.
Seneca

The god of greed is a cheat. His delights have the power to dazzle and excite but they can satisfy nobody.
John White

Grief
See also: Bereavement; Death; Sorrow; Tears
Nothing can make up for the absence of someone whom we love, and it would be wrong to try to find a substitute. It is nonsense to say that God fills the gap; he

does not fill it, but on the contrary, he keeps it empty and so helps us to keep alive our former communion with each other, even at the cost of pain.
Dietrich Bonhoeffer

Yes, thou art gone! and never more
Thy sunny smile shall gladden me;
But I may pass the old church door,
And pace the floor that covers thee.
May stand upon the cold, damp stone,
And think that, frozen, lies below
The lightest heart that I have known,
The kindest I shall ever know.
Yet, though I cannot see thee more,
'Tis still a comfort to have seen;
And though thy transient life is o'er,
'Tis sweet to think that thou hast been;
O think a soul so near divine,
Within a form so angel fair,
United to a heart like thine,
Has gladdened once our humble sphere.
Anne Brontë

There's little joy in life for me,
And little terror in the grave;
I've lived the parting hour to see
Of one I would have died to save.
Calmly to watch the failing breath,
Wishing each sigh might be the last;
Longing to see the shade of death
O'er those beloved features cast.
The cloud, the stillness that must part
The darling of my life from me;
And then to thank God from my heart,
To thank Him well and fervently;
Although I knew that we had lost
The hope and glory of our life;
And now, benighted, tempest-tossed,
Must bear alone the weary strife.
Charlotte Brontë, on the death of Anne Brontë

I tell you, hopeless grief is passionless.
Elizabeth Barrett Browning

Just as a bundle of green logs suffocates and puts out a bonfire causing clouds of smoke, so excessive grief often surrounds the soul with thick clouds and dries up the fount of tears.
John Climacus

Grief is itself a medicine
William Cowper

Grief is the agony of an instant; the indulgence in grief, the blunder of a life.
Benjamin Disraeli

Truly, it is in darkness that one finds the light, so when we are in sorrow, then this light is nearest of all to us.
Meister Eckhart

A man who craves esteem cannot be rid of the causes of grief.
Isaac from Syria

And no one ever told me about the laziness of grief. Not only writing but even reading a letter is too much. Even shaving. What does it matter now whether my cheek is rough or smooth?
C.S. Lewis

Give sorrow words: the grief that does not speak
Whispers the o'er-fraught heart, and bids it break.
William Shakespeare, Macbeth

Griefs exalt us, and troubles lift us.
C.H. Spurgeon

Outside the Psalms and the Book of Job, there is not a book quite like *A Grief Observed*, a book by a man who still believes in God but cannot find evidence for His goodness.
A.N. Wilson

Groups
It's hard to work in groups when you're omnipotent.
Q, Star Trek, the Next Generation

Growing old
Grow old along with me!
The best is yet to be,
The last of life, for which the first was made:
Our times are in his hand
Who said, "A whole I planned,

Youth shows but half; trust God: see all,
  nor be afraid!"
Robert Browning

At fifty, everyone has the face he deserves.
George Orwell

Growing up
When I was a boy of 14, my father was
so ignorant I could hardly stand to have
the old man around. But when I got to
be 21, I was astonished at how much the
old man had learned in seven years.
Mark Twain

Growth
See also: Progress

Growth, spiritual
Such as have need of milk, and not of
strong meat.
The Bible, Hebrews 5:12 KJV

Like newborn babies, crave pure spiritual
milk, so that by it you may grow up in
your salvation …
The Bible, 1 Peter 2:2

But grow in the grace and knowledge of
our Lord and Savior Jesus Christ.
The Bible, 2 Peter 3:18

The head grows by taking in but the heart
grows by giving out.
Author unknown

Sometimes we must be hurt in order to grow,
We must fail in order to know,
We must lose in order to gain,
Some lessons are learned best only through
  pain.
Sometimes our vision clears,
Only after our eyes are washed with tears.
Sometimes we have to be broken,
So we can be tender;
Sick, so we can rest and think better
On things more important than work or fun;
Trip near death, so we can assess how we've
  ran.
Sometimes we have to suffer lack,
So we can know God's provisions.

Feel another's pain,
So we can have a sense of mission.
So take heart, my friend,
If you don't understand today,
Instead of grumbling, ask God what he
  means to say.
In order to learn, you must endure
And learn to see the bigger picture.
In order to grow, you must stand
Look beyond the hurt, to God's loving
  hand
That takes what is good
And gives what is best
And on this blessed thought : *rest*.
As your anxious heart, with questions : *wait*.
God's hand only gives, what his loving
  heart dictates.
Author unknown

You cannot propel yourself forward by
patting yourself on the back.
Author unknown

Growth merely for the sake of growth is
the ideology of the cancer cell.
Edward Abbey

What you are must always displease you,
if you would attain that which you are
not.
Augustine of Hippo

If you are pleased with what you are, you
have stopped already. If you say, "It is
enough," you are lost. Keep on walking,
moving forward, trying for the goal. Don't
try to stop on the way, or to go back, or to
deviate from it.
Augustine of Hippo

Some tension is necessary for the soul to
grow, and we can put that tension to good
use. We can look for every opportunity to
give and receive love, to appreciate nature,
to heal our wounds and the wounds of
others, to forgive, and to serve.
Joan Borysenko

I say that man was meant to grow, not stop.
Robert Browning

If in the last few years you haven't discarded a major opinion or acquired a new one, check your pulse. You may be dead.
Gelet Burgess

If we're not growing, we must feel guilty, because we are not fulfilling Christ's command.
Evan Burrows, referring to the Salvation Army

Don't go through life, grow through life.
Eric Butterworth

Love not what you are, but what you may become.
Miguel de Cervantes

He who stops being better stops being good.
Oliver Cromwell

Develop a passion for learning. If you do, you will never cease to grow.
Anthony J. D'Angelo

The strongest principle of growth lies in the human choice.
George Eliot

There is nothing that is more dangerous to your own salvation, more unworthy of God and more harmful to your own happiness than that you should be content to remain as you are.
F. Fénelon

Nothing marks so much the solid advancement of a soul, as the view of one's wretchedness without anxiety and without discouragement.
F. Fénelon

We must always change, renew, rejuvenate ourselves; otherwise we harden.
Johann Wolfgang von Goethe

Everybody wants to be somebody: nobody wants to grow.
Johann Wolfgang von Goethe

Spiritual growth consists most in the

growth of the root, which is out of sight.
Matthew Henry

Some people's religion reminds me of a rocking horse, which has motion with no progress.
Rowland Hill

If you are looking for painless ways to grow toward each other and toward maturity, call off the search.
J. Grant Howard

As the sculptor devotes himself to wood and stone, I would devote myself to my soul.
Toyohiko Kagawa

It is as reasonable to suppose it the desire of all Christians to arrive at Christian perfection as to suppose that all sick men desire to be restored to perfect health; yet experience shows us, that nothing wants more to be pressed, repeated, and forced upon our minds, than the plainest rules of Christianity.
William Law

Many do not advance in Christian progress because they stick in penances and particular exercises, while they neglect the love of God, which is the end.
Brother Lawrence

Mere change is not growth. Growth is the synthesis of change and continuity, and where there is no continuity there is no growth.
C.S. Lewis

All growth that is not towards God is growing to decay.
George Macdonald

Growth is the only evidence of life.
J.H. Newman

I asked the Lord that I might grow,
In faith and love and every grace,
Might more of His salvation know,
And seek more earnestly His face.
It was He who taught me thus to pray,

And He I trust has answered prayer.
But it has been in such a way,
As almost drove me to despair.
I hoped that in some favored hour,
At once He'd answer my request.
And by his love's constraining power,
Subdue my sins and give me rest.
Instead of this, He made me feel,
The hidden evils of my heart.
And let the angry powers of hell,
Assault my soul in every part.
Yes, more with His own hand, he seemed,
Intent to aggravate my woe.
Crossed all the fair designs I schemed,
Blasted my gourds, and laid me low.
"Lord, why is this?" I trembling cried.
"Will You pursue this worm to death?"
"This is the way," the Lord replied,
"I answer prayer for grace and strength."
John Newton

Be not afraid of growing slowly, be afraid
only of standing still.
Chinese proverb

The quickest way to become an old dog is
to stop learning new tricks.
John Rooney

Our knowledge of God must lead to a
more intimate relationship with Him or
we run the risk of becoming Pharisees.
Douglas Rumford

Gradual growth in grace, growth in
knowledge, growth in faith, growth in
love, growth in holiness, growth in
humility, growth in spiritual-mindedness –
all this I see clearly taught and urged in
Scripture, and clearly exemplified in the
lives of many of God's saints. But sudden,
instantaneous leaps from conversion to
consecration I fail to see in the Bible.
J.C. Ryle

If we don't change, we don't grow. If we
don't grow, we are not really living.
Gail Sheehy

The mother eagle teachers her little ones to
fly by making their nest so uncomfortable

that they are forced to leave it and commit
themselves to the unknown world of air
outside. And just so does our God to us.
Hannah Whitall Smith

He who advances rapidly is the one who is
humble in heart, who thinks the most
humble thoughts and is contrite in mind,
and chooses more zealously to follow the
divine Scriptures.
Symeon the New Theologian

Twelve signs of grace and predestination:
That man does certainly belong to God
who believes and is baptized into all the
articles of the Christian faith
and studies to improve his knowledge in
the matters of God, so as may best make
him to live a holy life;
he that, in obedience to Christ, worships
God diligently, frequently, and constantly,
with natural religion, that is of prayer,
praises, and thanksgiving;
he that takes all opportunities to remember
Christ's death by a frequent sacrament, as
it can be had, or else by inward acts of
understanding, will, and memory (which is
the spiritual communion) supplies the
want of the external rite;
he that lives chastely; and is merciful;
and despises the world, using it as a man,
but never suffering it to rifle [to effect
strongly or injuriously] a duty;
and is just in his dealing, and diligent in
his calling;
he that is humble in his spirit;
and obedient to government;
and content in his fortune and
employment;
he that does his duty because he loves
God;
and especially if after all this he be
afflicted, and patient, or prepared to suffer
affliction for the cause of God;
the man that hath these twelve signs of
grace and predestination does as certainly
belong to God, and is His son as surely, as
he is His creature.
Jeremy Taylor

Progress in the Christian life is exactly

equal to the growing knowledge we gain of the Triune God in personal experience.
A. W. Tozer

How tragic that we in this dark day have had our seeking done for us by our teachers. Everything is made to center upon the initial act of "accepting" Christ (a term, incidentally, which is not found in the Bible) and we are not expected thereafter to crave any further revelation of God to our souls. We have been snared in the coils of a spurious logic which insists that if we have found Him we need no more seek Him. The experiential heart-theology of a grand army of fragrant saints is rejected in favor of a smug interpretation of Scripture which would certainly have sounded strange to an Augustine, a Rutherford or a Brainerd.
A. W. Tozer

The more we grow in grace, the more shall we flourish in glory. Though every vessel of glory shall be full, yet some vessels hold more.
Thomas Watson

Don't ask for an easier life; ask to be a stronger person. Sometimes you just have to take the leap, and build your wings on the way down.
Kobi Yamada

Grudge
The heaviest thing to carry is a grudge.
Author unknown

To carry a grudge is like being stung to death by one bee.
William H. Walton

Grumbling
See also: Contentment
Don't grumble against each other, brothers, or you will be judged. The Judge is standing at the door!
The Bible, James 5:9

And do not grumble, as some of them did – and were killed by the destroying angel.
The Bible, 1 Corinthians 10:10

Some people complain because God put thorns on roses, while others praise Him for putting roses among thorns.
Author unknown

To complain of the age we live in, to murmur at the present possessors of power, to lament the past, to conceive extravagant hopes of the future, are the common dispositions of the greatest part of mankind.
Edmund Burke

Complain as little as possible of your wrongs, for, as a general rule, you may be sure that complaining is sin: … because self-love always magnifies our injuries.
Francis de Sales

Anyone who complains or grumbles is not perfect, nor even a good Christian.
John of the Cross

I have always been a grumbler. I am designed for the part – sagging face, weighty underlip, rumbling, resonant voice. Money couldn't buy a better grumbling outfit.
J.B. Priestly

Murmuring is wasted breath, and fretting is wasted time.
C.H. Spurgeon

Nothing ousts the sense of God's presence so thoroughly as the soul's dialogues with itself – when these are grumblings, grievances, etc.
Friedrich von Hügel

Guidance
See also: Obedience
The Lord went before them by day in a pillar of a cloud, to lead them the way; and by night in a pillar of fire.
The Bible, Exodus 13:21 KJV

Thy word is a lamp unto my feet, and a light unto my path.
The Bible, Psalm 119:105 KJV

Where God guides, He provides.
Author unknown

And if any sudden call should occur, which we are not prepared to meet, let us not apply to others, till we first seek Christ.
Author unknown

I acted alone on God's orders.
Yigal Amir, assassin of Yitzak Rabin, Israeli Prime Minister

And I said to the man who stood at the gate of the year: "Give me a light. that I may tread safely into the unknown." And he replied: "Go out into the darkness and put your hand into the hand of God. That shall be to you better than light, and safer than a known way."
Minnie L. Haskins

It is morally impossible to exercise trust in God while there is failure to wait upon Him for guidance and direction.
D.E. Hoste

When we fail to wait prayerfully for God's guidance and strength, we are saying with our actions if not our lips, that we do not need him.
Charles Hummel

I am satisfied that when the Almighty wants me to do or not to do any particular thing, he finds a way of letting me know.
Abraham Lincoln

And I will place within them as a guide
my umpire Conscience,
whom if they will hear,
Light after light well used they shall attain,
And to the end persisting, safe arrive.
John Milton

Man proposes, God disposes.
Proverb

If you ask enough people, you can usually find someone who will advise you to do what you were going to do anyway.
Weston Smith

Hang this question up in your houses –

"What would Jesus do?" and then think of another – "How would Jesus do it?" For what Jesus would do, and how he would do it, may always stand as the best guide to us.
C.H. Spurgeon

It is not enough to hold that God did great things for our fathers: not enough to pride ourselves on the inheritance of victories of faith: not enough to build the sepulchers of those who were martyred by men unwilling, in their day of trial as we may be in our own, to hear new voices of a living God. Our duty is to see whether God is with us; whether we expect great things from Him; whether we do not practically place Him far off, forgetting that, if He is, He is about us, speaking to us words that have not been heard before, guiding us to paths on which earlier generations have not been able to enter.
Brooke Foss Westcott

Guilt

Guilt drags us into the past, and fear pulls us into the future.
Michael Card

You never lose the love of God. Guilt is the warning that temporarily you are out of touch.
Jack Dominian

Guilt is one of the cements that binds us together and keeps us human. If it occurs to you that you've done something to injure someone else, guilt compels you to do something to fix it, to repair the bond.
Dr Helen Block Lewis, a psychoanalyst and psychologist at Yale University

The offender never forgives.
Russian proverb

Pray for a strong and lively sense of sin; the greater the sense of sin, the less sin.
Samuel Rutherford

Suspicion always haunts the guilty mind.
William Shakespeare, King Henry VI, Part 2

Gullible

We will find our most fertile ground for infiltration of Marxism within the field of religion, because religious people are the most gullible and will accept almost anything if it is couched in religious terminology.
Lenin

Who is more foolish? The fool, or the fool that follows him?
George W. Lucas Star Wars

H

Habit
Habit is the second nature which destroys the first.
Blaise Pascal

Habits
A bad habit is like a comfortable bed – easy to get into but hard to get out of.
Author unknown

First we build our habits; then our habits build us.
Author unknown

Good habits are hard to acquire but easy to live with. Bad habits are easy to acquire but hard to live with.
Author unknown

Defeat habit with innovation.
Author unknown

Break a bad habit – drop it.
Author unknown

A habit is something you can do without thinking – which is why most of us have so many of them.
Frank A. Clark

Just as iron, even without willing it, is drawn by a magnet, so is a slave to bad habits dragged about by them.
John Climacus

We first make our habits, then our habits make us.
John Dryden

Ill habits gather by unseen degrees,
As brooks make rivers, rivers run to seas.
John Dryden

A nail is driven out by another nail. Habit is overcome by habit.
Desiderius Erasmus

Early to bed and early to rise,
Makes a man healthy, wealthy, and wise.
Benjamin Franklin

Who is strong? He that can conquer his bad habits.
Benjamin Franklin

It is easier to prevent ill habits than to break them.
Thomas Fuller

Habits are chains that are too small to be felt until they are too strong to be broken.
Samuel Johnson

The unfortunate thing about this world is that the good habits are much easier to give up than the bad ones.
W. Somerset Maugham

Small habits well pursued betimes,
May reach the dignity of crimes.
Hannah More

Nothing is stronger than habit.
Ovid

The strength of a man's virtue should not be measured by his special exertions, but by his habitual acts.
Blaise Pascal

What is most contrary to salvation is not sin, but habit.
Charles Péguy

Good habits result from resisting temptation.
Proverb

Habit is a shirt made of iron.
Czech proverb

Habits begin like threads in a spider's web, but end up like ropes.
Spanish proverb

Don't let your sins turn into bad habits.
Teresa of Avila

If you do not shun small defects, bit by bit you will fall into greater ones.
Thomas à Kempis

Habit is habit and not to be flung out of the window by any man, but coaxed downstairs a step at a time.
Mark Twain

Nothing so needs reforming as other people's habits.
Mark Twain

Habits, Overcoming
I never knew a man to overcome a bad habit gradually.
John R. Mott

Habit is overcome by habit.
Thomas à Kempis

Habits, Spiritual
Failure to establish good spiritual habits will lead to poor spiritual health.
Author unknown

Hair
The hair is the richest ornament of women.
Martin Luther

Halloween
Every act around Halloween is in honor of false gods, which are spirits in the realm of the Satanic. Thus, Halloween is seen primarily as a Satanic holiday.
Christian Broadcasting Network

Children … shouldn't have anything to do with the celebration that glorifies the power of God's enemies.
Albert Dager

Happiness
He that is of a merry heart hath a continual feast.
The Bible, Proverbs 15:15 KJV

Is anyone happy? Let him sing songs of praise.
The Bible, James 5:13

Happiness is what happens to us when we try to make someone else happy.
Author unknown

Happiness depends on happenings, but joy depends on Jesus.
Author unknown

Happiness is the perfume that you cannot pour without getting a few drops on yourself.
Author unknown

Choose to love – rather than hate.
Choose to smile – rather than frown.
Choose to build – rather than destroy.
Choose to persevere – rather than quit.
Choose to praise – rather than gossip.
Choose to heal – rather than wound.
Choose to give – rather than grasp.
Choose to act – rather than delay.
Choose to forgive – rather than curse.
Choose to pray – rather than despair.
Author unknown

It is not how much we have, but how much we enjoy, that makes happiness.
Author unknown

True happiness comes from the joy of deeds well done, the zest of creating things new.
Author unknown

True happiness … arises, in the first place, from the enjoyment of one's self, and, in the next, from friendship and conversation of a few selected companions.
Joseph Addison

Three grand essentials to happiness in this life are something to do, something to

love, and something to hope for.
Joseph Addison

A man's happiness – to do the things
proper to man.
Marcus Aurelius Antoninus

Happiness is an expression of the soul in
considered actions.
Aristotle

Where your pleasure is, there is your treasure;
where your treasure, there your heart; where
your heart, there your happiness.
Augustine of Hippo

No one is really happy merely because he
has what he wants, but only if he wants
things he ought to want.
Augustine of Hippo

The secret of happiness is not doing what
one likes, but in liking what one does.
J.M. Barrie

Happiness is good health and a bad memory.
Ingrid Bergman

HAPPINESS: An agreeable sensation
arising from contemplating the misery of
another.
Ambrose Bierce

There is no cosmetic for beauty like
happiness.
Countess of Blessington

This is my "depressed stance." When you're
depressed, it makes a lot of difference how
you stand. The worst thing you can do is
straighten up and hold your head high
because then you'll start to feel better. If
you're going to get any joy out of being
depressed, you've got to stand like this.
Charlie Brown

Complete happiness is knowing God.
John Calvin

You will never be happy if you continue to
search for what happiness consists of. You

will never live if you are looking for the
meaning of life.
Albert Camus

Happiness is the practice of the virtues.
Clement of Alexandria

There is no happiness in having or in
getting, but only in giving.
Henry Drummond

Happiness is not a possession to be prized,
it is a quality of thought, a state of mind.
Daphne du Maurier

There is only one way to happiness and
that is to cease worrying about things
which are beyond the power of our will.
Epictetus

In order to be utterly happy the only thing
necessary is to refrain from comparing this
moment with other moments in the past,
which I often did not fully enjoy because I
was comparing them with other moments
of the future.
Andre Gide

The happiness which brings enduring
worth to life is not the superficial
happiness that is dependent on
circumstances. It is the happiness and
contentment that fills the soul even in the
midst of the most distressing circumstances
and the most bitter environment. It is the
kind of happiness that grins when things
go wrong and smiles through the tears.
The happiness for which our souls ache is
one undisturbed by success or failure, one
which will root deeply inside us and give
inward relaxation, peace, and contentment,
no matter what the surface problems may
be. That kind of happiness stands in need
of no outward stimulus.
Billy Graham

A cheerful look makes a dish a Feast.
George Herbert

The day of individual happiness has passed.
Adolf Hitler

The search for happiness is one of the chief sources of unhappiness.
Eric Hoffer

Happiness comes of the capacity to feel deeply, to enjoy simply, to think freely, to risk life, to be needed.
Storm Jameson

Happiness is like jam: you can't spread it without getting some on yourself.
Barbara Johnson

When one door of happiness closes another opens; but often we look so long at the closed door that we do not see the one which has been opened for us.
Helen Keller

Many persons have a wrong idea of what constitutes true happiness. It is not attained through self-gratification but through fidelity to a worthy purpose.
Helen Keller

Happiness is the full use of your powers along lines of excellence.
John F. Kennedy

We are never so happy or so unhappy as we suppose.
Francis, Duc de La Rochefoucauld

God cannot give us a happiness apart from Himself, because there is no such thing.
C.S. Lewis

Do not let your happiness depend on something you may lose ... only [upon] the Beloved who will never pass away.
C.S. Lewis

God designed the human machine to run on Himself. He is the fuel our spirits were designed to burn ... That is why it is no good asking God to make us happy in our own way without bothering about religion. God cannot give us a happiness apart from Himself, because there is no such thing.
C.S. Lewis

People are just about as happy as they make up their minds to be.
Abraham Lincoln

The abolition of religion, as the illusory happiness of men, is a demand for their real happiness.
Karl Marx

God has so constituted our nature that we cannot be happy unless we are or think we are the means of good to others. We can scarcely conceive of greater wretchedness than must be felt by him who knows he is wholly useless in the world.
Erskine Mason

The first recipe for happiness is: Avoid too lengthy meditations on the past.
Andre Maurois

Those who seek happiness too intensely will have little of it.
Calvin Miller

Happiness is a matter of one's most ordinary everyday mode of consciousness being busy and lively and unconcerned with self.
Iris Murdoch

The foolish man seeks happiness in the distance, the wise grows it under his feet.
James Oppenheim

Men can only be happy when they do not assume that the object of life is happiness.
George Orwell

The reason people find it so hard to be happy is that they always see the past better than it was, the present worse than it is, and the future less resolved than it will be.
Marcel Pagnol

Thus we never live, but we hope to live; and always disposing ourselves to be happy, it is inevitable that we never become so.
Blaise Pascal

If man is not made for God, why is he happy only in God?
Blaise Pascal

To show a child what once delighted you, to find the child's delight added to your own, this is happiness.
J.B. Priestly

Be happy while you're living,
For you're a long time dead.
Scottish proverb

To be happy, you must first make others happy.
Swedish proverb

The secret to happiness is this: Let your interest be as wide as possible, and let your reactions to the things and persons that interest you be as far as possible friendly rather than hostile.
Bertrand Russell

A lifetime of happiness, no man could bear it.
George Bernard Shaw

What leads to unhappiness, is making pleasure the chief aim.
William Shenstone

There is no duty we so much underrate as the duty of being happy. By being happy we sow anonymous benefits upon the world.
Robert Louis Stevenson

Happiness is the perpetual possession of being well deceived.
Jonathan Swift

Consider these things, my soul, and close the door of your senses, so that you can hear what the Lord your God speaks within you. "I am your salvation," says your Beloved. "I am your peace and your life. Remain with Me and you will find peace. Dismiss all passing things and seek the eternal. What are all temporal things but snares? And what help will all creatures be able to give you if you are deserted by the Creator?"
Thomas à Kempis

If you want to be happy, be.
Alexei Tolstoy

You can't buy happiness, you can't buy health and you can't buy inner peace.
The Duke of Westminster, spoken when he was Britain's richest man

Talk happiness. The world is sad enough without your woe. No path is wholly rough.
Ella Wheeler Wilcox

Happiness, Lack of
Imperial power is an ocean of miseries.
Marcus Aurelius

If we only wanted to be happy it would be easy; but we want to be happier than other people, which is almost always difficult, since we think them happier than they are.
Montesquieu

In a word, I do not live: I am dead before my time. I have no interest in the world. Everything conspires to embitter my life. My life is a continual death.
Mme de Pompadour, Louis XV's mistress and favorite

Hardships
See also: Adversity; Affliction; Burdens; Difficulties; Suffering; Trials
"We must go through many hardships to enter the kingdom of God," they said.
The Bible, Acts 14:22

Endure hardship with us like a good soldier of Christ Jesus.
The Bible, 2 Timothy 2:3

Nothing about our faith makes us pain-proof. It does hurt. It does make us cry. And we must dry our eyes and continue our work until our time is finished.
Jesse Jackson

If God sends you a cross, take it up and follow Him.
Use it wisely, lest it be unprofitable.

Bear it patiently, lest it be intolerable.
If it be light, slight it not.
If it be heavy, murmur not.
Quarles

Hard times
See: Hardships

Harmony
Live in harmony with one another.
The Bible, Romans 12:16

Tune me, O Lord,
into one harmony
With thee, one full
responsive vibrant chord;
Unto thy praise, all love
and melody,
Tune me, O Lord.
Christina Rossetti

Harvest
We plough the fields and scatter
The good seed on the land,
But it is fed and watered
By God's Almighty hand.
Jane Montgomery Campbell

Haste
See: Rush

Hate
Do not hate your brother in your heart.
The Bible, Leviticus 19:17

Hate is blind as well as love.
Author unknown

I imagine that one of the reasons people
cling to their hates so stubbornly is because
they sense, once the hate is gone, they will
be forced to deal with pain.
James Baldwin

Hatred ceases by love.
Buddha

Love, friendship, respect, do not unite
people as much as common hatred for
something.
Anton Chekhov

Hate kills both the person who you hate,
but also yourself as well.
H.E. Fosdick

If you hate a person, you hate
something in them that is part of
yourself. What isn't part of ourselves
doesn't disturb us.
Hermann Hesse

Darkness cannot drive out darkness; only
light can do that. Hate cannot drive out
hate; only love can do that.
Martin Luther King, Jr

Hatred paralyzes life; love releases it.
Hatred confuses life; love harmonizes it.
Hatred darkens life; love illuminates it.
Martin Luther King, Jr

Hate is like acid. It can damage the vessel
in which it is stored as well as destroy the
object on which it is poured.
Ann Landers

Always remember that others may hate you,
but those who hate you don't win unless you
hate them. And then you destroy yourself.
Richard Mulhouse Nixon

Love and hatred are natural exaggerators.
Hebrew proverb

It belongs to human nature to hate those
you have injured.
Tacitus

I shall allow no man to belittle my soul by
making me hate him.
Booker T. Washington.

Haughty
Do thou restrain the haughty spirit in thy
breast, for better far is gentle courtesy.
Homer

One who is repentant cannot be haughty.
Mark the Ascetic

Headship
I cannot see that it is demeaning to women

to say that masculine "headship" is the God-given means by which their femininity is protected and enabled to blossom.
John Stott

Healing

God heals, and the doctor takes the fee.
George Herbert

We are all healers who can reach out and offer health, and we are all patients in constant need of help.
Henri Nouwen

Health

No wonder you are sick. You are not linking yourself enough to the resources that bring healing.
Selwyn Hughes

The part can never be well unless the whole is well.
Plato

He who enjoys good health is rich, though he knows it not.
Italian proverb

Heart

Keep thy heart with all diligence; for out of it are the issues of life.
The Bible, Proverbs 4:23 KJV

A happy heart makes the face cheerful, but heartache crushes the spirit.
The Bible, Proverbs 15:13

A man's heart deviseth his way; but the LORD directeth his steps.
The Bible, Proverbs 16:9

A merry heart doeth good like a medicine.
The Bible, Proverbs 17:22

My son, give me thine heart.
The Bible, Proverbs 23:26 KJV

Out of the abundance of the heart the mouth speaketh.
The Bible, Matthew 12:34

The right kind of heart is a kind heart like God's.
Author unknown

To handle yourself, use your head. To handle others, use your heart.
Author unknown

To my God a heart of flame;
To my fellow men a heart of love;
To myself a heart of steel.
Augustine of Hippo

See that your chief study be about your heart, that there God's image may be planted, and his interest advanced, and the interest of the world and flesh subdued, and the love of every sin cast out, and the love of holiness succeed.
Richard Baxter

God hears no more than the heart speaks; and if the heart be dumb, God will certainly be deaf.
Thomas Brooks

The heart must be kept tender and pliable; otherwise agnosticism converts to skepticism ... for apologetics is aimed at persuading doubters, not at refuting the defiant. He who demands a kind of proof that the nature of the case renders impossible, is determined that no possible evidence shall convince him.
Edward John Carnell

To put the world in order, we must first put the nation in order; to put the nation in order, we must put the family in order; to put the family in order, we must cultivate our personal life; and to cultivate our personal life, we must first set our hearts right.
Confucius

Only the heart knows how to find what is precious.
Fyodor Dostoevski

The first and the great work of a Christian is about his heart. Do not be content with seeming to do good in "outward acts"

while your heart is bad, and you are a stranger to the greater internal heart duties.
Jonathan Edwards

See that your chief study be about your heart:
that there God's image may be planted;
that there His interests be advanced;
that there the world and flesh are subdued;
that there the love of every sin is cast out;
that there the love of holiness grows.
Jonathan Edwards

It is only with the heart that one can see rightly; what is essential is invisible to the eye.
Antoine de Saint-Exupery

Oh, study your hearts, watch your hearts, keep your hearts!
John Flavel

Heart-work is hard work indeed. Get your heart broken for sin while you are actually confessing it; melted with free grace even while you are blessing God for it; to be really ashamed and humbled through the awareness of God's infinite holiness, and to keep your heart in this state not only in, but after these duties, will surely cost you some groans and travailing pain of soul.
John Flavel

Do your utmost to guard your heart, for out of it comes life.
Walter Hilton

The most tremendous judgment of God in this world is the hardening of the hearts of men.
John Owen

The worst prison would be a closed heart.
Pope John Paul II

The heart has eyes that the brain knows nothing of.
Charles Henry Parkhurst

It is the heart which perceives God and not the reason.
Blaise Pascal

Throw your heart over the fence and the rest will follow.
Norman Vincent Peale

What can I give Him,
Poor as I am?
If I were a shepherd,
I would bring a lamb,
If I were a Wise Man,
I would do my part –
Yet what can I give Him?
Give my heart.
Christina Rossetti

Unless the heart be kept peaceable, the life will not be happy. If calm does not reign over that inner lake within the soul which feeds the rivers of our life, the rivers themselves will always be in storm. Our outward acts will always tell that they were born in tempests, by being tempestuous themselves. We all desire to lead a joyous life; the bright eye and the elastic foot are things which each of us desire; to carry about a contented mind is that to which most men are continually aspiring. Let us remember that the only way to keep our life peaceful and happy is to keep the heart at rest, for come poverty, come wealth, come honor, come shame, come plenty, or come scarcity, if the heart be quiet, there will be happiness anywhere. But whatever the sunshine and the brightness, if the heart be troubled, the whole life must be troubled too.
C.H. Spurgeon

You must keep all earthly treasures out of your heart, and let Christ be your treasure, and let him have your heart.
C.H. Spurgeon

I often think of dear old John Bunyan, when he said he wished God had made him a toad, or a frog, or a snake, or anything rather than a man, for he felt he was so offensive. Oh! I can conceive a nest of vipers, and I think that they are obnoxious;

I can imagine a pool of all kinds of loathsome creatures, breeding corruption; but there is nothing one half so worthy of abhorrence as the human heart.
C.H. Spurgeon

Neither prayer, nor praise, nor the hearing of the word will be profitable to those who have left their hearts behind them.
C.H. Spurgeon

God wants the heart.
The Talmud

If your heart were sincere and upright, every creature would be unto you a looking-glass of life and a book of holy doctrine.
Thomas à Kempis

Heart, Divided

A man-pleaser cannot be true to God, because he is a servant to the enemies of his service; the wind of a man's mouth will drive him about as the chaff, from any duty, and to any sin.
Richard Baxter

Heaven

Lay up for yourselves treasures in heaven.
The Bible, Matthew 6:20 KJV

Strait is the gate, and narrow is the way.
The Bible, Matthew 7:14 KJV

In my Father's house are many mansions.
The Bible, John 14:2 KJV

Now we know that if the earthly tent we live in is destroyed, we have a building from God, an eternal house in heaven, not built by human hands.
The Bible, 2 Corinthians 5:1

But our citizenship is in heaven. And we eagerly await a Savior from there, the Lord Jesus Christ, who, by the power that enables him to bring everything under his control, will transform our lowly bodies so that they will be like his glorious body.
The Bible, Philippians 3:20,21

Set your affections on things above, not on things on the earth.
The Bible, Colossians 3:2

Now there is in store for me the crown of righteousness, which the Lord, the righteous Judge, will award to me on that day—and not only to me, but also to all who have longed for his appearing.
The Bible, 2 Timothy 4:8

He who thinks most of heaven will do most for earth.
Author unknown

God's retirement plan is out of this world.
Author unknown

I don't believe in an afterlife, so I don't have to spend my whole life fearing hell, or fearing heaven even more. For whatever the tortures of hell, I think the boredom of heaven would be even worse.
Isaac Asimov

We shall rest and we shall see, we shall see and we shall love, we shall love and we shall pray, in the end which is no end.
Augustine of Hippo

Heaven is won or lost on earth; the possession is there, but the preparation is here. Christ will judge all men in another state, as their works have been in this. First, "Well done, good and faithful servant;" then, "Enter thou into the joy of the Lord."
Richard Baxter

My knowledge of that life is small,
The eye of faith is dim;
But 'tis enough that Christ knows all,
And I shall be with him.
Richard Baxter

Jesus the very thought of Thee
With sweetness fills my breast;
But sweeter far Thy face to see
And in Thy presence rest.
Bernard of Clairvaux

Heaven: A place where the wicked cease from troubling you with talk of their personal affairs, and the good listen with attention while you expound your own.
Ambrose Bierce

Understand what heaven is: It is but the turning in of the will into the Love of God. Wheresoever thou findest God manifesting himself in love, there thou findest heaven, without travelling for it so much as one foot.
Jacob Boehme

My heaven is to please God and glorify him, and to give all to him, and to be wholly devoted to his glory; that is the heaven I long for.
David Brainerd

No coward soul is mine,
No trembler in the world's storm-troubled
  sphere:
I see haven's glories shine,
And faith shines equal, arming me from
  fear.
Emily Brontë

But let us draw toward the candle's end.
The fire, you see, doth wick and tallow
  spend;
So wastes man's life, until his glass is run,
And so the candle and the man are done.
The man now lays him down upon his bed;
The wick yields up its fire, and so is dead.
The candle now extinct is, but the man
By grace mounts up to glory, there to
  stand.
John Bunyan

Christ is the desire of nations, the joy of angels, the delight of the Father. What solace then must that soul be filled with that hath the possession of Him to all eternity!
John Bunyan

They who will have Heaven must run for it because the devil, the law, sin, death, and hell are following them. There is never a poor soul that goes to Heaven where the devil, the law, sin, death, and hell do not

chase after it, "…your adversary the devil walks about like a roaring lion, seeking whom he may devour"(1 Pet. 5:8); and I assure you the devil is nimble; he can run very quickly; he is light on his feet and has overtaken many; he has knocked them down and has given them an everlasting fall. Also, there is the law, which can shoot a great distance. Be careful to stay out of the reach of the law's great guns – the ten commandments. Hell also has a wide mouth; it can stretch itself further than you're aware of. As the angel said to Lot, "Escape for your life! Do not look behind you nor stay anywhere in the plain. Escape to the mountains lest you be destroyed" (Gen 19:17).
  So I say to you, take heed. Do not delay any longer, lest the devil, hell, death, or the fearful curses of the law overtake you and throw you down in the midst of your sins, so you will never rise and recover again. If this were well considered, then you, as well as I, would say they who would have Heaven must run for it.
John Bunyan

He was a burning and shining light. He was for the church, and for the world and for people. He stood as a lamp on a lamp-stand, for the illumination of the world. Perhaps his greatest resource was that he knew that he would go to his eternal home and find his Father waiting for him.
George Carey, at the thanksgiving service for David Watson

All the way to heaven is heaven.
Catherine of Siena

Heaven is a prepared place for a prepared people.
Lewis Sperry Chafer

It is a far, far better thing that I do, than I have ever done; it is a far, far better rest that I go to, than I have ever known.
Charles Dickens, end of A Tale of Two Cities

Bring us, O Lord God, at our last awakening into the house and gate of

heaven, to enter that gate and dwell in that house, where there shall be no darkness nor dazzling, but one equal light; no noise nor silence, but one equal music; no fears nor hopes, but one equal possession; no ends nor beginnings, but one equal eternity; in the habitations of your glory and dominion, world without end.
John Donne

To pretend to describe the excellence, the greatness or duration of the happiness of heaven by the most artful composition of words would be but to darken and cloud it; to talk of raptures and ecstasies, joy and singing, is but to set forth very low shadows of the reality.
Jonathan Edwards

The enjoyment of God is the only happiness with which our souls can be satisfied. To go to heaven, fully to enjoy God, is infinitely better than the most pleasant accommodations here. Fathers and mothers, husbands, wives, or children, or the company of earthly friends, are but shadows; but God is the substance. These are but scattered beams, but God is the sun. These are but streams. But God is the ocean.
Jonathan Edwards

Heaven is a cheap purchase, whatever it cost.
Thomas Fuller

Heaven will be the perfection we have always longed for. All the things that made Earth unlovely and tragic will be absent in Heaven.
Billy Graham

Bid faith look through the key-hole of the promise, and tell thee what it sees there laid up for him that overcomes; bid it listen and tell thee whether it cannot hear the shout of those crowned saints, as of those that are dividing the spoil, and receiving the reward of all their services and sufferings here on earth.
William Gurnall

I saw the heavens opened, and God sitting on his great white throne.
Handel, explaining how he was inspired during his writing of the Hallelujah chorus.

The main object of religion is not to get a man into heaven, but to get heaven into him.
Thomas Hardy

Heaven doesn't come to earth cheap. It never has! It takes prayer.
Norvel Hayes

Jesus himself is preparing all of us who know and love him for a most distant journey – more distant even than the trip to the moon. The Lord wants us to be where he is throughout eternity.
Colonel James B. Irwin
One of only twelve men who have walked on the moon. He walked on the surface of the moon on July 30, 1971 and stayed there for a record sixty-seven hours.

A continual looking forward to the eternal world is not a form of escapism or wishful thinking, but one of the things a Christian is meant to do.
C.S. Lewis

Has this world been so kind to you that you should leave with regret? There are better things ahead than any we leave behind.
C.S. Lewis

The only air of the soul, in which it can breathe and live, is the present God and the spirits of the just: that is our heaven, our home, our all-right place.
George Macdonald

The passing beauty and joys of the world point us towards another world, a New Jerusalem in which "there will be no more death or mourning or crying or pain, for the old order of things has passed away" (Revelation 21:4). In the meantime, we must live and work in the world. Yet we do so as people who know that they are on

their way home, and anticipate the joy of return and arrival.
Alister McGrath

We are here and it is now. Further than that, all human knowledge is moonshine.
H.L. Mencken

We talk about heaven being so far away. It is within speaking distance of those who belong there.
Dwight L. Moody

When I get to heaven, I shall see three wonders there. The first wonder will be to see many there whom I did not expect to see; the second wonder will be to miss many people who I did expect to see; the third and greatest of all will be to find myself there.
John Newton

Heaven

John Owen
We may hereby examine both our own notions of the state of glory and our preparations for it, and whether we are in any measure "made meet for the inheritance of the saints in light." Various are the thoughts of men about the future state,-the things which are not seen, which are eternal. Some rise no higher but unto hopes of escaping hell, or everlasting miseries, when they die. Yet the heathen had their Elysian fields, and Mohammed his sensual paradise. Others have apprehensions of I know not what glistening glory, that will please and satisfy them, they know not how, when they can be here no longer. But this state is quite of another nature, and the blessedness of it is spiritual and intellectual. Take an instance in one of the things before laid down. The glory of heaven consists in the full manifestation of divine wisdom, goodness, grace, holiness, – of all the properties of the nature of God in Christ. In the clear perception and constant contemplation

hereof consists no small part of eternal blessedness. What, then, are our present thoughts of these things? What joy, what satisfaction have we in the sight of them, which we have by faith through divine revelation? What is our desire to come unto the perfect comprehension of them? How do we like this heaven? What do we find in ourselves that will be eternally satisfied hereby? According as our desires are after them, such and no other are our desires of the true heaven, – of the residence of blessedness and glory. Neither will God bring us unto heaven whether we will or no. If, through the ignorance and darkness of our minds, – if, through the earthliness and sensuality of our affections, – if, through a fulness of the world, and the occasions of it, – if, by the love of life and our present enjoyments, we are strangers unto these things, we are not conversant about them, we long not after them, – we are not in the way towards their enjoyment. The present satisfaction we receive in them by faith, is the best evidence we have of an indefeasible interest in them. How foolish is it to lose the first-fruits of these things in our own souls, – those entrances into blessedness which the contemplation of them through faith would open unto us, – and hazard our everlasting enjoyment of them by an eager pursuit of an interest in perishing things here below! This, this is that which ruins the souls of most, and keeps the faith of many at so low an ebb, that it is hard to discover any genuine working of it.
John Owen

———

Hearts on earth say in the course of a joyful experience, "I don't want this ever to end." But it invariably does. The hearts of those in heaven say, "I want this to go on forever." And it will. There is no better news than this.
J.I. Packer

I am constrained to express my adoration of the Author of my existence for His forgiving mercy revealed to the world through Jesus

Christ, through whom I hope for never ending happiness in a future state.
Robert Treat Paine, Signer of the Declaration

Earthly crowns are dross to him who looks for a heavenly one.
Jane Porter

O my Lord Jesus Christ, if I could be in heaven without thee, it would be a hell; and if I could be in hell, and have thee still, it would be a heaven to me, for thou art all the heaven I want.
S. Rutherford

Heaven and Christ are the same thing.
S. Rutherford

Socrates, being asked what countryman he was, answered, "I am a citizen of the whole world." But ask a Christian what countryman he is, and he will answer, "A citizen of heaven."
William Secker

In heaven, God will not ask us why we sinned; He will ask us why we didn't repent.
Pope Shenouda III

My idea of heaven, is eating patés de foie gras to the sound of trumpets.
Revd Sydney Smith

There will be little else we shall want of heaven besides Jesus Christ. He will be our bread, our food, our beauty, and our glorious dress. The atmosphere of heaven will be Christ; everything in heaven will be Christ-like: yes, Christ is the heaven of His people.
C.H. Spurgeon

Ultimately, when we have fought a good fight and finished our course, and even if need be suffered death for the name of Christ, we shall emerge from the great tribulation and suffer no more. The King of the universe will grant us refuge in the shelter of His throne, where we may see Him and worship Him day and night in His temple, and the Lamb turned Shepherd will lead us with the rest of His sheep to fountains of living water, where we may slake our thirst for ever at the eternal springs.
John Stott

For the saints in the world to come, there can be no change in the object of their faith and hope and love. They have Christ, they have God, and they are satisfied. There can be no monotony in the contemplation and worship of the Infinite. Their great possession is unchangeable, but also inexhaustible; no change is possible where all is love and truth.
Henry Barclay Swete

The world rings changes, it is never constant but in its disappointments. The world is but a great inn, where we are to stay a night or two, and be gone; what madness is it so to set our heart upon our inn, as to forget our home?
Thomas Watson

The doctrine of the Kingdom of Heaven, which was the main teaching of Jesus, is certainly one of the most revolutionary doctrines that ever stirred and changed human thought.
H.G. Wells

The best is yet to be.
John Wesley

Entrance into heaven is not at the hour of death, but at the moment of conversion.
Benjamin Whichcote

Heaven and hell
Oh sirs, deal with sin as sin, and speak of heaven and hell as they are, and not as if you were in jest.
John Flavel

If the Lord should bring a wicked man to heaven, heaven would be hell to him; for he who loves not grace upon earth will never love it in heaven.
Christopher Love

Absence from Christ is hell; but the presence of Jesus is heaven.
C.H. Spurgeon

Heavenly minded
The Christians who did most for the present world were precisely those who thought most of the next. It is since Christians have begun thinking less of the other world that they have become so ineffective in this. Aim at heaven and you get earth thrown in; aim at earth and you get neither.
W.R. Inge

Hebrews, The letter to the
Chapter eleven of Hebrews is the Westminster Abbey of the Bible
Author unknown

The great theme of the letter to the Hebrews is the finality of Jesus Christ.
John Stott

Hell
Wide is the gate, and broad is the way, that leadeth to destruction.
The Bible, Matthew 7:13 KJV

Then I saw that there was a way to Hell, even from the gates of heaven.
John Bunyan

Hell is paved with priests' skulls.
John Chrysostom

The "pains of hell" are not the greatest part of hell. The "loss of heaven" is the weightiest woe of hell.
John Chrysostom

The doctrine of hell is not just some dusty, theological holdover from the unenlightened Middle Ages. It has significant social consequences. Without ultimate justice, people's sense of moral obligation dissolves; social bonds are broken. People who have no fear of God soon have no fear of man, and no respect for human laws and authority.
Chuck Colson

The most prominent place in hell is reserved for those who are neutral on the great issues of life.
Billy Graham

The only thing I could say for sure is that hell means separation from God. We are separated from His light, from His fellowship. That is going to hell. When it comes to a literal fire, I don't preach it because I'm not sure about it. When the Scripture uses fire concerning hell, that is possibly an illustration of how terrible it's going to be – not fire but something worse, a thirst for God that cannot be quenched.
Billy Graham

The national anthem of hell is, "I Did It My Way."
Peter Kreeft

The safest road to hell is a gradual one. This safe road has a gentle slope, without turns, without milestones, without signposts, without warnings.
C.S. Lewis

There are only two kinds of people in the end: those who say to God, "Thy will be done," and those to whom God says, in the end, "Thy will be done." All that are in hell, choose it. Without that self-choice there could be no hell. No soul that seriously and constantly desires joy will ever miss it. Those who seek find. To those who knock it is opened.
C.S. Lewis

The lost enjoy for ever the horrible freedom they have demanded, and are therefore self-enslaved.
C.S. Lewis

I willingly believe that the damned are, in one sense, successful, rebels to the end; that the doors of hell are locked on the inside.
C.S. Lewis

The Dominical utterances about hell are

addressed to the conscience and the will, not to our intellectual curiosity.
C.S. Lewis

The road to hell is paved with good intentions.
Proverb

Disbelieve hell, and you unscrew, unsettle, and unpin everything in Scripture.
J.C. Ryle

If I never spoke of hell, I should think I had kept back something that was profitable, and should look on myself as an accomplice of the devil.
J.C. Ryle

Hell is other people.
Jean-Paul Sartre

Annihilation is an everlasting punishment, though it is not unending torment.
William Temple

Helpfulness
See also: God's help
Vain is the help of man.
The Bible, Psalm 60:11 KJV

There is no exercise better for the heart than reaching down and lifting someone else up.
Author unknown

The truest help we can render an afflicted man is not to take his burden from him, but to call out his best energy, that he may be able to bear the burden.
Phillips Brooks

The greatest good you can do for another is not just share your riches, but reveal to them their own.
B. Disraeli

People who won't help others in trouble "because they got into trouble through their own fault" would probably not throw a lifeline to a drowning man until they

learned whether he fell in through his own fault or not.
Sydney J. Harris

If a friend is in trouble, don't annoy him by asking if there is anything you can do. Think up something appropriate and do it.
Edgar Watson Howe

Even if it's a little thing, do something for those who have need of help, something for which you get no pay but the privilege of doing it.
Albert Schweitzer

Hence we must support one another, console one another, mutually help, counsel, and advise.
Thomas à Kempis

Heresy
See also: Doctrine; Persecution
The Son had a beginning, but God is without beginning.
Arius, Arian heresy

You are not to suppose, brethren, that heresies could be produced through any little souls. None save great men have been the authors of heresies.
Augustine of Hippo

To assert that the earth revolves around the sun is as erroneous as to claim that Jesus was not born of a virgin.
Cardinal Bellarmine 1615, during the trial of Galileo

No man is to lower himself by showing tolerance towards any sort of heretic, least of all a Calvinist.
Cardinal Carafe, 1542

Every heresy has been an effort to narrow the church.
G.K. Chesterton

A heretic is a fellow who disagrees with you regarding something neither of you knows anything about.
William Cowper

The only remedy for a false view of the cross is the cross itself.
H.B. Dehqani-Tafit, former Bishop of Jerusalem and the Middle East

Heresy is another word for freedom of thought.
Graham Greene

Avoid heretics like wild beasts; for they are mad dogs who bite in secret. You must be on your guard against them; their bite is not easily cured.
Ignatius of Antioch

I therefore, yet not I, but the love of Jesus Christ, entreat you that ye use Christian nourishment only, and abstain from herbage of a different kind; I mean heresy. For those who mix up Jesus Christ with their own poison, speaking things which are unworthy of credit, like those who administer a deadly drug in sweet wine, which he who is ignorant of does greedily take, with a fatal pleasure leading to his own death.
Irenaeus

It is a destructive addition to add anything to Christ.
Richard Sibbes

It is a remarkable fact that all the heresies which have arisen in the Christian Church have had a decided tendency to "dishonor God and to flatter man."
C.H. Spurgeon

Heretics

Heretics in holding false opinions regarding God, do injury to the faith itself.
Augustine of Hippo

If a man blatantly denies the deity of Christ or that Christ has come in the flesh, we are not to even bid him godspeed. Thus, the Scriptures teach that we are to be separated from those who deny the deity of our Lord Jesus Christ. I am to treat him as an Anti-Christ and an enemy of the cross.
Billy Graham

Hero

Heroes are not the ones that never fail, but the ones who never give up.
Author unknown

Hesitation

He who hesitates is a damned fool.
Mae West (1892-1980)

Hinduism

As a Hindu I endured the self-discipline and much study for one purpose – to better myself, to achieve heaven by my own deeds. Christianity starts with man's weakness. It asks us to accept our selfishness and inabilities, then promises a new nature.
Professor Paul Krishna, a former Hindu

Hinduism believes in many gods, but again no heaven.
Luis Palau

Historians

It is astonishing that while Graeco-Roman historians have been growing in confidence, the twentieth-century study of the Gospel narratives, starting from no less promising material, has taken so gloomy a turn in the development of form-criticism that the more advanced exponents of it apparently maintain – so far as an amateur can understand the matter – that the historical Christ is unknowable and the history of his mission cannot be written. This seems very curious.
A.N. Sherwin-White, classical historian at Oxford University

History

History teaches us that man learns nothing from history.
Author unknown

He who learns nothing from the past will be punished by the future.
Author unknown

Human beings, who are almost unique in having the ability to learn from the experience of others, are also remarkable

for their apparent disinclination to do so.
Douglas Adams

The study of history is the beginning of
political wisdom.
Jean Bodin

Not to know what happened before one
was born is always to be a child.
Cicero

Study the past if you would divine the future.
Confucius

History is bunk.
Henry Ford

History is, indeed, little more than the
register of the crimes, follies, and
misfortunes of mankind.
Edward Gibbon

The study of history is a powerful antidote to
contemporary arrogance. It is humbling to
discover how many of our glib assumptions,
which seem to us novel and plausible, have
been tested before, not once but many times
and in innumerable guises; and discovered
to be, at great human cost, wholly false.
Paul Johnson

History is the version of past events that
people have decided to agree upon.
Napoleon

Dwell in the past and you'll lose an eye.
Forget the past and you'll lose both eyes.
Russian proverb

Those who cannot remember the past are
condemned to repeat it.
George Santayana

The best way to suppose what may come,
is to remember what is past.
George Savile

History and Jesus Christ
All history is incomprehensible without
Christ.
Ernest Renan

Holiness
*See also: Abiding; God's holiness;
Perfection; Union with Christ; Union
with God*
You become like what you look at.
Author unknown

It takes more of the power of the Spirit to
make the farm, the home, the office, the
store, the shop holy than it does to make
the Church holy. It takes more of the power
of the Spirit to make Saturday holy than to
make Sunday holy. It takes much more of
the power of the Spirit to make money for
God than to make a talk for God.
Cowards never won heaven. Do not claim
that you are begotten of God and have His
royal blood running in your veins unless you
can prove your lineage by this heroic spirit;
to dare to be holy in spite of men and devils.
Author unknown

When holiness loses its sweetness it is a
fierce thing to come in contact with.
Frank Bartleman

Remember your ultimate purpose, and
when you set yourself to your day's work or
approach any activity in the world, let
HOLINESS TO THE LORD be written
upon your hearts in all that you do.
Richard Baxter

Nothing but the name of Jesus can restrain
the impulse of anger, repress the swelling
of pride, cure the world of envy, bridle the
onslaught of luxury, extinguish the flame
of carnal desire – can temper avarice, and
put to flight impure and ignoble thoughts.
Bernard of Clairvaux

To be holy is to be morally blameless. It is
to be separated from sin and, therefore,
consecrated to God. The word signifies
"separation to God, and the conduct
befitting those so separated."
Jerry Bridges

The pursuit of holiness is a joint venture
between God and the Christian. No one can
attain any degree of holiness without God

working in his life, but just as surely no one will attain it without effort on his own part.
Jerry Bridges

Holiness is a process, something we never completely attain in this life.
Jerry Bridges

The more man becomes irradiated with the divinity of Christ, the more, not the less, truly he is man.
Phillips Brooks

There will come a time when in this world holiness shall be more general, and more eminent, than ever it hath been since Adam fell in paradise.
Thomas Brooks

Christian holiness is not a matter of painstaking conformity to the individual precepts of an external law code; it is rather a question of the Holy Spirit's producing His fruit in the life, reproducing those graces which were seen in perfection in the life of Christ.
F.F. Bruce

Christ is the most perfect image of God, into which we are so renewed as to bear the image of God, in knowledge, purity, righteousness, and true holiness.
John Calvin

The Christian must be consumed by the conviction of the infinite beauty of holiness and the infinite damnability of sin.
Thomas Carlyle

The Bible as a whole speaks more of God's holiness than of His love.
Walter Chantry

If you Christians would live like Jesus Christ, India would be at your feet tomorrow.
Bara Dada

Contemplating Jesus' sacrifice is the highest motive to holiness.
J.L. Dagg

He that sees the beauty of holiness, or true moral good, sees the greatest and most important thing in the world. Unless this is seen, nothing is seen that is worth seeing: for there is no other true excellence or beauty.
Jonathan Edwards

A true love of God must begin with a delight in his holiness, and not with a delight in any other attribute; for no other attribute is truly lovely without this.
Jonathan Edwards

As God delights in his own beauty, he must necessarily delight in the creature's holiness which is a conformity to and participation of it, as truly as [the] brightness of a jewel, held in the sun's beams, is a participation or derivation of the sun's brightness, though immensely less in degree.
Jonathan Edwards

A worldly spirit loves to talk a lot but do nothing, striving for the exterior signs of holiness that people can see, with no desire for true piety and interior holiness of spirit.
Francis of Assisi

The more we appropriate God into our lives the more progress we make on the road of Christian godliness and holiness.
Madame Guyon

Nothing can make a man truly great but being truly good and partaking of God's holiness.
Matthew Henry

There is no greater holiness than in procuring and rejoicing in another's good.
George Herbert

Things that are holy are revealed only to men who are holy.
Hippocrates

Holiness is the end of redemption, for Christ gave Himself for us that He might redeem us from all iniquity and purify

unto Himself a peculiar people zealous of good works.
Charles Hodge

Holiness involves friendship with God. There has to be a moment in our relationship with God when he ceases to be just a Sunday acquaintance and becomes a weekday friend.
Basil Hume

If on our daily course our mind
Be set to hallow all we find,
New treasures still of countless price
God will provide for sacrifice.
The trivial round, the common task
Will furnish all we ought to ask;
Room to deny ourselves – a road
To bring us daily nearer God.
John Keble

It is when we notice the dirt that God is most present in us.
C.S. Lewis

How little people know who think that holiness is dull. When one meets the real thing … it is irresistible. If even 10 per cent of the world's population had it, would not the whole world be converted and happy before a year's end?
C.S. Lewis

Holiness is not something we are called upon to do in order that we may become something; it is something we are to do because of what we already are.
M. Lloyd-Jones

I am a great enemy to flies; when I have a good book, they flock upon it and parade up and down it, and soil it. It is just the same with the devil. When our hearts are purest, he comes and soils them.
Martin Luther

In the final analysis our greatest problem with holiness is not that our concepts of holiness are feeble, but that our hearts are rebellious. We are selfish, that's our problem. And the fact that we often won't admit our selfishness shows how deep the pride goes.
Floyd McClung

Study universal holiness of life. Your whole usefulness depends on this.
Robert Murray M'Cheyne

A holy life will produce the deepest impression. Lighthouses blow no horns; they only shine.
Dwight L. Moody

The foundation of true holiness and true Christian worship is the doctrine of the gospel, what we are to believe. So when Christian doctrine is neglected, forsaken, or corrupted, true holiness and worship will also be neglected, forsaken, and corrupted.
John Owen

There is no duty we perform for God that sin does not oppose. And the more spirituality or holiness there is in what we do, the greater is its enmity to it. Thus those who seek most for God, experience the strongest opposition.
John Owen

The serene beauty of a holy life is the most powerful influence in the world next to the power of God.
Blaise Pascal

The perfume of holiness travels even against the wind.
Indian proverb

It matters but little whether this eminent state of holiness be gained by a bold, energetic, and determined exercise of faith and prayer, or by a more gradual process – whether it be instantaneous or gradual, or both the one and the other. The great matter is, with each and all of us, that we lose no time, but arise at once, and "press toward the mark for the prize of the high calling of God in Christ Jesus."
Thomas N. Ralston

I am convinced that the first step toward attaining a higher standard of holiness is to realize more fully the amazing sinfulness of sin.
J.C. Ryle

Sound Protestant and Evangelical doctrine is useless if it is not accompanied by a holy life.
J.C. Ryle

True holiness is much more than tears and sighs ... A holy violence, a conflict, a warfare, a fight, a soldier's life, a wrestling are spoken of as characteristic of the true Christian.
J.C. Ryle

True holiness does not consist merely of believing and feeling, but of doing and bearing, and a practical exhibition of active and passive grace. Our tongues, our tempers, our natural passions and inclinations – our conduct as parents and children, masters and servants, husbands and wives, rulers and subjects – our dress, our employment of time, our behavior in business, our demeanor in sickness and health, in riches and poverty – all, all these are matters which are fully treated by inspired writers.
J.C. Ryle

I have had a deep conviction for many years that practical holiness and entire self-consecration to God are not sufficiently attended to by modern Christians in this country.
J.C. Ryle

To love Jesus is to love holiness.
David Smithers

Holiness consists of doing the will of God with a smile.
Mother Teresa of Calcutta

No one can be enlightened unless he be first cleansed or purified or stripped. So also, no one can be united to God unless he be first enlightened. Thus there are three stages: first, the purification; secondly, the enlightening, thirdly, the union.
Theologia Germanica

The stiff and wooden quality about our religious lives is a result of our lack of holy desire.
A. W. Tozer

Social religion is perfected when private religion is purified.
A. W. Tozer

We have learned to live with unholiness and have come to look upon it as the natural and expected thing.
A. W. Tozer

To be holy is so zealously to desire, so vastly to esteem, and so earnestly to endeavor it, that we would not for millions of gold and silver, decline, nor fail , nor mistake in a tittle.
Thomas Traherne

There is nothing negative or killjoy about holiness.
David Watson

He called them that they might be holy, and holiness is the beauty produced by His workmanship in them.
Thomas Watson

The neglect of prayer is a grand hindrance to holiness.
John Wesley

My aim is to reform the nation, particularly the church, and to spread scriptural holiness over the land.
John Wesley

It is an undoubted truth that every doctrine that comes from God, leads to God; and that which doth not tend to promote holiness is not of God.
George Whitefield

Let him who would indeed be a Christian learn from the lives of eminent Christians

the best ways to overcome temptation and to grow in every aspect of holiness.
William Wilberforce

Progress in holiness can best be measured not by the length of time we spend in prayer, not by the number of times we go to church, not by the amount of money we contribute to God's work, not by the range and depth of our knowledge of the Bible, but rather by the quality of our personal relationships.
Stephen F. Winward

Holiness

Rules and Instructions for a Holy Life
Robert Leighton, DD, (1611-1684)
Archbishop of Glasgow

For disposing you the better to observe these rules, and profit by them, be pleased to take the following advices.

1. Put all your trust in the special and singular mercy of God, that he, for his mercy's sake and of his holy goodness, will help and bring you to perfection; not that absolute perfection is attainable here, but the meaning is, to high degrees of that spiritual and divine life, which is always growing, and tending toward the absolute perfection above but in some persons comes nearer to that, and riseth higher, even here, than in the most. If you, with hearty and fervent desires, do continually wish and long for it, and with most humble devotion, daily pray unto God, and call for it, and with all diligence do busily labor and travel to come to it, undoubtedly it shall be given you; for you must not think it sufficient to use exercises, as though they had such virtues in them, that of themselves alone they could make such as do use them perfect; for, neither those, nor any other, whatever they be, can of themselves, by their use only, bring unto perfection. But our merciful Lord God, of his own goodness, when you seek with hearty desires and fervent sighings, maketh you to find it when you ask daily with devout prayer, then he giveth it to you; and when you continually, with unwearied labor and travel, knock perseveringly, then he doth mercifully open unto you; and because that those exercises do teach you to seek, ask, and knock, yea, they are none other but very devout petitions, seekings, and spiritual pulsations for the merciful help of God; therefore they are very profitable means to come to perfection by God's grace.

2. Let no particular exercise hinder your public and standing duties to God and your neighbors, but for these rather intermit the other for a time, and then return to them as soon as you can.

3. If in time of your spiritual exercise you find yourself drawn to any better, or to as good a contemplation as that is, follow the track of that good motion so long as it shall last.

4. Always take care to follow such exercises of devout thoughts, withal putting in practice such lessons as they contain and excite to.

5. Though at first ye feel no sweetness in such exercises, yet be not discouraged, nor induced to leave them, but continue them faithfully, whatsoever pain or spiritual trouble ye feel; for doing them for God and his honor, and finding none other present fruit, yet you shall have an excellent reward for your diligent labor and your pure intentions.

And let not your falling short of these models and rules, nor your daily manifold imperfections and faults, dishearten you; but continue steadfast in your desires, purposes, and endeavors, and ever ask the best, aim at the best, and hope the best, being sorry that you can do no better, and they shall be a most acceptable sacrifice in the sight of God, "and in due time you shall reap, if you faint not": and of all such instructions, let your rule be to follow them as much as you can; but not too scrupulously thinking your labor lost if you do not exactly and strictly answer them in everything; purpose still better, and, by God's grace, all shall be well.

SECTION I

Rule 1. Exercise thyself in the knowledge and deep consideration of our Lord God, calling humbly to mind how excellent and incomprehensible he is; and this knowledge shalt thou rather endeavor to obtain by fervent desire and devout prayer than with high study and outward labor; it is the singular gift of God, and certainly very precious. Pray then,

2. "Most gracious Lord, whom to know is the very bliss and felicity of man's soul, and yet none can know thee, unless thou wilt open and show thyself unto him, vouchsafe of thy infinite mercy now and ever to enlighten my heart and mind to know thee, and thy most holy and perfect will, to the honor and glory of thy name. Amen."

3. Then lift up thy heart to consider, not with too great violence, but sobriety, the eternal and infinite of God, who created all things by his excellent wisdom – his unmeasurable goodness, and incomprehensible love; for he is very and only God, most excellent, most high, most glorious, the everlasting and unchangeable goodness, and eternal substance, a charity infinite, so excellent and ineffable in himself, that all dignity, perfection, and goodness that is possible to be spoke or thought of, cannot sufficiently express the smallest part thereof.

4. Consider that he is the natural place, the center, and rest of thy soul: if thou then think of the most blessed Trinity, muse not too much thereon, but, with devout and obedient faith, meekly and lowly adore and worship.

5. Consider Jesus the redeemer and husband of thy soul, and walk with him as becomes a chaste spouse, with reverence and lowly shamefulness, obedience and submission.

6. Then turn to the deep, profound consideration of thyself, thine own nothingness, and thy extreme defilement and pollution, thy natural aversion from God, and that thou must by conversion to him again, and union with him, be made happy.

7. Consider thyself and all creatures as nothing, in comparison of thy Lord: that so thou mayst not only be content, but desirous to be unknown, or, being known, to be contemned and despised of all men, yet without thy faults or deservings, as much as thou canst.

8. "O God, infuse into my heart thy heavenly light and blessed charity, that I may know and love thee above all things; and above all things loathe and abhor myself Grant that I may be so ravished in the wonder and love of thee, that I may forget myself and all things, feel neither prosperity nor adversity, may not fear to suffer all the pains of this world, rather than to be parted and pulled away from thee, whose perfections infinitely exceed all thought and understanding. Oh! let me find thee more inwardly and verily present with me than I am with myself, and make me most circumspect how I do use myself in the presence of thee, my holy Lord. 'Cause me always to remember how everlasting and constant is the love thou bearest toward me, and such a charity and continual care as though thou hadst "no more creatures in heaven or earth besides me. What am I? A vile worm and filth".'

9. Then aspire to a great contrition for thy sins, and hatred of them; and abhorring of thyself for them, then crave pardon in the blood of Jesus Christ, and then offer up thyself, soul and body, an oblation or sacrifice in and through him – as they did of old, laying wood on the altar, and then burning up all; so this shall be a sacrifice of sweet savor, and very acceptable to God.

10. Offer all that thou hast, to be nothing, to use nothing of all that thou hast about thee, and is called thine, but to his honor and glory. and resolve, through his grace, to use all the powers of thy soul, and every member of thy body, to his service, as formerly thou hast done to sin.

11. Consider the passion of thy Lord; how he was buffeted, scourged, reviled, stretched with nails on the cross, and hung on it three long hours, suffered all the contempt and shame, and all the inconceivable pain of it, for thy sake.

12. Then turn thy heart to him, humbly saying, "Lord Jesus, whereas I daily fall,

and am always ready to sin, vouchsafe me grace as oft as I shall, to rise again; let me never presume, but most meekly and humbly acknowledge my wretchedness and frailty, and repent, with a firm purpose to amend; and let me not despair because of my great frailty, but ever trust in thy most loving mercy, and readiness to forgive.

SECTION II

1. Thou shalt have much to do in mortifying of thy five senses, which must be all shut up in the crucified humility of Jesus Christ, and be as they were plainly dead.

2. Thou must now learn to have a continual eye inwardly to thy soul, and spiritual life, as thou hast used heretofore to have all thy mind and regard to outward pleasure and worldly things.

3. Thou must submit and give thyself up unto the discipline of Jesus, and become his scholar, resigning and compelling thyself altogether to obey him in all things: so that thy willing thou utterly and perfectly do cast away from thee, and do nothing without his licence at every word thou wilt speak, at every morsel thou wilt eat, at every stirring or moving of every article or member of thy body, thou must ask leave of him in thy heart, and ask thyself whether, having so done, that be according to his will and holy example, and with sincere intention of his glory, hence,

4. Even the most necessary actions of thy life, though lawful, yet must thus be offered up with a true intention unto God, in the union of the most holy works and blessed merits of Christ, saying: "Lord Jesus, bind up in the merits of thy blessed senses all my feeling and sensation, and all my wits and senses, that I never hereafter use them to any sensuality!"

5. Thus labor to come to this union and knitting up of thy senses in God and thy Lord Jesus, and remain so fast to the cross that thou never part from it, and still behave thy body and all thy senses as in the presence of thy Lord God, and commit all things to the most trusty providence of thy loving Lord, who will then order all things delectably and sweetly for thee; reckon all things besides for right naught, and thus mayst thou come unto wonderful illuminations, and spiritual influence from the Lord thy God.

6. If for his love, thou canst crucify, renounce, and forsake perfectly thyself, and all things; thou must so crucify thyself to all things, and love and desire God only, with thy care and whole heart, that in this most steadfast and strong knot and union unto the will of God, if he would create hell in thee here, thou mightest be ready to offer thyself, by his grace, for his eternal honor and glory, to suffer it, and that purely for his will and pleasure.

7. Thou must keep thy memory clean and pure, as it were a wedlock chamber, from all strange thoughts, fancies and imaginations, and it must be trimmed and adorned with holy meditations and virtues of Christ's holy crucified life and passion: that God may continually and ever rest therein.

Prayer

8. "Lord, instead of knowing thee, I have sought to know wickedness and sin; and whereas my will and desire were created to love thee, I have lost that love, and declined to the creatures; while my memory ought to be filled with thee, I have painted it with the imagery of innumerable fancies, not only of all creatures, but of all sinful wickedness. Oh! blot out these by thy blood, and imprint thine own blessed image in my soul, blessed Jesus, by that blood that issued out from thy most loving heart when thou hanged on the cross. So knit my will to thy most holy will, that I may have no other will but thine, and may be most heartily and fully content with whatsoever thou wilt do to me in this world; yea, if thou wilt, so that I hate thee not, nor sin against thee, but retain thy love, make me suffer the greatest pains."

SECTION III

Rule 1. Exercise thyself to the perfect abnegation of all things which may let or impede this union; mortify in thee every thing that is God, nor for God, or which he willeth and loveth not; resigning and yielding up to the high pleasure of God, all love and affection for transitory things; desire neither to have nor hold them, nor bestow or give them, but only for the pure love and honor of God: put away superfluous and unnecessary things, and affect not even things necessary. 2. Mortify all affection to, and seeking of thyself, which is so natural to men, in all the good they desire, and in all the good they do, and in all the evil they suffer; yea, by the inordinate love of the gifts and graces of God, instead of himself, they fall into spiritual pride, gluttony and greediness.

3. Mortify all affection to and delectation in meat and drink, and vain thoughts and fancies, which though they proceed not to consent, yet they defile the soul, and grieve the Holy Ghost, and do great damage to the spiritual life.

4. Imprint on thy heart the image of Jesus crucified, the impressions of his humility, poverty, mildness, and all his holy virtues; let thy thoughts of him turn into affection, and thy knowledge into love; for the love of God doth most purely work in the mortification of nature; the life of the spirit purifying the higher powers of the soul, begets the solitariness and departure from all creatures, and the influence and flowing into God.

5. Solitude, silence, and the strait keeping of the heart, are the foundations and grounds of a spiritual life.

6. Do all thy necessary and outward works without any trouble or carefulness of mind, and bear thy mind amidst all, always inwardly lifted up and elevated to God, following always more the inward exercise of love than the outward acts of virtue.

7. To this can no man come unless he be rid and delivered from all things under God, and be so swallowed up in God that he can contemn and despise himself and all things; for the pure love of God maketh the spirit pure and simple, and so free, that without any pain and labor, it can at all times turn and recollect itself in God.

8. Mortify all bitterness of heart toward thy neighbors, and all vain complacency in thyself, all vain-glory and desire of esteem, in words and deeds, in gifts and graces. To this thou shalt come by a more clear and perfect knowledge and consideration of thy own vileness; and by knowing God to be the fountain of all grace and goodness.

9. Mortify all affection toward inward, sensible, spiritual delight in grace, and the following devotion with sensible sweetness in the lower faculties or powers of the soul, which are no ways real sanctity and holiness in themselves, but certain gifts of God to help our infirmity.

10. Mortify all curious investigation or search, all speculation and knowledge of unnecessary things, human or divine; for the perfect life of a Christian consisteth not in high knowledge, but profound meekness; in holy simplicity, and in the ardent love of God; wherein we ought to desire to die to all affection to ourselves, and all things below God; yea, to sustain pain and dereliction, that we may be perfectly knit and united to God, and be perfectly swallowed up in him.

11. Mortify all undue scrupulousness of conscience, and trust in the goodness of God; for our doubting and scruples oft times arise from inordinate self-love, and therefore vex us; they do no good, neither work any real amendment in us; they cloud the soul, and darken faith, and cool love, and it is only the stronger beams of these that can dispel them; and the stronger that faith and divine confidence is in us, and the hotter divine love is, the soul is so much the more excited and enabled to all the parts of holiness, to mortifications of passions and lusts, to more patience in adversity, and to more thankfulness in all estates.

12. Mortify all impatience in all pains and troubles, whether from the hands of God or men, all desire of revenge, all resentment of injuries, and, by the pure love of God, love thy very persecutors as if they were thy dearest friends.

13. Finally, mortify thy own will in all things, with full resignation of thyself to suffer all dereliction outward and inward, all pain, and pressures, and desolations, and that for the pure love of God: for from self-love, and self-will, spring all sin, and all pain.

Prayer

14. "O Jesus, my Savior, thy blessed humility! impress it on my heart, make me most sensible of

thy infinite dignity, and of my own vileness, that I may hate myself as a thing of naught, and be

willing to be despised, and trodden upon by all, as the vilest mire of the streets, that I may still

retain these words, 'I am nothing, I have nothing, I can do nothing, and I desire nothing but one."

SECTION IV

1. Never do any thing with propriety and singular affection, being too earnest, or too much given to it; but with continual meekness of heart and mind, lie at the foot of God, and say, "Lord, I desire nothing, neither in myself nor in any creature, save only to know and execute thy blessed will," saying always in thy heart, "Lord, what wouldst thou have me to do? Transform my will into thine, fill full and swallow up, as it were, my affections with thy love, and with an insatiable desire to honor thee, and despise myself."

2. If thou aspire to attain to the perfect knitting and union with God, know that it requireth a perfect exploitation and denudation, or bare nakedness, and utter forsaking of all sin, yea, of all creatures, and of thyself particularly: even that thy mind and understanding, thy affections and desires, thy memory and fancy, be made bare of all things in the world, and all sensual pleasures in them; so as thou wouldst be content that the bread which thou eatest had no more savor than a stone, and yet, for his honor and glory that created the bread, thou art pleased that it savoreth so well; but yet from the delectation thou feelest in it, turn thy heart to his praises and love that made it.

3. The more perfectly thou livest in the abstraction and departure, and bare nakedness of thy mind from all creatures, the more nakedly and purely shalt thou have the fruition of the Lord thy God, and shalt live the more heavenly and angelical a life. Therefore,

4. Labor above all things most exactly to forsake all for him; and chiefly to forsake and contemn thyself, purely loving him; and in a manner forgetting thyself and all things for the vehement burning love of him, that thou wilt take no heed what is sweet or bitter, neither wilt thou consider time nor place, nor mark one person from another, for the wonder and love of thy Lord God, and the desire of his blessed will, pleasure and honor in all things; and whatsoever good thou dost, know and think that God doth it, and not thou.

5. Choose always, to the best of thy skill, what is most to God's honor, and most like unto Christ and his example and most profitable to thy neighbor, and most against thy own proper will, and least serviceable to thy own praise and exaltation.

6. If thou continue faithful in this spiritual work and travel, God at length, without doubt, will hear thy knocking, and will deliver thee from all thy spiritual trouble, from all the tumults. noise and encumbrance of cogitations and fancies, and from all earthly affections, which thou canst by no better means put away, than by continual and fervent desire of the love of God.

7. Do not at any time let or hinder his working, by following thine own will; for, behold how much thou dost the more perfectly forsake thine own will, and the love of thyself, and of all worldly things, so much the more deeply and safely shalt thou be knit unto God, and increase in his true and pure love.

SECTION V

1. If thou still above all things seek that union, thou must transfund and pour thy whole will into the high pleasure of God; and whatsoever befalls thee, thou must be without murmuring and retraction of heart, accepting it most joyfully for his love, whose will and work it is.

2. Let thy great joy and comfort evermore be, to have his pleasure done in thee, though in pains, sickness, persecutions, oppressions, or inward griefs and pressures of heart, coldness or barrenness of mind, darkening of thy will and senses, or any

temptations spiritual or bodily. And,

3. Under any of these be always wary thou turn not to sinful delights, nor to sensual and carnal pleasures, nor set thy heart on vain things, seeking comfort thereby, nor in any ways be idle, but always as thou canst, compel and force thyself to some good spiritual exercise or bodily work; and though they be then unsavory to thee, yet are they not the less, but the more acceptable to God.

4. Take all afflictions as tokens of God's love to thee, and trials of thy love to him, and purposes of kindness to enrich thee, and increase more plentifully in thee his blessed gifts and spiritual graces, if thou persevere faithfully unto the end, nor leaving off the vehement desire of his love, and thy own perfection.

5. Offer up thyself wholly to him, and fix the point of thy love upon his most blessed love, and there let thy soul and heart rest and delight, and be, as it were, resolved and melted most happily into the blessed Godhead; and then take that as a token, and be assured by it, that God will grant thy lovely and holy desire; then shalt thou feel, in a manner, no difference betwixt honor and shame, joy and sorrow; but whatsoever thou perceivest to appertain to the honor of thy Lord, be it ever so hard and unpleasant to thyself, thou wilt heartily embrace it, yea, with all thy might follow and desire it; yet, when thou hast done what is possible for thee, thou wilt think thou hast done nothing at all; yea, thou shalt be ashamed, and detest thyself, that thou hast so wretchedly and imperfectly served so noble and worthy a Lord; and therefore thou wilt desire and endeavor every hour to do and suffer greater and more perfect things than hitherto thou hast done, forgetting the things that are behind, and pressing forward, etc.

6. If thou hast in any measure attained to love and abide in God, then mayst thou keep the powers of thy soul and thy senses, as it were, shut up in God, from gadding out to any worldly thing or vanity, as much as possible, where they have so joyful a security and safeness: satiate thy soul in him, and in all other things still see his blessed presence.

7. Whatsoever befalleth thee, receive it not from the hand of any creature, but from him alone, and render back all to him, seeking in all things his pleasure and honor – the purifying and subduing thyself What can harm thee, when all must first touch God, within whom thou hast inclosed thyself?

8. When thou perceivest thyself thus knit to God, and thy soul more fast and joined nearer to him than to thine own body, then shalt thou know his everlasting, and incomprehensible, and ineffable goodness, and the true nobleness of thy soul that came from him, and was made to be reunited to him.

9. If thou wouldst ascend and come up to thy Lord God, thou must climb up by the wounds of his blessed humanity, that remain, as it were, for that use; and when thou art got up there, thou wouldst rather suffer death than willingly commit any sin.

10. Entering into Jesus, thou castest thyself in an infinite sea of goodness, that more easily drowns and happily swallows thee up than the ocean does a drop of water. Then shalt thou be hid and transformed in him, and shalt often be as thinking without thought, and knowing without knowledge, and loving without love, comprehended of him whom thou canst not comprehend.

SECTION VI

1. Too much desire to please men mightily prejudgeth the pleasing of God.

2. Too great earnestness and vehemency, and too greedy delight in bodily work and external doings, scattereth and loseth the tranquillity and calmness of the mind.

3. Cast all thy care on God, and commit all to his good pleasure; laud, and praise, and applaud him in all things small and great; forsake thy own will, and deliver up thyself freely and cheerfully to the will of God, without reserve or exception, in prosperity, in adversity, sweet or sour, to have or to want, to live or to die.

4. Disunite thy heart from all things, and unite it only to God.

5. Remember often, and devoutly, the life and passion, the death and resurrection of our Savior, Jesus.

6. Descant not on other men's deeds, but consider thine own; forget other men's faults, and remember thine own.

7. Never think highly of thyself, nor despise any other man.

8. Keep silence and retirement as much as thou canst, and through God's grace they will keep thee from snares and offences.

9. Lift up thy heart often to God, and desire in all things his assistance.

IO. Let thy heart be filled, and wholly taken up with the love of God, and of thy neighbor, and do all that thou dost in that sincere charity and love.

The Sum is:

1. Remember always the presence of God.
2. Rejoice always in the will of God. And,
3. Direct all to the glory of God.

SECTION VII

1. Little love, little trust; but a great love brings a great confidence.

2. That is a blessed hope that doth not slacken us in our duty, nor maketh us secure, but increaseth both a cheerful will, and gives greater strength to mortification and all obedience.

3. What neediest thou, or why travelest thou about so many things; think upon one, desire and love one and thou shalt find great rest. Therefore,

4. Wherever thou be, let this voice of God be still in thine ear: "My son, return inwardly to thy heart, abstract thyself from all things, and mind me only." Thus:

5. With a pure mind in God, clean and bare from the memory of all things, remaining unmoveably in him, thou shalt think and desire nothing but him alone; as though there were nothing else in the world but he and thou only together; that all thy faculties and powers being thus re-collected into God, thou mayst become one spirit with him.

6. Fix thy mind on thy crucified Savior, and remember continually his great meekness, love, and obedience, his pure chastity, his unspeakable patience, and all the holy virtues of his humanity.

7. Think on his mighty power and infinite goodness; how he created and redeemed thee, how he justifieth thee, and worketh in thee all virtues, graces, and goodness; and thus remember him, until thy memory turn into love and affection. Therefore,

8. Draw thy mind thus from all creatures, unto a certain silence, and rest from the jangling and company of all things below God; and when thou canst come to this, then is thy heart a place meet and ready for thy Lord God to abide in, there to talk with thy soul.

9. True humility gaineth and overcometh God Almighty, and maketh thee also apt and meet to receive all graces and gifts; but, alas! who can say that he hath this blessed meekness? it being so hard, so uncertain, so secret and unknown a thing to forsake and mortify perfectly and exactly thyself, and that most venomous worm of all goodness, vain-glory.

10. Commit all to the high providence of God, and suffer nothing to rest or enter into thy heart, save only God: all things in the earth are too base to take up thy love or care, or to trouble thy noble heart, thy immortal and heavenly mind. Let them care and sorrow or rejoice about these things who are of the world, for whom Christ would not pray.

11. Thou canst not please nor serve two masters at once; thou canst not love divers and contrary things; if, then, thou wouldst know what thou lovest, mark well what thou thinkest most upon. Leave earth, and have heaven; leave the world, and have God.

12. All sin and vice springeth from the property of our own will; all virtue and perfection cometh and groweth from the mortifying of it, and the resigning of it wholly to the pleasure and will of God.

Holy Communion

See also: Lord's suffer

In the celebration of this sacrament we receive the renewed assurance of the forgiveness of our sins, and of our fellowship with Christ; unite with one

another as members of His Body; and rejoice in the hope of His return in glory. Therefore, we will commune faithfully and thus renew our pledge of allegiance to Him.
Moravian Covenant for Christian living

Holy Spirit

The Spirit searches all things, even the deep things of God.
The Bible, 1 Corinthians 2:10

Do you not know that your body is a temple of the Holy Spirit, who is in you, whom you have received from God? You are not your own.
The Bible, 1 Corinthians 6:19

The Holy Spirit is not something that stands by itself, something that we can pray for and have as a thing in itself, it is born from Love and is of Love, all its treasures are of Love, and if we are to believe our Gospels it is received by Love and Love only.
Florence Allshorn

Happy the man whose words come from the Holy Spirit and not from himself.
Anthony of Padua

We share in the divine nature through our sharing of the Spirit.
Athanasius

The Holy Spirit, object of faith, is also an object of prayer: we must not only pray that we receive the Holy Spirit. We must pray to him.
Karl Barth

As a foolish church presupposes the Holy Spirit's presence and action in its own existence, in its offices and sacraments, ordinations, consecrations, and absolutions, so a foolish theology presupposes the Holy Spirit. Only where the Spirit is sighed, cried, and prayed for does he become present and newly active.
Karl Barth

The Spirit bears witness. Ecstasy and enlightenment, inspiration and intuition

are not necessary. Happy is the man who is worthy of these; but woe unto us if we wait for such experiences; woe unto us if we do not perceive that these things are of secondary importance.
Karl Barth

We are all strings in the concert of his joy; the spirit from his mouth strikes the note and the tune of our strings.
Jakob Boehme

There is no worse screen to block out the Spirit than confidence in our own intelligence.
John Calvin

If we recognize the Spirit of God as the unique fountain of truth, we shall never despise the truth wherever it may appear, unless we wish to do dishonor to the Spirit of God.
John Calvin

True discrimination between right and wrong does not then depend on the acuteness of our intelligence, but on the wisdom of the Spirit.
John Calvin

All of us who have received one and the same Spirit, that is, the Holy Spirit, are in a sense blended together with one another and with God. For if Christ, together with the Father's and his own Spirit, comes to dwell in each of us, though we are many, still the Spirit is one and undivided. He binds together the spirits of each and every one of us, and makes all appear as one in him. For just as the power of Christ's sacred flesh unites those in whom it dwells into one body, I think that in the same way the one and undivided Spirit of God, who dwells in all, leads all into spiritual unity.
Cyril of Alexandria

The Spirit of God is given to the true saints to dwell in them, as his proper lasting abode; and to influence their hearts, as a principle of new nature or as a divine

supernatural spring of life and action.
Jonathan Edwards

A general rule for the good use of time is to accustom oneself to live in a continual dependence on the Spirit of God.
F. Fénelon

For Paul the Spirit was an experienced reality.
H. Gunkel

Spiritual rest maketh no man idle, spiritual walking maketh no man weary.
Nathaniel Hardy

Those who have the gale of the Holy Spirit go forward even in sleep. If the vessel of our soul is still tossed with winds and storms, let us awake the Lord, who reposes in it, and He will quickly calm the sea.
Brother Lawrence

The Holy Spirit of grace desires to disturb your sleep. Blessed are you if you awaken.
Lars Linderot

The Holy Ghost has called me by the Gospel, and illuminated me with His gifts, and sanctified and preserved me in the true faith.
Martin Luther

Than anyone should be represented as just and God-fearing who does not have the Spirit would be the same as if Belial were called Christ.
Martin Luther

The unconverted do not like to hear much about the Holy Spirit.
Robert Murray M'Cheyne

His task is to bring about the unity of the human race in the Body of Christ, but he also imparts to this unity a personal, and hence diversified, character.
John Meyendorff

Thou, O Spirit, that dost prefer
Before all Temples th' upright heart and
pure.
John Milton

There is not a better evangelist in the world than the Holy Spirit.
Dwight L. Moody

All other ways of mortification are vain, all helps leave us helpless, it must be done by the Spirit.
John Owen

Pardon comes not to the soul alone; or rather, Christ comes not to the soul with pardon only! It is that which He opens the door and enters by, but He comes with a Spirit of life and power.
John Owen

Every time we say, "I believe in the Holy Spirit," we mean that we believe that there is a living God able and willing to enter human personality and change it.
J.B. Phillips

The testimony of the Spirit is that alone by which the true knowledge of God has been, is and can be only revealed.
The Chief Principles of the Christian Religion as Professed by the People Called the Quakers

The Pentecostal power, when you sum it all up, is just more of God's love. If it does not bring more love, it is simply a counterfeit.
William J. Seymour

We do not need to wait for the Holy Spirit to come: he came on the day of Pentecost. He has never left the church.
John Stott

I believe in the surprises of the Holy Spirit.
Leon Joseph Cardinal Suenens

I found that I believed in the action of the Holy Spirit, but in a limited sphere; in me the Spirit could not call forth from the organ all the melody he wished; some of the pipes did not function, because they had not been used.
Leon Joseph Suenens

God is especially present in the hearts of His people, by His Holy Spirit; and indeed the

hearts of holy men are temples in the truth of things, and in type and shadow they are heaven itself. For God reigns in the hearts of His servants; there is His Kingdom.
Jeremy Taylor

The Holy Spirit is not a blessing from God, He is God.
Colin Urquhart

The renewal of our natures is a work of great importance. It is not to be done in a day. We have not only a new house to build up, but an old one to pull down.
George Whitefield

I feel it's very important that we direct this "refreshing" and "enabling" move of the Spirit to the New Testament works of the church, that is to say, having been refreshed, we now must channel these people into work that would express that refreshing in solid, biblical context. I believe that if we channel this energy away from a "bless me" kind of focus to a "bless them" kind of focus we will indeed be utilizing this fresh anointing in a biblically appropriate fashion.
John Wimber

Holy Spirit, Baptism of
The baptism of the Holy Ghost will do for you what a phone booth did for Clark Kent – it will change you into a different human being.
Rod Parsley

I was baptized with the Holy Spirit when I took Him by simple faith in the Word of God.
R.A. Torrey

Holy Spirit, Deposit of
[He] … set his seal of ownership on us, and put his Spirit in our hearts as a deposit, guaranteeing what is to come.
The Bible, 2 Corinthians 1:22

Guard the good deposit that was entrusted to you–guard it with the help of the Holy Spirit who lives in us.
The Bible, 2 Timothy 1:14

Holy Spirit, Fruit of the
But the fruit of the Spirit is love, joy, peace, patience, kindness, goodness, faithfulness, gentleness and self-control.
The Bible, Galatians 5:22, 23

The Spirit of God first imparts love; he next inspires hope, and then gives liberty; and this is about the last thing we have in many of our churches.
Dwight L. Moody

Holy Spirit, Gifts of
There are different kinds of gifts, but the same Spirit.
The Bible, 1 Corinthians 12:4

But eagerly desire the greater gifts. And now I will show you the most excellent way.
The Bible, 1 Corinthians 12:31

Some people drive out devils … some can see into the future … others heal the sick through the laying on of hands … and even the dead have been raised before now and have remained with us for many years.
Irenaeus

To St Paul, the Church of Christ does not appear as some administrative organization, but as a living, organic ensemble of gifts, charisms, and services. The Holy Spirit is given to all Christians, and to each one in particular; and he in turn gives to each and every one gifts and charisms "which differ according to the grace bestowed upon us" (Rm 12:6).
Leon Joseph Suenens

We believe the Holy Spirit lives in us as believers and brings love, joy, peace, patience, kindness, goodness, faithfulness, humility and self-control into our lives. He works in and through us with His charismatic gifts.
The Toronto Airport Christian Fellowship

Just as important as knowing what gift God has given you is knowing which gifts He hasn't given you.
C. Peter Wagner

Jesus promised his disciples that they would do the same works that he did during his earthly ministry, and even "greater works" (John 14:17). He then went on to speak of the coming of the Holy Spirit. It was through the power and gifts of the Spirit that this promise was fulfilled.
David Watson

Holy Spirit, Indwelling of the
The philosophers of old made reason the sole ruler of man and listened only to her, as the arbiter of conduct. But Christian philosophy makes her move aside and give complete submission to the Holy Spirit, so that the individual no longer lives, but Christ lives and reigns in him (Galatians 2:20).
John Calvin

Ephesians 5:18 is not just an experience to be enjoyed but a command to be obeyed. If we do not open ourselves to a daily encounter with the Holy Spirit, then the inevitable conclusion is that we are disobedient Christians.
Dwight L. Moody

Holy Spirit, Led by
When led of the Spirit, the child of God must be as ready to wait as to go, as prepared to be silent as to speak.
Lewis Sperry Chafer

Holy Spirit, Life in the
Life in the Spirit is ... to be a ceaseless personal response to the call and claim of Jesus in each new situation by the individual disciple from within the Christ-centered fellowship.
John V. Taylor

Holy Spirit, Power of
The Holy Spirit is the secret of the power in my life. All I have to do is surrender my life to Him.
Kathryn Kuhlman

There is no human power that can replace the power of the Spirit.
Lewi Pethrus

Holy Spirit and free will
Our nature is so vitiated, and has such a propensity to sin, that unless it is renewed by the Holy Spirit, no man can do or will what is good of himself.
Confession of Basil

God works immediately by his Spirit in and on the wills of his saints.
John Owen

Holy Spirit and organization
On the mountains, torrents flow right along, cutting their own courses. But on the plains canals have to be dug out painfully by men so that the water might flow. So among those who live on the heights with God, the Holy Spirit makes its way through of its own accord, whereas those who devote little time to prayer and communion with God have to organize painfully.
Sadhu Sunder Singh

Holy Spirit and prayer
In the same way, the Spirit helps us in our weakness. We do not know what we ought to pray for, but the Spirit himself intercedes for us with groans that words cannot express. And he who searches our hearts knows the mind of the Spirit, because the Spirit intercedes for the saints in accordance with God's will.
The Bible, Romans 8:26,27

Holy Spirit and the Bible
I knew the Bible from beginning to end, but could find no consolation in Holy Writ; and my spirit, as if moving in a great storm, arose in God, carrying with it my whole heart, mind and will and wrestled with the love and mercy of God, that his blessing might descend upon me, that my mind might be illumined with his Holy Spirit, that I might understand his will and get rid of my sorrow.
Jacob Boehme

The Spirit breathes upon the Word,
And brings the truth to sight.
William Cowper

Holy Spirit and the Christian life

The best men in the estate of grace would be in darkness, and call their estate into question, if the Holy Ghost did not convince them, and answer all cavils for them; and therefore we must not only be convinced at first by the Spirit, but in our continued course of Christianity.
Richard Sibbes

Holy Spirit and the Church

If you do not join in what the church is doing, you have no share in this Spirit. ... For where the church is, there is the Spirit of God; and where the Spirit of God is, there is the church and every kind of grace.
Irenaeus

The Spirit is given through the Word, through proclamation of the gospel and sacrament, through Word and sacrament, and through Baptism. Where the Word is, the Spirit is at work. The Spirit does its work on earth through the church.
Lutheran Book of Condord

The great heresy of the Church of the present day is unbelief in this Spirit.
George Macdonald

A church in the land without the Spirit is rather a curse than a blessing.
C.H. Spurgeon

For the Holy Spirit did come on the day of Pentecost, and has never left his church.
John Stott

Holy Spirit and work

We need the Spirit of Christ, without whom all our works are only worthy of condemnation.
Martin Luther

For the attainment of divine knowledge, we are directed to combine a dependence on God's Spirit with our own researches. Let us, then, not presume to separate what God has thus united.
Charles Simeon

Holy Spirit as Teacher

Christ teaches by the Spirit of wisdom in the heart, opening the understanding to the Spirit of revelation in the word.
Matthew Henry

Holy Spirit guarantees heaven

Now it is God who has made us for this very purpose and has given us the Spirit as a deposit, guaranteeing what is to come.
The Bible, 2 Corinthians 5:5

Holy Spirit's ministry

Jesus has gone to prepare a place for us, and the Holy Spirit has been sent to prepare us for that place.
Author unknown

The Holy Spirit convicts of sin, man does not.
Oswald Chambers

The Holy Spirit's great task is to carry on the work for which Jesus sacrificed his throne and his life – the redemption of fallen humanity.
Alan Redpath

The marks of the Spirit's presence ... [are] biblical teaching, loving fellowship, living worship, and an ongoing, outgoing evangelism.
John Stott

The Holy Spirit is the source of community and the Spirit's work is more related to the building of the community than to the edification of the isolated individual.
Jim Wallis

The Holy Spirit not only unites us, but also ensures our infinite diversity in the Church.
Kallistos Ware

Home
See also: Hospitality

Unless the Lord builds the house, those who build it labor in vain.
Psalm 127.1 NRSV

The strength of a nation is derived from the integrity of its homes.
Confucius

Let a man behave in his own house as a guest.
Ralph Waldo Emerson

If you cannot exhibit true love at home, you cannot exhibit it in marriage.
Max and Vivian Rice

This is the true nature of home – it is the place of peace; the shelter, not only from injury, but from all terror, doubt and division.
John Ruskin

The goal of every married couple, indeed, every Christian home, should be to make Christ the Head, the Counselor and the Guide.
Paul Sadler

Homosexuality
We are not at liberty to urge the Christian homosexual to celibacy and to a spreading of his relationships, unless support for the former and opportunities for the latter are available in genuine love.
Dr David Atkinson

God loves homosexuals as much as anyone else. I think homosexuality is a sin, but no greater than idolatry and adultery. In my judgment, it's not that big.
Billy Graham

It is striking that every time homosexual practice is mentioned in the scriptures, it is condemned. There are only two ways one can neutralize the biblical witness against homosexual behavior: by gross misinterpretation or by moving away from a high view of Scripture.
Stanton L. Jones

Whether these matters are to be regarded as sport, or as earnest, we must not forget that this pleasure is held to have been granted by nature to male and female when conjoined for the work of procreation; the crime of male with male, or female with female, is an outrage on nature and a capital surrender to lust of pleasure.
Plato

Concerning homosexuality: This once brought hell out of heaven on Sodom.
C.H. Spurgeon

Honesty
Our lives improve only when we take chances – and the first and most difficult risk we can take is to be honest with ourselves.
Walter Anderson

Honesty is the first chapter of the book of wisdom.
Thomas Jefferson

An honest man's the noblest work of God.
Alexander Pope

Honor
Dignity does not consist in possessing honors, but in deserving them.
Aristotle

It ill becomes the servant to seek to be rich, and great, and honored in that world where his Lord was poor, and mean, and despised.
George Müller

Success without honor is an unseasoned dish; it will satisfy your hunger, but it won't taste good.
Joe Paterno

A godly mind prizes honor above worldly good.
Rembrandt

Honoring God
My heavenly bod [body] is just for God.
Samantha Fox, Headline in Sun newspaper in which Samantha Fox used to be their top topless Page Three Girl

Honors
Just as anyone who climbs a rotten ladder

risks his life, so are honors and power a danger for humility.
John Climacus

Hope

Though you have made me see troubles, many and bitter, you will restore my life again; from the depths of the earth you will again bring me up.
The Bible, Psalm 71:20

Hope deferred maketh the heart sick.
The Bible, Proverbs 13:12 KJV

Prisoners of hope.
The Bible, Zechariah 9:12 KJV

Be joyful in hope …
The Bible, Romans 12:11

For everything that was written in the past was written to teach us, so that through endurance and the encouragement of the Scriptures we might have hope.
The Bible, Romans 15:4

May the God of hope fill you with all joy and peace as you trust in him, so that you may overflow with hope by the power of the Holy Spirit.
The Bible, Romans 15:13

I pray also that the eyes of your heart may be enlightened in order that you may know the hope to which he has called you, the riches of his glorious inheritance in the saints, and his incomparably great power for us who believe.
The Bible, Ephesians 1:18,19

Praise be to the God and Father of our Lord Jesus Christ! In his great mercy he has given us new birth into a living hope through the resurrection of Jesus Christ from the dead …
The Bible, 1 Peter 1:3

Hope to the end.
The Bible, 1 Peter 1:13 KJV

Never deprive someone of hope – it may be all they have.
Author unknown

A religious hope does not only bear up the mind under her sufferings, but makes her rejoice in them.
Joseph Addison

If they can make penicillin out of moldy bread, they can sure make something out of you.
Muhammad Ali

When you say a situation or a person is hopeless, you are slamming the door in the face of God.
Charles Allen

The most hopeful people in the world are the young and the drunk. The first because they have little experience of failure, and the second because they have succeeded in drowning theirs.
Thomas Aquinas

Hope is a waking dream.
Aristotle

What can be hoped for which is not believed?
Augustine of Hippo

Cursed is everyone who places his hope in man.
Augustine of Hippo

Hope is a good breakfast, but it is a bad supper.
Francis Bacon

In God alone is there faithfulness and faith in the trust that we may hold to him, to his promise, and to his guidance. To hold to God is to rely on the fact that God is there for me, and to live in this certainty.
Karl Barth

The glory of the star, the glory of the sun – we must not lose either in the other. We must not be so full of the hope of heaven that we cannot do our work on the earth; we must not be so lost in the work of the earth that we shall not be inspired by the hope of heaven.
Phillips Brooks

The word "hope" I take for faith; and indeed hope is nothing else but the constancy of faith.
John Calvin

If seeds in the black earth can turn into such beautiful roses, what might not the heart of man become in its long journey toward the stars?
Gilbert Keith Chesterton

If you do not hope you will never discover what is beyond your hopes.
Clement of Alexandria

If we were logical, the future would be bleak indeed. But we are more than logical. We are human beings, and we have faith, and we have hope.
Jacques Cousteau

"Hope" is the thing with feathers –
That perches in the soul –
And sings the tunes without the words –
And never stops – at all.
Emily Dickinson

Totally without hope one cannot live. To live without hope is to cease to live.
Fyodor Dostoevsky

All human wisdom is summed up in two words – wait and hope.
Alexander Dumas

All earthly delights are sweeter in expectation than in enjoyment; all spiritual pleasures, more in fruition than in expectation.
Owen Feltham

Great hopes make great men.
Thomas Fuller

If it were not for hopes, the heart would break.
Thomas Fuller

Expecting something for nothing is the most popular form of hope.
Arnold Glasow

Hope is not the conviction that something will turn out well but the certainty that something makes sense, regardless of how it turns out.
Vaclav Havel

He that lives in hope danceth without musick.
George Herbert

Hope is the poor man's bread.
George Herbert

The word which God has written on the brow of every man is hope.
Victor Hugo

Every blade of grass, each leaf, each separate petal, is an inscription speaking of hope.
Richard Jefferies

It is more serious to lose hope than to sin.
John of Carpathos

Where there is no hope, there can be no endeavor.
Samuel Johnson

Whatever enlarges hope will also exalt courage.
Samuel Johnson

We love to expect, and when expectation is either disappointed or gratified, we want to be again expecting.
Samuel Johnson

Hope is itself a species of happiness, and perhaps the chief happiness which this world affords.
Samuel Johnson

The natural flights of the human mind are not from pleasure to pleasure, but from hope to hope.
Samuel Johnson

The future is as bright as the promises of God.
Adoniram Judson

There is no better or more blessed bondage than to be a prisoner of hope.
Roy Z. Kemp

We must accept finite disappointment, but we must never lose infinite hope.
Martin Luther King

We stand in life at midnight; we are always at the threshold of a new dawn.
Martin Luther King, Jr

When compassion for the common man was born on Christmas Day, with it was born new hope among the multitudes. They feel a great, ever-rising determination to lift themselves and their children out of hunger and disease and misery, up to a higher level. Jesus started a fire upon the earth, and it is burning hot today, the fire of a new hope in the hearts of the hungry multitudes.
Frank C. Laubach

My only hope is that I shall be clothed with the righteousness of Jesus Christ.
M. Lloyd-Jones

Everything that is done in the world is done by hope. No husbandman would sow a grain of corn if he hoped not it would grow up and become seed ...
Or no tradesman would set himself to work if he did not hope to reap benefit thereby.
Martin Luther

In our sad condition our only consolation is the expectancy of another life. Here below all is incomprehensible.
Martin Luther

There is no medicine like hope, no incentive so great, and no tonic so powerful as expectation of something tomorrow.
Orison Swett Marden

Hope saves a man in the midst of misfortunes.
Menander

Courage is like love; it must have hope for nourishment.
Napoleon

Nothing worth doing is completed in our lifetime; therefore we must be saved by hope.
Reinhold Niebuhr

Hope is a much greater stimulant of life than any happiness.
F. Nietzsche

Those who keep speaking about the sun while walking under a cloudy sky are messengers of hope, the true saints of our day.
Henri J. Nouwen

Let your hook be always cast; in the pool where you least expect it, there will be a fish.
Ovid

The Christmas message is that there is hope for a ruined humanity – hope of pardon, hope of peace with God, hope of glory – because at the Father's will Jesus Christ became poor, and was born in a stable so that thirty years later He might hang on a cross.
J.I. Packer

Notwithstanding the sight of all our miseries, which press upon us and take us by the throat, we have an instinct which we cannot repress, and which lifts us up.
Blaise Pascal

Practice hope. As hopefulness becomes a habit, you can achieve a permanently happy spirit.
Norman Vincent Peale

Hope is the pillar that holds up the world. Hope is the dream of a waking man.
Pliny the Elder

A hope based on a God who can interact with his world in ways more particular than just the general willing of its existence, is a hope which is a coherent possibility within the framework provided

by the scientific understanding of cosmic process.
John Polkinghorne

Hope springs eternal in the human breast:
Man never is, but always to be blest.
The soul, uneasy and confined from home,
Rests and expatiates in a life to come.
Alexander Pope

It is not the end of joy that makes old age so sad, but the end of hope.
Jean Paul Richter

I rejoice in the hope of that glory to be revealed, for it is no uncertain glory that we look for. Our hope is not hung upon such an untwisted thread as, "I imagine so," or "It is likely," but the cable, the strong tow of our fastened anchor, is the oath and promise of Him who is eternal verity. Our salvation is fastened with God's own hand, and with Christ's own strength, to the strong stake of God's unchangeable nature.
Samuel Rutherford

Our ground of hope is that God does not weary of mankind.
Ralph W. Sockman

Do not look to your hope, but to Christ, the source of your hope.
C.H. Spurgeon

Without Christ there is no hope.
C.H. Spurgeon

The longest day must have its close – the gloomiest night will wear on to a morning. An eternal, inexorable lapse of moments is ever hurrying the day of the evil to an eternal night, and the night of the just to an eternal day.
Harriet Beecher Stowe

Before the rain stops we hear a bird. Even under the heavy snow we see snowdrops.
Shunryu Suzuki

One day we will meet beside the river and our Lord will dry every tear. For now, we must live in the joy of that promise and recall that for every generation life is hard, but God is faithful.
Bodie Thoene

Hope, like faith, is nothing if it is not courageous; it is nothing if it is not ridiculous.
Thornton Wilder

Hope and fear
Fear cannot be without hope nor hope without fear.
Benedict de Spinoza

Hope and grace
Just as the sinner's despair of any hope from himself is the first prerequisite of a sound conversion, so the loss of all confidence in himself is the first essential in the believer's growth in grace.
A. W. Pink

Hopeless
There are no hopeless situations; there are only people who have grown hopeless about them.
Clare Boothe Luce

Did you ever get, where Bunyan pictures Christian as getting, right under the old dragon's foot? He is very heavy, and presses the very breath out of a fellow when he makes him his footstool. Poor Christian lay there with the dragon's foot on his breast, but he was just able to stretch out his hand and lay hold on his sword, which, by a good providence, lay within his reach. Then he gave Apollyon a deadly thrust, which made him spread his dragon wings and fly away. The poor crushed and broken pilgrim, as he gave the stab to his foe, cried, "Rejoice not over me, O mine enemy; though I fall, yet shall I rise again." Brother, do you the same. You that are near despair, let this be the strength that nerves your arm and steels your heart. "Jesus Christ of the seed of David was raised from the dead according to Paul's gospel."
C.H. Spurgeon

Hopelessness

Hell is hopelessness. It is no accident that above the entrance to Dante's hell is the inscription: "Leave behind all hope, you who enter here."
Fyodor Dostoevsky

Horoscopes

A deep night oppresses the whole world. This is what we have to dispel and dissolve. It is night not among heretics and among Greeks only, but also in the multitude on our side, in respect of doctrines and of life. For many Christians entirely disbelieve the resurrection; many fortify themselves with the horoscope; many adhere to superstitious observances, and to omens, and auguries.
John Chrysostom

Hospitality

Practice hospitality.
The Bible, Romans 12:13

Do not forget to entertain strangers, for by so doing some people have entertained angels without knowing it.
The Bible, Hebrews 13:2

Offer hospitality to one another without grumbling.
The Bible, 1 Peter 4:9

If a man be gracious and courteous to strangers, it shows he is a citizen of the world and that his heart is no island, cut off from other islands, but a continent that joins them.
Francis Bacon

Let all guests that come be received like Christ, for he will say, "I was a stranger and ye took me in" (Matthew 25:35). Let suitable honor be shown to all, but especially to pilgrims.
The Rule of St Benedict

To welcome a fellow man is to welcome the Shekhinah [divine presence].
Jewish proverb

To give our Lord a perfect hospitality, Mary and Martha must combine.
Teresa of Avila

Human

To be human means most fundamentally to be with God.
Karl Barth

Human nature
See also: Humanity; Mankind; Relationships

Those who belong to Christ Jesus have crucified the sinful nature with its passions and desires.
The Bible, Galatians 5:24

Put to death, therefore, whatever belongs to your earthly nature: sexual immorality, impurity, lust, evil desires and greed, which is idolatry.
The Bible, Colossians 3:5

It is easier to denature plutonium than to denature the evil from the spirit of man.
Albert Einstein

Human nature has ineffable dignity.
John Duns Scotus

Humanism

Humanism is the human case and the human cause, an age-old conviction about the human case which will induce men and women to espouse the human cause with head and heart and with two hands.
H.J. Blackman

The battle for humankind's future must be waged and won in the school classroom by teachers who correctly perceive their role as the proselytizers of a new faith. The classroom must and will become an arena of conflict between the old and the new – the rotting corpse of Christianity and the new faith of Humanism.
John Dynphy, New Ager

Humanity
See also: Human nature; Mankind; Relationships

You will be like God, knowing good and evil.
The Bible, Genesis 3:5

All flesh is grass.
The Bible, Isaiah 40:6 KJV

Can the Ethiopian change his skin, or the leopard his spots?
The Bible, Jeremiah 13:23 KJV

Thou hast made him a little lower than the angels.
The Bible, Psalm 8:5 KJV

I am fearfully and wonderfully made.
The Bible, Psalm 139:14 KJV

God made man to be somebody, not just to have things.
Author unknown

Bible's description of the human body:
a. At birth: "The Lord formed man from the dust of the earth" Genesis 2:7.
b. At death: "The dust returns to the ground it came from." Ecclesiastes 12:7.
Author unknown

People are funny; they spend money they don't have to buy things they don't need to impress people they don't like.
Author unknown

Biologist's view of the human body:
The human body has 206 bones, weighing only 20% of the body; 600 muscles. Its lungs have over 3 million tiny air sacs. Nearly 100,000 kilometers of arteries and capillaries transport 6 liters of blood around the body, over 1,000 times a day. 60% of the body is fluid and 95% of the body's weight consists of oxygen, nitrogen, carbon, hydrogen, phosphorus and calcium – six of the most common elements.
Author unknown

That's one small step for man, one giant leap for mankind.
Neil Armstrong

The times have never hurt anyone. Those who are hurt are human beings; those by whom they are hurt are also human beings. So, change human beings and the times will be changed.
Augustine of Hippo

I classify the human race into two branches: the one consists of those who live by human standards, the other of those who live according to God's will. I also call these two classes the two cities, speaking allegorically. By two cities I mean two societies of human beings, one of which is predestined to reign with God for all eternity, the other doomed to undergo eternal punishment with the devil.
Augustine of Hippo

Why presume so much on the capability of nature? It is wounded, maimed, vexed, lost. The thing wanted is genuine confession, not false defense.
Augustine of Hippo

We have before us the fiendishness of business competition and the world war, passion and wrongdoing, antagonism between classes and moral depravity within them, economic tyranny above and the slave spirit below.
Karl Barth

But man, in so far as he is the image of the divine being, that is, in so far as he is a symbol of divinity, has a precise and absolute meaning and significance. When his mind is turned towards the divine world he discovers everywhere an inner connection and meaning: the indications of another world are apparent to him.
N. Berdayev

The tree which moves some to tears of joy is, in the eyes of others, only a green thing which stands in the way. As a man, so he sees.
William Blake

Man is the great mystery of God, the microcosm, or complete abridgement of

the whole universe: he is the *mirandum Dei opus*, God's masterpiece, a living emblem and hieroglyphic of eternity and time.
Jacob Boehme

A pair of pincers set over a bellows and a stewpan, and the whole thing fixed upon stilts.
Samuel Butler's description of the human body.

No great man lives in vain. The history of the world is but the biography of great men.
Thomas Carlyle

A self-made man? Yes, and worships his creator.
Henry Austin Clapp

We are each of us angels with only one wing. And we can only fly embracing each other.
Luciano De Crescenzo

The greatest organized wrongs which the civilized world has seen perpetrated in modern times, upon the well-being of mankind, have been committed under the amiable name of humanity.
R.L. Dabney

It was the best of times, it was the worst of times, it was the age of wisdom, it was the age of foolishness, it was the epoch of belief, it was the epoch of incredulity, it was the season of Light, it was the season of Darkness, it was the spring of hope, it was the winter of despair, we had everything before us, we had nothing before us, we were all going direct to heaven, we were all doing direct the other way – in short, the period was so far like the present period, that some of its noisiest authorities insisted on its being received, for good or for evil, in the superlative degree of comparison only.
Charles Dickens, opening line of A Tale of Two Cities

No man is an Island, entire of itself; every man is a piece of the Continent, a part of the main; if a clod be washed away by the sea, Europe is the less, as well as if a promontory were, as well as if a manor of thy friends or of thine own were; any man's death diminishes me, because I am involved in Mankind; And therefore never send to know for whom the bell tolls; It tolls for thee.
John Donne

The release of atomic energy has not created a new problem. It has merely made more urgent the necessity of solving an existing one.
Albert Einstein

People wish to be settled: only as far as they are unsettled is there any hope for them.
Ralph Waldo Emerson

It's really a wonder that I haven't dropped all my ideals, because they seem so absurd and impossible to carry out. Yet I keep them, because in spite of everything I still believe that people are really good at heart.
Anne Frank

Most people who visit psychiatrists suffer from an inner deadness. They live in the midst of plenty and are joyless.
Erich Fromm

All that is human must retrograde if it does not advance.
Edward Gibbon

Man is the viceregent of God's world. He is also the rebel in God's world, and the object of God's love. The image of God is there, albeit so marred. The wonder of it all is that this image can be restored in Christ.
Michael Green

The proud man hath no God; the envious man hath no neighbor; the angry man hath not himself. What good then, in being a man, if one has neither himself nor a neighbor nor God?
Joseph Hall

Man is a make-believe animal – he is never so truly himself as when he is acting a part.
William Hazlitt

Man is the only animal that laughs and weeps, for he is the only animal that is struck with the difference between what things are, and what they ought to be.
William Hazlitt

Man is rational and therefore like God; he is created with free will and is master over his acts.
Irenaeus

I hate mankind, for I think myself to be one of them, and I know how bad I am.
Samuel Johnson

Christianity is the highest perfection of humanity.
Samuel Johnson

Human nature is like a drunk peasant. Lift him into the saddle on one side, over he topples on the other side.
Martin Luther

Men love to be encouraged by false hopes; the world is full of quack remedies for sin.
J. Gresham Machen

Only two great groups of animals, men and ants, indulge in highly organized mass warfare.
Charles H. Maskins

All the evidence of history suggests that man is indeed a rational animal, but with a nearly infinite capacity for folly. His history seems largely a halting but persistent effort to raise his reason above his animality. He draws blueprints for Utopia, but never quite gets it built.
Robert McNamara

We cannot live only for ourselves. A thousand fibers connect us with our fellow men!
Herman Melville

The misery of man is derived from his idolatry, from his partly conscious and partly unconscious effort to make himself, his race, and his culture God.
Reinhold Niebuhr

Which is it, is man one of God's blunders or is God one of man's?
Friedrich Wilhelm Nietzsche

On the whole, human beings want to be good, but not too good and not quite all the time.
George Orwell

Our nature consists in movement; absolute rest is death.
Blaise Pascal

Man is equally incapable of seeing the nothingness from which he emerges and the infinity in which he is engulfed.
Blaise Pascal

There are only two kinds of men: the righteous who believe themselves sinners, and the rest, sinners who believe themselves righteous.
Blaise Pascal

There is a God-shaped blank in every heart.
Blaise Pascal

What a chimera, then, is man! what a novelty, what a monster, what a chaos, what a subject of contradiction, what a prodigy! A judge of all things, feeble worm of the earth, depositary of the truth, cloaca of uncertainty and error, the glory and the shame of the universe!
Blaise Pascal

Man is but a reed, the weakest in nature, but he is a thinking reed.
Blaise Pascal

What is man in nature? Nothing in relation to the infinite, all in relation to nothing, a mean between nothing and everything.
Blaise Pascal

The world is a spiritual kindergarten, where thousands of bewildered infants are trying to spell GOD with the wrong blocks.
Edward Arlington Robinson

God made man a little lower than the angels, and he has been getting a little lower ever since.
Will Rogers

Man is an empty bubble on the sea of nothingness.
Jean-Paul Sartre

Man is a clever animal who behaves like an imbecile.
Albert Schweitzer

What a piece of work is a man! How noble in reason! how infinite in faculty! in form, in moving, how express and admirable! in action how like an angel! in apprehension how like a god! the beauty of the world, the paragon of animals!
William Shakespeare, Hamlet

Better contraceptives will control the population only if people will use them. A nuclear holocaust can be prevented only if the conditions under which nations make war can be changed. The environment will continue to deteriorate until pollution practices are abandoned. We need to make vast changes in human behavior.
B. F. Skinner

Man and woman are one body and soul.
The Talmud

We are not human beings having a spiritual experience, we are spiritual beings having a human experience.
Pierre Teilhard de Chardin

Everybody thinks of changing humanity and nobody thinks of changing himself.
Leo Tolstoy

Man is the only animal that blushes – or needs to.
Mark Twain

I sometimes think that God in creating man somewhat overestimated His ability.
Oscar Wilde

We are all in the gutter. But some of us are looking at the stars.
Oscar Wilde

Man is nothing so much as a lump of muddy earth plunged into a very clear, pure brook.
Ulrich Zwingli

Humanity, Christ's redemption of

Jesus Christ taught men the simple truth about themselves: that they were selfish; enslaved to their appetites; blind, sick, unhappy sinners; that it was laid upon himself to deliver, enlighten, bless, and heal them; and that this would be brought about by hatred of self, and by following him through poverty to the death of the cross.
Blaise Pascal

Humanity, compared with animals

This is the quality peculiar to man, wherein he differs from other animals, that he alone is endowed with perception to distinguish right from wrong, justice from injustice.
Aristotle

Man with all his noble qualities ... still bears in his bodily frame the indelible stamp of his lowly origin.
Charles Darwin

The question is this: Is man an ape or an angel? I, my lord, am on the side of the angels.
Benjamin Disraeli

It is dangerous to make man see how like he is to animals without keeping his greatness in view. It is dangerous also to show him his greatness and not his baseness; and still more to leave him ignorant of both. But it is most profitable to show him both.
Blaise Pascal

Brutes never meet in bloody fray,
Nor cut each other's throats for pay.
Jonathan Swift

Humanity, Depravity of

Man is very far gone from original righteousness.
Book of Common Prayer

Our nature is not only completely empty of goodness, but so full of every kind of wrong that it is always active.
John Calvin

Eichmann is in us, each of us.
Dinur

It is easier to denature plutonium that to denature the evil spirit of man.
Albert Einstein

The true problem lies in the hearts and thoughts of men. It is not a physical but an ethical one ... What terrifies us is not the explosive force of the atomic bomb but the power of the wickedness of the human heart.
Albert Einstein

The more I see of men, the better I like my dog.
H. Eves

Out of the crooked timber of humanity no straight thing can ever be made.
Immanuel Kant

It is men, not God, who have produced racks, whips, prisons, slavery, guns, bayonets, and bombs. It is by human avarice or human stupidity, not by the churlishness of nature, that we have poverty or overwork.
C.S. Lewis

No clever arrangement of bad eggs will make a good omelette.
C.S. Lewis

The natural man cannot want God to be God. Rather he wants himself to be God, and God not to be God.
Martin Luther

If I wrote down every thought I have ever thought and every deed I have ever done, men would call me a monster of depravity.
Somerset Maugham

There is no man so good who, if all his actions and thoughts were put to the test of the laws, would not deserve hanging ten times in his life.
Montaigne

Humanity, Depravity of

C.H. Spurgeon

"No man can come to me, except the Father which hath sent me draw him." John 6:44.

"Coming to Christ" is a very common phrase in Holy Scripture. It is used to express those acts of the soul wherein, leaving at once our self-righteousness, and our sins, we fly unto the Lord Jesus Christ, and receive his righteousness to be our covering, and his blood to be our atonement. Coming to Christ, then, embraces in it repentance, self-negation, and faith in the Lord Jesus Christ, and it sums within itself all those things which are the necessary attendants of these great states of heart, such as the belief of the truth, earnestness of prayer to God, the submission of the soul to the precepts of God's gospel, and all those things which accompany the dawn of salvation in the soul. Coming to Christ is just the one essential thing for a sinner's salvation. He that cometh not to Christ, do what he may, or think what he may, is yet in "the gall of bitterness and in the bonds of iniquity." Coming to Christ is the very first effect of regeneration. No sooner is the soul quickened than it at once discovers its lost estate, is horrified thereat, looks out for a refuge, and believing Christ to be a suitable one, flies to him and reposes in him. Where there is not this coming to Christ, it is certain that there is as yet no quickening; where there is no quickening, the soul is dead in trespasses and sins, and being dead it cannot enter into the kingdom of heaven. We have before us now an announcement very startling, some say very obnoxious. Coming to Christ, though described by some people as being the very easiest thing in all the world, is in our text declared to be a thing utterly and entirely impossible to any man, unless the Father shall draw him to Christ. It shall be our business, then, to enlarge upon this declaration. We doubt not that it will always be offensive to carnal nature, but, nevertheless, the offending of human nature is sometimes the first step towards bringing it to bow itself before God. And if this be the effect of a painful process, we can forget the pain and rejoice in the glorious consequences.

I shall endeavor this morning, first of all, to notice man's inability, wherein it consists. Secondly, the Father's drawings – what these are, and how they are exerted upon the soul. And then I shall conclude by noticing a sweet consolation which may be derived from this seemingly barren and terrible text.

I. First, then, MAN'S INABILITY. The text says, "No man can come to me, except the Father which hath sent me draw him." Wherein does this inability lie?

First, it does not lie in any physical defect. If in coming to Christ, moving the body or walking with the feet should be of any assistance, certainly man has all physical power to come to Christ in that sense. I remember to have heard a very foolish Antinomian declare, that he did not believe any man had the power to walk to the house of God unless the Father drew him. Now the man was plainly foolish, because he must have seen that as long as a man was alive and had legs, it was as easy for him to walk to the house of God as to the house of Satan. If coming to Christ includes the utterance of a prayer, man has no physical defect in that respect, if he be not dumb, he can say a prayer as easily as he can utter blasphemy. It is as easy for a man to sing one of the songs of Zion as to sing a profane and libidinous song. There is no lack of physical power

in coming to Christ. All that can be wanted with regard to the bodily strength man most assuredly has, and any part of salvation which consists in that is totally and entirely in the power of man without any assistance from the Spirit of God. Nor, again, does this inability lie in any mental lack. I can believe this Bible to be true just as easily as I can believe any other book to be true. So far as believing on Christ is an act of the mind, I am just as able to believe on Christ as I am able to believe on anybody else. Let his statement be but true, it is idle to tell me I cannot believe it. I can believe the statement that Christ makes as well as I can believe the statement of any other person. There is no deficiency of faculty in the mind: it is as capable of appreciating as a mere mental act the guilt of sin, as it is of appreciating the guilt of assassination. It is just as possible for me to exercise the mental idea of seeking God, as it is to exercise the thought of ambition. I have all the mental strength and power that can possibly be needed, so far as mental power is needed in salvation at all. Nay, there is not any man so ignorant that he can plead a lack of intellect as an excuse for rejecting the gospel. The defect, then, does not lie either in the body, or, what we are bound to call, speaking theologically, the mind. It is not any lack or deficiency there, although it is the vitiation of the mind, the corruption or the ruin of it, which, after all, is the very essence of man's inability.

Permit me to show you wherein this inability of man really does lie. It lies deep in his nature. Through the fall, and through our own sin, the nature of man has become so debased, and depraved, and corrupt, that it is impossible for him to come to Christ without the assistance of God the Holy Spirit. Now, in trying to exhibit how the nature of man thus renders him unable to come to Christ, you must allow me just to take this figure. You see a sheep; how willingly it feeds upon the herbage! You never knew a sheep sigh after carrion; it could not live on lion's food.

Now bring me a wolf; and you ask me whether a wolf cannot eat grass, whether it cannot be just as docile and as domesticated as the sheep. I answer, no; because its nature is contrary thereunto. You say, "Well, it has ears and legs; can it not hear the shepherd's voice, and follow him whithersoever he leadeth it ?" I answer, certainly; there is no physical cause why it cannot do so, but its nature forbids, and therefore I say it cannot do so. Can it not be tamed? cannot its ferocity be removed? Probably it may so far be subdued that it may become apparently tame; but there will always be a marked distinction between it and the sheep, because there is a distinction in nature. Now, the reason why man cannot come to Christ, is not because he cannot come, so far as his body or his mere power of mind is concerned, but because his nature is so corrupt that he has neither the will nor the power to come to Christ unless drawn by the Spirit. But let me give you a better illustration. You see a mother with her babe in her arms. You put a knife into her hand, and tell her to stab that babe to the heart. She replies, and very truthfully, "I cannot." Now, so far as her bodily power is concerned, she can, if she pleases; there is the knife, and there is the child. The child cannot resist, and she has quite sufficient strength in her hand immediately to stab it to its heart. But she is quite correct when she says she cannot do it. As a mere act of the mind, it is quite possible she might think of such a thing as killing the child, and yet she says she cannot think of such a thing; and she does not say falsely, for her nature as a mother forbids her doing a thing from which her soul revolts. Simply because she is that child's parent she feels she cannot kill it. It is even so with a sinner. Coming to Christ is so obnoxious to human nature that, although, so far as physical and mental forces are concerned, (and these have but a very narrow sphere in salvation) men could come if they would: it is strictly correct to say that they cannot and will not unless the Father who hath sent Christ doth draw them. Let us enter a little more deeply into the subject, and try to show you wherein this inability of man consists, in its more minute particulars.

First, it lies in the obstinacy of the human will. "Oh!" saith the Arminian, "men may be saved if they will." We reply, "My dear sir, we all believe that; but it is just the if they will that is the difficulty. We assert that no man will come to Christ unless he be drawn; nay, we do not assert it, but Christ himself declares it – "Ye will not come unto me that ye might have life;' and as long as that "ye will not come' stands on record in Holy Scripture, we shall not be brought to believe in any doctrine of the freedom of the human will." It is strange how people, when talking about free-will, talk of things which they do not at all understand. "Now," says one, "I believe men can be saved if they will." My dear sir, that is not the question at all. The question is, are men ever found naturally willing to submit to the humbling terms of the gospel of Christ? We declare, upon Scriptural authority, that the human will is so desperately set on mischief, so depraved, and so inclined to everything that is evil, and so disinclined to everything that is good, that without the powerful. supernatural, irresistible influence of the Holy Spirit, no human will ever be constrained towards Christ. You reply, that men sometimes are willing, without the help of the Holy Spirit. I answer – Did you ever meet with any person who was? Scores and hundreds, nay, thousands of Christians have I conversed with, of different opinions, young and old, but it has never been my lot to meet with one who could affirm that he came to Christ of himself, without being drawn. The universal confession of all true believers is this – "I know that unless Jesus Christ had sought me when a stranger wandering from the fold of God, I would to this very hour have been wandering far from him, at a distance from him, and loving that distance well." With common consent, all believers affirm the truth, that men will not come to Christ till the Father who hath sent Christ doth draw them.

2. Again, not only is the will obstinate, but the understanding is darkened. Of that we have abundant Scriptural proof. I am not now making mere assertions, but stating doctrines authoritatively taught in the Holy Scriptures, and known in the conscience of every Christian man – that the understanding of man is so dark, that he cannot by any means understand the things of God until his understanding has been opened. Man is by nature blind within. The cross of Christ, so laden with glories, and glittering with attractions, never attracts him, because he is blind and cannot see its beauties. Talk to him of the wonders of the creation, show to him the many-colored arch that spans the sky, let him behold the glories of a landscape, he is well able to see all these things; but talk to him of the wonders of the covenant of grace, speak to him of the security of the believer in Christ, tell him of the beauties of the person of the Redeemer, he is quite deaf to all your description; you are as one that playeth a goodly tune, it is true; but he regards not, he is deaf, he has no comprehension. Or, to return to the verse which we so specially marked in our reading, "The natural man receiveth not the things of the Spirit of God, for they are foolishness unto him: neither can he know them because they are spiritually discerned;" and inasmuch as he is a natural man, it is not in his power to discern the things of God. "Well," says one, "I think I have arrived at a very tolerable judgment in matters of theology; I think I understand almost every point." True, that you may do in the letter of it; but in the spirit of it, in the true reception thereof into the soul, and in the actual understanding of it, it is impossible for you to have attained, unless you have been drawn by the Spirit. For as long as that Scripture stands true, that carnal men cannot receive spiritual things, it must be true that you have not received them, unless you have been renewed and made a spiritual man in Christ Jesus. The will, then, and the understanding, are two great doors, both blocked up against our coming to Christ, and until these are

opened by the sweet influences of the Divine Spirit, they must be for ever closed to anything like coming to Christ.

3. Again, the affections, which constitute a very great part of man, are depraved. Man, as he is, before he receives the grace of God, loves anything and everything above spiritual things. If ye want proof of this, look around you. There needs no monument to the depravity of the human affections. Cast your eyes everywhere – there is not a street, nor a house, nay, nor a heart, which doth not bear upon it sad evidence of this dreadful truth. Why is it that men are not found on the Sabbath Day universally flocking to the house of God? Why are we not more constantly found reading our Bibles? How is it that prayer is a duty almost universally neglected? Why is it that Christ Jesus is so little beloved? Why are even his professed followers so cold in their affections to him? Whence arise these things? Assuredly, dear brethren, we can trace them to no other source than this, the corruption and vitiation of the affections. We love that which we ought to hate, and we hate that which we ought to love. It is but human nature, fallen human nature, that man should love this present life better than the life to come. It is but the effect of the fall, that man should love sin better than righteousness, and the ways of this world better than the ways of God. And again, we repeat it, until these affections be renewed, and turned into a fresh channel by the gracious drawings of the Father, it is not possible for any man to love the Lord Jesus Christ.

4. Yet once more – conscience, too, has been overpowered by the fall. I believe there is no more egregious mistake made by divines, than when they tell people that conscience is the vicegerent of God within the soul, and that it is one of those powers which retains its ancient dignity, and stands erect amidst the fall of its compeers. My brethren, when man fell in the garden, manhood fell entirely; there was not one single pillar in the temple of manhood that stood erect. It is true, conscience was not

destroyed. The pillar was not shattered; it fell, and it fell in one piece, and there it lies along, the mightiest remnant of God's once perfect work in man. But that conscience is fallen, I am sure. Look at men. Who among them is the possessor of a "good conscience toward God," but the regenerated man? Do you imagine that if men's consciences always spoke loudly and clearly to them, they would live in the daily commission of acts, which are as opposed to the right as darkness to light? No, beloved; conscience can tell me that I am a sinner, but conscience cannot make me feel that I am one. Conscience may tell me that such-and-such a thing is wrong, but how wrong it is conscience itself does not know. Did any man s conscience, unenlightened by the Spirit, ever tell him that his sins deserved damnation? Or if conscience did do that, did it ever lead any man to feel an abhorrence of sin as sin? In fact, did conscience ever bring a man to such a self-renunciation, that he did totally abhor himself and all his works and come to Christ? No, conscience, although it is not dead, is ruined, its power is impaired, it hath not that clearness of eye and that strength of hand, and that thunder of voice, which it had before the fall; but hath ceased to a great degree, to exert its supremacy in the town of Mansoul. Then, beloved, it becomes necessary for this very reason, because conscience is depraved, that the Holy Spirit should step in, to show us our need of a Savior, and draw us to the Lord Jesus Christ.

"Still," says one, "as far as you have hitherto gone, it appears to me that you consider that the reason why men do not come to Christ is that they will not, rather than they cannot." True, most true. I believe the greatest reason of man's inability is the obstinacy of his will. That once overcome, I think the great stone is rolled away from the sepulcher, and the hardest part of the battle is already won. But allow me to go a little further. My text does not say,"No man will come," but it says, "No man can come." Now, many interpreters believe that the can here, is but a strong expression conveying no more meaning than the word will. I feel assured that this is not correct. There is in man, not only unwillingness to be saved, but there is a spiritual powerlessness to come to Christ; and this I will prove to every Christian at any rate. Beloved, I speak to you who have already been quickened by the divine grace, does not your experience teach you that there are times when you have a will to serve God, and yet have not the power? Have you not sometimes been obliged to say that you have wished to believe. but you have had to pray, Lord, help mine unbelief?" Because, although willing enough to receive God's testimony, your own carnal nature was too strong for you, and you felt you needed supernatural help. Are you able to go into your room at any hour you choose, and to fall upon your knees and say,"Now, it is my will that I should be very earnest in prayer, and that I should draw near unto God ?" I ask, do you find your power equal to your will? You could say, even at the bar of God himself, that you are sure you are not mistaken in your willingness; you are willing to be wrapt up in devotion, it is your will that your soul should not wander from a pure contemplation of the Lord Jesus Christ, but you find that you cannot do that, even when you are willing, without the help of the Spirit. Now, if the quickened child of God finds a spiritual inability, how much more the sinner who is dead in trespasses and sin? If even the advanced Christian, after thirty or forty years, finds himself sometimes willing and yet powerless – if such be his experience, – does it not seem more than likely that the poor sinner who has not yet believed, should find a need of strength as well as a want of will?

But, again, there is another argument. If the sinner has strength to come to Christ, I should like to know how we are to understand those continual descriptions of the sinner's state which we meet with in God's holy Word? Now, a sinner is said to be dead in trespasses and sins. Will you affirm that death implies nothing more than the absence of a will? Surely a corpse is quite as unable as unwilling. Or again, do not all men see that there is a distinction between will and power: might not that corpse be sufficiently quickened to get a will, and yet be so powerless that it could not lift as much as its hand or foot? Have we never seen cases in which persons have been just sufficiently re-animated to give evidence of life, and have yet been so near death that they could not have performed the slightest action? Is there not a clear difference between the giving or the will and the giving of power? It is quite certain, however, that where the will is given, the power will follow. Make a man willing, and he shall be made powerful; for when God gives the will, he does not tantalize man by giving him to wish for that which he is unable to do; nevertheless he makes such a division between the will and the power, that it shall be seen that both things are quite distinct gifts of the Lord God.

Then I must ask one more question: if all that were needed to make a man willing, do you not at once degrade the Holy Spirit? Are we not in the habit of giving all the glory of salvation wrought in us to God the Spirit? But now, if all that God the Spirit does for me is to make me willing to do these things for myself, am I not in a great measure a sharer with the Holy Spirit in the glory? and may I not boldly stand up and say, "It is true the Spirit gave me the will to do it, but still I did it myself, and therein will I glory; for if I did these things myself without assistance from on high, I will not cast my crown at his feet; it is my own crown, I earned it, and I will keep it." Inasmuch as the Holy Spirit is evermore in Scripture set forth as the person who worketh in us to will and to do of his own good pleasure, we hold it to be a legitimate inference that he must do something more for us than the mere making of us willing, and that therefore there must be another thing besides want of will in a sinner – there must be absolute and actual want of power.

Now, before I leave this statement, let me address myself to you for a moment. I am often charged with preaching doctrines that may do a great deal of hurt. Well, I shall not deny the charge, for I am not careful to answer in this matter. I have my witnesses here present to prove that the things which I have preached have done a great deal of hurt, but they have not done hurt either to morality or to God's Church; the hurt has been on the side of Satan. There are not ones or twos but many hundreds who this morning rejoice that they have been brought near to God; from having been profane Sabbath-breakers, drunkards, or worldly persons, they have been brought to know and love the Lord Jesus Christ; and if this be any hurt may God of his infinite mercy send us a thousand times as much. But further, what truth is there in the world which will not hurt a man who chooses to make hurt of it? You who preach general redemption, are very fond of proclaiming the great truth of God's mercy to the last moment. But how dare you preach that? Many people make hurt of it by putting off the day of grace, and thinking that the last hour may do as well as the first. Why, if we never preached anything which man could misuse, and abuse, we must hold our tongues for ever. Still says one, "Well then, if I cannot save myself, and cannot come to Christ, I must sit still and do nothing." If men do say so, on their own heads shall be their doom. We have very plainly told you that there are many things you can do. To be found continually in the house of God is in your power; to study the Word of God with diligence is in your power; to renounce your outward sin, to forsake the vices in which you indulge, to make your life honest, sober, and righteous, is in your power. For this you need no help from the Holy Spirit; all this you can do yourself; but to come to Christ truly is not in your power, until you are renewed by the Holy Ghost. But mark you, your want of power is no excuse, seeing that you have no desire to come, and are living in wilful rebellion against God. Your want of power lies mainly in the obstinacy of nature. Suppose a liar says that it is not in his power to speak the truth, that he has been a liar so long, that he cannot leave it off; is that an excuse for him? Suppose a man who has long indulged in lust should tell you that he finds his lusts have so girt about him like a great iron net that he cannot get rid of them, would you take that as an excuse? Truly it is none at all. If a drunkard has become so foully a drunkard, that he finds it impossible to pass a public – house without stepping in, do you therefore excuse him? No, because his inability to reform, lies in his nature, which he has no desire to restrain or conquer. The thing that is done, and the thing that causes the thing that is done, being both from the root of sin, are two evils which cannot excuse each other, What though the Ethiopian cannot change his skin, nor the leopard his spots? It is because you have learned to do evil that you cannot now learn to do well; and instead, therefore, of letting you sit down to excuse yourselves, let me put a thunderbolt beneath the seat of your sloth, that you may be startled by it and aroused. Remember, that to sit still is to be damned to all eternity. Oh! that God the Holy Spirit might make use of this truth in a very different manner! Before I have done I trust I shall be enabled to show you how it is that this truth, which apparently condemns men and shuts them out, is, after all, the great truth, which has been blessed to the conversion of men.

II. Our second point is THE FATHER'S DRAWINGS. "No man can come to me, except the Father which hath sent me draw him." How then does the Father draw men? Arminian divines generally say that God draws men by the preaching of the gospel. Very true; the preaching of the gospel is the instrument of drawing men, but there must be some thing more than this. Let me ask to whom did Christ address these words? Why, to the people of Capernaum, where he had often preached, where he had uttered mournfully and plaintively the woes of the law and the invitations of the gospel. In that city he had done many mighty works and worked many miracles. In fact, such teaching and such miraculous attestation had he given to them, that he declared that Tyre and Sidon would have repented long ago in sack-cloth and ashes, if they had been blessed with such privileges. Now, if the preaching of Christ himself did not avail to the enabling these men to come to Christ, it cannot be possible that all that was intended by the drawing of the Father was simply preaching. No, brethren, you must note again, he does not say no man can come except the minister draw him, but except the Father draw him. Now there is such a thing as being drawn by the gospel, and drawn by the minister, without being drawn by God. Clearly, it is a divine drawing that is meant, a drawing by the Most High God – the First Person of the most glorious Trinity sending out the Third Person, the Holy Spirit, to induce men to come to Christ. Another person turns round and says with a sneer, "Then do you think that Christ drags men to himself, seeing that they are unwilling!" I remember meeting once with a man who said to me, Sir, you preach that Christ takes people by the hair of their heads and drags them to himself" I asked him whether he could refer to the date of the sermon wherein I preached that extraordinary doctrine, for if he could, I should be very much obliged. However, he could not. But said I, while Christ does not drag people to himself by the hair of their heads, I believe that, he draws them by the heart quite as powerfully as your caricature would suggest. Mark that in the Father's drawing there is no compulsion whatever; Christ never compelled any man to come to him against his will. If a man be unwilling to be saved, Christ does not save him against his will. How, then, does the Holy Spirit draw him? Why, by making him willing. It is true he does not use "moral suasion;" he knows a nearer method of reaching the heart. He goes to the secret fountain of the heart, and he knows how, by some mysterious operation, to turn the will in an opposite direction, so that, as Ralph Erskine paradoxically puts it, the man is saved "with full consent against his will;" that is, against his old will he is saved. But he is saved with full consent, for he is made willing in the day of God's power. Do not imagine that any man will go to heaven kicking and struggling all the way against the hand that draws him. Do not conceive that any man will be plunged in the bath of a Savior's blood while he is striving to run away from the Savior. Oh, no. It is quite true that first of all man is unwilling to be saved. When the Holy Spirit hath put his influence into the heart, the text is fulfilled – "draw me and I will run after thee." We follow on while he draws us, glad to obey the voice which once we had despised. But the gist of the matter lies in the turning of the will. How that is done no flesh knoweth; it is one of those mysteries that is clearly perceived as a fact, but the cause of which no tongue can tell, and no heart can guess. The apparent way, however, in which the Holy Spirit operates, we can tell you. The first thing the Holy Spirit does when he comes into a man's heart is this: he finds him with a very good opinion of himself: and there is nothing which prevents a man coming to Christ like a good opinion of himself. Why, says man, "I don't want to come to Christ. I have as good a righteousness as anybody can desire. I feel I can walk into heaven on my own rights." The Holy Spirit lays bare his heart, lets him see the loathsome cancer that is there eating away his life, uncovers to him all the blackness and defilement of that sink of hell, the human heart, and then the man stands aghast. "I never thought I was like this. Oh! those sins I thought were little, have swelled out to an immense stature. What I thought was a mole-hill has grown into a mountain; it was but the hyssop on the wall before, but now it has become a cedar of Lebanon. Oh," saith the man within himself, "I will try and reform; I will do good deeds enough to wash these black deeds out." Then comes the Holy Spirit and shows him that he cannot do this, takes away all his fancied power and strength, so that the man falls down on his knees in agony, and cries, "Oh! once I thought I could save myself by my good works, but now I find that

"Could my tears for ever flow,
Could my zeal no respite know,
All for sin could not atone,
Thou must save and thou alone.'"

Then the heart sinks, and the man is ready to despair. And saith he, "I never can be saved. Nothing can save me." Then, comes the Holy Spirit and shows the sinner the cross of Christ, gives him eyes anointed with heavenly eye-salve, and says, "Look to yonder cross. that Man died to save sinners; you feel that you are a sinner; he died to save you." And he enables the heart to believe, and to come to Christ. And when it comes to Christ, by this sweet drawing of the Spirit, it finds "a peace with God which passeth all understanding, which keeps his heart and mind through Jesus Christ our Lord." Now, you will plainly perceive that all this may be done without any compulsion. Man is as much drawn willingly, as if he were not drawn at all; and he comes to Christ with full consent, with as full a consent as if no secret influence had ever been exercised in his heart. But that influence must be exercised, or else there never has been and there never will be, any man who either can or will come to the Lord Jesus Christ.

III. And, now, we gather up our ends, and conclude by trying to make a practical application of the doctrine; and we trust a comfortable one. "Well," says one, "if what this man preaches be true, what is to become of my religion? for do you know I have been a long while trying, and I do not like to hear you say a man cannot save himself. I believe he can, and I mean to persevere; but if I am to believe what you say, I must give it all up and begin again." My dear friends, it will be a very happy thing if you do. Do not think that I shall be at all alarmed if you do so. Remember, what you are doing is building your house upon the sand, and it is but an act of charity if I can shake it a little for you. Let me assure you, in God's name, if your religion has no better foundation than your own strength, it will not stand you at the bar of God. Nothing will last to eternity, but that which came from eternity. Unless the everlasting God has done a good work in your heart, all you may have done must be unraveled at the last day of account. It is all in vain for you to be a church-goer or chapel-goer, a good keeper of the Sabbath, an observer of your prayers: it is all in vain for you to be honest to your neighbors and reputable in your conversation; if you hope to be saved by these things, it is all in vain for you to trust in them. Go on; be as honest as you like, keep the Sabbath perpetually, be as holy as you can. I would not dissuade you from these things. God forbid; grow in them, but oh, do not trust in them, for if you rely upon these things you will find they will fail you when most you need them. And if there be anything else that you have found yourself able to do unassisted by divine grace, the sooner you can get rid of the hope that has been engendered by it the better for you, for it is a foul delusion to rely upon anything that flesh can do. A spiritual heaven must be inhabited by spiritual men, and preparation for it must be wrought by the Spirit of God. "Well," cries another, "I have been sitting under a ministry where I have been told that I could, at my own option, repent and believe, and the consequence is that I have been putting it off from day to day. I thought I could come one day as well as another; that I had only to say, "Lord, have mercy upon me,' and believe, and then I should be saved. Now you have taken all this hope away for me, sir; I feel amazement and horror taking hold upon me." Again, I say, "My dear friend, I am very glad of it. This was the effect which I hoped to produce. I pray that you may feel this a great deal more. When you have no hope of saving yourself, I shall have hope that God has begun to save you. As soon as you say "Oh, I cannot come to Christ. Lord, draw me, help me,' I shall rejoice over you. He who has got a will, though he has not power, has grace begun in his heart, and God will not leave him until the work is finished." But, careless sinner, learn that thy salvation now hangs in God's hand. Oh, remember thou art entirely in the hand of God. Thou hast sinned against him, and if he wills to damn thee, damned thou art. Thou canst not resist his will nor thwart his purpose. Thou hast deserved his wrath, and if he chooses to pour the full shower of that wrath upon thy head, thou canst do nothing to avert it. If, on the other hand, he chooses

to save thee, he is able to save thee to the very uttermost. But thou liest as much in his hand as the summer's moth beneath thine own finger. He is the God whom thou art grieving every day. Doth it not make thee tremble to think that thy eternal destiny now hangs upon the will of him whom thou hast angered and incensed? Dost not this make thy knees knock together, and thy blood curdle? If it does so I rejoice, inasmuch as this may be the first effect of the Spirit's drawing in thy soul. Oh, tremble to think that the God whom thou hast angered, is the God upon whom thy salvation or thy condemnation entirely depends. Tremble and "kiss the Son lest he be angry and ye perish from the way while his wrath is kindled but a little,"

Now, the comfortable reflection is this: – Some of you this morning are conscious that you are coming to Christ. Have you not begun to weep the penitential tear? Did not your closet witness your prayerful preparation for the hearing of the Word of God? And during the service of this morning, has not your heart said within you, "Lord, save me, or I perish, for save myself I cannot?" And could you not now stand up in your seat, and sing,

"Oh, sovereign grace my heart subdue;
I would be led in triumph, too,
A willing captive of my Lord,
To sing the triumph of his Word"?

And have I not myself heard you say in your heart – "Jesus, Jesus, my whole trust Is in thee: I know that no righteousness of my own can save me, but only thou, O Christ – sink or swim, I cast myself on thee?" Oh, my brother, thou art drawn by the Father, for thou couldst not have come unless he had drawn thee. Sweet thought! And if he has drawn thee, dost thou know what is the delightful inference? Let me repeat one text, and may that comfort thee: "The Lord hath appeared of old unto me, saying, I have loved thee with an everlasting love: therefore with loving-kindness have I drawn thee." Yes, my poor weeping brother, inasmuch as thou art now coming to Christ, God has

drawn thee; and inasmuch as he has drawn thee, it is a proof that he has loved thee from before the foundation of the world. Let thy heart leap within thee, thou art one of his. Thy name was written on the Savior's hands when they were nailed to the accursed tree. Thy name glitters on the breast-plate of the great High Priest to-day; ay, and it was there before the day-star knew its place, or planets ran their round. Rejoice in the Lord ye that have come to Christ, and shout for joy all ye that have been drawn of the Father. For this is your proof, your solemn testimony, that you from among men have been chosen in eternal election, and that you shall be kept by the power of God, through faith, unto the salvation which is ready to be revealed.
C.H. Spurgeon

Humanity, Exalted estimates of
Man is naturally inclined to beneficence.
Marcus Aurelius

The world is full of wonders, but nothing so more wonderful than man.
Sophocles

Glory to Man in the Highest! For Man is the master of things.
Tennyson

Humanity, Insignificance of
Man is a little soul carrying around a corpse.
Epictetus

Man is but a breath and shadow.
Euripides

The life of man, solitary, poor, nasty, brutish, and short.
Thomas Hobbes

The state of man is inconstancy, boredom, anxiety.
Blaise Pascal

When a man is wrapped up in himself he makes a pretty small package.
John Ruskin

Humanity, Middle state of
Man is neither angel nor brute, and the unfortunate thing is that he who would act the angel acts the brute.
Blaise Pascal

Humanity, Nature of
Since human nature has that weakness by which it cannot always concentrate on grave and serious matters but demands other rest besides sleep, there must also be provision made for certain relaxations from work and useful studies and a certain recreation of the strength both of the spirit and of the body in play and games.
Martin Bucer

Man is by his constitution a religious animal.
Edmund Burke

It will be very generally found that those who sneer habitually at human nature, and affect to despise it, are among its worst and least pleasant samples.
Charles Dickens

Man … is a being born to believe.
Benjamin Disraeli

Human action can be modified to some extent, but human nature cannot be changed.
Abraham Lincoln

Romans 1:18 stands in its insistence that even in the most excellent men, however endowed with law, righteousness, wisdom, and all virtues, free will, their most excellent part, is nonetheless ungodly, and unrighteous, and merits God's wrath.
Martin Luther

It is the nature of man to believe and to love: if he has not the right objects for his belief and love, he will attach himself to wrong ones.
Blaise Pascal

Man – a being in search of meaning.
Plata

There is nothing in man by nature apart

from God, which is not vile and deceitful. In me (that is, in my flesh,) dwells no good thing.
If there be anything good in my nature, if I have been transformed by the renewing of my mind, if I am regenerate, if I have passed from death unto life, if I have been taken out of the family of Satan, and adopted into the family of God's dear Son, and if I am now no more an heir of wrath, but a child of heaven, then all these things are of God, and in no sense, and in no degree whatever are they of myself.
C.H. Spurgeon

Our nature is very bad in itself, but very good to them that use it well.
Jeremy Taylor

Humanity, Need of
Christ came to heal the sick, not the well or self-sufficient.
Professor Paul Krishna, a former Hindu

Humanity, Potential of
Humanity, potential with God
All great knowledge is this, for a man to know that he himself by himself is nothing; and that, whatever he is, he is from God and on account of God.
Augustine of Hippo

Our humanity were a poor thing were it not for the divinity which stirs within us.
Francis Bacon

MAN: An animal so lost in rapturous contemplation of what he thinks he is as to overlook what he indubitably ought to be.
Ambrose Bierce

Whatever else may be said of man, this one thing is clear: He is not what he is capable of being.
G.K. Chesterton

No man need stay the way he is.
Harry Emerson Fosdick

God created man in order to have someone on whom to shower his love.
Irenaeus of Lyons

Human rights
We hold these truths to be self-evident, that all men are created equal, that they are endowed by their Creator with certain unalienable rights, that among these are life, liberty and the pursuit of happiness.
American Declaration of Independence, 1776

All human beings are born free and equal in dignity and rights.
Universal Declaration of Human Rights, 1948

Humility:
See also: Pride
I am meek and lowly in heart.
The Bible, Matthew 11:29 kjv

For whoever exalts himself will be humbled, and whoever humbles himself will be exalted.
The Bible, Matthew 23:12

He humbled himself, and became obedient unto death, even the death of the cross.
The Bible, Philippians 2:8 kjv

Humble yourselves before the Lord, and he will lift you up.
The Bible, James 4:10

… clothe yourselves with humility …
The Bible, 1 Peter 5:5

Only a fool knows everything. A wise man knows how little he knows.
Author unknown

Many would be scantily clad if clothed in their humility.
Author unknown

It is the laden bough that hangs low, and the most fruitful Christian who is the most humble.
Author unknown

I would rather have a defeat with humility

than a victory with pride.
Author unknown, an anonymous Desert Father

Some never get started on their destiny because they cannot humble themselves to learn, grow, and change.
Author unknown

Humility is that holy place in which God bids us make the sacrifice of ourselves.
Author unknown, a Desert Father

The knowledge is truth and only found at the peak of humility, which is our food by which we grow in love to the truth.
Author unknown

Humility is like your underwear; it shouldn't show.
Author unknown

Humility is the only certain defense against humiliation.
Author unknown

A little humility is good for us all.
Author unknown

Man knows mighty little, and may some day learn enough of his own ignorance to fall down and pray.
Henry Adams

Humility exists only in those who are poor enough to see that they possess nothing of their own.
Angela of Foligno

Without humility of heart all the other virtues by which one runs toward God seem – and are – absolutely worthless.
Angela of Foligno

Abba Anthony said, "I saw the snares that the enemy spreads out over the world and I said groaning, "What can get through from such snares?" Then I heard a voice saying to me, "Humility."
Abba Anthony the Great

By the lowliness and humility of our Lord Jesus Christ, we climb up as on a true ladder to heaven into the heart of God, our dear Father, and we rest in his love.
Johann Arndt

If you plan to build a tall house of virtues, you must first lay deep foundations of humility.
Augustine of Hippo

When a certain rhetorician was asked what was the chief rule of eloquence he replied, "Delivery." What was the second rule? "Delivery." What was the third rule? "Delivery." So if you ask me about the precepts of the Christian religion, first, second, third and always I would answer, "Humility."
Augustine of Hippo

Unless humility precede, accompany, and follow up all the good we accomplish, unless we keep our eyes fixed on it, pride will snatch everything right out of our hands.
Augustine of Hippo

What makes humility so desirable is the marvelous thing it does to us; it creates in us a capacity for the closest possible intimacy with God.
Monica Baldwin

Christian humility is based on the sight of self, the vision of Christ, and the realization of God.
William Barclay

Life is a long lesson in humility.
James M. Barrie

It is a contradiction to be a true Christian and not humble.
Richard Baxter

Humility is the virtue by which a man recognizes his own unworthiness because he really knows himself.
Bernard of Clairvaux

It is no great thing to be humble when you are brought low; but to be humble when

you are praised is a great and rare attainment.
Bernard of Clairvaux

God's substance is humility. He who came to rescue us from the evil power, described himself as "meek and lowly".
Jacob Boehme

The true way to be humble is not to stoop until you are smaller than yourself, but to stand at your real height against some higher nature that will show you what the real smallness of your greatness is.
Phillips Brooks

Without humility there can be no humanity.
John Buchan

He that is down need fear no fall,
He that is low no pride.
John Bunyan

It is never said of those who are entangled in other sins that they have God resisting them, but only "God resisteth the proud."
Cassian

[The humble soul] knows that all that she is and every gift she has is from me, not from herself, and to me she attributes all.
Catherine of Siena, God speaking in a vision

The foundation of our philosophy is humility.
John Chrysostom

The higher we are placed, the more humbly we should walk.
Cicero

Christ is with the humble, not with those who set themselves up over his flock.
Clement of Rome

The signs of humility are poverty, withdrawal from the world, the concealment of one's wisdom, simplicity of speech, the seeking of alms, the disguising of one's nobility, the exclusion of free and

easy relationships, and no idle talk.
John Climacus

Holy humility said: "The one who loves me will not condemn someone, or pass judgment on anyone, or lord it over someone else, or show off his wisdom until he has been united with me."
John Climacus

Humility is a grace in the soul. It is indescribable wealth, a name and a gift from God.
John Climacus

If pride turned some of the angels into demons, then humility can doubtless make angels out of demons.
John Climacus

The Lord often humbles the vainglorious by causing some dishonor to befall them. And indeed the first step in overcoming vainglory is to remain silent and to accept dishonor gladly. The middle stage is to check every act of vainglory while it is still in thought. The end – insofar as one may talk of an end to an abyss – is to be able to accept humiliation before others without actually feeling it.
John Climacus

Just as darkness retreats before light, so all anger and bitterness disappear before the fragrance of humility.
John Climacus

There are men who wear out their bodies to no purpose in the pursuit of total dispassion, heavenly treasures, miracle working, and prophetic ability, and the poor fools do not realize that humility, not hard work, is the mother of such things.
John Climacus

Humility is nothing more than an accurate self-assessment, an awareness of oneself as one really is. And surely, anyone seeing himself for what he really is, must be truly humble.
The Cloud of Unknowing

What you lack and not what you have is the quickest path to humility.
The Cloud of Unknowing

Mr Lely, I desire you would use all your skill to paint my picture freely like me, and not flatter me at all; but remark all these roughnesses, pimples, warts and everything as you see me, otherwise I will never pay a farthing for it.
Oliver Cromwell

It is better for a man to be conquered by others on account of his humility, than to be victorious over them by means of pride.
A Desert Father

Humility is hard to acquire, and the deeper it is, the greater the struggle needed to gain it.
Diadochos of Photiki

Humiliation is the beginning of sanctification; and as without this, without holiness, no man shall see God, though he pore whole nights upon his Bible; so without that, without humility, no man shall hear God speak to his soul, though he hear three two-hour sermons every day.
John Donne

We must view humility as one of the most essential things that characterizes true Christianity.
Jonathan Edwards

Nothing sets a person so much out of the devil's reach as humility.
Jonathan Edwards

Pure Christian humility disposes a person to take notice of every thing that is good in others, and to make the best of it, and to diminish their failings.
Jonathan Edwards

True humility is not an abject, groveling, self-despising spirit; it is but a right estimate of ourselves as God sees us.
Tryon Edwards

The only wisdom we can hope to acquire is the wisdom of humility.
T.S. Eliot

"My children," my grandfather said, "you will never see anything worse than yourselves."
Ralph Waldo Emerson

The beginning of salvation is to despise yourself.
Evagrius

Humility is not a grace that can be acquired in a few months: it is the work of a lifetime.
F. Fénelon

There is no true and constant gentleness without humility. While we are so fond of ourselves, we are easily offended with others. Let us be persuaded that nothing is due to us, and then nothing will disturb us. Let us often think of our own infirmities, and we will become indulgent towards those of others.
F. Fénelon

When the corn is nearly ripe it bows the head and stoops lower than when it was green. When the people of God are near ripe for heaven, they grow more humble and self-denying.
John Flavel

They that know God will be humble; they that know themselves cannot be proud.
John Flavel

To do the wondrous work God had mind to do, he chose me. For God has chosen the foolish things of the world to confound the wise; the mean, contemptible, feeble things of the world to confound the noble and great; so that the grandeur of goodness should proceed from God, and not from his creature; so that no flesh should boast, but that God alone should be honored.
Francis of Assisi
In reply to Brother Masseo who had asked him:
"Why you? The whole world goes after you. But you

are not a handsome man, you have no great knowledge or wisdom, you are not noble. Why you?"

The devil sees nothing more abominable than a truly humble Christian, for that Christian is just the opposite of the devil's own image.
Hans Nielsen Hauge

A servant with this cause
Makes drudgery divine;
Who sweeps a room as for Thy laws
Makes that and th' action fine.
George Herbert

Let us learn humility from Christ, humiliation from David, and from Peter to cry over what has happened; but let us also learn to avoid the despair of Samson, Judas, and the wisest of men, Solomon.
Hesychois of Sinai

Humility says, "I am nothing, I have nothing."
Walter Hilton

Humility is to be exercised not so much in considering your own vileness and sinfulness, though in the beginning this consideration is good and beneficial, but rather in a quiet consideration of the infinite being and goodness of Jesus.
Walter Hilton

There was one who thought himself above me, and he was above me until he had that thought.
Elbert Hubbard

The tree of life is on high. Man climbs to it by the ladder of humility.
Hyperichius

No man has understanding if he is not humble, and whoever lacks humility is devoid of understanding. No man is humble if he is not peaceful, and he who is not peaceful is not humble. And no man is peaceful without rejoicing.
Isaac from Syria

Faithful service in a lowly place is true spiritual greatness.
D. Jackman

Humility and the fear of God are pre-eminent over all virtues.
John the Short

The door of God is humility. Our fathers, through the many insults which they suffered, entered the city of God.
John the Short

We may as well try to see without eyes, or live without breath, as to live in the spirit of religion without humility.
William Law

Woe be to them who disdain to humble themselves as little children, for the low gate of heaven will not permit them to enter through it.
Brother Lawrence

God said: The higher they are in heaven, the more humble they are in themselves, and the closer to Me and the more in love with Me.
Brother Lawrence

… the delight of being lowly; of saying of myself, "I am what I am, nothing more."
George Macdonald

I have seen unlearned men who were truly humble, and they became wiser than the wise. Another unlearned man, upon hearing them praised, instead of imitating their humility, prided himself on being unlearned and so fell into arrogance.
Mark the Ascetic

Don't be so humble – you are not that great.
Golda Meir, to a visiting diplomat

No man will learn anything at all, unless he first will learn humility.
Owen Meredith

Pride makes us artificial and humility

makes us real.
Thomas Merton

I have had more trouble with myself than with any other man I ever met.
Dwight L. Moody

We can never have more of true faith than we have of true humility.
Andrew Murray

Christ is the humility of God embodied in human nature; the Eternal Love humbling itself, clothing itself in the garb of meekness and gentleness, to win and serve and save us.
Andrew Murray

I am persuaded that love and humility are the highest attainments in the school of Christ and the brightest evidences that he is indeed our Master.
John Newton

A man ought to breathe humility as his nostrils breathe the air.
Pastor, a Desert Father

An able yet humble man is a jewel worth a kingdom.
William Penn

Jesus' life began in a borrowed stable and ended in a borrowed tomb.
Alfred Plummer

He who asks is a fool for five minutes, but he who does not ask remains a fool forever.
Chinese proverb

If thou desire the love of God and man, be humble, for the proud heart, as it loves none but itself, is beloved of none but itself.
Francis Quarles

The first test of a really great man is his humility.
John Ruskin

Humility is a strange flower; it grows best in winter weather, and under storms of affliction.
Samuel Rutherford

Humility is a virtue all men preach, none practice, and yet everybody is content to hear. The master thinks it good doctrine for his servants, the laity for the clergy, and the clergy for the laity.
John Seldon

In peace there's nothing so becomes a man
As modest stillness and humility.
William Shakespeare, King Henry V

The Churches must learn humility as well as teach it.
George Bernard Shaw, St. Joan

The proud man counts his newspaper clippings – the humble man his blessings.
Fulton J. Sheen

We cannot have one spark of real humility till we are abased before God, as guilty, helpless, and undone creatures, who have no hope but in the tender mercy of God in Christ Jesus.
Charles Simeon

Humility is not a mere insulated grace, if I may so speak, like patience, or meekness, or any other virtue, but a feeling which pervades the whole man, and is called forth into exercise with every grace.
Charles Simeon

Humility is strong, not bold; quiet, not speechless; sure, not arrogant.
Estelle Smith

You cannot expect anything from God unless you put yourself in the right place, that is, as a beggar at his footstool. Then will he hear you, and not until then.
C.H. Spurgeon

Humility is to make a right estimate of one's self; it is no humility for a man to think less of himself than he ought.
C.H. Spurgeon

Let us pray much for humility and
especially for humility in our days of peace
and success.
C.H. Spurgeon

As no ships can be built without nails, so
no man can be saved without humility.
Amma Syncletica

The source of humility is the habit of
realizing the presence of God.
William Temple

True humility,
The highest virtue, mother of them all.
Tennyson

For the foundation of this whole edifice is
humility. Therefore, sisters, if you wish to
lay good foundations, each of you must try
to be the least of all, and the slave of God,
and must seek a way and means to please
and serve all your companions. If you do
that your foundation will be so firmly laid
that your Castle will not fall.
Teresa of Avila

By meditating upon Christ's humility, we
shall see how far we are from being humble.
Teresa of Avila

Humility must always be doing its work
like a bee making its honey in the hive:
without humility all be lost.
Teresa of Avila
It is by humility that the Lord allows
Himself to be conquered so that He will
do all we ask of Him.
Teresa of Avila

Learn to humble yourself, you who are but
earth and clay
Thomas à Kempis

Unto the humble He revealeth His secrets,
and sweetly draweth nigh and inviteth him
unto Himself.
Thomas à Kempis

If you would learn anything and know it
profitably to the health of your soul, learn

to be unknown and be glad to be
considered despicable and as nothing.
Thomas à Kempis

Great peace is with the humble man, but
in the heart of a proud man are always
envy and anger.
Thomas à Kempis

Humility comes from the constant sense of
our own creatureliness.
R.C. Trench

Truly, with Augustine, our prayer should
ever be for humility and more humility.
Cornelius Van Til

Lord, help me to begin to begin.
*George Whitefield, whose indefatigable
preaching was the means of conversion of
thousands in England and America*

Talent is God-given; be humble.
John Wooden

There is no knowledge, no light, no wisdom
that you are in possession of, but what you
have received it from some source.
Brigham Young

Humility, False
Too humble is half proud
Hanan J. Ayalti

I am tired of hearing the words, "I can't."
Jeremiah said, "I am a child;" but the Lord
didn't pat him on the back and say,
"Jeremiah, that is very good, I like that in
you; your humility is beautiful." Oh no!
God didn't want any such mock humility.
He reproved and rebuked it. I do not like
the humility that is too humble to do as it
is bid. When my children are too humble
to do as they are bid, I pretty soon find a
way to make them. I say, "Go and do it!"
The Lord wants us to "go and do it."
Catherine Booth

What we suffer from today is humility in the
wrong place. Modesty has settled on the
organ of conviction; where it was never meant

to be. A man was meant to be doubtful about himself but undoubting about the truth. This has been exactly reversed.
G.K. Chesterton

I am well aware that I am the 'umblest person going … 'umble we are, 'umble we have been, 'umble we ever shall be.
Charles Dickens, spoken by Uriah Heepin David Copperfield

False humility is to believe that one is unworthy of God's goodness and does not dare to seek it humbly. True humility lies in seeing one's own unworthiness, giving up oneself to God, not doubting for a moment that he can perform the greatest results for us and in us.
F. Fénelon

Humility, Nature of
The reason why God is so great a lover of humility is because he is the great lover of truth. Now humility is nothing but truth, while pride is nothing but lying.
Vincent de Paul

True humility is a kind of self-annihilation, and this is the center of all virtues.
John Wesley

Humility and exorcism
Neither asceticism, nor vigils nor any kind of suffering are able to save, only true humility can do that.
   There was an anchorite (hermit) who was able to banish demons; and he asked them:
Hermit: What makes you go away? Is it fasting?
The demons: We do not eat or drink.
Hermit: Is it vigils?
The demons: We do not sleep.
Hermit: Is it separation from the world?
The demons: We live in the deserts.
Hermit: What power sends you away then?
The demons: Nothing can overcome us, but only humility.
Amma Theodora

Humility and love
Humility and love are precisely the graces

which the men of the world can understand, if they do not comprehend doctrines. They are the graces about which there is no mystery, and they are within reach of all classes. The poorest Christian can every day find occasion for practicing love and humility.
J. C. Ryle

Humility and revival
One of our troubles is we are not willing to humble ourselves. We are not willing to give up our opinions as to how things should be done. We want a revival to come just in our way. You never saw two revivals come just alike. We must let them come in God's way. People are ashamed to admit they need a revival.
Mordecai Ham

Humility and temptation
The devil has least power to fasten a temptation on him that is most humble.
Thomas Brooks

It is reported of Satan that he should say thus of a humble man: You do always overcome me; when I would exalt and promote you, you keep yourself in humility; and when I would throw you down, you lift up yourself in assurance of faith.
Thomas Brooks

Humor
Without humor you cannot run a sweetie-shop, let alone a nation.
John Buchan

True humor springs not more from the head than from the heart; it is not contempt, its essence is love.
Thomas Carlyle

For health and the constant enjoyment of life, give me a keen and ever-present sense of humor; it is the next best thing to an abiding faith in providence.
George B. Cheever

The size of man's understanding might be

justly measured by his mirth.
Samuel Johnson

Humor is the great thing, the saving thing. The minute it crops up, all our irritations and resentments slip away and a sunny spirit takes their place.
Mark Twain

Humor is mankind's greatest blessing.
Mark Twain

Hunger
You cannot reason with a hungry belly, since it has no ears.
Greek proverb

It is not the horse that draws the cart, but the oats.
Russian proverb

A hungry man is not a free man.
Adlai E. Stevenson

Hunger, Spiritual
Give me persons in love: they know what I mean. Give me those who yearn; give me those who are hungry; give me those far away in this desert, who are thirsty and sigh for the spring of the eternal country. Give me those kinds of people: they know what I mean. But if I speak to cold persons, they just do not know what I am talking about.
Augustine of Hippo

It is a sure mark of grace to desire more.
Robert Murray M'Cheyne

A man may study because his brain is hungry for knowledge, even Bible knowledge. But he prays because his soul is hungry for God.
Leonard Ravenhill

God will fill the hungry because He Himself has stirred up the hunger. As in the case of prayer, when God prepares the heart to pray, He prepares His ear to hear (Ps. 10: 17). So in the case of spiritual hunger, when God prepares the heart to

hunger, He will prepare His hand to fill.
Thomas Watson

Hurry
Hurry is not of the devil. It is the devil.
K. Jung

Husbands
See also: Wives
Husbands, love your wives, just as Christ also loved the church and gave himself up for her.
The Bible, Ephesians 5:25

However, each one of you also must love his wife as he loves himself, and the wife must respect her husband.
The Bible, Ephesians 5:33

Husbands, in the same way be considerate as you live with your wives, and treat them with respect as the weaker partner and as heirs with you of the gracious gift of life, so that nothing will hinder your prayers.
The Bible, 1 Peter 3:7

My husband used to make all the decisions in our family. But now that he's a Promise Keeper, we always talk first and then he makes the decision.
Author unknown
Wife of a Promise Keeper, a U.S. men's religious group focusing on men's commitments to their families

Being a husband is a whole-time job. That is why so many husbands fail. They cannot give their entire attention to it.
Arnold Bennett

If thou art a man of holiness, thou must look more for a portion of grace in thy wife, than a portion of gold with a wife; thou must look more after righteousness than riches; more after piety than money; more after the inheritance she hath in heaven, than the inheritance she hath on earth; more at her being new born, than at her being high born.
Thomas Brooks

It is necessary to be almost a genius to

make a good husband.
Honoré de Balzac

Husbands are like fires. They go out when unattended.
Zsa Zsa Gabor

A husband's power over his wife is paternal and friendly, not magisterial and despotic.
Jeremy Taylor

Hymn singing
Hymns were still a new thing in the worship of the Church of England, and the greatest change the Evangelicals made in the church services in the eighteenth century was the introduction of congregational singing.
Kenneth Hylson-Smith

Hymns
God is known in his works, not in our experience. That is why the Psalms recite God's works. Very often, in the contemporary praise music that uses the Psalms, the part of the Psalm that is a response is included, while the recitation of the works is excluded.
Author unknown

A good hymn book is a wonderful companion to the Bible.
Francis Schaeffer

Hypocrisy
See also: Hypocrites
Woe to you, teachers of the law and Pharisees, you hypocrites! You give a tenth of your spices – mint, dill and cummin. But you have neglected the more important matters of the law – justice, mercy and faithfulness. You should have practiced the latter, without neglecting the former.
The Bible, Matthew 23:23

Whited sepulchers, which indeed appear beautiful outward, but are within full of dead men's bones.
The Bible, Matthew 23:27

A bad man is worse when he pretends to be a saint.
Francis Bacon

Hypocrisy can plunge the mind of a man into a dark abyss, when he believes his own self-flattery instead of God's verdict.
John Calvin

Hypocrisy is the lubricant of society.
David Hull

It is no fault of Christianity that a hypocrite falls into sin.
Jerome

For neither Man nor Angel can discern
Hypocrisy, the only evil that walks
Invisible, except to God alone,
By his permissive will, through Heav'n
  and Earth.
And oft though wisdom wake, suspicion
  sleeps
At wisdom's Gate, and to simplicity
Resigns her charge, while goodness thinks
  no ill
Where no ill seems.
John Milton

Do not live one way in private, and another in public.
Quintilian

That one may smile, and smile, and be a villain.
William Shakespeare, Hamlet

Hypocrites
See also: Hypocrisy
I saw about a peck of counterfeit dollars once. Did I go to the window and throw away all my good dollars? No! Yet you reject Christianity because there are hypocrites, or counterfeit Christians.
William E. Biederwolf

Hypocrites in the Church? Yes, and in the lodge and at the home. Don't hunt through the Church for a hypocrite. Go home and look in the mirror. Hypocrites? Yes. See that you make the number one less.
Billy Sunday

I

Icons
See: Pictures

Ideas
One of the greatest pains to human nature
is the pain of a new idea.
Walter Bagehot

Neither man nor nation can exist without
a sublime idea.
Fyodor Dostoevsky

Only those who build on ideas build for
eternity.
Ralph Waldo Emerson

Whoso shrinks from ideas ends by having
nothing but sensations.
Goethe

Daring ideas are like chessmen moved
forward; they may be beaten, but they may
start a winning game.
Goethe

There is one thing stronger than all the
armies of the world, and that is an idea
whose time has come.
Victor Hugo

Great ideas need landing gear as well as wings.
C.D. Jackson

You do not destroy an idea by killing
people; you replace it with a better one.
Edward Keating

A man with a new idea is a crank, until the
idea succeeds.
Mark Twain

Ideals
An ideal is never yours until it comes out

of your finger tips.
Florence Allshorn

Ideals are like tuning forks: sound them
often to bring your life up to standard
pitch.
S.D. Gordon

It is from numberless diverse acts of
courage and belief that human history is
shaped. Each time a man stands up for an
ideal, or acts to improve the lot of others,
or strikes out against injustice, he sends
forth a tiny ripple of hope, and crossing
each other from a million different centers
of energy and daring those ripples build a
current which can sweep down the
mightiest walls of oppression and
injustice.
Robert F. Kennedy

Identification
I have been crucified with Christ and I no
longer live, but Christ lives in me. The life
I live in the body, I live by faith in the Son
of God, who loved me and gave himself for
me.
The Bible, Galatians 2:20

Jesus did not become identical to us; he
did become identified with us.
Donald English

Idleness
See also: Action; Effort
All hard work brings a profit, but mere talk
leads only to poverty.
The Bible, Proverbs 14:23

Idleness and luxury are the devil's jackals,
and find him abundant prey.
Author unknown

The ruin of most men dates from idle moments.
Author unknown

Make sure that you are not merely never idle, but rather that you are using your time in the most profitable way that you can and do not prefer a less profitable way before one of greater profit.
Richard Baxter

Let us use the gifts of God lest they be extinguished by our slothfulness.
John Calvin

Men were created to do something, that they might not be idle and unoccupied. God condemned in his person all idleness.
John Calvin

Diligence is the mother of good fortune, and idleness, its opposite, never brought a man to the goal of any of his best wishes.
Cervantes

Idleness and pride tax with a heavier hand than kings and parliaments. If we can get rid of the former, we may easily bear the latter.
Benjamin Franklin

Hunger is the constant companion of the idle man.
Hesiod

Ease and idleness are the destruction of the soul and they can injure her more than the demons.
Isaac from Syria

To do nothing is in every man's power.
Samuel Johnson

Never be entirely idle; but either be reading, or writing, or praying, or meditating, or endeavoring something for the public good.
Thomas à Kempis

The true, living faith, which the Holy Spirit instils into the heart, simply cannot be idle.
Martin Luther

Activity may lead to evil; but inactivity cannot be led to good.
Hannah More

Idle time is the devil's workshop.
Proverb

Satan finds work for idle hands to do.
Proverb

Idleness is the mother of want.
Greek proverb

Idleness is the key to Poverty's door.
Greek proverb

As worms breed in a pool of stagnant water, so evil thoughts breed in the mind of the idle.
Latin proverb

Be sure to keep busy, so the devil may always find you occupied.
Flavius Vegetius Renatus

Shun idleness even if you are wealthy.
Thales

Idleness, Sacred
Work is not always required of a man. There is such a thing as sacred idleness, the cultivation of which is now fearfully neglected.
George Macdonald

Idolatry
Therefore, my dear friends, flee from idolatry.
The Bible, 1 Corinthians 10:14

My sin was this, that not in him but in his creatures — myself and others — I sought for pleasures, honors, and truths, and so fell headlong into sorrows, confusions, errors.
Augustine of Hippo

Man's mind is like a store of idolatry and superstition; so much so that if a man believes his own mind it is certain that he will forsake God and forge some idol in his own brain.
John Calvin

Every one of us is, even from his mother's
womb, a master craftsman of idols.
John Calvin

Let nought that is worshiped be depicted
on walls.
Council of Elvira, c. AD 305

The dearest idol I have known,
Whate'er that idol be,
Help me to tear it from thy throne,
And worship only thee.
William Cowper

It is a horrid abomination to see in
Christian temples a painted image either of
Christ or of any saint.
Epiphanius, Bishop of Salamis

Whatever man loves, that is his god. For he
carries it in his heart; he goes about with it
night and day, he sleeps and wakes with it,
be it what it may – wealth or self, pleasure
or renown.
Martin Luther

That to which your heart clings is your
god.
Martin Luther

Anything that one imagines of God apart
from Christ is only useless thinking and
vain idolatry.
Martin Luther

You don't have to go to heathen lands
today to find false gods. America is full of
them. Whatever you love more than God
is your idol.
D.L. Moody

Idolatry is an attempt to use God for man's
purposes, rather than to give oneself to
God's service.
C.F.D. Moule

There is nothing so abominable in the eyes
of God and of men as idolatry, whereby
men render to the creature that honor
which is due only to the Creator.
Blaise Pascal

Idols
See: Idolatry

Ignorance

Ignorance is not innocence, but sin.
Robert Browning

A man may be theologically knowing and
spiritually ignorant.
Stephen Charnock

To be conscious that you are ignorant is a
great step to knowledge.
Benjamin Disraeli

His ignorance is encyclopedic.
Abba Eban

I have never met a man so ignorant that I
couldn't learn something from him.
Galileo

Nothing is as terrible to see as ignorance in
action.
Goethe

The recipe for perpetual ignorance is a very
simple and effective one: be satisfied with
your opinions and content with your
knowledge.
Elbert Hubbard

It is worse still to be ignorant of your
ignorance.
Jerome

Nothing in the world is more dangerous
than sincere ignorance and conscientious
stupidity.
Martin Luther King, Jr

Ignorance of God and of ourselves is the
great principle and cause of all our
disquietments; and this ariseth mostly not
from want of light and instruction, but for
want of consideration and application.
John Owen

Everybody is ignorant, only on different
subjects.
Will Rogers

Herein is the evil of ignorance, that he who is neither good nor wise is nevertheless satisfied with himself: he has no desire for that of which he feels no want.
Socrates

Illness
See also: Trials
Are any among you sick? They should call for the elders of the church and have them pray over them, anointing them with oil in the name of the Lord. The prayer of faith will save the sick, and the Lord will raise them up.
The Bible, James 5.14-15

All diseases of Christians are to be ascribed to demons.
Augustine of Hippo

Before all things and above all things, care must be taken of the sick, so that they may be served in very deed as Christ himself … But let the sick on their part consider that they are being served for God's honor, and not provoke their brethren who are serving them by their unreasonable demands.
Benedict, Rule

I cannot believe that my illness is natural. I suspect Satan, and therefore I am the more inclined to take it lightly.
Martin Luther, laid low with a sudden illness

In time of sickness the soul collects itself anew.
Latin proverb

Sickness helps to remind men of death.
  Sickness helps to make men think seriously of God, and their souls, and the world to come.
  Sickness helps to soften men's hearts, and teach them wisdom.
  Sickness helps to level and humble us.
  Sickness helps to try men's religion, of what sort it is.
  The storms of winter often bring out the defects in a man's dwelling, and sickness often exposes the gracelessness of a man's soul. Surely anything that makes us find out the real character of our faith is a good.
J.C. Ryle

Image of God
According to Scripture the essence of man consists in this, that he is the image of God. As such he is distinguished from all other creatures and stands supreme as the head and crown of the entire creation.
Louis Berkof

The rule of life for a perfect person is to be in the image and likeness of God.
Clement of Alexandria

Within each of us exists the image of God, however disfigured and corrupted by sin it may presently be. God is able to recover this image through grace as we are conformed to Christ.
Alister McGrath

The salvation of man includes his restoration into the image of God and the calling implicit in that image, to subdue the earth and to exercise dominion.
R.J. Rushdoony

The image of God is found essentially and personally in all mankind.
Jan Van Ruysbroeck

Imagination
Imagination gallops; judgment merely walks.
Author unknown

Choosing is only difficult for those with imagination.
Author unknown

If you can imagine yourself as something, you can become it.
Author unknown

I like to have a thing suggested rather than told in full. When every detail is given, the mind rests satisfied, and the imagination loses the desire to use its own wings.
Thomas Bailey Aldrich

Imagination is the highest kite you can fly.
Lauren Bacall

The soul without imagination is what an observatory would be without a telescope.
Henry War Beecher

What is now proved was once only imagined.
William Blake

The man who cannot wonder is but a pair of spectacles behind which there is no eye.
Thomas Carlyle

I am enough of an artist to draw freely upon my imagination.
Imagination is more important than knowledge.
Knowledge is limited.
Imagination encircles the world.
Albert Einstein

When I examine myself and my methods of thought, I come to the conclusion that the gift of fantasy has meant more to me than my talent for absorbing positive knowledge.
Albert Einstein

I am looking for a lot of men who have an infinite capacity to not know what can't be done.
Henry Ford

Our imagination is the only limit to what we can hope to have in the future.
Charles F. Kettering

Imagination cannot make fools wise; but she can make them happy, to the envy of reason, who can only make her friends miserable.
Blaise Pascal

Imagination decides everything.
Blaise Pascal

Put the world's greatest philosopher on a plank that is wider than need be: if there is a precipice below, although reason may convince him that he is safe, his imagination will prevail.
Blaise Pascal

Everything you can imagine is real.
Picasso

Wonder is the beginning of wisdom.
Greek proverb

I like nonsense, it wakes up the brain cells. Fantasy is a necessary ingredient in living, it's a way of looking at life through the wrong end of a telescope. Which is what I do, and that enables you to laugh at life's realities.
Dr Seuss

Some men see things as they are and say why? I dream things that never were and say, "Why not?"
George Bernard Shaw

Not all who wander are lost.
J.R.R. Tolkien.

You can't depend on your judgment when your imagination is out of focus.
Mark Twain

It is better to be high-spirited even though one makes more mistakes, than to be narrow-minded and all too prudent. Do not quench your inspiration and your imagination; do not become the slave of your model.
Vincent van Gogh

Imagination and humor
Imagination was given to man to compensate him for what he is not; a sense of humor to console him for what he is.
Francis Bacon

Imitation
Never take others for your example in the tasks you have to perform, however holy they may be, for the devil will set their imperfections before you. But imitate Christ, who is supremely perfect and supremely holy, and you will never err.
John of the Cross

Immorality
See also: Marriage
Let us behave decently, as in the daytime,

not in orgies and drunkenness, not in sexual immorality and debauchery, not in dissension and jealousy. Rather, clothe yourselves with the Lord Jesus Christ, and do not think about how to gratify the desires of the sinful nature.
The Bible, Romans 13:13,14

"Food for the stomach and the stomach for food" – but God will destroy them both. The body is not meant for sexual immorality, but for the Lord, and the Lord for the body.
The Bible, 1 Corinthians 6:13

Flee from sexual immorality. All other sins a man commits are outside his body, but he who sins sexually sins against his own body.
The Bible, 1 Corinthians 6:18

We should not commit sexual immorality.
The Bible, 1 Corinthians 10:8

God promises punishment not only to adulterers but to all kinds of fornicators because both depart from the holy ordinance of God, and indeed violate and overturn it by their promiscuity, since there is only one lawful union which is approved by the name and authority of God. Since promiscuous and unsettled lusts cannot be controlled without the remedy of marriage he commends it to us and calls it honorable.
John Calvin

It is worse to live like a beast than to be a beast.
William Gurnall

The unclean person makes himself a stigmatic; he brands his body, and leaves upon it a loathsome stain. Other sins comparatively are without the body, by it, not in it; this is both.
William Jenkyn

Immorality in the church
It is actually reported that there is sexual immorality among you, and of a kind that does not occur even among pagans: A man has his father's wife.
The Bible, 1 Corinthians 5:1

But now I am writing you that you must not associate with anyone who calls himself a brother but is sexually immoral or greedy, an idolater or a slanderer, a drunkard or a swindler. With such a man do not even eat.
The Bible, 1 Corinthians 5:11

Impartiality
There is no respect of persons with God.
The Bible, Romans 2:11 KJV

Immortality
Even Pliny, one of the most intelligent Latin writers, in his Natural History, says there were two things which were beyond the power of God – one was to give immortality to mortals, and the other was to give bodily life again to the dead.
J.C. Ryle

Spring – an experience in immortality.
Henry David Thoreau

Death cannot kill what never dies.
Thomas Traherne

Impossible
What are Christians put into the world for except to do the impossible in the strength of God.
General S.C. Armstrong

God loves with a great love the man whose heart is bursting with a passion for the impossible.
William Booth

I have learned to use the word "impossible" with the greatest caution.
Wernher Von Braun

Scientists have proven that it's impossible to long-jump 30 feet, but I don't listen to that kind of talk. Thoughts like that have a way of sinking into your feet.
Carl Lewis

We never test the resources of God until we attempt the impossible
F.B. Meyer

We have a God who delights in impossibilities.
Andrew Murray

Until we reach for the impossible through fervent, faith-filled prayer, we will never fulfill our created purpose!
David Smithers

Faith sees the invisible, believes the unbelievable, and receives the impossible.
Corrie ten Boom

Inaction

To the rich man, Lazarus was part of the landscape. If ever he did notice him, it never struck him that Lazarus had anything to do with him. He was simply unaware of his presence, or, if he was aware of it, he had no sense of responsibility for it. A man may well be condemned, not for doing something, but for doing nothing.
William Barclay

The hottest places in hell are reserved for those who in time of great moral crises maintain their neutrality.
Dante

Iron rusts from disuse; stagnant water loses its purity and in cold weather becomes frozen; even so does inaction sap the vigor of the mind.
Leonardo da Vinci

In Germany, they first came for the Communists, and I didn't speak up because I wasn't a Communist.
  Then they came for the Jews, and I didn't speak up because I wasn't a Jew.
  Then they came for the trade unionists, and I didn't speak up because I wasn't a trade unionist.
  Then they came for the Catholics, and I didn't speak up because I wasn't a Catholic.

Then they came for me – and by that time there was nobody left to speak up.
Marton Niemoller, German Lutheran pastor speaking about the Holocaust

Incarnation
See also: Christmas
More light than we can learn,
More wealth than we can treasure,
More love than we can earn,
More peace than we can measure,
Because one Child is born.
Author unknown

I think that the purpose and cause of the Incarnation was that God might illuminate the world by his wisdom and excite it to the love of Himself.
Peter Abelard

By his divine nature, Christ is simple,
By his human nature, he is complex.
Thomas Aquinas

He built himself a temple, a body that is, in the Virgin, and so made himself an instrument in which to dwell.
Athanasius

Our Lord took a body like ours and lived as a man in order that those who had refused to recognize him in his superintendence and captaincy of the whole universe might come to recognize from the works he did here below in the body, that what dwelt in this body was the Word of God.
Athanasius

He, indeed, assumed humanity that we might become God.
Athanasius

Maker of the sun,
He is made under the sun.
In the Father he remains,
From his mother he goes forth.
Creator of heaven and earth,
He was born on earth under heaven.
Unspeakably wise,
He is wisely speechless.
Filling the world,

He lies in a manger.
Ruler of the stars,
He nurses at his mother's breast.
He is both great in the nature of God,
and small in the form of a servant.
Augustine of Hippo

He was created of a mother whom he
created. He was carried by hands that he
formed. He cried in the manger in
wordless infancy, he the Word, without
whom all human eloquence is mute.
Augustine of Hippo

God is away beyond everything.
Celsus

He comes down to our level, adapting His
Godhead to our power to comprehend.
The Cloud of Unknowing

On Christmas Day two thousand years
ago, the birth of a tiny baby in an obscure
village in the Middle East was God's
supreme triumph of good over evil.
Charles Colson

Even when a baby seen in swaddling
clothes at the bosom of the Virgin who
bore him, Christ still filled the whole
creation as God and was co-regent with his
Father – for deity is measureless, sizeless,
and admits no bounds.
Cyril of Alexandria

The Only Begotten Word of God has saved
us by putting on our likeness. Suffering in
the flesh, and rising from the dead, he
revealed our nature as greater than death or
corruption. What he achieved was beyond
the ability of our condition, and what
seemed to have been worked out in human
weakness and by suffering was really
stronger than men and a demonstration of
the power that pertains to God.
Cyril of Alexandria

The Son of God is also known as the Word
of God. Once He incarnated Himself, He
became known as the Christ.
Cyril of Alexandria

The Word introduced Himself into that
which He was not, in order that the nature
of man also might become what it was not,
resplendent, by its union, with the
grandeur of divine majesty, which has been
raised beyond nature rather than that it has
cast the unchangeable God beneath its
nature.
Cyril of Alexandria

Christ did not pass through the Virgin as
through a channel, but actually took flesh
and was actually fed with her milk. He
really ate as we eat and drank as we drink.
For if the incarnation was a figment of the
imagination so is our salvation.
Cyril of Jerusalem

Christ uncrowned himself to crown us,
and put off his robes to put on our rags,
and came down from heaven to keep us
out of hell. He fasted forty days that he
might feast us to all eternity; he came from
heaven to earth that he might send us from
earth to heaven.
W. Dyer

How many observe Christ's birthday! How
few, his precepts! O! 'tis easier to keep
holidays than commandments.
Benjamin Franklin

The Self-Existent comes into being, the
Uncreate is created, That which cannot be
contained is contained.
Gregory of Nazianzus

The fact is that the greatest mystery of all –
the incarnation – comes at the very
beginning and is the central reason why we
believe in God. We cannot explain it: there
is the beginning of the mystery of faith.
But because of the evidence neither can we
explain it away: there is the beginning of
the rationality of faith.
Os Guinness

How can God stoop lower than to come
and dwell with a poor humble soul? which
is more than if he had said, such a one
should dwell with him; for a beggar to live

at court is not so much as the king to dwell
with him in his cottage.
William Gurnall

It was great condescension that He who
was God should be made in the likeness of
flesh; but much greater that He who was
holy should be made in the likeness of
sinful flesh.
Matthew Henry

Rejoice, that the immortal God is born, so
that mortal man may live in eternity.
John Huss

There is one physician, fleshly and
spiritual, begotten and unbegotten, God in
man, both of Mary and of God, first
passible and then impassible.
Ignatius

Surely royalty in rags, angels in cells, is not
descent compared to Deity in flesh!
Henry Law

The central miracle asserted by Christians
is the incarnation. They say that God
became man.
C.S. Lewis

Never can man and God meet.
Plato

This little Babe, so few days old,
Is come to rifle Satan's fold;
All hell doth at his presence quake,
Though he himself for cold do shake;
For in this weak unarmed wise
The gates of hell he will surprise.
Robert Southwell

Immanuel, God with us in our nature, in our
sorrow, in our lifework, in our punishment,
in our grave, and now with us, or rather we
with Him, in resurrection, ascension,
triumph, and Second Advent splendor.
C.H. Spurgeon

Our God contracted to a span
Incomprehensibly made man.
Charles Wesley

Christ, by highest heaven adored,
Christ, the everlasting Lord,
Late in time behold him come,
Offspring of a virgin's womb.
Veiled in flesh the Godhead see;
Hail, the incarnate Deity,
Pleased as Man with man to dwell,
Jesus our Immanuel!
Charles Wesley

Inconsistency

He does not believe, that does not live
according to his "belief."
Thomas Fuller

Indecision

We know what happens to people who stay
in the middle of the road. They get run
over.
Aneurin Bevan

Indecision may or may not be my
problem.
Jimmy Buffett

They are decided only to be undecided,
resolved to be irresolute, adamant for drift,
all-powerful for impotence.
Winston Churchill

There is no more miserable human being
than one in whom nothing is habitual but
indecision.
William James

Nothing is so exhausting as indecision, and
nothing is so futile.
Bertrand Russell

Indifference
See: Apathy

Indignation

Moral indignation is jealousy with a
halo.
H.G. Wells

Indispensable

The graveyards are full of indispensable
men.
Charles de Gaulle

Individual

The individual is the central, rarest, most precious capital resource in our society.
Peter F. Drucker

Any power must be an enemy of mankind which enslaves the individual by terror and force, whether it arises under the Fascist or the Communist flag. All that is valuable in human society depends upon the opportunity for development accorded to the individual.
Albert Einstein

One man with courage makes a majority.
Andrew Jackson

The worth of the state, in the long run, is the worth of the individuals composing it.
John Stuart Mill

I believe in the supreme worth of the individual and in his right to life, liberty, and the pursuit of happiness.
John D. Rockefeller

We forfeit three-fourths of ourselves in order to be like other people.
Arthur Schopenhauer

The greatest works are done by the ones. The hundreds do not often do much – the companies never; it is the units – the single individuals, that are the power and the might. Individual effort is, after all, the grand thing.
C.H. Spurgeon

Noah was the first of many individuals who, apparently single-handed, have been used by God to carry out his purpose and to make a crucial difference to the world. Even today people famous and people unknown are making a difference in the world simply by trying to obey God. They have refused to be bullied into believing that what they do makes no difference.
Stephen Travis

Indulgences

There is no divine authority for preaching that the soul flies out of purgatory immediately after the money clinks in the bottom of the chest. All those who believe themselves certain of their own salvation by means of letters of indulgence will be eternally damned, together with their teachers. Any Christian whatsoever, who is truly repentant, enjoys remission from penalty and guilt, and this is given him without letters of indulgence.
Martin Luther

Industry
See also: Idleness

Men who have attained things worth having in this world have worked while others idled, have persevered when others gave up in despair, have practiced early in life the valuable habits of self-denial, industry, and singleness of purpose. As a result, they enjoy later in life the success so often erroneously attributed to good luck.
Grenville Kleiser

Queen Victoria: Mr Paderewski [a world famous violinist], you are a genius.
Paderewski: That may be, Ma'am, but before I was a genius, I was a drudge.
Paderewski

Indwelling sin
See also: Temptation

Inequality

All animals are equal but some are more equal than others.
George Orwell, Animal Farm

Inerrancy

That the Roman church has never erred; nor will it err to all eternity; the Scriptures bearing witness.
Gregory the Great

Infallibility

I'm sorry we're late, we misread the timetables. But there – nobody's infallible.
Geoffrey Fisher
To Pope John XXIII, on the occasion of the first meeting of an Archbishop of Canterbury with a Pope since before the Reformation.

Infant baptism
See also: Baptism

The divine sign given to the child in baptism confirms the promise given to godly parents, and proclaims that the Lord is not only their God, but their children's. All this is to God's glory and increases the believer's love towards him, as they realize that his love is not only for them, but for their offspring.
John Calvin

Inferiority

No one can make you feel inferior without your consent.
Eleanor Roosevelt

Infertility
See: Adoption

Influence

Immortality lies not in the things you leave behind, but in the people your life has touched.
Author unknown

We can influence others as much as God has influenced us.
Bobbie-Jean Merck

Born in a manger and crucified as a malefactor, Jesus now controls the destinies of the civilized world, and rules a spiritual empire which embraces one-third of the inhabitants of the globe.
Philip Schaff

Ingratitude
See also: Gratitude

Thankless men are like swine feeding on acorns, which, though they fall upon their heads, never make them look up to the tree from which they come.
Jean Daille

Inheritance

The lines are fallen unto me in pleasant places; yea, I have a goodly heritage.
The Bible, Psalm 16:6 KJV

... an inheritance that can never perish, spoil or fade – kept in heaven for you ...
The Bible, 1 Peter 1:4

This is all the inheritance I can give to my dear family. The religion of Christ can give them one which will make them rich indeed.
Patrick Henry

Initiative

God always takes the initiative, from the act of creation on. The supreme example is the incarnation, the supreme example of taking history and time and the created world seriously. Instead of the passive Eastern God receiving man's search, man's spiritual efforts, Jesus is himself the western God barging into man's world physically.
Peter Kreeft

Men will never believe with a saving and real faith, unless God inclines the heart; and they will believe as soon as He inclines it.
Blaise Pascal

Christianity declares that God has taken the initiative in Jesus Christ to deliver us from our sin. This is the main theme of the Bible.
John Stott

Injustice

Injustice anywhere is a threat to justice everywhere.
Martin Luther King, Jr

When I was a boy, the Lakota owned the world.
The sun rose and set on their land. They sent ten thousand men to battle.
Where are the warriors today? Who slew them? Where are our lands? Who owns them?
What white man can say I ever stole his land or a penny of his money? Yet they say I am a thief.
What white woman, however lonely, was ever captive or insulted by me? Yet they say I am a bad Indian.
What white man has ever seen me drunk? Who has ever come to me hungry and left me unfed?

Who has ever seen me beat my wives or
abuse my children? What law have I
broken?
Is it wrong for me to love my own? Is it
wicked of me because my skin is red?
Because I am a Lakota?
Because I was born where my father lived?
Because I would die for my people and my
country?
Tatanka Yotanka, Sitting Bull

Inner life
We must have richness of soul.
Antiphanes

If better were within, better would come out.
Thomas Fuller

Inscriptions
Ye call me master, and obey me not;
Ye call me light, and seek me not;
Ye call me way, and walk me not;
Ye call me wise, and follow me not;
Ye call me fair, and love me not;
Ye call me rich, and ask me not;
Ye call me eternal, and seek me not;
Ye call me gracious, and trust me not;
Ye call me noble, and serve me not;
Ye call me mighty, and honor me not;
Ye call me just, and fear me not;
If I condemn you, blame me not.
Inscription in Lubek Cathedral, Germany
Author unknown

Insight
Where others see a shepherd boy, God may
see a king.
Author unknown

A moment's insight is sometimes worth a
life's experience.
Oliver Wendell Holmes

Insincerity
See also: Hypocrisy
The most exhausting thing in my life is
being insincere.
Anne Morrow Lindbergh

Inspiration
No man was ever great without some

degree of divine inspiration.
Cicero

Find inspiring people. Inspiring people are
vitamins for our spirit.
Sark

Institutions
An institution is the lengthened shadow of
one man.
Ralph Waldo Emerson

All national institutions of churches,
whether Jewish, Christian, or Turkish,
appear to me no other than human
inventions, set up to terrify and enslave
mankind, and monopolize power and
profit.
Thomas Paine

Instruction
He who scorns instruction will pay for it,
but he who respects a command is rewarded.
The Bible, Proverbs 13:13

Our critical day is not the very day of our
death, but the whole course of our life; I
thank him, that prays for me when my bell
tolls; but I thank him much more, that
catechizes me, or preaches to me, or
instructs me how to live.
John Donne

Insults
A fool shows his annoyance at once, but a
prudent man overlooks an insult.
The Bible, Proverbs 12:16

An injury is much sooner forgotten than
an insult.
Lord Chesterfield

A smiling face, and forgiveness, are the
best way to avenge an insult.
Spanish proverb

Integrity
Never esteem anything as of advantage to
thee that shall make thee break thy word
or lose thy self-respect.
Marcus Aurelius Antoninus

Integrity without knowledge is weak and useless, and knowledge without integrity is dangerous and dreadful.
Samuel Johnson

There is no such thing as a minor lapse of integrity.
Tom Peters

Integrity is the noblest possession.
Latin proverb

This above all: to thine own self be true,
And it must follow, as the night the day,
Thou canst not then be false to any man.
William Shakespeare, Hamlet

Intellect
We should take care not to make the intellect our god; it has, of course, powerful muscles, but no personality.
Albert Einstein

There is a great difference between a lofty spirit and a right spirit. A lofty spirit excites admiration by its profoundness; but only a right spirit achieves salvation and happiness by its stability and integrity. Do not conform your ideas to those of the world. Scorn the "intellectual" as much as the world esteems it. What men consider intellectual is a certain facility to produce brilliant thoughts. Nothing is more vain. We make an idol of our intellect as a woman who believes herself beautiful worships her face. We take pride in our own thoughts. We must reject not only human cleverness, but also human prudence, which seems so important and so profitable. Then we may enter – like little children, with candor and innocence of worldly ways – into the simplicity of faith; and with humility and a horror of sin we may enter into the holy passion of the cross.
F. Fénelon

Intelligence
The test of a first-rate intelligence is the ability to hold two opposed ideas in the mind at the same time, and still retain the ability to function.
F. Scott Fitzgerald

Intermarriage
Intermarriage [between people of different races] is a sin against the will of the Eternal Creator.
Adolf Hitler

Intolerance
I have seen gross intolerance shown in support of tolerance.
Samuel Taylor Coleridge

Introspection
Each one must ... act sincerely and without reflection, seeking with all his strength to love God, holding himself in his presence, and desiring to live unknown to himself.
François Malaval

Intuition
The only real valuable thing is intuition.
Albert Einstein

Often you just have to rely on your intuition.
Bill Gates, Microsoft

Invitations
When the ass was invited to the wedding feast, he said, "They need more wood and water."
Bosnian proverb

J

Jealousy

They stript Joseph out of his coat, his coat of many colors.
The Bible, Genesis 37:23

Jealousy sees with opera glasses, making little things big; dwarfs are changed into giants and suspicions into truths.
Cervantes

In jealousy there is more self-love than love.
La Rochefoucauld

O! beware, my lord, of jealousy;
It is the green-eyed monster which doth mock
The meat it feeds on.
William Shakespeare, Othello

Jehovah's Witnesses

Their official teaching
Bible

Only this organization functions for Jehovah's purpose and to his praise. To it alone God's Sacred Word, the Bible, is not a sealed book. How very much true Christians appreciate associating with the only organization on earth that understands the "deep things of God"! Furthermore, this organization alone is supplied with "gifts in men," such as evangelizers, shepherds and teachers.
Watchtower

Prophecy

For the time our Lord said, "Your house is left unto you desolate," AD 33, to AD 70 was 36? years; and so from AD 1878 to the end of AD 1914 is 36? years. And with the end of AD 1914, what God calls Babylon, and what men call Christendom, will have passed away."
Thy Kingdom Come, 1891

End of the world

The date of the close of that "battle" is definitely marked in Scripture as October, 1914. It is already in progress, its beginning dating from October, 1874.
Watchtower, Jan. 15, 1892

Return of Christ

The Scriptural proof is that the second presence of the Lord Jesus Christ began in 1874 AD *Prophecy*, 1929
Watchtower

It should be expected that the Lord would have a means of communication to his people on the earth, and he has clearly shown that the magazine called *The Watchtower* is used for that purpose.
Yearbook of Jehovah's Witnesses

Bible, Understanding the

We all need help to understand the Bible, and we cannot find the scriptural guidance we need outside the "faithful and discreet slave" organization.
Watchtower

People cannot see the Divine Plan in studying the Bible by itself. If he then lays them [*Scripture Studies*] aside and ignores them and goes to the Bible alone, though he has understood his Bible for ten years, our experience shows that within two years he goes into darkness. On the other hand, if he had merely read the *Scripture Studies* with their references, and had not read a page of the Bible, as such, he would be in

the light at the end of the two years, because he would have the light of the Scriptures.
Watchtower

Jerusalem
If I forget thee, O Jerusalem, let my right hand forget her cunning.
The Bible, Psalm 137:5 KJV

Jesus
See also: Christ
The name of Jesus is in my mind as a joyful song, in my ear a heavenly music, and in my mouth sweet honey.
Richard Rolle

Jews
A man is not a Jew if he is only one outwardly, nor is circumcision merely outward and physical. No, a man is a Jew if he is one inwardly; and circumcision is circumcision of the heart, by the Spirit, not by the written code.
The Bible, Romans 2:28,29

The apostle Paul affirms the salvation of the mass of Israel.
John Murray

The Jews are a frightened people. Nineteen centuries of Christian love have broken down their nerves.
Israel Zangwill

Jews and Gentiles
Jews have God's promise and if we Christians have it, too, then it is only as those chosen with them, as guests in their house, that we are new wood grafted onto their tree.
Karl Barth

I think myself that the shocking reply to the Syrophonician woman (it came alright in the end) is to remind all us Gentile Christians – who forget it easily enough and even flirt with anti-Semitism – that the Hebrews are spiritually senior to us, that

God did entrust the descendants of Abraham with the first revelation of Himself.
C.S. Lewis

By the death of Christ, "the middle wall of partition ... the law of the commandments contained in the ordinances" – which was at the same time a token of the enmity between God and sinners, and an occasion of distance and alienation between Jews and Gentiles – was abolished; and believing Jews and Gentiles were reconciled to God and united into one body.
Thomas M'Crie

Job
So great was the extremity of his pain and anguish that he did not only sigh but roar.
Matthew Henry

Job, Book of
One of the grandest things ever written with pen.
Thomas Carlyle

Magnificent and sublime as no other book in the Bible.
Martin Luther

The greatest poem of ancient and modern times.
Alfred Tennyson

I read the book of Job last night – I don't think God comes out well in it.
Virginia Woolf

John 3:16
The most famous sentence in the English language.
Author unknown

Joy
For, lo, the winter is past, the rain is over and gone; the flowers appear on the earth; the time of the singing of birds is come, and the voice of the turtle is heard in our land.
The Bible, The Song of Solomon 2:11,12

Be joyful always.
The Bible, 1 Thessalonians 5:16

Joy is peace dancing;
peace is joy resting.
Author unknown

J   Jesus
O   Others
Y   Yourself
If you use the joy rule and think of Jesus,
then others, then yourself; you will really
feel true joy.
Author unknown

Joy is everywhere.
Author unknown

Seek joy in what you give not in what you
get.
Author unknown

Man cannot live without joy; therefore
when he is deprived of true spiritual joys it
is necessary that he become addicted to
carnal pleasures.
Aquinas

There is a joy which is not given to the
ungodly, but to those who love Thee for
Thine own sake, whose joy Thou Thyself
art. And this is the happy life, to rejoice to
Thee, of Thee, for Thee; this it is, and
there is no other.
Augustine of Hippo

Find joy in simplicity, self-respect, and
indifference to what lies between virtue
and vice. Love the human race. Follow the
divine.
Marcus Aurelius

The whole point of the letter to the
Philippians is: I do rejoice – do you
rejoice?
Bengel

Desire joy and thank God for it. Renounce
it, if need be, for other's sake. That's joy
beyond joy.
Robert Browning

There is not one blade of grass, there is no
color in this world that is not intended to
make us rejoice.
John Calvin

To be simply ensconced in God is true joy.
C.C. Colton

Man is fond of counting his troubles but
he does not count his joys. If he counted
them up as he ought to, he would see that
every lot has enough happiness provided
for it.
Fyodor Dostoevsky

Christ is not only a remedy for your
weariness and trouble, but he will give you
an abundance of the contrary, joy and
delight.
Jonathan Edwards

Study always to have joy, for it befits not the
servant of God to show before his brother
or another sadness or a troubled face.
Francis of Assisi

Where there is poverty and joy, there is
neither greed nor avarice.
Francis of Assisi

Know that joy is rarer, more difficult, and
more beautiful than sadness. Once you
make this all-important discovery, you
must embrace joy as a moral obligation.
André Gide

Real joy comes not from ease or riches or
from praise of men, but from doing
something worthwhile.
Sir Wilfred Grenfell

Join the great company of those who make
the barren places of life fruitful with
kindness. Carry a vision of heaven in your
hearts, and you shall make your name, your
college, the world, correspond to that
vision. Your success and happiness lie within
you. External conditions are the accidents of
life, its outer wrappings. The great,
enduring realities are love and service. Joy is
the holy fire that keeps our purpose warm

and our intelligence aglow. Resolve to keep happy, and your joy and you shall form an invincible host against difficulty.
Helen Keller

All joy (as distinct from mere pleasure, still more amusement) emphasizes our pilgrim status; always reminds, beckons, awakens desire. Our best havings are wantings.
C.S. Lewis

I sometimes wonder whether all pleasures are not substitutes for joy.
C.S. Lewis

To pursue joy is to lose it. The only way to get it is to follow steadily the path of duty, without thinking of joy.
Alexander MacLaren

God and eternal things are my only pleasure.
Henry Martyn

Joy is the experience of knowing that you are unconditionally loved.
Henri Nouwen

This is the true joy in life – being used for a purpose recognized by yourself as a mighty one.
George Bernard Shaw

Joy is the wine that God is ever pouring
Into the hearts of those who strive with
   Him,
Lighting their eye to vision and airing,
Strengthening their arms to warfare glad
   and grim.
G. A. Studdert Kennedy

Rejoicing is clearly a spiritual command. To ignore it is disobedience.
Charles Swindoll

One filled with joy preaches without preaching.
Mother Teresa

All earthly joy begins pleasantly, but at the end it gnaws and kills.
Thomas à Kempis

Eternal joy is the end of the ways of God. The message of all religions is that the kingdom of God is peace and joy. And it is the message of Christianity. But eternal joy is not to be reached by living on the surface. It is rather attained by breaking through the surface, by penetrating the deep things of ourselves, of our world, and of God. The moment in which we reach the last depth of our lives is the moment in which we can experience the joy that has eternity within it, the hope that cannot be destroyed, and the truth on which life and death are built. For in the depth is truth; and in the depth is hope; and in the depth is joy.
Paul Tillich

Joy can be real only if people look upon their life as a service, and have a definite object in life outside themselves and their personal happiness.
Leo Tolstoy

Till you can sing and rejoice and delight in God, as misers do in gold, and kings in scepters, you never enjoy the world.
Thomas Traherne

The opposite of joy is not sorrow. It is unbelief.
Leslie Weatherhead

The religion of Christ is the religion of joy. Christ came to take away our sins, to roll off our curse, to unbind our chains, to open our prison house, to cancel our debt; in a word, to give us the oil of joy for mourning, the garment of praise for the spirit of heaviness. Is not this joy? Where can we find a joy so real, so deep, so pure, so lasting? There is every element of joy – deep, ecstatic, satisfying, sanctifying joy – in the gospel of Christ. The believer in Jesus is essentially a happy man. The child of God is, from necessity, a joyful man. His sins are forgiven, his soul is justified, his person is adopted, his trials are blessings, his conflicts are victories, his death is immortality, his future is a heaven of inconceivable, unthought-of, untold, and endless blessedness. With such a God,

such a Savior, and such a hope, is he not, ought he not, to be a joyful man?
Octavius Winslow

We have within ourselves
Enough to fill the present day with joy,
And overspread the future years with hope.
William Wordsworth

Joy and happiness
The Bible talks plentifully about joy, but it nowhere talks about a "happy Christian." Happiness depends on what happens; joy does not. Remember, Jesus Christ had joy, and He prays "that they might have my joy fulfilled in themselves."
Oswald Chambers

Joys
In joys and pleasures, immediately draw near to God in fear and truth, and you will be neither deceived nor involved in vanity.
John of the Cross

Judging others
The first to present his case seems right, till another comes forward and questions him.
The Bible, Proverbs 18:17

Accept him whose faith is weak, without passing judgment on disputable matters.
The Bible, Romans 14:1

Who are you to judge someone else's servant? To his own master he stands or falls.
The Bible, Romans 14:4

Be quick to judge yourself and not to judge others.
Author unknown

Most of us are umpires at heart; we like to call balls and strikes on somebody else.
Leo Aikman

It is not failure of others to appreciate your abilities that should trouble you, but rather your failure to appreciate theirs.
Confucius

We hand folks over to God's mercy, and show none ourselves.
George Eliot

It is the property of fools, to be always judging.
Thomas Fuller

I see no fault that I might not have committed myself.
Goethe

We evaluate others with a godlike justice, but we want them to evaluate us with a godlike compassion.
Sydney J. Harris

Judge not thy friend until thou standest in his place.
Rabbi Hillel

Never look at the good or evil of others.
John of the Cross

If we had no faults ourselves, we should not take so much delight in noticing those of others.
La Rochefoucauld

We judge ourselves by what we feel capable of doing, while others judge us by what we have already done.
Longfellow

I will not judge a person to be spiritually dead whom I have judged formerly to have had spiritual life, though I see him at present in a swoon as to all evidences of the spiritual life. And the reason why I will not judge him so is this – because if you judge a person dead, you neglect him, you leave him; but if you judge him in a swoon, though never so dangerous, you use all means for the retrieving of his life.
John Owen

Before I judge my neighbor, let me walk a mile in his moccasins.
Sioux proverb

We keep other people's vices in our eyes,

our own we keep on our back.
Seneca

I would rather bite my tongue till it bleed, than pass judgment upon any man. Judgment we should leave to God, for out of the habit of sitting in judgment upon one's neighbor grow self-satisfaction and arrogance, which are of the devil.
Tauler

If you judge people, you have no time to love them.
Mother Teresa

Do not be angry that you cannot make others as you would wish them to be, since you cannot make yourself as you wish to be.
Thomas à Kempis

Judgment
See also: God's Judgment

And the rain was upon the earth forty days and forty nights.
The Bible, Genesis 7:12 KJV

I will deal with them according to their conduct, and by their own standards I will judge them.
The Bible, Ezekiel 7:27

Thou art weighed in the balances, and art found wanting.
The Bible, Daniel 5:27 KJV

Moreover, the Father judges no one, but has entrusted all judgment to the Son, that all may honor the Son just as they honor the Father. He who does not honor the Son does not honor the Father, who sent him.
The Bible, John 5:22-23

Judge not according to the appearance.
The Bible, John 7:24 KJV

So then, each of us will give an account of himself to God.
The Bible, Romans 14:12

For we must all appear before the judgment seat of Christ, that each one may receive what is due him for the things done while in the body, whether good or bad.
The Bible, 2 Corinthians 5:10

… man is destined to die once, and after that to face judgment …
The Bible, Hebrews 9:27

God examines both rich and poor, not according to their lands and houses, but according to the riches of their hearts.
Augustine of Hippo

Whether the achievement of a man's life is great or small, significant or insignificant, he will one day stand before his eternal judge, and everything that he has done and performed will be no more than a mole hill, and then he will have nothing better to do than hope for something he has not earned: not for a crown, but quite simply for gracious judgment which he has not deserved. That is the only thing that will count then, achievement or not. "My kindness shall not depart from you." By this man lives. By this alone can he live.
Karl Barth

God hath appointed a day, wherein he will judge the world by Jesus Christ, when every man shall receive according to his deed; the wicked shall go into everlasting punishment; the righteous, into everlasting life.
James Boyce, Abstract of Principles, 1858

You have been once more warned today, while the door of the ark yet stands open. You have, as it were, once again heard the knocks of the hammer and axe in the building of the ark, to put you in mind that a flood is approaching. Take heed therefore that you do not still stop your ears, treat these warnings with a regardless heart, and still neglect the great work which you have to do, lest the flood of wrath suddenly come upon you, sweep you away, and there be no remedy.
Jonathan Edwards

[The death of Jesus] means the verdict which God will pronounce over us on the

day of judgment has been brought into the present. We therefore do not need to fear the Judgment Day.
Anthony Hoekema

Tomorrow's history has already been written. At the name of Jesus every knee must bow.
E. Kauffman

Everyone complains of his memory, and nobody complains of his judgment.
La Rochefoucauld

I can hardly recollect a single plan of mine, of which I have not since seen reason to be satisfied, that had it taken place in season and circumstance just as I proposed, it would, humanly speaking, have proved my ruin; or at least it would have deprived me of the greater good the Lord had designed for me. We judge of things by their present appearances, but the Lord sees them in their consequences, if we could do so likewise we should be perfectly of His mind; but as we cannot, it is an unspeakable mercy that He will manage for us, whether we are pleased with His management or not; and it is spoken of as one of his heaviest judgments, when He gives any person or people up to the way of their own hearts, and to walk after their own counsels.
John Newton

Jesus will judge us not only for what we did, but also for what we could have done and didn't.
George Otis

Examine what is said, not who speaks.
Arabian proverb

I am not sure exactly what heaven will be like, but I do know that when we die and it comes time for God to judge us, he will not ask, "How many good things have you done in your life?", rather he will ask, "How much love did you put into what you did?"
Mother Teresa

Truly, when the day of judgment comes, we shall not be examined as to what we have read, but what we have done, not how well we have spoken but how we have lived.
Thomas à Kempis

Just, The
The memory of the just is blessed.
The Bible, Proverbs 10:7 KJV

Justice
Do not pervert justice.
The Bible, Leviticus 19:15

Acquitting the guilty and condemning the innocent – the LORD detests them both.
The Bible, Proverbs 17:15

He who is only just is cruel. Who on earth could live were all judged justly?
Byron

Let justice be done, though the world perish.
Ferdinand I

Justice delayed is justice denied.
W.E. Gladstone

I tremble for my country when I reflect that God is just.
Thomas Jefferson

Justice is truth in action.
Joseph Joubert

True peace is not merely the absence of tension; it is the presence of justice.
Martin Luther King

Injustice anywhere is a threat to justice everywhere.
Martin Luther King

Justice is a temporary thing that must at last come to an end; but the conscience is eternal and will never die.
Martin Luther

There is no justice among men.
Czar Nicholas II

Justice and power must be brought together, so that whatever is just may be powerful, and whatever is powerful may be just.
Blaise Pascal

Injustice, swift, erect, and unconfin'd, Sweeps the wide earth, and tramples o'er mankind.
Alexander Pope

Justice is the foundations of kingdoms.
Latin proverb

He hurts the good who spares the bad.
Publius Syrus

Justice, racial
And then I got into Memphis and some began to talk about the threats of what would happen to me from some of our sick white brothers. But I don't know what will happen now. We've got some difficult days ahead. But it really doesn't matter with me now. Because I've been to the mountain-top and I don't mind. Like anybody, I would like to live a long life, longevity has its place, but I'm not concerned about that now. I just want to do God's will, and he's allowed me to go up to the mountain. And I've looked over and I've seen the Promised Land. I may not get there with you, but I want you to know tonight that we as a people will get to the Promised Land. So I'm happy tonight. I'm not fearing any man. Mine eyes have seen the glory of the coming of the Lord.
Martin Luther King, Jr (The night before he was assassinated.)

Our aim must be never to defeat or humiliate the white man, but to win his friendship and understanding. We must come to see that the end we seek is a society at peace with itself, a society that can live with its conscience. That will be a day not of the white man, not of the black man. That will be the day of man as man.
Martin Luther King, Jr

Justification
See also: Faith

This righteousness from God comes through faith in Jesus Christ to all who believe. There is no difference, for all have sinned and fall short of the glory of God, and are justified freely by his grace through the redemption that came by Christ Jesus.
The Bible, Romans 3:22-24

And that is what some of you were. But you were washed, you were sanctified, you were justified in the name of the Lord Jesus Christ and by the Spirit of our God.
The Bible, 1 Corinthians 6:11

You see that a person is justified by what he does and not by faith alone.
The Bible, James 2:24

Justification, Method and Fruits of

Martin Luther
Now I say, that the heir, as long as he is a child, differeth nothing from a servant, though he be Lord of all; but is under tutors and governors until the time appointed of the father. Even so we, when we were children, were in bondage under the elements of the world: but when the fullness of the time was come, God sent forth His son, made of a woman, made under the law, to redeem them that were under the law, that we might receive the adoption of sons. And because ye are sons, God hath sent forth the Spirit of His Son into your hearts, crying, Abba, Father. Wherefore thou art no more a servant, but a son, and if a son, then an heir of God through Christ" Galatians 4:1-7.
This text touches the very pith of Paul's chief doctrine. The cause why it is well understood but by few is, not that it is so obscure and difficult, but because there is so little knowledge of faith left in the world; without which it is not possible to understand Paul, who everywhere treats of

faith with such earnestness and force. I must, therefore, speak in such a manner that this text will appear plain; and that I may more conveniently illustrate it, I will speak a few words by way of preface.

First, therefore, we must understand the doctrine in which good works are set forth, far different from that which treats of justification; as there is a great difference between the substance and its working; between man and his work. Justification pertains to men, and not to works; for man is either justified and saved, or judged and condemned, and not works. Neither is it a controversy among the godly, that man is not justified by works, but righteousness must come from some other source than from his own works: for Moses, writing of Abel, says, "The Lord had respect unto Abel, and to his offering." First, He had respect to Abel himself, then to his offering; because Abel was first counted righteous and acceptable to God, and then for his sake his offering was accepted also, and not he because of his offering. Again, God had no respect to Cain, and therefore neither to his offering: therefore thou seest that regard is had first to the worker, then to the work.

From this it is plainly gathered that no work can be acceptable to God, unless he which worketh it was first accepted by Him: and again, that no work is disallowed of Him unless the author thereof be disallowed before. I think these remarks will be sufficient concerning this matter at present, by which it is easy to understand that there are two sorts of works, those before justification and those after it; and that these last are good works indeed, but the former only appear to be good. Hereof cometh such disagreement between God and those counterfeit holy ones; for this cause nature and reason rise and rage against the Holy Ghost; this is that of which almost the whole Scripture treats. The Lord in His Word defines all works that go before justification to be evil, and of no importance, and requires that man before all things be justified.

Again He pronounces all men which are unregenerate and have that nature which they received of their parents unchanged, to be unrighteous and wicked, according to that saying, "All men are liars," that is, unable to perform their duty, and to do those things which they ought to do; and "Every imagination of the thoughts of his heart are only evil continually"; whereby he is able to do nothing that is good, for the fountain of his actions, which is his heart, is corrupted. If he do works which outwardly seem good, they are no better than the offering of Cain.

Here again comes forth reason, our reverend mistress, seeming to be marvelously wise, but who indeed is unwise and blind, gainsaying her God, and reproving Him of lying; being furnished with her follies and feeble honor, to wit, the light of nature, free will, the strength of nature; also with the books of the heathen and the doctrines of men, contending that the works of a man not justified are good works, and not like those of Cain, yea, and so good that he that worketh them is justified by them; that God will have respect first to the works, then to the worker. Such doctrine now bears the sway everywhere in schools, colleges and monasteries. Now from this error comes another; they which attribute so much to works and do not accordingly esteem the worker, and sound justification, go so far that they ascribe all merit and righteousness to works done before justification, making no account of faith, alleging that which James saith, that without works faith is dead. This sentence of the apostle they do not rightly understand; making but little account of faith, they always stick to works, whereby they think to merit exceedingly, and are persuaded that for their work's sake they shall obtain the favor of God: by this means they continually disagree with God, showing themselves to be the posterity of Cain. God hath respect unto man, then unto the works of man; God alloweth the work for the sake of him that worketh, these require that for the work's sake the worker may be crowned.

But here, perhaps, thou wilt say, what is needful to be done? By what means shall I become righteous and acceptable to God? How shall I attain to this perfect justification? Those the gospel answers teaching that it is necessary that thou hear Christ, and repose thyself wholly on Him, denying thyself and distrusting thine own strength; by this means thou shalt be changed from Cain to Abel, and being thyself acceptable, shalt offer acceptable gifts to the Lord. It is faith that justifies thee, thou being endued therewith; the Lord remitteth all thy sins by the mediation of Christ His Son, in whom this faith believeth and trusteth. Moreover, He giveth unto such a faith His Spirit, which changes the man and makes him anew, giving him another reason and another will. Such a one worketh nothing but good works. Wherefore nothing is required unto justification but to hear Jesus Christ our Savior, and to believe in Him. Howbeit these are not the works of nature, but of grace.

He, therefore, that endeavors to attain to these things by works shutteth the way to the gospel, to faith, grace, Christ, God, and all things that help unto salvation. Again, nothing is necessary in order to accomplish good works, but justification; and he that hath attained it performs good works, and not any other. Hereof it sufficiently appears that the beginning, the things following, and the order of man's salvation are after this sort; first of all it is required that thou hear the Word of God; next that thou believe; then that thou work; and so at last become saved and happy. He that changes this order, without doubt is not of God. Paul also describes this, saying "Whosoever shall call upon the name of the Lord shall be saved. How then shall they call on Him in whom they have not believed? and, how shall they believe in Him of whom they have not heard?

and, how shall they hear without a preacher? and, how shall they preach except they be sent?"

Christ teaches us to pray the Lord of the harvest to send forth laborers into His harvest; that is, sincere preachers. When we hear these preach the true Word of God, we may believe; which faith justifies a man, and makes him godly indeed, so that he now calls upon God in the spirit of holiness, and works nothing but that which is good, and thus becomes a saved man. Thus he that believeth shall be saved; but he that worketh without faith is condemned as Christ saith, he that doth not believe shall be condemned, from which no works shall deliver him. Some say, I will now endeavor to become honest. It is meet surely that we study to lead an honest life, and to do good works. But if one ask them how we may apply ourselves unto honesty, and by what means we may attain it, they answer, that we must fast, pray, frequent temples, avoid sins, etc. Whereby one becomes a Carthusian monk, another chooses some other order of monks, and another is consecrated a priest; some torment their flesh by wearing hair-cloth, others scourge their bodies with whips, others afflict themselves in a different manner; but these are of Cain's progeny, and their works are no better than his; for they continue the same that they were before, ungodly, and without justification: there is a change made of outward works only, of apparel, of place, etc.

They scarce think of faith; they presume only on such works as seem good to themselves, thinking by them to get to heaven. But Christ said, "Enter in at the strait gate, for I say unto you, many seek to enter in, and can not." Why is this? because they know not what this narrow gate is; for it is FAITH, which altogether annihilates or makes a man appear as nothing in his own eyes, and requires him not to trust in his own works, but to depend upon the grace of God, and be prepared to leave and suffer all things.

Those holy ones of Cain's progeny think their good works are the narrow gate; and are not, therefore, extenuated or made less, whereby they might enter.

When we begin to preach of faith to those that believe altogether in works, they laugh and hiss at us, and say, "Dost thou count us as Turks and heathens, whom it behooves now first to learn faith? is there such a company of priests, monks, and nuns, and is not faith known? who knoweth not what he ought to believe? even sinners know that." Being after this sort animated and stirred up, they think themselves abundantly endued with faith, and that the rest is now to be finished and made perfect by works. They make so small and slender account of faith, because they are ignorant of what faith is, and that it alone doth justify. They call it faith, believing those things which they have heard of Christ, this kind of faith the devils also have and yet they are not justified. But this ought rather to be called an opinion of men. To believe those things to be true which are preached of Christ is not sufficient to constitute thee a Christian, but thou must not doubt that thou art of the number of them whom all the benefits of Christ are given and exhibited; which he that believes must plainly confess, that he is holy, godly, righteous, the son of God, and certain of salvation; and that by no merit of his own, but by the mere mercy of God poured forth upon him for Christ's sake; which he believes to be so rich and plentiful, as indeed it is, that although he be as it were drowned in sin, he is notwithstanding made holy, and become the son of God.

Wherefore, take heed that thou nothing doubt that thou art the son of God, and therefore made righteous by His grace; let all fear and care be done away. However, thou must fear and tremble that thou mayest persevere in this way unto the end; but thou must not do this as tho it consisted in thy own strength, for righteousness and salvation are of grace, whereunto only thou must trust. But when thou knowest that it is of grace alone, and that thy faith also is the gift of God, thou shalt have cause to fear, lest some temptation violently move thee from this faith.

Every one by faith is certain of this salvation; but we ought to have care and fear that we stand and persevere, trusting in the Lord, and not in our own strength. When those of the race of Cain hear faith treated of in this manner, they marvel at our madness, as it seems to them. God turn us from this way, say they, that we should affirm ourselves holy and godly; far be this arrogance and rashness from us; we are miserable sinners; we should be mad, if we should arrogate holiness to ourselves. Thus they mock at true faith, and count such doctrine as this execrable error; and thus try to extinguish the Gospel. These are they that deny the faith of Christ, and persecute it throughout the whole world; of whom Paul speaks: "In the latter times many shall depart from the faith," etc., for we see by these means that true faith lies everywhere oppressed; it is not preached, but commonly disallowed and condemned.

The pope, bishops, colleges, monasteries, and universities have more than five hundred years persecuted it with one mind and consent most obstinately, which has been the means of driving many to hell. If any object against the admiration, or rather the mad senselessness of these men, if we count ourselves even holy, trusting the goodness of God to justify us, or as David prayed, "Preserve Thou me, O Lord, for I am holy," or as Paul saith, "the Spirit of God beareth witness with our spirit that we are the children of God"; they answer that the prophet and apostle would not teach us in these words, or give us an example which we should follow, but that they, being particularly and specially enlightened, received such revelation of themselves. In this way they misrepresent the Scripture, which affirms that they are holy, saying that such doctrine is not written for us, but that it is rather peculiar miracles, which do not belong to all. This forged imagination we account of as having come from their sickly mind. Again, they believe that they shall be made righteous and holy by their own works, and that because of them God will give them salvation and eternal blessedness.

In the opinion of these men it is a Christian duty to think that we shall be righteous and sacred because of our works; but to believe that these things are given by the grace of God, they condemn as heretical; attributing that to their own works which they do not attribute to the grace of God. They that are endued with true faith, and rest upon the grace of the Lord, rejoice with holy joy, and apply themselves with pleasure to good works, not such as those of Cain's progeny do, as feigned prayers, fasting, base and filthy apparel, and such like trifles, but to true and good works whereby their neighbors are profited.

Perhaps some godly man may think, if the matter be so, and our work do not save us, to what end are so many precepts given us, and why doth God require that they be obeyed? The present text of the apostle will give a solution of this question, and upon this occasion we will give an exposition thereof. The Galatians being taught of Paul the faith of Christ, but afterward seduced by false apostles, thought that our salvation must be finished and made perfect by the works of the law; and that faith alone doth not suffice. These Paul calls back again from works unto faith with great diligence; plainly proving that the works of the law, which go before faith, make us only servants and are of no importance toward godliness and salvation; but that faith makes us the sons of God, and from thence good works without constraint forthwith plentifully flow.

But here we must observe the words of the apostle; he calls him a servant that is occupied in works without faith, of which we have already treated at large; but he calls him a son which is righteous by faith alone. The reason is this, although the servant applies himself to good works, yet he does it not with the same mind as doth the son; that is, with a mind free, willing, and certain that the inheritance and all the good things of the Father are his; but does it as he that is hired in another man's house, who hopes not that the inheritance shall come to him. The works indeed of the son and the servant are alike; and almost the same in outward appearance; but their minds differ exceedingly as Christ saith, "the servant abideth not in the house forever, but the son abideth ever."

Those of Cain's progeny want the faith of sons, which they confess themselves; for they think it most absurd, and wicked arrogance to affirm themselves to be the sons of God, and holy; therefore as they believe even so are they counted before God; they neither become holy nor the sons of God, nevertheless are they exercised with the works of the law; wherefore they are and remain servants forever. They receive no reward except temporal things; such as quietness of life, abundance of goods, dignity, honor, etc., which we see to be common among the followers of popish religion. But this is their reward, for they are servants, and not sons; wherefore in death they shall be separated from all good things, neither shall any portion of the eternal inheritance be theirs, who in this life would believe nothing thereof. We perceive, therefore, that servants and sons are not unlike in works, but in mind and faith they have no resemblance.

The apostle endeavors here to prove that the law with all the works thereof makes us but mere servants, if we have not faith in Christ; for this alone makes us sons of God. It is the word of grace followed by the Holy Ghost as is shown in many places, where we read of the Holy Ghost falling on Cornelius and his family while hearing the preaching of Peter. Paul teaches that no man is justified before God by the works of the law; for sin only cometh by the law. He that trusts in works condemns faith as the most pernicious arrogance and error of all others. Here thou seest plainly that such a man is not righteous, being destitute of that faith and belief which is necessary to make him acceptable before God and His Son; yea, he is an enemy to this faith, and therefore to righteousness also. Thus it is easy to understand that which Paul saith, that no man is justified before God by the works of the law.

The worker must be justified before God before he can work any good thing. Men judge the worker by the works; God judges the works by the worker. The first precept requires us to acknowledge and worship one God, that is, to trust Him alone, which is the true faith whereby we become the sons of God. Thou canst not be delivered from the evil of unbelief by thine own power, nor by the power of the law; wherefore all thy works which thou doest to satisfy the law can be nothing but works of the law; of far less importance than to be able to justify thee before God, who counteth them righteous only who truly believe in Him; for they that acknowledge Him the true God are His sons, and do truly fulfill the law. If thou shouldst even kill thyself by working, thy heart can not obtain this faith thereby, for thy works are even a hindrance to it, and cause thee to persecute it.

He that studieth to fulfill the law without faith is afflicted for the devil's sake; and continues a persecutor both of faith and the law, until he come to himself, and cease to trust in his own works; he then gives glory to God, who justifies the ungodly, and acknowledges himself to be nothing, and sighs for the grace of God, of which he knows that he has need. Faith and grace now fill his empty mind, and satisfy his hunger; then follow works which are truly good; neither are they works of the law, but of the spirit, of faith and grace; they are called in the Scripture the works of God, which He worketh in us.

Whatsoever we do of our own power and strength, that which is not wrought in us by His grace, without doubt is a work of the law, and avails nothing toward justification; but is displeasing to God, because of the unbelief wherein it is done. He that trusts in works does nothing freely and with a willing mind; he would do no good work at all if he were not compelled by the fear of hell, or allured by the hope of present good. Whereby it is plainly seen that they strive only for gain, or are moved with fear, showing that they rather hate the law from their hearts, and had rather there were no law at all. An evil heart can do nothing that is good. This evil heart can do nothing that is good. This evil propensity of the heart, and unwillingness to do good, the law betrays when it teaches that God does not esteem the works of the hand, but those of the heart.

Thus sin is known by the law, as Paul teaches; for we learn thereby that our affections are not placed on that which is good. This ought to teach us not to trust in ourselves, but to long after the grace of God, whereby the evil of the heart may be taken away, and we become ready to do good works, and love the law voluntarily; not for fear of any punishment, but for the love of righteousness. By this means one is made of a servant, a son; of a slave an heir.

We shall now come to treat more particularly of the text:

Verse 1. "The heir, as long as he is a child, differeth nothing from a servant, though he be lord of all." We see that the children unto whom their parents have left some substance are brought up no otherwise than if they were servants. They are fed and clothed with their goods, but they are not permitted to do with them, nor use them according to their own minds, but are ruled with fear and discipline of manners, so that even in their own inheritance they live no otherwise than as servants. After the same sort it is in spiritual things. God made with His people a covenant, when He promised that in the seed of Abraham, that is in Christ, all nations of the earth should be blest. That covenant was afterward confirmed by the death of Christ, and revealed and published abroad by the preaching gospel. For the gospel is an open and general preaching of this grace, that in Christ is laid up a blessing for all men that believe.

Before this covenant is truly opened and made manifest to men, the sons of God live after the manner of servants under the law; and are exercised with the works of the law, although they can not be justified by them; they are true heirs of heavenly things, of this blessing and grace of the covenant; although they do not as yet know or enjoy it. Those that are justified by grace cease from the works of the law, and come unto the inheritance of justification; they then freely work those things that are good, to the glory of God and benefit of their neighbors. For they have possessed it by the covenant of the Father, confirmed by Christ, revealed, published, and as it were delivered into their hands by the gospel, through the grace and mercy of God.

This covenant Abraham, and all the fathers which were endued with true faith, had no otherwise than we have; although before Christ was glorified this grace was not openly preached and published; they lived in like faith, and therefore obtained the like good things. They had the same grace, blessing, and covenant that we have; for there is one Father and God over all. Thou seest that Paul here, as in almost all other places, treats much of faith; that we are not justified by works, but by faith alone. There is no good thing which is not contained in this covenant of God; it gives righteousness, salvation, and peace. By faith the whole inheritance of God is at once received. From thence good works come; not meritorious, whereby thou mayest seek salvation, but which with a mind already possessing righteousness thou must do with great pleasure to the profit of thy neighbors. Verse 2. "But is under tutors and governors until the time appointed of the Father."

Tutors and governors are they which bring up the heir, and so rule him and order his goods that he neither waste his inheritance by riotous living, nor his goods perish or be otherwise consumed. They permit him not to use his goods at his own will or pleasure, but suffer him to enjoy them as they shall be needful and profitable to him. They keep him at home, and instruct him whereby he may long and comfortably enjoy his inheritance; but as soon as he arrives to the years of discretion and judgment, it can not but be grievous to him to live in subjection to the commands and will of another.

In the same manner stands the case of the children of God, which are brought up and instructed under the law, as under a master in the liberty of sons. The law profits them in this, that be the fear of it and the punishment which it threatens, they are driven from sin, at least from the outward work; by it they are brought to a knowledge of themselves, and that they do no good at all with a willing and ready mind as becomes sons; whereby they may easily see what is the root of this evil, and what is especially needful unto salvation; to wit, a new and living spirit to that which is good: which neither the law nor the works of the law is able to give; yea, the more they apply themselves to it, the more unwilling they find themselves to work those things which are good.

Here they learn that they do not satisfy the law, although outwardly they live according to its precepts. They pretend to obey it in works, although in mind they hate it; they pretend themselves righteous, but they remain sinners. These are like unto those of Cain's progeny, and hypocrites; whose hands are compelled to do good, but their hearts consent unto sin and are subject thereto. To know this concerning one's self is not the lowest degree toward salvation. Paul calls such constrained works the works of the law; for they flow not from a ready and willing heart; howbeit the law does not require works alone, but the heart itself; wherefore it is said in the first psalm of the blest man: "But his delight is in the law of the Lord: and in His law doth he meditate day and night." Such a mind the law requires, but it gives it not; neither can it of its own nature: whereby it comes to pass that while the law continues to exact it of a man, and condemns him as long as he hath such a mind, as being disobedient to God, he is in anguish on every side; his conscience being grievously terrified.

Then, indeed, is he most ready to receive the grace of God; this being the time appointed by the Father when his servitude shall end, and he enter into the liberty of the sons of God. For being thus in distress, and terrified, seeing that by no other means he can avoid the condemnation of the law, he prays to the Father for grace; he acknowledges his frailty, he confesses his sin, he ceases to trust in works, and humbles himself, perceiving that between him and a manifest sinner there is no difference at all except of works, that he hath a wicked heart, even as every other sinner hath. The condition of man's nature is such that it is able to give to the law works only, and not the heart; and unequal division, truly, to dedicate the heart, which, comparably excels all other things, to sin, and the hand to the law: which is offering chaff to the law, and the wheat to sin; the shell to God, and the kernel to Satan; whose ungodliness if one reprove, they become enraged, and would even take the life of innocent Abel, and persecute all those that follow the truth.

Those that trust in works seem to defend them to obtain righteousness; they promise to themselves a great reward for this, by persecuting heretics and blasphemers, as they say, who seduce with error, and entice many from good works. But those that God hath chosen, learn by the law how unwilling the heart is to conform to the works of the law; they fall from their arrogance, and are by this knowledge of themselves brought to see their own unworthiness. Hereby they receive that covenant of the eternal blessing and the Holy Ghost which renews the heart: whereby they are delighted with the law, and hate sin; and are willing and ready to do those things which are good. This is the time appointed by the Father, when the heir must no longer remain a servant, but a son, being led by a free spirit, he is no more kept in subjection under tutors and governors after the manner of a servant; which is even that which Paul teaches in the following:

Verse 3. "Even so we, when we were children, were in bondage under the elements of the world." By the word elements thou mayest here understand the first principles or law written; which is as it were the first exercises and instructions of holy learning; as it is said: "As concerning the time ye ought to be teachers, ye have need that one teach you again which be the first principles of the oracles of God." "Beware lest any man spoil you through philosophy and vain deceit, after the tradition of men, after the rudiments of the world." "How turn ye again to the weak and beggarly elements, whereunto ye desire again to be in bondage."

Here Paul calls the law rudiments; because it is not able to perform that righteousness which it requires. For whereas it earnestly requires a heart and mind given to godliness, nature is not able to satisfy it: herein it makes a man feel his poverty, and acknowledge his infirmity: it requires that of him by right which he has not, neither is able to have. "The letter killeth, but the Spirit giveth life." Paul calls them the rudiments of the world, which, not being renewed by the Spirit, only perform worldly things; to wit, in places, times, apparel, persons, vessels, and such like. But faith rests not in worldly things, but in the grace, word, and mercy of God: counting alike, days, meats, persons, apparel, and all things of this world.

None of these by themselves either help or hinder godliness or salvation. With those of Cain's progeny, faith neither agrees in name or anything else; one of them eats flesh, another abstains from it; one wears black apparel, another white; one keeps this day holy, and another that; every one has his rudiments, under which he is in bondage; all of them are addicted to the things of the world, which are frail and perishable. Against these Paul speaks, "Wherefore, if ye be dead with Christ from the rudiments of the world, why, as though living in the world, are ye subject to ordinances: touch not, taste not, handle not, which all are to perish with the using, after the commandments and doctrines of men? Which things have indeed a show of wisdom in will-worship and humility, and neglecting of the body; not in any honor to the satisfying of the flesh."

By this and other places above mentioned, it is evident that monasteries and colleges, whereby we measure the state of spiritual men as we call them, plainly disagree with the Gospel and Christian liberty: and therefore it is much more dangerous to live in this kind of life than among the most profane men. All their works are nothing but rudiments and ordinances of the world; neither are they Christians but in name, wherefore all their life and holiness are sinful and most detestable hypocrisy. The fair show of feigned holiness which is in those ordinances does, in a marvelous and secret manner, withdraw from faith more than those manifest and gross sins of which open sinners are guilty. Now this false and servile opinion faith alone takes away, and teaches us to trust in, and rest upon, the grace of God, whereby is given freely that which is needful to work all things.

Verses 4, 5. "But when the fullness of the time was come, God sent forth His Son, made of a woman, made under the law, that we might receive the adoption of sons." After Paul had taught us that righteousness and faith can not come to us by the law, neither can we deserve it by nature, he shows us by whom we obtain it; and who is the author of our justification. The apostle saith, "When the fullness of the time was come"; here Paul speaks of the time which was appointed by the Father to the Son, wherein He should live under tutors, etc. This time being come to the Jews, and ended, Christ came in the flesh; so it is daily fulfilled to others, when they come to the knowledge of Christ, and change the servitude of the law, for the faith of sons. Christ for this cause came unto us that believing in Him we may be restored to true liberty; by which faith they of ancient times also obtained the liberty of the Spirit.

As soon as thou believest in Christ, He comes to thee, a deliverer and Savior; and now the time of bondage is ended; as the apostle saith the fullness thereof is come.

Verse 6. "And because ye are sons, God hath sent forth the Spirit of His Son into your hearts, crying, Abba, Father." Here we see plainly that the Holy Ghost cometh to the saints, not by works, but by faith alone. Sons believe, while servants only work; sons are free from the law, servants are held under the law, as appears by those things that have been before spoken. But how comes it to pass that he saith "because ye are sons, God hath sent forth the Spirit," etc., seeing it as before said that by the coming of the Spirit we are changed from servants to sons: but here, as though we could be sons before the coming of the Spirit, he saith "because ye are sons," etc. To this question we must answer, that Paul speaks here in the same manner that he did before, that is, before the fullness of the time came, we were in bondage under the rudiments of the world: all that shall become sons are counted in the place of sons with God: therefore he saith rightly, "because ye are sons," that is, because the state of sons is appointed to you from everlasting, "God hath sent forth the Spirit of His Son," to wit, that He might finish it in you, and make you such as He hath long since of His goodness determined that He would make you.

Now if the Father give unto us His Spirit, He will make us His true sons and heirs, that we may with confidence cry with Christ, Abba, Father; being His brethren and fellow heirs. The apostle has well set forth the goodness of God which makes us partakers with Christ, and causes us to have all things common with Him, so that we live and are led by the same Spirit. These words of the apostle show that the Holy Ghost proceeds from Christ, as he calls Him His Spirit. So God hath sent forth the Spirit of His Son, that is, of Christ, for He is the Spirit of God, and comes from God to us, and not ours, unless one will say after this manner, "my Holy Spirit," as we say, "my God," "my Lord," etc. As He is said to be the Holy Spirit of Christ, it proves Him to be God of whom that Spirit is sent, therefore it is counted His Spirit.

Christians may perceive by this whether they have in themselves the Holy Ghost, to wit, the Spirit of sons; whether they hear His voice in their hearts; for Paul saith He crieth in the hearts which He possesseth, Abba, Father; he saith also, "We have received the Spirit of adoption, whereby we cry, Abba, Father." Thou hearest this voice when thou findest so much faith in thyself that thou dost assuredly, without doubting, presume that not only thy sins are forgiven thee, but also that thou art the beloved Son of God, who, being certain of eternal salvation, durst both call Him Father, and be delighted in Him with a joyful and confident heart. To doubt these things brings a reproach upon the death of Christ, as though He had not obtained all things for us.

It may be that thou shalt be so tempted as to fear and doubt, and think plainly that God is not a favorable Father, but a wrathful revenger of sins, as it happened with Job, and many other saints; but in such a conflict this trust and confidence that thou art a son ought to prevail and overcome. It is said "The Spirit itself maketh intercession for us with groanings which can not be uttered; and that He beareth witness with our spirit

that we are the children of God." How can it therefore be that our hearts should not hear this cry and testimony of the Spirit? But if thou dost not feel this cry, take heed that thou be not slothful and secure; pray constantly, for thou art in an evil state.

Cain saith, "My punishment is greater than I can bear. Behold, Thou hast driven me out this day from the face of the earth, and from Thy face shall I be hid; and it shall come to pass that every one that findeth me shall slay me." This is a dreadful and terribly cry, which is heard from all Cain's progeny, all such as trust to themselves and their own works, who put not their trust in the Son of God, neither consider that He was sent from the Father, made of a woman under the law, much less that all these things were done for their salvation. And while their ungodliness is not herewith content, they begin to persecute even the sons of God, and grow so cruel that, after the example of their father Cain, they can not rest until they slay their righteous brother Abel, wherefore the blood of Christ continually cries out against them nothing but punishment and vengeance; but for the heirs of salvation it cries by the Spirit of Christ for nothing but grace and reconciliation.

The apostle here uses a Syrian and Greek word, saying, Abba, Pater. This word Abba, in the Syrian tongue, signifies a father, by which name the heads of monasteries are still called; and by the same name, hermits in times past, being holy men, called their presidents; at last, by use, it was also made a Latin word. Therefore that which Paul saith is as much as Father, Father; or if thou hadst rather, "my Father."

Verse 7. "Wherefore thou art no more a servant, but a son, and if a son, then an heir of God through Christ." He saith, that after the coming of the Spirit, after the knowledge of Christ, "thou art not a servant." A son is free and willing, a servant is compelled and unwilling; a son liveth and resteth in faith, a servant in works. Therefore it appears that we can not obtain salvation of God by works, but before thou workest that which is acceptable to Him, it is necessary that thou receive salvation; then good works will freely flow, to the honor of thy heavenly Father, and to the profit of thy neighbors; without any fear of punishment, or looking for reward.

If this inheritance of the Father be thine by faith, surely thou art rich in all things, before thou hast wrought any thing. It is said, "Your salvation is prepared and reserved in heaven, to be showed in the last time," wherefore the works of a Christian ought to have no regard to merit, which is the manner of servants, but only for the use and benefit of our neighbors, whereby we may truly live to the glory of God. Lest that any think that so great an inheritance cometh to us without cost (although it be given to us without our cost or merit), yet it cost Christ a dear price, who, that He might purchase it for us, was made under the law, and satisfied it for us, both by life and also by death.

Those benefits which from love we bestow upon our neighbor, come to him freely, without any charges or labor of his, notwithstanding they cost us something, even as Christ hath bestowed those things which are His upon us. Thus hath Paul called back the Galatians from the teachers of works, which preaching nothing but the law, perverted the Gospel of Christ. Which things are very necessary to be marked of us also: for the Pope, with his prelates and monks hath for a long time intruded, urging his laws, which are foolish and pernicious, disagreeing in every respect with the Word of God, seducing almost the whole world from the gospel of Christ, and plainly extinguishing the faith of sons, as the Scripture hath in diverse places manifestly prophesied of His kingdom. Wherefore let every one that desires salvation, diligently take heed of him and his followers, no otherwise than Satan himself.
Martin Luther

Faith is neither the ground nor substance of our justification, but the hand, the instrument, the vessel which receives the divine gift proffered to us in the gospel.
Joel Beeke

Justification is God's gracious and full acquittal of sinners, who believe in Christ, from all sin, through the satisfaction that Christ has made; not for anything wrought in them or done by them; but on account of the obedience and satisfaction of Christ, they receiving and resting on Him and His righteousness by faith.
James Boyce

For, as regards justification, faith is something merely passive, bringing nothing of ours to the recovering of God's favor but receiving from Christ that which we lack.
John Calvin

It is entirely by the intervention of Christ's righteousness that we obtain justification before God. This is equivalent to saying that man is not just in himself, but that the righteousness of Christ is communicated to him by imputation, while he is strictly deserving of punishment.
John Calvin

Justification is the main hinge on which salvation turns.
John Calvin

The necessity of Christ's satisfaction to divine justice is, as it were, the center and hinge of all doctrines of pure revelation. Other doctrines are of little importance comparatively except as they have respect to this.
Jonathan Edwards

The perfect obedience of Christ, and His meritorious death, were both necessary as the ground of a sinner's justification. Neither would have been sufficient without the other. His obedience would not answer without His death; for the law which had been broken must be honored; and the penalty which had been incurred by the sinner must be endured by the

Substitute. Neither would His death answer without His obedience; for it is the obedient, and not the punished, that the law justifies; he who keeps the precept, and not he who endures the penalty. It is only by satisfying both claims on our behalf, that Christ "of God is made unto us wisdom, and righteousness, and sanctification, and redemption."
Christmas Evans

God's justification of those who trust him, according to the gospel, is a decisive transition, here and now, from a state of condemnation and wrath because of their sins to one of acceptance and favor by virtue of Jesus' flawless obedience culminating in his voluntary sin-bearing death.
The gospel of Jesus Christ: An evangelical celebration

When the article of justification has fallen, everything has fallen. This is the chief article from which all other doctrines have flowed. It alone begets, nourishes, builds, preserves, and defends the church of God. Without it the church of God cannot exist for one hour. It is the master and prince, the lord, the ruler, and the judge over all kinds of doctrines.
Martin Luther

I am justified and acceptable to God – even though there are in me sin, unrighteousness, and fear of death.
Martin Luther

There is something inexpressibly pleasing to a justified mind to know that God has all the honor in our salvation, and we have none; to know that God's honor is not violated, but on the contrary, shines more illustrious; to know that God's law is not injured, but magnified and made honorable; to know that we are safe, and God has all the glory.
Robert Murray M'Cheyne

The means by which we are justified is faith. Faith is like a channel through which the benefits of Christ flow to us. We are not justified on account of faith; we are justified through faith. It is the work of Christ, not our faith, which is the foundation of justification. Faith itself is a gift of God.
Alister McGrath

Justification is an act of God by which he declares sinners to be righteous by grace alone through faith alone because of Christ alone.
R.C. Sproul and James M. Boice

Justification is the pillar of Christianity. An error about justification is dangerous, like a defect in a foundation. Justification by Christ is a spring of the water of life. To have the poison of corrupt doctrine cast into this spring is damnable.
Thomas Watson

Justification and good deeds

What I have hitherto and constantly taught concerning this I know not how to change in the least, namely, that by faith, as St Peter says, we acquire a new and clean heart, and God will and does account us entirely righteous and holy for the sake of Christ, our Mediator. And although sin in the flesh has not yet been altogether removed or become dead, yet He will not punish or remember it. And such faith, renewal, and forgiveness of sins is followed by good works. And what there is still sinful or imperfect also in them shall not be accounted as sin or defect, even [and that, too] for Christ's sake; but the entire man, both as to his person and his works, is to be called and to be righteous and holy from pure grace and mercy, shed upon us [unfolded] and spread over us in Christ. Therefore we cannot boast of many merits and works, if they are viewed apart from grace and mercy, but as it is written, 1 Cor. 1. 31: He that glorieth, let him glory in the Lord, namely, that he has a gracious God. For thus all is well. We say, besides, that if good works do not follow, faith is false and not true.
Martin Luther

Justification and sanctification

We reject any view of justification which

divorces it from our sanctifying union with Christ and our increasing conformity to his image through prayer, repentance, cross-bearing, and life in the Spirit.

The gospel of Jesus Christ: An evangelical celebration

By grace we are what we are in justification, and work what we work in sanctification.

Richard Sibbes

Justification by faith

You cannot say that Luther invented the idea of justification by faith alone. Long before Luther it was taught by Augustine and Paul and Jesus and Moses. Even ... Adam and Eve realized soon after their sin that the fig leaves with which they tried to cover their shame were woefully inadequate. The gospel is given in Genesis 3:21 when Moses tells us that God clothed them. They needed something they couldn't provide for themselves; and God giving man what man needs to stand in His favorable presence is the essence of the gospel. Luther merely restated what true Christians have understood for centuries, that justification is by faith alone.

John MacArthur, Jr

Martin Luther described the doctrine of justification by faith as the article of faith that decides whether the church is standing or falling. By this he meant that when this doctrine is understood, believed, and preached, as it was in New Testament times, the church stands in the grace of God and is alive; but where it is neglected, overlaid, or denied ... the church falls from grace and its life drains away, leaving it in a state of darkness and death.

J.I. Packer

I can sympathize with Luther when he said, "I have preached justification by faith so often, and I feel sometimes that you are so slow to receive it, that I could almost take the Bible and bang it about your heads."

C.H. Spurgeon

The courage to be is the courage to accept oneself as accepted in spite of being unacceptable. This is the genuine meaning of the Paulinian-Lutheran doctrine of justification by faith.

Paul Tillich

K

Kindness

An anxious heart weighs a man down, but
a kind word cheers him up.
The Bible, Proverbs 12:25

… in the coming ages he might show the
incomparable riches of his grace, expressed
in his kindness to us in Christ Jesus.
The Bible, Ephesians 2:7

Be kind to unkind people – they need it
the most.
Author unknown

A smile is the universal language of kindness.
Author unknown

The right kind of heart is a kind heart like
God's.
Author unknown

The kindest word in all the world is the
unkind word, unsaid.
Author unknown

Kindness is a language that the dumb can
speak and the deaf can hear.
Author unknown

If you were arrested for being kind, would
there be enough evidence to convict you?
Author unknown

You can't speak a kind word too soon, for
you never know how soon it will be too late.
Author unknown

The person who sows seeds of kindness
enjoys a perpetual harvest.
Author unknown

It's what each of us sows, and how, that
gives to us character and prestige. Seeds of
kindness, goodwill, and human
understanding, planted in fertile soil,
spring up into deathless friendships, big
deeds of worth, and a memory that will
not soon fade out. We are all sowers of
seeds – and let us never forget it!
George Matthew Adams

No act of kindness, no matter how small,
is ever wasted.
Æsop

He who plants kindness gathers love.
St Basil

Great people are able to do great kindnesses.
Cervantes

The greatest thing a man can do for his
heavenly Father is to be kind to some of
his other children.
Henry Drummond

Do unto others even if they never ever do
unto you.
Mary Ellen Edmunds

You can never do a kindness too soon
because you never know how soon it will
be too late.
Ralph Waldo Emerson

Kindness is the noblest weapon to conquer
with.
Thomas Fuller

When I was young, I used to admire
intelligent people. Now I admire kind
people.
Abraham Heschel

Let us be kinder to one another.
Aldous Huxley's last words

A kind heart is a fountain of gladness, making everything in its vicinity freshen into smiles.
Washington Irving

Conquer evil men by your gentle kindness.
Isaac from Syria

Three things in human life are important.
The first is to be kind.
The second is to be kind.
The third is to be kind.
Henry James

He was so benevolent, so merciful a man that he would have held an umbrella over a duck in a shower of rain.
Douglas Jerrold

Getting money is not all a man's business: to cultivate kindness is a valuable part of the business of life.
Samuel Johnson

Kindness is in our power, even when fondness is not.
Samuel Johnson

Every act of kindness and compassion done by any man for his fellow Christian is done by Christ working within him.
Julian of Norwich

Neither genius, fame, nor love show the greatness of the soul. Only kindness can do that.
Jean Baptiste Henri Lacordaire

Kindness in words creates confidence
Kindness in thinking creates profoundness
Kindness in giving creates love.
Lao-tzu

If I can put one touch of rosy sunset into the life of any man or woman, I shall feel that I have worked with God.
John MacDonald

Just because an animal is large, it doesn't mean he doesn't want kindness; however big Tigger seems to be, remember that he wants as much kindness as Roo.
Pooh's Little Instruction Book, inspired by A.A. Milne

Kind words do not cost much. Yet they accomplish much.
Blaise Pascal

If there is any kindness I can show, or any good thing I can do to any fellow being, let me do it now, and not deter or neglect it, as I shall not pass this way again.
William Penn

Be kind, for everyone you meet is fighting a harder battle.
Plato

One kind word can warm three winter months.
Japanese proverb

Human kindness has never weakened the stamina or softened the fiber of a free people. A nation does not have to be cruel to be tough.
Franklin D. Roosevelt

Constant kindness can accomplish much. As the sun makes ice melt, kindness causes misunderstanding, mistrust and hostility to evaporate.
Albert Schweitzer

Wherever there is a human being, there is an opportunity for kindness.
Seneca

There are ten strong things.
Iron is strong, but fire melts it.
Fire is strong, but water quenches it.
Water is strong, but the clouds evaporate it.
Clouds are strong, but wind drives them away.
Man is strong, but fears cast him down.
Fear is strong, but sleep overcomes it.
Sleep is strong, yet death is stronger.
But loving kindness survives death.
The Talmud

Deeds of kindness weigh as much as all the commandments.
The Talmud

Spread love everywhere you go: First of all in your own house.
Let no one ever come to you without leaving better and happier.
Be the living expression of God's kindness; kindness in your face, kindness in your eyes, kindness in your smile, kindness in your warm greeting.
Mother Teresa

Kind words can be short and easy to speak, but their echoes are truly endless.
Mother Teresa

Never lose a chance of saying a kind word.
William Makepeace Thackeray

If you stop to be kind, you must swerve often from your path.
Mary Webb

The best portion of a good man's life,
His little nameless, unremembered acts
Of kindness and of love.
William Wordsworth

Kindness and wisdom
Kindness is more important than wisdom, and the recognition of this is the beginning of wisdom.
Theodore Isaac Rubin

King James Version
See also: Authorized Version
The Rules for Revision
Summary of the fourteen rules drawn up, apparently by King James himself, for the guidance of the revisers:
1. The Bishops' Bible to be followed "and as little altered as the original will permit."
2. The proper names "to be retained as near as may be ... as vulgarly used."
3. Old ecclesiastical words not to be changed, "as the word 'Church' not to be translated 'congregation'."
4. Words of varying interpretations to be rendered in accordance with patristic tradition and the analogy of faith.
5. No change to be made in the chapter divisions.
6. No notes except to explain Hebrew or Greek words.
7. Cross references to be inserted.
8. As each reviser completes the portion assigned to him, all his company should compare results and decide on the rendering to be chosen.
9. The completed work of each company to be sent to the other companies "to be considered of seriously and judiciously; for, his Majesty is very careful in this point."
10. Doubts thence arising to be settled "at the general meeting of the chief persons of each company, at the end of the work."
11. In really obscure passages the help of other learned people is to be sought.
12. The bishops are to look for men capable of assisting in the work.
13. The directors to be the deans of Westminster and Chester and the regius professors of Hebrew and Greek.
14. "These translations to be used when they agree better with the text than the Bishops' Bible: namely, Tindal's, Matthews', Coverdale's, Whitchurch's, the Geneva."
Hugh Pope

King James Version, *Famous Bible verses in the*

A Old Testament

Light
And God said, Let there be light: and there was light.
Genesis 1:3

Marriage
It is not good that the man should be alone.
Genesis 2:18

Shame
They sewed fig leaves together and made themselves aprons.
Genesis 3:7

Work
In the sweat of thy face shalt thou eat bread.
Genesis 3:19

Death
For dust thou art, and unto dust shalt thou return.
Genesis 3:19

Eve
The mother of all living.
Genesis 3:20

Society
Am I my brother's keeper?
Genesis 4:9

Judgement
And the rain was upon the earth forty days and forty nights.
Genesis 7:12

Punishment
Whoso sheddeth man's blood, by man shall his blood be shed.
Genesis 9:6

Worldliness
His wife looked back from behind him, and she became a pillar of salt.
Genesis 19:26

Jealousy
They stript Joseph out of his coat, his coat of many colors.
Genesis 37:23

Sorrow
… then shall ye bring down my gray hairs with sorrow to the grave.
Genesis 42:38

Stranger
I have been a stranger in a strange land.
Exodus 2:22

Promised Land
A land flowing with milk and honey.
Exodus 3:8

Guidance
The Lord went before them by day in a pillar of a cloud, to lead them the way; and by night in a pillar of fire.
Exodus 13:21

Neighborliness
Love thy neighbor as thyself.
Leviticus 19:18

Miracle
The Lord opened the mouth of the ass, and she said unto Balaam, What have I done unto thee, that thou hast smitten me these three times?
Numbers 22:28

Spiritual food
Man doth not live by bread only.
Deuteronomy 8:3

Revenge, Limited
Life shall go for life, eye for eye, tooth for tooth, hand for hand, foot for foot.
Deuteronomy 19:21

Revelation
The secret things belong unto the LORD.
Deuteronomy 29:29

Protection
He kept him as the apple of his eye.
Deuteronomy 32:10

God's strength
As thy days, so shall thy strength be.
Deuteronomy 33:25

Death
I am going the way of all the earth.
Joshua 23:14

Leadership
I arose a mother in Israel.
Judges 5:7

Faithfulness
Whither thou goest, I will go; and where thou lodgest, I will lodge: thy people shall be my people, and thy God my God.
Ruth 1:16

Godliness
A man after his own heart.
1 Samuel 13:14

Rebuke
Thou art the man.
2 Samuel 12:7

Psalms
The sweet psalmist of Israel.
2 Samuel 23:1

Decision
How long halt ye between two opinions?
1 Kings 18:21

God's presence
A still small voice.
1 Kings 19:12

Godliness
One that feared God, and eschewed evil.
Job 1:1

Satan
Satan came also.
Job 1:6

Gratitude
The LORD gave, and the LORD hath taken away; blessed be the name of the LORD.
Job 1:21

Life
All that a man hath will he give for his life.
Job 2:4

Afterlife
There the wicked cease from troubling, and there the weary be at rest.
Job 3:17

Trouble
Man is born unto trouble, as the sparks fly upward.
Job 5:7

Crafty
He taketh the wise in their own craftiness.
Job 5:13

Death
Thou shalt come to thy grave in a full age, like as a shock of corn cometh, in his season.
Job 5:26

Words
How forcible are right words!
Job 6:25

Life
My days are swifter than a weaver's shuttle.
Job 7:6

Death
I would not live alway.
Job 7:16

Afterlife
The land of darkness and the shadow of death.
Job 10:21

Wisdom
Wisdom shall die with you.
Job 12:2

Trouble
Man that is born of a woman is of few days, and full of trouble.
Job 14:1

Comforter
Miserable comforters are ye all.
Job 16:2

Wisdom
The price of wisdom is above rubies.
Job 28:18

Words
He multiplieth words without knowledge.
Job 35:16

Counsel
Who is this that darkeneth counsel by words without knowledge?
Job 38:2

Nature
The morning stars sang together, and all the sons of God shouted for joy.
Job 38:7

Worship
I have heard of thee by the hearing of the ear; but now mine eye seeth thee.
Job 42:5

Strength
His leaf also shall not wither.
Psalm 1:3

Light
Lift thou up the light of thy countenance upon us.
Psalm 4:6

Wisdom
Out of the mouth of babes and sucklings.
Psalm 8:2

Humanity
Thou hast made him a little lower than the angels.
Psalm 8:5

Atheist
The fool hath said in his heart, There is no God.
Psalm 14:1

Faithfulness
He that sweareth to his own hurt, and changeth not.
Psalm 15:4

Inheritance
The lines are fallen unto me in pleasant places; yea, I have a goodly heritage.
Psalm 16:6

Protection
Keep me as the apple of the eye, hide me under the shadow of thy wings.
Psalm 17:8

Death
The sorrows of death compassed me.
Psalm 18:4

God's power
He rode upon a cherub, and did fly: yea, he did fly upon the wings of the wind.
Psalm 18:10

Nature
The heavens declare the glory of God; and the firmament showeth his handiwork.
Psalm 19:1

God's provision
He maketh me to lie down in green pastures; he leadeth me beside the still waters.
Psalm 23:2

God's protection
Thy rod and thy staff they comfort me.
Psalm 23:4

God's provision
My cup runneth over.
Psalm 23:5

Argument
From the strife of tongues.
Psalm 31:20

Speaking
Keep thy tongue from evil, and thy lips from speaking guile.
Psalm 34:13

Life
Lord, make me to know mine end, and the measure of my days, what it is; that I may know how frail I am.
Psalm 39:4

Poor
Blessed is he that considereth the poor.
Psalm 41:1

Thirst, Spiritual
As the hart panteth after the water brooks.
Psalm 42:1

Advice
My tongue is the pen of a ready writer.
Psalm 45:1

Trouble
God is our refuge and strength, a very
present help in trouble.
Psalm 46:1

Help
Vain is the help of man.
Psalm 60:11

God's blessing
He shall come down like rain upon the
mown grass.
Psalm 72:6

Strength
They go from strength to strength.
Psalm 84:7

God's presence
A day in thy courts is better than a
thousand. I had rather be a doorkeeper in
the house of my God than to dwell in the
tents of wickedness.
Psalm 84:10

Mercy
Mercy and truth are met together:
righteousness and peace have kissed each
other.
Psalm 85:10

Time
A thousand years in thy sight are but as
yesterday when it is past, and as a watch in
the night.
Psalm 90:4

Life
We spend our years as a tale that is told.
Psalm 80:9

Life
The days of our years are threescore years

and ten; and if by reason of strength they
be fourscore years, yet is their strength
labor and sorrow; for it is soon cut off, and
we fly away.
Psalm 80:10

Wisdom
So teach us to number our days, that we
may apply our hearts unto wisdom.
Psalm 80:12

Trust
I will say of the Lord, He is my refuge and
my fortress: my God; in him will I trust.
Psalm 91:2

Righteous, The
The righteous shall flourish like the palm
tree: he shall grow like a cedar in
Lebanon.
Psalm 92:12

God's power
The Lord reigneth; let the earth rejoice.
Psalm 97:1

Life
As for man his days are as grass: as a flower
of the field so he flourisheth.
Psalm 103:15

Wine
Wine that maketh glad the heart of man.
Psalm 104:15

Work
Man goeth forth unto his work and to his
labor until the evening.
Psalm 104:23

Sea
They that go down to the sea in ships, that
do business in great waters.
Psalm 107:23

Lying
I said in my haste, All men are liars.
Psalm 116:11

Death
Precious in the sight of the Lord is the

death of his saints.
Psalm 116:15

Rejection
The stone which the builders refused is
become the head stone of the corner.
Psalm 118:22

Understanding
I have more understanding than all my
teachers: for thy testimonies are my
meditations.
Psalm 119:99

Guidance
A lamp unto my feet, and a light unto my
path.
Psalm 119:105

God's protection
The sun shall not smite thee by day, nor
the moon by night.
Psalm 121:6

Peace
Peace be within thy walls, and prosperity
within thy palaces.
Psalm 122:7

Sleep
He giveth his beloved sleep.
Psalm 127:2

Children
Happy is the man that hath his quiver full
of them.
Psalm 127:5

Unity
Behold, how good and how pleasant it is
for brethren to dwell together in unity.
Psalm 133:1

Sadness
We hanged our harps upon the willows.
Psalm 137:2

Jerusalem
If I forget thee, O Jerusalem, let my right
hand forget her cunning.
Psalm 137:5

Humanity
I am fearfully and wonderfully made.
Psalm 139:14

Trust
Put not your trust in princes.
Psalm 146:3

Sinners
My son, if sinners entice thee, consent
thou not.
Proverbs 1:10

Wisdom
Wisdom crieth without; she uttereth her
voice in the street.
Proverbs 1:20

Wisdom
Length of days is in her right hand; and in
her left hand riches and honor.
Proverbs 3:16

Wisdom
Her ways are ways of pleasantness, and all
her paths are peace.
Proverbs 3:17

Wisdom
Wisdom is the principal thing; therefore
get wisdom: and with all thy getting get
understanding.
Proverbs 4:7

Godly, The
The path of the just is as the shining light,
that shineth more and more unto the
perfect day.
Proverbs 4:18

Laziness
Go to the ant, thou sluggard; consider her
ways, and be wise.
Proverbs 6:6

Laziness
Yet a little sleep, a little slumber, a little
folding of the hands to sleep.
Proverbs 6:10

Wisdom
Wisdom is better than rubies.
Proverbs 8:11

Stealing
Stolen waters are sweet, and bread eaten in secret is pleasant.
Proverbs 9:17

Son
A wise son maketh a glad father.
Proverbs 10:1

Just, The
The memory of the just is blessed.
Proverbs 10:7

Advice
In the multitude of counselors there is safety.
Proverbs 11:14

Righteous, The
A righteous man regardeth the life of his beast; but the tender mercies of the wicked are cruel.
Proverbs 12:10

Hope
Hope deferred maketh the heart sick.
Proverbs 13:12

Fools
Fools make a mock at sin.
Proverbs 14:9

Death
The righteous hath hope in his death.
Proverbs 14:32

Righteousness
Righteousness exalteth a nation.
Proverbs 14:34

Gentleness
A soft answer turneth away wrath.
Proverbs 15:1

Cheerfulness
A merry heart maketh a cheerful countenance.
Proverbs 15:13

Happiness
He that is of a merry heart hath a continual feast.
Proverbs 15:15

Love
Better is a dinner of herbs where love is, than a stalled ox and hatred therewith.
Proverbs 15:17

Words
A word spoken in due season, how good is it!
Proverbs 15:23

Heart
A man's heart deviseth his way: but the Lord directeth his steps.
Proverbs 16:9

Pride
Pride goeth before destruction, and an haughty spirit before a fall.
Proverbs 16:18

Anger
He that is slow to anger is better than the mighty; and he that ruleth his spirit than he that taketh a city.
Proverbs 16:32

Lots
The lot is cast into the lap; but the whole disposing thereof is of the LORD.
Proverbs 16:33

Heart
A merry heart doeth good like a medicine.
Proverbs 17:22

Speaking
He that hath knowledge spareth his words.
Proverbs 17:27

Silence
Even a fool, when he holdeth his peace, is counted wise.
Proverbs 17:28

Wife
Whoso findeth a wife findeth a good thing.
Proverbs 18:22

Friends
A man that hath friends must show himself friendly: and there is a friend that sticketh closer than a brother.
Proverbs 18:24

Poor, The
He that hath pity upon the poor lendeth unto the LORD.
Proverbs 19:17

Drunkenness
Wine is a mocker, strong drink is raging.
Proverbs 20:1

Reputation
A good name is rather to be chosen than great riches.
Proverbs 22:1

Education
Train up a child in the way he should go: and when he is old he will not depart from it.
Proverbs 22:6

Debt
The borrower is servant to the lender.
Proverbs 22:7

Tradition
Remove not the ancient landmark.
Proverbs 22:28

Over-eating
Put a knife to thy throat, if thou be a man given to appetite.
Proverbs 23:2

Strength
A wise man is strong; yea, a man of knowledge increaseth strength.
Proverbs 24:5

Adversity
If thou faint in the day of adversity thy strength is small.
Proverbs 24:10

Words
A word fitly spoken is like apples of gold in pictures of silver.
Proverbs 25:11

Good news
As cold waters to a thirsty soul, so is good news from a far country.
Proverbs 25:25

Fools
Answer a fool according to his folly.
Proverbs 26:5

Pride
Seest thou a man wise in his own conceit? there is more hope of a fool than of him.
Proverbs 26:12

Future
Boast not thyself of tomorrow; for thou knowest not what a day may bring forth.
Proverbs 27:1

Rebuke
Open rebuke is better than secret love.
Proverbs 27:5

Rebuke
Faithful are the wounds of a friend.
Proverbs 27:6

Quarrelsome
A continual dropping in a very rainy day and a contentious woman are alike.
Proverbs 27:15

Friends
Iron sharpeneth iron; so a man sharpeneth the countenance of his friend.
Proverbs 27:17

Vision
Where there is no vision, the people perish.
Proverbs 29:18

Contentment
Give me neither poverty nor riches.
Proverbs 30:8

Work
She looketh well to the ways of her household, and eateth not the bread of idleness.
Proverbs 31:27

Beauty
Favor is deceitful, and beauty is vain.
Proverbs 31:30

Vanity
Vanity of vanities; all is vanity.
Ecclesiastes 1:2

Life
One generation passeth away, and another generation cometh.
Ecclesiastes 1:4

Life
There is no new thing under the sun.
Ecclesiastes 1:9

Vanity
All is vanity and vexation of spirit.
Ecclesiastes 1:14

Seasons
To everything there is a season, and a time to every purpose under the heaven.
Ecclesiastes 3:1

Unity
A threefold cord is not quickly broken.
Ecclesiastes 4:12

Words
Let thy words be few.
Ecclesiastes 5:2

Vows
Better is it that thou shouldest not vow, than that thou shouldest vow and not pay.
Ecclesiastes 5:5

Sleep
The sleep of a laboring man is sweet.
Ecclesiastes 5:12

Reputation
A good name is better than precious ointment.
Ecclesiastes 7:1

Feasting
It is better to go to the house of mourning than to go to the house of feasting.
Ecclesiastes 7:2

Fools
As the crackling of thorns under a pot, so is the laughter of a fool.
Ecclesiastes 7:6

Prosperity
In the day of prosperity be joyful, but in the day of adversity consider.
Ecclesiastes 7:14

Life
To eat, and to drink, and to be merry.
Ecclesiastes 8:15

Work
Whatsoever thy hand findeth to do, do it with thy might.
Ecclesiastes 9:10

Action
Cast thy bread upon the waters: for thou shalt find it after many days.
Ecclesiastes 11:1

Caution
He that observeth the wind shall not sow; and he that regardeth the clouds shall not reap.
Ecclesiastes 11:4

Light
Truly the light is sweet, and a pleasant thing it is for the eyes to behold the sun.
Ecclesiastes 11:7

Youth
Rejoice, O young man, in thy youth.
Ecclesiastes 11:9

Youth
Remember now thy Creator in the days of thy youth.
Ecclesiastes 12:1

Death
Then shall the dust return to the earth as it was; and the spirit shall return unto God who gave it.
Ecclesiastes 12:7

Study
Of making many books there is no end; and much study is a weariness of the flesh.
Ecclesiastes 12:12

Reverence
Let us hear the conclusion of the whole matter: Fear God, and keep his commandments: for this is the whole duty of man.
Ecclesiastes 12:13

Joy
For, lo, the winter is past, the rain is over and gone; the flowers appear on the earth; the time of the singing of birds is come, and the voice of the turtle is heard in our land.
The Song of Solomon 2:11, 12

Destruction
The little foxes, that spoil the vines.
The Song of Solomon 2:15

Love
Love is strong as death; jealousy is cruel as the grave.
The Song of Solomon 8:6

Love
Many waters cannot quench love, neither can the floods drown it.
The Song of Solomon 8:7

Sin
The whole head is sick, and the whole heart faint.
Isaiah 1:5

Peace
They shall beat their swords into ploughshares, and their spears into pruninghooks; nation shall not lift up sword against nation, neither shall they learn war any more.
Isaiah 2:4

Evil
Woe unto them that call evil good, and good evil.
Isaiah 5:20

Sinfulness
I am a man of unclean lips.
Isaiah 6:5

God's Spirit
The spirit of the LORD shall rest upon him, the spirit of wisdom and understanding, the spirit of counsel and might, the spirit of knowledge and of the fear of the LORD.
Isaiah 11:2

Future
The wolf also shall dwell with the lamb, and the leopard shall lie down with the kid.
Isaiah 11:6

Teaching
For precept must be upon precept, precept upon precept; line upon line, line upon line; here a little, and there a little.
Isaiah 28:10

Strength
Their strength is to sit still.
Isaiah 30:7

Transformation
The desert shall rejoice, and blossom as the rose.
Isaiah 35:1

Humanity
All flesh is grass.
Isaiah 40:6

Nations
The nations are as a drop of a bucket.
Isaiah 40:15

Gentleness
A bruised reed shall he not break, and the smoking flax shall he not quench.
Isaiah 42:3

Wicked, The
There is no peace, saith the LORD, unto the wicked.
Isaiah 48:22

Sacrifice
He is brought as a lamb to the slaughter.
Isaiah 53:7

Wicked, The
Let the wicked forsake his way, and the unrighteous man his thoughts.
Isaiah 55:7

Transformation
Give unto them beauty for ashes, the oil of joy for mourning, the garment of praise for the spirit of heaviness.
Isaiah 61:3

Life
We all do fade as a leaf.
Isaiah 64:6

Repent
Amend your ways and your doings.
Jeremiah 7:3

Comfort
Is there no balm in Gilead; Is there no physician there?
Jeremiah 8:22

Humanity
Can the Ethiopian change his skin, or the leopard his spots?
Jeremiah 13:23

Judgment
Thou art weighed in the balances, and art found wanting.
Daniel 5:27

Knowledge
Many shall run to and fro, and knowledge shall be increased.
Daniel 12:4

Retribution
They have sown the wind, and they shall reap the whirlwind.
Hosea 8:7

Visions
Your old men shall dream dreams, your young men shall see visions.
Joel 2:28

God's blessing
They shall sit every man under his vine and under his fig tree.
Micah 4:4

Despising
For who hath despised the day of small things?
Zechariah 4:10

Hope
Prisoners of hope.
Zechariah 9:12

Betrayal
I was wounded in the house of my friends.
Zechariah 13:6

Reverence
But unto you that fear my name shall the Sun of righteousness arise with healing in his wings.
Malachi 4:2

B New Testament

Tragedy
Rachel weeping for her children, and would not be comforted, because they are not.
Matthew 2:18

Witness
Ye are the light of the world. A city that is set on an hill cannot be hid.
Matthew 4:14

Witness
Ye are the salt of the earth: but if the salt have lost his savor, wherewith shall it be salted?
Matthew 5:13

Neighborliness
Ye have heard that it have been said, Thou shalt love thy neighbor, and hate thine enemy.
Matthew 5:43

Giving
Take heed that ye do not your alms before men, to be seen of them.
Matthew 6:1

Giving
When thou doest alms, let not thy left hand know what thy right hand doeth.
Matthew 6:3

Heaven
Lay up for yourselves treasures in heaven.
Matthew 6:20

Treasure
Where your treasure is, there will your heart be also.
Matthew 6:21

Service
Ye cannot serve God and mammon.
Matthew 6:24

Life
Take no thought for your life, what ye shall eat, or what ye shall drink.
Matthew 6:25

Worry
Consider the lilies of the field, how they grow; they toil not, neither do they spin.
Matthew 6:28

Worry
Take therefore no thought for the morrow; for the morrow shall take thought for the things of itself. Sufficient unto the day is the evil thereof.
Matthew 6:34

Witness
Neither cast ye your pearls before swine.
Matthew 7:6

Prayer
Ask, and it shall be given you; seek, and ye shall find; knock, and it shall be opened unto you.
Matthew 7:7

Prayer
Every one that asketh receiveth; and he that seeketh findeth.
Matthew 7:8

God's goodness
Or what man is there of you, whom if his son ask bread, will he give him a stone?
Matthew 7:9

Living
Therefore all things whatsoever ye would that men should do to you, do ye even so to them: for this is the law and the prophets.
Matthew 7:12

Hell
Wide is the gate, and broad is the way, that leadeth to destruction.
Matthew 7:13

Heaven
Strait is the gate, and narrow is the way, which leadeth unto life.
Matthew 7:14

Fruitfulness
By their fruits ye shall know them.
Matthew 7:20

Mission
The harvest truly is plenteous, but the laborers are few.
Matthew 9:37

Wisdom
Be ye therefore wise as serpents, and harmless as doves.
Matthew 10:16

God's care
The very hairs of your head are all numbered.
Matthew 10:30

Wisdom
Wisdom is justified of her children.
Matthew 11:19

Heart
Out of the abundance of the heart the mouth speaketh.
Matthew 12:34

Fear
Be of good cheer: it is I: be not afraid.
Matthew 14:27

Divorce
What therefore God hath joined together, let not man put asunder.
Matthew 19:6

Neighborliness
Love thy neighbor as thyself.
Matthew 19:19

Wealth
It is easier for a camel to go through the eye of a needle, than for a rich man to enter into the kingdom of God.
Matthew 19:24

Election
For many are called, but few are chosen.
Matthew 22:14

Taxes
Render therefore unto Cæsar the things which are Cæsar's.
Matthew 22:21

Leadership
Blind guides, which strain at a gnat, and swallow a camel.
Matthew 23:24

Hypocrisy
Whited sepulchers, which indeed appear beautiful outward, but are within full of dead men's bones.
Matthew 23:27

Faithfulness
Unto every one that hath shall be given, and he shall have abundance; but from

him that hath not shall be taken away even that which he hath.
Matthew 25:29

Prayer
The spirit indeed is willing, but the flesh is weak.
Matthew 26:41

Sabbath
The sabbath was made for man, and not man for the sabbath.
Mark 2:27

Division
If a house be divided against itself, that house cannot stand.
Mark 3:25

Christmas
Glory to God in the highest, and on earth peace, good will toward men.
Luke 2:14

Reputation
Woe unto you, when all men shall speak well of you!
Luke 6:26

Peace
Peace be to this house.
Luke 10:5

Action
Go, and do thou likewise.
Luke 10:37

Priorities
But one thing is needful; and Mary hath chosen that good part which shall not be taken away from her.
Luke 10:42

Self-satisfaction
Soul, thou hast much goods laid up for many years; take thine ease, eat, drink, and be merry.
Luke 12:19

Wisdom
The children of this world are in their

generation wiser than the children of light.
Luke 16:8

Stumbling block
It were better for him that a millstone were
hanged about his neck, and he cast into
the sea.
Luke 17:2

Worldliness
Remember Lot's wife.
Luke 17:32

Christ's presence
Did not our heart burn within us while he
talked with us?
Luke 24:32

Light
The true Light, which lighteth every man
that cometh into the world.
John 1:9

Judging
Judge not according to the appearance.
John 7:24

Truth
The truth shall make you free.
John 8:32

Poor
The poor always ye have with you.
John 12:8

Anxiety
Let not your heart be troubled.
John 14:1

Heaven
In my Father's house are many mansions.
John 14:2

Sacrifice
Greater love hath no man than this, that a
man lay down his life for his friends.
John 15:13

Giving
It is more blessed to give than to receive.
Acts 20:35

Paul
I appeal unto Cæsar.
Acts 25:11

Impartiality
There is no respect of persons with God.
Romans 2:11

Sin
The wages of sin is death.
Romans 6:23

Struggle, Spiritual
For the good that I would I do not: but the
evil which I would not, that I do.
Romans 7:19

Providence
All things work together for good to them
that love God.
Romans 8:28

Zeal
A zeal of God, but not according to
knowledge.
Romans 10:2

Hospitality
Given to hospitality.
Romans 12:13

Pride
Be not wise in your own conceits.
Romans 12:16

Retaliation
Recompense to no man evil for evil.
Provide things honest in the sight of all
men.
Romans 12:17

Peace
If it be possible, as much as lieth in you,
live peaceably with all men.
Romans 12:18

Revenge
If thine enemy hunger, feed him; if he
thirst, give him drink: for in so doing thou
shalt heap coals of fire on his head.
Romans 12:20

Goodness
Be not overcome of evil, but overcome evil with good.
Romans 12:21

Love
Owe no man anything, but to love one another.
Romans 13:8

Love
Love is the fulfilling of the law.
Romans 13:10

Election
God hath chosen the foolish things of the world to confound the wise; and God hath chosen the weak things of the world to confound the things that are mighty.
1 Corinthians 1:27

Spiritual life
I have planted, Apollos watered; but God gave the increase.
1 Corinthians 3:6

Worldliness
The fashion of this world passeth away.
1 Corinthians 7:31

Evangelism
I am made all things to all men.
1 Corinthians 9:22

Pride
Let him that thinketh he standeth take heed lest he fall.
1 Corinthians 10:12

Love
Though I speak with the tongues of men and of angels, and have not charity, I am become as sounding brass, or a tinkling cymbal.
1 Corinthians 13:1

Love
Though I have all faith, so that I could remove mountains, and have not charity, I am nothing.
1 Corinthians 13:2

Love
Charity suffereth long and is kind; charity envieth not; charity vaunteth not itself, is not puffed up.
1 Corinthians 13:4

Sight
Now we see through a glass, darkly.
1 Corinthians 13:12

Love
And now abideth faith, hope, charity, these three; but the greatest of these is charity.
1 Corinthians 13:13

Preaching
If the trumpet give an uncertain sound.
1 Corinthians 14:8

Worship
Let all things be done decently and in order.
1 Corinthians 14:40

Death
O death, where is thy sting? O grave, where is thy victory?
1 Corinthians 15:55

Spirit
Not of the letter, but of the spirit; for the letter killeth, but the spirit giveth life.
2 Corinthians 3:6

Faith
We walk by faith, not by sight.
2 Corinthians 5:7

Persecution
Forty stripes save one.
2 Corinthians 11:24

Strength
Strength is made perfect in weakness.
2 Corinthians 12:9

Fellowship
The right hands of fellowship.
Galatians 2:9

Backsliding
Ye are fallen from grace.
Galatians 5:4

Unstable
Carried about with every wind of doctrine.
Ephesians 4:14

Truth
Speak every man truth with his neighbor.
Ephesians 4:25

Anger
Be ye angry, and sin not: let not the sun go
down upon your wrath.
Ephesians 4:26

Death
To live is Christ, and to die is gain.
Philippians 1:21

Peace
The peace of God, which passeth all
understanding.
Philippians 4:7

Meditation
Whatsoever things are true, whatsoever
things are honest, whatsoever things are
just, whatsoever things are pure,
whatsoever things are lovely, whatsoever
things are of good report; if there be any
virtue, and if there be any praise, think on
these things.
Philippians 4:8

Contentment
I have learned, in whatsoever state I am,
therewith to be content.
Philippians 4:11

Heaven
Set your affections on things above, not on
things on the earth.
Colossians 3:2

Speech
Let your speech be alway with grace,
seasoned with salt.
Colossians 4:6

Love
Labor of love.
1 Thessalonians 1:3

Quietness
Study to be quiet.
1 Thessalonians 4:11

Discernment
Prove all things; hold fast that which is good.
1 Thessalonians 5:21

Law
The law is good, if a man use it lawfully.
1 Timothy 1:8

Greed
Not greedy of filthy lucre.
1 Timothy 3:3

Family, Care of
He hath denied the faith, and is worse
than an infidel.
1 Timothy 5:8

Wine
Drink no longer water, but use a little wine
for thy stomach's sake.
1 Timothy 5:23

Money, Love of
The love of money is the root of all evil.
1 Timothy 6:10

Good deeds
Rich in good works.
1 Timothy 6:18

Faithfulness
I have fought a good fight, I have finished
my course, I have kept the faith.
2 Timothy 4:7

Purity
Unto the pure all things are pure.
Titus 1:15

Growth, spiritual
Such as have need of milk, and not of
strong meat.
Hebrews 5:12

Faith
Faith is the substance of things hoped for, the evidence of things not seen.
Hebrews 11:1

Martyrs
Of whom the world was not worthy.
Hebrews 11:38

Christians in heaven
A cloud of witnesses.
Hebrews 12:1

Discipline
Whom the Lord loveth he chasteneth.
Hebrews 12:6

Hospitality
Be not forgetful to entertain strangers: for thereby some have entertained angels unawares.
Hebrews 13:2

God's faithfulness
Yesterday, and to day, and forever.
Hebrews 13:8

Temptation
Blessed is the man that endureth temptation: for when he is tried, he shall receive the crown of life.
James 1:12

Listening
Be swift to hear, slow to speak, slow to wrath.
James 1:19

Speech
How great a matter a little fire kindleth!
James 3:5

Speech
The tongue can no man tame; it is an unruly evil.
James 3:8

Devil
Resist the devil, and he will flee from you.
James 4:7

Hope
Hope to the end.
1 Peter 1:13

Reverence
Fear God. Honor the king.
1 Peter 2:17

Wives
Giving honor unto the wife, as unto the weaker vessel.
1 Peter 3:7

Unity
Be ye all of one mind.
1 Peter 3:8

Love
Charity shall cover the multitude of sins.
1 Peter 4:8

Devil
Be sober, be vigilant; because your adversary, the devil, as a roaring lion, walketh about, seeking whom he may devour.
1 Peter 5:8

Fear
There is no fear in love; but perfect love casteth out fear.
1 John 4:18

Faithfulness
Be thou faithful unto death.
Revelation 2:10

God's nature
I am Alpha and Omega, the beginning and the end, the first and the last.
Revelation 22:13

Kingdom of God
For the kingdom of God is not a matter of eating and drinking, but of righteousness, peace and joy in the Holy Spirit.
The Bible, Romans 14:17

Do you not know that the wicked will not inherit the kingdom of God? Do not be

deceived: Neither the sexually immoral nor idolaters nor adulterers nor male prostitutes nor homosexual offenders nor thieves nor the greedy nor drunkards nor slanderers nor swindlers will inherit the kingdom of God.
The Bible, 1 Corinthians 6:9,10

There is no point in us traveling abroad to find the kingdom of heaven, or crossing the sea in search of virtue. As the Lord has already told us, God's kingdom is within you.
Anthony of Egypt

Let the proud seek and love earthly kingdoms, but blessed are the poor in spirit for theirs is the kingdom of heaven.
Augustine of Hippo

To accept His kingdom and to enter it brings blessedness, because the best conceivable thing is that we should be in obedience to the will of God.
C.H. Dodd

To want all that God wants, always to want it, for all occasions and without reservations, this is the kingdom of God which is all within.
F. Fénelon

I will place no value on anything I have or possess unless it is in relationship to the kingdom of God.
David Livingstone

There is no structural organization of society which can bring about the coming of the kingdom of God on earth, since all systems can be perverted by the selfishness of man.
The Malvern Manifesto of the York province of the Church of England, 1941

The gospel of Jesus is *autobasilea*, the kingdom himself.
Origen

The kingdom of God and of his Christ is greater than the Church.
Wolfhart Pannenberg

If you do not wish for His kingdom, don't pray for it. But if you do, you must do more than pray for it; you must work for it.
J. Ruskin

If God could not be found on this side of the sea we would indeed journey across. Since, however, God is near to everyone who call on him, we are under no obligation to cross the sea. The kingdom of heaven can be reached from every land.
Samhthann

There can be no kingdom of God in the world without the kingdom of God in our hearts.
Albert Schweitzer

O World Invisible, we view thee,
O World intangible, we touch thee,
O World unknowable, we know thee,
Inapprehensible, we clutch thee!

Does the fish soar to find the ocean,
The eagle plunge to find the air –
That we ask of the stars in motion
If they have rumor of thee there?

Not where the wheeling systems darken,
And our benumbed conceiving soars! –
The drift of pinions, would we hearken,
Beats at our own clay-shuttered doors.

The angels keep their ancient places;
Turn but a stone, and start a wing!
'Tis ye, 'tis your estranged faces,
That miss the many-splendoured thing.

But (when so sad thou canst not sadder)
Cry; – and upon thy so sore loss
Shall shine the traffic of Jacob's ladder
Pitched betwixt Heaven and Charing
  Cross.

Yea, in the night, my Soul, my daughter,
Cry, – clinging Heaven by the hems;
And lo, Christ walking on the water,
Not of Genesareth, but Thames!
Francis Thompson

The only significance of life consists in

helping to establish the kingdom of God.
Leo Tolstoy

Kiss, Holy
Greet one another with a holy kiss.
The Bible, 1 Corinthians 16:20

At the close of the prayers we embrace one another with a kiss.
Justin Martyr

Kneeling Christian, *The*

By AN UNKNOWN CHRISTIAN

AUTHOR'S PREFACE

A traveler in China visited a heathen temple on a great feast-day. Many were the worshiper of the hideous idol enclosed in a sacred shrine. The visitor noticed that most of the devotees brought with them small pieces of paper on which prayers had been written or printed. These they would wrap up in little balls of stiff mud and fling at the idol. He enquired the reason for this strange proceeding, and was told that if the mud ball stuck fast to the idol, then the prayer would assuredly be answered; but if the mud fell off, the prayer was rejected by the god.

We may smile at this peculiar way of testing the acceptability of a prayer. But is it not a fact that the majority of Christian men and women who pray to a Living God know very little about real prevailing prayer? Yet prayer is the key which unlocks the door of God's treasure-house.

It is not too much to say that all real growth in the spiritual life-all victory over temptation, all confidence and peace in the presence of difficulties and dangers, all repose of spirit in times of great disappointment or loss, all habitual communion with God-depend upon the practice of secret prayer.

This book was written by request, and

with much hesitancy. It goes forth with much prayer. May He Who said, "Men ought always to pray, and not to faint," "teach us to pray."

CHAPTER 1: GOD'S GREAT NEED

"God Wondered." This is a very striking thought! The very boldness of the idea ought surely to arrest the attention of every earnest Christian man, woman and child. A wondering God! Why, how staggered we might well be if we knew the cause of God's "wonder"! Yet we find it to be, apparently, a very little thing. But if we are willing to consider the matter carefully, we shall discover it to be one of the greatest possible importance to every believer on the Lord Jesus Christ. Nothing else is so momentous – so vital – to our spiritual welfare. God "wondered that there was no intercessor" (Isa. lix. 16) – "none to interpose" (RV., marg.). But this was in the days of long ago, before the coming of the Lord Jesus Christ "full of grace and truth" – before the outpouring of the Holy Spirit, full of grace and power, "helping our infirmity," "Himself making intercession for us" and in us (Rom. viii. 26). Yes, and before the truly amazing promises of our Savior regarding prayer; before men knew very much about prayer; in the days when sacrifices for their sins loomed larger in their eyes than supplication for other sinners. Oh, how great must be God's wonder today! For how few there are among us who know what prevailing prayer really is! Every one of us would confess that we believe in prayer, yet how many of us truly believe in the power of, prayer? Now, before we go a step farther, may the writer most earnestly implore you not to read hurriedly what is contained in these chapters. Much – very much – depends upon the way in which every reader receives what is here recorded. For everything depends upon prayer.

Why are many Christians so often defeated? Because they pray so little. Why are many church-workers so often discouraged and disheartened? Because they pray so little.

Why do most men see so few brought "out of darkness to light" by their ministry? Because they pray so little.

Why are not our churches simply on fire for God? Because there is so little real prayer.

The Lord Jesus is as powerful today as ever before. The Lord Jesus is as anxious for men to be saved as ever before. His arm is not shortened that it cannot save: but He cannot stretch forth His arm unless we pray more – and more really.

We may be assured of this – the secret of all failure is our failure in secret prayer.

If God "wondered" in the days of Isaiah, we need not be surprised to find that in the days of His flesh our Lord "marveled." He marveled at the unbelief of some – unbelief which actually prevented Him from doing any mighty work in their cities (Mark vi. 6).

But we must remember that those who were guilty of this unbelief saw no beauty in Him that they should desire Him, or believe on Him. What then must His "marvel" be today, when He sees amongst us who do truly love and adore Him, so few who really "stir themselves up to take hold of God" (Isa. lxiv. 7). Surely there is nothing so absolutely astonishing as a practically prayerless Christian? These are eventful and ominous days. In fact, there are many evidences that these are "the last days" in which God promised to pour out His Spirit – the Spirit of supplication – upon all flesh (Joel ii. 28). Yet the vast majority of professing Christians scarcely know what "supplication" means; and very many of our churches not only have no prayer-meeting, but sometimes unblushingly condemn such meetings, and even ridicule them.

The Church of England, recognizing the importance of worship and prayer, expects her clergy to read prayers in Church every morning and evening.

But when this is done, is it not often in an empty church? And are not the prayers frequently raced through at a pace which precludes real worship? "Common prayer," too, often must necessarily be rather vague and indefinite.

And what of those churches where the old-fashioned weekly prayer-meeting is retained? Would not "weakly" be the more appropriate word? C. H. Spurgeon had the joy of being able to say that he conducted a prayer-meeting every Monday night "which scarcely ever numbers less than from a thousand to twelve hundred attendants." My brothers, have we ceased to believe in prayer? If you still hold your weekly gathering for prayer, is it not a fact that the very great majority of your church members never come near it? Yes, and never even think of coming near it. Why is this? Whose fault is it?

"Only a prayer-meeting" – how often we have heard the utterance! How many of those reading these words really enjoy a prayer-meeting? Is it a joy or just a duty? Please forgive me for asking so many questions and for pointing out what appears to be a perilous weakness and a lamentable shortcoming in our churches. We are not out to criticize – far less to condemn. Anybody can do that. Our yearning desire is to stir up Christians "to take hold of" God, as never before. We wish to encourage, to enhearten, to uplift.

We are never so high as when we are on our knees.

Criticize? Who dare criticize another? When we look back upon the past and remember how much prayerlessness there has been in one's own life, words of criticism of others wither away on the lips.

But we believe the time has come when a clarion call to the individual and to the Church is needed – a call to prayer.

Now, dare we face this question of prayer? It seems a foolish query, for is not prayer a part and parcel of all religions? Yet we venture to ask our readers to look at this matter fairly and squarely. Do I really believe that prayer is a power? Is prayer the greatest power on earth, or is it not? Does prayer indeed "move the Hand that moves the world"?

Do God's prayer-commands really concern Me? Do the promises of God concerning prayer still hold good? We have all been muttering "Yes – Yes – Yes" as we read these questions. We dare not say "No" to any one of them. And yet – !

Has it ever occurred to you that our Lord never gave an unnecessary or an optional command? Do we really believe that our Lord never made a promise which He could not, or would not, fulfil? Our Savior's three great commands for definite action were: –

Pray ye
Do this
Go ye!

Are we obeying Him? How often His command, "Do this," is reiterated by our preachers today! One might almost think it was His only command! How seldom we are reminded of His bidding to "Pray" and to "Go." Yet, without obedience to the "Pray ye," it is of little or no use at all either to "Do this" or to "Go."

In fact, it can easily be shown that all want of success, and all failure in the spiritual life and in Christian work, is due to defective or insufficient prayer. Unless we pray aright we cannot live aright or serve aright. This may appear, at first sight, to be gross exaggeration, but the more we think it over in the light Scripture throws upon it, the more convinced shall we be of the truth of this statement.

Now, as we begin once more to see what the Bible has to say about this mysterious and wonderful subject, shall we endeavor to read some of our Lord's promises, as though we had never heard them before. What will the effect be?

Some twenty years ago the writer was studying in a Theological College. One morning, early, a fellow-student – who is today one of England's foremost missionaries – burst into the room holding an open Bible in his hands. Although he was preparing for Holy Orders, he was at that time only a young convert to Christ.

He had gone up to the University "caring for none of these things." Popular, clever, athletic – he had already won a place amongst the smart set of his college, when Christ claimed him. He accepted the Lord Jesus as a personal Savior, and became a very keen follower of his Master. The Bible was, comparatively, a new book to him, and as a result he was constantly making "discoveries." On that memorable day on which he invaded my quietude he cried excitedly – his face all aglow with mingled joy and surprise – "Do you believe this? Is it really true?" "Believe what?" I asked, glancing at the open Bible with some astonishment. "Why, this – " and he read in eager tones St. Matthew xxi. 21, 22: "'If ye have faith and doubt not … all things whatsoever ye shall ask in prayer, believing, ye shall receive.' Do you believe it? Is it true?" "Yes," I replied, with much surprise at his excitement, "of course it's true – of course I believe it."

Yet, through my mind there flashed all manner of thoughts! "Well, that's a very wonderful promise," said he. "It seems to me to be absolutely limitless! Why don't we pray more?" And he went away, leaving me thinking hard. I had never looked at those verses quite in that way. As the door closed upon that eager young follower of the Master, I had a vision of my Savior and His love and His power such as I never had before. I had a vision of a life of prayer – yes, and "limitless" power, which I saw depended upon two things only – faith and prayer. For the moment I was thrilled. I fell on my knees, and as I bowed before my Lord what thoughts surged through my mind – what hopes and aspirations flooded my soul! God was speaking to me in an extraordinary way. This was a great call to prayer. But – to my shame be it said – I heeded not that call.

Where did I fail? True, I prayed a little more than before, but nothing much seemed to happen. Why? Was it because I did not see what a high standard the Savior requires in the inner life of those who would pray successfully?

Was it because I had failed to measure up my life to the "perfect love" standard so beautifully described in the thirteenth chapter of the first Epistle to the Corinthians?

For, after all, prayer is not just putting

into action good resolutions "to pray." Like David, we need to cry, "Create in me a clean heart, O God" (Psa. li.) before we can pray aright. And the inspired words of the Apostle of Love need to be heeded today as much as ever before: "Beloved, if our heart condemn us not, we have boldness toward God; and [then] whatsoever we ask, we receive of Him" (I John iii. 21).

"True – and I believe it." Yes, indeed, it is a limitless promise, and yet how little we realize it, how little we claim from Christ. And our Lord "marvels" at our unbelief. But if we could only read the Gospels for the first time, what an amazing book it would seem! Should not we "marvel" and "wonder"? And today I pass on that great call to you. Will you give heed to it? Will you profit by it? Or shall it fall on deaf ears and leave you prayerless?

Fellow-Christians, let us awake! The devil is blinding our eyes. He is endeavoring to prevent us from facing this question of prayer. These pages are written by special request. But it is many months since that request came.

Every attempt to begin to write has been frustrated, and even now one is conscious of a strange reluctance to do so. There seems to be some mysterious power restraining the hand. Do we realize that there is nothing the devil dreads so much as prayer? His great concern is to keep us from praying. He loves to see us "up to our eyes" in work – provided we do not pray. He does not fear because we are eager and earnest Bible students – provided we are little in prayer. Someone has wisely said, "Satan laughs at our toiling, mocks at our wisdom, but trembles when we pray." All this is so familiar to us – but do we really pray? If not, then failure must dog our footsteps, whatever signs of apparent success there may be.

Let us never forget that the greatest thing we can do for God or for man is to pray. For we can accomplish far more by our prayers than by our work. Prayer is omnipotent; it can do anything that God can do! When we pray God works. All fruitfulness in service is the outcome of

prayer – of the worker's prayers, or of those who are holding up holy hands on his behalf. We all know how to pray, but perhaps many of us need to cry as the disciples did of old, "Lord, teach us to pray."

O Lord, by Whom ye come to God,
The Life, the Truth, the Way,
The path of prayer Thyself hast trod;
Lord, teach us now to pray.

CHAPTER 10: HOW GOD ANSWERS PRAYER

For man fully to understand God and all His dealings with us is an utter impossibility. "O the depth of the riches both of the wisdom and the knowledge of God! How unsearchable are his judgments, and his ways past tracing out!" (Rom. xi. 33.) True, but we need not make difficulties where none exists. If God has all power and all knowledge, surely prayer has no difficulties, though occasionally there may be perplexities. We cannot discover God's method, but we know something of His manner of answering prayer.

But at the very outset may we remind ourselves how little we know about ordinary things? Mr. Edison, whose knowledge is pretty profound, wrote in August, 1921, "We don't know the millionth part of one per cent about anything. We don't know what water is. We don't know what light is. We don't know what gravitation is. We don't know what enables us to keep on our feet to stand up. We don't know what electricity is. We don't know what heat is. We don't know anything about magnetism. We have a lot of hypotheses, but that is all." But we do not allow our ignorance about all these things to deprive us of their use! We do not know much about prayer, but surely this need not prevent us from praying! We do know what our Lord has taught us about prayer. And we do know that He has sent the Holy Spirit to teach us all things (John xiv. 26). How, then, does God answer prayer? One way is just this: –

He reveals His mind to those who pray. His Holy Spirit puts fresh ideas into the minds of praying people. We are quite aware that the devil and his angels are busy enough putting bad thoughts into our minds. Surely, then, God and His holy angels can give us good thoughts? Even poor, weak, sinful men and women can put good thoughts into the minds of others. That is what we try to do in writing! We do not stop to think what a wonderful thing it is that a few peculiar-shaped black marks on this white paper can uplift and inspire, or depress and cast down, or even convict of sin! But, to an untutored savage, it is a stupendous miracle. Moreover, you and I can often read people's thoughts or wishes from an expression on the face or a glance of the eye. Even thought transference between man and man is a commonplace today. And God can in many ways convey His thoughts to us. A remarkable instance of this was related by a speaker last year at Northfield. Three or four years ago, he met an old whaling captain who told him this story.

"A good many years ago, I was sailing in the desolate seas off Cape Horn, hunting whales. One day we were beating directly south in the face of a hard wind. We had been tacking this way and that all the morning, and were making very little headway. About 11 o'clock, as I stood at the wheel, the idea suddenly came into my mind, "Why batter the ship against these waves? There are probably as many whales to the north as to the south. Suppose we run with the wind instead of against it? In response to that sudden idea I changed the course of the ship, and began to sail north instead of south. One hour later, at noon, the look-out at the masthead shouted "Boats ahead!"

Presently we overtook four lifeboats, in which were fourteen sailors, the only survivors of the crew of a ship which had burned to the water's edge ten days before. Those men had been adrift in their boats ever since, praying God frantically for rescue; and we arrived just in time to save them. They could not have survived another day."

Then the old whaler added, "I don't know whether you believe in religion or not, but I happen to be a Christian. I have begun every day of my life with prayer that God would use me to help someone else, and I am convinced that God, that day, put the idea into my mind to change the course of my ship. That idea was the means of saving fourteen lives."

God has many things to say to us. He has many thoughts to put into our minds. We are apt to be so busy doing His work that we do not stop to listen to His Word. Prayer gives God the opportunity of speaking to us and revealing His will to us. May our attitude often be: "Speak, Lord, Thy servant heareth."

God answers other prayers by putting new thoughts into the minds of those we pray for. At a series of services dealing with the victorious life, the writer one afternoon urged the congregation to "makeup" their quarrels if they really desired a holy life. One lady went straight home, and after very earnest prayer wrote to her sister, with whom, owing to some disagreement, she had had nothing to do for twenty years! Her sister was living thirty miles away. The very next morning the writer of that note received a letter from that very sister asking forgiveness and seeking reconciliation. The two letters had crossed in the post. While the one sister was praying to God for the other, God was speaking to that other sister, putting into her mind the desire for reconciliation.

You may say, Why did not God put that desire there before? It may be that He foresaw that it would be useless for the distant sister to write asking forgiveness until the other sister was also willing to forgive. The fact remains that, when we pray for others, somehow or other it opens the way for God to influence those we pray for. God needs our prayers, or He would not beg us to pray.

A little time back, at the end of a weekly prayer-meeting, a godly woman begged those present to pray for her husband, who would never go near a place of worship. The leader suggested that they should continue in prayer then and there. Most earnest prayers were offered up. Now, the husband was devoted to his wife, and frequently came to meet her. He did so that night, and arrived at the hall while the prayer-meeting was still in progress. God put it into his mind to open the door and wait inside – a thing he had never done before. As he sat on a chair near the door, leaning his head upon his hand, he overheard those earnest petitions. During the homeward walk he said, "Wife, who was the man they were praying for tonight?" "Oh," she replied, "it is the husband of one of our workers." "Well, I am quite sure he will be saved," said he; "God must answer prayers like that." A little later in the evening he again asked, "Who was the man they were praying for?" She replied in similar terms as before. On retiring to rest he could not sleep. He was under deep conviction of sin. Awaking his wife, he begged her to pray for him.

How clearly this shows us that when we pray, God can work! God could have prompted that man to enter that prayer-meeting any week. But had he done so it is a question whether any good at all would have come from it. When once those earnest, heartfelt petitions were being offered up on his behalf God saw that they would have a mighty influence upon that poor man.

It is when we pray that God can help us in our work and strengthen our resolves. For we can answer many of our own prayers. One bitter winter a prosperous farmer was praying that God would keep a neighbor from starving. When the family prayers were over, his little boy said, "Father, I don't think I should have troubled God about that. Why not?" he asked. "Because it would be easy enough for you to see that they don't starve!" There is not the slightest doubt that if we pray for others we shall also try to help them.

A young convert asked his vicar to give him some Christian work. "Have you a chum?" "Yes," replied the boy. "Is he a Christian?" "No, he is as careless as I was." "Then go and ask him to accept Christ as his Savior." "Oh, no!" said the lad, "I could never do that. Give me anything but that." "Well," said the vicar, "promise me two

things: that you will not speak to him about his soul, and that you will pray to God twice daily for his conversion." "Why, yes, I'll gladly do that," answered the boy. Before a fortnight was up he rushed round to the vicarage. "Will you let me off my promise? I must speak to my chum!" he cried. When he began to pray God could give him strength to witness. Communion with God is essential before we can have real communion with our fellow-man. My belief is that men so seldom speak to others about their spiritual condition because they pray so little for them.

The writer has never forgotten how his faith in prayer was confirmed when, as a lad of thirteen, he earnestly asked God to enable him on a certain day to secure twenty new subscribers for missions overseas. Exactly twenty new names were secured before night closed in. The consciousness that God would grant that prayer was an incentive to eager effort, and gave an unwonted courage in approaching others.

A cleric in England suggested to his people that they should each day pray for the worst man or woman and then go to them and tell them about Jesus. Only six agreed to do so. On arrival home he began to pray. Then he said, "I must not leave this to my people. I must take it up myself. I don't know the bad people. I'll have to go out and enquire." Approaching a rough-looking man at a street corner, he asked, "Are you the worst man in this district?" "No, I'm not." "Would you mind telling me who is?" "I don't mind. You'll find him at No. 7, down that street."

He knocked at No. 7 and entered. "I'm looking for the worst man in my parish. They tell me it might be you?" "Whoever told you that? Fetch him here, and I'll show him who's the worst man! No, there are lots worse than me." "Well, who is the worst man you know?" "Everybody knows him. He lives at the end house in that court. He's the worst man." So down the court he went and knocked at the door. A surly voice cried, "Come in!"

There were a man and his wife. "I hope you'll excuse me, but I'm the minister of the chapel along the round. I'm looking for the worst man in my district, because I have something to tell him. Are you the worst man?" The man turned to his wife and said, "Lass, tell him what I said to you five minutes ago." "No, tell him yourself." "What were you saying?" enquired the visitor. "Well, I've been drinking for twelve weeks. I've had the D.T's and have pawned all in the house worth pawning. And I said to my wife a few minutes ago, "Lass, this thing has to stop, and if it doesn't, I'll stop it myself – I'll go and drown myself." Then you knocked at the door! Yes, sir, I'm the very worst man. What have you got to say to me?" "I'm here to tell you that Jesus Christ is the greatest Savior, and that He can make out of the worst man one of the best. He did it for me, and He will do it for you." "D'you think He can do it even for me?" "I'm sure He can. Kneel down and ask Him."

Not only was the poor drunkard saved from his sins, but he is today a radiant Christian man, bringing other drunken people to the Lord Jesus Christ.

Surely none of us finds it difficult to believe that God can, in answer to prayer, heal the body, send rain or fair weather, dispel fogs, or avert calamities?

We have to do with a God whose knowledge is infinite. He can put it into the mind of a doctor to prescribe a certain medicine, or diet, or method of cure. All the doctor's skill is from God. "He knoweth our frame" – for He made it. He knows it far better than the cleverest doctor or surgeon. He made, and He can restore. We believe that God desires us to use medical skill, but we also believe that God, by His wonderful knowledge, can heal, and sometimes does heal, without human co-operation. And God must be allowed to work in His own way. We are so apt to tie God down to the way we approve of. God's aim is to glorify His name in answering our prayers. Sometimes He sees that our desire is right, but our petition wrong. St. Paul thought he could bring more glory to God if only the thorn in the flesh could be removed. God knew that he would be a better man and do better work with the thorn than without it. So God said No-No-No to his prayer, and then explained why!

So it was with Monica, who prayed so many years for the conversion of Augustine, her licentious son. When he was determined to leave home and cross the seas to Rome she prayed earnestly, even passionately, that God would keep him by her side, and under her influence. She went down to a little chapel on the seashore to spend the night in prayer close by where the ship lay at anchor. But, when morning came, she found that the ship had sailed even while she prayed! Her petition was refused, but her real desire was granted. For it was in Rome that Augustine met the sainted Ambrose, who led him to Christ. How comforting it is to know that God knows what is best!

But we should never think it unreasonable that God should make some things dependent upon our prayers. Some people say that if God really loves us He would give us what is best for us whether we ask Him or not. Dr. Fosdick has so beautifully pointed out that God has left man many things to do for himself. He promises seedtime and harvest. Yet man must prepare the soil, sow, and till, and reap in order to allow God to do His share. God provides us with food and drink. But He leaves us to take, and eat, and drink. There are some things God cannot, or at least will not, do without our help. God cannot do some things unless we think. He never emblazons His truth upon the sky. The laws of science have always been there. But we must think, and experiment, and think again if we would use those laws for our own good and God's glory.

God cannot do some things unless we work. He stores the hills with marble, but He has never built a cathedral. He fills the mountains with iron ore, but He never makes a needle or a locomotive. He leaves that to us. We must work.

If, then, God has left many things dependent upon man's thinking and working, why should He not leave some things dependent upon man's praying? He has done so. "Ask and ye shall receive." And there are some things God will not give us unless we ask. Prayer is one of the three ways in which man can co-operate with God; and the greatest of these is prayer.

Men of power are without exception men of prayer. God bestows His Holy Spirit in His fullness only on men of prayer. And it is through the operation of the Spirit that answers to prayer come. Every believer has the Spirit of Christ dwelling in him. For "if any have not the Spirit of Christ, he is none of his." But a man of prevailing prayer must be filled with the Spirit of God.

A lady missionary wrote recently that it used to be said of Praying Hyde that he never spoke to an unconverted man but that he was soundly converted. But if he ever did fail at first to touch a heart for God, he went back to his room and wrestled in prayer till he was shown what it was in himself that had hindered his being used by God. Yes, when we are filled with the Spirit of God, we cannot help influencing others God-ward. But, to have power with men, we must have power with God.

The momentous question for you and me is not, however, "How does God answer prayer?" The question is, "Do I really pray?" What a marvelous power God places at our disposal! Do we for a moment think that anything displeasing to God is worth our while holding on to? Fellow-Christian, trust Christ wholly, and you will find Him wholly true.

Let us give God the chance of putting His mind into us, and we shall never doubt the power of prayer again.

Author unknown

Knowing Christ

The knowledge of God without that of our wretchedness creates pride. The knowledge of our wretchedness without that of God creates despair. The knowledge of Jesus Christ is the middle way, because in him we find both God and our wretchedness.

Blaise Pascal

To know Christ was to know God (John 8:19; 14:7).
To see Christ was to see God (John 12:45; 14:9).
To believe in Christ was to believe in God (John 12:44; 14:1).
To receive Christ was to receive God (Mark 9:37).
To hate Christ was to hate God (John 15:23).
And to honor Christ was to honor God (John 5:23).

John Stott

Oh that Christ may be so known by us as a "living, bright reality" that our one desire, our one absorbing heart-passion, may be that we personally gain Christ – that we personally know Him as the apostle longed to do.

Hudson Taylor

Knowing God

The people who know God best are those who least presume to speak of him.

Angela of Foligno

Disciple: But how shall I comprehend this Ground of the Soul?
Master: If thou goest about to comprehend it, then it will fly away from thee; but if thou dost surrender thyself wholly up to it, then it will abide with thee, and become the Life of thy life, and be natural to thee.

Jacob Boehme

Not I, the I that I am, know these things, but God knows them in me.

Jacob Boehme

The first and most important thing we know about God is that we know nothing about him except what he himself makes known.

Emil Brunner

The saints of the past have never known God otherwise than by looking to him in his Son, as in a mirror.
John Calvin

For even if a man is deeply versed in the understanding and knowledge of all spiritual things ever created, he can never by such understanding come to know an uncreated spiritual thing … which is none else than God!
The Cloud of Unknowing

The image of God is worth more than all substances, and we give it for colors, for dreams, for shadows.
J. Donne

This is how men get to know God – by doing his will.
Henry Drummond

If we would reach the depth of God's nature, we must humble ourselves. He who would know God must first know himself.
Meister Eckhart

Oh, the fullness, pleasure, sheer excitement of knowing God on Earth!
Jim Elliot

God cannot be grasped with the mind. If he could be he would not be God.
Evagrius of Pontus

The promise [of seeing God] surpasses all beatitude. In Scripture, to see is to possess. Whoever sees God has obtained all the goods of which he can conceive.
Gregory of Nyssa

God is continually drawing us to himself in everything we experience.
Gerard Hughes

Among all created things, and things that can be apprehended by the understanding, there is no ladder whereby the understanding can attain to this high Lord.
John of the Cross

In order to come to union with the wisdom of God, the soul has to proceed rather by unknowing than by knowing.
John of the Cross

There are two big books, the book of nature and the book of super-nature, the Bible.
Johannes Keller

I, the pigmy creature of time, can know God the infinite, the absolute and the eternal.
M. Lloyd-Jones

To possess Him Who cannot be understood is to renounce all that can be understood.
Thomas Merton

When we speak of knowing God, it must be understood with reference to man's limited powers of comprehension. God, as He really is, is far beyond man's imagination, let alone his understanding. God has revealed only so much of Himself as our minds can conceive and the weakness of our nature can bear.
John Milton

The tragedy of much modern life is that the abandonment of the knowledge of God means that futility has taken over.
Leon Morris

Since God is not knowable in this world, where reason, opinion, and teaching lead us, by means of symbols, from the better known to the unknown, God is grasped only where persuades leave off and faith enters in. Through faith we are rapt in simplicity so that, while in a body incorporeally, because in spirit, and in the world not in a worldly manner but celestially, we may incomprehensibly contemplate Christ above all reason and intelligence, in the third heaven (2 Corinthians 12:2) of the simplest intellectuality.
Nicholas of Cusa

I often wonder if my knowledge about God has not become my greatest stumbling block to my knowledge of God.
Henri Nouwen

What were we made for? To know God.
What aim should we have in life? To know
God.
What is the eternal life that Jesus gives? To
know God.
What is the best thing in life? To know God.
What in humans gives God most pleasure?
Knowledge of himself.
J.I. Packer

Once you become aware that the main
business that you are here for is to know
God, most of life's problems fall into place
of their own accord.
J.I. Packer

It is equally dangerous to man to know
God without knowing his own
wretchedness, and to know his own
wretchedness without knowing God.
Blaise Pascal

The knowledge of God is very far from the
love of him.
Blaise Pascal

It is not only impossible but useless to
know God without Christ.
Blaise Pascal

Unknown makes unloved.
Dutch proverb

Man, made in the image of God, has a
purpose – to be in relationship to God, who
is there. Man forgets his purpose and thus
he forgets who he is and what life means.
Francis Schaeffer

We think we will receive the full
knowledge of God's truth by means of
worldly wisdom, and fancy that the mere
reading of the God-inspired writings of the
saints is to comprehend Orthodoxy, and
that this is an exact and certain knowledge
of the Holy Trinity. Nor is this all, but the
more august among us foolishly suppose
that the contemplation which comes to
pass only through the Spirit in those who
are worthy is the same as the thoughts
produced by their own reasoning. How

ridiculous! How callous!
Symeon the New Theologian

My son, says our Lord, hear My words and
follow them, for they are most sweet, far
passing the wisdom and learning of all
philosophers and all the wise men of the
world. My words are spiritual and cannot
be comprehended fully by man's
intelligence. Neither are they to be adapted
or applied according to the vain pleasure of
the hearer, but are to be heard in silence,
with great humility and reverence, with
great inward affection of the heart and in
great rest and quiet of body and soul.
Thomas à Kempis

The Bible assumes that every rational
human being knows of the existence of
God, therefore it simply states in its
opening line: "In the beginning God."
A.W. Tozer

Knowledge
See also: Learning; Reason; Wisdom
Many shall run to and fro, and knowledge
shall be increased.
The Bible, Daniel 12:4 KJV

Knowledge puffs up, but love builds up.
The Bible, 1 Corinthians 8:1

Knowledge becomes wisdom only after it
has been put to practical use.
Author unknown

Those of you who think you know
everything are very annoying to those of us
who do.
Author unknown

The more you know, the less you need to
show.
Author unknown

Once we had wisdom,
then we had knowledge,
now it's mostly just information.
Author unknown

Knowledge is proud that he has learned so

much; wisdom is humble that he knows no
more.
Author unknown

We both exist and know that we exist, and
rejoice in this existence and this
knowledge.
Augustine of Hippo

Lord, teach me to know Thee, and to
know myself.
Augustine of Hippo

Knowledge is power.
Francis Bacon

A man is but what he knows.
Francis Bacon

The desire of power in excess caused the
angels to fall; the desire of knowledge in
excess caused man to fall.
Francis Bacon

To know a thing is nothing in your eyes,
unless some other person is aware of your
knowledge.
Bernard of Clairvaux

We should not seek to learn anything just
so that we can pander to our pride, indulge
our curiosity, but only so that we can edify
ourselves and our neighbors.
Bernard of Clairvaux

Knowledge is the small part of ignorance
that we arrange and classify.
Ambrose Bierce

Knowledge is like money: the more he
gets, the more he craves.
Josh Billings

The best treasure that a man can attain
unto in this world is true knowledge; even
the knowledge of himself.
Jacob Boehme

Reader, remember this: if thy knowledge
do not now affect thy heart, it will at last,
with a witness, afflict thy heart; if it do not

now endear Christ to thee, it will at last
provoke Christ the more against thee; if it
do not make all the things of Christ to be
very precious in thy eyes, it will at last
make thee the more vile in Christ's eyes.
Thomas Brooks

He who lives up to a little knowledge shall
have more knowledge.
Thomas Brooks

Never mistake knowledge for wisdom.
One helps you make a living and the other
helps you make a life.
Sandra Carey

A man may be theologically knowing and
spiritually ignorant.
Stephen Charnock

One may understand the cosmos, but never
the ego; the self is more distant than any star.
G.K. Chesterton

Knowledge is the only instrument of
production that is not subject to
diminishing returns.
J.M. Clark

Real knowledge is to know the extent of
one's ignorance.
Confucius

To know, is to know that you know
nothing. That is the meaning of true
knowledge.
Confucius

The essence of knowledge is, having it, to
apply it; not having it, to confess your
ignorance.
Confucius

Knowledge is proud that she knows so
much; Wisdom is humble that she knows
no more.
William Cowper

A smattering of everything, and a
knowledge of nothing.
Charles Dickens

To be conscious that you are ignorant is a great step to knowledge.
Benjamin Disraeli

We don't know a millionth of one per cent about anything.
Thomas Alva Edison

Seek not to grow in knowledge chiefly for the sake of applause, and to enable you to dispute with others; but seek it for the benefit of your souls.
Jonathan Edwards

The more I learn, the more I realize I don't know.
Albert Einstein

He that knows least commonly presumes most.
Thomas Fuller

What man does not understand, he does not possess.
Goethe

True knowledge lies in knowing how to live.
Baltasar Gracián

My goal is simple. It is complete understanding of the universe, why it is as it is and why it exists as all.
Stephen Hawking

Knowledge is vain and fruitless which is not reduced to practice.
Matthew Henry

Wonder, rather than doubt, is the root of knowledge.
Abraham Heschel

The thing is, in this life you can know a great deal about something, and still be wrong.
Sir Len Hutton

It is better to know some of the questions than all of the answers.
Aldous Huxley

If a little knowledge is dangerous, where is the man who has so much as to be out of danger?
Thomas Henry Huxley

A student may easily exhaust his life in comparing divines and moralists without any practical regard to morals and religion; he may be learning not to live but to reason ... while the chief use of his volumes is unthought of, his mind is unaffected, and his life is unreformed.
Samuel Johnson

All wish to know, but none want to pay the price.
Juvenal

Knowledge is happiness, because to have knowledge – broad, deep knowledge – is to know true ends from false, and lofty things from low.
Helen Keller

Knowledge is love and light and vision.
Helen Keller

Believers who have most knowledge, are not therefore necessarily the most spiritual.
John Newton

Learned men are the cisterns of knowledge, not the fountainheads.
James Northcote

We must guard against becoming so engrossed in the specific nature of the roots and bark of the trees of knowledge as to miss the meaning and grandeur of the forest they compose.
George S. Patton

He that knows not and knows not that he knows not is a fool: shun him.
He that knows not and knows that he knows not is a child: teach him.
He that knows and knows not that he knows is asleep: wake him.
He that knows and knows that he knows is a wise man: follow him.
Arabic proverb

As we acquire more knowledge, things do not become more comprehensible, but more mysterious.
Albert Schweitzer

I am never afraid of what I know.
Anna Sewell, Black Beauty

The larger the island of knowledge, the longer the shoreline of wonder.
Ralph W. Sockman

True knowledge exists in knowing that you know nothing.
And in knowing that you know nothing, that makes you the smartest of all.
Socrates

One must spend time in gathering knowledge to give it out richly.
Edward C. Steadman

The more I know, the more I know how little I know. The less you know, the more you think you know.
Bill Stenberg

Knowledge is gained by learning; trust by doubt; skill by practice; and love by love.
Thomas Szasz

Shun too great a desire for knowledge, for in it there is much fretting and delusion. Intellectuals like to appear learned and to be called wise. Yet there are many things the knowledge of which does little or no good to the soul, and he who concerns himself about other things than those which lead to salvation is very unwise.
Thomas à Kempis

Modern mankind can go anywhere, do everything and be completely curious about the universe. But only a rare person now and then is curious enough to want to know God.
A. W. Tozer

I was gratified to be able to answer promptly, and I did. I said I didn't know.
Mark Twain

I know everything except myself.
François Villon

Knowledge without repentance will be but a torch to light men to hell.
Thomas Watson

When I was young I was sure of everything; in a few years, having been mistaken a thousand times, I was not half so sure of most things as I was before; at present, I am hardly sure of anything but what God has revealed to me.
John Wesley

The learned tradition is not concerned with truth, but with the learned adjustment of learned statements of antecedent learned people.
Alfred North Whitehead

Only the shallow know themselves.
Oscar Wilde

Knowledge, Warnings concerning
Knowledge without integrity is dangerous and dreadful.
Samuel Johnson

Cease from an excessive desire of knowing, for you will find much distraction and delusion in it.
Thomas à Kempis

Knowledge and love
Knowledge is not the most important thing in the world. Love is essential.
F. Fénelon

Human things must be known to be loved: but Divine things must be loved to be known.
Blaise Pascal

Beware that you are not swallowed up in books! An ounce of love is worth a pound of knowledge.
John Wesley

L

Laity

The blessings promised us by Christ were not promised to those alone who were priests; woe unto the world, indeed, if all that deserved the name of virtue were shut up in a cloister.
Héloise

Lamb of God

The precious Lamb of God gave up his precious fleece for us.
Christopher Nesse

Last days

But mark this: There will be terrible times in the last days.
The Bible, 2 Timothy 3:1

Last words

Truth sits upon the lips of dying men.
Matthew Arnold

Last words of famous people

This is the last of earth! I am content.
John Quincy Adams

See in what peace a Christian can die.
Joseph Addison

"What think ye of Heaven and Glory that is at the back of the cross?" The hope of this makes me look upon pale death as a lovely messenger to me. I bless the Lord for my lot this day … Friends, give our Lord credit; He is aye good, but 0! He is good in a day of trial, and He will be sweet company through the ages of eternity.
Archibald Alison

I am not come hither to deny my Lord and Master.
Anne Askew, July 16, 1545, burned at the stake after torture on the rack, at the age of 25

Nothing, but death.
Jane Austen, when asked by her sister, Cassandra, if there was anything she wanted.

I can't sleep.
James M. Barrie

I have pain (there is no arguing against sense), but I have peace, I have peace.
Richard Baxter

Now comes the mystery.
Henry Ward Beecher

Friends applaud, the Comedy is over.
Ludwig von Beethoven

I beg you, dearest brethren, love one another.
Bernard of Clairvaux

While women weep, as they do now, I'll fight; while men go to prison, in and out, in and out, as they do now, I'll fight; where there is a drunkard left, while there is a poor lost girl upon the streets, where there remains one dark soul without the light of God – I'll fight! I'll fight to the very end.
William Booth, end of his last speech

I am about to – or I am going to – die; either expression is used.
Dominique Bouhours, French grammarian

Be of good comfort, brother, for we shall have a merry supper with the Lord this night.
John Bradford, 1510-1555, to fellow martyr, John Leaf, at the stake, Smithfield

I was a little better than speechless all day. O my God, I am speedily coming to thee! Hasten the day, O Lord, if it be thy blessed will. Oh, come, Lord Jesus, come quickly.
David Brainerd

Oh, I am not going to die, am I? He will not separate us, we have been so happy.
Charlotte Brontë, spoken to her husband of nine months, Rev. Arthur Nicholls

This is a beautiful country.
John Brown

Beautiful.
Elizabeth Barrett Browning, in reply to her husband who had asked how she felt

I am going to a place where few kings and great men will come.
Buchanan, tutor to James I

I don't feel good.
Luther Burbank

"Though I have endeavored to avoid sin, and to please God to the utmost of my power, yet, from the consciousness of perpetual infirmities, I am still afraid to die. [His chaplain replied: "My Lord, you have forgotten that Jesus Christ is a Savior."] True, but how shall I know that he is a Savior for me? ["My Lord," answered the chaplain, "it is written, 'Him that cometh to me I will in no wise cast out.'"] True, and I am surprised that, although I have read that scripture a thousand times over, I have never felt its virtue till this moment; and now I die happy.
Joseph Butler

Thou, Lord, bruisest me, but I am abundantly satisfied, since it is from thy hand.
John Calvin

When I am gone, speak less of Dr Carey and more of Dr Carey's Savior.
William Carey, the missionary

This is the most joyful day that ever I saw in my pilgrimage on earth. My joy is now begun which I see shall never be interrupted … It is nearly thirty years since He made it sure … I have followed holiness, I have taught truth, and I have been most in the main things … This day I am to seal with my blood all the truths that ever I preached … I had a great sweetness of spirit and great submission as to my taking, the Providence of God was so eminent in it; and I could not but think that God judged it necessary for His glory to bring me to such an end, seeing he loosed me from such a work. The Lord knows I go up this ladder with less fear, confusion or perturbation of mind, than ever I entered a pulpit to preach.
Donald Cargill, 27 July 1681

I know now that patriotism is not enough; I must have no hatred and no bitterness toward anyone.
Edith Cavell

In the end, everything is a gag.
Charlie Chaplin

The issue is now clear. It is between light and darkness and everyone must choose his side.
G.K. Chesterton

Goodbye, Everybody!
Hart Crane, poet, who committed suicide by jumping overboard during a steamship voyage

This was the hand that wrote it, therefore it shall suffer the first punishment.
Archbishop Thomas Cranmer, burnt at the stake in 1555

Lord, however Thou dispose of me, continue and go on to do good for them. Pardon Thy foolish people! Forgive their sins and do not forsake them, but love and bless them. Give them consistency of judgment, one heart, and mutual love; and go on to deliver them, and with the work of reformation; and make the name of Christ glorious in the world. Teach those

who look too much on Thy instruments, to depend more upon Thyself … And pardon the folly of this short prayer. And give me rest for Jesus Christ's sake, to whom, with Thee and Thy Holy Spirit, be all honor and glory, now and forever! Amen.
Oliver Cromwell

Show my head to the people, it is worth seeing.
George Danton, to his executioner

These are the last words of David:
'When one rules over men in
  righteousness,
when he rules in the fear of God,
he is like the light of morning at sunrise
on a cloudless morning,
like the brightness after rain
that brings the grass from the earth.
… But evil men are all to be cast aside like
  thorns,
which are not gathered with the hand.
Whoever touches thorns
uses a tool of iron or the shaft of a spear;
they are burned up where they lie."
David, The Bible, 2 Samuel 23:1, 4, 6-7

… the fog is rising.
Emily Dickinson

Weep not, I shall not die; and as I leave the land of the dying I trust to see the blessings of the Lord in the land of the living.
Edward the Confessor

I have sinned against my brother the ass. … Welcome, Sister Death!
Francis of Assisi

More light!
Johann Wolfgang von Goethe

Here die I, Richard Grenville, with a joyful and quiet mind, that I have ended my life as a true soldier ought to do that hath fought for his country, Queen, religion and honor. Whereby my soul most joyfully departeth out of this body, and shall always leave behind it an everlasting fame of a valiant and true soldier that hath done his duty as he was bound to do.
Richard Grenville

I am more fortunate than the Great Marquis, [Archibald Campbell, Marquis of Argyle] for my Lord was beheaded, but I am to be hanged on a tree as my Savior was. I take God to record upon my soul, I would not exchange this scaffold with the palace and miter of the greatest prelate in Britain. Blessed be God who has shown mercy to me such a wretch, and has revealed His Son in me, and made me a minister of the everlasting gospel, and that He hath deigned, in the midst of much contradiction from Satan, and the world, to seal my ministry upon the hearts of not a few of His people, and especially in the station where I was last, I mean the congregation and presbytery of Stirling. Jesus Christ is my Life and my Light, my Righteousness, my strength, and my Salvation and all my desire. Him! O Him, I do with all the strength of my soul commend to you. Bless Him, O my soul, from henceforth even forever. Lord, now lettest Thou Thy servant depart in peace for mine eyes have seen Thy salvation. "Art not Thou from everlasting, O Lord my God. I shall not die but live." The Covenants! The Covenants! They shall yet be Scotland's reviving. Be not afraid at His sweet, lovely and desirable cross, for although I have not been able because of my wounds to lift up or lay down my head, but as I was helped, yet I was never in better case all my life. He has not given me one challenge since I came to prison, for anything less or more; but on the contrary He has so wonderfully shined on me with the sense of His redeeming, strengthening, assisting, supporting, through-bearing, pardoning and reconciling love, grace and mercy, that my soul doth long to be freed of bodily infirmities and earthly organs, that so I may flee to His Royal Palace even the Heavenly Habitation of my God, where I am sure of a crown put on my head, and a palm put in my hand, and a new song in

my mouth, even the song of Moses and of the Lamb, that so I may bless, praise, magnify and extol Him for what He hath done to me and for me. Wherefore I bid farewell to all my dear fellow-sufferers for the testimony of Jesus, who are wandering in dens and caves. Farewell, my children, study holiness in all your ways, and praise the Lord for what He hath done for me, and tell all my Christian friends to praise Him on my account. Farewell, sweet Bible, and wanderings and contendings for truth. Welcome, death. Welcome, the City of my God where I shall see Him and be enabled to serve Him eternally with full freedom. Welcome, blessed company, the angels and spirits of just men made perfect. But above all, welcome, welcome, welcome, our glorious and alone God, Father, Son and Holy Ghost; into Thy hands I commit my spirit for Thou art worthy. Amen.
James Guthrie, 1 June 1661

Now farewell, lovely and sweet Scriptures, which were aye my comfort in the midst of all my difficulties! Farewell, faith! Farewell, hope! Farewell, wanderers, who have been comfortable to my soul, in the hearing of them commend Christ's love! Farewell, brethren! Farewell, sisters! Farewell, Christian acquaintances! Farewell, sun, moon and stars! And, now, welcome my lovely, heartsome Christ Jesus, into whose hands I commit my spirit throughout all eternity. I may say, few and evil have the days of the years of my life been, I being about twenty years of age.
Marion Harvie, executed 26 January 1681

Dieu me pardonnera. C'est son métier. (God will forgive me. It's his job.)
Heinrich Heine

You have been used to take notice of the sayings of dying men. This is mine: that a life spent in the service of God, and communion with him, is the most comfortable and pleasant life that anyone can live in this world.
Matthew Henry

How thankful I am for death! It is the passage to the Lord and giver of eternal life. O welcome, welcome death! Thou mayest well be reckoned among the treasures of the Christian! To live is Christ, but to die is gain! Lord, now lettest thou thy servant depart in peace, according to thy most holy and comfortable Word; for mine eyes have seen thy precious salvation.
James Hervey

I shall be glad then to find a hole to creep out of the world at.
Thomas Hobbes

Let nothing cause thy heart to fail;
Launch out thy boat, hoist up thy sail,
Put from the shore;
And be sure thou shalt attain
Unto the port that shall remain
For evermore.
John Hooper, written the night before his execution as a heretic in 1555

And now, in keeping with Channel 40's policy of always bringing you the latest in blood and guts, in living color, you're about to see another first – an attempted suicide.
Chris Hubbock, who shot herself during a broadcast

You are now going to burn a goose [the meaning of Huss's name in Bohemian], but in a century you will have a swan whom you can neither roast nor boil. O holy simplicity!
John Huss, to his executioner [Martin Luther, who came about a hundred years after him, had a swan for his coat of arms.]
John Huss

Let us pass over the river and rest under the shade of the trees.
General T.J. "Stonewall" Jackson; wounded by his own men

This is the fourth?
Thomas Jefferson

Seven last sayings of Jesus:

"Father, forgive them, for they know not what they do" Luke 23:34.
"Today shalt thou be with me in paradise" Luke 23:43.
"Woman, behold thy Son" John 19:26.
"My God, my God, why hast thou forsaken me?" Mark 15:34
"I thirst" John 19:28
"It is finished" John 19:30
"Father, into thy hands I commend my spirit"
Luke 23:46 (KJV)

God bless you!
Samuel Johnson

I am not tired of my work, neither am I tired of the world; yet when Christ calls me home, I shall go with the gladness of a boy bounding away from school.
Adoniram Judson

You have conquered, O Galilean.
The emperor Julian

Such is life.
Ned Kelly, before being hung at Old Melbourne Gaol

Live in Christ, live in Christ, and the flesh need not fear death.
John Knox

Be of good comfort, Master Ridley, and play the man; we shall this day light such a candle, by God's grace, in England, as I trust shall never be put out ... Father of heaven, receive my soul!
Hugh Latimer

Away with these filthy garments. I feel a sacred fire kindled in my soul, which will destroy everything contrary to itself, and burn as a flame of divine love to all eternity.
William Law

I give my dying testimony to the truth of Christianity. The promises of the gospel are my support and consolation. They, alone, yield me satisfaction in a dying hour. I am not afraid to die. The gospel of Christ has raised me above the fear of death; for I know that my redeemer liveth.
John Leland

Abe, I'm going to leave you now and I shall not return. I want you to be kind to your mother and live as I have taught you. Love your heavenly Father and keep his commandments.
Thomas Lincoln, father of nine-year-old Abraham Lincoln

Do not pray for healing. Do not hold me back from the glory.
Dr D. Martyn Lloyd-Jones, words written on a scrap of paper a few days before his death (on March 1, 1981) after he had lost the power of speech. Dr Martyn Lloyd-Jones had pastored Westminster Chapel, London, from 1939 to 1968.

God so loved the world that he gave his only begotten Son, that whosoever believeth in him should not perish but have everlasting life. [Repeated three times.]
Martin Luther

I'm so thankful for active obedience of Christ. No hope without it.
J. Gresham Machen

Go on, get out. Last words are for fools who haven't said enough.
Karl Marx, dying words to his housekeeper

God gave me a message to deliver and a horse to ride. Alas, I have killed the horse and now I cannot deliver the message.
Robert Murray M'Cheyne, as he lay dying, aged 29

You will tell the others I am going home a little sooner than I thought. Then tell them not to talk about the servant but to talk about the Savior.
F.B. Meyer

Earth is receding; heaven is approaching. This is my crowning day!
D.L. Moody

Too kind – too kind!
Florence Nightingale, when presented on her deathbed with the Order of Merit

My soul doth magnify the Lord! my soul doth magnify the Lord! I have longed these sixteen years to seal the precious cause and interest of precious Christ with my blood. And now, now He hath answered and granted my request, and has left me no more ado but to come here and pour forth my last prayers, sing forth my last praise to Him in time on this sweet and desirable scaffold, mount that ladder, and then I shall quickly get home to my Father's House, see, enjoy, serve and sing forth the praises of my glorious Redeemer, for evermore world without end.
John Nisbet

See now, I commend my soul to God for whom I am an ambassador because he chose me for this task, despite my obscurity, to be one of the least among his servants. This is my confession before I die.
St Patrick

Lord, help my poor soul.
Edgar Allan Poe

Drink to me.
Pablo Picasso

Even such is time which takes in trust
Our youth, our joys, and all we have
And pays us but with age and dust:
Who in the dark and silent grave
When we have wandered all our ways
Shuts up the glory of our days.
And from the earth and grave and dust
The Lord shall raise me up, I trust.
Walter Raleigh, written on the day before he was beheaded

So little done, so much to do.
Cecil Rhodes

Why yes: a bulletproof vest.
James Rodges, murderer, when asked for his final request before facing the firing squad

Eternal Being! The soul that I am going to give you back is as pure, at this moment, as it was when it proceeded from you: render it partaker of your felicity!
Jean-Jacques Rousseau

Neither my imprisonment nor fear of death have been able to discompose me in any degree. On the contrary I have found the assurances of the love and mercy of God, in and through my blessed Redeemer, in whom I only trust. And I do not question but I am going to partake of that fulness of joy which is in his presence; the hopes of which do so wonderfully delight me, that I think this is the happiest time of my life, though others may look upon it as the saddest.
William Russell

If he should slay me ten thousand times, ten thousand times I'll trust. I feel, I feel, I believe in joy and rejoice; I feed on manna. O for arms to embrace him! O for a well-tuned harp!
Samuel Rutherford

Sir Walter Scott expressed the wish, as he lay dying, that I should read to him, and when I asked him from what book, he said, "Need you ask? There is but one." I chose the fourteenth chapter of St John's Gospel. Then Sir Walter Scott said, "Well, this is great comfort."
J.G. Lockhart, Life of Sir Walter Scott

They couldn't hit an elephant at this dist ...
John B. Sedgwick, general, 1864

Love my memory; cherish my friends; but above all, govern your will and affection by the will and word of your Creator; in my beholding the end of this world, with all her vanities.
Philip Sidney

I wish to be alone, with my God, and to lie before him as a poor, wretched, hell-deserving sinner ... But I would also look to him as my all-forgiving God – and as my all-sufficient God and as my all-atoning God – and as my covenant-keeping God … I would lie here to the last, at the foot of the cross, looking unto Jesus; and go as such into the presence of my God … Jesus Christ is all in all for my soul, and now you must be all for my body. I cannot tell you any longer what I want. My principles were not founded on fancies or enthusiasm; there is a reality in them, and I find them sufficient to support me in death.

Charles Simeon

Farewell, all created enjoyments, pleasures and delights; farewell, sinning and suffering; farewell, praying and believing, and welcome, heaven and singing. Welcome, joy in the Holy Ghost; welcome, Father, Son and Holy Ghost; into Thy hands I commend my spirit. I have one word more to say, and that is, to all that have any love to God and His righteous cause, that they will set time apart, and sing a song of praise to the Lord, for what He has done to my soul, and my soul says, "To Him be the praise."

Walter Smith, 27 July 1681

Crito, I owe a cock to Æsculapius; will you remember to pay the debt?

Socrates, as he died of poisoning (a cock used to be sacrificed as a thanksgiving offering to the god of healing, Æsculapius)

My son, may you be more fortunate that your father; in all else be like him; then you will be no base man.

Sophocles

What is the answer? In that case, what is the question?

Gertrude Stein

And they stoned Stephen as he was calling on God and saying, "Lord Jesus, receive my spirit."

Stephen, Acts 7:59

I have taken a look into eternity. Oh, if I could come back and preach again, how differently would I preach from what I have done before!

Summerfield

"I am so weak that I can hardly write, I cannot read my Bible, I cannot even pray, I can only lie still in God's arms like a little child, and trust."

Hudson Taylor

The hour I have long wished for is now come.

Teresa of Avila

I am ready to die for my Lord, that in my blood the Church may obtain liberty and peace.

Thomas à Becket, Archbishop of Canterbury

The sky is clear; there is no cloud; come, Lord Jesus, come quickly.

Augustus Toplady

Don't let it end like this. Tell them I said something.

Pancho Villa

I am abandoned by God and man … Doctor, I will give you half of what I am worth, if you will give me six months' life. (The doctor answered, "Sir, you cannot live six weeks.) Then I shall go to hell, and you will go with me!

Voltaire

I still live.

Daniel Webster

Go away … I'm alright.

H.G. Wells

I shall be satisfied with thy likeness – satisfied, satisfied.

Charles Wesley

The best of all is, God is with us. Farewell!

John Wesley

My doctor at last has given what has been his real diagnosis of my illness for weeks – an inoperable case of cancer. Now if he had been a Christian he wouldn't have been so dilatory or shaken, for he would have known, as you and I do, that life or death is equally welcome when we live in the will and presence of the Lord. If the Lord has chosen me to go to Him soon, I go gladly. Please do not give a moment's grief for me. I do not say a cold goodbye but rather a warm Auf Wiedersehen till I see you again – in the blessed land where I may be allowed to draw aside a curtain when you enter. With a heart full of love for every individual of you.

(Signed) Effie Jane Wheeler

I am tired in the Lord's work, but not tired of it.

George Whitefield

Ah, well, then I suppose I shall have to die beyond my means.

Oscar Wilde

———

Laughter
See also: Humor

Laugh at your problems. Everyone else does!

Author unknown

You are never fully dressed until you wear a smile.

Author unknown

Those who can't laugh at themselves leave the job to others.

Author unknown

Laughter is a bodily exercise precious to health.

Aristotle

Laughter is the closest thing to the grace of God.

Karl Barth

Laughter is the shortest distance between two people.

Victor Borge

Always laugh when you can; it is cheap medicine. Merriment is a philosophy not well understood. It is the sunny side of existence.

Lord Byron

No man who has once heartily and wholly laughed can be altogether irreclaimably bad.

Thomas Carlyle

The man who cannot laugh is not only fit for treasons, strategems, and spoils; but his whole life is already a treason and a stratagem.

Thomas Carlyle

The most wasted day is that in which we have not laughed.

Chamfort

Laughter is inner jogging.

Norman Cousins

Laughter is, after speech, the chief thing that holds society together.

Max Eastman

Laughter can relieve tension, soothe the pain of disappointment, and strengthen the spirit for the formidable tasks that always lie ahead.

Dwight D. Eisenhower

Once you get people laughing, they're listening and you can tell them almost anything.

Herbert Gardner

There is nothing in which people more betray their character than in what they laugh at.

Goethe

Man is the only animal that laughs and weeps; for he is the only animal that is struck with the difference between what things are and what they might have been.

William Hazlitt

Laughter is the sun that drives winter from the human face.

Victor Hugo

The faculty of laughter is not in the brain but in the heart.
Laurent Joubert

Teach us delight in simple things,
And Mirth that has no bitter springs;
Forgiveness free of evil done,
And Love to all men 'neath the sun.
Rudyard Kipling

With the fearful strain that is on me day and night, if I did not laugh, I should die.
Abraham Lincoln

If you're not allowed to laugh in heaven, I don't want to go there.
Martin Luther

It is pleasing to the dear God whenever thou rejoicest or laughest from the bottom of thy heart.
Martin Luther

It is the heart that is not yet sure of its God that is afraid to laugh in His presence.
George MacDonald

We know the degree of refinement in men by the matter they laugh at and the ring of the laugh.
George Meredith

I have an idea that laughter is able to mediate between the infinite magnitude of our tasks and the limitation of our strength.
Jürgen Moltmann

Perhaps I know best why it is man alone who laughs; he alone suffers so deeply that he had to invent laughter.
Friedrich Nietzsche

We cannot really love anybody with whom we never laugh.
Agnes Repplier

The young man who has not wept is a savage, and the old man who will not laugh is a fool.
George Santayana

It better befits a man to laugh at life than to lament over it.
Seneca

Life does not cease to be funny when people die; any more than it ceases to be serious when people laugh.
George Bernard Shaw

Of all the things God created, I am often most grateful He created laughter.
Charles Swindoll

A good laugh is sunshine in a house.
William Makepeace Thackeray

The human race has one really effective weapon, and that is laughter.
Mark Twain

Nature has made us frivolous to console us for our miseries.
Voltaire

Law
See also: Paul

The law is good, if a man use it lawfully.
The Bible, 1 Timothy 1:8

For whoever keeps the whole law and yet stumbles at just one point is guilty of breaking all of it.
The Bible, James 2:10

Fifteen million laws have been passed to try to enforce the Golden Rule and the Ten Commandments.
Author unknown

Man is an able creature, but he has made 32,600,000 laws and hasn't yet improved on the Ten Commandments.
Author unknown

God enjoins what we cannot do, in order that we may know what we have to ask of him.
Augustine of Hippo

The utility of the law is, that it convinces man of his weakness, and compels him to

apply for the medicine of grace, which is in Christ.
Augustine of Hippo

The law was given, in order to convert a great into a little man – to show that you have no power of your own for righteousness; and might thus, poor, needy, and destitute, flee to grace.
Augustine of Hippo

The law is the light and the commandment the lantern.
William Austin, Puritan

Upon these foundations, the law of nature and the law of revelation (Holy Scripture), depend all human laws; that is to say no human laws should be suffered to contradict these.
William Blackstone

The law sends us to the gospel, that we may be justified, and the gospel sends us to the law again to enquire what is our duty, being justified.
Samuel Bolton

There is but one law for all, namely, that law which governs all law, the law of our Creator, the law of humanity, justice, equity – the law of nature, and of nations.
Edmund Burke

If men will not be governed by the Ten Commandments, they shall be governed by the ten thousand commandments.
G.K. Chesterton

What is hateful to you, do not do to another. This is the whole law and else is explanation.
Rabbi Hillel

It may be true that the law cannot make a man love me. But it can keep him from lynching me, and I think that's pretty important.
Martin Luther King

I submit that an individual who breaks a law that conscience tells him is unjust, and willingly accepts the penalty by staying in jail in order to arouse the conscience of the community over its injustice, is in reality expressing the very highest respect for law.
Martin Luther King, Jnr

The law opens not nor makes visible God's grace and mercy, or the righteousness whereby we obtain everlasting life and salvation; but our sins, our weakness, death, God's wrath and judgment.
Martin Luther

The observance of the divine laws constitutes the most effective preventative medicine against disease.
Rabbi Musk

The glory of the gospel is, not that it destroys the law, but that it makes it cease to be a bondage; not that it gives us freedom from it, but in it; and the notion of the gospel which I have been describing as cold and narrow is, not that of supposing Christianity a law, but a supposing it to be scarcely more than a law, and thus leaving us where it found us … They have not merely the promise of grace; they have its presence. They have not merely the conditional prospect of a reward; for a blessing, nay, unspeakable, fathomless, illimitable, infinite, eternal blessings are poured into their very hearts, even as a first step and an earnest from God our Savior, of what He will do for those who love Him. They "are passed from death unto life," and are the children of God and heirs of heaven.
J.H. Newman

Ignorance of the nature and design of the law is at the bottom of most religious mistakes. This is the root of self-righteousness. The grace of God, received by faith, will dispose us to obedience in general; but, through remaining darkness and ignorance, we are much at a loss as to particulars. We are therefore sent to the law, that we may learn how to walk worthy of God, who has

called us to his kingdom and glory; and every precept has its proper place and use.
John Newton

The world, indeed, seems to be weary of the just, righteous, holy ways of God, and of that exactness in walking according to His institutions and commands which it will be one day known that He doth require. But the way to put a stop to this declension is not by accommodating the commands of God to the corrupt courses and ways of men. The truths of God and the holiness of His precepts must be pleaded and defended, though the world dislike them here and perish hereafter. His law must not be made to lackey after the wills of men, nor be dissolved by vain interpretations, because they complain they cannot – indeed, because they will not – comply with it. Our Lord Jesus Christ came not to destroy the law and the prophets, but to fulfil them, and to supply men with spiritual strength to fulfil them also. It is evil to break the least commandment; but there is a great aggravation of that evil in them that shall teach men so to do.
John Owen

Good people do not need laws to tell them to act responsibly, while bad people will find a way around the laws.
Plato

Man is not answerable to an abstract law, but to God. Behind the law is the Lawgiver. Therefore, to find fault with the law is to find fault with the Lawgiver. The law is not the arbitrary edicts of a capricious despot, but the wise, holy, loving precepts of one who is jealous for His glory and for the good of His people.
Ernest Reisinger

The law by which God rules us, is as dear to Him as the gospel by which He saves us.
William Secker, Puritan

The heart is like a dark cellar, full of lizards, cockroaches, beetles, and all kinds of reptiles and insects, which in the dark we see not. But the law takes down the shutters and lets in the light, and we see the evil.
C.H. Spurgeon

The propitious smiles of heaven can never be expected on a nation that disregards the eternal rules of order and right which Heaven itself has ordained.
George Washington

Law and gospel

When you see that men have been wounded by the law, then it is time to pour in the gospel oil. It is the sharp needle of the law that makes way for the scarlet thread of the gospel.
Samuel Bolton

Law and grace

The "Law" required what it could not give. "Grace" gives that which it requires.
Author unknown

The law orders; grace supplies the power of acting.
Augustine of Hippo

If the Spirit of grace is absent, the law is present only to convict and kill.
Augustine of Hippo

That thy walk with God in the way of obedience is not to fulfil the law, as a covenant of works. Thou art not required to do this. Thou canst not do it. Immanuel, thy divine surety, took it upon Himself. Because it was impossible for thee, a fallen creature, to keep the law, so as to be justified by it, He therefore came in person to fulfil it. He honored its precepts by His infinite obedience. He magnified its penalties by His inestimable sacrifice. And this is thy justifying righteousness. Through faith in the life and death of the God-man thou art not only freed from guilt and condemnation, from curse and hell, but art also entitled to life and glory. The law is now on thy side, and is become thy friend. It acquits thee. It

justifies thee. It will give thee the reward promised to obedience. The law in the hand of thy Savior has nothing but blessings to bestow upon thee. Thou art to receive it at His mouth and to obey Him: but not from any legal hopes of heaven, or from any slavish fears of hell: for then thou wouldst come under the covenant of works again. Whereas thou art not under the law, but under grace, mind thy privilege and pray for grace to live up to it. Thou art not under the law, bound to keep it perfectly in thine own person, or in case of failing, condemned by it, and under its fearful curse. Thou art under grace, a state of grace through faith in the obedience and sufferings of thy blessed surety, and under the power of grace constrained and motivated by the love of Christ.
William Romaine

Law and the Christian

Luther said: "A Christian man is a most free lord of all, subject to none. A Christian man is a most dutiful servant of all, subject to all." "Subject to none" in respect of his liberty; "subject to all" in respect of his charity. This, for Paul, is the law of Christ because this was the way of Christ. And in this way, for Paul, the divine purpose underlying Moses' law is vindicated and accomplished.
F.F. Bruce

According to Paul, the believer is not under law as a rule of life. When Paul says, "Sin will have no dominion over you, since you are not under law but under grace" (Romans 6:14), it is the on-going course of Christian life that he has in view, not simply the initial justification by faith.
F.F. Bruce

In the maxims of the law, God is seen as the rewarder of perfect righteousness and the avenger of sin. But in Christ, his face shines out, full of grace and gentleness to poor, unworthy sinners.
John Calvin

Laws

Lex mala, lex nulla. An evil law, is no law.
Thomas Aquinas

Laws of God

God has instituted three estates. These God has commanded not to let sin go unpunished. The first estate is that of the parents. They should exercise a strict control over their house and rule the children and the household. The second estate is that of the government. A magistrate bears the sword in order to compel the disobedient and the wayward by force to conform to the law or suffer its penalty. The third estate is that of the church. It governs by the Word. So God has protected the human race by this threefold authority against the devil, our flesh, and the world, to the end that offenses may not develop but be prevented.
Martin Luther

Good people do not need laws to tell them to act responsibly, while bad people will find a way around the laws.
Plato

Laziness

Go to the ant, thou sluggard; consider her ways, and be wise.
The Bible, Proverbs 6:6 KJV

Yet a little sleep, a little slumber, a little folding of the hands to sleep.
The Bible, Proverbs 6:10 KJV

Perseverance in prayer is the annihilation of sloth.
John Climacus

Sloth should not be confused with exhaustion or illness.
W. H. Griffith Thomas

The lazier a man is, the more he plans to do tomorrow.
Norwegian proverb

I don't think there ever was a lazy man in this world. Every man has some sort of

gift, and he prizes that gift beyond all others. He may be a professional billiard-player, or a Paderewski, or a poet – I don't care what it is. But whatever it is, he takes a native delight in exploiting that gift, and you will find it is difficult to beguile him away from it. Well, there are thousands of other interests occupying other men, but those interests don't appeal to the special tastes of the billiard champion or Paderewski. They are set down, therefore, as too lazy to do that or do this – to do, in short, what they have no taste or inclination to do. In that sense, then I am phenomenally lazy. But when it comes to writing a book I am not lazy. My family find it difficult to dig me out of my chair.
Mark Twain

I like the word "indolence." It makes my laziness seem classy.
Bern Williams

Leadership
... I, Deborah, arose, arose a mother in Israel ...
The Bible, Judges 5:7

Blind guides, which strain at a gnat, and swallow a camel.
The Bible, Matthew 23:24 KJV

When in doubt, mumble; when in trouble, delegate; when in charge, ponder.
James H. Boren

Spiritual power is the outpouring of spiritual life, and like all life, from that of the moss and lichen on the wall to that of the archangel before the throne, is from God. Therefore those who aspire to leadership must pay the price, and seek it from God.
Samuel Brengle

When we talk about questions of authority or leadership in our churches, we must do so in a way which empowers our own leadership, our own holiness, our own sense of discernment, and the gift of

obedience, which means listening.
Lavinia Byrne

There are only three kinds of people in the world – those that are movable, those that are immovable, and those that move them.
Li Hung Chang, when General Charles Gordon asked about the nature of leadership

The man who wants to lead the orchestra must turn his back on the crowd.
James Crook

Leadership is found in becoming the servant of all.
Richard Foster

If you command wisely, you'll be obeyed cheerfully.
Thomas Fuller

Faith in the ability of a leader is of slight service unless it be united with faith in his justice.
George W. Goethals

Although potential leaders are born, effective leaders are made.
Bennie E. Goodwin

We never find a presbyter in the singular in the New Testament. He is always a member of a team. In the modern church, the ordained man is almost always on his own in the community, unless he is lucky enough to have a colleague, or to be a member of a team ministry. We expect the ordained man to be almost omni-competent, and complain at his deficiencies. This is an extremely serious error.
E.M.B. Green

The great leader is seen as the servant first.
Robert K. Greenleaf

There is great force hidden in a gentle command.
George Herbert

You must be careful how you walk, and where you go, for there are those following

you who will set their feet where yours are set.
Robert E. Lee

You can't lead anyone else further than you have gone yourself.
Gene Mauch

FATSOS
Faithful to God, to his Word and to the leadership.
Available to God in the use of their time and opportunities.
Teachable by the leaders, circumstances and the Spirit.
Sound in New Testament Christianity, both orthodoxy and orthopraxy.
Outgoing in social skills, so as to maximise their impact.
Spirit-led in the development of character and obedience to Jesus.
John McClure, Vineyard Fellowship leader

Leaders should be the chief repenters.
Jack Miller

I'd rather get ten men to do the job than to do the job of ten men.
Dwight L. Moody

I start with the premise that the function of leadership is to produce more leaders, not more followers.
Ralph Nader

I made all my generals out of mud.
Napoleon

Never tell people how to do things. Tell them what to do and they will surprise you with their ingenuity.
General George S. Patton, Jr

Not the cry, but the flight of the wild duck, leads the flock to fly and follow.
Chinese proverb

It is the part of a good shepherd to shear his flock, not to skin it.
Latin proverb

Without a shepherd, sheep are not a flock.
Russian proverb

True greatness, true leadership, is achieved not by reducing men to one's service but in giving oneself in selfless service to them.
Oswald Sanders

[Christian leadership is] a blending of natural and spiritual qualities.
Oswald Sanders

Christian leadership ... appears to break down into five main ingredients – clear vision, hard work, dogged perseverance, humble service and iron discipline.
John R. W. Stott

Until self-effacing men return again to spiritual leadership, we may expect a progressive deterioration in the quality of popular Christianity year after year till we reach the point where the grieved Holy Spirit withdraws – like the Shekinah from the temple.
A. W. Tozer

A leader is best when he is neither seen nor heard,
Not so good when he is adored and glorified,
Worst when he is hated and despised.
Lao Tzu

Success without a successor is failure.
Noel Vose

Learning
Unless we accept lifelong learning as a habit, we're shortening our lives.
Author unknown

If you don't learn from your mistakes, there's no sense making them.
Author unknown

He who will not use the thoughts of other men's brains, proves that he has no brains of his own.
Author unknown

Live to learn ... forget ... and learn again.
Author unknown

Learning is not a spectator sport.
Author unknown

Nothing is lost or wasted if we learn from it.
Author unknown

Learning is not attained by chance. It must be sought for with ardor and attended to with diligence.
Abigail Adams

The wise learn many things from their enemies.
Aristophanes

For the things we have to learn before we can do them, we learn by doing them.
Aristotle

See how the unlearned start up and take heaven by storm whilst we with all our learning grovel upon the earth.
Augustine of Hippo

To spend too much time in studies is sloth.
Francis Bacon

Truth which is merely told is quick to be forgotten; truth which is discovered lasts a lifetime.
William Barclay

It is what we think we know already that prevents us from learning.
Claude Bernard

The man who knows not God is vain, though he should be conversant with every branch of learning.
John Calvin

Without Christ, sciences in every department are vain, and that the man who knows not God is vain, though he should be conversant with every branch of learning. Nay more, we may affirm this, too, with truth, that these choice gifts of God – expertness of mind, acuteness of

judgment, liberal sciences, and acquaintance with languages, are in a manner profaned in every instance in which they fall to the lot of wicked men.
John Calvin

The first step towards knowledge is to know that we are ignorant.
Richard Cecil

The university brings out all abilities including incapability.
Anton Chekov

One's mind is like a knife. If you don't sharpen it, it gets rusty.
Nien Cheng

Never seem wiser, nor more learned, than the people you are with. Wear your learning, like your watch, in a private pocket: and do not pull it out and strike it merely to show that you have one.
Lord Chesterfield

The greatest lesson in life is to know that even fools are right sometimes.
Winston Churchill

Personally I'm always ready to learn, although I do not always like being taught.
Winston Churchill

Eating words has never given me indigestion.
Winston Churchill

A man who has committed a mistake and doesn't correct it, is committing another mistake.
Confucius

Learning is not compulsory... neither is survival.
W. Edwards Deming

Each man must look to himself to teach him the meaning of life. It is not something molded.
Antoine de Saint-Exupery

Each human mind is a galaxy of intelligences, wherein shines the light of a billion stars.
Timothy Ferris

Anyone who stops learning is old, whether twenty or eighty. Anyone who keeps learning stays young. The greatest thing in life is to keep your mind young.
Henry Ford

You cannot teach a man anything. You can only help him discover it within himself.
Galileo

I have learned silence from the talkative, tolerance from the intolerant, and kindness from the unkind, yet, I'm ungrateful to those teachers.
Kahlil Gibran

You live and learn. Or you don't live long.
Robert A. Heinlein

In a time of drastic change, it is the learners who inherit the future. The learned find themselves equipped to live in a world which no longer exists.
Eric Hoffer

God alone, through his Word, instructs the heart, so that it may come to the serious knowledge how wicked it is, and corrupt and hostile to God.
Martin Luther

If I have seen farther than others, it is because I was standing on the shoulders of giants.
Isaac Newton

We are usually convinced more easily by reasons we have found ourselves than by those which have occurred to others.
Blaise Pascal

Knowledge which is acquired under compulsion has no hold on the mind.
Plato

Bodily exercise, when compulsory, does no

harm to the body; but knowledge which is acquired under compulsion obtains no hold on the mind.
Plato

Trees and fields tell me nothing: men are my teachers.
Plato

A wise man will learn something even from the words of a fool.
Chinese proverb

One picture is worth more than a thousand words.
Chinese proverb

He who asks is a fool for five minutes, but he who does not ask remains a fool forever.
Chinese proverb

Don't limit a child to your own learning, for he was born in another time.
Rabbinic saying

The only kind of learning which significantly influences behavior is self-discovered or self-appropriated learning – truth that has been assimilated in experience.
Carl R. Rogers

The wisest mind has something yet to learn.
George Santayana

As long as you live, keep learning how to live.
Seneca

A man learns to skate by staggering about making a fool of himself; indeed, he progresses in all things by making a fool of himself.
George Bernard Shaw

Knowledge is gained by learning; trust by doubt; skill by practice; and love by love.
Thomas Szasz

The illiterate of the 21st century will not be those who cannot read and write, but those

who cannot learn, unlearn, and relearn.
Alvin Toffler

For learning to take place with any kind of efficiency students must be motivated. To be motivated, they must become interested. And they become interested when they are actively working on projects which they can relate to their values and goals in life.
Gus Tuberville, President, William Penn College

You do well to learn above all the religion of Jesus Christ.
George Washington

Learning after unpromising beginnings
A boy was expelled from his Latin class for slow learning. He resolved to excel in English where he was slow in Latin. He was Winston Churchill.
  A six-year-old boy was sent home from school with a note saying he was too stupid to learn. His name was Thomas Edison.
  Sir Walter Scott's teacher called him a hopeless dunce.
  Louis Pasteur was reckoned the slowest learner in his chemistry class.

Learning from all sources
I make it my rule to lay hold of light and embrace it, though it be held forth by a child or an enemy.
Jonathan Edwards

You will find many things help honest living, and you should not refuse whatever an author (even though a gentile) teaches well. It is profitable to taste all manner of learning of the gentiles, if it is done with caution and judgment discreetly – and furthermore with speed and like someone intending only to pass through the country and not to stay or live there. In conclusion, and this is the most important, everything must be applied and referred to Christ.
Erasmus

It is allowable to learn even from an enemy.
Latin proverb

Improve yourself by others' experience: so shall you quickly acquire what others labor and long for.
Socrates

From the errors of others a wise man corrects his own.
Publilius Syrus

Leisure
Neither in your actions be sluggish, nor in your conversation without method, nor wandering in your thoughts, nor let there be inward contention in your soul, nor be so busy in life as to have no leisure.
Marcus Aurelius

What is this life if, full of care,
We have no time to stand and stare.
W.H. Davies

He hath no leisure who useth it not.
George Herbert

Leisure is the mother of philosophy.
Thomas Hobbes

We are suddenly threatened with a liberation that taxes our inner resources of self-employment and imaginative participation in society.
Marshall McLuhan

If all the year were playing holidays,
To sport would be as tedious as to work;
But when they seldom come, they wished
  for come.
William Shakespeare, King Henry IV, Part 1

If you are losing your leisure, look out! You are losing your soul.
Logan Pearsall Smith

Leprosy
I care about people with disabilities and that's why I am 100 per cent behind the work of American Leprosy Missions. Our friends at ALM are laboring among the world's least and last – persons with disabilities – giving them help and hope in Christ.
Joni Eareckson Tada

The Bible tells us that Jesus not only healed those with leprosy, He touched them. That, to me, is the most important aspect of the wonderful work done by American Leprosy Missions. They don't just heal people with leprosy, they touch them with the love and hope of Jesus. Can we do any less?
Ruth Bell Graham

[Lepers are treated] as if they were, in effect, dead men.
Josephus

If the children receive the cure in time, they don't have to suffer at all; if they don't receive the cure, their suffering will never end.
C. Everett Koop, U.S. Surgeon General (retired)

No other disease reduces a human being for so many years to so hideous a wreck.
E. W. G. Masterman

Letter-writing
Everyone reveals his own soul in his letters. In every other form of composition it is possible to discern the writer's character, but in none so clearly as the epistolary.
Demetrius

Letters
In 1568 Scobland, Hues and Coomans were arrested in Antwerp, in the Netherlands. In a letter from prison they wrote: "Since it is the will of the Almighty that we should suffer for his name, we patiently submit; though the flesh may rebel against the spirit, yet the truths of the gospel shall support us, and Christ shall bruise the serpent's head.

We are comforted, for we have faith; we fear not affliction, for we have hope; we forgive our enemies, for we have charity.

Do not worry about us, we are happy because of God's promises and exult in being thought worthy to suffer for Christ's sake.

We do not desire release, but fortitude; we ask not for liberty, but for the power of perseverance; we wish for no change but that which places a crown of victory on our heads."
Scobland, Hues and Coomans

Liberalism
Liberalism is totalitarianism with a human face.
Thomas Sowell

Liberty
See also: Freedom
The God who gave us life, gave us liberty at the same time.
Thomas Jefferson

A liberty to that only which is good, just, and honest.
John Winthrop

Lies
See also: Cover up
Do not lie.
The Bible, Leviticus 19:11

A lie which is all a lie
May be met and fought outright.
But a lie which is part of truth
Is a harder matter to fight.
Author unknown

We lie loudest when we lie to ourselves.
Author unknown

Those who are given white lies soon become color blind.
Author unknown

The least initial deviation from the truth is multiplied later a thousandfold.
Aristotle

A lie consists in speaking a falsehood with the intention of deceiving.
Augustine of Hippo

Never chase a lie. Let it alone, and it will run itself to death. I can work out a good character much faster than anyone can lie me out of it.
Lyman Beecher

People never lie so much as after a hunt, during a war or before an election.
Otto von Bismarck

Lying to ourselves is more deeply ingrained than lying to others.
Dostoevsky

The camera cannot lie. But it can be an accessory to untruth.
Harold Evans

Dare to be true: nothing can need a lie;
A fault which needs it most, grows two
   thereby.
George Herbert

By means of shrewd lies, unremittingly repeated, it is possible to make people believe that heaven is hell – and hell heaven. The greater the lie, the more readily it will be believed.
Adolph Hitler

Sin has many tools, but a lie is the handle which fits them all.
Oliver Wendell Holmes

The great advantage of telling the truth is that one is so much more likely to sound convincing.
Susan Howatch

White lies are non-existent, for a lie is wholly a lie; falsehood is the personification of evil; Satan has two names: he is called Satan, and he is called the Father of Lies.
Victor Hugo

Lying is the acme of evil.
Victor Hugo

He who permits himself to tell a lie once, finds it much easier to do it a second and third time, till at length it becomes habitual; he tells lies without attending to it, and truth without the world's believing him. This falsehood of the tongue leads to that of the heart, and in time depraves all its good dispositions.
Thomas Jefferson

It is always the best policy to tell the truth, unless, of course, you are an exceptionally good liar.
Jerome K. Jerome

Of all the liars in the world, sometimes the worst are your own fears.
Rudyard Kipling

RULE A: Don't.
RULE A1: Rule A does not exist.
RULE A2: Do not discuss the existence or non-existence of Rules A, A1 or A2.
R.D. Laing

A little lie is like a little pregnancy – it doesn't take long before everyone knows.
C.S. Lewis

A lie is a snowball: the further you roll it, the bigger it becomes.
Martin Luther

Lying covers a multitude of sins – temporarily.
Dwight L. Moody

People do not believe lies because they have to, but because they want to.
Malcolm Muggeridge

A little inaccuracy sometimes saves a ton of explanation.
H.H. Munro (Saki)

The most common sort of lie is the one uttered to one's self.
Nietzsche

I was a pilot flying an airplane and it just so happened that where I was flying made what I was doing spying.
Francis Gary Power, U-2 reconnaissance pilot held by the Soviets for spying, in an interview after he was returned to the US

Half-truths are like half a brick – they can be thrown farther.
Hyman von Rickover

The essence of lying is in deception, not in

words; a lie may be told in silence, by equivocation, by the accent on a syllable, by a glance of the eye attaching a peculiar significance to a sentence; and all these kinds of lies are worse and baser by many degrees than a lie plainly worded; so that no form of blinded conscience is so far sunk than that which comforts itself for having deceived because the deception was by gesture or silence, instead of utterance.
John Ruskin

Man has an inexhaustible faculty for lying, especially to himself.
George Santayana

Oh what a tangled web we weave, When first we practice to deceive!
Sir Walter Scott

The President has kept all of the promises he intended to keep.
Clinton aide George Stephanopolous speaking on Larry King Live

A lie is an abomination unto the Lord, and a very present help in trouble.
Adlai Stevenson

A lie which is half truth is the blackest of lies.
Alfred, Lord Tennyson

When in doubt, tell the truth.
Mark Twain

A little lie can travel half way round the world while Truth is still lacing up her boots.
Mark Twain

Lies are the mortar that binds the savage individual man into the social masonry.
H.G. Wells

Life
See also: A-Z of Life; Ages of man
To eat, and to drink, and to be merry.
The Bible, Ecclesiastes 8:15 KJV

All that a man hath will he give for his life.
The Bible, Job 2:4 KJV

My days are swifter than a weaver's shuttle.
The Bible, Job 7:6 KJV

LORD, make me to know mine end, and the measure of my days, what it is; that I may know how frail I am.
The Bible, Psalm 39:4 KJV

As for man his days are as grass; as a flower of the field so he flourisheth.
The Bible, Psalm 103:15 KJV

One generation passeth away, and another generation cometh.
The Bible, Ecclesiastes 1:4 KJV

There is no new thing under the sun.
The Bible, Ecclesiastes 1:9 KJV

We all do fade as a leaf.
The Bible, Isaiah 64:6 KJV

Take no thought for your life, what ye shall eat, or what ye shall drink.
The Bible, Matthew 6:25 KJV

I have come that they may have life, and have it to the full.
The Bible, John 10:10

Life is a journey, not a destination.
Author unknown.

Between the wish and the thing life lies waiting.
Author unknown

The Winner is always a part of the answer;
The Loser is always a part of the problem.
The Winner always has a program;
The Loser always has an excuse.
The Winner says, "Let me do it for you;"
The Loser says, "That's not my job."
The Winner sees an answer for every
  problem;
The Loser sees a problem in every answer.
The Winner says, "It may be difficult but
  it's possible;"
The Loser says, "It may be possible but it's
too difficult."
Author Unknown

If life is a comedy to him who thinks and a tragedy to him who feels, it is a victory to him who believes.
Author unknown

Life is a daring adventure, or it is nothing.
Author unknown

Is life worth living? That depends on the liver.
Author unknown.

It may be that your whole purpose in life is simply to serve as a warning to others.
Author unknown

Life can seem ungrateful and not always kind,
Life can pull at your heartstrings and play with your mind,
Life can be blissful and happy and free,
Life can put beauty in the things that you see,
Life can place challenges right at your feet,
Life can make good of the hardships we meet,
Life can overwhelm you and make your head spin,
Life can reward those determined to win,
Life can be hurtful and not always fair,
Life can surround you with people who care,
Life clearly does offer its ups and its downs,
Life's days can bring you both smiles and frowns,
Life teaches us to take the good with the bad,
Life is a mixture of happy and sad …
SO
Take the life that you have and give it your best,
Think positive, be happy, let God do the rest,
Take the challenges that life has laid at your feet,
Take pride and be thankful for each one you meet,
To yourself give forgiveness if you stumble and fall,

Take each day that is dealt you and give it your all,
Take the love that you're given and return it with care,
Have faith that when needed it will always be there,
Take time to find the beauty in the things that you see,
Take life's simple pleasures, let them set your heart free,
The idea here is simply to even the score,
As you are met and faced with life's Tug of War.
Author unknown

I don't know what I want, and I won't be happy until I get it.
Author unknown.

I asked God for all things, that I might enjoy life.
God gave life, that I might enjoy all things.
Author unknown

The only things you live to regret are the risks you didn't take.
Author unknown.

Life would be so much easier if everyone read the manual.
Author unknown

No wise man wants a soft life.
King Alfred the Great

Here is a test to see if your mission on earth is finished. If you are alive, it isn't.
Francis Bacon

Whatever you are doing, in company or alone, do it all to the glory of God (1 Corinthians 10:31). Otherwise, it is unacceptable to God.
Richard Baxter

The law of God and also the way to life is written in our hearts; it lies in no man's supposing, nor in any historical opinion, but in a good will and well doing.
Jacob Böhme

The great danger facing all of us is not that we shall make an absolute failure of life, nor that we shall fall into outright viciousness, nor that we shall be terribly unhappy, nor that we shall feel that life has no meaning at all – not these things. The danger is that we may fail to perceive life's greatest meaning, fall short of its highest good, miss its deepest and most abiding happiness, be unable to tender the most needed service, be unconscious of life ablaze with the light of the Presence of God – and be content to have it so – that is the danger: that some day we may wake up and find that always we have been busy with husks and trappings of life and have really missed life itself. For life without God, to one who has known the richness and joy of life with Him, is unthinkable, impossible. That is what one prays one's friends may be spared – satisfaction with a life that falls short of the best, that has in it no tingle or thrill that comes from a friendship with the Father.
Phillips Brooks

In the book of life, the answers aren't in the back.
Charlie Brown

Whose life is a bubble, and in length a span.
Thomas Browne

Life is one long process of getting tired.
Samuel Butler

In the end, everything is a gag.
Charlie Chaplin

Youth is a blunder; manhood a struggle; old age a regret.
Benjamin Disraeli

Life is not a holiday, but an education. And the one eternal lesson for us all is how better we can love.
Henry Drummond

The life of the individual only has meaning insofar as it aids in making the life of every living thing nobler and more beautiful.

Life is sacred, that is to say, it is the supreme value to which all other values are subordinate.
Albert Einstein

In three words I can sum up everything I've learned about life: It goes on.
Robert Frost

We are born crying, live complaining, and die disappointed.
Thomas Fuller

There is more to life than increasing its speed.
Gandhi

Life is love.
Goethe

Don't take life too serious. You'll never escape it alive anyway.
Elbert Hubbard

The greatest use of life is to spend it for something that will outlast it.
William James

Life is a mystery to be lived, not a problem to be solved.
Van Kaam

Life is a great big canvas; throw all the paint on it you can.
Danny Kaye

Life is either a daring adventure or nothing.
Helen Keller

Life can only be understood backwards, but it must be lived forwards.
S. Kierkegaard

We make a living by what we get. We make a life by what we give.
Martin Luther King, Jr

Life is something to do when you can't get to sleep.
Fran Lebowitz

Life is what happens while you are making other plans.
John Lennon

The game of life is not so much in holding a good hand as in playing a poor hand well.
H.T. Leslie

The next best thing to being wise oneself is to live in a circle of those who are.
C.S. Lewis.

Better to love God and die unknown than to love the world and be a hero; better to be content with poverty than to die a slave to wealth; better to have taken some risks and lost than to have done nothing and succeeded at it.
Erwin W. Lutzer

The Lord Jesus came into this world not primarily to say something, not even to be something, but to do something; He came not merely to lead men through his example out into a "larger life," but to give life, through His death and resurrection, to those who were dead in trespasses and sins.
J. Gresham Machen

Pythagoras used to say that life resembles the Olympic Games: a few men strain their muscles to carry off a prize; others bring trinkets to sell to the crowd for gain; and some there are, and not the worst, who seek no other profit than to look at the show and see how and why everything is done; spectators of the life of other men in order to judge and regulate their own.
Michel de Montaigne

The value of life lies not in the length of days, but in the use we make of them.
Michel de Montaigne

Life is a foreign language; all men mispronounce it.
Christopher Morley

Our life is but a span.
New England Primer

Life is a hard fight, a struggle, a wrestling with the principle of evil, hand to hand, foot to foot. Every inch of the way is disputed. The night is given us to take breath, to pray, to drink deep at the fountain of power. The day, to use the strength which has been given us, to go forth to work with it till the evening.
Florence Nightingale

You will soon break the bow if you keep it always stretched.
Phaedrus

Everything passes, everything perishes, everything palls.
French proverb

There are three material things essential to life. These are pure air, water, and earth. There are three immaterial things essential to life. These are admiration, hope, and love.
Admiration – the power of discerning and taking delight in what is beautiful in visible form and lovely in human character; and, necessarily, striving to produce what is beautiful in form and to become what is lovely in character.
Hope – the recognition, by true foresight, of better things to be reached hereafter, whether by ourselves or others; necessarily issuing in the straight-forward and undisappointable effort to advance, according to our proper power, the gaining of them.
Love – both of family and neighbor, faithful and satisfying.
John Ruskin

Life is nothing but a competition to be the criminal rather than the victim.
Bertrand Russell

Everything has been figured out, except how to live.
Jean-Paul Sartre

There must be more to life than having everything.
Maurice Sendak

As is a tale, so is life: not how long it is, but how good it is, is what matters.
Seneca

Life is long, if we know how to use it.
Seneca

Life is as tedious as a twice-told tale
Vexing the dull ear of a drowsy man.
Shakespeare, King John

Tomorrow, and tomorrow, and tomorrow,
Creeps in this petty pace from day to day,
To the last syllable of recorded time,
And all our yesterdays have lighted fools
The way to dusty death. Out, out, brief
   candle!
Life's but a walking shadow, a poor player,
That struts and frets his hour upon the
   stage,
And then is heard no more: it is a tale
Told by an idiot, full of sound and fury,
Signifying nothing.
William Shakespeare, Macbeth

The web of our life is of a mingled yarn,
good and ill together.
William Shakespeare, Alls Well That Ends Well

[Life] is a tale
Told by an idiot – full of sound and fury,
Signifying nothing.
William Shakespeare, Macbeth

The unexamined life is not worth living.
Socrates

Each small task of everyday life is part of the total harmony of the universe.
Theresa of Lisieux

Life's a continuous business, and so is success, and requires continuous effort.
Margaret Thatcher

It is vanity to desire a long life and to take no heed of a good life.
Thomas à Kempis

There are only two tragedies in life: one is not getting what one wants, and the other is getting it.
Oscar Wilde

Life, Meaning of
See also: Meaninglessness

Are we to regard it as the product of pure chance, and believe that everything happens at random without rhyme or reason?
Colin Brown

What we call the world is intrinsically unintelligible, apart from the existence of God.
Fredrick Copleston

The issue is whether the world is explicable solely in terms of itself, i.e., is the world itself ultimate, or is there a being other than the world to which the world is related?
David H. Freeman

When we try to think about this infinitely fascinating universe in which we live we find that we are faced in the end with the mystery of existence, of why there is a universe at all.
John Hick

I never asserted so absurd a proposition as that anything might arise without a cause.
David Hume

The first question which should rightly be asked is: Why is there something rather than nothing?
Gottfried Wilhelm Leibniz

The question, "Why is there something rather than nothing?" is regarded even by some skeptical philosophers as a significant one.
H.D. Lewis

Nothing in this world is able to explain its own existence; thus, there must be a God in order to explain the world in which we find ourselves.
John Warwick Montgomery

Man cannot find the ultimate explanation

of his own being anywhere but in God himself.
Edward Sillem

… the riddle of all riddles …
Paul Tillich

It is not how things are in the world that is mystical, but that it exists.
Ludwig Wittgenstein

The solution of the riddle of life in space and time lies outside space and time.
Ludwig Wittgenstein

Life, Sanctity of

We may ask: "How much did it weigh?" and, "Does it have any hair?" When the Athabaskan Indians hear of a birth they ask, "Who came?" From the beginning, there is a respect for the newborn as a full person.
Lisa Delpit

I have no wit, no words, no tears;
My heart within me like a stone
Is numbed too much for hopes or fears.
Look right, look left, I dwell alone;
I lift mine eyes, but dimmed with grief
No everlasting hills I see;
My life is in the falling leaf:
O Jesus, quicken me.
Christina Rossetti

There are two ways, one of life and one of death, and there is a great difference between the two ways.
Didache

Life after death

But though life's valley be a vale of tears,
A brighter scene beyond that vale appears.
William Cowper

This life is the cradle in which we are prepared for the other one.
Joubert

We know and feel that we are eternal.
Benedict Spinoza

Life and death

Thou hast no life to lose, because thou hast given it already to Christ, nor can man take away that without God's leave.
William Gurnall

Life of faith

Order your soul; reduce your wants; live in charity; associate in Christian community; obey the laws; trust in Providence.
Augustine of Hippo

There is no more blessed way of living, than the life of faith upon a covenant-keeping God – to know that we have no care, for he cares for us; that we need have no fear, except to fear him; that we need have no troubles, because we have cast our burdens upon the Lord, and are conscious that he will sustain us.
C.H. Spurgeon

Lifestyle

Having been freed by the sacrifice of our Lord Jesus Christ, in obedience to his call, in heartfelt compassion for the poor, in concern for evangelism, development and justice, and in solemn anticipation of the Day of Judgment, we humbly commit ourselves to develop a just and simple lifestyle, to support one another in it and to encourage others to join with us in the commitment.
An Evangelical Commitment to Simple Lifestyle, International Consultation on Simple Lifestyle, 1980
Ronald Sider, John Stott

All of us are shocked by the poverty of millions and disturbed by the injustices which cause it. Those of us who live in affluent circumstances accept our duty to develop a simple lifestyle, in order to contribute more generously to both relief and evangelism.
The Lausanne Covenant

Light

And God said, Let there be light: and there was light.
The Bible, Genesis 1:3 KJV

Lift thou up the light of thy countenance
upon us.
The Bible, Psalm 4:6 KJV

Truly the light is sweet, and a pleasant
thing it is for the eyes to behold the sun.
The Bible, Ecclesiastes 11:7 KJV

The true Light, which lighteth every man
that cometh into the world.
The Bible, John 1:9 KJV

So let us put aside the deeds of darkness
and put on the armor of light.
The Bible, Romans 13:12

Do not believe that you are a light to
yourself. The Light is that which
illumines every person coming into this
world.
Augustine of Hippo

He who lives up to a little light shall have
more light.
Thomas Brooks

A sense of the beauty of Christ is the
beginning of true saving faith in the life of
a true convert. This is quite different from
any vague feeling that Christ loves him or
died for him. These sort of fuzzy feelings
can cause a sort of love and joy, because
the person feels a gratitude for escaping the
punishment of their sin. In actual fact,
these feelings are based on self-love, and
not on a love for Christ at all. It is a sad
thing that so many people are deluded by
this false faith. On the other hand, a
glimpse of the glory of God in the face of
Jesus Christ causes in the heart a supreme
genuine love for God. This is because the
divine light shows the excellent loveliness
of God's nature. A love based on this is far,
far above anything coming from self-love,
which demons can have as well as men.
The true love of God which comes from
this sight of His beauty causes a spiritual
and holy joy in the soul; a joy in God, and
exulting in Him. There is no rejoicing in
ourselves, but rather in God alone.
The sight of the beauty of divine things

will cause true desires after the things of
God. These desires are different from the
longings of demons, which happen because
the demons know their doom awaits them,
and they wish it could somehow be
otherwise. The desires that come from this
sight of Christ's beauty are natural free
desires, like a baby desiring milk. Because
these desires are so different from their
counterfeits, they help to distinguish
genuine experiences of God's grace from
the false.
Jonathan Edwards

I have walked with people whose eyes are
full of light but who see nothing in sea or
sky, nothing in city streets, nothing in
books.
   It were far better to sail forever in the
night of blindness with sense, and feeling,
and mind, than to be content with the
mere act of seeing.
   The only lightless dark is the night of
darkness in ignorance and insensibility.
Helen Keller

Darkness cannot drive out darkness; only
light can do that. Hate cannot drive out
hate; only love can do that.
Martin Luther King, Jr

As we let our light shine, we unconsciously
give other people the permission to do the
same.
Nelson Mandela

An age is called Dark, not because the light
fails to shine, but because people refuse to
see it.
James A. Michener

What in me is dark
Illumine, what is low raise and support;
That, to the height of this great argument,
I may assert Eternal Providence,
And justify the ways of
God to men.
John Milton

I should like my light to shine, even if only
very fitfully, like a match struck in a dark,

cavernous night and then flickering out.
Malcolm Muggeridge
In reply to the question: What do you most want
to do with the rest of your life?

We can forgive a child who is afraid of the
dark; the real tragedy of life is when men
are afraid of the light.
Plato

If there is light in the soul,
There will be beauty in the person.
If there is beauty in the person,
There will be harmony in the house.
If there is harmony in the house,
There will be order in the nation.
If there is order in the nation,
There will be peace in the world.
A Chinese proverb

There are two kinds of light – the glow
that illuminates, and the glare that
obscures.
James Thurber

Lead me from the unreal to the real!
Lead me from darkness to light!
Lead me from death to immortality!
Upanishad

O Lord, forgive what I have been,
sanctify what I am, and order what I shall
be.
Thomas Wilson

Limits
The main thing is to be honest with
yourself, know and recognize your limits
and attain maximum achievement within
them. I would for example get more
satisfaction from climbing Snowdon,
which I know I could, than from
attempting Everest, which I couldn't.
Stirling Moss

We must learn our limits. We are all
something, but none of us are everything.
Blaise Pascal

Listening
See also: **Speech**

Everyone should be quick to listen, slow to
speak ...
The Bible, James 1:19

His thoughts were slow,
His words were few and never formed to
glisten.
But he was a joy to all his friends,
You should have heard him listen!
Author unknown

My wife said I never listen to her. At least I
think that's what she said.
Author unknown

A wise old owl sat in an oak.
The longer he sat, the less he spoke.
The less he spoke, the more he heard.
Why can't we be like that wise old bird?
Author unknown

Blessed are those who listen, for they shall
learn.
Author unknown

Women like silent men. They think they're
listening.
Marcel Archard

The world is dying for want, not of good
preaching, but of good hearing.
George Dana Boardman

What people really need is a good listening
to.
Mary Lou Casey

The most important thing in
communication is to hear what isn't being
said.
Peter F. Drucker

We have two ears and one mouth so that
we can listen twice as much as we speak.
Epictetus

The most effective remedy for self-love and
self-absorption is the habit of humble
listening.
E. Herman

The only way to entertain some folks is to listen to them.
K. Hubbard

The surest rule [for excelling in conversation] is to listen much, speak little, and say nothing that you may be sorry for.
La Rochefoucauld

Lots of people talk to animals. Not that many listen though. That's the problem.
A.A. Milne, Winnie the Pooh

A good listener is not only popular everywhere, but after a while he gets to know something.
Wilson Mizner

You cannot truly listen to anyone and do anything else at the same time.
M. Scott Peck

None so deaf as those who won't hear.
Proverb

It takes two to speak the truth – one to speak, the other to hear.
Henry David Thoreau

The first duty of love is to listen.
Paul Tillich

Be a good listener. Your ears will never get you into trouble.
Frank Tyger

If a man were invited to a feast, and there being music at the feast, he should so listen to the music, that he did not mind his meat, you would say, Sure he is not hungry; so when men are for jingling words, and like rather gallantry of speech than spirituality of matter, it is a sign that they have surfeited stomachs, and itching ears.
Thomas Watson

Helping others, that's the main thing. The only way for us to help ourselves is to help others and to listen to each other's stories.
Eli Wiesel

Listening to God

God is our true Friend, who always gives us the counsel and comfort we need. Our danger lies in resisting Him; so it is essential that we acquire the habit of hearkening to His voice, or keeping silence within, and listening so as to lose nothing of what He says to us. We know well enough how to keep outward silence, and to hush our spoken words, but we know little of interior silence. It consists in hushing our idle, restless, wandering imagination, in quieting the promptings of our worldly minds, and in suppressing the crowd of unprofitable thoughts which excite and disturb the soul.
François Fénelon

God never ceases to speak to us, but the noise of the world without and the tumult of our passions within bewilder us and prevent us from listening to him.
F. Fénelon

Literature

Literature exists to teach what is useful, to honor what deserves honor, to appreciate what is delightful. The useful, honorable, and delightful things are superior to it: it exists for their sake; its own use, honor, or delightfulness is derivative from theirs.
C.S. Lewis

Little things
See also: Faithfulness

Be great in little things.
Augustine of Hippo

Attention to little things is a great thing.
John Chrysostom

Exactness in little duties is a wonderful source of cheerfulness.
F.W. Faber

I am only one. I can't do everything, but that won't stop me from doing the little I can do.
Everett Hale

Do little things as if they were great,

because of the majesty of the Lord Jesus Christ, who dwells in thee; and do great things as if they were little and easy, because of his omnipotence.
Blaise Pascal

Liturgy

Charismatic spontaneity and liturgical conformity to the truth of Christ are not enemies, but allies in securing our well-ordered freedom. The task of the whole church in regard to its worship is to discover a new and creative relationship between liturgical tradition and charismatic liberation. Neither can be what God has called it to be without the other.
Tom Smail

Living
See also: Behavior; Life Mottoes

Therefore all things whatsoever ye would that men should do to you, do ye even so to them: for this is the law and the prophets.
The Bible, Matthew 7:12 KJV

Take time to think:
it is the course of power.
Take time to play:
it is the secret of perpetual youth.
Take time to read:
it is the fountain of wisdom.
Take time to laugh:
it is the music of the soul.
Take time to give:
it is too short a day to be selfish.
Author unknown

Plan to be here forever, but live as if it were your last day.
Author unknown

Things worth remembering:
The value of time.
The success of perseverance.
The pleasure of working.
The dignity of simplicity.
The worth of character.
The improvement of talent.
The influence of example.
The obligation of duty.
The wisdom of economy.

The virtue of patience.
The joy of originating.
The power of darkness.
Author unknown

1. Count your blessings, not your troubles.
2. Learn to live one day at a time.
3. Learn to say, "I love you," "thank you," and, "I appreciate you."
4. Learn to be a giver and not a getter.
5. Seek the good in everyone and everything.
6. Pray every day.
7. Do at least one good deed every day.
8. Learn to count. Put God first.
9. Let nothing bother you.
10. Practice the "Do it now" habit.
11. Fill your life with good.
12. Learn to laugh and learn to cry.
13. Learn to practice the Happiness habit.
14. Learn to fear nothing and no one.
15. Learn to let go and let God.
Author Unknown

There is no such thing as a sudden heart-attack. It takes years of preparation.
Author unknown

It is better to live for God than to be perpetually talking about Him.
Author unknown

Our lives are a manifestation of what we think about God.
Author unknown

Most men forget God all day and ask Him to remember them at night.
Author unknown

You can't direct the wind, but you can adjust your sails.
Author unknown

It's not how much you make, but how you manage what you make that will make you rich.
Author unknown

Live dangerously, but in the hands of God.
Author unknown

For attractive lips, speak words of
kindness.
For beautiful eyes, seek out the good in
other people.
To lose weight, let go of stress and the need
to control others.
To improve your ears, listen to the word of
God.
Touch someone with your love.
Rather than focus on the thorns of life,
smell the roses and count your blessings.
For poise, walk with knowledge and
self-esteem.
To strengthen your arms, hug at least three
people a day.
To strengthen your heart, forgive yourself
and others.
Don't worry and hurry so much.
Rather walk this earth lightly and yet leave
your mark.
Author unknown

What you live is what you believe!
Author unknown

We commit the Golden Rule to memory
and forget to commit it to life.
Author unknown

Anybody who brags about what he is going
to do tomorrow probably did the same
thing yesterday.
Author unknown

Let us live while we live.
Author unknown

If you want to truly be great, you must
learn to heal, because hurting people is
easy.
Author unknown

Only the things we do for God's kingdom
have eternal meaning.
Author unknown

People can be divided into three groups:
1) Those who make things happen,
2) Those who watch things happen, and
3) Those who wonder what's happening.
Author unknown

So live that after the minister has ended his
remarks, those present will not think they
have attended the wrong funeral.
Author unknown

If God came back tomorrow, would it
change the way I think, act, and live today?
Author unknown

It is easier to fight for one's principles than
to live up to them.
Alfred Adler

Mark how fleeting and paltry is the estate
of man – yesterday in embryo, to-morrow
a mummy or ashes. So for the
hair's-breadth of time assigned to thee live
rationally, and part with life cheerfully, as
drops the ripe olive, extolling the season
that bore it and the tree that matured it.
Marcus Aurelius Antoninus

Though thou be destined to live three
thousand years and as many myriads
besides, yet remember that no man loseth
other life than that which he liveth, nor
liveth other than that which he loseth.
Marcus Aurelius Antoninus

Not everything that is more difficult is
more meritorious.
Thomas Aquinas

The quality of life is determined by its
activities.
Aristotle

May your Creed be for you as a mirror.
Look at yourself in it, to see if you believe
everything you say you believe. And rejoice
in your faith each day.
Augustine of Hippo

The most important things to do in the
world are to get something to eat, something
to drink and somebody to love you.
Brendan Behan

Everything that God has effected has been
perfected in Love, Humility and Peace.
Human beings, therefore, should esteem

Love, embrace Humility and grasp Peace.
Hildegard of Bingen

Every man dies, not every man truly
lives.
Braveheart

One should hallow all that one does in
one's natural life. One eats in holiness,
tastes the taste of food in holiness, and the
table becomes an altar. One works in
holiness, and he raises up the sparks which
hide themselves in all tools. One walks in
holiness across the fields, and the soft
songs of all herbs, which they voice to
God, enter into the song of our soul.
Martin Buber

Don't take life too seriously. You'll never
get out alive.
Bugs Bunny

I'd rather be a failure at something I love
than a success at something I hate.
George Burns

How far you go in life depends on your
being tender with the young,
compassionate with the aged, sympathetic
with the striving, and tolerant of the weak
and strong. Because someday in your life
you will have been all of these.
George Washington Carver

In dwelling, live close to the ground.
In thinking, keep to the simple.
In conflict, be fair and generous.
In governing, don't try to control.
In work, do what you enjoy.
In family life, be completely present.
Tao Te Ching

You're either part of the solution or part of
the problem.
Eldridge Cleaver

The superior man has nine things which
are subjects with him of thoughtful
consideration.
In regard to the use of his eyes, he is
anxious to see clearly.

In regard to the use of his ears, he is
anxious to hear distinctly.
In regard to his countenance, he is anxious
that it should be benign.
In regard to his demeanor, he is anxious
that it should be respectful.
In regard to his speech, he is anxious that it
should be sincere.
In regard to his doing of business, he is
anxious that he should be reverently
careful.
In regard to what he doubts about, he is
anxious to question others.
When he is angry, he thinks of the
difficulties his anger may involve him in.
When he sees gain to be got, he thinks of
righteousness.
Contemplating good, and pursuing it, as if
he could not reach it; contemplating evil
and shrinking from it, as he would from
thrusting the hand into boiling water.
Confucius

What you do not want done to yourself,
do not do to others.
Confucius

The most important thing in the Olympic
Games is not winning but taking part …
The essential thing in life is not
conquering but fighting well.
*Pierre de Coubertin, speech to officials of the
Olympic Games, 24 July 1908*

It is better to wear out than to rust out.
Richard Cumberland

Try to do to others as you would have
them do to you, and do not be discouraged
if they fail sometimes.
Charles Dickens

Live while you live, the epicure would say,
And seize the pleasures of the present day;
Live while you live, the sacred preacher
cries,
And give to God each moment as it flies.
Lord, in my views, let both united be:
I live in pleasure when I live to thee.
*Philip Dodderidge, Epigram on his Family
Arms.*

RESOLVED: To live with all might while I do live.
Jonathan Edwards

Only a life lived for others is worth living.
Albert Einstein

A person starts to live when he can live outside himself.
Albert Einstein

What do we live for if it is not to make life less difficult for each other?
George Eliot

Finish each day and be done with it. You have done what you could; some blunders and absurdities have crept in; forget them as soon as you can. Tomorrow is a new day; you should begin it serenely and with too high a spirit to be encumbered with your old nonsense.
Ralph Waldo Emerson

Make the best use of what is in your power, and take the rest as it happens.
Epictetus

What I gave, I have; what I spent, I had; what I kept, I lost.
Old epitaph

Live as though today you may die a martyr's death.
Charles de Faucauld

Don't forget until too late that the business of life is not business, but living.
B.C. Forbes

The best thing to give an enemy is forgiveness;
To an opponent, tolerance;
To a friend, your ear;
To your child, a good example;
To a father, reverence;
To your mother, conduct that will make her proud of you;
To yourself, respect;
And to all, charity.
Benjamin Franklin

If you wouldst live long, live well; for folly and wickedness shorten life.
Benjamin Franklin

Think of these things: whence you came, where you are going, and to whom you must account.
Benjamin Franklin

It's not your blue blood, your pedigree or your college degree. It's what you do with your life that counts.
Millard Fuller

He does not believe, that does not live according to his belief.
Thomas Fuller

Resolve to be tender with the young, compassionate with the aged, sympathetic with the striving, and tolerant with the weak and the wrong. Sometime in your life you will have been all of these.
Bob Goddard

One ought, every day at least, to hear a little song, read a good poem, see a fine picture and, if possible, speak a few reasonable words.
Goethe

Keep cool, but don't freeze.
Heilmann's Mayonnaise

I'm the one that has to die when it's time for me to die, so let me live my life, the way I want to.
Jimi Hendrix

The Lord has many fine farms from which he receives but little rent. Thanksgiving is a good thing: thanks-living is better.
Philip Henry

Great deeds are usually wrought at great risks.
Herodotus

How many people eat, drink, and get married; buy, sell, and build; make contracts and attend to their fortune; have

friends and enemies, pleasures and pains,
are born, grow up, live and die – but asleep!
Joubert

It's not how long you live, it's how well you
live.
Martin Luther King

All mortals tend to turn into the thing
they are pretending to be.
C.S. Lewis

You cannot bring about prosperity by
discouraging thrift.
You cannot strengthen the weak by
weakening the strong.
You cannot help the wage earner by
pulling down the wage payer.
You cannot further brotherhood by
encouraging class hatred.
You cannot help the poor by destroying
the rich.
You cannot establish sound security on
borrowed money.
You cannot keep out of trouble by
spending more than you earn.
You cannot build character and courage by
taking away man's initiative and
independence.
You cannot help men permanently by
doing for them what they could and
should do for themselves.
Abraham Lincoln

Look not mournfully into the past. It comes
not back again. Wisely improve the present.
It is thine. Go forth to meet the shadowy
future, without fear, and with a manly heart.
Henry Wadsworth Longfellow

Life is given not as a lasting possession, but
merely for use.
Lucretius

Make sure the thing you're living for is
worth dying for.
Charles Mayes

Live so as to be missed when dead.
*Robert Murray M'Cheyne, who was only 28
years old when he died*

Be careful for nothing, prayerful for
everything, thankful for anything.
Dwight L. Moody

Every happening, great and small, is a
parable whereby God speaks to us, and the
art of life is to get the message.
Malcolm Muggeridge

We are living in a world today where
lemonade is made from artificial flavors and
furniture polish is made from real lemons.
Alfred E. Newman

I compare the troubles which we have to
undergo in the course of the year to a great
bundle of sticks, far too large for us to lift.
But God does not require us to carry the
whole at once. He mercifully unties the
bundle, and gives us first one stick, which
we are to carry today, and then another,
which we are to carry tomorrow, and so on.
This we might easily manage, if we would
only take the burden appointed for us each
day; but we choose to increase our troubles
by carrying yesterday's stick over again
today, and adding tomorrow's burden to
our load, before we are required to bear it.
John Newton

We should consider every day lost on
which we have not danced at least once.
And we should call every truth false which
was not accompanied by at least one laugh.
Friedrich Nietzsche

Do not let the good things in life rob you
of the best things.
Buster Rothman

Live simply that others might simply live.
Elizabeth Seaton

Our care should not be to have lived long
as to have lived enough.
Seneca

The best things in life are nearest : Breath in
your nostrils, light in your eyes, flowers at
your feet, duties at your hand, the path of
right just before you. Then do not grasp at

the stars, but do life's plain, common work as it comes, certain that daily duties and daily bread are the sweetest things in life.
Robert Louis Stevenson

Let us live as people who are prepared to die, and die as people who are prepared to live.
James S. Stewart

Integrate what you believe into every single area of your life.
Meryl Streep

May you live all the days of your life.
Jonathan Swift

The best doctors in the world are Doctor Diet, Doctor Quiet and Doctor Merryman.
Jonathan Swift

Life is 10 per cent what happens to you, 90 per cent how you respond to it.
Chuck Swindoll

You should not live one way in private, another in public.
Publilius Syrus

Remember that you have only one soul; that you have only one death to die; that you have only one life, which is short and has to be lived by you alone; and there is only one glory, which is eternal. If you do this, there will be many things about which you care nothing.
Teresa of Avila

The world is a looking glass, and gives back to every man the reflection of his own face. Frown at it and it will in turn look sourly upon you; laugh at it and with it, and it is a jolly kind companion.
William Makepeace Thackeray

Live each season as it passes; breathe the air, drink the drink, taste the fruit, and resign yourself to the influences of each.
Henry David Thoreau

My policy is to learn from the past, focus on the present, and dream about the future.
Donald Trump

Let us so live that when we come to die even the undertaker will be sorry.
Mark Twain

Manifest plainness,
Embrace simplicity,
Reduce selfishness,
Have few desires.
Lao Tzu

O Lord, forgive what I have been, sanctify what I am, and order what I shall be.
Thomas Wilson

Living, God's help for

I asked for knowledge – power to control things;
I was granted understanding – to learn to love persons.
I asked for strength to be a great man;
I was make weak to become a better man.
I asked for wealth to make friends;
I became poor, to keep friends.
I asked for all things to enjoy life;
I was granted life, to enjoy all things.
I cried for pity; I was offered sympathy.
I craved for healing of my own disorders;
I received insight into another's suffering.
I prayed to God for safety – to tread the trodden path;
I was granted danger, to lose the track and find the Way.
I got nothing that I prayed for;
I am among all men, richly blessed.
Author unknown

Live in such a manner that death may not find you unprepared.
Thomas à Kempis

Teach me to live, that I may dread
The grave as little as my bed;
Teach me to die, that so I may
Rise glorious at the awful day.
Thomas Ken

Lives of great men all remind me
We can make our lives sublime,
And, departing, leave behind us
Footprints on the sands of time.
Henry Wadsworth Longfellow

Living and human relationships

May I be no man's enemy, and may I be the
friend of that which is eternal and abides.
May I never quarrel with those nearest to
me; and if I do, may I be reconciled quickly.
May I love, seek, and attain only what is
good.
May I wish for all men's happiness and
envy no one.
May I never rejoice in the ill fortune of
someone who has wronged me.
May I win no victory that harms either me
or my opponent.
Eusebius

Live among men as if the eye of God was
upon you; pray to God as if men were
listening to you.
Seneca

Living day by day

Look to this day. ... In it lie all the realities
and verities of existence, the bliss of
growth, the splendor of action, the glory of
power. For yesterday is but a dream and
tomorrow is only a vision. But today, well
lived, makes every yesterday a dream of
happiness and every tomorrow a vision of
hope.
Sanskrit proverb

Living for God

Live in the world as if God and your soul
only were in it; that your heart may be
captive to no earthly thing.
John of the Cross

The Son of God has redeemed us solely to
this end: that we should, by a right life and
devotion, live to the glory of God. This is
the one and only rule and standard of
living.
William Law

I have held many things in my hands, and

I have lost them all; but whatever I have
placed in God's hands, that I still possess.
Martin Luther

If I had a thousand lives, China should
have them. No! Not China, but Christ.
Can we do too much for him?
Hudson Taylor

Forth in thy name, O Lord, I go,
My daily labor to pursue;
Thee, only thee, resolved to know,
In all I think, or speak, or do.

The task thy wisdom hath assigned
O let me cheerfully fulfil:
In all thy works thy presence find,
And prove thy good and perfect will.
Charles Wesley

Logic

"Contrariwise," continued Tweedledee, "if
it was so, it might be; and if it were so, it
would be; but as it isn't, it ain't. That's
logic."
Lewis Carroll Society

Loneliness

I am like a desert owl, like an owl among
the ruins.
The Bible, Psalm 102:6

When I fancied that I stood alone I was
really in the ridiculous position of being
backed up by all of Christendom.
G.K. Chesterton

I have never been alone but that my heart
did ache, my eyes fill with tears, and my
hands tremble for a peace and a joy that I
never found.
Isadora Duncan, ballet dancer

No soul is desolate as long as there is a
human being for whom it can feel trust
and reverence.
George Eliot

What loneliness is more lonely than
distrust?
George Eliot

Loneliness is never more cruel than when it is felt in close propinquity with someone who has ceased to communicate.
Germaine Greer

Loneliness is the first thing which God's eye named not good.
John Milton

I hope no missionary will ever be as lonely as I have been.
Lottie Moon

People are lonely because they build walls instead of bridges.
Joseph Fort Newton

A city is a large community where people are lonesome together.
Herbert Prochnow

Loneliness and the feeling of being unwanted is the most terrible type of poverty.
Mother Theresa

There is no one left to call me Victoria.
Queen Victoria, after the death of her husband

I am sixty-five, and I am lonely and have never found peace.
H.G. Wells, on his sixty-fifth birthday

Longing for God
You called, you cried, you shattered my deafness, you sparkled, you blazed, you drove away my blindness, you shed your fragrance, and I drew in my breath, and I pant for you.
Augustine of Hippo

Blest are the pure in heart,
For they shall see our God;
The secret of the Lord is theirs,
Their soul is Christ's abode.
John Keble

Acute desire must be present or there will be no manifestation of Christ to His people. He waits to be wanted. Too bad

that with many of us He waits so long, so very long, in vain.
A.W. Tozer

Longings
There is not a heart but has its moments of longing, yearning for something better.
Henry Ward Beecher

Longsuffering
But longsuffering is great and strong, and has a mighty and vigorous power, and is prosperous in great enlargement, gladsome, exultant, free from care, glorifying the Lord at every season, having no bitterness in itself, remaining always gentle and tranquil. This longsuffering therefore dwelleth with those whose faith is perfect.
Hermas

Looking
Happy is he and more than wise
Who sees with wondering eyes and clean
This world through all the grey disguise
Of sleep and custom in between.
G.K. Chesterton

The place from which all spirituality must begin is the created world around us.
Ian Ramsay

The basic command of religion is not, "Do this!" or "Do not do that!" but simply "Look!"
P. Toynbee

One of the principal truths of Christianity, a truth which goes by almost unrecognized today, is that the looking is what saves us.
Simone Weil

Looking at Jesus
If I look at myself, I am depressed.
If I look at those around me, I am often disappointed.
If I look at my circumstances, I am discouraged.
But if I look at Jesus, I am constantly, consistently, and eternally fulfilled!
Author unknown

Lordship of Christ

As Christ is the root by which a saint grows, so is he the rule by which a saint walks.
Author unknown

He values not Christ at all who does not value Christ above all.
Augustine of Hippo

The Lord who vacated his tomb has not vacated his throne.
G.R. Beasley-Murray

Jesus cannot be our Savior unless he is first our Lord.
Hugh C. Burt

Christ is either both Savior and Lord, or he is neither Savior nor Lord.
John R. DeWitt

You cannot have the gifts of Christ apart from the government of Christ.
A. Lindsay Glegg

A Christ supplemented is a Christ supplanted.
William Henricksen

Seek Christ, and you will find him, and with him everything else thrown in.
C.S. Lewis

When Jesus Christ utters a word, he opens his mouth so wide that it embraces all heaven and earth, even though that word be but in a whisper.
Martin Luther

When we come to Jesus for salvation, we come to the one who is Lord over all. Any message omitting this truth cannot be called the gospel according to Jesus.
John E. MacArthur, Jr

Christ is either Lord of all or he is not Lord at all.
J. Hudson Taylor

If Christ does not reign over the mundane events of our lives, he does not reign at all.
Paul Tripp

To present Christ's lordship as an option leaves it squarely in the category of stereo equipment for a new car.
Dallas Willard

Lord's Prayer

The Lord's Prayer is the most perfect of prayers ... In it we ask, not only for the things we can rightly desire, but also in the sequence that they should be desired. This prayer teaches us not only to ask for things, but also in what order we should desire them.
Thomas Aquinas

[The Lord's Prayer] is truly the summary of the whole gospel.
Tertullian

The Lord's prayer contains the sum total of religion and morals.
Duke of Wellington

The Lord's Prayer in Aramaic, the language spoken by Jesus.
aboon dabashmaya
ethkadash shamak
tetha malkoothak
newe tzevyanak
aykan dabashmaya af bara
hav lan lakma dsoonkanan
yamanawashbook lan
kavine aykana daf hanan shabookan
lhayavine
oolow talahn lanesyana
ela fatsan men beesha

Lord's Supper
See also: Holy Communion; Mass; Means of grace

You cannot drink the cup of the Lord and the cup of demons too; you cannot have a part in both the Lord's table and the table of demons.
The Bible, 1 Corinthians 10:21

For whenever you eat this bread and drink this cup, you proclaim the Lord's death

until he comes. Therefore, whoever eats the bread or drinks the cup of the Lord in an unworthy manner will be guilty of sinning against the body and blood of the Lord. A man ought to examine himself before he eats of the bread and drinks of the cup.
The Bible, 1 Corinthians 11:26-28

The Church of England has wisely forborne to use the term Real Presence in all the books set forth by her authority. We neither find it recommended in the Liturgy, nor the Articles, nor the Homilies, nor the Church Catechism, nor Nowell's Catechism. For though it be once in the Liturgy, and once more in the Articles of 1552, it is mentioned in both places as a phrase of the Papists, and rejected for their abuse of it. So that if any Church of England man use it, he does more than the Church directs him; if any reject it, he has the Church's example to warrant him.
Dean Aldrich

The proper effect of the Eucharist is the transformation of man into God.
Thomas Aquinas

Whereas it is ordained in this Office for the Administration of the Lord's Supper, that the Communicants should receive the same kneeling; (which order is well meant, for a signification of our humble and grateful acknowledgment of the benefits of Christ therein given to all worthy Receivers, and for the avoiding of such profanation and disorder in the Holy Communion, as might otherwise ensue;) yet, lest the same kneeling should by any persons, either out of ignorance and infirmity, or out of malice and obstinacy, be misconstrued and depraved; It is hereby declared, That thereby no adoration is intended, or ought to be done, either unto the Sacramental Bread or Wine there bodily received, or unto any corporal presence of Christ's natural Flesh and Blood. For the Sacramental Bread and Wine remain still in their very natural substances, and therefore may not be adored; (for that were Idolatry, to be abhorred of all faithful Christians;) and the

natural Body and Blood of our Savior Christ are in Heaven, and not here; it being against the truth of Christ's natural Body to be at one time in more places than one.
Book of Common Prayer, Rubric at the end of the Communion Service

The Lord's Supper is an ordinance of Jesus Christ to be administered with the elements of bread and wine, and to be observed by His Churches until the end of the world. It is in no sense a sacrifice, but is designed to commemorate his death, to confirm the faith and other graces of Christians, and to be a bond, pledge and renewal of their communion with him, and of their church fellowship.
James Boice

Although [at the Lord's Supper] my mind can think beyond what my tongue can utter, yet even my mind is conquered and overwhelmed by the greatness of the thing. Therefore nothing remains but to break forth in wonder at this mystery, which plainly neither the mind is able to conceive nor the tongue to express.
John Calvin

As concerning the form of doctrine used in this Church of England in the Holy Communion, that the Body and Blood of Christ be under the forms of bread and wine, when you shall show the place where this form of words is expressed, then shall you purge yourself from that which in the meantime I take to be a plain untruth.
Thomas Cranmer

But every Lord's day, do ye gather yourselves together, and break bread, and give thanksgiving after having confessed your transgressions, that your sacrifice may be pure. But let no one that is at variance with his fellow come together with you, until they be reconciled, that your sacrifice may not be profaned. For this is that which was spoken by the Lord.
Didache

The Lord's Supper (re)-presents the death of Christ and proclaims that death in and through the shared celebration.
James D.G. Dunn

'Twas God the word that spake it,
He took the bread and brake it;
And what the word did make it,
That I believe, and take it.
Elizabeth I, when asked what she believed about the presence of Christ in the sacrament of the Lord's Supper

The four views which have unhappily divided the Christian world on the subject of the sacrament [i.e., Holy Communion, the Lord's Supper or the Mass] are the following:
1. The Romish doctrine, or transubstantiation. This maintains the absolute change of the elements into the actual body and blood of Christ; so that though the elements of bread and wine remain present to the senses, they are no longer what they seem, being changed into the body, blood, and divinity of Christ.
2. The Lutheran view, called consubstantiation. This maintains that after consecration the body and blood of Christ are substantially present, but nevertheless that the bread and wine are present, unchanged.
3. The Anglican view – that Christ is present in the sacrament only after the spiritual manner, and that his body and blood are eaten by the faithful after a spiritual, and not after a carnal manner, to the maintenance of their spiritual life and their growth in grace.
4. The Zwinglian, which declares the sacrament to be no channel of grace, but only a commemorative feast, admitting only a figurative presence of Christ's body and blood.
  Alas! that prisons should have been peopled, and thousands immolated on the pyre, for the sake of opinions; and that nothing but death could atone for the horrible crime of individual judgment, instead of allowing each to stand or fall to their own master.
John Foxe

To eat or drink unworthily is not to eat and drink with a consciousness of unworthiness, for such a sense of ill desert is one of the conditions of acceptable communion. It is not the whole, but the consciously sick whom Christ came to heal. Nor is it to eat with doubt and misgiving of our being duly prepared to come to the Lord's table; for such doubts, although an evidence of a weak faith, indicate a better state of mind than indifference or false security. In the Larger Catechism of our Church, in answer to the question, whether one who doubts of his being in Christ, may come to the Lord's supper, it is said,
"One who doubteth of his being in Christ, or of his due preparation to the sacrament of the Lord's supper, may have true interest in Christ, though he be not yet assured thereof, and in God's account hath it, if he be duly affected with the apprehension of the want of it, and unfeignedly desires to be found in Christ, and to depart from iniquity. In which case (because promises are made, and this sacrament is appointed, for the relief even of weak and doubting Christians) he is to bewail his unbelief, and labor to have his doubts resolved, and so doing, he may and ought to come to the Lord's supper, that he may be further strengthened."
  To eat or drink unworthily is in general to come to the Lord's table in a careless, irreverent spirit, without the intention or desire to commemorate the death of Christ as the sacrifice for our sins, and without the purpose of complying with the engagements which we thereby assume. The way in which the Corinthians ate unworthily was, that they treated the Lord's table as though it were their own; making no distinction between the Lord's supper and an ordinary meal; coming together to satisfy their hunger, and not to feed on the body and blood of Christ; and refusing to commune with their poorer brethren. This, though one, is not the only way in which men may eat and drink unworthily. All that is necessary to observe is, that the warning is directly against the

careless and profane, and not against the timid and the doubting.
Charles Hodge

The real presence of Christ's most blessed body and blood is not to be sought for in the sacrament, but in the worthy receiver of the sacrament.
Richard Hooker

Take great care to keep one Eucharist, for there is one flesh of our Lord Jesus Christ and one cup to unite us by his blood.
Ignatius of Antioch (being the first occasion on which the word Eucharist [thanksgiving] was applied to the Lord's Supper)

I desire God's bread, which is the flesh of Christ who was from David's seed; and for drink I desire his blood, which is love incorruptible.
Ignatius of Antioch

There is a change in the bread and wine, and such a change as no power but the omnipotency of God can make, in that that which before was bread should now have the dignity to exhibit Christ's body. And yet the bread is still bread, and the wine is still wine. For the change is not in the nature but in the dignity.
Hugh Latimer

In short, the Mass itself and anything that proceeds from it, and anything that is attached to it, we cannot tolerate, but must condemn, in order that we may retain the holy Sacrament pure and certain, according to the institution of Christ, employed and received through faith.
Martin Luther

The words of the priests do not transform the bread into Christ's body or the wine into His blood. Christ is present no matter what words are spoken or ceremonies performed.
Martin Luther

The sacrament is the eaten word of God.
Martin Luther

The sacraments have been given to us in order to stimulate our faith. In fact, they are means of grace mainly because they are means of faith. And the Lord's Supper is a means of faith because it sets forth in dramatic visual symbolism the good news that Christ died for our sins in order that we might be forgiven.
John Stott

The flesh feeds on the body and blood of Christ so that the soul may be fattened on God.
Tertullian

This meal is for sinners only.
David Watson

Author of life divine,
Who hast a table spread,
Furnished with mystic wine
And everlasting bread,
Preserve the life thyself hast given,
And feed and train us up for heaven.
John Wesley

Lord's Supper, *Preparation for*

John Willison
A proposal for young communicants, for expressly renewing the baptismal engagements, before their first admission to the Lord's table.
The Young Communicant's Catechism

Question 1. What moves you to seek access to the Lord's table?
Answer. The Lord's command, and because I desire to renew my baptismal engagements, and declare myself a Christian by my own free choice and consent, and would join myself unto the Lord by my own voluntary act and deed.
Q. 2. Why do you desire to do so?
A. Because, when I got the first seal of the covenant, namely, baptism, I knew not

what was done for me, nor was I capable to consent to my parents' deed; but now, when I am come to some knowledge and capacity, I am willing to declare, that I make religion my free choice, and reasonable service.

Q. 3. Why do you come so early? Will it not be soon enough to mind religion in old age?

A. No; for besides that I may die young, these who neglect religion, and give themselves up to the world, or the flesh in their youth, do fall into hardness of heart, from which few recover.

Q. 4. What is the most proper season to seek acquaintance with Christ and religion?

A. The time of youth, because in this age the heart is more easily melted, and the habits of vice are not so riveted as afterward; and because God has a special delight in early piety.

Q. 5. What views then have you got of your natural state and condition?

A. I do see it to be a most sinful, wretched, and helpless case; I am condemned to perish under a load of guilt and wrath, having broke the covenant of works, which I cannot fulfill, offended the justice of God, which I cannot satisfy, and lost the image of God, and my precious soul, which I cannot recover. O what shall I do to be saved?

Q. 6. Where do you look for relief?

A. Only to Jesus Christ, who hath, in his free love to lost sinners, undertaken as Surety and Mediator in the new covenant, which is exhibited and sealed to believers at the Lord's table.

Q. 7. What views have you got of that covenant which is there sealed?

A. I see the way of salvation laid down in it through the suretyship and righteousness of Jesus Christ, to be an excellent contrivance, well-ordered in all things and sure. I look upon it as a device every way worthy of God, and of infinite wisdom, and I do heartily approve of it, consent to it, and desire to come and venture my soul and eternal salvation upon it.

Q. 8. What think you of the love of God, that was the spring of this new covenant?

A. I view it as wonderful and amazing; I admire the love of the Father, in contriving and sending his beloved Son to execute it; I admire the love of the Son of God, in undertaking to be a Surety and sacrifice for lost sinners of Adam's race, when the sinning angels were passed by, and left to perish forever; and I admire the love of the Holy Ghost, in undertaking to apply that redemption to lost elect sinners, by working in them conviction, conversion, and faith in Jesus Christ.

Q. 9. With what disposition do you come to renew your baptismal covenant?

A. I desire to sense my guilt in breaking this covenant, in running away from Christ's flag, in going over to Satan's camp, and in standing so long out against Christ's calls and offers; and I desire now to return to the Lord as a penitent prodigal, and a mourning backslider, with my face toward Zion, weeping as I go, willing to renew my baptismal vows with others, saying, Come, let us join ourselves to the Lord in an everlasting covenant never to be forgotten. And, in a word, I desire to go to a broken Christ with a broken heart.

Q. 10. What is that baptismal vow or covenant, which you design to renew?

A. According to my engagement and dedication in baptism, I desire expressly to own and acknowledge the only living and true God as my God in Christ, as he offers himself in the covenant of grace; and to give up myself, soul and body to him, to be for him and not for another. And I design, in the most solemn manner, to go and renounce all the enemies of the Holy Trinity, namely, the devil, the world, and the flesh; and to declare my acceptance of God the Father as my Father, of God the Son as my Redeemer, and of God the Holy Ghost as my Sanctifier; in whose blessed name I was baptized, and to whose service and glory I was dedicated.

Q. 11. What do you think of Jesus Christ, the Mediator of the covenant?

A. I think him a matchless Person, and an excellent and all-sufficient Savior; and I am content to accept him in all his offices, namely, as a Prophet to instruct and teach me, as a Priest to atone and intercede for me, and as a King to rule in me and over me.

Q. 12. What do you think of your own righteousness and strength with respect to your salvation?

A. I look upon my own righteousness and strength as insufficient to answer the demands of God's law, and therefore I renounce them, and flee to a Surety for both, saying, In the Lord Jesus only have I righteousness and strength; and I am content and resolved to make use of a borrowed strength for my performing of duty, and of a borrowed righteousness for my acceptance in duty.

Q. 13. How do you like this self-denying way of saving lost souls?

A. I am well pleased with it, as it makes me an eternal debtor to free grace, as it doth exclude all boasting and glorying in the creature, and ascribes all the glory of my salvation to Christ only; as it takes the crown off the head of self, and puts it upon the head of glorious Christ.

Q. 14. How do you relish the kingly office of Jesus Christ?

A. I am well pleased therewith, and content to take Christ as a King to govern me by his laws, as well as a Priest to save me by his blood; nay, I am desirous he may come in as a King, and execute his kingly office in my soul; that he may set up his throne in my heart, subdue indwelling sin, and conquer all my rebellious lusts and corruption.

Q. 15. What view have you of the Holy Ghost, the third person in the Trinity, and of his office in the business of saving souls?

A. I look upon him as the blessed applier of Christ's purchase unto me, and do accept him as such; and I am willing to give up myself to him, to convince, enlighten, renew, sanctify and guide me; and I believe he is as willing and ready to make the application, as Christ was to make the purchase; and therefore I desire to trust him for this blessed effect.

Q. 16. What think you of the things of this world as a portion to the soul?

A. I look upon all its profits, honors, and pleasures, to be insufficient to suit the soul's desires, and that they are nothing but vanity and vexation of spirit; and therefore I will never set my heart upon the world as my portion: it is only the enjoyment of God reconciled in Christ, that can afford complete satisfaction to my soul; and this only I choose for my happiness and portion.

Q. 17. What do you think of the world to come?

A. I look upon it, and the things thereof, as awful, certain, and very near. I look upon hell as the eternal habitation of unbelievers; but I view heaven as the country and dwelling place of the followers of the Lamb, with whom I desire to join, to seek that country, and dwell with them forever.

Q. 18. What do you think of a holy and religious life?

A. I think a religious life, or a life spent in the service of God, and in communion with him, the most pleasant and comfortable life that a man can live in the world.

Q. 19. How do you think to attain to holiness for living this life?

A. I look upon Jesus Christ as the Purchaser of holiness as well as of happiness, as he, who, by his death, hath obtained the Holy Spirit to effectuate the new birth, and form the image of God in his people; and therefore desire to come to Christ and his blood for sanctification, as well as for justification; for conformity and likeness to God, as well as for access to fellowship and communion with God, and I will plead, that he may send his Holy Spirit unto my soul, for producing holiness, and all the graces of the Spirit.

Q. 20. What view have you got of the promises of the covenant, and their usefulness?

A. I look upon them as the ground of all my faith and hope, and I desire to make daily use of them, and to plead them with God for strength to perform every duty, and for perseverance in all the steps of my pilgrimage; and I resolve to have recourse to him in every strait and difficulty.

Q. 21. As you profess willingness to accept God in Christ as your God, are ye not also willing to dedicate yourself to him for his use and service?

A. Yes, I am willing (I hope through grace) to give up and surrender unto the Lord myself, and all that belongs unto me, my soul and body, with all their powers, faculties, senses, members, and enjoyments, to be instruments of his glory, and to be disposed of him for his use and service at his pleasure.

Q. 22. How do you instruct your willingness to give up and surrender the powers and faculties of your soul unto the Lord?

A. I think I am willing to dedicate and give up my understanding to the Lord, to contemplate his perfections, and know his will; my memory to him, to retain and treasure up his gracious promises and counsels; my will to him, to choose and refuse every thing according to his will, and to comply therewith in all things, and my conscience to him, to be his deputy, to accuse and excuse according to his direction.

Q. 23. Do you also resign and give up the passions and affections of your soul unto the Lord?

A. Yes, I give up and dedicate my passion of grief to the Lord, to mourn for every thing that is offensive to him; my hatred, to abhor every thing that is hateful to him; my desires, to long for his presence; my love, to embrace and entertain him; my delight and joy, to solace myself, and to acquiesce cheerfully in him as my soul's portion and happiness.

Q. 24. In what respects do you resign your bodily senses and members to the Lord?

A. I give up my eyes, to read his word, and behold his wondrous works; my ears to hear his word, and attend to his counsels; my taste, smell, and feeling, to discern and relish his sweetness and excellence in the creatures; my tongue, to proclaim his praise, and commend his ways and service; my hands to help his people; and my feet to walk in paths pleasing to him.

Q. 25. How do you resign your enjoyments and comforts to the Lord?

A. I resign my time, my health, my talents, my opportunities, my relations, my gifts, my interest, my power, my wisdom, my substance, my honor, my reputation, and all I have in the world, unto the Lord, to be employed and disposed of by him for his glory, as he thinks proper.

Q. 26. What view have you now of sin, and of these sins you once esteemed as your right hand and right eye?

A. I see and abhor them as the enemies and crucifiers of my Lord Jesus, and as the very nails and spear that pierced him, and desire to throw them out of my heart, and to cut off every right hand and pluck out every right eye, and to renounce all ungodliness and all beloved lusts, and count no sin too dear to part with for Jesus Christ my Lord.

Q. 27. What do you think now of companions in sin and their invitations to join them in sin?

A. I am convinced of their folly, and resolve never to follow the multitude to do evil, nor to join them in any of the common sins of the age, and steadfastly (through grace) to avoid the snares, and resist the temptations of evil company; saying, with David, Depart from me, ye evil doers, for I will keep the commandments of my God.

Q. 28. What thoughts have you of the people of God and these who bear his image?

A. I look upon them as God's precious jewel, the excellent ones of the earth, and the most desirable company in the world.

Q. 29. But what will you think of them when you see them few and despised?

A. I resolve through grace to join Christ's little flock, his praying, and sin-hating flock, though they be few in number; desire to love them above all others, and to accept them as my fellow travelers to the heavenly Zion, and that notwithstanding their being despised or reproached by the world.

Q. 30. But what do you think of the cross, and of sharp persecution, that sometimes accompany the confessing of Christ?

A. I desire to take Christ with his cross, as well as with his crown; and to welcome the world's hatred, reproaches, injuries, or any kind of trouble or persecution I may meet with for confessing Christ, his truth, and ways.

Q. 31. What think ye of the holy scriptures?

A. I believe they are inspired by God's Holy Spirit, I value them above all books, I accept them thankfully as a guide through the wilderness, a light to my feet, and a lamp to my paths, and a treasure of comforts and cordials suitable for me in all cases and difficulties, which I desire always to search into and study to be acquainted with.

Q. 32. What do you think of the Lord's Day?

A. I regard it as holy and honorable; and as a standing testimony of the perfection of Christ's sacrifice; I look upon it as the best day of the week, as being Christ's weekly market day, for needy souls, which I resolve to improve carefully for getting provision for my soul through the rest of the week.

Q. 33. What do you think of gospel ordinances?

A. I look upon the word, sacraments, prayer, and praise, to be God's institutions, and means of conveying grace to souls. I thankfully accept them, as needful helps in the way to heaven, and as meeting places between God and my soul; and I desire to make it my main errand in attending them to meet with him therein.

Q. 34. What do you think of the Lord's Supper that you have in view?

A. I look upon it as Christ's banqueting house, and spiritual feast, which in his love he hath provided for refreshing and strengthening his people's souls, while traveling through this wilderness: desire to bless God for it, and to accept it as a rare privilege, a quickener of grace, a memorial of redeeming love, and a pledge of Christ's second coming.

Q. 35. What do you think of the duty of prayer?

A. I look upon it not only as my great duty, but also as an honorable privilege, seeing hereby I have access to converse with God; and therefore I resolve, through grace, to live a life of prayer and acquaintance with God, in and through Christ, all my days, and that I will always go to God and consult with him in all cases and difficulties.

Q. 36. What do you think of the rest of the duties of Christianity, and of all these which the moral law enjoins?

A. I look upon the law (which Christ hath adopted into the covenant of grace, as a rule of life to his people) to be holy, just, and good; and the duties enjoined by it to be most reasonable, calculated for the glory of God and his people's good. The gospel, which is the doctrine of grace, doth strongly enforce this law, by teaching us sobriety with respect to ourselves, righteousness with respect to our neighbor, and godliness with respect to God; and the love of Christ doth mightily constrain us to the diligent performance of all these moral duties.

Q. 37. What do you think of the rods and afflictions which attend the children of God?

A. I believe they are fatherly chastisements for our good; and that they are wisely and seasonably ordered by him, who hedges up his people's way with thorns, that they may not find their crooked paths, and therefore I desire to submit to the rod, as the needful discipline of Christ's house, and to welcome his convictions and reproofs, as well as his comforts and smiles; and to bless him for afflictions as well as for mercies.

Q. 38. What do you think of the life of faith?

A. I believe it to be the most happy life, and that it ought to be the daily life of God's people while in this world. And I desire to study and learn this noble life of faith, and of dependence upon the Son of God, and to make daily use of his blood and righteousness to cover my guilt, and of his grace and strength to enable me to perform duty, conquer sin, resist temptation, and bear affliction.

Q. 39. What do you think of the spiritual warfare which Christ calls you to?

A. I look upon that war as just and honorable; and therefore do come in a volunteer at the sound of the gospel trumpet, to enlist myself a soldier under Christ's banner, I do forever abandon the devil's camp, and am willing to swear allegiance to Christ Jesus, to take up arms for him, and to fight against his enemies, the world, the devil, and the flesh, all the days of my life. I resolve never to make peace with these enemies, nor agree to a cessation of arms. I will never wittingly nor willingly reset, nor give harbor to, the bosom traitors of indwelling lusts and corruptions; but under the conduct of my glorious Captain, and in his strength, I will carry on the war, till I attain to that complete victory which is promised to all believers in Christ.

Q. 40. What do you think of these who are deserters and runaways from Christ's standard?

A. I look upon them as guilty of the greatest madness, and exposed to the greatest wrath, seeing Christ's soul can take no pleasure in these who draw back from him; and therefore I purpose, through grace, to keep close by my Captain, and to adhere to his cause and interest all the days of my life.

Q. 41. In whose strength is it that you engage to all these parts and articles of the covenant?

A. Only in the strength of Jesus Christ my Head and Surety, who hath undertaken for me, and promised to make his grace forthcoming to me. Wherefore I altogether distrust my own strength and resolution, and betake myself to borrowed strength. I resolve never to trust in my promise to Christ, but in Christ's promise to me, that he will never leave me, nor forsake me.

Q. 42. Will you satisfy yourself with a public profession and engaging to these things before men?

A. No; I will, through grace, profess and declare all these things also in secret before God. And I will give my consent to all the parts and articles of God's covenant of grace, in the most serious and self-denied manner: and I will, by grace, bind and engage myself to them, by entering into secret transaction, or personal covenant with God, through Christ, before I come to take the seal of God's covenant. And afterwards I will adventure, in his strength, to approach to his holy table, to ratify and seal this bargain before men and angels.

John Willison (1680-1750)
Minister at Dundee, Scotland, was a prominent voice against the spiritual laxity of the mid-eighteenth-century Church of Scotland.

Lord's Supper ineffective by itself
We do not become good just by eating. What causes our deprivation is wickedness and sin; what causes our abundance is righteousness and doing good deeds.
Origen

Lord's Supper to be received worthily
If you have received worthily, you are what you have received.
Augustine of Hippo

We call this food the thanksgiving [Eucharist], and the only people allowed to receive it are those who believe our teaching and have received the washing for the remission of sins and for regeneration; and who live according to the commands of Christ.
Justin Martyr

Loss
He loseth nothing that loseth not God.
George Herbert

Nothing is really lost by a life of sacrifice; everything is lost by failure to obey God's call.
Henry P. Liddon

In the arithmetic of love, one plus one equals everything, and two minus one equals nothing.
Mignon McLaughlin

Life's greatest tragedy is to lose God and not to miss him.
F.W. Norwood

Lost souls
There is no one so far lost that Jesus cannot find him and cannot save him.
Andrew Murray

Lots
The lot is cast into the lap; but the whole disposing thereof is of the LORD.
The Bible, Proverbs 16:33 KJV

Love
See also: God's love

Better is a dinner of herbs where love is, than a stalled ox and hatred therewith.
The Bible, Proverbs 15:17 KJV

Love is strong as death; jealousy is cruel as the grave.
The Song of Solomon 8:6 KJV

Many waters cannot quench love; rivers cannot wash it away.
The Bible, Song of Songs 8:7

Love must be sincere.
The Bible, Romans 12:9

Owe no man any thing, but to love one another.
The Bible, Romans 13:8 KJV

Love is the fulfilling of the law.
The Bible, Romans 13:10 KJV

Follow the way of love.
The Bible, 1 Corinthians 14:1

And over all these virtues put on love, which binds them all together in perfect unity.
The Bible, Colossians 3:14

Labor of love.
The Bible, 1 Thessalonians 1:3 KJV

May the Lord make your love increase and overflow for each other and for everyone else, just as ours does for you.
The Bible, 1 Thessalonians 3:12

The goal of this command is love, which comes from a pure heart and a good conscience and a sincere faith.
The Bible, 1 Timothy 1:5

Charity shall cover the multitude of sins.
The Bible, 1 Peter 4:8 KJV

Love means having to say you're sorry every five minutes.
Author unknown

Love is the doorway through which the human soul passes from selfishness to service and from solitude to kinship with all mankind.
Author unknown

Love is the only service that power cannot command and money cannot buy.
Author unknown

Love always seeks to help, never to hurt.
Author unknown

You aren't loved because you're valuable. You're valuable because God loves you.
Author unknown

Love is not blind, it sees more not less; But because it sees more it chooses to see less.
Author unknown

If there is anything better than to be loved, it is loving.
Author unknown

God's love is unconditional. Be sure that yours is too!
Author unknown

You can't treat love like something you buy.
Author unknown

Love means loving the unlovable – or it is no virtue at all.
Author unknown

Love is like a rose. It's all good-smelling, but if you hold it too tight, it can stab you, make you bleed, and scar you for life.
Alfonso Aguila

In real love you want the other person's good. In romantic love you want the other person.
Margaret Anderson

Increase my capacity for love and decrease my impulses to throw stones, actual or mental.
George Appleton

To love is to will the good of another.
Thomas Aquinas

Love is the fulfilment of all our works.
There is the goal; that is why we run: we
run toward it, and once we reach it, in it
we shall find rest.
Augustine of Hippo

Love, and do what you will.
Augustine of Hippo

To my God a heart of flame;
To my fellow man a heart of love;
To myself a heart of steel.
Augustine of Hippo

People are renewed by love. As sinful
desire ages them, so love rejuvenates
them.
Augustine of Hippo

The single desire that dominated my
search for delight was simply to love and to
be loved.
Augustine of Hippo

Love is the beauty of the soul.
Augustine of Hippo

He loves Thee too little, who loves
anything together with Thee, which he
loves not for Thy sake
Augustine of Hippo

It is impossible to love and be wise.
Francis Bacon

The desire of power in excess caused the
angels to fall; the desire of knowledge in
excess caused man to fall; but in charity
there is no excess, neither can angel or man
come in danger by it.
Francis Bacon

Love takes off masks that we fear we
cannot live without and now we cannot
live within.
James Baldwin

We are able to love others only when we

love ourselves.
Brent A. Barlow

If they can see you love them, you can say
anything to them.
Richard Baxter

I had everything, from flights on Concord
to the best hotels. Everything but love.
And I was very lonely.
Boris Becker

He alone loves the Creator perfectly who
manifests a pure love for his neighbor.
Venerable Bede

First learn to love yourself, then you can
love me.
Bernard of Clairvaux

Love transcends all that human Sense and
Reason can reach to.
Jacob Boehme

Know this: though love is weak and hate is
strong, yet hate is short, and love is very
long.
Kenneth Boulding

In labors of love, every day is payday.
Gaines Brewster

He who lives up to a little love shall have
more love.
Thomas Brooks

Whoever loves true life, will love true love.
Elizabeth Barrett Browning

Take away love and earth is a tomb.
Robert Browning

What's earth with all its art, verse, music,
worth compared with love, found, gained
and kept?
Robert Browning

Love does not die easily. It is a living thing.
It thrives in the face of all life's hazards,
save one – neglect.
James D. Bryden

It is astonishing how little one feels poverty when one loves.
John Bulwer

Love is always open arms. With arms open you allow love to come and go as it will, freely, for it'll do so anyway. If you close your arms about love, you'll find you are left only holding yourself.
Leo Buscaglia

Sometimes it's a form of love just to talk to somebody that you have nothing in common with and still be fascinated by their presence.
David Byrne

We were born to love, we live to love, and we will die to love still more.
Joseph Cafasso

Whatever a person maybe like, we must still love them because we love God.
John Calvin

If I put my own good name before the other's highest good, then I know nothing of Calvary love.
Amy Carmichael

Anything will give up its secrets if you love it enough. Not only have I found that when I talk to the little flower or to the little peanut they will give up their secrets, but I have found that when I silently commune with people they give up their secrets also – if you love them enough.
George Washington Carver

If thou wish to reach the perfection of love, it befits thee to set thy life in order.
Catherine of Siena

For I created your soul with a capacity for loving – so much so that you cannot live without love. Indeed, love is your food.
Catherine of Siena, God speaking to Catherine in a vision

Love is nature's second son.
George Chapman

Love is blind.
Geoffrey Chaucer

Love is not blind; that is the last thing it is. Love is bound; and the more it is bound the less it is blind.
G.K. Chesterton

The way to love anything is to realize that it might be lost.
G.K. Chesterton

The message that "love" will solve all of our problems is repeated incessantly in contemporary culture – like a philosophical tom tom. It would be closer to the truth to say that love is a contagious and virulent disease which leaves a victim in a state of near imbecility, paralysis, profound melancholia, and sometimes culminates in death.
Quentin Crisp

My very soul was flooded with celestial light. For the first time I realized that I had been trying to hold the world in one hand and the Lord in the other.
Frances Crosby

Real love is a force more formidable than any other. It is invisible – it cannot be seen or measured, yet it is powerful enough to transform you in a moment, and offer you more joy than any material possession could.
Barbara DeAngelis

A loving heart is the truest wisdom.
Charles Dickens

How do you know when love is gone ? If you said that you would be there at seven and you get there by nine, and he or she has not called the police yet, it's gone.
Marlene Dietrich

We are all born for love. It is the principle of existence, and its only end.
Benjamin Disraeli

Love, all alike, no season knows, nor clime, Nor hours, days, months, which are the

rags of time.
John Donne

You will find, as you look back upon your life, that the moments when you really lived are the moments when you have done things in the spirit of love.
Henry Drummond

Love is not a thing of enthusiastic emotion. It is a rich, strong, manly, vigorous expression of the whole round Christian character – the Christ-like nature in its fullest development. And the constituents of this great character are only to be built up by ceaseless practice.
Henry Drummond

The pain associated with emotional trials and worries can almost always be lessened by a little love.
Chris Edmunds

I have found it impossible to carry the heavy burden of responsibility and to discharge my duties as king as I would wish to do without the help of the woman I love.
Edward, Duke of Windsor

And at the end of the world, when the church of Christ shall be settled in its last, and most complete, and its eternal state, and all common gifts, such as convictions and illuminations, and all miraculous gifts, shall be eternally at an end, yet then divine love shall not fail, but shall be brought to its most glorious perfection in every individual member of the ransomed church above. Then, in every heart, that love which now seems as but a spark, shall be kindled to a bright and glowing flame, and every ransomed soul shall be as it were in a blaze of divine and holy love, and shall remain and grow in this glorious perfection and blessedness through all eternity!
Jonathan Edwards

But it is doubtless true, and evident from these Scriptures, that the essence of all true religion lies in holy love; and that in this divine affection, and an habitual disposition to it, and that light which is the foundation of it, and those things which are the fruits of it, consists the whole of religion.
Jonathan Edwards

Love is the sum of all virtue, and love disposes us to do good.
Jonathan Edwards

Gravitation can not be held responsible for people falling in love.
Albert Einstein

The greatest gift is a portion of thyself.
Ralph Waldo Emerson

Love is all we have, the only way that each can help the other.
Euripides

The history of the world suggests that without love of God there is little likelihood of a love for man that does not become corrupt.
Francois Fénelon

Ecstasy cannot last, but it can carve a channel for something lasting.
E.M. Forster

We cannot help conforming ourselves to what we love.
Francis of Sales

You learn to love by loving.
Francis of Sales

There are many who want me to tell them of secret ways of becoming perfect and I can only tell them that the sole secret is a hearty love of God, and the only way of attaining that love is by loving. You learn to speak by speaking, to study by studying, to run by running, to work by working; and just so you learn to love God and man by loving. Begin as a mere apprentice and the very power of love will lead you on to become a master of the art.
Francis of Sales

Immature love says: "I love you because I need you." Mature love says "I need you because I love you."
Erich Fromm

Love is an act of faith, and whoever is of little faith is also of little love.
Erich Fromm

Nature teaches us to love our friends, but religion our enemies.
Thomas Fuller

It's an extra dividend when you like the girl you're in love with.
Clarke Gable

Love never claims, it ever gives; love never suffers, never resents, never revenges itself. Where there is love there is life; hatred leads to destruction.
Mahatma Gandhi

We look forward to the time when the power to love will replace the love of power. Then will our world know the blessings of peace.
William Gladstone

To be loved for what one is, is the greatest exception. The great majority love in others only what they lend him, their own selves, their version of him.
Goethe

Treat a man as he is and he will remain as he is. Treat a man as he can and should be and he will become as he can and should be.
Johann Wolfgang von Goethe

Love has power to give in a moment what toil can scarcely reach in an age.
Johann Wolfgang Von Goethe

Love does not dominate; it cultivates.
Johann Wolfgang von Goethe

Love, love, love – all the wretched cant of it, masking egotism, lust, masochism, fantasy under a mythology of sentimental postures.
Germaine Greer

Love's finest speech is without words.
Hadewijch of Brabant

Whoever loves, allows themselves willingly to be corrected, without seeking excuses, in order to be freer in love.
Hadewijch of Brabant

Oh, you who are trying to learn the marvel of Love through the copy book of Reason, I'm very much afraid you will never really see the point.
Hafiz of Shiraz

Love understands love; it needs no talk.
Frances Ridley Havergal

Love is a condition in which the happiness of another person is essential to your own.
Robert Heinlein

The test of love is in how one relates not to saints and scholars but to rascals.
Abraham Joshua Heschel

If I know what love is, it is because of you.
Herman Hesse

The most precious possession that ever comes to a man in this world is a woman's heart.
Josiah G. Holland

Love of man necessarily arises out of love of God.
John Hooper

To love another person is to see the face of God.
Victor Hugo

The greatest happiness of life is the conviction that we are loved – loved for ourselves, or rather, loved in spite of ourselves.
Victor Hugo

Love knows nothing of order.
Jerome

Just as water extinguishes a fire, so love

wipes away sin.
John of the Cross

When evening comes, you will be examined in love. Learn to love as God desires to be loved and abandon your own ways of acting.
John of the Cross

The soul that walks in love neither tires others nor grows tired.
John of the Cross

Love doesn't make the world go round. Love is what makes the ride worthwhile.
Franklin P. Jones

I remember the morning that I first asked the meaning of the word "love …" Miss Sullivan put her arm gently round me and spelled into my hand, "I love Helen." "What is love?" I asked …
"Love is something like the clouds that were in the sky before the sun came out," she replied … "You cannot touch the clouds, you know; but you feel the rain and know how glad the flowers and the thirsty earth are to have it after a hot day. You cannot touch love either; but you feel the sweetness that it pours into everything. Without love you would not be happy or want to play."
The beautiful truth burst upon my mind – I felt that these were invisible lines stretched between my spirit and the spirits of others.
Helen Keller

To love another person is to help them love God.
Søren Kierkegaard

Agape (love) means understanding, redeeming good will for all persons. It is an overflowing love which is purely spontaneous, unmotivated, groundless, and creative. It is not set in motion by any quality or function of its object. It is the love of God operating in the human heart.
Martin Luther King, Jr

Love is the only force capable of transforming an enemy into a friend.
Martin Luther King, Jr

Man while he loves is never quite depraved.
Charles Lamb

There are few people who would not be ashamed of being loved when they love no longer.
Francis, Duc de La Rochefoucauld

Love is infallible; it has no errors, for all errors are the want of love.
William Law

Those that go searching for love only make manifest their own lovelessness, and the loveless never find love, only the loving find love, and they never have to seek for it.
D.H. Lawrence

Romantic love is mental illness. But it's a pleasurable one. It's a drug. It distorts reality, and that's the point of it. It would be impossible to fall in love with someone that you really saw.
Fran Lebowitz

Love doesn't just sit there like a stone, it has to be made, like bread; remade all the time, made new.
Ursula K. LeGuin

To love is to be vulnerable.
C.S. Lewis

A perfect man would never act from a sense of duty… Duty is only a substitute for love, like a crutch which is a substitute for a leg. Most of us need the crutch at times; but of course it is idiotic to use the crutch when our own legs can do the journey on their own.
C.S. Lewis

When I have learnt to love God better than my earthly dearest, I shall love my earthly dearest better than I do now.
C.S. Lewis

Love is something more stern and splendid than mere kindness.
C.S. Lewis

Love gives itself; it is not bought.
Henry Wadsworth Longfellow

If the man and woman walk off into the sunset hand-in-hand in the last reel, it adds $10 million to the box office.
George Lucas, advice to Steven Spielberg

Love is the only fire that is hot enough to melt the iron obstinacy of a creature's will.
Alexander MacLaren

What power can poverty have over a home where loving hearts are beating with a consciousness of untold riches of the head and heart?
Orison Swett Marden

No one perfectly loves God who does not perfectly love some of his creatures.
Marguerite de Valois

Love that seeks to do men good is cowardice when it refuses to prevent them from doing wrong.
Shailer Matthews

If love is the soul of Christian existence, it must be at the heart of every other Christian virtue. Thus, for example, justice without love is legalism; faith without love is ideology; hope without love is self-centeredness; forgiveness without love is self-abasement; fortitude without love is recklessness; generosity without love is extravagance; care without love is mere duty; fidelity without love is servitude. Every virtue is an expression of love. No virtue is really a virtue unless it is permeated, or informed, by love.
Richard P. McBrien

It is by loving and by being loved that one can come nearest to the soul of another.
George McDonald

Just as bitterness produces more bitterness in others, so love begets love.
Alan Loy McGinnis

In the arithmetic of love, one plus one equals everything, and two minus one equals nothing.
Mignon McLaughlin

Joy is love exalted; peace is love in repose; long-suffering is love enduring; gentleness is love in society; goodness is love in action; faith is love on the battlefield; meekness is love in school; and temperance is love in training.
D.L. Moody

Age does not protect you from love. But love, to some extent, protects you from age.
Jeanne Moreau

Nothing we do, however virtuous, can be accomplished alone; therefore we are saved by love.
Reinhold Niebuhr

The significance of the law of love is precisely that it is not just another law, but a law which transcends all law.
Reinhold Niebuhr

The perfectionist ethic of Jesus demands that love be poured forth whether or not we suffer from injustice.
Reinhold Niebuhr

If you want to be loved, be loveable.
Ovid

You'll discover that real love is millions of miles past falling in love with anyone or anything.
Sara Paddison

When you love someone you love him as he is.
Charles Péguy

Do not try to go to God alone. If you do, he will certainly ask you an embarrassing

question: "Where are your brothers and sisters?"
Charles Péguy

Love is bold, respect is timid.
A. Perez

Those who love deeply never grow old; they may die of old age, but they die young.
Sir Arthur Wing Pinero

Love cannot be equated with sacrificial action! It cannot be equated with any action!
John Piper

How vast a memory has love!
Alexander Pope

He who has no charity, deserves no mercy.
English proverb

Love teaches even asses to dance.
French proverb

Charity sees the need, not the cause.
German proverb

He who loves, trusts.
Italian proverb

Love me when I least deserve it, because that's when I really need it.
Swedish proverb

Only love enables humanity to grow, because love engenders life and it is the only form of energy that lasts forever.
Michel Quoist

This is the miracle that happens every time to those who really love; the more they give, the more they possess.
Rainer Maria Rilke

Love came down at Christmas,
Love all lovely, Love divine;
Love was born at Christmas;
Star and angels gave the sign.

Worship we the Godhead,
Love incarnate, love divine;

Worship we our Jesus:
But wherewith for sacred sign.

Love shall be our token;
Love be yours and love be mine;
Love to God and all men,
Love for plea and gift and sign.
Christina Rossetti

She sat and wept, and with her untressed hair
She wiped the feet she was blest to touch;
And He wiped off the soiling despair
From her sweet soul – because she loved so much.
Dante Gabriel Rossetti

The root of the matter, if we want a stable world, is a very simple and old-fashioned thing, a thing so simple that I am almost ashamed to mention it for fear of the derisive smile with which wise cynics will greet my words. The thing I mean is love, Christian love, or compassion. If you feel this, you have a motive for existence, a reason for courage, an imperative necessity for intellectual honesty.
Bertrand Russell

I think it is possible on earth to build a young, new Jerusalem, a little, new heaven of this surpassing love. God, either send me more of this love, or take me quickly over the water, where I may be filled with his love.
Samuel Rutherford

Love does not consist in gazing at each other, but in looking outward together in the same direction.
Antoine de Saint-Exupéry
Only through love can we attain communion with God.
Albert Schweitzer

True love's the gift which God has given
To man alone beneath the heaven.
Walter Scott

Love is not love
Which alters when it alteration finds.
William Shakespeare, Sonnets

Doubt thou the stars are fire;
Doubt that the sun doth move;
Doubt truth to be a liar;
But never doubt I love.
William Shakespeare, Hamlet

The course of true love never did run
smooth.
*William Shakespeare, The Merry Wives of
Windsor*

Love sought is good, but given unsought is
better.
William Shakespeare, Twelfth Night

Love is the only weapon we need.
H.R.L. Sheppard

They love indeed who quake to say they
love.
Philip Sidney

Alas, oh, love is dead! How could it perish
thus? No one has cared for it: It simply
died of frost.
Angelus Silesius

One word frees us of all the weight and
pain in life.
That word is love.
Sophocles

Not where I breathe, but where I love, I live.
Robert Southwell

So let us love, dear Love, like as we ought;
Love is the lesson which the Lord us
taught.
Edmund Spenser

Go measure the heavens with your span;
go weigh the mountains in the scales;
go take the ocean's water and calculate each
   drop;
go count the sand upon the sea's wide
   shore;
and when you have accomplished all of
   this,
then you can tell how much He loves you!
He has loved you long!
He has loved you well!

He will love you forever!
C.H. Spurgeon

Love: that's self-love á deux.
Madame de Stael

Love is the greatest thing that God can
give us for Himself is love: and it is the
greatest thing we can give to God.
Jeremy Taylor

Love is the most universal, the most
tremendous, and the most mysterious of
the cosmic forces.
Pierre Teilhard de Chardin

The day will come when, after harnessing
space, the winds, the tides, and gravitation,
we shall harness for God the energies of
love. And on that day, for the second time
in the history of the world, we shall have
discovered fire.
Pierre Teilhard de Chardin

The future of the thinking world is
organically bound up with the turning of
forces of hate into forces of charity.
Teilhard de Chardin

Love of God is the root, love of our
neighbor the fruit of the Tree of Life.
Neither can exist without the other, but
the one is cause and the other effect.
William Temple

Charity begins at home.
Andria Terence

Accustom yourself continually to make
many ats of love, for they enkindle and
melt the soul.
Teresa of Avila

Spread love everywhere you go: First of all
in your own house ... let no one ever come
to you without leaving better and happier.
Be the living expression of God's kindness;
kindness in your face, kindness in your
eyes, kindness in your smile, kindness in
your warm greeting.
Mother Teresa

Jesus said love one another. He didn't say love the whole world.
Mother Teresa

We can do no great things; only small things with great love.
Mother Teresa

The hunger for love is much more difficult to remove than the hunger for bread.
Mother Teresa

If you judge people, you have no time to love them.
Mother Teresa

It is our care for the helpless, our practice of loving kindness, that brands us in the eyes of many of our opponents. "Look!" they say. "How they love one another! Look how they are prepared to die for one another."
Tertullian

It is best to love wisely, no doubt; but to love foolishly is better than not to be able to love at all.
William Makepeace Thackeray

Nothing is sweeter than Love, nothing stronger, nothing higher, nothing wider, nothing more pleasant, nothing fuller nor better in heaven and earth.
Thomas à Kempis

He does much who loves much.
Thomas à Kempis

Love is swift, sincere, pious, joyful, generous, strong, patient, faithful, prudent, long-suffering, courageous, and never seeking its own; for wheresoever a person seeketh his own, there he falleth from love.
Thomas à Kempis

Love feels no burden, thinks nothing of trouble, attempts what is above its strength, pleads no excuse of impossibility; for it thinks all things lawful for itself, and all things possible.
Thomas à Kempis

There is no love which does not become help.
Paul Tillich

Love is life. All, everything that I understand, I understand only because I love.
Leo Tolstoy

Love can forbear, and love can forgive, but love can never be reconciled to an unlovely object. He can never therefore be reconciled to your sin, because sin itself is incapable of being altered; but He may be reconciled to your person, because that may be restored.
Thomas Traherne

To love someone deeply gives you strength. Being loved by someone deeply gives you courage.
Lao Tzu

Love is an act of endless forgiveness, a tender look which becomes a habit.
Peter Ustinov

It is only by feeling your love that the poor will forgive you for the gifts of bread.
St Vincent de Paul

Love is a canvas furnished by Nature and embroidered by imagination.
Voltaire

The most wonderful of all things in life, I believe, is the discovery of another human being with whom one's relationship has a glowing depth, beauty and joy as the years increase. This inner progressiveness of love between two human beings is a most marvelous thing, it cannot be found by looking for it or by passionately wishing for it. It is a sort of Divine accident.
Sir Hugh Walpole

It is possible to love your friends, your competitors, and even your enemies. It is hard, bitterly hard, but there is a long distance between hard and impossible.
Herbert Welch

Love, Christian

If I speak in the tongues of men and of angels, but have not love, I am only a resounding gong or a clanging cymbal.
If I have the gift of prophecy and can fathom all mysteries and all knowledge, and if I have a faith that can move mountains, but have not love, I am nothing.
If I give all I possess to the poor and surrender my body to the flames, but have not love, I gain nothing.
Love is patient, love is kind. It does not envy, it does not boast, it is not proud.
It is not rude, it is not self-seeking, it is not easily angered, it keeps no record of wrongs.
Love does not delight in evil but rejoices with the truth.
It always protects, always trusts, always hopes, always perseveres.
Love never fails. But where there are prophecies, they will cease; where there are tongues, they will be stilled; where there is knowledge, it will pass away.
For we know in part and we prophesy in part, but when perfection comes, the imperfect disappears.
When I was a child, I talked like a child, I thought like a child, I reasoned like a child. When I became a man, I put childish ways behind me.
Now we see but a poor reflection as in a mirror; then we shall see face to face. Now I know in part; then I shall know fully, even as I am fully known.
And now these three remain: faith, hope and love. But the greatest of these is love.
The Bible, 1 Corinthians 13

The four degrees of the Christian's love.
1. Man loves himself for his own sake.
2. Man loves God but for his own advantage.
3. Man loves God for God's sake.
4. Man loves himself for the sake of God.
Bernard of Clairvaux

You will find all that is lacking in your heart in the heart of Jesus, dying on the cross. Then you will be enabled to love those whom you would naturally, in your pride, hate and crush.
F. Fénelon

Love is superior to all extraordinary gifts. It is better than the gift of tongues; than the gifts of prophecy and knowledge; and than the gift of miracles. All outward works of charity without it are worthless. Love has this superiority, first, because of its inherent excellence; and secondly, because of its perpetuity.
Charles Hodge

Since disciples of Jesus are to be known by the love they have to one another (John 13:35), we will cherish Christian love as of prime importance.
Moravian Covenant for Christian living

Love, Consistency of

Love will teach us all things: but we must learn how to win love; it is got with difficulty: it is a possession dearly bought with much labor and in long time; for one must love not sometimes only, for a passing moment, but always. There is no man who does not sometimes love: even the wicked do that.
Fyodor Dostoevsky

Love, Genuine

The Church of God needs to remember that fellowship with God necessitates separation from all who fail to fulfill the responsibilities of fellowship in light. We are not only to yield to love; we are to guard its holiness. It is possible to be led astray from the activity of true love by yielding to a false charity. At the very center of love is light. That is not true love which sacrifices doctrine and principle. God has never acted in love at the expense of light.
W. Graham Scroggie

Love, Lack of

All this famine of love, how it saddens my soul. There is not a drop of love anywhere.
Tayohiko Kagawa

Love, Learning

Love is a great teacher.
Augustine of Hippo

I loved not yet … I sought what I might love, in love with loving.
Augustine of Hippo

They who will learn love, will always be its scholars.
Byron

Love, Platonic
Platonic love is a delusion; it does not exist in nature.
Ninon de Lenclos

Love, Purity of
An instant of pure love is more precious to God and the soul, and more profitable to the church, than all other good works together, though it may seem as if nothing were done.
John of the Cross

Love one another in truth and purity, as children, impulsively, uncalculatingly.
Edward Wilson

Love, Response to
Alexander, Caesar, Charlemagne and I founded empires; but upon what did we rest the creations of our genius? Upon force. Jesus Christ alone founded his empire upon love; and at this hour millions of men would die for him.
Napoleon

We are too ready to retaliate rather than to forgive or to gain by love and information. Let us, then, try what love will do: for if men do once see we love them, we should find they would not harm us.
William Penn

Love begets love.
Latin proverb

Love, Sexual
Heaven has no rage like love to hatred turned,
Nor hell a fury like a woman scorned.
William Congreve

All mankind loves a lover.
Ralph Waldo Emerson

She who has never loved has never lived.
John Gay

There is not stronger tie upon a woman than the knowledge that she is loved.
Mme de Motteville

Love is the selfishness of two.
De la Salle

Love, Types of
Charity means love. It is called Agape in the New Testament to distinguish it from Eros (sexual love), Storge (family affection) and Philia (friendship). So there are four kinds of love, all good in their proper place, but Agape is the best because it is the kind of love God has for us and is good in all circumstances.
C.S. Lewis

Love and action
True affection is ingeniously inventive.
F. Fénelon

He that hath love in his breast hath spurs in his side.
George Herbert

Our Lord does not care so much for the importance of our works as for the love with which they are done.
Teresa of Avila

God regards with how much love a person performs a work, rather than how much he does.
Thomas à Kempis

Love and death
Love is strong as death; but nothing else is as strong as either; and both, love and death, meet in Christ. How strong and powerful upon you, then, should that instruction be, that comes to you from both these, the love and death of Jesus Christ!
John Donne

Love and faith

Love is an act of faith, and whoever is of little faith is also of little love.
Erich Fromm

Love and fear

There is no fear in love; but perfect love casteth out fear.
The Bible, 1 John 4:18 KJV

Those who love to be feared, fear to be loved; they themselves are of all people the most abject; some fear them, but they fear everyone.
Francis of Sales

True love can fear no one.
Seneca

Love and God's nature

He who is filled with love is filled with God himself.
Augustine of Hippo

Human love is a reflection of something in the divine nature itself.
A.E. Brooke

Love and hate

What you love and what you hate reveal what you are.
Dr Bob Jones Sr

Love must be learned again and again… Hate needs no instruction, but waits only to be provoked.
Katherine Anne Porter

Love and humility

Love seeks not to possess, but to be possessed.
R.H. Benson

Love and knowledge

Human things must be known to be loved: but divine things must be loved to be known.
Blaise Pascal

Beware you are not swallowed up in books! An ounce of love is worth a pound of knowledge.
John Wesley

Love and lust

The desire of love is to give. The desire of lust is to get.
Author unknown

Love and prayer

Love is kindled in a flame, and ardency is its life. Flame is the air which true Christian experience breathes. It feeds on fire; it can withstand anything rather than a feeble flame; but when the surrounding atmosphere is frigid or lukewarm, it dies, chilled and starved to its vitals. True prayer must be aflame.
E.M. Bounds

It is not a matter of thinking a great deal but of loving a great deal, so do whatever arouses you most to love.
Teresa of Avila

Love and self

Love seeketh not itself to please
Nor for itself hath any care.
But for another gives its ease
And builds a heaven in hell's despair.
William Blake

Love and suffering

The one who will be found in trial capable of great acts of love, is ever the one who is doing considerate small ones.
F.W. Robertson

Love for Christ

Thomas Doolittle

Love is the everlasting grace that will continue in use and increase, even when other graces will have ceased. Some graces are particularly suited to our present state of imperfection in this world. At the present time, we live by faith, repent and mourn for sin, live in hope of the glory which will be revealed, and wait until we possess the mansions above. We patiently wait for all the good that is promised to us, but not yet conferred upon us. However, in the future faith will be turned into sight, hope into enjoyment, desires into gratification, and waiting into possession. When this happens, we will believe no more, hope no more, desire no more, and wait no more. But even then we will continue in love– indeed, we will love more than ever, more abundantly, perfectly, and continually, without pause or alteration. We will love eternally. One reason why love is considered the greatest of the three Christian virtues, is that it will last the longest. "And now abide faith, hope, love, these three; but the greatest of these is love." 1 Cor 13:13.

So it is that those who love Christ sincerely here, will love him perfectly hereafter, and be forever blessed in that love. But those who do not love him in this world, cannot love him in the next. For the lack of such love, they shall be accursed forever.

Love shows the true character of a man, according to the object which he loves more than anything else: for as is the love, so is the man. According to his love, so might you confidently designate the man. If he is a lover of honor, he is an ambitious man; a lover of pleasure, a sensual man; and if he chiefly love the world, he is a covetous man. If a man loves righteousness, he is a religious man; if the things above, a heavenly-minded man; and if he love Christ with a pre-eminent love, he is a sincere man: "Rightly do they love you.," Song of Songs 1:4.

If Christ has our love, he has our all; and Christ never has what he deserves from us, till he has our love. True love withholds nothing from Christ, when it is sincerely set upon him. If we actually love him, he will have our time, and he will have our service, and he will have the use of all our resources, and gifts, and graces; indeed, then he shall have our possessions, freedom, and our very lives, whenever he calls for them. In the same way, when God loves any of us, he will withhold nothing from us that is good for us. He does not

hold back his own only begotten Son, Rom.8:32. When Christ loves us, he gives us everything we need– his merits to justify us, his Spirit to sanctify us, his grace to adorn us, and his glory to crown us. Therefore, when any of us love Christ sincerely, we lay everything down at his feet, and give up all to be at his command and service: "And they loved not their lives unto the death," Rev. 12:11.
Thomas Doolittle

Love for Christians
Be devoted to one another in brotherly love. Honor one another above yourselves.
The Bible, Romans 12:10

And let us consider one another; to provoke unto love and good works.
The Bible, Hebrews 10:24

Everyone who has been born of God must love those who have been similarly ennobled.
A.E. Brooke

The beloved John in his old age [see Jerome's commentary on Galatians 3:6] kept on saying to his disciples "Little children, love one another." They became so fed up with just hearing this that they eventually asked him why he kept on repeating the same thing: "Because it is the Lord's command and if it comes to pass, that suffices."
Philipp Jakob Spener

The love of God and the God of love constrain you to love one another that it may at last be said of Christians as it was at first, "Behold how they love one another."
Ralph Venning

Love for Christians

Andrew Murray
And let us consider one another. He that enters into the Holiest enters into the

home of eternal love; the air he breathes there is love; the highest blessing he can receive there is a heart in which the love of God is shed abroad in power by the Holy Ghost, and which is on the path to be made perfect in love. That thou mayest know how thou oughtest to behave thyself in the house of God – remember this, Faith and hope shall pass away but love abideth ever. The chief of these is love.

Let us consider one another. When first we seek the entrance into the Holiest, the thought is mostly of ourselves. And when we have entered in, in faith, it is as if it is all we can do to stand before God, and wait on Him for what He has promised to do for us. But it is not long before we perceive that the Holiest and the Lamb are not for us alone; that there are others within with whom it is blessed to have fellowship in praising God; that there are some without who need our help to be brought in. It is into the love of God that we have had access given us; that love enters our hearts; and we see ourselves called to live like Christ in entire devotion to those around us.

Let us consider one another. All the redeemed form one body. Each one is dependent on the other, each one is for the welfare of the other. Let us beware of the self-deception that thinks it possible to enter the Holiest, into the nearest intercourse with God, in the spirit of selfishness. It cannot be. The new and living way Jesus opened up is the way of self-sacrificing love. The entrance into the Holiest is given to us as priests, there to be filled with the Spirit and the love of Christ and to go out and bring God's blessing to others.

Let us consider one another. The same Spirit that said, Consider Christ Jesus – take time, and give attention to know Him well – says to us, Consider one another – take time, and give attention to know the needs of your brethren around you. How many are there whose circumstances are so unfavorable, whose knowledge is so limited, whose whole life is so hopeless. For them there is but one thing to be done; We that are strong ought to hear the infirmities of the weak, and not to please ourselves. Each one who begins to see what the blessedness is of a life in the full surrender to Christ, should offer himself to Christ, to be made His messenger to the feeble and the weary. Consider one another, to provoke unto love and good works. Love and good works: These are to be the aim of the Church in the exercise of its fellowship. Everything that can hinder love is to be sacrificed and set aside. Everything that can promote, and prove, and provoke others to, love is to be studied and performed. And with love good works too. The Church has been redeemed by Christ, to prove to the world what power He has to cleanse from sin, to conquer evil, to restore to holiness and to goodness. Let us consider one another, in every possible way, to provoke, to stir up, to help to love and good works.

The chief thought is this: Life in the Holiest must be a life of love. As earnest as the injunction, Let us draw nigh in fullness of faith, Let us hold fast the confession of our hope, is this, Let us consider one another to provoke unto love and good works. God is love. And all He has done for us in His Son, as revealed in this Epistle, is love. And Christ is love. And there can be no real access to God as a union with Him in His holy will, no real communion with Him, but in the Spirit of love. Our entering into the Holiest is mere imagination, if we do not yield ourselves to the love of God in Christ, to be filled and used for the welfare and joy of our fellow-men.

O Christian! study what love is. Study it in the word, in Christ, in God. As thou seest Him to be an ever-flowing fountain of all goodness, who has His very being and glory in this, that He lives in all that exists, and communicates to all His own blessedness and perfection as far as they are capable of it, thou wilt learn to acknowledge that he that loveth not hath not known God. And thou wilt learn, too, to admit more deeply and truly than ever before, that no effort of thy will can bring forth love; it must be given thee from above. This will become to thee one of the chief joys and beauties of the Holiest of All, that there thou canst wait on the God of love to fill thee with His love. God hath the power to shed abroad His love in our hearts, by the Holy Spirit given unto us. He has promised to give Christ so dwelling in our heart by faith, that we shall be rooted and grounded in love, and know and have in us something of a love that passeth knowledge. The very atmosphere of the Holiest is love. Just as I breathe in the air in which I live, so the soul that abides in the presence of God breathes the air of the upper world. The promise held out to us, and the hour of its fulfillment, will come, when the love of God will be perfected in us, and we are made perfect in love. Nowhere can this be but in the Holiest; but there most surely. Let us draw nigh in the fullness of faith, and consider one another. While we are only thinking of others to bring God's love to them, we shall find God thinking of us, and filling us with it.

What a difference it would make in the world if every believer were to give himself with his whole heart to live for his fellow-men! What a difference to his own life, as he yielded himself to God's saving love in its striving for souls! What a difference to all our Christian agencies, suffering for want of devoted, whole-hearted helpers! What a difference to our churches, as they rose to know what they have been gathered for! What a difference to thousands of lost ones, who would learn with wonder what love there is in God's children, what power and blessing in that love! Let us consider one another
Andrew Murray

Love for God

Choose to love the Lord your God and to obey him and to commit yourself to him, for he is your life.
The Bible, Deuteronomy 30:20 NLT

Love to God purifies and ennobles every taste and desire, intensifies every affection, and brightens every worthy pleasure.
Author unknown

For when love is pure, you consider yourself as worthless, see yourself as dead and as nothing, and present yourself to God as dead and putrid.
Anglea of Foligno

Late have I loved thee, O Beauty so ancient and so new ... For behold, thou wert within me and I outside.
Augustine of Hippo

Where there is love, there is a trinity: a lover, a beloved and a spring of love.
Augustine of Hippo

Suppose, brethren, a man should make a ring for his betrothed, and she should love the ring more wholeheartedly than the betrothed who made it for her? Certainly, let her love his gift: but, if she should say, "The ring is enough, I do not want to see his face again," what would we say of her? The pledge is given her by the betrothed just that, in his pledge, he himself may be loved. God, then, has given you all these things. Love Him who made them.
Augustine of Hippo

He loves too little, who loves anything together with Thee, which he loves not for Thy sake.
Augustine of Hippo

To love God entirely, the soul must be pure and strong, staying faithful to God in times of trouble, alert against dishonesty and fraud. In this way man will not just find the supreme good, he will himself become like the supreme good – because he will be transformed into the image of God.
Augustine of Hippo

The reason for loving God is God himself and how he should be loved is to love him without limit.
Bernard of Clairvaux

The way to the Love of God is Folly to the World, but is Wisdom to the

Children of God. Hence, whenever the World perceiveth this Holy Fire of Love in God's Children, it concludeth immediately that they are turned Fools, and are besides themselves. But to the Children of God, that which is despised of the World is the Greatest Treasure; yea, so great a Treasure it is, as no Life can express, nor Tongue so much as name what this enflaming, all-conquering Love of God is. It is brighter than the Sun; it is sweeter than any Thing that is called sweet; it is stronger than all Strength; it is more nutrimental than Food; more cheering to the Heart than Wine, and more pleasant than all the Joy and Pleasantness of this World.
Jacob Boehme

My brothers, the love of God is a hard love. It demands total self-surrender.
Albert Camus

Not by traveling, Lord,
men come to you,
but by the way of love.
Amy Carmichael

The reason why God's servants love creatures so much is that they see how much Christ loves them, and it is one of the properties of love to love what is loved by the person we love.
Catherine of Siena

Love him totally who gave himself totally for you love.
Claire of Assisi

The nearer we draw to God in our love for him, the more we are united together by love for our neighbor; and the greater our union with our neighbor, the greater is our union with God.
Dorotheus of Gaza

The more a true saint loves God with a truly gracious love, the more he desires to love Him, and the more miserable he is at his lack of love to Him.
Jonathan Edwards

The will to love God is the whole of religion.
F. Fénelon

True love rests in the depths of the heart.
F. Fénelon

There is no true love to God which is not habitually supreme.
Edward Griffin

Love cannot think any evil of God, nor endure to hear any speak evil of him, but it must take God's part.
William Gurnall

I love my God, but with no love of mine
For I have none to give;
I love Thee, Lord, but all that love is Thine,
For by Thy life I live.
I am as nothing, and rejoice to be
Emptied and lost and swallowed up in Thee.
Madame Guyon

To be one with love is an awesome calling and those who long for it should spare no effort.
Hadewijch

Love consists not in feeling great things but in having great detachment and in suffering for the Beloved.
John of the Cross

Who falls for love of God shall rise a star.
Ben Jonson

To approach God requires neither art nor science, but only a heart resolutely determined to apply itself to nothing but Him, or for His sake, and to love Him only.
Brother Lawrence

Our only business is to love and delight ourselves in God.
Brother Lawrence

A little courage helps more than much knowledge, a little human sympathy more than much courage, and the least tincture

of the love of God more than all.
C. S. Lewis

Every Christian would agree that a man's spiritual health is exactly proportional to his love for God.
C.S. Lewis

To love God is to hate oneself and to know nothing apart from God.
Martin Luther

To love God is the greatest of virtues; to be loved by God is the greatest of blessings.
Portuguese proverb

Let us make God the beginning and the end of our love, for he is the fountain from which all good things flow and into him alone they flow back. Let him therefore be the beginning of our love.
Richard Rolle

The commandment of God is, that we love Our Lord in all our heart, in all our soul, in all our thought. In all our heart; that is, in all our understanding without erring. In all our soul; that is, in all our will without gainsaying. In all our thought; that is, that we think on Him without forgetting. In this manner is very love and true, that is work of man's will. For love is a willful stirring of our thoughts unto God, so that it receive nothing that is against the love of Jesus Christ, and therewith that it be lasting in sweetness of devotion; and that is the perfection of this life.
Richard Rolle

That we ought to love Him we are never in doubt, but whether we do love Him, we may well begin to question. A deep yearning in our innermost being "to know Him more clearly, love Him more dearly and follow Him more nearly" is probably all to which we dare lay claim.
Helen Roseveare

Our work is the love of God.
Jan Van Ruysbroeck

As our love is the best thing we have, and none deserves it more than God, so let him have our love, yea, the strength of our love, that we may love him with all our souls, and with all our mind, and with all our strength.
Richard Sibbes

Our love for God is tested by whether we seek Him or His gifts.
Ralph Sockman

The devil does not understand real love and affection; but the child of God can tell the devil to his face that he loves God if he covers him with sores and sets him on the dunghill, and by God's good help he means to cling to God through troubles tenfold heavier than those he has had to bear, should they come upon him.
C.H. Spurgeon

If you knew the whole Bible by heart, and the sayings of all the philosophers, what good would it do you without the love of God, without grace?
Thomas à Kempis

All is vanity but to love God and serve Him.
Thomas à Kempis

It behooves the lover of Jesus to forsake all other love besides Him, for He will be loved alone, above all others. The love of creatures is deceptive and disappointing, but the love of Jesus is faithful and always abiding. He who clings to any creature must of necessity fail as the creature fails. But he who cleaves abidingly to Jesus shall be made firm in Him forever.
Thomas à Kempis

He who loves God with all his heart dreads neither death, torment, judgment, nor hell, for perfect love opens a sure passage to God.
Thomas à Kempis

Whom should we love, if not him who loved us, and gave himself for us? If the bliss even of angels and glorified souls, consists greatly in seeing, and praising, the

Son of God; surely, to love, to trust, and to celebrate the friend of sinners, must be a principal ingredient in the happiness of saints not yet made perfect.
Augustus Toplady

The Soul is shriveled up and buried in a grave that does not love.
Thomas Traherne

Love to God is armor of proof against error. For want of hearts full of love, men have heads full of error; unholy opinions are for want of holy affections.
Thomas Watson

Love for God

John Newton

It is a point I long to know,
Often it causes anxious thought,
"Do I love the Lord, or no?
Am I His, or am I not?"
If I love, why am I thus?
Why this dull and lifeless frame?
Hardly sure could they be worse,
Who have never heard His name.
Could my heart so hard remain?
Prayer a task and burden prove?
Every trifle give me pain,
If I knew a Savior's love?
When I turn my eyes within,
All is dark and vain and wild.
Filled with unbelief and sin,
Can a deem myself a child?
If I pray, or hear, or read,
Sin is mixed with all I do.
You that love the Lord indeed,
Tell me, is it thus with you?
Yet I mourn my stubborn will.
Find my sin a grief and thrall.
Should I grieve for what I feel,
If I did not love at all?
Could I joy His saints to meet,
And choose the way I once abhorred?
Find at times the promise sweet,
If I did not love the Lord?
Lord decide the doubtful case.

You who are Your people's Sun.
Shine upon Your work of grace,
If indeed it has begun.
Let me love You more and more.
If I love at all, I pray.
If I have not loved before,
Help me to begin today.
John Newton

Love for people

If physical objects give you pleasure, praise God for them and return love to their Maker.... If souls please you, they are being loved in God.
Augustine of Hippo

Love from God

Love suffering on Calvary is far greater than love alive with excitement on Mount Tabor.
F. Fénelon

The love of the Father is like a sudden rain shower that will pour forth when you least expect it, catching you up into wonder and praise.
Richard J. Foster

A soul enkindled with love is a gentle, meek, humble, and patient soul.
John of the Cross

Love: Christ's love

Robert Murray M'Cheyne

"For the love of Christ constraineth us; because we thus judge, that if one died for all, then were all dead" 2 Corinthians 5:14. Of all the features of St. Paul's character, untiring activity was the most striking. From his early history, which tells us of his personal exertions in wasting the infant Church, when he was a "blasphemer, and a persecutor, and injurious," it is quite obvious that this was the prominent characteristic of his natural mind. But when it pleased the

Lord Jesus Christ to show forth in him all along suffering, and to make him "a pattern to them which should afterwards believe on Him," it is beautiful and most instructive to see how the natural features of this daringly bad man became not only sanctified, but invigorated and enlarged; so true it is that they that are in Christ are a new creation. Old things pass away, and all things become new. "Troubled on every side, yet not stressed; perplexed, but not in despair; persecuted, but not forsaken; cast down, but not destroyed" – this was a faithful picture of the life of the converted Paul.

Knowing the terror of the Lord, and the fearful situation of all who were yet in their sins, he made it the business of his life to persuade men – striving if, by any means, he might commend the truth to their consciences. "For (saith he) whether we be beside ourselves, it is to God; or whether we be sober, it is for your cause." (Verse 13.) Whether the world think us wise or mad, the cause of God and of human souls is the cause in which we have embarked all the energies of our being. Who, then, is not ready to inquire into the secret spring of all these supernatural labors? Who would not desire to have heard from the lips of Paul what mighty principle it was that impelled him through so many toils and dangers? What magic has taken possession of this mighty mind, or what unseen planetary, influence, with unceasing power, draws him on through all discouragements-indifferent alike to the world's dread laugh, and the fear of man, which bringeth a snare – careless alike of the sneer of the skeptical Athenian, of the frown of the luxurious Corinthian, and the rage of the narrow minded Jew? What saith the apostle himself? for we have his own explanation of the mystery in the words before us: "The love of Christ constraineth us."

That Christ's love to man is here intended, and not our love to the Savior, is quite obvious, from the explanation which follows, where his dying for all is pointed to as the instance of his love. It was the view of that strange compassion of the Savior, moving him to die for his enemies – to bear double for all our sins – to taste death for every man – it was this view which gave him the impulse in every labor-which made all suffering light to him, and every commandment not grievous. He "ran with patience the race that was set before him." Why? Because, "looking unto Jesus," he lived a man "crucified unto the world, and the world crucified unto him." By what means? By looking to the cross of Christ. As the natural sun in the heavens exercises a mighty and unceasing attractive energy on the planets which circle round it, so did the Sun of Righteousness, which had indeed arisen on Paul with a brightness above that of noon-day, exercise on his mind a continual and an almighty energy, constraining him to live henceforth no more unto himself, but to him that died for him and rose again. And observe, that it was no temporary, fitful energy, which it exerted over his heart, and life, but an abiding and a continued attraction; for he doth not say that the love of Christ did once constrain him; or that it shall yet constrain him; or that in times of excitement, in seasons of prayer, or peculiar devotion, the love of Christ was wont to constrain him; but he saith simply, that the love of Christ constraineth him. It is the ever-present, ever-abiding, ever moving power, which forms the main-spring of all his world; so that, take that away, and his energies are gone, and Paul is become weak as other men.

Is there no one before me whose heart is longing to do just such a master-principle? Is there no one of you, brethren, who has arrived at that most interesting of all the stages of salvation in which you are panting after a power to make you new? You have entered in at the strait gate of believing. You have seen that there is no peace to the unjustified; and therefore you have put on Christ for your righteousness; and already you feel something of the joy and peace of believing. You can look back on your past life, spent without God in the world, and without Christ in the world, and without the Spirit in the world-you can see yourself a condemned outcast, and you say:

"Though I should wash my hands in snow-water, yet mine own clothes would abhor me." You can do all this, with shame and self-reproach it is true, but yet without dismay, and without despair; for your eye has been lifted believingly to him who was made sin for us, and you are persuaded that, as it pleased God to count all your iniquities to the Savior, so he is willing, and hath always been willing, to count all the Savior's righteousness to you.

Without despair, did I say? nay, with joy and singing; for if, indeed, thou believest with all thine heart, then thou art come to the blessedness of the man unto whom God imputeth righteousness without work-which David describes, saying: "Blessed are they whose iniquities are forgiven, and whose sins are covered. Blessed is the man to whom the Lord imputeth not sin." This is the peace of the justified man. But is this peace a state of perfect blessedness? Is there nothing left to be desired? I appeal to those of you who know what it is to be just by believing. What is it that still clouds the brow-that represses the exulting of the spirit? Why might we not always join in the song of thanksgiving, "Bless the Lord, O my soul, and forget not all his benefits: who forgiveth all thine iniquities"? If we have received double for all our sins, why should it ever be needful for us to argue as doth the Psalmist: "Why art thou cast down, O my soul; and why art thou disquieted in me? Ah! my friends, there is not a man among you, who has really believed, who has not felt the disquieting thought of which I am now speaking.

There may be some of you who have felt it so painfully, that it has obscured, as with a heavy cloud, the sweet light of Gospel the shining in of the reconciled countenance upon the soul. The thought is this, "I am a justified man; but, alas! I am not a sanctified man. I can look at my past life without despair; but how can I look forward to what is to come?"

There is not a more picturesque moral landscape in the universe than such a soul presents. Forgiven all trespasses that are past, the eye looks inwards with a clearness and an impartiality unknown before, and there it gazes upon its long-fostered affections for sin, which like ancient rivers, have worn a deep channel into the heart, hitherto irresistible and overwhelming, like the tides of the ocean. Ah! what a scene is here-what anticipations of the future! Were it not that the hope of the glory of God is one of the chartered rights of the justified man, who would be surprised if this view of terror were to drive a man back, like the dog to his vomit, or the sow that was washed to wallow again in the mire? Now it is to the man precisely in this situation, crying out at morning and at evening, How shall I be made new?-what good shall the forgiveness of my past sins do me, if I be not delivered from the love of sin? it is to that man that we would now, with all earnestness and affection, point out the example of Paul, and the secret power which wrought in him. "The love of Christ (says Paul) constraineth us." We, too, are men of like passions with yourselves: that same sight which you view with dismay within you, was in like manner revealed to us in all its discouraging power. Nay, ever and anon the same hideous view of our own hearts is opened up to us. But we have an encouragement which never fails. The love of the bleeding Savior constraineth us. The Spirit is given to them that believe; and that almighty Agent hath one argument that moves us continually – THE LOVE OF CHRIST.

My present object, brethren, is to show how this argument, in the hand of the Spirit, does move the believer to live unto God – how so simple a truth as the love of Christ to man, continually presented to the mind by the Holy Ghost, should enable any man to live a life of Gospel holiness; and if there be one man among you whose great inquiry is, How shall I be saved from sin-how shall I walk as a child of God?

1. The love of Christ to man constraineth believer to live a holy life, because that truth take away all dead and hatred of God. When Adam was unfallen, God was

everything to his soul; and everything was good and desirable to him, only in so far as it had to do with God. Every vein of his body, so fearfully and wonderfully made – every leaf that rustled in the bowers of Paradise-every new sun that rose, rejoicing like a strong man to ran his race-brought him in every day new subjects of godly thought and of admiring praise; and it was only for that reason that he could delight to look on them. The flowers that appeared on the earth-the singing of birds, and the voice of the turtle heard throughout the happy land the fig tree putting forth her green figs, and the vines with the tender grapes giving a good smell – all these combined to bring in to him at every pore a rich and varied tribute of pleasantness. And why? Just because they brought into the soul rich and varied communications of the manifold grace of Jehovah. For, just as you may have seen a child on earth devoted to its earthly parent – pleased with everything when he is present, and valuing every gift just as it shows more of the tenderness of that parent's heart – so was it with that genuine child of God. In God he lived, and moved, and had his being; and not more surely would the blotting out the sun in the heavens have taken away that light which is so pleasant to the eyes, than would the hiding of the face of God from him have taken away the light of his soul, and left nature a dark and desolate wilderness. But when Adam fell, the fine gold became dim – the system of his thoughts and likings was just reversed. Instead of enjoying God in everything, and everything in God, everything now seemed hateful and disagreeable to him, just in as far as it had to do with God.

When man sinned, he began to fear God and also to hate him; and fled to all sin, just to flee from Him whom he hated, So that, just as you may have seen a child who has grievously transgressed against a loving parent, doing all it can to hide from that parent-hurrying from his presence, and plunging into other thoughts and occupations, just to rid itself of the thought of its justly offended father-in the very same way when fallen Adam heard the voice of the Lord God walking in the garden in the cool of the day-that voice which, before he sinned, was heavenly music in his ears – then did Adam and his wife hide themselves from the presence of the Lord, among the trees of the garden. And in the same way does every natural man run from the voice and presence of the Lord-not to hide under the thick embowering leaves of Paradise, but to bury himself in cares, and business, and pleasures, and ravelings. Any occupation is tolerable, if God be not in the thoughts. Now I am quite sure that many of you may hear this charge against the natural man with incredulous indifference, if not with indignation. You do not feel that you hate God, or dread his presence; and, therefore, you say it cannot be true. But, brethren, when God says of your heart that it is "desperately wicked," yea, unsearchably wicked who can know it? When God claims for himself the privilege of knowing and trying the heart is it not presumptuous in such ignorant beings as we are, to say that that is not true, with respect to our hearts, which God affirms to be true, merely because we are not conscious of it? God saith that "the carnal mind is enmity against God." The very grain and substance of an unconverted mind is hatred against God – absolute, implacable hatred against Him in whom we live, and move, and have our being. It is quite true that we do not feel this hatred within us; but that is only an aggravation of our sin and of our danger. We have so choked up the avenues of self-examination, there are so many turnings and windings, before we can arrive at the true motives of our actions that our dread and hatred of God, which first moved man to sin, and which are still the grand impelling forces whereby Satan goads on the children of disobedience. These are wholly concealed from our view, and you cannot persuade a natural man that they are really there. But the Bible testifies, that out of these two deadly roots – dread of God and hatred of God-grows up the thick forest of sins with which the earth is blackened and overspread. And if there be one among you, brethren, who has been awakened by God to know what is in his heart, I take that man this day to witness, that his bitter cry, in the view of all his sins, has ever been: "Against thee, thee only, have I sinned."

If, then, dread of God, and hatred of God, be the cause of all our sins, how shall we be cured of the love of sin, but by taking away the cause? How do you most effectually kill the noxious weed? is it not by striking at the root? In the love of Christ to man, then-in that strange unspeakable gift of God, when he laid down his life for his enemies-when he died the just for the unjust, that he might bring us to God – do not you see an object which, if really believed by the sinner, takes away all his dread and all his hatred of God? The root of sin is severed from the stock. In His bearing double for all our sins, we see the curse carried away-we see God reconciled. Why should we fear any more? Not fearing, why should we hate God any more? Not hating God, what desirableness can we see in sin any more? Putting on the righteousness of Christ, we are again placed as Adam was – with God as our friend. We have no object in sinning; and, therefore, we do not care to sin. In the 6th chapter of Romans, Paul seems to speak of the believer sinning, as if the very proposition was absurd: "How shall we that are dead to sin" – that is, who in Christ have already borne the penalty – how shall we live any longer therein?" And again he saith very boldly: "Sin shall not have dominion over you." It is impossible in the nature of things. "For ye are not under the law, but under grace," ye are no longer under the curse of a broken law, dreading and hating God; ye are under grace-under a system of peace and friendship with God.

But is there anyone ready to object to me, that if these things be so-if nothing more than that a man be brought into peace with God is needful to a holy life and conversation-how comes it that believers do still sin? I answer, It is indeed too true that believers do sin; but it is just as true that unbelief is the cause of their sinning.

If, brethren, you and I were to live with our eye so closely on Christ bearing double for all our sins-freely offering to all a double righteousness for all our sins; and if this constant view of the love of Christ maintained within us-as assuredly it would, if we looked with a straight forward eye-the peace of God which passeth all understanding-the peace that rests on nothing in us, but upon the completeness that is in Christ-then, brethren, I do say, that frail and helpless as we are, we should never sin-we should not have the slightest object in sinning. But, ah! my friends, this is not the way with us. How often in the day is the love of Christ quite out of view! How often is it obscured to us – sometimes hid from us by God himself, to teach us what we are. How often are we left without the real sense of the completeness of his offering-the perfectness of his righteousness, and without the will or the confidence to claim an interest in him! Who can wonder, then, that, where there is so much unbelief, dread and hatred of God should again and again creep in, and sin should often display its poisonous head? The matter is very plain, brethren, if only we had spiritual eyes to see it. If we live a life of faith on the Son of God, then we shall assuredly live a life of holiness. I do not say, we ought to do so; but I say we shall, as a matter of necessary consequence. But, in as far as we do not live a life of faith, in so far we shall live a life of unholiness. It is through faith that God purifies the heart; and there is no other way.

Is there any of you, then, brethren, desirous of being made new-of being delivered from the slavery of sinful habits and affections? We can point you to no other remedy than the love of Christ. Behold how he loved you! See what he bore for you-put your finger, as it were, into the prints of the nails, and thrust your hand into his aide; and be no more faithless, but believing. Under a sense of your sins, flee to the Savior of sinners. As the timorous dove flies to hide itself in the crevices of the rock, so do you flee to hide yourself in the wounds of your Savior; and when you have found him like the shadow of a great rock in a weary land-when you sit under his shadow with great delight-you will find that he hath slain all the enmity-that he hath accomplished all your warfare. God is now for you. Planted together with Christ in the likeness of his death, you shall be also in the likeness of his resurrection. Dead unto sin, you shall be alive unto God.

2. The love of Christ to man constraineth the believer to live a holy life, because that truth not only takes away our fear and hatred, but stirs up our love. When we are brought to see the reconciled face of God in peace-that is a great privilege. But how can we look upon that face, reconciling and reconciled, and not love him who hath so loved us? Love begets love. We can hardly keep from esteeming those on earth who really love us, however worthless they may be. But, ah! my friends, when we are convinced that God loves us, and convinced in such a way as by the giving up of his Son for us all, how can we but love him in whom are all excellences-everything to call forth love? I have already shown you that the Gospel is a restorative scheme; it brings us back to the same state of friendship with God which Adam enjoyed, and thus takes away the desire of sin. But now I wish to show you that the Gospel does far more than restore us to the state from which we fell. If rightly and consistently embraced by us, it brings us into a state far better than Adam's. It constrains us by a far more powerful motive. Adam had not this strong love of God to man shed abroad in his heart; and, therefore, he had not this constraining power to make him live to God. But our eyes have seen this great sight. Before us Christ hath been evidently set forth crucified. If we have truly believed, his love hath brought us into peace, through pardon; and because we are pardoned and at peace with God, the Holy Ghost is given us. What to do? Why, just to shed abroad this truth over our hearts – to show us more and more of this love of God to us, that we may be drawn to love him who hath so loved us-to live to him

who died for us and rose again.

It is truly admirable, to see how the Bible way of making us holy is suited to our nature. Had God proposed to frighten us into a holy life, how vain would have been the attempt! Men have always an idea, that if one came from the dead to tell us of the reality of the doleful regions where dwell, in endless misery, the spirits of the damned, that that would constrain us to live a holy life; but, alas! brethren, what ignorance does this show of our mysterious nature! Suppose that God should this hour unveil before our eyes the secrets of those dreadful abodes where hope never comes; nay, suppose, if it were possible, that you were actually made to feel for a season the real pains of the lake of living agony, and the worm that never dies; and then that you were brought back to the earth, and placed in your old situation, among your old friends and companions; do you really think that there would be any chance of your walking as a child with God? I doubt not you would be frightened out of your positive sins; the cup of godless pleasure would drop from your hand-you would shudder at an oath-you would tremble at a falsehood; because you had seen and felt something of the torment which awaits the drunkard, and the swearer, and the liar, in the world beyond the grave; but do you really think that you would live to God any more than you did-that you would serve him better than before? It is quite true you might be driven to give larger charity; yea, to give all your goods to feed the poor, and your body to be burned; you might live strictly and soberly, most fearful of breaking one of the commandments, all the rest of your days; but this would not be living to God; you would not love him one whit more. Ah! brethren, you are sadly blinded to your curiously formed hearts, if you do not know that love cannot be forced; no man was ever frightened into love, and, therefore, no man was ever frightened into holiness.

But thrice blessed be God, he hath invented a way more powerful than hell and all its terrors-an argument mightier far than even a sight of those torments-he hath invented a way of drawing us to holiness. By showing us the love of his Son, he calleth forth our love, He knew our frame-he remembered that we were dust-he knew all the peculiarities of our treacherous hearts; and, therefore, he suited his way of sanctifying to the creature to be sanctified. And thus, the Spirit doth not make use of terror to sanctify us, but of love: " "The love of Christ constraineth us." He draws us by "the cords of love – by the bands of a man." What parent does not know that the true way to gain the obedience of a child, is to gain the affections of the child? And think you God, who gave us this wisdom, doth not himself know it? Think you he would set about obtaining the obedience of his children, without first of all gaining their affections? To gain our affections, brethren, which by nature rove over the face of the earth, and center anywhere but in him, God hath sent his Son into the world to bear the curse of our sins. "Though he was rich, yet for our sakes he became poor, that we, through his poverty, might be made rich."

And, oh! if there is but one of you who will consent this day, under a sense of undoneness, to flee for refuge to the Savior, to find in him the forgiveness of all sins that are past, I know well, that from this day forth you will be like that poor woman which was a sinner, which stood at Christ feet behind him, weeping, and began to wash his feet with tears, and did wipe them with the hairs of her head; and kissed his feet, and anointed them with the ointment. Forgiven much, you will love much – loving much, you will live to the service of Him whom you love. This is the grand master-principle of which we spoke; this is the secret spring of all the holiness of the saints. The life of holiness is not what the world falsely represents it-a life of preciseness and painfulness, in which a man crosses every affection of his nature. There is no such thing as self-denial, in the Popish sense of that word, in the religion of the Bible. The system of restrictions and self-crossings, is the very, system which Satan hath set up as a counterfeit of God's way of sanctifying. It is thus that Satan frightens away thousands from Gospel Peace and Gospel holiness; as if to be a sanctified man were to be a man who crossed every desire of his being-who did everything that was disagreeable and uncomfortable to him. My friends, our text distinctly shows you that it is not so. We are constrained to holiness by the love of Christ; the love of him who loved us, is the only cord by which we are bound to the service of God. The scourge of our affections is the only scourge that drives us to duty. Sweet bands, and gentle scourges! Who would not be under their power?

And, finally, brethren, if Christ's love to us be the object which the Holy Ghost makes use of, at the very first, to draw us to the service of Christ, it is by means of the same object that he draws us onwards, to persevere even unto the end. So that if you are visited with seasons of coldness and indifference if you begin to be weary, or lag behind in the service of God, behold! here is the remedy: Look again to the bleeding Savior. That Sun of Righteousness is the grand attractive center, round which all his saints move swiftly, and in smooth harmonious concert – "not without song." As long as the believing eye is fixed upon his love, the path of the believer is easy and unimpeded; for that love always constraineth. But lift off the believing eye, and the path becomes impracticable – the life of holiness a weariness. – Whosoever, then, would live a life of persevering holiness, let him keep his eye fixed on the Savior. As long as Peter looked only to the Savior, he walked upon the sea in safety, to go to Jesus; but when he looked around, and saw the wind boisterous, he was afraid, and, beginning to sink, cried, "Lord, save me!" Just so will it be with you. As long as you look believingly to the Savior, who loved you and gave himself for you, so long you may tread the waters of life's troubled sea, and the soles of your feet shall not be wet; but venture to look around upon the winds and waves that threaten you on every hand, and, like Peter, you begin to sink, and cry, "Lord, save me!" How justly,

then, may we address to you the Savior's rebuke to Peter: "0 thou of little faith, wherefore didst thou doubt?" Look again to the love of the Savior, and behold that love which constraineth thee to live no more to thyself, but to him that died for thee and rose again.
Robert Murray M'Cheyne

Loyalty

Intreat me not to leave thee, or to return from following after thee: for whither thou goest, I will go; and where thou lodgest, I will lodge: thy people shall be my people, and thy God my God.
The Bible, Ruth 1:16

Our loyalty is due not to our species but to God ... it is spiritual, not biological, kinship that counts.
C.S. Lewis

Loyalty to organizations and movements has always tended over time to take the place of loyalty to the person of Christ.
Francis Schaeffer

Luck

There is no such thing as "luck." It is God's grace.
Author unknown

Lukewarmness

... because you are lukewarm – neither hot nor cold – I am about to spit you out of my mouth.
The Bible, Revelation 3:16

Lukewarmness I account as great a sin in love as in religion.
Abraham Cowley

Anyone who does things lukewarmly is close to falling.
John of the Cross

Stagnation in the church is the devil's delight!
C.H. Spurgeon

I do not think the devil cares how many churches you build, if only you have lukewarm preachers and people in them.
C.H. Spurgeon

It seems to me that my text (Rev. 3:17,18) accounts for the lukewarmness of the Laodiceans. They were lukewarm because they imagined themselves rich when they were poor. Two conditions will help us to escape lukewarmness. The one is to be really rich in grace; for they that have much grace will not be lukewarm. Grace is as a fire in the soul, and he that hath much of it, so as to become an advanced Christian, cannot but have a heart boiling with earnestness. The other way is to have but little grace, but to be painfully aware of it, to be deeply conscious of soul-poverty, to sigh and cry because you are not what you should be. There is no lukewarmness in a strong desire caused by a bitter sense of need. The poor man, poor in spirit, conscious of his imperfections and failures, is never a lukewarm man, but with sighs and cries coming out of a heart that is all on fire with a desire to escape out of such a sad condition, he besieges the throne of God that he may obtain more grace. These Laodicean people were unhappily in such a state that you could not get at them. They were not so poor that they knew they were poor, and therefore when the poverty-stricken were addressed, they said, "These things are not for us: we are increased in goods." They were blind, but they thought they saw; they were naked, and yet they prided themselves on their princely apparel, and hence it was hard to reach them. Had they even been outwardly worse, had they openly sinned, had they defiled their garments with overt transgression, then the Spirit might have pointed out the blot and convicted them there and then but what was to be done when the mischief was hidden and internal? Had they been utterly cold and frost-bitten, then he might have thawed them into living warmth; but such was their puffed-up notion of themselves that one could not convince them of sin, or

awaken them to any sense of fear, and it seemed likely that after all the Lord must needs spew them out of his mouth as things he could not endure. How far this may be true of any one of us may God of his infinite mercy help us to judge each one for himself.
C.H. Spurgeon

Beware of a supine, lukewarm, libertine spirit. Watch unto prayer, guard against negligence. Advance not to the uttermost bounds of your liberty.
Augustus Toplady

Lust is the craving for salt of a man who is dying of thirst.
Frederick Buechner

My child, be not lustful, for the path of lust leads to sexual promiscuity; neither be obscene in speech nor have roving eyes, for from all of these are born adulteries.
The Didache

Sin is that power which transforms desire from something neutral or positive into something harmful, from "desire" into "lust." It is the power which turns desire in upon itself in destructive self-indulgence.
James S.G. Dunn

He that but looketh on a plate of ham and eggs to lust after it hath already committed breakfast with it in his heart.
C.S. Lewis

Capricious, wanton, bold, and brutal lust
Is meanly selfish; when resisted, cruel;
And, like the blast of pestilential winds,
Taints the sweet bloom of nature's fairest
  forms.
John Milton

The original meaning of the word lust is "strong desire" and not necessarily a sinful desire, since there are certain desires of our physical nature – such as hunger and thirst – which we have in common with the animal world and which, in themselves, are natural and not sinful. It is only their abuse that is evil. Hunger is natural lust. Gluttony is a sinful lust. Thirst is a natural lust. Intemperance is a sinful lust.
W. H. Griffith Thomas

With the lusts of passion I have darkened the beauty of my soul, and turned my whole mind entirely into dust.
The Lenten Triodion

Luxury

Luxury and gluttony is a sin exceeding contrary to the love of God: it is idolatry: it hath the heart, which God should have; and therefore gluttons are commonly and well-called belly-gods, and god-bellies, because that love, that care, that delight, that service and diligence which God should have is given by the glutton to his belly and his throat.
Richard Baxter

Luxury causes great care and produces great carelessness as to virtue.
Cato

A man can never learn what divine power is, while he abides in comfort and spacious living.
Isaac from Syria

Luxury is more deadly than any foe.
Juvenal

Lying
Lying: see Lies

M

Male chauvinism

The German saying which restricts the province of women to *Kinder, Küche und Kirche* (children, kitchen and church) is an example of blatant male chauvinism.
John Stott

Man

Man is only a reed, the weakest thing in nature; but he is a reed that thinks.
Blaise Pascal

Mankind

See: Humanity

Mark's Gospel

Mark's Gospel is for disciples.
John Stott

Marriage

See also: Divorce, Families; Husbands; Wives

It is not good that the man should be alone.
The Bible, Genesis 2:18 KJV

For this reason a man will leave his father and mother and be united to his wife, and they will become one flesh.
The Bible, Genesis 2:24

Marriage should be honored by all, and the marriage bed kept pure, for God will judge the adulterer and all the sexually immoral.
The Bible, Hebrews 13:4

Marriage is not a metaphysical status which cannot be destroyed; it is rather a moral commitment which should be honored.
Dr David Atkinson

Marriage: A community consisting of a master, a mistress, and two slaves, making in all, two.
Ambrose Bierce

[God intended marriage for] the mutual society, help and comfort that the one ought to have of the other both in prosperity and adversity.
Book of Common Prayer

An archaeologist is the best husband any woman can have; the older she gets, the more interested he is in her.
Agatha Christie, who was married to an archaeologist

Young husbands should say to their wives: I have taken you in my arms, and I love you, and I prefer you to my life itself. For the present life is nothing, and my most ardent dream is to spend it with you in such a way that we may be assured of not being separated in the life reserved for us. I place your love above all things, and nothing would be more bitter or painful to me than to be of a different mind than you.
John Chrysostom

Statistically, you're much better off marrying than living together.
Dr Nancy Clatworthy

All that can be called happy in the life of man, is summed up in the state of marriage; that is the center to which all lesser delights of life tend, as a point in the circle.
Daniel Defoe

Be the mate God designed you to be.
Anthony T. Evans

Only six marriages in a hundred are truly fulfilling.
Howard Hendricks

Marriage is an exclusive union between one man and one woman, publicly acknowledged, permanently sealed, and physically consummated.
Selwyn Hughes

The Bible opens and closes with a wedding.
Selwyn Hughes

There is no more lovely, friendly or charming relationship, communion or company, than a good marriage.
Martin Luther

We regard Christian marriage as an indissoluble union, which requires the life-long loyalty of the man and the woman towards each other.
Moravian Covenant for Christian living

Wedlock is padlock.
John Ray

Marriage is lonelier than solitude.
Adrienne Rich

Better communication means an improved relationship.
Gary Smalley

My advice to you is get married: if you find a good wife you'll be happy; if not, you'll become a philosopher.
Socrates

Two pure souls fused into one by an impassioned love – friends, counselors – a mutual support and inspiration to each other amid life's struggles, must know the highest human happiness; this is marriage; and this is the only cornerstone of an enduring home.
Elizabeth Cady Stanton

The marital love is a thing pure as light, sacred as a temple, lasting as the world.
Jeremy Taylor

Marriage is according to the will of God and the dictates of human nature, physical, mental and social.
W. H. Griffith Thomas

To say that you can love one person all your life is just like saying that one candle will continue burning as long as you live.
Leo Tolstoy

Marriage was ordained for a remedy and to increase the world and for the man to help the woman and the woman the man, with all love and kindness.
William Tyndale

I have many reasons to make me love thee, whereof I will name two, first because thou lovest God, and secondly because that thou lovest me.
Margaret Winthrop, Letter to John Winthrop

Marriage

Richard Baxter
Direct. I. The first duty of husbands is to love their wives (and wives their husbands). Eph 5.25,28,29,33. "Husbands, love your wives, even as Christ also loved the church, and gave himself for it. – So ought men to love their wives as their own bodies; he that loveth his wife, loveth himself. For no man ever yet hated his own flesh; but nourisheth and cherisheth it, even as the Lord the church. – Let every one of you in particular so love his wife, even as himself." See Gen 2.24.

Some directions for maintaining love are as follows:
1. Choose a good spouse in the first place. A spouse who is truly good and kind. Full of virtue and holiness to the Lord.
2. Don't marry till you are sure that you can love entirely.
3. Be not too hasty, but know beforehand all the imperfections which may tempt you to despise your future mate.

4. Remember that justice commands you to love one that has forsaken all the world for you. One who is contented to be the companion of your labors and sufferings, and be a sharer in all things with you, and that MUST be your companion until death.

5. Remember that women are ordinarily affectionate, passionate creatures, and as they love much themselves, so they expect much love from you.

6. Remember that you are under God's command; and to deny marital love to your wives, is to deny a duty which God has urgently imposed on you. Obedience therefore should command your love.

7. Remember that you are "one flesh"; you have drawn her to forsake father and mother, and to cleave to you;

8. Take more notice of the good, that is in your wives, than of her faults. Let not the observation of their faults make you forget or overlook their virtues.

9. Don't magnify her imperfections until they drive you crazy.

Excuse them as far as is right in the Lord. Consider the frailty of the sex. Consider also your own infirmities, and how much your wives must bear with you.

10. Don't stir up the evil of your spouse, but cause the best in them to be lived out.

11. Overcome them with love; and then they will be loving to you, and consequently lovely. Love will cause love, as fire kindleth fire. A good husband is the best means to make a good and loving wife.

12. Live before them the life of a prudent, lowly, loving, meek, self-denying, patient, harmless, holy heavenly Christian.

Direct. II. Husbands and wives must live together. 1 Cor 7:2-5

Direct III. Abhor not only adultery itself, but all that leads to unchasteness and the violation of your marriage_covenant. [Mat 5.31,32; 19:9; John 8,4-5, of adultery; Heb 13.4; Prov 22.14; Hos 4.2-3; Prov 2.17; 1 Cor 6.15,19; Mal. 2.15; Prov 6.32,35; Deu 23.2; Lev 21.9; 18:28; Num 25.9; Jer 5.7-9]

Direct. IV. Husband and wife must delight in the love and company, and lives of each other. When husband and wife take pleasure in each other, it unites them in duty, it helps them with ease to do their work, and bear their burdens; and is a major part of the comfort of marriage. [Prov 5.18,19]

Direct. V. It is your solemn duty to live in quietness and peace. To avoid every occasion of fierce anger and discord.

[I. Directions showing the great necessity of avoiding dissension.]

1. The duty of your marriage-union requires unity. Can you not agree with your own flesh?

2. Division with your spouse will pain and upset your whole life … Just as you do not wish to hurt your own self and are quick to care for your own wounds; so you should take notice of any break in the peace of your marriage and quickly seek to heal it.

3. Fighting chills love, fighting makes your spouse undesirable to you in your mind. Wounding is separating; to be tied together through marital bonds while your hearts are estranged is to be tormented. To be inwardly adversaries, while outwardly husband and wife turns your home and delight into a prison.

4. Dissension between the husband and the wife disrupts the whole family life; they are like oxen unequally yoked, no work can be accomplished for all the striving with one another.

5. It greatly makes you unfit for the worship of God; you are not able to pray together nor to discuss heavenly things together, nor can you be mutual helpers to each other's souls.

6. Dissension makes it impossible to manage your family properly.

7. Your dissension will expose you to the malice of Satan, and give him advantage for many, many temptations.

[II. Directions for avoiding dissensions.]

1. Keep alive your love for one another. Love your spouse dearly and fervently.

Love will suppress wrath; you cannot be bitter over little things with someone you dearly love; much less will you descend to harsh words, aloofness, or any form abuse.

2. Both husband and wife must mortify their pride and strong self-centered feelings. These are the feelings which cause intolerance and insensitivity. You must pray and labor for a humble, meek, and quiet spirit. A proud heart is troubled and provoked by every word that seems to assault your self-esteem.

3. Do not forget that you are both diseased persons, full of infirmities; and therefore expect the fruit of those infirmities in each other; and do not act surprised about it, as if you had never known of it before. Decide to be patient with one another; remembering that you took one another as sinful, frail, imperfect persons, and not as angels, or as blameless and perfect.

4. Remember still that your are one flesh; and therefore be no more offended with the words or failings of each other, than you would be if they were your own. Be angry with your wife for her faults no more than you are angry with yourself for your own. Have such an anger and displeasure against a fault, as will work to heal it; but not such as will cause festering and aggravation of the diseased part. This will turn anger into compassion, and will cause you to administer care for the cure.

5. Agree together beforehand, that when one of you is sinfully angry and upset the other shall silently and gently bear it until you have come to your sanity.

6. Have an eye to the future and remember that you must live together until death, and must be the companions of each other's lives, and the comforts of each other's lives, and then you will see how absurd it is for you to disagree and upset each other.

7. As far as you are able, avoid all occasions of wrath and quarreling, about the matters of your families.

8. If you are so angry that you cannot calm yourself at least control your tongue and do not speak hurtful and taunting words, talking it out hotly fans the fire, and increases the flame; (Do not ventilate your anger as you only feed your fleshly vengeance) Be silent, and you will much sooner return to your serenity and peace.

9. Let the calm and rational spouse speak carefully and compellingly reason with the other (unless it be with a person so insolent as will make things worse). Usually a few sober, grave admonitions, will prove as water to the boiling pot. Say to your angry wife or husband, "You know this should not be between us; love must put it to rest, and it must be repented of. God does not approve of it, and we shall not approve of it when this heat is over. This frame of mind is contrary to a praying frame, and this language contrary to a praying language; we must pray together; let us do nothing contrary to prayer now: sweet water and bitter come not from one spring", etc. Some calm and condescending words of reason, may stop the torrent, and revive the reason which passion had overcome.

10. When you have sinfully acted towards your spouse confess to one another; and ask for forgiveness of each other, and join in prayer to God for pardon; and this will act as a preventative in you the next time: you will surely be ashamed to do that which you have confessed and asked forgiveness for of God and man.

Direct. VI. One of the most important duties of a husband to his wife and a wife to her husband is to carefully, skillfully, and diligently help each other in the knowledge and worship, and obedience of God that they might be saved and grow in their Christian Life.

1. This is not love, when you neglect each other's soul. Do you believe that you have immortal souls, and an endless life of joy or misery to live? Then you *must* know that your great concern and business is, to care for those souls, and for the endless life. Therefore if your love does not help one another in this which is your main concern, it is of little worth, and of little use. Every thing in this world is as valuable as it is useful. A useless or unprofitable love, is a

worthless love. It is a trifling, or a childish, or a beastly love, which helps you but in trifling, childish, or beastly things. Do you love your wife, and will leave her in the power of Satan, or will not help to save her soul? What! love her, and yet let her go to hell? and rather let her be damned than you will be at the pains to endeavor her salvation? Never say you love them, if you will not labor for their salvation.

What then shall we say of them that do not only deny their help, but are hinderers of the holiness and salvation of each other! [1 Kings 11.4, Acts 5.2, Job 2.9] And yet (the Lord have mercy on the poor miserable world!) how common a thing is this among us! If the wife be ignorant and ungodly, she will do her worst to make or keep her husband in the same state as she is herself; and if God put any holy inclinations into his heart, she will be like water to the fire, to quench it or to keep it subdued; and if he will not be as sinful and miserable as herself, he shall have little rest. And if God open the eyes of the wife of a bad man, and show her the necessity of a holy life, and she resolves to obey the Lord, and save her soul, what an enemy and tyrant will her husband be to her (if God does not restrain him); so that the devil himself will do no more to prevent the saving of their souls than ungodly husbands and wives do against each other.

2. Consider also that you are not living up to the design of marriage, if you are not helping each other's souls.

3. Consider also, if you neglect each other's souls, what enemies you are to one another, and how you are preparing for your everlasting sorrows: when you should be preparing for your joyful meeting in heaven, you are laying up for yourselves everlasting horror.

Therefore without a moment's hesitation determine to live together as heirs of heaven, and to be a helper to one other's souls. To assist you in this holy pursuit I will give you these following directions, which if you will faithfully practice, may make you to be special blessings to each other.

Direct. I. Before you can help to save each other's souls you must be sure of your own. You must have a deep and living understanding of the great eternal matters of which you are required to speak to others about. If you have no compassion for your own soul and will sell it for a moment of ease and pleasure, surely then you have no compassion for your spouse's soul.

Direct. II. Take every opportunity which your nearness provides to be speaking seriously to each other about the matters of God, and your salvation.(30) Discussing those things of this world no more than required. And then talk together of the state and duty of your souls towards God, and of your hopes of heaven, as those that take these for their greatest business. And don't speak lightly, or unreverently, or in a rude and disputing manner; but with gravity and sobriety, as those that are discussing the most important things in the whole world. [Mark 8:36]

Direct. III. When either husband or wife is speaking seriously about holy things, let the other be careful to cherish, and not to extinguish the conversation.

Direct IV. Watch over the hearts and lives of one another, judging the condition of each other's souls, and the strength or weakness of each others sins and graces, and the failings of each others lives, so that you may be able to apply to one another the most suitable help.

Direct. V. Do not flatter one another from a foolish love. Neither meanly criticize one another. Do all in true, Godly love. Some are so blinded to the faults of husband, wife or child that they do not see the sin and wickedness in them. They are deluded concerning their eternal souls. This is the same as it is with self-loving sinners and their own souls, willfully deceiving themselves to their damnation. This flattering of yourselves or others, is but the devil's charm to keep you from effectual repentance and salvation. On the other hand, some cannot speak to one another of their faults, without such bitterness, or contempt, which will cause them to refuse the medicine that could save them. If the everyday warnings you make to strangers must all be offered in love, much more between the husband and wife.

Direct. VI. Keep up your love to one another, do not grow distant. For if you do, you will despise each other's counsels and reproofs.

Direct. VII. Do not discourage your spouse from instructing you by refusing to receive and learn from their corrections.

Direct. VIII. Help each other by reading together the most convicting, cutting, life-giving books. The ones most spiritual. Do not waste your time on light, weak, milk-toast ministries and books. Make friendships together with the holiest persons. This is not neglecting your duty to one another, but that all the helps working together may be the more effectual.

Direct. IX. Don't Conceal the state of your souls, nor hide your faults from one another. You are as one flesh, and should have one heart: and as it is dangerous for a man to be ignorant of his own soul so it is very hurtful to husband or wife to be ignorant of one another, in those areas where they have need of help.

Direct X. Avoid as much as possible different opinions in religion.

Direct. XI. If different religious understandings come between you, be sure that you manage it with holiness, humility, love, and peace, and not with carnality, pride, uncharitableness, or contention.

Direct. XII. Do not either blindly indulge each others faults nor be too critical of each other's state, allowing Satan to alienate your affections from one another.

Direct. XIII. If you are married to one that is an ungodly person, yet keep up all the love which is due for the relation's sake.

Direct XIV. Join together in frequent and fervent prayer. Prayer forces the mind into sobriety, and moves the heart with the presence and majesty of God. Pray also for each other when you are in secret, that God may do that work which you most desire, upon each other's hearts.

Direct. XV. Lastly, help each other by an exemplary life. Be yourself, what you desire your husband or wife should be; excel in meekness, and humility, and charity, and dutifulness, and diligence, and self_denial, and patience.

Direct. VII. Another important duty in marriage is, to help in the health and comfort of each other's bodies. Not to pamper each other's flesh, or cherish the vices of pride, or sloth, or gluttony, or the sensual pleasures in each other; but to increase the health and vigor of the body, making it fit for the service of the soul and God.

1. In health, you must be careful to provide for each other (not so much pleasing as) wholesome food, and to keep each other from that which is hurtful to your health; warning each other from the dangers of gluttony and idleness, the two great murderers of mankind.

2. Also in sickness, you are to be caring of each other; and not to spare any costs or pains, by which the health of each other may be restored, or your souls confirmed, and your comforts cherished.

Direct. VIII. Another duty of husbands and wives is, to be helpful to each other in their worldly business and estates. Not for worldly ends, nor with a worldly mind; but in obedience to God, who will have them labor, as well as pray, for their daily bread, and has determined that in the sweat of their brows they shall eat their bread; and that six days they shall labor and do all that they have to do; and that he that will not work must not eat.

Direct IX. Also you must be careful to guard the honor of one another. You must not divulge, but conceal, the failings of each other; The reputation of each other must be as dear to you as your own. It is a sinful and unfaithful practice of many, both husbands and wives, who among their friends are discussing the faults of each other, which they are required in tenderness to cover up. MANY peevish persons will aggravate all the faults of their spouse behind their backs.

Direct X. IT is your marriage duty to assist one another in the education of your children.

Direct XI. It is your marriage duty to assist each other in charity.

Direct XII. *Lastly*, it is a great *duty* of husbands and wives, to help and comfort one other in preparing for a safe and happy death.

1. In the time of health, you must often and seriously remind each other of the time when death will make the separation; and live together daily as those that are still expecting the parting hour....Reprove everything in one another, which would be an unwelcome memory at death. If you see each other dull and slow in heavenliness, or living in vanity, worldliness, or sloth, as if you had forgotten that you must shortly die, stir up one another to do all without delay which the approach of such a day requireth.

2. And when death is at hand, oh then what abundance of tenderness, and seriousness, and skill, and diligence, is needful for one, that hath the last office of love to perform, to the departing soul of so near a friend! Oh then what need will there be of your most wise, and faithful, and diligent help! They that are utterly unprepared and unfit to die themselves, can do little to prepare or help another. But they that live together as the heirs of heaven, and converse on earth as fellow travelers to the land of promise, may help and encourage the souls of one another, and joyfully part at death, as expecting quickly to meet again in life eternal.
Richard Baxter

Marriage, Christian
Nowhere in the New Testament is a wife exhorted to obey her husband.
Mary Evans

Marriage, Preparation for
We consider it essential, therefore, that all persons contemplating marriage should receive premarital counseling and that our young people should be instructed, beginning in adolescence, in the meaning and obligation of true Christian marriage; this instruction to be given through the Church and the home.
Moravian Covenant for Christian living

Premarital preparations should include planning for the sexual union God designed for couples. Many couples feel so passionate about each other they assume that they will naturally have a blissful sexual experience. The truth is that achieving mutual satisfaction requires work, time, and experience.
Brian and Deborah Newman

You cannot shortcut the growth process God has set up. You must "leave" home in a healthy way if you are ever to attain a fulfilling marriage relationship.
John Trent

Marriage and celibacy
Wholly abstain or wed.
George Herbert

Of whom the world was not worthy.
The Bible, Hebrews 11:38 KJV

Martyrdom
It is not the pain but the purpose that makes the martyr.
Augustine of Hippo

Lord, if any have to die this day, let it be me, for I am ready.
Billy Bray

I will not purchase corruptible life at so dear a rate; and indeed, if I had a hundred lives, I would willingly lay down all in defense of my faith.
Christopher Buxton

Have great love for trials and think of them as but a small way of pleasing your Bridegroom, who did not hesitate to die for you.
John of the Cross

Martyrdom does not end something; it is only the beginning.
Indira Gandhi

The tyrant dies and his rule ends, the martyr dies and his rule begins.
Søren Kierkegaard

No one makes us afraid or leads us into captivity as we have set our faith on Jesus. For though we are beheaded, and crucified, and exposed to beasts and chains and fire and all other forms of torture, it is plain that we do not forsake the confession of our faith, but the more things of this kind which happen to us the more are there others who become believers and truly religious through the name of Jesus.
Justin Martyr

When I was delighting in the doctrines of Plato, and heard the Christians slandered, and saw them fearless of death … I perceived that it was impossible that they could be living in wickedness and pleasure.
Justin Martyr

You can kill us, but not hurt us.
Justin Martyr

Love makes the whole difference between an execution and a martyrdom.
Evelyn Underhill

Let me be given to the wild beasts, for by their means I can attain to God. I am God's wheat, and I am being ground by the teeth of the beasts so that I may be like pure bread.
Ignatius of Antioch

Now do I begin to be a disciple of my Master, Christ.
Ignatius of Antioch, traveling cheerfully to the place where he was to be thrown to the lions.

Eighty-six years have I served Jesus and he has done me no wrong. How can I blaspheme my King who saved me?
Polycarp

I have committed my cause to the great judge of all mankind, so I am not moved by threats, nor are your swords more ready to strike than is my soul for martyrdom.
Thomas à Beckett

Martyrs of the Reformation

John Foxe

JOHN BRADFORD
'I pray you stretch out your gentleness that I may feel it, for hitherto I have not.'

John Bradford determined to devote his life to the Scriptures, and the ministry of the Word. In order to carry out his plan, he went to Cambridge University, where he applied himself with such diligence, that in a few years the degree of Master of Arts was conferred on him. He was then made a Fellow of Pembroke College, and was befriended by Martin Bucer, who strongly urged him to use his talents in preaching. Bradford replied that he could not preach, ask he did not consider himself qualified for such an office; to which his friend would answer, "If thou hast not fine wheat bread, yet give the poor people barely bread, or whatsoever else the Lord hath committed unto thee."

Bradford was appointed by Dr Ridley as a prebendary of St Paul's, where he labored diligently for three years, after which he was called upon to show his allegiance to his Savior by following him to prison and to death.

It was in the first year of Queen Mary's reign that the Bishop of Bath, Dr Bourne, preached at Paul's Cross on the merits of Popery, which raised the indignation of the people to such a pitch, that they would have pulled him out from the pulpit by force, had not the bishop, seeing the danger, called to Mr Bradford, who was standing near, to come forward and take his place. Bradford obeyed the request, and so greatly was he respected and beloved, that he soon quelled the rising tumult, and dismissed the people quietly to their homes. Within three days he was summoned before the queen's council, and accused of having saved Bourne's life, and having put himself forward to preach in the bishop's stead; being found guilty, he was committed to the Tower.

For two years he remained closely confined there; and then he was brought before the lord chancellor, and other councillors, to be examined on the accusation of seditious behavior at Paul's Cross.

On entering the council room, the chancellor told him he had been justly imprisoned for his arrogancy in preaching without authority; "but now," he said, "the time for mercy has come, and the queen's highness hath by us sent for you, to declare and give the same, if you will with us return; and if you will do as we have done, you shall find as we have found.'

To this Bradford answered, "My lords, I know that I have been long imprisoned, and – with humble reverence be it spoken – unjustly, for that I did nothing seditiously, falsely, or arrogantly, in word or fact, by preaching or otherwise, but rather sought truth, peace, and all godly quietness, as an obedient and faithful subject, both in going about to serve the present Bishop of Bath, then Mr Bourne, the preacher at the Cross,

and in preaching for quietness accordingly." The chancellor angrily made answer: I know thou hast a glorious tongue, and goodly shows thou makest; but all is lies thou speakest. And again, I have not forgot how stubborn thou wast when thou wast before us in the Tower, whereupon thou wast committed to prison concerning religion.'

The conversation continued as follows:

BRADFORD: My lord, I stand as before you, so before God, and one day we shall all stand before him; the truth then will be the truth, though now ye will not take it so. Yea, my lord, I dare say that my lord of Bath, Mr Bourne, will witness with me, that I sought his safeguard with the peril of mine own life. I thank God, therefore.

BISHOP BONNER: That is not true, for I myself did see thee take upon thee too much.

BRADFORD: No; I took nothing upon me undesired, and that of Mr Bourne himself, as, were he present, I dare say he would affirm. For he desired me both to help him to pacify the people, and also not to leave him until he was in safety.

The councillors and bishops then began to question him on religious opinions, that they might find some reason to sentence him to death; and after much argument, the lord chancellor again offered him mercy, to which Bradford nobly and simply answered that mercy with God's mercy would be welcome, but otherwise he would have none. On this the chancellor rang a bell, and when the under-marshal entered, said to him, "You shall take this man with you, and keep him close, without conference with any man but by your knowledge, and suffer him not to write any letters, for he is of another manner of charge to you now than he was before." And so the first examination ended, Bradford testifying by his looks, as well as his words, that he was ready and willing, yea, even desirous, to lay down his life in confirmation of his faith and doctrine.

In about a week he was again brought before the council, when the chancellor having made a long speech, Bradford thus answered: "My lords, as I now stand in your sight before you, so I humbly beseech your honors to consider that you sit in the seat of the Lord, who, as David doth witness, is in the congregation of judges, and sitteth in the midst of them judging: and as you would have your place to be by us taken as God's place, so demonstrate yourselves to follow him in your sitting; that is, seek not guiltless blood, neither hunt by questions to bring into a snare them which are out of the same. At this present I stand before you guilty or guiltless; then proceed and give sentence accordingly: if guiltless, then give me the benefit of a subject, which hitherto I could not have."

Here the lord chancellor said that Bradford began with a true sentence, saying that the Lord is in the midst of them that judge: "But," said he, "this and all thy gesture declareth but hypocrisy and vain-glory." He then continued, endeavoring to clear himself from the charge of seeking to shed innocent blood, stating that Bradford's act at Paul's Cross was arrogant and presumptuous, and a taking upon himself to lead the people, which could not but tend to much disquietness. He then accused him of having written seditious letters when in the Tower, and of having endeavored to pervert the people, and finally questioned him closely as to his belief in the presence of Christ in the sacrament.

To this Bradford replied, "My lord, I have now been a year and almost three quarters in prison, and in all this time you have never questioned my hereabouts, when I might have spoke my conscience frankly without peril; but now you have a law to hang up and put to death, if a man answer freely and not to your liking, and so now you come to demand this question. Ah! my lord, Christ used not this way to bring men to faith; nor did the prophets nor apostles."

Here the lord chancellor, affecting astonishment and horror, replied that neither did he use such means, that he had ofttimes been charged with showing too much gentleness and forbearance. The Bishop of London, and nearly all the rest of the audience, the broke out into affirmations of his gentleness and mildness. Mr Bradford answered, "Then, my lord, I pray you stretch out your gentleness that I may feel it, for hitherto I have not."

The lord chancellor being now informed that his dinner was ready, arose, and Bradford was again led to his prison.

At seven the next morning, Mr Thomas Hussey came into the room where he was confined, and, saying that he came to see and speak to him through love, said, "So wonderfully did you behave yourself before chancellor and other bishops yesterday, that even the greatest enemies you have say they have no matter against you; therefore I advise you to desire a time, and men to confer with, so by that means you may escape danger, which is otherwise nearer to you than you suppose."

Bradford refused to make any such request, which would give occasion to people to think that he doubted the doctrine he confessed. While they were still talking Dr Seton entered the room, and began to speak of Ridley and Latimer, who, he said, were unable to answer anything, and had desired to confer with others, hinting that Bradford had better follow their example. Bradford, however, refused his suggestions as he had Mr Hussey's, whereupon they both became enraged, calling him arrogant and vain-glorious.

Soon after they had quitted his cell, the prisoner was again brought before his judges, when, after a long discussion, during which he displayed as much gentleness as they did ferocity, the sentence of excommunication was read, when he knelt down an thanked God that he was thought worthy to suffer for his sake. It was proposed that he should be sent to Manchester, his native town, to be burnt; and while they were settling whether or not it should be so, he was once again committed to prison.

He remained there nearly five months; when one afternoon the keeper's wife came to him, and in much trouble, said, "Oh, Mr Bradford, I come to bring you heavy news."

"What is that?" asked he.

"Tomorrow," she replied, "you must be

burnt; and your chain is now a- buying, and you must soon go to Newgate."

Bradford, taking off his cap, and lifting up his eyes to heaven, exclaimed, "I thank God for it."

Then, after thanking the woman for the kindness she had always shown him, he went to his room, and remained in private prayer for some time. At midnight he was removed to Newgate, and the next morning conducted by a large body of armed men to Smithfield, where he suffered death by being burnt alive, in company with a young man only twenty years of age, being joyful to the last moment of his life that he was thought worthy to die for his Savior.

The Book of Martyrs, John Foxe

Mary, Virgin
See also: Virgin birth

... not as the mother of grace, but as the daughter of grace.

Bengel

Not that she is above him who is truly God, or even equal to him. To think or say such a thing would be blasphemous.

Louis de Montfort

If the angel Gabriel addressed her as "highly favored," and if her cousin Elizabeth called her "blessed ... among women," we should not be shy to think and speak of her in the same terms, because of the greatness of her Son.

John Stott

Mass
See also: Lord's Supper

The sacrifices of masses, in the which it was commonly said, that the priest did offer Christ for the quick and the dead, to have remission of pain or guilt, were blasphemous fables, and dangerous deceits.

Book of Common Prayer

No part of Christian religion was ever so vilely contaminated and abused by profane wretches, as this pure holy, plain action and institution of our Savior; witness the Popish horrid monster of transubstantiation, and their idolatrous mass.

John Owen

Matthew's Gospel

"The kingdom of heaven" is the great theme of Matthew's Gospel.

John Stott

Maturity
See also: Growth

Love slays what we have been that we may be what we are not.

Augustine of Hippo

He is only advancing in life, whose heart is getting softer, his blood warmer, his brain quicker, and his spirit entering into living peace.

John Ruskin

Maturity, Christian

Perseverance must finish its work so that you may be mature and complete, not lacking anything.

The Bible, James 1:4

Maxims

It is unbecoming for young men to utter maxims.

Aristotle

Meals

Whiles thou eatest or drinkest let not the memory of thy God that feeds thee pass from thy mind; but praise, bless, and glorify him in like morsel, so that thy heart be more in God's praising than in thy meat, and thy soul be not parted from God at any hour.

Richard Rolle

Meaning of life

There is within every soul a thirst for happiness and meaning.

Thomas Aquinas

Only religion is able to answer the

question of the purpose of life. One can hardly go wrong in concluding that the idea of a purpose in life stands and falls with the religious system.
Sigmund Freud

The only reason why man as man has individual significance is that Christ died for him.
George MacLeod

Meaninglessness
Either our moral values tell us something about the nature and purpose of reality or they are subjective and therefore meaningless.
D.M. Baillie

Birth: the first and direst of all disasters.
Ambrose Bierce

Life is one long process of getting tired.
Samuel Butler

Drank every cup of joy, drank early, deeply drank, drank draughts which common millions might have drunk, then died of thirst because there was no more drink.
Byron

To kill God is to become god oneself: it is to realize on this earth the eternal life of which the gospel speaks.
Albert Camus

If there are no gods all our toil is without meaning.
Euripides

More people today have the means to live, but no meaning to live for.
Victor Frankl

Human thought cannot conceive any system of final truth that can give a patient what he needs in order to live.
Carl Jung

Life is one long struggle in the dark.
Lucretius

The universe is indifferent. Who created

it? Why are we here on this puny mud-heap, spinning in infinite space? I have not the slightest idea, and I am quite convinced that no one has the least idea.
André Maurois

I have to read at least one detective book a day to drug myself against the nuclear threat.
Bertrand Russell

Why shouldn't things be largely absurd, futile, and transitory? They are so, and we are so, and they and we go very well together.
George Santayana

All existing things are born for no reason, continue through weakness and die by accident. It is meaningless that we are born; it is meaningless that we die.
Jean-Paul Sartre

All the world's a stage,
And all the men and women merely players;
They have their exits and their entrances;
… Last scene of all,
That ends this strange eventful history,
Is second childishness and mere oblivion;
Sans teeth, sans eyes, sans taste, sans everything.
William Shakespeare, As You Like It

Life's but a walking shadow, a poor player,
That struts and frets his hour upon the
  stage,
And then is heard no more; it is a tale
Told by an idiot, full of sound and fury,
Signifying nothing.
William Shakespeare, Macbeth

Life is as tedious as a twice-told tale,
Vexing the dull ear of a drowsy man.
William Shakespeare, King John

As flies to wanton boys, are we to the gods;
They kill us for their sport.
William Shakespeare, King Lear

No mortal is happy of all on whom the sun looks down.
Theognis

The mass of men lead lives of quiet desperation.
Henry David Thoreau

Life is a bad joke.
Voltaire

Mediator

For there is one God and one mediator between God and men, the man Christ Jesus, who gave himself as a ransom for all men – the testimony given in its proper time.
The Bible, 1 Timothy 2:5,6

Christ's work as Mediator was unique: it was to restore us to divine favor and to make us sons of God, instead of sons of men; heirs of a heavenly kingdom instead of heirs of hell.
John Calvin

Meditation
See also: Contemplation

Whatsoever things are true, whatsoever things are honest, whatsoever things just, whatsoever things pure, whatsoever things lovely, whatsoever things of good report; if there be any virtue, and if there be any praise, think on these things.
The Bible, Philippians 4:8 KJV

If by meditation, thou does not find an increase in all thy graces, and do not grow beyond the stature of common Christians, and art not made more serviceable in thy place, and more precious in the eyes of all discerning persons; if thy soul enjoy not more communion with God, and thy life be not fuller of comfort, and hast it not readier by thee at a dying hour; then cast away these directions, and exclaim against me forever as a deceiver.
Richard Baxter

Wilt thou love God, as he thee! then digest,
My soul, this wholesome meditation,
How God the Spirit by angels waited on
In heaven, doth make his Temple in thy heart.
John Donne

When you meditate, imagine that Jesus Christ in person is about to talk to you about the most important thing in the world. Give him your complete attention.
F. Fénelon

It is preferable to be very humble and ashamed of the faults one has committed than to be satisfied with one's meditation and puffed up with the idea that one is very advanced in spiritual matters.
F. Fénelon

Spend an hour every day, some time before the midday meal, in meditation; and the earlier the better, because your mind will then be less distracted, and fresh after a night's sleep.
Francis of Sales

If meditation is to be fruitful, it must be followed by devoted prayer, and the sweetness of contemplation may be called the effect of prayer.
Guigo II the Carthusian

Meditation is no panacea.
Martin Israel

My spirit has become dry because it forgets to feed on you.
John of the Cross

Those who draw water from the wellspring of meditation know that God dwells close to their hearts.
Toyohiko Kagawa

We should not take a simple look at the cross, but rather meditate and be satisfied with it.
Pishoy Kamel

All the troubles of life come upon us because we refuse to sit quietly for a while each day in our rooms.
Blaise Pascal

In the rush and noise of life, as you have intervals, step home within yourselves and be still. Wait upon God, and feel his good

presence; this will carry you evenly through your day's business.
William Penn

Work of sight is done.
Now do heart work
On the pictures within you.
Rainer Maria Rilke

It is not the busy skimming over religious books or the careless hastening through religious duties which makes for a strong Christian faith. Rather, it is unhurried meditation on the gospel truths and the exposing of our minds to these truths that yield the fruit of a sanctified character.
Maurice Roberts

Let us leave the surface and, without leaving the world, plunge into God.
Teilhard de Chardin

To think well is to serve God in the interior court: To have a mind composed of divine thoughts, and set frame, to be like Him within.
Thomas Traherne

Mediums
Do not turn to mediums or seek out spiritists.
The Bible, Leviticus 19:31

Meekness
In meekness and lowliness consisteth the kingdom of heaven.
Jacob Boehme

Choose the meekness of Moses (Num. 12:3) and you will find your heart which is a rock changed into a spring of water (Ex. 17:5-6, Ps. 105:41).
Amma Syncletica

[The motto of the meek person is:] In himself, nothing; in God, everything.
A. W. Tozer

Selfish men may possess the earth; it is the meek only who inherit from the heavenly Father, free from all defilements and perplexities of unrighteousness.
John Woolman

Melancholy
See also: Depression
Give no place to despondency. This is a dangerous temptation of the adversary. Melancholy contracts and withers the heart.
Madame Guyon

Memory
God gave us memories so we could have roses in the winter.
Author unknown

Mercy
Mercy and truth are met together: righteousness and peace have kissed each other.
The Bible, Psalm 85:10 KJV

Mercy is compassion in action.
Author unknown

Two works of mercy set a man free: forgive and you will be forgiven, and give and you will receive.
Augustine of Hippo

Do you wish to receive mercy? Show mercy to your neighbor.
John Chrysostom

Messenger
Jacob Boehme was not a messenger of anything new in religion, but the mystery of all that was old and true in religion and nature, was opened up to him, the depth of the riches, both of the wisdom and knowledge of God.
William Law

Methodism
A Methodist is one who loves the Lord his God with all his heart, with all his soul, with all his mind, and with all his strength. God is the joy of his heart, and the desire of his soul.
John Wesley

Millionaires
Millionaires seldom smile.
Andrew Carnegie

Mind
The Christian mind has succumbed to the secular drift with a degree of weakness and nervelessness unmatched in Christian history.
Harry Blamires

It is not enough to have a good mind. The main thing is to use it well.
René Descartes

The human mind is so constructed that it resists vigor and yields to gentleness.
Francis of Sales

It is riches of the mind only that make a man rich and happy.
Thomas Fuller

The mind is its own place, and in itself Can make a heaven of hell, a hell of heaven.
John Milton

Choose to have a vigorous mind rather than a vigorous body.
Pythagoras

Mind, Renewed
Do not conform any longer to the pattern of this world, but be transformed by the renewing of your mind. Then you will be able to test and approve what God's will is *M* his good, pleasing and perfect will.
The Bible, Romans 12:2

Ministers of religion
See also: Women's ministry
It will, I believe, be everywhere found, that as the clergy are, or are not what they ought to be, so are the rest of the nation.
Jane Austin

The leading defect in Christian ministers is want of a devotional habit.
Richard Cecil

The Lord opened unto me that being bred at Oxford or Cambridge was not enough to fit and qualify men to be ministers of Christ.
George Fox

Prayer and temptation, the Bible and meditation make a true minister of the gospel.
Martin Luther

[The Mayflower pilgrims] held (in opposition to the church) that the priesthood is not a distinct order, but an office temporarily conferred by the vote of the congregation.
John Masefield

What village parson would not like to be a pope?
Voltaire

Ministers of religion, Authority of
Be eager to act always in godly agreement; with the bishop presiding as the counterpart of God, the presbyters as the counterpart of the council of the apostles, and the deacons (most dear to me) who have been entrusted with a service [*diaconate*] under Jesus Christ, who was with the Father before all ages and appeared at the end of time.
Ignatius of Antioch

One ought to think as follows about ministers. The office does not belong to Judas but to Christ alone. When Christ said to Judas, "Go baptize," Christ himself was the baptizer and not Judas because the command comes from above even if it passes down through a stinking pipe. Nothing is taken from the office on account of the unworthiness of a minister.
Martin Luther

Ministers of religion, Choice of
When appointing priests we should choose only those of spotless and upright character as our leaders.
Cyprian of Carthage

Appoint bishops and deacons worthy of the Lord – mild men, who are not out to

get money, men who are genuine and approved; for they are your prophets and teachers.
Didache

Ministry

There can be no future for the Church unless we have collaborative styles of ministry.
George Carey

A man set on fire is an apostle of his age. And the only one who can kindle the spark of light and fire on the hearth where it has died down is He who has revealed Himself as the God of fire, our Lord Jesus Christ. "Our God is a consuming fire"…Tell me, is your ministry a burning and shining light, or a smoking wick, slowly dying out to ashes? … It is a strange custom that we should supply a minister with a glass of water; if only we could supply him with a bonfire in the pulpit, a spiritual bonfire. We need the dynamic of a flaming ministry that will set the Church on fire.
Samuel M. Zwemer

Minorities

Keep in mind that throughout the centuries humanity has been led by daring minorities.
Helder Camara

Miracles

The Lord opened the mouth of the ass, and she said unto Balaam, What have I done unto thee, that thou hast smitten me these three times?
The Bible, Numbers 22:28

Miracles do not happen.
Matthew Arnold

Miracles are not contrary to nature, but only contrary to what we know about nature.
Augustine of Hippo

I never have any difficulty believing in miracles, since I experienced the miracle of a change in my own heart.
Augustine of Hippo

God never wrought miracles to convince atheism, because his ordinary works convince it.
Francis Bacon

We are not to look for manifestations of divine power to make natural faith easier.
R.M. Benson

We must first make up our minds about Christ before coming to conclusions about the miracles attributed to him.
F.F. Bruce

If a man is a fool for believing in a Creator, then he is a fool for believing in a miracle; but not otherwise.
G.K. Chesterton

Miracles are the swaddling clothes of infant churches.
Thomas Fuller

A miracle is an event beyond the power of any known physical law to produce; it is a spiritual occurrence produced by the power of God, a marvel, a wonder.
Billy Graham

It is not necessary for me to go far afield in search of miracles. I am a miracle myself. My physical birth and my soul's existence are miracles. First and foremost, the fact that I was even born is a miracle.
Toyohiko Kagawa

Miracles are those acts which establish the central beliefs of the Hebrew-Christian tradition.
Calvin Miller

It is noteworthy that one of the words very frequently used of these miracles in the Gospels is the ordinary term, works (*erga*). They were the natural and necessary outcome of His life, the expression in act of what He Himself was.
Griffith Thomas

As for me, I know of nothing but miracles.
Walt Whitman

Miracles, Purpose of

At strategic moments God again and again manifested himself to men by miracles so they had outward, confirming evidence that the words they heard from God's servants were true.
Billy Graham

Miracles of Jesus

The miracles of Jesus were the ordinary works of his Father, wrought small and swift that we might take them in.
George Macdonald

Misery

Change is mandatory, stress is manageable, but misery is optional!
Author unknown

It is a miserable state of mind to have few things to desire and many things to fear.
Francis Bacon

Misery loves company.
John Ray

Misjudgment

I think there is a world market for maybe five computers.
Thomas Watson (1874-1956), Chairman of IBM, 1943

Mission

The harvest truly is plenteous, but the laborers are few.
The Bible, Matthew 9:37

The church exists by mission, as fire exists by burning.
Emil Brunner

When God wills to convert the heathen world, young man, he'll do it without consulting you or me.
The advice which William Carey was given, and which led him in 1792 to start a fund for the Baptist Missionary Society

I will go down, if you will hold the ropes.
William Carey's prayer, likening his missionary work to exploring a mine

The crowning wonder of God's scheme is that he entrusted it to men. It is the supreme glory of humanity that the machinery for its redemption should have been placed within itself.
Henry Drummond

We cannot hesitate to believe that the great mission of Christianity was in reality accomplished by means of informal missionaries.
Adolf Harnack

You have a world to win.
Karl Marx, conclusion of Communist Manifesto

My parish is the gutter.
David Wilkerson

Missionaries

I wasn't God's first choice for what I've done in China.
Gladys Aylward

There are three indispensable requirements for a missionary: 1. Patience. 2. Patience. 3. Patience.
Hudson Taylor

God had an only Son, and he was a missionary and a physician.
David Livingstone

Missionary call

We were enabled to renounce a life of usefulness in another and more distant land.
Thomas Barnardo's description of his call to work in London's East End, when he had previously thought he was being called to be a missionary in China

The awareness of a need and the capacity to meet that need: this constitutes a call.
John R. Mott

Millions have never heard of Jesus. We ought not to ask, "Can I prove that I *ought* to go?" but, "Can I prove that I *ought not* to go?"
C.H. Spurgeon

Cannibals Need Missionaries.
Poster outside a Liverpool hall, advertising a meeting at which C.T. Studd heard of the need of Africa for missionaries.

Go not to those who want you, but to those who want you most.
John Wesley

Mistakes
See also: Confession of sin; Faults; Perfection
Never let mistakes or wrong directions, of which every man falls into many, discourage you. There is precious instruction to be got by finding where we were wrong.
Thomas Carlyle

I beseech you, in the bowels of Christ, think it possible you may be mistaken.
Oliver Cromwell

Great blunders are often made, like large ropes, of a multitude of fibers.
Victor Hugo

There is nothing progressive about being pig-headed and refusing to admit a mistake.
C.S. Lewis

The man who makes no mistakes does not usually make anything.
Edward John Phelps

A life making mistakes is not only more honorable but more useful than a life spent doing nothing.
George Bernard Shaw

A man should never be ashamed to own he has been in the wrong, which is but saying, in other words, that he is wiser today than he was yesterday.
Jonathan Swift

He that never changed any of his opinions, never corrected any of his mistakes: and he, who was never wise enough, to find out any mistakes in himself, will not be charitable enough, to excuse what he

reckons mistakes in others.
Benjamin Whichcote

Misunderstood
To be great is to be misunderstood.
Ralph Waldo Emerson

Mobs
The mob has many heads but no brains.
Proverb

Moderation
Moderation is the silken string running through the pearl chain of all virtues.
Joseph Hall

To go beyond the bounds of moderation is to outrage humanity.
Blaise Pascal

Modesty
He who speaks without modesty will find it difficult to make his words good.
Confucius

Modesty is the citadel of beauty and virtue.
Demades

Great modesty often hides great merit.
Benjamin Franklin

Modesty in human beings is praised because it is not a matter of nature, but of will.
Lactantius

It's good to be clever, but not to show it.
French proverb

Beauty is truly beauty when its comrade is a modest mind.
Greek proverb

Modesty is a becoming ornament in a young man.
Plautus

Modesty once gone never returns.
Seneca

Money
See also: Wealth

Treat money like your God
And it will plague you like the devil.
Author unknown

The surface above gold mines is generally
very barren.
Author unknown

Money is like muck, not good except it be
spread.
Francis Bacon

Every evil, harm, and suffering in this life
… comes from the love of riches.
Catherine of Siena

Money often costs too much.
Ralph Waldo Emerson

Dally not with money or women.
George Herbert

Money is life to wretched mortals.
Hesiod

You can tell what God thinks of money
when you see the people he gives it to.
Abraham Lincoln

Money is always either our master or our
slave.
Latin proverb

Nothing that is God's can be obtained with
money.
Tertullian

Making of money is necessary for daily
living, but money-making is apt to
degenerate into money-loving and then the
deceitfulness of riches enters into and
spoils our spiritual life.
W.H. Griffith Thomas

Get all you can, save all you can and give
all you can.
John Wesley

Money, Love of

People who want to get rich fall into
temptation and a trap and into many
foolish and harmful desires that plunge
men into ruin and destruction. For the
love of money is a root of all kinds of evil.
Some people, eager for money, have
wandered from the faith and pierced
themselves with many griefs.
The Bible, 1 Timothy 6:9,10

It has been said that the love of money is
the root of all evil. The want [lack] of
money is so quite as truly.
Samuel Butler

To be clever enough to get a great deal of
money, one must be stupid enough to
want it.
G.K. Chesterton

The love of money is the parent of all
wickedness.
Philoctetes

Nothing I am sure has such a tendency to
quench the fire of religion as the possession
of money.
J.C. Ryle

Morality

But among you there must not be even a
hint of sexual immorality, or of any kind of
impurity, or of greed, because these are
improper for God's holy people.
The Bible, Ephesians 5:3

Better, though difficult, the right way to go
Than wrong, tho' easy, where the end is
woe.
John Bunyan

All is relative.
Auguste Comte

How is it that nobody has dreamed up
any moral advances since Christ's
teaching?
Michael Green

Give up money, give up fame, give up
science, give up the earth itself and all it
contains, rather than do an immoral act.
Thomas Jefferson

If no set of moral ideas were truer or better than any other, there would be no sense in preferring civilized morality to savage morality, or Christian morality to Nazi morality.
C.S. Lewis

The moment you say that one set of moral ideas can be better than another, you are, in fact, measuring them both by a standard, saying that one of them conforms to that standard more nearly than the other.
C.S. Lewis

A piano has not got two kinds of notes on it, the "right" notes and the "wrong" ones. Every single note is right at one time and wrong at another.
C.S. Lewis

Lord, give us faith that right makes might.
Abraham Lincoln

Each individual, however benighted, recognizes something in him that tells him that he ought to do the thing that is right morally and ought to shun the wrong.
Henry M. Morris

Right is right, even if everyone is against it; and wrong is wrong, even if everyone is for it.
William Penn

If our rationality and morality do not come from God they come from chance permutations of some basic stuff or from the working of mindless forces. In either case, they have no validity.
Richard Purtill

A moral ideal can exist nowhere and nowhow but in a Mind; an absolute moral ideal can exist only in a Mind from which all Reality is derived. Our Moral ideal can only claim objective validity in so far as it can rationally be regarded as the revelation of a moral ideal eternally existing in the mind of God.
Hasting Rashdall

If God exists man cannot be free. But man is free, therefore God cannot exist. Since God does not exist all things are morally permissible.
Jean-Paul Sartre

The Golden Rule is that there are no golden rules.
George Bernard Shaw

The recognition of an objective moral law drives us to the belief in God.
David Elton Trueblood

Mormons

Their official teaching

CHRIST'S CONCEPTION AND BIRTH
Christ was born into the world as the literal Son of this Holy Being; he was born in the same personal, real, and literal sense that any mortal son is born to a mortal father. There is nothing figurative about his paternity; he was begotten, conceived and born in the normal and natural course of events,...Christ is the Son of Man, meaning that his Father (the Eternal God!) is a Holy Man.
Bruce McConkie, a member of the first council of the Seventy, a very high and important position.

PRESIDENT
The Church and kingdom to which we belong will become the kingdom of our God and his Christ, and brother Brigham Young will become President of the United States.
Herber C. Kimball, member of the First Presidency

PROPHECY
God promised in the year 1832 that we should, before the generation then living had passed away, return and build up the City of Zion in Jackson County. We believe in these promises as much as we believe in any promise ever uttered by the mouth of Jehovah. The Latter-day Saints

just as much expect to receive a fulfillment of that promise during the generation that was in existence in 1832 as they expect that the sun will rise and set to-morrow. Why? Because God cannot lie. He will fulfill all His promises. He has spoken, it must come to pass.

Orson Pratt, a Mormon apostle in the 1800's

CHRISTIANITY IS OF THE DEVIL

Myself and hundreds of the Elders around me have seen its [Christianity] pomp, parade, and glory; and what is it? It is a sounding brass and a tinkling symbol; it is as corrupt as hell; and the Devil could not invent a better engine to spread his work than the Christianity of the nineteenth century.

John Taylor, the third President of the Mormon Church, said Christianity

GOD INCREASES IN KNOWLEDGE

If there were a point where a man in his progression could not proceed any further, the very idea would throw a gloom over every intelligent and reflecting mind. God himself is increasing in knowledge, power and dominion, and will do so, worlds without end. It is just so with us.

Wilford Woodruff, the fourth President

ATONEMENT WITH YOUR OWN BLOOD

There is not a man or woman, who violates the covenants made with their God, that will not be required to pay the debt. The blood of Christ will never wipe that out, your own blood must atone for it.

Brigham Young

JOSEPH SMITH WAS A PROPHET

… and he that confesseth not that Jesus has come in the flesh and sent Joseph Smith with the fullness of the Gospel to this generation, is not of God, but is Antichrist.

Bible and Brigham Young's writings

I say now, when they [his discourses] are copied and approved by me they are as good Scripture as is couched in this Bible.

Brigham Young

BRIGHAM YOUNG IS NEVER WRONG

I am here to answer. I shall be on hand to answer when I am called upon, for all the counsel and for all the instruction that I have given to this people. If there is an Elder here, or any member of this Church, called the Church of Jesus Christ of Latter-day Saints, who can bring up the first idea, the first sentence that I have delivered to the people as counsel that is wrong, I really wish they would do it; but they cannot do it, for the simple reason that I have never given counsel that is wrong; this is the reason.

Brigham Young

POLYGAMY

Now if any of you will deny the plurality of wives, and continue to do so, I promise that you will be damned.

Brigham Young

The only men who become Gods, even the Sons of God, are those who enter into polygamy.

Brigham Young

JOSEPH SMITH

No man or woman in this dispensation will ever enter into the celestial kingdom of God without the consent of Joseph Smith.

Brigham Young

CHRIST'S BIRTH

I have given you a few leading items upon this subject, but a great deal more remains to be told. Now, remember from this time forth, and for ever, that Jesus Christ was not begotten by the Holy Ghost.

Brigham Young

ADAM

Now hear it, O inhabitants of the earth, Jew and Gentile, Saint and sinner! When our father Adam came into the garden of Eden, he came into it with a celestial body, and brought Eve, one of his wives, with him. He helped to make and organize this world. He is Michael, the Archangel, the Ancient of Days! about whom holy men have written and spoken – He is our

Father, and our God, and the only God with whom we have to do._ Every man upon the earth, professing Christians or non professing, must hear it, and will know it sooner or later.
Brigham Young

PROPHECY
In the days of Joseph [Smith] it was considered a great privilege to be permitted to speak to a member of Congress, but twenty-six years will not pass away before the Elders of this Church will be as much thought of as the kings on their thrones.
Brigham Young

RACE
You see some classes of the human family that are black, uncouth, uncomely, disagreeable and low in their habits, wild, and seemingly deprived of nearly all the blessings of the intelligence that is generally bestowed upon mankind....Cain slew his brother. Cain might have been killed, and that would have put a termination to that line of human beings._ This was not to be, and the Lord put a_ mark upon him, which is the flat nose and black skin.
Brigham Young

Morning
Your first words every morning should be, Here I am, send me.
John Mason

Mortification
As soon as the soul dies to itself and becomes aware of how much it is loved, the life of grace is given to it and it lives in Christ.
Angela of Foligno

Upon this entire surrender and yielding up of thy will, the love of God in thee becometh the life of thy nature; it killeth thee not, but quickeneth thee, who art now dead to thyself in thine own will.
Jacob Boehme

Mothers
See also: Children; Fathers; Parenting
It is impossible that the son of these tears should perish.
Augustine of Hippo

The mother's heart is the child's schoolroom.
Henry Ward Beecher

What the mother sings to the cradle goes all the way down to the coffin.
Henry Ward Beecher

The great academy, a mother's knee.
Thomas Carlyle

You have omitted to mention the greatest of my teachers – my mother.
Winston Churchill, on being asked to check a list of those who had taught him

Pride is one of the seven deadly sins; but it cannot be the pride of a mother in her children, for that is a compound of two cardinal virtues – faith and hope.
Charles Dickens

Most of the stones for the buildings of the City of God, and all the best of them, are made by mothers.
Henry Drummond

Holy as heaven a mother's tender love, the love of many prayers and many tears which changes not with dim, declining years.
Caroline Norton

God could not be everywhere and therefore he made mothers.
Jewish proverb

Though motherhood is the most important of all the professions – requiring more knowledge than any other department in human affairs – there was no attention given to preparation for this office.
Elizabeth Cady Stanton

Motives
The end justifies the means.
Hermann Busenbaum

Mottoes

The doctor's job: to cure occasionally; to help frequently; to comfort always.
Motto from an American country doctor's surgery

All for one, and one for all.
Alexandre Dumas

Liberty! Equality! Fraternity!
Motto of the French Revolution

Mottoes, corporate

Have you got any rivers they say are uncrossable?
Have you got any mountains you can't tunnel through?
We specialize in the wholly impossible,
Doing the job that no man can do.
Motto of the American engineers

Mottoes, *Corporate*

No absolutely destitute child ever refused admission.
Motto of Dr Barnardo's Homes

Always faithful
United States Marine Corps

Through struggle to the stars.
Motto of the Royal Air Force

To the greater glory of God.
Motto of the Society of Jesus

Unless the Lord is with us, our efforts are in vain.
Motto (in the Latin form Nisi Dominus, frustra) of the city of Edinburgh

Let Glasgow flourish by the preaching of the Word.
Motto of the city of Glasgow

Evil to him who evil thinks.
Motto of the Order of the Garter

Be prepared.
Motto of the Scouts.

Either learn or depart, there is no third choice here.
Motto of Winchester College

National mottos

In God We Trust
In God We Trust first appeared on U.S. coins after April 22, 1864, when Congress passed an act authorizing the coinage of a 2-cent piece bearing this motto. On July 30, 1956, it became the national motto.

The Olympic motto is *Citius, Altius, Fortius;* Faster, Higher, Stronger.
Olympic Games

Mottoes, State

State of Arizona
Ditat Deus (God enriches)

State of Colorado
Nil sine Numine (Nothing without Providence)

State of Connecticut
Qui transtulit sustinet (He who transplanted still sustains)

State of Hawii
Ua Mau Ke Ea O Ka Aina I Ka Pono (The life of the land is perpetuated in righteousness)

State of Kansas
Ad astra per aspera (To the stars through difficulties)

State of Kentucky
United we stand, divided we fall

State of New York
Excelsior (Ever upward)

State of Ohio
With God, all things are possible

State of Rhode Island
Hope

Mottoes, Family and personal

Union makes strength
Motto of the King of the Belians

Speaking the truth in love.
Motto (from Ephesians 4:15) used on letters to friends of Professor Blackie

My heart I give you, Lord, eagerly and entirely.
Motto of John Calvin

What God wills, I will.
Motto of Lord Dormer

Find a way or make one.
Motto of Henry Ford

In God is my hope.
Motto of the Gerard family

Virtue is the only nobility.
Motto of the Earl of Guildford

To a valiant heart nothing is impossible.
Motto of Henry IV of France

Never speak of others' faults nor your own virtues.
Motto of Bob Hope

Night is coming
Motto of Samuel Johnson, Walter Scott and Robert Murray M'Cheyne

Send me where workers are most needed and difficulties are greatest.
Motto of Robert Morrison

At the all-powerful disposal of God.
Motto of the Earl of Mount Edgecumbe

You may be whatever you resolve to be.
Thomas J. (Stonewall) Jackson

Hope in God.
Motto of the Duke of Northumberland

Fidelity is of God.
Motto of Viscount Powerscourt

The first principle God's honor, the second man's happiness, the means prayer and unremitting diligence.
Motto of Lord Shaftesbury

I serve.
Motto since 1346 of the Prince of Wales

Love loyalty
Motto of the Marquis of Winchester

I have one passion, and it is He, only He.
Motto of Count von Zinzendorf

Heart speaks to heart.
Motto of J.H. Newman

God only do I seek.
Motto of the Marquis of Northampton

Mourning
The true way to mourn the dead is to take care of the living who belong to them.
Edmund Burke

Mourning which is according to God's will is an anguished heart that passionately seeks what it thirsts for, and when it fails to attain it, pursues it diligently and follows behind it lamenting bitterly.
John Climacus

Silent sorrow is only the more fatal.
Racine

Murder
No actions are bad in themselves, even murder can be justified.
Dietrich Bonhoeffer

The five most important motives for murder are: Fear – jealousy – money –

revenge – and protecting someone you love.
Frederick Knott – Max Halliday, Dial M for Murder

The poor man raises his sons, but the daughters, if one is poor, we expose.
Stobaeus

Murphy's law
1. Nothing is as easy as it looks.
2. Everything takes longer than you think.
3. If anything can go wrong, it will.
Author unknown

Music
Music, the greatest good that mortals know,
And all of heaven we have below.
Joseph Addison

God has preached the gospel through music.
Martin Luther

Music is the thing of the world that I love most.
Samuel Pepys

Music, Effects of
Music is for the soul what wind is for the ship, blowing her onwards in the direction in which she is steered.
William Booth

Music strikes in me a profound contemplation of the First Composer.
Thomas Browne

Music and the devil
I see no reason why the devil should have all the good tunes.
Rowland Hill

Music is hateful and intolerable to the devil. I truly believe, and do not mind saying, that there is no art like music, next to theology. It is the only art, next to theology, that can calm the agitations of the soul, which plainly shows that the devil, the source of anxiety and sadness, flees from the sound of music as he does

from religious worship. That is why the scriptures are full of psalms and hymns, in which praise is given to God. That is why, when we gather round God's throne in heaven, we shall sing his glory. Music is the perfect way to express our love and devotion to God. It is one of the most magnificent and delightful presents God has given us.
Martin Luther

Mystery
For there is no other mystery of God, except Christ.
Augustine of Hippo

The simple, absolute and immutable mysteries of the divine Truth are hidden in secret. For this darkness, though of deepest obscurity, is yet radiantly clear; and, though beyond touch and sight, it more than fills our unseeing minds with splendors of transcendent beauty. And we behold that darkness beyond being, concealed under all natural light.
Dionysius the Areopagite

It was the experience of mystery – even if mixed with fear – that engendered religion.
Albert Einstein

A religion without mystery must be a religion without God.
Jeremy Taylor

Mysticism
Mysticism keeps men sane.
G.K. Chesterton

The dark night of the soul through which the soul passes on its way to the Divine Light.
John of the Cross

A most sublime and sweet knowledge of God and of His attributes overflows into the understanding from the contact of the attributes of God with the substance of the soul.
John of the Cross

For what is mysticism? Is it not the
attempt to draw near to God, not by rites
or ceremonies, but by inward disposition?
Is it not merely a hard word for "The
Kingdom of Heaven is within"? Heaven is
neither a place nor a time.
Florence Nightingale

In joy of inward peace, or sense
Of sorrow over sin,
He is his own best evidence
His witness is within.
J.G. Whittier

Mysticism, Christian
Christian mysticism is the attempt to
realize in the thought and feeling the
immanence of the temporal in the eternal
and of the eternal in the temporal.
Dean Inge

Mystics
Holidays, relaxation, and the simple
pleasure of life are as important for the
mystic as they are for other people.
Martin Israel

Myths
They will turn their ears away from the
truth and turn aside to myths.
The Bible, 2 Timothy 4:4

N

Name of Jesus

The name Jesus is not only light but food. It is oil without which food for the soul is dry, and salt without which it is insipid. It is honey in the mouth, melody in the ear and joy in the heart. It has healing power. Every discussion where his name is not heard is pointless.
Bernard of Clairvaux

How sweet the name of Jesus sounds
In a believer's ear!
It soothes his sorrows, heals his wounds,
And drives away his fear.
John Newton

Narcissist

A narcissist is someone better looking than you are.
Gore Vidal

Nations

The nations are as a drop of a bucket.
The Bible, Isaiah 40:15 KJV

By three things will a nation endure: truth, justice, and peace.
Rabbinical saying

Nature
See also: Creation

The morning stars sang together, and all the sons of God shouted for joy.
Job 38:7 KJV

The heavens declare the glory of God; and the firmament showeth his handiwork.
The Bible, Psalm 19:1 KJV

All things bright and beautiful,
All things great and small,
All things wise and wonderful,

The Lord God made them all.
Cecil Frances Alexander

In all things of nature there is something marvelous.
Aristotle

Nature, to be commanded, must be obeyed.
Francis Bacon

You will find something more in woods than in books. Trees and stones will teach you what you cannot learn from masters.
Bernard of Clairvaux

Every creature is a divine word because it proclaims God.
Bonaventure

Nature is but a name for an effect whose cause is God.
William Cowper

We can almost smell the aroma of God's beauty in the fresh spring flowers. His breath surrounds us in the warm summer breezes.
Gale Heide

[Speaking of his studies and discoveries:] O God, I am thinking your thoughts after you.
Johann Kepler

Every formula which expresses a law of nature is a hymn of praise to God.
Maria Mitchell, inscription on Bust in the Hall of Fame

The more I study nature, the more I am amazed at the Creator.
Louis Pasteur

Anyone can count the seeds in an apple,
but only God can count the number of
apples in a seed.
Robert H. Schuller

And this our life, exempt from public
  haunt,
Finds tongues in trees, books in the
  running brooks,
Sermons in stones, and good in everything.
William Shakespeare, As You Like It

Nature, as far as in her lies,
Imitates God and turns her face
To every land beneath the skies,
Counts nothing that she meets with base
But lives and loves in every place.
Tennyson

Nature and belief in God
For the atheist maintains that he sees
nothing but contradictions in nature. He,
therefore, rejects from his world of ideas
any thought of a creator behind nature.
However, we dare not forget that even the
tiniest island of order in the largest sea of
chaos demands a creator of that small
remaining order.
A.E. Wilder-Smith, British scientist

Nature as revealing God
I love to think of nature as an unlimited
broadcasting station through which God
speaks to us every hour, if we will only
tune in.
George Washington Carver

It is a remarkable fact than no canonical
writer has ever used Nature to prove
God.
Blaise Pascal

Jesus taught men to see the operation of
God in the regular and the normal – in the
rising of the sun and the falling of the rain
and the growth of the plant.
William Temple

For the beauty of the earth,
For the beauty of the skies,
For the love which from our birth

Over and around us lies:
Father, unto thee we raise
This our sacrifice of praise.
F.S. Pierpoint

Need of God
O God, never suffer us to think that we
can stand by ourselves, and not need thee.
John Donne

Neighbor
… love your neighbor as yourself.
The Bible, Leviticus 19:18

Neighbor, Love for
Charity begins at home, and justice begins
next door.
Charles Dickens

Those who do not love their neighbor
abhor God.
John of the Cross

Do not waste your time bothering about
whether you love your neighbor; act as if
you did … When you are behaving as if
you love someone, you will presently come
to love him.
C.S. Lewis

I am to become a Christ to my neighbor
and be for him what Christ is for me.
Martin Luther

The love of our neighbor is the only door
out of the dungeon of self.
George Macdonald

Neighbor, Love for, and love for God
The love of God is the first and great
commandment. But love of our neighbor
is the means by which we obey it. Since we
cannot see God directly, God allows us to
catch sight of him through our neighbor.
By loving our neighbor we purge our eyes
to see God. So love your neighbor and you
will discover that in doing so you come to
know God.
Augustine of Hippo

He alone loves the Creator perfectly who

manifests a pure love for his neighbor.
Bede

In order to love our neighbor properly we must seek God's help. It is not possible to love our neighbor with a pure heart without loving God first. We cannot pass on God's love if we do not possess God's love ourselves.
Bernard of Clairvaux

You can never love your neighbor without loving God.
Bossuet

Though we do not have our Lord with us in bodily presence, we have our neighbor, who, for the ends of love and loving service, is as good as our Lord himself.
Teresa of Avila

Neighbor, Love for, and the "Golden Rule"

Do to others as you would have them do to you.
The Bible, Luke 6:31

Is not *reciprocity* such a word [that can act as a rule for all life]? What you do not want done to yourself, do not do to others.
Confucius

What you hate to suffer, do not do to anyone else.
Isocrates

What is hateful to thyself do not unto thy neighbor.
The Talmud

Neighborliness

Love your neighbor, but don't pull down the hedge.
Swiss proverb

There is no principle of the heart that is more acceptable to God than a universal, ardent love for all mankind, which seeks and prays for their happiness.
William Law

New Testament

I have put a New Testament among your books ... because it is the best book that ever was, or will be, known in the world; and because it teaches you the best lessons by which any human creature, who tries to be truthful and faithful to duty, can possibly be guided.
Charles Dickens, when his youngest child was about to leave England for Australia

One does well to put on gloves when reading the New Testament; the proximity of so much impurity almost compels this. ... I have searched it vainly for even a single congenial trait ... everything in it is cowardice and self-deception.
Friedrich Nietzsche

New Testament, Reliability of

The evidence for our New Testament writings is ever so much greater than the evidence for many writings of classical authors, the authenticity of which no one dreams of questioning.
F.F. Bruce

Ninety-five Theses

Martin Luther

Disputation on the Power and Efficacy of Indulgences commonly known as the 95 Theses

Out of love and concern for the truth, and with the object of eliciting it, the following heads will be the subject of a public discussion at Wittenberg under the presidency of the reverend father, Martin Luther, Augustinian, Master of Arts and Sacred Theology, and duly appointed Lecturer on these subjects in that place. He requests that whoever cannot be present personally to debate the matter orally will do so in absence in writing.

1. When our Lord and Master, Jesus Christ, said "Repent", He called for the entire life of believers to be one of penitence.

2. The word cannot be properly

understood as referring to the sacrament of penance, i.e. confession and satisfaction, as administered by the clergy.

3. Yet its meaning is not restricted to penitence in one's heart; for such penitence is null unless it produces outward signs in various mortifications of the flesh.

4. As long as hatred of self abides (i.e. true inward penitence) the penalty of sin abides, viz., until we enter the kingdom of heaven.

5. The pope has neither the will nor the power to remit any penalties beyond those imposed either at his own discretion or by canon law.

6. The pope himself cannot remit guilt, but only declare and confirm that it has been remitted by God; or, at most, he can remit it in cases reserved to his discretion. Except for these cases, the guilt remains untouched.

7. God never remits guilt to anyone without, at the same time, making humbly submissive to the priest, His representative.

8. The penitential canons apply only to men who are still alive, and, according to the canons themselves, none applies to the dead.

9. Accordingly, the Holy Spirit, acting in the person of the pope, manifests grace to us, by the fact that the papal regulations always cease to apply at death, or in any hard case.

10. It is a wrongful act, due to ignorance, when priests retain the canonical penalties on the dead in purgatory.

11. When canonical penalties were changed and made to apply to purgatory, surely it would seem that tares were sown while the bishops were asleep.

12. In former days, the canonical penalties were imposed, not after, but before absolution was pronounced; and were intended to be tests of true contrition.

13. Death puts an end to all the claims of the Church; even the dying are already dead to the canon laws, and are no longer bound by them.

14. Defective piety or love in a dying person is necessarily accompanied by great fear, which is greatest where the piety or love is least.

15. This fear or horror is sufficient in itself, whatever else might be said, to constitute the pain of purgatory, since it approaches very closely to the horror of despair.

16. There seems to be the same difference between hell, purgatory, and heaven as between despair, uncertainty, and assurance.

17. Of a truth, the pains of souls in purgatory ought to be abated, and charity ought to be proportionately increased.

18. Moreover, it does not seem proved, on any grounds of reason or Scripture, that these souls are outside the state of merit, or unable to grow in grace.

19. Nor does it seem proved to be always the case that they are certain and assured of salvation, even if we are very certain ourselves.

20. Therefore the pope, in speaking of the plenary remission of all penalties, does not mean "all" in the strict sense, but only those imposed by himself.

21. Hence those who preach indulgences are in error when they say that a man is absolved and saved from every penalty by the pope's indulgences;

22. Indeed, he cannot remit to souls in purgatory any penalty which canon law declares should be suffered in the present life.

23. If plenary remission could be granted to anyone at all, it would be only in the cases of the most perfect, i.e. to very few.

24. It must therefore be the case that the major part of the people are deceived by that indiscriminate and high-sounding promise of relief from penalty.

25. The same power as the pope exercises in general over purgatory is exercised in particular by every single bishop in his bishopric and priest in his parish.

26. The pope does excellently when he grants remission to the souls in purgatory on account of intercessions made on their behalf, and not by the power of the keys (which he cannot exercise for them).

27. There is no divine authority for preaching that the soul flies out of the purgatory immediately the money clinks in the bottom of the chest.

28. It is certainly possible that when the money clinks in the bottom of the chest avarice and greed increase; but when the

church offers intercession, all depends in the will of God.

29. Who knows whether all souls in purgatory wish to be redeemed in view of what is said of St. Severinus and St. Pascal?

30. No one is sure if the reality of his own contrition, much less of receiving plenary forgiveness.

31. One who — *bona fide* — buys indulgence is a rare as a — *bona fide* — penitent man, i.e. very rare indeed.

32. All those who believe themselves certain of their own salvation by means if letters of indulgence, will be eternally damned, together with their teachers.

33. We should be most carefully on our guard against those who say that the papal indulgences are an inestimable divine gift, and that a man is reconciled to God by them.

34. For the grace conveyed by these indulgences relates simply to the penalties of the sacramental "satisfactions" decreed merely by man.

35. It is not in accordance with Christian doctrines to preach and teach that those who buy off souls, or purchase confessional licences, have no need to repent of their own sins.

36. Any Christian whatsoever, who is truly repentant, enjoys plenary remission from penalty and guilt, and this is given him without letters of indulgence.

37. Any true Christian whatsoever, living or dead, participates in all the benefits of Christ and the Church; and this participation is granted to him by God without letters of indulgence.

38. Yet the pope's remission and dispensation are in no way to be despised, form as already said, they proclaim the divine remission.

39. It is very difficult, even for the most learned theologians, to extol to the people the great bounty contained in the indulgences, while, at the same time, praising contrition as a virtue.

40. A truly contrite sinner seeks out, and loves to pay, the penalties of his sins; whereas the very multitude of indulgences dulls men's consciences, and tends to make them hate the penalties.

41. Papal indulgences should only be preached with caution, lest people gain a wrong understanding, and think that they are preferable to other good works: those of love.

42. Christians should be taught that the pope does not at all intend that the purchase of indulgences should be understood as at all comparable with the works of mercy.

43. Christians should be taught that one who gives to the poor, or lends to the needy, does a better action than if he purchases indulgences.

44. Because, by works of love, love grows and a man becomes a better man; whereas, by indulgences, he does not become a better man, but only escapes certain penalties.

45. Christians should be taught that he who sees a needy person, but passes him by although he gives money for indulgences, gains no benefit from the pope's pardon, but only incurs the wrath of God.

46. Christians should be taught that, unless they have more than they need, they are bound to retain what is only necessary for the upkeep of their home, and should in no way squander it on indulgences.

47. Christians should be taught that they purchase indulgences voluntarily, and are not under obligation to do so.

48. Christians should be taught that, in granting indulgences, the pope has more need, and more desire, for devout prayer on his own behalf than for ready money.

49. Christians should be taught that the pope's indulgences are useful only if one does not rely on them, but most harmful if one loses the fear of God through them.

50. Christians should be taught that, if the pope knew the exactions of the indulgence-preachers, he would rather the church of St. Peter were reduced to ashes than be built with the skin, flesh, and bones of the sheep.

51. Christians should be taught that the pope would be willing, as he ought if necessity should arise, to sell the church of St. Peter, and give, too, his own money to

many of those whom the pardon-merchants conjure money.

52. It is vain to rely on salvation by letters if indulgence, even if the commissary, or indeed the pope himself, were to pledge his own soul for their validity.

53. Those are enemies of Christ and the pope who forbid the word of God to be preached at all in some churches, in order that indulgences may be preached in others.

54. The word of God suffers injury if, in the same sermon, an equal or longer time is devoted to indulgences than to that word.

55. The pope cannot help taking the view that if indulgences (very small matters) are celebrated by one bell, one pageant, or one ceremony, the gospel (a very great matter) should be preached to the accompaniment of a hundred bells, a hundred processions, a hundred ceremonies.

56. The treasures of the church, out of which the pope dispenses indulgences, are not sufficiently spoken of or known among the people of Christ.

57. That these treasures are note temporal are clear from the fact that many of the merchants do not grant them freely, but only collect them.

58. Nor are they the merits of Christ and the saints, because, even apart from the pope, these merits are always working grace in the inner man, and working the cross, death, and hell in the outer man.

59. St. Laurence said that the poor were the treasures of the church, but he used the term in accordance with the custom of his own time.

60. We do not speak rashly in saying that the treasures of the church are the keys of the church, and are bestowed by the merits of Christ.

61. For it is clear that the power of the pope suffices, by itself, for the remission of penalties and reserved cases.

62. The true treasure of the church is the Holy gospel of the glory and the grace of God.

63. It is right to regard this treasure as most odious, for it makes the first to be the last.

64. On the other hand, the treasure of indulgences is most acceptable, for it makes the last to be the first.

65. Therefore the treasures of the gospel are nets which, in former times, they used to fish for men of wealth.

66. The treasures of the indulgences are the nets to-day which they use to fish for men of wealth.

67. The indulgences, which the merchants extol as the greatest of favors, are seen to be, in fact, a favorite means for money-getting.

68. Nevertheless, they are not to be compared with the grace of God and the compassion shown in the Cross.

69. Bishops and curates, in duty bound, must receive the commissaries of the papal indulgences with all reverence;

70. But they are under a much greater obligation to watch closely and attend carefully lest these men preach their own fancies instead of what the pope commissioned.

71. Let him be anathema and accursed who denies the apostolic character of the indulgences.

72. On the other hand, let him be blessed who is on his guard against the wantonness and licence of the pardon-merchant's words.

73. In the same way, the pope rightly excommunicates those who make any plans to the detriment of the trade in indulgences.

74. It is much more in keeping with his views to excommunicate those who use the pretext of indulgences to plot anything to the detriment of holy love and truth.

75. It is foolish to think that papal indulgences have so much power that they can absolve a man even if he has done the impossible and violated the mother of God.

76. We assert the contrary, and say that the pope's pardons are not able to remove the least venial of sins as far as their guilt is concerned.

77. When it is said that not even St. Peter, if he were now pope, could grant a greater grace, it is blasphemy against St. Peter and the pope.

78. We assert the contrary, and say that he, and any pope whatever, possesses greater graces, viz., the gospel, spiritual powers,

gifts of healing, etc., as is declared in I Corinthians 12 [:28].

79. It is blasphemy to say that the insignia of the cross with the papal arms are of equal value to the cross on which Christ died.

80. The bishops, curates, and theologians, who permit assertions of that kind to be made to the people without let or hindrance, will have to answer for it.

81. This unbridled preaching of indulgences makes it difficult for learned men to guard the respect due to the pope against false accusations, or at least from the keen criticisms of the laity;

82. They ask, e.g.: Why does not the pope liberate everyone from purgatory for the sake of love (a most holy thing) and because of the supreme necessity of their souls? This would be morally the best of all reasons. Meanwhile he redeems innumerable souls for money, a most perishable thing, with which to build St. Peter's church, a very minor purpose.

83. Again: Why should funeral and anniversary masses for the dead continue to be said? And why does not the pope repay, or permit to be repaid, the benefactions instituted for these purposes, since it is wrong to pray for those souls who are now redeemed?

84. Again: Surely this is a new sort of compassion, on the part of God and the pope, when an impious man, an enemy of God, is allowed to pay money to redeem a devout soul, a friend of God; while yet that devout and beloved soul is not allowed to be redeemed without payment, for love's sake, and just because of its need of redemption.

85. Again: Why are the penitential canon laws, which in fact, if not in practice, have long been obsolete and dead in themselves,-why are they, to-day, still used in imposing fines in money, through the granting of indulgences, as if all the penitential canons were fully operative?

86. Again: since the pope's income to-day is larger than that of the wealthiest of wealthy men, why does he not build this one church of St. Peter with his own money, rather than with the money of indigent believers?

87. Again: What does the pope remit or dispense to people who, by their perfect penitence, have a right to plenary remission or dispensation?

88. Again: Surely a greater good could be done to the church if the pope were to bestow these remissions and dispensations, not once, as now, but a hundred times a day, for the benefit of any believer whatever.

89. What the pope seeks by indulgences is not money, but rather the salvation of souls; why then does he not suspend the letters and indulgences formerly conceded, and still as efficacious as ever?

90. These questions are serious matters of conscience to the laity. To suppress them by force alone, and not to refute them by giving reasons, is to expose the church and the pope to the ridicule of their enemies, and to make Christian people unhappy.

91. If therefore, indulgences were preached in accordance with the spirit and mind of the pope, all these difficulties would be easily overcome, and indeed, cease to exist.

92. Away, then, with those prophets who say to Christ's people, "Peace, peace," where in there is no peace.

93. Hail, hail to all those prophets who say to Christ's people, "The cross, the cross," where there is no cross.

94. Christians should be exhorted to be zealous to follow Christ, their Head, through penalties, deaths, and hells;

95. And let them thus be more confident of entering heaven through many tribulations rather than through a false assurance of peace.

Martin Luther

___

Non-violence

Non-violence is the article of faith.
Mahatma Gandhi

In my opinion non-violence is not passivity in any shape or form. Non-violence as I understand it is the most active force in the world.
Mahatima Gandhi

Violence as a way of achieving racial justice is both impractical and immoral. It is impractical because it is a descending spiral ending in destruction for all. The old law of an eye for an eye leaves everyone blind. It is immoral because it seeks to humiliate the opponent rather than win his understanding; it seeks to annihilate rather than convert. Violence is immoral because it thrives on hatred rather than love. It destroys community and makes brotherhood impossible. It leaves society in monologue rather than dialogue. Violence ends by defeating itself. It creates bitterness in the survivors and brutality in the destroyers.
Martin Luther King, Jr

Preach and pray, but do not fight.
Martin Luther, advising those reformers who might have become revolutionaries

This house will in no circumstances fight for its King and country.
Motion passed at the Oxford Union, Oxford University, 9 February 1933

The Spirit of Christ, which leads us into all Truth, will never move us to fight and war against any man with outward weapons, neither for the kingdom of Christ, nor for the kingdoms of this world.
Quaker Declaration, 1660

Novelty
It is in the nature of man to long for novelty.
Pliny the Elder

Obedience

See also: Faith; Service

And when they brought them, they set them before the high council. And the high priest asked them, saying, "Did we not strictly command you not to teach in his name? And look, you have filled Jerusalem with your doctrine, and intend to bring this Man's blood on us!" But Peter and the apostles answered and said: "We ought to obey God rather than men."
The Bible, Acts 5:27-29 NKJV

Circumcision is nothing and uncircumcision is nothing. Keeping God's commands is what counts.
The Bible, 1 Corinthians 7:19

Do not merely listen to the word, and so deceive yourselves. Do what it says.
The Bible, James 1:22

Obedience to God is always for our good and his glory.
Author unknown

You can never go wrong when you chose to obey Christ.
Author unknown

The cost of obedience is small compared with the cost of disobedience.
Author unknown

Wicked men obey from fear; good men, from love.
Aristotle

When your commands are obeyed, it is from you that we receive the power to obey them.
Augustine of Hippo

It does not require great learning to be a Christian and be convinced of the truth of the Bible. It requires only an honest heart and a willingness to obey God.
Albert Barnes

The strength and happiness of a man consists in finding out the way in which God is going, and going that way too.
Henry Ward Beecher

Put aside your own will so as to go to war under Christ the Lord, the real King, picking up the keen and glittering weapons of obedience.
Benedict, Rule

Unless he obeys, a man cannot believe.
Dietrich Bonhoeffer

The test of progress is obedience.
A.E. Brooke

How absurd would it be that in satisfying men you should incur the displeasure of him for whose sake you obey men themselves!
John Calvin

The golden rule for understanding in spiritual matters is not intellect, but obedience.
Oswald Chambers

Obedience is the complete renunciation of one's own soul, demonstrated, however, by actions. More exactly, it is the death of the senses in a living soul.
John Climacus

Obedience is the burial of the will and the resurrection of humility.
John Climacus

As soon as we lay ourselves entirely at His feet, we have enough light given to us to guide our own steps. We are like the foot soldier, who hears nothing of the councils that determine the course of the great battle he is in, but hears plainly enough the word of command that he must himself obey.
George Eliot

It is a vain thought to flee from the work that God appoints us, instead of seeking it in loving obedience.
George Eliot

Happy the soul which by a sincere self-renunciation, holds itself ceaselessly in the hands of its Creator, ready to do everything which He wishes; which never stops saying to itself a hundred times a day, "Lord, what would you have me do?"
F. Fénelon

How many observe Christ's birthday! How few, his precepts! O! 'tis easier to keep holidays than commandments.
Benjamin Franklin

Obedience is the only virtue that plants the other virtues in the heart and preserves them after they have been planted.
Gregory the Great

A Christian is just as much under obligation to obey God's will in the most secular of his daily businesses as he is in his closet or at the communion table.
A.A. Hodge

Ye call me master, and obey me not;
Ye call me light, and seek me not;
Ye call me way, and walk me not;
Ye call me wise, and follow me not;
Ye call me fair, and love me not;
Ye call me rich, and ask me not;
Ye call me eternal, and seek me not;
Ye call me gracious, and trust me not;
Ye call me noble, and serve me not;
Ye call me mighty, and honor me not;
Ye call me just, and fear me not;

If I condemn you, blame me not.
In the cathedral at Lubek, Germany

God desires the least degree of obedience and submissiveness more than all those services you think of rendering him.
John of the Cross

It is so hard to believe because it is so hard to obey.
Søren Kierkegaard

Obedience is the road to freedom, humility the road to pleasure, unity the road to personality.
C.S. Lewis

I was not born to be free. I was born to adore and to obey.
C.S. Lewis

Nothing is really lost by a life of sacrifice; everything is lost by failure to obey God's call.
Henry P. Liddon

You may as well quit reading and hearing the Word of God, and give it to the devil, if you do not desire to live according to it.
Martin Luther

I find that doing the will of God leaves me with no time for disputing about his plans.
George Macdonald

When God gives a command or a vision of truth, it is never a question of what he will do, but what we will do.
Henrietta Mears

That thou art happy, owe to God; That thou continuest such, owe to thyself, That is, to thy obedience.
John Milton

Every virtue is a form of obedience to God. Every evil word or act is a form of rebellion against him.
Stephen Neill

If two angels were to receive at the same moment a commission from God, one to

go down and rule earth's grandest empire, the other to go and sweep the streets of its meanest village, it would be a matter of entire indifference to each which service fell to his lot, the post of ruler or the post of scavenger; for the joy of the angels lies only in obedience to God's will, and with equal joy they would lift a Lazarus in his rags to Abraham's bosom, or be a chariot of fire to carry an Elijah home.
John Newton

Then are we servants of God, then are we the disciples of Christ, when we do what is commanded us and because it is commanded us.
John Owen

There is no greater life than always to will the divine will.
Marguerite Porete

No man is a successful commander who has not first learned to obey.
Chinese proverb

A man is not far from the gates of heaven when he is fully submissive to the Lord's will.
C.H. Spurgeon

I know the power obedience has of making things easy which seem impossible.
Teresa of Avila

Learn to obey, you who are but dust!
Thomas à Kempis

It is much safer to obey, than to govern.
Thomas à Kempis

The lips are how to obey the brain when the heart is mutinous.
Voltaire

Obedience and understanding
The tiniest fragment of obedience, and heaven opens up and the profoundest truths of God are yours straight away. God will never reveal more truth about himself till you obey what you know already.
Oswald Chambers

Objections
There is nothing new in people objecting to Paul's doctrine of salvation. People were objecting to it in the first century and they have been objecting to it ever since. Today's objections to this teaching have nothing to do with modern learning, modern knowledge, modern science – nothing at all. People have always objected to it.
Martyn Lloyd-Jones

Observation
Nothing has such power to broaden the mind as the ability to investigate systematically and truly all that comes under thy observation in life.
Marcus Aurelius Antoninus

To acquire knowledge, one must study; but to acquire wisdom, one must observe.
Marilyn Vos Savant

Observing Christian festivals
One man considers one day more sacred than another; another man considers every day alike. Each one should be fully convinced in his own mind. He who regards one day as special, does so to the Lord. He who eats meat, eats to the Lord, for he gives thanks to God; and he who abstains, does so to the Lord and gives thanks to God.
The Bible, Romans 14:5-6

Obstacles
If you can find a path with no obstacles, it probably doesn't lead anywhere.
Author unknown

Obstacles cannot crush me. Every obstacle yields to stern resolve. He who is fixed to a star does not change his mind.
Leonardo da Vinci

Most of our obstacles would melt away if, instead of cowering before them, we should make up our minds to walk boldly through them.
Orison Swett Marden

Obstacles are those frightful things you see when you take your eyes off the goal.
Hannah More

Occult
The occult may be fascinating, but it is not edifying.
Douglas Groothuis

Although detestable to God, delightful to the devil, unhealthy to humans and impotent to save (Isaiah 47:12-15), the occult draws adherents like metal to a magnet because it gives rein to the religious instinct deep within a person but does not make upon him any claims for love, holiness, or service to others.
Douglas Groothuis

Offence, Giving
But the man who has doubts is condemned if he eats, because his eating is not from faith; and everything that does not come from faith is sin.
The Bible, Romans 14:23

Old age
See also: Age; Ages of man
Do not regret growing older. It is a privilege denied to many.
Author unknown

To grow old is to pass from passion to compassion.
Albert Camus

Old age isn't so bad when you consider the alternative.
Maurice Chevalier 1888-1972

You old people, don't think you are becoming better just because you are becoming deader.
Dr Manfred Gutzke

In the evening of our lives we shall be examined in love.
John of the Cross

He that lives, must grow old; and he that would rather grow old than die, has God

to thank for the infirmities of old age.
Samuel Johnson

Accept it, adjust to it, adorn it.
Guy King

Grey hairs are a proof of age, but not of wisdom.
Menander

My memory is nearly gone, but I remember two things: that I am a great sinner, and that Christ is a great Savior.
John Newton, aged 82

What you and I become in the end will be just more and more of what we are deciding and trying to be right now.
John Powell

We fool ourselves. We pray for a long life, and fear old age.
Chinese proverb

[During the Boxer Rebellion of 1900, the China Inland Mission was suffering great losses, and every telegram brought more tragic news of Christians being killed, property being confiscated, and workers scattered. The mission's founder, the elderly J. Hudson Taylor, was in Switzerland and under orders to rest because of ill health. His heart ached for his coworkers in China. When things were at their worst, he said,] "I cannot read; I cannot think; I cannot even pray; but I can trust."
Hudson Taylor

Nobody grows old merely by living a number of years. We grow old by deserting our ideals.
Samuel Ullman

Old age, Respect for
Learn all you can from old people. They've been down the road you must travel.
Author unknown

Respect grey hairs.
Greek proverb

Old age and action
Keeping useful keeps us youthful.
Author unknown

We never grow old. We get old when we stop growing.
Author unknown

Old age and maturing
To know how to grow old is the master work of wisdom, and one of the most difficult chapters in the great art of living.
Henri Frédéric Amiel

Old Testament
In the Old Testament the New is concealed, in the New Testament the Old is revealed.
Augustine of Hippo

I beg every devout Christian not to despise the simplicity of language and the stories found in the Old Testament. He should remember that, however simple the Old Testament may seem, it contains the words, works, judgments and actions of God himself. Indeed the simplicity makes fools of the wise and clever, and allows the poor and simple to see the ways of God. Therefore submit your thoughts and feelings to the stories you read, and let yourself be carried like a child to God.
Martin Luther

The Old Testament does not occupy itself with how Israel thought of God. Its concern is with how Israel ought to think of God. The fundamental note of the Old Testament is revelation.
Benjamin B. Warfield

Old Testament, Trustworthiness of
For forty-five years continuously, since I left college, I have devoted myself to the one great study of the Old Testament, in all its languages, in all its archaeology, in all its translations, and as far as possible in everything bearing upon its text and history.

The result of my forty-five years of study of the Bible has led me all the time to a firmer faith that in the Old Testament we have a true historical account of the Israelite people.
Robert Dick Wilson

Old Testament and Christianity
The followers of Jesus seem to have described themselves by various names in early days. Many of these names were redolent of Old Testament phraseology. "The saints" or "holy people" was a common name, implying that they regarded themselves as the pious remnant or true Israel ... They themselves constituted a separated "synagogue" or community within the larger community of Judaism. But while the term "synagogue" enjoyed some currency among them for some decades, it was gradually ousted by its synonym *ekklesia* – church... In the Septuagint, *ekklesia* was used to render the Hebrew word *qahal*, the "congregation" of Israel, the nation in its theocratic character, organized as a religious community. The choice of this term was a further indication of the early Christians' conviction that they were the legitimate successors of the true Israel, bound by God to himself in covenant-relationship from the days when Israel first became a nation.
F.F. Bruce

Old Testament and Jesus
Christ adopted towards the Scriptures of the Old Testament an attitude of reverent assent and submission, and he maintained this position through his life and ministry, including the post-resurrection period.
John Stott

Older men
Teach the older men to be temperate, worthy of respect, self-controlled, and sound in faith, in love and in endurance.
The Bible, Titus 2:2

Older women
Likewise, teach the older women to be reverent in the way they live, not to be slanderers or addicted to much wine, but to teach what is good. Then they can train

the younger women to love their husbands and children, to be self-controlled and pure, to be busy at home, to be kind, and to be subject to their husbands, so that no one will malign the word of God.

The Bible, Titus 2:3-5

Omens

My child, be no dealer in omens, since it leads to idolatry, nor an enchanter nor an astrologer nor a magician, neither be willing to look at them; for from all these things idolatry is engendered.

Didache

On Loving God

Bernard of Clairvaux

CHAPTER I

Why we should love God and the measure of that love

You want me to tell you why God is to be loved and how much. I answer, the reason for loving God is God Himself; and the measure of love due to Him is immeasurable love. Is this plain? Doubtless, to a thoughtful man; but I am debtor to the unwise also. A word to the wise is sufficient; but I must consider simple folk too. Therefore I set myself joyfully to explain more in detail what is meant above.

We are to love God for Himself, because of a twofold reason; nothing is more reasonable, nothing more profitable. When one asks, Why should I love God? he may mean, What is lovely in God? or What shall I gain by loving God? In either case, the same sufficient cause of love exists, namely, God Himself.

And first, of His title to our love. Could any title be greater than this, that He gave Himself for us unworthy wretches? And being God, what better gift could He offer than Himself? Hence, if one seeks for God's claim upon our love here is the chiefest: Because He first loved us (I John 4:19).

Ought He not to be loved in return, when we think who loved, whom He loved, and how much He loved? For who is He that loved? The same of whom every spirit testifies: "Thou art my God: my goods are nothing unto Thee" (Ps. 16:2, Vulg.). And is not His love that wonderful charity which "seeketh not her own"? (I Cor.13:5). But for whom was such unutterable love made manifest? The apostle tells us: "When we were enemies, we were reconciled to God by the death of His Son" (Rom. 5:10). So it was God who loved us, loved us freely, and loved us while yet we were enemies. And how great was this love of His? St. John answers: "God so loved the world that He gave His only-begotten Son, that whosoever believeth in Him should not perish, but have everlasting life" (John 3:16). St. Paul adds: "He spared not His own Son, but delivered Him up for us all" (Rom. 8:32); and the son says of Himself, "Greater love hath no man than this, that a man lay down his life for his friends" (John 15:13).

This is the claim which God the holy, the supreme, the omnipotent, has upon men, defiled and base and weak. Some one may urge that this is true of mankind, but not of angels. True, since for angels it was not needful. He who succored men in their time of need, preserved angels from such need; and even as His love for sinful men wrought wondrously in them so that they should not remain sinful, so that same love which in equal measure He poured out upon angels kept them altogether free from sin.

CHAPTER II

On loving God

How much God deserves love from man in recognition of His gifts, both material and spiritual: and how these gifts should be cherished without neglect of the Giver

Those who admit the truth of what I have said know, I am sure, why we are bound to love God. But if unbelievers will not grant it, their ingratitude is at once confounded by His innumerable benefits, lavished on our race, and plainly discerned by the senses. Who is it that gives food to all flesh, light to every eye, air to all that breathe? It would be foolish to begin a catalogue, since I have just called them innumerable: but I name, as notable instances, food, sunlight and air; not because they are God's best gifts, but because they are essential to bodily life. Man must seek in his own higher nature for the highest gifts; and these are dignity, wisdom and virtue. By dignity I mean free-will, whereby he not only excels all other earthly creatures, but has dominion over them. Wisdom is the power whereby he recognizes this dignity, and perceives also that it is no accomplishment of his own. And virtue impels man to seek eagerly for Him who is man's Source, and to lay fast hold on Him when He has been found.

Now, these three best gifts have each a twofold character. Dignity appears not only as the prerogative of human nature, but also as the cause of that fear and dread of man which is upon every beast of the earth. Wisdom perceives this distinction, but owns that though in us, it is, like all good qualities, not of us. And lastly, virtue moves us to search eagerly for an Author, and, when we have found Him, teaches us to cling to Him yet more eagerly. Consider too that dignity without wisdom is nothing worth; and wisdom is harmful without virtue, as this argument following shows: There is no glory in having a gift without knowing it. But to know only that you have it, without knowing that it is not of yourself that you have it, means self-glorying, but no true glory in God. And so the apostle says to men in such cases, "What hast thou that thou didst not receive? Now, if thou didst receive it, why dost thou glory as if thou hadst not received it? (I Cor. 4:7). He asks, Why dost thou glory? but goes on, as if thou hadst not received it, showing that the guilt is not in glorying over a possession, but in glorying as though it had not been received. And rightly such glorying is called vain-glory, since it has not the solid foundation of truth. The apostle shows how to discern the true glory from the false, when he says, He that glorieth, let him glory in the Lord, that is, in the Truth, since our Lord is Truth (I Cor. 1:31; John 14:6).

We must know, then, what we are, and that it is not of ourselves that we are what we are. Unless we know this thoroughly, either we shall not glory at all, or our glorying will be vain. Finally, it is written, "If thou know not, go thy way forth by the footsteps of the flock" (Cant. 1:8). And this is right. For man, being in honor, if he know not his own honor, may fitly be compared, because of such ignorance, to the beasts that perish. Not knowing himself as the creature that is distinguished from the irrational brutes by the possession of reason, he commences to be confounded with them because, ignorant of his own true glory which is within, he is led captive by his curiosity, and concerns himself with external, sensual things. So he is made to resemble the lower orders by not knowing that he has been more highly endowed than they.

We must be on our guard against this ignorance. We must not rank ourselves too low, and with still greater care we must see that we do not think of ourselves more highly than we ought to think, as happens when we foolishly impute to ourselves whatever good may be in us. But far more than either of these kinds of ignorance, we must hate and shun that presumption which would lead us to glory in goods not our own, knowing that they are not of ourselves but of God, and yet not fearing to rob God of the honor due unto Him. For mere ignorance, as in the first instance, does not glory at all; and mere wisdom, as in the second, while it has a kind of glory, yet does not glory in the Lord. In the third evil case, however, man sins not in ignorance but deliberately, usurping the glory which belongs to God. And this arrogance is a more grievous and deadly fault than the ignorance of the second, since it contemns God, while the other knows Him not. Ignorance is brutal, arrogance is devilish. Pride only, the chief of all iniquities, can make us treat gifts as if they were rightful attributes of our nature, and, while receiving benefits, rob our Benefactor of His due glory.

Wherefore to dignity and wisdom we must add virtue, the proper fruit of them both. Virtue seeks and finds Him who is the

Author and Giver of all good, and who must be in all things glorified; otherwise, one who knows what is right yet fails to perform it, will be beaten with many stripes (Luke 12:47). Why? you may ask. Because he has failed to put his knowledge to good effect, but rather has imagined mischief upon his bed (PS. 36:4); like a wicked servant, he has turned aside to seize the glory which, his own knowledge assured him, belonged only to his good Lord and Master. It is plain, therefore, that dignity without wisdom is useless and that wisdom without virtue is accursed. But when one possesses virtue, then wisdom and dignity are not dangerous but blessed. Such a man calls on God and lauds Him, confessing from a full heart, "Not unto us, O Lord, not unto us, but unto Thy name give glory" (Ps. 115:1). Which is to say, "O Lord, we claim no knowledge, no distinction for ourselves; all is Thine, since from Thee all things do come."

But we have digressed too far in the wish to prove that even those who know not Christ are sufficiently admonished by the natural law, and by their own endowments of soul and body, to love God for God's own sake. To sum up: what infidel does not know that he has received light, air, food--all things necessary for his own body's life--from Him alone who giveth food to all flesh (Ps. 136:25), who maketh His sun to rise on the evil and on the good, and sendeth rain on the just and on the unjust (Matt. 5:45). Who is so impious as to attribute the peculiar eminence of humanity to any other except to Him who saith, in Genesis, "Let us make man in Our image, after Our likeness"? (Gen. 1:26). Who else could be the Bestower of wisdom, but He that teacheth man knowledge? (Ps. 94:10). Who else could bestow virtue except the Lord of virtue? Therefore even the infidel who knows not Christ but does at least know himself, is bound to love God for God's own sake. He is unpardonable if he does not love the Lord his God with all his heart, and with all his soul, and with all his mind; for his own innate justice and common sense cry

out from within that he is bound wholly to love God, from whom he has received all things. But it is hard, nay rather, impossible, for a man by his own strength or in the power of free-will to render all things to God from whom they came, without rather turning them aside, each to his own account, even as it is written, "For all seek their own" (Phil. 2:21); and again, "The imagination of man's heart is evil from his youth" (Gen. 8:21).

CHAPTER VIII
Of the first degree of love: wherein man loves God for self's sake
Love is one of the four natural affections, which it is needless to name since everyone knows them. And because love is natural, it is only right to love the Author of nature first of all. Hence comes the first and great commandment, "Thou shalt love the Lord thy God." But nature is so frail and weak that necessity compels her to love herself first; and this is carnal love, wherewith man loves himself first and selfishly, as it is written, "That was not first which is spiritual but that which is natural; and afterward that which is spiritual" (I Cor. 15:46). This is not as the precept ordains but as nature directs: "No man ever yet hated his own flesh" (Eph. 5:29). But if, as is likely, this same love should grow excessive and, refusing to be contained within the restraining banks of necessity, should overflow into the fields of voluptuousness, then a command checks the flood, as if by a dike: "Thou shalt love thy neighbor as thyself". And this is right: for he who shares our nature should share our love, itself the fruit of nature. Wherefore if a man find it a burden, I will not say only to relieve his brother's needs, but to minister to his brother's pleasures, let him mortify those same affections in himself, lest he become a transgressor. He may cherish himself as tenderly as he chooses, if only he remembers to show the same indulgence to his neighbor. This is the curb of temperance imposed on thee, O man, by the law of life and conscience, lest thou shouldest follow thine own lusts

to destruction, or become enslaved by those passions which are the enemies of thy true welfare. Far better divide thine enjoyments with thy neighbor than with these enemies. And if, after the counsel of the son of Sirach, thou goest not after thy desires but refrainest thyself from thine appetites (Ecclus. 18:30); if according to the apostolic precept having food and raiment thou art therewith content (I Tim. 6:8), then thou wilt find it easy to abstain from fleshly lusts which war against the soul, and to divide with thy neighbors what thou hast refused to thine own desires. That is a temperate and righteous love which practices self-denial in order to minister to a brother's necessity. So our selfish love grows truly social, when it includes our neighbors in its circle.

But if thou art reduced to want by such benevolence, what then? What indeed, except to pray with all confidence unto Him who giveth to all men liberally and upbraideth not (James 1:5), who openeth His hand and filleth all things living with plenteousness (Ps. 145:16). For doubtless He that giveth to most men more than they need will not fail thee as to the necessaries of life, even as He hath promised: "Seek ye the Kingdom of God, and all those things shall be added unto you" (Luke 12:31). God freely promises all things needful to those who deny themselves for love of their neighbors; and to bear the yoke of modesty and sobriety, rather than to let sin reign in our mortal body (Rom. 6:12), that is indeed to seek the Kingdom of God and to implore His aid against the tyranny of sin. It is surely justice to share our natural gifts with those who share our nature.

But if we are to love our neighbors as we ought, we must have regard to God also: for it is only in God that we can pay that debt of love aright. Now a man cannot love his neighbor in God, except he love God Himself; wherefore we must love God first, in order to love our neighbors in Him. This too, like all good things, is the Lord's doing, that we should love Him, for He hath endowed us with the possibility of love. He who created nature sustains it; nature is so constituted that its Maker is its protector for ever. Without Him nature could not have begun to be; without Him it could not subsist at all. That we might not be ignorant of this, or vainly attribute to ourselves the beneficence of our Creator, God has determined in the depths of His wise counsel that we should be subject to tribulations. So when man's strength fails and God comes to his aid, it is meet and right that man, rescued by God's hand, should glorify Him, as it is written, "Call upon Me in the time of trouble; so will I hear thee, and thou shalt praise Me" (Ps. 50:15). In such wise man, animal and carnal by nature, and loving only himself, begins to love God by reason of that very self-love; since he learns that in God he can accomplish all things that are good, and that without God he can do nothing.

CHAPTER IX

Of the second and third degrees of love

So then in the beginning man loves God, not for God's sake, but for his own. It is something for him to know how little he can do by himself and how much by God's help, and in that knowledge to order himself rightly towards God, his sure support. But when tribulations, recurring again and again, constrain him to turn to God for unfailing help, would not even a heart as hard as iron, as cold as marble, be softened by the goodness of such a Savior, so that he would love God not altogether selfishly, but because He is God? Let frequent troubles drive us to frequent supplications; and surely, tasting, we must see how gracious the Lord is (Ps. 34:8). Thereupon His goodness once realized draws us to love Him unselfishly, yet more than our own needs impel us to love Him selfishly: even as the Samaritans told the woman who announced that it was Christ who was at the well: "Now we believe, not because of thy saying: for we have heard Him ourselves, and know that this is indeed the Christ, the savior of the world" (John 4:42). We likewise bear the same witness to our own fleshly nature, saying,

"No longer do we love God because of our necessity, but because we have tasted and seen how gracious the Lord is". Our temporal wants have a speech of their own, proclaiming the benefits they have received from God's favor. Once this is recognized it will not be hard to fulfill the commandment touching love to our neighbors; for whosoever loves God aright loves all God's creatures. Such love is pure, and finds no burden in the precept bidding us purify our souls, in obeying the truth through the Spirit unto unfeigned love of the brethren (I Peter 1:22). Loving as he ought, he counts that command only just. Such love is thankworthy, since it is spontaneous; pure, since it is shown not in word nor tongue, but in deed and truth (I John 3:18); just, since it repays what it has received. Whoso loves in this fashion, loves even as he is loved, and seeks no more his own but the things which are Christ's, even as Jesus sought not His own welfare, but ours, or rather ourselves. Such was the psalmist's love when he sang: "O give thanks unto the Lord, for He is gracious" (Ps. 118:1). Whosoever praises God for His essential goodness, and not merely because of the benefits He has bestowed, does really love God for God's sake, and not selfishly. The psalmist was not speaking of such love when he said: "So long as thou doest well unto thyself, men will speak good of thee" (Ps. 49:18). The third degree of love, we have now seen, is to love God on His own account, solely because He is God.

CHAPTER X

Of the fourth degree of love: wherein man does not even love self save for God's sake

How blessed is he who reaches the fourth degree of love, wherein one loves himself only in God! Thy righteousness standeth like the strong mountains, O God. Such love as this is God's hill, in the which it pleaseth Him to dwell. "Who shall ascend into the hill of the Lord?" "O that I had wings like a dove; for then would I flee away and be at rest." "At Salem is His tabernacle; and His dwelling in Sion." "Woe is me, that I am constrained to dwell with Mesech!" (Ps. 24:3; 55:6; 76:2; 120:5). When shall this flesh and blood, this earthen vessel which is my soul's tabernacle, attain thereto? When shall my soul, rapt with divine love and altogether self-forgetting, yea, become like a broken vessel, yearn wholly for God, and, joined unto the Lord, be one spirit with Him? When shall she exclaim, "My flesh and my heart faileth; but God is the strength of my heart and my portion for ever" (Ps. 73:26). I would count him blessed and holy to whom such rapture has been vouchsafed in this mortal life, for even an instant to lose thyself, as if thou wert emptied and lost and swallowed up in God, is no human love; it is celestial. But if sometimes a poor mortal feels that heavenly joy for a rapturous moment, then this wretched life envies his happiness, the malice of daily trifles disturbs him, this body of death weighs him down, the needs of the flesh are imperative, the weakness of corruption fails him, and above all brotherly love calls him back to duty. Alas! that voice summons him to re-enter his own round of existence; and he must ever cry out lamentably, "O Lord, I am oppressed: undertake for me" (Isa. 38:14); and again, "O wretched man that I am! who shall deliver me from the body of this death?" (Rom. 7:24).

Seeing that the Scripture saith, God has made all for His own glory (Isa. 43:7), surely His creatures ought to conform themselves, as much as they can, to His will. In Him should all our affections center, so that in all things we should seek only to do His will, not to please ourselves. And real happiness will come, not in gratifying our desires or in gaining transient pleasures, but in accomplishing God's will for us: even as we pray every day: "Thy will be done in earth as it is in heaven" (Matt. 6:10). O chaste and holy love! O sweet and gracious affection! O pure and cleansed purpose, thoroughly washed and purged from any admixture of selfishness, and sweetened by contact with the divine will! To reach this state is to become godlike. As a drop of water poured into wine loses itself, and takes the color and savor of wine; or as a bar of iron, heated red-hot, becomes like fire itself, forgetting its own nature; or as the air, radiant with sun-beams, seems not so much to be illuminated as to be light itself; so in the saints all human affections melt away by some unspeakable transmutation into the will of God. For how could God be all in all, if anything merely human remained in man? The substance will endure, but in another beauty, a higher power, a greater glory. When will that be? Who will see, who possess it? "When shall I come to appear before the presence of God?" (Ps. 42:2). "My heart hath talked of Thee, Seek ye My face: Thy face, Lord, will I seek" (Ps. 27:8). Lord, thinkest Thou that I, even I shall see Thy holy temple?

In this life, I think, we cannot fully and perfectly obey that precept, "Thou shalt love the Lord thy God with all thy heart, and with all thy soul, and with all thy strength, and with all thy mind" (Luke 10:27). For here the heart must take thought for the body; and the soul must energize the flesh; and the strength must guard itself from impairment. And by God's favor, must seek to increase. It is therefore impossible to offer up all our being to God, to yearn altogether for His face, so long as we must accommodate our purposes and aspirations to these fragile, sickly bodies of ours. Wherefore the soul may hope to possess the fourth degree of love, or rather to be possessed by it, only when it has been clothed upon with that spiritual and immortal body, which will be perfect, peaceful, lovely, and in everything wholly subjected to the spirit. And to this degree no human effort can attain: it is in God's power to give it to whom He wills. Then the soul will easily reach that highest stage, because no lusts of the flesh will retard its eager entrance into the joy of its Lord, and no troubles will disturb its peace. May we not think that the holy martyrs enjoyed this grace, in some degree at least, before they laid down their victorious bodies? Surely that was immeasurable strength of love which enraptured their souls, enabling them to laugh at fleshly torments and to yield their lives gladly. But even though the frightful pain could not destroy their peace of mind, it must have impaired somewhat its perfection.

Bernard of Clairvaux

Opinionated

An obstinate man does not hold opinions – they hold him.

Author unknown

Opinions

The man who never alters his opinions is like standing water, and breeds reptiles of the mind.

William Blake

Opinions, Other people's

I am not sure which of the two occupies the lower sphere, he who hungers for money or he who thirsts for applause.

J.H. Jowett

Opportunity

Opportunities are seldom labeled.

Author unknown

If you're not lighting any candles, don't complain about the dark.

Author unknown

There are a lot of ways to become a failure, but never taking a chance is the most successful.

Author unknown

A wise man will make more opportunities than he finds.

Francis Bacon

When one door closes another door opens; but we so often look so long and so regretfully upon the closed door, that we do not see the ones which open for us.

Alexander Graham Bell

The lure of the distant and the difficult is deceptive. The great opportunity is where you are.
John Burroughs

All life is a chance. So take it! The person who goes the furthest is the one who is willing to do and dare.
Dale Carnegie

You may not realize it when it happens, but a kick in the teeth may be the best thing in the world for you.
Walt Disney

In the middle of difficulty lies opportunity.
Albert Einstein

If you lose an opportunity you will be like one who lets the bird fly away; you will never get it back.
John of the Cross

Opportunities flit by while we sit regretting the chances we have lost, and the happiness that comes to us we heed not, because of the happiness that is gone.
Jerome K. Jerome

We must use time creatively… and forever realize that the time is always ripe to do right.
Martin Luther King, Jr

There is no security on this earth; there is only opportunity.
General Douglas MacArthur

Ability is of little account without opportunity.
Napoleon Bonaparte

Let your hook always be cast. In the pool where you least expect it, will be a fish.
Ovid

Three things come not back – the spoken word, the spent arrow, and the lost opportunity.
Proverb

Opportunities multiply as they are seized.
Sun Tzu

Every man is guilty of all the good he didn't do.
Voltaire

Opportunity is often difficult to recognize; we usually expect it to beckon us with beepers and billboards.
William Arthur Ward

Of all sad words of tongue or pen, the saddest are these: "It might have been!"
John Greenleaf Whittier

Opposition
Great spirits have always encountered violent opposition from mediocre minds.
Albert Einstein

Opposition to Christianity
The term "conspiracy" should not be applied to us but rather to those who plot to foment hatred against decent and worthy people, those who shout for the blood of the innocent and plead forsooth in justification of their hatred the foolish excuse that the Christians are to blame for every public disaster and every misfortune that befalls the people. If the Tiber rises to the walls, if the Nile fails to rise and flood the fields, if the sky withholds its rain, if there is earthquake or famine or plague, straightaway the cry arises: "The Christians to the lions!"
Tertullian

Opposition to God
It is not by nature that man is hostile and opposed to God. He is of course in fact so opposed, but only by acts of rejection, by an abuse of nature. But all man's perversity cannot make wrong what God has wrought as good by nature.
Karl Barth

Oppression
He that would make his own liberty secure must guard even his enemy from oppression; for if he violates this duty he

establishes a precedent that will reach to himself.
Thomas Paine

Optimism
See also: Pessimism
Pessimism is an investment in nothing; optimism is an investment in hope.
Author unknown

As you travel on through life,
Whatever be your goal,
Keep your eye upon the doughnut
And not upon the hole.
Author unknown

Let not thy mind run on what thou lackest as much as on what thou hast already.
Marcus Aurelius Antoninus

No Christian can be a pessimist, for Christianity is a system of radical optimism.
William R. Inge

Optimism is the faith that leads to achievement. Nothing can be done without hope and confidence.
Helen Keller

Optimism is an intellectual choice.
Diana Schneider

There is no sadder sight than a young pessimist.
Mark Twain

Optimist
When the heart weeps for what it has lost, the spirit laughs for what it has found.
Author unknown

A pessimist sees the difficulty in every opportunity; an optimist sees the opportunity in every difficulty.
Winston Churchill

Positive anything is better than negative nothing.
Elbert Hubbard

The optimist thinks that this is the best of all possible worlds, and the pessimist knows it.
J. Robert Oppenheimer

A pessimist is what an optimist calls a realist.
Proverb

The optimist already sees the scar over the wound; the pessimist still sees the wound beneath the scar.
Ernst Schroder

Ordeals, personal
I was at that time alone. It was the day of my sister's marriage, and the rest of the family were staying overnight in Glasgow. [It was also just after his own fiancée had called off their engagement, on account of Mattheson's blindness.] Something happened to me which was known only to myself, and which caused me the most severe mental suffering. The hymn was the fruit of that suffering. It was the quickest bit of work I ever did in my life. I had the impression rather of having it dictated to me by some inward voice than of working it out myself. I am quite sure that the whole work was completed in five minutes, and equally sure it never received at my hands any retouching or correction.
George Mattheson's hymn, "O Love, that wilt not let me go" was written in the manse at Inellan on the evening of June 6th, 1882.

O Love, that wilt not let me go,
I rest my weary soul in Thee;
I give Thee back the life I owe,
That in Thine ocean depths its flow
 May richer, fuller be.

O Light, that followest all my way,
I yield my flickering torch to Thee;
My heart restores its borrowed ray,
That in Thy sunshine's blaze its day
 May brighter, fairer be.
O Joy, that seekest me through pain,
I cannot close my heart to Thee;
I trace the rainbow through the rain,
And feel the promise is not vain

That morn shall tearless be.

O Cross, that liftest up my head,
I dare not ask to fly from Thee;
I lay in dust life's glory dead,
And from the ground there blossoms red
 Life that shall endless be.

Later on, George Mattheson, sensing the
meaning behind his suffering, wrote:
"My God, I have never thanked thee for
my thorn. I have been looking forward to a
world where I shall get compensated for
my cross – but I have never thought of my
cross as itself a present glory. Teach me the
glory of my cross. Teach me the value of
my thorn. Show me that my tears made
my rainbow."
George Mattheson

Order
Good order is the foundation of all good
things.
Edmund Burke

Order is heaven's first law.
Alexander Pope

Original sin
Original sin may be defined as the hereditary
corruption and depravity of our nature. This
reaches every part of the soul, makes us
abhorrent to God's wrath and produces in us
what Scripture calls works of the flesh.
John Calvin

Certain new theologians dispute original
sin, which is the only part of Christian
theology which can really be proved.
G.K. Chesterton

The glad news brought by the gospel was
the good news of original sin.
Francis of Assisi

Original sin is the only rational solution of
the undeniable fact of the deep, universal
and early manifested sinfulness of men in
all ages, of every class, and in every part of
the world.
Charles Hodge

We repudiated all versions of the doctrine
of original sin, of there being instances of
irrational springs of wickedness in most men.
John Maynard Keynes

Original sin is in us, like the beard. We are
shaved today and look clean, and have a
smooth chin; tomorrow our beard has
grown again, nor does it cease growing
while we remain on earth.
Martin Luther

Everything is good when it leaves the
hands of the Creator; everything
degenerates in the hands of men.
Jean-Jacques Rousseau

Originality
Originality is the fine art of remembering
what you hear but forgetting where you
heard it.
Peter Laurance

The more intelligent one is, the more men
of originality one finds. Ordinary people
find no difference between men.
Blaise Pascal

Other religions
The Bible offers no hope that sincere
worshipers of other religions will be saved
without personal faith in Jesus Christ.
*The gospel of Jesus Christ: An evangelical
celebration*

Superficial minds see a resemblance
between Christ and the founders of
empires, and the gods of other religions.
That resemblance does not exist. There is
between Christianity and whatever other
religion the distance of infinity.
Napoleon Bonaparte

We confirm that we believe that: Jesus
Christ is the only way of salvation; and
that: The bible offers no hope that sincere
worshipers of other religions will be saved
without personal faith in Jesus Christ.
*Jerry Falwell, D. James Kennedy, Pat Robertson,
and Charles Stanley, signed a joint statement in
June, 1999*

Outcasts

The modern church rejects the outcasts of
society where as these very outcasts were
the very ones who were drawn to Jesus.
Philip Yancy

Outsiders

Be wise in the way you act toward outsiders;
make the most of every opportunity.
The Bible, Colossians 4:5

Over-eating

Put a knife to thy throat, if thou be a man
given to appetite.
The Bible, Proverbs 23:2 KJV

Overseer

Now the overseer must be above reproach,
the husband of but one wife, temperate,
self-controlled, respectable, hospitable, able
to teach, not given to drunkenness, not
violent but gentle, not quarrelsome, not a
lover of money.
The Bible, 1 Timothy 3:2-3

Since an overseer is entrusted with God's
work, he must be blameless – not
overbearing, not quick-tempered, not
given to drunkenness, not violent, not
pursuing dishonest gain. Rather he must
be hospitable, one who loves what is good,
who is self-controlled, upright, holy and
disciplined. He must hold firmly to the
trustworthy message as it has been taught,
so that he can encourage others by sound
doctrine and refute those who oppose it.
The Bible, Titus 1:7-9

Be shepherds of God's flock that is under
your care, serving as overseers – not
because you must, but because you are
willing, as God wants you to be; not
greedy for money, but eager to serve; not
lording it over those entrusted to you, but
being examples to the flock.
The Bible, 1 Peter 5:2,3

Overweight

"How long does getting thin take?" Pooh
asked anxiously.
A. A. Milne

P

Pacifism
See also: Non-violence

My study of Gandhi convinced me that true pacifism is not non-resistance to evil, but non-violent resistance to evil. Between the two positions, there is a world of difference. Gandhi resisted evil with as much vigor and power as the violent resister, but true pacifism is not unrealistic submission to evil power. It is rather a courageous confrontation of evil by the power of love.

There comes a time when one must take a position that is neither safe, nor politic, nor popular but one must take it because it's right. At the center of non-violence stands the principle of love. Peace is not merely a distant goal that we seek, but a means by which we arrive at that goal.
Martin Luther King, Jr

The cause of peace has had a share of my efforts, taking the ultra non-resistance ground – that a Christian cannot consistently uphold, and actively support, a government based on the sword, or whose ultimate resort is to the destroying weapon.
Lucretia Mott

Pagans

I used to think that pagans in far-off countries were lost – were going to hell – if they did not have the gospel of Jesus Christ preached to them. I no longer believe that … I believe there are other ways of recognizing the existence of God – through nature, for instance – and plenty of other opportunities, therefore, of saying yes to God.
Billy Graham

Pain
See also: Healing

There was a faith-healer of Deal,
Who said, "Although pain isn't real,
If I sit on a pin
And it punctures my skin,
I dislike what I fancy I feel."
Author unknown

We cannot learn without pain.
Aristotle

Real pain can alone cure us of imaginary ills.
Jonathan Edwards

Pain is no evil, unless it conquer us.
Charles Kingsley

When pain is to be borne, a little courage helps more than much knowledge, a little human sympathy more than much courage, and the least tincture of the love of God more than all.
C.S. Lewis

God whispers to us in our pleasures, speaks to us in our conscience, but shouts in our pains: It is His megaphone to rouse a deaf world.
C.S. Lewis

Pain makes men think,
Thinking gives men wisdom;
And wisdom confers peace.
Boris Pasternak

No pain, no palm; no thorns, no throne; no gall, no glory; no cross, no crown.
William Penn

Illness is the most heeded of doctors: to goodness and wisdom we only make promises; pain we obey.
Proust

Let me not beg for the stilling of my pain,
but for the heart to conquer it.
Rabindranath Tagore

Palm Sunday

Look at Christ. He rides not upon a horse
which is a steed of war. He comes not with
appalling pomp and power but sits upon
an ass, which is a gentle beast to bear
burdens and work for men. From this we
see that Christ comes not to terrify, to
drive, and oppress, but to help and take for
himself our load.
Martin Luther

Pantheism

If God's being is an aspect of my own, "the
depth in me," all attempts to worship him
become self-worship.
J.I. Packer

Parables

I sometimes wonder what hours of prayer
and thought lie behind the apparently
simple and spontaneous parables of the
gospel.
J.B. Phillips

Paradigms

The six major paradigms, according to
Hans Küng are as follows:
1. The apocalyptic paradigm of primitive
Christianity
2. The Hellenistic paradigm of the patristic
period
3. The medieval Roman Catholic
paradigm
4. The Protestant (Reformation) paradigm
5. The modern Enlightenment paradigm
6. The emerging ecumenical paradigm
Hans Küng

Parenting
See also: Children; Fathers; Mothers, Parents

Training a child to follow Christ is easy for
parents all they have to do is lead the way.
Author unknown

Be the soul support of your children.
Author unknown

You train a child until age ten. After that,
you only influence them.
Author unknown

Love is spelled T-I-M-E
Author unknown

Sandwich every bit of criticism between
two layers of praise.
Mary Kay Ash

If you can give your son or daughter only
one gift, let it be Enthusiasm.
Bruce Barton

The best inheritance a parent can give his
children is a few minutes of his time each
day.
O.A. Battista

It is very difficult and expensive to undo
after you are married the things that your
mother and father did to you while you
were putting your first six birthdays behind
you.
Bureau of Social Hygiene study, 1928

Children can stand vast amounts of
sternness. It is injustice, inequity and
inconsistency that kill them.
Robert Capon

Most overnight success usually takes about
fifteen years.
Little drops of water, little grains of sand,
Make the mighty ocean and the beauteous
land.
And the little moments, humble though
they be,
Make the mighty ages of eternity.
Julia Carney

There are two lasting bequests we can give
our children: One is roots. The other is
wings.
Hodding Carter, Jr

Praise your children openly, reprove them
secretly.
W. Cecil

Nothing I've ever done has given me more joys and rewards than being a father to my children.
Bill Cosby

The greatest teacher is not experience; it is example.
John Croyle

Train up a fig-tree in the way it should go, and when you are old sit under the shade of it.
Charles Dickens

Children miss nothing in sizing up their parents. If you are only half convinced of your beliefs, they will quickly discern that fact.
James Dobson

In the man whose childhood has known caresses and kindness, there is always a fiber of memory that can be touched to gentle issues.
George Eliot

I learned the way a monkey learns, by watching its parents.
Queen Elizabeth II

I grew up to have my father's looks, my father's speech patterns, my father's posture, my father's opinions, and my mother's contempt for my father.
Jules Feiffer

Telling lies and showing off to get attention are the mistakes I made and don't want my kids to make.
Jane Fonda

Let your children go if you want to keep them.
M. Forbes

It's always been my feeling that God lends you your children until they're about eighteen years old. If you haven't made your points with them by then, it's too late.
Betty Ford

There is nothing in a caterpillar that tells you it's going to be a butterfly.
Buckminster Fuller

Enjoy one another and take the time to enjoy family life together. Quality time is no substitute for quantity time. Quantity time is quality time.
Billy Graham

Do you love me because I'm beautiful, or am I beautiful because you love me?
Oscar Hammerstein II

A child should be loved for who he is, not for what he does.
David Jeremiah

Never worry too much about the things you can replace, worry only about the things you can't replace.
Winnie Johnson

Whatever you do to your child's body, you are doing to your child's mind.
Penelope Leach

There is only one way to bring up a child in the way he should go and that is to travel that way yourself.
Abraham Lincoln

Him that I love, I wish to be free even from me.
Anne Morrow Lindbergh

One should not only serve youth but should also avoid offending them by word or deed. One should give them the best of training that they may learn to pray.
Martin Luther

If obedience is not rendered in the homes, we shall never have a whole city, country, principality, or kingdom well governed. For this order in the homes is the first rule; it is the source of all other rule and government.
Martin Luther

If we would only give, just once, the same amount of reflection to how we want our

children to remember us that we give to the question of what to do with two weeks' vacation, we would overnight become better parents and over time become the kind of family that we always dreamed we'd be.
Rich Melheim

Some people work to give their kids a car so they can get away. I'd rather work to give my kids a home that they'd like to stick around so their friends have a place to hang out with their new cars.
Rich Melheim

If a child lives with criticism, he learns to condemn.
If a child lives with hostility, he learns to fight.
If a child lives with ridicule, he learns to be shy.
If a child lives with shame, he learns to feel guilty.
If a child lives with tolerance, he learns to be patient.
If a child lives with encouragement, he learns confidence.
If a child lives with praise, he learns to appreciate.
If a child lives with fairness, he learns justice.
If a child lives with security, he learns to have faith.
If a child lives with approval, he learns to like himself.
If a child lives with acceptance and friendship, he learns to find love in the world.
Dorothy Nolte

If you bungle raising your children, I don't think whatever else you do well matters very much.
Jacqueline Kennedy Onassis

It takes a village to raise a child.
African proverb

Oh, to be only half as wonderful as my child thought I was when he was small, and only half as stupid as my teenager now thinks I am.
Rebecca Richards

The tasks connected with the home are the fundamental tasks of humanity.
Theodore Roosevelt

You don't raise heroes, you raise sons. And if you treat them like sons, they'll turn out to be heroes.
Walter Schirra

Your children are a mirror which reflects back on you the kind of image you cast.
Fulton Sheen

Trust yourself. You know more than you think you do.
Dr Benjamin Spock

Train your child in the way in which you know you should have gone yourself.
C.H. Spurgeon

If we never have headaches through rebuking our children, we shall have plenty of heartaches when they grow up.
C.H. Spurgeon

I have found the best way to give advice to your children is to find out what they want and then advise them to do it.
Harry S. Truman

The thing that impresses me most about America is the way parents obey their children.
Duke of Windsor

When you lead your sons and daughters in the good way, let your words be tender and caressing, in terms of discipline that wins the heart's assent.
Elijah Ben Solomon Zalman

Parenting and culture
In recent years our culture has sent hostile signals about the job of parenting, even though few men and women will ever do anything more important than nurturing and raising the next generation of children.
James Dobson and Gary L. Bauer

Parents

See also: Children, Parenting

The typical parent spends less than one hour per week in meaningful interaction with each of his or her children.
George Barna

Honor your parents both in your thoughts, and speech, and behavior. Think not dishonorably or contemptuously of them in your hearts. Speak not dishonorably, rudely, unreverently, or saucily, either to them or of them. Behave not yourselves rudely and unreverently before them. Yea, though your parents be never so poor in the world, or weak of understanding, yea, though they were ungodly, you must honor them notwithstanding all this; though you cannot honor them as rich, or wise, or godly, you must honor them as your parents.
Richard Baxter

We take care of our possessions for our children. But of the children themselves we take no care at all. What an absurdity is this! Form the soul of thy son aright, and all the rest will be added hereafter.
John Chrysostom

Every parent especially ought to feel, every hour of the day, that, next to making his own calling and election sure, this is the end for which he is kept alive by God, this is his task on earth.
R.L. Dabney

The neglect of moral training is monstrous, involving an outrage of the clearest sentiments of Nature and flagrant injustice to the offspring.
R.L. Dabney

A hundred years from now it will not matter what my bank account was, the sort of house I lived in, or the kind of car I drove. But the world may be different because I was important in the life of a child.
Kathy Davis

The most important things we can give our kids are our time, our lives, and our values – and values are caught more than they are taught.
Tim Hansel

No matter how old a mother is she watches her middle-aged children for signs of improvement.
Florida Scott Maxwell

If you are not willing to make time for your children, then every other piece of advice you get is meaningless.
Josh McDowell

God loves your children through you, but if you're not available, how can he love them?
Josh McDowell

Acceptance and appreciation tells the child that he or she is of tremendous worth. And I can only express my acceptance and appreciation through being affectionate – and available.
Josh McDowell

Many things we need can wait. The child cannot. Now is the time his bones are being formed; his blood is being made; his mind is being developed. To him we cannot say tomorrow. His name is today.
Gabriela Mistral

I pray you so live, that when you stand over your child's dead body, you may never hear a voice coming up from that clay, "Father, your negligence was my destruction. Mother, your prayerlessness was the instrument of my damnation."
C.H. Spurgeon

When parents instruct not their children, they seldom prove blessings. God often punishes the carelessness of parents with undutifulness in their children.
Thomas Watson

Passion

[Passions] are evil if love is evil and good if it is good.
Augustine of Hippo

We may affirm absolutely that nothing great in the world has ever been accomplished without passion.
Georg Hegel

Rule your passions, or they will rule you.
Horace

The spiritual combat in which we kill our passions in order to put on the new man is the most difficult of all the arts.
Nilus

However vast a man's spiritual resources, he is capable of but one great passion.
Blaise Pascal

When the passions become masters, they are vices.
Blaise Pascal

Nothing is so intolerable to man as being fully at rest, without a passion, without business, without entertainment, without care.
Blaise Pascal

It is more grievous to be a slave to one's passions than to be ruled by a despot.
Pythagoras

A wise man will be master of his passions, a fool their slave.
Publius Syrus

Passion, Christ's

I, the Eternal Wisdom, was mocked as a fool in a white garment before Herod, My fair body was rent and torn without mercy by the rude stripes of whips, My lovely countenance was drenched in spittle and blood, and in this condition I was condemned, and miserably and shamefully led forth with My cross to death. They shouted after Me very furiously, so that: Crucify, crucify the miscreant! resounded to the skies.
Henry Suso

Past

Never live in the past, but always learn from it.
Author unknown

Pastor
See also: Ministers of religion

A powerless pastor is a prayerless pastor.
Author unknown

We must feel toward our people as a father toward his children; yea, the most tender love of a mother must not surpass ours. We must even travail in birth, till Christ be formed in them. They should see that we care for no outward thing, neither liberty, nor honor, nor life, in comparison to their salvation.
Richard Baxter

[The five tasks of pastoral care are]
to seek and to find all the lost;
to bring back those that are scattered;
to heal the wounded;
to strengthen the sickly;
to protect the healthy and to put them to pasture.
Martin Bucer

Christ is with those of humble mind, not with those who exalt themselves over his flock.
Clement of Rome

If a church wants a better pastor, it can get one by praying for the one it has.
Robert E. Harris

Pastors can hardly do a greater disservice to people than to convince those bound for hell that they are en route to heaven.
Tom Hovestol

Go round your parish, as it were, upon your knees.
Edward King

Patience
See also: Disappointment; Rush

The great believers have been the unwearied waiters.
Author unknown

Waiting is God's school, wherein we learn some of His most valuable lessons for us.
Author unknown

Be as patient with others as God has been with you.
Author unknown

Patience carries a lot of wait.
Author unknown

Happy homes are built with blocks of patience.
Author unknown

The greatest prayer is patience.
Author unknown

Patience and perseverence have a magical effect before which difficulties disappear and obstacles vanish.
John Quincy Adams

Patience is the companion of wisdom.
Augustine of Hippo

Patience with others is Love,
Patience with self is Hope,
Patience with God is Faith.
Adel Bestavros

Faith takes up the cross, love binds it to the soul, patience bears it to the end.
Horatius Bonar

Patience will achieve more than force.
Edmund Burke

Patience is the queen of the virtues.
John Chrysostom

It is true to say that patience in sickness and other forms of trouble pleases God much more than any splendid devotion that you might show in health.
The Cloud of Unknowing

Patient waiting is often the highest way of doing God's will!
Jeremy Collier

The greatest power is often simple patience.
E. Joseph Cossman

Patience is a necessary ingredient of genius.
Benjamin Disraeli

Everything comes if a man will only wait.
Benjamin Disraeli

Beware the fury of a patient man.
John Dryden

Adopt the pace of nature; her secret is patience.
Ralph Waldo Emerson

If you patiently accept what comes, you will always pray with joy.
Evagrios the Solitary

We must wait for God, long, meekly, in the wind and wet, in the thunder and lightning, in the cold and the dark. Wait, and he will come. He never comes to those who do not wait.
F. W. Faber

Where there is patience and humility, there is neither anger nor vexation.
Francis of Assisi

True patience is to suffer the wrongs done to us by others in an unruffled spirit and without feeling resentment. Patience bears with others because it loves them; to bear with them and yet to hate them is not the virtue of patience but a smokescreen for anger.
Gregory the Great

If we truly preserve patience in our souls, we are martyrs without being killed.
Gregory the Great

True patience grows with the growth of love.
Gregory the Great

Patience is our martyrdom.
Gregory the Great

What cannot be amended is made easier by patience.
Horace

When God ripens apples, he isn't in a hurry and doesn't make a noise.
D. Jackman

Patience is more worth than miracles doing.
Margery Kempe

I can well wait a century for a reader, since God has waited six thousand years for a discoverer.
Johannes Kepler

Patience and time do more than strength or passion.
Jean de La Fontaine

Patience serves as a protection against wrongs as clothes do against cold. For if you put on more clothes as the cold increases, it will have no power to hurt you. So in like manner you must grow in patience when you meet with great wrongs, and they will be powerless to vex your mind.
Leonardo da Vinci

Rest in the Lord; wait patiently for Him. In Hebrew, "Be silent in God, and let Him Moule thee." Keep still, and He will Moule thee to the right shape.
Martin Luther

The principal part of faith is patience.
George Macdonald

Consider the hour-glass; there is nothing to be accomplished by rattling or shaking; you have to wait patiently until the sand, grain by grain, has run from one funnel into the other.
John Christian Morgenstern

May I be patient! It is so difficult to make real what one believes, and to make these trials, as they are intended, real blessings.
John Henry Newman

Patience and diligence, like faith remove mountains.
William Penn

All things come to those who wait.
Proverb

The weak man is impetuous, the strong is patient.
Proverb

If you are patient in one day of anger, you will escape a hundred days of sorrow.
Chinese proverb

Patience is power; with time and patience the mulberry leaf becomes silk.
Chinese proverb

An ounce of patience is worth a pound of brains.
Dutch proverb

Patience is a bitter plant, but it has a sweet fruit.
German proverb

There are times when God asks nothing of His children except silence, patience, and tears.
Charles Seymour Robinson

Obedience is the fruit of faith; patience, the bloom on the fruit.
Christina Rossetti

How poor are they that have not patience!
William Shakespeare

He is not truly patient who will endure only as much as he pleases and from whom he pleases. A truly patient person bears all, and it matters not whether he is wronged by someone whose social standing is superior, inferior, or equal to his own.
Thomas à Kempis

He who waits on God never waits too long.
Chuck Wagner

Patience in suffering

Brothers, as an example of patience in the face of suffering, take the prophets who spoke in the name of the Lord. As you know, we consider blessed those who have persevered. You have heard of Job's perseverance and have seen what the Lord finally brought about.
The Bible, James 5:10,11

Patriotism

Heroism on command, senseless violence, and all the loathsome nonsense that goes by the name of patriotism – how passionately I hate them!
Albert Einstein

Patriotism is the last refuge of the scoundrel.
Samuel Johnson

Patriotism is the willingness to kill and be killed for trivial reasons.
Bertrand Russell

Patronizing

Never look down on anybody unless you are helping him up.
Jesse Louis Jackson

Paul

A man small in size, bald-headed, bandy-legged, well built, with eyebrows meeting, rather long-nosed, full of grace – for sometimes he seemed like a man, and sometimes he had the countenance of an angel.
[Apocrypha] Acts of Paul and Thecla

Among the many innovative features which shaped Christian theology for all time are the key terms which Paul introduced. Above all we should think of "gospel," "grace," and "law."
Paul's image of the gospel is the good news of Christ focusing in his death and resurrection.
  The word grace epitomizes the character of God's dealing with humankind.
The word love means the motive of divine giving and in turn the motive for human living.
James Dunn

Paul stakes all his life upon the truth of what he says about the death and resurrection of Jesus.
J. Gresham Machen

Peace

Therefore, since we have been justified through faith, we have peace with God through our Lord Jesus Christ.
The Bible, Romans 5:1

The shortest path to domestic peace and marital peace is communication.
Author unknown

No God, no peace. Know God, know peace.
Author unknown

All men desire peace; few desire the things which make for peace.
Author unknown

The shortest path to world peace is world trade.
Author unknown

If there is righteousness in the heart there will be beauty in the character.
If there is beauty in the character, there will be harmony in the home.
If there is harmony in the home, there will be order in the nation.
When there is order in the nation, there will be peace in the world.
Author unknown

A crust eaten in peace is better than a banquet partaken in anxiety.
Aesop

I was in Chelsea police station where I was charged with perjury and conspiracy to pervert public justice. I spent the next five hours alone in a police cell while waiting for the various formalities such as finger-printing and photographs. I used that time to pray, to meditate and to read all sixteen chapters of St Mark's Gospel, something I had long meant to do at one sitting. This should have been a time of deep despair. The worst day of my life. Not so. For I had

such an overwhelming sense of God's presence in the cell with me that I was at peace.
Jonathan Aitken, former member of the British Cabinet, imprisoned for perjury

If a man does not say in his heart, in the world there is only myself and God, he will not gain peace.
Abba Alonius

[Peace is] the tranquillity of order.
Augustine of Hippo

The peace of the rational soul is the ordered agreement of knowledge and action.
Augustine of Hippo

Peace: In international affairs, a period of cheating between two periods of fighting.
Ambrose Bierce

And I smiled to think God's greatness flowed around our incompleteness, Round our restlessness His rest.
Elizabeth Barrett Browning

My soul can see no other remedy pleasing to God than peace. Peace, peace, therefore, for the love of Christ crucified!
Catherine of Siena

Great peace is found in little busy-ness.
Geoffrey Chaucer

The world would have peace if the men of politics would only follow the gospel.
Bridget of Sweden

The real differences around the world today are not between Jews and Arabs; Protestants and Catholics; Muslims, Croats, and Serbs. The real differences are between those who embrace peace and those who would destroy it. Between those who look to the future and those who cling to the past. Between those who open their arms and those who are determined to clench their fists.
William Jefferson Clinton

Matthew Arnold counted as the greatest single line in all poetry that saying of Dante's poetic insight: "In Thy will is our peace."
Dante

The peace which believers enjoy, is a participation of the peace which their glorious Lord and Master himself enjoys, by virtue of the same blood by which Christ himself has entered into rest. It is in a participation of this same justification; for believers are justified with Christ. As he was justified when he rose from the dead, and as he was made free from our guilt, so believers are justified in him and through him; as being accepted of God in the same righteousness. It is the favor of the same God and heavenly Father that they enjoy peace.
Jonathan Edwards

Peace and justice are two sides of the same coin.
Dwight D. Eisenhower

I couldn't live in peace if I put the shadow of a wilful sin between myself and God.
George Eliot

Peace cannot be achieved through violence, it can only be attained through understanding.
Ralph Waldo Emerson

Nothing can bring you peace but yourself.
Ralph Waldo Emerson

Nothing can bring you peace but yourself.
Ralph Waldo Emerson

While the emperor may give peace from war on land and sea, he is unable to give peace from passion, grief and envy. He cannot even give peace of heart, for which man yearns more than even for outward peace.
Epictetus

There is never any peace for those who resist God.
François Fénelon

Peace does not dwell in outward things, but within the soul; we may preserve it in the midst of the bitterest pain, if our will remains firm and submissive.

Peace in this life springs from acquiescence to, not in an exemption from, suffering.

François Fénelon

Lord, make me an instrument of thy
  peace.
Where there is hatred, let me sow love;
Where there is injury, pardon;
Where there is doubt, faith;
Where there is despair, hope;
Where there is darkness, light;
Where there is sadness, joy.
O Divine Master, grant that I may not so
  much seek
To be consoled as to console;
Not so much to be understood as to
  understand;
Not so much to be loved as to love;
For it is in giving that we receive;
It is in pardoning that we are pardoned;
It is in dying that we are born to eternal
  life.

Attributed to Francis of Assisi

Even peace may be purchased at too high a price.

Benjamin Franklin

Christ alone can bring lasting peace – peace with God – peace among men and nations – and peace within our hearts.

Billy Graham

Like a river glorious is God's perfect peace,
Over all victorious in its bright increase;
Perfect, yet it floweth fuller every day,
Perfect, yet it groweth deeper all the way.
Stayed upon Jehovah, hearts are fully blest;
Finding, as he promised, perfect peace and rest.

Frances Ridley Havergal

Peace is such a precious jewel that I would give anything for it but truth.

Matthew Henry

Keep your heart in peace; let nothing in this world disturb it: everything has an end.

John of the Cross

Peace reigns where our Lord reigns.

Julian of Norwich

But peace does not rest in the charters and covenants alone. It lies in the hearts and minds of all people. So let us not rest all our hopes on parchment and on paper, let us strive to build peace, a desire for peace, a willingness to work for peace in the hearts and minds of all of our people. I believe that we can. I believe the problems of human destiny are not beyond the reach of human beings.

John F. Kennedy

But natural love and conscience shall come together, and turn law into an honest workman. Such love shall arise, and such peace and perfect truth among the people, that the Jews, amazed that men should be so truthful, will be filled with joy, thinking that Moses or the Messiah has come to earth.

And any man who carries a sword, a lance, an axe, a dagger, or any kind of weapon, shall be put to death, unless he sends it to the smithy to be turned into a scythe, a sickle, or a ploughshare. "They shall beat their swords into ploughshares, and their spears into pruning hooks." And men will pass their time in digging or ploughing, spinning yarn or spreading dung, or else there will be nothing for them to do.

And the only kind of hunting left to priests will be for the souls of the dead; and they will hammer at their Psalms from morn till night. For if any of them hunt with hawks and hounds, they shall lose their boasted livings.

No king or knight or officer or mayor shall tyrannize over the people, or summon them to serve on juries and compel them to take oaths. But each criminal will be punished according to his crime, heavily or lightly as truth shall decide. And the King's Court, the Common Court, the Church Court, and the Chapter shall all be one Court, with a single judge, one true-tongue, an honest man who never opposed me. There shall be no more battles, and any blacksmith who forges a weapon shall perish by it.

"Nation shall not lift up sword against nation, neither shall they learn war any more."
William Langland

Peace if possible, truth at all costs.
Martin Luther

Who except God can give you peace? Has the world ever been able to satisfy the heart?
Gerard Majella

We have peace with God by the righteousness of Christ, and peace of conscience by the fruits of righteousness in ourselves.
Thomas Manton

We are not at peace with others because we are not at peace with ourselves, and we are not at peace with ourselves because we are not at peace with God.
Thomas Merton

Peace hath her victories
No less renowned than war.
John Milton

Many love to walk in a very careless, unwise profession. So long as they can hold out in the performance of outward duties, they are very regardless of the greatest evangelical privileges – of those things which are the marrow of divine promises – all real endeavors of a vital communion with Christ. Such are spiritual peace, refreshing consolations, ineffable joys, and the blessed composure of assurance. Without some taste and experience of these things, profession is heartless, lifeless, useless; and religion itself a dead carcass without an animating soul. The peace which some enjoy is a mere stupidity. They judge not these things to be real which are the substance of Christ's present reward; and a renunciation whereof would deprive the church of its principal supportments and encouragements in all its sufferings. It is a great evidence of the power of unbelief, when we can satisfy ourselves without an experience in our own hearts of the great things, in this kind of joy, peace, consolation, assurance, that are promised in the gospel. For how can it be supposed that we do indeed believe the promises of things future – namely, of heaven, immortality, and glory, the faith whereof is the foundation of all religion – when we do not believe the promises of the present reward in these spiritual privileges? And how shall we be thought to believe them, when we do not endeavor after an experience of the things themselves in our own souls, but are even contented without them? But herein men deceive themselves. They would very desirously have evangelical joy, peace, and assurance, to countenance them in their evil frames and careless walking And some have attempted to reconcile these things, unto the ruin of their souls. But it will not be. Without the diligent exercise of the grace of obedience, we shall never enjoy the grace of consolation.
John Owen

The more we sweat in peace the less we bleed in war.
Vijaya Lakshmi Pandit

If you take little account of yourself, you will have peace, wherever you live.
Abba Poemen

A harvest of peace is produced from a seed of contentment.
Indian proverb

A man who cannot find tranquillity within himself will search for it in vain elsewhere.
La Rochefoucauld

It isn't enough to talk about peace. One must believe in it. And it isn't enough to believe in it. One must work at it.
Eleanor Roosevelt

Peace without truth is a false peace;
it is the very peace of the devil.
J.C. Ryle

Peace is not an absence of war, it is a
virtue, a state of mind, a disposition for
benevolence, confidence, justice.
Baruch Spinoza

Men of peace usually are brave.
Spock, "The Savage Curtain", stardate 5906.5

Peace does not mean the end of all our
striving,
Joy does not mean the drying of our tears.
Peace is the power that comes to souls arriving
Up to the light where God Himself appears.
G.A. Studdert Kennedy

If we ever are to attain to true divine peace,
and be completely united to God, all that
is not absolutely necessary, either bodily or
spiritually, must be cast off; everything that
could interpose itself to an unlawful extent
between us and Him, and lead us astray:
for He alone will be Lord in our hearts,
and none other; for divine love can admit
of no rival.
Johannes Tauler

If we have no peace, it is because we have
forgotten that we belong to each other.
Mother Teresa

Let nothing disturb thee,
Nothing affright thee;
All things are passing;
God never changeth.
Patient endurance
Attaineth to all things;
Who God possesseth
In nothing is wanting;
Alone God sufficeth.
Teresa of Avila, Teresa's Bookmark

Let nothing good or bad upset the balance
of your life.
Thomas à Kempis

Son, now will I teach you the way of peace
and true freedom. (Lord, do as you say; for

this is delightful for me to hear.) Study,
son, to do the will of another rather than
your own. Choose always to have less
rather than more. Seek always the lowest
place; and to be inferior to everyone.
Wish always and pray that the will of
God may be wholly fulfilled in you.
Behold, such a person enters the land of
peace and rest.
Thomas à Kempis

We should have great peace if we did not
busy ourselves with what others say and
do.
Thomas à Kempis

First put yourself at peace, and then you
may the better make others be at peace. A
peaceful and patient man is of more profit
to himself and to others, too, than a
learned man who has no peace.
Thomas à Kempis

What peace and inward quiet should he
have who would cut away from himself all
busyness of mind, and think only on
heavenly things.
Thomas à Kempis

The labor of self-love is a heavy one
indeed. Think for yourself whether much
of your sorrow has not arisen from
someone speaking slightingly of you. As
long as you set yourself up as a little god to
which you must be loyal, how can you
hope to find inward peace?
A.W. Tozer

It is understanding that gives us an ability
to have peace. When we understand the
other fellow's viewpoint, and he
understands ours, then we can sit down
and work out our differences.
Harry S. Truman

If God be our God, He will give us peace
in trouble. When there is a storm without,
He will make peace within. The world can
create trouble in peace, but God can create
peace in trouble.
Thomas Watson

It is our duty to keep the peace, as well as to keep the faith.
Douglas Wilson

My soul, there is a country
Far beyond the stars,
Where stands a wingèd sentry
All skillful in the wars,
There above noise, and danger,
Sweet peace sits crown'd with smiles.
George Herbert

Peace of God and the death of Jesus
When Christ came into the world, peace was sung; and when he went out of the world, peace was bequested.
Francis Bacon

Peace, perfect peace, in this dark world of sin?
The blood of Jesus whispers peace within.
E.H. Bickersteth

A great many people are trying to make peace, but that has already been done. God has not left it for us to do; all we have to do is to enter into it.
Dwight L. Moody

Peacemaker
If you are not a peacemaker, at least do not be a troublemaker.
Isaac from Syria

Peacemaking
I would sooner reconcile all Europe than two women.
Louis XIV

The making of peace people are blessed for is the building of nests amidst our "sea of troubles" (like the halcyons).
John Ruskin

Pentecostalism
The very truths that gave birth to the Pentecostal movement are today generally rejected as too strong.
Frank Bartleman

Pentecostalism wishes to be taken seriously as a Christian movement. Its assessment is due.
Frederick Dale Brunner

This Pentecostal movement is something which God has started at high speed, but the faster we go the greater the need of holiness. The more power we have, the more we need to have every obstacle cleared out of the way. That which cannot be noticed in an old dead church can wreck a revival in a Pentecostal church. May God give us holiness with our Pentecost, for we surely need it. No revival can continue with the blessing of God upon it that does not have a high standard of holiness.
Donald Gee

People
See also: Humanity
You never met a mere mortal. Remember the people you see are eternal; if you knew what they'd become you'd fall down and worship.
C.S. Lewis

Never, never pin your whole faith on any human being.
C.S. Lewis

There are no ordinary people.
C.S. Lewis

I love mankind; it's people I can't stand.
Charles Schultz

Perception
Look to the essence of a thing, whether it be a point of doctrine, of practice, or of interpretation.
Marcus Aurelius Antoninus

When you have first learned God, or His will, you can address yourself cheerfully to the study of His works. If you do not see yourselves and all things as living, moving, and having their being in God, you see nothing, whatever you may think you see.
Richard Baxter

All our knowledge has its origin in our perceptions.
Leonardo da Vinci

Perfection
See also: Holiness; Mistakes
Perfection consists not in doing extraordinary things, but in doing ordinary things extraordinarily well. Neglect nothing; the most trivial action may be performed to God.
Angelique Arnauld

Perfection does not consist in macerating or killing the body, but in killing our perverse self-will.
Catherine of Siena

Perfection is achieved, not when there is nothing more to add, but when there is nothing left to take away.
Antoine de Saint Exupery

Christian perfection has but one limit, that of having none.
Gregory of Nyssa

The farther a man knows himself to be from perfection, the nearer he is to it!
Gerard Groote

The crucified state is necessary for us, is good, is best and safest and will bring us more sooner to the height of perfection.
Jean Nicholas Grou

The surest hindrance of success is to have too high a standard of refinement in our own minds, or too high an opinion of the judgment of the public. He who is determined not to be satisfied with anything short of perfection will never do anything to please himself or others.
Hazlitt

There is no such thing as completed or perfect holiness in this life. Progress yes! Perfection no!
Erroll Hulse

Perfection does not lie in the virtues that the soul knows it has, but in the virtues that our Lord sees in it. This is a closed book; hence one has no reason for presumption, but must remain prostrate on the ground with respect to self.
John of the Cross

If you desire to be perfect, sell your will, give it to the poor in spirit, come to Christ in meekness and humility, and follow him to Calvary and the sepulcher.
John of the Cross

Twelve stars for reaching the highest perfection: love of God, love of neighbor, obedience, chastity, poverty, attendance at choir, penance, humility, mortification, prayer, silence, peace.
John of the Cross

No saint on earth can be fully perfect and pure.
Martin Luther

A glad spirit attains to perfection more quickly than any other.
Philip Neri

None of us has lived up to the teachings of Christ.
Eleanor Roosevelt

The plain truth is that there is no literal and absolute perfection among true Christians, so long as they are in the body.
J.C. Ryle

Have we ever seen holier man then the martyred John Bradford, or Hooker, or Usher, or Baxter, or Rutherford, or M'Cheyne? Yet no one can read the writings and letters of these men without seeing that they felt themselves "debtors to mercy and grace" every day, and the very last thing they ever laid claim to was perfection!
J.C. Ryle

I have yet to learn that there is a single passage in Scripture which teaches that a literal perfection, a complete and entire

freedom from sin, in thought, or word, or deed, is attainable, or has ever been attained, by any child of Adam in this world.
J.C. Ryle

The fact that perfection is beyond our reach, should not diminish the fervor of our desire after it.
C.H. Spurgeon

Either in spirit, or motive, or lack of zeal, or lack of discretion, we are faulty.
C.H. Spurgeon

An absolutely holy man is a being whom I expect to see in heaven, but not in this poor fallen world.
C.H. Spurgeon

Perfection stands in a man offering all his heart wholly to God, not seeking himself or his own will, either in great things or in small, in time or in eternity, but abiding always unchanged and always yielding to God equal thanks for things pleasing and displeasing, weighing them all in one same balance, as in His love.
Thomas à Kempis

[Perfection] is the devoting, not a part but all our soul, body and substance to God.
John Wesley

The only way to perfection is, to live in the presence of God.
Thomas Wilson

Demand perfection of yourself and you'll seldom attain it. Fear of making a mistake is the biggest single cause of making one. Relax – pursue excellence, not perfection.
Bud Winter

Perfection in the church

If the Lord himself teaches that the Church will struggle with the burden of countless sinners until the day of judgment, it is obviously futile to look for a Church totally free from faults.
John Calvin

Permissiveness

If God had believed in permissiveness, he would have given us Ten Suggestions.
Sign outside a church in Rhode Island

Perplexities

In perplexities – when we cannot tell what to do, when we cannot understand what is going on around us – let us be calmed and steadied and made patient by the thought that what is hidden from us is not hidden from Him.
Frances Ridley Havergal

Persecution
See also: Martyrdom

The arrogant mock me without restraint, but I do not turn from your law.
The Bible, Psalm 119:51

Bloodthirsty men hate a man of integrity and seek to kill the upright.
The Bible, Proverbs 29:10

He drew his bow and made me the target for his arrows. He pierced my heart with arrows from his quiver. I became the laughing-stock of all my people; they mock me in song all day long.
The Bible, Lamentations 3:12-14

They persecuted me, they will persecute you also.
The Bible, John 15:20

I consider that our present sufferings are not worth comparing with the glory that will be revealed in us.
The Bible, Romans 8:18

Up to this moment we have become the scum of the earth, the refuse of the world.
The Bible, 1 Corinthians 4:13

Forty stripes save one.
The Bible, 2 Corinthians 11:24 KJV

In fact, everyone who wants to live a godly life in Christ Jesus will be persecuted.
The Bible, 2 Timothy 3:12

Women received back their dead, raised to life again. Others were tortured and refused to be released, so that they might gain a better resurrection. Some faced jeers and flogging, while still others were chained and put in prison. They were stoned; they were sawn in two; they were put to death by the sword. They went about in sheepskins and goatskins, destitute, persecuted and mistreated – the world was not worthy of them. They wandered in deserts and mountains, and in caves and holes in the ground.
The Bible, Hebrews 11:35-38

But how is it to your credit if you receive a beating for doing wrong and endure it? But if you suffer for doing good and you endure it, this is commendable before God. To this you were called, because Christ suffered for you, leaving you an example, that you should follow in his steps.
The Bible, 1 Peter 2:20, 21

In our case [as Christians] we are hated for our name.
Athenagoras

Against the persecution of a tyrant the godly have no remedy but prayer.
John Calvin

Jesus promised his disciples three things – that they would be completely fearless, absurdly happy and in constant trouble.
G.K. Chesterton

Great spirits have often encountered violent opposition from weak minds.
Albert Einstein

Paul was Nero's prisoner, but Nero was much more God's.
William Gurnall

When your enemies see that you are so determined that neither sickness, fancies, poverty, life, death, nor sins discourage you, but that you will continue to seek the love of Jesus and nothing else, by continuing your prayer and other spiritual

works, they will grow enraged and will not spare you the most cruel abuse.
Walter Hilton

Christians have become the targets of opportunity to the thug regimes around the world, and they are many. What's going on now is monumental, and it's affecting millions, tens of millions, of people. We're talking not about discrimination, but persecution of the worst sort: slavery, starvation, murder, looting, burning, torture.
Michael Horowitz

If it were an art to overcome heresy with fire, the executioners would be the most learned doctors on earth.
Martin Luther

If the devil were wise enough and would stand by in silence and let the gospel be preached, he would suffer less harm. For when there is no battle for the gospel it rusts and it finds no cause and no occasion to show its vigor and power. Therefore, nothing better can befall the gospel than that the world should fight it with force and cunning.
Martin Luther

You can kill us, but you can't hurt us.
Justin Martyr

Let us therefore become imitators of His endurance; and if we should suffer for His name's sake, let us glorify Him. For He gave this example to us in His own person, and we believed this.
Polycarp

"Eighty and six years have I now served Christ, and he has never done me the least wrong; how, then, can I blaspheme my King and my Savior?"
Polycarp
In reply to the Roman Proconsul commanding him to swear allegiance to Caesar, saying, "Swear, and I will set thee at liberty; reproach Christ."

One of the shocking untold stories of our time, is that more Christians have died this

century simply for being Christians than in any century since Christ was born.
A.M. Rosenthal, The New York Times

The servant of Christ must never be surprised if he has to drink of the same cup with his Lord.
J.C. Ryle

In the midst of the flame and the rack I have seen men not only groan, that is little; not only not complain, that is little; not only not answer back, that too is little; but I have seen them smile, and smile with a good heart.
Seneca

Persecution for righteousness' sake is what every child of God must expect.
Charles Simeon

The true Christian is like sandalwood, which imparts its fragrance to the axe which cuts it, without doing any harm in return.
Sundar Singh

It is sad that the United States has capitulated to China on fundamental human rights issues as China continues its maltreatment of innocent civilians whose only desire is to gather for prayer and Bible study. If the silence continues, it is only a matter of time until a form of quasi-democracy spreads worldwide where economic wealth is elevated as god and religious conviction is trodden down.
Steven L. Snyder, President of International Christian Concern

Persecution in the early church
Through zeal and envy, the most faithful and righteous pillars of the church have been persecuted even to the most grievous deaths.
Clement of Rome

They are put to death, and they gain new life.
Eusebius

The church of Christ has been founded by shedding its own blood, not that of others; by enduring outrage, not by inflicting it.
Jerome

Persecutions have made the church of Christ grow; martyrdoms have crowned it.
Jerome

[Nero] laid the guilt, and inflicted the most cruel punishments, upon a set of people who were held in abhorrence for their crimes, and popularly called Christians ... Their sufferings at their execution were aggravated by insult and mockery, for some were disguised in the skins of wild beasts and worried to death by dogs, some were crucified, and others were wrapped in pitched shirts and set on fire when the day closed, that they might serve as lights to illuminate the night. Nero lent his own gardens for these executions
Tacitus

Perseverance
See also: Persistence
He will keep you strong to the end, so that you will be blameless on the day of our Lord Jesus Christ.
The Bible, 1 Corinthians 1:8

We are hard pressed on every side, but not crushed; perplexed, but not in despair; persecuted, but not abandoned; struck down, but not destroyed.
The Bible, 2 Corinthians 4:8,9

You need to persevere so that when you have done the will of God, you will receive what he has promised.
The Bible, Hebrews 10:36

In the confrontation between the stream and the rock, the stream always wins – not through strength but through perseverance.
Author unknown

The differences between a successful person and others is not a lack of strength, not a lack of knowledge, but rather in a lack of will.
Author unknown

A champion is someone who gets up even when they can't.
Author unknown

We're born with "go" up to our eyeballs. It's "stop" and "can't" that we learn.
Author unknown

A quitter never wins, a winner never quits.
Author unknown

Trying times are no time to quit trying.
Author unknown

Slow and steady wins the race.
Æsop

We ought to persevere to the end in good works.
Anselm

The difference between perseverance and obstinacy is, that one often comes from a strong will, and the other from a strong won't.
Henry Ward Beecher

It is not the going out of the port, but the coming in, that determines the success of a voyage.
Henry Ward Beecher

Perseverance is the sister of patience, the daughter of constancy, the friend of peace, the cementer of friendships, the bond of harmony and the bulwark of holiness.
Bernard of Clairvaux

Seeing that a Pilot steers the ship in which we sail, who will never allow us to perish even in the midst of shipwrecks, there is no reason why our minds should be overwhelmed with fear and overcome with weariness.
John Calvin

If the biographer gives me credit for being a plodder, he will describe me justly. Anything beyond this will be too much. I can plod. I can persevere in any definite pursuit. To this I owe everything.
William Carey.
Carey's reply, as an old man, to his nephew who asked if he might write his biography.

Permanence, perseverance and persistence in spite of all obstacles, discouragements, and impossibilities: It is this, that in all things distinguishes the strong soul from the weak.
Thomas Carlyle

Most of the important things in the world have been accomplished by people who have kept on trying when there seemed to be no help at all.
Dale Carnegie

I learned that one can never go back, that one should not ever try to go back – that the essence of life is going forward. Life is really a one-way street, isn't it?
Agatha Christie

Nothing in the world can take the place of persistence. Talent will not; nothing is more common than unsuccessful individuals with talent. Genius will not; unrewarded genius is almost a proverb. Education will not; the world is full of educated derelicts. Persistence and determination alone are omnipotent.
Calvin Coolidge

Can one be purchased for God and then not belong to Him?
Curtis Crenshaw

The secret of success is constancy of purpose.
Benjamin Disraeli

Through perseverance many people win success out of what seemed destined to be certain failure.
Benjamin Disraeli

There must be a beginning to any great matter, but the continuing to the end until it be thoroughly finished yields the true glory.
Francis Drake

It is always too soon to quit.
Dr V. Raymond Edman

Perseverance is not a long race; it is many short races one after another.
Walter Elliott

History has demonstrated that the most notable winners usually encountered heartbreaking obstacles before they triumphed. They won because they refused to become discouraged by their defeats.
B.C. Forbes

Energy and persistence conquer all things.
Benjamin Franklin

The best way out is always through.
Robert Frost

The value of good work depends on perseverance. You live a good life in vain if you do not continue it until you die.
St Gregory

Only a sweet and virtuous soul,
Like seasoned timber, never gives.
George Herbert

'Tis a lesson you should heed,
Try, try again.
If at first you don't succeed,
Try, try again.
William Edward Hickson

Great works are performed, not by strength, but by perseverance; yonder palace was raised by single stones, yet you see its height and spaciousness. He that shall walk with vigor three hours a day, will pass in seven years a space equal to the circumference of the globe.
Samuel Johnson

When I find that so much of my life has stolen unprofitably away, and that I can descry by retrospection scarcely a few single days properly and vigorously employed, why do I yet try to resolve again? I try, because reformation is necessary and despair is criminal. I try, in humble hope of the help of God.
Samuel Johnson

All the performances of human art, at which we look with praise or wonder, are instances of the resistless force of perseverance; it is by this that the quarry becomes a pyramid, and that distant countries are united with canals. If a man was to compare the single stroke of the pickaxe, or of one impression of the spade, with the general design and the last result, he would be overwhelmed by the sense of their disproportion; yet those petty operations, incessantly continued, in time surmount the greatest difficulties, and mountains are leveled and oceans bounded by the slender force of human beings.
Samuel Johnson

Few things are impossible to diligence and skill. Great works are performed, not by strength, but perseverance.
Samuel Johnson

Be of good cheer. Do not think of today's failures, but of the success that may come tomorrow. You have set yourselves a difficult task, but you will succeed if you persevere; and you will find joy in overcoming obstacles. Remember, no effort that we make to attain something beautiful is ever lost.
Helen Keller

The drop of rain maketh a hole in the stone, not by violence, but by oft falling.
Hugh Latimer

All things are possible to him who believes, yet more to him who hopes, more still to him who loves, and most of all to him who practices and perseveres in these three virtues.
Brother Lawrence

We can do all things with the grace of God, which He never refuses to them who ask it earnestly. Knock, persevere in knocking, and I answer for it that He will open to you.
Brother Lawrence

I am a slow walker, but I never walk backwards.
Abraham Lincoln

With malice toward none; with charity for all; with firmness in the right, as God gives us to see the right – let us strive on to finish the work we are in.
Abraham Lincoln

Perseverance is a great element of success. If you only knock long enough and loud enough at the gate, you are sure to wake up somebody.
Henry Wadsworth Longfellow

To persevere is to succeed.
Thomas Sutcliffe Mort

Victory belongs to the most persevering.
Napoleon

Lack of will power has caused more failure than lack of intelligence or ability.
Flower A. Newhouse

If I have ever made any valuable discoveries, it has been owing more to patient attention, than to any other talent.
Isaac Newton

God hath work to do in this world; and to desert it because of its difficulties and entanglements, is to cast off His authority. It is not enough that we be just, that we be righteous, and walk with God in holiness; but we must also serve our generation, as David did before he fell asleep. God hath a work to do; and not to help Him is to oppose Him.
John Owen

Let me tell you the secret that has led me to my goal. My strength lies solely in my tenacity.
Louis Pasteur

Nothing of great value in life comes easily.
Norman Vincent Peale

There are only two creatures that can surmount the pyramids, the eagle and the snail.
Eastern proverb

You're looking at a man who spent two years trying to learn to wiggle his big toe.
Franklin Roosevelt,
When asked how he could do so much without being tired, referring to his recovery after polio

To endure is the first thing that a child ought to learn, and that which he will have the most need to know.
Jean Jacques Rousseau

I exhort you and beseech you in the compassion of Christ, faint not, weary not. There is a great necessity of heaven; you must have it. Think it not easy; for it is a steep ascent to eternal glory; many are lying dead by the way, that were slain with security.
Samuel Rutherford

By perseverance the snail reached the ark.
C.H. Spurgeon

The saints are the sinners who keep on going.
Robert Louis Stevenson

When God calls a man, He does not repent of it. God does not, as many friends do, love one day, and hate another; or as princes, who make their subjects favorites, and afterwards throw them into prison. This is the blessedness of a saint; his condition admits of no alteration. God's call is founded on His decree, and His decree is immutable. Acts of grace cannot be reversed. God blots out his people's sins, but not their names.
Thomas Watson

Let therefore none presume on past mercies, as if they were out of danger.
John Wesley

Our motto must continue to be perseverance. And ultimately I trust the

Almighty will crown our efforts with success.
William Wilberforce
Message to the Anti-Slavery Society, during his
forty-five year battle to outlaw the slave trade.

Perseverence of Christians
The doctrine of the final perseverance of
the saints has as its corollary the salutary
teaching that the saints are the people who
persevere to the end.
F.F. Bruce

There is no question in the Scripture about
the eternal security of those truly
regenerated by the Holy Spirit. One
should be careful at this point to note that
this is no "once saved always saved no
matter what you do" doctrine. Indeed,
"faith without works" is not the sign of
spiritual sickness (or backsliding), but
death (Jas. 2:17). The biblical doctrine,
therefore, is once saved always saved and
that you will keep on doing what God says
because you are dead to sin and alive to
Christ (Rom. 6:2). All pretenders will
receive judgment (Matt. 7:21-23). All
regenerates will persevere.
Leonard Coppes

That doctrine of the final perseverance of
the saints is, I believe, as thoroughly bound
up with the standing or falling of the
gospel as is the article of justification by
faith. Give that up, and I see no gospel left.
C.H. Spurgeon

Persistence
See also: Perseverance
And let us not be weary in well doing: for
in due season we shall reap, if we faint not.
The Bible, Galatians 6:9 KJV

Even if you're on the right track – you'll
get run over if you just sit there.
Author unknown

Never give in, never give in, never, never,
never, never – in nothing, great or small,
large or petty – never give in except to
convictions of honor and good sense.
Winston Churchill

It does not matter how slowly you go, so
long as you do not stop.
Confucius

Persistent people begin their success where
others end in failures.
Edward Eggleston

Vitality shows in not only the ability to
persist but the ability to start over.
F. Scott Fitzgerald

Little strokes fell great oaks.
Benjamin Franklin

Press on. Nothing in the world can take
the place of persistence.
Ray A. Kroc

It's not whether you get knocked down. It's
whether you get up again.
Vince Lombardi

When you have completed 95 per cent of
your journey, you are only halfway there.
Japanese proverb

When you get to the end of your rope, tie
a knot and hang on.
Franklin Delano Roosevelt

You may have to fight a battle more than
once to win it.
Margaret Thatcher

Personal evangelism
The greatest service that one person can do
another.
William Temple, describing evangelism

Perspective
To see a world in a grain of sand
And a heaven in a wild flower:
Hold infinity in the palm of your hand,
And eternity in an hour.
William Blake

Pessimism
See also: Optimism
We live in an era in which pessimism has
become the norm, rather than the

exception … Cultural pessimism draws heavily on the philosophy of Friedrich Nietzsche and on his sweeping condemnation of the European society of his day as "sick" and "decadent."
Arthur Herman

Pessimist
No pessimist ever discovered the secrets of the stars or sailed to an uncharted land or opened a new heaven to the human spirit.
Helen Keller

Peter, Apostle
Peter couldn't open his mouth without putting his foot in it. He also had feet of clay.
Author unknown

Philanthropy
Philanthropy is commendable, but it must not cause the philanthropist to overlook the circumstances of economic injustice which make philanthropy necessary.
Martin Luther King, Jr

Philosophy
Philosophy: A study that lets us be unhappy more intelligently.
Author unknown

Unintelligible answers to insoluble problems.
Henry Adams

It is true, that a little philosophy inclineth man's mind to atheism, but depth in philosophy bringeth men's minds about to religion.
Francis Bacon

All are lunatics, but he who can analyze his delusions is called a philosopher.
Ambrose Bierce

There is nothing so absurd but some philosopher has said it.
Marcus Tullius Cicero

The first step towards philosophy is incredulity.
Diderot

Philosophers have only interpreted the world differently; the point is, however, to change it.
Karl Marx

Philosophy has shown itself over and over again to be full of arguments but lacking in conclusions.
Hugh Sylvester

When he who hears doesn't know what he who speaks means, and when he who speaks doesn't know what he himself means – that's philosophy.
Voltaire

Pictures
I kiss my child not only because I love it; I kiss in order to love it. A religious picture not only expresses my awakened faith; it is a help to my faith's awakening.
Baron von Hügel

Piety
True piety is acting what one knows.
Matthew Arnold

Piety and morality are but the same spirit differently manifested. Piety is religion with its face toward God; morality is religion with its face toward the world.
Tryon Edwards

Paul does not forbid you to use rites and ceremonies, but it is not his wish that he who is free in Christ should be bound by them. He does not condemn the law of works if only one uses it lawfully. Without these things perhaps you will not be pious; but they do not make you pious.
Desiderius Erasmus

Multitudes are substituting zeal for piety, liberality for mortification, and a social for a personal religion.
John Angell James

Earth has nothing more tender than a woman's heart when it is the abode of piety.
Martin Luther

Pilgrim

We are Christians and strangers on this earth. Let none of us be frightened; our native land is not this world.
Augustine of Hippo

Make two homes for yourself, my daughter. One actual home and another spiritual home, which you carry with you always.
Catherine of Siena

Keep yourself as a pilgrim and a stranger here in this world, as one to whom the world's business counts but little. Keep your heart free, and always lift it up to God.
Thomas à Kempis

Pilgrimage

Here God gives his people some taste, that they may not faint; and he gives them but a taste, that they may long to be at home, that they may keep humble, that they may sit loose from things below, that they may not break and despise bruised reeds, and that heaven may be more sweet to them at last.
Thomas Brooks

Blest be the day that I began
A pilgrim to be;
And blessèd also be that man
That thereto movèd me.

Fullness to such, a burden is,
That go on pilgrimage:
Here little, and hereafter bliss,
Is best from age to age.
John Bunyan

As I walk'd through the wilderness of this world …
John Bunyan

Who would true valor see,
Let him come hither;
One here will constant be,
Come wind, come weather.
There's no discouragement
Shall make him once relent
His first avowed intent
To be a pilgrim
John Bunyan

They live in their own countries, but as travelers. They share everything as citizens, they suffer everything as foreigners. Every foreign land is their own country, their own country a foreign land. They pass their life here on earth, but are citizens of heaven. They obey the laws of the land, but they out-do the laws in their own lives.
Diognetus

It was always our custom that when we arrived at our intended destination to first of all say a prayer, then to read a section of Scripture. Then we sang an appropriate psalm and then said a prayer again. With God's help we always kept to this custom at each place we visited.
Egeria

Begin your journey in God's name; but be sure to have with you two necessary instruments, Humility and Charity. These are contained in the words above mentioned, which must always be present to your mind, "I am naught, I have naught, I desire only one thing and that is our Lord Jesus, and to be with Him at peace in Jerusalem."
Walter Hilton

Pioneers

Never be a pioneer. It's the early Christian that gets the fattest lion.
Saki

Pity

When a man suffers himself, it is called misery; when he suffers in the suffering of another, it is called pity.
Augustine of Hippo

Plagiarism

Whatever is well said by another, is mine.
Seneca

Planning

Fail to plan is knowingly planning to fail.
Author unknown

Planning is bringing the future into the present so you can do something about it now.
Alan Lakein

Luck is the residue of design.
Branch Rickey – former owner of the Brooklyn Dodger Baseball Team

The loftier the building the deeper the foundation must be.
Thomas à Kempis

Play

Wherever they go, and whatever happens to them on the way, in that enchanted place on the top of the forest, a little boy and his Bear will always be playing.
A.A. Milne, closing lines of Winnie-the-Pooh

The real joy of life is in its play. Play is anything we do for the joy and love of doing it, apart from any profit, compulsion, or sense of duty. It is the real living of life with the feeling of freedom and self-expression. Play is the business of childhood, and its continuation in later years is the prolongation of youth.
Walter Rauschenbach

Pleasing God

1. You will be most careful to understand the Scripture, to know what doth please and displease God.
2. You will be more careful in the doing of every duty, to fit it to the pleasing of God than men.
3. You will look to your hearts, and not only to your actions; to your ends, and thoughts, and the inward manner and degree.
4. You will look to secret duties as well as public and to that which men see not, as well as unto that which they see.
5. You will reverence your consciences, and have much to do with them, and will not slight them: when they tell you of God's displeasure, it will disquiet you; when they tell you of his approval, it will comfort you.
6. Your pleasing men will be charitable for their good, and pious in order to the pleasing of God, and not proud and ambitious for your honor with them, nor impious against the pleasing of God.
7. Whether men be pleased or displeased, or how they judge of you, or what they call you, will seem a small matter to you, as their own interest, in comparison to God's judgment. You live not on them. You can bear their displeasure, censures, and reproaches, if God be but pleased. These will be your evidences.
Richard Baxter

Pleasure

Our mind is where our pleasure is, our heart is where our treasure is, our love is where our life is, but all these, our pleasure, treasure, and life, are reposed in Jesus Christ.
Thomas Adams

No pleasure is worth giving up for the sake of two more years in a geriatric home at Weston-Super-Mare.
Kingsley Amis

Remember that God would give you more pleasure, and not less, and that he will give you as much of the delights of sense as is truly good for you, so you will take them in their place, in subordination to your heavenly delights. And is not this to increase and multiply your pleasure? Are not health, and friends, and food, and convenient habitation, much sweeter as the fruit of the love of God, and the foretastes of everlasting mercies, and as our helps to heaven, and as the means to spiritual comfort, than of themselves alone? All your mercies are from God: he would take none from you, but sanctify them, and give you more.
Richard Baxter

The devil invites men to the water of death.
Catherine of Siena

Where pleasure prevails, all the greatest virtues will lose their power.
Cicero

In order to arrive at having pleasure in everything, desire to have pleasure in nothing.
John of the Cross

He remains a fool his whole life long
Who loves not women, wine and song.
Martin Luther

God made all pleasures innocent.
Caroline Sheridan Norton

Pleasure is the bait of sin.
Plato

There are certain elements of daily life
which are not sinful in themselves, but
which have a tendency to lead to sin if they
are abused. Abuse literally means extreme
use, and in many instances overuse of
things lawful becomes sin. Pleasure is
lawful in use but unlawful in its overuse.
Dr W.H. Griffith Thomas

What fools are they who, for a drop of
pleasure, drink a sea of wrath.
Thomas Watson

Poetry
If I had my life again, I would have made a
rule to read some poetry and listen to some
music at least once every week; for perhaps
the parts of my brain now atrophied would
thus have been kept active through use.
Charles Darwin

Happy who in his verse can gently steer
From grave to light, from pleasant to severe.
John Dryden

Poetry and Hums aren't things which you
get, they're things which get you. And all
you can do is to go where they can find you.
Winnie the Pooh, A.A. Milne

Politeness
There is a politeness of the heart, and it is
allied to love. It produces the most
agreeable politeness of outward behavior.
Goethe

Politeness is the blossom of our humanity.
Joubert

Politeness is worth much and costs little.
Spanish proverb

Politics
See also: Government
In politics, what begins in fear usually ends
in folly.
S.T. Coleridge

Many Christians, like most of the
populace, believe the political illusion; that
is, that political structures can cure all our
ills. The fact is, however, that government,
by its very nature, is limited in what it can
accomplish. What it does best is perpetuate
its own power and bolster its own
bureaucracies.
Charles Colson

He serves his party best who serves the
country best.
*Rutherford B. Hayes: Inaugural Address,
March 5, 1877*

What luck for the rulers that men do not
think.
Adolf Hitler

When a man assumes a public trust, he
should consider himself as public property.
Thomas Jefferson

In politics stupidity is not a handicap.
Napoleon

You cannot create a new world except by
creating a new heart and a new purpose in
common man.
John Percival

What is morally wrong can never be
politically right.
Lord Shaftesbury

A man who acts from the principles I
profess reflects that he is to give an account
of his political conduct at the judgment
seat of Christ.
William Wilberforce

Politics and the Bible
It is impossible to rightly govern the world
without God and the Bible. Do not ever
let anyone claim to be a true American

patriot if they ever attempt to separate religion from politics.
George Washington

Polygamy

A Mormon challenged Mark Twain to cite any passage of scripture forbidding polygamy. "Nothing easier," replied Twain. "No man can serve two masters."
Edmund Fuller

Poor, The

Blessed is he that considereth the poor.
The Bible, Psalm 41:1 KJV

He that hath pity upon the poor lendeth unto the Lord.
The Bible, Proverbs 19:17 KJV

The poor always ye have with you.
The Bible, John 12:8 KJV

Listen, my dear brothers: Has not God chosen those who are poor in the eyes of the world to be rich in faith and to inherit the kingdom he promised those who love him?
The Bible, James 2:5

Christ hungers now, my brethren; it is he who deigns to hunger and thirst in the persons of the poor.
Caesarius of Arles

I shall never cease to give all I can to those in need until I find myself reduced to such a state of poverty that there will scarcely remain to me five feet of earth for my grave or a penny for my funeral.
Cajetan of Thiene

Not to enable the poor to share in our goods is to steal from them and deprive them of life. The goods we possess are not ours, but theirs.
John Chrysostom

When we attend to the needs of those in want, we give them what is theirs, not ours. More than performing works of mercy, we are paying a debt of justice.
Gregory the Great

The cry of the poor must either be heard by us, or it will ascend up against us into the ears of the Lord of Sabaoth.
F.D. Maurice

Systems by which the rich are made richer, and the poor poorer, should find no favor among people professing to "fear God and hate covetousness."
Lucretia Mott

When we serve the poor and the sick, we serve Jesus. We must not fail to help our neighbors, because in them we serve Jesus.
Rose of Lima

Because of God's own care for the poor, and because of their exploitation by the unscrupulous and their neglect by the church, they should now receive a "positive" or "reverse" discrimination.
John Stott

What the poor need, even more than food and clothing and shelter (though they need these, too, desperately), is to be wanted.
Mother Teresa

Poor in Spirit

He that is poor in spirit is lowly in heart. Rich men are commonly proud and scornful, but the poor are submissive. The poor in spirit roll themselves in the dust in the sense of their unworthiness. "I abhor myself in dust" (Job 42:6). He that is poor in spirit looks at another's excellencies and his own infirmities. He denies not only his sins but his duties. The more grace he has, the more humble he is, because he now sees himself a greater debtor to God. If he can do any duty, he acknowledges it is Christ's strength more than his own. As the ship gets to the haven more by the benefit of the wind than the sail, so when a Christian makes swift progress, it is more by wind of God's Spirit than the sail of his own endeavor. The poor in spirit, when he acts most like a saint, confesses himself to be "the chief of sinners." He blushes more at the defect of his graces than others do at

the excess of their sins. He dares not say he has prayed or wept. He lives, yet not he, but Christ lives in him.
Thomas Watson

Pope

That of the pope alone all princes shall kiss his feet.
Gregory the Great

The Roman pontiff alone can with right be called universal.
Gregory the Great

I do not believe that in order to be a believing Christian you have to believe in the pope also.
Martin Luther

I would have made a good pope.
Richard M. Nixon

Popularity

The fumes of popularity have turned the brains of many a man.
C.H. Spurgeon

The adulation of multitudes has laid thousands low.
C.H. Spurgeon

Possessions

God made man to be somebody, not just to have things.
Author unknown

It is our nature's law that makes a man set higher value on the things he has not got than upon those he has, so that he loathes his actual possessions in longing for the things that are not his.
Bernard of Clairvaux

The riches and goods of Christians are not common, as touching the right, title, and possession of the same, as certain Anabaptists do falsely boast.
Book of Common Prayer

Nobody can fight properly and boldly for the faith if he clings to a fear of being

stripped of earthly possessions.
Peter Damian

All my possessions are for a moment of time.
Elizabeth I, Queen of England

Christianity teacheth me that what I charitably give alive, I carry with me dead; and experience teacheth me that what I leave behind, I lose. I will carry that treasure with me by giving it, which the worldling loseth by keeping it; so, while his corpse shall carry nothing but a winding cloth to his grave, I shall be richer under the earth than I was above it.
Joseph Hall

It is easier to renounce worldly possessions than it is to renounce the love of them.
Walter Hilton

The desire for possessions is dangerous and terrible, knowing no satiety; it drives the soul which it controls to the heights of evil.
Abba Isidore of Pelusia

The true ascetic counts nothing his own but his harp.
Joachim of Fiore

These are things that make it difficult to die.
Samuel Johnson, being shown round a castle and its grounds

I will place no value on anything I have or may possess, except in relation to the kingdom of Christ.
David Livingstone

At least I left shoes in my closets and not skeletons. And besides, I didn't have 3,000 pairs of shoes. I only had 1,060.
Imelda Marcos

If you have anything that you prize very highly, hold it very loosely, for you may easily lose it.
C.H. Spurgeon

We have very little, so we have nothing to be preoccupied with. The more you have, the more you are occupied, the less you give. But the less you have, the more free you are.
Mother Teresa

The blessed ones who possess the kingdom are they who have repudiated every external thing and have rooted from their hearts all sense of possessing.
A. W. Tozer

There can be no doubt that possessive clinging to things is one of the most harmful habits in the Christian life. Because it is so natural, it is rarely recognized for the evil that it is. But its outworkings are tragic.
A. W. Tozer

Potential
Treat people as if they were what they ought to be and you help them become what they are capable of being.
Goethe

Poverty
See also: Possessions; Wealth
Franciscan poverty is a poverty not only of having but of being itself. As such it entails the annihilation of the false self, the emptying to the point of nothingness, in order to become totally free and filled with the abundance of God's uncreated love and wisdom.
Angela of Foligno

What is the use of being kind to a poor man?
Cicero

Better to go to heaven in rags than to hell in embroidery.
Thomas Fuller

Poverty is no sin.
George Herbert

A decent provision for the poor is the true test of civilization.
Samuel Johnson

The inevitable consequence of poverty is dependence.
Samuel Johnson

Resolve not to be poor. Poverty is a great enemy of human happiness.
Samuel Johnson

No society can surely be flourishing and happy, of which the far greater part of the members are poor and miserable.
Adam Smith

Gold cannot sustain grace; and on the other hand, rags cannot make it flourish.
C.H. Spurgeon

Poverty is no virtue; wealth is no sin.
C.H. Spurgeon

The strong soul becomes much more stable thanks to voluntary poverty.
Amma Syncletica

Poverty for us is freedom.
Mother Teresa

The real disgrace of poverty is not in admitting the fact but in declining to struggle against it.
Thucydides

The more is given the less people will work for themselves, and the less they work the more their poverty will increase.
Leo Tolstoy

Power
Now to him who is able to do immeasurably more than all we ask or imagine, according to his power that is at work within us, to him be glory in the church and in Christ Jesus throughout all generations, forever and ever. Amen!
The Bible, Ephesians 3:20-21

Power doesn't corrupt people. People corrupt power.
Author unknown

Don't forget the golden rule. He who has the gold makes the rules.
Author unknown

Power is never good, unless the one who has it is good.
King Alfred

Power tends to corrupt, and absolute power corrupts absolutely. Great men are almost always bad men. There is no worse heresy than that the office sanctifies the holder of it.
Lord Acton

God has every bit of me.
William Booth's account of why his life displayed such spiritual power

Power gradually extirpates from the mind every humane and gentle virtue.
Edmund Burke

Never underestimate the power of very stupid people in large groups.
John Kenneth Galbraith

All the resources of the Godhead are at our disposal!
Jonathan Goforth

The power that is supported by force alone will have cause often to tremble.
Lajos Kossuth

Nearly all men can stand adversity, but if you want to test a man's character, give him power.
Abraham Lincoln

The essence of government is power; and power, lodged as it must be in human hands, will ever be liable to abuse.
James Madison

There are in the world two powers – the sword and the spirit. And the spirit has always vanquished the sword.
Napoleon

The measure of a man is what he does with power.
Pittacus

Power, Love of
The love of liberty is the love of others; the love of power is the love of ourselves.
William Hazlitt

Powerlessness
The best antidote for a powerless Church is the influence of a praying man.
David Smithers

Practice
The only way to become master of any skill is first to become its slave. And that takes practice, practice, practice.
Paderewski, on being asked by a youngster how he too could master the piano

Practice is the best of all instructors.
Publilius Syrus

Practicing the presence of God
Q: "What must one do in order to please God?"
A: "Whoever you may be, always have God before your eyes."
Abba Anthony the Great

Make every effort then to let God be great and to ensure that all your good intentions and endeavors are directed to him in all that you do and in all that you refrain from doing.
Meister Eckhart

I worshiped God as often as I could, keeping my mind in His holy presence, and recalling it as often as I found it had wandered from Him. I found no small pain in this exercise, and yet I continued it, notwithstanding all the difficulties that occurred, without troubling or disquieting myself when my mind had wandered involuntarily. I made this my business not only at the appointed times of prayer, but all the day long; for at all times, every hour, every minute, even in the height of my business, I drove away from my mind

everything that was capable of interrupting my thoughts of God.
Brother Lawrence

Let it be your business to keep your mind in the presence of the Lord.
Brother Lawrence

When the remembrance of God lives in the heart and there maintains the fear of Him, then all goes well; but when this remembrance grows weak or is kept only in the head, then all goes astray.
Theophan the Recluse

We should always honor and reverence Him as if we were always in His bodily presence.
Thomas à Kempis

We must break the evil habit of ignoring the spiritual. We must shift our interest from the seen to the unseen.
A. W. Tozer

Many have found the secret of which I speak and, without giving much thought to what is going on within them, constantly practice this habit of inwardly gazing upon God.
A. W. Tozer

Praise

I will bless the LORD at all times; his praise shall continually be in my mouth.
The Bible, Psalm 34.1 NRSV

Let them praise his name with dancing and make music to him with tambourine and harp.
The Bible, Psalm 149:3

Sing to the LORD, for he has done glorious things; let this be known to all the world.
The Bible, Isaiah 12:5

… a garment of praise instead of a spirit of despair.
The Bible, Isaiah 61:3

Praise our God, all you his servants, you who fear him, both small and great!
The Bible, Revelation 19:5

There is nothing that pleases the Lord so much as praise.
Author unknown

God can never receive too much praise.
Author unknown

Mans chief work is the praise of God.
Augustine of Hippo

Let us sing how the eternal God, the author of all marvels, first created the heavens for the sons of men as a roof to cover them, and how their almighty Protector gave them the earth to live in.
Caedmon

If I was a nightingale I would sing like a nightingale; if a swan, like a swan. But since I am a rational creature my role is to praise God.
Epictetus

The prophetic spirit orders that God be praised with cymbals of jubilation and with the rest of the musical instruments which the wise and studious have created, since all the arts are brought to life by that breath of life which God breathed into the body of man: and therefore it is just that God be praised in all things.
Hildegard of Bingen

If any one would tell you the shortest, surest way to all happiness and all perfection, he must tell you to make it a rule to yourself to thank and praise God for everything that happens to you. For it is certain that whatever seeming calamity happens to you, if you thank and praise God for it, you turn it into a blessing. Could you, therefore, work miracles, you could not do more for yourself than by this thankful spirit; for it heals with a word, and turns all that it touches into happiness.
William Law

I was not born to be free. I was born to adore and to obey.
C.S. Lewis

A man should utter a hundred daily benedictions.
Rabbi Meir

Let us, with a gladsome mind,
Praise the Lord, for he is kind:
For his mercies aye endure,
Ever faithful, ever sure.
Let us blaze his name abroad,
For of gods he is the God:
He, with all-commanding might,
Filled the new-made world with light:
All things living he doth feed,
His full hand supplies their need:
He his chosen race did bless
In the wasteful wilderness:
Let us then with gladsome mind
Praise the Lord, for he is kind.
John Milton

When we wake up each morning, if praise of the Risen Christ were to fill our hearts … then in the monotony of daily life, an inner surge of vitality would reveal our hidden longing.
Brother Roger

One day all Christians will join in a doxology and sing God's praises with perfection. But even today, individually and corporately, we are not only to sing the doxology, but to be the doxology.
Francis Schaeffer

Look at the very birds on earth – how they shame us!
Dear little creatures, if you watch them when they are singing, you will sometimes wonder how so much sound can come out of such diminutive bodies.
How they throw their whole selves into the music, and seem to melt themselves away in song!
How the wing vibrates, the throat pulsates, and every part of their body rejoices to assist the strain!

This is the way in which we ought to praise God.
C.H. Spurgeon

Praising God is one of the highest and purest acts of religion. In prayer we act like men; in praise we act like angels.
Thomas Watson

In vain the first-born seraph tries to sound the depths of love divine.
Charles Wesley

The sweetest of all sounds is praise.
Xenophon

Praise of others

As long as one can admire and love, then one is young for ever.
Pablo Casals

Praise often turns losers into winners.
Author unknown

As we must account for every idle remark, so we must account for every idle silence.
Benjamin Franklin

The applause of a single human being is of great importance.
Samuel Johnson

Usually we praise only to be praised.
La Rouchefoucauld

Glory paid to ashes comes too late.
Martial

A slowness to applaud betrays a cold temper or an envious spirit.
Hannah More

Praise of self

Speaking ill of others is a cheap, dishonest way to praise ourselves.
Author unknown

Prayer

See also Church and prayer; Comforters;
Godliness; Faith and prayer; Fasting;
Holiness; Impossible; Love and prayer;
Prayer, Neglect of; Prayerlessness;
Revival; Warfare, Spiritual; Witness

Prayer

John Calvin

Institutes of Christian Religion

BOOK III.,CHAPTER XX.OF PRAYER:
A PERPETUAL EXERCISE OF FAITH
THE DAILY BENEFITS DERIVED FROM IT.

1. FROM the previous part of the work we clearly see how completely destitute man is of all good, how devoid of every means of procuring his own salvation. Hence, if he would obtain succor in his necessity, he must go beyond himself, and procure it in some other quarter. It has farther been shown that the Lord kindly and spontaneously manifests himself in Christ, in whom he offers all happiness for our misery, all abundance for our want, opening up the treasures of heaven to us, so that we may turn with full faith to his beloved Son, depend upon him with full expectation, rest in him, and cleave to him with full hope. This, indeed, is that secret and hidden philosophy which cannot be learned by syllogisms: a philosophy thoroughly understood by those whose eyes God has so opened as to see light in his light (Ps. xxxvi. 9.) But after we have learned by faith to know that whatever is necessary for us or defective in us is supplied in God and in our Lord Jesus Christ, in whom it hath pleased the Father that all fulness should dwell, that we may thence draw as from an inexhaustible fountain, it remains for us to seek and in prayer implore of him what we have learned to be in him. To know God as the sovereign disposer of all good, inviting us

to present our requests, and yet not to approach or ask of him, were so far from availing us, that it were just as if one told of a treasure were to allow it to remain buried in the ground. Hence the Apostle, to show that a faith unaccompanied with prayer to God cannot be genuine, states this to be the order: As faith springs from the Gospel, so by faith our hearts are framed to call upon the name of God, (Rom. x. 14.) And this is the very thing which he had expressed some time before, viz., that the – Spirit of adoption – , which seals the testimony of the Gospel on our hearts, gives us courage to make our requests known unto God, calls forth groanings which cannot be uttered, and enables us to cry, Abba, Father, (Rom. viii. 26.) This last point, as we have hitherto only touched upon it slightly in passing, must now be treated more fully.

2. To – prayer – , then, are we indebted for penetrating to those riches which are treasured up for us with our heavenly Father. For there is a kind of intercourse between God and men, by which, having entered the upper sanctuary, they appear before Him and appeal to his promises, that when necessity requires they may learn by experiences that what they believed merely on the authority of his word was not in vain. Accordingly, we see that nothing is set before us as an object of expectation from the Lord which we are not enjoined to ask of Him in prayer, so true it is that prayer digs up those treasures which the Gospel of our Lord discovers to the eye of faith. The necessity and utility of this exercise of prayer no words can sufficiently express. Assuredly it is not without cause our heavenly Father declares that our only safety is in calling upon his name, since by it we invoke the presence of his providence to watch over our interests, of his power to sustain us when weak and almost fainting, of his goodness to receive us into favor, though miserably loaded with sin; in fine, call upon him to manifest himself to us in all his perfections. Hence, admirable peace and tranquillity are given to our

consciences; for the straits by which we were pressed being laid before the Lord, we rest fully satisfied with the assurance that none of our evils are unknown to him, and that he is both able and willing to make the best provision for us.

3. But some one will say, Does he not know without a monitor both what our difficulties are, and what is meet for our interest, so that it seems in some measure superfluous to solicit him by our prayers, as if he were winking, or even sleeping, until aroused by the sound of our voice? Those who argue thus attend not to the end for which the Lord taught us to pray. It was not so much for his sake as for ours. He wills indeed, as is just, that due honor be paid him by acknowledging that all which men desire or feel to be useful, and pray to obtain, is derived from him. But even the benefit of the homage which we thus pay him redounds to ourselves. Hence the holy patriarchs, the more confidently they proclaimed the mercies of God to themselves and others felt the stronger incitement to prayer. It will be sufficient to refer to the example of Elijah, who being assured of the purpose of God had good ground for the promise of rain which he gives to Ahab, and yet prays anxiously upon his knees, and sends his servant seven times to inquire, (1 Kings xviii. 42;) not that he discredits the oracle, but because he knows it to be his duty to lay his desires before God, lest his faith should become drowsy or torpid. Wherefore, although it is true that while we are listless or insensible to our wretchedness, he wakes and watches for use and sometimes even assists us unasked; it is very much for our interest to be constantly supplicating him; first, that our heart may always be inflamed with a serious and ardent desire of seeking, loving and serving him, while we accustom ourselves to have recourse to him as a sacred anchor in every necessity; secondly, that no desires, no longing whatever, of which we are ashamed to make him the witness, may enter our minds, while we learn to place all our wishes in his sight, and thus pour out our heart before him; and, lastly, that we may be prepared to receive all his benefits with true gratitude and thanksgiving, while our prayers remind us that they proceed from his hand. Moreover, having obtained what we asked, being persuaded that he has answered our prayers, we are led to long more earnestly for his favor, and at the same time have greater pleasure in welcoming the blessings which we perceive to have been obtained by our prayers. Lastly, use and experience confirm the thought of his providence in our minds in a manner adapted to our weakness, when we understand that he not only promises that he will never fail us, and spontaneously gives us access to approach him in every time of need, but has his hand always stretched out to assist his people, not amusing them with words, but proving himself to be a present aid. For these reasons, though our most merciful Father never slumbers nor sleeps, he very often seems to do so, that thus he may exercise us, when we might otherwise be listless and slothful, in asking, entreating, and earnestly beseeching him to our great good. It is very absurd, therefore, to dissuade men from prayer, by pretending that Divine Providence, which is always watching over the government of the universes is in vain importuned by our supplications, when, on the contrary, the Lord himself declares, that he is "nigh unto all that call upon him, to all that call upon him in truth, (Ps. cxlv. 18.) No better is the frivolous allegation of others, that it is superfluous to pray for things which the Lord is ready of his own accord to bestow; since it is his pleasure that those very things which flow from his spontaneous liberality should be acknowledged as conceded to our prayers. This is testified by that memorable sentence in the psalms to which many others corresponds: "The eyes of the Lord are upon the righteous, and his ears are open unto their cry," (Ps. xxxiv. 15.) This passage, while extolling the care which Divine Providence spontaneously exercises

over the safety of believers, omits not the exercise of faith by which the mind is aroused from sloth. The eyes of God are awake to assist the blind in their necessity, but he is likewise pleased to listen to our groans, that he may give us the better proof of his love. And thus both things are true, "He that keepeth Israel shall neither slumber nor sleep," (Ps. cxxi. 4;) and yet whenever he sees us dumb and torpid, he withdraws as if he had forgotten us.

4. Let the first rule of right prayer then be, to have our heart and mind framed as becomes those who are entering into converse with God. This we shall accomplish in regard to the mind, if, laying aside carnal thoughts and cares which might interfere with the direct and pure contemplation of God, it not only be wholly intent on prayer, but also, as far as possible, be borne and raised above itself. I do not here insist on a mind so disengaged as to feel none of the gnawings of anxiety; on the contrary, it is by much anxiety that the fervor of prayer is inflamed. Thus we see that the holy servants of God betray great anguish, not to say solicitude, when they cause the voice of complaint to ascend to the Lord from the deep abyss and the jaws of death. What I say is, that all foreign and extraneous cares must be dispelled by which the mind might be driven to and fro in vague suspense, be drawn down from heaven, and kept groveling on the earth. When I say it must be raised above itself, I mean that it must not bring into the presence of God any of those things which our blind and stupid reason is wont to devise, nor keep itself confined within the little measure of its own vanity, but rise to a purity worthy of God.

5. Both things are specially worthy of notice. First, let every one in professing to pray turn thither all his thoughts and feelings, and be not (as is usual) distracted by wandering thoughts; because nothing is more contrary to the reverence due to God than that levity which bespeaks a mind too much given to license and devoid of fear. In this matter we ought to labor the more earnestly the more difficult we experience it to be; for no man is so intent on prayer as not to feel many thoughts creeping in, and either breaking off the tenor of his prayer, or retarding it by some turning or digression. Here let us consider how unbecoming it is when God admits us to familiar intercourse to abuse his great condescension by mingling things sacred and profane, reverence for him not keeping our minds under restraint; but just as if in prayer we were conversing with one like ourselves forgetting him, and allowing our thoughts to run to and fro. Let us know, then, that none duly prepare themselves for prayer but those who are so impressed with the majesty of God that they engage in it free from all earthly cares and affections. The ceremony of lifting up our hands in prayer is designed to remind us that we are far removed from God, unless our thoughts rise upward: as it is said in the psalm, "Unto thee, O Lord, do I lift up my soul," (Psalm xxv. 1.) And Scripture repeatedly uses the expression to – raise our prayers – meaning that those who would be heard by God must not grovel in the mire. The sum is, that the more liberally God deals with us, condescendingly inviting us to disburden our cares into his bosom, the less excusable we are if this admirable and incomparable blessing does not in our estimation outweigh all other things, and win our affection, that prayer may seriously engage our every thought and feeling. This cannot be unless our mind, strenuously exerting itself against all impediments, rise upward.

Our second proposition was, that we are to ask only in so far as God permits. For though he bids us pour out our hearts, (Ps. lxii. 8) he does not indiscriminately give loose reins to foolish and depraved affections; and when he promises that he will grant believers their wish, his indulgence does not proceed so far as to submit to their caprice. In both matters grievous delinquencies are everywhere committed. For not only do many without modesty, without reverence, presume to invoke God concerning their frivolities, but impudently bring forward their dreams, whatever they may be, before the tribunal of God. Such is the folly or stupidity under which they labor, that they have the hardihood to obtrude upon God desires so vile, that they would blush exceedingly to impart them to their fellow men. Profane writers have derided and even expressed their detestation of this presumption, and yet the vice has always prevailed. Hence, as the ambitious adopted Jupiter as their patron; the avaricious, Mercury; the literary aspirants, Apollo and Minerva; the warlike, Mars; the licentious, Venus: so in the present day, as I lately observed, men in prayer give greater license to their unlawful desires than if they were telling jocular tales among their equals. God does not suffer his condescension to be thus mocked, but vindicating his own light, places our wishes under the restraint of his authority. We must, therefore, attend to the observation of John: "This is the confidence that we have in him, that if we ask any thing according to his will, he heareth us," (1 John v. 14.)

But as our faculties are far from being able to attain to such high perfection, we must seek for some means to assist them. As the eye of our mind should be intent upon God, so the affection of our heart ought to follow in the same course. But both fall far beneath this, or rather, they faint and fail, and are carried in a contrary direction. To assist this weakness, God gives us the guidance of the Spirit in our prayers to dictate what is right, and regulate our affections. For seeing "we know not what we should pray for as we ought," "the Spirit itself maketh intercession for us with groanings which cannot be uttered," (Rom. viii. 26) not that he actually prays or groans, but he excites in us sighs, and wishes, and confidence, which our natural powers are not at all able to conceive. Nor is it without cause Paul gives the name of – groanings which cannot be uttered – to the prayers which believers send forth under the guidance of the Spirit. For those who are truly exercised in prayer are not

unaware that blind anxieties so restrain and perplex them, that they can scarcely find what it becomes them to utter; nay, in attempting to lisp they halt and hesitate. Hence it appears that to pray aright is a special gift. We do not speak thus in indulgence to our sloths as if we were to leave the office of prayer to the Holy Spirit, and give way to that carelessness to which we are too prone. Thus we sometimes hear the impious expression, that we are to wait in suspense until he take possession of our minds while otherwise occupied. Our meaning is, that, weary of our own heartlessness and sloth, we are to long for the aid of the Spirit. Nor, indeed, does Paul, when he enjoins us to pray – in the Spirit – , (1 Cor. xiv. 15,) cease to exhort us to vigilance, intimating, that while the inspiration of the Spirit is effectual to the formation of prayer, it by no means impedes or retards our own endeavors; since in this matter God is pleased to try how efficiently faith influences our hearts.

6. Another rule of prayer is, that in asking we must always truly feel our wants, and seriously considering that we need all the things which we ask, accompany the prayer with a sincere, nay, ardent desire of obtaining them. Many repeat prayers in a perfunctory manner from a set form, as if they were performing a task to God, and though they confess that this is a necessary remedy for the evils of their condition, because it were fatal to be left without the divine aid which they implore, it still appears that they perform the duty from custom, because their minds are meanwhile cold, and they ponder not what they ask. A general and confused feeling of their necessity leads them to pray, but it does not make them solicitous as in a matter of present consequence, that they may obtain the supply of their need. Moreover, can we suppose anything more hateful or even more execrable to God than this fiction of asking the pardon of sins, while he who asks at the very time either thinks that he is not a sinner, or, at least, is not thinking that he is a sinner; in other words, a fiction

by which God is plainly held in derision? But mankind, as I have lately said, are full of depravity, so that in the way of perfunctory service they often ask many things of God which they think come to them without his beneficence, or from some other quarter, or are already certainly in their possession. There is another fault which seems less heinous, but is not to be tolerated. Some murmur out prayers without meditation, their only principle being that God is to be propitiated by prayer. Believers ought to be specially on their guard never to appear in the presence of God with the intention of presenting a request unless they are under some serious impression, and are, at the same time, desirous to obtain it. Nay, although in these things which we ask only for the glory of God, we seem not at first sight to consult for our necessity, yet we ought not to ask with less fervor and vehemency of desire. For instance, when we pray that his name be hallowed–that hallowing must, so to speak, be earnestly hungered and thirsted after.

7. If it is objected, that the necessity which urges us to pray is not always equal, I admit it, and this distinction is profitably taught us by James: "Is any among you afficted? let him pray. Is any merry? let him sing psalms," (James v. 13.) Therefore, common sense itself dictates, that as we are too sluggish, we must be stimulated by God to pray earnestly whenever the occasion requires. This David calls a time when God "may be found," (a seasonable time;) because, as he declares in several other passages, that the more hardly grievances, annoyances, fears, and other kinds of trial press us, the freer is our access to God, as if he were inviting us to himself. Still not less true is the injunction of Paul to pray "always," (Eph. vi. 18;) because, however prosperously according to our view, things proceed, and however we may be surrounded on all sides with grounds of joy, there is not an instant of time during which our want does not exhort us to prayer. A man abounds in wheat and wine; but as he cannot enjoy a morsel of bread, unless by the continual bounty of God, his granaries or cellars will not prevent him from asking for daily bread. Then, if we consider how many dangers impend every moment, fear itself will teach us that no time ought to be without prayer. This, however, may be better known in spiritual matters. For when will the many sins of which we are conscious allow us to sit secure without suppliantly entreating freedom from guilt and punishment? When will temptation give us a truce, making it unnecessary to hasten for help? Moreover, zeal for the kingdom and glory of God ought not to seize us by starts, but urge us without intermission, so that every time should appear seasonable. It is not without cause, therefore, that assiduity in prayer is so often enjoined. I am not now speaking of perseverance, which shall afterwards be considered; but Scripture, by reminding us of the necessity of constant prayer, charges us with sloth, because we feel not how much we stand in need of this care and assiduity. By this rule hypocrisy and the device of lying to God are restrained, nay, altogether banished from prayer. God promises that he will be near to those who call upon him in truth, and declares that those who seek him with their whole heart will find him: those, therefore, who delight in their own pollution cannot surely aspire to him.

One of the requisites of legitimate prayer is repentance. Hence the common declaration of Scripture, that God does not listen to the wicked; that their prayers, as well as their sacrifices, are an abomination to him. For it is right that those who seal up their hearts should find the ears of God closed against them, that those who, by their hardheartedness, provoke his severity should find him inflexible. In Isaiah he thus threatens: "When ye make many prayers, I will not hear: your hands are full of blood," (Isaiah i. 15.) In like manner, in Jeremiah, "Though they shall cry unto me, I will not hearken unto them," (Jer. xi. 7, 8, 11;) because he regards it as the highest insult for the wicked to boast of his covenant while profaning his sacred name by their whole lives. Hence he complains in Isaiah: "This people draw near to me with their mouth, and with their lips do honor me; but have removed their heart far from men" (Isaiah xxix. 13.) Indeed, he does not confine this to prayers alone, but declares that he abominates pretense in every part of his service. Hence the words of James, "Ye ask and receive note because ye ask amiss, that ye may consume it upon your lusts," (James iv. 3.) It is true, indeed, (as we shall again see in a little,) that the pious, in the prayers which they utter, trust not to their own worth; still the admonition of John is not superfluous: "Whatsoever we ask, we receive of him, because we keep his commandments," (1 John iii. 22;) an evil conscience shuts the door against us. Hence it follows, that none but the sincere worshipers of God pray aright, or are listened to. Let every one, therefore, who prepares to pray feel dissatisfied with what is wrong in his condition, and assume, which he cannot do without repentance, the character and feelings of a poor suppliant.

8. The third rule to be added is: that he who comes into the presence of God to pray must divest himself of all vainglorious thoughts, lay aside all idea of worth; in short, discard all self-
confidence, humbly giving God the whole glory, lest by arrogating any thing, however little, to himself, vain pride cause him to turn away his face. Of this submission, which casts down all haughtiness, we have numerous examples in the servants of God. The holier they are, the more humbly they prostrate themselves when they come into the presence of the Lord. Thus Daniel, on whom the Lord himself bestowed such high commendation, says, "We do not present our supplications before thee for our righteousness but for thy great mercies. O Lord, hear; O Lord, forgive; O Lord, hearken and do; defer not, for thine own sake, O my God: for thy city and thy people are called by thy name." This he does not indirectly in the usual manner, as if he were one of the individuals in a crowd: he rather confesses his guilt apart, and as a suppliant betaking himself to the asylum of pardon, he distinctly declares that he was confessing his own sin, and the sin of his people Israel, (Dan. ix. 18-20.) David also sets us an example of this humility: "Enter not into judgment with thy servant: for in thy sight shall no man living be justified," (Psalm cxliii. 2.) In like manner, Isaiah prays, "Behold, thou art wroth; for we have sinned: in those is continuance, and we shall be saved. But we are all as an unclean thing, and all our righteousnesses are as filthy rags; and we all do fade as a leaf; and our iniquities, like the wind, have taken us away. And there is none that calleth upon thy name, that stirreth up himself to take hold of thee: for thou hast hid thy face from us, and hast consumed us, because of our iniquities. But now, O Lord, thou art our Father; we are the clay, and thou our potter; and we all are the work of thy hand. Be not wroth very sore, O Lord, neither remember iniquity for ever: Behold, see, we beseech thee, we are all thy people." (Isa. lxiv. 5-9.) You see how they put no confidence in any thing but this: considering that they are the Lord's, they despair not of being the objects of his care. In the same way, Jeremiah says, "O Lord, though our iniquities testify against us, do thou it for thy name's sake," (Jer. xiv. 7.) For it was most truly and piously written by the uncertain author (whoever he may have been) that wrote the book which is attributed to the prophet Baruch, "But the soul that is greatly vexed, which goeth stooping and feeble, and the eyes that fail, and the hungry soul, will give thee praise and righteousness, O Lord. Therefore, we do not make our humble supplication before thee, O Lord our God, for the righteousness of our fathers, and of our kings." "Hear, O Lord, and have mercy; for thou art merciful: and have pity upon us, because we have sinned before thee," (Baruch ii. 18, 19; iii. 2.)

9. In fine, supplication for pardon, with humble and ingenuous confession of guilt, forms   both   the   preparation   and

commencement of right prayer. For the holiest of men cannot hope to obtain any thing from God until he has been freely reconciled to him. God cannot be propitious to any but those whom he pardons. Hence it is not strange that this is the key by which believers open the door of prayer, as we learn from several passages in The Psalms. David, when presenting a request on a different subject, says, "Remember not the sins of my youth, nor my transgressions; according to thy mercy remember me, for thy goodness sake, O Lord," (Psalm xxv. 7.) Again, "Look upon my affliction and my pain, and forgive my sins," (Psalm xxv. 18.) Here also we see that it is not sufficient to call ourselves to account for the sins of each passing day; we must also call to mind those which might seem to have been long before buried in oblivion. For in another passage the same prophet, confessing one grievous crime, takes occasion to go back to his very birth, "I was shapen in iniquity, and in sin did my mother conceive me," (Psalm li. 5;) not to extenuate the fault by the corruption of his nature, but as it were to accumulate the sins of his whole life, that the stricter he was in condemning himself, the more placable God might be. But although the saints do not always in express terms ask forgiveness of sins, yet if we carefully ponder those prayers as given in Scripture, the truth of what I say will readily appear; namely, that their courage to pray was derived solely from the mercy of God, and that they always began with appeasing him. For when a man interrogates his conscience, so far is he from presuming to lay his cares familiarly before God, that if he did not trust to mercy and pardon, he would tremble at the very thought of approaching him. There is, indeed, another special confession. When believers long for deliverance from punishment, they at the same time pray that their sins may be pardoned; for it were absurd to wish that the effect should be taken away while the cause remains. For we must beware of imitating foolish patients who, anxious only about curing accidental symptoms, neglect

the root of the disease. Nay, our endeavor must be to have God propitious even before he attests his favor by external signs, both because this is the order which he himself chooses, and it were of little avail to experience his kindness, did not conscience feel that he is appeased, and thus enable us to regard him as altogether lovely. Of this we are even reminded by our Savior's reply. Having determined to cure the paralytic, he says, "Thy sins are forgiven thee;" in other words, he raises our thoughts to the object which is especially to be desired, viz. admission into the favor of God, and then gives the fruit of reconciliation by bringing assistance to us. But besides that special confession of present guilt which believers employ, in supplicating for pardon of every fault and punishment, that general introduction which procures favor for our prayers must never be omitted, because prayers will never reach God unless they are founded on free mercy. To this we may refer the words of John, "If we confess our sins, he is faithful and just to forgive us our sins and to cleanse us from all unrighteousness," (1 John i. 9.) Hence, under the law it was necessary to consecrate prayers by the expiation of blood, both that they might be accepted, and that the people might be warned that they were unworthy of the high privilege until, being purged from their defilements, they founded their confidence in prayer entirely on the mercy of God.

10. Sometimes, however, the saints in supplicating God, seem to appeal to their own righteousness, as when David says, "Preserve my soul; for I am holy," (Ps. lxxxvi. 2.) Also Hezekiah, "Remember now, O Lord, I beseech thee how I have walked before thee in truth, and with a perfect heart, and have done that which is good in thy sight," (Is. xxxviii. 2.) All they mean by such expressions is, that regeneration declares them to be among the servants and children to whom God engages that he will show favor. We have already seen how he declares by the Psalmist that his eyes "are upon the righteous, and his ears are open unto their

cry," (Ps. xxxiv. 16:) and again by the apostle, that "whatsoever we ask of him we obtain, because we keep his commandments," (John iii. 22.) In these passages he does not fix a value on prayer as a meritorious work, but designs to establish the confidence of those who are conscious of an unfeigned integrity and innocence, such as all believers should possess. For the saying of the blind man who had received his sight is in perfect accordance with divine truth, And God heareth not sinners (John ix. 31;) provided we take the term sinners in the sense commonly used by Scripture to mean those who, without any desire for righteousness, are sleeping secure in their sins; since no heart will ever rise to genuine prayer that does not at the same time long for holiness. Those supplications in which the saints allude to their purity and integrity correspond to such promises, that they may thus have, in their own experience, a manifestation of that which all the servants of God are made to expect. Thus they almost always use this mode of prayer when before God they compare themselves with their enemies, from whose injustice they long to be delivered by his hand. When making such comparisons, there is no wonder that they bring forward their integrity and simplicity of heart, that thus, by the justice of their cause, the Lord may be the more disposed to give them succor. We rob not the pious breast of the privilege of enjoying a consciousness of purity before the Lord, and thus feeling assured of the promises with which he comforts and supports his true worshipers, but we would have them to lay aside all thought of their own merits and found their confidence of success in prayer solely on the divine mercy.

11. The fourth rule of prayer is, that notwithstanding of our being thus abased and truly humbled, we should be animated to pray with the sure hope of succeeding. There is, indeed, an appearance of contradiction between the two things, between a sense of the just vengeance of God and firm confidence in his favor, and yet they are perfectly accordant, if it is the mere goodness of God that raises up those who are overwhelmed by their own sins. For, as we have formerly shown (chap. iii. sec. 17 2) that repentance and faith go hand in hand, being united by an indissoluble tie, the one causing terror, the other joy, so in prayer they must both be present. This concurrence David expresses in a few words: "But as for me, I will come into thy house in the multitude of thy mercy, and in thy fear will I worship toward thy holy temple," (Ps. v. 7.) Under the goodness of God he comprehends faith, at the same time not excluding fear; for not only does his majesty compel our reverence, but our own unworthiness also divests us of all pride and confidence, and keeps us in fear. The confidence of which I speak is not one which frees the mind from all anxiety, and soothes it with sweet and perfect rest; such rest is peculiar to those who, while all their affairs are flowing to a wish are annoyed by no care, stung with no regret, agitated by no fear. But the best stimulus which the saints have to prayer is when, in consequence of their own necessities, they feel the greatest disquietude, and are all but driven to despair, until faith seasonably comes to their aid; because in such straits the goodness of God so shines upon them, that while they groan, burdened by the weight of present calamities, and tormented with the fear of greater, they yet trust to this goodness, and in this way both lighten the difficulty of endurance, and take comfort in the hope of final deliverance. It is necessary therefore, that the prayer of the believer should be the result of both feelings, and exhibit the influence of both; namely, that while he groans under present and anxiously dreads new evils, he should, at the same times have recourse to God, not at all doubting that God is ready to stretch out a helping hand to him. For it is not easy to say how much God is irritated by our distrust, when we ask what we expect not of his goodness. Hence, nothing is more accordant to the nature of prayer

than to lay it down as a fixed rule, that it is not to come forth at random, but is to follow in the footsteps of faith. To this principle Christ directs all of us in these words, "Therefore, I say unto you, What things soever ye desire, when ye pray, believe that ye receive them, and ye shall have them," (Mark xi. 24.) The same thing he declares in another passage, "All things, whatsoever ye shall ask in prayer, believing, ye shall receive," (Matth. xxi. 22.) In accordance with this are the words of James, "If any of you lack wisdom, let him ask of God, that giveth to all men liberally, and upbraideth not, and it shall be given him. But let him ask in faith, nothing wavering," (James i. 5.) He most aptly expresses the power of faith by opposing it to wavering. No less worthy of notice is his additional statement, that those who approach God with a doubting, hesitating mind, without feeling assured whether they are to be heard or not, gain nothing by their prayers. Such persons he compares to a wave of the sea, driven with the wind and tossed. Hence, in another passage he terms genuine prayer "the prayer of faith," (James v. 15.) Again, since God so often declares that he will give to every man according to his faith he intimates that we cannot obtain any thing without faith. In short, it is faith which obtains every thing that is granted to prayer. This is the meaning of Paul in the well known passage to which dull men give too little heed, "How then shall they call upon him in whom they have not believed? and how shall they believe in him of whom they have not heard?" "So then faith cometh by hearing, and hearing by the word of God," (Rom. x. 14,17.) Gradually deducing the origin of prayer from faith, he distinctly maintains that God cannot be invoked sincerely except by those to whom, by the preaching of the Gospel, his mercy and willingness have been made known, nay, familiarly explained.

12. This necessity our opponents do not at all consider. Therefore, when we say that believers ought to feel firmly assured, they think we are saying the absurdest thing in the world. But if they had any experience in true prayer, they would assuredly understand that God cannot be duly invoked without this firm sense of the Divine benevolence. But as no man can well perceive the power of faith, without at the same time feeling it in his heart, what profit is there in disputing with men of this character, who plainly show that they have never had more than a vain imagination? The value and necessity of that assurance for which we contend is learned chiefly from prayer. Every one who does not see this gives proof of a very stupid conscience. Therefore, leaving those who are thus blinded, let us fix our thoughts on the words of Paul, that God can only be invoked by such as have obtained a knowledge of his mercy from the Gospel, and feel firmly assured that that mercy is ready to be bestowed upon them. What kind of prayer would this be? "O Lord, I am indeed doubtful whether or not thou art inclined to hear me; but being oppressed with anxiety I fly to thee that if I am worthy, thou mayest assist me." None of the saints whose prayers are given in Scripture thus supplicated. Nor are we thus taught by the Holy Spirit, who tells us to "come boldly unto the throne of grace, that we may obtain mercy, and find grace to help in time of need," (Heb. iv. 16;) and elsewhere teaches us to "have boldness and access with confidence by the faith of Christ," (Eph. iii. 12.) This confidence of obtaining what we ask, a confidence which the Lord commands, and all the saints teach by their example, we must therefore hold fast with both hands, if we would pray to any advantage. The only prayer acceptable to God is that which springs (if I may so express it) from this presumption of faith, and is founded on the full assurance of hope. He might have been contented to use the simple name of faith, but he adds not only confidence, but liberty or boldness, that by this mark he might distinguish us from unbelievers, who indeed like us pray to God, but pray at random. Hence, the whole Church thus prays "Let thy mercy O Lord, be upon us,

according as we hope in thee," (Ps. xxxiii. 22.) The same condition is set down by the Psalmist in another passage, "When I cry unto thee, then shall mine enemies turn back: this I know, for God is for me," (Ps. lvi. 9.) Again, "In the morning will I direct my prayer unto thee, and will look up," (Ps. v. 3.) From these words we gather, that prayers are vainly poured out into the air unless accompanied with faith, in which, as from a watchtower, we may quietly wait for God. With this agrees the order of Paul's exhortation. For before urging believers to pray in the Spirit always, with vigilance and assiduity, he enjoins them to take "the shield of faith," "the helmet of salvation, and the sword of the Spirit, which is the word of God," (Eph. vi. 16-18.)

Let the reader here call to mind what I formerly observed, that faith by no means fails though accompanied with a recognition of our wretchedness, poverty, and pollution. How much soever believers may feel that they are oppressed by a heavy load of iniquity, and are not only devoid of every thing which can procure the favor of God for them, but justly burdened with many sins which make him an object of dread, yet they cease not to present themselves, this feeling not deterring them from appearing in his presence, because there is no other access to him. Genuine prayer is not that by which we arrogantly extol ourselves before God, or set a great value on any thing of our own, but that by which, while confessing our guilt, we utter our sorrows before God, just as children familiarly lay their complaints before their parents. Nay, the immense accumulation of our sins should rather spur us on and incite us to prayer. Of this the Psalmist gives us an example, "Heal my soul: for I have sinned against thee," (Ps. xli. 4.) I confess, indeed, that these stings would prove mortal darts, did not God give succor; but our heavenly Father has, in ineffable kindness, added a remedy, by which, calming all perturbation, soothing our cares, and dispelling our fears he condescendingly allures us to himself; nay, removing all doubts, not to say obstacles,

makes the way smooth before us.

13. And first, indeed in enjoining us to pray, he by the very injunction convicts us of impious contumacy if we obey not. He could not give a more precise command than that which is contained in the psalms: "Call upon me in the day of trouble," (Ps. l. 15.) But as there is no office of piety more frequently enjoined by Scripture, there is no occasion for here dwelling longer upon it. "Ask," says our Divine Master, "and it shall be given you; seek, and ye shall find; knock, and it shall be opened unto you," (Matth. vii. 7.) Here, indeed, a promise is added to the precept, and this is necessary. For though all confess that we must obey the precept, yet the greater part would shun the invitation of God, did he not promise that he would listen and be ready to answer. These two positions being laid down, it is certain that all who cavillingly allege that they are not to come to God directly, are not only rebellious and disobedient but are also convicted of unbelief, inasmuch as they distrust the promises. There is the more occasion to attend to this, because hypocrites, under a pretense of humility and modesty, proudly contemn the precept, as well as deny all credit to the gracious invitation of God; nay, rob him of a principal part of his worship. For when he rejected sacrifices, in which all holiness seemed then to consist, he declared that the chief thing, that which above all others is precious in his sight, is to be invoked in the day of necessity. Therefore, when he demands that which is his own, and urges us to alacrity in obeying, no pretexts for doubt, how specious soever they may be, can excuse us. Hence, all the passages throughout Scripture in which we are commanded to pray, are set up before our eyes as so many banners, to inspire us with confidence. It were presumption to go forward into the presence of God, did he not anticipate us by his invitation. Accordingly, he opens up the way for us by his own voice, "I will say, It is my people: and they shall say, The Lord is my God," (Zech. xiii. 9.) We see how he anticipates his worshipers, and desires them to follow,

and therefore we cannot fear that the melody which he himself dictates will prove unpleasing. Especially let us call to mind that noble description of the divine character, by trusting to which we shall easily overcome every obstacle: O thou that hearest prayer, unto thee shall all flesh come," (Ps. lxv. 2.) What can be more lovely or soothing than to see God invested with a title which assures us that nothing is more proper to his nature than to listen to the prayers of suppliants? Hence the Psalmist infers, that free access is given not to a few individuals, but to all men, since God addresses all in these terms, "Call upon me in the day of trouble: I will deliver thee, and thou shalt glorify me," (Ps. l. 15.) David, accordingly, appeals to the promise thus given in order to obtain what he asks: "Thou, O Lord of hosts, God of Israel, hast revealed to thy servant, saying, I will build thee an house: therefore hath thy servant found in his heart to pray this prayer unto thee" (2 Sam. vii. 27.) Here we infer, that he would have been afraid but for the promise which emboldened him. So in another passage he fortifies himself with the general doctrine, "He will fulfil the desire of them that fear him," (Ps. cxlv. 19.) Nay, we may observe in The Psalms how the continuity of prayer is broken, and a transition is made at one time to the power of God, at another to his goodness, at another to the faithfulness of his promises. It might seem that David, by introducing these sentiments, unseasonably mutilates his prayers; but believers well know by experience, that their ardor grows languid unless new fuel be added, and, therefore, that meditation as well on the nature as on the word of God during prayer, is by no means superfluous. Let us not decline to imitate the example of David, and introduce thoughts which may reanimate our languid minds with new vigor.

14. It is strange that these delightful promises affect us coldly, or scarcely at all, so that the generality of men prefer to wander up and down, forsaking the fountain of living waters, and hewing out to themselves broken cisterns, rather than embrace the divine liberality voluntarily offered to them (Jer. ii.13). "The name of the Lord," says Solomon, "is a strong tower; the righteous runneth into it, and is safe." (Pr. xviii.10) Joel, after predicting the fearful disaster which was at hand, subjoins the following memorable sentence: "And it shall come to pass, that whosoever shall call on the name of the Lord shall be delivered." (Joel ii. 32) This we know properly refers to the course of the Gospel. Scarcely one in a hundred is moved to come into the presence of God, though he himself exclaims by Isaiah, "And it shall come to pass, that before they call, I will answer; and while they are yet speaking, I will hear." (Is. lxv. 24) This honor he elsewhere bestows upon the whole Church in general, as belonging to all the members of Christ: "He shall call upon me, and I will answer him: I will be with him in trouble; I will deliver him, and honor him." (Ps. xci.15) My intention, however, as I already observed, is not to enumerate all, but only select some admirable passages as a specimen how kindly God allures us to himself, and how extreme our ingratitude must be when with such powerful motives our sluggishness still retards us. Wherefore, let these words always resound in our ears: "The Lord is nigh unto all them that call upon him, to all that call upon him in truth," (Ps. cxlv. 18.) Likewise those passages which we have quoted from Isaiah and Joel, in which God declares that his ear is open to our prayers, and that he is delighted as with a sacrifice of sweet savor when we cast our cares upon him. The special benefit of these promises we receive when we frame our prayer, not timorously or doubtingly, but when trusting to his word whose majesty might otherwise deter us, we are bold to call him Father, he himself deigning to suggest this most delightful name. Fortified by such invitations it remains for us to know that we have therein sufficient materials for prayer, since our prayers depend on no merit of our own, but all their worth and hope of success are founded and depend on the promises of God, so that they need no

other support, and require not to look up and down on this hand and on that. It must therefore be fixed in our minds, that though we equal not the lauded sanctity of patriarchs, prophets, and apostles, yet as the command to pray is common to us as well as them, and faith is common, so if we lean on the word of God, we are in respect of this privilege their associates. For God declaring, as has already been seen, that he will listen and be favorable to all, encourages the most wretched to hope that they shall obtain what they ask; and, accordingly, we should attend to the general forms of expression, which, as it is commonly expressed, exclude none from first to last; only let there be sincerity of heart, self-dissatisfaction humility, and faith, that we may not, by the hypocrisy of a deceitful prayer, profane the name of God. Our most merciful Father will not reject those whom he not only encourages to come, but urges in every possible way. Hence David's method of prayer to which I lately referred: "And now, O Lord God, thou art that God, and thy words be true, and thou hast promised this goodness unto thy servant, that it may continue for ever before thee" (2 Sam. vii. 28.) So also, in another passage, "Let, I pray thee, thy merciful kindness be for my comfort, according to thy word unto thy servant," (Psalm cxix. 76.) And the whole body of the Israelites, whenever they fortify themselves with the remembrance of the covenant, plainly declare, that since God thus prescribes they are not to pray timorously, (Gen. xxxii. 13.) In this they imitated the example of the patriarchs, particularly Jacob, who, after confessing that he was unworthy of the many mercies which he had received of the Lord's hand, says, that he is encouraged to make still larger requests, because God had promised that he would grant them. But whatever be the pretexts which unbelievers employ, when they do not flee to God as often as necessity urges, nor seek after him, nor implore his aid, they defraud him of his due honor just as much as if they were fabricating to themselves new gods and idols, since in this way they deny that God is the author of all their blessings. On the contrary, nothing more effectually frees pious minds from every doubt, than to be armed with the thought that no obstacle should impede them while they are obeying the command of God, who declares that nothing is more grateful to him than obedience. Hence, again, what I have previously said becomes still more clear, namely, that a bold spirit in prayer well accords with fear, reverence, and anxiety, and that there is no inconsistency when God raises up those who had fallen prostrate. In this way forms of expression apparently inconsistent admirably harmonize. Jeremiah and David speak of humbly laying their supplications before God (Jer. xlii. 9; Dan. ix. 18.) In another passage Jeremiah says "Let, we beseech thee, our supplication be accepted before thee, and pray for us unto the Lord thy God, even for all this remnant." (Jer. xlii. 2) On the other hand, believers are often said to – lift up prayer – . Thus Hezekiah speaks, when asking the prophet to undertake the office of interceding (2 Kings xix. 4.) And David says, "Let my prayer be set forth before thee as incense; and the lifting up of my hands as the evening sacrifice." (Ps. cxli. 2) The explanation is, that though believers, persuaded of the paternal love of God, cheerfully rely on his faithfulness, and have no hesitation in imploring the aid which he voluntarily offers, they are not elated with supine or presumptuous security; but climbing up by the ladder of the promises, still remain humble and abased suppliants.

As for me, far be it from me that I should sin against the LORD by failing to pray for you.
The Bible, 1 Samuel 12:23

Ask, and it shall be given you; seek, and ye shall find; knock, and it shall be opened unto you.
The Bible, Matthew 7:7 KJV

Every one that asketh receiveth; and he that seeketh findeth.
The Bible, Matthew 7:8 KJV

The spirit indeed is willing, but the flesh is weak.
The Bible, Matthew 26:41 KJV

So I tell you, whatever you ask for in prayer, believe that you have received it, and it will be yours.
Mark 11:24 NRSV

I will do whatever you ask in my name, so that the Father may be glorified in the Son. If in my name you ask me for anything, I will do it.
The Bible, John 14:13-14

The Spirit helps us in our weakness; for we do not know how to pray as we ought, but that very Spirit intercedes with sighs too deep for words. And God, who searches the heart, knows what is the mind of the Spirit, because the Spirit intercedes for the saints according to the will of God.
The Bible, Romans 8:26-27 NRSV

Be … faithful in prayer.
The Bible, Romans 12:11

I urge you, brothers, by our Lord Jesus Christ and by the love of the Spirit, to join me in my struggle by praying to God for me.
The Bible, Romans 15:30

I pray that you may have the power to comprehend, with all the saints, what is the breadth and length and height and depth; and to know the love of God that surpasses knowledge, so that you may be filled with all the fullness of God.
The Bible, Ephesians 3:18-19 NRSV

And pray in the Spirit on all occasions with all kinds of prayers and requests. With this in mind, be alert and always keep on praying for all the saints.
The Bible, Ephesians 6:18

Devote yourselves to prayer, being watchful and thankful.
The Bible, Colossians 4:2

Epaphras, who is one of you and a servant of Christ Jesus, sends greetings. He is always wrestling in prayer for you, that you may stand firm in all the will of God, mature and fully assured.
The Bible, Colossians 4:12

Night and day we pray most earnestly that we may see you again and supply what is lacking in your faith.
The Bible, 1 Thessalonians 3:10

I want men everywhere to lift up holy hands in prayer, without anger or disputing.
The Bible, 1 Timothy 2:8

First of all, then, I urge that supplications, prayers, intercessions and thanksgivings should be made for everyone, for kings and all who are in high positions, so that we may lead a quiet and peaceable life in all godliness and dignity.
1 Timothy 2:1-2 NRSV

The prayer of a righteous man is powerful and effective.
The Bible, James 5:16

Therefore be clear minded and self-controlled so that you can pray.
The Bible, 1 Peter 4:7

Pray in the Holy Spirit.
The Bible, Jude 20

A prayer warrior is a person who is convinced that God is omnipotent – that God has the power to do anything, to change anyone, and to intervene in any circumstance. A person who truly believes this refuses to doubt God.
Author unknown

Wishing will never be a substitute for prayer.
Author unknown

If Christians spent as much time praying as grumbling, they would soon have nothing to grumble about.
Author unknown

I got up early one morning
And rushed right into the day;
I had so much to accomplish
That I didn't have time to pray.
Problems just tumbled about me,
And heavier came each task;
"Why doesn't God help me?" I wondered.
He answered, "You didn't ask."
I wanted to see joy and beauty,
But the day toiled on gray and bleak;
I wondered why God didn't show me.
He said, "But you didn't seek."
I tried to come into God's presence;
I used all my keys in the lock.
God gently and lovingly chided,
"My child, you didn't knock."
I woke up early this morning,
And paused before entering the day;
I had so much to accomplish
That I had to take time to pray.
Author unknown

To get nations back on their feet, we must get down on our knees first.
Author unknown

Pray and doubt, do without.
Pray and believe, humbly receive.
Author unknown

The time to get your spiritual instrument in tune is early in the morning before the concert of the day begins.
Author unknown

Life is fragile ... handle with prayer.
Author unknown

Each day is a gift to be opened with prayer.
Author unknown

Ask
All that we ask
All that we ask or think
Above all that we ask or think
Abundantly above all that we ask or think

Able to do abundantly above all that we ask or think.
Some Bible verses can be built up into pyramids, and like the Egyptian pyramids, are for our meditation and contemplation.
Author unknown

One of the best ways to get on your feet is to first get on your knees.
Author unknown

Seven days without prayer makes one weak.
Author unknown

Don't pray for tasks equal to your powers. Pray for powers equal to your tasks.
Author unknown

Prayer changes things? No! Prayer changes people, and people change things.
Author unknown

The child of many prayers shall never perish.
An old Christian, to Monica, mother of Augustine of Hippo

Some people treat God like they do a lawyer; they go to Him only when they are in trouble.
Author unknown

Prayer is not a last extremity, it's a first necessity.
Author unknown

Pray as if it's all up to God, work as if it's all up to you.
Author unknown

Prayer will put backbone where your wishbone is.
Author unknown

Prayer consists of:
P-etition: "Daniel made his petition three times a day" (Daniel 6:13)
R-everence: "Let us offer to God acceptable worship, with reverence and awe" (Hebrews 12:28)
A-doration: "My lips will praise thee" (Psalm 63:3)

Y-earning: "Blessed are those who hunger and thirst for righteousness" (Matthew 5:6)
E-xpectation: "Elijah ... prayed fervently that it might not rain" (James 5:17)
R-equests: "Let your requests be made known to God" (Philippians 4:6)
Author unknown

If an army advances on its stomach, a church advances on its knees.
Author unknown

If your prayers were always answered, you'd have a reason to doubt the wisdom of God.
Author unknown

Do not make prayer a monologue – make it a conversation.
Author unknown

I often say my prayers, but do I ever pray?
And do the wishes of my heart, go with the words I say?
I might as well kneel down, and worship gods of stone,
As offer to the living God, a prayer of words alone.
Author unknown

The more a man bows his knee before God, the straighter he stands before men.
Author unknown

Don't seek the blessing, seek the blesser.
Author unknown

When you can't put your prayers into words, God hears your heart.
Author unknown

Wishing will never be a substitute for prayer.
Author unknown

Prayer does not change God's mind, it changes ours.
Author unknown

Prayer is faith in God, not faith in prayer.
Author unknown

Prayer is relationship.
Author unknown

He who rises from prayers a better person ... his prayers are answered.
Author unknown

You should pray, therefore, in spirit, seeing that God is spirit.
Abraham of Nathpar

We would often be sorry if our wishes were gratified.
Aesop

There is no effort comparable to prayer to God. In fact, whenever you want to pray, hostile demons try to interrupt you. Of course they know that nothing but prayer to God entangles them. Certainly when you undertake any other good work, and persevere in it, you obtain rest. But prayer is a battle all the way to the last breath.
Abba Agathon

Our prayers are answered not when we are given what we ask but when we are challenged to be what we can be.
Morris Alder

Prayer is no more inconsistent with the unchangeable purposes of God, than the use of any other means; for God in forming his purposes had respect to all appropriate means of producing the intended ends, and among these prayer has an important place.
Archibald Alexander

The reason why we obtain no more in prayer is because we expect no more. God usually answers us according to our own hearts.
Richard Alleine

The purpose of prayer is nothing other than to manifest God and self. And this manifestation of God and self leads to a state of perfect and true humility. It is in this profound state of humility, and from it, that divine grace deepens and grows in

the soul. The more divine grace deepens humility in the soul, the more divine grace can grow in this depth of humility. The more divine grace grows, the deeper the soul is grounded, and the more it is settled in a state of true humility.
Angela of Foligno

It is clear that he does not pray, who, far from uplifting himself to God, requires that God shall lower Himself to him, and who resorts to prayer not to stir the man in us to will what God wills, but only to persuade God to will what the man in us wills.
Thomas Aquinas

I have no doubt that the world stands because of the prayers of Christians.
Aristides of Athens

He prayed for His enemies, and you do not even pray for your friends.
Johann Arndt

Know that you are freed from all desires when you have reached such a point that you pray to God for nothing except what you can pray for openly.
Athenodorus

Man is a beggar before God.
Augustine of Hippo

The pure prayer that ascends from a faithful heart will be like incense rising from a hallowed altar.
Augustine of Hippo

What can be more excellent than prayer; what is more profitable to our life; what sweeter to our souls; what more sublime, in the course of our whole life, than the practice of prayer!
Augustine of Hippo

Prayer is the protection of holy souls; a consolation for the guardian angel; an insupportable torment to the devil; a most acceptable homage to God; the best and most perfect praise for penitents and religious; the greatest honor and glory; the preserver of spiritual health.
Augustine of Hippo

He whose attitude towards Christ is correct does indeed ask "in his name" and receives what he asks for, if it is something which does not stand in the way of his salvation. He gets it, however, only when he ought to receive it, for certain things are not refused us, but their granting is delayed to a fitting time.
Augustine of Hippo

Holy prayer is the column of all virtues; a ladder to God; the support of widows, the foundation of faith; the crown of religious; the sweetness of the married life.
Augustine of Hippo

Do you wish to pray in the temple? Pray in your own heart. But begin by being God's temple, for He will listen to those who invoke Him in His temple.
Augustine of Hippo

When you pray to God in psalms and hymns, think over in your hearts the words that come from your lips.
Augustine, The Rule of St Augustine

Prayer is the spirit speaking truth to Truth.
Phil James Bailey

The man who says his prayers in the evening is a captain posting his sentries. After that, he can sleep.
Charles Baudelaire

Let prayer by yourself alone (or with your partner) take place before the collective prayer of the family. If possible let it be first, before any work of the day.
Richard Baxter

You shall find this to be God's usual course: not to give his children the taste of his delights till they begin to perspire in seeking after them.
Richard Baxter

If you are swept off your feet, it's time to get on your knees.
Fred Beck

In the morning, prayer is the key that opens to us the treasures of God's mercies and blessings; in the evening, it is the key that shuts us up under His protection and safeguard.
Henry Ward Beecher

Prayer covers the whole of a man's life. There is no thought, feeling, yearning or desire, however low, trifling, or vulgar we may deem it, which, if it affects our real interest or happiness, we may not lay before God and be sure of sympathy. His nature is such that our often coming does not tire him. The whole burden of the whole life of every man may be rolled on to God and not weary him, though it has wearied the man.
Henry Ward Beecher

He who ceases to pray ceases to prosper.
William Gurney Benham

Wherever you are, pray secretly within yourself. If you are far from a house of prayer, give not yourself trouble to seek for one, for you yourself are a sanctuary designed for prayer. If you are in bed, or in any other place, pray there; your temple is there.
Bernard of Clairvaux

Prayer is a wine which makes glad the heart of man.
Bernard of Claivaux

Praying: To ask that the laws of the universe be annulled in behalf of a single petitioner confessedly unworthy.
Ambrose Bierce

We must not talk about prayer, we must pray in right earnest.
Andrew A. Bonar

Brethren, why so many meetings with our fellow men and so few meetings with God?
Andrew Bonar

We have not been men of prayer.
Andrew Bonar

Above all, it is not necessary that we should have any unexpected, extraordinary experiences in meditation. This can happen, but if it does not, it is not a sign that the meditation period has been useless. Not only at the beginning, but repeatedly, there will be times when we feel a great spiritual dryness and apathy, an aversion, even an inability to meditate. We dare not be balked by such experiences. Above all, we must not allow them to keep us from adhering to our meditation period with great patience and fidelity.
Dietrich Bonhoeffer

Pray as if everything depended upon your prayer.
William Booth

You must pray with all your might. That does not mean saying your prayers, or sitting gazing about in church or chapel with eyes wide open while someone else says them for you. It means fervent, effectual, untiring wrestling with God … This kind of prayer be sure the devil and the world and your own indolent, unbelieving nature will oppose. They will pour water on this flame.
William Booth

God's cause is committed to men; God commits Himself to men. Praying men are the vice-regents of God; they do His work and carry out His plans.
E.M. Bounds

The men who have done the most for God in this world have been early on their knees.
E.M. Bounds

No erudition, no purity of diction, no width of mental outlook, no flowers of eloquence, no grace of person can atone for lack of fire. Prayer ascends by fire. Flame gives prayer access as well as wings,

acceptance as well as energy. There is no incense without fire; no prayer without flame.
E.M. Bounds

Prayer is not learned in the classroom but in the closet.
E.M. Bounds

Prayer is weakness leaning on omnipotence.
W.S. Bowden

Some time in February, 1739, I set apart a day for secret fasting and prayer, and spent the day in almost incessant cries to God for mercy, that he would open my eyes to see the evil of sin, and the way of life by Jesus Christ. And God was pleased that day to make considerable discoveries of my heart to me.
David Brainerd

In the forenoon, I felt the power of intercession for the advancement of the kingdom of my dear Lord and Savior in the world; and withal, a most sweet resignation, and even consolation and joy in the thoughts of suffering hardships, distresses, and even death itself, in the promotion of it. In the afternoon God was with me of a truth. Oh, it was a blessed company indeed! My soul was drawn out very much for the world; I think I had more enlargement for sinners, than for the children of God; though I felt as if I could spend my life in cries for both.
David Brainerd

The great battles, the battles that decide our destiny and the destiny of generations yet unborn, are not fought on public platforms, but in the lonely hours of the night and in moments of agony.
Samuel Logan Brengle

I do not pray for a lighter load, but for a stronger back.
Phillips Brooks

Prayer is not conquering God's reluctance, but taking hold of God's willingness.
Phillips Brooks

Pray not for crutches but for wings.
Phillips Brooks

"Continuing instant in prayer" Romans 12:12. The Greek is a metaphor taken from hunting dogs that never give over the game till they have their prey.
Thomas Brooks

Pray often.
John Bunyan

If thou wouldst more fully express thyself before the Lord, study, first, thy filthy estate; secondly, God's promises; thirdly, the heart of Christ.
John Bunyan

In prayer it is better to have a heart without words than words without a heart.
John Bunyan

Prayer opens the heart to God, and it is the means by which the soul, though empty, is filled by God.
John Bunyan

It is expedient then that the understanding should be occupied in prayer, as well as the heart and mouth: "I will pray with the Spirit, and I will pray with the understanding also."
John Bunyan

He who runs from God in the morning will scarcely find him the rest of the day.
John Bunyan

To pray with understanding, is to pray as being instructed by the Spirit in the understanding of the want of those things which the soul is to pray for.
John Bunyan

Thou art not a Christian that art not a praying person.
John Bunyan

By prayer the Christian can open his heart to God, as to a friend, and obtain fresh testimony of God's friendship to him.
John Bunyan

The truths that I know best I have learned on my knees. I never know a thing well, till it is burned into my heart by prayer.
John Bunyan

When I go aside in order to pray, I find my heart unwilling to approach God; and when I tarry in prayer my heart is unwilling to abide in Him. Therefore I am compelled first to pray to God to move my heart into Himself, and when I am in Him, I pray that my heart remain in Him.
John Bunyan

Prayer is a shield to the soul, a sacrifice to God, and a scourge for Satan.
John Bunyan

Prayer is a sincere, sensible, affectionate pouring out of the soul to God, through Christ in the strength and assistance of the Spirit, for such things as God has promised.
John Bunyan

He that hath his understanding well exercised, to discern between good and evil, and in it placed a sense either of the misery of man, or the mercy of God; that soul hath no need of the writings of other men to teach him by forms of prayer.
John Bunyan

Pray often, for prayer is a shield to the soul, a sacrifice to God, and a scourge to Satan. Prayer will cease a man from sin; or sin will cease a man from prayer.
John Bunyan

They never sought in vain that sought the Lord aright!
Robert Burns

You know the value of prayer; it is precious beyond all price. Never, never neglect it.
Thomas Buxton

Seeing we are the true temples of God, we must pray in ourselves if we would invoke God in his holy temple.
John Calvin

God tolerates even our stammering, and pardons our ignorance whenever something inadvertently escapes us – as, indeed, without this mercy there would be no freedom to pray.
John Calvin

Prayer is ordained to this end that we should confess our needs to God, and bare our hearts to him, as children lay their troubles in full confidence before their parents.
John Calvin

There is a communion of men with God by which, having entered the heavenly sanctuary, appeal to him in person concerning his promises in order to experience, where necessity so demands, that what they believed was not in vain, although he had promised it in word alone.
John Calvin

The reason why Paul enjoins, "Pray without ceasing; in everything give thanks" (1 Thessalonians 5:17-18), is, because he would have us with the utmost assiduity, at all times, in every place, in all things, and under all circumstances, direct our prayers to God, to expect all the things which we desire from him, and when obtained ascribe them to him; thus furnishing perpetual grounds for prayer and praise.
John Calvin

The first rule of right prayer is to have our heart and mind framed as becomes those who are entering into converse with God.
John Calvin

Prayer – secret, fervent, believing prayer – lies at the root of all personal godliness.
Carey's brotherhood

Prayer is and remains always a native and deepest impulse of the soul of man.
Thomas Carlyle

The influence of prayer on the human mind and body is as demonstrable as that of secreting glands. Its results can be measured in terms of increased physical buoyancy, greater intellectual vigor, moral stamina, and a deeper understanding of the realities underlying human relationships.
Dr Alex Carrel

God is Spirit, and accepts prayer only with the spirit."
John Cassian

Follow the leading of simplicity in prayer, there can never be excess of it, for God loves to see us like little children in his presence.
Jean-Pierre de Caussade

Prayer does not enable us to do a greater work for God. Prayer is a greater work for God.
Thomas Chalmers

Jesus Christ carries on intercession for us in heaven; the Holy Ghost carries on intercession in us on earth; and we the saints have to carry on intercession for all men.
Oswald Chambers

Keep praying in order to get a perfect understanding of God Himself.
Oswald Chambers

Whoso will pray, he must fast and be clean, And fast his soul, and make his body lean.
Geoffrey Chaucer

It is a very good thing to ask. For if through conversing with a person of great power no small benefit is gained, what great benefit will one not gain from converse with God? ... He is surely able to grant us our requests even before we ask him; nevertheless He holds off and waits, so that we may have an occasion for being justly deserving of His providence.
John Chrysostom

It is possible to offer fervent prayer even while walking in public or strolling alone, or seated in your shop ... while buying or selling ... or even while cooking.
John Chrysostom

Whether or not our prayer is heard depends not on the number of words, but on the fervor of our souls.
John Chrysostom

Prayer requires more of the heart than of the tongue.
Adam Clarke

We know the utility of prayer from the efforts of the wicked spirits to distract us during the divine office; and we experience the fruit of prayer in the defeat of our enemies.
John Climacus

God wants us to pray, and will tell us who to begin and where we are.
The Cloud of Unknowing

Be not afraid to pray... to pray is right.
Pray if thou canst with hope; but ever pray
Though hope be weak, or sick with long
 delay.
Whatever is good to wish, ask that of heaven;
But if for any wish thou darest not pray,
Then pray to God to cast that wish away.
Hartley Coleridge

He prayeth best, who loveth best
All things both great and small;
For the dear God who loveth us,
He made and loveth all.
Samuel Taylor Coleridge

The act of praying is the very highest energy of which the human mind is capable; praying, that is, with the total concentration of the faculties. The great mass of worldly men and of learned men are absolutely incapable of prayer.
Samuel Taylor Coleridge

There is absolutely no substitute for this secret communion with God. The public Church services, or even the family altar,

cannot take the place of the "closet" prayer.
Gordon Cove

Christ taught that we should pray alone and silently, and by ourselves; and, so to speak, conversing alone with God alone, with pure and undistracted mind (see Mt. 6:5-7).
Cyril of Alexandria

For those who have hidden fellowship with God, life is a continuous feast.
S.G. Degraff

When I awake in the morning, which is always before it is light, I address myself to him, and converse with him, speak to him while I am lighting my candle and putting on my clothes.
Philip Doddridge

If the only prayer we say is "thank you" that would be enough.
Meister Eckhart

If some Christians that have been complaining of their ministers had said and acted less before men and had applied themselves with all their might to cry to God for their ministers – had, as it were, risen and stormed heaven with their humble, fervent, and incessant prayers for them – they would have been much more in the way of success.
Jonathan Edwards

We should not pray only for those whom we like. It is easy to pray for the leader whom we respect or with whom we agree. It is much harder to pray for the leader whose personality is offensive, whose ethics are questionable, who takes the "wrong" position on every issue, or who is in the "wrong" party. Yet these leaders are also ministers of God. They don't necessarily deserve our vote, but they do deserve our respect and prayers.
John Eidsmoe

The air which we breathe, the bread which we eat, the heart which throbs in our

bosoms, are not more necessary for man that he may live as a human being, than is prayer for the Christian that he may live as a Christian.
John Eudes

There are some favors the Almighty does not grant either the first, or the second, or the third time you ask him, because he wishes you to pray for a long time and often. He wills this delay to keep you in a state of humility and self-contempt and make you realize the value of his graces.
John Eudes

Persevere with patience in your prayer, and repulse the cares and doubts that arise within you.
Evagrios the Solitary

If you long for prayer, renounce all to gain all.
Evagrios the Solitary

Tell God all that is in your heart, as one unloads one's heart, its pleasures and its pains, to a dear friend. Tell Him your troubles, that He may comfort you; tell Him your joys, that He may sober them; tell Him your longings, that He may purify them; tell Him your dislikes, that He may help you conquer them; talk to Him of your temptations, that He may shield you from them: show Him the wounds of your heart, that He may heal them; lay bare your indifference to good, your depraved tastes for evil, your instability.
François Fénelon

If you are to pray in a profitable way it is best for you, from the start, to think of yourself as a poor, naked, miserable wretch, dying of hunger, who knows about one person who can help you and relieve you of your suffering.
F. Fénelon

Of all the duties enjoined by Christianity, none is more essential and yet more neglected, than prayer.
François Fénelon

Some men will spin out a long prayer telling God who and what he is, or they pray out a whole system of divinity. Some people preach, others exhort the people, till everybody wishes they would stop, and God wishes so, too, most undoubtedly.
Charles G. Finney

What a person is in his closet, alone before the all-seeing God, that he is and no more.
Don Fortner

Real prayer comes not from gritting our teeth, but from falling in love.
Richard Foster

Most men pray for power, the strength to do things. Few people pray for love, the quality to be someone.
Robert D. Foster

When God wants to perform in us and through us and with us some act of great charity, he first proposes it to us by his inspiration, then we favor it, and finally we consent to it.
Francis of Sales

The greatest thing anyone can do for God and for man is to pray. You can do more than pray after you have prayed, but you cannot do more than pray until you have prayed.
S.D. Gordon

Heaven is full of answers to prayers for which no one ever bothered to ask.
Billy Graham

Just pray for a tough hide and a tender heart.
Ruth Graham

We must remember God more often than we draw breath.
Gregory of Nazianzus

To pray in the Spirit is the inward principle of prayer. It comprehends both the spirit of the person praying, and the

Spirit of God by which our spirits are fitted for, and acted in, prayer.
William Gurnall

You have now, Christian, the armor of God; but take heed thou forgettest not to engage the God of this armor by humble prayer for your assistance, lest for all this you be worsted in the fight.
William Gurnall

The only way to heaven is prayer.
Madame Guyon

You may as soon find a living man without breath as a living saint without prayer.
Matthew Henry

Prayer, the Church's banquet, Angel's age,
God's breath in man returning to his birth,
The soul in paraphrase, the heart in
  pilgrimage,
The Christian plummet sounding heav'n and earth.
George Herbert

Prayer is the soul's blood.
George Herbert

In prayer the lips ne'er act the winning
  part,
Without the sweet concurrence of the
  heart.
Robert Herrick

A soul without prayer is a soul without a home.
Abraham Joshua Heschel

You must pray. To pray is just as important for your spiritual life as food is for your body.
Benny Hinn

God is not moved by need, he is moved by faith.
Benny Hinn

Should it not be recognized that the practice of prayer and intercession needs to be taught to young believers, or rather

developed in young believers, quite as much, if not more so than other branches of the curriculum? Unless, however, we ourselves are, through constant persevering practice, truly alive unto God in this holy warfare, we shall be ineffective in influencing others. I am quite sure the rule holds that the more we pray the more we want to pray; the converse also being true.
D.E. Hoste

Hudson Taylor practically recognized that much time must be spent in seeking God's guidance, if a right understanding was to be obtained of the problems and difficulties that confronted him, in carrying on the work of the Mission.
D.E. Hoste

Certain thoughts are prayers. There are moments when whatever be the attitude of the body, the soul is on its knees.
Victor Hugo

Prayer is the return of the repentant to God.
Ignatius of Loyola

Pray as if everything depended on God and act as if everything depended on oneself.
Ignatius of Loyola

We pray with words until the words are cut off and we are left in a state of wonder.
Isaac the Syrian

Before the war begins, seek out your ally; before you fall ill, seek out your physician; and before grievous things come upon you, pray, and in the time of your tribulations you will find Him, and He will listen to you.
Isaac the Syrian

He did not pray to men, but to God. He seemed to realize that he was speaking to heaven's king.
A minister describing "Stonewall" Jackson

To saints their very slumber is a prayer.
St Jerome

It is ours to offer what we can, His to supply what we cannot.
St Jerome

The attributes of prayer must be: love of God, sincerity, and simplicity. We must pray in spirit, because God is a spirit, and not flesh; with truth, and not falsely, because God is the Truth.
John of Kronstadt

Take God for your spouse and friend and walk with him continually, and you will not sin and will learn to love, and the things you must do will work out prosperously for you.
John of the Cross

Whoever flees prayer flees all that is good.
John of the Cross

My spirit is dry within me because it forgets to feed on you.
John of the Cross

I would rather teach one man to pray than ten men to preach.
J.H. Jowett

It is in the field of prayer that life's critical battles are lost or won. In prayer we bring our spiritual enemies into the presence of God and we fight them there.
J.H. Jowett

Prayer unites the soul to God.
Julian of Norwich

It is more honor to God, and more very delight, that we faithfully pray to Himself of His goodness and cleave thereunto by His grace, and with true understanding, and steadfast by love, than if we took all the means that heart can think. For if we took all those means it is too little, and not full honor to God. But in His goodness is all the whole, and there faileth right nought … For the goodness of God is the highest prayer, and it cometh down to the lowest part of our need.
Julian of Norwich

Our Lord is the ground from whom our prayer grows and in his love and grace he himself gives us our prayer.
Julian of Norwich

Your greatest lack is that you do not know how to pray.
Toyohiko Kagawa

Prayer does not change God, but it changes him who prays.
Soren Kierkegaard

The very act of prayer honors God and gives glory to God, for it confesses that God is what he is.
Charles Kingsley

A sense of real want is at the very root of prayer.
John Laidlaw

The main lesson about prayer is just this: Do it! Do it! Do it!
John Laidlaw

Beloved, it is not our long prayers but our believing God that gets the answer.
John G. Lake

A short prayer finds its way to heaven.
William Langland

There is nothing that makes us love a man so much as praying for him.
William Law

If you were to rise early every morning, as an instance of self-denial, as a method of renouncing indulgence, as a means of redeeming your time and of fitting your spirit for prayer, you would find mighty advantages from it. This method, though it seem such a small circumstance of life, would in all probability be a means [toward] great piety. It would keep it constantly in your head that softness and idleness were to be avoided and that self-denial was a part of Christianity.
William Law

He that seeks God in everything is sure to find God in everything. When we thus live wholly unto God, God is wholly ours and we are then happy in all the happiness of God; for by uniting with Him in heart, and will, and spirit, we are united to all that He is and has in Himself.
William Law

He who has learned to pray has learned the greatest secret of a holy and happy life.
William Law

Prayer is my chief work, by it I carry on all clsc.
William Law

Do not always scrupulously confine yourself to certain rules, or particular forms of devotion; but act with a general confidence in God, with love and humility.
Brother Lawrence

You will tell me that I am always saying the same thing: it is true, for this is the best and easiest method I know; and as I use no other, I advise all the world to it. We must know before we can love. In order to know God, we must often think of Him; and when we come to love Him, we shall then also think of Him often, for our heart will be with our treasure.
Brother Lawrence

When I apply myself to prayer, I feel all my spirit and all my soul lift itself up without any care or effort of mine, and it continues as it were suspended and firmly fixed in God, as in its center and place of rest.
Brother Lawrence

Lift up your heart to Him, sometimes even at your meals, and when you are in company; the least little remembrance will always be acceptable to Him. You need not cry very loud; he is nearer to us than we are aware of.
Brother Lawrence

One single grateful thought raised to heaven is the most perfect prayer.
G.E. Lessing

We must lay before Him what is in us, not what ought to be in us.
C.S. Lewis

Prayer is request. The essence of request, as distinct from compulsion, is that it may or may not be granted. And if an infinitely wise Being listens to the requests of finite and foolish creatures, of course He will sometimes grant and sometimes refuse them.
C.S. Lewis

The great masters and teachers in Christian doctrine have always found in prayer their highest source of illumination.
H.P. Liddon

I have been driven many times to my knees by the overwhelming conviction that I had absolutely no other place to go.
Abraham Lincoln

Fastings and vigils without a special object in view are time run to waste.
David Livingstone

If we only spent more of our time in looking at Him we should soon forget ourselves.
Martyn Lloyd-Jones

Pleading the promises of God is the whole secret of prayer, I sometimes think.
Martyn Lloyd-Jones

Prayer, in many ways, is the supreme expression of our faith in God.
Martyn Lloyd-Jones

Thomas Goodwin wrote about pleading the promises of God: "Sue him for it, sue him for it." Do not leave him alone. Pester him, as it were, with his own promise. Tell him that what he has said he is going to do.
Martyn Lloyd-Jones

Grant that I may not pray alone with the mouth; help me that I may pray from the depths of my heart.
Martin Luther

I have so much to do that I spend several hours in prayer before I am able to do it.
Martin Luther

When Luther's puppy happened to be at the table, he looked for a morsel from his master, and watched with open mouth and motionless eyes. Luther said, "Oh, if I could only pray the way this dog watches the meat! All his thoughts are concentrated on the piece of meat. Otherwise he has no thought, wish, or hope."
Martin Luther

Whenever I happen to be prevented by the press of duties from observing the hour of prayer, the entire day is bad for me.
Martin Luther

None can believe how powerful prayer is, and what it is able to effect, but those who have learned it by experience.
Martin Luther

No one prays for anything who has not been deeply alarmed.
Martin Luther

Pray, and let God worry.
Martin Luther

The fewer the words, the better the prayer.
Martin Luther

All who call on God in true faith, earnestly from the heart, will certainly be heard, and will receive what they have asked and desired, although not in the hour or in the measure, or the very thing which they ask; yet they will obtain something greater and more glorious than they had dared to ask.
Martin Luther

Where there is not faith and confidence in prayer, the prayer is dead.
Martin Luther

Do not attempt to assess the quality of your prayer. God alone can judge its value.
Macarius of Optino

There is a communion with God that asks for nothing, yet asks for everything … He who seeks the Father more than anything He can give, is likely to have what he asks, for he is not likely to ask amiss.
George Macdonald

The purpose of all prayer is to find God's will and to make that will our prayer.
Catherine Marshall

Oh, that I may be a man of prayer!
Henry Martyn

In my first prayer for deliverance from worldly thoughts, depending on the power and promises of God, for fixing my soul while I prayed, I was helped to enjoy such abstinence from the world for nearly an hour.
Henry Martyn, journal entry, describing a day of prayer and fasting

Prayer is asking for rain; faith is carrying the umbrella.
John Mason

It is true friendship to teach one another to pray. It is a believing mother's part to teach her little children to pray. But the Holy Spirit's love is greater than this, he not only puts the words in our mouth, but he puts the desire in our heart.
Robert Murray M'Cheyne

I ought to spend the best hours of the day in communion with God. It is my noblest and most fruitful employment.
Robert Murray M'Cheyne

That prayer has great power which a person makes with all his might. It makes a sour heart sweet, a sad heart merry, a poor heart rich, a foolish heart wise, a timid heart brave, a sick heart well, a blind heart full of sight, a cold heart ardent. It draws down the great God into the little heart; it drives the hungry soul up into the fullness of God; it brings together two lovers, God and the soul, in a wondrous place where they speak much of love.
Mechthild of Magheburg

Trouble and perplexity drive me to prayer, and prayer drives away perplexity and trouble.
Philip Melanchthon

There is always time to look up to Him for His smile.
F.B. Meyer

Don't put people down, unless it's on your prayer list.
Stan Michalski

There are two ways of praying. One asks and hopes; the other craves and waits until he has obtained. It is just this "until" that characterizes the latter.

One seeks God and finds Him; the other strives with God and triumphs. The first observes seriously his daily devotions; the second stays on his knees hours a day, through the night.

The first fits in with the ordinary course of life; the second watches, fasts, cries, weeps, sweats blood.

The first we have known since we learned to know the Lord; the second … "Lord, teach us to pray."
M. Monod

Some people think God does not like to be troubled with our constant coming and asking. The way to trouble God is not to come at all.
D.L. Moody

The Christian on his knees sees more than the philosopher on tiptoe.
D.L. Moody

Farewell, my dear child, and pray for me, and I shall for you and all your friends that we may merrily meet in heaven.
Thomas More [His last letter to his daughter Margaret Roper]

Some people pray just to pray and some people pray to know God.
Andrew Murray

Where there is much prayer, there will be much of the Spirit; where there is much of

the Spirit, there will be ever-increasing prayer.
Andrew Murray

Beware in your prayers, above everything
else, of limiting God, not only by unbelief,
but by fancying that you know what He
can do. Expect unexpected things "above
all that we ask or think."
Andrew Murray

Prayer is not monologue, but dialogue.
God's voice in response to mine is its most
essential part.
Andrew Murray

Let us advance upon our knees.
Joseph Neesima

When we speak with God, our power of
addressing him, of holding communion
with him, and listening to his still small
voice, depends on our will being one and
the same with his.
Florence Nightingale

Do not be always wanting everything to
turn out as you think it should, but rather
as God pleases, then you will be
undisturbed and thankful in your prayer.
Abba Nilus

No heart can conceive that treasury of mercies
which lies in this one privilege, in having
liberty and ability to approach unto God at
all times, according to His mind and will.
John Owen

Be on your guard against the tricks of the
demons. While you are praying purely and
calmly, sometimes they suddenly bring
before you some strange and alien form,
making you imagine in your conceit that
the Deity is there. They are trying to
persuade you that the object suddenly
disclosed to you is the Deity.
The Philokalia

The Word of God represents all the
possibilities of God as at the disposal of
true prayer.
A. T. Pierson

God has no greater controversy with His
people today than this, that with boundless
promises to believing prayer, there are so
few who actually give themselves unto
intercession.
A. T. Pierson

Nothing is too great and nothing is too
small to commit into the hands of the Lord.
A. W. Pink

A person without prayer is like a tree
without roots.
Pope Pius XII

We have not been commanded to work, to
keep watch and to fast constantly, but it
has been laid down that we are to pray
without ceasing.
Evagrius Ponticus

Do not be troubled if you do not
immediately receive from God what you
ask him; for he desires to do something
even greater for you, while you cling to
him in prayer.
Evagrius Ponticus

Prayer is the pillow of religion.
Arab proverb

To work is to pray
Benedictine proverb

Many things are lost for want of asking.
English proverb

What men usually ask for when they pray
to God is, that two and two may not make
four.
Russian proverb

Prayer may be equally with words or without:
it may be "Jesu," "my God and my all."
E.B. Pusey

Catherine of Siena made a cell in her heart.
Afterwards, in a most busy life she could
keep quite close to God and without the
least distraction.
E.B. Pusey

Practice in life whatever you pray for and God will give it to you more abundantly.
E.B. Pusey

Have some arrow prayers to pray during the day, or a psalm. A good watchmaker is one who makes watches and prays: a good housemaid is one who sweeps and prays.
E.B. Pusey

If you can't pray a door open, don't pry it open.
Lyell Rader

Talk less with men, talk more with God.
Leonard Ravenhill

A sinning man will stop praying. A praying man will stop sinning.
Leonard Ravenhill

A man may study because his brain is hungry for knowledge, even Bible knowledge. But he prays because his soul is hungry for God.
Leonard Ravenhill

A man who is intimate with God will never be intimidated by men.
Leonard Ravenhill

Quit playing, start praying.
Leonard Ravenhill

When we find anything promised in the Word of God, we are not to neglect to seek it because it is promised: but we are to pray for it on that very account.
B.T. Roberts

The feeling of need and not the force of habit will make thee a sincere suppliant.
Evan Roberts

Secret prayer is the spring-time of life.
Evan Roberts

Dry wells send us to the fountain.
Samuel Rutherford

I have benefited by my praying for others; for by making an errand to God for them, I have gotten something for myself.
Samuel Rutherford

I urge upon you communion with Christ, a growing communion.
Samuel Rutherford

Words are but the body, the garment, the outside of prayer; sighs are nearer the heart work.
Samuel Rutherford

Do not be upset if ye come from prayer without sense of joy. Downcasting, sense of guiltiness, and hunger, are often best for us.
Samuel Rutherford

Prayer is absolutely necessary to a man's salvation.
J.C. Ryle

There is no part of religion so neglected as private prayer.
J.C. Ryle

In the Bible I can find that nobody will be saved by his prayers, but I cannot find that without prayer anybody will be saved.
J.C. Ryle

A habit of prayer is one of the surest marks of a true Christian.
J.C. Ryle

Truly we have learned a great lesson when we have learned that "saying prayers" is not praying!
J.C. Ryle

Prayer is that act in Christianity in which there is the greatest encouragement.
J.C. Ryle

Prayer obtains fresh and continued outpourings of the Spirit.
J.C. Ryle

Prayer is the surest remedy against the devil and besetting sins.
J.C. Ryle

Prayer is the most important subject in practical religion.
J.C. Ryle

The name of Jesus is a never-failing passport to our prayers. In that name a man may draw near to God with boldness, and ask with confidence. God has engaged to hear him.
J.C. Ryle

What is the reason that some believers are so much brighter and holier than others? I believe the difference, in nineteen cases out of twenty, arises from different habits about private prayer. I believe that those who are not eminently holy pray little, and those who are eminently holy pray much.
J.C. Ryle

Neglect of prayer is one great cause of backsliding.
J.C. Ryle

I once thought, in my ignorance, that most people said their prayers, and many people prayed. I have lived to think differently. I have come to the conclusion that the great majority of professing Christians do not pray at all.
J.C. Ryle

Prayer is not a matter of getting what we want the most. Prayer is a matter of giving ourselves to God and learning his laws, so that he can do through us what he wants the most.
Agnes Sanford

Prayer is the means by which we obtain all the graces that rain down upon us from the divine Fountain of Goodness and Love.
Laurence Scupoli

The essence of prayer does not consist in asking God for something but in opening our hearts to God, in speaking with Him, and living with Him in perpetual communion.
Sadhu Sundar Singh

Prayer makes things possible for men which they find otherwise impossible.
Sundar Singh

Prayer does not mean asking God for all kinds of things we want; it is rather the desire for God Himself, the only Giver of Life, Prayer is not asking, but union with God. Prayer is not a painful effort to gain from God help in the varying needs of our lives. Prayer is the desire to possess God Himself, the Source of all life. The true spirit of prayer does not consist in asking for blessings, but in receiving Him who is the giver of all blessings, and in living a life of fellowship with Him.
Sadhu Sundar Singh

God has created both the mother's milk and the child's desire to drink it. But the milk does not flow of itself into the child's mouth. No, the child must lie in its mother's bosom and suck the milk diligently. God has created the spiritual food which we need. He has filled the soul of man with desire for this food, with an impulse to cry out for it and to drink it in. The spiritual milk, the nourishment of our souls, we receive through prayer. By means of fervent prayer we must receive it into our souls. As we do this we become stronger day by day, just like the infant at the breast.
Sadhu Sundar Singh

For the first two or three years after my conversion, I used to ask for specific things. Now I ask for God ... So ask not for gifts but for the Giver of gifts: not for life but for the Giver of life – then life and the things needed for life will be added unto you.
Sadhu Sundar Singh

Oh, how few find time for prayer! There is time for everything else, time to sleep and time to eat, time to read the newspaper and the novel, time to visit friends, time

for everything else under the sun, but – no time for prayer, the most important of all things, the one great essential!
Oswald Smith

Some years ago in China, at a meeting of missionaries and Chinese pastors, one of the Chinese pastors made a striking address. He said that he and his brethren were more than grateful to those who brought them the word of life and the gospel of the Lord Jesus Christ, but yet, he said, there was one thing more which missionaries should teach their spiritual children. This new thing was to pray with authority, so that they might know how to take their stand in faith before the throne and rebuke the forces of evil, holding steady and firm, and gain the victory over them. That same need is tremendously evident today in the experiences of all that are seeking to walk closely with the Lord, and to stand for Him in the face of increasing opposition. Some have spoken of this as "throne prayer" – praying with one's hand touching the throne of God.
T. Stanley Soltau

The fiend chooses for his most furious attacks the times when we feel most unable to pray.
Nilus Sorsky

The best way to get to know a new friend is to spend time with him, to talk with him. And the best way to get to know God better is to spend time with Him, to talk to Him. That's what prayer is – simply talking to God.
Stephen L. Spanoudis

Groanings which cannot be uttered are often prayers which cannot be refused.
C.H. Spurgeon

Whether we like it or not, asking is the rule of the kingdom. If you may have everything by asking in His Name, and nothing without asking, I beg you to see how absolutely vital prayer is.
C. H. Spurgeon

Your prayers at the best are nothing but a beggar's cry. You still stand as beggars at the gate of mercy, asking for the dole of God's charity, for the love of Jesus.
C.H. Spurgeon

As artists give themselves to their models, and poets to their classical pursuits, so must we addict ourselves to prayer.
C.H. Spurgeon

On your knees wrestle against your besetting sins.
C.H. Spurgeon

Oh! it is a glorious fact, that prayers are noticed in heaven.
C.H. Spurgeon

Frequently we pray that God would not forsake us in the hour of trial and temptation, but we too much forget that we have need to use this prayer at all times. There is no moment of our life, however holy, in which we can do without His constant upholding. Whether in light or in darkness, in communion or in temptation, we alike need the prayer, "Forsake me not, O Lord." "Hold Thou me up, and I shall be safe."
C.H. Spurgeon

To pray is to cast off your burdens, it is to tear away your rags, it is to shake off your diseases, it is to be filled with spiritual vigor, it is to reach the highest point of Christian health.
C.H. Spurgeon

We may be certain that whatever God has made prominent in His Word, He intended to be conspicuous in our lives. If He has said much about prayer, it is because He knows we have much need of it.
C.H. Spurgeon

Prayers are heard in heaven very much in proportion to our faith.
C.H. Spurgeon

God always has an open ear and a ready hand, if you have an open and ready heart. Take your groanings and your sighs to God and he will answer you.
C.H. Spurgeon

Prayer is the lisping of the believing infant, the shout of the fighting believer, the requiem of the dying saint falling asleep in Jesus.
C.H. Spurgeon

To pray is to mount on eagle's wings above the clouds and get into the clear heaven where God dwells.
C.H. Spurgeon

I know of no better thermometer to your spiritual temperature than this, the measure of the intensity of your prayer.
C.H. Spurgeon

To pray is to grasp heaven in one's arms, to embrace the Deity within one's soul, and to feel one's body made a temple of the Holy Spirit.
C.H. Spurgeon

The finest of God's blessings is to be found in secret prayer.
C.H. Spurgeon

A groan is a matter about which there is no hypocrisy.
C.H. Spurgeon

We should speak to God from our own hearts, and talk to him as a child talks to his father.
C.H. Spurgeon

If you learn it upon your knees you will never unlearn it.
C.H. Spurgeon

Only that prayer which comes from our heart can get to God's heart.
C.H. Spurgeon

Prayer has a mighty power to sustain the soul in every season of its distress and sorrow.
C.H. Spurgeon

David said, "I found it in my heart to pray this prayer unto Thee, O Lord." How many of us seem to begin to pray without really thinking about prayer! We rush, without preparation or thought, into the presence of God. But David did not make that mistake; he found his prayer in his heart. Prayer is the product of a humble heart, a believing heart, and a heart renewed by grace. I pray that the Lord will give us a heart to pray.
C.H. Spurgeon

If ye keep watch over your hearts, and listen for the voice of God and learn of Him, in one short hour ye can learn more from Him than ye could learn from man in a thousand years.
Johannes Tauler

I used to ask God to help me.
Then I asked if I might help Him.
I ended up by asking Him to do his work through me.
James Hudson Taylor

Prayer is the ascent of the mind to God. It is an abstract and summary of Christian religion. Prayer is an act of religion and divine worship, confessing His power and His mercy; it celebrates His attributes, and confesses His glories, and reveres His Person, and implores His aid, and gives thanks for His blessings; it is an act of humility, condescension, and dependence, expressed in the prostration of our bodies and humiliation of our spirits; it is an act of charity, when we pray for others; it is an act of repentance, when it confesses and begs pardon for our sins, and exercises every grace according to the design of the man, and the matter of the prayer.
Jeremy Taylor

Is prayer your steering wheel or your spare tire?
Corrie ten Boom

Battering the gates of heaven with the storms of prayer.
Lord Alfred Tennyson

More things are wrought by prayer
Than this world dreams of. Wherefore, let
thy voice
Rise like a fountain for me night and day.
For what are men better than sheep or
goats
That nourish a blind life within the brain,
If, knowing God, they lift not hands of
prayer
Both for themselves and those who call
them friend?
For so the whole round earth is every way
Bound by gold chains about the feet of God.
Alfred, Lord Tennyson

Mental prayer is nothing else … but being
on terms of friendship with God,
frequently conversing in secret with Him.
St Teresa of Avila

The life of prayer is just love to God, and
the custom of being ever with Him.
St Teresa of Avila

There is but one road which reaches God
and that is prayer; if anyone shows you
another, you are being deceived.
Teresa of Avila

In recollective prayer, the individual
doesn't seek to influence God to do this or
that for him in the material world. Instead
he seeks God Himself. God, God, God,
and nothing but God. Consequently the
hallmark of this prayer is an ongoing effort
to keep God in mind, to recall His
continual presence.
Teresa of Avila

The soul which gives itself to prayer –
whether a lot or only a little – must
absolutely not have limits set on it.
Teresa of Avila

More tears are shed over answered prayers
than unanswered ones.
Mother Teresa

The more you pray, the easier it becomes. The
easier it becomes, the more you will pray.
Mother Teresa

Interviewer: You love people whom others
regard as human debris. What is your
secret? Mother Teresa: My secret is simple.
I pray.
Mother Teresa

Love to pray. Feel often during the day the
need for prayer, and take trouble to pray.
Prayer enlarges the heart until it is capable
of containing God's gift of Himself. Ask
and seek and your heart will grow big
enough to receive Him.
Mother Teresa

The true monk should have prayer and
psalmody continually in his heart.
Abba Theonas

Prayer is the test of everything; prayer is
also the source of everything; prayer is the
driving force of everything; prayer is also
the director of everything. If prayer is
right, everything is right. For prayer will
not allow anything to go wrong.
Theophan the Recluse

For me, prayer is a surge of the heart; it is a
simple look turned toward heaven, it is a
cry of recognition and of love, embracing
both trial and joy.
Thérèse of Lisieux

He who can inwardly lift his mind up to
God, and can regard outward things little,
needs not to seek for time or place to pray.
Thomas à Kempis

Out of a very intimate acquaintance with
D.L. Moody, I wish to testify that he was a
far greater pray-er than he was preacher.
R.A. Torrey

D.L. Moody knew and believed in the
deepest depths of his soul that nothing was
too hard for the Lord, and that prayer
could do anything that God could do.
R.A. Torrey

We sometimes fear to bring our troubles to
God, because they must seem small to
Him who sitteth on the circle of the earth.

But if they are large enough to vex and endanger our welfare, they are large enough to touch His heart of love. For love does not measure by a merchant's scales, nor with a surveyor's chain. It hath a delicacy... unknown in any handling of material substance.
R.A. Torrey

We Christians must simplify our lives or lose untold treasures on earth and in eternity. Modern civilization is so complex as to make the devotional life all but impossible. The need for solitude and quietness was never greater than it is today.
A.W. Tozer

God never denied that soul anything that went as far as heaven to ask for it.
John Trapp

Prayer should never be regarded as a science or reduced to a system – that ruins it, because it is essentially a living and personal relationship, which tends to become more personal and also more simple, as one goes on.
E. Underhill

Who fetched the angel? The angel fetched Peter out of prison, but it was prayer that fetched the angel.
Thomas Watson

If God doth not give us what we crave, He will give us what we need.
Thomas Watson

A godly man is a praying man.
Thomas Watson

A godly man is a praying man. As soon as grace is poured in, prayer is poured out. Prayer is the soul's traffic with heaven; God comes down to us by His Spirit, and we go up to Him by prayer.
Thomas Watson

God does nothing but by prayer, and everything with it.
John Wesley

The end of prayer is the perfection of the whole Christian body.
B.F. Westcott

Be much in secret prayer. Converse less with man, and more with God.
George Whitefield

Once we spent a whole night in prayer and praise: and many a time, at midnight and at one in the morning, after I have been wearied almost to death in preaching, writing and conversation, and going from place to place, God imparted new life to my soul, and enabled me to intercede with Him for an hour and a half and two hours together.
George Whitefield

O prayer! Prayer! It brings and keeps God and man together. It raises man up to God and brings God down to man. If you would keep your walk up with God, pray, pray without ceasing.
George Whitefield

When the gods choose to punish us, they merely answer our prayers.
Oscar Wilde

You may pray for an hour and still not pray. You may meet God for a moment and then be in touch with Him all day.
Fredrik Wisloff

Prayer is less about changing the world than it is about changing ourselves.
David J. Wolpe

If a man wants God to hear his prayer quickly, then before he prays for anything else, even his own soul, when he stands and stretches out his hands towards God, he must pray with all his heart for his enemies.
Abba Zeno

Prayer is self-discipline. The effort to realize the presence and power of God stretches the sinews of the soul and hardens its muscles. To pray is to grow in

grace. To tarry in the presence of the King leads to new loyalty and devotion on the part of the faithful subjects. Christian character grows in the secret-place of prayer.
Samuel M. Zwemer

The energies of the universe, nay, of God Himself, are at the disposal of those who pray – to the man who stirreth up himself to take hold of God.
Samuel Zwemer

True prayer will achieve just as much as it costs us.
Samuel M. Zwemer

When we pray for each other on earth we do so believing that all things are given to us through Christ alone.
Huldrych Zwingli

Prayer, Answered
There are 667 prayers recorded in the Bible, and the answers to 454 are recorded.
Author unknown

God will either give you what you ask, or something far better.
Robert Murray M'Cheyne

On the ground of our own goodness we cannot expect to have our prayers answered. But Jesus is worthy, and for His sake we may have our prayers answered. But if we trust in Christ, if we hide in Him, if we put Him forward and ourselves in the background, depend on Him and plead His name, we may expect to have our prayers answered.
George Müller

When I stop praying, the coincidences stop happening.
William Temple

Prayer, Definitions of
Prayer, in its simplest definition, is merely a wish turned God-ward.
Author unknown

Prayer is taking our troubles to God. Faith is leaving them there.
Author unknown

What you love you worship; true prayer, real prayer, is nothing but loving: what you love, that you pray to.
Augustine of Hippo

Prayer. The chief exercise of faith, by which we daily receive God's benefits.
John Calvin

Prayer is conversation with God.
Clement of Alexandria

Prayer is the raising of one's mind and heart to God or the requesting of good things from God.
John Damascus

As soon as we are with God in faith and in love, we are in prayer.
F. Fénelon

Prayer is the guide to perfection. For the one way to become perfect is to walk in the presence of God.
Madame Guyon

Prayer is the application of the heart to God, and the internal exercise of love.
Madame Guyon

Prayer is the overflowing of the heart in the presence of God.
Madame Guyon

Prayer is love in need appealing to love in power.
Robert Moffatt

Prayer is the burden of a sigh,
The falling of a tear,
The upward glancing of an eye
When none but God is near.
James Montgomery

Prayer is a cry of hope.
Alfred de Musset

Prayer is the laying aside of thoughts.
Evagrius Ponticus

Prayer is an effort to lay hold of God himself, the author of life.
Sundar Singh

Prayer is the breathing in of the Holy Spirit.
Sundar Singh

Prayer, Effect of
The influence of prayer on the human mind and body is as demonstrable as that of secreting glands. Its results can be measured in terms of increased physical buoyancy, greater intellectual vigor, moral stamina, and a deeper understanding of the realities underlying human relationships.
Dr Alex Carrel

Prayer, Expectant
Beware in your prayers, above everything else, of limiting God, not only by unbelief, but by fancying that you know what He can do. Expect unexpected things, "above all that we ask or think." Each time, before you intercede, be quiet first, and worship God in His glory. Think of what He can do, and how He delights to hear the prayers of His redeemed people. Think of your place and privilege in Christ, and expect great things!
Andrew Murray

Prayer, Extempore
We pray without a prompter because from the heart.
Tertullian

Prayer, Feeble
Though our private desires are ever so confused, though our private requests are ever so broken, and though our private groanings are ever so hidden from men, yet God eyes them, records them, and puts them upon the file of heaven, and will one day crown them with glorious answers and returns.
Thomas Brooks

Prayer, Fiery
Prayer is not a collection of balanced phrases; it is the pouring out of the soul. What is love if it be not fiery? What are prayers if the heart be not ablaze? They are the battles of the soul. In them men wrestle with principalities and powers.
Samuel Chadwick

Prayer, Hidden
All prayer is hidden. It is behind a closed door. The best spade diggers go down into deep ditches out of sight. There are numbers of surface workers, but few who in self-obliteration toil alone with God.
Seth Joshua

There is a sense in which every man when he begins to pray to God should put his hand upon his mouth.
Martyn Lloyd-Jones

Prayer, Intercessory
Prayer must carry on our work as much as preaching; he preacheth not heartily to his people, that will not pray for them.
Richard Baxter

To make intercession for men is the most powerful and practical way in which we can express our love for them.
John Calvin

Prayer, Length of
If I fail to spend two hours in prayer each morning, the devil gets the victory through the day. I have so much business I cannot get on without spending three hours daily in prayer.
Martin Luther

I suspect I have been allotting habitually too little time to religious exercises, as private devotion and religious meditation, scripture-reading, etc. Hence I am lean and cold and hard. I had better allot two hours or an hour and a half daily. I have been keeping too late hours, and hence have had but a hurried half-hour in a morning to myself. Surely the experience of all good men confirms the proposition that without

a due measure of private devotions the will grows lean.
William Wilberforce

Prayer, Method of

Enter into the inner chamber of your mind. Shut out all things save God and whatever may aid you in seeking God; and having barred the door of your chamber, seek him.
Anselm

We must understand that the only ones who prepare themselves for prayer adequately are those who are so impressed with God's majesty that they can be free from all earthly worries and affections.
John Calvin

The first rule of true prayer is to have heart and mind in the right mood for talking with God.
John Calvin

No one should give the answer that it is impossible for a man occupied with worldly cares to pray always. You can set up an altar to God in your mind by means of prayer. And so it is fitting to pray at your trade, on a journey, standing at a counter or sitting at your handicraft.
John Chrysostom

You must literally prostrate yourself before him in the quietness of your own room, and through this outward physical action express the humiliation of your soul as you view the terrible sight of your own faults.
F. Fénelon

Take time to be holy;
Speak oft with thy Lord.
W.D. Longstaff

Prayer, Morning

First Thoughts
Let God have your first awaking thoughts; lift up your hearts to Him reverently and thankfully for the rest enjoyed the night before and cast yourself upon Him for the day which follows.

Familiarize yourself so consistently to this that your conscience may check you when common thoughts shall first intrude. Think of the mercy of a night's rest and of how many that have spent that night in hell; how many in prison; how many in cold, hard lodgings; how many suffering from agonizing pains and sickness, weary of their beds and of their lives. Think of how many souls were that night called from their bodies terrifyingly to appear before God and think how quickly days and nights are rolling on! How speedily your last night and day will come! Observe that which is lacking in the preparedness of your soul for such a time and seek it without delay.
Richard Baxter

Prayer, Neglect of

All decays begin in the closet; no heart thrives without much secret converse with God, and nothing will make amends for the want of it.
John Berridge

The western church has lost the prayer stamina of the mission churches in Asia, Africa, South America, Indonesia, and those of the underground church in many parts of the world. Yes, we are great organizers, but poor pray-ers.
Paul E. Billheimer

The leading defect of Christian ministers is want of a devotional habit.
Richard Cecil

A great many people do not pray because they do not feel any sense of need.
Oswald Chambers

They who pray not, know nothing of God, and know nothing of the state of their own souls.
Adam Clarke

A minister who prays not, who is not in love with prayer, is not a minister of the Church of God. He is a dry tree, which occupies in vain a place in Christ's garden.

He is an enemy, and not a father, of the people. He is a stranger, who has taken the place of the shepherd, and to whom the salvation of the flock is an indifferent thing.
Thomas Coke

God has a good deal more to give than most of us are getting. "Knee-ology" is a much-neglected branch of Christian ethics. The Church loses immeasurably in strength and accelerated power by failing to test the wonderful promises of God in prayer. Oh, for somebody who can really pray.
C.E. Cornell

Of all the duties enjoined by Christianity none is more essential and yet more neglected than prayer.
F. Fénelon

The worst sin is prayerlessness.
P.T. Forsyth

It is a sin against God not to pray for the Israel of God, especially for those of them that are under our charge. Good men are afraid of the guilt of omissions.
Matthew Henry

Who goes to bed and does not pray
Maketh two nights to every day.
George Herbert

He who neglects prayer, thinking he has another doorway for repentance, is deceived by the devil.
Isaac the Syrian

He that flees from prayer flees from all that is good.
John of the Cross

Next to the wonder of seeing my Savior will be, I think, the wonder that I made so little use of the power of prayer.
D.L. Moody

A man cannot lead others where he is not willing to go himself. Therefore, beware of the prayerless church leader who no longer

readily admits his own need for more of the person and power of Jesus Christ. Only a seeking, praying heart can truly encourage spiritual hunger in others!
David Smithers

Prayerlessness is a sin.
Corrie ten Boom

If we are too busy to pray, we are too busy to have power. We have a great deal of activity, but we accomplish little; many services but few conversions; much machinery but few results.
R.A. Torrey

The neglected heart will soon be a heart overrun with worldly thoughts; the neglected life will soon become a moral chaos.
A.W. Tozer

Jesus Christ went more willingly to the cross than we do to the throne of grace.
Thomas Watson

Prayer, Occasions and times of

If I have accomplished anything in the world, I attribute it to the fact that the first hour of every day of my life for years has been given to communion with God in secret prayer and the study of his word. Do you suppose I come to a Cabinet meeting without first having talked it over with God?
Earl Cairns

You can only pray all the time everywhere if you bother to pray some of the time somewhere.
J. Dalrymple

Prayer should be the key of the day and the lock of the night.
Thomas Fuller

Affliction teacheth a wicked person sometime to pray: prosperity never.
Ben Jonson

Endeavor seven times a day to withdraw from business and company and lift up thy

soul to God in private retirement.
Adoniram Judson

Let your first "Good morning" be to your
Father in heaven.
Karl G. Maeser

I ought to pray before seeing anyone.
Robert Murray M'Cheyne

Vows made in storms are forgotten in
calm.
Proverb

When the clock strikes it is good to say a
prayer.
Jeremy Taylor

Prayer, Perseverance in
God's acquaintance is not made hurriedly.
He does not bestow his gifts on the casual
or hasty comer and goer. To be much alone
with God is the secret of knowing him and
of influence with him.
E.M. Bounds

The secret of the constancy of grace and
virtue lies in the perseverance in prayer.
John Cassian

Do not forget prayer. Every time you pray,
if your prayer is sincere, there will be new
feeling and new meaning in it, which will
give you fresh courage.
Fyodor Dostoevsky

Pray inwardly, even if you do not enjoy it.
It does good, though you feel nothing, see
nothing, yes, even though you think you
are doing nothing. For when we are dry,
empty, sick or weak, at such a time is your
prayer most pleasing, though you find little
enough to enjoy in it. This is true of all
believing prayer.
Julian of Norwich

Hold yourself in prayer before God, like a
dumb or paralytic beggar at a rich man's
gate: let it be your business to keep your
mind in the presence of God.
Brother Lawrence

It is not enough for the believer to begin to
pray, nor to pray correctly; nor is it enough
to continue for a time to pray. We must
patiently, believingly continue in prayer
until we obtain an answer. Further, we have
not only to continue in prayer until the
end, but we have also to believe that God
does hear us and will answer our prayers.
Most frequently we fail in not continuing
in prayer until the blessing is obtained, and
in not expecting the blessing.
George Müller

Storm the throne of grace and persevere
therein, and mercy will come down.
John Wesley

Prayer, Power of
Prayer moves the hand that moves the
world.
Author unknown

Prayer is a powerful thing, for God has
bound and tied himself thereto.
Martin Luther

None can believe how powerful prayer is,
and what it is able to effect, but those who
have learned it by experience.
Martin Luther

I fear John Knox's prayers more than an
army of ten thousand men.
Mary Queen of Scots

Thou art coming to a king,
Large petitions with thee bring;
For his grace and power are such,
None can ever ask too much.
John Newton

It is possible to move men, through God,
by prayer alone.
Hudson Taylor

Prayer is the secret of power.
Evan Roberts

God does nothing redemptively in the
world – except through prayer.
John Wesley

Prayer, Preparation for

It is necessary to rouse the heart to pray, otherwise it will become quite dry.
John of Kronstadt

Each time, before you intercede, be quiet first, and worship God in His glory. Think of what He can do, and how He delights to hear the prayers of His redeemed people. Think of your place and privilege in Christ, and expect great things!
Andrew Murray

If we would pray aright, the first thing we should do is to see to it that we really get an audience with God, that we really get into His very presence. Before a word of petition is offered, we should have the definite consciousness that we are talking to God, and should believe that He is listening and is going to grant the thing that we ask of Him.
R.A. Torrey

Prayer, Prevailing

There is no power like that of prevailing prayer – of Abraham pleading for Sodom, Jacob wrestling in the stillness of the night, Moses standing in the breach, Hannah intoxicated with sorrow, David heart-broken with remorse and grief, Jesus in sweat and blood. Add to this list from the records of the church your personal observation and experience, and always there is cost of passion unto blood. Such prayer prevails. It turns ordinary mortals into men of power. It brings power. It brings fire. It brings rain. It brings life. It brings God.
Samuel Chadwick

I have never known a person sweat blood; but I have known a person pray till the blood started from his nose. And I have known persons to pray till they were all wet with perspiration, in the coldest weather in winter. I have known persons pray for hours, till their strength was all exhausted with the agony of their minds. Such prayers prevailed with God.
Charles G. Finney

Five grand conditions of prevailing prayer were ever before his mind:
1 Entire dependence upon the merits and mediation of the Lord Jesus Christ, as the only ground of any claim for blessing.
2 Separation from all known sin.
3 Faith in God's word of promise.
4 Asking in accordance with his will.
5 Importunity in supplication. There must be *waiting* on God and waiting for God.
A.T. Pierson, George Müller of Bristol

Prayer, *Public*

John Newton

It is much to be desired, that our hearts might be so affected with a sense of divine things and so closely engaged when we are worshiping God, that it might not be in the power of little circumstances to interrupt and perplex us, and to make us think the service wearisome and the time which we employ in it tedious. But as our infirmities are many and great, and the enemy of our souls is watchful to discompose us, if care is not taken by those who lead in social prayer, the exercise which is approved by the judgment may become a burden and an occasion of sin.

LENGTH OF PRAYERS

The chief fault of some good prayers is, that they are too long; not that I think we should pray by the clock, and limit ourselves precisely to a certain number of minutes; but it is better of the two, that the hearers should wish the prayer had been longer, than spend half the time in wishing it was over. This is frequently owing to an unnecessary enlargement upon every circumstance that offers, as well as to the repetition of the same things. If we have been copious in pleading for spiritual blessings, it may be best to be brief and summary in the article of intercession for others, or if the frame of our spirits, or the circumstances of affairs, lead us to be more large and particular in laying the cases of others before the Lord respect should be had to this intention in the former part of the prayer.

There are, doubtless, seasons when the Lord is pleased to favor those who pray with a peculiar liberty: they speak because they feel; they have a wrestling spirit and hardly know how to leave off. When this is the case, those who join with them are seldom wearied, though the prayer should be protracted something beyond the usual limits. But I believe it sometimes happens, both in praying and in preaching, that we are apt to spin out our time to the greatest length, when we have in reality the least to say. Long prayers should in general be avoided, especially where several persons are to pray successively; or else even spiritual hearers will be unable to keep up their attention. And here I would just notice an impropriety we sometimes meet with, that when a person gives expectation that he is just going to conclude his prayer, something not thought of in its proper place occurring that instant to his mind, leads him as it were to begin again. But unless it is a matter of singular importance, it would be better omitted for that time.

PREACHING IN PRAYERS

The prayers of some good men are more like preaching than praying. They rather express the Lord's mind to the people, than the desires of the people to the Lord. Indeed this can hardly be called prayer. It might in another place stand for part of a good sermon, but will afford little help to those who desire to pray with their hearts. Prayer should be sententious, and made up of breathings to the Lord, either of confession, petition, or praise. It should be not only Scriptural and evangelical, but experimental, a simple and unstudied expression of the wants and feelings of the soul. It will be so if the heart is lively and affected in the duty, it must be so if the edification of others is the point in view.

METHOD IN PRAYER

Several books have been written to assist in the gift and exercise of prayer, and many useful hints may be borrowed from them. But a too close attention to the method therein recommended, gives an air of study and formality, and offends against that simplicity which is so essentially necessary to a good prayer, that no degree of acquired abilities can compensate for the want of it. It is possible to learn to pray mechanically, and by rule; but it is hardly possible to do so with acceptance and benefit to others. When the several parts of invocation, adoration, confession, petition, etc., follow each other in a stated order, the hearer's mind generally goes before the speaker's voice, and we can form a tolerable conjecture what is to come next. On this account we often find that unlettered people who have had little or no help from books, or rather have not been fettered by them, can pray with an unction and savor in an unpremeditated way, while the prayers of persons of much superior abilities, perhaps even of ministers themselves, are, though accurate and regular, so dry and starched, then they afford little either of pleasure or profit to spiritual mind. The spirit of prayer is the fruit and token of the Spirit of adoption.

The studied addresses with which some approach the throne of grace remind us of a stranger's coming to a great man's door; he knocks and waits, sends in his name, and goes through a course of ceremony, before he gains admittance, while a child of the family uses no ceremony at all, but enters freely when he pleases, because he knows he is at home. It is true, we ought always to draw near the Lord with great humiliation of spirit, and a sense of our unworthiness. But this spirit is not always best expressed or promoted by a pompous enumeration of the names and titles of the God with whom we have to do, or by fixing in our minds beforehand the exact order in which we propose to arrange the several parts of our prayer. Some attention to method may be proper, for the prevention of repetitions; and plain people may be a little defective in it sometimes; but this defect will not be half so tiresome and disagreeable as a studied and artificial exactness.

PECULIARITIES OF MANNER

Many – perhaps most – people who pray in public have some favorite word or expression which recurs too often in their prayers, and is frequently used as a mere expletive, having no necessary connection with the sense of what they are speaking. The most disagreeable of these is when the name of the blessed God, with the addition perhaps of one or more epithets, as Great, Glorious, Holy, Almighty, etc., is introduced so often and without necessity, as seems neither to indicate a due reverence in the person who uses It, nor suited to excite reverence in those who hear. I will not say that this is taking the Name of God in vain, in the usual sense of the phrase: it is, however, a great impropriety, and should be guarded against. It would be well if they who use redundant expressions had a friend to give them a caution so that they might with a little care be retrenched; and hardly any person can be sensible of the little peculiarities he may inadvertently adopt, unless he is told of them.

There are several things likewise respecting the voice and manner of prayer, which a person may with due care correct in himself, and which, if generally corrected, would make meetings for prayer more pleasant than sometimes they are... Very loud speaking is a fault, when the size of the place and the number of the hearers do not render it necessary. The end of speaking (in public) is to be heard: and when that end is attained a greater elevation of the voice is frequency hurtful to the speaker, and is more likely to confuse a hearer than fix his attention. I do not deny but allowance must be made for constitution, and the warmth of the passions, which dispose some persons to speak louder than others. Yet such will do well to restrain themselves as much as they can. It may seem indeed to indicate great earnestness, and that the heart is much affected; yet it is often but false fire. It may be thought speaking "with power", but a person who is favored with the Lord's presence may pray with power in a moderate voice; and there may be very little of the power of the Spirit, though the voice should be heard in the street and neighborhood.

The other extreme of speaking too low is not so frequent; but, if we are not heard, we might as well altogether hold our peace. It exhausts the spirits and wearies the attention, to be listening for any length of time to a very low voice. Some words or sentences will be lost, which will render what is heard less intelligible and agreeable. If the speaker can be heard by the person furthest distant from him, the rest will hear of course.

The tone of the voice is likewise to be regarded. Some have a tone in prayer so very different from their usual way of speaking, that their nearest friends, if not accustomed to them, could hardly know them by their voice. Sometimes the tone is changed, perhaps more than once, so that if our eyes did not give us more certain information than our ears, we might think two or three persons had been speaking by turns. It is a pity that when we approve what is spoken we should be so easily disconcerted by an awkwardness of delivery: yet so it often is, and probably so it will be, in the present weak and imperfect state of human nature. It is more to be lamented than wondered at, that sincere Christians are sometimes forced to confess: "He is a good man, and his prayers as to their substance are spiritual and judicious, but there is something so displeasing in his manner that I am always uneasy when I hear him".

INFORMALITY IN PRAYER

Contrary to this, and still more offensive, is a custom that some have of talking to the Lord in prayer. It is their natural voice indeed, but it is that expression of it which they use upon the most familiar and trivial occasions. The human voice is capable of so many inflections and variations, that it can adapt itself to the different sensations of the mind, as joy, sorrow, fear, desire, etc. If a man was pleading for his life, or expressing his thanks to the king for a pardon, common sense and decency would teach

him a suitableness of manner; and anyone who could not understand his language might know by the sound of his words that he was not making a bargain or telling a story. How much more, when we speak to the King of kings, should the consideration of his glory and our own vileness, and of the important concerns we are engaged in before him, impress us with an air of seriousness and reverence, and prevent us from speaking to him as if he was altogether such an one as ourselves! The liberty to which we are called by the gospel does not at all encourage such a pertness and familiarity as would be unbecoming to use towards a fellow-worm, who was a little advanced above us in worldly dignity. I shall be glad if these hints may be of any service to those who desire to worship God in spirit and in truth, and who wish that whatever has a tendency to damp the spirit of devotion, either in themselves or in others, might be avoided.
John Newton

Prayer, Purpose of
The point of asking is that you may get to know God better.
Oswald Chambers

Prayer is not designed to inform God, but to give man a sight of his misery; to humble his heart, to excite his desire, to inflame his faith, to animate his hope, to raise his soul from earth to heaven.
Adam Clarke

Prayer, Secret of real
How many Christians there are who cannot pray, and who seek by effort, resolve, joining prayer circles, etc., to cultivate in themselves the "holy art of intercession," and all to no purpose. Here for them and for all is the only secret of a real prayer life – "Be filled with the Spirit," who is "the Spirit of grace and supplication."
J. Stuart Holden

Prayer, Spirit of
When God is about to give His people the expected good, He pours out a Spirit of prayer, and it is a good sign that He is coming towards them in mercy.
Matthew Henry

Prayer, Unanswered
God denies a Christian nothing, but with a design to give him something better.
Richard Cecil

I have had prayers answered – most strangely so sometimes – but I think our heavenly Father's loving-kindness has been even more evident in what He has refused me.
Lewis Carroll

Prayer, Value of
There is no way that Christians, in a private capacity, can do so much to promote the work of God and advance the kingdom of Christ as by prayer.
Jonathan Edwards

Every great movement of God can be traced to a kneeling figure.
D.L. Moody

Prayer and action
It is in vain to expect our prayers to be heard, if we do not strive as well as pray.
Aesop

Prayer is not a substitute for work, thinking, watching, suffering, or giving; prayer is a support for all other efforts.
George Butyric

When you pray for potatoes, grab a hoe.
David Jamieson's Mom

Prayer and action, therefore, can never be seen as contradictory or mutually exclusive. Prayer without action grows in powerless pietism, and action without prayer degenerates into questionable manipulation. If prayer leads us into a deeper unity with the compassionate

Christ, it will always give rise to concrete acts of service.
Henri J.M. Nouwen

Whatsoever we beg of God, let us also work for it.
Jeremy Taylor

Prayer and Bible reading
Look at the lives of those men and the time they gave to Scripture reading and prayer and various other forms of self-examination and spiritual exercises. They believed in the culture and the discipline of the spiritual life and it was because they did so that God rewarded them by giving them these gracious manifestations of himself and these mighty experiences which warmed their hearts.
D. Martyn Lloyd-Jones

That hours of the day, less or more time, for the Word and prayer, be given to God; not sparing the twelfth hour, or mid-day, howbeit it should then be the shorter time.
Samuel Rutherford

Prayer and boldness
What a spirit – what a confidence was in his very expression! With such a reverence he petitioned, as one begging of God, and yet with such hope and assurance, as if he spoke with a loving father or friend.
Author unknown. Someone who heard Martin Luther praying

Prayer and conflict
There are few children of God who do not often find the season of prayer a season of conflict. The devil has a special rage against us when he sees us on our knees.
J.C. Ryle

Prayer and fasting
Prayer is reaching out and after the unseen; fasting, letting go of all that is seen and temporal. Fasting helps express, deepens, confirms the resolution that we are ready to sacrifice anything, even ourselves, to attain what we seek for the kingdom of God.
Andrew Murray

Prayer and grace
Prayer is an ordinance of God, in which a man draws very near to God; and therefore it calleth for so much the more of the assistance of the grace of God to help a soul to pray as becomes one that is in the presence of him.
John Bunyan

Prayer and lethergy
Christ was in an agony at prayer, Luke 22: 44. Many when they pray are rather in a lethargy, than in an agony. When they are about the world they are all fire; when they are at prayer, they are all ice.
Thomas Watson

Prayer and mercy
Prayer is the midwife of mercy, that helps to bring it forth.
Matthew Henry

Prayer and ministers
Prayer is the first thing, the second thing, the third thing necessary to a minister. Pray, then, my dear brother; pray, pray, pray.
Edward Payson

Prayer and preaching
I would rather teach one man to pray than ten men to preach.
J.H. Jowett

May God help me, if you cease to pray for me! Let me know the day, and I must cease to preach.
C.H. Spurgeon

Shall I give you yet another reason why you should pray? I have preached my very heart out. I could not say any more than I have said. Will not your prayers accomplish that which my preaching fails to do? Is it not likely that the Church has been putting forth its preaching hand but not its praying hand? Oh dear friends! Let us agonize in prayer.
C.H. Spurgeon

Prayer and revival
The prayer that sparks revival begins long

before the countryside seems to awaken from its slumber in sin. It starts when men fall on their knees and cry out to God. That's where true intimacy with God takes place and we begin the journey of being transformed into the image of Christ. And as men are transformed, the course of a nation can be changed.
Wellington Boone

When God has something very great to accomplish for his church it is his will that there should precede it, the extraordinary prayers of his people. When God is about to accomplish great things for his church, he begins with as remarkable outpouring of his spirit of grace and a desire to pray. If we are not to expect that the devil should go out of a particular person, who is in the grip of bodily possession, without extraordinary prayer, or prayer and fasting; how much less should we expect to have him cast out of the land without it.
Jonathan Edwards

Workers that are strangers to knee work may work up a temporary excitement, but never will be able to secure the copious outpourings of genuine revival power.
Martin Wells Knapp

Why should anybody pray for revival? Out of a concern for the glory of God.
Martyn Lloyd-Jones

Prayer and Satan
It is the great work of the devil to do his best, or rather worst, against the best prayers.
John Bunyan

Satan dreads nothing but prayer.
Samuel Chadwick

The one concern of the devil is to keep the saints from praying. He fears nothing from prayerless studies/work/Christian activity. He laughs at our toil, mocks our wisdom, but trembles when we pray.
Samuel Chadwick

And Satan trembles when he sees
The weakest saint upon his knees.
William Cowper

The devil is aware that one hour of close fellowship, hearty converse with God in prayer, is able to pull down what he hath been contriving and building many a year.
Flavel

Satan's tactics seem to be as follows: He will first of all oppose our breaking through to the place of a real living faith, by all means in his power. He detests the prayer of faith, for it is an authoritative "notice to quit." We often have to strive and wrestle in prayer before we attain this quiet, restful faith. And until we break right through and join hands with God we have not attained to a real faith at all. However, once we attain to a real faith, all the forces of hell are impotent to annul it. The real battle begins when the prayer of faith has been offered.
J.O. Fraser

Satan cannot deny but that great wonders have been wrought by prayer. As the spirit of prayer goes up, so his kingdom goes down. Satan's stratagems against prayer are three. First, if he can, he will keep thee from prayer. If that be not feasible, secondly, he will strive to interrupt thee in prayer. And, thirdly, if that plot takes not, he will labor to hinder the success of thy prayer.
William Gurnall

Satan rocks the cradle when we sleep at our devotions.
Joseph Hall

Prayer and service
Prayer is striking the winning blow. Service is gathering up the results.
S.D. Gordon

Prayer and sincerity
Sincerity carries the soul in all simplicity to open its heart to God.
John Bunyan

Prayer and the church

Prayer is a strong wall and fortress of the church; it is a goodly Christian weapon.
Martin Luther

Prayer and the heart's desire

Your desire is your prayer; and your desire is without ceasing; your prayer will also be without ceasing.
Augustine of Hippo

Prayer is not merely expressing our present desires. Its purpose is to exercise and train our desires, so that we want what he is getting ready to give us. His gift is very great, and we are small vessels for receiving it. So prayer involves widening our hearts to God.
Augustine of Hippo

The best prayers have more often groans than words.
John Bunyan

Prayer and the Holy Spirit

There is no man nor church in the world that can come to God in prayer, but by the assistance of the Holy Spirit.
John Bunyan

The Holy Ghost has two offices: first, he is a Spirit of grace, that makes God gracious unto us, and receive us as his acceptable children, for Christ's sake. Secondly, he is a Spirit of prayer, that prays for us, and for the whole world, to the end that all evil may be turned from us, and that all good may happen to us.
Martin Luther

Where there is much prayer, there will be much of the Spirit; where there is much of the Spirit, there will be ever-increasing prayer.
Andrew Murray

Prayer obtains fresh and continued outpourings of the Spirit. He alone begins the work of grace in a man's heart. He alone can carry it forward and make it prosper. But the good Spirit loves to be entreated. And those who ask most will have most of his influence.
J.C. Ryle

Of all the evidences of the real work of the Spirit, a habit of hearty private prayer is one of the most satisfactory that can be named.
J.C. Ryle

Prayer and the will of God

You cannot alter the will of God, but the man of prayer can discover God's will.
Sundar Singh

Prayer and wandering thoughts

I throw myself down in my chamber, and I call in, and invite God, and his angels thither, and when they are there, I neglect God and his angels, for the noise of a fly, for the rattling of a coach, for the whining of a door.
John Donne

It is a shameful thing to quit our conversation with God to think of trifles and fooleries.
Brother Lawrence

We ought to reject them as soon as we perceive their irrelevance to the matter at hand, or to our salvation, and return to our communion with God.
Brother Lawrence

Prayerlessness
See also: Prayer, Neglect of

Bibles read without prayer, sermons heard without prayer, engagements to marriage without prayer, travel undertaken without prayer, homes chosen without prayer, friendships formed without prayer, the daily act of private prayer itself hurried over or gone through without heart – these are the kind of downward steps by which many a Christian descends to a condition of spiritual paralysis, or reaches the point where God allows him to have a tremendous fall.
J.C. Ryle

A prayerless soul is a Christless soul.
C.H. Spurgeon

Nothing brings such leanness into a man's soul as lack of prayer.
C.H. Spurgeon

No man can progress in grace if he forsakes prayer.
C.H. Spurgeon

It is well said that neglected prayer is the birth-place of all evil.
C.H. Spurgeon

Prayer meeting

Prayer meetings are dead affairs when they are merely asking sessions; there is adventure, hope and life when they are believing sessions, and the faith is corporately, practically and deliberately affirmed.
Norman Grubb

Prayer program

A church without an intelligent, well-organized, and systematic prayer program is simply operating a religious treadmill.
Paul E. Billheimer

Prayers, Arrow

Remember your mercies, Lord.
Be gracious to me, O God.
In you I hope all day long.
In your love remember me.
In you I place all my trust.
Awake, O my soul, awake!
God is worthy of our praise.
Create a clean heart in me.
Have mercy on me, O God.
Holy is the Lamb of God.
Jesus is the Lamb of God.
Glory to the Lamb of God.
Holy, holy, holy Lord.
My cup is overflowing.
Joy cometh in the morning.
I have been given mercy.
Taste and see that the Lord is good.
You are my strength and my song.
I will never forget you.
His eye is on the sparrow.
The Lord keeps the little ones.
How good is the Lord to all.

Fill me with joy and gladness.
Let the healing waters flow
Oh, that we might know the Lord!
I have grasped you by the hand
His love is everlasting.
I have called you by your name.
My peace is my gift to you.
Let go and let God.

Have some arrow prayers to pray during the day, or a psalm.
A good watchmaker is one who makes watches and prays: a good housemaid is one who sweeps and prays.
E.B. Pusey

In the midst of worldly employments, there should be some thoughts of sin, death, judgment, and eternity, with at least a word or two of ejaculatory prayer to God.
Samuel Rutherford

Prayers, Bible prayers, Old Testament

I will sing to the Lord, for he has triumphed gloriously;
horse and rider he has thrown into the sea.
The Lord is my strength and my might,
and he has become my salvation;
this is my God, and I will exalt him. …
Who is like you, O Lord, among the gods?
Who is like you, majestic in holiness,
awesome in splendor, doing wonders?
Moses, Exodus 15:1-2, 11 NRSV

My heart exults in the Lord;
my strength is exalted in my God.
My mouth derides my enemies,
because I rejoice in my victory.
There is no Holy One like the Lord;
no one besides you;
there is no Rock like our God.
…The barren has borne seven,
but she who has many children is forlorn.
…The Lord will judge the ends of the earth;
he will give strength to his king,
and exalt the power of his anointed.
Hannah's prayer, 1 Samuel 2:1-2, 5, 10 NRSV

You are great, O Lord God; for there is no one like you, and there is no God besides

you, according to all that we have heard with our ears.
David's prayer, 2 Samuel 7:22 NRSV

The Lord is my rock, my fortress, and my deliverer,
my God, my rock, in whom I take refuge,
my shield and the horn of my salvation,
my stronghold and my refuge,
my savior; you save me from violence.
David, 2 Samuel 22:1-3 NRSV

The spirit of the Lord speaks through me,
his word is upon my tongue.
The God of Israel has spoken,
the Rock of Israel has said to me:
One who rules over people justly,
ruling in the fear of God,
is like the light of morning,
like the sun rising on a cloudless morning,
gleaming from the rain on the grassy land.
David, 2 Samuel 23:2-4 NRSV

But will God indeed dwell on the earth? Even heaven and the highest heaven cannot contain you, much less this house that I have built! Have regard to your servant's prayer and his plea, O LORD my God, heading the cry and the prayer that your servant prays to you today; that your eyes may be open night and day towards this house, the place of which you said, "My name shall be there', that you may heed the prayer that your servant prays towards this place. Hear the plea of your servant and of your people Israel when they pray towards this place; O hear in heaven your dwelling-place; heed and forgive."
Solomon, at the dedication of the temple, 1 Kings 8:27-30 NRSV

Blessed are you, O Lord, the God of our ancestor Israel, for ever and ever.
Yours, O Lord, are the greatness, the power, the glory, the victory, and the majesty;
for all that is in the heavens and on the earth is yours; yours is the kingdom, O Lord, and you are exalted as head above all.
David, 1 Chronicles 29:10-11 NRSV

You show me the path of life.
In your presence there is fullness of joy;
in your right hand are pleasures for evermore.
Psalm 16:11 NRSV

I love you, O LORD, my strength.
Psalm 18:1 NRSV

The LORD is my shepherd, I shall not want.
He makes me lie down in green pastures;
he leads me beside still waters;
he restores my soul.
He leads me in right paths
for his name's sake.
Even though I walk through the darkest valley,
I fear no evil;
for you are with me;
your rod and your staff-
they comfort me.
You prepare a table before me
in the presence of my enemies;
you anoint my head with oil;
my cup overflows.
Surely goodness and mercy shall follow me
all the days of my life,
and I shall dwell in the house of the Lord
my whole life long.
Psalm 23 NRSV

To you, O LORD, I lift up my soul.
…Make me to know your ways, O LORD;
teach me your paths.
Lead me in your truth, and teach me,
for you are the God of my salvation;
for you I wait all day long.
Be mindful of your mercy, O LORD, and
of your steadfast love,
for they have been from of old.
Psalm 25:1,4-6 NRSV

The Lord is my light and my salvation;
whom shall I fear?
The Lord is the stronghold of my life;
of whom shall I be afraid?
I believe that I shall see the goodness of the Lord in the land of the living.
Wait for the Lord; be strong, and let y our heart take courage: wait for the Lord!
Psalm 27:1, 13-14 NRSV

For with you is the fountain of life;
in your light we see light.
Psalm 36:9 NRSV

Why are you cast down, O my soul,
and why are you disquieted within me?
Hope in God; for I shall again praise him,
my help and my God.
Psalm 42:11 NRSV

Be still and know that I am God.
Psalm 46:10 NRSV

Be merciful to me, O God, be merciful to
me, for in you my soul takes refuge; in the
shadow of your wings I will take refuge,
until the destroying storms pass by.
Psalm 57:1 NRSV

Hear my cry, O God;
listen to my prayer.
From the end of the earth I call to you,
when my heart is faint.
Lead me to the rock
that is higher than I;
for you are my refuge,
a strong tower against the enemy.
Psalm 61:1-3 NRSV

O God, you are my God, I seek you,
my soul thirsts for you; my flesh faints for
you, as in a dry and weary land where
there is no water.
Psalm 63:1 NRSV

God be merciful unto us, and bless us :
and shew us the light of his countenance,
and be merciful unto us;
That thy way may be known upon earth :
thy saving health among all nations.
Let the peoples praise thee, O God : yea,
let all the peoples praise thee.
O let the nations rejoice and be glad : for
thou shalt judge the folk righteously, and
govern the nations upon earth.
Let the people praise thee, O God : yea, let
all the people praise thee.
Then shall the earth bring forth her
increase : and God, even our own God,
shall give us his blessing.
God shall bless us : and all the ends of the
world shall fear him.
*Deus misereatur, Psalm 67, Book of Common
Prayer*

How lovely is your dwelling-place,
O LORD of hosts!
My soul longs, indeed it faints
for the courts of the Lord;
my heart and my flesh sing for joy
to the living God.
Event he sparrow finds a home,
and the swallow a nest for herself,
where she may lay her young,
at your altars, O LORD of hosts,
my King and my God.
Happy are those who love in your house,
ever singing your praise.
Happy are those whose strength is in you,
in whose heart are the highways of Zion.
As they go through the valley of Baca
they make it a place of springs;
the early rain also covers it with pools.
They go from strength to strength;
the God of gods will be seen in Zion.
Psalm 84:1-7 NRSV

O sing unto the Lord a new song : for he
hath done marvelous things.
With his own right hand, and with his
holy arm : hath he gotten himself the
victory.
The Lord declared his salvation : his
righteousness hath he openly showed in
the sight of the heathen.
He hath remembered his mercy and truth
toward the house of Israel : and all the
ends of the world have seen the salvation
of our God.
Show yourselves joyful unto the Lord, all
ye lands : sing, rejoice, and give thanks.
Praise the Lord upon the harp : sing to the
harp with a psalm of thanksgiving.
With trumpets also and shawms : O shew
yourselves joyful before the Lord the
King.
Let the sea make a noise, and all that
therein is : the round world, and that dwell
therein.
Let the floods clap their hands, and let the
hills be joyful together before the Lord :
for he cometh to judge the earth.

With righteousness shall he judge the world : and the peoples with equity.
Cantate Domino, Psalm 98, Book of Common Prayer

O come, let us sing unto the Lord : let us heartily rejoice in the strength of our salvation.
Let us come before his presence with thanksgiving : and show ourselves glad in him with Psalms.
For the Lord is a great God : and a great King above all gods.
In his hand are all the corners of the earth : and the strength of the hills is his also.
The sea is his, and he made it : and his hands prepared the dry land.
O come, let us worship and fall down : and kneel before the Lord our Maker.
For he is the Lord our God : and we are the people of his pasture, and the sheep of his hand.
To day if ye will hear his voice, harden not your hearts : as in the provocation, and as in the day of temptation in the wilderness;
When your fathers tempted me : proved me, and saw my works.
Forty years long was I grieved with this generation, and said : It is a people that do err in their heart, and they have not known my ways.
Unto whom I sware in my wrath that they should not enter into my rest.
Glory be to the Father, and to the Son : and to the Holy Ghost;
As it was in the beginning, is now, and ever shall be : world without end. Amen.
Psalm 95, Book of Common Prayer

O be joyful in the Lord, all ye lands : serve the Lord with gladness, and come before his presence with a song.
Be ye sure that the Lord he is God; it is he that hath made us, and not we ourselves : we are his people, and the sheep of his pasture.
O go your way into his gates with thanksgiving, and into his courts with praise : be thankful unto him, and speak good of his Name.
For the Lord is gracious, his mercy is everlasting : and his truth endureth from generation to generation.
Jubilate Deo, Psalm 100, Book of Common Prayer

Incline your ear, O my God, and hear. Open your eyes and look at our desolation and the city that bears your name. We do not present our supplication before you on the ground of your great mercies. O Lord, hear; O Lord, forgive; O Lord, listen and act and do not delay! For your own sake, O my God, because your city and your people bear your name!
Daniel 9:18-19 NRSV

Though the fig tree does not blossom, and no fruit is on the vines;
though the produce of the olive fails and the fields yield no food;
though the flock is cut off from the fold and there is no herd in the stalls,
yet I will rejoice in the Lord;
I will exult in the God of my salvation.
Habakkuk 3:17-18 NRSV

Prayers, Bible prayers, New Testament
Glory to God in the highest heaven, and on earth peace among those whom he favors!
Luke 2:14 NRSV

Our Father in heaven,
hallowed be your name.
Your kingdom come.
Your will be done,
on earth as it is in heaven.
Give us this day our daily bread.
And forgive us our debts,
as we also have forgiven our debtors.
And do not bring us to the time of trial,
but rescue us from the evil one.
Matthew 6:9-13 NRSV

My soul doth magnify the Lord : and my spirit hath rejoiced in God my Savior.
For he hath regarded : the lowliness of his handmaiden.
For behold, from henceforth : all generations shall call me blessed.
For he that is mighty hath magnified me : and holy is his Name.

And his mercy is on them that fear him : throughout all generations.
He hath showed strength with his arm : he hath scattered the proud in the imagination of their hearts.
He hath put down the mighty from their seat : and hath exalted the humble and meek.
He hath filled the hungry with good things : and the rich he hath sent empty away.
He remembering his mercy hath holpen his servant Israel : as he promised to our forefathers, Abraham and his seed, for ever.
Magnificat, Luke 1:46-55, Book of Common Prayer

Blessed the Lord God of Israel : for he hath visited and redeemed his people;
And hath raised up a mighty salvation for us : in the house of his servant David;
As he spake by the mouth of his holy Prophets : which have been since the world began;
That we should be saved from our enemies : and from the hand of all that hate us.
To perform the mercy promised to our forefathers : and to remember his holy Covenant;
To perform the oath which he sware to our forefather Abraham : that he would give us;
That we being delivered out of the hand of our enemies : might serve him without fear;
In holiness and righteousness before him : all the days of our life.
And thou, Child, shalt be called the Prophet of the Highest : for thou shalt go before the face of the Lord to prepare his ways;
To give knowledge of salvation unto his people : for the remission of their sins,
Through the tender mercy of our God : whereby the day-spring from on high hath visited us;
To give light to them that sit in darkness, and in the shadow of death : and to guide our feet into the way of peace.
Glory be to the Father, and to the Son : and to the Holy Ghost;
As it was in the beginning, is now, and ever shall be : world without end. Amen.
Benedictus, Luke 1:68-79, The Book of Common Prayer

Lord, now lettest thou thy servant depart in peace : according to thy word.
For mine eyes have seen : thy salvation,
Which thou hast prepared : before the face of all people;
To be a light to lighten the Gentiles : and to be the glory of thy people Israel.
Nunc dimittis, Luke 2:29-32, Book of Common Prayer

I thank you, Father, Lord of heaven and earth, because you have hidden these things from the wise and the intelligent and have revealed them to infants; yes, Father, for such was your gracious will.
Luke 10:21 NRSV

Father, if you are willing, remove this cup from me; yet, not my will but yours be done.
Luke 22:42 NRSV

Father, I thank you for having heard me. I knew that you always hear me, but I have said this for the sake of the crowd standing here, so that they may believe that you sent me.
John 11:41-42 NRSV

Father, glorify your name.
John 12:28 NRSV

The prayers of Jesus on the cross
Father, forgive them; for they know not what they do.
Luke 23:34 KJV

My God, my God, why hast thou forsaken me?
Matthew 27:46 KJV

It is finished.
John 19:30 KJV

Father, into thy hands I commend my spirit.
Luke 23:46 KJV

And now, Lord, look at their threats, and grant to your servants to speak your word with all boldness, while you stretch out your hand to heal, and signs and wonders

are performed through the name of your holy servant Jesus.
Acts 4:29-30 NRSV

Lord Jesus, receive my spirit. ... Lord, do not hold this sin against them.
Stephen, as he was being martyred.
Acts 7:59-60 NRSV

Now may the God of peace, who brought back from the dead our Lord Jesus, the great shepherd of the sheep, by the blood of the eternal covenant, make you complete in everything good so that you may do his will, working among us that which is pleasing in his sight, through Jesus Christ, to whom be the glory for ever and ever. Amen.
Hebrews 13:20-21 NRSV

Blessed be the God and Father of our Lord Jesus Christ! By his great mercy we have been born anew to a living hope through the resurrection of Jesus Christ from the dead, and to an inheritance which is imperishable, undefiled, and unfading, kept in heaven for you, who by God's power are guarded through faith for a salvation ready to be revealed in the last time.
1 Peter 1:3-5 NRSV

Now to him who is able to keep you from falling, and to make you stand without blemish in the presence of his glory with rejoicing, to the only God our Savior, through Jesus Christ our Lord, be glory, majesty, power, and authority, before all time and now and for ever. Amen.
Jude 24-25 NRSV

To him who loves us and freed us from our sins by his blood, and made us to be a kingdom, priests serving his God and Father, to him be glory and dominion for ever and ever. Amen.
Revelation 1:5-6 NRSV

You are worthy, our Lord and God, to receive glory and honor and power, for you created all things, and by your will they existed and were created.
Revelation 4:11 NRSV

Amen! Blessing and glory and wisdom and thanksgiving and honor and power and might be to our God for ever and ever! Amen.
Revelation 7:12 NRSV

Great and amazing are your deeds,
Lord God the Almighty!
Just and true are your ways,
King of the nations!
Lord, who will not fear
and glorify your name?
For you alone are holy.
All nations will come
and worship before you.
for your judgements have been revealed.
Revelation 15:3-4 NRSV

Prayers, Bible, Prayers of Paul

What am I to do, Lord?
Acts 22:10 NRSV

O the depth of the riches and wisdom and knowledge of God! How unsearchable are his judgements and how inscrutable his ways! "For who has known the mind of the Lord? Or who has been his counselor?"
"Or who has given a gift to him,
to receive a gift in return?"
For from him and through him and to him are all things. To him be the glory for ever. Amen.
Romans 11:33-36 NRSV

May the God of hope fill you with all joy and peace in believing, so that you may abound in hope by the power of the Holy Spirit.
Romans 15:13 NRSV

Blessed be the God and Father of our Lord Jesus Christ, the Father of mercies and the God of all consolation, who consoles us in all our affliction, so that we may be able to console those who are in any affliction with the consolation with which we ourselves are consoled by God.
2 Corinthians 1:3-4 NRSV

The grace of the Lord Jesus Christ, the love of God, and the communion of the

Holy Spirit be with all of you.
2 Corinthians 13:13 NRSV

Grace to you and peace from God our
Father and the Lord Jesus Christ, who gave
himself for our sins to set us free from the
present evil age, according to the will of
our God and Father, to whom be the glory
for ever and ever. Amen.
Galatians 1:3-4 NRSV

Blessed be the God and Father of our Lord
Jesus Christ, who has blessed us in Christ
with every spiritual blessing in the heavenly
places, just as he chose us in Christ before
the foundation of the world to be holy and
blameless before him in love.
Ephesians 1:3-4 NRSV

Now may our God and Father himself and
our Lord Jesus direct our way to you.
1 Thessalonians 3:11 NRSV

May the God of peace himself sanctify you
entirely; and may your spirit and soul and
body be kept sound and blameless at the
coming of our Lord Jesus Christ.
1 Thessalonians 5:23 NRSV

Now may our Lord Jesus Christ himself and
God our Father, who loved us and through
grace gave us eternal comfort and good
hope, comfort your hearts and strengthen
them in every good work and word.
2 Thessalonians 2:16-17 NRSV

Prayers, Bible prayers, short
Speak, for your servant is listening.
Samuel, 1 Samuel 3:10 NRSV

Let the words of my mouth and the
meditation of my heart be acceptable to
you, O LORD, my rock and my redeemer.
Psalm 19:14 NRSV

Wait for the Lord; be strong, and let your
heart take courage; wait for the LORD!
Psalm 27:14 NRSV

O send out your light and your truth;
let them lead me;

let them bring me to your holy hill
and to your dwelling.
Psalm 43:3 NRSV

O God, you know my folly; the wrongs I
have done are not hidden from you.
Psalm 69:5 NRSV

Be pleased, O God, to deliver me.
O Lord, make haste to help me!
Psalm 70:1 NRSV

Will you not revive us again,
so that your people may rejoice in you?
Psalm 85:6 NRSV

Bless the Lord, O my soul,
and all that is within me,
bless his holy name.
Psalm 103:1 NRSV

Lord, save me!
Peter, Matthew 14:30 NRSV

Lord, help me.
A Canaanite woman, Matthew 15:25 NRSV

I believe, help my unbelief!
Father of boy possessed by an unclean spirit,
Mark 9:24 NRSV

Here am I, the servant of the Lord; let it be
with me according to your word.
Mary, Luke 1:38 NRSV

God, be merciful to me, a sinner!
Praying tax-collector, Luke 18:13 NRSV

Jesus, remember me when you come into
your kingdom.
Penitent dying thief, Luke 23.42

My Lord and my God!
Thomas, John 20:28 NRSV

Come, Lord Jesus!
Revelation 22.20

The grace of the Lord Jesus be with all the
saints. Amen.
Revelation 22:20 NRSV

Prayers, Blessings

People were bringing little children to him [Jesus] in order that he might touch them; and the disciples spoke sternly to them. But when Jesus saw this, he was indignant and said to them, "Let the children come to me; do not stop them; for it is to such as these that the kingdom of God belongs. Truly I tell you, whoever does not receive the kingdom of God as a little child will never enter it." And he took them up in his arms, laid his hands on them, and blessed them.
The Bible, Mark 10.13-16 NRSV

May God the Father bless us, may Christ take care of us; the Holy Spirit enlighten us all the days of our life. The Lord our defender and keeper of body and soul, both now and for ever, to the ages of ages.
Aedelwald

The everlasting Father bless us with his blessing everlasting.
The Primer, 1559

God bless all those that I love;
God bless all those that love me.
God bless all those that love those that I love
And all those that love those that love me.
From an old New England sampler

To the Holy Spirit who sanctifies us, with the Father who made and created us, and the Son who redeemed us, be given all honour and glory, world without end.
Thomas Cranmer

Bless all who worship thee,
From the rising of the sun
Unto the going down of the same.
Of thy goodness, give us;
With thy love, inspire us;
By thy spirit, guide us;
By thy power, protect us;
In thy mercy, receive us,
Now and always.
Fifth century

Unto God's gracious mercy and protection we commit you. The Lord bless you and keep you. The Lord make his face shine

upon you, and be gracious to you. The Lord lift his countenance upon you, and give you peace.
The Aaronic blessing, Numbers 6.24-26

May the grace of Christ our Saviour,
And the Father's boundless love,
With the Holy Spirit's favour,
Rest upon us from above.
John Newton

Son of God, Lord Jesus Christ, crucified on a cross for us and raised up from the grave, to you we pray. Receive us into your eternal church and keep us always. In the light of your Word, with your Holy Spirit, guide us.
Philip Melanchthon

May God, the Lord, bless us with all heavenly benediction, and make us pure and holy in his sight.
May the riches of his glory abound in us.
May he instruct us with the word of truth, inform us with the gospel of salvation and enrich us with his love, through Jesus Christ, our Lord.
Gelasian Sacramentary

The grace of God the Father and the peace of our Lord Jesus Christ, through the fellowship of the Holy Spirit, dwell with us for ever.
John Calvin

May the eternal God bless and keep us, guard our bodies, save our souls, direct our thoughts, and bring us safe to the heavenly country, our eternal home, where Father, Son and Holy Spirit ever reign, one God for ever and ever.
Sarum Breviary

The almighty God, Father of our Lord and Saviour, Jesus Christ, mercifully protect you, strengthen you, and guide you.
Philip Melanchthon

May the love of the Lord Jesus draw us to himself;
may the power of the Lord Jesus strengthen us in his service;

may the joy of the Lord Jesus fill our
souls.
May the blessing of God almighty, the
Father, the Son, and the Holy Spirit, be
among you and remain with you always.
After William Temple

The great Bishop of our souls, Jesus our
Lord, so strengthen and assist your
troubled hearts with the mighty comfort of
the Holy Spirit, that neither earthly
tyrants, nor worldly torments, may have
power to drive you from the hope and
expectation of that kingdom, which for the
elect was prepared from the beginning, by
our heavenly Father, to whom be all praise
and honour, now and ever.
John Knox

Go forth into the world in peace;
be of good courage;
hold fast that which is good;
render to no man evil for evil;
strengthen the fainthearted;
support the weak;
help the afflicted;
honour all men;
love and serve the Lord,
rejoicing in the power of the Holy Spirit.
And the blessing of God Almighty, the
Father, the Son, and the Holy Ghost, be
upon you, and remain with you for ever.
The Proposed Prayer Book, 1928

May the almighty God, Father of our
Saviour Jesus Christ, who through his
gospel is gathering an eternal church
among men and women, strengthen you in
body and soul, and graciously keep and
guide you, world without end.
Philip Melanchthon

May the Almighty Lord, who bore the
reproach of the cross, bless all this family
present here. Amen.
May he, who hung on the tree, himself
lead us to the heavenly kingdom. Amen.
May he place us at the right hand of the
Father, who was made the cause of our
peace. Amen.
Through the mercy of our God, who is

blessed and reigns, and governs all things,
world without end.
Mozarabic Breviary

The blessing of the Lord rest and remain
upon all his people,
in every land and of every tongue;
the Lord meet in mercy all who seek him;
the Lord comfort all who suffer and
mourn;
the Lord hasten his coming,
and give us his people peace by all means.
Handley Moule

The peace of God, which passeth all
understanding, keep your hearts and
minds in the knowledge and love of God,
and of his Son Jesus Christ our Lord: and
the blessing of God Almighty, the Father,
the Son, and the Holy Ghost, be amongst
you and remain with you always.
*The Book of Common Prayer, The Order for
Holy Communion*

God the Father bless me;
Jesus Christ defend and keep me;
the power of the Holy Spirit enlighten me
and sanctify me,
this night and for ever.
The Treasury of Devotion

The mighty God of Jacob be with you to
defeat his enemies, and give you the favour
of Joseph.
The wisdom and spirit of Stephen be with
your heart and with your mouth, and
teach your lips what to say, and how to
answer all things.
He is our God, if we despair in ourselves
and trust in him; and his is the glory.
William Tyndale

The Lord bless you and keep you.
May he show his face to you and have
mercy on you.
May he turn his countenance to you and
give you peace.
The Lord bless you, Brother Leo.
Francis of Assisi
*Francis' blessing to Brother Leo, which Brother
Leo always carried with him.*

Blessing and honour, thanksgiving and praise
more than we can utter unto thee,
O most adorable Trinity, Father, Son and Holy Ghost,
by all angels, all men, all creatures
for ever and ever. Amen and Amen.
Thomas Ken

May the blessing of God Almighty, the Father, the Son, and the Holy Spirit, rest on us and on all our work and worship done in his name. May he give us light to guide us, courage to support us, and love to unite us, now and for evermore.
Author unknown

Go in peace; and may the blessing of God the Father, the Son, and the Holy Spirit rest on you and remain with you, this day (night) and for evermore.
Author unknown

May the road rise to meet you,
may the wind be always at your back,
may the sun shine warm upon your face,
may the rain fall softly on your fields,
may God hold you in the hollow of his hand.
Traditional Gaelic prayer

May the love of the Father enfold us,
the wisdom of the Son enlighten us,
the fire of the Spirit inflame us;
and may the blessing of the triune God rest on us,
and abide with us,
now and evermore.
Author unknown

Prayers, Doxologies

To God the Father, who has made us and all the world;
to God the Son, who has redeemed us and all mankind;
to God the Holy Spirit, who sanctifies us and all the elect people of God;
to the one living and true God be all glory for ever and ever.
Author unknown

Bless us, O God the Father, who has created us.
Bless us, O God the Son, who has redeemed us.
Bless us, O God the Holy Spirit, who sanctifies us.
O Blessed Trinity, keep us in body, soul, and spirit to everlasting life.
Author unknown

To God the Father, who first loved us, and made us accepted in the Beloved;
to God the Son, who loved us, and washed us from our sins in his own blood;
to God the Holy Ghost, who sheds the love of God abroad in our hearts:
to the one true God be all love and all glory, for time and eternity.
Thomas Ken

Praise God, from whom all blessings flow;
Praise him, all creatures here below;
Praise him above ye heavenly host;
Praise Father, Son and Holy Ghost.
Thomas Ken

Prayers, Family

HOW A FATHER SHOULD TEACH HIS HOUSEHOLD TO CONDUCT MORNING AND EVENING DEVOTIONS.
Morning Devotions
As soon as you get out of bed in the morning, you should bless
yourself with the sign of the Holy Cross and say:

May the will of God, the Father, the Son and the Holy Spirit be done! Amen.

Then, kneeling or standing, say the creed and pray the Lord's Prayer. If you wish, you may then pray this little prayer as well:

My Heavenly Father, I thank You, through Jesus Christ, Your beloved Son, that You kept me safe from all evil and danger last night. Save me, I pray, today as well, from every evil and sin, so that all I do and the way that I live will please you. I put myself in your care, body and soul and all that I have. Let Your holy angels be with me, so that the evil enemy will not gain power over me. Amen.

After that, with joy go about your work and perhaps sing a song inspired by the Ten Commandments or your own thoughts.

Luther's Little Instruction Book
(The Small Catechism of Martin Luther)
Appendix 1: Devotions
The Evening Devotions

When you go to bed in the evening, you should bless yourself with the sign of the Holy Cross and say:

May the will of God, the Father, the Son and the Holy Spirit be done! Amen.

Then, kneeling or standing, say the creed and pray the Lord's Prayer. If you wish, then you may pray this little prayer as well:

My Heavenly Father, I thank You, through Jesus Christ, Your beloved Son, that You have protected me, by Your grace. Forgive, I pray, all my sins and the evil I have done. Protect me, by Your grace, tonight. I put myself in your care, body and soul and all that I have. Let Your holy angels be with me, so that the evil enemy will not gain power over me. Amen.

After this, go to sleep immediately with joy.

Luther's Little Instruction Book
(The Small Catechism of Martin Luther)

Famous prayers

I asked God for strength that I might achieve;
I was made weak that I might learn humbly to obey.
I asked for help that I might do greater things;
I was given infirmity that I might do better things.
I asked for riches that I might be happy;
I was given poverty that I might be wise.
I asked for all things that I might enjoy life;
I was given life that I might enjoy all things.

I was given nothing I asked for;
But everything that I had hoped for.
Despite myself, my prayers were answered;
I am among all men most richly blessed.
An unknown Confederate soldier

The Lord is not my servant, I am His. Let my prayers reflect this.
Author unknown

O direct my life towards thy commandments,
Hallow my soul,
purify my body,
correct my thoughts,
cleanse my desires,
soul, and body, mind and spirit,
heart and reins.
Renew me thoroughly, O God,
for, if Thou wilt, Thou canst.
Bishop Lancelot Andrewes

O Lord our God, grant us grace to desire Thee with our whole heart; that, so desiring, we may seek, and seeking find Thee; and so finding Thee may love Thee; and loving Thee, may hate those sins from which Thou hast redeemed us.
Anselm

Almighty God, unto whom all hearts are open, all desires known, and from whom no secrets are hid: Cleanse the thoughts of our hearts by the inspiration of thy Holy Spirit, that we may perfectly love thee, and worthily magnify thy holy Name; through Jesus Christ our Lord. Amen.
Book of Common Prayer

We do not presume to come to this thy Table, O merciful Lord, trusting in our own righteousness, but in thy manifold and great mercies. We are not worthy so much as to gather up the crumbs under thy Table. But thou art the same Lord whose property is always to have mercy. Grant us therefore, gracious Lord, so to eat the flesh of thy dear Son Jesus Christ, and to drink his blood, that we may evermore dwell in him, and he in us. Amen.
Book of Common Prayer

Grant, Almighty God, as at the present time thou dost deservedly chastise us for our sins, according to the example of thine ancient people, that we may turn our face to thee with true penitence and humility: May we throw ourselves suppliantly and prostrately before thee; and, despairing of ourselves, place our only hope in thy pity which thou hast promised.
John Calvin

Keep us, Lord, so awake in the duties of our callings that we may sleep in Thy peace and wake in Thy glory.
John Donne

Praise to the Trinity
Praise to the Trinity
Who is sound and life.
Creator and sustainer
Of all beings.
The angels praise You,
Who in the splendor
Of your hidden mysteries
Pour out life abundant.
Hildegard of Bingen

I have now spent fifty-five years in resolving: having, from the earliest time almost that I can remember, been forming plans of a better life. I have done nothing. The need of doing, therefore, is pressing, since the time of doing is short. O GOD, grant me to resolve aright, and to keep my resolutions, for Jesus Christ's sake. Amen.
Samuel Johnson

If this obstacle is from Thee, Lord, I accept it; but if it is from Satan, I refuse him and all his works in the name of Calvary.
Isobel Kuhn

Do not always scrupulously confine yourself to certain rules, or particular forms of devotion, but act with a general confidence in God, with love and humility
Brother Lawrence

Oh, Lord God, Thou hast made me a pastor and teacher in the Church. Thou seest how unfit I am to administer rightly this great and responsible Office; and had I been without Thy aid and counsel I would surely have ruined it all long ago. Therefore, do I invoke Thee. How gladly do I desire to yield and consecrate my heart and mouth to this ministry! I desire to teach the congregation. I, too, desire ever to learn and keep Thy Word my constant companion, and to meditate thereupon earnestly. Use me as Thy instrument in Thy service, Only do not Thou forsake me, for if I am left to myself, I will certainly bring it all to destruction. Amen.
Martin Luther. Luther's prayer when he was ordained

Grant that I may not pray alone with the mouth; help me that I may pray from the depths of my heart.
Martin Luther

Thanks be to thee, O Lord Jesus Christ, for all the benefits which Thou hast given us; for all the pains and insults which Thou hast borne for us. O most merciful redeemer, friend and brother, may we know thee more clearly, love Thee more dearly, and follow Thee more nearly; For Thine own sake.
St. Richard of Chichester

The peace of God, which passeth all understanding, keep your hearts and minds in the knowledge and love of God, and of his Son Jesus Christ our Lord: and the blessing of God Almighty, the Father, the Son, and the Holy Ghost, be amongst you and remain with you always. Amen.
The Book of Common Prayer, The Order for Holy Communion

Lord Jesus Christ, Son of God, have mercy on me, a sinner.
The Jesus Prayer.

EASTER WINGS
Lord, who createdst man in wealth and store,
Though foolishly he lost the same,
Decaying more and more,
Till he became
Most poor:

With thee
Oh let me rise
As larks, harmoniously,
And sing this day thy victories:
Then shall the fall farther the flight in me.
My tender age in sorrow did begin:
And still with sickness and shame
Thou did'st so punish sin,
That I became
Most thin
With thee
Let me combine,
And feel this day the victory,
For, if I imp my wing on thine,
Affliction shall advance the flight in me.

George Herbert, The Temple

Lord, make me an instrument of your peace.
Where there is hatred, let me sow love,
where there is injury, pardon,
where there is doubt, faith,
where there is despair, hope,
where there is darkness, light,
where there is sadness, joy.
O Divine Master, grant that we may not so
much seek
to be consoled as to console,
not so much to be understood as to
understand,
not so much to be loved as to love. For it is
in giving that we receive,
it is in pardoning that we are pardoned,
it is in dying that we are born to eternal life.

Attributed to Francis of Assisi

We beg you, Lord, to help and defend us.
Deliver the oppressed,
have compassion on the despised,
raise the fallen,
reveal yourself to the needy,
heal the sick,
bring back those who have strayed from you,
feed the hungry,
lift up the weak,
remove the prisoners' chains.
May every nation come to know that you
are God alone,
that Jesus is your Son,
that we are your people, the sheep of your
pasture.

Clement of Rome

O Lord, convert the world – and begin
with me.

Chinese student's prayer

Be present, O merciful God, and protect
us through the silent hours of this night, so
that we who are wearied by the changes
and chances of this fleeting world, may
repose on your eternal changelessness;
through Jesus Christ our Lord.

Office of Compline

Save us, Lord, while waking, and guard us
while sleeping, that awake we may watch
with Christ, and asleep we may rest in peace.

Office of Compline

O God, from whom all holy desires, all
good counsels, and all just works do
proceed: Give unto thy servants that peace
which the world cannot give; that both our
hearts may be set to obey thy
commandments, and also that by thee we,
being defended from the fear of our
enemies, may pass our time in rest and
quietness; through the merits of Jesu
Christ our Saviour.

*The Book of Common Prayer, 1549, Evensong,
Second Collect*

My dearest Lord,
be thou a bright flame before me,
be thou a guiding star above me,
be thou a smooth path beneath me,
be thou a kindly shepherd behind me,
today – tonight – and forever.

Columba

O Lord, support us all the day long, until
the shadows lengthen, and the evening
comes, and the busy world is hushed, and
the fever of life is over, and our work is
done. Then, Lord, in your mercy grant us
a safe lodging, and a holy rest, and peace at
the last; through Jesus Christ our Lord.

*Used by J.H. Newman. Based on a 16th century
prayer*

O Lord, forgive what I have been, sanctify
what I am, and order what I shall be.

Author unknown

Our Father, which art in heaven, Hallowed be thy Name. Thy kingdom come. Thy will be done in earth, As it is in heaven. Give us this day our daily bread. And forgive us our trespasses, As we forgive them that trespass against us. And lead us not into temptation, But deliver us from evil. For thine is the kingdom, The power, and the glory, For ever and ever. Amen.
Book of Common Prayer

Grant to us your servants: to our God – a heart of flame; to our fellow men – a heart of love; to ourselves – a heart of steel.
Augustine of Hippo

God, give us the serenity to accept what cannot be changed;
give us the courage to change what should be changed;
give us the wisdom to distinguish one from the other.
Attributed to Reinhold Neibuhr, also known as The Serenity Prayer

Let nothing disturb you
nothing frighten you,
all things are passing;
patient endurance
attains all things.
One whom God possesses   lacks nothing,
for God alone suffices.
Bookmark of Teresa of Avila

Dearest Lord, teach me to be generous;
teach me to serve you as you deserve;
to give and not to count the cost,
to fight and not to heed the wounds,
to toil and not to see for rest,
to labour and not to seek reward,
except to know that I do your will.
Ignatius Loyola

Almighty God, in whom we live and move and have our being, you have made us for yourself and our hearts are restless until in you they find their rest. Grant us purity of heart and strength of purpose, that no selfish passion may hinder us from knowing your will, no weakness from

doing it; but that in your light we may see light clearly, and in your service we may find our perfect freedom; through Jesus Christ our Lord.
Augustine of Hippo

Grant me, I beseech thee, almighty and merciful God, fervently to desire, wisely to search out, truly to acknowledge, and perfectly to fulfil, all that is well-pleasing to thee. Order thou my worldly condition to the honour and glory of thy name; and of all that thou requirest me to do, grant me the knowledge, the desire, and the ability, that I may so fulfil it as I ought, and as is expedient for the welfare of my soul
Thomas Aquinas

O Lord, thou knowest how busy I must be this day. If I forget thee, do not thou forget me.
General Lord Astley, before the battle of Edgehill

Thanks be to you, my Lord Jesus Christ,
for all the benefits you have won for me.
For all the pains and insults you have borne for me.
O most merciful Redeemer, Friend, and Brother,
may I know you more clearly,
love you more dearly,
and follow you more nearly,
day by day.
Richard of Chichester

Father,
give us wisdom to perceive you,
intellect to understand you,
diligence to seek you,
patience to wait for you,
eyes to behold you,
a heart to meditate on you
and a life to proclaim you,
through the power of the Spirit
of our Lord Jesus Christ.
Benedict

O Lord, remember not only the men and women of good will, but also those of ill will. But do not remember all the suffering they have inflicted on us; remember the

fruits we have brought, thanks to this
suffering – our comradeship, our loyalty,
our courage, our generosity, the greatness
of heart which has grown out of all this,
and when they come to judgment let all
the fruits which we have borne be their
forgiveness.
*Prayer found near the body of a dead child in
the Revensbruck concentration camp*

Blessing and honour, thanksgiving and
praise
more than we can utter,
more than we can conceive,
be unto you, O most holy and glorious
Trinity,
Father, Son and Holy Spirit,
by all angels, all people, all creatures
for ever and ever. Amen and Amen.
Lancelot Andrewes

I bind to myself the name,
the strong name of the Trinity;
by invocation of the same,
The Three in One, and One in Three.
Of whom all nature has creation;
eternal Father, Spirit, Word:
Praise to the Lord of my salvation,
Salvation is of Christ the Lord.
St Patrick

Christ be with me, Christ within me,
Christ behind me, Christ before me,
Christ beside me, Christ to win me,
Christ to comfort and restore me,
Christ beneath me, Christ above me,
Christ in quiet, Christ in danger,
Christ in hearts of all that love me,
Christ in mouth of friend and stranger.
The Breastplate of St Patrick

Lord Jesus Christ, you said that you are the
Way, the Truth, and the Life.
Help us not to stray from you, for you are
the Way;
nor to distrust you, for you are the Truth;
nor to rest on any other than you, as you
are the Life.
You have taught us what to believe, what
to do, what to hope, and where to take our
rest.

Give us grace to follow you, the Way, to
learn from you, the Truth, and live in you,
the Life.
Desiderius Erasmus

Soul of Christ, sanctify me.
Body of Christ, save me.
Blood of Christ, inebriate me.
Water from the side of Christ, wash me.
Passion of Christ, strengthen me.
O good Jesus, hear me.
Hide me within your wounds
and never allow me to be separated from
you.
From the wicked enemy defend me.
In the hour of my death call me,
and bid me come to you,
so that with your saints I may praise you
for ever and ever.
The "Anima Christi", fourteenth century

God be in my head,
and in my understanding;
God be in my eyes,
and in my looking;
God be in my mouth,
and in my speaking;
God be in my heart,
and in my thinking;
God be at my end,
and at my departing.
Book of Hours, 1514

We praise thee, O God : we acknowledge
thee to be the Lord.
All the earth doth worship thee : the
Father everlasting.
To thee all Angels cry aloud : the Heavens,
and all the Powers therein.
To thee Cherubim and Seraphim :
continually do cry,
Holy, Holy, Holy : Lord God of Sabaoth;
Heaven and earth are full of the Majesty :
of thy glory.
The glorious company of the Apostles :
praise thee.
The goodly fellowship of the Prophets :
praise thee.
The noble army of Martyrs : praise thee.
The holy Church throughout all the world
: doth acknowledge thee;

The Father : of an infinite Majesty;
Thine honourable, true : and only Son;
Also the Holy Ghost : the Comforter.
Thou art the King of Glory : O Christ.
Thou art the everlasting Son : of the Father.
When thou tookest upon thee to deliver man : thou didst not abhor the Virgin's womb.
When thou hadst overcome the sharpness of death : thou didst open the Kingdom of Heaven to all believers.
Thou sittest at the right hand of God : in the glory of the Father.
We believe that thou shalt come : to be our Judge.
We therefore pray thee, help thy servants : whom thou hast redeemed with thy precious blood.
Make them to be numbered with thy Saints : in glory everlasting.
O Lord, save thy people : and bless thine heritage.
Govern them : and lift them up for ever.
Day by day : we magnify thee;
And we worship thy Name : ever world without end.
Vouchsafe, O Lord : to keep us this day without sin.
O Lord, have mercy upon us : have mercy upon us.
O Lord, let thy mercy lighten upon us : as our trust is in thee.
O Lord, in thee have I trusted : let me never be confounded.
Te Deum Laudamus, fourth/fifth century, The Book of Common Prayer

I rise today with the power of God to guide me,
the might of God to uphold me,
the wisdom of God to teach me,
the eye of God to watch over me,
the ear of God to hear me,
the word of God to give me speech,
the hand of God to protect me,
the path of God to lie before me,
the shield of God to shelter me,
the host of God to defend me
against the snares of the devil and the temptations of the world,
against every man who meditates injury to me,
whether far or near.
The breastplate of St Patrick

Almighty God, who hast given us grace at this time with one accord to make our common supplications unto thee; and dost promise, that when two or three are gathered together in thy Name thou wilt grant their requests; Fulfil now, O Lord, the desires and petitions of thy servants, as may be most expedient for them; granting us in this world knowledge of thy truth, and in the world to come life everlasting. Amen.
John Chrysostom

Prayers, Short
Grace be with you.
The Bible, 2 Timothy 4.22

Let this day, O Lord, add some knowledge or good deed to yesterday.
Lancelot Andrewes

Lord, give me what you are requiring of me.
Augustine of Hippo

You have made us for yourself and our hearts are restless until in you they find their rest.
Augustine of Hippo

O God, give me strength.
Gladys Aylward

Help me, O God, like Jesus to be growing all the time.
William Barclay

O God, keep me from being difficult to live with.
William Barclay

Protect me, dear Lord;
My boat is so small,
And your sea is so big.
Breton fisherman's prayer

Let our chief goal, O God, be your glory,
and to enjoy you for ever.
John Calvin

Lord, let your glory be my goal, your word
my rule, and then you will be done.
King Charles I

Change the world, O Lord, beginning
with me.
A Chinese student

Glory to God for all things.
John Chrysostom

O God, make us children of quietness and
heirs of peace.
Clement of Rome

O Lord, never allow us to think we can
stand by ourselves and not need you, our
greatest need.
John Donne

My God and My All! The Meditation
Prayer of St. Francis of Assisi:

Teach me to pray. Pray yourself in me.
F. Fénelon

Lord Jesus Christ, Son of God, have mercy
on me, a sinner.
The Jesus Prayer.
The Eastern Orthodox Church teaches that this
prayer is to be said many times regularly during the
day.

Lord, make me according to your heart.
Brother Lawrence

Lord, give us faith that right makes
might.
Abraham Lincoln

Lord, make me see your glory in every
place.
Michelangelo

The things, good Lord, that we pray for,
give us the grace to labor for.
Thomas More

I ask not to see; I ask not to know; I ask
only to be used.
J.H. Newman

O God, help us not to despise or oppose
what we do not understand.
William Penn

Teach us to pray often, that we may pray
oftener.
Jeremy Taylor

Pray God, keep us simple.
W.M. Thackeray

Lord, make your will our will in all things.
Charles Vaughan

Jesus, strengthen my desire to work and
speak and think for you.
John Wesley

O Lord, let us not live to be useless, for
Christ's sake.
John Wesley

Prayers, Written
So many confess their weakness, in
denying to confess it, who, refusing to be
beholden to a set form of prayer, prefer to
say nonsense, rather than nothing, in their
extempore expressions. More modesty, and
no less piety, it had been for such men to
have prayed longer with set forms that they
might pray better without them.
Thomas Fuller

Written forms of prayer are not only useful
and proper, but indispensably necessary to
begin with.
Hannah More

Prayers of the famous

Lord, give us faith that right makes might.
Abraham Lincoln

Lord, make me see your glory in every place.
Michelangelo

O Lord my God, I have hope in thee;
O my dear Jesus, set me free.
Though hard the chains that fasten me
And sore my lot, yet I long for thee.
I languish and groaning bend my knee,
Adoring, imploring, O set me free.
Mary Queen of Scots, on the eve of her execution

Strengthen us, O God, to relieve the oppressed, to hear the groans of poor prisoners, to reform the abuses of all professions; that many be made not poor to make a few rich; for Jesus Christ's sake.
Oliver Cromwell

Go with each of us to rest; if any awake, temper them the dark hours of watching; and when the day returns, return to us, our sun and comforter, and call us up with morning faces and with morning hearts, eager to labor, eager to be happy, if happiness should be our portion, and if the day be marked for sorrow, strong to endure it.
R.L. Stevenson, written on the eve of his unexpected death

Make me remember, O God, that every day is Thy gift and ought to be used according to Thy command, through Jesus Christ our Lord.
Samuel Johnson

O Lord God, grant us always, whatever the world may say, to content ourselves with what you say, and to care only for your approval, which will outweigh all worlds; for Jesus Christ's sake.
General Charles Gordon

O Lord God, when Thou givest to Thy servants to endeavor any great matter, grant us also to know that it is not the beginning, but the continuing of the same to the end, until it be thoroughly finished, which yieldeth the true glory; through Him who for the finishing of Thy work laid down his life, our Redeemer, Jesus Christ.
Source unknown, based on a saying of Sir Francis Drake

Take from us, O God, all pride and vanity, all boasting and self-assertiveness, and give us the true courage that shows itself by gentleness; the true wisdom that shows itself by simplicity; and the true power that shows itself by modesty; through Jesus Christ our Lord.
Charles Kingsley

Grant, O Lord, that we may keep a constant guard on our thoughts and passions, that they may never lead us into sin; that we may live in perfect love with all humankind, in affection to those who love us, and in forgiveness to those, if any there are, who hate us. Give us good and virtuous friends. In the name of our blessed Lord and Savior Jesus Christ.
Warren Hastings

O my sweet Savior Christ, who in your undeserved love towards humankind so kindly suffered the painful death of the cross, do not allow me to be cold or lukewarm in love again towards you.
Thomas More

O Savior, pour upon me thy Spirit of meekness and love,
Annihilate the selfhood in me, be thou all my life.
William Blake

O merciful God, fill our hearts, we pray, with the graces of your Holy Spirit; with love, joy, peace, patience, gentleness, goodness, faithfulness, humility and self-control. O Lord, in confidence of your great mercy and goodness to all who truly repent and resolve to do better, I most humbly implore the grace and assistance of the Holy Spirit to enable me to become every day better.
Grant me the wisdom and understanding to know my duty, and the heart and will to do it.

Endue me, O Lord, with the true fear and love of you, and with a prudent zeal for your glory.
Increase in me the graces of charity and meekness, of truth and justice, of humility and patience, and a firmness of spirit to bear every condition with constancy of mind.
King William III

I beseech Thee, good Jesus, that as Thou hast graciously granted to me here on earth sweetly to partake of the words of Thy wisdom and knowledge, so Thou wilt vouchsafe that I may some time come to Thee, the fountain of all wisdom, and always appear before Thy face; who livest and reignest, world without end.
Venerable Bede

Merciful God, be thou now unto me a strong tower of defense. Give me grace to await thy leisure, and patiently to bear what you doest unto me, nothing doubting or mistrusting thy goodness towards me. Therefore do with me in all things as thou wilt: Only arm me, I beseech thee, with thy armor, that I may stand fast; above all things taking to me the shield of faith, praying always that I may refer myself wholly to thy will, being assuredly persuaded that all thou doest cannot but be well. And unto thee be all honor and glory.
Lady Jane Grey, before her execution

Give me my scallop-shell of quiet,
My staff of faith to walk upon,
My scrip of joy, immortal diet,
My bottle of salvation,
My gown of glory, hope's true gage;
And thus I'll take my pilgrimage.
Blood must be my body's balmer;
No other balm will there be given;
Whilst my soul, like quiet palmer,
Travelleth towards the land of heaven;
  Over the silver mountains,
  Where spring the nectar fountains:
    There will I kiss
    The bowl of bliss,
And drink mine everlasting fill
Upon every milken hill.
My soul will be a-dry before;

But, after, it will thirst no more.
From thence to heaven's Bribeless hall
Where no corrupted voices brawl,
No Conscience molten into gold,
Nor forged accusers bought and sold,
No cause deferred, nor vain spent journey,
For there Christ is the King's Attorney:
Who pleads for all without degrees,
And he hath Angels, but no fees.
When the grand twelve million Jury,
Of our sins with dreadful fury,
'Gainst our souls black verdicts give,
Christ pleads his death, and then we live,
Be thou my speaker, taintless pleader,
Unblotted Lawyer, true proceeder,
Thou movest salvation even for alms:
Not with a bribed Lawyer's palms.
And this is my eternal plea,
To him that made Heaven, Earth and Sea,
Seeing my flesh must die so soon,
And want a head to dine next noon,
Just at the stroke when my veins start and spread
Set on my soul an everlasting head.
Then am I ready like a palmer fit,
To tread those blest paths which before I writ.
Sir Walter Raleigh, written when he was a prisoner in the Tower of London, awaiting execution. The scallop-shell was a symbol of pilgrimage in the Middle Ages.

Almighty God, the Protector of all who trust in you, without whose grace nothing is strong, nothing is holy, increase and multiply on us your mercy, that through your holy inspiration we may think the things that are right and by your power may carry them out, through Jesus Christ our Lord.
Martin Luther

Almighty and most merciful Father, look down on us your unworthy servants through the mediation and merits of Jesus Christ, in whom only are you well pleased. Purify our hearts by your Holy Spirit, and as you add days to our lives, so good Lord, add repentance to our days; that when we have passed this mortal life we may be partakers of your everlasting kingdom;

through the merits of Jesus Christ our Lord.
King Charles I

Lord God Almighty, shaper and ruler of all
creatures, we pray that by your great mercy
and by the token of the holy cross you will
guide us to your will. Make our minds
steadfast, strengthen us against temptation,
and keep us from all unrighteousness.
Shield us against our enemies, seen and
unseen. Teach us to inwardly love you
before all things with a clean mind and a
clean body. For you are our Maker and
Redeemer, our help and comfort, our trust
and hope, for ever.
King Alfred

O Lord Jesus Christ, you have made me
and redeemed me and brought me to
where I now am: you know what you wish
to do with me; do with me according to
your will, for your tender mercies' sake.
King Henry VI

Our Father, here I am, at your disposal,
your child,
to use me to continue your loving the world,
by giving Jesus to me and through me,
to each other and to the world.
Let us pray for each other that we allow
Jesus to love in us
and through us with the love with which
his Father loves us.
Mother Teresa

Jesus, your light is shining within us,
let not my doubts and my darkness speak
to me;
Jesus, your light is shining within us,
let my heart always welcome your love.
Brother Roger

Teach me, my Lord Jesus, instruct me, that
I may learn from you what I ought to
teach about you.
William Laud

O Lord, I am yours. Do what seems good
in your sight, and give me complete
resignation to your will.
David Livingstone

In my Redeemer's name,
I give myself to thee;
And, all unworthy as I am,
My God will cherish me.
Anne Brontë

Give us grace, almighty Father, to address
you with all our hearts as well as with our
lips.
You are present everywhere: from you no
secrets can be hidden.
Teach us to fix our thoughts on you,
reverently and with love, so that our
prayers are not in vain, but are acceptable
to you, now and always, through Jesus
Christ our Lord.
Jane Austin

O almighty God, the searcher of all hearts,
who has declared that who draw near to
you with their lips when their hearts are far
from you are an abomination to you:
cleanse, we beseech you, the thoughts of
our hearts by the inspiration of your Holy
Spirit, that no wandering, vain, or idle
thoughts may put out of our minds that
reverence and godly fear that becomes all
those who come into your presence.
Jonathan Swift

Praying to saints
Of the Invocation of Saints.
The invocation of saints is also one of the
abuses of Antichrist conflicting with the
chief article, and destroys the knowledge of
Christ. Neither is it commanded nor
counseled, nor has it any example [or
testimony] in Scripture, and even though
it were a precious thing, as it is not [while,
on the contrary, it is a most harmful
thing], in Christ we have everything a
thousandfold better [and surer, so that we
are not in need of calling upon the saints].
And although the angels in heaven pray for
us (as Christ Himself also does), as also do
the saints on earth, and perhaps also in
heaven, yet it does not follow thence that
we should invoke and adore the angels and
saints, and fast, hold festivals, celebrate

Mass in their honor, make offerings, and establish churches, altars, divine worship, and in still other ways serve them, and regard them as helpers in need [as patrons and intercessors], and divide among them all kinds of help, and ascribe to each one a particular form of assistance, as the Papists teach and do. For this is idolatry, and such honor belongs alone to God. For as a Christian and saint upon earth you can pray for me, not only in one, but in many necessities. But for this reason I am not obliged to adore and invoke you, and celebrate festivals, fast, make oblations, hold masses for your honor [and worship], and put my faith in you for my salvation. I can in other ways indeed honor, love, and thank you in Christ. If now such idolatrous honor were withdrawn from angels and departed saints, the remaining honor would be without harm and would quickly be forgotten. For when advantage and assistance, both bodily and spiritual, are no more to be expected, the saints will not be troubled [the worship of the saints will soon vanish], neither in their graves nor in heaven. For without a reward or out of pure love no one will much remember, or esteem, or honor them [bestow on them divine honor].
Martin Luther

Preachers

He had nothing to say and said it endlessly.
Author unknown

Oh, if we did but study half as much to affect and amend our own hearts, as we do those of our hearers, it would not be with many of us as it is.
Richard Baxter

The test of a preacher is that his congregation goes away saying, not, "What a lovely sermon!" but, "I will do something."
Billy Graham

I believe that there are too many accommodating preachers ... Jesus Christ did not say, "Go into the world and tell the

world that it is quite right." The gospel is something completely different. In fact, it is directly opposed to the world.
C.S. Lewis

How is it that there are not many who are led by sermons to forsake open sin? Do you know what I think? That it is because preachers have too much worldly wisdom. They are not like the Apostles, flinging it all aside and catching fire with love of God; and so their flames give little heat.
Teresa of Avila

Preaching

For Christ did not send me to baptize, but to preach the gospel – not with words of human wisdom, lest the cross of Christ be emptied of its power.
The Bible, 1 Corinthians 1:17

For since in the wisdom of God the world through its wisdom did not know him, God was pleased through the foolishness of what was preached to save those who believe.
The Bible, 1 Corinthians 1:21

Until I come, devote yourself to the public reading of Scripture, to preaching and to teaching.
The Bible, 1 Timothy 4:13

Preach the Word; be prepared in season and out of season; correct, rebuke and encourage – with great patience and careful instruction.
The Bible, 2 Timothy 4:2

Sermonettes make Christianettes
Author unknown

He was a marvelous preacher. At the end of his sermon, there was a tremendous awakening.
Author unknown

Comfort the afflicted, and afflict the comfortable.
Author unknown
Probably first applied to newspapers, in the saying,

"The duty of a newspaper is to comfort the afflicted and afflict the comfortable."
The former Archbishop of Canterbury, Michael Ramsey, adapted this saying, as follows: "The duty of the church is to comfort the disturbed and to disturb the comfortable."

Preaching is the primary work of the Church.
Author unknown

A speech, to be immortal, need not be eternal.
Author unknown

It is a disgraceful and dangerous thing for an infidel to hear a Christian, while presumably giving the meaning of Holy Scripture, talking nonsense. If they find a Christian mistaken in a field which they themselves know well, and hear him maintaining his foolish opinions about the Scriptures how then are they going to believe those Scriptures in matters concerning the resurrection of the dead, the hope of eternal life, and the kingdom of heaven?
Augustine of Hippo

I preached as never sure to preach again, And as a dying man to dying men.
Richard Baxter

My Lord, I have nothing to do in this world, but to seek and serve thee; I have nothing to do with a heart and its affections but to breathe after thee; I have nothing to do with my tongue and pen, but to speak to thee, and for thee, and to publish thy glory and thy will.
Richard Baxter

It is a fearful thing to be an unsanctified professor, but much more to be an unsanctified preacher.
Richard Baxter

I argue for preaching that speaks to the whole person and to all of life.
Alan Boesak

Preaching is not the performance of an hour. It is the outflow of a life. It takes twenty years to make a sermon, because it takes twenty years to make a man.
E.M Bounds

The pulpits of the great cities in Christendom are filled largely by two classes of men, viz.: critics who believe too little to preach and men who fear the critics too much to preach.
Warren Akin Candler

I may not practice what I preach, but God forbid that I preach what I practice.
G.K. Chesterton

Preaching is not a natural but acquired power, though a man may reach a high standard, even then his power may forsake him unless he cultivate it by constant application and exercise.
John Chrysostom

Whoever does not find in holy Scriptures, and the works of the fathers, wherewithal to affect his hearers, is not worthy of mounting the pulpit.
Pope Clement XIV

No preacher can at one and the same time give the impression that he is clever and that Jesus is great and wonderful.
James Denney

Whenever you touch reality in the spiritual realm, you touch things that are so vital that any normal, healthy person cannot fail to be moved. If we have today such ministry in our churches that men and women cannot be moved, there is something wrong with our preaching.
Donald Gee

All that God does in time, or will do to all eternity, is only telling his people how much he loved them from everlasting.
John Gill

Preaching duty, is preaching the law; preaching the free grace of God, and salvation by Christ, is preaching the gospel; to say otherwise, is to turn the gospel into law and to blend and confound both together.

John Gill

When I go to hear a preacher preach, I may not agree with what he says, but I want him to believe it.

Goethe

The subject matter here is called "the word of God." Although that which is spoken by ministers is only the sound of a man's voice, yet that which true ministers of God preach in exercising their ministerial function is the word of God. Thus it is said of the apostles, "They spoke the word of God," Acts 4:31, and it is said of the people of Antioch, that "almost the whole city came together to hear the word of God," Acts 13:44.

That which ministers do or ought to preach is called the word of God in four respects.

1. In regard to the primary author of it, which is God. God did immediately inspire extraordinary ministers, and thereby informed them in his will. "For the prophecy came not in old time by the will of man, but holy men of God spoke as they were moved by the Holy Ghost," 2 Peter 1:21. Therefore they would commonly use these introductory phrases, "The word of the Lord," Hosea 1:1; "Thus says the Lord," Isa 7:7; and an apostle says, "I have received of the Lord, that which also I delivered unto you," 1 Cor. 11:23. As for ordinary ministers, they have God's word written and left upon record for their use, "For all Scripture is given by inspiration of God," 2 Tim. 3:16. They therefore that ground what they preach upon the Scripture, and deliver nothing but what is agreeable to it, preach the word of God.

2. In regard to the subject-matter which they preach, which is the will of God; as the apostle exhorts, to "understand what the will of the Lord is," Eph. 5:17, and to "prove what is that good, that acceptable,

and perfect will of God," Rom. 12:2.

3. In regard to the purpose of preaching, which is the glory of God, and making known "the manifold wisdom of God," Eph. 3:10.

4. In regard to the mighty effect and power of it, for preaching God's word is "the power of God unto salvation, Rom. 1:16. Preaching the word of God is "mighty through God to bring every thought to the obedience of Christ," 2 Cor. 10:4,5. For "the word of God is quick and powerful," etc., Heb. 4:12.

So close ought ministers to hold to God's word in their preaching, that they should not dare to swerve away from it in anything. The apostle pronounces a curse against him, whosoever he is, that shall preach any other word, Gal. 1:8,9. Therefore we have just cause to avoid such teachers as preach contrary to this doctrine, Rom. 16:17, 2 John 10. The whole body of Roman Catholicism is to be rejected for this reason. So are the manifold errors and heresies which have been broached in former ages, and in this our age. The feigning of new light and immediate inspiration in these days is a mere pretense.

William Gouge

It is God's word that does convert, quicken, comfort, and build up, or, on the other side, wound and beat down. What is the reason that there was so great an alteration made by the ministry of Christ and his disciples, by the apostles and others after them, indeed, by Luther, and other ministers of reformed churches? They did not preach traditions of elders like the scribes; nor men's inventions like the Roman Catholics do. They preached the pure word of God. The more purely God's word is preached, the more deeply it pierces and the more kindly it works.

William Gouge

A vacillating unbeliever has no respect for the man who lacks the courage to preach what he believes.

Billy Graham

A reporter once asked Billy Graham, "Why did you become an evangelist?"

"Let me ask you a question," replied Billy Graham. "Suppose I discovered a chemical which would make any person radiant and happy, giving meaning to his life here, and assure him of eternal life hereafter? Then suppose that I decided to keep that secret to myself. Wouldn't you say: "Billy, you're a criminal"? If I didn't know that faith in Christ is vital, transforming, that it gives direction to life and makes life worth living, I'd go back to my little North Carolina farm and spend the rest of my days tilling the soil. But I have seen too many lives untangled and rehabilitated, too many homes reconstructed, too many people find peace and joy through simple, humble confession and faith in Christ, ever to doubt that he is the answer. I am an evangelist for the same reason that the apostle Paul was: 'Woe unto me, if I preach not the gospel.'"

A survey was made of 4000 laymen in 114 evangelical churches across the U.S. They were asked, "Do you feel the preaching on Sunday relates to what's going on in your life?" Over 83% saw virtually no connection between what they heard on Sunday morning and what they faced on Monday morning.
Howard Hendricks

The worst speak something good; if all
  want sense,
God takes a text, and preacheth Pa-ti-ence.
George Herbert

An irritable man cannot preach.
Rabbi Hillel

The chief virtue that language can have is clearness, and nothing detracts from it so much as the use of unfamiliar words.
Hippocrates

Without preaching, which sows the word of God, the whole world would be barren and without fruit.
Humbert of Romans

When you are preaching in a church do not seek for applause but for lamentation; the tears of your hearers are your praise. A preacher's sermon should be based on his reading of Scripture.
Jerome

As a result [of the ignorance of Scripture], we have numberless ranters in our pulpits who do not deserve to be called preachers of the Word of God, as they seldom quote Scripture. They thus deprive the people of solid nourishment and leave them in ignorance of the science of salvation.
Bernard Lamy, 1699

Latimer! Latimer! Latimer! Be careful what you say. Henry the king is here.
[Pause] Latimer! Latimer! Latimer! Be careful what you say. The King of kings is here.
Hugh Latimer, preaching before Henry VIII

Teaching the Word is such an awesome task that a godly man shrinks from it. Nothing but the overwhelming sense of being called, and of compulsion, should ever lead anyone to preach.
Martyn Lloyd-Jones

Logic on fire = preaching.
Martyn Lloyd-Jones

A preacher must be both soldier and shepherd. He must nourish, defend, and teach; he must have teeth in his mouth, and be able to bite and fight.
Martin Luther

A good preacher should have these qualities and virtues.
1. He should teach systematically.
2. He should have a ready wit.
3. He should be eloquent.
4. He should have a good voice.
5. A good memory.
6. He should know when to stop.
7. He should be sure of his doctrine.
8. He should go out and grapple with body and blood, wealth and honor, in the word.

9. He should let himself be mocked and jeered at by everybody.
Martin Luther

I simply taught, preached, wrote God's word: otherwise I did nothing. And then, while I slept, or drank Wittenberg beer with my friend Philip or my friend Amsdorf, the word so greatly wakened the papacy that no prince or emperor ever inflicted such damage upon it. I did nothing. The word did it all.
Martin Luther

The preached gospel is offensive in all places of the world, rejected and condemned.
Martin Luther

If I profess with the loudest voice and clearest exposition every portion of God's word except precisely that little point which the world and the devil are attacking, I am not confessing Christ, however boldly I may be professing Christ. Where the battle rages, there the loyalty of the soldier is tested.
Martin Luther

Unless the gospel is preached with contemporary relevance it has not been preached.
Martin Luther

Men tell us that our preaching should be positive and not negative, that we can preach the truth without attacking error. But if we follow that advice we shall have to close our Bible and desert its teachings. The New Testament is a polemic book almost from beginning to end. It is when men have felt compelled to take a stand against error that they have risen to the really great heights in the celebration of the truth.
J. Gresham Machen

The truly educated man will speak to the understanding of the most unlearned man of his audience.
Karl G. Maeser

I do not think we should use television as the measure of all attention spans. I have heard people of all ages listen for hours as a speaker or two gives them stories, harangues, and marching orders for their various causes. And they would listen to every word. Could it be that the attention span problem for sermons is that the setting is too much like a television-viewing setting that calls for passivity? If the church became a movement again, and if we felt a life-and-death urgency about getting the message out and getting it right, we would probably not be discussing how long we should go on.
Martin E. Marty

Study universal holiness of life. Your whole usefulness depends on this, for your sermons last but an hour or two: your life preaches all week. If Satan can only make a covetous minister a lover of praise, of pleasure, of good eating, he has ruined your ministry. Give yourself to prayer, and get your texts, your thoughts, your words, from God.
Robert Murray M'Cheyne

How often do we preach sermons, or make addresses, and attend meetings, with no other thought than to secure the recognition and praise of those to whom we "minister".
F.B. Meyer

One lesson I learned that night is that I must preach to press Christ upon the people then and there, and try to bring them to a decision on the spot. Ever since that night I have determined to make more of Christ than in the past.
D.L. Moody
[Moody describing the fire which, by burning down the hall where he had just asked people to think about Christ, prevented them coming back with their decision.]

The first condition for powerful preaching is the presence in the Christian ministry of a commitment to sound learning and hard study.
Iain Murray

The gospel is not merely the doctrine of salvation as it lies in the holy Scripture, but that public and authoritative dispensation of this doctrine, which the Lord Jesus Christ has committed to his true ministers; who having been themselves, by the power of his grace, brought out of darkness into marvelous light, are by his Holy Spirit qualified and sent forth to declare to their fellow-sinners what they have seen, and felt, and tasted, of the word of life. Their commission is, to exalt the Lord alone, to stain the pride of all human glory. They are to set forth the evil and demerit of sin, the strictness, spirituality, and sanction of the law of God, the total apostasy of mankind; and from these premises to demonstrate the utter impossibility of a sinner's escaping condemnation by any works or endeavors of his own; and then to proclaim a full and free salvation from sin wrath, by faith in the name, blood, obedience, and mediation of God manifest in the flesh; together with a denunciation of eternal misery to all who shall finally reject the testimony which God has given of his Son. Though these several branches of the will of God respecting sinners, and other truths in connection with them, are plainly revealed and repeatedly inculcated (driven in) in the Bible; and though the Bible is to be found in almost every house, yet we see, in fact, it is a sealed book, little read, little understood, and therefore but little regarded, except in those places which the Lord is pleased to favor with ministers who can confirm them from their own experience, and who, by a sense of his constraining love, and the worth of souls, are animated to make the faithful discharge of their ministry the one great business of their lives: who aim not to possess the wealth, but to promote the welfare of their hearers; are equally regardless of the frowns or smiles of the world; and count not their lives dear, so that they may be wise and successful in winning souls to Christ.
John Newton

Preaching should break a hard heart, and heal a broken heart.
John Newton

A sermon is not made with an eye upon the sermon, but with both eyes upon the people and all the heart upon God.
John Owen

Christ had no interest in gathering vast crowds of professed adherents who would melt away as soon as they found out what following Him actually demanded of them. In our own presentation of Christ's gospel, therefore, we need to lay a similar stress on the cost of following Christ, and make sinners face it soberly before we urge them to respond to the message of free forgiveness. In common honesty, we must not conceal the fact that free forgiveness in one sense will cost everything.
J.I. Packer

He is the best speaker who can turn the ear into an eye.
Arabian proverb

Of late years, the Church has not succeeded very well in preaching Christ; she has preached Jesus, which is not quite the same thing.
Dorothy Sayers

Not a little preaching is much more imposition than exposition.
W. Graham Scroggie

All originality and no plagiarism makes for dull preaching.
C.H. Spurgeon

Certain earnest preachers are incessantly exciting the people but seldom, if ever, instructing them.

They carry much fire and very little light. A feather floats on the wind, but it has no inherent power to move. Consequently, when the gale is over, it falls to the ground. Such is the religion of excitement.

In contrast the eagle has life within itself, and its wings bear it aloft and onward whether the breeze favors it or not. Such is religion when sustained by a conviction of the truth.
C.H. Spurgeon

Whatever subject I preach, I do not stop until I reach the Savior, the Lord Jesus, for in Him are all things.

Charles Spurgeon

Only as the Spirit of God shall bless men by you, shall they receive a blessing through you.

C.H. Spurgeon

We shall not adjust our Bible to the age; but before we have done with it, by God's grace, we shall adjust the age to the Bible.

C.H. Spurgeon

There is a limit, for, "The Lord knoweth them that are His," but in the preaching of the gospel we are not bound by the decree which is secret, but by our marching orders, "Go ye into all the world, and preach the gospel to every creature; he that believeth and is baptized shall be saved." He who bade me preach to every creature did not bid me exempt one soul from my message.

C.H. Spurgeon

I believe Martin Luther would have faced the infernal fiend himself without a fear; and yet we have his own confession that his knees often knocked together when he stood up to preach. He trembled lest he should not be faithful to God's word. To preach the whole truth is an awful charge.

C.H. Spurgeon

The only power that is effectual for the highest design of preaching is the power which does not lie in your word nor in my word, but in THE WORD OF GOD! It is God's Word, not our comments on God's Word, which saves souls. Dear brethren, if you seek to do good in this world and want a powerful weapon to work with, stick to the gospel, the living gospel. There is power in the gospel of Christ Jesus our Lord to meet the sin and death of human nature. Nothing can convince of sin, reveal inability, nor reveal the sufficiency of Christ but the Word of God! "Where the word of the King is, there is power." Nothing can

resist it. The Word of God is that by which sin is slain and grace is born in the heart. It is the light that brings life with it. It brought us to Christ at the first, and it still leads us to look to Christ until we grow like Him. God's children are not sanctified by legal methods but by the Word.

C.H. Spurgeon

Try to get saturated with the gospel. I always find that I can preach best when I … lie down in it and let it soak into me … become saturated with spices, and you will smell of them.

C.H. Spurgeon

Preaching is not child's play:
it is not a thing to be done without labor and anxiety;
it is solemn work;
it is awful work,
if you view it in its relation to eternity.

C.H. Spurgeon

Avowed atheists are not a tenth as dangerous as those preachers who scatter doubt and stab at faith.

C.H. Spurgeon

The finest sermon can do no more than expound the Word of God. He that preaches an hour together against drunkenness with the tongue of men or angels, hath spoke no other word of God but this, "Be not drunk with wine, wherein there is excess."

Jeremy Taylor

We deny that the power of the gospel rests in the eloquence of the preacher, the technique of the evangelist, or the persuasion of rational argument (1 Cor. 1:21; 2:1–5).

The gospel of Jesus Christ: An evangelical celebration

Truth when it is in the plainest dress is the most comely. When men preach rather words than matter, they catch people's ears, not their souls; they do but court, not convert.

Thomas Watson

Once in seven years I burn all my sermons; for it is a shame, if I cannot write better sermons now than I did seven years ago.
John Wesley

In answer to the question, "How must the Word of God be preached?" John Wycliffe once answered, "Appropriately, simply, directly, and from a devout, sincere heart."
John Wycliffe

Preaching, Manner of

The most reverent preacher that speaks as if he saw the face of God doth more affect my heart though with common words, than an irreverent man with the most exquisite preparations.
Richard Baxter

Whatever you do, let the people see that you are in good earnest. You cannot break men's hearts by jesting with them, or telling them a smooth tale, or patching up a gaudy oration.
Richard Baxter

I preach as though Christ was crucified yesterday; rose again from the dead today; and is coming back to earth tomorrow.
Martin Luther

The pastor who wants to keep his church full of people should first of all preach the gospel. Then he should preach the gospel keeping the following three adverbs in his mind: earnestly, interestingly, and fully.
C.H. Spurgeon

Preaching, Open air

I could scarcely reconcile myself at first to this strange way of preaching in the fields, of which Whitefield set me an example on Sunday; having been all my life so tenacious of every point relating to decency and order, that I should have thought the saving of souls almost a sin, if it had not been done in a church.
John Wesley's Journal

I love a commodious room, a soft cushion and a handsome pulpit, but field preaching saves souls.
John Wesley

Preaching, Purpose of

Doctrine should be such as should make men in love with the lesson, and not with the teacher.
Francis Bacon

Every sermon should be an agony of soul, a passion to beget Christ in the souls of men.
John Chrysostom

People want to be comforted. They need consolation – really need it, and do not merely long for it.
R.W. Dale

The test of a preacher is that his congregation goes away saying, not, "What a lovely sermon!" but, "I will do something!"
Francis of Sales

Preaching is thirty minutes in which to raise the dead.
John Ruskin

To humble the sinner,
to exalt the Savior,
and to promote holiness.
Charles Simeon

Some are dead; you must rouse them.
Some are troubled; you must comfort them.
Others are burdened; you must point them to the burden-bearer.
Still more are puzzled; you must enlighten them.
Still others are careless and indifferent; you must warn and woo them.
C.H. Spurgeon

Preaching, Simplicity of

In the United States the vocabulary of an average person is 600 words, whereas that of the average preacher is 5,000 words. So the average person in the pew does not know what the man in the pulpit is saying.

That's why I fight to keep it simple.
Billy Graham

Martyn Lloyd-Jones recounts how he once led a university mission, in 1941, at Oxford. He was invited to preach on the Sunday night, the first service of the mission in St Mary's Church, from the pulpit where John Henry Newman, later Cardinal Newman, once regularly preached. After the service students were invited to put any questions they had to the preacher. The room was packed and the first question came from a law student who was also a leading light in the famous Oxford University Union Debating Society – where future barristers and statesmen learnt about the art of public debating. The law student said to Martyn Lloyd-Jones, "Your sermon could equally well have been delivered to a congregation of farm laborers." He sat down to a burst of laughter and applause.
    Lloyd-Jones replied, "I do not see your difficulty. For while you may regard me as a heretic, I have always thought of undergraduates and indeed graduates of Oxford University as being just ordinary common human clay and miserable sinners like everyone else. I hold the view that your needs are precisely the same as those of the agricultural laborer or anyone else. I preached as I did quite deliberately."

A preacher should have the skill to teach the unlearned simply, roundly and plainly; for teaching is more important than exhorting. When I preach I regard neither doctors nor magistrates, of whom I have about forty in the congregation. I have all my eyes on the servant maids and the children. And if the learned men are not well pleased with what they hear, well, the door is open.
Martin Luther

No one can be a good preacher to the people, who is not willing to preach in a manner that seems childish and vulgar to some.
Martin Luther

You will never attain simplicity in preaching without plenty of trouble. Pains and trouble, I say emphatically, pains and trouble. When Turner, the great painter, was asked by someone how it was he mixed his colors so well, and what it was that made them so different from those of other artists, he replied: "Mix them? Mix them? Mix them? Why, with brains, sir." I am persuaded that, in preaching, little can be done except by trouble and pains.
J.C. Ryle

Be sparing in allegorizing or spiritualizing.
John Wesley

We use the language of the market.
George Whitefield

Preaching and love
Whoever preaches with love preaches effectively.
Francis of Sales

To love to preach is one thing, to love those to whom we preach is quite another.
Francis of Sales

Preaching and practice
With their doctrine they build, and with their lives they destroy.
Augustine of Hippo

It is no use walking anywhere to preach unless we preach as we walk.
Francis of Assisi

We must study hard how to live well as how to preach well.
Richard Baxter

He preaches well that lives well.
Phillips Brooks' definition of great preaching

Every preacher should sound out more by his deeds than by his words. He should, by his good life, make footprints for men to follow rather than, by speaking, merely show them the way to walk in.
Gregory the Great

No man preaches his own sermon well to others if he doth not first preach it to his own heart.
John Owen

Practice yourself what you preach.
Plautus

Preaching and the gospel message
I would like to see no questions asked as to what denomination a chaplain belongs, but let the question be, "Does he preach the gospel?"
"Stonewall" Jackson, on the recruitment of army chaplains

Preaching and the gospel message
The celebrated lawyer, Blackstone, had the curiosity early in the reign of George III, to go from church to church to hear every clergyman of note in London. He says that he did not hear a single discourse which had more Christianity in it than the writings of Cicero, and that it would have been impossible for him to discover, from what he had heard, whether the preacher were a follower of Confucius, of Muhammad or of Christ!
J.C. Ryle

Preaching and the gospel message
Brethren, first and above all things, keep to plain evangelical doctrines; whatever else you do or do not preach, be sure incessantly to bring forth the soul-saving truth of Christ and him crucified.
C.H. Spurgeon

Preaching and the Holy Spirit
If the Holy Spirit does not come, and give spiritual life, we may preach until we have not another breath left, but we shall not raise from the tomb of sin even the soul of a little child, or bring a single sinner to the feet of Christ.
C.H. Spurgeon

Predestination
See also: Calvinism; Election
And we know that in all things God works for the good of those who love him, who have been called according to his purpose. For those God foreknew he also predestined to be conformed to the likeness of his Son, that he might be the firstborn among many brothers.
The Bible, Romans 8:28,29

The elect are whosoever will, and the non-elect, whosoever won't.
Henry Ward Beecher

Those of mankind that are predestinated unto life, God, before the foundation of the world was laid, according to his eternal and immutable purpose, and the secret counsel and good pleasure of his will, hath chosen in Christ, unto everlasting glory, out of his free grace and love alone.
Loraine Beottner

Predestination (n): The doctrine that all things occur according to program. This doctrine should not be confused with that of foreordination, which means that all things are programmed, but does not affirm their occurrence, that being only an implication from other doctrines by which this is entailed. The difference is great enough to have deluged Christendom with ink, to say nothing of the gore. With the distinction of the two doctrines kept well in mind, and a reverent belief in both, one may hope to escape perdition if spared.
Ambrose Bierce

They that do continue to reject and slight the Word of God are such, for the most part, as are ordained to be damned.
John Bunyan

Reprobation is before the person cometh into the world, or hath done good or evil. This is evidenced by Rom 9:11. Here you find twain in their mother's womb, and both receiving their destiny, not only before they had done good or evil, but before they were in a capacity to do it, they being yet unborn – their destiny, I say, the one unto, the other not unto the blessing of eternal life; the one elect, the other

reprobate; the one chosen, the other refused.
John Bunyan

Whoever heaps odium upon the doctrine of predestination openly reproaches God, as if he had unadvisedly let slip something hurtful to the church.
John Calvin

God preordained a part of the human race, without any merit of their own, to eternal salvation, and another part, in just punishment of their sin, to eternal damnation.
John Calvin

When they inquire into predestination, they are penetrating the sacred precincts of divine wisdom. If anyone with carefree assurance breaks into this place, he will not succeed in satisfying his curiosity and he will enter a labyrinth from which he can find no exit. For it is not right for man unrestrainedly to search out things that the Lord has willed to be hidden in Himself; nor is it right for him to investigate from eternity that sublime wisdom, which God would have us revere but not understand, in order that through this also He should fill us with wonder. He has set forth by His Word the secrets of His will that He has decided to reveal to us. These He decided to reveal in so far as He foresaw that they would concern and benefit us.
John Calvin

The only people who believe are those who had been appointed to eternal life. God only grants the gift of faith to those who are predestined to salvation. He chose us, and to those he has he gives the power to believe.
John Calvin

Predestination we call the eternal decree of God by which he determined in himself what he would have to become of every individual of mankind. For they are not all created with a similar destiny, but eternal

life is foreordained for some and eternal death for others.
John Calvin

God invites all indiscriminately by outward preaching.
John Calvin

For Scripture is the school of the Holy Spirit, in which, as nothing is omitted that is both necessary and useful to know, so nothing is taught but what is expedient to know. Therefore we must guard against depriving believers of anything disclosed about predestination in Scripture, lest we seem either wickedly to defraud them of the blessing of their God or to accuse and scoff at the Holy Spirit for having published what it is in any way profitable to suppress.
John Calvin

Scripture clearly proves that God, by his eternal and unchanging will, determined once and for all those whom he would one day admit to salvation and those whom he would consign to destruction. His decision about the elect is based on his free mercy with no reference to human deserving. Equally, those whom he dooms to destruction are shut off from eternal life by his perfect, but incomprehensible, judgment.
John Calvin

God draws, but he draws the willing one.
John Chrysostom

Those who love God are within the predetermined purpose of God, their final acquittal and glorification assured.
James Dunn

God, by an eternal and immutable decree, out of his mere love, for the praise of his glorious grace, to be manifested in due time, hath elected some angels to glory, and in Christ hath chosen some men to eternal life, and the means thereof; and also, according to his sovereign power, and the unsearchable counsel of his own will (whereby he extendeth or withholdeth favor as he pleases), hath passed by, and

foreordained the rest to dishonor and wrath, to for their sin inflicted, to the praise of the glory of his justice.
Larger Westminster Catechism (1688)

Although it is true that no one can be saved unless he is predestined, and has faith and grace, we must be very careful how we speak and treat these subjects.
Ignatius Loyola

To those who are elect and have the Spirit, predestination is the very sweetest of all doctrines, but to the worldly-wise it is the bitterest and hardest of all. The reason God saves in this way is to show that he saves not by our merits but by election pure and simple, and by his unchanging will. We are saved by his unchanging love.
Martin Luther

The perfect infallible preparation for grace, the only one, is eternal election and the predestination of God.
Martin Luther

All things whatsoever arise from, and depend upon, the divine appointments, whereby it was preordained who should receive the Word of Life, and who should disbelieve it, who should be delivered from their sins, and who should be hardened in them, who should be justified and who should be condemned. This is the very truth which razes the doctrine of free will from its foundations, to wit, that God's eternal love of some men and hatred of others is immutable and cannot be reversed.
Martin Luther

When God predestines someone, He predestines him to holiness, not licentiousness (Eph. 1:4). If anyone says that it does not matter what he does because God has predestined him, then he cannot say that he has been predestined; for predestined people never act in such a sinful way.
Edwin Palmer

He who cannot believe is cursed, for he reveals by his unbelief that God has not chosen to give him grace.
Blaise Pascal

When I teach the doctrine of predestination I am often frustrated by those who obstinately refuse to submit to it. I want to scream, "Don't you realize you are resisting the Word of God?" ... If my understanding of predestination is correct, then at best I am being impatient with people who are merely struggling as I once did, and at worst I am being arrogant and patronizing toward those who disagree with me.
R.C. Sproul

The Reformed Faith has held to the existence of an eternal, divine decree which, antecedently to any difference or desert in men themselves separates the human race into two portions and ordains one to everlasting life and the other to everlasting death.
R.C. Sproul

Oh! we love the sublime doctrine of eternal absolute predestination.
C.H. Spurgeon

An objection has been raised which is very ancient indeed, and has a great appearance of force. It is raised not so much by skeptics, as by those who hold a part of the truth; it is this – that prayer can certainly produce no result, because the decrees of God have settled everything, and those decrees are immutable. Now we have no desire to deny the assertion that the decrees of God have settled all events. It is our full belief that God has foreknown and predestinated everything that happened in heaven above or in the earth beneath, and that the foreknown station of a reed by the river is fixed as the station of a king, and "the chaff from the hand of the winnower is steered as the stars in their courses."
  Predestination embraceth the great and the little, and reacheth unto all things; the question is, wherefore pray? Might it not as logically be asked, wherefore breathe, eat,

move, or do anything? We have an answer which satisfies us, namely, that our prayers are in the predestination, and that God has as much ordained his people's prayers as anything else, and when we pray we are producing links in the chain of ordained facts. Destiny decrees that I should pray – I pray; destiny decrees that I shall be answered, and the answer comes to me.

Moreover, in other matters we never regulate our actions by the unknown decrees of God; as for instance, a man never questions whether he shall eat or drink, because it may or may not be decreed that he shall eat or drink; a man never enquires whether he shall work or not on the ground that it is decreed how much he shall do or how little; as it is inconsistent with common sense to make the secret decrees of God a guide to us in our general conduct, so we feel it would be in reference to prayer, and therefore still we pray.

But we have a better answer than all this. Our Lord Jesus Christ comes forward, and he says to us this morning, "My dear children, the decrees of God need not trouble you, there is nothing in them inconsistent with your prayers being heard. "I say unto you, ask, and it shall be given you." Now, who is he that says this? Why it is he that has been with the Father from the beginning – "The same was in the beginning with God" and he knows what the purposes of the Father are and what the heart of God is, for he has told us in another place, "The Father himself loveth you."

Now since he knows the decrees of the Father, and the heart of the Father, he can tell us with the absolute certainty of an eye-witness that there is nothing in the eternal purposes in conflict with this truth, that he that asketh receiveth, and he that seeketh findeth. He has read the decrees from the beginning to end: hath he not taken the book, and loosed the seven seals thereof, and declared the ordinances of heaven? He tells you there is nothing there inconsistent with your bended knee and streaming eye, and with the Father's opening the windows of heaven to shower upon you the blessings which you seek. Moreover, he is himself God: the purposes of heaven are his own purposes, and he who ordained the purpose here gives the assurance that there is nothing in it to prevent the efficacy of prayer. "I say unto you." O ye that believe in him, your doubts are scattered to the winds, ye know that he heareth your prayer.

C.H. Spurgeon

I am persuaded that the doctrine of predestination is one of the "softest pillows" upon which the Christian can lay his head, and one of the "strongest staffs" upon which he may lean, in his pilgrimage along this rough road.

C.H. Spurgeon

Without doubt, the doctrine of election and reprobation must stand or fall together ... I frankly acknowledge I believe the doctrine of Reprobation, that God intends to give saving grace, through Jesus Christ, only to a certain number; and that the rest of mankind, after the fall of Adam, being justly left of God to continue in sin, will at last suffer that eternal death which is its proper wages.

George Whitefield

Predestination

B.B. Warfield

A great man of the last generation began the preface of a splendid little book he was writing on this subject, with the words: "Happy would it be for the church of Christ and for the world, if Christian ministers and Christian people could be content to be disciples -- learners." He meant to intimate that if only we were all willing to sit simply at the feet of the inspired writers and take them at their word, we should have no difficulties with predestination. The difficulties we feel with regard to predestination are not derived from the Word. The Word is full of it, because it is full of God, and when we say God and mean God – God in all that God is – we have said Predestination.

Our difficulties with Predestination arise from a, no doubt not unnatural, unwillingness to acknowledge ourselves to be wholly at the disposal of another. We wish to be at our own disposal. We wish "to belong to ourselves," and we resent belonging, especially belonging absolutely, to anybody else, even if that anybody else be God. We are in the mood of the singer of the hymn beginning, "I was a wandering sheep," when he declares of himself, "I would not be controlled." We will not be controlled. Or, rather, to speak more accurately, we will not admit that we are controlled.

I say that it is more accurate to say that we will not admit that we are controlled. For we are controlled, whether we admit it or not. To imagine that we are not controlled is to imagine that there is no God. For when we say God, we say control. If a single creature which God has made has escaped beyond his control, at the moment that he has done so he has abolished God. A God who could or would make a creature whom he could not or would not control, is no God. The moment he should make such a creature he would, of course, abdicate his throne. The universe he had created would have ceased to be his universe; or rather it would cease to exist – for the universe is held together only by the control of God.

Even worse would have happened, indeed, than the destruction of the universe. God would have ceased to be God in a deeper sense than that he would have ceased to be the Lord and Ruler of the world. He would have ceased to be a moral being. It is an immoral act to make a thing that we cannot or will not control. The only justification for making anything is that we both can and will control it. If a man should manufacture a quantity of an unstable high-explosive in the corridors of an orphan asylum, and when the stuff went off should seek to excuse himself by saying that he could not control it, no one would count his excuse valid. What right had he to manufacture it, we should say, unless he could control it? He relieves himself of none of the responsibility for the havoc wrought, by pleading inability to control his creation.

To suppose that God has made a universe – or even a single being – the control of which he renounces, is to accuse him of similar immorality. What right has he to make it, if he cannot or will not control it? It is not a moral act to perpetrate chaos. We have not only dethroned God; we have demoralized him.

Of course, there is no one that thinks at all who will imagine such a vanity. We take refuge in a vague antinomy. We fancy that God controls the universe just enough to control it, and that he does not control it just enough not to control it. Of course God controls the universe, we perhaps say – in the large; but of course he does not control everything in the universe – in particular.

Probably nobody deceives himself with such palpable paltering in a double sense. If this is God's universe, if he made it and made it for himself, he is responsible for everything that takes place in it. He must be supposed to have made it just as he wished it to be – or are we to say that he could not make the universe he wished to make, and had to put up with the best he could do?

And he must be supposed to have made it precisely as he wished it to be, not only statically but dynamically considered, that is, in all its potentialities and in all its developments down to the end. That is to say, he must be supposed to have made it precisely to suit himself, as extended not only in space but in time. If anything occurs in it as projected through time – just as truly as if anything is found in it as extended in space which is not just as he intended it to be – why, then we must admit that he could not make such a universe as he would like to have, and had to put up with the best he could get. And, then, he is not God. A being who cannot make a universe to his own liking is not

God. A being who can agree to make a universe which is not to his liking, most certainly is not God.

But though such a being obviously is not God, he does not escape responsibility for the universe which he actually makes – whether as extended in space or in time – and that in all its particulars. The moment this godling (not now God) consented to put up with the actual universe – whether as extended in space or as projected through time, including all its particulars without exception – because it was the best he could get, it became his universe. He adopted it as his own, and made it his own even in those particulars which in themselves he would have liked to have otherwise. These particulars, as well as all the rest, which in themselves please him better, have been determined on by him as not only allowable, but as actually to exist in the universe which, by his act, is actually realized.

That is to say they are predestinated by him, and because predestinated by him actually appear in the universe that is made We have got rid of God, indeed; but we have not got rid of the predestination, to get rid of which we have been willing to degrade our God into a godling.

We have passed insensibly from the idea of control to the idea of predestination. That is because there is no real difference between the two ideas at bottom. If God controls anything at all, of course he has intended to control it before he controls it. Exactly the control which he exerts, of course has intended to exert all long.

No one can imagine so inadvertent a God, that he always acts "on the spur of the moment," so to speak, with no manner of intention determining his action. Providence and predestination are ideas which run into one another. Providence is but predestination in its execution; predestination is but providence in its intention. When we say the one, we say the other, and the common idea which gives its content to both is control.

It is purely this idea of control which people object to when they say they object to predestination; not the idea of previousness, but purely the idea of control. They would object just much if the control was supposed to be exercised without any previous intention at all.

They ought to object much more. For a control exercised without intention would be a blind control. It would have no end in view to justify it; it would have no meaning; it would be sheerly irrational, immoral, maddening. That is what we call Fate. Say intention, however, and we say person; and when we say person we say purpose. A meaning is now given to the control that is exercised; an end is held before it.

And if the person who exercises the control be an intelligent being, the end will be a wise end; if he be a moral being it will be a good end; if he be infinitely wise and holy, just and good, it will be an infinitely wise and holy, just and good end, and it will be wrought out by means as wise and holy, just and good as itself.

To say predestination is to say all this. It is to introduce order into the universe. It is to assign an end and a worthy end to it. If enables us to speak of a far off divine event to which the whole creation is moving. It enables us to see that whatever occurs, great or small, has a place to fill in this universal teleology; and thus has significance given it, and a justification supplied to it. To say predestination is thus not only to say God; it is also to say Theodicy.

No matter what we may say of predestination in moments of puzzlement, as we stand in face of the problems of life – the problem of the petty, the problem of suffering, the problem of sin – it is safe to say that at the bottom of our minds we all believe in it. We cannot help believing in it – if we believe in God; and that, in its utmost extension, as applying to everything about us which comes to pass.

Take any occurrence that happens, great or small – the fall of an empire or the fall of a sparrow, which our Lord himself tells us never once happens "without our Father." It surely cannot be imagined that God is ignorant of its happening – nay, even if it be so small a thing as the fall of a pin.

God assuredly is aware of everything that happens in his universe. There are no dark corners in it into which his all-seeing eye cannot pierce; there is nothing that occurs in it which is hidden from his universal glance. But certainly neither can it be imagined that anything which occurs in his universe takes him by surprise. Assuredly God has been expecting it to happen, and in happening it has merely justified his anticipations.

Nor yet can he be imagined to be indifferent to its happening, as if, though he sees it coming, he does not care whether it happens or not. That is not the kind of God our God is; he is a God who infinitely cares, cares even about the smallest things. Did not our Savior speak of the sparrows and the very hairs of our heads to teach us this?

Well, then, can it be imagined that, though infinitely caring, God stands impotently over against the happenings in his universe, and cannot prevent them? Is he to be supposed to be watching from all eternity things which he does not wish to happen, coming, coming, ever coming, until at last they come – and he is unable to stop them? Why, if he could not prevent their happening any other way he need not have made the universe; or he might have made it differently. There was nothing to require him to make this universe – or any universe at all – except his own good pleasure; and there is nothing to compel him to allow anything which he does not wish to happen, to occur in the universe which he has made for his own good pleasure.

Clearly things cannot occur in God's universe, the occurrence of which is displeasing to him. He does not stand helplessly by, while they occur against his wish. Whatever occurs has been foreseen by him from all eternity, and it succeeds in occurring only because its occurrence meets his wish.

It may not be apparent to us what wish of his it meets, what place it fills in the general scheme of things to which it is his pleasure to give actuality, what its function is in his all-inclusive plan. But we know that it could not occur unless it had such a function to perform, such a place to fill, a part to play in God's comprehensive plan. And knowing that, we are satisfied. Unless, indeed, we cannot trust God with his own plan, and feel that we must insist that he submit it to us, down to the last detail, and obtain our approval of it, before he executes it.

Least of all will the religious man doubt the universal predestination of God. Why, what makes him a religious man is, among other things, that he sees God in everything.

A glass window stands before us. We raise our eyes and see the glass; we note its quality, and observe its defects; we speculate on its composition. Or we look straight through it on the great prospect of land and sea and sky beyond. So there are two ways of looking at the world. We may see the world and absorb ourselves in the wonders of nature. That is the scientific way. Or we may look right through the world and see God behind it. That is the religious way.

The scientific way of looking at the world is not wrong any more than the glass-manufacturer's way of looking at the window. This way of looking at things has its very important uses. Nevertheless the window was placed there not to be looked at but to be looked through; and the world has failed of its purpose unless it too is looked through and the eye rests not on it but on its God. Yes, its God; for it is of the essence of the religious view of things that God is seen in all that is and in all that occurs. The universe is his, and in all its movements speaks of him, because it does only his will.

If you would understand the religious man's conception of the relation of God to his world, observe him on his knees. For prayer is the purest expression of religion and in prayer we see religion come to its rights.

Did ever a man pray thus: "O God, Thou knowest that I can do as I choose and Thou canst not prevent me, Thou knowest that my fellow men are, like me, beyond Thy control, Thou knowest that nature itself goes its own way and Thou canst but stand helplessly by and watch whither it tends"?

No, the attitude of the soul in prayer is that of entire dependence for itself, and of complete confidence in God's all-embracing government. We ask him graciously to regulate our own spirit, to control the acts of our fellow men, and to direct the course of the whole world in accordance with his holy and beneficent will. And we do right. Only, we should see to it that we preserve this conception of God in his relation to his world, when we rise from our knees; and make it the operative force of our whole life.

I know, it is true, an eminent theologian who will shake his head at this. God cannot control the acts of free agents, he says, and it is folly to ask him to do so. If we go gunning with an unskillful friend, he may awkwardly shoot us; and it is useless to ask God to protect us; he simply cannot do it. If we are at work at a dangerous machine by the side of a careless companion, he may destroy us at any moment, and it is useless to ask God to avert the mishap; God cannot do it.

If this were so, we certainly would be in a parlous case. Or rather the world would long ago have broken down into chaos.

Every religious man knows full well that it is not so. Every religious man knows that God can and will and does control everything that he has made in all their actions, and that therefore – despite all adverse appearances – it is all well with the world.

All well with the world, which is moving steadily forward in its established orbit; and all well with us who put our trust in God. For has he not himself told us that all things – all things, mind you – are working together for good to those that love him? And how, pray, could that be, except that they all do his bidding in all their actions?

Benjamin B. Warfield

Predestination and election

Predestination to Life is the everlasting purpose of God, whereby (before the foundations of the world were laid) he hath constantly decreed by his counsel secret to us, to deliver from curse and damnation those whom he hath chosen in Christ out of mankind, and to bring them to Christ to everlasting salvation, as vessels made to honor. Wherefore, they which be endued with so excellent a benefit of God be called according to God's purpose by his Spirit working in due season: they through grace obey the calling: they be justified freely: they be made sons of God by adoption: they be made like the image of his only-begotten Son Jesus Christ: they walk religiously in good works, and at length, by God's mercy, they attain to everlasting felicity.

As the godly consideration of Predestination, and our Election in Christ, is full of sweet, pleasant, and unspeakable comfort to godly persons, and such as feel in themselves the working of the Spirit of Christ, mortifying the works of the flesh, and their earthly members, and drawing up their mind to high and heavenly things, as well because it doth greatly establish and confirm their faith of eternal salvation to be enjoyed through Christ, as because it doth fervently kindle their love towards God: So, for curious and carnal persons, lacking the Spirit of Christ, to have continually before their eyes the sentence of God's Predestination, is a most dangerous downfall, whereby the devil doth thrust them either into desperation, or into wretchedness of most unclean living, no less perilous than desperation. Furthermore, we must receive God's promises in such wise, as they be generally set forth to us in holy Scripture: and, in our doings, that will of God is to be followed, which we have expressly declared unto us in the Word of God.

Book of Common Prayer, The Thirty Nine Articles

Predestination and free will

Predestination to life is the everlasting purpose of God, whereby (before the foundations of the world were laid) He hast

continually decreed by his counsel secret to us, to deliver from curse and damnation those whom he hath chosen in Christ out of mankind, and to bring them by Christ to everlasting salvation, as vessels made to honor. Wherefore they which be endued with so excellent a benefit of God be called according to God's purpose by his Spirit working in due season: they through grace obey the calling: they be justified freely: they be made sons of God by adoption: they be made like the image of his only-begotten Son Jesus Christ: they walk religiously in good works, and at length, by God's mercy, they attain to everlasting felicity.
C.H. Spurgeon

Some have doubted whether predestination is consistent with the free agency of man. We believe that man does as he pleases, yet notwithstanding he always does as God decrees.
C.H. Spurgeon

Prejudice
Education will broaden a narrow mind, but there is no cure for a big head.
Author unknown

The eye sees only what the mind is prepared to comprehend.
Henri Bergson

Prejudices, it is well known, are most difficult to eradicate from the heart whose soil has never been loosened or fertilized by education; they grow there, firm as weeds among stones.
Charlotte Brontë

Common sense is the collection of prejudices acquired by age eighteen.
Albert Einstein

I am free of all prejudices. I hate everyone equally.
W.C. Fields

Prejudice is the child of ignorance.
William Hazlitt

Beware lest we mistake our prejudices for our convictions.
Dr Harry Ironside

A great many people think they are thinking when they are merely rearranging their prejudices.
William James

Prejudice not being founded on reason cannot be removed by argument.
Samuel Johnson

All looks yellow to a jaundiced eye.
Alexander Pope

Opinions founded on prejudice are always sustained with the greatest violence.
Hebrew proverb

It is never too late to give up your prejudices.
Henry David Thoreau

The true ground of most men's prejudice against the Christian doctrine is because they have no mind to obey it.
John Tillotson

We want the facts to fit the preconceptions. When they don't, it is easier to ignore the facts than to change the preconceptions.
Jessamyn West

Prelate
Prelate (n): A church officer having a superior degree of holiness and a fat preferment. One of heaven's aristocracy. A gentleman of God.
Ambrose Bierce

Preoccupation
Those who are much occupied with the care of the body usually give little care to the soul.
Proverb

Preparation
It's easier to prepare and prevent, than to repair and repent.
Author unknown

Failing to prepare is preparing to fail.
Author unknown

The Six P Principle:
Prior Proper Preparation Prevents Poor
Performance
Author unknown

The fight is won or lost far away from
witnesses – behind the lines, in the gym
and out there on the road, long before I
dance under those lights.
Muhammad Ali

Not knowing when the dawn will come, I
open every door.
Emily Dickinson

The best impromptu speeches are the ones
written well in advance.
Ruth Gordon

Have thy tools ready. God will provide
thee work.
Charles Kingsley

In all matters we should hope and pray for
the best; nevertheless, we should be
prepared for the worst.
Martin Luther

Dig the well before you are thirsty.
Chinese proverb

Presence of God
See also: God's presence
God makes of *all* things mysteries and
sacraments of love, why should not every
moment of our lives be a sort of
communion with the divine love?
Jean Pierre de Caussade

The Lord is my Pace-setter, I shall not rush.
He makes me stop and rest for quiet intervals,
He provides me with images of stillness,
which restore my serenity.
He leads me in ways of efficiency, through
calmness of mind,
And His guidance is peace.
Even though I have a great many things to
accomplish each day

I will not fret, for His presence is here,
His timelessness, His all-importance will
keep me in balance.
He prepares refreshment and renewal in
the midst of my activity
By anointing my mind with His oils of
tranquillity;
My cup of joyous energy overflows.
Surely harmony and effectiveness shall be
the fruits of my hours,
For I shall walk at the pace of my Lord,
and dwell in His house for ever.
Variation on the theme of the twenty-third
Psalm by a Japanese student, Toki Miyashina

What hell may be, I know not. This I know,
I cannot lose the presence of the Lord.
One arm, Humility, takes hold upon
His dear humanity; the other, Love,
Clasps His divinity. So where I go
He goes; and better fire-walled hell with Him
Than golden-gated Paradise without.
(Unknown friend of Tauler)
Said Tauler,
My prayer is answered. God hath sent the
man,
Long sought, to teach me, by his simple
trust,
Wisdom the weary Schoolmen never knew.
John Tauler

Presence of Jesus
I ask for the angels of heaven to be among us.
I ask for the abundance of peace.
I ask for full vessels of charity.
I ask for rich treasures of mercy.
I ask for cheerfulness to preside over all.
I ask for Jesus to be present.
Brigid of Ireland

Present, The
Every man's life lies within the present; for
the past is spent and done with, and the
future is uncertain.
Marcus Aurelius

Nothing is worth more than this day.
Goeth

There is only one time that is important –
NOW! It is the most important time

because it is the only time we have any
power over.
Leo Tolstoy

I have realized that the past and the future
are real illusions, that they exist only in the
present, which is what there is and all there
is.
Alan Watts

Present moment, The
If you abandon all restraint, carry your
wishes to their furthest limits, open your
heart boundlessly, there is not a single
moment when you will not find all you
could possibly desire. The present moment
holds infinite riches beyond your wildest
dreams.
Jean-Pierre de Caussade

Pride
See also: Humility; Ministers
When pride comes, then comes disgrace,
but with humility comes wisdom.
The Bible, Proverbs 11:2

Pride goeth before destruction, and an
haughty spirit before a fall.
The Bible, Proverbs 16:18 KJV

Seest thou a man wise in his own conceit?
There is more hope of a fool than of him.
The Bible, Proverbs 26:12 KJV

Do not be proud, but be willing to
associate with people of low position.
The Bible, Romans 12:16

Let him that thinketh he standeth take
heed lest he fall.
The Bible, 1 Corinthians 10:12 KJV

Pride is the only disease known to man
that makes everyone sick except the one
who has it.
Author unknown

God's whole employment is to lift up the
humble and to cast down the proud.
Author unknown

Swallowing your pride seldom leads to
indigestion.
Author unknown

Pride is what we have. Vanity is what
others have.
Author unknown

A man is usually as young as he feels, but
seldom as important.
Author unknown

Remember that pride leads to hell, but
humility to heaven! God always beats
down the proud, and lifts up the humble.
Isaac Ambrose

As pride is the resemblance of the devil
and what brought him to ruin, so humility
is the resemblance of Christ, which exalted
Him to honors.
Isaac Ambrose

Pride can exist only in those who believe
that they possess something. The fallen
angel and the first man became proud and
fell only because they imagined and
believed that they possessed something.
For neither angel nor man nor anything
else has being; only one has it, God.
Angela of Foligno

The demons are aware that the devil fell
from heaven through pride, so they attack
first those who are advanced in the way, by
trying to set them against each other
through pride. In this way they attempt to
cut us off from God.
Antony of Egypt

Other sins find their vent in the
accomplishment of evil deeds, whereas
pride lies in wait for good deeds, to destroy
them.
Augustine of Hippo

Those who wish to be praised in themselves
are proud.
Augustine of Hippo

They think they will be proud if they have

anything. It has been made clear to us where God wishes us to be in the depths and where he wishes us to be in the heights. He wishes us to be humble to avoid pride, and he wishes us to be on high to grasp wisdom.
Augustine of Hippo

One of our most heinous and palpable sins is pride. This is a sin that hath too much interest in the best of us, but which is more hateful and inexcusable in us than in other men.
Richard Baxter

Pride is a vice that ill suits those that would lead others in a humble way to heaven. Let us take heed, lest when we have brought others so far, the gates should prove too narrow for ourselves. For God, who thrust out a proud angel, will not tolerate a proud preacher, either. For it is pride that is at the root of all other sins: envy, contention, discontent, and all hindrances that would prevent renewal. Where there is pride, all want to lead and none want to follow or to agree.
Richard Baxter

I see that my chief obstacle to holiness is pride. I will overcome it!
Andrew Beltrami

Pride is tasteless, colorless, and sizeless. Yet it is the hardest thing to swallow.
August B. Black

Pride alienates man from heaven; humility leads to heaven.
Bridget of Sweden

Proud people breed sad sorrows for themselves.
Emily Brontë

He that is down need fear no fall;
He that is low, no pride.
John Bunyan

The greatest fault is to be conscious of none.
Thomas Carlyle

The core of pride is impatience and its offshoot is the lack of any discernment.
Catherine of Siena

Sisters beware of all pride, vain ambition, envy, greed, and of taking part in the cares and busy ways of the world.
Clare of Assisi

A proud monk needs no demon. He has turned into one, an enemy to himself.
John Climacus

Pride is utter poverty of soul disguised as riches, imaginary light where in fact there is darkness.
John Climacus

Like the sun which shines on all alike, vainglory beams on every occupation. What I mean is this. I fast, and turn vainglorious. I stop fasting so that I will draw no attention to myself, and I become vainglorious over my prudence. I dress well or badly, and am vainglorious in either case. I talk or I hold my peace, and each time I am defeated. No matter how I shed this prickly thing, a spike remains to stand up against me.
John Climacus

Men can heal lust. Angels can heal malice. God alone can cure pride.
John Climacus

Of all the marvelous works of the Deity, perhaps there is nothing that angels behold with such supreme astonishment as a proud man.
C.C. Colton

He was like a cock who thought the sun had risen to hear him crow.
George Eliot

They that know God will be humble; they that know themselves cannot be proud.
John Flavel

Pride says, "I am the Lord my God, and I shall have no other gods besides me," and,

"I shall love the Lord my Self with all my heart, soul, strength and mind."
Douglas Groothuis

The charity that hastens to proclaim its good deeds, ceases to be charity, and is only pride and ostentation.
William Hutton

Peter was first given the keys, but then he was allowed to fall into the sin of denying Christ; and so his pride was humbled by his fall.
John of Carpathos

A cold, self-righteous prig who goes regularly to church may be far nearer to hell than a prostitute.
C.S. Lewis

Pride always means enmity – it is enmity.
C.S. Lewis

According to Christian teachers, the essential vice, the utmost evil, is Pride. Unchastity, anger, greed, drunkenness, and all that, are mere fleabites in comparison: it was through Pride that the devil became the devil: Pride leads to every other vice: it is the complete anti-God state of mind.
C.S. Lewis

Haughtiness towards men is rebellion to God.
Moses Maimonides

Pride makes us artificial and humility makes us real.
Thomas Merton

God sends no one away empty except those who are full of themselves.
Dwight L. Moody

The gospel insists that what stands between humans and God is pride – the stubborn refusal to derive our worth from God's love alone.
Peter C. Moore

Pride becomes the root of our rage against a God who condescends to do for us what

we cannot do for ourselves.
Peter C. Moore

Pride, or the loss of humility, is the root of every sin and evil.
Andrew Murray

I pray God to keep me from being proud.
Samuel Pepys

Boasting is the voice of pride in the heart of the strong. Self-pity is the voice of pride in the heart of the weak.
John Piper

Be not proud of race, face, place, or grace.
Samuel Rutherford

The proud man counts his newspaper clippings – the humble man his blessings.
Fulton J. Sheen

Pride is a stab at Deity; it is an attack upon the undivided glory of God.
C.H. Spurgeon

As long as a man's soul is lifted up with pride, he will never truly know anything about faith, and never come to live by faith.
C.H. Spurgeon

Oh! man, hate pride, flee from it, abhor it, do not let it dwell with you!
C.H. Spurgeon

Pride may be set down as "the sin" of human nature.
C.H. Spurgeon

Pride is the shirt of the soul, put on first and put off last.
George Swinnock

Pride deprives us of God's help, making us over-reliant on ourselves and arrogant towards other people.
Thalassios

Learn to break your own will. Be zealous

against yourself! Allow no pride to dwell in you.

Thomas à Kempis

Pride, Spiritual

Spiritual pride in its own nature is so secret, that it is not so well discerned by immediate intuition on the thing itself, as by the effects and fruits of it; some of which I would mention, together with the contrary fruits of pure Christian humility.

Spiritual pride disposes to speak of other persons' sins, their enmity against God and his people, the miserable delusion of hypocrites, and their enmity against vital piety, and the deadness of some saints, with bitterness, or with laughter and levity, and an air of contempt; whereas pure Christian humility rather disposes, either to be silent about them, or to speak of them with grief and pity.

Spiritual pride is very apt to suspect others; whereas an humble saint is most jealous of himself; he is so suspicious of nothing in the world as he is of his own heart. The spiritually proud person is apt to find fault with other saints, that they are low in grace; and to be much in observing how cold and dead they are; and being quick to discern and take notice of their deficiencies. But the eminently humble Christian has so much to do at home, and sees so much evil in his own heart, and is so concerned about it, that he is not apt to be very busy with other hearts; he complains most of himself, and complains of his own coldness and lowness in grace. He is apt to esteem others better than himself, and is ready to hope that there is nobody but what has more love and thankfulness to God than he, and cannot bear to think that others should bring forth no more fruit to God's honor than he.

Some who have spiritual pride mixed with high discoveries and great transports of joy, disposing them in an earnest manner to talk to others, are apt, in such frames, to be calling upon other Christians about them, and sharply reproving them for their being so cold and lifeless. There are others, who in their raptures are overwhelmed with a sense of their own vileness; and, when they have extraordinary discoveries of God's glory, are all taken up about their own sinfulness; and though they also are disposed to speak much and very earnestly, yet it is very much in blaming themselves, and exhorting fellow-Christians, but in a charitable and humble manner. Pure Christian humility disposes a person to take notice of every thing that is good in others, and to make the best of it, and to diminish their failings; but to give his eye chiefly on those things that are bad in himself, and to take much notice of every thing that aggravates them.

In a contrariety to this, it has been the manner in some places, or at least the manner of some persons, to speak of almost every thing that they see amiss in others, in the most harsh, severe, and terrible language. It is frequent with them to say of others' opinions, or conduct, or advice – or of their coldness, their silence, their caution, their moderation, their prudence, that they are from the devil, or from hell; that such a thing is devilish, or hellish, or cursed, and that such persons are serving the devil, or the devil is in them, that they are soul-murderers, and the like; so that the words devil and hell are almost continually in their mouths. And such kind of language they will commonly use, not only towards wicked men, but towards them whom they themselves allow to be the true children of God, and also towards ministers of the gospel and others who are very much their superiors. And they look upon it as a virtue and high attainment thus to behave themselves. Oh, say they, we must be plain hearted and bold for Christ, we must declare war against sin wherever we see it, we must not mince the matter in the cause of God and when speaking for Christ. And to make any distinction in persons, or to speak the more tenderly, because that which is amiss is seen in a superior, they look upon as very mean for a follower of Christ when speaking in the cause of his Master.

What a strange device of the devil is here, to overthrow all Christian meekness and gentleness, and even all show and appearance of it, and to defile the mouths of the children of God, and to introduce the language of common sailors among the followers of Christ, under a cloak of high sanctity and zeal, and boldness for Christ! And it is a remarkable instance of the weakness of the human mind, and how much too cunning the devil is for us!
Jonathan Edwards

Pride and its correction
Pride is like a beard. It just keeps growing. The solution? Shave it every day.
Author unknown

When you become like a child, your pride will melt away and you will be like Christ himself in the stable at Bethlehem.
Martin Luther

Our pride must have winter weather to rot it.
Samuel Rutherford

Pride and its source
Pride comes from a deeply buried root – it comes from the devil himself. Where pride is fostered a person will be insincere, harsh, bitter, cutting, disdainful.
F. Fénelon

Pride and what it leads to
The source of sin is pride.
Augustine of Hippo

Pride made the soul desert God, to whom it should cling as the source of life, and to imagine itself instead as the source of its own life.
Augustine of Hippo

Pride causes us to use our gifts as though they came from ourselves, not benefits received from God, and to usurp our benefactor's glory.
Bernard of Clairvaux

Excessive scruple is only hidden pride.
Goethe

The more proud anyone is himself, the more impatient he becomes at the slightest instance of it in other people. And the less humility anyone has, the more he demands and is delighted with it in other people.
William Law

You can have no greater sign of a confirmed pride than when you think you are humble enough.
William Law

Pride and what it leads to
If you harden your heart with pride, you soften your brain with it too.
Jewish proverb

Pride is at the bottom of all great mistakes.
John Ruskin

What is the sign of a proud man? He never praises anyone.
The Zohar

Priests
The blessings promised us by Christ were not promised to those alone who were priests; woe unto the world, indeed, if all that deserved the name of virtue were shut up in a cloister.
Héloise

Principle
Faithfully faithful to every trust,
Honestly honest in every deed,
Righteously righteous and justly just:
This is the whole of the good man's creed.
Author unknown

Principle is ever my motto, not expediency.
Benjamin Disraeli

In matters of principle, stand like a rock; in matters of taste, swim with the current.
Thomas Jefferson

Moderation in temper is always a virtue; but moderation in principle is always a vice.
Thomas Paine

I believe that every right implies a responsibility; every opportunity an obligation; every possession a duty.
John D. Rockefeller, Jr

Principles
We must adjust to changing times and still hold to unchanging principles.
Jimmy Carter, quoting his high school teacher Julia Coleman

The Christian must stand fixed to his principles, and not change his habit; but freely show what countryman he is by his holy constancy in the truth.
William Gurnall

Those who stand for nothing fall for anything.
Alex Hamilton

We hold these truths to be self-evident, that all men are created equal; that they are endowed by their Creator with inherent and inalienable rights; that among these, are life, liberty, and the pursuit of happiness; that to secure these rights, governments are instituted among men, deriving their just powers from the consent of the governed; that whenever any form of government becomes destructive of these ends, it is the right of the people to alter or abolish it, and to institute new government, laying its foundation on such principles, and organizing its powers in such form, as to them shall seem most likely to effect their safety and happiness.
Declaration of Independence as originally written by Thomas Jefferson, 1776.

The ultimate measure of a man is not where he stands in moments of comfort, but where he stands at times of challenge and controversy.
Martin Luther King, Jr

My husband often told the children that if a man had nothing that was worthy dying for, then he was not fit to live.
Coretta Scott King

I am not bound to win but I am bound to be true. I am not bound to succeed but I am bound to live up to what light I have. I must stand with anybody that stands right; stand with him while he is right and part with him when he goes wrong.
Abraham Lincoln

No man is better than his principles.
Drake Raft

Priorities
But seek first his kingdom and his righteousness, and all these things will be given you as well.
The Bible, Matthew 6:33

But one thing is needful; and Mary hath chosen that good part which shall not be taken away from her.
The Bible, Luke 10:42 KJV

There are three essential priorities I want to commend:
1. To build confidence in the message and work of the Church.
2. To grapple with the challenge of evangelism.
3. To deepen our internal unity.
George Carey

In biblical days prophets were astir while the world was asleep; today the world is astir while church and synagogue are busy with trivialities.
Abraham Joshua Heschel

You can't get second things by putting them first; you can get second things only by putting first things first.
C.S. Lewis

When first things are put first, second things are not suppressed but increased.
C.S. Lewis

The moment you wake up each morning, all your wishes and hopes for the day rush at you like wild animals. And the first job each morning consists in shoving it all back; in listening to that other voice,

taking that other point of view, letting that other, larger, stronger, quieter life come flowing in.
C.S. Lewis

It's a good idea not to major in minor things.
Anthony Robbins

Don't be afraid to give up the good to go for the great.
Kenny Rogers

Do not let the good things in life rob you of the best things.
Buster Rothman

Lord, we don't mind who is second as long as Thou art first.
W.E. Stangter

First things first, but not necessarily in that order.
Doctor Who

Prison
Punishment is not for revenge, but to lesson crime and reform the criminal.
Elizabeth Fry

Stone walls do not a prison make,
Nor iron bars a cage.
Richard Lovelace

Though my body is enslaved, still my thoughts are free.
Sophocles

Prisoners
Remember my chains.
The Bible, Colossians 4:18

Remember those in prison as if you were their fellow-prisoners, and those who are mistreated as if you yourselves were suffering.
The Bible, Hebrews 13:3

Problems
See also: Adversity; Afflictions; Burdens; Difficulties; Trials
The problem is not the problem; the problem is your attitude about the problem.
Author unknown.

Have you prayed about your problem as much as you have talked about it?
Author unknown

It's easy enough to be pleasant
when everything goes like a song;
but the man who's worthwhile
is the man who can smile
when everything goes dead wrong.
Author unknown

A problem is a chance for you to do your best.
Duke Ellington

They conquer who believe they can.
Ralph Waldo Emerson

You must live with people to know their problems, and live with God in order to solve them.
P.T. Forsyth

Learn to take your every problem to the Bible. Within its pages you will find the correct answer.
Billy Graham

When you find yourself in a hole, stop digging.
U.S. Grant

Your difficulties are not almighty. The Lord alone is almighty.
S. Hughes

Don't duck the most difficult problems. That just insures that the hardest part will be left when you're most tired. Get the big one done – it's downhill from then on.
Norman Vincent Peale

Don't talk to others about your problem, speak to the problem about your God!
Carl-Gustaf Severin

I am persuaded that all of your problems are conceived and born in the sinful belief that

something or someone other than Jesus Christ can quench the thirst of our souls.
C. Samuel Storms

Problems, Facing
Not everything that is faced can be changed. But nothing can be changed until it is faced.
James Baldwin

Proclamation
The quickest way to slay error is to proclaim the truth. The surest mode of extinguishing falsehood is to boldly advocate Scripture principles. Scolding and protesting will not be so effectual in resisting the progress of error as the clear proclamation of the truth in Jesus.
C.H. Spurgeon

Procrastination
Elijah went before the people and said, "How long will you waver between two opinions? If the Lord is God, follow him; but if Baal is God, follow him." But the people said nothing.
The Bible, 1 Kings 18:21

The reason some people don't go very far in life is because they sidestep opportunity and shake hands with procrastination.
Author unknown

Procrastination is the thief of time.
Author unknown

Never put off until tomorrow what you can put off indefinitely.
Author unknown

Procrastination is the assassination of motivation.
Author unknown

The devil's favorite tool is tricking people to put things off. Outsmart him. Do it now.
Author unknown

Give me chastity and continence, but not yet.
Augustine of Hippo

God has promised forgiveness to your repentance, but He has not promised tomorrow to your procrastination.
Augustine of Hippo

He who hesitates is probably right.
Bogovich

Never do today what you can put off till tomorrow.
Matthew Browne

Delay always breeds danger; and to protract a great design is often to ruin it.
Miguel de Cervantes

There is practically nothing that men do not prefer to God. A tiresome detail of business, an occupation utterly pernicious to health, the employment of time in ways one does not dare to mention. Anything rather than God.
François Fénelon

Never leave that till tomorrow which you can do today.
Benjamin Franklin

You cannot repent too soon, because you do not know how soon it may be too late.
Thomas Fuller

Lose this day loitering, 'twill be the same story tomorrow, and the next more dilatory, For indecision bring its own delays, and days are lost lamenting o'er lost days.
Goethe

The man who procrastinates is always struggling with misfortunes.
Hesiod

Tear thyself from delay.
Horace

When, as a child, I laughed and wept,
Time crept.
When, as a youth, I dreamed and talked,
Time walked.
What I became a full-grown man,

Time ran.
And later, as I older grew,
Time flew.
Soon I shall find, while traveling on,
Time gone.
Will Christ have saved my soul by then?
Amen
Inscription on clock in Chester Cathedral

There is no more miserable human being than one in whom nothing is habitual but indecision.
William James

Putting off an easy thing makes it hard, and putting off a hard one makes it impossible.
George H. Lonmer

How soon not now, becomes never.
Martin Luther

He who awaits much can expect little.
Gabriel Garcia Marquez

Procrastination is the art of keeping up with yesterday.
Don Marquis

Tomorrow's life is too late, so live today.
Martial

A duty dodged is like a debt unpaid; it is only deferred, and we must come back and settle the account at last.
Joseph F. Newton

Delay is the deadliest form of denial.
C. Northcote Parkinson

Procrastination is my sin.
It brings me naught but sorrow.
I know that I should stop it.
In fact, I will – tomorrow!
Gloria Pitzer

A ripe crop must not wait for tomorrow.
Latin proverb

Throughout history, it has been the inaction of those who could have acted, the indifference of those who should have known better, the silence of the voice of justice when it mattered most, that has made it possible for evil to triumph.
Haile Selassie

While we are postponing, life speeds by.
Seneca

In delay there lies no plenty.
William Shakespeare, Twelfth Night

It is better to cleanse ourselves of our sins now, and to give up our vices, than to reserve them for cleansing at some future time.
Thomas à Kempis

Never put off till tomorrow what you can do the day after tomorrow.
Mark Twain

He who hesitates is last.
Mae West

Production
Production is not the application of tools to material, but of logic to work.
Peter Drucker

Professional
A professional is a person who can do his best at a time when he doesn't particularly feel like it.
Alistair Cooke

Progress
See also: Growth
I may not be who I want to be,
And I may not be who I am going to be,
But thank God I am not who I was.
Author unknown

Don't be yourself. Be superior to the fellow you were yesterday.
Author unknown

People should not consider so much what they are to do, as what they are.
Meister Eckhart

He who limps is still walking.
Stanislaw J. Lec

We all want progress, but if you're on the wrong road, progress means doing an about-turn and walking back to the right road; in that case, the man who turns back soonest is the most progressive.
C.S. Lewis

You're not very smart if you're not a little kinder and wiser than yesterday.
Abraham Lincoln

Pygmies placed on the shoulders of giants see more than the giants themselves.
Lucan

If I have seen further it is by standing on the shoulders of giants.
Isaac Newton

If necessity is the mother of invention, discontent is the father of progress.
David Rockefeller

It must shake up our conscience that we become all the more inhuman the more we grow into supermen.
Albert Schweitzer

The reasonable man adapts himself to the world; the unreasonable one persists in trying to adapt the world to himself. Therefore all progress depends on the unreasonable man.
George Bernard Shaw

True progress is not found in breaking away from the old ways, but in abiding in the teaching of Christ and His Spirit in the Church. There is an apparent contradiction here, for how can we abide, and yet advance? It is a paradox, like much else in Scripture; but Christian experience proves it true. Those make the best progress in religion who hold fast by the faith once for all delivered to the saints, and not those who drift away from their moorings, rudderless upon a sea of doubt.
Henry Barclay Swete

Promised Land

A land flowing with milk and honey.
The Bible, Exodus 3:8

Promises of God

For no matter how many promises God has made, they are "Yes" in Christ. And so through him the "Amen" is spoken by us to the glory of God.
The Bible, 2 Corinthians 1:20

Tackle life's problems by trusting God's promises.
Author unknown

Our thinking: It's impossible
God's promise: All things are possible (Luke 18:27)
"I'm too tired"
   I will give you rest (Matthew 11:28-30)
"Nobody really loves me"
I love you (John 3:16; John 13:34)
"I can't go on"
   My grace is sufficient (II Corinthians 12:9; Psalm 91:15)
"I can't figure things out"
   I will direct your steps (Proverbs 3:5-6)
"I can't do it"
   You can do all things (Philippians 4:13)
"I'm not able"
 I am able (II Corinthians 9:8)
"It's not worth it"
 It will be worth it (Romans 8:28)
"I can't forgive myself"
 I forgive you (I John 1:9; Romans 8:1)
"I can't manage"
   I will supply all your needs (Philippians 4:19)
"I'm afraid"
   I have not given you a spirit of fear (II Timothy 1:7)
"I'm always worried and frustrated"
   Cast all your cares on Me (I Peter 5:7)
"I don't have enough faith"
   I've given everyone a measure of faith (Romans 12:3)
"I'm not smart enough"
   I give you wisdom (I Corinthians 1:30)
"I feel all alone"
   I will never leave you or forsake you (Hebrews 13:5)
Author unknown

God's lips know not how to lie, but he will accomplish all his promises.
Æschylus

Jesus is the yes to every promise of God.
William Barclay

The acid test of our faith in the promises of God is never found in the easy-going, comfortable ways of life, but in the great emergencies, the times of storm and of stress, the days of adversity, when all human aid fails.
Ethel Bell

The main hinge on which faith turns is this: we must not imagine that the Lord's promises are true objectively but not in our experience. We must make them ours by embracing them in our hearts.
John Calvin

They are a foundation of our faith, and we have them as such; and also of our hope. On these we are to build all our expectations from God; and in all temptations and trials we have them to rest our souls upon.
Matthew Henry

If God promises something, then faith must fight a long and bitter fight, for reason or the flesh judges that God's promises are impossible. Therefore faith must battle against reason and its doubts. The devil, too, approaches us with promises, and indeed such as seem very plausible. It certainly requires at times a keen mind rightly to distinguish between God's true and the devil's false promises. The promises of the devil are seemingly very pleasant and acceptable. Faith is something that is busy, powerful and creative, though properly speaking, it is essentially an enduring rather than a doing. It changes the mind and heart. While reason holds to what is present, faith apprehends the things that are not seen. Contrary to reason, faith regards the invisible things as already materialized. This explains why faith, unlike hearing is not found in many, for only few believe, while the great majority cling to the things that are present and can be felt and handled rather than to the Word.

This, then, is the mark of the true divine promises, that they are contrary to reason so that it refuses to believe them. The promises of the devil, on the contrary, are in full agreement with reason and are readily and uncritically accepted. God's promises which are true and faithful, lead to the cross, and by the cross to His eternal blessing. Therefore reason is offended at them in two ways. It regards as nothing what is invisible and far away in the future, and it detests the cross as a calamity that is everlasting and without end. That is the reason why despite the riches of the divine promises, few believe them. These are such whose hearts are led by the Holy Spirit so that, as Abraham, they defy all foes and cling to the Word of God who calls them. Before Abraham came to Canaan he was blessed in many ways, but in the land of promise, he, despite his strong faith was forced to go into another country to escape the fury of the famine. God does this purposely to try the faith of His saints. However after a short time, He restores to them not only earthly prosperity, as Abraham became very wealthy, but He also gives them a greater faith and a deeper experience of His divine grace and mercy. For this reason Paul says in Romans 5:3 that though God's saints sigh under their cross, yet they glory in their tribulations when they discover how wonderfully God directs their life.

God thus proves Himself the Protector of all that put their trust in Him. He tries their faith by chastisements, but never forsakes them. Finally, He gloriously delivers them and at the same time benefits others with them.
Martin Luther

God's promises are like the stars; the darker the night, the brighter they shine.
David Nicholas

Every promise God has ever made finds its fulfillment in Jesus.
Joni Eareckson Tada

There is a living God; he has spoken in the Bible. He means what he says and will do all he has promised.
Hudson Taylor

Prophecy

For to us a child is born, to us a son is given, and the government will be on his shoulders. And he will be called Wonderful Counselor, Mighty God, Everlasting Father, Prince of Peace.
The Bible, Isaiah 9:6

But there is a God in heaven who reveals mysteries. He has shown ... what will happen.
The Bible, Daniel 2:28

Write the vision, and make it plain upon tables, that he may run that readeth it.
The Bible, Habakkuk 2:2 KJV

Above all, you must understand that no prophecy of Scripture came about by the prophet's own interpretation. For prophecy never had its origin in the will of man, but men spoke from God as they were carried along by the Holy Spirit.
The Bible, 2 Peter 1:20,21

Only the supernatural mind can have prior knowledge to the natural mind. If then the Bible has foreknowledge, historical and scientific, beyond the permutation of chance it truly then bears the fingerprint of God.
G.B. Hardy

Prophecy fulfilled by Jesus

This is what I told you while I was still with you: Everything must be fulfilled that is written about me in the Law of Moses, the Prophets and the Psalms.
The Bible, Luke 24:44

Prophets

"The vision ... that Isaiah ... saw" Isaiah 1:1. The Hebrew word for "saw", literally means a "vision," but often signifies a "prophecy." This word, as it stands in this verse, unquestionably denotes that there is nothing in this book which was not made

known to Isaiah himself. We learn from this word that the prophets did not speak on their own accord, but were enlightened by God, to see those things which they themselves would not have otherwise been able to understand.
John Calvin

All the prophets are to give thanks as much as they want.
Didache

Not everyone who speaks in a spirit is a prophet; he is only a prophet if he walks in the ways of the Lord.
Didache

The false and the genuine prophet will be known by their ways. If a prophet teaches the truth but does not practice what he teaches, he is a false prophet.
Didache

Propitiation

We propitiate only a person: we expiate only a fact or act or thing.
Horace Bushnell

Prosperity
See also: Wealth

In the day of prosperity be joyful, but in the day of adversity consider.
The Bible, Ecclesiastes 7:14 KJV

Prosperity is not without many fears and distastes; adversity not without many comforts and hopes.
Francis Bacon

For a hundred that can bear adversity there is hardly one that can bear prosperity.
Thomas Carlyle

Few are made better by prosperity, whom afflictions make worse.
William Gurnall

Prosperity is a great teacher; adversity is a greater. Possession pampers the mind; privation trains and strengthens it.
William Hazlitt

Adversity makes men, and prosperity makes monsters.
Victor Hugo

It is prosperity that we cannot endure.
Martin Luther

Wherever riches have increased, the essence of religion has decreased in the same proportion. Therefore I do not see how it is possible in the nature of things for any revival of religion to continue long. For religion must necessarily produce both industry and frugality, and these cannot but produce riches. But as riches increase, so will pride, anger, and love of the world in all its branches.
John Wesley

Protection
He kept him as the apple of his eye.
The Bible, Deuteronomy 32:10 KJV

Keep me as the apple of the eye, hide me under the shadow of thy wings.
The Bible, Psalm 17:8 KJV

Protest
When the church concludes that biblical faith or righteousness requires it to take a public stand on some issue, then it must obey God's Word and trust him with the consequences.
Dr Edward Norman

Protestants
The chief contribution of Protestantism to human thought is its massive proof that God is a bore.
H.L. Mencken

The faith of the Protestants, in general, embraces only those truths, as necessary to salvation, which are clearly revealed in the oracles of God. Whatever is plainly declared in the Old and New Testaments is the object of their faith. They believe neither more nor less than what is manifestly contained in, and provable by, the Holy Scriptures ... The written Word is the whole and sole rule of their faith, as well as practice. They believe

whatsoever God has declared, and profess to do whatsoever He hath commanded. This is the proper faith of Protestants: by this they will abide, and no other.
John Wesley

Proverbs
A proverb is a short sentence with long experience.
Author unknown

Wise sayings are lamps that light our way, from darkness to the light of day.
Henry Ward Beecher

Fire your ambition and courage by studying the priceless advice in the proverbs and wise sayings. They're the shortest road to wisdom you'll ever find.
Alexander Graham Bell

These wise sayings seem to have some strange power to discover our rich, hidden talents – those hidden seeds of greatness that God plants inside every one of us.
Thomas Carlyle

In the proverbs, a drop of ink makes thousands think.
Bennet Cerf

Every man like myself, who never went to college, can largely make up for that lack by reading the wise sayings of the great men of the past, who gladly left their wisdom and experience in proverbs for us who follow them.
Winston Churchill

Proverbs introduce us to ourselves – to that bigger, grander man we never knew, beating beneath that dwarf of a man we always knew. That bigger man often haunts us until we express him.
Ralph Waldo Emerson

In this hectic age, when most of us are unsure, confused and troubled, the surest anchors, guides and advisers are the wise sayings of great men of the past.
Clifton Fadiman

Time has weeded out of the great books all the unnecessary details and left us the gist, the essentials – the proverbs. They are the wisdom of the ages in the fewest words.
Goethe

Learning from the wise sayings of great men is like riding to success on the shoulders of giants.
Elbert Hubbard

Mankind would lose half its wisdom built up over the centuries if it lost its great sayings. They contain the best parts of the best books.
Thomas Jefferson

Proverbs give us quality, not quantity. An hour of reading proverbs is usually worth weeks, even months or years, of ordinary reading. Here is wisdom, not knowledge.
Montaigne

Wise men make proverbs, but fools repeat them.
Samuel Palmer

A country can be judged by the quality of its proverbs.
German proverb

Now back to my real people – to my 2,000 page book of wise sayings, proverbs, and epigrams.
Eleanor Roosevelt, leaving a political rally

One of the greatest treasures is a collection of wise sayings and proverbs for sharpening the mind.
P. Toynbee

I use all the brains I have and borrow all I can from the classics and wise sayings.
Thomas Woodrow Wilson

Proverbs, Book of
The principles of the Proverbs of Solomon are piety, charity, justice, benevolence, and true prudence. Their universal purity proves that they are the word of God.
John Calvin

Proverbs from around the world

Abundance
Abundance, like want, ruins many.
Romanian proverb

Action
If the wind will not serve, take to the oars.
Latin proverb

Better to light a candle than to curse the darkness.
Chinese proverb

Talk doesn't cook rice.
Chinese proverb

He who deliberates fully before taking a step will spend his entire life on one leg.
Chinese proverb

I have so much to do that I am going to bed.
Savoyard proverb

To talk much and arrive nowhere is the same as climbing a tree to catch a fish.
Ancient Chinese proverb

If there is no wind, row.
Latin proverb

Action and words
Deeds, and not fine speeches, are the proof of love.
Spanish proverb

Adversity
Adversity makes a man wise, not rich.
Romanian proverb

Smooth seas do not make skillful sailors.
Old African proverb

When the storm passes over, the grass will stand up again.
Kikuyu proverb

Affliction
The gem cannot be polished without friction, nor man perfected without trials.
Chinese proverb

The hammer shatters glass but forges steel.
Russian proverb

Ambition
It is not enough to aim, you must hit.
Italian proverb

Anger
He that overcomes his anger conquers his greatest enemy.
Latin proverb

The best answer to anger is silence.
German proverb

Little folk are soon angry.
Scots proverb

If you are patient in one moment of anger, you will avoid one hundred days of sorrow.
Chinese proverb

Anger is as a stone cast into a wasp's nest.
Malabar proverb

Appearances
Just because the river is quiet does not mean the crocodiles have left.
Malay proverb

Ask
Many things are lost for want of asking.
English proverb

Authority
If you wish to know what a man is, place him in authority.
Yugoslav proverb

Beauty
Beauty is a flower, fame a breath.
Latin proverb

Bereavement
To lose a friend is the greatest of all losses.
Latin proverb

Charity
Charity sees the need, not the cause.
German proverb

He that has no charity deserves no mercy.
English proverb

Conscience
There is no pillow so soft as a clear conscience.
French proverb

Courage
Great things are done more through courage than through wisdom.
German proverb

Criticism
If one man calls you a horse, ignore him;
If two men call you a horse, consider it;
If three men call you a horse, buy a saddle.
Persian proverb

Devil
The devil comes where money is; where it is not he comes twice.
Swedish proverb

Discernment
If you believe everything you read, you'd better not read.
Japanese proverb

Doubt
Who knows nothing doubts nothing.
French proverb

The wise are prone to doubt.
Greek proverb

With great doubts come great understanding; with little doubts come little understanding.
Chinese proverb

Education
It takes a village to raise a child.
African proverb

All the flowers of all the tomorrows are in the seeds of today.
Chinese proverb

Empathy
Shared joy is double joy and shared sorrow is half-sorrow.
Swedish proverb

Environment
Only after the last tree has been cut down,
Only after the last river has been poisoned,
Only after the last fish has been caught,
Only then will you find that money cannot be eaten.
Cree Indian proverb

Evil
Every evil comes to us on wings and goes away limping.
French proverb

One does evil enough when one does nothing good.
German proverb

Two wrongs do not make a right.
English proverb

Avoid the evil, and it will avoid thee.
Gaelic proverb

Failure
Fall seven times, stand up eight.
Japanese proverb

Faith
A person consists of his faith. Whatever is his faith, even so is he.
Indian proverb

Faith
Faith is like a bird that feels dawn breaking and sings while it is still dark.
Scandinavian proverb

Food
Man is what he eats.
German proverb

A fat paunch breeds no fine thoughts.
Greek proverb

Forgiveness
If God were not willing to forgive sin,
heaven would be empty.
German proverb

Forgiving
He who forgives ends a quarrel.
African proverb

He never pardons those he injures.
Italian proverb

Formalism
There are no formalities between the closest of friends.
Japanese proverb

Friendship
A faithful friend is an image of God.
French proverb

Friends are lost by calling often and calling seldom.
Scottish proverb

Do not use a hatchet to remove a fly from your friend's forehead.
Chinese proverb

Those who possess good friends are truly rich.
Spanish proverb

A friend in need is a friend indeed.
English proverb

Friends are needed both for joy and for sorrow.
Yiddish proverb

Gambling
A wager is a fool's argument.
French proverb

Generosity
What I kept, I lost;
What I spent, I had;
What I gave, I have.
Persian proverb

Giving
No purchase is as good as a gift.
French proverb

Many a man digs his grave with his teeth.
Puritan proverb

Goals
Unless we change direction, we are likely to end up where we are going.
Chinese proverb

God, as Creator
No rain, no mushrooms. No God, no world.
African proverb

God's knowledge
There are three things that only God knows: the beginning of things, the cause of things and the end of things.
Welsh proverb

Goodness
Conquer a man who never gives by gifts;
Subdue untruthful men by truthfulness;
Vanquish an angry man by gentleness;
And overcome the evil man by goodness.
Indian proverb

Gossip
Whoever gossips to you will gossip of you.
Spanish proverb

Gratitude
We never know the worth of water till the well is dry.
French proverb

Gratitude is the heart's memory.
French proverb

Gratitude and ingratitude
Ingratitude is the sepulcher of love.
Portuguese proverb

Growth
Be not afraid of growing slowly, be afraid only of standing still.
Chinese proverb

Guilt
The offender never forgives.
Russian proverb

Habits
Habit is a shirt made of iron.
Czech proverb

Habits begin like threads in a spider's web, but end up like ropes.
Spanish proverb

Happiness
To be happy, you must first make others happy.
Swedish proverb

Be happy while you're living,
For you're a long time dead.
Scottish proverb

Hate
Love and hatred are natural exaggerators.
Hebrew proverb

Health
He who enjoys good health is rich, though he knows it not.
Italian proverb

History
Dwell in the past and you'll lose an eye.
Forget the past and you'll lose both eyes.
Russian proverb

Holiness
The perfume of holiness travels even against the wind.
Indian proverb

Hospitality
To welcome a fellow man is to welcome the Shekinah [divine presence].
Jewish proverb

Humility
He who asks is a fool for five minutes, but he who does not ask remains a fool forever.
Chinese proverb

Hunger
It is not the horse that draws the cart, but the oats.
Russian proverb

You cannot reason with a hungry belly, since it has no ears.
Greek proverb

Idleness
Idleness is the key to Poverty's door.
Greek proverb

Idleness is the mother of want.
Greek proverb

As worms breed in a pool of stagnant water, so evil thoughts breed in the mind of the idle.
Latin proverb

Illness
In time of sickness the soul collects itself anew.
Latin proverb

Imagination
Wonder is the beginning of wisdom.
Greek proverb

Insults
A smiling face, and forgiveness, are the best way to avenge an insult.
Spanish proverb

Integrity
Integrity is the noblest possession.
Latin proverb

Invitations
When the ass was invited to the wedding feast, he said, "They need more wood and water."
Bosnian proverb

Judgment
Examine what is said, not who speaks.
Arabian proverb

Judging others
Before I judge my neighbor, let me walk a mile in his moccasins.
Sioux proverb

Justice
Justice is the foundation of kingdoms.
Latin proverb

Kindness
One kind word can warm three winter months.
Japanese proverb

Knowledge of God
Unknown makes unloved.
Dutch proverb

Laziness
The lazier a man is, the more he plans to do tomorrow.
Norwegian proverb

Leadership
He who knows not, and knows not that he knows not, is a fool – shun him.
He who knows not, and knows that he knows not, is a child – teach him.
He who knows, and knows not that he knows, is asleep – wake him.
He who knows, and knows that he knows, is wise – follow him.
Persian proverb

It is the part of a good shepherd to shear his flock, not to skin it.
Latin proverb

Without a shepherd, sheep are not a flock.
Russian proverb

Not the cry, but the flight of the wild duck, leads the flock to fly and follow.
Chinese proverb

Learning
A wise man will learn something even from the words of a fool.
Chinese proverb

One picture is worth more than a thousand words.
Chinese proverb

Learning from all sources
It is allowable to learn even from an enemy.
Latin proverb

Life
Everything passes, everything perishes,
everything palls.
French proverb

Light
If there is light in the soul,
There will be beauty in the person.
If there is beauty in the person,
There will be harmony in the house.
If there is harmony in the house,
There will be order in the nation.
If there is order in the nation,
There will be peace in the world.
Chinese proverb

Living
Look to this day ... In it lie all the realities
and verities of existence, the bliss of
growth, the splendor of action, the glory of
power. For yesterday is but a dream and
tomorrow is only a vision. But today, well
lived, makes every yesterday a dream of
happiness and every tomorrow a vision of
hope.
Sanskrit proverb

Love
He who loves, trusts.
Italian proverb

Love teaches even asses to dance.
French proverb

Love me when I least deserve it, because
that's when I really need it.
Swedish proverb

Love begets love.
Latin proverb

Love for God
To love God is the greatest of virtues; to
be loved by God is the greatest of
blessings.
Portuguese proverb

Modesty
It's good to be clever, but not to show it.
French proverb

Beauty is truly beauty when its comrade is
a modest mind.
Greek proverb

Money
Money is always either our master or our
slave.
Latin proverb

Money really adds no more to the wise
than clothes can to the beautiful.
Jewish proverb

Motherhood
God could not be everywhere and
therefore he made mothers.
Jewish proverb

Neighborliness
Love your neighbor, but don't pull down
the hedge.
Swiss proverb

Obedience
No man is a successful commander who
has not first learned to obey.
Chinese proverb

Old age
We fool ourselves. We pray for a long life,
and fear old age.
Chinese proverb

Patience
Patience is power; with time and patience
the mulberry leaf becomes silk.
Chinese proverb

An ounce of patience is worth a pound of
brains.
Dutch proverb

Patience is a bitter plant, but it has a sweet
fruit.
German proverb

Peace
A harvest of peace is produced from a seed
of contentment.
Indian proverb

Peace and truth
I love peace, but I love truth even more.
Latin proverb

Perseverance
There are only two creatures that can surmount the pyramids, the eagle and the snail.
Eastern proverb

Persistence
When you have completed 95 per cent of your journey, you are only halfway there.
Japanese proverb

Politeness
Politeness is worth much and costs little.
Spanish proverb

Prayer
Prayer is the pillow of religion.
Arab proverb

What men usually ask for when they pray to God is, that two and two may not make four.
Russian proverb

To work is to pray
Benedictine proverb

Prcaching
He is the best speaker who can turn the ear into an eye.
Arabian proverb

Prejudice
Opinions founded on prejudice are always sustained with the greatest violence.
Hebrew proverb

Preparation
Dig the well before you are thirsty.
Chinese proverb

Pride
If you harden your heart with pride, you soften your brain with it too.
Jewish proverb

Procrastination
A ripe crop must not wait for tomorrow.
Latin proverb

Providence
God writes straight with crooked lines.
Spanish proverb

Repentance
Years of repentance are necessary in order to blot out a sin in the eyes of men, but one tear of repentance suffices with God.
French proverb

Rest
How beautiful it is to do nothing, and then rest afterward.
Spanish proverb

Revenge
The smallest revenge will poison the soul.
Jewish proverb

Blood that has been shed does not rest.
Jewish proverb

Seeing
Men are born with two eyes and one tongue in order that they may see twice as much as they say.
Romanian proverb

Self
If a man is cruel to himself, how can we expect him to be compassionate to others?
Jewish proverb

Sharing
Shared joy is double joy and shared sorrow is half-sorrow.
Swedish proverb

Slander
The tongue of him who utters slander, and the ear of him who listens to it, are brothers.
Portuguese proverb

Smiling
The smile you send out returns to you.
Indian proverb

Sorrow
A day of sorrow is longer than a month of joy.
Chinese proverb

Speaking
Speech is silver, silence is golden.
Persian proverb

Starting
The man who removes a mountain begins by carrying away small stones.
Chinese proverb

Well begun is half done.
English proverb

Suffering
Suffer in order to know, and toil in order to have.
Spanish proverb

Teachers
To teach is to learn.
Japanese proverb

Tears
What soap is to the body, tears are for the soul.
Jewish proverb

The good are always prone to tears.
Greek proverb

Truth
Speak the truth, but leave immediately after.
Slovenian proverb

There are three truths: my truth, your truth, and the truth.
Chinese proverb

Plato is my friend, Socrates is my friend, but truth is greater.
Latin proverb

Victory
He conquers who overcomes himself.
Latin proverb

Will
Where there's a will, there's a way.
English proverb

Great souls have wills; feeble ones have only wishes.
Chinese proverb

Wisdom
A wise man makes his own decisions, an ignorant man follows public opinion.
Chinese proverb

Even though you know a thousand things, ask the man who knows one.
Turkish proverb

It is better to weep with wise men than to laugh with fools.
Spanish proverb

Wit
Wit without discretion is a fool with a sword.
Spanish proverb

Witness
A candle lights others and consumes itself.
Jewish proverb

Words
Words must be weighed, not counted.
Polish proverb

Work
God is a busy worker, but he loves help.
Basque proverb

Pray to God, but hammer away.
Spanish proverb

Everyone must row with the oars he has.
English proverb

If you want your dreams to come true, don't sleep.
Yiddish proverb

An ant on the move does more than a dozing ox.
Mexican proverb

Who begins too much accomplishes little.
German proverb

Worry
Worry gives a small thing a big shadow.
Swedish proverb

Providence
*See also: Anxiety; Chance; Dying;
God's providence; Worry*
All things work together for good to them
that love God.
The Bible, Romans 8:28

The longer one lives, the more one realizes
that everything depends upon chance, and
the harder it is to believe that this
omnipotent factor in human affairs arises
simply from the blind interplay of events.
Chance, Fortune, Luck, Destiny, Fate,
Providence, seem to me only different ways
of expressing the same thing, to wit, that a
man's own contribution to his life story is
continually dominated by an external
superior power.
Author unknown

The true recipe for a miserable existence is
to quarrel with Providence.
James W. Alexander

God overrules all mutinous accidents,
brings them under his laws of fate, and
makes them all serviceable to His purpose.
Marcus Aurelius

There are no accidents in the life of the
Christian.
Rowland Bingham

1. Beware of drawing an excuse for your
sin from the providence of God; for it is
most holy, and is in no way any cause of
any sin you commit. Every sin is an act of
rebellion against God; a breach of his holy
law, and deserves his wrath and curse; and
therefore cannot be authorized by an
infinitely-holy God, who is of purer eyes
than to behold iniquity without

detestation and abhorrence. Though he has
by a permissive decree allowed moral evil
to be in the world, yet that has no
influence on the sinner to commit it. For it
is not the fulfilling of God's decree, which
is an absolute secret to every mortal, but
the gratification of their own lusts and
perverse inclinations, that men intend and
mind in the commission of sin.
2. Beware of murmuring and fretting
under any dispensations of providence that
you meet with; remembering that nothing
falls out without a wise and holy
providence, which knows best what is fit
and proper for you. And in all cases, even
in the middle of the most afflicting
incidents that happen to you, learn
submission to the will of God, as Job did,
when he said upon the end of a series of
the heaviest calamities that happened to
him, "The Lord gave, and the Lord has
taken away, blessed be the name of the
Lord," Job, 1. 21. In the most distressing
case, say with the disciples, "The will of
the Lord be done," Acts, 21:14.
3. Beware of anxious cares and fearfulness
about your material well-being in the
world. This our Lord has cautioned his
followers against, Matt. 6:31. "Take no
thought, [that is, anxious and perplexing
thought] saying, What shall we eat? or,
What shall we drink? or, Wherewithal shall
we be clothed?" Never let the fear of man
stop you from duty, Matt. 10:28, 29; but
let your souls learn to trust in God, who
guides and superintends all the events and
administrations of providence, by whatever
hands they are performed.
4. Do not think little of means, seeing
God works by them; and he that has
appointed the end, orders the means
necessary for gaining the end. Do not rely
upon means, for they can do nothing
without God, Matt. 4:4. Do not despair if
there be no means, for God can work
without them, as well as with them; Hosea
1:7. "I will save them by the Lord their
God, and will not save them by bow, nor
by sword, nor by battle, by horses, nor by
horsemen." If the means be unlikely, he
can work above them, Rom. 4:19. "He

considered not his own body now dead, neither yet the deadness of Sarah's womb." If the means be contrary, he can work by contrary means, as he saved Jonah by the whale that devoured him. That fish swallowed up the prophet, but by the direction of providence, it vomited him out upon dry land.

Lastly, happy is the people whose God is the Lord: for all things shall work together for their good. They may sit secure in exercising faith upon God, come what will. They have good reason for prayer; for God is a prayer-hearing God, and will be enquired of by his people as to all their concerns in the world. And they have ground for the greatest encouragement and comfort in the middle of all the events of providence, seeing they are managed by their covenant God and gracious friend, who will never neglect or overlook his dear people, and whatever concerns them. For he has said, "I will never leave you, nor forsake you," Heb. 13:5.
Thomas Boston

God from eternity, decrees or permits all things that come to pass, and perpetually upholds, directs and governs all creatures and all events; yet so as not in any wise to be the author or approver of sin nor to destroy the free agency and responsibility of intelligent creatures
James Boyce

Fate is not the ruler, but the servant of Providence.
Edward George Bulwer-Lytton

I recognized that our Lord had caused me to run aground at this place so that I might establish a settlement here. And so many things came to hand here that the disaster was a blessing in disguise.
Christopher Columbus

God moves in a mysterious way His wonders to perform; He plants His footsteps in the sea, And rides upon the storm.

Deep in unfathomable mines Of never-failing skill, He treasures up His bright designs, And works His sovereign will.

Blind unbelief is sure to err and scan His work in vain; God is His own interpreter, and He will make it plain.
William Cowper

God never does anything to you that isn't for you.
Elizabeth Elliott

I have lived a long time and the longer I live the more convincing proofs I see that God governs in the affairs of men.
Benjamin Franklin

The almighty and everywhere present power of God; whereby, as it were by his hand, he upholds and governs heaven, earth, and all creatures; so that herbs and grass, rain and drought, fruitful and barren years, meat and drink, health and sickness, riches and poverty, yea, and all things come, not by chance, but by his fatherly hand.
Heidelberg Catechism

Providence is the care God takes of all existing things.
John of Damascus

Knowing that I am not the one in control gives great encouragement. Knowing the One who is in control is everything.
Alexander Michael

That power Which erring men call chance.
John Milton

What in me is dark Illumine, what is low raise and support, That to the height of this great argument I may assert eternal Providence, And justify the ways of God to men.
John Milton

God often takes a course for accomplishing His purposes directly contrary to what our narrow views would prescribe. He brings a death upon our feelings, wishes and prospects when He is about to give us the desire of our hearts.
John Newton

We serve a gracious Master who knows how to overrule even our mistakes to His glory and our own advantage.
John Newton

God writes straight with crooked lines.
Spanish proverb

Man proposes but God disposes.
Thomas à Kempis

We distrust the providence of God when, after we have used all our best endeavors and begged His blessing upon them, we torment ourselves about the wise issue and event of them.
John Tillotson

A firm faith in the universal providence of God is the solution of all earthly problems. It is almost equally true that a clear and full apprehension of the universal providence of God is the solution of most theological problems.
B.B. Warfield

We are immortal until our work on earth is done.
George Whitefield

Provision
Where God guides, He provides.
Author unknown

Prudence
A simple man believes anything, but a prudent man gives thought to his steps.
The Bible, Proverbs 14:15

[Prudence is] right reason in action.
Thomas Aquinas

Prudence must precede all our actions.
Basil

Titian has a painting in the National Gallery, London, called "An Allegory of Prudence." Prudence has three heads, a youth's which looks towards the future, a mature man's which looks at the present, and an old man's which looks back on the past with the wisdom of experience. Titian has written over their heads: "From the [example of] the past the man of the present acts prudently so as not to imperil the future."
Os Guinness

We must not trust every word of others or feeling within ourselves, but cautiously and patiently try the matter, to see whether it is of God.
Thomas à Kempis

The richest endowments of the mind are temperance, prudence, and fortitude. Prudence is a universal virtue, which enters into the composition of all the rest; and where she is not, fortitude loses its name and nature.
Vincent Voiture

Psalm
What is more pleasing than a psalm? A psalm is a blessing on the lips of the people, praise of God, the assembly's homage, a general acclamation, a word that speaks for all, the voice of the Church, a confession of faith in song.
Ambrose

Psalm 23
The Lord is my shepherd, that's all I want.
Small child misquoting Psalm 23

Psalm 23 and the TV
The TV is my shepherd, my spiritual life shall want,
It makes me to sit down and do nothing for the cause of Christ.
It demandeth my spare time.
It restoreth my desire for the things of the world.
It keepeth me from studying the truth of God's Word.
It leadeth me in the path of failure to attend God's house.

Yea, though I live to be a hundred, I will
fear no rental;
My "Telly" is with me, its sound and vision
comfort me.
It prepareth a program for me, even in the
presence of visitors.
Its volume shall be full.
Surely comedy and commercials shall
follow me all the days of my life,
And I will dwell in spiritual poverty
forever.
Author unknown

Psalm 119

The general scope and design of this
psalm is to magnify the Divine law, and
make it honorable. There are ten words by
which Divine revelation is called in this
psalm, and each expresses what God
expects from us, and what we may expect
from him.
1. God's law; this is enacted by him as our
Sovereign.
2. His way; this is the rule of his
providence.
3. His testimonies; they are solemnly
declared to the world.
4. His commandments; given with
authority.
5. His precepts; not left as indifferent
matters to us.
6. His word, or saying; it is the declaration
of his mind.
7. His judgments; framed in infinite
wisdom.
8. His righteousness; it is the rule and
standard of what is right.
9. His statutes; they are always binding.
10. His truth or faithfulness; it is eternal
truth, it shall endure for ever.
C.H. Spurgeon

Psalms

The sweet psalmist of Israel.
2 Samuel 23:1

Every psalm either points directly to
Christ, in his person, his character, and
offices; or may lead the believer's thoughts
to Him.
Author unknown

I find that the Psalms are like a mirror, in
which one can see oneself and the
movements of one's own heart.
Athanasius

No part of the Old Testament is more
frequently quoted or referred to in the New.
Matthew Henry

The most valuable thing the Psalms do for
me is to express that same delight in God
which made David dance.
C.S. Lewis

Psychiatry

God may choose to use an able psychiatrist
to help you with some of the problems you
are facing. Therefore, you should not feel
that you are wrong in seeking the help of a
psychiatrist or trained psychologist if that
will help you deal with some deep-seated
emotional problems. Seek one who will
not discourage your faith in God. Your
pastor can perhaps suggest a Christian
psychiatrist in your area.
Billy Graham

Public opinion

The man tenacious of purpose fears
neither the despot's tyranny nor that of the
mob.
Author unknown

I do not believe in the collective wisdom of
individual ignorance.
Thomas Carlyle

In matters of conscience, the law of the
majority has no place.
Mahatma Gandhi

We are all of us, more or less, the slaves of
opinion.
William Hazlitt

The world is governed by opinion.
Thomas Hobbes

Follow the wise few rather than the vulgar
many.
Proverb

The voice of the people is the voice of God.
Latin proverb

The first quality of a ruler is the ability to endure unpopularity.
Seneca

Its name is Public Opinion. It is held in reverence. It settles everything. Some think it is the voice of God.
Mark Twain

Punishment
Whoso sheddeth man's blood, by man shall his blood be shed.
The Bible, Genesis 9:6 KJV

All who are strangers to the true God, however excellent they may be, deserve punishment if only because they contaminate the pure gifts of God.
Augustine of Hippo

Man punishes the action, but God the intention.
Thomas Fuller

Distrust all in which the impulse to punish is powerful.
Friedrich Nietzsche

Purgatory
See also: Heaven
The Romish doctrine concerning purgatory, pardons, worshiping, and adoration, as well of images as of relics, and also invocation of saints, is a fond thing vainly invented, and grounded upon no warranty of scripture, but rather repugnant to the word of God.
Book of Common Prayer

First, purgatory. Here they carried their trade into purgatory by masses for souls, and vigils, and weekly, monthly, and yearly celebrations of obsequies, and finally by the Common Week and All Souls Day, by soul-baths so that the Mass is used almost alone for the dead, although Christ has instituted the Sacrament alone for the living. Therefore purgatory, and every solemnity, rite, and commerce connected with it, is to be regarded as nothing but a specter of the devil. For it conflicts with the chief article [which teaches] that only Christ, and not the works of men, are to help [set free] souls. Not to mention the fact that nothing has been [divinely] commanded or enjoined upon us concerning the dead. Therefore all this may be safely omitted, even if it were no error and idolatry.

The Papists quote here Augustine and some of the Fathers who are said to have written concerning purgatory, and they think that we do not understand for what purpose and to what end they spoke as they did. St Augustine does not write that there is a purgatory nor has he a testimony of Scripture to constrain him thereto, but he leaves it in doubt whether there is one, and says that his mother asked to be remembered at the altar or Sacrament. Now, all this is indeed nothing but the devotion of men, and that, too, of individuals, and does not establish an article of faith, which is the prerogative of God alone.

Our Papists, however, cite such statements [opinions] of men in order that men should believe in their horrible, blasphemous, and cursed traffic in masses for souls in purgatory [or in sacrifices for the dead and oblations], etc. But they will never prove these things from Augustine. Now, when they have abolished the traffic in masses for purgatory, of which Augustine never dreamt, we will then discuss with them whether the expressions of Augustine without Scripture [being without the warrant of the Word] are to be admitted, and whether the dead should be remembered at the Eucharist. For it will not do to frame articles of faith from the works or words of the holy Fathers; otherwise their kind of fare, of garments, of house, etc., would have to become an article of faith, as was done with relics. [We have, however, another rule, namely] The rule is: The Word of God shall establish articles of faith, and no one else, not even an angel.
Martin Luther

God has placed two ways before us in His Word: salvation by faith, damnation by unbelief. He does not mention purgatory at all. Nor is purgatory to be admitted, for it obscures the benefits and grace of Christ.
Martin Luther

The Bible teaches plainly, that as we die, whether converted or unconverted, whether believers or unbelievers, whether godly or ungodly, so shall we rise again when the last trumpet sounds. There is no repentance in the grace: there is no conversion after the last breath is drawn.
J.C. Ryle

Puritanism
Puritanism: The fear that someone, somewhere is happy.
H.L. Mencken

Puritans
His whole life he accounted a warfare, wherein Christ was his captain, his arms, and tears. The cross his Banner and his motto, "he who suffers conquers."
John Gerea, The Character of an Old English Puritane or Nonconformist, 1646

On many questions and specially in view of the marriage bed, the Puritans were the indulgent party ... they were much more Chestertonian than their adversaries. The idea that a Puritan was a repressed and repressive person would have astonished Sir Thomas More and Luther about equally.
C.S. Lewis

What the Puritans gave the world was not thought, but action.
Wendell Phillips

Ministers never write or preach so well as when under the cross; the Spirit of Christ and of glory then rests upon them. It was this, no doubt, that made the Puritans ... such burning lights and shining lights.
   When cast out by the black Bartholomew-act [the 1662 Act of Uniformity] and driven from their respective charges to preach in barns and

fields, in the highways and hedges, they in an especial manner wrote and preached as men having authority. Though dead, by their writings they yet speak; a peculiar unction attends them to this very hour.
George Whitefield

Puritans, Need for
Why do we need the Puritans? The answer, in one word, is maturity. Maturity is a compound of wisdom, goodwill, resilience, and creativity. The Puritans exemplified maturity; we don't.
J.I. Packer

Purity
See also: Holiness
Since we have these promises, dear friends, let us purify ourselves from everything that contaminates body and spirit, perfecting holiness out of reverence for God.
The Bible, 2 Corinthians 7:1

Keep yourself pure.
The Bible, 1 Timothy 5:22

Unto the pure all things are pure.
The Bible, Titus 1:15 KJV

I thought that continence arose from one's own powers, which I did not recognize in myself. I was foolish enough not to know that no one can be continent unless you grant it. For you would surely have granted it if my inner groaning had reached your ears and I with firm faith had cast my cares on you.
Augustine of Hippo

Nobody is more dangerous than he who imagines himself pure in heart; for his purity, by definition, is unassailable.
James Baldwin

Since then we are a holy portion, let us accomplish all that pertains to holiness; fleeing from slander, vile and impure embraces, drunkenness and rebellion and filthy lusts, detestable adultery and foul arrogance.
Clement of Rome

Solitude and silence help to maintain purity.
John Climacus

How to be pure? By steadfast longing for
the one good, that is, God.
Meister Eckhart

There cannot be perfect transformation
without perfect pureness.
John of the Cross

God desires the smallest degree of purity of
conscience in you more than all the works
you can perform.
John of the Cross

Still to the lowly soul
He doth himself impart,
And for his dwelling and his throne
Chooseth the pure in heart.

Lord, we thy presence seek;
May ours this blessing be;
Give us a pure and lowly heart,
A temple meet for thee.
John Keble

Oh! To be clean as a mountain river!
Clean as the air above the clouds, or on
the middle seas! As the throbbing ether
that fills the gulf between star and star!
Nay, as the thought of the Son of Man
Himself.
George MacDonald

Young Timothy
Learnt sin to fly.
New England Primer

Purity of heart means to love God above all
things and at the same time to see him
everywhere in all things.
Teilhard de Chardin

My strength is as the strength of ten,
Because my heart is pure.
Lord Alfred Tennyson

By looking at Christ's purity we shall see
our foulness.
Teresa of Avila

Make and keep me pure within.
Charles Wesley

Purpose
See also: Ambition; Goals
The purpose of life ... is a life of purpose.
Author unknown

Everyone who breathes, high and low,
educated and ignorant, young and old,
man and woman, has a mission, has a
work. We are not sent into this world for
nothing; we are not born at random; we
are not here, that we may go to bed at
night, and get up in the morning, toil for
our bread, eat and drink, laugh and joke,
sin when we have a mind, and reform
when we are tired of sinning, rear a family
and die. God sees every one of us; He
creates every soul ... for a purpose.
John Henry Newman

The chief end of man is to glorify God and
enjoy Him forever.
The Shorter Catechism, 1646

The main thing in this world is not being
sure what God's will is, but seeking it
sincerely, and following what we do
understand of it. The only possible answer
to the destiny of man is to seek without
respite to fulfil God's purpose.
P. Tournier

Q

Quarrels

You should either avoid quarrels altogether or else put an end to them as quickly as possible; otherwise, anger may grow into hatred, making a plank out of a splinter, and turn the soul into a murderer.
Augustine, The Rule of St Augustine

Quakers

Justice Bennett of Derby was the first that called us Quakers, because I bade them tremble at the word of the Lord. That was in the year 1650.
George Fox

He [Oliver Cromwell] said: "I see there is a people risen, that I cannot win either with gifts, honors, offices or places; but all other sects and people I can."
George Fox

Quarrelsome

A continual dropping in a very rainy day and a contentious woman are alike.
The Bible, Proverbs 27:15 KJV

Questions

Be patient with all that is unresolved in your heart and try to love the questions themselves. Do not seek the answers that cannot be given you because you wouldn't be able to live them. Live the questions now.
Author unknown

The first key to wisdom is assiduous and frequent questioning. For by doubting we come to inquiry, and by inquiry we arrive at truth.
Peter Abelard

A prudent question is one half of wisdom.
Francis Bacon

The important thing is not to stop questioning.
Albert Einstein

I keep six honest serving men
(They taught me all I knew);
Their names are What and Why and
When. And How and Where and Who.
Rudyard Kipling

Judge a man by his questions rather than by his answers.
Voltaire

Quietness

See also: Silence; Stillness
Study to be quiet.
The Bible, 1 Thessalonians 4:11 KJV

If we have not quiet in our minds, outward comfort will do no more for us than a golden slipper on a gouty foot.
John Bunyan

O God, make us children of quietness, and heirs of peace.
Clement of Rome

Sometimes quiet is disquieting.
Seneca

The holy time is quiet as a nun.
William Wordsworth

Quotations

It is a good thing for an uneducated man to read books of quotations.
Winston Churchill

The wisdom of the wise and the experience of the ages are perpetuated by quotations.
Benjamin Disraeli

I hate quotations.
Ralph Waldo Emerson

Next to the originator of a good sentence is
the first quoter of it.
Ralph Waldo Emerson

Quotations are useful, ingenious, and
excellent, when not overdone, and aptly
applied.
Edouard Fournier

Everything has been said before, but since
nobody listens we have to keep going back
and beginning all over again.
André Gide

I quote others only the better to express
myself.
Montaigne

To make good use of a thought found in a
book requires almost as much cleverness as
to originate it. Cardinal du Perron said
that the apt quotation of a line of Virgil
was worthy of the highest talent.
Stendhal

R

Race
See also: Intermarriage
God knew what he was doing when he made me black. On a piano you cannot play a good tune using only the white notes: you must use the black and white notes together. God wants to play tunes with both his white notes and his black ones.
Dr Aggrey

All who are not of good race in this world are chaff.
Adolf Hitler

The Americans ought to be ashamed of themselves for letting their medals be won by Negroes.
Adolf Hitler

I have a dream that my four little children will one day live in a nation where they will not be judged by the color of their skin but by the content of their character.
Martin Luther King

I want to be the white man's brother, not his brother-in-law.
Martin Luther King

My only concern was to go get home after a hard day's work.
Rosa Parks
Referring to her refusal, in 1955, to give up her seat on a bus in Montgomery, Alabama, to a white person who was standing. This act sparked the bus boycott and the leadership of Martin Luther King Jr

A heavy guilt rests upon us for what the whites of all nations have done to the colored peoples. When we do good to them, it is not benevolence – it is atonement.
Albert Schweitzer

Rainbows
My heart leaps up when I behold
A rainbow in the sky.
William Wordsworth

Rat race
The trouble with the rat race is that even if you win, you're still a rat.
Lily Tomlin

Reading
See also: Bible reading
Some books are to be tasted, others to be swallowed, and some few to be chewed and digested.
Francis Bacon

Read not to contradict and confute, nor to believe and take for granted, nor to find talk and discourse, but to weigh and consider.
Francis Bacon

To read without reflecting is like eating without digesting.
Edmund Burke

Seek in reading and you will find in meditation; knock in prayer and it will be opened to you in contemplation.
John of the Cross

Show me an army of leaders and I'll show you an army of readers.
Napoleon

Much reading is an oppression of the mind, and extinguishes the natural candle, which is the reason of so many senseless scholars in the world.
William Penn

Reading is to the mind what exercise is to

the body.
Richard Steele

Reading, Devotional

Idleness is the enemy of the soul. And therefore, at fixed times, the brothers ought to be occupied in manual labor; and again, at fixed times, in sacred reading.
Rule of Benedict

Read, mark, learn, and inwardly digest.
Book of Common Prayer

Christian devotional reading helps us find intimate union with God, its motivation being to love God with all our heart, mind, and will.
Jonathan Edwards

Read to refill the wells of inspiration.
Harold J. Ockenga

If you would benefit, read with humility, simplicity and faith, and never seek the fame of being learned.
Thomas à Kempis

In all things I sought quiet, and found it not save in retirement and in books.
Thomas à Kempis

Reality

Beware that you do not lose the substance by grasping at the shadow.
Æsop

I am certain of nothing but the holiness of the heart's affections, and the truth of imagination.
John Keats

Reality is usually something you could not have guessed.
C.S. Lewis

I stopped believing in Santa Claus when my mother took me to see him in a department store, and he asked for my autograph.
Shirley Temple

Reality is nothing but a collective hunch.
Lily Tomlin

I do not know whether I was then a man dreaming I was a butterfly, or whether I am now a butterfly dreaming I am a man.
Chuang-Tzu

Reason

Since grace does not scrap nature but brings it to perfection, so also natural reason should assist faith, as the natural loving bent of the will leads to charity.
Thomas Aquinas

God destines us for an end beyond the grasp of reason.
Thomas Aquinas

He that will not reason is a bigot;
he that cannot reason is a fool;
and he that dares not reason is a slave.
William Drummond

Without the capacity of rational argument, all our proof of God ceases.
Jonathan Edwards

I do not feel obliged to believe that the same God who has endowed us with sense, reason, and intellect has intended us to forgo their use.
Galileo Galilei

If you make use of your reason, you are like one who eats substantial food; but if you are moved by the satisfaction of your will, you are like one who eats insipid fruit.
John of the Cross

There is a difficulty about disagreeing with God. He is the source from which all your reasoning power comes.
C.S. Lewis

Reason is God's crowning gift to man.
Sophocles

Reason, Limitations of

Human reason cannot begin to answer the great questions as to what God is in

himself, and what he is in relation to us.
John Calvin

Reason is the greatest enemy faith has: it
never comes to the aid of spiritual things,
but – more frequently than not – struggles
against the divine Word, treating with
contempt all that emanates from God.
Martin Luther

If the greatest philosopher in the world
find himself on a plank wider than actually
necessary, but hanging over a precipice, his
imagination will prevail, though his reason
convince him of his safety.
Blaise Pascal

Reason acts slowly and with so many
views, on so many principles, which it
must always keep before it, that it
constantly slumbers and goes astray from
not having its principles to hand. The
heart does not act thus; it acts in a
moment, and is always ready to act. We
must then place faith in the heart or it will
always be vacillating.
Blaise Pascal

We know truth not only by reason but also
by the heart, and it is from this last that we
know first principles.
Blaise Pascal

The ultimate purpose of reason is to bring
us to the place where we can see that there
is a limit to reason.
Blaise Pascal

Rebuke
Thou art the man.
The Bible, 2 Samuel 12:7 KJV

A rebuke impresses a man of discernment
more than a hundred lashes a fool.
The Bible, Proverbs 17:10 KJV

Open rebuke is better than secret love.
The Bible, Proverbs 27:5 KJV

Faithful are the wounds of a friend.
The Bible, Proverbs 27:6 KJV

This testimony is true. Therefore, rebuke
them sharply, so that they will be sound in
the faith and will pay no attention to
Jewish myths or to the commands of those
who reject the truth.
The Bible, Titus 1:13,14

Receiving
See: Acceptance

Reclusive life
[The two general directions for the life of a
recluse are] to keep the heart smooth and
without any scar of evil, and to practice
bodily discipline, which serves the first
end, and of which Paul said that it
profiteth little.
Simon of Ghent, bishop of Salisbury, d. 1315

Recognition
I believe that honor and money nearly
always go together. Seldom or never is a
poor man honored by the world; however
worthy of honor he may be, he is apt
rather to be despised by it.
Teresa of Avila

Recollection
Preserve a habitual remembrance of eternal
life, recalling that those who hold
themselves the lowest and poorest and least
of all will enjoy the highest dominion and
glory in God.
John of the Cross

There are three signs of inner recollection:
first, a lack of satisfaction in passing things;
second, a liking for solitude and silence, and
an attentiveness to all that is more perfect;
third, the considerations, meditations and
acts that formerly helped the soul now
hinder it, and it brings to prayer no other
support than faith, hope, and love.
John of the Cross

Reconciliation
… God was reconciling the world to
himself in Christ, not counting men's sins
against them. And he has committed to us
the message of reconciliation.
The Bible, 2 Corinthians 5:19

All who strive for reconciliation seek to listen rather than to convince, to understand rather than to impose themselves.
Brother Roger

Redemption
See: Christ, Cross; Death of; Salvation

Reformation, Church
The Bishop of Rome hath no jurisdiction in this Realm of England.
Book of Common Prayer

The church needs a reformation. This reformation is not, however, the concern just of the pope, nor of the cardinals. It is the concern of all Christendom, or better still, of God alone. Only he knows the hour of this reformation.
Martin Luther

Reformation, Personal
Repentance may begin instantly, but reformation often requires a sphere of years.
Henry Ward Beecher

Reformers
The best reformers the world has ever seen are those who commence on themselves.
George Bernard Shaw

Regeneration
See also: Accepting God; Becoming a Christian; Conversion
For you have been born again, not of perishable seed, but of imperishable, through the living and enduring word of God.
The Bible, 1 Peter 1:23

The manner of regeneration cannot be fully comprehended by believers in this life. Notwithstanding which, they rest satisfied with knowing and experiencing that by this grace of God they are enabled to believe with the heart, and to love their Savior.
Canons of the Synod of Dort

A light from above entered and permeated my heart, now cleansed from its defilement. The Spirit came from heaven, and changed me into a new man by the second birth. Almost at once in a marvelous way doubt gave way to assurance, and what I had thought impossible could be done.
Cyprian

God's ultimate purpose is birth. He is not content until he brings his Son to birth in us.
Meister Eckhart

The very first and indispensable sign is self-loathing and abhorrence.
Charles Simeon, asked about the principal mark of regeneration

Regret
Regret for time wasted can become a power for good in the time that remains, if we will only stop the waste and the idle, useless regretting.
Arthur Brisbane

Rejection
The stone which the builders refused is become the head stone of the corner.
The Bible, Psalm 118:22 KJV

Rejoicing
Rejoice in the Lord always. I will say it again. Rejoice!
The Bible, Philippians 4:4

Relationships
See also: Anger; Kindness; Praise of others
Use your head to handle yourself, your heart to handle others.
Author unknown

Almost all of our relationships begin and most of them continue as forms of mutual exploitation, a mental or physical barter, to be terminated when one or both parties run out of goods.
W.H. Auden

The easiest kind of relationship for me is with ten thousand people. The hardest is with one.
Joan Baez

A man's feelings of good will toward others is the strongest magnet for drawing good will from others.
Chesterfield

It is better to be hated for what you are than loved for what you are not.
André Gide

If you want people to be glad to meet you, you must be glad to meet them – and show it.
Johann Wolfgang von Goethe

We are interested in others if they are interested in us.
Horace

Well, it seems to me that the best relationships – the ones that last – are frequently the ones that are rooted in friendship. You know, one day you look at the person and you see something more than you did the night before. Like a switch has been flicked somewhere. And the person who was just a friend is … suddenly the only person you can ever imagine yourself with.
Scully, X-files

You can never establish a personal relationship without opening up your own heart.
Paul Tournier

Religion
See also: Atheism; Christianity; Faith
It may be said with some certainty that no religion or religious philosophy is any better than its conception of God.
Mark Albrecht

Religion is unbelief. It is a concern, indeed we must say that it is the one great concern of godless man … It is the attempted replacement of a divine work by a human manufacture.
Karl Barth

Man is by his constitution a religious animal.
Edmund Burke

Men will wrangle for religion; write for it; fight for it; anything but – live for it.
C.C. Colton

Religion is an illusion and it derives its strength from the fact that it falls in with our instinctual desires.
Sigmund Freud

Religion without piety hath done more mischief in the world than all other things put together.
Thomas Fuller

My position is that all the great religions are fundamentally equal.
Mahatma Gandhi

Religion often partakes of the myth of progress that shields us from the terrors of an uncertain future.
Frank Herbert

Man makes religion, religion does not make man.
Karl Marx

Religion is the opium of the people.
Karl Marx

Religion is the sigh of the oppressed creature, the sentiment of a heartless world, and the soul of soulless condition.
Karl Marx

The first requisite for the happiness of the people is the abolition of religion.
Karl Marx

My country is the world, and my religion is to do good.
Tom Paine

Men never do evil so completely and cheerfully as when they do it from religious conviction.
Blaise Pascal

Every religion is false which, as to its faith, does not worship one only God as the origin of all things, and, as to its morality,

does not worship one only God as the goal of all things.
Blaise Pascal

Religion is so great a thing that it is right that those who will not take the trouble to seek it, if it be obscure, should be deprived of it.
Blaise Pascal

The true nature of religion is ...
immediate consciousness of the Deity as he is found in ourselves and in the world.
Friedrich Schleiermacher

We have just enough religion to make us hate, but not enough to make us love one another.
Jonathan Swift

Religions
To maintain that all religions are paths leading to the same goal, as is so frequently done today, is to maintain something that is not true. Not only on the dogmatic, but also on the mystical plane, too, there is no agreement. It is then only too true that the basic principles of Eastern and Western, which in practice means Indian and Semitic, thought are, I will not say irreconcilably opposed; they are simply not starting from the same premises.
Professor Zaehner, Hindu scholar

Religious fanaticism
Defoe says that there were a hundred thousand country fellows in his time ready to fight to the death against popery, without knowing whether popery was a man or a horse.
William Hazlitt

Religious practice
There's a kind of religious practice without any inward experience which is of no account in the sight of God. It is good for nothing.
Jonathan Edwards

Remarriage
A woman is bound to her husband as long as he lives. But if her husband dies, she is free to marry anyone she wishes, but he must belong to the Lord.
The Bible, 1 Corinthians 7:39

The primary question is how it [the church] may find some arrangement that will give adequate form both to its beliefs about the permanence of marriage and to its beliefs about the forgiveness of the penitent sinner.
Professor Oliver O'Donovan, Regius Professor of Moral and Pastoral Theology at Oxford

Remember
Remember Jesus Christ, raised from the dead, descended from David.
The Bible, 2 Timothy 2:8

People need to be reminded more often than they need to be instructed.
Samuel Johnson

Remembrance Day
See: Death

Remorse
Dread remorse when you are tempted to err, Miss Eyre: remorse is the poison of life.
Charlotte Brontë

Renewal
Therefore we do not lose heart. Though outwardly we are wasting away, yet inwardly we are being renewed day by day.
The Bible, 2 Corinthians 4:16

... he saved us, not because of righteous things we had done, but because of his mercy. He saved us through the washing of rebirth and renewal by the Holy Spirit ...
The Bible, Titus 3:5

Renunciation
A firm faith is the mother of the renunciation of the world; the opposite, obviously, produces the opposite effect. Unwavering hope is the door to the renunciation of every earthly affection; the opposite, obviously produces the opposite effect.

The love of God is the basis of detachment from the world; and here too the opposite, obviously, has the opposite effect.
John Climacus

To renounce all is to gain all; to descend is to rise; to die is to live.
Karl Rahner

The Protestant Church has perhaps taught too exclusively the duty of consecrating to God the life we are born into, and left too little room for the truth that in the present evil world there must be great renunciations as well if there are to be great Christian careers.
John Sung

Repentance
Amend your ways and your doings.
The Bible, Jeremiah 7:3 KJV

Repentance

John Bunyan
"The sacrifices of God are a broken spirit; a broken and a contrite heart, O God, Thou wilt not despise." Psalm 51:17
Psalm 51 is David's penitential psalm. It may be fitly so called, because it is a Psalm by which is manifest the unfeigned sorrow which he had for his horrible sin, in defiling of Bathsheba, and slaying Uriah her husband; a relation at large of which you have in the 11th and 12th of the second of Samuel.
Many workings of heart, as this psalm showeth, this poor man had, so soon as conviction did fall upon his spirit: one while he cries for mercy, then he confesses his heinous offences. Then he bewails the depravity of his nature; sometimes he cries out to be washed and sanctified, and then again he is afraid that God will cast him away from his presence, and take his Holy Spirit utterly from him: and thus he goes on till he comes to the text, and there he stayeth his mind. Finding in himself that

heart and spirit which God did not dislike: "The sacrifices of God." says he. "are a broken spirit;" as it he should say. I thank God I have that. "A broken and a contrite heart," saith he. "O God, thou wilt not despise;" as if he should say. I thank God I have that.
The words consist of two parts: 1. An Assertion. 2. A Demonstration of that Assertion. The Assertion is this, "The sacrifices of God are a broken spirit." The Demonstration is this. "Because a broken and a contrite heart God will not despise."
In the Assertion, we have two things present themselves to our consideration: 1. That a broken spirit is to God a sacrifice. 2. That it is to God, as that which answereth to or goeth beyond all sacrifices: The sacrifices of God are a broken spirit." The demonstration of this is plain, for that heart God will not despise; "a broken and a contrite heart. O God, thou wilt not despise."
Whence I draw this conclusion, That a spirit rightly broken, a heart truly contrite, is to God an excellent thing; that is, a thing that goeth "beyond all external duties whatever; for that is intended by this saying. "The sacrifices," because it answereth to all sacrifices which we can offer to God: yea. it serveth in the room of all: alt our sacrifices without this are nothing; this alone is all.
There are four things that are very acceptable to God.
The First is, The sacrifice of the body of Christ for our sins; of this you read, Heb. 10; for there you have it preferred to all burnt offerings and sacrifices; it is this that pleaseth God; it is this that sanctifieth and so setteth the people acceptable in the sight of God.
Secondly, unfeigned love to God is counted better than all sacrifices, or external parts of worship: "And to love the lord thy God with all the heart, with all the understanding, and with all the soul, and with all the strength, and to love his neighbor as himself, is more than all whole burnt-offerings and sacrifices." Mark 12:33.
Thirdly. To walk holily and humbly and obediently towards and before God, is another: Mic. 6: 6-8. "Hath the Lord as

great delight in burnt-offerings and sacrifices, as in obeying the voice of the Lord? Behold, to obey is better than sacrifice, and to hearken, than the fat of rams," I Sam. 15:22.

Fourthly. And this in our text is the fourth, "The sacrifices of God are a broken spirit: a broken and a contrite heart. O God, thou wilt not despise."

But note by the way, that this broken, and contrite head, is thus excellent only to God: "O God." saith he "thou wilt not despise it:" by which is implied, the world has not this esteem or respect for such a heart, or for one that is of a broken and a contrite spirit: no, no: a man, a woman, that is blessed with a broken heart is so far off from getting by that esteem with the world, that they are but burdens, and trouble houses wherever they are or go; such people carry with them molestation and disquietment; they are in carnal families, as David was to the King of Gath, "troublers of the house." 1 Sam. 21

Their sighs, their tears, their day and night groans. Their cries and prayers and solitary carriages put all the carnal family out of order: hence you have them brow-beaten by some, contemned by others; yea and their company fled from and deserted by others. But mark the text, "A broken and a contrite heart. O God, thou wilt not despise," but rather accept; for not to despise is, with God, to esteem and set a high price upon.

But we will demonstrate by several particulars. That a broken spirit, a spirit rightly broken, a heart truly contrite, is to God an excellent thing.

First, This is evident from the comparison. "Thou desirest not sacrifice, else would I give it: thou delightest not in burnt-offerings: the sacrifices of God are a broken spirit," etc. Mark, he rejecteth sacrifices, offerings and sacrifices; that is, all Levitical ceremonies under the law, and all external performances under the gospel; but accepteth a broken heart. It is therefore manifest by this, were there nothing else to be said, that proves, that a heart truly broken, truly contrite, is to God an excellent thing: for, as you see, such a heart is set before all sacrifice, and yet they were the ordinances of God, and things that he commanded. But, lo! a broken spirit is above them all. A contrite heart goes beyond them, yea beyond them, when put all together. Thou wilt not have the one, thou wilt not despise the other. O brethren! a broken and contrite heart is an excellent thing. Have I said, a broken heart, a broken and a contrite heart is esteemed above all sacrifices? I will add.

Secondly, It is of greater esteem with God, than is either heaven or earth, and that is more than to be set before external duties. "Thus saith the Lord. Heaven is my throne, and the earth is my footstool: where is the house that ye build me, or where is the place of my rest? For all these things hath mine hands made. And all these things have been. saith the Lord: but to this man will I look, even to him that is poor and of a contrite spirit, and trembleth at my word," Isa. 66:1.2.

Mark, God saith, he hath made all these things; but he doth not say that he will look to them, that is, take complacency and delight in them; no, there is that wanting in all that be hath made, that should take up and delight his heart: but now, let a broken-hearted sinner come before him, yea, he ranges the world throughout to find such an one, and having found him, "To this man," saith he, "will I look." I say again, that such a man, to him, is of more value than is either heaven or earth: "They," saith he, wax old, they shall perish and vanish away; but this man, he continues, he, (as is presented to us in another place. Under another character,) "he shall abide for ever." Heb. 1.10-12; 1 John 11.17.

"To this man will I look?' with this man be delighted; for to look doth sometimes signify. "Thou hast ravished my heart, my sister, my spouse, saith Christ to his humble-hearted: "thou hast ravished my heart with one of thine eyes." (while it is as a conduit to let the rivers out of thy broken heart.) "I am taken," saith he, "with one chain of thy neck" Song 4:9. Here, you see, he looks and is ravished. He looks and is taken; as it saith in another place, "The king is held in the galleries." Song 7: 5 That is, is taken with his beloved, "with the dove's eyes" of his beloved, (1:15,) with the contrite spirit of his people.

But it is not thus reported of him with respect to heaven or earth; them he sets more lightly by; "them unto fire against the day of judgment and perdition of ungodly men," 2 Pet. 3: 7. But the broken in heart are His beloved, his jewels.

Wherefore what I have said as to this, must go for the truth of God. To wit, that a broken-hearted sinner, a sinner with a contrite spirit, is of more esteem with God than is either heaven or earth. He saith, he hath made them; but he doth not say, he will look to them: he saith, they are his throne and footstool; but he doth not say, they have taken or ravished his heart; no, it is those that are of a contrite spirit do this.

But there is yet more in the words. "To this man will I look;" that is, For this man will I care; about this man will I camp; I will put this man under my protection; for so to look to one, doth sometimes signify; and I take the meaning in this place to be such. Prov.27:23; Jer. 39:12; 44:4.

"The Lord upholdeth all that fall, and raiseth up all that are bowed down." And the broken-hearted are of this number; wherefore he careth for, campeth about, and hath set his eyes upon such an one for good. This therefore is a second demonstration to prove that the man that hath his spirit rightly broken, his heart truly contrite, is of great esteem with God.

Thirdly, yet further, God doth not only prefer such an one, as has been said, before heaven and earth, but he loveth, he desireth to have that man for an intimate, for a companion: he must dwell, he must cohabit with him that is of a broken heart, with such as are of a contrite spirit. "For thus saith the high and lofty One that inhabiteth eternity, whose name is holy. I dwell in the high and holy place. with him also that is of a contrite and humble spirit," Isa. 57:15.

Behold here both the majesty and condescension of the high and lofty One; his majesty, in that he is high, and the inhabiter of eternity. "I am the high and lofty One," saith he; "I inhabit eternity." Verily, this consideration is enough to make the broken-hearted man creep into a mouse hole to hide himself from such a majesty. But behold his heart, his condescending mind: I am for dwelling also "with him that hath a broken heart, with him that is of a contrite spirit," that is the man that I would converse with, that is the man with whom I will cohabit, that is he, saith God. I will choose for my companion. For to desire to dwell with one, supposeth all these things; and verily, of all the men in the world, none have acquaintance with God, none understand what communion with him, and what his teachings mean, but such as are of a broken and contrite heart: "He is nigh to them that are of a broken spirit," Psa. 34:18. These are intended in the 14th Psalm, where it is said, "The Lord looked down from heaven, to see if any did understand and seek God," that he might find somebody in the world with whom he might converse; for indeed there is none else that either understand, or that can attend to hearken to him. God, as I may say, is forced to break men's hearts, before he can make them willing to cry to him, or be willing that he should have any concerns with them, the rest shut their eyes, stop their ears, withdraw their hearts, or say unto God, "Be gone," Job 21. But now the broken heart can attend it, he has leisure, yea, leisure and will, and understanding and all; and therefore he is a fit man to have to do with God. There is also room in this man's house, in this man's heart, in this man's spirit, for God to dwell, for God to walk, for God to set up a kingdom.

Here therefore is suitableness. "Can two walk together," saith God. "except they be agreed?" Amos 3:3 . The broken-hearted desireth God's company: "When wilt thou come unto me?" saith he. The broken-hearted loveth to hear God speak and talk to him. Here is a suitableness: "Cause me." saith he, "to hear joy and gladness, that the bones which thou hast broken may rejoice," Psa. 11.8.

But here lies the glory, in that the high and lofty One, the God that inhabiteth eternity, and that has a high and holy place for his habitation, should choose to dwell with, and to be a companion of the broken in heart, and of them that are of a contrite spirit: yea, and here is also great comfort for such.

John Bunyan, The Excellency of a Broken Heart, the last book Bunyan wrote

---

Repentance

He shows himself worthy, in that he confesses himself unworthy.
Augustine of Hippo

Before God can deliver us we must undeceive ourselves.
Augustine of Hippo

When thou leavest that which loveth thee, and lovest that which hateth thee; then thou mayest abide continually in repentance.
Jacob Boehme

Repentance ranges from regretting obvious sins like murder, adultery, abuse, swearing, and stealing to the realization that not loving (loving your brother as yourself) is a murder. "Whoever hates his brother is a murderer,"(1 John 3:15), and that an evil look is adultery and the love of praise is stealing God's glory.
John Chrysostom

Repentance is not the work of man, as the prophet Jeremiah said, "Make me repent my Lord and I shall repent."
John Chrysostom

To do so no more is the truest repentance.
Martin Luther

A noble mind disdains not to repent.
Alexander Pope

Years of repentance are necessary in

order to blot out a sin in the eyes of men, but one tear of repentance suffices with God.
French proverb

When preaching has failed to reform a man, try a little ridicule.
Santeuil

One of the most fundamental marks of true repentance is a disposition to see our sins as God sees them.
Charles Simeon

Reprobation
See: Predestination

Reproof

If you reprove someone, you yourself get carried away by anger and you are satisfying your own passion; do not lose yourself, therefore, in order to save another.
Abba Macarius the Great

Reputation

A good name is better than precious ointment.
The Bible, Ecclesiastes 7:1 KJV

Woe unto you, when all men shall speak well of you!
The Bible, Luke 6:26 KJV

Rescue
See: Deliverance

Resolutions

Resolved: that every man should live to the glory of God.
Resolved second: that whether others do this or not I will.
Martin Luther

Respect

Show proper respect to everyone ...
The Bible, 1 Peter 2:17

Without respect, love cannot go far or rise high: it is an angel with but one wing.
Alexandre Dumas

He that respects not is not respected.
George Herbert

Responsibility
Character – the willingness to accept responsibility for one's own life – is the source from which self-respect springs.
Joan Didion

When the freedom they wished for most was freedom from responsibility, then Athens ceased to be free and was never free again.
Edith Hamilton

Do you realize the responsibility I carry? I'm the only person standing between Richard Nixon and the White House.
John F. Kennedy

Rest
You have created us for yourself, and our heart cannot be stilled until it finds rest in you.
Augustine of Hippo

How beautiful it is to do nothing, and then rest afterward.
Spanish proverb

Restoration
The house of my soul is too small for you to come to it. May it be enlarged by you. It is in ruins, restore it.
Augustine of Hippo

Restoring others
Brothers, if someone is caught in a sin, you who are spiritual should restore him gently. But watch yourself, or you also may be tempted.
The Bible, Galatians 6:1

Results
Leave results to God.
Elizabeth Barrett Browning

Resurrection
See also: Life after death
He was raised on the third day according to the Scriptures.
The Bible, 1 Corinthians 15:4

But if it is preached that Christ has been raised from the dead, how can some of you say that there is no resurrection of the dead? If there is no resurrection of the dead, then not even Christ has been raised. And if Christ has not been raised, our preaching is useless and so is your faith.
The Bible, 1 Corinthians 15:12-14

For since death came through a man, the resurrection of the dead comes also through a man. For as in Adam all die, so in Christ all will be made alive.
The Bible, 1 Corinthians 15:21,22

So will it be with the resurrection of the dead. The body that is sown is perishable, it is raised imperishable; it is sown in dishonor, it is raised in glory; it is sown in weakness, it is raised in power; it is sown a natural body, it is raised a spiritual body. If there is a natural body, there is also a spiritual body.
The Bible, 1 Corinthians 15:42-44

On Easter day tomorrow has become today.
Author unknown

I know of no one fact in the history of mankind which is proved by better evidence of every sort, to the understanding of a fair enquirer, than the great sign which God has given us that Christ died and rose from the dead.
Thomas Arnold

The claims of Jesus Christ, namely his resurrection, has led me as often as I have tried to examine the evidence to believe it as a fact beyond dispute.
Lord Caldecote, former Lord Chief Justice of England

Although we have complete salvation through his death, because we are reconciled to God by it, it is by his resurrection, not his death, that we are said to be born to a living hope (1 Peter 1:3).
John Calvin

Christ has turned all our sunsets into dawns.
Clement of Alexander

Let us look at the resurrection which happens regularly. Day and night show us a resurrection; night goes to sleep, day rises: day departs, night arrives.
Clement of Rome

Christianity does not hold the resurrection to be one among many tenets of belief. Without faith in the resurrection there would be no Christianity at all ... Once disprove it, and you have disposed of Christianity.
Michael Green

There are but two essential requirements: first: Has any one cheated death and proved it? Second: Is it available to me? Here is the complete record.
Confucius' tomb – occupied
Buddha's tomb – occupied
Mohammed's tomb – occupied
Jesus' tomb – empty.
Argue as you will. There is no point in following a loser.
G.B. Hardy

Without the resurrection there will not be a Christianity – Christianity stands or falls with the resurrection, and this single factor makes Christianity remarkably one of a kind.
Steve Kumar

If the thing happened, it was the central event in the history of the earth.
C.S. Lewis

Jesus' supreme credential to authenticate his claim to deity was his resurrection from the dead. Five times in the course of his life he predicted he would die. He also predicted how he would die and that three days later he would rise from the dead and appear to his disciples.
Paul E. Little

I know pretty well what evidence is; and, I tell you, such evidence as that for the resurrection has never broken down yet.
Lord Lyndhurst.

High Steward of Cambridge University, regarded as one of the greatest legal minds in the history England

It thus appears that from the dawn of her history the Christian Church not only believed in the resurrection of her Lord, but that her belief upon the point was interwoven with her whole existence.
William Milligan

[The origin of Christianity must] remain an unsolved enigma for any historian who refuses to take seriously the only explanation offered by the Church itself.
Professor C.F.D. Moule

Our old history ends with the cross; our new history begins with the resurrection.
Watchman Nee

The purpose of revelation is restoration, the renewal in us of that likeness to God which man lost by sin.
Stephen Neill

No single example can be produced of belief in the resurrection of an historical personage such as Jesus was: none at least on which anything was ever founded. The Christian resurrection is thus a fact without historical analogy.
James Orr

The empty tomb of Christ has been the cradle of the Church.
Pressensé

No resurrection, no Christianity.
Michael Ramsey

Perhaps the transformation of the disciples of Jesus is the greatest evidence of all for the resurrection.
John Stott

Christ himself deliberately staked his whole claim to the credit of men upon his resurrection. When asked for a sign he pointed to this sign as his single and sufficient credential.
B.B. Warfield

Indeed, taking all the evidence together, it is not too much to say that there is no single historic incident better or more variously supported than the resurrection of Christ.
B.F. Westcott

Resurrection, Bodily

We affirm that the bodily resurrection of Christ from the dead is essential to the biblical gospel (1 Cor. 15:14).
The gospel of Jesus Christ: An evangelical celebration

The seed dies into new new life and so does man.
George Macdonald

Resurrection, Last command of risen Jesus

Therefore go and make disciples of all nations.
The Bible, Matthew 28:19

Resurrection of Christians

By his power God raised the Lord from the dead, and he will raise us also.
The Bible, 1 Corinthians 6:14

Listen, I tell you a mystery: We will not all sleep, but we will all be changed – in a flash, in the twinkling of an eye, at the last trumpet. For the trumpet will sound, the dead will be raised imperishable, and we will be changed.
The Bible, 1 Corinthians 15:51,52

… we know that the one who raised the Lord Jesus from the dead will also raise us with Jesus and present us with you in his presence.
The Bible, 2 Corinthians 4:14

Retirement

If I followed my own inclination I would sit in my armchair and take it easy for the rest of my life. But I dare not do it. I must work as long as life lasts.
Lord Shaftesbury

Retribution

They have sown the wind, and they shall reap the whirlwind.
The Bible, Hosea 8:7

Revelation

The secret things belong unto the Lord.
The Bible, Deuteronomy 29:29 KJV

I am God, and there is none like me. I make known the end from the beginning, from ancient times, what is still to come.
The Bible, Isaiah 46:9,10 KJV

No one has ever seen God, but God the One and Only, who is at the Father's side, has made him known.
The Bible, John 1:18

Self-will cannot comprehend anything of God.
Jacob Boehme

The only possible answer to modern man's quest for the ultimate meaning of history and for an absolute ethical standard would have to lie in a revelation from outside the world.
John W. Montgomery

Instead of complaining that God had hidden himself, you will give him thanks for having revealed so much of himself.
Blaise Pascal

The world's best geographer cannot show us the way to God, and the world's best psychiatrist cannot give us a final answer to the problem of our guilt. There are matters contained in Holy Writ that "unveil" for us that which is not exposed to the natural course of human investigation.
Sproul

What is offered to man's apprehension in any specific revelation is not truth concerning God but the living God Himself.
William Temple

Revelations

All the principles of godliness are

undermined by fanatics who substitute revelations for Scripture.
John Calvin

The work of the Spirit promised to us is not to create new and unfamiliar revelations, or to coin some novel type of teaching by which we may be led away from the received doctrine of the gospel, but to seal on our minds the very doctrine which the gospel recommends.
John Calvin

All visions, revelations, heavenly feelings and whatever is greater than these, are not worth the least act of humility, being the fruits of that charity which neither values nor seeks itself, which thinketh well, not of itself, but of others. Many souls, to whom visions have never come, are incomparably more advanced in the way of perfection than others to whom many have been given.
John of the Cross

And sometimes those that men think were revelations, are deceits and illusions, and therefore it is not expedient to give readily credence to every stirring, but soberly abide.
Margery Kempe

Revenge

Do not seek revenge …
The Bible, Leviticus 19:18

Do not take revenge, my friends, but leave room for God's wrath, for it is written: "It is mine to avenge; I will repay," says the Lord.
The Bible, Romans 12:19

If thine enemy hunger, feed him; if he thirst, give him drink: for in so doing thou shalt heap coals of fire on his head.
The Bible, Romans 12:20 KJV

Do not repay evil with evil or insult with insult, but with blessing, because to this you were called so that you may inherit a blessing.
The Bible, 1 Peter 3:9

Revenge is sweet, but forgiveness is sweeter.
Author unknown

A man that studieth revenge keeps his own wounds green.
Francis Bacon

Revenge never healed a wound.
Guarini

Revenge is the abject pleasure of an abject mind.
Juvenal

That old law about "an eye for an eye" leaves everybody blind.
Martin Luther King, Jr

Revenge is often like biting a dog because the dog bit you.
Austin O'Malley

Blood that has been shed does not rest.
Jewish proverb

The smallest revenge will poison the soul.
Jewish proverb

Revenge is an inhuman word.
Seneca

It costs more to revenge injuries than to bear them.
Thomas Wilson

Revenge, limited

Eye for eye, tooth for tooth, hand for hand, foot for foot.
The Bible, Deuteronomy 19:21

Reverence

Let us hear the conclusion of the whole matter: Fear God, and keep his commandments; for this is the whole duty of man.
The Bible, Ecclesiastes 12:13 KJV

But unto you that fear my name shall the Sun of righteousness arise with healing in his wings.
The Bible, Malachi 4:2 KJV

Fear God. Honor the king.
1 Peter 2:17 KJV

Fear the Lord and you will do everything well.
Shepherd of Hermas

Revival

Extract from: The Distinguishing Marks of a Work of the Spirit of God, Jonathan Edwards

Beloved, believe not every spirit, but try the spirits whether they are of God: because many false prophets are gone out into the world (1 John 4:1).

JUDGING BETWEEN THE TRUE AND THE FALSE

In the apostolic age, there was the greatest outpouring of the Spirit of God that ever was, both as to his extraordinary influences and gifts, and his ordinary operations, in convincing, converting, enlightening, and sanctifying the souls of men. But as the influences of the true Spirit abounded, so counterfeits did also abound: the devil was abundant in mimicking, both the ordinary and extraordinary influences of the Spirit of God, as is manifest by innumerable passages of the apostles' writings. This made it very necessary that the church of Christ should be furnished with some certain rules, distinguishing and clear marks, by which she might proceed safely in judging of the true from the false without danger of being imposed upon. The giving of such rules is the plain design of this chapter, where we have this matter more expressly and fully treated of than anywhere else in the Bible. The apostle, of set purpose, undertakes to supply the church of God with such marks of the true Spirit as may be plain and safe, and well accommodated to use and practice; and that the subject might be clearly and sufficiently handled, he insists upon it throughout the chapter, which makes it wonderful that what is said here is no more

taken notice of in this extraordinary day, when there is such an uncommon and extensive operation on the minds of people, such a variety of opinions concerning it, and so much talk about the work of the Spirit.

THE INDWELLING OF THE SPIRIT

The apostle's discourse on this subject is introduced by an occasional mention of the indwelling of the Spirit, as the sure evidence of an interest in Christ. "And he that keepeth his commandments dwelleth in him, and he in him; and hereby we know that he abideth in us, by the Spirit which he hath given us." From this we may infer that the apostle's purpose is not only to give marks by which to distinguish the true Spirit from the false, in his extraordinary gifts of prophecy and miracles, but also in his ordinary influences on the minds of his people, in order that they may be united to Christ, and be built up in him. This is also manifest from the marks themselves that are given, which we shall consider later.

CREDULITY AND COUNTERFEITS

The words of the text are an introduction to this discourse of the distinguishing signs of the true and false Spirit. Before the apostle proceeds to lay down these signs, he exhorts Christians, first, against being over-credulous, and forward to admit every specious appearance as a work of a true Spirit. "Beloved, believe not every spirit, but try the spirits whether they are of God." And, second, he shows that there were many counterfeits, "because many false prophets are gone out into the world". These not only claimed to have the Spirit of God in his extraordinary gifts of inspiration, but also to be the great friends and favorites of heaven, to be eminently holy persons, and to have much of the ordinary saving, sanctifying influences of the Spirit of God on their hearts. Hence we are to look upon these words as a direction to examine and try their claims to the Spirit of God in both these respects.

THE SCRIPTURE IS OUR GUIDE

My purpose therefore at this time is to show what are the true, certain, and distinguishing evidences of a work of the Spirit of God, by which we may safely proceed in judging any operation we find in ourselves, or see in others. And here I would observe that we are to take the *Scriptures* as our guide in such cases. This is the great and standing rule which God has given to his church, in order to guide them in things relating to the great concerns of their souls; and it is an infallible and sufficient rule. There are undoubtedly sufficient marks given to guide the church of God in this great affair of judging of spirits, without which it would lie open to woeful delusion, and would be remedilessly exposed to be imposed on and devoured by its enemies. And we need not be afraid to trust these rules. Doubtless that Spirit who indited the Scriptures knew how to give us good rules, by which to distinguish his operations from all that is falsely claimed to be from him. And this, as I observed before, the Spirit of God has here done of set purpose, and done it more particularly and fully than anywhere else; so that in my present discourse I shall go nowhere else for rules or marks for the trial of spirits, but shall confine myself to those that I find in this chapter.

But before I proceed to speak about these particularly, I would prepare my way by first observing *negatively,* in some instances, what are *not* signs or evidences of a work of the Spirit of God.

Nine Negative signs
1. The very unusual and extraordinary character of a work

WHAT THE CHURCH HAS BEEN USED TO IS NOT A RULE BY WHICH WE ARE TO JUDGE

Nothing can be certainly concluded from a work being carried on in a very unusual and extraordinary way, provided the variety or difference is such as may still be included within the limits of scriptural rules. What the church has been used to is not a rule by which we are to judge, because there may be new and extraordinary works of God, and he has hitherto evidently worked in an extraordinary manner. He has brought to pass new things, strange works; and has worked in such a manner as to surprise both men and angels. And as God has done thus in times past, so we have no reason to think but that he will still do so. The prophecies of Scripture give us reason to think that God has things to accomplish which have never yet been seen. No deviation from what has hitherto been usual, let it be never so great, is an argument that a work is not from the Spirit of God, if it is no deviation from his prescribed rule. The Holy Spirit is sovereign in his operation; and we know that he uses a great variety; and we cannot tell how great a variety he may use, within the compass of the rules he himself has fixed. We ought not to limit God where he has not limited himself.

Therefore it is not reasonable to determine that a work is not from God's Holy Spirit because of the extraordinary degree in which the minds of persons are influenced. If they seem to have an extraordinary conviction of the dreadful nature of sin, and a very uncommon sense of the misery of a Christless condition – or extraordinary views of the certainty and glory of divine things – and are proportionably moved with very extraordinary affections of fear and sorrow, desire, love, or joy; or if the apparent change is very sudden, and the work carried on with very unusual swiftness – and the persons affected are very numerous, and many of them are very young, with other unusual circumstances, not infringing upon scriptural marks of a work of the Spirit – these things are no argument that the work is not of the Spirit of God. The extraordinary and unusual degree of influence, and power of operation, if in its nature it fits the rules and marks given in Scripture, is rather an argument in its favor; for by how much higher the degree which in its nature is agreeable to the rule, so much the more is there of conformity to the rule; and so much the more evident that conformity. When things are in small degrees, though they may really follow the rule, it is not so easily seen whether their nature agrees with the rule.

PEOPLE ARE VERY APT TO HAVE DOUBTS ABOUT THINGS THAT ARE STRANGE

People are very apt to have doubts about things that are strange; especially elderly persons, who doubt that things are right which they have never been used to in their day, and have not heard of in the days of their fathers. But if it is a good argument that a work is not from the Spirit of God if it is very unusual, then it was so in the apostles' days. The work of the Spirit then was carried on in a manner that, in very many respects, was altogether new – such as had never been seen or heard since the world stood. The work was then carried on with more visible and remarkable power than ever; nor had there been seen before such mighty and wonderful effects of the Spirit of God in sudden changes and such great engagedness and zeal in great multitudes – such a sudden alteration in towns, cities, and countries; such a swift progress, and vast extent of the work – and many other extraordinary circumstances might be mentioned. The great unusualness of the work surprised the Jews; they knew not what to make of it, but could not believe it to be the work of God; many looked upon the persons that were the subjects of it as bereft of reason; as you may see in Acts 2:13 and 26:24, and in 1 Corinthians 4:10.

And we have reason from Scripture prophecy to suppose that at the commencement of that last and greatest outpouring of the Spirit of God that is to come in the latter ages of the world, the manner of the work will be very extraordinary, and such as has never yet been seen; so that there shall be occasion to say, as in Isaiah 56:8, "Who hath heard such a thing? Who hath seen such things? Shall the earth be made to bring forth in one day? Shall a nation be born at once? for as soon as Zion travailed, she brought forth

her children." It may be reasonably expected that the extraordinary manner of the work then will bear some proportion to the very extraordinary events, and that glorious change in the state of the world, which God will bring to pass by it.

2. How the body is affected

A WORK IS NOT TO BE JUDGED BY TEARS, TREMBLING, GROANS, LOUD OUTCRIES, AGONIES OF BODY, OR THE FAILING OF BODILY STRENGTH

The influence people are under is not to be judged of one way or the other by such effects on the body; and the reason is, because the Scripture nowhere gives us any such rule. We cannot conclude that people are under the influence of the Spirit because we see such effects upon their bodies, because this is not given as a mark of the true Spirit; nor on the other hand have we any reason to conclude from any such outward appearances that persons are not under the influence of the Spirit of God, because there is no rule of Scripture given us to judge of spirits by, that does either expressly or indirectly exclude such effects on the body, nor does reason exclude them.

It is easily accounted for from the consideration of the nature of divine and eternal things, and the nature of man, and the laws of the union between soul and body, how a right influence, a true and proper sense of things, should have such effects on the body, even those that are of the most extraordinary kind, such as taking away the bodily strength, or throwing the body into great agonies, and extorting loud outcries. None of us does not suppose that the misery of hell is doubtless so dreadful, and eternity so vast, that if a person should have a clear apprehension of that misery as it is, it would be more than his feeble frame could bear, and especially if at the same time he saw himself in great danger of it, and to be utterly uncertain whether he would be delivered from it, and have no security from it one day or hour. If we consider human nature, we must not wonder that when person have a great sense of that which is so amazingly dreadful, and also have a great view of their own wickedness and God's anger, that things seem to them to forebode speedy and immediate destruction. We see the nature of man to be such that when he is in danger of some terrible calamity to which he is greatly exposed, he is ready upon every occasion to think that it is coming *now*.

THE MANIFESTATION OF GOD'S WRATH OVERWHELMS HUMAN STRENGTH

When people's hearts are full of fear, in time of war, they are ready to tremble at the shaking of a leaf, and to expect the enemy every minute, and to say within themselves, "*Now* I shall be slain." If we should suppose that a person saw himself hanging over a great pit, full of fierce and glowing flames, by a thread that he knew to be very weak, and not sufficient to bear his weight, and knew that multitudes had been in such circumstances before, and that most of them had fallen and perished, and saw nothing within reach that he could take hold of to save him, what distress would he be in! How ready to think that *now* the thread was breaking, that now, *this minute,* he would be swallowed up in those dreadful flames! And would he not be ready to cry out in such circumstances? How much more those that see themselves in this manner hanging over an infinitely more dreadful pit, or held over it in the hand of God, who at the same time they see to be exceedingly provoked! No wonder that the wrath of God, when manifested only a little to the soul, overbears human strength.

So it may easily be accounted for, that a true sense of the glorious excellence of the Lord Jesus Christ, and of his wonderful dying, love, and the exercise of a truly spiritual love and joy, should be such as very much to overcome the bodily strength. We are all ready to admit that no one can see God and live, and that it is only a very small part of that apprehension of the glory and love of Christ, which the saints enjoy in heaven, that our present frame can bear; therefore it is not at all strange that God should sometimes give his saints such foretastes of heaven as to diminish their bodily strength.

SOME EXTRAORDINARY THINGS ARE NOT MENTIONED IN THE NEW TESTAMENT

Some people object against such extraordinary appearances, that we have no instances of them recorded in the New Testament, under the extraordinary effusions of the Spirit. Were this allowed, I can see no force in the objection, if neither reason nor any rule of Scripture exclude such things – especially considering what was observed under the last heading. I do not know that we have any express mention inn the New Testament of any person's weeping, or groaning, or sighing through fear of hell, or a sense of God's anger; but is there anybody so foolish as to argue from this, that anyone in whom these things appear is not being convicted by the Spirit of God? And the reason why we do not argue thus is because these are easily accounted for from what we know of the nature of man, and from what the Scripture informs us in general concerning the nature of eternal things, and the nature of the convictions of God's Spirit; so that there is no need that anything should be said in particular concerning these external, circumstantial effects. Nobody supposes that there is any need of express scripture for every external, accidental manifestation of the inward motion of the mind: and though such circumstances are not particularly recorded in sacred history, there is a great deal of reason to think, from the general accounts we have, that it could not be otherwise than that such things must be in those days.

THE JAILER FELL DOWN AND TREMBLED

And there is also reason to think that such great outpouring of the Spirit was not wholly without those more extraordinary effects on people's bodies. The jailer in particular seems to have been an instance of that nature, when he, in the utmost distress and amazement, came trembling, and fell down before Paul and Silas. His falling down at that time does not seem to be intentionally putting himself into a posture of supplication, or humble address to Paul and Silas; for he seems not to have said anything to them then; but he first brought them out, and then he says to them, "Sirs, what must I do to be saved?" (Acts 16:29-30). But his falling down seems to be from the same cause as his trembling.

THE EXAMPLE OF THE PSALMIST

The psalmist gives an account of his crying out aloud, and a great weakening of his body under convictions of s#conscience, and a sense of the guilt of sin: "When I kept silence my bones waxed old, through my roaring all the day long; for day and night thy hand was heavy upon me: my moisture is turned into the drought of summer" (Ps. 32:3-4). We may at least argue so much from it, that such an effect of conviction of sin may well in some cases be supposed; for the psalmist would not represent his case by what would be absurd, and to which no degree of that exercise of mind he spoke of would have any tendency.

THE DISCIPLES CRIED OUT FOR FEAR

We read of the disciples that when they saw Christ coming to them in the storm, and took him for some terrible enemy, threatening their destruction in that storm, "they cried out for fear" (Matt. 14:26). Why then should it be thought strange that people should cry out for fear when God appears to them as a terrible enemy, and they see themselves in great danger of being swallowed up in the bottomless gulf of eternal misery?

THE SONG OF SONGS

The spouse, once and again, speaks of herself as overpowered with the love of Christ, so as to weaken her body, and make her faint: "Stay me with flagons, comfort me with apples; for I am sick of love... . I charge you, O ye daughters of Jerusalem, if ye find my Beloved, that ye tell him that I am sick of love" (S. of S. 2:5, 8). From this

we may at least argue that such an effect may well be supposed to arise from such a cause in the saints in some cases, and that such an effect will sometimes be seen in the church of Christ.

It is a weak objection to say that the impressions of enthusiasts have a great effect on their bodies. That the Quakers used to tremble is no argument that Saul, afterwards called Paul, and the jailer did not tremble from real convictions of conscience. Indeed, all such objections from effects on the body, whether greater or less, seem to be exceedingly frivolous. Those who argue from them proceed in the dark – they do not know what ground they go upon, nor by what rule they judge. The root and course of things is to be looked at, and the nature of the operations and affections are to be inquired into, and examined by the rule of God's word, and not the motions of the blood and animal spirits.

3. "A great deal of noise about religion"

It is no argument that an operation on people's minds is not the work of the Spirit of God, that it occasions a great deal of noise about religion.

For though true religion is contrary to that of the Pharisees – which was ostentatious, and delighted to set itself forth to the view of men for their applause – yet such is human nature that it is morally impossible for there to be a great concern, strong affection, and a general engagedness of mind among a people, without causing a notable, visible, and open commotion and alteration among that people. – Surely, it is no argument that people's minds are not under the influence of God's Spirit, that they are very much moved; for indeed spiritual and eternal things are so great, and of such infinite concern, that there is a great absurdity in men's being only moderately moved and affected by them; and surely it is no argument that they are affected with these things in some measure as they deserve, or in some proportion to their importance. And when was there ever any such thing since the world, stood, as a people in general being greatly affected in any affair whatsoever, without noise or stir? The nature of man will not allow it.

THEY TURNED THE WORLD UPSIDE DOWN

Indeed, Christ says: "The kingdom of God cometh not with observation" (Luke 17:20). That is, it will not consist in what is outward and visible; it will not be like earthly kingdoms, set up with outward pomp, in some particular place which will be the special royal city and seat of the kingdom. As Christ explains in the words which come next: "Neither shall they say, Lo here, or lo there; for behold the kingdom of God is within you." " Not that the kingdom of God will be set up in the world on the ruin of Satan's kingdom, without a very observable great effect: a mighty change in the state of things, to the observation and astonishment of the whole world. Just such an effect as this is foretold in the prophecies of Scripture, and by Christ himself in this very passage, and indeed in his own explanation of these words: "For as the lightning that lighteneth out of one part under heaven, shineth unto another part under heaven, so shall also the Son of man be in his day" (verse 24). This is to distinguish Christ's coming to set up his kingdom from the coming of false Christs, which he tells us will be in a private manner in the deserts and in the secret chambers; whereas this event of setting up the kingdom of God would be open and public in the sight of the whole world with clear manifestation, like lightning that cannot be hidden but glares in everyone's eyes and shines from one side of heaven to the other. And we find that when Christ's kingdom came, by that remarkable outpouring of the Spirit in the apostles' days, it occasioned a great stir everywhere. What a mighty opposition was there in Jerusalem on occasion of that great effusion of the Spirit! And so in Samaria, Antioch, Ephesus, Corinth, and other places! News of the affair filled the world, and caused some people to say of the apostles that they had turned the world upside down (Acts 17:6).

4. People's imaginations are affected

It is no argument that an operation on people's minds is not the work of the Spirit of God, that many who are subject to it have great impressions made on their imaginations. That people have many impressions on their imaginations does not prove that they have nothing else.

It is easy to account for there being much of this nature among a people, where a great many, of all kinds, have their minds engaged with intense thought and strong feelings about invisible things. Indeed, it would be strange if this did not happen. Such is our nature that we cannot think about invisible things without a degree of imagination. I dare appeal to any man, of the greatest powers of mind, whether he is able to fix his thoughts on God or Christ, or the things of another world, without imaginary ideas attending his meditations? And the more engaged the mind is, and the more intense the contemplation and affection, still the more lively and strong the imaginary idea will ordinarily be; especially when attended with surprise. And this is the case when the mental prospect is very new, and takes strong hold of the passions, such as fear or joy; and when the state and views of the mind suddenly changes from a contrary extreme, such as from that which was extremely dreadful to that which is extremely delightful. And it is no wonder that many people do not easily distinguish between that which is imaginary and that which is intellectual and spiritual; and that they are apt to lay too much weight on the imaginary part, and are most ready to speak of that in the account they give of their experiences, especially people of less understanding and distinguishing capacity.

THE IMAGINATION IS A GOD-GIVEN FACULTY

As God has given us such a faculty as the imagination, and so made us that we cannot think of things spiritual and invisible without some exercise of this faculty; so it appears to me that such is our state and nature that this faculty is really subservient and helpful to the other faculties of the mind, when a proper use is made of it; though often, when the imagination is too strong, and the other faculties weak, it overbears, and disturbs them in their exercise. It seems clear to me, in many instances with which I have been acquainted, that God has really made use of this faculty to truly divine purposes; especially in some that are more ignorant. God seems to condescend to their circumstances, and deal with them as babes; as of old he instructed his church, whilst in a state of ignorance and minority, by types and outward representations. I can see nothing unreasonable in such a position. Let others who have much occasion to deal with souls in spiritual concerns, judge whether experience does not confirm it.

It is no argument that a work is not of the Spirit of God, that some who are the subjects of it have been in a kind of ecstasy, in which they have had their minds transported into a train of strong and pleasing imaginations, and a kind of visions, as though they were rapt up to heaven, and there saw glorious sights. I have been acquainted with some such instances, and I see no need of bringing in the help of the devil into the account that we give of these things, nor yet of supposing them to be of the same nature as the visions of the prophets, or St Paul's rapture into paradise. Human nature, under these intense exercises and affections, is all that need be brought into the account.

THE WHOLE SOUL IS RAVISHED

If it may be well accounted for, that people under a true sense of the glorious and wonderful greatness and excellence of divine things, and soul-ravishing views of the beauty and love of Christ, should have the strength of nature overpowered, as I have already shown that it may; then I think it is not at all strange that amongst great numbers that are thus affected and overborne, there should be some persons of particular constitutions that have their imaginations effected like this. The effect is no other than what bears a proportion and analogy to other effects of the strong exercise of their minds. It is no wonder, when the thoughts are so fixed, and the affections so strong – and the whole soul so engaged, ravished, and swallowed up – that all other parts of the body are so affected as to be deprived of their strength, and the whole frame ready to dissolve. Is it any wonder that, in such a case, the brain in particular (especially in some constitutions), which we know is most especially affected by intense contemplations and exercises of mind, should be so affected that its strength and spirits should be diverted for a while, and taken off from impressions made on the organs of external sense, and wholly employed in a train of pleasing delightful imaginations, corresponding with the present frame of the mind? Some people are ready to interpret such things wrongly, and to lay too much weight on them, as prophetic visions, divine revelations, and sometimes indications from heaven of what is to happen (which, in some instances I have known, have been disproved in the event). But yet it appears to me that such things are evidently sometimes from the Spirit of God, though indirectly; that is, their extraordinary frame of mind, and that strong and lively sense of divine things which is the occasion of them, is from his Spirit; and also as the mind continues in its holy frame, and retains a divine sense of the excellence of spiritual things even in its rapture; which holy frame and sense is from the Spirit of God, though the imaginations that attend it are only accidental, and therefore there is commonly something or other in them that is confused, improper, and false.

5. The influence of example

It is no sign that a work is not from the Spirit of God that example is a great means of it.

It is surely no argument that an effect is nor from God, that means are used in producing it; for we know that it is God's manner to make use of means in carrying on his work in the world, and it is no more an argument against the divinity of an effect, that this means is made use of, than if it was by any other means. It is agreeable to Scripture that people should be influenced by one another's good example. The Scripture directs us to set good examples to that end (Matt. 5:16; 1 Pet. 3:1; 1 Tim. 4:12; Titus 2:7), and also directs us to be influenced by the good examples of others, and to follow them (2 Cor. 8:1-7; Heb. 6:12; Phil. 3:17; 1 Cor. 4:16 and 11:1; 2 Thess. 3:9-11; 1 Thess. 1:7). By this it appears that example is one of God's means; and certainly it is no argument that a work is not of God, that his own means are made use of to effect it.

And as it is a *scriptural* way of carrying on God's work, by example, so it is a *reasonable* way. It is no argument that men are not influenced by reason, that they are influenced by example. This way of people holding forth truth to one another has a tendency to enlighten the mind, and to convince reason. None will deny but that for people to communicate things to one another by words may rationally be supposed to tend to enlighten each other's minds; but the same thing may be communicated by actions, and much more fully and effectually. Words are of no use unless they convey our own ideas to others; but actions, in some cases, may do it much more fully.

There is a language in actions; and in some cases it is much more clear and convincing than in words. It is therefore no argument against the goodness of the effect, that people are greatly affected by seeing others so; indeed, though the impression may be made only by seeing the tokens of great and extraordinary affection in others in their behavior, taking for granted what they are affected with, without hearing them say one word. There may be language sufficient in such a case in their behavior alone, to convey their minds to others, and to communicate their sense of things more than can possibly be done by words alone. If a person should see another under extreme bodily torment, he might receive much clearer ideas, and more convincing evidence of what he suffered by his actions in his misery, than he could do only by the words of an unaffected, indifferent relater. In like manner he might receive a greater idea of anything that is excellent and very delightful, from the behavior of one that is in actual enjoyment, than by the dull narration of one who is inexperienced and insensible himself.

I desire that this matter may be examined by the strictest reason. Is it not manifest that effects produced in people's minds are rational, since not only weak and ignorant people are much influenced by example, but also those who make the greatest boast of strength of reason, are more influenced by reason held forth in this way than almost any other way? Indeed, the religious affections of many when raised by this means (such as by hearing the word preached, or any other means) may prove flashy, and soon vanish, as Christ represents the stony-ground hearers; but the affections of some thus moved by example are abiding, and prove to result in salvation.

There never yet was a time of remarkable pouring out of the Spirit, and great revival of religion, but that example had a main hand. So it was at the reformation, and in the apostles' days in Jerusalem and Samaria and Ephesus, and other parts of the world, as will be most manifest to anyone who attends to the accounts we have in the Acts of the Apostles. As in those days one person was moved by another, so one city or town was influenced by the example of another: "So that ye were ensamples to all that believe in Macedonia and Achaia, for from you sounded out the word of the Lord, not only in Macedonia and Achaia, but also in every place your faith to God-ward is spread abroad" (1 Thess. 1:7-8).

The word of God applied by example

It is no valid objection against example being so much used, that the Scripture speaks of the words as the principal means of carrying on God's work; for the word of God is the principal means, nevertheless, by which other means operate and are made effectual. Even the sacraments have no effect except by the word; and so it is that example becomes effectual; for all that is visible to the eye is unintelligible and vain without the word of God to instruct and guide the mind. It is the word of God that is indeed held forth and applied by example, as the word of the Lord sounded forth to other towns in Macedonia and Achaia by the example of those who believed in Thessalonica.

That example should be a great means of propagating the church of God seems to be indicated in Scripture in several ways: it is indicated by Ruth's following Naomi out of the land of Moab, into the land of Israel, when she resolved that she would not leave her, but would go wherever she went, and would lodge where she lodged; and that Naomi's people would be her people, and Naomi's God, her God. Ruth, who was the ancestral mother of David, and of Christ, was undoubtedly a great type of the church; and for this reason her story is inserted in the canon of Scripture. In her leaving the land of Moab, and its gods, to come and put her trust under the shadow of the wings of the God of Israel, we have a type of the conversion not only of the Gentile church but of every sinner, that is naturally an alien and stranger, but in his conversion forgets his own people, and father's house, and becomes a fellow-citizen with the saints and a true Israelite.

The same seems to be indicated in the effect which the example of the love-sick spouse has on the daughters of Jerusalem, i.e., visible Christians, who are first awakened by seeing the spouse in such extraordinary circumstances, and then converted (see Song of Songs 5:8-9 and 6:1). And this is undoubtedly one way that "the Spirit and the bride say, come" (Rev. 22:17) – i.e., the Spirit in the bride. It is foretold that the work of God will be very much carried on by this means in the last great outpouring of the Spirit that will introduce the glorious day of the church, so often spoken of in Scripture: "And the inhabitants of one city shall go to another,

saying, Let us go speedily to pray before the Lord, and to seek the Lord of hosts: I will go also. Yea, many people, and strong nations, shall come to seek the Lord of hosts in Jerusalem, and to pray before the Lord. Thus saith the Lord of hosts, In those days it shall come to pass, that ten men shall take hold of the skirt of him that is a Jew, saying, We will go with you for we have heard that God is with you" (Zech. 8:21-3).

6. Serious mistakes

It is no sign that a work is not from the Spirit of God, that many people who seem to be the subjects of it are guilty of great imprudences and irregularities in their conduct.

We are to consider that the end for which God pours out his Spirit is to make men holy, and not to make them politic. It is no wonder that, in a mixed multitude of all sorts – wise and unwise, young and old, of weak and strong natural abilities, under strong impressions of mind – there are many who behave imprudently. There are but few who know how to conduct themselves under strong feelings of any kind, whether of a temporal or spiritual nature; to do so requires a great deal of discretion, strength, and steadiness of mind. A thousand imprudences will not prove a work to be not of the Spirit of God; indeed, if there are not only imprudences but many things prevailing that are irregular, and really contrary to the rule of God's holy word. That it should be like this may be accounted for by the exceeding weakness of human nature, together with the remaining darkness and corruption of those that are the subjects of the saving influence of God's Spirit, and have a real zeal for God.

THE CHURCH AT CORINTH

We have a remarkable instance, in the New Testament, of a people who partook largely of that great effusion of the Spirit in the apostles' days, among whom there nevertheless abounded imprudence and great irregularities; namely, the church at

Corinth. There is scarcely any church more celebrated in the New Testament for being blessed with large measures of the Spirit of God, both in his ordinary influences, in convincing and converting sinners, and also in his extraordinary and miraculous gifts; yet what manifold imprudences, great and sinful irregularities, and strange confusion did they run into, at the Lord's supper, and in the exercise of church discipline! To which may be added their indecent manner of attending other parts of public worship, their jarring and contention about their teachers, and even the exercise of their extraordinary gifts of prophecy, speaking with tongues, and the like, in which they spoke and acted by the immediate inspiration of the Spirit of God.

THE APOSTLE PETER WAS GUILTY OF A GREAT AND SINFUL ERROR

And if we see great imprudences, and even sinful irregularities, in some who are great instruments to carry on the work, it will not prove it not to be the work of God. The apostle Peter himself, who was a great, eminently holy, and inspired apostle – and one of the chief instruments of setting up the Christian church in the world – when he was actually engaged in this work was guilty of a great and sinful error in his conduct; of which the apostle Paul speaks in Galatians 2:11-13: "But when Peter was come to Antioch, I withstood him to the face, because he was to be blamed; for before that certain men came from James, he did eat with the Gentiles, but when they were come, he withdrew, and separated himself, fearing them that were of the circumcision; and the other Jews dissembled likewise with him; insomuch, that Barnabas also was carried away with their dissimulation." If a great pillar of the Christian church – one of the chief of those who are the very foundation son which, next to Christ, the whole church is said to be built – was guilty of such an irregularity, is it any wonder if other lesser instruments, who have not that extraordinary conduct of the divine Spirit he had, should be guilty of many irregularities?

CENSURING OTHERS

And in particular, it is no evidence that a work is not of God, if many who are either the subjects or the instruments of it are guilty of too great forwardness to censure others as unconverted. For this may be through mistakes they have embraced concerning the marks by which they are to judge of the hypocrisy and carnality of others; or from not duly apprehending the latitude the Spirit of God uses in the methods of his operations; or, from not making due allowance for that infirmity and corruption that may be left in the hearts of the saints; as well as through lack of a due sense of their own blindness and weakness, and remaining corruption, by which spiritual pride may have a secret vent this way, under some disguise, and not be discovered. If we admit that truly pious men may have a great deal of remaining blindness and corruption, and may be liable to mistakes about the marks of hypocrisy, as undoubtedly all will agree, then it is not unaccountable that they should sometimes run into such errors as these. It is easy, and upon some accounts more easy to be accounted for, why the remaining corruption of good men should sometimes have an unobserved vent like this, than in most other ways; and without doubt (however lamentable) many holy men have erred in this way.

ZEAL NEEDS TO BE STRICTLY WATCHED AND SEARCHED

Lukewarmness in religion is abominable, and zeal an excellent grace; yet above all other Christian virtues, this needs to be strictly watched and searched; for it is that with which corruption, and particularly pride and human passion, is exceedingly apt to mix unobserved. And it is observable that there never was a time of great reformation, to cause a revival of zeal in the church of God, that has not been attended in some notable instances with irregularity, and undue severity in one way or another. Thus in the apostles' days, a great deal of zeal was spent about unclean foods, with heat of spirit in Christians against one another, both parties condemning and censuring one another as not true Christians; when the apostle had charity for both, as influenced by a spirit of real piety: "he that eats," he says, "to the Lord he eats, and giveth God thanks; and he that eateth not, to the Lord he eateth not, and giveth God thanks." So in the church of Corinth, they had got into a way of extolling some ministers, and censuring others, and were puffed up against one another: but yet these things were no sign that the work then so wonderfully carried on was not the work of God. And after this, when religion was still greatly flourishing in the world, and a spirit of eminent holiness and zeal prevailed in the Christian church, the zeal of Christians ran out into a very improper and undue severity, in the exercise of church discipline towards delinquents. In some cases they would by no means admit them into their charity and communion though they appeared never so humble and penitent. And in the days of Constantine the Great, the zeal of Christians against heathenism overflowed into a degree of persecution. Similarly in that glorious revival of religion, at the reformation, zeal in many instances appeared in a very improper severity, and even a degree of persecution; indeed, in some of the most eminent reformers, such as the great Calvin in particular. And many in those days of the flourishing of vital religion were guilty of severely censuring others who differed from them in opinion in some points of divinity.

7. Errors of judgment and delusions

Nor are many errors of judgement, and some delusions of Satan intermixed with the work, any argument that the work in general is not of the Spirit of God.

However great a spiritual influence may be, it is not to be expected that the Spirit of God should be given now in the same manner as to the apostles, infallibly to guide them in points of Christian doctrine, so that what they taught might be relied on as a rule to the Christian church. And if

many delusions of Satan appear at the same time that a great religious concern prevails, it is not an argument that the work in general is not the work of God, any more than it was an argument in Egypt that there were no true miracles wrought there by the hand of God, because Jannes and Jambres wrought false miracles at the same time by the hand of the devil. Indeed, the same persons may be the subjects of much of the influences of the Spirit of God, and yet in some things be led away by the delusions of Satan, and this be no more of paradox than many other things that are true of real saints, in the present state, where grace dwells with so much corruption, and the new man and the old man subsist together in the same person; and the kingdom of God and the kingdom of the devil remain for a while together in the same heart. Many godly persons have undoubtedly in this and other ages exposed themselves to woeful delusions by an aptness to lay too much weight on impulses and impressions, as if they were immediate revelations from God, to signify something future, or to direct them where to go, and what to do.

8. Some counterfeits

If some who were thought to be wrought upon fall away into gross errors, or scandalous practices, it is no argument that the work in general is not the work of the Spirit of God.

That there are some counterfeits is no argument that nothing is true: such things are always expected in a time of reformation. If we look into church history, we shall find no instance of any great revival of religion but what has been attended with many such things. Instances of this nature in the apostles' days were innumerable; some fell away into gross heresies, others into vile practices, though they seemed to be the subjects of a work of the Spirit – and were accepted for a while amongst those that were truly so as their brethren and companions – and were not suspected till they went out from them. And some of these were teachers and officers – and eminent persons in the Christian church – whom God had endowed with miraculous gifts of the Holy Spirit; as appears from the beginning of Hebrews 6.

JUDAS

An instance of these was Judas, who was one of the twelve apostles, and had long been constantly united to, and intimately conversant with, a company of disciples of true experience, without being discovered or suspected, till he revealed himself by his scandalous practice. He had been treated by Jesus himself, in all external things, as if he had truly been a disciple, even investing him with the character of apostle, sending him out to preach the gospel, and enduing him with miraculous gifts of the Spirit. For though Christ knew him, yet he did not then clothe himself with the character of omniscient Judge and searcher of hearts, but acted the part of a minister of the visible church (for he was his Father's minister); and therefore did not reject him till he had revealed himself by his scandalous practice; thereby giving an example to guides and rulers of the visible church, not to take it upon themselves to act the part of searcher of hearts, but to be influenced in their administrations by what is visible and open.

There were some Instances then of such apostates, who were esteemed eminently full of the grace of God's Spirit. An instance of this nature probably was Nicolas, one of the seven deacons, who was looked upon by the Christians in Jerusalem, in the time of that extraordinary outpouring of the Spirit, as a man full of the Holy Spirit, and was chosen out of the multitude of Christians for that office for that reason (Acts 6:3, 5); yet he afterwards fell away and became the head of a sect of vile heretics, of gross practices, called from his name the sect of the Nicolaitans (Revelation 2:6, 15).

REFORMATION APOSTATES

So in the time of the reformation, How great was the number of those who for a while seemed to join with the reformers, yet fell away into the grossest and most absurd errors, and abominable practices. And it is particularly observable that in times of great pouring out of the Spirit to revive religion in the world, a number of those who for a while seemed to partake in it, have fallen off into whimsical and extravagant errors, and gross enthusiasm, boasting of high degrees of spirituality and perfection, censuring and condemning others as carnal. Thus it was with the Gnostics in the apostles' times; and thus it was with several sects at the reformation, as Anthony Burgess observes:

The first worthy reformers, and glorious instruments of God, found a bitter conflict herein, so that they were exercised not only with formalists, and traditionary papists on the one side, but men that pretended themselves to be more enlightened than the reformers were, on the other side: hence they called those that did adhere to the Scripture, and would try revelations by it, Literists and Vowelists, as men acquainted with the words and vowels of Scripture, having nothing of the Spirit of God: and wheresoever in any town, the true doctrine of the gospel brake forth to the displacing of popery, presently such opinions arose, like tares that came up among the good wheat; whereby great divisions were raised, and the reformation made abominable and odious to the world; s if that had been the sun to give heat and warmth to those worms and serpents to crawl out of the ground. Hence they inveighed against Luther, and said he had only promulgated a carnal gospel.

Some of the leaders of those wild enthusiasts had been for a while highly esteemed by the first reformers, and peculiarly dear to them.

Thus also in England, at the time when vital religion much prevailed in the days of King Charles I, the interregnum, and Oliver Cromwell, such things as these abounded. And so in New England in her purest days, when vital piety flourished, such kind of things as these broke out. Therefore the devil's sowing such tares is no proof that a true work of the Spirit of God is not gloriously carried on.

Making people aware of hell

It is no argument that a work is not from the Spirit of God, that it seems to be promoted by ministers insisting very much on the terrors of God's holy law, and that with a great deal of pathos and earnestness. If there really is a hell of such dreadful and never-ending torments as is generally supposed, of which multitudes are in great danger – and into which the greater part of men in Christian countries do actually from generation to generation fall, for lack of a sense of its terribleness, and so for lack of taking due care to avoid it – then why is it not proper for those who have the care of souls to take great pains to make men aware of it? Why should they not be told as much of the truth as can be? If I am in danger of going to hell, I should be glad to know as much as I possibly can of the dreadfulness of it. If I am very prone to neglect due care to avoid it, the person who does me the best kindness is he who does most to represent to me the truth of the case, setting forth my misery and danger in the liveliest manner.

I ask everyone whether this is not the very course they would take in case of exposure to any great temporal calamity. If any of you who are heads of families saw your children in a house all on fire, and in imminent danger of soon being consumed in the flames, yet seemed to be very unaware of its danger, and neglected to escape after you had often called them – would you go on to speak only in a cold and indifferent manner? Would you not cry aloud, and call earnestly, and tell them the danger they were in, and their folly in delaying, in the most lively manner of which you were capable? Would not nature itself teach this, and oblige you to do so? If you continued to speak only in a cold manner, as you usually do in ordinary conversation about indifferent matters, would not those about you begin to think

that you were bereft of reason yourself? This is not the way of mankind in temporal affairs of great moment, that require earnest heed and great haste, and about which they are greatly concerned. They do not usually speak to others of their danger, and warn them just a little, or in a cold and indifferent manner. Nature teaches men otherwise. If we who have the care of souls knew what hell was, had seen the state of the damned or by any other means had become aware how dreadful their case was – and at the same time knew that most people went there, and saw our hearers not aware of their danger – it would be morally impossible for us to avoid most earnestly setting before them the dreadfulness of that misery, and their great exposedness to it, and even to cry aloud to them.

PREACHING ABOUT HELL IN A COLD MANNER
When ministers preach about hell, and warn sinners to avoid it, in a cold manner – though they may say in words that it is infinitely terrible – they contradict themselves. For actions, as I observed before, have a language as well as words. If a preacher's words represent the sinner's state as infinitely dreadful, while his behavior and manner of speaking contradict it – showing that the preacher does not think so – he defeats his own purpose; for the language of his actions in such a case is much more effectual than the bare meaning of his words. Not that I think that the law only should be preached: ministers may preach other things too little. The gospel is to be preached as well as the law, and the law is to be preached only to make way for the gospel, and in order that it may be preached more effectually. The main work of ministers is to preach the gospel: "Christ is the end of the law for righteousness". So a minister would miss it very much if he should insist so much on the terrors of the law as to forget his Lord, and neglect to preach the gospel; but the law is still very much to be insisted on, and the preaching of the gospel will probably be in vain without it.

And certainly such earnestness and affection in speaking is beautiful, as becomes the nature and importance of the subject. Not but that there may be such a thing as an indecent boisterousness in a preacher, something besides which the matter and manner do not well agree together. Some people talk of it as an unreasonable thing to frighten people to heaven; but I think it is a reasonable thing to endeavor to frighten people away from hell. They stand upon its brink, and are just ready to fall into it, and are unaware of their danger. Is it not a reasonable thing to frighten a person out of a house on fire? The word "fright" is commonly used for sudden, causeless fear, or groundless surprise; but surely a fear for which there is good reason is not to be criticized by any such name.

Evidence in Scripture

Having given some examples of things that are not evidence that a work wrought among a people is not a work of the Spirit of God, I now proceed to show positively what are the sure, distinguishing scripture evidences and marks of a work of the Spirit of God, by which we may proceed in judging any operation we find in ourselves, or see among a people, without danger of being misled. And in this, as I said before, I shall confine myself to those marks which are given us by the apostle in 1 John 4, where this matter is dealt with particularly, and more plainly and fully than anywhere else in the Bible. And in speaking about these marks, I shall take them in the order in which I find them in the chapter.

1. Jesus is seen to be the Son of God

When the operation is such as to raise their esteem of that Jesus who was born of the Virgin, and was crucified outside the gates of Jerusalem; and seems more to confirm and establish their minds in the truth of what the gospel declares to us of his being the Son of God, and the Savior of men, this is a sure sign that it is from the Spirit of God. The apostle gives us this sign in verses 2 and 3: "Hereby know ye the Spirit of God; and every spirit that confesseth that Jesus Christ is come in the flesh is of God; and every spirit that confesseth not that Jesus Christ is come in the flesh is not of God." This implies a confessing not only that there was such a person who appeared in Palestine and did and suffered those things that are recorded of him, but that he was the Christ, i.e. the Son of God, anointed to be Lord and Savior, as the name Jesus Christ implies.

Confessing that Jesus is the Son of God

That thus much is implied in the apostle's meaning is confirmed by verse 15, where the apostle is still on the same subject of signs of the true Spirit: "Whosoever shall confess that Jesus is the Son of God, God dwelleth in him, and he in God." And it is to be observed that the word *confess*, as it is often used in the New Testament, signifies more than merely *allowing*: it implies an establishing and confirming of a thing by testimony, and declaring it with manifestation of esteem and affection. "Whosoever therefore shall *confess* me before men, him will I *confess* also before my Father which is in heaven" (Matt. 10:32). "I will *confess* to thee among the Gentiles, and sing unto thy name" (Rom. 15:9). "That every tongue shall *confess* that Jesus Christ is Lord, to the glory of God the Father" (Phil. 2:11). And that this is the force of the expression as the apostle John uses it in this passage is confirmed in the next chapter, verse 1: "Whosoever believeth that Jesus is the Christ, is born of God, and every one that loveth him that begat, loveth him also that is begotten of him." And by that parallel passage of the apostle Paul, where we have the same rule given to distinguish the true Spirit from all counterfeits: "Wherefore I give you to understand that no man speaking by the Spirit of God, calleth Jesus accursed [or will show an ill or mean esteem of him]; and that no man can say that Jesus is the Lord, but by the Holy Ghost" (1 Cor. 21:3).

So if the spirit that is at work among a

people is plainly observed to work so as to convince them of Christ, and lead them to him – to confirm their minds in the belief of the history of Christ as he appeared in the flesh – and that he is the Son of God, and was sent by God to save sinners; That he is the only Savior, and that they stand in great need of him; and if he seems to beget in them higher and more honorable thoughts of him than they used to have and to incline their affections more to him; it is a sure sign that it is the true and right Spirit; however incapable we may be of determining whether that conviction and affection is in that manner, or to that degree, as to be saving or not.

But the words of the apostle are remarkable; the person to whom the Spirit gives testimony, and for whom he raises their esteem, must be that Jesus who appeared in the flesh, and not another Christ in his stead; nor any mystical, fantastical Christ, such as the light within. The spirit of Quakers extols this, while it diminishes their esteem of and dependence upon an outward Christ – or Jesus as he came in the flesh – and leads them off form him; but the spirit that gives testimony for that Jesus, and leads to him, can be no other than the Spirit of God. The devil has the most bitter and implacable enmity against that person, especially in his character of the Savior of men; he mortally hates the story and doctrine of his redemption; he never would go about to beget in men more honorable thoughts of him, and lay greater weight on his instructions and commands. The Spirit that inclines men's hearts to the seed of the woman is not the spirit of the serpent that has such an irreconcilable enmity against him. He that heightens men's esteem of the glorious Michael, That prince of the angels, is not the spirit of the dragon that is at war with him.

Working against Satan's kingdom

When the spirit that is at work operates against the interests of Satan's kingdom, which lies in encouraging and establishing sin, and cherishing men's worldly lusts; this is a sure sign that it is a true, and not a false spirit.

This sign we have given us in verses 4 and 5: "Ye are of God, little children, and have overcome them; because greater is he that is in you, than he that is in the world. They are of the world, therefore speak they of the world, and the world heareth them." Here is a plain antithesis: it is evident that the apostle is still comparing those that are influenced by the two opposite kinds of spirits, the true and the false, and showing the difference; the one is of God, and overcomes the spirit of the world; the other is of the world, and speaks and savors the things of the world. The spirit of the devil is here called "he that is in the world". Christ says, "My kingdom is not of this world". But it is otherwise with Satan's kingdom; he is "the god of this world".

What the apostle means by *the world,* or "the things that are of the world", we learn by his own words in 1 John 2:15-16: "Love not the world, neither the things that are in the world: if any man love the world, the love of the Father is not in him: for all that is in the world, the lust of the flesh, and the lust of the eyes, and the pride of life, is not of the Father, but is of the world." So by the world the apostle evidently means everything that appertains to the interest of sin, and comprehends all the corruptions and lusts of men, and all those acts and objects by which they are gratified.

So we may safely determine from what the apostle says that the spirit that is at work among a people, after such a manner as to lessen their esteem of the pleasures, profits, and honors of the world, and to take off their hearts from an eager pursuit after these things; and to engage them in a deep concern about a future state and eternal happiness which the gospel reveals – and puts them upon earnestly seeking the kingdom of God and his righteousness; and the spirit that convinces them of the dreadfulness of sin, the guilt it brings, and the misery to which it exposes – this must be the Spirit of God.

WAKING UP THE CONSCIENCE

It is not to be supposed that Satan would convince men of sin, and awaken the conscience; it can no way serve his end to make that candle of the Lord shine the brighter, and to open the mouth of that viceregent of God in the soul. It is for his interest, whatever he does, to lull conscience asleep, and keep it quiet. To have That, with its eyes and mouth open in the soul, will tend to clog and hinder all his desires of darkness, and evermore to disturb his affairs, to cross his interest, and disquiet him, so that he can achieve nothing he wants without being molested. Would the devil, when he is trying to establish men in sin, take such a course, in the first place, to enlighten and awaken the conscience to see the dreadfulness of sin, and make them exceedingly afraid of it, and aware of their misery by reason of their past sins, and their great need of deliverance from their guilt? Would he make them more careful, inquisitive, and watchful to discern what is sinful, and to avoid future sins, and so be more afraid of the devil's temptations, and more careful to guard against them? What do those men do with their reason, who suppose that the Spirit that operates thus is the spirit of the devil?

Possibly some may say that the devil may even awaken men's consciences to deceive them, and make them think they have been the subject of a saving work of the Spirit of God, while they are indeed still in the gall of bitterness. But to this it may be replied that the man who has an awakened con science is the least likely to be deceived by anyone in the world; it is the drowsy, unaware, stupid conscience that is most easily blinded. The more aware conscience is in a diseased soul, the less easily is it quieted without a real healing. The more aware conscience is made of the dreadfulness of sin, and of the greatness of a man's own guilt, the less likely he is to rest in his own righteousness, or to be pacified with nothing but shadows. A man that has been thoroughly terrified with a sense of his own danger and misery is not easily flattered and made to believe himself safe, without any good grounds. To awaken conscience, and convince it of the evil of sin, cannot tend to establish it, but certainly tends to make way for sin and Satan's being cut out.

THE SPIRIT OF THE DEVIL

Therefore this is a good argument that the Spirit that operates in this way cannot but the spirit of the devil – unless we suppose that Christ did not know how to argue, when he told the Pharisees (who supposed that the Spirit by which he worked was the spirit of the devil) That Satan would not cast out Satan (Matt. 12:25-6). And therefore, if we see people made aware of the dreadful nature of sin, and of the displeasure of God against it; of their own miserable condition as they are in themselves, by reason of sin, and earnestly concerned for their eternal salvation – and aware of their need of God's pity and help, and committed to seek it in the use of the means that God has appointed – we may certainly conclude that it is from the Spirit of God, whatever effects this concern has on their bodies – even if it causes them to cry out aloud, or to shriek, or to faint; or if it throws them into convulsions, or whatever other way the blood and spirits are moved.

The influence of the Spirit of God is yet more abundantly manifest if people have their hearts drawn away from the world, and weaned from the objects of their worldly lusts, and away from worldly pursuits, by the feelings they have for those spiritual enjoyments of another world, That are promised in the gospel.

Greater regard for the Scriptures

The spirit that operates in such a manner as to cause in men a greater regard for the Holy Scriptures, and establishes them more in their truth and divinity, is certainly the Spirit of God.

The apostle gives us this rule in verse 6: "We are of God; he that knoweth God heareth us; he that is not of God heareth not us: hereby know we the spirit of truth, and the spirit of error." *We are of God;* That is, "We the apostles are sent forth by God, and appointed by him to teach the world, and to deliver those doctrines and instructions which are to be their rule; *he that knoweth God, heareth us… .*"

The apostle's argument here equally reaches all that in the same sense are *of God;* That is, all those that God has appointed and inspired to deliver to his church its rule of faith and practice; all the prophets and apostles, whose doctrine God has made the foundation on which he has built his church, as in Ephesians 2:20 – in a word, all the penmen of the Holy Scriptures. The devil would never attempt to beget in people a regard for that divine word which God has given to be the great and standing rule for the direction of his church in all religious matters, and all concerns of their souls, in all ages. A spirit of delusion will not incline people to seek direction at the mouth of God. "To the law and to the testimony" is never the cry of those evil spirits that have no light in them; for it is God's own direction to discover their delusions. "And when they shall say unto you, Seek unto them that have familiar spirits, and unto wizards that peep and that mutter: should not a people seek unto their God? for the living to the dead? To the law and to the testimony; if they speak not according to this word, it is because there is no light in them" (Isa. 8:19-20). The devil does not say the same as Abraham did – "They have Moses and the prophets, let them hear them" – nor the same as the voice from heaven did concerning Christ – "Hear ye him". Would the spirit of error, in order to deceive people, beget in them a high opinion of the infallible rule, and incline them to think a lot about it, and be very conversant with it? Would the prince of darkness, in order to promote his kingdom of darkness, lead men to the sun? The devil has always shown a mortal spite and hatred towards that holy book the Bible; he has done all in his power to extinguish that light, and to lead people away from it. He knows it to be that light by which his kingdom of darkness is to be overthrown. He has had

for many ages experience of its power to defeat his purposes, and baffle his designs; it is his constant plague.

It is the main weapon which Michael uses in his war with him; it is the sword of the Spirit, That pierces him and conquers him. It is that great and strong word with which God punishes Leviathan, That crooked serpent. It is that sharp sword that we read of in Revelation 19:15, That proceeds out of the mouth of him that sat on the horse, with which he smites his enemies. Every text is a dart to torment the old serpent. He has felt the stinging dart thousands of times; therefore he is against the Bible, and hates every word in it; and we may be sure he will never attempt to raise people's esteem of it or feeling for it. And accordingly we see it common in enthusiasts, That they depreciate this written rule, and set up the light within or some other rule above it.

The Spirit of truth leading people to the truth

Another rule to judge spirits by may be drawn from the names given to the opposite spirits, in the last words of verse 6: "the spirit of truth and the spirit of error".

These words exhibit the two opposite characters of the Spirit of God, and other spirits that counterfeit his operations. And therefore, if by observing the manner of the operation of a spirit that is at work among a people, we see that it operates as a spirit of truth, leading people to truth, convincing them of those things that are true, we may safely determine that it is a right and true spirit. For instance, if we observe that the spirit at work makes people more aware than they used to be that there is a God, and that he is a great and a sin-hating God; That life is short, and very uncertain; and that there is another world; That they have immortal souls, and must give account of themselves to God, That they are exceedingly sinful by nature and practice; That they are helpless in themselves; and confirms them in other things that agree with some sound doctrine; the spirit that works in such a way operates as a spirit of truth; he represents things as they truly are. He brings people to the light; for whatever makes truth manifest is light; as the apostle Paul observes: "But all things that are reproved [or discovered, as it is in the margin] are made manifest by the light; for whatsoever doth make manifest is light" (Ephesians 5:13).

And therefore we may conclude that it is not the spirit of darkness that thus reveals the truth and makes it clear. Christ tells us that Satan is a liar, and the father of lies; and his kingdom is a kingdom of darkness. It is upheld and promoted only by darkness and error. Satan has all his power and dominion by darkness. Hence we read of the power of darkness (Luke 22:53 and Col. 1:13). And devils are called "the rulers of the darkness of this world". Whatever spirit removes our darkness, and brings us to the light, undeceives us, and, by convincing us of the truth, does us a kindness. If I am brought to a sight of truth, and made aware of things as they really are, my duty is immediately to thank God for it, without stopping first to inquire by what means I have such a benefit.

A spirit of love for both God and man

If the spirit that is at work among a people operates as a spirit of love to God and man, it is a sure sign that it is the Spirit of God. The apostle insist on this sign from verse 6 to the end of the chapter: "Beloved, let us love on another; for love is of God, and every one that loveth is born of God, and knoweth God: he that loveth not, knoweth not God; for God is love... ." Here it is evident that the apostle is still comparing those tow sorts of people that are influenced by the opposite kinds of spirits; and he mentioned love as a mark by which we may know who has the true spirit. This is especially evident from verses 12 and 13: "If we love on another, God dwelleth in us, and his love is perfected in us: hereby know we that we dwell in him, and he in us, because he hath given us of his Spirit."

In these verses love is spoken of as if it were that in which the very nature of the Holy Spirit consisted; or as if *divine love* dwelling in us, and the *Spirit of God* dwelling in us, were the same thing. It is the same in the last two verses of the previous chapter, and verse 16 of this chapter. Therefore this last mark which the apostle gives of the true Spirit he seems to speak of as the most eminent; and so insists much more largely upon it than upon all the rest; and speaks expressly of both love to God and love to men – of *love to men* in verses 7, 11, and 12; and of *love to God* in verses 17, 18, and 19; and of both together in the last two verses; and of love to men as arising from love to God, in these last two verses.

Therefore, when the spirit that is at work amongst the people tends this way, and brings many of them to high and exalting thoughts of the Divine Being, and his glorious perfections; and works in them an admiring, delightful sense of the excellence of Jesus Christ; representing him as the chief among ten thousand, and altogether lovely; and makes him precious to the soul, winning and drawing the heart with those motives and incitements to love, of which the apostle speaks in that passage of Scripture we are upon, namely the wonderful, free love of God in giving his only-begotten Son to die for us, and the wonderful love of Christ to us, who had no love to him, but were his enemies – this must be the Spirit of God. "In this was manifested the love of God towards us, because God sent his only-begotten Son into the world, That we might live through him. Herein is love; not that we loved God, but that he loved us, and sent his Son to be the propitiation for our sins" (verses 9-10). "And we have known, and believed, the love that God hath to us" (verse 16). "We love him because he first loved us" (verse 19).

The spirit that excites people to love on these motives, and makes the attributes of God as revealed in the gospel, and manifested in Christ, delightful objects of contemplation; and makes the soul long after God and Christ – after their presence and communion, acquaintance with them, and conformity to them – and to live so as to please and honor them – the spirit that quells contentions among men, and gives a spirit of peace and good will, excites to acts of outward kindness, and earnest desires of the salvation of souls – and causes a delight in those that appears as the children of God, and followers of Christ; I say, when a spirit operates in this way among a people, there is the highest kind of evidence of the influence of a true and divine spirit.

COUNTERFEIT LOVE

Indeed there is a counterfeit love, That often appears among those who are led by a spirit of delusion. There is commonly in the wildest enthusiasts a kind of union and affection arising from self-love, occasioned by their agreeing in those things in which they greatly differ from all others, and from which they are objects of the ridicule of all the rest of mankind. This naturally will cause them so much the more to prize those peculiarities that make them the objects of others" contempt. Thus the ancient Gnostics, and the wild fanatics that appeared at the beginning of the reformation, boasted of their great love to one another; one sect of them, in particular, calling themselves the *family of love*. But this is quite another thing than that Christian love I have just described: it is only the working of a natural self-love, and no true benevolence, any more than the union and friendship which may be among a company of pirates that are at war with all the rest of the world. There is enough said in this passage about the nature of a truly Christian love, thoroughly to distinguish it from all such counterfeits. It is love that arises from apprehension of the wonderful riches of the free grace and sovereignty of God's love to us, in Christ Jesus; being attended with a sense of our own utter unworthiness, as in ourselves the enemies and haters of God and Christ, and with a renunciation of all our own excellence and righteousness. See verses 9-11 and 19.

THE CHRISTIAN VIRTUE OF HUMILITY

The surest character of true divine supernatural love – distinguishing it from counterfeits that arise from a natural self-love – is that the Christian virtue of *humility* shine sin it; That which above all other renounces, abases, and annihilates what we term *self*. Christian love, or true charity, is a humble love. "Charity vaunteth not itself, is not puffed up, doth not behave itself unseemly, seeketh not her own, is not easily provoked" (1 Cor. 13:4-5). When therefore we see love in people attended with a sense of their own littleness, vileness, weakness, and utter insufficiency; and so with self-diffidence, self-emptiness, self-renunciation, and poverty of spirit; these are the manifest tokens of the Spirit of God. He that thus dwells in love, dwells in God, and God in him. What the apostle speaks of as a great evidence of the true Spirit, is God's love or Christ's love: "his love is perfected in us" (verse 12). What kind of love that is, we may see best in what appeared in Christ's example. The love that appeared in that Lamb of God was not only a love to friends, but to enemies, and a love attended with a meek and humble spirit. "Learn of me," he says, "for I am meek and lowly in heart."

Love and humility are two of the most contrary things in the world to the spirit of the devil, for the character of that evil spirit, above all things, consists in pride and malice.

Thus I have spoken particularly about the various marks the apostle gives us of a work of the true Spirit. There are some of these things which the devil *would not* do if he could: thus he would not awaken the conscience, and make people aware of their miserable state because of sin, and aware of their great need of a Savior; and he would not confirm people in the belief that Jesus is the Son of God, and the Savior of sinners, or raise people's value and esteem of him: he would not beget in men's minds an opinion of the necessity, usefulness, and truth of the Holy Scriptures, or incline them to make much use of them; nor would he show people the truth in things that concern their souls' interest; to undeceive them and lead them out of darkness into light, and give them a view of things as they really are. And there are other things that the devil *neither can nor will* do; he will not give people a spirit of divine love, or Christian humility and poverty of spirit; nor *could* he is he wanted to. He cannot give those things he does not himself have: these things are as contrary as possible to his nature. And therefore when there is an extraordinary influence or operation appearing on the minds of a people, if these things are found in it, we are safe in determining that it is the work of God, whatever other circumstances it may be attended with, whatever instruments are used, whatever methods are taken to promote it; whatever means a sovereign God, whose judgements are a great deep, employs to carry it on; and whatever motion there may be of the animal spirits, whatever effects may be wrought on men's bodies.

These marks that the apostle have given us are sufficient to stand alone, and support themselves. They plainly show the finger of God, and are sufficient to outweigh a thousand such little objections as many make from oddities, irregularities, errors in conduct, and the delusions and scandals of some who claim to believe.

But some people may raise as an objection to the sufficiency of the marks what the apostle Paul says in 2 Corinthians 11:13-14: "For such are false apostles, deceitful workers, transforming themselves into the apostles of Christ; and no marvel, for Satan himself is transformed into an angel of light."

FALSE PROPHETS, FALSE APOSTLES

To this, I answer that this can be no objection against the sufficiency of these marks to distinguish the true from the false spirit, in those false apostles and prophets in whom the devil was transformed into an angel of light, because it is principally with a view to them that the apostle gives these marks; as appears by the words of the text, "Believe not every spirit, but try the spirits, whether they are of God". This is the reason he gives — because many false prophets are gone out into the world: "There are many gone out into the world who are the ministers of the devil, who transform themselves into the prophets of God, in whom the spirit of the devil is transformed into an angel of light; therefore try the spirits by these rules that I shall give you, That you may be able to distinguish the true spirit from the false, under such a crafty disguise."

Those *false prophets* the apostle John speaks of are doubtless the same sort of men as those *false apostles* and deceitful workers that the apostle Paul speaks of, in whom the devil was transformed into an angel of light; and therefore we may be sure that these marks are especially adapted to distinguish between the true Spirit, and the devil transformed into an angel of light, because they are given especially for that end; That is the apostle's declared purpose and design, to give marks by which the true Spirit may be distinguished from that sort of counterfeits.

And if we look over what is said about these false prophets, and false apostles (as there is much said about them in the New Testament), and take notice in what manner the devil was transformed into an angel of light in them, we shall not find anything that in the least injures the sufficiency of these marks to distinguish the true Spirit from such counterfeits. The devil transformed himself into an angel of light, as there was in them a show and great boast of extraordinary knowledge in divine things (Col. 2:8; 1 Tim. 1:6-7 and 6:3-5; 2 Tim. 2:14-18; Titus 1:10, 16). Hence their followers called themselves Gnostics, from their great pretended knowledge: and the devil in them mimicked the miraculous gifts of the Holy Spirit, in visions, prophecies, miracles, etc. Hence they are called false apostles, and false prophets (Matt. 24:24). Again, there was a false show of, and lying pretensions to, great holiness and devotion in words (Rom. 16:17-18; Eph. 4:14). Hence they are called deceitful workers, and wells and clouds without water (2 Cor. 11:13; 2 Pet. 2:17; Jude 12). There was also in them a show of extraordinary piety and righteousness in their superstitious worship

(Col. 2:16-23). So they had a false, proud, and bitter zeal (Gal. 4:17-18; 1 Tim. 1:6 and 6:4-5). And likewise a false show of humility, in affecting an extraordinary outward meanness and dejection, when indeed they were "vainly puffed up in their fleshly mind"; and made a righteousness of their humility, and were exceedingly lifted up with their eminent piety (Col. 2:18, 23). But how do such things as these in the least injure those things that have been mentioned as the distinguishing evidences of the true Spirit? Besides such vain shows which may be from the devil, there are common influences of the Spirit, which are often mistaken for saving grace; but these are out of the question, because though they are not saving, they are still the work of the true Spirit.
Jonathan Edwards

[The eighteenth-century Evangelical Revival] did more to transfigure the moral character of the general populace, than any other movement British history can record.
J. Wesley Bready

All great revivals have been preceded and carried out by persevering, prevailing knee-work in the closet.
Samuel Logan Brengle

Lord, revive your church and begin with me.
Chinese Christian

A revival is nothing else than a new beginning of obedience to God.
Charles G. Finney

A revival may be expected whenever Christians are found willing to make the sacrifices necessary to carry it on. They must be willing to sacrifice their feelings, their business, their time, to help forward the work.
Charles G. Finney

Revival is a clean-cut breakthrough of the Spirit, a sweep of Holy Ghost power, bending the hearts of hardened sinners as the wheat before the wind, breaking up the fountains of the great deep, sweeping the whole range of the emotions, as the master hand moves across the harp strings, from the tears and cries of the penitent to the holy laughter and triumphant joy of the cleansed.
Norman Grubb

If our goal is revival, we will be quite unbalanced when it comes. If our goal is God, we will be able to walk with Him calmly and steadfastly through years of waiting and through the joys and victories of a season of refreshing. Christ crucified and risen is not only the Door, and the Way, but the End also. It is our personal relationship to Him which counts more than anything else. Oh, the need for men and women who know their God! The Church of Christ will only arise militant, triumphant, an "exceeding great army," when individuals get rightly related to God.
Nancy B. Morris

From the Day of Pentecost until now, there has not been any one great spiritual awakening in any land which has not begun in a union of prayer though only among two or three, and no such outward or upward movement has continued after such prayer meetings have declined.
A. T. Pierson

Kneel down and with a piece of chalk draw a complete circle all around you – and pray to God to send a revival on everything inside the circle. Stay there until he answers, and you will have revival.
Gypsy Smith, when asked how to have a revival

Revival, Barrier to

Perhaps the greatest barrier to revival on a large scale is the fact that we are too interested in a great display. We want an exhibition; God is looking for a man who will throw himself entirely on God. Whenever self-effort, self-glory, self-seeking or self-promotion enters into the work of revival, then God leaves us to ourselves.
Ted S. Rendall

Revival and humility

Revival will call for much love and humility, because it may please God to use one man more extensively than another. The fleece of one denomination may appear to be wet with the dews of heaven while another is only damp with it. In some cases God may use the least gifted of men – at least some would so judge them – and in the least likely of churches find a channel for His grace. May God preserve us from a spirit which would prefer to see no revival at all if it did not come in our form, after our pattern, and through our instrumentality.
John T. Carson

Revival and prayer

The disappearance of the "prayer meeting" from the life of many churches is something which occasions widespread regret, even among many who would not normally attend. Indeed, the prayer meeting in which the laity participated freely is a legacy from the 1859 (Ulster) Revival …These prayer meetings were not in many cases in existence before the revival set in. The very establishment of them in the first instance, was an evidence that it was spring-time again in the Church of Christ, and the restoration of them today would be for her reviving once more.
John T. Carson

Revival and preaching

Preachers who never have revivals never weary of calling attention to everything objectionable in the methods of those who have powerful revivals … O ye fault-finders, beware lest when your Lord come, ye be found smiting your fellow servants, instead of working with them!
B. T. Roberts

Revolution

Rebellion to tyrants is obedience to God.
John Bradshaw

Whoever wishes to live a quiet life should not have been born in the twentieth century.
Leon Trotsky

Reward

When God crowns our merits, it is nothing other than his own gifts that he crowns.
Augustine of Hippo

Ridicule

It is easier to ridicule than to commend.
Thomas Fuller

Righteous, The

The righteous shall flourish like the palm-tree: he shall grow like a cedar in Lebanon.
The Bible, Psalm 92:12 KJV

A righteous man regardeth the life of his beast; but the tender mercies of the wicked are cruel.
The Bible, Proverbs 12:10 KJV

Righteousness
See also: Faith

Righteousness exalteth a nation.
The Bible, Proverbs 14:34 KJV

He who pursues righteousness and love finds life, prosperity and honor.
The Bible, Proverbs 21:21

For in the gospel a righteousness from God is revealed, a righteousness that is by faith from first to last, just as it is written: "The just will live by faith."
The Bible, Romans 1:17

God made him who had no sin to be sin for us, so that in him we might become the righteousness of God.
The Bible, 2 Corinthians 5:21

… not having a righteousness of my own that comes from the law, but that which is through faith in Christ – the righteousness that comes from God and is by faith.
The Bible, Philippians 3:9

The most important ingredient of righteousness is to render to God the service and homage due to him. He is shamefully cheated whenever we do not submit to his authority.
John Calvin

God "justifies the wicked" (ungodly: Rom. 4:5) by imputing (reckoning, crediting, counting, accounting) righteousness to them and ceasing to count their sins against them (Rom. 4:1–8).
The gospel of Jesus Christ: An evangelical celebration

The righteousness of God is not acquired by acts frequently repeated, as Aristotle taught, but is imparted by faith.
Martin Luther

Paul teaches us that the righteousness of God revealed in the gospel is passive, given to us in Christ. As this truth dawned, I felt I was born again, and was entering in at the gates of paradise itself. There and then the whole face of scripture changed. Just as much as I had hated the phrase "the righteousness of God," I now loved it – it seemed the sweetest and most joyous phrase ever written.
Martin Luther

My hope is built on nothing less
Than Jesus' blood and righteousness.
Edward Mote

No condemnation now I dread.
Jesus, and all in him, is mine;
Alive in him, my living Head,
And clothed in righteousness divine,
Bold I approach the eternal throne,
And claim the crown, through Christ, my own.
Charles Wesley

Risk
See also: Action; Choice
Be daring, be different, be impractical; be anything that will assert integrity of purpose and imaginative vision against the play-it-safers, the creatures of the commonplace, the slaves of the ordinary.
Cecil Beaton

One doesn't discover new lands without consenting to lose sight of the shore for a very long time.
André Gide

One can never consent to creep when one feels an impulse to soar.
Helen Keller

Often the difference between a successful man and a failure is not one's better abilities or ideas, but the courage that one has to bet on his ideas, to take a calculated risk – and to act.
Maxwell Maltz

If you want a place in the sun, you must leave the shade of the family tree.
Osage saying

Every man has the right to risk his own life in order to save it.
Jean-Jacques Rousseau

I can say, "I am terribly frightened and fear is terrible and awful and it makes me uncomfortable, so I won't do that because it's uncomfortable." Or I could say, "Get used to being uncomfortable. It is uncomfortable doing something that's risky." But so what? Do you want to stagnate and just be comfortable?
Barbra Streisand

Fortune sides with him who dares.
Virgil

Roman Catholic Church
Rome has spoken; the case is concluded.
Augustine of Hippo

The Roman church was founded by God alone.
Gregory the Great

Roman Catholic Doctrine

Antichrist
It is a common opinion of the Fathers that the Antichrist will be a Jew from the tribe of Dan.
Irenaeus

Baptism

Men are bound to that without which they cannot obtain salvation. Now it is manifest that no one can obtain salvation, but through Christ; wherefore the Apostle says (Rom. 5:18): "As by the offense of one unto all men unto condemnation; so also by the justice of one, unto all men unto justification of life." But for this end is Baptism conferred on a man, That being regenerated thereby, he may be incorporated in Christ, by becoming His member: wherefore it is written (Gal. 3:27): "As many of you as have been baptized in Christ, have put on Christ." Consequently it is manifest that all are bound to be baptized: and that without Baptism there is no salvation for men."

Thomas Aquinas

Calvin says that infants born of parents who have the faith are saved, even though they should die without Baptism. But this is false: for David was born of parents who had the faith, and he confessed that he was born in sin. This was also taught by the Council of Trent in the Fifth Session, number Four: there the fathers declared that infants dying without Baptism, although born of baptized parents, are not saved, and are lost, not on account of the sin of their parents, but for the sin of Adam in whom all have sinned.

Alphonsus Maria Liguori

All the faithful must confess only one Baptism which regenerates all the baptized, just as there is one God and one faith. We believe that this Sacrament, celebrated in water and in the name of the Father, Son, and Holy Ghost, is necessary for children and grown-up people alike for salvation.

Ecumenical Council of Vienne

If anyone says that baptism is optional, That is, not necessary for salvation, let him be anathema.

Council of Trent

Catholic

Such is the nature of Catholicism that it does not admit of more or less, but must be held as a whole or as a whole rejected: "This is the Catholic faith, which unless a man believe faithfully and firmly, he cannot be saved" (Athanasian Creed). There is no adding any qualifying terms to the profession of Catholicism: it is quite enough for each one to proclaim "Christian is my name and Catholic is my surname," only let him endeavor to be in reality what he calls himself.

Pope Benedict XV

Church

There is but one universal Church of the faithful, outside which no one at all is saved.

Pope Innocent III

[The Church is] the one and only path to salvation.

Pope John Paul II

[I condemn as] absolutely contrary to Catholic teaching the notion that persons living in error and outside the True Faith and Catholic unity can reach eternal life.

Pius IX

The mystery of salvation is revealed to us and is continued and accomplished in the Church…and from this genuine and single source, like "humble, useful, precious and chaste" water, it reaches the whole world. Dear young people and members of the faithful, like Brother Francis we have to be conscious and absorb this fundamental and revealed truth, consecrated by tradition: "There is no salvation outside the Church." From her alone there flows surely and fully the life-giving force destined in Christ and in His Spirit, to renew the whole of humanity, and therefore directing every human being to become a part of the Mystical Body of Christ.

Pope John Paul II

According to the words of St. Augustine, who takes up an image dear to the ancient Fathers, the ship of the Church must not fear, because it is guided by Christ and by

His Vicar. "Although the ship is tossed about, it is still a ship. It alone carries the disciples and receives Christ. Yes, it is tossed on the sea, but, without it, one would immediately perish." Only in the Church is salvation. "Without it one perishes."
Pope John Paul I

Strong in this faith, unshakably established on this Peter, We turn the eyes of Our soul both to the heavy obligations of this holy primacy and at the same time to the strength divinely imparted to Our heart. In peace We wait for those to be silent who are loudly proclaiming that the Catholic Church has had her day, That her teaching is hopelessly reactionary, That she will soon be reduced either to conformity with the data of science and a civilization without God, or to withdrawal from the society of men. And while We wait, it is Our duty to recall to everyone, great and small, as the Holy Pontiff Gregory did in ages past, the absolute necessity which is ours to have recourse to this Church to effect our eternal salvation, to obtain peace, and even prosperity in our life here below.
Pope Pius X

This is our last lesson to you: receive it, engrave it in your minds, all of you: by God's commandment salvation is to be found nowhere but in the Church; the strong and effective instrument of salvation is none other than the Roman Pontificate.
Pope Leo XIII

By the ministry of this Church so gloriously founded by Him, He willed to perpetuate the mission which He had Himself received from the Father; and on the one hand, having put within her all the means necessary for man's salvation, on the other hand, He formally enjoined upon men the duty of obeying His Church as Himself, and religiously taking her as a guide of their whole lives. "He that heareth you, heareth Me; he that despiseth you, despiseth me." (Luke 10:16) Therefore, it is from the Church alone that the law of

Christ must be asked: and, consequently, if for man Christ is the way, the Church, too, is the way, the former of Himself and by His nature, the latter by delegation and communication of power. Consequently, all who wish to reach salvation outside the Church, are mistaken as to the way and are engaged in a vain effort.
Pope Leo XIII

The most Holy Roman Church firmly believes, professes and preaches that none of those existing outside the Catholic Church, not only pagans, but also Jews and heretics and schismatics, can have a share in life eternal; but that they will go into the eternal fire which was prepared for the devil and his angels, unless before death they are joined with Her; and that so important is the unity of this ecclesiastical body that only those remaining within this unity can profit by the sacraments of the Church unto salvation, and they alone can receive an eternal recompense for their fasts, their almsgivings, their other works of Christian piety and the duties of a Christian soldier. No one, let his almsgiving be as great as it may, no one, even if he pour out his blood for the Name of Christ, can be saved, unless he remain within the bosom and the unity of the Catholic Church.
Pope Eugene IV

Evangelicals
Take a view of this evangelical people, the Protestants. Perhaps 'tis my misfortune, but I never yet met with one who does not appear changed for the worse. Some persons whom I knew formerly innocent, harmless, and without deceit, no sooner have I seen them joined to that sect (the Protestants), than they began to talk of wenches, to play at dice, to leave off prayers, being grown extremely worldly, most impatient, revengeful, vain, like vipers, tearing one another. I speak by experience.
Erasmus

Freemasonry
It is evident that in a general way, this

doctrine of Freemasonry is not only a heresy, nor even the totality of all heresies, which find in it a haven; it is a fact that Masonry goes beyond the limits of what constitutes what is generally ascribed to the word heresy, for it allows full play to the commission of outrageous perversion. Freemasonry is indeed the abyss of all errors, the well of perdition.

Monseigneur Gay

There exists in the world a certain number of sects which although seemingly different one from another as to name, ritual, form and origin are, however, similar due to the analogy of their aim and chief principles. Indeed, they are identical to Freemasonry which is, for them all, the central point from which they proceed and toward which they converge.

Pope Leo XIII

Let us remember that Christianity and Freemasonry are essentially incompatible, to such an extent, That to become united with one means being divorced from the other. Let us, therefore, expose Freemasonry as the enemy of God, of the Church and of our Motherland.

Pope Leo XIII

It is necessary to fight Freemasonry with those weapons of divine faith which in past ages vanquished paganism.

Pope Leo XIII

Grail, Holy

When the mystery of the Holy Grail is revealed, one realizes it is in no way an esoteric enigma; what it encloses is the most dramatic, romantic and sublime story humanity has ever known: the story of the Word made Man and Eucharist.

Professor Salvador Antuñano Alea

Hell

The state or place of those condemned to eternal punishment.

William Byrne

Ignorance

To be ignorant of what we are bound to know is sinful.

George Haydock

Incarnation

After grace had been revealed both the learned and simple folk are bound to explicit faith in the mysteries of Christ, chiefly as regards those which are observed and publicly proclaimed, such as the articles which refer to the Incarnation.

Thomas Aquinas

Justification

But when the Apostle says that man is justified by faith and freely, these words are to be understood in that sense in which the uninterrupted unanimity of the Catholic Church has held and expressed them, namely, That we are therefore said to be justified by faith, because faith is the beginning of human salvation, the foundation and root of all justification, without which it is impossible to please God and to come to the fellowship of His sons.

Council of Trent

Now, they are disposed to that justice when, aroused and aided by divine grace, receiving faith by hearing, they are moved freely toward God, believing to be true what has been divinely revealed and promised, especially that the sinner is justified by God by His grace, through the redemption that is in Christ Jesus; and when, understanding themselves to be sinners, they, by turning themselves from the fear of divine justice, by which they are salutarily aroused, to consider the mercy of God, are raised to hope, trusting that God will be propitious to them for Christ's sake; and they begin to love Him as the fountain of all justice, and on that account are moved against sin by a certain hatred and detestation, That is, by that repentance that must be performed before baptism; finally, when they resolve (desire) to receive baptism, to begin a new life and to keep the commandments of God.

Council of Trent

Mary, Blessed Virgin

The great sign which the Apostle Saint John contemplated in the heavens, the woman clothed with the sun (cf. Apoc. 12:1), is rightly, in the Holy Liturgy of the Catholic Church, interpreted of the Blessed Virgin Mary, by the grace of Christ the Redeemer, Mother of all men.
Pope Paul VI

Mary, Immaculate conception

The Most Holy Virgin Mary was, in the first moment of her conception, by a unique gift of grace and privilege of Almighty God, in view of the merits of Jesus Christ, the Redeemer of mankind, preserved free from all stain of original sin.
Pope Pius IX

Mary, Mother of God

The Holy Virgin is the Mother of God since according to the flesh she brought forth the Word of God made flesh.
Council of Ephesus, 431

We acknowledge the resurrection of the dead, of which Jesus Christ our Lord became the firstling; he bore a body not in appearance but in truth derived from Mary the Mother of God.
Alexander of Alexandria

The Father bears witness from heaven to his Son. The Holy Spirit bears witness, coming down bodily in the form of a dove. The Archangel Gabriel bears witness, bringing the good tidings to Mary. The Virgin Mother of God bears witness.
Cyril of Jerusalem

Perpetual virginity

After giving birth to Jesus, Mary remained a virgin for the rest of her life. Joseph never had relations with her, and she never physically bore any other children.
Benedict brothers

Let those, therefore, who deny that the Son is by nature from the Father and proper to His essence, deny also that He took true human flesh from the Ever-Virgin Mary.
Athanasius

I have heard from someone that certain people dare to say of Mary that after she bore the Savior she had sexual relations with a man. I am not surprised. The ignorance of those who have no exact knowledge of the sacred scriptures and who have not applied themselves to the histories turns from one thing to another and distracts the one who wishes to trace something of the truth with his own mind.
Epiphanius

It helps us to understand the terms first-born and only-begotten when the Evangelist tells that Mary remained a virgin "until she brought forth her first-born son"; for neither did Mary, who is to be honored and praised above all others, marry anyone, nor did she ever become the Mother of anyone else, but even after childbirth she remained always and forever and immaculate virgin.

Mary's assumption, Definition of

Mary, the immaculate perpetually Virgin Mother of God, after the completion of her earthly life, was assumed body and soul into the glory of heaven.
Pope Pius XII, 1950

Mary's assumption

Therefore the Virgin is immortal to this day, seeing that he who had dwelt in her transported her to the regions of her assumption.
Timothy of Jerusalem

And from that time forth all knew that the spotless and precious body had been transferred to paradise.
John the Theologian

Mary's intercession, Definition of

Though she enjoys the glory of heaven, the Virgin Mary is still lovingly concerned with the struggles of Christ's Body on earth. So she constantly prays for our

needs with a mother's love.
Benedict brothers

Mary's intercession

With the Mediator, you are the Mediatrix of the entire world.
Ephraem

The Lord said to his mother, "Let your heart rejoice and be glad, for every favor and every gift has been given to you from my Father in heaven and from me and from the Holy Spirit. Every soul that calls upon your name shall not be ashamed, but shall find mercy and comfort and support and confidence, both in the world that now is and in that which is to come, in the presence of my Father in the heavens."
John the Theologian

Hail you who acceptably intercede as a Mediatrix for mankind.
Antipater of Bostra

Perseverence

If any one saith, That he will for certain, of an absolute and infallible certainty, have that great gift of perseverance unto the end, unless he have learned this by special revelation; let him be anathema.
The Council of Trent

Pope

They, therefore, walk in the path of dangerous errors who believe that they can accept Christ as the head of the Church, while not adhering loyally to His Vicar on earth. They have taken away the visible bonds of unity and left the Mystical Body of the Redeemer so obscured and so maimed, That those who are seeking the haven of eternal salvation can neither see it nor find it.
Pope Pius XII

And you, venerable brothers, will not fail, in your teaching, to recall to the flocks entrusted to you these grand and salutary truths; we cannot render to God the devotion that is due Him and that is pleasing to Him nor is it possible to be united to Him except through Jesus Christ; and it is not possible to be united to Jesus Christ except in the Church and through the Church, His Mystical Body, and, finally, it is not possible to belong to the Church except through the bishops, successors of the Apostles, united to the Supreme Pastor, the successor of Peter.
Pope John XXIII

It is shown also that it is necessary for salvation to be subject to the Roman Pontiff.
Thomas Aquinas

The Savior Himself is the door of the sheepfold: "I am the door of the sheep." Into this fold of Jesus Christ, no man may enter unless he be led by the Sovereign Pontiff; and only if they be united to him can men be saved, for the Roman Pontiff is the Vicar of Christ and His personal representative on earth.
Pope John XXIII

Popes

Furthermore, in this one Church of Christ no man can be or remain who does not accept, recognize and obey the authority and supremacy of Peter and his legitimate successors. Did not the ancestors of those who are now entangled in the errors of Photius and the reformers, obey the Bishop of Rome, the chief shepherd of souls? Alas their children left the home of their fathers, but it did not fall to the ground and perish for ever, for it was supported by God. Let them therefore return to their common Father, who, forgetting the insults previously heaped on the Apostolic See, will receive them in the most loving fashion. For if, as they continually state, they long to be united with Us and ours, why do they not hasten to enter the Church, "the Mother and mistress of all Christ's faithful?" Let them hear Lactantius crying out: "The Catholic Church is alone in keeping the true worship. This is the fount of truth, this is the house of Faith, this is the temple of God: if any man enter not here, or if any man go forth from it, he is a stranger to

the hope of life and salvation. Let none delude himself with obstinate wrangling. For life and salvation are here concerned, which will be lost and entirely destroyed, unless their interests are carefully and assiduously kept in mind."
Pope Pius XI

Prayer
And by the way,
Speaking of how to pray,
Dogmas come first, not liturgies.
Leonard Feeney

Predestination
If any one saith, That a man, who is born again and justified, is bound of faith to believe that he is assuredly in the number of the predestinate; let him be anathema.
The Council of Trent

Punishment
God in His supreme goodness and clemency, by no means allows anyone to be punished with eternal punishments who does not have the guilt of voluntary fault.
Pius IX

Purgatory
We believe ... That the souls, by the purifying compensation are purged after death.
Council of Lyons II (1274):

"If they have died repentant for their sins and having love of God, but have not made satisfaction for things they have done or omitted by fruits worthy of penance, then their souls, after death, are cleansed by the punishment of Purgatory...the suffrages of the faithful still living are efficacious in bringing them relief from such punishment, namely the Sacrifice of the Mass, prayers and almsgiving and other works of piety which, in accordance with the designation of the Church, are customarily offered by the faithful for each other." 12
Council of Florence (1438-1443):

"We constantly hold that purgatory exists, and that the souls of the faithful there detained are helped by the prayers of the faithful."
Council of Trent (1545-1563)

1021: "Each will be rewarded immediately after death in accordance with his works and faith."
1023: "Those who die in God's grace and friendship and are perfectly purified [with no need of purgatory] live for ever with Christ"
The Roman Catholic Catechism states:

Return of Christ
We command all those who exercise the function of preaching, or will do so in the future, not to presume, either in their sermons or in their affirmations, to fix a date for future evils, whether for the coming of Antichrist or for the Day of Judgment, seeing that the Truth has said: "It is not for you to know the times or the moments, which the Father put in His own power." Those, therefore, who have had the audacity to make such statements in the past have lied, and it is well known That, on their account, the authority of those who preach wisely has greatly suffered.
Pope Leo X

Sacraments
If anyone says that the sacraments of the New Law are not necessary for salvation but are superfluous, and that without them or without the desire of them men obtain from God through faith alone the grace of justification, though all are not necessary for each one, let him be anathema.
Council of Trent

Salvation
We declare, say, define, and pronounce that it is absolutely necessary for the salvation of every human creature to be subject to the Roman Pontiff.
Pope Boniface VIII

There can be, and actually are, individuals who are actually justified in the grace of

God who attain to supernatural salvation in God's sight ... yet who do not belong to the Church ... as a visible historical reality.
Karl Rahner

But the unity of the Church exists primarily because of the unity of faith; for the Church is nothing else than the aggregate of the faithful. And because without faith it is impossible to please God, for this reason there is no room for salvation outside the Church. Now the salvation of the faithful is consummated through the sacraments of the Church, in which [sacraments] the power of the Passion of Christ is effective.
Thomas Aquinas

A man cannot have salvation except in the Catholic Church. Outside the Catholic Church he can have everything except salvation. He can have honor, he can have Sacraments, he can sing Allelulia, he can answer Amen, he can possess the Gospel, he can preach faith in the name of the Father and of the Son and of the Holy Spirit: but never except in the Catholic Church will he be able to find salvation.
Augustine of Hippo

Romans, Paul's letter to the
It is the profoundest piece of writing in existence.
Samuel Taylor Coleridge

Rule of faith
[The following rule is attributed to St Columba, 521-597, and reflects the spirit of early Irish monasticism.]
Be alone in a separate place near a chief city, if thy conscience is not prepared to be in common with the crowd.
Be always single-minded in your imitation of Christ and the Evangelists.
Whatsoever little or much thou possessest of anything, whether clothing, or food, or drink, let it be at the command of the senior and at his disposal, for it is not befitting a religious to have any distinction of property with his own free brother.
Let a fast place, with one door, enclose thee.
A few religious men to converse with thee of God and his Testament; to visit thee on days of solemnity; to strengthen thee in the Testaments of God, and the narratives of the Scriptures.
A person too who would talk with thee in idle words, or of the world; or who murmurs at what he cannot remedy or prevent, but who would distress thee more should he be a tattler between friends and foes, thou shalt not admit him to thee, but at once give him thy benediction should he deserve it.
Let thy servant be a discreet, religious, not tale-telling man, who is to attend continually on thee, with moderate labor of course, but always ready.
Yield submission to every rule that is of devotion.
A mind prepared for red martyrdom [That is death for the faith].
A mind fortified and steadfast for white martyrdom. [That is ascetic practices].
Forgiveness from the heart of every one.
Constant prayers for those who trouble thee.
Fervor in singing the office for the dead, as if every faithful dead was a particular friend of thine.
Hymns for souls to be sung standing.
Let thy vigils be constant from eve to eve, under the direction of another person.
Three labors in the day, viz., prayers, work, and reading.
The work to be divided into three parts, viz., thine own work, and the work of thy place, as regards its real wants; secondly, thy share of the brethren's work; lastly, to help the neighbors, viz., by instruction or writing, or sewing garments, or whatever labor they may be in want of, as the Lord says, "You shall not appear before me empty."
Everything in its proper order; for no one is crowned except he who has striven lawfully.
Follow alms-giving before all things.

Take not of food till thou art hungry.
Sleep not till thou feelest desire.
Speak not except on business.
Every increase which comes to thee in
lawful meals, or in wearing apparel, give it
for pity to the brethren that want it, or to
the poor in like manner.
The love of God with all thy heart and all
thy strength.
The love of thy neighbor as thyself.
Abide in the Testament of God throughout
all times.
Thy measure of prayer shall be until thy
tears come;
Or thy measure of work of labor till thy
tears come;
Or thy measure of thy work of labor, …
until thy perspiration often comes, if thy
tears are not free.
Rule of St Columba

Rules
See also: Words to live by
How to behave in an elevator
1. Face forward.
2. Fold hands in front.
3. Do not make eye contact.
4. Watch the numbers.
5. Don't talk to anyone you don't know.
6. Stop talking with anyone you do know
when anyone you don't know enters the
elevator.
7. Avoid brushing bodies.
Layne Longfellow

The best rules to form a young man are: to
talk a little, to hear much, to reflect alone
upon what has passed in company, to
distrust one's own opinions, and value
others' that deserve it.
William Temple

Rush
Great haste makes great waste. Adopt the
pace of nature. Her pace is patience.
Author unknown

Go placidly amid the noise and the haste,
and remember what peace there may be in
silence.
Max Ehrmann

Good and quickly seldom meet.
George Herbert

Haste in every business brings failures.
Herodotus

God never imposes a duty without giving
time to do it.
John Ruskin

The perpetual hurry of business and
company ruins me in soul if not in body.
William Wilberforce

S

Sabbath
See also: Sunday
The Sabbath was made for man, and not
man for the Sabbath.
The Bible, Mark 2:27

The conscionable keeping of the Sabbath,
is the Mother of all Religion.
Lewis Bayly

The Sabbath is God's special present to the
working man, and one of its chief objects
is to prolong his life, and preserve efficient
his working tone. The savings bank of
human existence is the weekly Sabbath.
William G. Blaikie

The external observance of the Sabbath
rest is a Jewish ceremonial ordinance and
no longer binding on Christians.
Sabbatarians surpass the Jews three times
over in a crass and carnal Sabbatarian
superstition.
John Calvin

If Sunday were anywhere made holy merely
for the day's sake or its observance set on a
Jewish foundation, "then I order you to
walk on it, to ride on it, to dance on it, to
feast on it, to do anything that shall remove
this encroachment on Christian Liberty."
Martin Luther

Sacraments
See also: Baptism; Lord's Supper
A sacrament is a visible sign of a sacred
thing, or a visible form of an invisible grace.
Augustine of Hippo

The spiritual virtue of a sacrament is like
light: although it passes among the impure,
it is not polluted.
Augustine of Hippo

An outward and visible sign of an inward
and spiritual grace.
Book of Common Prayer

A sacrament is God's witness to us of his
favor towards us, by means of an outward
sign.
John Calvin

The sacraments can only fulfil their
function when accompanied by the Spirit
within, whose power alone can penetrate
the heart and stir the emotions.
John Calvin

We have two sacraments which are
certainly of our Blessed Savior's institution,
for which we are thankful and with which
we are satisfied. Had our Savior instituted
more sacraments, we should have been
more thankful and should have had greater
obligations to gratitude. ... Though we
reject those five additional sacraments of
the Church of Rome, yet we do it not
because they are sacraments we do not like,
but because they are not sacraments at all.
Edward Gee

What is Jordan that I should wash in it?
What is the preaching that I should attend
on it, while I hear nothing but what I
knew before? What are these beggarly
elements of water, bread, and wine? Are
not these the reasonings of a soul that
forgets who appoints the means of grace?
William Gurnall

Sacraments are the powerful instruments
of God to eternal life. For as our natural
body consists in the union of the body
with the soul, so our life supernatural is in
the union of the soul with God.
Richard Hooker

The use of sacraments is but only in this life, yet so that here they concern a far better life than this and are for that cause accompanied with "grace which worketh salvation." Sacraments are the powerful instruments of God to eternal life.
Richard Hooker

The sun, too, shines into cesspools and is not polluted.
Diogenes Laertius

There should be no sacraments except those found in the Bible: I can find only two, the Lord's Supper and Baptism.
Martin Luther

Grace sometimes precedes the sacrament, sometimes follows it, and sometimes does not even follow it.
Theodoret

Sacraments, Validity of
The spiritual virtue of a sacrament is like light,--although it passes among the impure, it is not polluted.
Augustine of Hippo

Sacrifice
He is brought as a lamb to the slaughter.
The Bible, Isaiah 53:7

Greater love hath no man than this, that a man lay down his life for his friends.
The Bible, John 15:13

Not what we stand for but what we fall for is the true test of strength.
Author unknown

Every action done so as to cling to God in communion of holiness, and thus achieve blessedness, is a true sacrifice.
Augustine of Hippo

It is in spending oneself that one becomes rich.
Sara Bernhardt

It is normal to give away a little of one's life in order not to lose it all.
Albert Camus

To gain that worth having, it may be necessary to lose everything else.
Bernadette Devlin

No sacrifice is worth the name unless it is a joy. Sacrifice and a long face go ill together.
Mahatma Gandhi

We can offer up much in the large, but to make sacrifices in the little things is what we are seldom equal to.
Goethe

If one has not given everything, one has given nothing.
Georges Guynemer

Nothing is really lost by a life of sacrifice; everything is lost by failure to obey God's call.
Henry P. Liddon

People talk of the sacrifice I have made in spending so much of my life in Africa. Can that be called a sacrifice which is simply paid back as a small part of a great debt owing to our God, which we can never repay? It is emphatically no sacrifice. Say rather it is a privilege.
David Livingstone

I never made a sacrifice. We ought not to talk of "sacrifice" when we remember the great sacrifice which he made who left his Father's throne on high to give himself for us.
David Livingstone

No sacrifice can be too great to make for him who gave his life for me.
C. T. Studd

Unless a life is lived for others, it is not worthwhile.
Mother Teresa of Calcutta

See from his head, his hands, his feet,
Sorrow and love flow mingled down;
Did e'er such love and sorrow meet,
Or thorns compose so rich a crown.
Isaac Watts
[Matthew Arnold thought that this was "the finest hymn in the English language."]

John Julian, the author of the massive Dictionary of Hymnology rates it as "one of the four hymns which stand at the head of all hymns in the English language."

Eric Routley believed it to be "the most penetrating of all hymns, the most demanding, the most imaginative."

Isaac Watts gave it the title: "Crucifixion to the world by the cross of Christ," basing it on the text from Galatians 6:14.]

Sadness

We hanged our harps upon the willows.
The Bible, Psalm 137:2 KJV

Instead of allowing yourself to be so unhappy, just let your love grow as God wants it to grow; just seek goodness in others, love more persons more; love them more impersonally, more unselfishly, without thought of return. The return, never fear, will take care of itself.
Henry Drummond

Saint

Saint: A dead sinner revised and edited.
Ambrose Bierce

The saint is a saint because he received the Holy Spirit, who took up his abode with him and inwardly married himself to the soul.
Abraham Kuyper

Every saint is a pattern; but no saint is a pattern of everything.
Henri de Tourville

What is the Church if not the assembly of all the saints?
Nicetas

There is an unknowing that is higher than all knowledge, a darkness that is supremely bright; and in this dazzling darkness divine things are given to the saints.
Gregory Palamas

During their lifetime saints are a nuisance.
George Bernard Shaw

Salvation
See also: Atonement; Christ, Death of; Cross

Salvation is found in no one else, for there is no other name under heaven given to men by which we must be saved.
The Bible, Acts 4:12 KJV

For it is by grace you have been saved, through faith — and this not from yourselves, it is the gift of God — not by works, so that no one can boast. For we are God's workmanship.
The Bible, Ephesians 2:8-10

... continue to work out your salvation with fear and trembling ...
The Bible, Philippians 2:12

Therefore, my dear friends, as you have always obeyed—not only in my presence, but now much more in my absence—continue to work out your salvation with fear and trembling, for it is God who works in you to will and to act according to his good purpose.
The Bible, Philippians 2:12,13

Here is a trustworthy saying that deserves full acceptance: Christ Jesus came into the world to save sinners — of whom I am the worst.
The Bible, 1 Timothy 1:15

Salvation is so simple we can overlook it, so profound we can never comprehend it.
Author unknown

Once saved, always saved.
Author unknown. A motto of the Reformation

You cannot climb to salvation on atheistic steppes.
Author unknown

Salvation is entirely the result of the sovereign will and election of God and nothing to do with us at all.
Author unknown

It was not by dialectic that it pleased God to save His people; "for the kingdom of

God consisteth in simplicity of faith, not in wordy contention."
St. Ambrose

Lord my God, you have formed and reformed me.
Anselm

Three things are necessary for the salvation of man: To know what he ought to believe, to know what he ought to desire, and to know what he ought to do.
Thomas Aquinas

He who created you without you will not justify you without you.
Augustine of Hippo

Salvation is God's way of making us real people.
Augustine of Hippo

Justification is the criminal pardoned; sanctification, the patient healed. The union of both constitutes present salvation.
Joel Beeke

The early Christians believed that salvation is a gift from God but that God gives his gift to whomever he chooses. And he chooses to give it to those who love and obey him.
D.W. Bercot

Man of Sorrows! what a name
For the Son of God, who came
Ruined sinners to reclaim!
Hallelujah, what a Savior!
Philip Paul Bliss

Holy Scripture containeth all things necessary to salvation.
Book of Common Prayer KJV

There are, even today, a great many people who understand that man needs salvation, but there are very few who are convinced that he needs forgiveness and redemption... Sin is understood as imperfection, sensuality, worldliness -- but not as guilt.
Emil Brunner

I remember that one day, as I was considering of the enmity that was in me to God, that Scripture came in my mind, He hath, "made peace through the blood of His cross" Colossians 1:26. By which I was made to see that God and my soul were friends by His blood. I saw that the justice of God and my sinful soul could embrace and kiss each other through the blood. This was a good day to me; I hope I shall not forget it.
John Bunyan

The fulfillment of the Lord's mercy does not depend upon believers' works, but... he fulfills the promise of salvation for those who respond to his call with upright life, because in those who are directed to the good by his Spirit he recognizes the only genuine insignia of his children.
John Calvin

Since no man is excluded from calling upon God the gate of salvation is set open to all. There is nothing else to hinder us from entering, but our own unbelief.
John Calvin

Salvation is the work of God for man; it is not the work of man for God.
Lewis Sperry Chafer

Anyone can devise a plan by which good people go to heaven. Only God can devise a plan whereby sinners, which are His enemies, can go to heaven.
Lewis Sperry Chafer

Fight to escape from your own cleverness. If you do, then you will find salvation and uprightness through Jesus Christ our Lord.
John Climacus

The Lord is loving unto man, and swift to pardon, but slow to punish. Let no man therefore despair of his own salvation.
Cyril of Alexandria

Before an individual can be saved, he must first learn that he cannot save himself.
M.R. DeHaan

As I do no good action here, merely for the interpretation of good men, though that be one good and justifiable reason of my good actions: so I must do nothing for my salvation hereafter, merely for the love I bear to mine own soul, though that also be one good and justifiable reason of that action; but the primary reason in both, as well as the actions that establish a good name, as the actions that establish eternal life, must be the glory of God.
John Donne

There is no more urgent and critical question in life than that of your personal relationship with God and your eternal salvation.
Billy Graham

No more soul-destroying doctrine could well be devised than the doctrine that sinners can regenerate themselves, and repent and believe just when they please. As it is a truth both of Scripture and of experience that the unrenewed man can do nothing of himself to secure his salvation, it is essential that he should be brought to practical conviction of that truth. When thus convinced, and not before, he seeks help from the only source whence it can be obtained.
Charles Hodge

To follow the Savior is to participate in salvation, to follow the light is to perceive the light.
Irenaeus

Christ came to save all through his own person.
Irenaeus

For this is why the Word became man, and the Son of God became the Son of man: so that man, by entering into communion with the Word and thus receiving divine sonship, might become a son of God.
Irenaeus

The deaf may hear the Savior's voice,
The fettered tongue its chains may break;
But the deaf heart, the dumb by choice,

The laggard soul that will not wake,
The guilt that scorns to be forgiven --
These baffle e'en the spells of heaven.
John Keble

The salvation of one soul is worth more than the framing of a Magna Charta of a thousand worlds.
John Keble

We must first be made good before we can do good; we must first be made just before our works can please God.
Hugh Latimer

A world of nice people, content in their own niceness, looking no further, turned away from God, would be just as desperately in need of salvation as a miserable world – and might even be more difficult to save.
C.S. Lewis

Christians are not men and women who are hoping for salvation, but those who have experienced it.
M. Lloyd-Jones

If man could have saved himself there would have been no need for the Son of God to come on earth. Indeed, his coming is proof that people cannot save themselves.
M. Lloyd-Jones

Everyone needs to be saved, however great, however illustrious. We are all sinners. We are all born in sin.
M. Lloyd-Jones

Is it not wonderful news to believe that salvation lies outside ourselves?
Martin Luther

If every a man could be saved by monkery, that man was I.
Martin Luther

The beginning of our salvation is from God the Father, the dispensation is from the Son, and the application from the Holy Ghost.
Thomas Manton

Most of God's people are contented to be saved from the hell that is without; they are not so anxious to be saved from the hell that is within.
Robert Murray M'Cheyne

To know Christ is not to speculate about the mode of his incarnation, but to know his saving benefits.
Philip Melanchthon

Salvation consists wholly in being saved from ourselves, or that which we are by nature.
Andrew Murray

Salvation comes through a cross and a crucified Christ.
Andrew Murray

Only in Jesus Christ do we have assurance of salvation, forgiveness of sins, entrance into God's family, and the guarantee of heaven forever when we die.
Luis Palau

We need to rethink our reformed soteriology so that every limb and every branch in the tree is coursing with the sap of Augustinian delight. We need to make plain that total depravity is not just badness, but blindness to beauty and deadness to joy; and unconditional election means that the completeness of our joy in Jesus was planned for us before we ever existed; and that... irresistible grace is the commitment and power of God's love to make sure we don't hold on to suicidal pleasures, but will set us free from by the sovereign power of superior delights; and that the perseverance of the saints is the almighty work of God to keep us, through all affliction and suffering, for an inheritance of pleasures at God's right hand forever.
John Piper

My only hope of salvation is in the infinite, transcendent love of God manifested to the world by the death of his Son upon the cross. Nothing but His blood will wash away my sins. I rely exclusively upon it. Come, Lord Jesus! Come quickly!
Benjamin Rush, Signer of the Declaration

That a man can have salvation without "asking" for it, I cannot see in the Bible. That a man will receive pardon of his sins, who will not so much as lift up his heart inwardly, and say, "Lord Jesus, give it to me," this I cannot find.
J.C. Ryle

John Bunyan understood the Gospel when he wrote that tract, *The Jerusalem Sinner Saved*. He knew that every sinner is a Jerusalem sinner who has crucified the Lord of Glory; and to whom, notwithstanding all this, the grace of God is exceedingly abundant with faith and love which is in Christ Jesus.
Adolph Saphir

I am not saved so that I may be born again. I am born again so that I may be saved.
R.C. Sproul

God just doesn't throw a life preserver to a drowning person. He goes to the bottom of the sea, and pulls a corpse from the bottom of the sea, takes him up on the bank, breathes into him the breath of life and makes him alive. That's what the Bible says happens in your salvation.
R.C. Sproul

We say Christ so died that he infallibly secured the salvation of a multitude that no man can number, who through Christ's death not only may be saved, but are saved, must be saved, and cannot by any possibility run the hazard of being anything but saved.
C.H. Spurgeon

Rock of Ages, cleft for me,
Let me hide myself in thee.
A.M. Toplady

Salvation is from our side a choice; from the divine side it is a seizing upon, an apprehending, a conquest by the Most

High God. Our accepting and willing are reactions rather than actions.
A. W. Tozer

The fundamental principles of Christianity are these two: the doctrine of justification, and that of the new birth; the former relating to that great work God does for us, in forgiving our sins; the latter to the great work of God in us, in renewing our fallen nature.
John Wesley

Seek not to explore the heights of the divine majesty, but to find salvation in the saving deeds of God our Savior
William of St Thierry

Salvation, Gift of
For it is by grace you have been saved, through faith--and this not from yourselves, it is the gift of God – not by works, so that no one can boast.
The Bible, Ephesians 2:8,9

Salvation, Need for
We must not suppose that if we succeeded in making everyone nice we should have saved their souls. A world of nice people, content in their own niceness, looking no further, turned away from God, would be just as desperately in need of salvation as a miserable world.
C.S. Lewis

Salvation and grace alone
Salvation is wholly of grace, not only undeserved but undesired by us until God is pleased to awaken us to a sense of our need of it. And then we find everything prepared that our wants require or our wishes conceive; yea, that He has done exceedingly beyond what we could either ask or think. Salvation is wholly of the Lord and bears those signatures of infinite wisdom, power, and goodness which distinguish all His works from the puny imitations of men. It is every way worthy of Himself, a great, a free, a full, a sure salvation. It is great whether we consider the objects (miserable, hell-deserving sinners), the end (the restoration of such

alienated creatures to His image and favor, to immortal life and happiness) or the means (the incarnation, humiliation, sufferings and death of His beloved Son). It is free, without exception of persons or cases, without any conditions or qualifications, but such as He, Himself, performs in them and bestows upon them.
John Newton

Salvation and the church
To me, to whom God hath revealed his Son, in a Gospel, by a Church, there can be no way of salvation, but by applying that Son of God, by that Gospel, in that Church.
John Donne

Sanctification
See also: Holiness
To sanctify you wholly is to complete the work of purification and renovation begun in your regeneration.
Joseph Benson

He is not a Christian that thinks he is a finished Christian and is insensible how far short he falls. That man without doubt, has never so much as begun to be renewed, nor did he ever taste what it is to be a Christian.
Bernard of Clairvaux

Those who have been regenerated are also sanctified, by God's word and Spirit dwelling in them. This satisfaction is progressive through the supply of divine strength which all saints seek to obtain, pressing after a heavenly life in cordial obedience to all Christ's commands.
James Boyce

The change that takes place in a man when he is converted and sanctified, is not that his love for happiness is diminished but only that it is regulated with respect to its exercises and influences, and the course and objects it leads to when God brings a soul out of a miserable state and condition into a happy state of conversion, he gives him happiness that before he had not (namely

in God), but he does not at the same time take away any of his love of happiness.
Jonathan Edwards

Sanctify yourself and you will sanctify society.
Francis of Assisi

No sweat, no sanctification.
Russ Gaippe

Justification is at once an accomplished fact, but sanctification is gradual.
Abraham Kuyper

Sanctification is a gracious work of God, whereby in a supernatural way he gradually divests from sin the inclinations and dispositions of the regenerate and clothes them with holiness.
Abraham Kuyper

Our sanctification did not depend upon changing our works, but in doing that for God's sake which we commonly do for our own.
Brother Lawrence

Sanctification is that condition in which the sin principle is dealt with.
M. Lloyd-Jones

This life therefore is not righteousness but growth in righteousness; not health but healing, not being but becoming, not rest but exercise. We are not what we shall be but we are growing toward it; the process is not yet finished but it is going on; this is not the end but it is the road. All does not yet gleam in glory but all is being purified.
Martin Luther

A soul may be in as thriving a state when thirsting, seeking and mourning after the Lord as when actually rejoicing in him; as much in earnest when fighting in the valley as when singing upon the mount.
John Newton

Jesus, like any good fisherman, first catches the fish; then he cleans them.
Mark Potter

Sanctification, in its place and proportion, is quite as important as justification.
J.C. Ryle

Contend to the death for the truth that no man is a true Christian who is not converted and is not a holy man. But allow that a man be converted, have a new heart, and be a holy man, and yet be liable to infirmity, doubts, and fears.
J.C. Ryle

We must remember throughout our lives that in God's sight there are no little people and no little places. Only one thing is important: to be consecrated persons in God's place for us, at each moment.
Francis A. Schaeffer

The renewal of our natures is a work of great importance. It is not to be done in a day. We have not only a new house to build up, but an old one to pull down.
George Whitefield

Sanctification and glory
Sanctification is glory begun. Glory is sanctification completed.
F.F. Bruce

Sanity
Great wits are sure to madness near allied, And thin partitions do their bounds divide.
John Dryden

Show me a sane man and I will cure him for you.
Carl Gustav Jung

Satan
See also: Devil
Satan came also.
The Bible, Job 1:6 KJV

The god of this age has blinded the minds of unbelievers, so that they cannot see the light of the gospel of the glory of Christ, who is the image of God.
The Bible, 2 Corinthians 4:4

For we wanted to come to you--certainly I, Paul, did, again and again--but Satan stopped us.
The Bible, 1 Thessalonians 2:18

The coming of the lawless one will be in accordance with the work of Satan displayed in all kinds of counterfeit miracles, signs and wonders, and in every sort of evil that deceives those who are perishing.
The Bible, 2 Thessalonians 2:9,10

Satan looks back and sees the believer's sin. God looks back and sees the cross.
Author unknown

The best protection against Satan's lies is to know God's truth.
Author unknown

Satan promises the best, but pays with the worst; he promises honor, and pays with disgrace; he promises pleasure, and pays with pain; he promises profit, and pays with loss; he promises life, and pays with death. But God pays as he promises; all his payments are made in pure gold.
Thomas Brooks

Satan, who acts by an untiring power, and who will never let the saints rest till they are taken up to an everlasting rest in the bosom of Christ, is so powerful and subtle that he will often make the greatest and dearest mercies to become our greatest snares.
Thomas Brooks

Study Satan's tricks, and acquaint yourself with his tactics. Paul takes for granted that every Christian understands them in some measure: "We are not ignorant of his devices," he says (II Cor. 2:11). Can this be said of you? Do you know how subtle and clever your enemy is? What pleasant company that he can pretend to be? "Sit down at my gaming table," says Satan. "Here are some tempting prizes: your earthly estate, your life, your liberty." Now you must agree, these things are good and lawful. But here is Satan's gimmick: he expands the rule of his game so that if you play for him, you will certainly violate the irrevocable and unchangeable laws of God. If you cannot have good things by plain dealing but must resort to sleight of hand, you know the prize is counterfeit and will turn to dung in your hands. How utterly foolish to fast shuffle with God by compromising His truth. You may think you have won a hand or two, but when the game is over, you will find yourself bankrupt.

If Satan can entice you to sin for what he assures you is a worthy prize, you are in serious trouble, but the worst is yet to come. Once he has you sitting at his table, he will begin in earnest to teach you the tricks of his trade. This diabolical dealer will show you how to slip your sins under the table, telling you no one-not even God-will see. He has been teaching this trick since Adam, who thought he could hide behind a fig leaf. What did Joseph's brothers do when they had left him for dead but hide their deed under the coat they had bloodied? And how did Potiphar's wife respond when Joseph turned away from her adulterous gaze? She hid her sin (again in his coat) and accused him of her own wickedness.

Beware of playing such games of chance with God. No coat is large enough to hide your sin; no hand is quick enough to slip it under the table and miss the all-seeing eye of God. If He does not call you to account for it in this life, you can be sure you will answer for it in the next. The gravest discipline God can dispense this side of eternity is to leave a sinner to his own pursuits when he is hell bound in the company of Satan. One of the dangers of playing the devil's games is that you come to like them. They are as addictive as wine, and create an insatiable thirst. Practice the devil's tricks long enough, and your blackened soul will begin to devise mischief of its own, to help satisfy your ravishing appetite for sin. No sins speak of a higher attainment in wickedness than those which are the result of deliberate, premeditated plotting. Set your heart

toward wickedness, and Satan will lend you his own chariot and drive you himself to perform the deed.
William Gurnall

Christ will bear no equal, and Satan no superior; and therefore, hold in with both thou canst not.
William Gurnall

Like a good chess player, Satan is always trying to manoeuver you into a position where you can save your castle only by losing your bishop.
C.S. Lewis

Satan strikes either at the root of faith or at the root of diligence.
John Livingstone

The natural response to denials of Satan's existence is to ask, Who then runs his business?
J.I. Packer

Satan never sells his poisons naked – he always gilds them before he vends them.
C.H. Spurgeon

Satan and prayer
Satan does not care how many people read about prayer if only he can keep them from praying.
Paul E. Billheimer

No one is a firmer believer in the power of prayer than the devil; not that he practices it, but he suffers from it.
Guy H. King

When we go to God by prayer, the devil knows we go to fetch strength against him, and therefore he opposeth us all he can.
Richard Sibbes

Satisfaction
The rattle without the breast, will not satisfy the child;
the house without the husband, will not satisfy the wife;

the world without Christ, will not satisfy the soul.
Thomas Brooks

Forsaking the food that gives strength to man's heart, I have fed upon the pleasure that gives passing satisfaction.
The Lenten Triodion

Do not give your heart to that which does not satisfy your heart.
Abba Poemen

Savior
See also: Sin-bearer
Jesus, the savior of mankind.
Meaning of the common Latin letters "I.H.S." (Iesus hominum salvator)

Sayings of Jesus

(NRSV, UNLESS STATED OTHERWISE)
Come unto me
Come unto me, all ye that labor and are heavy laden, and I will give you rest.
Matthew 11:28 KJV

Take my yoke upon you
Take my yoke upon you, and learn of me; for I am meek and lowly in heart: and ye shall find rest for your souls.
For my yoke is easy, and my burden is light.
Matthew 11:29-30 KJV

The Lord's prayer
Our Father which art in heaven,
Hallowed be thy name.
Thy kingdom come.
Thy will be done in earth, as it is in heaven.
Give us this day our daily bread.
And forgive us our debts, as we forgive our debtors.
And lead us not into temptation, but deliver us from evil:
For thine is the kingdom, and the power, and the glory, for ever. Amen.
Matthew 6:9-13 KJV

The Lord's prayer
Our Father in heaven:
May your holy name be honored;
may your Kingdom come;
may your will be done on earth as it is in heaven.
Give us today the food we need.
Forgive us the wrongs we have done,
as we forgive the wrongs that others have done to us.
Do not bring us to hard testing,
but keep us safe from the Evil One.
Matthew 6:9-13 GNB

Believing prayer
Whatever you ask for in prayer with faith, you will receive.
Matthew 21:22

Ask, seek, knock
Ask, and it will be given to you;
search, and you will find;
knock, and the door will be opened for you.
For everyone who asks receives,
and everyone who searches finds,
and for everyone who knocks, the door will be opened.
Matthew 7:7-8

Good gifts from heaven
Is there anyone among you who, if your child asks for bread, will give a stone? Or if the child asks for a fish, will give a snake? If you then, who are evil, know how to give good gifts to your children, how much more will your Father in heaven give good things to those who ask him!
Matthew 7:9-11

The golden rule
In everything do to others as you would have them do to you; for this is the law and the prophets.
Matthew 7:12

Love your enemies
You have heard that it was said, "You shall love your neighbor and hate your enemy." But I say to you, Love your enemies and pray for those who persecute you, so that you may be children of your Father in heaven.
Matthew 5:43-45

Be perfect
For if you love those who love you, what reward do you have? Do not even the tax-collectors do the same? And if you greet only your brothers and sisters, what more are you doing than others? Do not even the Gentiles do the same? Be perfect, therefore, as your heavenly Father is perfect.
Matthew 5:46-48

A generous heart
Give, and it will be given to you.
A good measure, pressed down, shaken together, running over, will be put into your lap; for the measure you give will be the measure you get back.
Luke 6:38

Giving in secret
So whenever you give alms, do not sound a trumpet before you, as the hypocrites do in the synagogues and in the streets, so that they may be praised by others. Truly I tell you, they have received their reward.
But when you give alms, do not let your left hand know what your right hand is doing, so that your alms may be done in secret; and your Father who sees in secret will reward you.
Matthew 6:2-4

Forgive
For if you forgive others their trespasses, your heavenly Father will also forgive you; but if you do not forgive others, neither will your Father forgive your trespasses.
Matthew 6:14-15

Forgiveness and love
The one to whom little is forgiven, loves little.
Luke 7:47

I am the truth
I am the way, and the truth, and the life. No one comes to the Father except through me.
John 14:6

Truth and freedom

If you continue in my word, you are truly my disciples; and you will know the truth, and the truth will make you free.
John 8:31-32

I am the bread of life

The bread of God is that which comes down from heaven and gives life to the world.... .
I am the bread of life. Whoever comes to me will never be hungry, and whoever believes in me will never be thirsty
John 6:33, 35

Man shall not live by bread alone
One does not live by bread alone, but by every word that comes from the mouth of God.
Matthew 4:4

I am the light

I am the light of the world. Whoever follows me will never walk in darkness but will have the light of life.
John 8:12

Light and darkness

The eye is the lamp of the body. So, if your eye is healthy, your whole body will be full of light; but if your eye is unhealthy, your whole body will be full of darkness. If then the light in you is darkness, how great is the darkness!
Matthew 6:22-23

I am the gate

I am the gate for the sheep.... .
Whoever enters by me will be saved, and will come in and go out and find pasture.
John 10:7, 9

Abundant life

I came that they may have life, and have it abundantly.
John 10:10

The good shepherd
I am the good shepherd. The good shepherd lays down his life for the sheep...
I know my own and my own know me.
John 10: 11, 14

Searching for one lost sheep

Which one of you, having a hundred sheep and losing one of them, does not leave the ninety-nine in the wilderness and go after the one that is lost until he finds it?
When he has found it, he lays it on his shoulders and rejoices. And when he comes home, he calls together his friends and neighbors, saying to them, "Rejoice with me, for I have found my sheep that was lost."
Just so, I tell you, there will be more joy in heaven over one sinner who repents than over ninety-nine righteous people who need no repentance.
Luke 15:4-7

Life

I am the resurrection and the life.
John 11:25

Life, and not death

Those who believe in me, even though they die, will live, and everyone who lives and believes in me will never die.
John 11:25-26

I am the true vine

I am the true vine, and my Father is the vine-grower. He removes every branch in me that bears no fruit. Every branch that bears fruit he prunes to make it bear more fruit.... .
I am the vine, you are the branches. Those who abide in me and I in them bear much fruit, because apart from me you can do nothing.
John 15:1-2, 5

A fruitful life

If you abide in me, and my words abide in you, ask for whatever you wish, and it will be done for you. My Father is glorified by this, that you bear much fruit and become my disciples.
John 15:7-8

No greater love

No one has greater love than this, to lay down one's life for one's friends.
John 15:13

Loved by the Father

For this reason the Father loves me, because I lay down my life in order to take it up again.
John 10:17

Giving

It is more blessed to give than to receive.
Acts 20:35

An eye for an eye

You have heard that it was said, "An eye for an eye and a tooth for a tooth." But I say to you, Do not resist an evildoer. But if anyone strikes you on the right cheek, turn the other also.
Matthew 5:38-39

The second mile

If anyone wants to sue you and take your coat, give your cloak as well; and if anyone forces you to go one mile, go also the second mile. Give to everyone who begs from you, and do not refuse anyone who wants to borrow from you.
Matthew 5:40-42

Treasures on earth, treasures in heaven

Do not store up for yourselves treasures on earth, where moth and rust consume and where thieves break in and steal; but store up for yourselves treasures in heaven, where neither moth nor rust consumes and where thieves do not break in and steal. For where your treasure is, there your heart will be also.
Matthew 6:19-21

The choice: God or wealth?

No one can serve two masters; for a slave will either hate the one and love the other, or be devoted to the one and despise the other. You cannot serve God and wealth.
Matthew 6:24

Trusting God

All things can be done for the one who believes.
Mark 9:23

Mustard seed faith

If you had faith the size of a mustard seed, you could say to this mulberry tree, "Be uprooted and planted in the sea", and it would obey you.
Luke 17:6

Look at the birds

Therefore I tell you, do not worry about your life, what you will eat or what you will drink, or about your body, what you will wear. Is not life more than food, and the body more than clothing? Look at the birds of the air; they neither sow nor reap nor gather into barns, and yet your heavenly Father feeds them. Are you not of more value than they? And can any of you by worrying add a single hour to your span of life?
Matthew 6:25-27

Consider the lilies of the field

Consider the lilies of the field, how they grow; they neither toil nor spin, yet I tell you, even Solomon in all his glory was not clothed like one of these. But if God so clothes the grass of the field, which is alive today and tomorrow is thrown into the oven, will he not much more clothe you – you of little faith?
Matthew 6:28-30

Do not judge

Do not judge, so that you may not be judged. For with the judgement you make you will be judged, and the measure you give will be the measure you get.
Matthew 7:1-2

The speck and the log

Why do you see the speck in your neighbor's eye, but do not notice the log in your own eye? Or how can you say to your neighbor, "Let me take the speck out of your eye", while the log is in your own eye? You hypocrite, first take the log out of your own eye, and then you will see clearly to take the speck out of your neighbor's eye.
Matthew 7:3-5

A sword, not peace

Do not think that I have come to bring peace to the earth; I have not come to bring peace, but a sword.
Matthew 10:34

Deeds, not words

Not everyone who says to me, "Lord,
Lord", will enter the kingdom of heaven,
but only one who does the will of my
Father in heaven.
Matthew 7:21

Salt

You are like salt for all mankind.
Matthew 5:13 gnb

Light

You are like light for the whole world.
Matthew 5:14 gnb

Let your light shine

Your light must shine before people, so
that they will see the good things you do
and praise your Father in heaven.
Matthew 5:16 gnb

The poor in spirit

Blessed are the poor in spirit:
for theirs is the kingdom of heaven.
Matthew 5:3 KJV

Mourning

Blessed are they that mourn:
for they shall be comforted.
Matthew 5:4 KJV

The meek

Blessed are the meek:
for they shall inherit the earth.
Matthew 5:5 KJV

Hungry for God

Blessed are they which do hunger
and thirst after righteousness:
for they shall be filled.
Matthew 5:6 KJV

The merciful

Blessed are the merciful:
for they shall obtain mercy.
Matthew 5:7 KJV

The pure in heart

Blessed are the pure in heart:
for they shall see God.
Matthew 5:8 KJV

The peacemakers

Blessed are the peacemakers:
for they shall be called the children of God.
Matthew 5:9 KJV

Persecuted for righteousness' sake

Blessed are they which are persecuted for
righteousness sake: for theirs is the
kingdom of heaven.
Blessed are ye, when men shall revile you,
and persecute you, and shall say all manner
of evil against you falsely, for my sake.
Rejoice, and be exceeding glad: for great is
your reward in heaven: for so persecuted
they the prophets which were before you.
Matthew 5:10-12 KJV

The kingdom of God

Let the little children come to me; do not
stop them; for it is to such as these that the
kingdom of God belongs. Truly I tell you,
whoever does not receive the kingdom of
God as a little child will never enter it.
Mark 10:14-15

Born again

No one can see the Kingdom of God
unless he is born again.
John 3:3 GNB

To would-be followers of Jesus

Foxes have holes, and birds of the air have
nests; but the Son of Man has nowhere to
lay his head …
Let the dead bury their own dead; but as
for you, go and proclaim the kingdom of
God.
Luke 9:58, 60

Putting one's hand to the plough

No one who puts a hand to the plough
and looks back is fit for the kingdom of
God.
Luke 9:62

From death to life

Anyone who hears my word and believes
him who sent me has eternal life, and does
not come under judgement, but has passed
from death to life.
John 5:24

People loved darkness rather than light

And this is the judgement, that the light has come into the world, and people loved darkness rather than light because their deeds were evil. For all who do evil hate the light and do not come to the light, so that their deeds may not be exposed. But those who do what is true come to the light, so that it may be clearly seen that their deeds have been done in God.

John 3:19-21

Whom to fear

I tell you, my friends, do not fear those who kill the body, and after that can do nothing more. But I will warn you whom to fear: fear him who, after he has killed, has authority to cast into hell.

Luke 12:4-5

Sparrows

Are not five sparrows sold for two pennies? Yet not one of them is forgotten in God's sight. But even the hairs of your head are all counted. Do not be afraid; you are of more value than many sparrows.

Luke 12:6-7

A stumbling-block

If any of you put a stumbling-block before one of these little ones who believe in me, it would be better for you if a great millstone were fastened around your neck and you were drowned in the depth of the sea.

Matthew 18:6

Compassion

You can be sure that whoever gives even a drink of cold water to one of the least of these my followers because he is my follower, will certainly receive a reward.

Matthew 10:42 GNB

Serving one another

You call me Teacher and Lord — and you are right, for that is what I am. So if I, your Lord and Teacher, have washed your feet, you also ought to wash one another's feet. For I have set you an example, that you also should do as I have done to you.

John 13:13-15

Humility

For everyone who makes himself great will be humbled, and everyone who humbles himself will be made great.

Luke 14:11

God so loved the world

For God so loved the world that he gave his only Son, so that everyone who believes in him may not perish but may have eternal life.

John 3:16

Belief in Jesus

This is the work of God, that you believe in him whom he has sent.... .
This is indeed the will of my Father, that all who see the Son and believe in him may have eternal life; and I will raise them up on the last day.

John 6:29, 40

A challenging call

If any want to become my followers, let them deny themselves and take up their cross and follow me.

Mark 8:34

Gaining the whole world

For those who want to save their life will lose it, and those who lose their life for my sake, and for the sake of the gospel, will save it. For what will it profit them to gain the whole world and forfeit their life? Indeed, what can they give in return for their life?

Mark 8:35-37

Words without actions

Why do you call me, "Lord, Lord," and yet don't do what I tell you? Anyone who comes to me and listens to my words and obeys them — I will show you what he is like ...

Luke 6:46-47 GNB

A house without foundations

... He is like a man who, in building his house, dug deep and laid the foundation on rock. The river overflowed and hit that house but could not shake it, because it was well built. But anyone who hears my words

and does not obey them is like a man who built his house without laying a foundation; when the flood hit that house it fell at once – and what a terrible crash that was!
Luke 6:48-49 GNB

Godless teachers
Every plant that my heavenly Father has not planted will be uprooted.... They are blind guides of the blind. And if one blind person guides another, both will fall into a pit.
Matthew 15:13-14

What defiles a person?
Do you not see that whatever goes into the mouth enters the stomach, and goes out into the sewer? But what comes out of the mouth proceeds from the heart, and this is what defiles. For out of the heart come evil intentions, murder, adultery, fornication, theft, false witness, slander. These are what defile a person, but to eat with unwashed hands does not defile.
Matthew 15:17-20

Not to be served but to serve
The Son of Man came not to be served but to serve, and to give his life a ransom for many.
Matthew 20:28

Faithful service
Whoever serves me must follow me, and where I am, there will my servant be also. Whoever serves me, the Father will honor.
John 12:26

On this rock I will build my church
Blessed are you, Simon Son of Jonah! For flesh and blood has not revealed this to you, but my Father in heaven. And I tell you, you are Peter, and on this rock I will build my church, and the gates of Hades will not prevail against it.
Matthew 16:17-18

The keys of the kingdom
I will give you the keys of the kingdom of heaven, and whatever you bind on earth will be bound in heaven, and whatever you loose on earth will be loosed in heaven.
Matthew 16:19

Jesus' family
Who are my mother and my brothers? [And looking at those who sat around him, he said,] Here are my mother and my brothers! Whoever does the will of God is my brother and sister and mother.
Mark 3:33-35

For or against?
Whoever is not with me is against me, and whoever does not gather with me scatters.
Luke 11:23

The sabbath
The sabbath was made for humankind, and not humankind for the sabbath; so the Son of Man is lord even of the sabbath.
Mark 2:27-28

The first will be last
But many who are first will be last, and the last will be first.
Matthew 19:30

Who needs a doctor?
Those who are well have no need of a physician, but those who are sick; I have come to call not the righteous but sinners to repentance.
Luke 5:31-32

Don't be afraid
Do not be afraid, little flock, for it is your Father's good pleasure to give you the kingdom.
Luke 12:32

Where your treasure is ...
Sell your possessions, and give alms. Make purses for yourselves that do not wear out, an unfailing treasure in heaven, where no thief comes near and no moth destroys. For where your treasure is, there your heart will be also.
Luke 12:33-34

I stand at the door and knock
Behold, I stand at the door, and knock: if any man hear my voice, and open the door, I will come in to him, and will sup with him, and he with me.
Revelation 3:20 KJV

The narrow gate

Enter the narrow gate; for the gate is wide and the road is easy that leads to destruction, and there are many who take it. For the gate is narrow and the road is hard that leads to life, and there are few who find it.

Matthew 7:13-14

Troubled hearts

Do not let your hearts be troubled. Believe in God, believe also in me.

John 14:1

In my Father's house

In my Father's house there are many dwelling-places. If it were not so, would I have told you that I go to prepare a place for you? And if I go and prepare a place for you, I will come again and will take you to myself, so that where I am, there you may be also.

John 14:2-3

Jesus predicts his death

See, we are going up to Jerusalem, and the Son of Man will be handed over to the chief priests and scribes, and they will condemn him to death; then they will hand him over to the Gentiles to be mocked and flogged and crucified; and on the third day he will be raised.

Matthew 20:18-19

Jerusalem, Jerusalem!

Jerusalem, Jerusalem! You kill the prophets and stone the messengers God has sent you! How many times have I wanted to put my arms round all your people, just as a hen gathers her chicks under her wings, but you would not let me!

Matthew 23:37 GNB

Peace

I have said this to you, so that in me you may have peace. In the world you face persecution. But take courage; I have conquered the world!

John 16:33

Peace I leave with you

Peace I leave with you; my peace I give to you. I do not give to you as the world gives. Do not let your hearts be troubled, and do not let them be afraid.

John 14:27

Love God

The first [commandment] is, "Hear, O Israel: the Lord our God, the Lord is one; you shall love the Lord your God will all your heart, and with all your soul, and with all your mind, and with all your strength."

Mark 12:29-30

Love your neighbor

The second [commandment] is this, "You shall love your neighbor as yourself."

Mark 12:31

Loved by Jesus

As the Father hath loved me, so have I loved you: continue ye in my love.

John 15:9 KJV

Love one another

This is my commandment, That ye love one another, as I have loved you.

John 15:12 KJV

For I was hungry ...

For I was hungry and you gave me food, I was thirsty and you gave me something to drink, I was a stranger and you welcomed me, I was naked and you gave me clothing, I was sick and you took care of me, I was in prison and you visited me.

Matthew 25:35-36

The least of these

Truly I tell you, just as you did it to one of the least of these who are members of my family, you did it to me.

Matthew 25:40

Freedom

So if the Son makes you free, you will be free indeed.

John 8:36

The Spirit of the Lord is upon me

The Spirit of the Lord is upon me,
    because he has anointed me
    to bring good news to the poor.

He has sent me to proclaim release to the captives
> and recovery of sight to the blind,
> to let the oppressed go free,
to proclaim the year of the Lord's favor.
Luke 4:18-19

Global salvation
Indeed, God did not send the Son into the world to condemn the world, but in order that the world might be saved through him. Those who believe in him are not condemned; but those who do not believe are condemned already, because they have not believed in the name of the only Son of God.
John 3:17-18

This is eternal life
And this is eternal life, that they may know you, the only true God, and Jesus Christ whom you have sent.
John 17:3

Not alone
For where two or three are gathered in my name, I am there among them.
Matthew 18:20

The harvest is plentiful
The harvest is plentiful, but the laborers are few; therefore ask the Lord of the harvest to send out laborers into his harvest.
Luke 10:2

Your heavenly Father knows
So do not start worrying: "Where will my food come from? or my drink? or my clothes?" (These are the things the pagans are always concerned about.) Your Father in heaven knows that you need all these things.
Matthew 6:31-32 GNB

Do not worry about tomorrow
Instead, be concerned above everything else with the Kingdom of God and with what he requires of you, and he will provide you with all these other things. So do not worry about tomorrow; it will have enough worries of its own. There is no need to add to the troubles each day brings.
Matthew 6:33-34 GNB

Like sheep among wolves
See, I am sending you out like sheep into the midst of wolves; so be wise as serpents and innocent as doves.
Matthew 10:16

Divine words
Beware of them, for they will hand you over to councils and flog you in their synagogues; and you will be dragged before governors and kings because of me, as a testimony to them and the Gentiles. When they hand you over, do not worry about how you are to speak or what you are to say; for what you are to say will be given to you at that time; for it is not you who speak, but the Spirit of your Father speaking through you.
Matthew 10:17-20

Thoughts
You have heard that it was said, "You shall not commit adultery." But I say to you that everyone who looks at a woman with lust has already committed adultery with her in his heart.
Matthew 5:27-28

A radical prescription
If your right eye causes you to sin, tear it out and throw it away; it is better for you to lose one of your members than for your whole body to be thrown into hell. And if your right hand causes you to sin, cut it off and throw it away; it is better for you to lose one of your members than for your whole body to go into hell.
Matthew 5:29-30

Streams of live-giving water
Whoever is thirsty should come to me and drink. As the scripture says, "Whoever believes in me, streams of life-giving water will pour out from his heart."
John 7:37-38 GNB

Thirst quenched
Whoever drinks this water will be thirsty again, but whoever drinks the water that I will give him will never be thirsty again. The water that I will give him will become

in him a spring which will provide him with life-giving water and give him eternal life.
John 4:13-14 GNB

How not to pray
When you pray, do not be like the hypocrites! They love to stand up and pray in the houses of worship and on the street corners, so that everyone will see them. I assure you, they have already been paid in full.
Matthew 6:5 GNB

How to pray
But when you pray, go to your room, close the door, and pray to your Father, who is unseen. And your Father, who sees what you do in private, will reward you. When you pray, do not use a lot a meaningless words, as the pagans do, who think that their gods will hear them because their prayers are long. Do not be like them. Your Father already knows what you need before you ask him.
Matthew 6:6-8 GNB

Fishers of men
Follow me, and I will make you fish for people.
Matthew 4:19

Go ... and make disciples
All authority in heaven and on earth has been given to me. Go therefore and make disciples of all nations, baptizing them in the name of the Father and of the Son and of the Holy Spirit, and teaching them to obey everything that I have commanded you.
Matthew 28:18-20a

Jesus' presence
And remember, I am with you always, to the end of the age.
Matthew 28:20b

Sayings Through the Centuries

SAINT CYPRIAN, 258 A.D. – "His money owns him rather than he owns it."

SAINT JOANNES CHYSOSTOMUS, 407 A.D. – "For to sin, indeed is human: but to persevere in sin, is not human: but altogether satanic."

BISHOP HUGH LATIMER, 1595 – "You rich men ... remember that thy riches be not thy own, but thou art but a steward over them."

MICHAEL MONTAIGNE, 1595 – "He who fears he will suffer, already suffers from his fear."

WILLIAM PENN, 1701 – "Oh God, Help us not to despise or oppose what we do not understand."

BARON MONTESQUIEU, 1748 – "Disrespect for women has invariably been the surest sign of moral corruption."

CESARE BONESANA, 1764 – "It is better to prevent crimes than to punish them."

JAMES MADISON, 1788 – "If men were angels, no government would be necessary."

ERASMUS DARWIN, 1789 – "He who allows oppression-shares the crime."

GEORGE WASHINGTON, 1796 – "The basis of our political systems is the right of the people to make and alter their constitutions of government."

FRANCIS SCOTT KEY, 1814 – "Then conquer we must, when our cause is just. And our motto, In God is our Trust."

HORACE MANN, 1850 – Be ashamed to die until you have won some victory for humanity."

ABRAHAM LINCOLN, 1863 – "Years ago our fathers brought forth on this continent, a new nation conceived in liberty and dedicated to proposition that all men are created equal. It is for us the living that government; of the people, by the people, for the people, shall not perish."

LORD ACTON, 6/11/1895 – "When a rich man becomes poor it is a misfortune, it is not a moral evil. When a poor man becomes destitute, it is a moral evil teeming with consequences and injurious to morality and society."

BOOKER T. WASHINGTON, 1896 – "I beg of you to remember that whenever our life touches yours, we help or hinder. Whenever your life touches ours, you make us stronger or weaker. There is no escape. Man drags man down, or man lifts up man."

HELEN KELLER, 1902 – "There is no king who has not had a slave among his ancestors, and no slave who has not had a king among his."

GEORGE BERNARD SHAW, 1906 – "Nothing is ever done in this world until men are prepared to kill one another, if it is not done."

S.G. TALLENTYRE, 1906 – "I disapprove of what you say, but I will defend to the death your right to say it."

HENRY ADAMS, 1907 – "A teacher affects eternity. He can never tell where his influence stops."

JOSEPH PULITZER, 4/10/1907 – "Always fight for progress and reform, never tolerate injustice and corruption, always remain devoted to the public welfare, never be afraid to attack wrong."

WOODROW WILSON, 1913 – "The Government of the U.S. at present is a foster child of the special interests."

TEDDY ROOSEVELT, 11/15/1913 – "I put human rights above property rights."

LENIN, 1919 – "With all the liberating laws, woman continues to be a domestic slave because petty housework crushes, strangles, stultifies and degrades her."

H.G. WELLS, 1920 – "Human history becomes more and more a race between education and catastrophe."

SIGMUND FREUD, 1927 – "It is only by the influences of individuals who can set an example whom the masses recognize as their leaders that they can be induced to submit to the labors and renunciations on which the existence of civilization depends."

SINCLAIR LEWIS, 1930 – "God damn the society that will permit such poverty! God damn the religions that stand for such a putrid system." F.D.R., 6/27/1936 – "I see one third of a nation ill-housed, ill-clad, ill- nourished. This generation of Americans has a rendezvous with destiny."

JOSEPH STALIN, 1936 – "What can be the "personal freedom" of an unemployed person who goes hungry."

JAMES AGEE, 1941 – "In every child who is born, the potentiality of the human race is born again."

GEORGE ORWELL, 1947 – "To accept civilization as it is , practically means accepting decay."

HAROLD CLAYTON UREY, 1950 – "There is no constructive solution to the world's problems, except eventually a world government capable of establishing law over the entire surface of the Earth."

ERICH FROMM, 1955 – "Man today is confronted with the most fundamental choice: not that between "capitalism" and "communism", but that between robotism (of both the "capitalism" and "communist" variety), or humanistic communitarian socialism."

EDWARD EISENHOWER, 4/19/1956 – "We seek victory not over any nation or people but over ignorance, poverty, disease, and human degradation wherever they may be found."

U.S. SUPREME COURT, 1956 – "There can be no equal justice, where the kind of trail a man gets depends on the amount of money he has."

MALCOLM X, 1960 – "Power never takes a back step – only in the face of more power. Power recognizes only power."

ANDRE' MALRAUX, 12/9/1961 – "The road from political idealism to political realism is strewn with the corpses of our dead selves."

J.F.KENNEDY, 1/10/1961 – "The world is very different now. For man holds in his mortal hands the power to abolish all forms of human poverty, and all forms of human life."

MARTIN LUTHER KING, JR., 1963 – "The question is not whether we will be extremists, but what kind of extremists we will be. The nation and world are in dire need of creative extremists."

J.F.KENNEDY, 1963 – "We choose to do things not because they are easy, but because they are hard; that goal will serve to organize and measure the best of our energies and skills. That challenge is one that we are willing to accept, one we are unwilling to postpone, and which we intend to win.

LINUS PAULING, 1965 – "The time has now come for the nations of the world to submit to the just requisition of their conduct by international law."

ALBERT SZENT-CYROG, 2/23/1970 – "You have only to wish it, and you can have a world without hunger, disease, cancer, and toil – anything you wish, wish anything and it can be done. Or else, we can exterminate ourselves… at present we are on the road to extermination. The present world crises can be solved only by a general human revolution against outdated concepts…due to the greed and lust for power of relatively small groups. The conspiracy of the few against the many. In much of the world half the children go to sleep hungry and we spend a trillion dollars on rubbish. We are all criminals."

BURRHUS FREDERIC SKINNER, 1971 – "The environment will continue to deteriorate until pollution practices are abandoned. We need to make vast changes in human behavior."

HAMMOND WORLD ATLAS, 1988 – "The sophistication of technology have yet to control effectively the by products of manufactured "miraculous" materials. These new materials, still subject to the order of nature's cycles, penetrate the biosphere and eventually come to roost in modern man's own vulnerable body. A compromise between technology and nature must take place, our "Plundered Planet" cries out for the day of reckoning!"

Schleiermacher

Schleiermacher set himself in sharp opposition to the intellectualism and moralism of the Age of Reason. He accused it of misunderstanding and debasing religion, of confusing it with and transforming it into metaphysics and morality. Thereby the Enlightenment had obscured the unique independent essence of religion.

Rudolf Otto

Science

The earth is flat, and anyone who disputes this claim is an atheist who deserves to be punished.
Muslim religious edict, 1993 Sheik Abdel-Aziz Ibn Baaz Supreme religious authority, Saudi Arabia

Science has promised us truth. It has never promised us either peace or happiness.
Gustave Le Bon

Ours is a world of nuclear giants and ethical infants. If we continue to develop our technology without wisdom or prudence, our servant may prove to be our executioner.
General Omar Bradley

No science is immune to the infection of politics and the corruption of power.
Jacob Bronowski

Knowledge of the sciences is so much smoke apart from the heavenly science of Christ.
John Calvin

It has become appallingly obvious that our technology has exceeded our humanity.
Albert Einstein

The religion that is afraid of science dishonors God and commits suicide.
Ralph Waldo Emerson

I do not feel obliged to believe that the same God who has endowed us with sense, reason, and intellect has intended us to forgo their use.
Galileo Galilei

Since the Holy Spirit did not intend to teach us whether heaven moves or stands still, nor whether the earth is located at its center or off to one side, then so much the less was it intended to settle for us any other conclusion of the same kind.
Now if the Holy Spirit has purposely neglected to teach us propositions of this sort as irrelevant to the highest goal (that is, to our salvation), how can anyone affirm that it is obligatory to take sides on them?

I would say here something that was heard from an ecclesiastic of the most eminent degree: "The intention of the Holy Spirit is to teach us how one goes to heaven, not how heaven goes."
Galileo

Science may have found a cure for most evils; but it has found no remedy for the worst of them all- the apathy of human beings.
Helen Keller

Our scientific power has outrun our spiritual power. We have guided missiles and misguided men.
Martin Luther King, Jr.

The scientists split the atom; now the atom is splitting us.
Quentin Reynolds

Science and belief in God

Now it is more respectable among philosophers than it has been for a generation to talk about the possibility of God's existence.
Time Magazine

Science and Christianity

In this modern world of ours many people seem to think that science has somehow made such religious ideas as immortality untimely or old fashioned. I think science has a real surprise for the skeptics. Science, for instance, tells us that nothing in nature, not even the tiniest particle, can disappear without a trace. Nature does not know extinction. All it knows is transformation. If God applies this fundamental principle to the most minute and insignificant parts of His universe, doesn't it make sense to assume that He applies it to the masterpiece of His creation, the human soul?
Dr. Warner von Braun, founder of U.S. space exploration program

I regard my research as a loving duty to seek the truth in all things, in so far as God has granted.
Nicolas Copernicus, astronomer

Since peace is alone in the gift of God; and as it is He who gives it, why should we be afraid? His unspeakable gift in His beloved Son is the ground of no doubtful hope.
Letter written by Michael Faraday, to a fellow scientist

Science and religion no more contradict each other than light and electricity.
William Hiram Foulkes

There are problems to whose solution I would attach an infinitely greater importance than to those of mathematics, for example touching ethics, or our relation to God, or concerning our destiny and our future; but their solution lies wholly beyond us and completely outside the province of science.
C.F. Gauss

Looking at the earth from this vantage point [of the moon], looking at this kind of creation and to not believe in God, to me, is impossible. To see (earth) laid out like that only strengthens my beliefs.
John Glenn

Therefore … , invoking the most holy name of our Lord Jesus Christ and of His Most Glorious Mother Mary, We pronounce this Our final sentence: We pronounce, judge, and declare, that you, the said Galileo … have rendered yourself vehemently suspected by this Holy Office of heresy. … From which it is Our pleasure that you be absolved, provided that with a sincere heart and unfeigned faith, in Our presence, you abjure, curse, and detest, the said error and heresies, and every other error and heresy contrary to the Catholic and Apostolic Church of Rome.
Indictment of 1630, from the Holy Tribunal

Science commits suicide when it adopts a creed.
T.H. Huxley

If I can't believe that the spacecraft I fly assembled itself, how can I believe that the universe assembled itself? I'm convinced only an intelligent God could have built a universe like this.
Jack Lousma, astronaut

No sciences are better attested than the religion of the Bible.
Isaac Newton

There is but one God the Father of whom are all things and we in him and one Lord Jesus Christ by whom are all things and we by him.
Isaac Newton

The rational order that science discerns is so beautiful and striking that it is natural to ask why it should be so. It could only find an explanation in a cause itself essentially rational. This would be provided by the Reason of the Creator … we know the world also to contain beauty, moral obligation and religious experience. These also find their ground in the Creator in his joy, his will and his presence.
John Polkinghorne

Christianity believes that God has created an external world that is really there; and because He is a reasonable God, one can expect to be able to find the order of the universe by reason.
Francis A. Schaeffer

The significance and joy in my science comes in those occasional moments of discovering something new and saying to myself, "So that's how God did it." My goal is to understand a little corner of God's plan.
Henry "Fritz" Schaefer.
The Graham Perdue Professor of Chemistry and director of the Center for Computational Quantum Chemistry at the University of Georgia.

It seems to me that when confronted with the marvels of life and the universe, one must ask why and not just how. The only possible answers are religious. I find a need for God in the universe and in my own life.
Arthur L. Schawlow.
Professor of Physics at Stanford University who

shared the 1981 Physics Nobel Prize with Bloembergen and Siegbahn for their contribution to the development of laser spectroscopy.

Science and faith

Father, we thank you, especially for letting me fly this flight ... for the privilege of being able to be in this position, to be in this wondrous place, seeing all these many startling, wonderful things that you have created.

L. Gordon Cooper, Jr. Prayer while orbiting the earth in a space capsule.

Speculations I have none. I'm resting on certainties. "For I know whom I have believed, and am persuaded that he is able to keep that which I have committed unto him against that day."

Michael Faraday, nearing death, quoting from 2 Timothy 1:12 KJV

Scientology

The best way to make money is to start a religion.

Remark by Scientology founder, Ron Hubbard, in 1948.

Scripture

See also: Bible

(All Scripture is given to:)
S-anctify: "Sanctify then through thy truth" (John 17:17)
C-orrect: "Profitable for correction" (2 Timothy :16)
R-ejoice: "Rejoicing the heart" (Psalm 19:8)
I-nstruct: "Instruction in righteousness" (2 Timothy 3:16)
P-urity: "Purified your souls in obey the truth" (1 Peter 1:22)
T-each: "Teach my thy statutes" (Psalm 119:12)
U-nite: "Unite my heart to fear thy name" (Psalm 86:11)
R-eprove:"By them is thy servant warned" (Psalm 19:11)
be E-aten: "Thy words were found and I did eat them" (Jeremiah 15:16)

Author unknown

The holy and inspired Scriptures are sufficient of themselves for the preaching of the Truth.

Athanasius

Scripture will ultimately suffice for a saving knowledge of God only when its certainty is founded upon the inward persuasion of the Holy Spirit. Indeed, these human testimonies which exist to confirm it will not be vain if, as secondary aids to our feebleness, they follow that chief and highest testimony. But those who wish to prove to unbelievers that Scripture is the Word of God are acting foolishly, for only by faith can this be known.

John Calvin

Scripture, Authority of

It is for Christ's sake that we believe in the Scriptures, but it is not for the Scriptures' sake that we believe in Christ.

Martin Luther

Scripture, Inspiration of

The inspiration of Scripture is a harmony of the active mind of the writer and the sovereign direction of the Holy Spirit to produce God's inerrant and infallible Word to mankind.

Brian Edwards

Scriptures

The Scriptures of the Old and New Testaments were given by inspiration of God, and are the only sufficient, certain and authoritative rule of all saving knowledge, faith, and obedience.

James Boyce, Abstract of Principles, 1858

Sea

They that go down to the sea in ships, that do business in great waters.

The Bible, Psalm 107:23

Searching for God

See also: Longing for God

Whosoever walks toward God one cubit, God runs toward him twain.

Author unknown

Desire only God, and you heart will be satisfied.
Augustine of Hippo

If the pleasures of love can attract a man to a woman, if hunger and loneliness can make a man travel miles in search of food and shelter, how much more will the desire for truth and holiness make a man seek God.
Augustine of Hippo

We taste Thee, O Thou Living Bread,
And long to feast upon Thee still:
We drink of Thee, the Fountainhead
And thirst our souls from Thee to fill.
St Bernard

The kingdom of heaven is not for the well-meaning but for the desperate.
James Denney

If we seek God for our own good and profit, we are not seeking God.
Johannes Eckhart

It is God's will that we have three things in our seeking:
1. The first is that we seek earnestly and diligently, without sloth, and, as it may be through His grace, without unreasonable heaviness and vain sorrow.
2. The second is, that we abide Him steadfastly for His love, without murmuring and striving against Him, to our life's end: for it shall last but awhile.
3. The third is that we trust in Him mightily of full assured faith. For it is His will that we know that He shall appear suddenly and blissfully to all that love Him.
Julian of Norwich

Seeking with faith, hope and love pleases our Lord and finding him pleases the soul, filling it full of joy. And so I learnt that as long as God allows us to struggle on this earth, seeking is as good as seeing.
Julian of Norwich

Human beings need not despair and go on an eternal search for the Eternal, for the Eternal has come to the temporal.
Steve Kumar

There's a God we want and there's a God who is and they are not the same God. The turning point comes when we stop seeking the God we want and start seeking the God who is.
Patrick Morley

There are three kinds of people in the world; those who have sought God and found Him and now serve Him, those who are seeking Him but have not yet found Him, and those who neither seek Him nor find Him. The first are reasonable and happy, the second reasonable and unhappy, and the third unreasonable and unhappy.
Blaise Pascal

Religion is so great a thing that it is right that those who will not take the trouble to seek it if it be obscure, should be deprived of it.
Blaise Pascal

Seek the true faith, by all manner of means, but do not spend a whole life in finding it, lest you be like a workman who wastes the whole day in looking for his tools.
C.H. Spurgeon

When I was coming to Christ, I thought I was doing it all myself, and though I sought the Lord earnestly, I had no idea the Lord was seeking me. The thought struck me, "How did you come to be a Christian?" I sought the Lord. "But how did you come to seek the Lord?" The truth flashed across my mind in a moment – I should not have sought Him unless there had come some previous influence in my mind to make me seek Him.
C.H. Spurgeon

If you seek your Lord Jesus in all things you will truly find Him, but if you seek yourself you will find yourself, and that will be to your own great loss.
Thomas à Kempis

He who seeks any other thing in religion than God alone and the salvation of his soul will find nothing there but trouble and sorrow.
Thomas à Kempis

Much of our difficulty as seeking Christians stems from our unwillingness to take God as He is and adjust our lives accordingly. We insist upon trying to modify Him and bring Him nearer to our own image.
A. W. Tozer

We pursue God because, and only because, He has first put an urge within us that spurs us to the pursuit.
A. W. Tozer

So long as we imagine it is we who have to look for God, we must often lose heart. But it is the other way about – He is looking for us.
Simon Tugwell

He who begins by seeking God within himself may end by confusing himself with God.
B.B. Warfield

Religion is the first thing and the last thing, and until a man has found God, and been found by God, he begins at no beginning and works to no end.
H.G. Wells

Seasons
To everything there is a season, and a time to every purpose under the heaven.
The Bible, Ecclesiastes 3:1

Secrecy
Secrecy is the beginning of tyranny.
Robert Heinlein

Sects
The greatest vicissitude of things amongst men is the vicissitude of sects and religions.
Francis Bacon

Secularism
If we were asked to produce one word which would characterize the twentieth century ... the one word [would be] secular. ... Secularization occurs when supernatural religion – that is, religion based on "belief in God or a future state" – becomes private, optional and problematic.
David L. Edwards

I can see little consistency in a type of Christian activity which preaches the gospel on the street corners and at the ends of earth, but neglects the children of the covenant by abandoning them to a cold and unbelieving secularism.
J. Gresham Machen

I believe that pluralistic secularism, in the long run, is a more deadly poison than straightforward persecution.
Frank Schaeffer

Security
The saints in heaven are happier but no more secure than are true believers here in this world.
Loraine Boethner

Security is when everything is settled. When nothing can happen to you. Security is the denial of life.
Germaine Greer

Those who desire to give up freedom in order to gain security, will not have, nor do they deserve, either one.
Thomas Jefferson

Only in growth, reform, and change, paradoxically enough, is true security to be found.
Anne Morrow Lindbergh

One of the outstanding glories of the gospel is its promise of eternal security to all who truly believe it. The gospel presents no third-rate Physician who is competent to treat only the milder cases, but One who ... is capable of curing the most desperate cases.
A. W. Pink

Seeing
Men are born with two eyes and one tongue in order that they may see twice as much as they say.
Rumanian proverb

Seeking for God
See: Longing for God; Searching for God; Service

Self
Be Good To You Be Yourself – Truthfully
Accept Yourself – Gracefully
Value Yourself – Joyfully
Forgive Yourself – Completely
Treat Yourself – Generously
Balance Yourself – Harmoniously
Bless Yourself – Abundantly
Trust Yourself – Confidently
Love Yourself – Wholeheartedly
Empower Yourself – Prayerfully
Give Yourself – Enthusiastically
Express Yourself – Radiantly
Author unknown

Who sits in solitude and is quiet has escaped from three wars: hearing, speaking, seeing; yet against one thing shall he continually battle: that is, his own heart.
St. Antony

That favorite subject, Myself
James Boswell

But how shall we expect charity towards others, when we are uncharitable to ourselves? Charity begins at home, is the voice of the world; yet is every man his greatest enemy, and, as it were, his own executioner.
Thomas Browne

If a man conquer in battle a thousand times a thousand, and another conquer himself, he who conquers himself is the greater conqueror.
Buddha

God, harden me against myself.
Amy Carmichael

He who conquers himself is the mightiest warrior.
Confucius

I am having more trouble with myself than any other man I have ever met.
Raymond Dale

Some conjurors say that three is the magic number, and some say number seven. It's neither, my friend, neither. It's number one.
Charles Dickens

There is one work which is right and proper for us to do, and that is the eradication of self. But however great this eradication and reduction of self may be, it remains insufficient if God does not complete it in us. For our humility is only perfect when God humbles us through ourselves.
Meister Eckhart

The true value of a human being can be found in degrees to which he has attained liberation from the self.
Albert Einstein

A person's attitude toward himself has a profound influence on his attitude toward God, his family, his friends, his future, and many other significant areas of his life.
Bill Gothard

It is only by a total death to self we can be lost in God.
Madame Guyon

To fight against sin is to fight against the devil, the world and oneself. The fight against oneself is the worst fight of all.
Martin Luther

I am more afraid of my own heart than of the pope and all his cardinals. I have within me the great pope, Self.
Martin Luther

There is no smaller package than a person all wrapped up in himself.
Peter C. Moore

Self is the root, the branches, the tree, of all the evil of our fallen state.
Andrew Murray

All greatness grows great by self-abasement, and not by exalting itself.
Nestorius

There is a principle of self, which disposes us to despise those who differ from us; and we are often under its influence, when we think we are only demonstrating a becoming zeal in the cause of God.
John Newton

Whenever I climb I am followed by a dog called Ego.
Friedrich Nietzsche

"I" is hateful.
Blaise Pascal

To conquer self is the best and noblest victory; to be vanquished by one's own nature is the worst and most ignoble defeat.
Plato

If I long to improve my brother, the first step toward doing so is to improve myself.
Christina Rossetti

No man is free who is a slave to the flesh.
Seneca

When you get your own way, you nurse a hideous idol called self. But when you give up your own way, you get God.
Janet Erskin Stewart

Real glory springs from the silent conquest of ourselves.
Joseph P. Thompson

Of Self and Me, the more of sin and wickedness and the more the Self, the I, the Me, the Mine, that is, self-seeking and selfishness, abate in a man, the more doth God's I, that is, God Himself, increase.
Theologian Germanica

The I, the Self and the like must all be given up and done away.
Theologian Germanica

Self is the opaque veil that hides the face of God from us. It can be removed only in spiritual experience, never by mere instruction.
A. W. Tozer

Self, Death of

The only way to achieve mortification is through inner recollection. The soul must meditate on Jesus Christ and so cease to concentrate on anything external and be consumed with the inner spiritual life and drawing close to God.
Madame Guyon

You will be dead so long as you refuse to die.
George Macdonald

There was a day when I died, utterly died, died to George Müller, his opinions, preferences, tastes and will, died to the world, its approval or censure, died to the approval or blame even of my brethren and friends, and since then I have studied to show myself approved unto God.
George Müller

The one true way of dying to self is the way of patience, meekness, humility, and resignation to God.
Andrew Murray

Self, Value of

If a man is cruel to himself, how can we expect him to be compassionate to others?
Jewish proverb

In the world to come I shall not be asked, "Why were you not Moses?" but God will ask me, "Why were you not Zusya?"
Rabbi Zusya

Self-assessment

The greatest of all faults is to imagine that you have none.
Author unknown

How you view yourself will determine how far you will go in life.
Author unknown

Psychological studies show that people consistently rate themselves higher than their peers evaluate them.
Charles Colson

No truly great man ever thought himself so.
William Hazlitt

Self-belief

He can who thinks he can, and he can't who thinks he can't. This is an inexorable, indisputable law.
Henry Ford

And above all things, never think that you're not good enough yourself. A man should never think that. My belief is that in life people will take you at your own reckoning
Anthony Trollope

Self-centeredness

Egotist: a person more interested in himself than in me.
Ambrose Bierce

So long as we are full of self, we are shocked at the faults of others. Let us think often of our own sin, and we shall be lenient to the sins of others.
François Fénelon

Above all the grace and the gifts that Christ gives to his beloved is that of overcoming self.
Francis of Assisi

No man is free who is a slave to the flesh.
Seneca

Self-confidence

The armor-bearer of sin is self-confidence.
Author unknown

We are not mightier than Samson, wiser than Solomon, more knowledgeable about God than David, and we do not love God better than did Peter, prince of the

Apostles. So let us not have confidence in ourselves; for he who has confidence in himself will fall headlong.
Hesychios of Sinai

Getting ahead in a difficult profession requires avid faith in yourself. You must be able to sustain yourself against staggering blows. There is no code of conduct to help beginners. That is why some people with mediocre talent, but with great inner drive, go much further than people with vastly superior talent.
Sophia Loren

Self-consciousness

I believe unself-consciousness is characteristic of the fruit of the Holy Spirit.
Billy Graham

Self-control
See also: Temperance

But since we belong to the day, let us be self-controlled …
The Bible, 1 Thessalonians 5:8

… be self-controlled …
The Bible, 1 Peter 1:13

The power of man has grown in every sphere, except over himself.
Winston Churchill

Self-control is the mother of spiritual health.
John Climacus

Control your appetites before they control you.
John Climacus

No man is free who is not a master of himself.
Epictetus

If you are to be self-controlled in your speech you must be self-controlled in your thinking.
F. Fénelon

A man cannot govern a nation if he cannot govern a city; he cannot govern a city if he

cannot govern a family; he cannot govern a family unless he can govern himself; and he cannot govern himself unless his passions are subject to reason.
Hugo Grotius

It's not the mountain we conquer but ourselves.
Edmund Hillary

Be charitable and indulgent to every one but thyself.
Joubert

He who reigns within himself, and rules passions, desires, and fears, is more than a king.
John Milton

I have conquered an empire but I have not been able to conquer myself.
Peter the Great

There has never been, and cannot be, a good life, without self-control.
Leo Tolstoy

Anything which increases the authority of the body over the mind is an evil thing.
Susannah Wesley, writing to her student son John

To enjoy freedom we have to control ourselves.
Virginia Woolfe

Self-deception
Nothing is easier than self-deceit. For what each man wishes, that he also believes to be true.
Demosthenes

The ingenuity of self-deception is inexhaustible.
Hannah More

The greatest magnifying glasses in the world are a man's own eyes when they look upon his own person.
Alexander Pope

Self-denial
1. Watch your appetites as to meat and drink, both quantity and quality. Gluttony is a common, unobserved sin: the flesh no way enslaves men more than by the appetite; as we see in drunkards and gluttons, that can no more forbear than one that thirtieth in a burning fever.
2. Take heed of the lust of uncleanness, and all degrees of it, and approaches to it; especially immodest embraces and behavior.
3. Take heed of ribald, filthy talk, and love songs, and of such incensing snares.
4. Take heed of too much sleep and idleness.
5. Take heed of taking too much delight in your riches, and lands, your buildings, and delectable conveniences.
6. Take heed lest honors, or worldly greatness, or men's applause, become your too great pleasure.
7. And lest you grow to make it your delight, to think on such things when you are alone, or talk idly of them in company with others.
8. And take heed lest the success and prosperity of your affairs do too much please you, as him, Luke xii. 20.
9. Take not up any inordinate pleasure in your children, relations, or nearest friends.
10. Take heed of a delight in vain, unprofitable, sinful company.
11. Or in fineness of apparel, to set you out to the eyes of others.
12. Take heed of a delight in romances, playbooks, feigned stories, useless news, which corrupt the mind, and waste your time.
13. Take heed of a delight in any recreations which are excessive, needless, devouring time, discomposing the mind, enticing to further sin, hindering any duty, especially our delight in God. They are miserable souls that can delight themselves in no more safe or profitable things, than cards, and dice, and stage plays, and immodest dancings.
Richard Baxter

God nowhere tells us to give up things for the sake of giving them up. He tells us to

give them up for the sake of the only thing worth having – life with Himself.
Oswald Chambers

There are plenty to follow our Lord half-way, but not the other half. They will give up possessions, friends and honors, but it touches them too closely to disown themselves.
Meister Eckhart

There is no greater valor or sterner fight than that for self-effacement, self-oblivion.
Meister Eckhart

The great Christian duty is self-denial, which consists in two things: first, in denying worldly inclinations and its enjoyments, and second, in denying self-exultation and renouncing one's self-significance by being empty of self.
Jonathan Edwards

All the graces of a Christian spring from the death of self.
Madame Guyon

Deny your desires and you will find what your heart longs for. For how do you know if any desire of yours is according to God's will?
John of the Cross

In the beginning of the spiritual life we ought to be faithful in doing our duty and denying ourselves.
Brother Lawrence

A self-denial that is truly supernatural must aspire to offer God what we have renounced ourselves.
Thomas Merton

One's own desires are never satisfied when they have all they wish; but they are satisfied as soon as the wish is renounced.
Blaise Pascal

Self-denial is not a virtue; it is only the effect of prudence on rascality.
George Bernard Shaw

Those who determine not to put self to death will never see the will of God fulfilled in their lives.
Sundar Singh

Self-discovery

One must know oneself. If this does not serve to discover truth, it at least serves as a rule of life and there is nothing better.
Blaise Pascal

I discovered something which I had never confronted before, that there were immense forces of darkness and hatred within my own heart. At particular moments of fatigue or stress, I saw forces of hate rising up inside me, and the capacity to hurt someone who was weak and was provoking me! That, I think, was what caused me the most pain: to discover who I really am, and to realize that maybe I did not want to know who I really was!
Jean Vanier

Self-examination

When we see men of a contrary character, we should turn inwards and examine ourselves.
Confucius

Whoever, therefore, is guided by good sense, does not look at the sins of others, nor busies himself about the faults of his neighbor, but closely scans his own misdoings.
Cyril of Alexandria

Consider well what your strength is equal to, and what exceeds your ability.
Horace

Frequent combing gives the hair more luster and makes it easier to comb; a soul that frequently examines its thoughts, words, and deeds, which are its hair, doing all things for the love of God, will have lustrous hair.
John of the Cross

The unexamined life is not worth living.
Socrates

You will never be an inwardly religious and devout man unless you pass over in silence the shortcomings of your fellow men, and diligently examine your own weaknesses.
Thomas à Kempis

Self-importance
Half of the harm that is done in this world is due to people who want to feel important.
T.S. Eliot

Self-improvement
There is only one corner of the universe you can be certain of improving and that is your own self.
Aldous Huxley

Self-justification
Just as water and fire cannot be combined, so self-justification and humility exclude one another.
Mark the Ascetic

Self-knowledge
See also: Knowledge
Let me know myself, Lord, and I shall know Thee.
Augustine of Hippo

For the gift to see ourselves as others see us.
Prayer of Robbie Burns

A man can know nothing of mankind without knowing something of himself. Self-knowledge is the property of that man whose passions have their full play, but who ponders over their results.
Benjamin Disraeli

To be conscious that you are ignorant is a great step to knowledge.
Benjamin Disraeli

There are three things extremely hard: steel, a diamond, and to know one's self.
Benjamin Franklin

The longest journey is the journey within.
Dag Hammarskjold

It has ever been allowed that to know one's self is the most valuable part of knowledge.
Eliza Haywood

Know thyself.
Inscription over the entrance of the temple of Apollo at Delphi

Everything that irritates us about others can lead us to an understanding of ourselves.
Carl Jung

If people can be educated to see the lowly side of their own natures, it may be hoped that they will also learn to understand and to love their fellow men better. A little less hypocrisy and a little more tolerance towards oneself can only have good results in respect for our neighbor; for we are all too prone to transfer to our fellows the injustice and violence we inflict upon our own natures.
Carl Jung

What can we gain by sailing to the moon if we are not able to cross the abyss that separates us from ourselves? This is the most important of all voyages of discovery, and without it, all the rest are not only useless, but disastrous.
Thomas Merton

One's own self is well hidden from one's own self: of all mines of treasure, one's own is the last to be dug up.
Friedrich Nietzsche

Know thyself, presume not God to scan;
The proper study of mankind is man.
Alexander Pope

When you realize that you have nothing and know nothing, then you will become rich in the Lord.
Theognostus

An humble knowledge of thyself is a surer way to God than a deep search after learning.
Thomas à Kempis

Knowing others is wisdom, knowing yourself is enlightenment.
Lao Tzu

Self-pity
Never feel self-pity, the most destructive emotion there is. How awful to be caught up in the terrible squirrel cage of self.
Millicent Fenwick

Self pity comes when you lose the intimacy with Jesus.
Stefan Salmonsson

Self-pleasing
1. God's glory must be the ultimate end.
2. The matter must be lawful and not forbidden.
3. Therefore it must not be to the hindrance of duty.
4. Nor to the drawing of us to sin.
5. Nor to the hurt of our health.
6. Nor too highly valued, nor too dearly bought.
7. The measure must be moderate rate.
Where any of these are wanting, it is sin: and where flesh-pleasing is habitually in the bent of heart and life preferred before the pleasing of God, it proves the soul in captivity to the flesh, and in a damnable condition.
Richard Baxter

Self-reliance
Depend not on another, but lean instead on thyself ... . True happiness is born of self-reliance.
The laws of Manu

Self-respect
Self-respect permeates every aspect of your life.
Joe Clark

He that respects himself if safe from others;
He wears a coat of mail that none can pierce.
Henry Wordsworth Longfellow

Self-righteousness
The man who is furthest from God is the man who thanks God he is not like others.
William Barclay

If there be ground for you to trust in your own righteousness, then, all that Christ did to purchase salvation, and all that God did to prepare the way for it is in vain.
Jonathan Edwards

Open sin kills its thousands of souls. Self-righteousness kills its tens of thousands.
J.C. Ryle

I prefer a sinful man who knows he has sinned and repents, to a man who has not sinned and considers himself to be righteous.
Abba Sarmatas

Whoever is acquainted with the nature of mankind in general, or the propensity of his own heart in particular, must acknowledge, that self-righteousness is the last idol that is rooted out of the heart... . therefore, as the apostle excellently observes, we go about, we fetch a circuit, to establish a righteousness of our own, and, like the Pharisees of old, will not wholly submit to that righteousness which is of God through Christ our Lord.
George Whitefield

Self-sacrifice
For anything worth having one must pay the price; and the price is always work, patience, love, self-sacrifice.
John Burroughs

Self-preservation is the first law of human nature.
Jean-Jacques Rousseau

If you wish peace and concord with others, you must learn to break your will in many things.
Thomas à Kempis

Self-satisfaction
Soul, thou hast much goods laid up for many years; take thine ease, eat, drink, and be merry.
The Bible, Luke 12:19 KJV

Be always displeased with what thou art, if your desirest to attain to what thou art

not; for where thou hast pleased thyself, there thou abidest. But if thou have enough thou perisheth. Always add, always walk, always proceed. Neither stand still, nor go back, nor deviate.
Augustine of Hippo

"I am not satisfied with my faith," says one. No, of course you aren't; nor will you ever be, at least I hope not! The Bible does not say, "Therefore being satisfied with our faith we have peace with God;" it says, "being justified by faith, we have peace with God."
"I am not satisfied with my love." What? Did you expect, on this earth, to be satisfied with any grace found in you? Was it your love for Christ or His love for you that gave you peace at first?
Now then, there is but one thing with which Almighty God is satisfied entirely satisfied and that is THE PERSON AND WORK OF HIS SON! It is with Christ that we must be satisfied, not with ourselves, nor anything about us! When we cease from all our labors, and all our righteousness, and ENTER INTO HIS REST, pardon and peace will come without delay.
Horatius Bonar

Self-seeking
Who pants for glory finds but short repose:
A breath revives him, or a breath o'erthrows.
Alexander Pope

Love is never self-seeking, for in whatever a person seeks himself there he falls from love.
Thomas à Kempis

Self-sufficiency
We are all weak, finite, simple human beings, standing in the need of prayer. None need it so much as those who think they are strong, those who know it not, but are deluded by self-sufficiency.
Harold C. Phillips

Do not be self-sufficient but place your trust in God.
Thomas à Kempis

Self-surrender
A year of self-surrender will bring larger blessings than fourscore year of selfishness.
Author unknown

It requires heroic courage and self-surrender to hold firmly to a simple faith and to keep singing the same tune confidently while grace itself seems to be singing a different one in another key, giving us the impression that we have been misled and are lost.
Jean-Pierre de Caussade

Self-understanding
See: Self-knowledge

Selfishness
He that falls in love with himself, will have no rivals.
Benjamin Franklin

It is well to remember that the entire universe, with one trifling exception, is composed of others.
John Andrew Holmes

A man's worst difficulties begin when he is able to do as he likes.
Thomas Henry Huxley

No indulgence of passion destroys the spiritual nature so much as respectable selfishness.
George Macdonald

The things that will destroy America are peace at any price, prosperity at any cost, safety first instead of duty first, the love of soft living, and the getting-rich-quick theory of life.
Theodore Roosevelt

He who lives only to benefit himself confers a benefit on the world when he dies.
Tertullian

Selflessness
If you take little account of yourself, you will have peace, wherever you live.
Abba Poemen

Sensuality

The Ten Marks of a Flesh-Pleaser
The signs of a flesh-pleaser or sensualist are these:

1. When a man in his desire to please his appetite, does not do it with a view to a higher end, that is to say to the preparing himself for the service of God; but does it only for the delight itself.
2. When he looks more eagerly and industriously after the prosperity of his body than of his soul.
3. When he will not refrain from his pleasures, when God forbids them, or when they hurt his soul, or when the necessities of his soul call him away from them. But he must have his delight whatever it costs him, and is so set upon it, that he cannot deny it to himself.
4. When the pleasures of his flesh exceed his delights in God, and his holy word and ways, and the expectations of endless pleasure. And this not only in the passion, but in the estimation, choice, and action. When he had rather be at a play, or feast, or other entertainment, or getting good bargains or profits in the world, than to live in the life of faith and love, which would be a holy and heavenly way of living.
5. When men set their minds to scheme and study to make provision for the pleasures of the flesh; and this is first and sweetest in their thoughts.
6. When they had rather talk, or hear, or read of fleshly pleasures, than of spiritual and heavenly delights.
7. When they love the company of merry sensualists, better than the communion of saints, in which they may be exercised in the praises of their Maker.
8. When they consider that the best place to live and work is where they have the pleasure of the flesh. They would rather be where they have things easy, and lack nothing for the body, rather than where they have far better help and provision for the soul, though the flesh be pinched for it.
9. When he will be more eager to spend money to please his flesh than to please God.
10. When he will believe or like no doctrine but "easy-believism," and hate mortification as too strict "legalism." By these, and similar signs, sensuality may easily be known; indeed, by the main bent of the life.
Richard Baxter

No one is free who is a slave to his body.
Seneca

Sentimentality

Sentimentality is no indication of a warm heart. Nothing weeps more copiously than a chunk of ice.
Author unknown

Separation

Do not be yoked together with unbelievers. For what do righteousness and wickedness have in common? Or what fellowship can light have with darkness?
The Bible, 2 Corinthians 5:21 KJV

And what is all this contention and separation for? Oh, they will tell you it is for the true and sincere worship of God; that they may serve Him purely without human additions or inventions ... Alas, my brethren, was there ever any schism in the world that did not plead the same?
Ezekiel Hopkins

The Church of God needs to remember that fellowship with God necessitates separation from all who fail to fulfill the responsibilities of fellowship in light.
W. Graham Scroggie

For Christians to be linked in association with ministries who do not preach the gospel of Christ is to incur moral guilt.
C.H. Spurgeon

It is absolutely impossible to maintain the truth without practicing discipline and separation.
O. Timothy

Serenity

Grant me the serenity to accept things I cannot change; the courage to change things I can and wisdom to know the difference.
Reinhold Niebhur

Let nothing good or bad upset the balance of your life.

Thomas à Kempis

Seriousness

Seriousness is not a virtue. It would be a heresy, but a much more sensible heresy, to say that seriousness is a vice. It is really a natural trend to lapse into taking oneself seriously, because it is the easiest thing to do. It is much easier to write a good *Times* leading article than a good joke in *Punch*. For solemnity flows out of men naturally; but laughter is a leap. It is easy to be heavy; hard to be light. Satan fell by the force of gravity.

G.K. Chesterton

Sermons, *Listening to*

Dear Mrs. S.

As it is our trial to live in a day wherein so many contentions and winds of strange doctrine abound, I hope you will watch and pray that you may not have itching ears, inclining you to hearken after the novel, singular, and erroneous sentiments of men of unstable minds, who are not sound in the faith. I have known some who have gone to hear such men, not for the sake of edification, but to hear what they had to say. They thought themselves too well established in the truth to be hurt by it. But the experiment (without a just and lawful call) is presumptuous and dangerous. In this way many have been hurt, or overthrown. Error is like poison; the subtlety, quickness, and force of its operation is often amazing. As we pray not to be led into temptation, we should take care not to run into it wilfully. If the Lord has shown you what is right, it is not worth your while to know how many ways there are of being wrong.

Next: I advise you, when you hear a Gospel sermon, and it is not in all respects to your satisfaction, do not be too hasty to lay the whole blame upon the preacher. The Lord's ministers feel (it is to be hoped) their own weakness and defects, and the greatness and difficulty of their work. They are conscious that their warmest endeavors to proclaim the Savior's glory are too cold, and their most urgent messages to the consciences of men are too faint. Indeed, they have much to be ashamed of; but it will be useful for you, who are their listener, to consider whether the fault may not possibly be in yourself. Perhaps you thought too highly of the man, and expected too much from him; or perhaps you thought too little of him, and expected too little. In the former case, the Lord justly disappointed you; in the latter, you received according to your faith. Perhaps you neglected to pray for him. Accordingly, though he might be useful to others, it is not at all strange that he was not useful to you.

Lastly, as a hearer, you have a right to try all doctrines by the word of God; it is your duty to do so. Faithful ministers will remind you of this. They will not wish to hold you in a blind obedience to what they say, upon their own authority. They would not be lords over your conscience, but helpers of your joy. Prize your liberty in the Gospel, which sets you free from the doctrines and commandments of men, but do not abuse it to the purposes of pride and self. There are hearers who make themselves, and not the Scripture, the standard of their judgment. They attend not so much to be instructed, as to pass their sentence. To them, the pulpit is the bar at which the minister stands to take his trial before them; it is a bar at which few escape censure, from judges both severe and inconsistent. For as these censors are not all of a mind, and perhaps agree in nothing so much as in the opinion they have of their own wisdom, it has often happened that in the course of one and the same sermon, the minister has been condemned as a legalist and an antinomian, as too high in his notions, and too low, as having to little action, and too much. Oh! this hateful spirit, that prompts hearers to pronounce ex cathedra as if they were infallible!

I pray God to preserve you from such a spirit, and to guide you in all things.

John Newton

ON HEARING SERMONS

I am glad to find that the Lord has at length been pleased to fix you in a favored situation, where you have frequent opportunities of hearing the Gospel. This is a great privilege; but like all other outward privileges, it requires grace and wisdom to make a due improvement of it. The great plenty of ordinances you enjoy, though in itself a blessing, is attended with snares, which, unless they are carefully guarded against, may hinder rather than promote your edification. I gladly embrace the occasion you afford me, of offering you my advice upon this subject.

Faithful ministers of the Gospel are all the servants and ambassadors of Christ. They are called and furnished by his Holy Spirit; they speak in his name; and their success in the discharge of their office, whether it is more or less, depends entirely upon his blessing. Thus far they are all upon a par. But in the measure of their ministerial abilities, and in the peculiar turn of their preaching, there is a great variety. There are "diversities of gifts from the same Spirit; and he distributes to every man severally according to his own will." Some are more happy in alarming the careless, others in administering consolation to the wounded conscience. Some are set more especially for the establishment and confirmation of the Gospel doctrines; others are skillful in solving points of application. Others are more excellent in enforcing practical godliness; and others again, having been led through depths of temptation and spiritual distress, are best acquainted with the various workings of the heart, and know best how to speak a word in season to weary and exercised souls. Perhaps no true minister of the Gospel is wholly at a loss upon any of these points. But few, if any, are remarkably and equally excellent in

managing them all. As to their manner; some are more popular and appealing, but at the same time more general and diffuse; while in others the lack of life and earnestness in delivery is compensated by the closeness, accuracy, and depth of their compositions.

In this variety of gifts, the Lord has a gracious regard to the different tastes, dispositions, and wants of his people. By their combined efforts, the complete system of God's truth is illustrated, and the good of his church promoted to the highest advantage. His ministers, like officers assigned to different stations in an army, have not only the good of the whole in view, but each one his particular post to maintain. This would be more evidently the case, if the remaining depravity of our hearts did not give Satan too great an advantage in his subtle attempts to hurt and ensnare us. But, alas! how often has he prevailed to infuse a spirit of envy or dislike in ministers towards each other, and to withdraw hearers from their proper concerns by dividing them into parties. He stirs them up to contend for a Paul, an Apollos, or a Cephas, for their own favorites, to the disparagement of others, who are equally dear to the Lord, and faithful in his service! You may think my preamble long, but I shall draw my counsel chiefly from it.

As the gifts and talents of ministers are different, I advise you to choose for your stated pastor and teacher one whom you find most suitable, upon the whole, to your own taste, and whom you are likely to hear with the most pleasure and advantage. Use some deliberation and much prayer in this matter. Entreat the Lord, who knows better than you do yourself, to guide you where your soul may be best fed. When your choice is fixed, you will do well to make a point of attending his ministry regularly at the stated times of worship on the Lord's day. I do not say that no circumstance will justify your going elsewhere on certain occasions, but I think more seldom you are absent the better. What I have observed of many, who run about unseasonably after new preachers, has reminded me of Proverbs 27:8: "As a bird that wandereth from her nest, so is the man that wandereth from his place." Such unsettled hearers seldom thrive: they usually grow wise in their own conceits, have their heads filled with notions, acquire a dry, critical, and censorious spirit; and are more intent upon disputing who is the best preacher, than upon obtaining benefit to themselves from what they hear.

John Newton

"Take heed what you hear," Mark 4:24. We must hear nothing with approval except what we know to be the word of God. We must, therefore, be well acquainted with the Scriptures ourselves, and by them test the things which we hear, whether they are the word of God or not, as the men of Berea did, Acts 17:11. "Take heed how you hear," Luke 18:18. That which we know to be grounded upon the Scriptures we must receive, "not as the word of men, but, as it is in truth, the word of God," 1 Thess. 2:13. We must with reverence attend to it; we must in our hearts believe, and we must in our lives obey it.

William Gouge

As an aside, no music is more sweet to a gospel preacher than the rustle of Bible pages in the congregation. Many times when I have been in the pulpit and I have read a passage of Scripture, nobody has followed me to see if I was quoting correctly. I strongly urge you to take your Bibles with you when you go to church. What is the best way of hearing the Word? Is it not to search and see whether what the preacher says is really according to the Word of God? Thus, I entreat you to search the Scriptures to see if what is being taught to you is true.

C.H. Spurgeon

Do we prize it in our judgments? Do we receive in into our hearts? Do we fear the loss of the Word preached more than the loss of peace and trade? Again, do we attend to the Word with reverential devotion? When the judge is giving the charge on the bench, all attend. When the Word is preached, the great God is giving us his charge. Do we listen to it as to a matter of life and death? This is a good sign that we love the Word.

Thomas Watson

Service
See also: Impossible; Leadership; Relevance; Vision

Ye cannot serve God and mammon.
The Bible, Matthew 6:24 KJV

But he that is the greatest among you shall be your servant. And whosoever shall exalt himself shall be abased; and he that shall humble himself shall be exalted.
The Bible, Matthew 23:11, 12 KJV

Therefore, my dear brothers, stand firm. Let nothing move you. Always give yourselves fully to the work of the Lord, because you know that your labor in the Lord is not in vain.
The Bible, 1 Corinthians 15:58

If anyone serves, he should do it with the strength God provides, so that in all things God may be praised through Jesus Christ.
The Bible, 1 Peter 4:11

The Lord doesn't ask about your ability, only your availability; and, if you prove your dependability, the Lord will increase your capability.
Author unknown

The service we render to others is really the rent we pay for our room on this earth.
Author unknown

Say well is good, but do well is better;
Do well seems the spirit, say well the letter;
Say well is godly and helps to please,
But do well is godly and gives the world ease.
Author unknown

I sought my soul,
But my soul I could not see.
I sought my God,
But my God eluded me.
I sought my brother,
And I found all three.
Author unknown

God doesn't call the equipped, he equips
the called.
Author unknown

The greatest reward for serving others
is the satisfaction found in your own
heart.
Author unknown

The head grows by taking in but the heart
grows by giving out.
Author unknown

In thought, faith;
In word, wisdom;
In deed, courage;
In life, service.
Author unknown

To give real service you must add
something which cannot be bought or
measured with money, and that is sincerity
and integrity.
Donald A. Adams

We don't follow him in order to be loved;
we are loved so we follow him.
Neil Anderson

In the time we have it is surely our duty to
do all the good we can to all the people we
can in all the ways we can.
William Barclay

Signs of living to please God
See therefore that you live upon God's
approval as that which you chiefly seek,
and will suffice you: which you may
discover by these signs.
1. You will be most careful to understand
the Scripture, to know what doth please
and displease God.
2. You will be more careful in the doing of

every duty, to fit it to the pleasing of God
than men.
3. You will look to your hearts, and not only
to your actions; to your ends, and thoughts,
and the inward manner and degree.
4. You will look to secret duties as well as
public and to that which men see not, as
well as unto that which they see.
5. You will reverence your consciences, and
have much to do with them, and will not
slight them: when they tell you of God's
displeasure, it will disquiet you; when they
tell you of his approval, it will comfort you.
6. Your pleasing men will be charitable for
their good, and pious in order to the
pleasing of God, and not proud and
ambitious for your honor with them, nor
impious against the pleasing of God.
7. Whether men be pleased or displeased,
or how they judge of you, or what they call
you, will seem a small matter to you, as
their own interest, in comparison to God's
judgment. You live not on them. You can
bear their displeasure, censures, and
reproaches, if God be but pleased. These
will be your evidences.
Richard Baxter

The advantages of pleasing God
1. If you seek first to please God and are
satisfied therein, you have but one to
please instead of multitudes; and a
multitude of masters are hardlier pleased
than one.
2. And it is one that putteth upon you
nothing that is unreasonable, for quantity
or quality.
3. And one that is perfectly wise and good,
not liable to misunderstand your case and
actions.
4. And one that is most holy, and is not
pleased in iniquity or dishonesty.
5. And he is one that is impartial and most
just, and is no respecter of persons, Acts x. 34.
6. And he is one that is a competent
judge, that hath fitness and authority,
and is acquainted with your hearts, and
every circumstance and reason of your
actions.
7. And he is one that perfectly agreeth with
himself, and putteth you not upon

contradictions or impossibilities.

8. And he is one that is constant and unchangeable; and is not pleased with one thing to-day, and another contrary to-morrow; nor with one person this year, whom he will be weary of the next.

9. And he is one that is merciful, and requireth you not to hurt yourselves to please him: nay, he is pleased with nothing of thine but that which tendeth to thy happiness, and displeased with nothing but that which hurts thyself or others, as a father that is displeased with his children when they defile or hurt themselves.

10. He is gentle, though just, in his censures of thee; judging truly, but not with unjust rigor, nor making your actions worse than they are.

11. He is one that is not subject to the passions of men, which blind their minds, and carry them to injustice.

12. He is one that will not be moved by tale-bearers, whisperers, or false accusers, nor can be perverted by any misinformation.
Richard Baxter

The best cure for worry, depression, melancholy, brooding, is to go deliberately forth and try to lift with one's sympathy the gloom of somebody else.
Arnold Bennett

Our true worth does not consist in what human being think of us. What we really are is what God knows us to be.
John Berchmans

Life begets life. Energy begets energy. It is by spending oneself that one becomes rich.
Sarah Bernhardt

What is sought from Christians is the motivation for selfless service, which once distinguished the Christian heritage.
Professor Klaus Bockmühl

I longed to be a flame of fire continually glowing in the divine service and building

up of Christ's kingdom to my last and dying breath.
David Brainerd's Diary

As long as I see any thing to be done for God, life is worth having; but O how vain and unworthy it is to live for any lower end!
David Brainerd's Journal

No person among us deserves any other reward for performing a brave and worthy action, but the consciousness of having served his nation.
Joseph Bryant, Thayendanegea of the Mohawk Tribe

Our lives will harmonize best with God's will and the demands of the Law when they serve other people best.
John Calvin

Service to a just cause rewards the worker with more real happiness and satisfaction than any other venture of life.
Carrie Chapman Catt

At the age of fourteen she made the three-fold resolution, to please her Consort, [Empress] Elizabeth, and the Nation.
Catherine II of Russia, Epitaph, written by herself

We are not built for ourselves, but for God. Not for service for God, but for God.
Oswald Chambers

Most arts require long study and application; but the most useful of all, that of pleasing, only the desire.
Lord Chesterfield

He who wishes to secure the good of others has already secured his own.
Confucius

No man was ever honored for what he received. Honor has been the reward for what he gave.
Calvin Coolidge

No one is useless in this world who lightens the burdens of another.
Charles Dickens

They might not need me; but they might.
I'll let my head be just in sight;
A smile as small as mine might be
Precisely their necessity.
Emily Dickinson

If I can stop one heart from breaking,
I shall not live in vain;
If I can ease one life the aching,
Or cool one pain,
Or help one fainting robin
Unto his nest again,
I shall not live in vain.
Emily Dickinson

You will find, as you look back upon your life, that the moments that stand out are the moments when you have done things for others.
Henry Drummond

Only a life lived for others is worth living.
Albert Einstein

My whole life, whether it be long or short, shall be devoted to your [the public's] service and the service of our great imperial family to which we all belong. But I shall not have strength to carry out this resolution alone unless you join in it with me.
Elizabeth II, on becoming Queen of England

Blessed is the servant who loves his brother as much when he is sick and useless as when he is well and can be of service to him. And blessed is he who loves his brother as well when he is afar off as when he is by his side, and who would say nothing behind his back he might not, in love, say before his face.
St. Francis of Assisi

The martyrs of love suffer infinitely more in remaining in this life so as to serve God, than if they died a thousand times over in

testimony to their faith, their love, and their fidelity.
Jeanne François de Chantal

What we must decide is how we are valuable rather than how valuable we are.
Edgar Z. Friedenberg

We must not hope to be mowers,
And to gather the ripe old ears,
Unless we have first been sowers
And watered the furrows with tears.
It is not just as we take it,
This mystical world of ours,
Life's field will yield as we make it
A harvest of thorns or of flowers.
Johann Wolfgang von Goethe

The most eloquent prayer is the prayer through hands that heal and bless. The highest form of worship is the worship of unselfish Christian service. The greatest form of praise is the sound of consecrated feet seeking out the lost and helpless.
Billy Graham

No one can write his real religious life with pen or pencil. It is written only in actions, and its seal is our character, not our orthodoxy. Whether we, our neighbor, or God is the judge, absolutely the only value of our religious life to ourselves or to anyone is what it fits us for and enables us to do.
Wilfred T. Grenfell

Tied to the value of the person is the principle of servanthood. We value what we freely serve.
Douglas Groothuis

Those prepared to do love's service will receive her rewards: new comfort and new strength.
Hadewijch

A noble deed is a step toward God.
J.G. Holland

Down in their hearts, wise men know this truth: the only way to help yourself is to help others.
Elbert Hubbard

It is a sin to do less then your best.
Dr. Bob Jones Sr.

If Christ were here, he would help them, and so must I.
Toyohiko Kagawa, on his mission to help the slum-dwellers of Kobe

So long as you can sweeten another's pain, life is not in vain.
Helen Keller

Life is an exciting business, and it is most exciting when it is lived for others.
Helen Keller

And so, my fellow Americans, ask not what your country can do for you; ask what you can do for your country.
John F. Kennedy

I won't have any money to leave behind. I won't have the fine and luxurious things of life to leave behind. But I just want to leave a committed life behind.
Martin Luther King, Jr.

Wash what is dirty, water what is dry, heal what is wounded. Bend what is stiff, warm what is cold, guide what goes off the road.
Stephen Langton

We may think God wants actions of a certain kind, but God wants people of a certain kind.
C.S. Lewis

Here is the truly Christian life, here is faith really working by love: when a man applies himself with joy and love to the works of that freest servitude, in which he serves others voluntarily and for naught; himself abundantly satisfied in the fulness and richness of his own faith.
Martin Luther

A faithful and good servant is a real godsend; but truly it is a rare bird in the land.
Martin Luther

In the kingdom of God service is not a stepping-stone to nobility: it is nobility, the only kind of nobility that is recognized.
T.W. Manson

One of God's specialities is to make somebodies out of nobodies.
Henrietta Mears

The value of life lies not in the length of days, but in the use we make of them; a man may live long yet live very little.
Montaigne

A servant of God has but one Master.
George Müller

We are here to add what we can to life, not to get what we can from it.
William Osler

Two men please God: who serves Him with all his heart because he knows Him; who seeks Him with all his heart because he knows Him not.
Nikita Ivanovich Panin

Do little things as though they were great, because of the majesty of Jesus Christ who does them in us, and who lives our life: and do the greatest things as though they were little and easy, because of His omnipotence.
Blaise Pascal

Every successful business in the world is in existence because its founder recognized in a problem or need an opportunity to be of service to others. Every problem or need in your life is in reality an opportunity to call forth inner resources of wisdom, love, strength, and ability.
J. Sig Paulson

I expect to pass through the world but once. Any good therefore that I can do, or any kindness or abilities that I can show to any fellow creature, let me do it now. Let me not defer or neglect it, for I shall not pass this way again.
William Penn

In the New Testament it is the work and not the workers that is glorified.
Alfred Plummer

Wherefore gird up your loins and serve God in fear and truth, forsaking the vain and empty talking and the error of the many, for ye have believed on Him that raised our Lord Jesus Christ from the dead and gave unto him glory and a throne on His right hand.
Polycarp

If we are going to reign as kings, we must serve as priests.
Derek Prince

True happiness consists in making others happy.
Hindu proverb

A man never stands as tall as when he kneels to help a child.
Knights of Pythagoras

One thing, and only one, in this world has eternity stamped upon it. Feelings pass; resolves and thoughts pass; opinions change. What you have done lasts – lasts in you. Through ages, through eternity, what you have done for Christ, that, and only that, you are.
F. W. Robertson

When you cease to make a contribution, you begin to die.
Eleanor Roosevelt

Do what you can, with what you have, where you are.
Theodore Roosevelt

As soon as public service ceases to be the chief business of the citizens, and they would rather serve with their money than with their persons, the State is not far from its fall.
J.J. Rousseau

Unless we perform divine service with every willing act of our life, we never perform it at all.
John Ruskin

Life becomes harder for us when we live for others, but it also becomes richer and happier.
Albert Schweitzer

I don't know what your destiny will be, but one thing I know, the only ones among you who will be really happy are those who have sought and found how to serve.
Albert Schweitzer

Always keep your eyes open for the little task, because it is the little task that is important to Jesus Christ. The future of the kingdom of God does not depend on the enthusiasm of this or that powerful person; those great ones are necessary too, but it is equally necessary to have a great number of little people who will do a little thing in the service of Christ.
Albert Schweitzer

One hour of life, crowded to the full with glorious action, and filled with noble risks, is worth whole years of those mean observances of paltry decorum, in which men steal through existence, like sluggish waters through a marsh, without either honor or observation.
Sir Walter Scott

Some want to live within the sound of church or chapel bell; I want to run a rescue shop within a yard of hell.
C.T. Studd

Think not that God will be always caressing His children, or shine upon their head, or kindle their hearts as He does at the first. He does so only to lure us to Himself, as the falconer lures the falcon with its gay hood. We must stir up and rouse ourselves and be content to leave off learning, and no more enjoy feeling and warmth, and must now serve the Lord with strenuous industry and at our own cost.
John Tauler

A visitor saw a nurse attending the sores of a leprosy patient. "I would not do that for a million dollars," she said. The nurse

answered, "Neither would I, but I do it for Jesus for nothing."
Corrie Ten Boom

Let us touch the dying, the poor, the lonely and the unwanted according to the graces we have received and let us not be ashamed or slow to do the humble work.
Mother Teresa

We are all pencils in the hand of a writing God, who is sending love letters to the world.
Mother Teresa

Christ has no body now on earth but yours;
yours are the only hands with which he can do his work,
yours are the only feet with which he can go about the world,
yours are the only eyes through which his compassion
can shine forth upon a troubled world.
Christ has no body now on earth but yours.
Teresa of Avila

Do not be ashamed to serve others for the love of Jesus Christ and to seem poor in this world.
Thomas à Kempis

The vocation of every man and woman is to serve other people.
Leo Tolstoy

The service of the less gifted brother is as pure as that of the more gifted, and God accepts both with equal pleasure.
A. W. Tozer

Do all the good you can,
By all the means you can,
In all the ways you can,
In all the places you can,
At all the times you can,
To all the people you can,
As long as ever you can.
John Wesley

The object of love is to serve, not to win.
Woodrow Wilson

Service and humility
We may easily be too big for God to use, but never too small.
Dwight L. Moody

The measure of a man is not how many servants he has but now many men he serves.
Dwight L. Moody

When God wants to do his great works he trains somebody to be quiet enough and little enough, then he uses that person.
Hudson Taylor

… they who fain would serve thee best
Are conscious most of wrong within.
Henry Twells

Service and love for God
If you want to be of use, get rightly related to Jesus Christ, and he will make you of use unconsciously every moment you live.
Oswald Chambers

It is possible to be so active in the service of Christ as to forget to love him.
P.T. Forsyth

Service means the activity of the spiritual life. It is man's spontaneous love offering to God.
Sundar Singh

Service and pride
How many of us, who are engaged in the Lord's holy service, are secretly cherishing some proud aspiration of excelling other men, of making a name for ourselves, of securing money or fame!
F.B. Meyer

Service in small things
All service ranks the same with God.
Robert Browning

To take up the cross of Christ is no great action done once for all; it consists in the continual practice of small duties which are distasteful to us.
J.H. Newman

Remember that there must be someone to cook the meals, and count yourselves happy in being able to serve like Martha.
Teresa of Avila

Small service is true service while it lasts:
Of humblest friends, bright creature, scorn not one:
The daisy, by the shadow that it casts,
Protects the lingering dew-drop from the sun.
William Wordsworth, verse written for a small child

Sex
See also: Adultery; Love; Sexuality
Nowhere does the Bible teach that sex in itself is a sin, although many interpreters of the Bible would try to make it appear so. The Bible teaches that the wrong use of sex is sinful. For sex, the act by which all life on this earth is created, should be a wonderful, meaningful, and satisfying human experience.
Billy Graham

For the past twenty years you and I have been fed all day long on good solid lies about sex.
C.S. Lewis

The monstrosity of sexual intercourse outside marriage is that those who indulge in it are trying to isolate one kind of union (the sexual) from all other kinds of union which were intended to go along with it and make up the total union.
C.S. Lewis

Within marriage, sex is beautiful, fulfilling, creative. Outside of marriage, it is ugly, destructive, and damning.
John MacArthur

Sex in marriage
The wife's body does not belong to her alone but also to her husband. In the same way, the husband's body does not belong to him alone but also to his wife. Do not deprive each other except by mutual consent and for a time, so that you may devote yourselves to prayer. Then come together again so that Satan will not tempt you because of your lack of self-control.
The Bible, 1 Corinthians 7:4,5

Sexuality
Same-sex friendships are to be encouraged, like those in the Bible between Ruth and Naomi, David and Jonathan, and Paul and Timothy.
John Stott

In God's view I suspect we are all sexual deviants. I doubt if there is anyone who has not had a lustful thought that deviated from God's perfect ideal of sexuality.
Merville Vincent

Shallowness
See: Preaching; Truth

Shame
They sewed fig leaves together and made themselves aprons.
Genesis 3:7

Little shame, little conscience, and much industry will make a man rich.
Thomas Fuller

The emotion of shame has been valued not as an emotion but because of the insight to which it leads.
C.S. Lewis

I think that man is lost indeed who has lost the sense of shame.
Plautus

Be not ashamed of your faith; remember it is the ancient gospel of martyrs, confessors, reformers and saints. Above all, it is "the truth of God", against which the gates of Hell cannot prevail.
C.H. Spurgeon

I never wonder to see men wicked, but I often wonder to see them not ashamed.
Jonathan Swift

Man is the only animal that blushes. Or needs to.
Mark Twain

Shamelessness
You should never trust a person who doesn't blush.
Turgenev

Sharing
Joys divided are increased.
Josia Gilbert Holland

Shared joy is double joy and shared sorrow is half-sorrow.
Swedish Proverb

You can read Kant by yourself if you wanted to; but you must share a joke with someone else.
Robert Louis Stevenson

Sickness
See also: Illness; Trials
Is any one of you sick? He should call the elders of the church to pray over him and anoint him with oil in the name of the Lord. And the prayer offered in faith will make the sick person well; the Lord will raise him up. If he has sinned, he will be forgiven. Therefore confess your sins to each other and pray for each other so that you may be healed.
The Bible, James 5:14-16

If you should get ill, through circumstances beyond your control, beat it patiently and wait patiently upon God's mercy. That is all you need to do. It is true to say that patience in sickness and other forms of trouble pleases God much more than any splendid devotion that you might show in health.
The Cloud of Unknowing

All mental disorders, all sicknesses, all perversions, all destruction, all wars find their original root in sin.
Billy Graham

Sight
See also: Vision

Now we see through a glass, darkly.
The Bible, 1 Corinthians 13:12 KJV

The eye sees only what the mind is prepared to comprehend.
Henri Bergson

If the blind put their hand in God's, they find their way more surely than those who see but have not faith or purpose.
Helen Keller

Lord, purge our eyes to see
Within the seed a tree,
Within the glowing egg a bird,
Within the shroud a butterfly,
Till, taught by such, we see
Beyond all creatures, thee.
Christina Rossetti

Sight, Spiritual
So it is through tears of penitence, through striving after righteousness, and through constant compassionate living, that spiritual eyesight is made clear.
Bernard of Clairvaux

Detachment from visible things is to open your eyes to the invisible.
John Climacus

Signs and wonders
It is perfectly clear that in New Testament times, the gospel was authenticated in this way by signs, wonders and miracles of various characters and descriptions ... Was it only meant to be true of the early church? ... The Scriptures never anywhere say that these things were only temporary – never! There is no such statement anywhere.
Martyn Lloyd-Jones

Silence
See also: Patience
Even a fool, when he holdeth his peace, is counted wise.
The Bible, Proverbs 17:28

If you don't speak out, your silence will speak for you.
Author unknown

Blessed are those who have nothing to say and cannot be persuaded to say it.
Author unknown

The finest thing that we can say of God is to be silent concerning him from the wisdom of inner riches.
Augustine of Hippo

There are times when silence has the loudest voice.
Leroy Brownlow

A dog barks when his master is attacked. I would be a coward if I saw that God's truth is attacked and yet would remain silent.
John Calvin

Silence is the element in which great things fashion themselves together.
Thomas Carlyle

Silence is deep as eternity, speech is shallow as time.
Thomas Carlyle

Silence is the mother of prayer. It frees the prisoner; it guards the divine flame; it watches over reasoning; it protects the sense of penitence.
John Climacus

Silence is the true friend that never betrays.
Confucius

Let thy speech be better than silence, or be silent.
Dionysus the Elder

Silence is true wisdom's best reply.
Eurpides

Outward silence is indispensable for the cultivation and improvement of inner silence.
Madame Guyon

It is better to keep silence and to be, than to talk and not to be.
Ignatius of Loyola

'Tis better to remain silent and be thought a fool, than open one's mouth and remove all doubt.
Samuel Johnson

Our lives begin to end the day we become silent about things that matter.
Martin Luther King Jr.

There is an eloquent silence: it serves sometimes to approve, sometimes to condemn; there is a mocking silence; there is a respectful silence.
Francois De La Rochefoucauld

It is the wise head that makes the still tongue.
W.J. Lucas

In order to see birds it is necessary to become a part of the silence.
Robert Lynd

True silence is the rest of the mind. It is to the spirit what sleep is to the body—nourishment and refreshment.
William Penn

When something important is going on, silence is a lie.
A.M. Rosenthal

Silence is more musical than any song.
Christina Rossetti

There should be in the soul halls of space, avenues of leisure, and high porticoes of silence, where God walks.
Jeremy Taylor

The beginning of prayer is silence.
Mother Teresa

Well-timed silence hath more eloquence than speech.
Martin Fraquhar Tupper

Simplicity

Make everything as simple as possible, but not simpler.
Albert Einstein

We should never finish if we wanted constantly to sound the bottom of our hearts; and in wanting to escape from self in the search of God, we should be too preoccupied with self in such frequent examinations. Let us go on in simplicity of heart, in peace and joy, which are the fruits of the Holy Spirit.
F. Fénelon

From the very outset every penny shall be consecrated to God. I think there is an art of simplicity. It will need no end of thinking out, and it is worth learning.
Temple Gairdner

Purity of heart and simplicity are of great force with almighty God, who is in purity most singular, and of nature most simple.
Gregory the Great

Simplicity is truth's most becoming garb.
Dr. Bob Jones Sr.

Simplify in order to live intensely in the present moment… Simplify and share as a way of identifying with Christ Jesus.
Brother Roger

Hold fast to simplicity of heart and innocence. Yes, be as babes who do not know the wickedness that destroys grown people's lives.
Shepherd of Hermas

It's easy to be clever. But the really clever thing is to be simple.
Jule Styne

Blissful are the simple, for they shall have much peace.
Thomas à Kempis

Our life is quite simply frittered away by detail. Simplify. Simplify.
Thoreau

Sin
See also: Mortification
But if you will not do so, behold, you have sinned against the LORD, and be sure your sin will find you out.
The Bible, Numbers 32:23 KJV

The whole head is sick, and the whole heart faint.
The Bible, Isaiah 1:5 KJV

The wages of sin is death.
The Bible, Romans 3:23 KJV

Sin wouldn't be so attractive if the wages were paid immediately.
Author unknown

The follies of youth become the vices of manhood and the disgrace of old age.
Author unknown

If there is no sorrow for sin, there will be no joy in salvation.
Author unknown

God is not against us because of our sin. He is with us against our sin.
Author unknown

You can never conquer sin with an excuse.
Author unknown

Man calls it an accident;
God calls it an abomination.
Man calls it a blunder;
God calls it blindness.
Man calls it a defect;
God calls it a disease.
Man calls it a chance;
God calls it a choice.
Author unknown

Lust and hate are sins as well as adultery and murder.
Mortimer J. Adler

Sin and repentance are the only grounds for hope and joy. The grounds for reconciled, joyful relationships. You can be born again.
John Alexander

Oh, better were it for you to die in a jail, in a ditch, in a dungeon, than to die in your sins.
Joseph Alleine

Your worthiness gives you no help, and your unworthiness does not harm you. As one drop of water is as compared to the great ocean, so are my sins as compared with God's incomprehensible grace in Christ.
Johann Arndt

In weighing our sins let us not use a deceitful balance, weighing at our own discretion what we will, and how we will, calling this heavy and that light: but let us use the divine balance of the holy Scriptures, as taken from the treasury of the Lord, and by it weigh every offence, nay, not weigh, but rather recognize what has been already weighed by the Lord.
Augustine of Hippo

Love the sinner but hate the sin.
Augustine of Hippo

Of our own we have nothing but sin.
Augustine of Hippo

I inquired what iniquity was, and found it to be no substance, but the perversion of the will, turned aside from Thee, O God, the Supreme, towards these lower things.
Augustine of Hippo

Shall we call it our pride or our laziness, or shall we call it the deceit of our life? Let us call it for once the great defiance which turns us again and again into the enemies of God and of our fellowmen, even of our own selves.
Karl Barth

Not only the worst of my sins, but the best of my duties speak me a child of Adam.
William Beveridge

Your virtues can never cancel out your vices. Good deeds can never remove bad ones. If a person gets right with God, it is not by works, so that no one can boast. No religious efforts or experiences: christening,

confirmation, baptism, holy communion, churchgoing, prayers, gifts, sacrifices of time and effort, Bible reading, or anything else can cancel out a single sin... . All sin, every sin, must be punished and when Jesus took the place of sinners, he became as accountable for their sins as if he had been responsible for them... . All the Bible's teaching points to the death of Christ. What makes his death so important? The answer is that he died as a Substitute, a Sin-bearer, and a Savior.
John Blanchard

If the guilt of sin is so great that nothing can satisfy it but the blood of Jesus; and the filth of sin is so great that nothing can fetch out the stain thereof but the blood of Jesus, how great, how heinous, how sinful must the evil of sin be.
William Bridge

Our attitude towards sin is more self-centered than God-centered. We are more concerned about our own "victory" over sin than we are about the fact that our sin grieve the heart of God.
Jerry Bridges

One leak will sink a ship; and one sin will destroy a sinner.
John Bunyan

Take heed of little sins.
John Bunyan

Take heed of secret sins. They will undo thee if loved and maintained: one moth may spoil the garment; one leak drown the ship; a penknife stab and kill a man as well as a sword; so one sin may damn the soul; nay, there is more danger of a secret sin causing the miscarrying of the soul than open profaneness, because not so obvious to the reproofs of the world; therefore take heed that secret sinnings eat not out good beginnings.
Jeremiah Burroughs

Though Satan instils his poison, and fans the flames of our corrupt desires within us,

we are yet not carried by any external force to the commission of sin, but our own flesh entices us, and we willingly yield to its allurements.
John Calvin

The deadliest sin were the consciousness of no sin.
Thomas Carlyle

It may be a secret sin on earth, but it is open scandal in heaven.
Lewis Sperry Chafer

The gospel of Jesus Christ must be the bad new of the conviction of sin before it can be the Good News of redemption. The truth is revealed in God's Holy Word; life can be lived only in absolute and disciplined submission to its authority.
Charles Colson

That which we call sin in others is experiment for us.
Ralph Waldo Emerson

The smallest things become great when God requires them of us; they are small only in themselves; they are always great when they are done for God, and when they serve to unite us with Him eternally.
François Fénelon

If the death of Christ was that which satisfied God for our sins, there is infinite evil in sin, since it would not be expiated but by an infinite satisfaction. Fools make a mock at sin, and there are few in the world who are fully sensible of its evil – but certainly, if God should exact of thee the full penalty, thy eternal sufferings could not satisfy for the evil there is in one vain thought. You may think it severe, that God should subject his creatures to everlasting sufferings for sin, and never be satisfied with them any more. But when you have well considered, that the Being against whom you sin is the infinitely blessed God, and how God dealt with the angels that fell, you will change your mind. Oh the depth of the evil of sin! If ever you wish to see how great and horrid an evil sin is, measure it in your thoughts, either by the infinite holiness and excellency of God, who is wronged by it; or by the infinite sufferings of Christ, who died to satisfy for it; and then you will have deeper apprehensions of its enormity.
If the death of Christ satisfied God, and thereby redeemed us from the curse; then the redemption of souls is costly; souls are precious and of great value with God. "Ye know that ye were not redeemed with corruptible things, as silver and gold, from your vain conversation received by tradition; but with the precious blood of the Son of God, as of a lamb without spot." (I Peter 1: 18,19). Only the blood of God is an equivalent for the redemption of souls. Gold and silver may redeem from human, but not from hellish bondage. The whole creation is not a value for the redemption of one soul. Souls are very dear; he that paid for them found them so: yet how cheaply do sinners sell their souls. If Christ's death satisfied God for our sins, how unparalleled is the love of God to poor sinners! If Christ, by dying, has made full satisfaction, then God can consistently pardon the greatest of sinners that believe in Jesus.
John Flavel

A fault, once denied, is twice committed.
Thomas Fuller

God's wounds cure, sin's kisses kill.
William Gurnall

Men love everything but righteousness and fear everything but God.
Vance Havner

Sin is like the poison of a mamba snake. It's exceedingly deadly. It kills. Every sin if permitted will become imperious in its demands and every lust will aim at its maximum expression. Sin is like the devil its originator. It is limitless in its capacity for evil.
Erroll Hulse

It is not only that sin consists in doing evil, but in not doing the good that we know.
H.A. Ironside

What death is to the body,
Sin is to the soul, but worse.
Jacopone da Todi

To argue from mercy to sin is the devil's logic.
James Janeway

Unbelief is the shield of every sin.
William Jenkyn

Out of timber so crooked as that from which man is made nothing entirely straight can be built.
Immanuel Kant

We are free to sin, but not to control sin's consequences.
J. Kenneth Kimberlin

In essence, sin is the abuse of free will, the misuse of what is good.
Steve Kumar

We have a strange illusion that mere time cancels sin.
C.S. Lewis

If we say we have not sinned, we are denying the doctrine of the Bible.
M. Lloyd-Jones

Sin cannot tear you away from him [Christ], even though you commit adultery a hundred times a day and commit as many murders.
Martin Luther

Let us not think ourselves more just than was the poor sinner and murderer on the cross.
Martin Luther

Either sin is with you, lying on your shoulders, or it is lying on Christ, the Lamb of God. Now if it is lying on your back, you are lost; but if it is resting on

Christ, you are free, and you will be saved. Now choose what you want.
Martin Luther

Everything that used to be a sin is now a disease.
Bill Maher

First we practice sin, then defend it, then boast of it.
Thomas Manton

Let them fear death who do not fear sin.
Thomas Manton

Religion would not have many enemies, if it were not an enemy to their vices.
Massillon

The basis of all sin is selfishness.
David O. McKay

Man's disobedience
brought into this World a world of woe,
Sin and her shadow Death, and Misery,
Death's Harbinger.
John Milton

God will forgive the sinner, but he will still judge the sin.
Beth Moore

There is no man so good who, were he to submit all his thoughts and actions to the law, would not deserve hanging ten times in his life.
Michel Eyquem de Montaigne

You'll never be able to speak against sin if you're entertained by it.
John Muncee

All human sin seems so much worse in its consequences than in its intentions.
Reinhold Niebuhr

Let no man think to kill sin with few, easy, or gentle strokes. He who hath once smitten a serpent, if he follow not on his blow until it be slain, may repent that ever he began the quarrel. And so he who

undertakes to deal with sin, and pursues it not constantly to the death.
John Owen

Do you mortify? Do you make it your daily work? Be always at it whilst you live; cease not a day from this work; be killing sin or it will be killing you.
John Owen

The vigor and power and comfort of our spiritual life depends on our mortification of deeds of the flesh.
John Owen

The custom of sinning takes away the sense of it, the course of the world takes away the shame of it.
John Owen

The indulgence of one sin opens the door to further sins. The indulgence of one sin diverts the soul from the use of those means by which all other sins should be resisted.
John Owen

When sin lets us alone we may let sin alone; but as sin is never less quiet than when it seems to be most quiet, and its waters are for the most part deep when they are still, so ought our contrivances against it to be vigorous at all times and in all conditions, even where there is least suspicion.
John Owen

The deceitfulness of sin is seen in that it is modest in its first proposals but when it prevails it hardens mens' hearts, and brings them to ruin.
John Owen

If we do not preach about sin and God's judgement on it, we cannot present Christ as Savior from sin and the wrath of God.
J.I. Packer

The first truth is that we are all invalids in God's hospital. In moral and spiritual terms, we are all sick and damaged, diseased and deformed, scarred and sore,

lame and lopsided, to a far, far, greater extent than we realize.
J.I. Packer

All sin comes from not putting supreme value on the glory of God – this is the very essence of sin.
John Piper

With the Fall all became abnormal.
Francis A. Schaeffer

The inward area is the first place of loss of true Christian life, of true spirituality, and the outward sinful act is the result.
Francis A. Schaeffer

In all their jollity in this world, the wicked are but as a book fairly bound, which when it is opened is full of nothing but tragedies. So when the book of their consciences shall be once opened, there is nothing to be read but lamentations and woes.
Richard Sibbes

Oh, how horrible our sins look when they are committed by someone else!
Chuck Smith

Any cloth may cover our sores, but the finest silk will not cover our sins.
Henry Smith

Sin can bring pleasure, but never happiness.
R.C. Sproul

Sin is cosmic treason against a perfectly pure Sovereign. It is an act of supreme ingratitude toward the One to whom we owe everything, to the One who has given us life itself.
R.C. Sproul

The death of Christ shall be the death of iniquity, the cross of Christ shall be the crucifixion of transgression.
C.H. Spurgeon

A sight of his crucifixion crucifies sin!
C.H. Spurgeon

Sin is sovereign till sovereign grace dethrones it.
C.H. Spurgeon

Christian, you are never out of danger of sinning.
C.H. Spurgeon

Sin goes in a disguise, and thence is welcome; like Judas, it kisses and kills; like Joab, it salutes and slays.
George Swinnock

No sin is small.
Jeremy Taylor

Whatever we do that creates deadness is a sin.
John V. Taylor

I can contribute nothing to my own salvation, except the sin from which I need to be redeemed.
William Temple

It is true that we cannot be free from sin, but at least let our sins not be always the same.
Teresa of Avila

A man by his sin may waste himself, which is to waste that which on earth is most like God. This is man's greatest tragedy, God's heaviest grief.
A.W. Tozer

The pleasure of sin is soon gone, but the sting remains.
Thomas Watson

When sin is your burden, Christ will be your delight.
Thomas Watson

Sin has the devil for its father, shame for its companion, and death for its wages.
Thomas Watson

Sin, Awareness of
I have had a vastly greater sense of my own wickedness and the badness of my heart than ever I had before my conversion
Jonathan Edwards

In youth, in middle age, and now after many battles, I find nothing in my but corruption.
John Knox

It is an accustomed action with her, to seem thus washing her hands: I have known her continue in this a quarter of an hour. ... "Out, out, damned spot! Out, I say! ... Here's the smell of the blood still: all the perfumes of Arabia will not sweeten this little hand. Oh, oh, oh!" ... What a sigh is there! The heart is sorely charged. ... This disease is beyond my practice.
William Shakespeare, Lady Macbeth being observed by her doctor

Sin, Besetting
All my life I have been seeking to climb out of the pit of my besetting sins and I cannot do it and I never will unless a hand is let down to draw me up.
Seneca

Sin, Burden of
However many and however great and burdensome your sins may be, with God there is greater mercy.
Tikhon of Zadonsk

Sin, Confession of
We have left undone those things which we ought to have done; and we have done those things which we ought not to have done.
Book of Common Prayer, Morning Prayer

Have mercy upon us miserable sinners.
Book of Common Prayer, The Litany

Sometimes when I went on and discussing silly sins with my confessor, he said, "You are a fool. God is not incensed against you, but you are incensed against God. God is not angry with you, but you are angry with God."
Martin Luther

Sin,
Conviction of

Robert Murray M'Cheyne
"And when he [the Comforter] is come, he will convince the world of sin, and of righteousness, and of judgment."
John xvi. 8.

When friends are about to part from one another, they are far kinder than ever they have been before. It was so with Jesus. He was going to part from his disciples, and never till now did his heart flow out toward them in so many streams of heavenly tenderness. Sorrow had filled their heart, and therefore divinest compassion filled his heart. "I tell you the truth, it is expedient for you that I go away."

Surely it was expedient for himself that he should go away. He had lived a life of weariness and painfulness, not having where to lay his head, and surely it was pleasant in his eyes that he was about to enter into his rest. He had lived in obscurity and poverty – he gave his back to the smiters, and his cheeks to them that plucked off the hair; and now, surely, he might well look forward with joy to his return to that glory which he had with the Father before ever the world was, when all the angels of God worshiped him; and yet he does not say: It is expedient for me that I go away. Surely that would have been comfort enough to his disciples. But no; he says: "It is expedient for you." He forgets himself altogether, and thinks only of his little flock which he was leaving behind him: "It is expedient for you that I go away." O most generous of Saviors! He looked not on his own things, but on the things of others also. He knew that it is far more blessed to give than it is to receive.

The gift of the Spirit is the great argument by which he here persuades them that his going away would be expedient for them. Now, it is curious to remark that he had promised them the Spirit before, in the beginning of his discourse. In chap. xiv. 16-18, he says: "I will pray the Father, and he shall give you another Comforter, that he may abide with you for ever; even the Spirit of truth; whom the world cannot receive, because it seeth him not, neither knoweth him: but ye know him; for he dwelleth with you, and shall be in you. I will not leave you comfortless: I will come to you." And again: "But the Comforter, which is the Holy Ghost, whom the Father will send in my name, he shall teach you all things, and bring all things to your remembrance, whatsoever I have said unto you." (Verse 26.) In that passage he promises the Spirit for their own peculiar comfort and joy. He promises him as a treasure which they, and they only, could receive: "For the world cannot receive him, because it neither sees nor knows him;" and yet, saith he, "he dwelleth with you, and shall be in you." But in the passage before us the promise is quite different. He promises the Spirit here, not for themselves, but for the world – not as a peculiar treasure, to be locked up in their own bosoms, which they might brood over with a selfish joy, but as a blessed power to work, through their preaching, on the wicked world around them – not as a well springing up within their own bosoms unto everlasting life, but as rivers of living water flowing through them to water this dry and perishing world.

He does not say: When he is come he will fill your hearts with peace and joy to overflowing; but: "When he is come, he will convince the world of sin, and of righteousness, and of judgment." But a little before he had told them that the world would hate and persecute them: "If ye were of the world, the world would love his own; but because ye are not of the world, but I have chosen you out of the world, therefore the world hateth you." (John XV. 19.) This was but poor comfort, when that very world was to be the field of their labors; but now he shows them what a blessed gift the Spirit would be; for he would work, through their preaching, upon the very hearts that hated and persecuted them: "He shall convince the world of sin." This has always been the case. In Acts ii. we are told that when the Spirit came on the apostles the crowd mocked them, saying: "These men are full of new wine;" and yet, when Peter preached, the Spirit wrought through his preaching on the hearts of these very scoffers. They were pricked in their hearts, and cried: "Men and brethren, what must we do?" and the same day three thousand souls were converted. Again, the jailer at Philippi was evidently a hard, cruel man towards the apostles; for he thrust them into the inner prison, and made their feet fast in the stocks; and yet the Spirit opens his hard heart, and he is brought to Christ by the very apostles whom he hated. Just so it is, brethren, to this day. The world does not love the true ministers of Christ a whit better than they did.

The world is the same world that it was in Christ's day. That word has never yet been scored out of the Bible: "Whosoever will live godly in the world, must suffer persecution." We expect, as Paul did, to be hated by the most who listen to us. We are quite sure, as Paul was, that the more abundantly we love you, most of you will love us the less; and yet, brethren, none of these things move us. Though cast down, we are not in despair; for we know that the Spirit is sent to convince the world; and we do not fear but some of you who are counting us all enemy, because we tell you the truth, may even this day, in the midst of all your hatred and cold indifference, be convinced of sin by the Spirit, and made to cry out: "Sirs, what must I do to be saved?"

I. The first work of the Spirit is to convince of sin.

1. Who it is that convinces of sin: "He shall convince the world of sin, because they believe not in me." It is curious to remark, that wherever the Holy Ghost is spoken of in the Bible, he is spoken of in terms of gentleness and love. We often read of the wrath of God the Father, "The wrath of God is revealed from heaven against all ungodliness and unrighteousness of men."

And we often read of the wrath of God the Son: "Kiss the Son, lest he be angry, and ye perish from the way" or, "Revealed from heaven taking vengeance." But we nowhere read of the wrath of God the Holy Ghost. He is compared to a dove, the gentlest of all creatures. He is warm and gentle as the breath: " Jesus breathed on them, and said, Receive ye the Holy Ghost." He is gentle as the falling dew: "I will be as the dew unto Israel." He is soft and gentle as oil; for he is called "The oil of gladness." The fine oil wherewith the high priest was anointed was a type of the Spirit. He is gentle and refreshing as the springing well: "The water that I shall give him shall be in him a well of water springing up unto everlasting life." He is called "The Spirit of grace and of supplications." He is nowhere called the Spirit of wrath. He is called the "Holy Ghost, which is the Comforter." Nowhere is he called the Avenger. We are told that he groans within the heart of a believer, "helping his infirmities;" so that he greatly helps the believer in prayer. We are told also of the love of the Spirit – nowhere of the wrath of the Spirit. We are told of his being grieved: "Grieve not the Holy Spirit;" of his being resisted: "Ye do always resist the Holy Ghost;" of his being quenched: "Quench not the Spirit." But these are all marks of gentleness and love. Nowhere will you find one mark of anger or of vengeance attributed to him; and yet, brethren, when this blessed Spirit begins his work of love, mark how he begins – he convinces of sin. Even he, all-wise, almighty, all-gentle and loving, though he be, cannot persuade a poor sinful heart to embrace the Savior, without first opening up his wounds, and convincing him that he is lost.

Now, brethren, I ask of you, Should not the faithful minister of Christ just do the very same? Ah! brethren, if the Spirit, whose very breath is all gentleness and love – whom Jesus hath sent into the world to bring men to eternal life – if he begins his work in every soul that is to be saved by convincing of sin, why should you blame the minister of Christ if he be in the very same way? Why should you say that we are harsh, and cruel, and severe, when we begin to deal with your souls by convincing you of sin? Am I become your enemy, because I tell you the truth?" When the surgeon comes to cure a corrupted wound – when he tears off the vile hands had wrapped around it – when he bandages which lays open the deepest recesses of your wound, and shows you all its venom and its virulence – do you call him cruel? May not his hands be all the time the hands of gentleness and love? Or, when a house is all on fire the flames are bursting out from every window – when some courageous man ventures to alarm the sleeping inmates – bursts through the barred door – tears aside the close drawn curtains, and with eager hand shakes the sleeper – bids him awake and flee – a moment longer, and you may be lost you call him cruel? or do you say this messenger of mercy spoke too loud – too plain? Ah, no. "Skin for skin, all that a man hath will he give for his life." Why, then, brethren, will you blame the minister of Christ when he begins by convincing you of sin? Think you that the wound of sin is less venomous or deadly than a wound in the flesh? Think you the flames of hell are less hard to bear than the flames of earth? The very Spirit of love begins by convincing you of sin; and are we less the messengers of love because we begin by doing the same thing? Oh, then, do not say that we are become your enemy because we tell you the truth?

II. What is this conviction of sin? I would begin to show this by showing you what it is not.

1. It is not the mere smiting of the natural conscience. Although man be utterly fallen, yet God has left natural conscience behind in every heart, to speak for him. Some men, by continual sinning, sear even the conscience as with a hot iron, so that it becomes dead and past feeling; but most men have so much natural conscience remaining, that they cannot commit open sin without their conscience smiting them. When a man commits murder or theft, no eye may have seen him, and yet conscience makes a coward of him. He trembles and is afraid – he feels that he has sinned, and he fears that God will take vengeance. Now, brethren, that is not the conviction of sin here spoken of – that is a natural work which takes place in every heart; but conviction of sin is a supernatural work of the Spirit of God. If you have had nothing more than the ordinary smiting of conscience, then you have never been convinced of sin.

2. It is not any impression upon the imagination. Sometimes, when men have committed great sin, they have awful impressions of God's vengeance made upon their imaginations. In the nighttime they almost fancy they see the flames of hell burning beneath them; or they seem to hear doleful cries in their ears telling of coming woe; or they fancy they see the face of Jesus all clouded with anger; or they have terrible dreams, when they sleep, of coming vengeance. Now, this is not the conviction of sin which the Spirit gives. This is altogether a natural work upon the natural faculties, and not at all a supernatural work of the Spirit. If you have had nothing more than these imaginary terrors, you have had no work of the Spirit.

3. It is not a mere head knowledge of what the Bible says against sin. Many unconverted men read their Bibles, and have a clear knowledge that their case is laid down there. They are sensible men. They know very well that they are in sin, and they know just as well that the wages of sin is death. One man lives a swearer, and he reads the words, and understands them perfectly: "Swear not at all" – "The Lord will not hold him guiltless that taketh his name in vain." Another man lives in the lusts of the flesh, and he reads the Bible, and understands these words perfectly: "No unclean person hath any inheritance in the kingdom of Christ and of God." Another man lives in habitual forgetfulness of God – never thinks of God from sunrise to sunset, and yet he reads: "The wicked shall be turned into hell, and all the people that forget God." Now, in this way most

unconverted men have a head knowledge of their sin, and of the wages of sin; yet, brethren, this is far from conviction of sin. This is a mere natural work in the head. Conviction of sin is a work upon the heart. If you have had nothing more than this head knowledge that you are sinners, then you have never been convinced of sin.

4. Conviction of sin is not to feel the loathsomeness of sin. This is what a child of God feels. A child of God has seen the beauty and excellency of God, and therefore sin is loathsome in his eyes. But no unconverted person has seen the beauty and excellency of God; therefore, even the Spirit cannot make him feel the loathsomeness of sin. Just as when you leave a room that is brilliantly lighted, and go out into the darkness of the open air, the night looks very dark; so when a child of God has been within the veil – in the presence of his reconciled God – in full view of the Father of lights, dwelling in light inaccessible and full of glory – then, when he turns his eye inwards upon his own sinful bosom, sin appears very dark, very vile, and very loathsome. But an unconverted soul never has been in the presence of the reconciled God; and therefore sin cannot appear dark and loathsome in his eyes. Just as when you have tasted something very sweet and pleasant, when you come to taste other things, they appear very insipid and disagreeable; so when a child of God has tasted and seen that God is gracious, the taste of sin in his own heart becomes very nauseous and loathsome to him. But an unconverted soul never tasted the sweetness of God's love; he cannot, therefore, feel the vileness and loathsomeness of sin. This, then, is not the conviction of sin here spoken of.

What, then, is this conviction of sin? Ans. It is a just sense of the dreadfulness of sin. It is not a mere knowledge that we have many sins, and that God's anger is revealed against them all; but it is a heart-feeling that we are under sin. Again: it is not a feeling of the loathsomeness of sin – that is felt only by the children of God; but it is a feeling of the dreadfulness of sin – of the

dishonor it does to God, and of the wrath to which it exposes the soul. Oh, brethren! conviction of sin is no slight natural work upon the heart. There is a great difference between knowing a thing and having a just sense of it. There is a great difference between knowing that vinegar is sour, and actually tasting and feeling that it is sour. There is a great difference between knowing that fire will burn us, and actually feeling the pain of being burned. Just in the same way, there is all the difference in the world between knowing the dreadfulness of your sins and feeling the dreadfulness of your sins. It is all in vain that you read your Bibles and hear us preach, unless the Spirit use the words to give sense and feeling to your dead hearts. The plainest words will not awaken you as long as you are in a natural condition. If we could prove to you, with the plainness of arithmetic, that the wrath of God is abiding on you and your children, still you would sit unmoved – you would go away and forget it before you reached your own door. Ah, brethren! he that made your heart can alone impress your heart. It is the Spirit that convinceth of sin.

1. Learn the true power of the read and preached Word. It is but an instrument in the hand of God. it has no power of itself, except to produce natural impressions. It is a hammer – but God must break your hearts with it. It is a fire – but God must kindle up your bosoms with it. Without him we may give you a knowledge of the dreadfulness of your condition, but he only can give you a just sense and feeling of the dreadfulness of your condition. The most powerful sermon in the world can make nothing more than a natural impression; but when God works through it, the feeblest word makes a supernatural impression. Many a poor sermon has been the means by which God hath converted a soul. Children of God, O that you would pray night and day for the lifting up of the arm of God!

2. Learn that conversion is not in your own power. It is the Spirit alone who convinces of sin, and he is a free agent. He is a

sovereign Spirit, and has nowhere promised to work at the bidding of unconverted men. He hath many on whom he will have mercy; and whom he will he hardeneth. Perhaps you think you may take your fill of sin just now, and then come and repent, and be saved; but remember the Spirit is not at your bidding. He is not your servant. Many hope to be converted on their death-bed; and they come to their death-bed, and yet are not converted. If the Spirit be working with you now, do not grieve him – do not resist him do not quench him; for he may never come back to you again.

III. I come to the argument which the Spirit uses. There are two arguments by which the Spirit usually gives men a sense of the dreadfulness of sin.

1. *The Law*: "The law is our schoolmaster to bring us to Christ – "Now we know that what things soever the law saith, it saith to them that are under the law, that every mouth may be stopped, and all the world become guilty before God." The sinner reads the law of the great God who made heaven and earth. The Spirit of God arouses his conscience to see that the law condemns every part of his life. The law bids him love God. His heart tells him he never loved God – never had a thought of regard toward God. The Spirit convinces him that God is a jealous God – that his honor is concerned to uphold the law, and destroy the sinner. The Spirit convinces him that God is a just God – that he can by no means clear the guilty. The Spirit convinces him that he is a true God that he must fulfil all his threatenings: "Have I said it, and shall I not do it?" The sinner's mouth is stopped, and he stands guilty before God.

2. The second argument is *the Gospel*: "Because they believe not on Jesus." This is the strongest of all arguments, and therefore is chosen by Christ here. The sinner reads in the Word that "he that believeth on the Son hath everlasting life;" and now the Spirit convinces him that he never believed on the Son of God indeed,

he does not know what it means. For the first time the conviction comes upon his heart: "He that believeth not the Son, shall not see life; but the wrath of God abideth on him." The more glorious and divine that Savior is, the more is the Christless soul convinced that he is lost; for he feels that he is out of that Savior. He sees plainly that Christ is an almighty ark riding over the deluge of God's wrath – he sees how safe and happy the little company are that are gathered within; but this just makes him gnash his teeth in agony, for he is not within the ark, and the waves and billows are coming over him. He hears that Christ hath been stretching out the hands all the day to the chief of sinners, not willing that any should perish; but then he never cast himself into these arms, and now he feels that Christ may be laughing at His calamity, and mocking when his fear cometh. O yes, my friends! how often on the death-bed, when the natural fears of conscience are aided by the Spirit of God – how often, when we speak of Christ – his love – his atoning blood – the refuge to be found in him – how safe and happy all are that are in him – how often does the dying sinner turn it all away with the awful question: But am I in Christ? The more we tell of the Savior, the more is their agony increased; for they feel that is the Savior they have refused. Ah! what a meaning does that give to these words: "The Spirit convinceth of sin, because they believe not on me."

1. Now, my friends, there are many of you who know that you never believed on Jesus, and yet you are quite unmoved. You sit without any emotion – you eat your meals with appetite, and doubtless sleep sound at night. Do you wish to know the reason? You have never been convinced of sin. The Spirit hath never begun his work in your heart. Oh! if the Spirit of Jesus would come on your hearts like a mighty rushing wind, what a dreadful thought it would be to you this night, that you are lying out of Christ! You would lose your appetite for this world's food – you would not be able to rest in your bed – you would

not dare to live on in your sins. All your past sins would rise behind you like apparitions of evil. Wherever you went you would meet the word: "Without Christ, without hope, and without God in the world;" and if your worldly friends should try to hush your fears, and tell you of your decencies, and that you were not so bad as your neighbors, and that many might fear if you feared, ah! how you would thrust them away, and stop your ears, and cry: There is a city of refuge, to which I have never fled; therefore there must be a blood avenger. There is an ark; therefore there must be a coming deluge. There is a Christ; therefore there must be a hell for the Christless.

2. Some of you may be under conviction of sin – you feel the dreadfulness of being out of Christ, and you are very miserable. Now, (1) Be thankful for this work of the Spirit: "Flesh and blood hath not revealed it unto thee, but my Father." God hath brought you into the wilderness just that he might allure you, and speak to your heart about Christ. This is the way he begins the work in every soul he saves. Nobody ever came to Christ but they were fast convinced of sin. All that are now in heaven began this way. Be thankful you are not dead like those around you.

(2) Do not lose these convictions. Remember they are easily lost. Involve yourself over head and ears in business, and work even on the Sabbath – day, and you will soon drive all away. Indulge a little in sensual pleasure – take a little diversion with companions, and you will soon be as happy and careless as they. If you love your soul, flee these things – do not stay – flee away from them. Read the books that keep up your anxiety – wait on the ministers that keep up that anxiety. Above all, Cry to the Spirit, who alone was the author of it, that he would keep it up. Cry night and day that he may never let you rest out of Christ. Oh I would you sleep over hell?

(3) Do not rest in these convictions. You are not saved yet. Many have come thus far and perished after all – many have been convinced, not converted – many lose their convictions, and wallow in sin again. "Remember Lot's wife." You are never safe till you are within the fold. Christ is the door. "Strive to enter in at the strait gate; for many shall seek to enter in and shall not be able."
Robert Murray M'Cheyne

Sin, Dealing with

When you attack the roots of sin, fix your thought more on the God you desire than on the sin you abhor.
Walter Hilton

Sin is not a monster to be mused on, but an impotence to be got rid of.
Martin Luther

Sin, Deceitfulness of

There are three false notions whereby the deceitfulness of sin deludes the souls of men:

1. That it is one sin alone wherein alone they would be indulged. Let them be spared in this one thing, and in all others they will be exact enough … . One sin willingly lived in is as able to destroy a man's soul as a thousand.

2. They judge that although they cannot shake off their sin, yet they will continue still to love God and abound in the duties of His worship … . Where God is not loved above all, He is not loved at all.

3. They determine that at such or such a season or time, after such satisfaction given unto their lusts or pleasures, they will utterly give over, so as that iniquity shall not be their ruin… . He that will not now give over, say what he will and pretend what he will, never intends to give over, nor is it probable, in an ordinary way, that ever he will do so.
John Owen

Sin, Defeating

Every method put to use to mortify sin which is not by the Holy Spirit is doomed to failure. Every system which attempts to deal with sin without Christ and the Holy Spirit is legalistic and miserable.
John Owen

You are not able to subdue the least sin apart from Christ. But, by the help of the Holy Spirit, there is nothing that can master you.
C.H. Spurgeon

Sin, Definition of

Sin is believing the lie that you are self-created, self-dependent, and self-sustained.
Augustine of Hippo

Sin is essentially a departure from God.
Martin Luther

I see and approve the better things; I follow the worse.
Ovid

Sin is to live according to one's own will and cast aside the will of God.
Sundar Singh

Sin, Deliverance from

We have sinned, fearfully sinned, and that we may be delivered from it and its consequences, two things are needed – two and not one. The two things are repentance and faith.
John Dickie

Sin, Dominion of

We will never cease to be plagued with sin; but we will never again be brought under the dominion of sin.
Author unknown

Sin, Effects of

The gods will punish the man whose heart is full of sin.
Euripides

As long as we meddle with any kind of sin we shall never clearly see the blessed face of our Lord.
Julian of Norwich

Commit a sin twice and it will not seem a crime.
Rabbinical saying

Sin, Harboring

I can offer no worship wholly pleasing to God if I know that I am harboring elements in my life that are displeasing to Him. I cannot truly and joyfully worship God on Sunday and not worship Him on Monday.
A.W. Tozer

Sin, *Hatred of*

Richard Baxter
Direct. I
Labor to know God, and to be affected with his attributes, and always to live as in his sight. – No man can know sin perfectly, because no man can know God perfectly. You can no further know what sin is than you know what God is, whom you sin against; for the formal malignity of sin is relative, as it is against the will and attributes of God. The godly have some knowledge of the malignity of sin, because they have some knowledge of God that is wronged by it. The wicked have no practical, prevalent knowledge of the malignity of sin, because they have no such knowledge of God. They that fear God will fear sinning; they that in their hearts are bold irreverently with God, will, in heart and life, be bold with sin: the atheist, who thinks there is no God thinks there is no sin against him. Nothing in world will tell us so plainly and powerfully of the evil of sin, as the knowledge of the greatness, wisdom goodness, holiness, authority, justice, truth, &c. of God. The sense of his presence, therefore, will revive our sense of sin's malignity.
Direct. II
Consider well of the office, the bloodshed, and the holy life of Christ. – His office is to expiate sin, and to destroy it. His blood was shed for it: his life condemned it. Love Christ, and you will hate that which caused his death. Love him, and you will love to be made like him, and hate that which is so contrary to Christ. These two great lights will show the odiousness of darkness.
Direct. III
Think well both how holy the office and work of the Holy Ghost is, and how great a

mercy it is to us. – Shall God himself, the heavenly light, come down into a sinful heart, to illuminate and purify it? And yet shall I keep my darkness and defilement, in opposition to such wonderful mercy? Though all sin against the Holy Ghost be not the unpardonable blasphemy, yet all is aggravated hereby.

Direct. IV

Know and consider the wonderful love and mercy of God, and think what he has done for you; and you will hate sin, and be ashamed of it. It is an aggravation which makes sin odious even to common reason and ingenuity, that we should offend a God of infinite goodness, who has filled up our lives with mercy. It will grieve you if you have wronged an extraordinary friend: his love and kindness will come into your thoughts, and make you angry with your own unkindness. Here look over the catalogue of God's mercies to you, for soul and body. And here observe that Satan, in hiding the love of God from you, and tempting you under the pretense of humility to deny his greatest, special mercy, seeks to destroy your repentance and humiliation, also, by hiding the greatest aggravation of your sin.

Direct. V

Think what the soul of man is made for, and should be used to, even to love, obey, and glorify our Maker; and then you will see what sin is, which disables and perverts it. – How excellent, and high, and holy a work are we created for and called to! And should we defile the temple of God? And serve the devil in filthiness and folly, when we should receive, and serve, and magnify our Creator?

Direct. VI

Think well what pure and sweet delights a holy soul may enjoy from God, in his holy service; and then you will see what sin is, which robs him of these delights, and prefers fleshly lusts before them. – O how happily might we perform every duty, and how fruitfully might we serve our Lord, and what delight should we find in his love and acceptation, and the foresight of everlasting blessedness, if it were not for

sin; which brings down the soul from the doors of heaven, to wallow with swine in a beloved dunghill!

Direct. VII

Bethink you what a life it is which you must live for ever, if you live in heaven; and what a life the holy ones there now live; and then think whether sin, which is so contrary to it, be not a vile and hateful thing. – Either you would live in heaven, or not. If not, you are not those I speak to. If you would, you know that there is no sinning; no worldly mind, no pride, no passion, no fleshly lust or pleasures there. Oh, did you but see and hear one hour, how those blessed spirits are taken up in loving and magnifying the glorious God in purity and holiness, and how far they are from sin, it would make you loathe sin ever after, and look on sinners as on men in bedlam wallowing naked in their dung. Especially, to think that you hope yourselves to live for ever like those holy spirits; and therefore sin does ill beseem you.

Direct. VIII

Look but to the state and torment of the damned, and think well of the difference betwixt angels and devils, and you may know what sin is. – Angels are pure; devils are polluted: holiness and sin do make the difference. Sin dwells in hell, and holiness in heaven. Remember that every temptation is from the devil, to make you like himself; as every holy motion is from Christ, to make you like himself. Remember when you sin, that you are learning and imitating of the devil, and are so far like him, John 8:44. And the end of all is, that you may feel his pains. If hell – fire be not good, then sin is not good.

Direct. IX

Look always on sin as one that is ready to die, and consider how all men judge of it at the last. – What do men in heaven say of it? And what do men in hell say of it? And what do men at death say of it? And what do converted souls, or awakened consciences, say of it? Is it then followed with delight and fearlessness as it is now? Is it then applauded? Will any of them speak well of it? Nay, all the world speaks evil of sin in the general now, even when they love and commit the several acts. Will you sin when you are dying?

Direct. X

Look always on sin and judgment together. – Remember that you must answer for it before God, and angels, and all the world; and you will the better know it.

Direct. XI

Look now but upon sickness, poverty, shame, despair, death, and rottenness in the grave, and it may a little help you to know what sin is. These are things within your sight or feeling; you need not faith to tell you of them. And by such effects you might have some little knowledge of the cause.

Direct. XII

Look but upon some eminent, holy persons upon earth, and upon the mad, profane, malignant world; and the difference may tell you in part what sin is. – Is there not an amiableness in a holy, blameless person, that lives in love to God and man, and in the joyful hopes of life eternal? Is not a beastly drunkard or whoremonger, and a raging swearer, and a malicious persecutor, a very deformed, loathsome creature? Is not the mad, confused, ignorant, ungodly state of the world a very pitiful sight? What then is the sin that all this consists in?

Though the principal part of the cure is in turning the will to the hatred of sin, and is done by this discovery of its malignity; yet I shall add a few more directions for the executive part, supposing that what is said already has had its effect.

Direct. I

When you have found out your disease and danger, give up yourselves to Christ as the Savior and Physician of souls, and to the Holy Ghost as your Sanctifier, remembering that he is sufficient and willing to do the work which he has undertaken. – It is not you that are to be saviors and sanctifiers of yourselves (unless as you work under Christ). But he that has undertaken it, takes it for his glory to perform it.

Direct. II

Yet must you be willing and obedient in applying the remedies prescribed you by Christ, and observing his directions in order to your cure. And you must not be tender, and coy, and fine, and say his is too bitter, and that is too sharp; but trust his love, and skill, and care, and take it as he prescribes it, or gives it you, without any more ado. Say not, It is grievous, and I cannot take it: for he commands you nothing but what is safe, and wholesome, and necessary, and if you cannot take it, must try whether you can bear your sickness, and death, and the fire of hell! Are humiliation, confession, restitution, mortification, and holy diligence worse than hell?

Direct. III

See that you take not part with sin, and wrangle not, or strive not against your Physician, or any that would do you good. – Excusing sin, and heading for and extenuating it, and striving against the Spirit and conscience, and wrangling against ministers and godly friends, and hating reproof, are not the means to be cured and sanctified.

Direct. IV

See that malignity in every one of your particular sins, which you can see and say is in sin in general. – It is a gross deceit of yourselves, if you will speak a great deal of the evil of sin, and see none of this malignity in your pride, and your worldliness, and your passion and peevishness, and our malice and uncharitableness, and your lying, backbiting, slandering, or sinning against conscience for worldly commodity or safety. What self-contradiction is it for a man in prayer to aggravate sin, and when he is reproved for it, to justify or excuse it! This is like him that will speak against treason, and the enemies of the king, but because the traitors are his friends and kindred, will protect or hide them, and take their parts.

Direct. V

Keep as far as you can from those temptations which feed and strengthen the, sins which you would overcome. – Lay siege to your sins, and starve them out, by keeping away the food and fuel which is their maintenance and life.

Direct. VI

Live in the exercise of those graces and duties which are contrary to the sins which you are most in danger of. – For grace and duty are contrary to sin, and kill it, and cure us of it, as the fire cures us of cold, or health of sickness.

Direct. VII

Hearken not to weakening unbelief and distrust, and cast not away the comforts of God, which are your cordials and strength. – It is not a frightful, dejected, despairing frame of mind, that is fittest to resist sin; but it is the encouraging sense of the love of God, and thankful sense of grace received (with a cautious fear).

Direct. VIII

Be always suspicious of carnal self – love, and watch against it. – For that is the burrow or fortress of sin, and the common patron of it; ready to draw you to it, and ready to justify it. We are very prone to be partial in our own cause; as the case of Judah with Tamar, and David when Nathan reproved him in a parable, show. our own passions, our own pride, our own censures, or backbitings, or injurious dealings, our own neglects of duty, seem small, excusable, if not justifiable things to us; whereas we could easily see the faultiness of all these in another, especially in an enemy: when yet we should be best acquainted with ourselves, and we should most love ourselves, and therefore hate our own sins most.

Direct. IX

Bestow your first and chiefest labor to kill sin at the root; to cleanse the heart, which is the fountain; for out of the heart come the evils of the life. – Know which are the master-roots; and bend your greatest care and industry to mortify those: and they are especially these that follow;

1. Ignorance.
2. Unbelief.
3. Inconsiderateness.
4. Selfishness and pride.
5. Fleshliness, in pleasing a brutish appetite, lust, or fantasy.

6. Senseless hard – heartedness and sleepiness in sin.

Direct. X

Account the world and all its pleasures, wealth, and honors, no better than indeed they are, and then Satan will find no bait to catch you. Esteem all as dung with Paul, Phil. 3:8; and no man will sin and sell his soul, for that which he accounts but as dung.

Direct. XI

Keep up above in a heavenly conversation, and then your souls will be always in the light, and as in the sight of God, and taken up with those businesses and delights which put them out of relish with the baits of sin.

Direct. XII

Let christian watchfulness be your daily work; and cherish a preserving, though not a distracting and discouraging fear.

Direct. XIII

Take heed of the first approaches and beginnings of sin. Oh how great a matter does a little of this fire kindle! And if you fall, rise quickly by sound repentance, whatever it may cost you.

Direct. XIV

Make God's word your only rule and labor diligently to understand it.

Direct. XV

And in doubtful cases, do not easily depart from the unanimous judgment of the generality of the most wise and godly of all ages.

Direct. XVI

In doubtful cases be not passionate or rash, but proceed deliberately, and prove things well, before you fasten on them.

Direct. XVII

Be acquainted with your bodily temperature, and what sin it most inclines you to, and what sin also your calling or living situation leave you most open to, that there your watch may be the stricter.

Direct. XVIII

Keep in a life of holy order, such as God has appointed you to walk in. For there is no preservation for stragglers that keep not rank and file, but forsake the order which God commands them. – And this order lies principally in these points:

1. That you keep in union with the universal church. Separate not from Christ's body upon any pretense whatever. With the church as regenerate, hold spiritual communion, in faith, love, and holiness with the church as congregate and visible, hold outward communion, in profession and worship.

2. If you are not teachers, live under your particular, faithful pastors, as obedient disciples of Christ.

3. Let the most godly, if possible, be your familiars.

4. Be laborious in an outward calling.

Direct. XIX

Turn all God's providences, whether of prosperity or adversity, against your sins. – If he gives you health and wealth, remember he thereby obliges you to obedience, and calls for special service from you. If he afflict you, remember that it is sin that he is offended at, and searches after; and therefore take it as his medicine, and see that you hinder not, but help on its work, that it may purge away your sin.

Direct. XX

Wait patiently on Christ till he has finished the cure, which will not be till this trying life be finished. – Persevere in attendance on his Spirit and means; for he will come in season, and will not tarry. "Then shall we know, if we follow on to know the Lord: his going forth is prepared as the morning, and he shall come unto us as the rain: as the latter and former rain upon the earth," Hos. 6:3. Though you have oft said, "There is no healing," Jer. 14:19; "He will heal your backslidings, and love you freely," Hos. 14:4. "Unto you that fear his name, shall the Sun of righteousness arise, with healing in his wings," Mal. 4:2: " and blessed are all they that wait for him," Isa. 30:18.

Thus I have given such directions as may help for humiliation under sin, or hatred of it, and deliverance from it.

Richard Baxter

Sin, Hatred of

The more a Christian hates sin, the more he desires to hate it.
Jonathan Edwards

A man may know his hatred of evil to be true, first, if it is universal- he that hates sin truly, hates all sin.
Secondly, true hatred of sin is fixed – there is no appeasing it but by abolishing the thing hated.
Thirdly, true hatred of sin is a more rooted affection than anger – anger may be appeased, but hatred of sin remains and sets itself against the whole kind.
Fourthly, if our hatred of sin is true, we hate all evil, in ourselves foremost, and secondarily in others.
Fifthly, he that hates sin truly, hates the greatest sin in the greatest measure; he hates all evil in a just proportion.
Sixthly, our hatred to sin is right if we can endure admonition and reproof for sin, and not be enraged – therefore, those that swell against reproof do not appear to hate sin.
Richard Sibbes

We cannot bear sin – when it is near us, we feel like a wretch chained to a rotting carcass; we groan to be free from the hateful thing.
C.H. Spurgeon

Sin, Hiding

He who conceals his sins does not prosper, but whoever confesses and renounces them finds mercy.
The Bible, Proverbs 28:13

Sin, Indwelling

I more fear what is within me than what comes from without.
Martin Luther

When a sinner comes first to Christ, he often thinks he will now bid an eternal farewell to sin: now I shall never sin any more. He feels already at the gate of heaven. But a little breath of temptation soon discovers his heart, and he cries out, "I see another law."
Robert Murray M'Cheyne

The choicest believers, who are assuredly freed from the condemning power of sin, ought yet to make it their business all their days to mortify the indwelling power of sin.
John Owen

The best and brightest of God's saints is but a poor mixed being.
J.C. Ryle

God's Holy Spirit and man's sin cannot live together peacefully. They may both be in the same heart, but they cannot both reign there, nor can they both be quiet there; for "the sinful nature desires what is contrary to the Spirit, and the Spirit what is contrary to the sinful nature;" they cannot rest, instead there will be a perpetual warring in the soul, so that the Christian will have to cry, "What a wretched man I am! Who will rescue me from this body of death?" But in due time: the Spirit will drive out all sin, and will present us blameless before the throne of his Majesty with exceeding great joy.
C.H. Spurgeon

Sin, Seriousness of

The very animals whose smell is most offensive to us have no idea that they are offensive, and are not offensive to one another. And man, fallen man, has just no idea what a vile thing sin is in the sight of God.
J.C. Ryle

No sin is small. No grain of sand is small in the mechanism of a watch.
Jeremy Taylor

Sin, Struggle against

We know that the law is spiritual; but I am unspiritual, sold as a slave to sin. I do not understand what I do. For what I want to do I do not do, but what I hate to do. And if I do what I do not want to do, I agree that the law is good. As it is, it is no longer I myself who do it, but it is sin living in me.
The Bible, Romans 7:14-17

Sin and salvation

God is none other than the Savior of our wretchedness. So we can only know God well by knowing our iniquities... Those who have known God without knowing their wretchedness have not glorified him, but have glorified themselves.
Blaise Pascal

Sin and sins

The corruption [of original sin] is constantly called sin by Paul (Galatians 5:19) while the things which spring from it such as adultery, fornication, theft, hatred, murder and revelings, he calls sins. Sins are the fruit of sin.
John Calvin

Sin and the Bible

Sin can keep you from the Bible – or the Bible can keep you from sin.
Author unknown

Sin forsaken

Sin forsaken is one of the best evidences of sin forgiven.
J.C. Ryle

Sin-bearer

See also: Savior

Sinfulness

I am a man of unclean lips.
The Bible, Isaiah 6:5 KJV

Singing

I wept at the beauty of your hymns and canticles, and was powerfully moved at the sweet sound of your Church singing. These sounds flowed into my ears, and the truth streamed into my heart.
Augustine of Hippo

The shepherds sing, and shall I be silent?
George Herbert

God respects me when I work, but he loves me when I sing.
Rabindranath Tagore

Single

Our lives hold meaning because God loves us and because we are His. Our lives do not depend upon someone else loving us, respecting us, noticing us or pledging their eternal devotion to us.
William Backus and Marie Chapian

Within the life of the church, the paths of the single and the married should not be allowed to diverge. The shared life of the Christian community must become a context in which the differing gifts can be used for each other. There is much still to be learned about this. Are the homes of married Christians an added support for the single? Is the availability of the single Christian put at the disposal of his married friends, for "babysitting" duties and the like. And what is true of the mutual support of married and single needs to be true in a wider way of the care exercised by the married and the single for each other, so that nobody's home life becomes completely cut off from support and help.
Oliver O'Donovan

There is never a place in the Bible where it says that marriage makes you happy. It says over and over again that God makes you happy.
Dick Purnell

Single-mindedness

If the heart is devoted to the mirage of the world, to the creature instead of the Creator, the disciple is lost... However urgently Jesus may call us, His call fails to find access to our hearts. Our hearts are closed, for they have already been given to another.
Dietrich Bonhoeffer

Only the man who follows the command of Jesus single-mindedly and unresistingly let his yoke rest upon him, finds his burden easy, and under its gentle pressure receives the power to persevere in the right way.
D. Bonhoeffer

Who keeps one end in view makes all things serve.
Robert Browning

Love will be pleased with the lover if he accepts no other comfort and trusts in her alone.
Hadewijch

You can have anything you want—if you want it badly enough. You can be anything you want to be, do anything you set out to accomplish if you hold to that desire with singleness of purpose.
Abraham Lincoln

I've learned to hold everything loosely because it hurts when God pries my fingers from it.
Corrie ten Boom

Blessed are the single-hearted; for they shall enjoy much peace.
Thomas à Kempis

Sinner

Man has not become a stranger to God in his sin. His position vis-à-vis God remains what it was when God created him. To dispute this would be to deny the continuity of the human subject as a creature, sinner and redeemed sinner.
Karl Barth

He that hath slight thoughts of sin never had great thoughts of God.
John Owen

There are only two kinds of men: the righteous who believe themselves sinners, and the rest, sinners who believe themselves righteous.
Blaise Pascal

Sinners and Jesus

Jesus hates sin but loves the sinner.
Billy Graham

Sinning

While the Christian commits a sin he hates it; whereas the hypocrite loves it while he

forbears it.
William Gurnall

The indulgence of one sin opens the door to further sins. The indulgence of one sin diverts the soul from the use of those means by which all other sins should be resisted.
John Owen

That known, discovered, and revealed sins, that are against the conscience, be avoided, as most dangerous preparatives to hardness of heart.
Samuel Rutherford

Smaller sins, if not guarded against, in time will issue in the greatest.
Charles Simeon

Sinning, Result of
We feel no pain in the act of sin, but the soul after it is sad and the conscience disturbed.
Martin Luther

Sins, Besetting
If any temptation prevails against you and you fall into any sins in addition to habitual failures, immediately lament it and confess it to God; repent quickly whatever the cost. It will certainly cost you more if you continue in sin and remain unrepentant.
   Do not make light of your habitual failures, but confess them and daily strive against them, taking care not to aggravate them by unrepentance and contempt.
Richard Baxter

Sins, Secret
As dogs have bones they hide and secretly steal forth to gnaw on them, so men have sins they hide under their tongues as sweet bits.
Thomas Goodwin

Sisters
For there is no friend like a sister
In calm or stormy weather;
To cheer one on the tedious way,
To fetch one if one goes astray,

To lift one if one totters down,
To strengthen whilst one stands.
Christina Rossetti

Skepticism
Secular skepticism about the world is wholly negative, for it opens no doors and offers no comfort. Christian skepticism is a by-product of faith and hope in another order that can itself transform this one.
Harry Blamires

Skepticism has not founded empires, established principles, or changed the world's heart. The great doers of history have always been men of faith.
Edwin Hubbel Chapin

Slander
"Do not go about spreading slander ..."
The Bible, Leviticus 19:16

It is better to eat meat and drink wine and not to eat the flesh of one's brethren through slander.
Abba Hyperechius

To vilify a great man is the readiest way in which a little man can himself attain greatness.
Edgar Allan Poe

The tongue of him who utters slander, and the ear of him who listens to it, are brothers.
Portuguese proverb

If he who was holy, harmless, and undefiled, was foully slandered, who can expect to escape? If the head of the house has been called Beelzebub, how much more the members of his household!
J.C. Ryle

The slanderous tongue kills three; the slandered, the slanderer, and the person listening to the slander.
The Talmud

Slavery
Slaves are the excrement of mankind.
Cicero

Slavery was established by decree of Almighty God.
Jefferson Davis

Whenever I hear anyone arguing for slavery, I feel a strong impulse to see it tried on him personally.
Abraham Lincoln

That execrable villainy, which is the scandal of religion, of England, and of human nature.
John Wesley

Sleep
He giveth his beloved sleep.
The Bible, Psalm 127:2 KJV

The sleep of a laboring man is sweet.
The Bible, Ecclesiastes 5:12 KJV

If you find it hard to sleep, stop counting sheep and talk to the shepherd.
Author unknown

Measure the time of your sleep appropriately so that you do not waste your precious morning hours sluggishly in your bed. Let the time of your sleep be matched to your health and labor, and not to slothful pleasure.
Richard Baxter

If you can't sleep, then get up and do something instead of lying there and worrying. It's the worry that gets you, not the loss of sleep.
Dale Carnegie

Small beginnings
Young people say, What is the sense of our small effort? They cannot see that they must lay one brick at a time; we can be responsible only for the one action at the present moment. But we can beg for an increase of love in our hearts that will vitalize and transform all our individual actions, and know that God will take them and multiply them, as Jesus multiplied the loaves and fishes.
Dorothy Day

Smiling
A smile is a gently curved line that sets a lot of things straight.
Author unknown

A smile is an inexpensive way to improve your looks.
Author unknown

Of all the things we wear, a smile and good humor are most important. Without them we are not properly dressed.
Author unknown

Most smiles are started by other smiles. Smile first.
Author unknown

Smile it only takes 13 muscles, a frown takes 64.
Author unknown

There is a special kind of sunshine in a smile.
Author unknown

A smile is one of the most appealing attributes a person can have.
Brent Barlow

Before you put on a frown make absolutely sure there are no smiles available.
Jim Beggs

There is a smile of Love,
And there is a smile of Deceit,
And there is a smile of smiles
In which these two smiles meet.
William Blake

Smile, it is the key that fits the lock of everybody's heart.
Anthony J. D'Angelo

Wear a smile and have friends; wear a scowl and have wrinkles. What do we live for if not to make the world less difficult for each other?
George Eliot

The smile you send out returns to you.
Indian proverb

Let us make one point... that we meet each other with a smile, when it is difficult to smile.... Smile at each other, make time for each other in your family.
Mother Teresa

Sneer

It is as hard to do your duty when men are sneering at you as when they are shooting at you.
Woodrow Wilson

Snob

Always hold your head up but be careful to keep your nose at a friendly level.
Max L. Forman

Social action

While women weep, as they do now, I'll fight; while children go hungry, as they do now I'll fight; while men go to prison, in and out, in and out, as they do now, I'll fight; while there is a drunkard left, while there is a poor lost girl upon the streets, while there remains one dark soul without the light of God, I'll fight – I'll fight to the very end!
William Booth

It is impossible to comfort men's hearts with the love of God when their feet are perishing with cold.
William Booth

If Christians followed the teachings of a benign dead man, their lives would display an innocuous piety. But when Christians stand up for righteousness and justice, they evidence the power of the living God.
Charles Colson

It means caring for AIDS patients though many think us fools. It means respecting the rule of law though our culture is increasingly lawless. It means visiting the prisoners who offend that law though our culture would prefer to forget them. In every way that matters, Christianity is an affront to the world; it is counter cultural.
Charles Colson

None are true saints except those who have the true character of compassion and concern to relieve the poor, indignant, and afflicted.
Jonathan Edwards

God is able to make a way out of no way and transform dark yesterdays into bright tomorrows. This is our hope for becoming better men and women. This is our mandate for seeking to make a better world.
Martin Luther King, Jr.

It is our shame and disgrace today that so many Christians – I will be more specific : so many of the soundest and most orthodox Christians – go through this world in the spirit of the priest and the Levite in our Lord's parable , seeing human needs all around them, but (after a pious wish , and perhaps a prayer , that God might meet them) averting their eyes , and passing by on the other side. That is not the Christmas Spirit.
J.I. Packer

The numbers stand in long rows like tombstones, monuments to lives lost to neglect: 100 million people have no shelter whatsoever, 770 million people do not get enough food for an active working life, 500 million suffer from iron-deficiency anemia, 1.3 billion do not have safe water to drink, 800 million live in absolute poverty, 880 million adults cannot read or write, 10 million babies are born malnourished every year and 14 million children die of hunger.
Ruth Sivard

If God's generous love indwells us, we shall relate what we "have" (possessions) to what we "see" (need) and take action.
John Stott

Although it is right to campaign for social justice and to expect to improve society further, in order to make it more pleasing to God, we know that we should never perfect it.
John R. W. Stott

If we have to choose between making men Christian and making the social order more Christian, we must choose the former. But there is no such antithesis. There is no hope of establishing a more Christian social order except through the labor and sacrifice of those in whom the Spirit of Christ is active, and the first necessity for progress is more and better Christians taking full responsibility as citizens for the political, social and economic system under which they and their fellows life.
William Temple

When I was hungry, you gave me food to eat.
When I was thirsty, you gave me your cup to drink.
Whatsoever you do to the least of these of my children, that you do unto me.
Now enter the house of my Father.
When I was homeless, you opened your doors.
When I was naked, you gave me your coat.
When I was weary, you helped me find rest.
When I was anxious, you calmed my fears.
When I was little, you taught me to read.
When I was lonely, you gave me your love.
When I was in prison, you came to my cell.
When on a sick bed, you cared for my needs.
In a strange country, you made me at home.
Seeking employment, you found me a job.
Hurt in a battle, you bound up my wounds.
Searching for kindness, you held out your hand.
When I was a Negro or Chinese or White,
Mocked and insulted you carried my cross.
When I was aged, you bothered to smile.
When I was restless, you listened and cared.
You saw me covered with spittle and blood,
You knew my features, though grimy with sweat.
When I was laughed at, you stood by my side.
When I was happy, you shared in my joy.
Mother Teresa

The Gospel in its free course goes hand-in-hand with the cup of cold water.
Sherwood Eliot Wirt

Social reform
Born-again Christians were in the forefront off every major social reform in America during the 1830s. They spear-headed the abolitionist movement, the temperance movement, the peace movement, and the early feminist movement.
Charles G. Finney

It is vain to assert the dignity of human beings, if we do not try to transform them.
Jacques Maritain

To expect to reform the poor while the opulent are corrupt, is to throw odors into the stream while the springs are poisoned.
Hannah Moore

Social sin
The doctrines and miracles of our Savior have required nearly two thousand years to convert but a small part of the human race, and even among Christian nations what gross errors still exist!
Robert E. Lee

Society
See also: Morality
Am I my brother's keeper?
The Bible, Genesis 4:9

Jesus endorsed the authority of those Old Testament prophets who vehemently rebuked social injustice; and he consistently identified himself with the poor and weak, with social outcasts and those who were regarded as morally disreputable.
J.N.D. Anderson

I think it's deplorable that when our culture is sinking into the morass of humanism that we're fighting with each other rather than fighting with the world.
Greg Bahnsen

We have a real problem in this country when it comes to values. We have become the kind of societies that civilized countries used to send missionaries to.
William Bennett

The sinfulness of human nature does not mean that social reforms and improvements are impossible. It only means that there can be no perfect and absolute social order before the transfiguration of the world.
Nikolai Berdyaev

I consider the greatest dangers of the twentieth-century to be:
1. Religion without the Holy Ghost.
2. Christianity without Christ.
3. Forgiveness without regeneration.
4. Morality without God.
5. Heaven without hell.
General William Booth

The world is made of people who never quite get into the first team and who just miss the prizes at the flower show.
Jacob Bronowski

The 7 Modern Sins:
Politics without principles,
Pleasures without conscience,
Wealth without work,
Knowledge without character,
Industry without morality,
Science without humanity,
Worship without sacrifice.
Canon Frederic Donaldson

A man of a right spirit is not a man of narrow and private views, but is greatly interested and concerned for the good of the community to which he belongs, and particularly of the city or village in which he resides, and for the true welfare of the society of which he is a member.
Jonathan Edwards

The Christian should participate in social and political efforts in order to have an influence in the work, not with the hope of making a paradise (of the earth), but simply to make it more tolerable – not to diminish the opposition between this world and the kingdom of God, but simply to modify the opposition between the disorder of this world and the order of preservation that God wants it to have – not to bring in the kingdom of God, but so that the gospel might be proclaimed in order that all men might truly hear the good news.
Jacques Ellul

Great men are they who see that spiritual is stronger than any material force, that thoughts rule the world.
Ralph Waldo Emerson

All evangelicals [should] stand openly and firmly for racial equality, human freedom, and all forms of social justice throughout the world.
Carl F.H. Henry

The pillars of truth and the pillars of freedom–they are the pillars of society.
Henrik Ibsen

If a free society cannot help the many who are poor, it cannot save the few who are rich.
John F. Kennedy

There is a spirit and a need and a man at the beginning of every great human advance. Each of these must be right for that particular moment of history, or nothing happens.
Coretta Scott King

There will be no true freedom without virtue, no true science without religion, no true industry without the fear of God and love to your fellow citizens.
Charles Kingsley

It's no measure of health to be well adjusted to a profoundly sick society.
Krishnamarti

The Christian cannot be satisfied so long as any human activity is either opposed to Christianity or out of all connection to Christianity. Christianity must pervade not merely all nations, but also all of human thought. The Christian, therefore, cannot be indifferent to any branch of earnest human endeavor. It must be brought into some relation to the gospel. It must be studied either in order to be demonstrated

as false, or else in order to be made useful in advancing the kingdom of God. The kingdom must be advanced not merely extensively, but also intensively. The Church must seek to conquer not merely every man for Christ, but also the whole of man.
J. Gresham Machen

Madness is rare in individuals; but in groups, political parties, nations, and eras it's the rule.
Friedrich Nietzsche

The chief product of an automated society is a widespread and deepening sense of boredom.
Cyril Parkinson

To give up the task of reforming society is to give up one's responsibility as a free man.
Alan Paton

From God we receive both our freedom and morality. A godless society will have neither.
Drake Raft

God is the judge of all social systems.
Oscar Romero

The basic problem of the Christians in this country in the last eighty years or so, in regard to society and in regard to government, is that they have seen things in bits and pieces instead of totals.
Francis A. Schaeffer

Christians are not utopians. Although we know the transforming power of the gospel and the wholesome effects of Christian salt and light, we also know that evil is ingrained in human nature and human society.
John R. W. Stott

Personal salvation — salvation in first gear — is still the way in [to the social problems of the city of Calcutta]. It is the key to unlock the door of determinism and make possible the "salvation" of corporate organizations and institutions — salvation

in second gear — by providing those who can transcend the situation.
John V. Taylor

Christians are the trustees of a revelation who go out into the world calling men to accept and follow it. Their duty is to declare its judgment upon social facts and lay down principles which should govern the order of society.
William Temple

The Bible must be considered as the great source of all the truth by which men are to be guided in government as well as in all social transactions.
Noah Webster

Society, Change in
Renewals and revolutions begin quietly, like faith itself. They start growing from one tiny seed, the staggering thought: things don't have to be like this.
John V. Taylor

Society, Reform of
The church's influence on society is best described in terms of "reform" rather than "redemption".
John Stott

Solitude
Solitude scares me. It makes me think about love, death, and war. I need distraction from anxious, black thoughts.
Brigitte Bardot

There is no test for the soul like solitude. Do you shrink from solitude? Perhaps the cause for your neglect of the "closet" is a guilty conscience? You are afraid to enter into the solitude. You know that however cheerful you appear to be you are not really happy. You surround yourself with company lest, being alone, truth should invade your delusion.
Gordon Cove

True religion disposes persons to be much alone in solitary places for holy meditation and prayer.
Jonathan Edwards

By all means use sometimes to be alone.
George Herbert

There is no solitude except interior solitude.
Thomas Merton

It is in deep solitude and silence that I find the gentleness with which I can truly love my brother and my sister.
Thomas Merton

There are many who live in the mountains and behave as if they were in the town, and they are wasting their time. It is possible to be a solitary in one's mind while living in a crowd, and it is possible for one who is a solitary to live in the crowd of his own thoughts.
Amma Syncletica

Settle yourself in solitude and you will come upon Him in trouble.
Teresa of Avila

Our language has wisely sensed the two sides of being alone. It has created the word "loneliness" to express the pain of being alone. And it has created the word "solitude" to express the glory of being alone.
Paul Tillich

Solitude is to the mind what diet is to the body.
Vauvenargues

Son
A wise son maketh a glad father.
The Bible, Proverbs 10:1 KJV

Sorcery
Do not practice divination or sorcery.
The Bible, Leviticus 19:26

Absolutely reject all divination, fortune-telling, sacrifices to the dead, prophecies in groves or by fountains, amulets, incantations, sorcery (ie: evil spells), and all those sacrilegious practices that used to go on in your country.
Gregory III

Sorrow
See also: Depression
Bring down my gray hairs with sorrow to the grave.
The Bible, Genesis 42:38

Sorrow is better than laughter: for by the sadness of the countenance the heart is made better.
The Bible, Ecclesiastes 7:3

Sorrow looks back, worry looks around, but faith looks up.
Author unknown

Sorrow can be alleviated by good sleep, a bath and a glass of wine.
Thomas Aquinas

We are tossed on a tide that puts us to the proof, and if we could not sob our troubles in your ear, what hope should we have left to us?
Augustine of Hippo

Sorrow makes men sincere.
Henry Ward Beecher

I was stunned. I felt as if the whole world were coming to a standstill. Opposite me on the wall was a picture of Christ on the cross. I thought I could understand it as never before. She talked like a heroine, like an angel to me. I could only kneel with her and try to pray.
William Booth, describing the day his wife told him she had cancer

Sorrow makes us all children again, destroys all differences of intellect.
Ralph Waldo Emerson

As gold is purified in the furnace, so the faithful heart is purified by sorrow.
Guarini

Thy sorrows outbid thy heart, thy fears outbid thy sorrows, and thy thoughts go beyond thy fears; and yet here is the comfort of a poor soul: in all his misery and wretchedness, the mercy of Lord

outbids all these, whatsoever may, can, or shall befall thee.
Thomas Hooker

Earth hath no sorrow that heaven cannot heal.
Thomas Moore

How sweet the name of Jesus sounds
In a believer's ear:
It soothes his sorrow, heals his wounds,
And drives away his fears.
John Newton

A day of sorrow is longer than a month of joy.
Chinese Proverb

Joys are our wings, sorrows our spurs.
Jean Paul Richter

Our trusting the Lord does not mean that there are not times of tears. I think it is a mistake as Christians to act as though trusting the Lord and tears are not compatible.
Francis Schaeffer

Sorrow, Remedies for
Time is a physician that heals every grief.
Diphilus

The best remedy for grief is the counsel of a kind and honest friend.
Euripides

Sorry
Sorry is such a simple word, so why is it so hard to say?
Terri Wetterberg

Soul
For you were like sheep going astray, but now you have returned to the Shepherd and Overseer of your souls.
The Bible, 1 Peter 2:25

The soul is more honorable than the substance of the body, seeing that it is God's image and inspiration. Still, the body is its instrument and its colleague in all that is best.
Cyril of Alexandria

The soul is in itself a most lovely and perfect image of God.
John of the Cross

Many Christians write to me, but I do not believe the way they do. They are really weird sometimes. I usually ignore them. They only want to save my soul. I need to save my life.
Arlene Raven

I began to think of the soul as if it were a castle made of a single diamond or of very clear crystal, in which there are many rooms, just as in heaven there are many mansions (cf. John 14:2). Now if we think carefully over this, sisters, the soul of the righteous man is nothing but a paradise, in which, as God tells us, he takes his delight (cf. Proverbs 8:31).
Teresa of Avila

Signs from the soul come silently, as silently as the sun enters the darkened world.
Tibetan Saying

We are truly indefatigable in providing for the needs of the body, but we starve the soul.
Ellen Wood

Speaking
Keep thy tongue from evil, and thy lips from speaking guile.
The Bible, Psalm 34:13 KJV

He that hath knowledge spareth his words.
The Bible, Proverbs 17:27 KJV

But now you must rid yourselves of all such things as these: anger, rage, malice, slander, and filthy language from your lips.
The Bible, Colossians 3:8

Speaking much is a sign of vanity.
Author unknown

It's when the fish opens his mouth that he gets caught.
Author unknown

Too many of us speak twice before we think.
Author unknown

Keep your words soft and sweet. You never know when you're going to have to eat them.
Author unknown

Wisdom is knowing when to speak your mind and when to mind your speech.
Author unknown

The tongue weighs practically nothing, But so few people can hold it!
Author unknown

Having a sharp tongue can cut your own throat.
Author unknown

When ideas fail, words come in very handy.
Goethe

The broad masses of a population are more amenable to the appeal of rhetoric than to any other force.
Adolf Hitler

A sharp tongue is the only edged tool that grows keener with constant use.
Washington Irving

A sharp tongue is worse than a sharp sword.
Proverb

Speech is silver, silence is golden.
Persian proverb

People who know little are usually great talkers, while people who know much say little.
Jean Jacques Rousseau

Not only to say the right thing in the right place, but far more difficult, to leave unsaid the wrong thing at the tempting moment.
George Sala

Those who have had anything useful to say have said it far too often, and those who have had nothing to say have been no more reticent.
B.F. Skinner

A bore is a man who, when you ask him how he is, tells you.
Bert Leston Taylor

Kind words can be short and easy to speak but their echoes are truly endless
Mother Theresa

It usually takes more than three weeks to prepare a good impromptu speech.
Mark Twain

"I was saying," continued the Rocket, "I was saying – What was I saying?"
"You were talking about yourself," replied the Roman Candle.
"Of course; I knew I was discussing some interesting subject when I was so rudely interrupted."
Oscar Wilde

Spirit-filled
Spirit-filled souls are ablaze for God. They love with a love that glows. They serve with a faith that kindles. They serve with a devotion that consumes. They hate sin with fierceness that burns. They rejoice with a joy that radiates. Love is perfected in the fire of God.
Samuel Chadwick

Spirit of the age
We want quick change; cheap grace; inspirational platitudes; bumper sticker theology; easy faith. We want Christianity Lite. We want the Nice News not necessarily the Good News.
George Grant

Spiritual
Great men are they who see that spiritual is stronger than any material force.
Ralph Waldo Emerson

Spiritual battle
The devil does not sleep, nor is the flesh yet dead; therefore, you must never cease your preparation for battle, because on the right and on the left are enemies who never rest.
Thomas à Kempis

Spiritual darkness

So soon as I perceived the happiness of any state, or its beauty, or the necessity of a virtue, it seemed to me that I fell incessantly into the contrary vice: as if this perception, which though very rapid was always accompanied by love, were only given to me that I might experience its opposite. I was given an intense perception of the purity of God; and so far as my feelings went, I myself became more and more impure: for in reality this state is very purifying, but I was far from understanding this.... My imagination was in a state of appalling confusion, and gave me no rest. I could not speak of Thee, oh my God, for I became utterly stupid; nor could I even grasp what was said when I heard Thee spoken of.... I found myself hard towards God, insensible to His mercies; I could not perceive any good thing that I had done in my whole life. The good appeared to me evil; and--that which is terrible--it seemed to me that this state must last for ever.
Madame Guyon

Spiritual depression

The ultimate cause of all spiritual depression is unbelief. For if it were not for unbelief even the devil could do nothing. It is because we listen to the devil instead of listening to God that we go down before him and fall before his attacks.
D. Martyn Lloyd-Jones

If we only spent more of our time in looking at Him we should soon forget ourselves.
D. Martyn Lloyd-Jones

Spiritual exercises
See also: Holiness

Look at the lives of those men and the time they gave to Scripture reading and prayer and various other forms of self-examination and spiritual exercises. They believed in the culture and the discipline of the spiritual life and it was because they did so that God rewarded them by giving them these gracious manifestations of himself and these mighty experiences which warmed their hearts.
D. Martyn Lloyd-Jones

Spiritual food

Man doth not live by bread only.
The Bible, Deuteronomy 8:3 KJV

Spiritual gifts

What was special about the new dispensation was that, first of all, these gifts were not confined to any one group of people but extended to all – male and female, young and old. Secondly, these supernatural endowments were wonderfully diverse.
Charles Hodge

Each of us, as members of the Body of Christ, has been given at least one spiritual gift.
Bruce Kemper

Spiritual hunger

I want deliberately to encourage this mighty longing after God. The lack of it has brought us to our present low estate. The stiff and wooden quality about our religious lives is a result of our lack of holy desire.
A. W. Tozer

Spiritual life

I have planted, Apollos watered; but God gave the increase.
The Bible, 1 Corinthians 3:6

Do not lose heart, then, my brother, in pursuing your spiritual life.
Thomas à Kempis

Spiritual warfare

In heaven we shall appear, not in armor, but in robes of glory. But here these are to be worn night and day; we must walk, work, and sleep in them, or else we are not true soldiers of Christ.
William Gurnall

We must not confide in the armor of God, but in the God of this armor, because all our weapons are only "mighty through God".
William Gurnall

We must engage in spiritual warfare. We must put on the whole armor of God (Eph 6:12). We must put to death the misdeeds of the body.
John Owen

Spirituality
Man is a spiritual being, and the proper work of his mind is to interpret the world according to his higher nature.
Robert Bridges

You no more need a day off from spiritual concentration in matters of your life than your heart needs a day off from beating. As you cannot take a day off morally and remain moral, you cannot take a day off spiritually and remain spiritual.
Oswald Chambers

Spiritual delight is not enjoyment found in things that exists outside the soul.
Isaac from Syria

Spirituality needs theology. Spirituality needs understanding, and it is such understanding that theology supplies. A spirituality without theology can become superstition or fanaticism or the quest for excitement.
John Macquarrie

It is in the ordinary duties and labors of life that the Christian can and should develop his spiritual union with God.
Thomas Merton

Christian spirituality does not begin with us talking about our experience; it begins with listening to God call us, heal us, forgive us.
Eugene H. Peterson

I doubt if there is any problem – political or economic – that will not melt before the fire of a spiritual awakening.
Franklin Roosevelt

The inward area is the first place of loss of true Christian life, of true spirituality, and the outward sinful act is the result.
Francis A. Schaeffer

When we major in minors and blow insignificant trifles out of proportion, we imitate the Pharisees. When we make Dancing and Movies the test of spirituality, we are guilty of substituting a cheap morality for a genuine one. We do these things to obscure the deeper issues of righteousness. Anyone can avoid dancing or going to Movies. These require no great effort or moral courage. What is difficult is to control the tongue, to act with integrity, to show forth the fruit of the Spirit.
R.C. Sproul

The highest conceivable state of spirituality is produced by a concentration of all the powers and passions of the soul upon the person of Christ.
C.H. Spurgeon

True spirituality manifests itself in certain dominant desires.
1. First is the desire to be holy rather than happy.
2. A man may be considered spiritual when he wants to see the honor of God advanced through his life even if it means that he himself must suffer temporary dishonor or loss.
3. The spiritual man wants to carry his cross.
4. Again, a Christian is spiritual when he sees everything from God's viewpoint.
5. Another desire of the spiritual man is to die right rather than to live wrong.
6. The desire to see others advance at his expense.
7. The spiritual man habitually makes eternity-judgments instead of time-judgments.
A.W. Tozer

We are not producing saints.
A.W. Tozer

Stagnation
Stagnation in the church is the devil's delight!
C.H. Spurgeon

Starting
See also: Achievement; Faith and action; Idleness; Success

Every accomplishment starts with the decision to try.
Author unknown

Begin; to have begun makes the work half done. Half still remains; again begin this, and you will complete the task.
Ausonius

It came to me that as they lay brick on brick, so I could still lay word on word, sentence on sentence.
Thomas Carlyle
Facing the prospect of having to rewrite his entire book on the French Revolution after the only manuscript had been destroyed.

A journey of a thousand miles begins with a single step.
Confucius

It is only the first step that costs.
Madame du Deffand, on the distance St Denis is reputed to have walked carrying his head.

What you can do, or dream you can, begin it.
Boldness has genius, power and magic in it.
Only engage, and then the mind grows heated;
Begin it and the task will be completed.
Goethe

The beginning is the half of the whole.
Hesiod

The beginning is the most important part of the work.
Plato

The man who removes a mountain begins by carrying away small stones.
Chinese Proverb

He who deliberates fully before taking a step will spend his entire life on one leg.
Chinese proverb

Well begun is half done.
English proverb

If you don't place your foot on the rope, you'll never cross the chasm.
Liz Smith

The greatest amount of wasted time is the time not getting started.
Dawson Trotman

A journey of a thousand miles must begin with a single step.
Lao Tzu

Starvation
There are people in the world so hungry, that God cannot appear to them except in the form of bread.
Mahatma Gandhi

State
Remind the people to be subject to rulers and authorities, to be obedient, to be ready to do whatever is good ...
The Bible, Titus 3:1

As servants are not bound to obey their masters if they command anything which is against the laws and ordinances of kings, subjects in like manner owe no obedience to kings which will make them to violate the law of God.
Junius Brutus

The bottom line is that at a certain point there is not only the right, but the duty, to disobey the state.
Francis A. Schaeffer

When the crowd urged the fearful Pilate to execute Jesus, they said: "If you release this man, you are not Caesar's friend." That was perfectly true, for Caesar demanded all that a person had; but the belief that there were some things that belonged to God instead brought the sword to such pretensions. That is why the persecution of Christians was inevitable as long as the state was thought to be all-inclusive.
Herbert Schlossberg

Statistics
To understand God's thoughts we must

study statistics, for these are the measure of his purpose.
Florence Nightingale

There are three kinds of lies: lies, damned lies, and statistics.
Mark Twain

Stealing
Stolen waters are sweet, and bread eaten in secret is pleasant.
The Bible, Proverbs 9:17

Strength
The Lord is the stronghold of my life.
The Bible, Psalm 27:1

Stewardship
The faith Christian
S-ees
T-hat
E-very
W-eek
A
R-egular
D-onation
S-upports
H-is
I-ndividual
P-arish
Author unknown

The living church ought to be dependent on its living members.
Thomas Barnardo

All the blessings we enjoy are Divine deposits, committed to our trust on this condition, that they should be dispensed for the benefit of our neighbors.
John Calvin

Why need the church resort to unscriptural methods to raise money? Somebody neglects to pray.
C.E. Cornell

The tithe is simply in not a sufficiently radical concept to embody the carefree unconcern for possessions that marks life in the kingdom of God.
Richard J. Foster

We deem it a sacred responsibility and genuine opportunity to be faithful stewards of all God has entrusted to us: our time, our talents, and our financial resources. We view all of life as a sacred trust to be used wisely.
Moravian Covenant for Christian living

Stillness
To the quiet mind all things are possible.
Meister Eckhart

The very best and highest attainment in this life is to remain still and let God act and speak in you.
Meister Eckhart

Be still and cool in thy own mind and spirit.
George Fox

This spiritual prayer is more interior than the tongue, more deeply interiorized than anything on the lips, more interiorized than any words or vocal song. When someone prays this kind of prayer he has sunk deeper than all speech, and he stands where spiritual beings and angels are to be found; like them, he utters "holy" without any words.
John the Solitary

Stillness has to do with seeing … the opening our eyes to another dimension, to the mystery of God that lies all about us.
M. Mayne

Stoicism
Begin with a cup or a household utensil; if it breaks, say, "I don't care." Go on to a horse or pet dog; if anything happens to it, say, "I don't care." Go on to yourself, and if you are hurt or inured in any way, say, "I don't care." If you go on long enough, and if you try hard enough, you will come to a stage when you can watch your nearest and dearest suffer and die, and say, "I don't care."
Epictetus

The Stoics make of the heart a desert, and
called it peace.
T.R. Glover

Strategy
Beware of small expenses; small leaks can
sink a big ship.
Benjamin Franklin

Perception is strong and sight weak. In
strategy it is important to see distant things
as if they were close and to take a distanced
view of close things.
Miyamoto Musashi

One who sets the entire army in motion to
chase an advantage will not attain it.
Sun Tzu

Strength
His leaf also shall not wither.
The Bible, Psalm 1:3 KJV

They go from strength to strength.
The Bible, Psalm 84:7

A wise man is strong; yea, a man of
knowledge increaseth strength.
The Bible, Proverbs 24:5 KJV

Strength is made perfect in weakness.
The Bible, 2 Corinthians 12:9 KJV

I can do everything through him who gives
me strength.
The Bible, Philippians 4:13

It is not armor as armor, but as armor of
God, that makes the soul impregnable.
William Gurnall

When we have, through Christ, obtained
mercy for our persons, we need not fear
but that we shall have suitable and
seasonable help for our duties.
John Owen

The way to grow strong in Christ is to
become weak in yourself.
C.H. Spurgeon

Strength, Inner
I love the confidence that makeup gives me.
Tyra Banks

Strength and love
They shall be strong and capable of any
task that will win them the love of love, to
help the sick or the healthy, the blind, the
crippled or the wounded.
Hadewijch

Struggle
Never forget that only dead fish swim with
the stream
Malcolm Muggeridge

Whoever fights monsters should see to it that
in the process he does not become a monster.
Nietzsche, Friedrich

Struggle, Spiritual
For the good that I would I do not; but the
evil which I would not, that I do.
The Bible, Romans 8:19 KJV

Stubbornness
Stubbornness should have been my middle
name.
Martin Luther

Study
See also: Books; Knowledge; Learning
Of making many books there is no end;
and much study is a weariness of the flesh.
The Bible, Ecclesiastes 12:12 KJV

Some books are to be tasted, others to be
swallowed, and some few to be chewed and
digested.
Francis Bacon

If I knew that the Lord was coming back in
three years time, I would spend two years
studying, and only one year in preaching.
Donald Barnhouse

All the remaining time of my life [i.e., after
leaving Wearmouth] I spent in that,
monastery [of Jarrow], wholly applying
myself to the study of Scripture, and amidst
observance of regular discipline and the daily

care of singing in the church. I always took delight in learning, teaching and writing.
Bede

It is important that students bring a certain ragamuffin, barefoot, irreverence to their studies; they are not here to worship what is known, but to question it.
J. Bronowski

The delight of opening a new pursuit, or a new course of reading, imparts the vivacity and novelty of youth even to old age.
Benjamin Disraeli

One of my great regrets is that I have not studied enough. I wish I had studied more and preached less.
Billy Graham

Let the root of thy study, and the mirror of thy life be primarily the gospel, for therein is the life of Christ portrayed.
Gerrit de Groote

You are the same today as you will be five years from now except for two things ... the people you meet and the books you read.
Charles E. Jones

Study is the bane of childhood, the oil of youth, the indulgence of adulthood, and a restorative in old age.
Walter Savage Landor

For the attainment of divine knowledge we are directed to combine a dependence on God's Spirit with our own researches. Let us, then, not presume to separate what God has thus united.
Charles Simeon

Employ your time in improving yourself by other men's writings so that you shall come easily by what others have labored hard for.
Socrates

I believe, right worshipful, that you are not ignorant of what has been determined concerning me [by the Council of Brabant]; therefore I entreat your Lordship, and that by the Lord Jesus, that if I am to remain here [in Vilvoorde] during the winter, you will request the Procurer to be kind enough to send me from my goods, which he has in his possession, a warmer cap, for I suffer extremely from cold in the head, being afflicted with a perpetual catarrh, which is considerably increased in the cell.

A warmer coat also, for that which I have is very thin; also a piece of cloth to patch my leggings: my overcoat has been worn out; my shirts are also worn out. He has a woolen shirt of mine, if he will be kind enough to send it. I have also with him leggings of thicker cloth for the putting on above; he also has warmer caps for wearing at night. I wish also his permission to have a candle in the evening, for it is wearisome to sit alone in the dark.

But above all, I entreat and beseech your clemency to be urgent with the Procurer that he may kindly permit me to have my Hebrew Bible, Hebrew Grammar, and Hebrew Dictionary, that I may spend my time with that study. And in return, may you obtain your dearest wish, provided always it be consistent with the salvation of your soul. But if any other resolutions have been come to concerning me, before the conclusion of the winter, I shall be patient, abiding the will of God to the glory of the grace of my Lord Jesus Christ, whose spirit, I pray, may ever direct your heart. Amen.
W. Tindalus (William Tyndale)
Tyndale's Letter from Prison, from Vilvoorde Castle, Antwerp

Stumble

Do not cause anyone to stumble, whether Jews, Greeks or the church of God ...
The Bible, 1 Corinthians 10:32

Stumbling block

It were better for him that a millstone were hanged about his neck, and he cast into the sea.
The Bible, Luke 17:2

Submission

Owing to the false opinion of his own excellence which every person entertains, there is no one who patiently endures that others should rule over him. The Apostle cuts off, by a single word, all disputes of this kind, by demanding that all who live "under the yoke" shall submit to it willingly.
John Calvin

Our satisfaction lies in submission to the divine embrace.
Jan Van Ruysbroeck

Substitution

On the cross Jesus was guilty of nothing but God treated Jesus as if he had committed personally every sin ever committed by every person who would ever believe…though in fact he committed none of them. That's what substitution means.
John McArthur

Success

See also: Achievement; Faith and action; God's will; Idleness; Starting

For every person who climbs the ladder of success, there are a dozen waiting for the elevator.
Author unknown

We should work to become, not to acquire.
Author unknown

Success comes in cans, failure comes in can'ts.
Author unknown

Every great achievement was once considered impossible.
Author unknown

Success depends on your backbone, not your wishbone.
Author unknown.

Success is more attitude then aptitude.
Author unknown.

The two hardest things to handle in life are failure and success.
Author unknown

If at first you do succeed, try something harder.
Author unknown

The road to success runs uphill, so don't expect to break any speed records.
Author unknown

Success is never final; and failure never fatal.
Author unknown.

The man on top of the mountain did not fall there.
Author unknown

No one ever attains success by simply doing what is required of him.
Charles Kendall Adams

Eighty percent of success is showing up.
Woody Allen

The more I see of the real champions and succeeders in this world, the more I become convinced that natural aptitude and talent are not the secrets to their success. Rather it is the ability to overcome obstacles, including the obstacles we place in our own paths, that makes the difference between success and failure.
Robert L. Backman

People rarely succeed unless they have fun in what they are doing.
Dale Carnegy

The key to whatever success I have today is: Don't ask. Do.
Vikki Carr

If successful, don't crow; if defeated, don't croak.
Samuel Chadwick

Success is never final.
Winston Churchill

Size is not a measure of success. Faithfulness is the measure of success. Biblical fidelity is the measure of success.
Chuck Colson

The secret of success is constancy to purpose.
Benjamin Disraeli

Success is the child of audacity.
Benjamin Disraeli

If you don't know how to succeed, first learn how to try to succeed. Then just keep trying.
Chris Edmunds

If A equals success, then the formula is A=X+Y+Z, where X is "work," Y is "play," and Z is "keep your mouth shut."
Albert Einstein.

Try not to become a man of success but rather try to become a man of value.
Albert Einstein

Success is relative: it's what we can make of the mess we have made of things.
T.S. Eliot

Coming together is a beginning; keeping together is progress; working together is success.
Henry Ford

Success has ruined many a man.
Benjamin Franklin

We will either find a way, or make one.
Hannibal

Success is the sole earthly judge of right and wrong.
Adolf Hitler

Little minds are tamed and subdued by misfortune; but great minds rise above them.
Washington Irving

The men whom I have seen succeed best in life have always been cheerful and hopeful men, who went about their business with a smile on their faces, and took the changes and chances of this mortal life like men, facing rough and smooth alike as it came.
Charles Kingsley

Life is made up of small pleasures. Happiness is made up of those tiny successes–the big ones come too infrequently. If you don't have all of those zillions of tiny successes, the big ones don't mean anything.
Norman Lear

It is not your business to succeed, but to do right: when you have done so, the rest lies with God.
C.S. Lewis

The heights that great men reached and kept were not attained by sudden flight, but they, while their companions slept, toiled ever upward through the night.
Longfellow

The desire for success lubricates secret prostitutions in the soul.
Norman Mailer

If you achieve success, you will get applause, and if you get applause, you will hear it. My advice to you concerning applause is this: Enjoy it but never quite believe it.
Robert Montgomery

If you wish to be a success in the world, promise everything, deliver nothing.
Napoleon

I owe all my success in life to having been always a quarter of an hour beforehand.
Lord Nelson

The secret of success is to know something nobody else knows.
Aristotle Onassis

Success without honor is an unseasoned dish; it will satisfy your hunger, but it won't taste good.
Joe Paterno

Formula for success: Underpromise and overdeliver.
Tom Peters

Success tends to go not to the person who is error-free, because he also tends to be

risk-averse. Rather it goes to the person who recognizes that life is pretty much a percentage business. It isn't making mistakes that's critical; it's correcting them and getting on with the principal task.
Donald Rumsfeld, Secretary of Defense

When love and skill work together expect a masterpiece.
John Ruskin

The time of success is a time of danger to the Christian soul.
J.C. Ryle

How ready Christians are to be puffed up with success!
J.C. Ryle

The only place where success comes before work is in the dictionary.
Vidal Sassoon

In the midst of our triumphs let us cry to God for humility.
C.H. Spurgeon

Success usually comes to those who are too busy to be looking for it.
David Henry Thoreau

It is not enough to succeed. Others must fail.
Gore Vidal

If you can't excel with talent, triumph with effort.
Dave Weinbaum

Do, or do not. There is no "try".
Yoda (The Empire Strikes Back)

Suffering
See also: Adversity; Affliction; Burdens; Difficulties; Hardships; Pain; Trials
I know that my Redeemer lives, and that in the end he will stand upon the earth. And after my skin has been destroyed, yet in my flesh I will see God.
The Bible, Job 19:25,26

… we also rejoice in our sufferings, because we know that suffering produces perseverance; perseverance, character; and character, hope.
The Bible, Romans 5:3,4

Suffering like Jesus comes before reining with Jesus.
Author unknown

A religious hope does not only bear up the mind under her sufferings, but makes her rejoice in them.
Joseph Addison

Wisdom comes through suffering.
Æschylus

Sufferings are lessons.
Æsop

When I learn that your body is worn out by fierce and incessant pain that brings you almost to the point of death, the news saddens me and humanly speaking fills me with grief. However, the thought that this is precisely the way your soul is being made ripe for eternity refreshes me and I watch your growth in holiness with spiritual happiness.
Your reverence is surely well aware that afflictions and the suffering of the body burn away the rust of sin and perfect the life of the just. Holy Scripture assures us that God scourges every son whom he receives (see Hebrews 12:6); it tells us further that tribulation brings endurance, and endurance brings character, and character brings hope, and hope does not disappoint us (see Romans 5:3-4).
This teaches us beyond all doubt that we will find joy in suffering in proportion as we have lived in hope and as we have labored for the perfection of our inheritance as sons of God.
St Anselm

Suffering isn't ennobling; recovery is.
Christiaan H. Barnard

God is weak and powerless in the world, and that is precisely the way, the only way,

in which he is with us and helps us. Only the suffering God can help.
Dietrich Bonhoeffer

To endure the cross is not tragedy; it is the suffering which is the fruit of an exclusive allegiance to Jesus Christ.
Dietrich Bonhoeffer

A Christian is someone who shares the sufferings of God in the world.
D. Bonhoeffer

Knowledge by suffering entereth.
Elizabeth Barrett Browning

He has seen but half the universe who never has been shown the house of pain.
Emerson

You will not be free of suffering, but a peaceful suffering is twice as easy to bear as suffering in turmoil.
F. Fénelon

Either he will shield you from suffering or he will give you unfailing strength to bear it. Be at peace, then, and put aside all anxious thoughts.
Francis de Sales

Be persecuted, but persecute not; be crucified, but crucify not; be wronged, but wrong not; be slandered, but slander not.
Isaac from Syria

What does anyone know who doesn't know how to suffer for Christ?
John of the Cross

The purest suffering produces the purest understanding.
John of the Cross

Man is never helped in his suffering by what he thinks for himself, but only by revelation of a wisdom greater than his own. It is this which lifts him out of his distress.
C.G. Jung

Although the world is full of suffering, it is full also of the overcoming of it.
Helen Keller

Suffering is the evidence against God, the reason not to trust him. Jesus is the evidence for God, the reason to trust him.
Peter Kreeft

God, who foresaw your tribulation, has specially armed you to go through it, not without pain but without stain.
C.S. Lewis

It is only under the shadow of the cross that we can appreciate the true weight of our own cross, and accept it each day from his hand, to carry it with love, with gratitude, and with joy.
Theodore Monod

Pain nourishes courage. You can't be brave if you've only had wonderful things happen to you.
Mary Tyler Moore

Neither suffering nor ease should find us without a suitable Christian response in prayer and song. Our religion should cover all experience, finding expression in prayer or praise as the occasion may demand. Calvin puts it well when he comments that James means "that there is no time in which God does not invite us to himself."
Alec Motyer

I think if this life is the end, and there is no God to wipe away all tears from all eyes, why, I could go mad.
John Henry Newman

Pain makes man think. Thought makes man wise. Wisdom makes life endurable.
John Patrick

Suffer in order to know, and toil in order to have.
Spanish proverb

Suffering is a stern teacher but a good one.
Proverb

Suffering would be altogether intolerable if there were no God. Atheism answers that the fact of suffering proves that there is no God. But this does not reduce the world's sufferings by one hair-breadth, it only takes away hope.
F.J. Sheed

The bitter herbs of Gethsemane have often taken away the bitters of your life; the scourge of Gabbatha hath often scourged away your cares, and the groans of Calvary have put all other groans to flight.
C.H. Spurgeon

I beg you then, do not misconstrue your sufferings of body and mind – they may be tokens of mercy; they certainly are not indicators of any special wrath.
C.H. Spurgeon

Unhurt people are not much good in the world.
Enid Starkie

A clay pot sitting in the sun will always be a clay pot. It has to go through the white heat of the furnace to become porcelain.
Mildred W. Struven

Tell me how much you know of the sufferings of your fellow men and I will tell you how much you have loved them.
Helmut Thielicke

Jesus has many who love his kingdom in heaven, but few who bear his cross. He has many who desire comfort, but few who desire suffering. He finds many to share his feast, but few his fasting. All desire to rejoice with him, but few are willing to suffer for his sake. Many follow Jesus to the breaking of bread, but few to the drinking of the cup of his passion. Many admire the miracles but few follow him to the humiliation of his cross. Many love Jesus as long as no hardship touches them.
Thomas à Kempis

It is by those who have suffered that the world has been advanced.
Leo Tolstoy

Suffering is overrated.
Bill Veeck

Taking us through suffering, not out of it, is one of the primary means that the Spirit uses today in bringing us to God.
Daniel Wallace

Christ himself came down and took possession of me… I had never foreseen the possibility of that, of a real contact, person to person, here below, between a human being and God… in this sudden possession of me by Christ, neither my sense nor my imagination had any part: I only felt in the midst of my suffering the presence of a love.
Simone Weil

Gladly shall I come whenever bodily strength will allow to join my testimony with yours in Olney pulpit, that God is love. As yet I have not recovered from the fatigues of my American expedition. My shattered bark is scarce worth docking any more. But I would fain wear, not rust, out. Oh! my dear Mr. Newton, indeed and indeed I am ashamed that I have done and suffered so little for Him that hath done and suffered so much for ill and hell-deserving me.
George Whitefield, letter to John Newton

Don't look forward to the day you stop suffering, because when it comes you'll *know* you're dead.
Tennessee Williams

Suffering

Letter from John Newton
Mrs H.
Long and often I have thought of writing to you; now the time is come. May the Lord help me to send a word in season! I

know not how it may be with you, but He does and to Him I look to direct my thoughts accordingly. I suppose you are still in the school of the cross, learning the happy art of extracting real good out of seeming evil, and to grow tall by stooping. The flesh is a sad untoward dunce in this school; but grace makes the spirit willing to learn by suffering; yea, it cares not what it endures, so sin may be mortified, and a conformity to the image of Jesus be increased. Surely, when we see the most and the best of the Lord's children so often in heaviness, and when we consider how much He loves them, and what He has done and prepared for them, we may take it for granted that there is a need-be for their sufferings. For it would be easy to His power, and not a thousandth part of what His love intends to do for them should He make their whole life here, from the hour of their conversion to their death, a continued course of satisfaction and comfort, without anything to distress them from within or without. But were it so, should we not miss many advantages?

In the first place, we should not then be very conformable to our Head, nor be able to say, "As He was, so are we in this world." Methinks a believer would be ashamed to be so utterly unlike his Lord. What! the master always a man of sorrow and acquainted with grief, and the servant always happy and full of comfort! Jesus despised, reproached, neglected, opposed, and betrayed, and His people admired and caressed; He living in the want of all things, and they filled with abundance; He sweating blood for anguish, and they strangers to distress! How unsuitable would these things be! How much better to be called to the honor of experiencing a measure of His sufferings! A cup was put into His hand on our account, and His love engaged Him to drink it for us. The wrath which it contained He drank wholly Himself; but He left us a little affliction to taste, that we might pledge Him, and remember how He loved us, and how much more He endured for us than He will ever call us to endure for Him.

Again, how could we, without sufferings, manifest the nature and truth of Gospel-grace! What place should we then have for patience, submission, meekness, forbearance, and a readiness to forgive, if we had nothing to try us, either from the hand of the Lord, or from the hand of men! A Christian without trials would be like a mill without wind or water; the contrivance and design of the wheel-work within would be unnoticed and unknown, without something to put it in motion from without. Nor would our graces grow, unless they were called out to exercise; the difficulties we meet with not only prove, but strengthen, the graces of the spirit. If a person were always to sit still, without making use of legs or arms, he would probably wholly lose the power of moving his limbs at last; but by walking and working he becomes strong and active. So, in a long course of ease, the powers of the new man would certainly languish; the soul would grow soft, indolent, cowardly, and faint; and therefore the Lord appoints His children such dispensations as make them strive and struggle, and pant; they must press through a crowd, swim against a stream, endure hardships, run, wrestle, and fight; and thus their strength grows in the using.

By these things, likewise, they are made more willing to leave the present world, to which we are prone to cleave too closely in our hearts when our path is very smooth. Had Israel enjoyed their former peace and prosperity in Egypt, when Moses came to invite them to Canaan, I think they would hardly have listened to him. But the Lord suffered them to be brought into great trouble and bondage, and then the news of deliverance was more welcome, yet still they were but half willing, and they carried a love to the flesh-pots of Egypt with them into the wilderness. We are like them: though we say this world is vain and sinful, we are too fond of it; and though we hope for true happiness only in Heaven, we are often well content to stay longer here. But the Lord sends afflictions one after another to quicken our desires, and to convince us that this cannot be our rest. Sometimes if you drive a bird from one branch of a tree he will hop to another a little higher, and from thence to a third; but if you continue to disturb him, he will at last take wing, and fly quite away. Thus we, when forced from one creature-comfort, perch upon another, and so on; but the Lord mercifully follows us with trials, and will not let us rest upon any; by degrees our desires take a nobler flight, and can be satisfied with nothing short of Himself; and we say, "To depart and be with Jesus is best of all!" I trust you find the name and grace of Jesus more and more precious to you; His promises more sweet, and your hope in them more abiding; your sense of your own weakness and unworthiness daily increasing; your persuasion of his all-sufficiency, to guide, support, and comfort you, more confirmed. You owe your growth in these respects in a great measure to His blessing upon those afflictions which He has prepared for you, and sanctified to you. May you praise Him for all that is past, and trust Him for all that is to come! I am, &c.

John Newton

Suffering and miracles
Suffering for God is better than working miracles.

John of the Cross

Suffering for Christ
However, if you suffer as a Christian, do not be ashamed, but praise God that you bear that name.

The Bible, 1 Peter 4:16

Suffering with Christ
... rejoice that you participate in the sufferings of Christ ...

The Bible, 1 Peter 4:13

Suffragettes
See: Women's rights; Votes for women

Suicide
Any one who kills a human being, himself

or another, is guilty of murder.

Augustine of Hippo

It is significant that in Holy Scripture no passage can be found enjoining or permitting suicide either in order to hasten our entry into immortality or to void or avoid temporal evils.

Augustine of Hippo

The final philosophical question is the question of suicide.

Albert Camus

Sunday
See also: Sabbath
Sunday clears away the rust of the whole week.

Joseph Addison

The Lord's Day is a Christian institution for regular observance, and should be employed in exercises of worship and spiritual devotion, both public and private, resting from worldly employments and amusements, works of necessity and mercy only excepted.

James Boyce, Abstract of Principles, 1858

Sundays observe; think when the bells do chime, 'T is angels' music.

George Herbert

The due observance of Sunday as a day of rest, of worship, and of religious teaching, has a direct bearing on the moral well-being of the Christian community.

Encyclical Letter, Lambeth Conference, 1888

Let men in whose hearts are the ways of God seriously consider the use that hath been made, under the blessing of God, of the conscientious observation of the Lord's day, in the past and present ages, unto the promotion of holiness, righteousness, and religion universally, in the power of it; and if they are not under invincible prejudices, it will be very difficult for them to judge that it is a plant which our heavenly Father hath not planted.

John Owen

The Lord's Day, from morning to night, should be spent always either in private or public worship.
Samuel Rutherford

Do not let Sunday be taken from you … If your soul has no Sunday, it becomes an orphan.
Albert Schweitzer

The Lord's Day is called this, because on that day the joy of our Lord's resurrection is celebrated.
Isidore of Seville

Sunday, Keeping
We, therefore, will be careful to avoid unnecessary labor on Sunday and plan that the recreations in which we engage on that day do not interfere with our own attendance or that of others at divine worship.
Moravian Covenant for Christian living

Sunday school
A Sunday school is a prison in which children do penance for the evil conscience of their parents.
H. L. Mencken

Sundial
Give God thy heart, thy service and thy gold;
The day wears on and time is waxing old.
Inscription on a sundial, in a garden close to Gloucester Cathedral, England

Superiority
Perhaps no sin so easily besets us as a sense of self-satisfied superiority to others.
William Osler

Supernatural
Whenever we find the presence of the Holy Spirit, we will always find the supernatural.
Kathryn Kuhlman

Superstition
Superstition is the religion of the feeble minds.
Edmund Burke

Superstition is godless religion.
Joseph Hall

It always surprises me that some things are so surprising that they even surprise people that nothing surprises any more.
Erik Das

Surprise
Everything in Christ astonishes me.
Napoleon Bonaparte

Surrender
The greatness of a man's power is the measure of his surrender.
William Booth

In order to arrive at having pleasure in everything,
Desire to have pleasure in nothing.
In order to arrive at possessing everything,
Desire to possess nothing.
In order to arrive at being everything,
Desire to be nothing.
In order to arrive at knowing everything,
Desire to know nothing.
John of the Cross

There can be no personal freedom where there is not an initial personal surrender.
Howard Thurman

Swearing
Above all, my brothers, do not swear—not by heaven or by earth or by anything else. Let your "Yes" be yes, and your "No," no, or you will be condemned.
The Bible, James 5:12

Profanity is the weapon of the witless.
Author unknown

Symbols
Symbols: the translucence of the eternal through and in the temporal.
S. T. Coleridge

Sympathy
Sympathy is your pain in my heart.
Author unknown

Next to love, sympathy is the divinest
passion of the human heart.
Edmund Burke

Teach me to feel another's woe,
To hide the fault I see;
That mercy I to others show,
That mercy show to me.
Alexander Pope

Syncretism
I am a Christian and a Hindu and a
Moslem and a Jew!
Gandhi

Systematic theology
Be Bible Christians, and not system
Christians.
Charles Simeon

T

Tact

Tact is the art of making a point without making an enemy.
Author unknown

Tact is rubbing out another's mistake instead or rubbing it in.
Author unknown

Tact is the unsaid part of what you're thinking.
Author unknown

Silence is not always tact and it is tact that is golden, not silence.
Samuel Butler

Tact is the intelligence of the heart. Mention not a halter in the house of him that was hanged.
George Herbert

Tact is the ability to describe others as they see themselves.
Abraham Lincoln

Talents
See also: Ability

Teach your students to use what talents they have; the woods would be silent if no bird sang except those that sing best.
Author unknown

Use your gifts faithfully, and they shall be enlarged; practice what you know, and you shall attain to higher knowledge.
Matthew Arnold

All our talents increase in the using, and every faculty, both good and bad, strengthens by exercise.
Anne Brontë

You must know that every man cannot be excellent, yet he may be useful. An iron key may unlock the door of a golden treasure; yea, iron can do things gold cannot do!
Thomas Brooks

Your talent is God's gift to you. What you do with it is your gift back to God.
Leo Buscaglia

Those talents which God has bestowed upon us are not our own goods but the free gifts of God; and any persons who become proud of them show their ungratefulness.
John Calvin

Talent is God given; be humble.
Fame is man-given; be grateful.
Conceit is self-given; be careful.
John Wooden

Use what talents you possess: the woods would be very silent if no bird sang there except those that sang best.
Henry Van Dyke

Talking
See also: Speech

Taxes

Render therefore unto Cæsar the things which are Cæsar's.
The Bible, Matthew 22:21 KJV

We will be subject to the civil authorities as the powers ordained of God, in accordance with the admonitions of Scripture (Rom. 13:1; I Peter 2:13-14) and will in nowise evade the taxes and other obligations which are lawfully required of us (Rom. 13:7).
Moravian Covenant for Christian living

Teaching
See also: Education

For precept must be upon precept, precept upon precept; line upon line, line upon line; here a little, and there a little.
The Bible, Isaiah 28:10 KJV

Give a man a fish and he will eat for a day; teach him how to fish and he will eat forever.
Author unknown

We need to be teachers not suppliers.
Author unknown

A teacher affects eternity; he can never tell, where his influence stops.
Henry B. Adams

Those that know, do. Those that understand, teach.
Aristotle

Those who educate children well are more to be honored than parents, for these only gave life, those the art of living well.
Aristotle

There is no such whetstone, to sharpen a good wit and encourage a will to learning, as is praise.
Roger Ascham

Screw the truth into men's minds.
Richard Baxter

Our critical day is not the very day of our death, but the whole course of our life; I thank them, that pray for me when my bell tolls; but I thank them much more, that catechize me, or preach to me, or instruct me how to live.
John Donne

The art of teaching is the art of assisting discovery.
Mark Van Doren

I never teach my pupils; I only attempt to provide the conditions in which they can learn.
Albert Einstein

It is the supreme art of the teacher to awaken joy in creative expression and knowledge.
Albert Einstein

You cannot teach a man anything; you can only help him to find it within himself.
Galileo

The teacher if he is indeed wise does not bid you to enter the house of his wisdom but leads you to the threshold of your own mind.
Kahlil Gibran

A teacher who can arouse a feeling for one single action, for one single good poem, accomplishes more than he who fills our memory with rows on rows of natural objects, classified with name and form.
van Goethe

The biggest enemy to learning is the talking teacher.
John Holt

You can't teach what you don't know and you can't lead where you don't go.
Jesse Jackson

To teach is to learn twice.
Joseph Joubert

We must know how to teach God's Word aright, discerningly.
Martin Luther

I touch the future. I teach.
Christa McAuliffe

Never tell people how to do things. Tell them what to do and they will surprise you with their ingenuity.
General George S. Patton, Jr.

To instruct your neighbor is the same thing as reproving him.
Abba Poemen

It is a sin to bore a kid.
Jim Rayburn

Sound Bible exposition is an imperative must in the Church of the living God. Without it no church can be a New Testament church in any strict meaning of that term. But exposition may be carried on in such a way as to leave the hearers devoid of any true spiritual nourishment whatever. For it is not mere words that nourish the soul, but God Himself, and unless and until the hearers find God in personal experience they are not the better for having heard the truth.
A. W. Tozer

It is now common practice in most evangelical churches to offer the people, especially the young people, a maximum of entertainment and a minimum of serious instruction.
A.W. Tozer

The mediocre teacher tells. The good teacher explains. The superior teacher demonstrates. The great teacher inspires.
William A. Ward

Teaching

Catechism of the Church of Geneva
GENEVA, 2nd December, 1545.

TO THE READER.
It has ever been the practice of the Church, and one carefully attended to, to see that children should be duly instructed in the Christian religion. That this might be done more conveniently, not only were schools opened in old time, and individuals enjoined properly to teach their families, but it was a received public custom and practice, to question children in the churches on each of the heads, which should be common and well known to all Christians. To secure this being done in order, there was written out a formula, which was called a Catechism or Institute. Thereafter the devil miserably rending the Church of God, and bringing upon it fearful ruin, (of which the marks are still too visible in the greater part of the world,) overthrew this sacred policy, and left nothing behind but certain trifles, which only beget superstition, without any fruit of edification. Of this description is that confirmation, as they call it, full of gesticulations which, worse than ridiculous, are fitted only for apes, and have no foundation to rest upon. What we now bring forward, therefore, is nothing else than the use of things which from ancient times were observed by Christians, and the true worshiper of God, and which never were laid aside until the Church was wholly corrupted.

CATECHISM OF THE CHURCH OF GENEVA OF FAITH.
Master.—What is the chief end of human life?
Scholar.—To know God by whom men were created.
M.—What reason have you for saying so?
S.—Because he created us and placed us in this world to be glorified in us. And it is indeed right that our life, of which himself is the beginning, should be devoted to his glory.
M.—What is the highest good of man?
S.—The very same thing.
M.—Why do you hold that to be the highest good?
S.—Because without it our condition is worse than that of the brutes.
M.—Hence, then, we clearly see that nothing worse can happen to a man than not to live to God.
S.—It is so.
M.—What is the true and right knowledge of God?
S.—When he is so known that due honor is paid to him.
M.—What is the method of honoring him duly?
S.—To place our whole confidence in him; to study to serve him during our whole life by obeying his will; to call upon him in all our necessities, seeking salvation and every good thing that can be desired in him; lastly, to acknowledge him both with heart and lips, as the sole Author of all blessings.

M.—To consider these points in their order, and explain them more fully-What is the first head in this division of yours?

S.—To place our whole confidence in God.

M.—How shall we do so?

S.—When we know him to be Almighty and perfectly good.

M.—Is this enough?

S.—Far from it.

M.—Wherefore?

S.—Because we are unworthy that he should exert his power in helping us, and show how good he is by saving us.

M.—What more then is needful?

S.—That each of us should set it down in his mind that God loves him, and is willing to be a Father, and the author of salvation to him.

M.—But whence will this appear?

S.—From his word, in which he explains his mercy to us in Christ, and testifies of his love towards us.

M.—Then the foundation and beginning of confidence in God is to know him in Christ?

S.—Entirely so.

The Apostles' Creed

M.—I should now wish you to tell me in a few words, what the sum of this knowledge is?

S.—It is contained in the Confession of Faith, or rather Formula of Confession, which all Christians have in common. It is commonly called the Apostles' Creed, because from the beginning of the Church it was ever received among all the pious, and because it either fell from the lips of the Apostles, or was faithfully gathered out of their writings.

M.—Repeat it.

S.—I believe in God the Father Almighty, maker of heaven and earth; and in Jesus Christ, his only Son, our Lord, who was conceived by the Holy Ghost, born of the Virgin Mary, suffered under Pontius Pilate, was crucified, dead, and buried: he descended into hell; the third day he arose again from the dead; he ascended into heaven, and sitteth on the right hand of God the Father Almighty, from thence he shall come to judge the quick and the dead. I believe in the Holy Ghost; the holy Catholic Church; the communion of saints; the forgiveness of sins; the resurrection of the body; and the life everlasting. Amen.

M.—To understand each point more thoroughly, into how many parts shall we divide this confession?

S.—Into four leading ones.

M.—Mention them to me.

S.—The first relates to God the Father; the second to his Son Jesus Christ, which also embraces the whole sum of man's redemption; the third to the Holy Spirit; the fourth to the Church, and the Divine blessings conferred upon her.

God the Father

M.—Since there is no God but one, why do you here mention three, the Father, Son, and Holy Spirit?

S.—Because in the one essence of God, it behoves us to look on God the Father as the beginning and origin, and the first cause of all things; next the Son, who is his eternal Wisdom; and, lastly, the Holy Spirit, as his energy diffused indeed over all things, but still perpetually resident in himself.

M.—You mean then that there is no absurdity in holding that these three persons are in one Godhead, and God is not therefore divided?

S.—Just so.

M.—Now repeat the first part.

S.—"I believe in God the Father Almighty, maker of heaven and earth."

M.—Why do you call him Father?

S.—Primarily with reference to Christ who is his eternal Wisdom, begotten of him before all time, and being sent into this world was declared to be his Son. We infer, however, that as God is the Father of Jesus Christ, he is our Father also.

M.—In what sense do you give him the name of Almighty?

S.—Not as having a power which he does not exercise, but as having all things under his power and hand; governing the world by his Providence, determining all things by his will, ruling all creatures as seems to him good.

M.—You do not then suppose an indolent power in God, but consider it such that his hand is always engaged in working, so that nothing is done except through Him, and by his decree.

S.—It is so.

M.—Why do you add "Creator of heaven, and earth?"

S.—As he has manifested himself to us by works, (Rom. i. 20,) in these too we ought to seek him. Our mind cannot take in his essence. The world itself is, therefore, a kind of mirror in which we may view him in so far as it concerns us to know.

M.—Do you not understand by "heaven and earth" all creatures whatever that exist?

S.—Yes, verily; under these two names all are included, because they are either heavenly or earthly.

M.—But why do you call God a Creator merely, while it is much more excellent to defend and preserve creatures in their state, than to have once made them?

S.—This term does not imply that God created his works at once, and then threw off the care of them. It should rather be understood, that as the world was once made by God, so it is now preserved by him, and that the earth and all other things endure just in as far as they are sustained by his energy, and as it were his hand. Besides, seeing that he has all things under his hand, it follows, that He is the chief ruler and Lord of all. Therefore, by his being "Creator of heaven and earth," we must understand that it is he alone who by wisdom, goodness, and power, guides the whole course and order of nature: who at once sends rain and drought, hail and other storms, as well as calm, who of his kindness fertilizes the earth, and on the contrary, by withholding his hand, makes it barren: from whom come health and disease; to whose power all things are subject, and whose nod they obey.

M.—But what shall we say of wicked men and devils? Shall we say that they too are under him?

S.—Although he does not govern them by his Spirit, he however curbs them by his power as a bridle, so that they cannot even move unless in so far as he permits them. Nay, he even makes them the ministers of his will, so that unwilling and against their own intention, they are forced to execute what to him seems good.

M.—What good redounds to you from the knowledge of this fact?

S.—Very much. It would go ill with us could devils and wicked men do any thing without the will of God, and our minds could never be very tranquil while thinking we were exposed to their caprice. Then only do we rest safely when we know that they are curbed by the will of God, and as it were kept in confinement, so that they cannot do any thing unless by his permission: the more especially that God has engaged to be our guardian, and the prince of our salvation.

His Son Jesus Christ

M.—Let us now come to the second part.

S.—It is that we believe "in Jesus Christ his only Son our Lord."

M.—What does it chiefly comprehend?

S.—That the Son of God is our Savior, and it at the same time explains the method by which he has redeemed us from death, and purchased life.

M.—What is the meaning of the name Jesus which you give to him?

S.—It has the same meaning as the Greek word *Soter*. The Latins have no proper name by which its force may be well expressed. Hence the term Savior *Salvator* was commonly received. Moreover, the angel gave this appellation to the Son of God, by the order of God himself (Matt. i. 21.)

M.—Is this more than if men had given it?

S.—Certainly. For since God wills that he be called so, he must absolutely be so.

M.—What, next, is the force of the name Christ?

S.—By this epithet, his office is still better expressed-for it signifies that he was anointed by the Father to be a King, Priest, and Prophet.

M.—How do you know that?

S.—First, Because Scripture applies anointing to these three uses; secondly, Because it often attributes the three things which we have mentioned to Christ.

M.—But with what kind of oil was he anointed?

S.—Not with visible oil as was used in consecrating ancient kings, priests, and prophets, but one more excellent, namely, the grace of the Holy Spirit, which is the thing meant by that outward anointing.

M.—But what is the nature of this kingdom of his which you mention?

S.—Spiritual, contained in the word and Spirit of God, which carry with them righteousness and life.

M.—What of the priesthood?

S.—It is the office and prerogative of appearing in the presence of God to obtain grace, and of appeasing his wrath by the offering of a sacrifice which is acceptable to him.

M.—In. what sense do you call Christ a Prophet?

S.— Because on coming into the world he declared himself an ambassador to men, and an interpreter, and that for the purpose of putting an end to all revelations and prophecies by giving a full exposition of his Father's will.

M.—But do you derive any benefit from this?

S.—Nay, all these things have no end but our good. For the Father hath bestowed them on Christ that he may communicate them to us, and all of us thus receive out of his fulness.

M.—State this to me somewhat more fully.

S.— He was filled with the Holy Spirit, and loaded with a perfect abundance of all his gifts, that he may impart them to us,-that is, to each according to the measure which the Father knows to be suited to us. Thus from him, as the only fountain, we draw whatever spiritual blessings we possess.

M.—What does his kingdom bestow upon us?

S.—By means of it, obtaining liberty of conscience to live piously and holily, and, being provided with his spiritual riches, we are also armed with power sufficient to overcome the perpetual enemies of our souls-sin, the world, the devil, and the flesh.

M.—To what is the office of priest conducive?

S.—First, by means of it he is the mediator who reconciles us to the Father; and, secondly, access is given us to the Father, so that we too can come with boldness into his presence, and offer him the sacrifice of ourselves, and our all. In this way he makes us, as it were, his colleagues in the priesthood.

M.—There is still prophecy.

S.—As it is an office of teaching bestowed on the Son of God in regard to his own servants, the end is that he may enlighten them by the true knowledge of the Father, instruct them in truth, and make them household disciples of God.

M.—All that you have said then comes to this, that the name of Christ comprehends three offices which the Father hath bestowed on the Son, that he may transfuse the virtue and fruit of them into his people?

S.—It is so.

M.—Why do you call him the only Son of God, seeing that God designs to bestow this appellation upon us all?

S.—That we are the sons of God we have not from nature, but from adoption and grace only, in other words, because God puts us in that place, (John i. 1;) but the Lord Jesus who was begotten of the substance of the Father, and is of one essence with the Father, (Eph. i. 2,) is by the best title called the only Son of God, because he alone is his Son by nature, (Heb. i. 1.)

M.—You mean then, that this honor is proper to him, as being due to him by right of nature, whereas it is communicated to us by gratuitous favor, as being his members?

S.—Exactly. Hence with a view to this communication he is called the First-born among many brethren. (Rom. viii. 29.)

M.—In what sense do you understand him to be "our Lord ?"

S.—Inasmuch as He was appointed by the Father to have us under his power, to administer the kingdom of God in heaven and on earth, and to be the Head of men and angels. (Col. i. 15, 18.)

M.—What is meant by what follows?

S.—It shows the manner in which the Son was anointed by the Father to be our Savior-namely, that having assumed our nature, he performed all things necessary to our salvation as here enumerated.

M.—What mean you by the two sentences-"Conceived of the Holy Ghost, born of the Virgin Mary ?"

S.—That he was formed in the womb of the virgin, of her substance, to be the true seed of David, as had been foretold by the Prophets, and that this was effected by the miraculous and secret agency of the Spirit without human connection. (Ps. cxxxii. 11 ; Matt. i. I ; Luke i. 32.)

M.—Was it of consequence then that he should assume our nature?

S.—Very much so; because it was necessary that the disobedience committed by man against God should be expiated also in human nature. Nor could he in any other way be our Mediator to make reconciliation between God and man. (Rom. iii. 24; 1 Tim. ii. 5; Heb. iv. 15; v. 7.)

M.—You say that Christ behoved to become man, that he might, as it were, in our person accomplish the work of salvation?

S.—So I think. For we must borrow of him whatever is wanting in ourselves: and this cannot be done in any other way.

M.—But why was that effected by the Holy Spirit, and not by the common and usual form of generation?

S.—As the seed of man is entirely corrupt, it was necessary that the operation of the Holy Spirit should interfere in the generation of the Son of God, that he might not be affected by this contagion, but endued with the most perfect purity.

M.—Hence then we learn that he who sanctifies us is free from every stain, and was possessed of purity, so to speak, from the original womb, so that he was wholly sacred to God, being unpolluted by any taint of the human race?

S.—That is my understanding.

M.—How is he our Lord?

S.—He was appointed by the Father to rule us, and having obtained the empire and dominion of God both in heaven and on earth, to be recognized as the head of angels and good men. (Eph. i. 21 ; Col. i. 18.)

M.—Why do you leap at once from his birth to his death, passing over the whole history of his life?

S.—Because nothing is treated of here but what so properly belongs to our salvation, as in a manner to contain the substance of it.

M.—Why do you not say in one word simply "was dead," (died,) but also add the name of the governor under whom he suffered?

S.—That has respect not only to the credit of the statement, but also to let us know that his death was connected with condemnation.

M.—Explain this more clearly.

S.—He died to discharge the penalty due by us, and in this way exempt us from it. But as we all being sinners were obnoxious to the judgment of God, he, that he might act as our substitute, was pleased to come into presence of an earthly judge, and condemned by his mouth, that we might be acquitted before the celestial tribunal of God.

M.—But Pilate pronounces him innocent, and therefore does not condemn him as a malefactor. (Matt. xxvii. 24.)

S.—It is necessary to attend to both things. The judge bears testimony to his innocence, to prove that he suffered not for his own misdeeds but ours, and he is formally condemned by the sentence of the same judge, to make it plain that he endured the sentence which he deserved as our surety, that thus he might free us from guilt.

M.—Well answered. Were he a sinner he would not be a fit surety to pay the penalty of another's sin; and yet that his condemnation might obtain our acquittal, he behoved to be classed among transgressors?

S.—I understand so.

M.—Is there any greater importance in his having been crucified than if he had suffered any other kind of death?

S.—Very much greater, as Paul also reminds us, (Gal iii. 13,) when he says, that he hung upon a tree to take our curse upon himself and free us from it. For that kind of death was doomed to execration. (Deut. xxi. 23.)

M.—What? Is not an affront put upon the Son of God when it is said that even before God he was subjected to the curse?

S.—By no means; since by undergoing he abolished it, and yet meanwhile he ceased not to be blessed in order that he might visit us with his blessing.

M.—Go on.

S.—Since death was the punishment imposed on man because of sin, the Son of God endured it, and by enduring overcame it. But to make it more manifest that he underwent a real death, he chose to be placed in the tomb like other men.

M.—But nothing seems to be derived to us from this victory, since we still die?

S.—That is no obstacle. Nor to believers is death now any thing else than a passage to a better life.

M.—Hence it follows that death is no longer to be dreaded as if it were a fearful thing, but we should with intrepid mind follow Christ our leader, who as he did not perish in death, will not suffer us to perish?

S.—Thus should we act.

M.—It is immediately added, "he descended into hell." What does this mean?

S.—That he not only endured common death, which is the separation of the soul from the body, but also the pains of death, as Peter calls them. (Acts ii. 24.) By this expression I understand the fearful agonies by which his soul was pierced.

M.—Give me the cause and the manner of this.

S.—As in order to satisfy for sinners he came himself before the tribunal of God, it was necessary that he should suffer excruciating agony of conscience, as if he had been forsaken of God, nay as it were, had God hostile to him. He was in this agony when he exclaimed, "My God, my God, why hast thou forsaken me?" (Matt. xxvii. 46.)

M.— Was his Father then offended with him?

S.—By no means. But he exercised this severity against him in fulfilment of what had been foretold by Isaiah, that "he was smitten by the hand of God for our sins and wounded for our transgressions." (Is. liii. 4, 5.)

M.—But seeing he is God, how could he be seized with any such dread, as if he were forsaken of God?

S.—We must hold that it was in respect to the feelings of his human nature that he was reduced to this necessity: and that this might be, his divinity for a little while was concealed, that is, did not put forth its might.

M.—How, on the other hand, is it possible that Christ, who is the salvation of the world, should have been subjected to this doom?

S.—He did not endure it so as to remain under it. For though he was seized with the terrors I have mentioned, he was not overwhelmed. Rather wrestling with the power of hell he subdued and crushed it.

M.—Hence we infer that the torture of conscience which he bore differs from that which excruciates sinners "when pursued by the hands of an angry God. For what was temporary in him is perpetual in them, and what was in him only the prick of a sting, is in them a mortal sword, which, so to speak, wounds the heart.

S.—It is so. The Son of God when beset by this anguish, ceased not to hope in the Father. But sinners condemned by the justice of God, rush into despair, murmur against him, and even break forth into open blasphemies.

M.—May we hence infer what benefit believers receive from the death of Christ?

S.—Easily. And, first, we see that it is a sacrifice by which he expiated our sins before God, and so having appeased the wrath of God, restored us to his favor. Secondly, That his blood is a layer by which our souls are cleansed from all stains. Lastly, That the remembrance of our sins was effaced so as never to come into the view of God, and that thus the handwriting which established our guilt was blotted out and canceled.

M.—Does it not gain us any other advantage besides?

S.—Yes, indeed. For by its benefit, if we are members of Christ, our old man is crucified, and the body of sin is destroyed, so that the lusts of a depraved flesh no longer reign in us.

M.—Proceed with the other articles.

S.—The next is, "On the third day he rose again from the dead." By this he declared himself the conqueror of sin and death. By his resurrection he swallowed up death, broke the fetters of the devil, and annihilated all his power.

M.—How manifold are the benefits resulting to us from the resurrection?

S.—Threefold. For by it righteousness was acquired for us; it is also a sure pledge to us of our immortality; and even now by virtue of it we are raised to newness of life, that by living purely and holily we may obey the will of God.

M.—Let us follow out the rest.

S.—"He ascended into heaven."

M.—Did he ascend so that he is no more on the earth?

S.—He did. For after he had performed all the things which the Father had given him to do, and which were for our salvation, there was no need of his continuing longer on earth.

M.—What good do we obtain from this ascension?

S.—The benefit is twofold. For inasmuch as Christ entered heaven in our name, just as he had come down to earth on our account, he also opened up an access for us, so that the door, previously shut because of sin, is now open. Secondly, he appears in the presence of God as our advocate and intercessor.

M.—But did Christ in going to heaven withdraw from us, so that he has now ceased to be with us?

S.—Not at all. On the contrary, he has engaged to be with us even to the end of the world. (Matt. xxviii. 20.)

M.—When we say he dwells with us, must we understand that he is bodily present?

S.—No. The case of the body which was received into heaven is one thing; that of the virtue which is everywhere diffused is another. (Luke xxiv. 51; Acts i. 11.)

M.— In what sense do you say that he "sitteth on the right hand of the Father?"

S.—These words mean that the Father bestowed upon him the dominion of heaven and earth, so that he governs all things. (Matt. xxviii. 18.)

M.— But what is meant by "right hand," and what by "sitteth?"

S.—It is a similitude taken from princes, who are wont to place those on their right hand whom they make their viceregents.

M.— You therefore mean nothing more than Paul says, namely, that Christ has been appointed head of the Church, and raised above all principalities, has obtained a name which is above every name. (Eph. i. 22; Phil. ii. 9.)

S.—It is as you say.

M.—Let us pass on.

S.—"From thence he will come to judge the quick and the dead." The meaning of these words is, that he will come openly from heaven to judge the world, just as he was seen to ascend. (Acts i. 11.)

M.—As the day of judgment is not to be before the end of the world, how do you say that some men will then be alive, seeing it is appointed unto all men once to die? (Heb. ix.

S.—Paul answers this question when he says, that those who then survive will undergo a sudden change, so that the corruption of the flesh being abolished, they will put on incorruption. (1 Cor. xv. 51; 1 Thess. iv. 17.)

M.—You understand then that this change will be like death; that there will be an abolition of the first nature, and the beginning of a new nature?

S.—That is my meaning.

M.—Does it give any delight to our conscience that Christ will one day be the judge of the world?

S.—Indeed singular delight. For we know assuredly that he will come only for our salvation.

M.—We should not then tremble at this judgment, so as to let it fill us with dismay?

S.—No, indeed; since we shall only stand at the tribunal of a judge who is also our advocate, and who has taken us under his faith and protection.

The Holy Spirit

M.—Let us come now to the third part.

S.—It relates to faith in the Holy Spirit.

M.—What do we learn by it?

S.—The object is to let us know that God, as he hath redeemed and saved us by his Son, will also by his Spirit make us capable of this redemption and salvation.

M.—How?

S.—As we have purification in the blood of Christ, so our consciences must be sprinkled by it in order to be washed. (1 Peter i. 2; 1 John i. 7.)

M.—This requires a clearer explanation.

S.—I mean that the Spirit of God, while he dwells in our hearts, makes us feel the virtue of Christ. (Rom. viii. 11.) For when our minds conceive the benefits of Christ, it is owing to the illumination of the Holy Spirit; to his persuasion it is owing that they are sealed in our hearts. (Eph. i. 13.) In short, he alone makes room in us for them. He regenerates us and makes us to be new creatures. Accordingly, whatever gifts are offered us in Christ, we receive by the agency of the Spirit.

The Church

M.— Let us proceed.

S.—Next comes the fourth part, in which we confess that we believe in one Holy Catholic Church.

M.—What is the Church?

S.—The body and society of believers whom God hath predestined to eternal life.

M.—Is it necessary to believe this article also?

S.—Yes, verily, if we would not make the death of Christ without effect, and set at nought all that has hitherto been said. For the one effect resulting from all is, that there is a Church.

M.—You mean then that we only treated of the cause of salvation, and showed the foundation of it when we explained that by the merits and intercession of Christ, we are taken into favor by God, and that this grace is confirmed in us by virtue of the Spirit. Now, however, we are explaining the effect of all these things, that by facts our faith may be made more firm?

S.—It is so.

M.—In what sense do you call the Church holy?

S.—All whom God has chosen he justifies, and forms to holiness and innocence of life, (Rom. viii. 30,) that his glory may be displayed in them. And this is what Paul means when he says that Christ sanctified the Church which he redeemed, that it might be a glorious Church, free from all blemish. (Eph. v. 25.)

M.—What is meant by the epithet Catholic or Universal?

S.—By it we are taught, that as all believers have one head, so they must all be united into one body, that the Church diffused over the whole world may be one-not more. (Eph. iv. 15; 1 Cor. xii. 12.)

M.—And what is the purport of what immediately follows concerning the communion of saints?

S.—That is put down to express more clearly the unity which exists among the members of the Church. It is at the same time intimated, that whatever benefits God bestows upon the Church, have a view to the common good of all; Seeing they all have communion with each other.

M.—But is this holiness which you attribute to the Church already perfect?

S.—Not yet, that is as long as she has her warfare in this world. For she always labors under infirmities, and will never be entirely purged of the remains of vice, until she adheres completely to Christ her head, by whom she is sanctified.

M.—Can this Church be known in any other way than when she is believed by faith?

S.—There is indeed also a visible Church of God, which he has described to us by certain signs and marks, but here we are properly speaking of the assemblage of those whom he has adopted to salvation by his secret election. This is neither at all times visible to the eye nor discernible by signs.

M.—What comes next?

S.—I believe in "the forgiveness of sins."

M.—What meaning do you give to the word forgiveness?

S.—That God of his free goodness forgives and pardons the sins of believers that they may not be brought to judgment, and that the penalty may not be exacted from them.

M.—Hence it follows, that it is not at all by our own satisfaction we merit the pardon of sins, which we obtain from the Lord?

S.—That is true; for Christ alone gave the satisfaction by paying the penalty.

M.—Why do you subjoin forgiveness of sins to the Church?

S.—Because no man obtains it without being previously united to the people of God, maintaining unity with the body of Christ perseveringly to the end, and thereby attesting that he is a true member of the Church.

M.—In this way you conclude that out of the Church is nought but ruin and damnation?

S.—Certainly. Those who make a departure from the body of Christ, and rend its unity by faction, are cut off from all hope of salvation during the time they remain in this schism, be it however short.

M.—Repeat the remainder.

S.—I believe in "the resurrection of the body and the life everlasting."

M.—To what end is this article set down in the Confession of Faith?

S.—To remind us that our happiness is not situated on the earth. The utility and use of this knowledge is twofold. First, we are taught by it that we are to live in this world as foreigners, continually thinking of departure, and not allowing our hearts to be entangled by earthly thoughts. Secondly, however the fruit of the grace of Christ bestowed upon us may escape our notice, and be hidden from our eyes, we must not despond, but patiently wait for the day of revelation.

M.—In what order will this resurrection take place?

S.—Those who were formerly dead will recover their bodies, the same bodies as before, but endued with a new quality, that is, no longer liable to death or corruption. (1 Cor. xv. 53.) Those who survive God will miraculously raise up by a sudden change.

M.—But will this be common to the righteous and the wicked?

S.—There will be one resurrection of all, but the condition will be different: some will rise to salvation and blessedness, others to death and extreme misery.

M.—Why then is eternal life only here mentioned, and is there no mention of hell?

S.—Because nothing is introduced here that does not tend to the consolation of pious minds; accordingly, only the rewards are enumerated which the Lord hath prepared for his servants, and nothing is added as to the doom of the wicked, whom we know to be aliens from the kingdom of God.

M.—As we understand the foundation on which faith ought to rest, it will be easy to extract from it a true definition of faith.

S.—It will. It may be defined-a sure and steadfast knowledge of the paternal goodwill of God toward us, as he declares in the gospel that for the sake of Christ he will be our Father and Savior.

M.—Do we conceive faith of ourselves, or do we receive it from God?

S.—Scripture teaches that it is the special gift of God, and this experience confirms.

M.—What experience do you mean?

S.—Our mind is too rude to be able to comprehend the spiritual wisdom of God which is revealed to us by faith, and our hearts are too prone either to diffidence or to a perverse confidence in ourselves or creatures, to rest in God of their own accord. But the Holy Spirit by his illumination makes us capable of understanding those things which would otherwise far exceed our capacity, and forms us to a firm Persuasion, by sealing the promises of salvation on our hearts.

M.—What good accrues to us from this faith, when we have once obtained it?

S.—It justifies us before God, and this justification makes us the heirs of everlasting life.

M.—What! are not men justified by good works when they study to approve themselves to God, by living innocently and holily?

S.—Could any one be found so perfect, he might justly be deemed righteous, but as we are all sinners, guilty before God in many ways, we must seek elsewhere for a worthiness which may reconcile us to him.

M.—But are all the works of men so vile and valueless that they cannot merit favor with God?

S.—First, all the works which proceed from us, so as properly to be called our own, are vicious, and therefore they can do nothing but displease God, and be rejected by him.

M.—You say then that before we are born again and formed anew by the Spirit of God, we can do nothing but sin, just as a bad tree can only produce bad fruit? (Matt. vii. 18.)

S.—Altogether so. For whatever semblance works may have in the eyes of men, they are nevertheless evil, as long as the heart to which God chiefly looks is depraved.

M.—Hence you conclude, that we cannot by any merits anticipate God or call forth his beneficence; or rather that all the works which we try or engage in, subject us to his anger and condemnation?

S.—I understand so; and therefore mere mercy, without any respect to works, (Titus iii. 5,) embraces and accepts us freely in Christ, by attributing his righteousness to us as if it were our own, and not imputing our sins to us.

M.—In what way, then, do you say that we are justified by faith?

S.—Because, while we embrace the promises of the gospel with sure heartfelt confidence, we in a manner obtain possession of the righteousness of which I speak.

M.—This then is your meaning-that as righteousness is offered to us by the gospel, so we receive it by faith?

S.—It is so.

M.—But after we have once been embraced by God, are not the works which we do under the direction of his Holy Spirit accepted by him?

S.—They please him, not however in virtue of their own worthiness, but as he liberally honors them with his favor.

M.—But seeing they proceed from the Holy Spirit, do they not merit favor?

S.—They are always mixed up with some defilement from the weakness of the flesh, and thereby vitiated.

M.—Whence then or how can it be that they please God?

S.—It is faith alone which procures favor for them, as we rest with assured confidence on this-that God wills not to try them by his strict rule, but covering their defects and impurities as buried in the purity of Christ, he regards them in the same light as if they were absolutely perfect.

M.—But can we infer from this that a Christian man is justified by works after he has been called by God, or that by the merit of works he makes himself loved by God, whose love is eternal life to us?

S.—By no means. We rather hold what is written-that no man can be justified in his sight, and we therefore pray, Enter not into judgment with us." (Ps. cxliii. 2.)

M.—We are not therefore to think that the good works of believers are useless?

S.—Certainly not. For not in vain does God promise them reward both in this life and in the future. But this reward springs from the free love of God as its source; for he first embraces us as sons, and then burying the remembrance of the vices which proceed from us, he visits us with his favor.

M.—But can this righteousness be separated from good works, so that he who has it may be void of them?

S.—That cannot be. For when by faith we receive Christ as he is offered to us, he not only promises us deliverance from death and reconciliation with God, but also the gift of the Holy Spirit, by which we are regenerated to newness of life; these things must necessarily be conjoined so as not to divide Christ from himself.

M.—Hence it follows that faith is the root from which all good works spring, so far is it from taking us off from the study of them?
S.—So indeed it is; and hence the whole doctrine of the gospel is comprehended under the two branches, faith and repentance.
M.—What is repentance?
S.—Dissatisfaction with and a hatred of sin and a love of righteousness, proceeding from the fear of God, which things lead to self-denial and mortification of the flesh, so that we give ourselves up to the guidance of the Spirit of God, and frame all the actions of our life to the obedience of the Divine will.
M.—But this second branch was in the division which was set down at first when you showed the method of duly worshiping God.
S.—True; and it was at the same time added, that the true and legitimate rule for worshiping God is to obey his will.
M.—Why so?
S.—Because the only worship which he approves is not that which it may please us to devise, but that which he hath of his own authority prescribed.

The law, that is, the ten commandments of god.

M.—What is the rule of life which he has given us?
S.—His law.
M.—What does it contain?
S.—It consists of two parts; the former of which contains four commandments, the latter six. Thus the whole law consists of ten commandments in all
M.—Who is the author of this division?
S.—God himself; who delivered it to Moses written on two tables, and afterwards declared that it was reduced into ten sentences. (Exod. xxiv. 12; xxxii. 15; xxxiv. 1; Deut. iv. 13; x. 4.)
M.—What is the subject of the first table?
S.—The offices of piety towards God.
M.—Of the second?
S.—How we are to act towards men, and what we owe them.

First commandment

M.—Repeat the first commandment or head.

S.—Hear, 0 Israel, I am Jehovah thy God, who brought thee out of the land of Egypt, out of the house of bondage: thou shalt have no other gods before me.
M.—Now explain the meaning of the words.
S.—At first he makes a kind of preface to the whole law. For when he calls himself Jehovah, he claims right and authority to command. Then in order to procure favor for his law, he adds, that he is our God. These words have the same force as if he had called himself our Preserver. Now as he bestows this favor upon us, it is meet that we should in our turn show ourselves to be an obedient people.
M.—But does not what he immediately subjoins, as to deliverance and breaking the yoke of Egyptian bondage, apply specially to the people of Israel, and to them alone?
S.—I admit this as to the act itself; but there is another kind of deliverance which applies equally to all men. For he has delivered us all from the spiritual bondage of sin, and the tyranny of the devil.
M.—Why does he mention that matter in a preface to his law?
S.—To remind us that we will be guilty of the greatest ingratitude if we do not devote ourselves entirely to obedience to him.
M.—And what does he require under this first head?
S.—That we maintain his honor entire and for himself alone, not transferring any part of it elsewhere.
M.—What is the honor peculiar to him which it is unlawful to transfer elsewhere?
S.—To adore him, to put our confidence in him, to call upon him, in short to pay him all the deference suitable to his majesty.
M.—Why is the clause added, "Before my face ?"
S.—As nothing is so hidden as to escape him, and he is the discerner and judge of secret thoughts, it means that he requires not the honor of outward affection merely, but true heartfelt piety.

Second commandment

M.—Let us pass to the second head.

S.—Thou shalt not sculpture to thyself the image, or form any of those things which are either in heaven above or on the earth beneath, or in the waters under the earth. Thou shalt not adore nor serve them.

M.—Does it entirely prohibit us from sculpturing or painting any resemblance?

S.—No; it only forbids us to make any resemblance's for the sake of representing or worshiping God.

M.—Why is it unlawful to represent God by a visible shape?

S.—Because there is no resemblance between him who is an eternal Spirit and incomprehensible, and a corporeal, corruptible, and lifeless figure. (Deut. iv. 15; Acts xvii. 29; Rom. i. 23.)

M.—You think then that an insult is offered to his majesty when he is represented in this way?

S.—Such is my belief.

M.—What kind of worship is here condemned?

S.—When we turn to a statue or image intending to pray, we prostrate ourselves before it: when we pay honor to it by the bending of our knees, or other signs, as if God were there representing himself to us.

M.—We are not to understand then that simply any kind of picture or sculpture is condemned by these words. We are only prohibited from making images for the purpose of seeking or worshiping God in them, or which is the same thing, for the purpose of worshiping them in honor of God, or abusing them in any way to superstition and idolatry.

S.—True.

M.—Now to what end shall we refer this head?

S.—As under the former head he declared that he alone should be worshiped and served, so he now shows what is the correct form of worship, that he may call us off from all superstition, and other vicious and carnal fictions.

M.—Let us proceed.

S.—He adds the sanction that he is Jehovah our God, a strong and jealous God, who avengeth the iniquity of the fathers upon the children of them who hate him, even to the third and fourth generation.

M.—Why does he make mention of his strength?

S.—He thereby intimates that he has power enough to vindicate his glory.

M.—What does he intimate by the term jealousy?

S.—That he cannot bear an equal or associate. For as he has given himself to us out of his infinite goodness, so he would have us to be wholly his. And the chastity of our souls consists in being dedicated to him, and wholly cleaving to him, as on the other hand they are said to be polluted with idolatry, when they turn aside from him to superstition.

M.—In what sense is it said that he avengeth the iniquity of fathers on children?

S.—To strike the more terror into us, he not only threatens to inflict punishment on those who offend him, but that their offspring also will be cursed.

M.—But is it consistent with the justice of God to punish any one for another's fault?

S.—If we consider what the condition of mankind is, the question is answered. For by nature we are all liable to the curse, and we have nothing to complain of in God when he leaves us in this condition. Then as he demonstrates his love for the righteous, by blessing their posterity, so he executes his vengeance against the wicked, by depriving their children of this blessing.

M.—Go on.

S.—To allure us by attractive mildness, he promises that he will take pity on all who love him and observe his commands, to a thousand generations.

M.—Does he mean that the innocence of a pious man will be the salvation of all his posterity, however wicked?

S.—Not at all, but that he will exercise his benignity to believers to such a degree, that for their sakes he will show himself benign also to their children, by not only giving them prosperity in regard to the present life, but also sanctifying their souls, so as to give them a place among his flock.

M.—But this does not always appear.

S.—I admit it. For as he reserves to himself liberty to show mercy when he pleases to the children of the ungodly, so he has not so astricted his favor to the children of believers as not to repudiate at pleasure those of them whom he will. (Rom. ix.) This, however, he so tempers as to show that his promise is not vain or fallacious.

M.—But why does he here say a thousand generations, whereas, in the case of punishment, he mentions only three or four?

S.—To intimate that he is more inclined to kindness and beneficence than to severity. This he also declares, when he says that he is ready to pardon, but slow to wrath. (Ex. xxxiv. 6; Ps. ciii. 8; cxlv. 8.)

Third commandment

M.—Now for the third commandment.

S.—Thou shalt not take the name of Jehovah thy God in vain.

M.—What is the meaning?

S.—He forbids us to abuse the name of God, not only by perjury, but by swearing without necessity.

M.—Can the name of God be lawfully used in making oath?

S.—It may indeed, when used on a fit cause: first, in asserting the truth; and secondly, when the business is of such importance as to make it meet to swear, in maintaining mutual love and concord among men..

M.—But does it not go farther than to restrain oaths, by which the name of God is profaned, or his honor impaired?

S.—The mention of one species admonishes us in general, never to utter the name of God unless with fear and reverence, and for the purpose of honoring it. For while it is thrice holy, we ought to guard, by all means, against seeming to hold it in contempt, or giving others occasion to contemn.

M.—How is this to be done?

S.—By never speaking or thinking of God and his works without honor.

M.—What follows?

S.—A sanction, by which he declares that he shall not be guiltless who taketh his name in vain.

M.—As he, in another place, declares that he will punish the transgressors of his law, what more is contained here?

S.—He hereby meant to intimate how much he values the glory of his name, and to make us more careful of it, when we see that vengeance is ready for any who may profane it.

Fourth commandment

M.—Let us come to the fourth commandment.

S.—Remember the Sabbath day, to keep it holy. Six days shalt thou labor, and do all thy work: But the seventh is the Sabbath of the Lord thy God: in it thou shalt not do any work, thou, nor thy son, nor thy daughter, thy manservant, nor thy maidservant, nor thy cattle, nor thy stranger that is within thy gates: For in six days the Lord made heaven and earth, the sea, and all that in them is, and rested the seventh day: wherefore the Lord blessed the Sabbath day, and hallowed it.

M.—Does he order us to labor on six days, that we may rest on the seventh ?

S.—Not absolutely; but allowing man six days for labor, he excepts the seventh, that it may be devoted to rest.

M.—Does he interdict us from all kind of labor?

S.—This commandment has a separate and peculiar reason. As the observance of rest is part of the old ceremonies, it was abolished by the advent of Christ.

M.—Do you mean that this commandment properly refers to the Jews, and was therefore merely temporary?

S.—I do, in as far as it is ceremonial.

M.—What then? Is there any thing under it beyond ceremony?

S.—It was given for three reasons.

M.—State them to me.

S.—To figure spiritual rest; for the preservation of ecclesiastical polity; and for the relief of slaves.

M.—What do you mean by spiritual rest?

S.—When we keep holiday from our own

works, that God may perform his own works in us.

M.—What, moreover, is the method of thus keeping holiday?

S.—By crucifying our flesh, – that is, renouncing our own inclination, that we may be governed by the Spirit of God.

M.—Is it sufficient to do so on the seventh day?

S.—Nay, continually. After we have once begun, we must continue during the whole course of life.

M.—Why, then, is a certain day appointed to figure it?

S.—There is no necessity that the reality should agree with the figure in every respect, provided it be suitable in so far as is required for the purpose of figuring.

M.—But why is the seventh day prescribed rather than any other day?

S.—In Scripture the number seven implies perfection. It is, therefore, apt for denoting perpetuity. It, at the same time, indicates that this spiritual rest is only begun in this life, and will not be perfect until we depart from this world.

M.—But what is meant when the Lord exhorts us to rest by his own example?

S.—Having finished the creation of the world in six days, he dedicated the seventh to the contemplation of his works. The more strongly to stimulate us to this, he set before us his own example. For nothing is more desirable than to be formed after his image.

M.—But ought meditation on the works of God to be continual, or is it sufficient that one day out of seven be devoted to it?

S.—It becomes us to be daily exercised in it, but because of our weakness, one day is specially appointed. And this is the polity which I mentioned.

M.—What order, then, is to be observed on that day?

S.—That the people meet to hear the doctrine of Christ, to engage in public prayer, and make profession of their faith.

M.—Now explain what you meant by saying that the Lord intended by this commandment to provide also for the relief of slaves.

S.—That some relaxation might be given to those under the power of others. Nay, this, too, tends to maintain a common polity. For when one day is devoted to rest, every one accustoms himself to labor during the other days.

M.—Let us now see how far this command has reference to us.

S.—In regard to the ceremony, I hold that it was abolished, as the reality existed in Christ. (Col. ii. 17.)

M.—How?

S.—Because, by virtue of his death, our old man is crucified, and we are raised up to newness of life. (Rom. vi. 6.)

M.—What of the commandment then remains for us?

S.—Not to neglect the holy ordinances which contribute to the spiritual polity of the Church; especially to frequent sacred assemblies, to hear the word of God, to celebrate the sacraments, and engage in the regular prayers, as enjoined.

M.— But does the figure give us nothing more?

S.—Yes, indeed. We must give heed to the thing meant by it; namely, that being engrafted into the body of Christ, and made his members, we cease from our own works, and so resign ourselves to the government of God.

Fifth commandment

M.—Let us pass to the second table.

S.—It begins, "Honor thy father and thy mother."

M.—What meaning do you give to the word "honor?"

S.—That children be, with modesty and humility, respectful and obedient to parents, serving them reverentially, helping them in necessity, and exerting their labor for them. For in these three branches is included the honor which is due to parents.

M.— Proceed.

S.—To the commandment the promise is added, "That thy days may be prolonged on the land which the Lord thy God will give thee."

M.—What is the meaning?

S.—That, by the blessing of God, long life will be given to those who pay due honor to parents.

M.—Seeing this life is so full of troubles, why does God promise the long continuance of it as a blessing?

S.—How great soever the miseries to which it is liable, yet there is a blessing from God upon believers, when he nourishes and preserves them here, were it only for this one reason, that it is a proof of his paternal favor.

M.—Does it follow conversely, that he who is snatched away from the world quickly, and before mature age, is cursed of God?

S.—By no means. Nay, rather it sometimes happens that the more a man is loved by God the more quickly is he removed out of this life.

M.— But in so acting, how does he fulfil his promise?

S.—Whatever earthly good God promises we must receive under this condition, viz., in so far as is expedient for the good and salvation of our soul. For the arrangement would be very absurd if the care of the soul did not always take precedence.

M.—What of those who are contumacious to parents?

S.—They shall not only be punished at the last judgment, but here also God will take vengeance on their bodies, either by taking them hence in the middle of their days, or bringing them to an ignominious end, or in other manners.

M.—But does not the promise speak expressly of the land of Canaan?

S.—It does so in as far as regards the Israelites, but the term ought to have a wider and more extensive meaning to us. For seeing that the whole earth is the Lord's, whatever be the region we inhabit he assigns it to us for a possession. (Ps, xxiv. 1; lxxxv. 5; cxv. 16.)

M.—Is there nothing more of the commandment remaining?

S.—Though father and mother only are expressed, we must understand all who are over us, as the reason is the same.

M.—What is the reason?

S.—That the Lord has raised them to a high degree of honor; for there is no authority whether of parents, or princes, or rulers of any description, no power, no honor, but by the decree of God, because it so pleases him to order the world.

Sixth commandment

M.—Repeat the sixth commandment.

S.—Thou shalt not kill.

M.—Does it forbid nothing but the perpetration of murder?

S.—Yes, indeed. For seeing it is God who speaks, he here gives law not only to outward works, but also to the affections of the mind, and indeed to them chiefly.

M.—You seem to insinuate that there is some kind of secret murder from which God here recalls us.

S.—I do. For anger, and hatred, and any desire to hurt, is murder in the sight of God.

M.—Is it enough if we do not hate any one?

S.—By no means. Since the Lord, by condemning hatred and restraining us from any harm by which our neighbor may be injured, shows at the same time that he requires us to love all men from the heart, and study faithfully to defend and preserve them.

Seventh commandment

M.—Now for the seventh commandment.

S.—Thou shalt not commit adultery.

M.—Explain what the substance of it is.

S.—That all kinds of fornication are cursed in the sight of God, and therefore as we would not provoke the anger of God against us we must carefully abstain from it.

M.—Does it require nothing besides?

S.—Respect must always be had to the nature of the Law-giver, who, we have said, not only regards the outward act, but looks more to the affections of the mind.

M.—What more then does it comprehend?

S.—Inasmuch as both our bodies and our souls are temples of the Holy Spirit, (1 Cor. iii. 16; vi. 19,) we must observe a chaste purity with both, and accordingly be chaste not only by abstaining from outward flagitiousness, but also in heart, speech, bodily gesture, and action, (2 Cor. vi. 16;) in short, our body must be free from all lasciviousness, our mind from all lust, and no part of us be polluted by the defilements of unchastity.

Eighth commandment

M.—Let us come to the eighth commandment.

S.—Thou shalt not steal.

M.—Does it only prohibit the thefts which are punished by human laws, or does it go farther?

S.—Under the name of theft, it comprehends all kinds of wicked acts of defrauding and circumventing by which we hunt after other men's goods. Here, therefore, we are forbidden either to seize upon our neighbor's goods by violence, or lay hands upon them by trick and cunning, or get possession of them by any other indirect means whatever.

M.—Is it enough to withhold your hand from the evil act, or is covetousness also here condemned?

S.—We must ever return to this-that the law given, being spiritual, intends to check not only outward thefts, but all counsels and wishes which incommode others in any way; and especially covetousness itself; that we may not long to enrich ourselves at the expense of our brethren.

M.—What then must be done to obey this commandment?

S.—We must endeavor to let every man have his own in safety.

Ninth commandment

M.—What is the ninth commandment?

S.—Thou shalt not bear false witness against thy neighbor.

M.—Does it prohibit perjury in court only, or any kind of lying against our neighbors?

S.—Under one species the general doctrine is comprehended, that we are not to charge our neighbor falsely, nor by our evil speaking and detraction hurt his good name, or harm him in his goods.

M.—But why does it expressly mention public perjury?

S.—That it may inspire us with a greater abhorrence of this vice. For it insinuates that if a man accustom himself to evil speaking and calumny, the descent to perjury is rapid if an opportunity is given to defame his neighbor.

M.—Does it mean to keep us from evil speaking only, or also from false suspicion and unjust and uncharitable judgment?

S.—It here condemns both, according to the view already stated. For whatever it is wrong to do before men, it is wrong to wish before God.

M.—Explain then what it means in substance.

S.—It enjoins us not to think ill of our neighbors, or be prone to defame them, but in the spirit of kindness and impartiality to think well of them as far as the truth will permit, and study to preserve their reputation entire.

Tenth commandment

M.—Repeat the last commandment.

S.—Thou shalt not covet thy neighbor's house, thou shalt not covet thy neighbor's wife, nor his man-servant, nor his maid-servant, nor his ox, nor his ass, nor any thing that is thy neighbor's.

M.—Seeing that the whole law is spiritual, as you have so often said before, and the above commandments are set down not only to curb outward acts, but also correct the affections of the mind, what more is added here?

S.—The Lord meant to regulate and govern the will and affections by the other commandments, but here he imposes a law even on thoughts which carry some degree of covetousness along with them, and yet come not the length of a fixed purpose.

M.—Do you say that the least degrees of covetousness which creep in upon believers and enter their minds are sins, even though they resist rather than assent?

S.—It is certainly clear that all vitious thoughts, even though consent is not added, proceed from the depravity of our nature. But I only say this-that this commandment condemns vicious desires which tickle and solicit the heart of man, without however drawing him on to a firm and deliberate act of will.

M.—You understand then that the evil affections in which men acquiesce, and by which they allow themselves to be overcome, were prohibited before, but that the thing now required of us is such strict integrity that our hearts are not to admit any perverse desire by which they may be stimulated to sin?

S.—Exactly so.

M.—Can we now frame a short compendium of the whole law?

S.—Very easily, since we can reduce it to two heads. The former is to love God with all our heart, and soul; and strength-the latter, to love our neighbors as ourselves.

M.—What is comprehended under the love of God?

S.—To love him as God should be loved-that is, recognizing him as at once our Lord, and Father, and Preserver. Accordingly, to the love of God is joined reverence for him, a willingness to obey him, trust to be placed in him.

M.—What do you understand by the whole heart, the whole soul, and the whole strength?

S.—Such vehemence of zeal, that there be no place at all in us for any thoughts, desires, or pursuits, adverse to this love.

M.—What is the meaning of the second head?

S.—As we are by nature so prone to love ourselves, that this feeling overcomes all others, so love to our neighbor ought to have such ascendency in us as to govern us in every respect, and be the rule of all our purposes and actions.

M.—What do you understand by the term neighbor?

S.—Not only kindred and friends, or those connected with us by any necessary tie, but also those who are unknown to us, and even enemies.

M.—But what connection have they with us?

S.—They are connected by that tie by which God bound the whole human race together. This tie is sacred and inviolable, and no man's depravity can abolish it.

M.—You say, then, that if any man hate us, the blame is his own, and yet he is nevertheless our neighbor, and as such is to be regarded by us, because the divine arrangement by which this connection between us was ratified stands inviolable?

S.—It is so.

M.—Seeing that the law of God points out the form of duly worshiping him, must we not live according to its direction?

S.—We must indeed. But we all labor under infirmity, owing to which no man fulfils, in every respect, what he ought.

M.—Why then does God require a perfection which is beyond our ability?

S.—He requires nothing which we are not bound to perform. But provided we strive after that form of living which is here prescribed, although we be wide of the mark, that is, of perfection, the Lord forgives us what is wanting.

M.—Do you speak of all men in general, or of believers only?

S.—He who is not yet regenerated by the Spirit of God, is not fit to begin the least iota of the law. Besides, even were we to grant that any one is found to obey the law in any respect, we do not think that he has performed his part before God. For the law pronounces all cursed who have not fulfilled all the things contained in it. (Deut. xxvii. 26; Gal. iii. 10.)

M.—Hence we must conclude, that as there are two classes of men, so the office of the law is twofold?

S.—Exactly. For among unbelievers it does nothing more than shut them out from all excuse before God. And this is what Paul means when he calls it the ministry of death and condemnation. In regard to believers it has a very different use. (Rom. i. 32; 2 Cor. iii. 6.)

M.—What?

S.—First, while they learn from it that they cannot obtain righteousness by works, they are trained to humility, which is the true preparation for seeking salvation in Christ. Secondly, inasmuch as it requires of them much more than they are able to perform, it urges them to seek strength from the Lord, and at the same time reminds them of their perpetual guilt, that they may not presume to be proud. Lastly, it is a kind of curb, by which they are kept in the fear of the Lord. (Rom. iii. 20; Gal. ii. 16; iii. 11; iv. 5.)

M.—Therefore, although in this earthly pilgrimage we never satisfy the law, we cannot judge that it is superfluous to require this strict perfection from us. For it shows the mark at which we ought to aim, the goal towards which we ought to press, that each of us, according to the measure of grace bestowed upon him, may endeavor to frame his life according to the highest rectitude, and, by constant study, continually advance more and more.

S.—That is my view.

M.—Have we not a perfect rule of righteousness in the law?

S.—So much so, that God wishes nothing else from us than to follow it; and, on the other hand, repudiates and holds void whatever we undertake beyond its prescription. For the only sacrifice which he accepts is obedience. (1 Sam. xv. 22.)

M.—To what end, then, the many admonitions, precepts, exhortations, which both Prophets and Apostles are continually employing? (Jer. vii. 12.)

S.—They are nothing but mere expositions of the law, which lead us by the hand to the obedience of the law, rather than lead us away from it.

M.—But he gives no command concerning the private case of each individual?

S.—When he orders us to render to every one his due, it is obvious to infer what the private part of each is in his own order and condition of life, and expositions of particular precepts, as has been said, he scattered throughout Scripture. For what the Lord has summarily comprised here in a few words, is given with more fulness and detail elsewhere.

Prayer

M.—As the second part of Divine Worship, which consists in service and obedience, has been sufficiently discussed, let us now proceed to the third part.

S.—We said it was invocation, by which we flee to God in any necessity.

M.—Do you think that he alone is to be invoked?

S.—Certainly; for he requires this as the proper worship of his Divinity.

M.—If it is so, how can we beseech men to assist us?

S.—There is a great difference between the two things. For when we invoke God, we testify that we expect no good from any other quarter, and that we place our whole defense in no other, and yet we ask the assistance of men, as far as he permits, and has bestowed on them the power of giving it.

M.—You say, then, that in having recourse to the faith and help of men, there is nothing that interferes with our invocation of God, seeing that our reliance is not fixed on them, and we beseech them on no other ground, than just because God, by furnishing them with the means of well-doing, has in a manner destined them to be the ministers of his beneficence, and is pleased by their hands to assist us, and draw out, on our account, the resources which he has deposited with them?

S.—Such is my view. And, accordingly, whatever benefits we receive from them, we should regard as coming from God, as in truth it is he alone who bestows all these things upon us by their instrumentality.

M.—But are we not to feel grateful to men whenever they have conferred any kindness upon us. This the mere equity of nature and law of humanity dictates?

S.—Certainly we are; and were it only for the reason that God honors them by sending to us, through their hands, as rivulets, the blessings which flow from the inexhaustible fountain of his liberality. In this way he lays us under obligation to them, and wishes us to acknowledge it. He, therefore, who does not show himself grateful to them by so doing, betrays his ingratitude to God.

M.—Are we hence at liberty to infer, that

it is wrong to invoke angels and holy servants of the Lord who have departed this life?

S.—We are not at liberty; for God does not assign to saints the office of assisting us. And in regard to angels, though he uses their labor for our salvation, he does not wish us to ask them for it.

M.—You say, then, that whatever does not aptly and fitly square with the order instituted by God, is repugnant to his will?

S.—I do. For it is a sure sign of unbelief not to be contented with the things which God gives to us. Then if we throw ourselves on the protection of angels or saints, when God calls us to himself alone, and transfer to them the confidence which ought wholly to be fixed upon God, we fall into idolatry, seeing we share with them that which God claimed entirely for himself.

M.—Let us now consider the manner of prayer. Is it sufficient to pray with the tongue, or does prayer require also the mind and heart?

S.—The tongue, indeed, is not always necessary, but true prayer can never be without understanding and affection.

M.—By what argument will you prove this to me?

S.—Since God is a Spirit, he requires men to give him the heart in all cases, and more especially in prayer, by which they hold communion with him. Wherefore he promises to be near to those only who call upon him in truth: on the other hand, he abominates and curses all who pray to him deceitfully, and not sincerely. (Psalm cxlv. 18; Isaiah xxix. 13.)

M.—All prayers, then, conceived only by the tongue, will be vain and worthless?

S.—Not only so, but will be most displeasing to God.

M.—What kind of feeling does God require in prayer?

S.—First, that we feel our want and misery, and that this feeling beget sorrow and anxiety in our minds. Secondly, that we be inflamed with an earnest and vehement desire to obtain grace from God. These things will also kindle in us an ardent longing to pray.

M.—Does this feeling flow from the temper natural to man, or does it proceed from the grace of God?

S.—Here God must come to our aid. For we are altogether stupid in regard to both. (Rom. viii. 25.) It is the Spirit of God who excites in us groanings which cannot be uttered, and frames our minds to the desires which are requisite in prayer, as Paul says. (Gal. iv. 6.)

M.—Is it the meaning of this doctrine, that we are to sit still, and, in a kind of vacillating state, wait for the motions of the Spirit, and not that each one is to urge himself to pray?

S.—By no means. The meaning rather is, that when believers feel themselves cold or sluggish, and somewhat indisposed to pray, they should forthwith flee to God, and beseech him to inflame them by the fiery darts of his Spirit, that they may be rendered fit to pray.

M.—You do not, however, mean that there is to be no use of the tongue in prayer?

S.—Not at all. For it often helps to sustain the mind, and keep it from being so easily drawn off from God. Besides, as it, more than other members, was created to display the glory of God, it is right that it be employed to this purpose, to the whole extent of its capacity. Moreover, vehemence of desire occasionally impels a man to break forth into utterance with the tongue without intending it.

M.—If so, what profit have those who pray in a foreign tongue not understood by them?

S.—It is nothing else than to sport with God. Christians, therefore, should have nothing to do with this hypocrisy. (1 Cor. xiv. 15.)

M.—But when we pray do we do it fortuitously, uncertain of success, or ought we to feel assured that the Lord will hear us?

S.—The foundation of our prayer should always be, that the Lord will hear us, and that we shall obtain whatever we ask, in so far as is for our good. For this reason Paul tells us, that true prayer flows from faith. (Rom. x. 14.) For no man will ever duly call upon him, without previously resting with firm reliance on his goodness.

M.—What then will become of those who pray in doubt, and without fixing in their minds what profit they are to gain by praying, nay, are uncertain whether or not their prayers will be heard by God?

S.—Their prayers are vain and void, not being supported by any promise. For we are ordered to ask with sure faith, and the promise is added, that whatever we shall ask, believing, we shall receive. (Matt. xxi. 22; Mark xi. 24; James i. 6.)

M.—It remains to be seen wherein we have such great confidence, that while unworthy, on so many accounts, of appearing in the presence of God, we however dare to place ourselves before him.

S.—First, we have promises by which we must simply abide, without. making any reference to our own worthiness. Secondly, if we are sons, God animates and instigates us by his Spirit, so that we doubt not to betake ourselves to him in a familiar manner, as to a father. As we are like worms, and are oppressed by the consciousness of our sins, God, in order that we may not tremble at his glorious majesty, sets forth Christ as a Mediator, through whom we obtain access, and have no doubt at all of obtaining favor. (Psalm iv. 15; xci. 15; cxlv. 18; Isaiah xxx. 19; lxv. 1; Jer. xxix. 12; Joel ii 32; Rom. viii. 25; x. 13.)

M.—Do you understand that we are to pray to God only in the name of Christ?

S.—I so understand. For it is both so enjoined in distinct terms, and the promise is added, that he will by his intercession obtain what we ask. (1 Tim. ii. 5; 1 John ii. 1.)

M.—He is not then to be accused of rashness or presumption, who, trusting to this Advocate, makes a familiar approach to God, and holds forth to God and to himself Christ as the only one through whom he is to be heard? (Heb. iv. 14.)

S.—By no means: For he who thus prays conceives his prayers as it were at the lips of Christ, seeing he knows, that by the intercession of Christ, his prayer is assisted and recommended.

M.—Let us now consider what the prayers of believers ought to contain. Is it lawful to ask of God whatever comes into our mind, or is a certain rule to be observed?

S.—It were a very preposterous method of prayer to indulge our own desires and the judgment of the flesh. We are too ignorant to be able to judge what is expedient for us, and we labor under an intemperance of desire, to which it is necessary that a bridle be applied.

M.—What then requires to be done?

S.—The only thing remaining is for God himself to prescribe a proper form of prayer, that we may follow him while he leads us by the hand, and as it were sets words before us.

M.—What rule has he prescribed?

S.—The doctrine on this subject is amply and copiously delivered in the Scriptures. But to give us a surer aim, he framed, and, as it were, dictated a form in which he has briefly comprehended and digested under a few heads whatever it is lawful, and for our interest to ask.

M.—Repeat it.

S.—Our Lord Jesus Christ being asked by his disciples in what way they ought to pray, answered, when ye would pray, say ye, (Matt. vi. 9; Luke xi. 2,) "Our Father, which art in heaven, hallowed be thy name. Thy kingdom come. Thy will be done in earth, as it is in heaven. Give us this day our daily bread. And forgive us our debts, as we forgive our debtors. And lead us not into temptation; but deliver us from evil: For thine is the kingdom, and the power, and the glory, for ever. Amen."

M.—That we may the better understand what it contains, let us divide it into heads.

S.—It contains six parts, of which the three first respect the glory of God alone as their proper end, without any reference to us: the other three relate to us and our interest.

M.—Are we then to ask God for any thing from which no benefit redounds to us?

S.—He indeed of his infinite goodness so arranges all things that nothing tends to his glory without being also salutary to us.

Therefore when his name is sanctified, he causes it to turn to our sanctification also; nor does his kingdom come without our being in a manner sharers in it. But in asking all these things, we ought to look only to his glory without thinking of advantage to ourselves.

M.—According to this view, three of these requests have a connection with our own good, and yet their only aim ought to be, that the name of God may be glorified.

S.—It is so; and thus the glory of God ought also to be considered in the other three, though they are properly intended to express desire for things which belong to our good and salvation.

M. Let us now proceed to an explanation of the words; and, first, Why is the name of Father, rather than any other, here given to God?

S.—As security of conscience is one of the most essential requisites for praying aright, God assumes this name, which suggests only the idea of pure kindness, that having thus banished all anxiety from our minds, he may invite us to make a familiar approach to him.

M.—Shall we then dare to go to him directly without hesitation as children to parents?

S.—Wholly so: nay, with much surer confidence of obtaining what we ask For as our Master reminds us, (Matt. vii. 11,) If we being evil cannot however refuse good things to our children, nor bear to send them empty away, nor give them poison for bread, how much greater kindness is to be expected from our heavenly Father, who is not only supremely good, but goodness itself?

M.—May we not from this name also draw the inference which we mentioned at the outset, viz., that to be approved, all our prayers should be founded on the intercession of Christ? (John xv. 7; Rom. viii. 15.)

S.—And indeed a most valid inference. For God regards us as sons, only in so far as we are members of Christ.

M.—Why do you call God "our Father" in common, rather than "my Father" in particular?

S.—Each believer may indeed call him his own Father, but the Lord used the common epithet that he might accustom us to exercise charity in our prayers, and that we might not neglect others, by each caring only for himself.

M.—What is meant by the additional clause, that God is in heaven?

S.—It is just the same as if I were to call him exalted, mighty, incomprehensible.

M.—To what end this, and for what reason?

S.—In this way we are taught when we pray to him to raise our minds aloft, and not have any carnal or earthly thoughts of him, nor measure him by our own little standard, lest thinking too meanly of him, we should wish to bring him into subjection to our will, instead of learning to look up with fear and reverence to his glorious Majesty. It tends to excite and confirm our confidence in him, when he is proclaimed to be the Lord and Governor of heaven, ruling all things at his pleasure.

M.—Repeat to me the substance of the first petition.

S.—By the name of God, Scripture denotes the knowledge and fame with which he is celebrated among men. We pray then that his glory may be promoted everywhere, and in all.

M.—But can any thing be added to his glory, or taken from it?

S.—In itself it neither increases nor is diminished. But we pray as is meet, that it may be illustrious among men- that in whatever God does, all his works may appear, as they are, glorious, that he himself may by all means be glorified.

M.—What understand you by the kingdom of God in the second petition?

S.—It consists chiefly of two branches-that he would govern the elect by his Spirit-that he would prostrate and destroy the reprobate who refuse to give themselves up to his service, thus making it manifest that nothing is able to resist his might.

M.—In what sense do you pray that this kingdom may come?

S.—That the Lord would daily increase the numbers of the faithful-that he would ever and anon load them with new gifts of his Spirit, until he fill them completely: moreover, that he would render his truth more clear and conspicuous by dispelling the darkness of Satan, that he would abolish all iniquity, by advancing his own righteousness.

M.—Are not all these things done every day?

S.—They are done so far, that the kingdom of God may be said to be commenced. We pray, therefore, that it may constantly increase and be carried forward, until it attain its greatest height, which we only hope to take place on the last day on which God alone, after reducing all creatures to order, will be exalted and preeminent, and so be all in all. (1 Cor. xv. 28.)

M.—What mean you by asking that the will of God may be done?

S.—That all creatures may be subdued into obedience to him, and so depend on his nod, that nothing may be done except at his pleasure.

M.—Do you think then that any thing can be done against his will?

S.—We not only pray that what he has decreed with himself may come to pass, but also that all contumacy being tamed and subjugated, he would subject all wills to his own, and frame them in obedience to it.

M.—Do we not by thus praying surrender our own wills?

S.—Entirely: nor do we only pray that he would make void whatever desires of ours are at variance with his own will, but also that he would form in us new minds and new hearts, so that we may wish nothing of ourselves, but rather that his Spirit may preside over our wishes, and bring them into perfect unison with God.

M.—Why do you pray that this may be done on earth as it is in heaven?

S.—As the holy angels, who are his celestial creatures, have it as their only object to obey him in all things, to be always obedient to his word, and prepared voluntarily to do him service, we pray for such prompt obedience in men, that each may give himself up entirely to him in voluntary subjection.

M.—Let us now come to the second part. What mean you by the "daily" bread you ask for?

S.—In general every thing that tends to the preservation of the present life, not only food or clothing, but also all other helps by which the wants of outward life are sustained; that we may eat our bread in quiet, so far as the Lord knows it to be expedient.

M.—But why do you ask God to give what he orders us to provide by our own labor?

S.—Though we are to labor, and even sweat in providing food, we are not nourished either by our own labor, or our own industry, or our own diligence, but by the blessing of God by which the labor of our hands, that would otherwise be in vain, prospers. Moreover we should understand, that even when abundance of food is supplied to our hand, and we eat it, we are not nourished by its substance, but by the virtue of God alone. It has not any inherent efficacy in its own nature, but God supplies it from heaven as the instrument of his own beneficence. (Deut. viii. 3; Matt. iv. 4.)

M.—But by what right do you call it your bread when you ask God to give it?

S.—Because by the kindness of God it becomes ours, though it is by no means due to us. We are also reminded by this term to refrain from coveting the bread of others, and to be contented with that which has come to us in a legitimate manner as from the hand of God.

M.—Why do you add both "daily" and "this day ?"

S.—By these two terms we are taught moderation and temperance, that our wishes may not exceed the measure of necessity.

M.—As this prayer ought to be common to all, how can the rich, who have abundance at home, and have provision laid up for a long period, ask it to be given them for a day?

S.—The rich, equally with the poor, should remember that none of the things which they have will do them good, unless God grant them the use of them, and by his grace make the use fruitful and efficacious. Wherefore while possessing all things, we have nothing except in so far as we every hour receive from the hand of God what is necessary and sufficient for us.

M.—What does the fifth petition contain?

S.—That the Lord would pardon our sins.

M.—Can no mortal be found so righteous as not to require this pardon?

S.—Not one. When Christ gave this form of prayer, he designed it for the whole Church. Wherefore he who would exempt himself from this necessity, must leave the society of the faithful. And we have the testimony of Scripture, namely, that he who would contend before God to clear himself in one thing, will be found guilty in a thousand. (Job ix. 3.) The only refuge left for all is in his mercy.

M.—How do you think that sins are forgiven us?

S.—As the words of Christ express, namely, that they are debts which make us liable to eternal death, until God of his mere liberality deliver us.

M.—You say then that it is by the free mercy of God that we obtain the pardon of sins?

S.—Entirely so. For were the punishment of only one sin, and that the least, to be ransomed, we could not satisfy it. All then must be freely overlooked and forgiven.

M.—What advantage accrues to us from this forgiveness?

S.—We are accepted, just as if we were righteous and innocent, and at the same time our consciences are confirmed in a full reliance on his paternal favor, assuring us of salvation.

M.—Does the appended condition, viz., that he would for. give us as we forgive our debtors, mean that we merit pardon from God by pardoning men who have in any way offended us?

S.—By no means. For in this way forgiveness would not be free nor founded alone on the satisfaction which Christ made for us on the cross. But as by forgetting the injuries done to ourselves, we, while imitating his goodness and clemency, demonstrate that we are in fact his children, God wishes us to confirm it by this pledge; and at the same time shows us, on the other hand, that if we do not show ourselves easy and ready to pardon, nothing else is to be expected of him than the highest inexorable rigor of severity.

M.—Do you say then that all who cannot from the heart forgive offences are discarded by God and expunged from his list of children, so that they cannot hope for any place of pardon in heaven?

S.—So I think, in accordance with the words, "With what measure ye mete it shall be measured to you again."

M.—What comes next?

S.—"Lead us not into temptation, but deliver us from evil."

M.—Do you include all this in one petition?

S.—It is only one petition ; for the latter clause is an explanation of the former.

M.—What does it contain in substance?

S.—That the Lord would not permit us to rush or fall into sin-that he would not leave us to be overcome by the devil and the desires of our flesh, which wage constant war with us-that he would rather furnish us with his strength to resist, sustain us by his hand, cover and fortify us by his protection, so that under his guardianship and tutelage we may dwell safely.

M.—How is this done?

S.—When governed by his Spirit we are imbued with such a love and desire of righteousness, as to overcome the flesh, sin, and Satan; and, on the other hand, with such a hatred of sin as may keep us separated from the world in pure holiness. For our victory consists in the power of the Spirit.

M.—Have we need of this assistance?

S.— Who can dispense with it? The devil is perpetually hovering over us, and going about as a roaring lion seeking whom he may devour. (1 Pet.. v. 8.) And let us consider what our weakness is. Nay, all would be over with us every single moment did not God equip us for battle with his own weapons, and strengthen us with his own hand.

M.—What do you mean by the term Temptation?

S.—The tricks and fallacies of Satan, by which he is constantly attacking us, and would forthwith easily circumvent us, were we not aided by the help of God. For both our mind, from its native vanity, is liable to his wiles, and our will, which is always prone to evil, would immediately yield to him.

M.—But why do you pray God not to lead you into temptation, which seems to be the proper act of Satan, not of God?

S.—As God defends believers by his protection; that they may neither be oppressed by the wiles of Satan, nor overcome by sin, so those whom he means to punish he not only leaves destitute of his grace, but also delivers to the tyranny of Satan, strikes with blindness, and gives over to a reprobate mind, so that they are completely enslaved to sin and exposed to all the assaults of temptation.

M.—What is meant by the clause which is added, "For thine is the kingdom, and the power, and the glory, for ever ?"

S.—We are here again reminded that our prayers must lean more on the power and goodness of God than on any confidence in ourselves. Besides, we are taught to close all our prayers with praise.

M.—Is it not lawful to ask any thing of God that is not comprehended in this form?

S.—Although we are free to pray in other words, and in another manner, we ought, however, to hold that no prayer can please God which is not referable to this as the only rule of right Prayer.

The Word of God

M.—The order already adopted by us requires that we now consider the fourth part of divine worship.

S.—We said that this consists in acknowledging God as the author of all good, and in extolling his goodness, justice, wisdom, and power with praise and thanksgiving, that thus the glory of all good may remain entirely with him.

M.—Has he prescribed no rule as to this part?

S.—All the praises extant in Scripture ought to be our rule.

M.—Has the Lord's Prayer nothing which applies here?

S.—Yes. When we pray that his name may be hallowed, we pray that he may be duly glorified in his works-that he may be regarded, whether in pardoning sinners, as merciful; or in exercising vengeance, as just; or in performing his promises, as true: in short, that whatever of his works we see may excite us to glorify him. This is indeed to ascribe to him the praise of all that is good.

M.—What shall we infer from these heads which have hitherto been considered by us?

S.—What truth itself teaches, and was stated at the outset, viz., that this is eternal life to know one true God the Father, and Jesus Christ whom he hath sent, (John xvii. 3,)-to know him, I say, in order that we may pay due honor and worship to him, that he may be not only our Lord but also our Father and Savior, and we be in turn his children and servants, and accordingly devote our lives to the illustration of his glory.

M.—How can we attain to such blessedness?

S.—For this end God has left us his holy word; for spiritual doctrine is a kind of door by which we enter his heavenly kingdom.

M.—Where are we to seek for this word?

S.—In the Holy Scriptures, in which it is contained.

M.—How are you to use it in order to profit by it?

S.—By embracing it with entire heartfelt persuasion, as certain truth come down from heaven-by being docile, and subjecting our minds and wills in obedience to it- by loving it sincerely-by having it once for all engraven on our hearts, and there rooted so as to produce fruit in our life-finally, by being formed after its rule. Then shall it turn to our salvation, as it was intended.

M.—Are all these things put in our own power?

S.—None of them at all; but every thing

which I have mentioned it belongs to God only to effect in us by the gift of his Spirit.

M.—But are we not to use diligence, and zealously strive to profit in it by reading, hearing, and meditating?

S.—Yea, verily: seeing that every one ought to exercise himself in the daily reading of it, and all should be especially careful to attend the sermons when the doctrine of salvation is expounded in the assembly of the faithful.

M.—You affirm then that it is not enough for each to read privately at home, and that all ought to meet in common to hear the same doctrine?

S.—They must meet when they can-that is, when an opportunity is given.

M.—Are you able to prove this to me?

S.—The will of God alone ought to be amply sufficient for proof; and the order which he hath recommended to his church is not what two or three only might observe, but all should obey in common. Moreover, he declares this to be the only method of edifying as well as preserving. This, then, should be a sacred and inviolable rule to us, and no one should think himself entitled to be wise above his Master.

M.—Is it necessary, then, that pastors should preside over churches?

S.—Nay; it is necessary to hear them, and listen with fear and reverence to the doctrine of Christ as propounded from their lips.

M.—But is it enough for a Christian man to have been instructed by his pastor once, or ought he to observe this course during life?

S.—It is little to have begun, unless you persevere. We must be the disciples of Christ to the end, or rather without end. But he has committed to the ministers of the Church the office of teaching in his name and stead.

The Sacraments

M.—Is there no other medium, as it is called, than the Word by which God may communicate himself to us?

S.—To the preaching of the Word he has added the Sacraments.

M.—What is a Sacrament?

S.—An outward attestation of the divine benevolence towards us, which, by a visible sign, figures spiritual grace, to seal the promises of God on our hearts, and thereby better confirm their truth to us.

M.—Is there such virtue in a visible sign that it can establish our consciences in a full assurance of salvation?

S.—This virtue it has not of itself, but by the will of God, because it was instituted for this end.

M.—Seeing it is the proper office of the Holy Spirit to seal the promises of God on our minds, how do you attribute this to the sacraments?

S.—There is a wide difference between him and them. To move and affect the heart, to enlighten the mind, to render the conscience sure and tranquil, truly belongs to the Spirit alone; so that it ought to be regarded as wholly his work, and be ascribed to him alone, that no other may have the praise; but this does not at all prevent God from employing the sacraments as secondary instruments, and applying them to what use he deems proper, without derogating in any respect from the agency of the Spirit.

M.—You think, then, that the power and efficacy of a sacrament is not contained in the outward element, but flows entirely from the Spirit of God?

S.—I think so; viz., that the Lord hath been pleased to exert his energy by his instruments, this being the purpose to which he destined them: this he does without detracting in any respect from the virtue of his Spirit.

M.—Can you give me a reason why he so acts?

S.—In this way he consults our weakness. If we were wholly spiritual, we might, like the angels, spiritually behold both him and his grace; but as we are surrounded with this body of clay, we need figures or mirrors to exhibit a view of spiritual and heavenly things in a kind of earthly manner; for we could not otherwise attain to them. At the same time, it is our interest to have all our senses exercised in the promises of God, that they may be the better confirmed to us.

M.—If it is true that the sacraments were instituted by God to be helps to our necessity, is it not arrogance for any one to hold that he can dispense with them as unnecessary?

S.—It certainly is; and hence, if any one of his own accord abstains from the use of them, as if he had no need of them, he contemns Christ, spurns his grace, and quenches the Spirit.

M.—But what confidence can there be in the sacraments as a means of establishing the conscience, and what certain security can be conceived from things which the good and bad use indiscriminately?

S.—Although the wicked, so to speak, annihilate the gifts of God offered in the sacraments in so far as regards themselves, they do not thereby deprive the sacraments of their nature and virtue.

M.—How, then, and when does the effect follow the use of the sacraments?

S.—When we receive them in faith, seeking Christ alone and his grace in them.

M.—Why do you say that Christ is to be sought in them?

S.—I mean that we are not to cleave to the visible signs so as to seek salvation from them, or imagine that the power of conferring grace is either fixed or included in them, but rather that the sign is to be used as a help, by which, when seeking salvation and complete felicity, we are pointed directly to Christ.

M.—Seeing that faith is requisite for the use of them, how do you say that they are given us to confirm our faith, to make us more certain of the promises of God?

S.—It is by no means sufficient that faith is once begun in us. It must be nourished continually, and increase more and more every day. To nourish, strengthen, and advance it, the Lord instituted the sacraments. This indeed Paul intimates, when he says that they have the effect of sealing the promises of God. (Rom. iv. 11.)

M.—But is it not an indication of unbelief not to have entire faith in the promises of God until they are confirmed to us from another source?

S.—It certainly argues a weakness of faith under which the children of God labor. They do not, however, cease to be believers, though the faith with which they are endued is still small and imperfect; for as long as we continue in this world remains of distrust cleave to our flesh, and these there is no other way of shaking off than by making continual progress even unto the end. It is therefore always necessary to be going forward.

M.—How many are the sacraments of the Christian Church?

S.—There are only two, whose use is common among all believers.

M.—What are they?

S.—Baptism and the Holy Supper.

M.—What likeness or difference is there between them?

S.—Baptism is a kind of entrance into the Church; for we have in it a testimony that we who are otherwise strangers and aliens, are received into the family of God, so as to be counted of his household; on the other hand, the Supper attests that God exhibits himself to us by nourishing our souls.

M.—That the meaning of both may be more clear to us, let us treat of them separately. First, what is the meaning of Baptism?

S.—It consists of two parts. For, first, Forgiveness of sins; and, secondly, Spiritual regencration, is figured by it. (Eph. v. 26 ; Rom. vi. 4.)

M.—What resemblance has water "with these things, so as to represent them?

S.—Forgiveness of sins is a kind of washing, by which our souls are cleansed from their defilements, just as bodily stains are washed away by water.

M.—What do you say of Regeneration?

S.—Since the mortification of our nature is its beginning, and our becoming new creatures its end, a figure of death is set before us when the water is poured upon the head, and the figure of a new life when instead of remaining immersed under water, we only enter it for a moment as a kind of grave, out of which we instantly emerge.

M.—Do you think that the water is a washing of the soul?

S.—By no means; for it were impious to snatch away this honor from the blood of Christ, which was shed in order to wipe away all our stains, and render us pure and unpolluted in the sight of God. (1 Pet. i. 19; 1 John i. 7.) And we receive the fruit of this cleansing when the Holy Spirit sprinkles our consciences with that sacred blood. Of this we have a seal in the Sacrament.

M.—But do you attribute nothing more to the water than that it is a figure of ablution?

S.—I understand it to be a figure, but still so that the reality is annexed to it; for God does not disappoint us when he promises us his gifts. Accordingly, it is certain that both pardon of sins and newness of life are offered to us in baptism, and received by us.

M.—Is this grace bestowed on all indiscriminately?

S.—Many precluding its entrance by their depravity, make it void to themselves. Hence the benefit extends to believers only, and yet the Sacrament loses nothing of its nature.

M.—Whence is Regeneration derived?

S.—From the Death and Resurrection of Christ taken together. His death hath this efficacy, that by means of it our old man is crucified, and the vitiosity of our nature in a manner buried, so as no more to be in vigor in us. Our reformation to a new life, so as to obey the righteousness of God, is the result of the resurrection.

M.—How are these blessings bestowed upon us by Baptism?

S.—If we do not render the promises there offered unfruitful by rejecting them, we are clothed with Christ, and presented with his Spirit.

M.—What must we do in order to use Baptism duly?

S.—The right use of Baptism consists in faith and repentance; that is, we must first hold with a firm heartfelt reliance that, being purified from all stains by the blood of Christ, we are pleasing to God: secondly, we must feel his Spirit dwelling in us, and declare this to others by our actions, and we must constantly exercise ourselves in aiming at the mortification of our flesh, and obedience to the righteousness of God.

M.—If these things are requisite to the legitimate use of Baptism, how comes it that we baptize Infants?

S.—It is not necessary that faith and repentance should always precede baptism. They are only required from those whose age makes them capable of both. It will be sufficient, then, if, after infants have grown up, they exhibit the power of their baptism.

M.—Can you demonstrate by reason that there is nothing absurd in this?

S.—Yes; if it be conceded to me that our Lord instituted nothing at variance with reason. For while Moses and all the Prophets teach that circumcision was a sign of repentance, and was even as Paul declares the sacrament of faith, we see that infants were not excluded from it. (Deut. xxx. 6; Jer. iv. 4; Rom. iv. 11.)

M.—But are they now admitted to Baptism for the same reason that was valid in circumcision?

S.—The very same, seeing that the promises which God anciently gave to the people of Israel are now published through the whole world.

M.—But do you infer from thence that the sign also is to be used?

S.—He who will duly ponder all things in both ordinances, will perceive this to follow. Christ in making us partakers of his grace, which had been formerly bestowed on Israel, did not condition, that it should either be more obscure or in some respect less abundant. Nay, rather he shed it upon us both more clearly and more abundantly.

M.—Do you think that if infants are denied baptism, some thing is thereby deducted from the grace of God, and it must be said to have been diminished by the coming of Christ?

S.—That indeed is evident; for the sign being taken away, which tends very much to testify the mercy of God and confirm the promises, we should want an admirable consolation which those of ancient times enjoyed.

M.—Your view then is, that since God, under the Old Testament, in order to show himself the Father of infants, was pleased that the promise of salvation should be engraven on their bodies by a visible sign, it were unbecoming to suppose that, since the advent of Christ, believers have less to confirm them, God having intended to give us in the present day the same promise which was anciently given to the Fathers, and exhibited in Christ a clearer specimen of his goodness?

S.—That is my view. Besides, while it is sufficiently clear that the force, and so to speak, the substance of Baptism are common to children, to deny them the sign, which is inferior to the substance, were manifest injustice.

M.—On what terms then are children to be baptized?

S.—To attest that they are heirs of the blessing promised to the seed of believers, and enable them to receive and produce the fruit of their Baptism, on acknowledging its reality after they have grown up.

M.—Let us now pass to the Supper. And, first, I should like to know from you what its meaning is.

S.—It was instituted by Christ in order that by the communication of his body and blood, he might teach and assure us that our souls are being trained in the hope of eternal life.

M.—But why is the body of our Lord figured by bread, and his blood by wine?

S.—We are hence taught that such virtue as bread has in nourishing our bodies to sustain the present life, the same has the body of our Lord spiritually to nourish our souls. As by wine the hearts of men are gladdened, their strength recruited, and the whole man strengthened, so by the blood of our Lord the same benefits are received by our souls.

M.—Do we therefore eat the body and blood of the Lord?

S.—I understand so. For as our whole reliance for salvation depends on him, in order that the obedience which he yielded to the Father may be imputed to us just as if it were ours, it is necessary that he be possessed by us; for the only way in which he communicates his blessings to us is by making himself ours.

M.—But did he not give himself when he exposed himself to death, that he might redeem us from the sentence of death, and reconcile us to God?

S.—That is indeed true; but it is not enough for us unless we now receive him, that thus the efficacy and fruit of his death may reach us.

M.—Does not the manner of receiving consist in faith?

S.—I admit it does. But I at the same time add, that this is done when we not only believe that he died in order to free us from death, and was raised up that he might purchase life for us, but recognize that he dwells in us, and that we are united to him by a union the same in kind as that which unites the members to the head, that by virtue of this union we may become partakers of all his blessings.

M.— Do we obtain this communion by the Supper alone?

S.—No, indeed. For by the gospel also, as Paul declares, Christ is communicated to us. And Paul justly declares this, seeing we are there told that we are flesh of his flesh and bones of his bones-that he is the living bread which came down from heaven to nourish our souls-that we are one with him as he is one with the Father, &c. (1 Cor. i. 6; Eph. v. 30; John vi. 51; John xvii. 21.)

M.—What more do we obtain from the sacrament, or what other benefit does it confer upon us?

S.—The communion of which I spoke is thereby confirmed and increased; for although Christ is exhibited to us both in baptism and in the gospel, we do not however receive him entire, but in part only.

M.—What then have we in the symbol of bread?

S.—As the body of Christ was once sacrificed for us to reconcile us to God, so now also is it given to us, that we may certainly know that reconciliation belongs to us.

M.—What in the symbol of wine?

S.—That as Christ once shed his blood for the satisfaction of our sins, and as the price of our redemption, so he now also gives it to us to drink, that we may feel the benefit which should thence accrue to us.

M.—According to these two answers, the holy Supper of the Lord refers us to his death, that we may communicate in its virtue?

S.—Wholly so; for then the one perpetual sacrifice, sufficient for our salvation, was performed. Hence nothing more remains for us but to enjoy it.

M.—The Supper then was not instituted in order to offer up to God the body of his Son?

S.—By no means. He himself alone, as priest for ever, has this privilege; and so his words express when he says, "Take, eat." He there commands us not to offer his body, but only to eat it. (Heb. v. 10; Matt. xxvi. 26.)

M.—Why do we use two signs?

S.—Therein the Lord consulted our weakness, teaching us in a more familiar manner that he is not only food to our souls, but drink also, so that we are not to seek any part of spiritual life anywhere else than in him alone.

M.—Ought all without exception to use both alike?

S.—So the commandment of Christ bears: and to derogate from it in any way, by attempting anything contrary to it, is wicked.

M.—Have we in the Supper only a figure of the benefits which you have mentioned, or are they there exhibited to us reality?

S.—Seeing that our Lord Jesus Christ is truth itself; there cannot be a doubt that he at the same time fulfils the promises which he there gives us, and adds the reality to the figures. Wherefore I doubt not that as he testifies by words and signs, so he also makes us partakers of his substance, that thus we may have one life with him.

M.—But how can this be, when the body of Christ is in heaven, and we are still pilgrims on the earth?

S.—This he accomplishes by the secret and miraculous agency of his Spirit, to whom it is not difficult to unite things otherwise disjoined by a distant space.

M.—You do not imagine then, either that the body is in-closed in the bread or the blood in the wine?

S.—Neither is inclosed. My understanding rather is, that in order to obtain the reality of the signs, our minds must be raised to heaven, where Christ is, and from whence we expect him as Judge and Redeemer, and that it is improper and vain to seek him in these earthly elements.

M.—To collect the substance of what you have said-You maintain that there are two things in the Supper, viz., bread and wine, which are seen by the eyes, handled by the hands, and perceived by the taste, and Christ by whom our souls are inwardly fed as with their own proper aliment?

S.—True; and so much so that the resurrection of the body also is there confirmed to us by a kind of pledge, since the body also shares in the symbol of life.

M.—What is the right and legitimate use of this Sacrament?

S.—That which Paul points out, "Let a man examine himself;" before he approach to it. (1 Cor. xi. 28.)

M.—Into what is he to inquire in this examination?

S.—Whether he be a true member of Christ.

M.—By what evidence may he come to know this?

S.—If he is endued with faith and repentance, if he entertains sincere love for his neighbor, if he has his mind pure from all hatred and malice.

M.—Do you require that a man's faith and charity should both be perfect?

S.—Both should be entire and free from all hypocrisy, but it were vain to demand an absolute perfection to which nothing should be wanting, seeing that none such will ever be found in man.

M.—Then the imperfection under which we still labor does not forbid our approach?

S.—On the contrary, were we perfect, the Supper would no longer be of any use to us. It should be a help to aid our weakness, and a support to our imperfection.

M.—Is no other end besides proposed by these two Sacraments?

S.—They are also marks and as it were badges of our profession. For by the use of them we profess our faith before men, and testify our consent in the religion of Christ.

M.—Were any one to despise the use of them, in what light should it be regarded?

S.—As an indirect denial of Christ. Assuredly such a person, inasmuch as he deigns not to confess himself a Christian, deserves not to be classed among Christians.

M.—Is it enough to receive both once in a lifetime?

S.—It is enough so to receive baptism, which may not be repeated. It is different with the Supper.

M.—What is the difference?

S.—By baptism the Lord adopts us and brings us into his Church, so as thereafter to regard us as part of his house-hold. After he has admitted us among the number of his people, he testifies by the Supper that he takes a continual interest in nourishing us.

M.—Does the administration both of baptism and of the Supper belong indiscriminately to all?

S.—By no means. It is confined to those to whom the office of teaching has been committed. For the two things, viz., to feed the Church with the doctrine of piety and administer the sacrament, are united together by an indissoluble tie.

M.—Can you prove this to me by the testimony of Scripture?

S.—Christ gave special commandment to the Apostles to baptize. In the celebration of the Supper he ordered us to follow his example. And the Evangelists relate that he himself in dispensing it, performed the office of a public minister. (Matt. xxviii. 19; Luke xxii. 19.)

M.—But ought pastors, to whom the dispensing of it has been committed, to admit all indiscriminately without selection?

S.—In regard to baptism, as it is now bestowed only on infants, there is no room for discrimination; but in the Supper the minister ought to take heed not to give it to any one who is clearly unworthy of receiving it.

M.—Why so?

S.—Because it cannot be done without insulting and profaning the Sacrament.

M.—But did not Christ admit Judas, impious though he was, to the Communion?

S.—I admit it; as his impiety was still secret. For though it was not unknown to Christ, it had not come to light or the knowledge of men. (Matt. xxvi. 25.)

M.—What then can be done with hypocrites?

S.—The pastor cannot keep them back as unworthy, but must wait till such time as God shall reveal their iniquity, and make it manifest to all.

M.—But if he knows or has been warned that an individual is unworthy?

S.—Even that would not be sufficient to keep him back from communicating, unless in addition to it there was a legitimate investigation and decision of the Church.

M.—It is of importance, then, that there should be a certain order of government established in churches?

S.—It is: they cannot otherwise be well managed or duly constituted. The method is for elders to be chosen to preside as censors of manners, to guard watchfully against offences, and exclude from communion all whom they recognize to be unfit for it, and who could not be admitted without profaning the Sacrament.

Teaching

The Westminster Shorter Catechism with Scripture Proofs

[The Westminster Shorter Catechism was completed in 1647 by the Westminster Assembly and continues to serve as part of the doctrinal standards of many Presbyterian churches. The biblical proof texts were prepared by a special committee of the General Assembly of the Orthodox Presbyterian Church.]

Q. 1. What is the chief end of man?
A. Man's chief end is to glorify God, [a] and to enjoy him for ever [b].
[a]. Ps. 86:9; Isa. 60:21; Rom. 11:36; I Cor. 6:20; 10:31; Rev. 4:11
[b]. Ps. 16:5-11; 144:15; Isa. 12:2; Luke 2:10; Phil. 4:4; Rev. 21:3-4

Q. 2. What rule hath God given to direct us how we may glorify and enjoy him?
A. The Word of God, which is contained in the Scriptures of the Old and New Testaments, [a] is the only rule to direct us how we may glorify and enjoy him [b].
[a]. Matt. 19:4-5 with Gen. 2:24; Luke 24:27, 44; I Cor. 2:13; 14:37; II Pet. 1:20-21; 3:2, 15-16
[b]. Deut. 4:2; Ps. 19:7-11; Isa. 18:20; John 15:11; 20:30-31; Acts 17:11; II Tim. 3:15-17; I John 1:4

Q. 3. What do the Scriptures principally teach?
A. The Scriptures principally teach what man is to believe concerning God, [a] and what duty God requires of man [b].
[a]. Gen. 1:1; John 5:39; 20:31; Rom. 10:17; II Tim. 3:15
[b]. Deut. 10:12-13; Josh. 1:8; Ps. 119:105; Mic. 6:8; II Tim. 3:16-17

Q. 4. What is God?
A. God is a Spirit [a], infinite [b], eternal [c], and unchangeable [d] in his being [e], wisdom [f], power [g], holiness [h], justice [i], goodness [j], and truth [k].
[a]. Deut. 4:15-19; Luke 24:39; John 1:18; 4:24; Acts 17:29
[b]. I Kings 8:27; Ps. 139:7-10; 145:3; 147:5; Jer. 23:24; Rom. 11:33-36
[c]. Deut. 33:27; Ps. 90:2; 102:12, 24-27; Rev. 1:4,8
[d]. Ps. 33:11; Mal. 3:6; Heb. 1:12; 6:17-18; 13:8; Jas. 1:17
[e]. Ex. 3:14; Ps. 115:2-3; I Tim. 1:17; 6:15-16
[f]. Ps. 104:24; Rom. 11:33-34; Heb. 4:13; I John 3:20
[g]. Gen. 17:1; Ps. 62:11; Jer. 32:17; Mat. 19:26; Rev. 1:8
[h]. Heb. 1:13; I Pet. 1:15-16; I John 3:3,

5; Rev. 15:4
[i]. Gen. 18:25; Ex. 34:6-7; Deut. 32:4; Ps. 96:13; Rom. 3:5, 26
[j]. Ps. 103:5; 107:8; Matt. 19:17; Rom. 2:4
[k]. Ex. 34:6; Deut. 32:4; Ps. 86:15; 117:2; Heb. 6:18

Q. 5. Are there more Gods than one?
A. There is but one only [a], the living and true God [b].
[a]. Deut. 6:4; Isa. 44:6; 45:21-22; I Cor. 8:4-6
[b]. Jer. 10:10; John 17:3; I Thess. 1:9; I John 5:20

Q. 6. How many persons are there in the Godhead?
A. There are three persons in the Godhead; the Father, the Son, and the Holy Ghost [a]; and these three are one God, the same in substance, equal in power and glory [b].
[a]. Matt. 3:16-17; 28:19; II Cor. 13:14; I Pet. 1:2
[b]. Ps. 45:6; John 1:1; 17:5; Acts 5:3-4; Rom. 9:5; Col. 2:9; Jude 24-25

Q. 7. What are the decrees of God?
A. The decrees of God are, his eternal purpose, according to the counsel of his will, whereby, for his own glory, he hath foreordained whatsoever comes to pass [a].
[a]. Ps. 33:11; Isa. 14:24; Acts 2:23; Eph. 1:11-12

Q. 8. How doth God execute his decrees?
A. God executeth his decrees in the works of creation and providence [a].
[a]. Ps. 148:8; Isa. 40:26; Dan. 4:35; Acts 4:24-28; Rev. 4:11

Q. 9. What is the work of creation?
A. The work of creation is, God's making all things of nothing, by the word of his power [a], in the space of six days, and all very good [b].
[a]. Gen. 1:1; Ps. 33:6, 9; Heb. 11:3
[b]. Gen. 1:31

Q. 10. How did God create man?
A. God created man male and female, after

his own image [a], in knowledge [b],
righteousness, and holiness [c], with
dominion over the creatures [d].
[a]. Gen. 1:27
[b]. Col. 3:10
[c]. Eph. 4:24
[d]. Gen. 1:28; see Ps. 8

Q. 11. What are God's works of
providence?
A. God's works of providence are, his most
holy [a], wise [b], and powerful [c]
preserving [d] and governing [e] all his
creatures, and all their actions [f].
[a]. Ps. 145:17
[b]. Ps. 104:24
[c]. Heb. 1:3
[d]. Neh. 9:6
[e]. Eph. 1:19-22
[f]. Ps. 36:6; Prov. 16:33; Matt. 10:30

Q. 12. What special act of providence did
God exercise toward man in the estate
wherein he was created?
A. When God had created man, he
entered into a covenant of life with him,
upon condition of perfect obedience;
forbidding him to eat of the tree of the
knowledge of good and evil, upon pain of
death [a].
[a]. Gen. 2:16-17; Jas. 2:10

Q. 13. Did our first parents continue in
the estate wherein they were created?
A. Our first parents, being left to the
freedom of their own will, fell from the
estate wherein they were created, by
sinning against God [a].
[a]. Gen. 3:6-8, 13; II Cor. 11:3
Q. 14. What is sin?
A. Sin is any want of conformity unto, or
transgression of, the law of God [a].
[a]. Lev. 5:17; Jas. 4:17; I John 3:4

Q. 15. What was the sin whereby our first
parents fell from the estate wherein they
were created?
A. The sin whereby our first parents fell
from the estate wherein thy were created,
was their eating the forbidden fruit [a].
[a]. Gen. 3:6

Q. 16. Did all mankind fall in Adam's first
transgression?
A. The covenant being made with Adam
[a], not only for himself, but for his
posterity; all mankind, descending from
him by ordinary generation, sinned in
him, and fell with him, in his first
transgression [b].
[a]. Gen. 2:16-17; Jas. 2:10
[b]. Rom. 5:12-21; I Cor. 15:22

Q. 17. Into what estate did the fall bring
mankind?
A. The fall brought mankind into an estate
of sin and misery [a].
[a]. Gen. 3:16-19, 23; Rom. 3:16; 5:12;
Eph. 2:1

Q. 18. Wherein consists the sinfulness of
that estate whereinto man fell?
A. The sinfulness of that estate whereinto
man fell, consists in the guilt of Adam's
first sin [a], the want of original
righteousness [b], and the corruption of
his whole nature [c], which is commonly
called original sin; together with all actual
transgressions which proceed from it [d].
[a]. Rom. 5:12, 19
[b]. Rom. 3:10; Col. 3:10; Eph. 4:24
[c]. Ps. 51:5; John 3:6; Rom. 3:18; 8:7-8;
Eph. 2:3
[d]. Gen. 6:5; Ps. 53:1-3; Matt. 15:19;
Rom. 3:10-18, 23; Gal. 5:19-21; Jas.
1:14-15

Q. 19. What is the misery of that estate
whereinto man fell?
A. All mankind by their fall lost
communion with God [a], are under his
wrath [b] and curse [c], and so made liable
to all miseries in this life [d], to death [e]
itself, and to the pains of hell for ever [f].
[a]. Gen. 3:8, 24; John 8:34, 42, 44; Eph.
2:12; 4:18
[b]. John 3:36; Rom. 1:18; Eph. 2:3; 5:6
[c]. Gal. 3:10; Rev. 22:3
[d]. Gen. 3:16-19; Job 5:7; Ecc. 2:22-23;
Rom. 8:18-23
[e]. Ezek. 18:4; Rom. 5:12; 6:23
[f]. Matt. 25:41, 46; II Thess. 1:9; Rev.
14:9-11

Q. 20. Did God leave all mankind to perish in the estate of sin and misery?
A. God having, out of his mere good pleasure, from all eternity, elected some to everlasting life [a,] did enter into a covenant of grace, to deliver them out of the estate of sin and misery, and to bring them into an estate of salvation by a Redeemer [b].
[a]. Acts 13:48; Eph. 1:4-5; II Thess. 2:13-14
[b]. Gen. 3:15; 17:7; Ex. 19:5-6; Jer. 31:31-34; Matt. 20:28; I Cor. 11:25; Heb. 9:15

Q. 21. Who is the Redeemer of God's elect?
A. The only Redeemer of God's elect is the Lord Jesus Christ [a], who, being the eternal Son of God [b], became man [c] and so was, and continueth to be, God and man in two distinct natures, and one person, forever [d].
[a]. John 14:6; Acts 4:12; I Tim. 2:5-6
[b]. Ps. 2:7; Matt. 3:17; 17:5; John 1:18
[c]. Isa. 9:6; Matt. 1:23; John 1:14; Gal. 4:4
[d]. Acts 1:11; Heb. 7:24-25

Q. 22. How did Christ, being the Son of God, become man?
A. Christ, the Son of God, became man, by taking to himself a true body, and a reasonable soul [a], being conceived by the power of the Holy Ghost, in the womb of the virgin Mary, and born of her [b] yet without sin [c].
[a]. Phil. 2:7; Heb. 2:14, 17
[b]. Luke 1:27, 31, 35
[c]. II Cor. 5:21; Heb. 4:15; 7:26; I John 3:5

Q. 23. What offices doth Christ execute as our Redeemer?
A. Christ, as our Redeemer, executeth the offices of a prophet [a], of a priest [b], and of a king [c], both in his estate of humiliation and exaltation.
[a]. Deut. 18:18; Acts 2:33; 3:22-23; Heb. 1:1-2
[b]. Heb. 4:14-15; 5:5-6
[c]. Isa. 9:6-7; Luke 1:32-33; John 18:37; I Cor. 15:25

Q. 24. How doth Christ execute the office of a prophet?
A. Christ executeth the office of a prophet, in revealing to us, by his Word [a] and Spirit [b,] the will of God for our salvation [c].
[a]. Luke 4:18-19, 21; Acts 1:1-2; Heb. 2:3
[b]. John 15:26-27; Acts 1:8; I Pet. 1:11
[c]. John 4:41-42; 20:30-31

Q. 25. How doth Christ execute the office of a priest?
A. Christ executeth the office of a priest, in his once offering up of himself a sacrifice to satisfy divine justice [a], and reconcile us to God [b]; and in making continual intercession for us [c].
[a]. Isa. 53; Acts 8:32-35; Heb. 9:26-28; 10:12
[b]. Rom. 5:10-11; II Cor. 5:18; Col. 1:21-22
[c]. Rom. 8:34; Heb. 7:25; 9:24

Q. 26. How doth Christ execute the office of a king?
A. Christ executeth the office of a king, in subduing us to himself, in ruling and defending us [a], and in restraining and conquering all his and our enemies [b].
[a]. Ps. 110:3; Matt. 28:18-20; John 17:2; Col. 1:13
[b]. Ps. 2:6-9; 110:1-2; Matt. 12:28; I Cor. 15:24-26; Col. 2:15

Q. 27. Wherein did Christ's humiliation consist?
A. Christ's humiliation consisted in his being born, and that in a low condition [a], made under the law [b], undergoing the miseries of this life [c], the wrath of God [d], and the cursed death of the cross [e]; in being buried, and continuing under the power of death for a time [f].
[a]. Luke 2:7; II Cor. 8:9; Gal. 4:4
[b]. Gal. 4:4
[c]. Isa. 53:3; Luke 9:58; John 4:6; 11:35; Heb. 2:18
[d]. Ps. 22:1 (Matt. 27:46); Isa. 53:10; I John 2:2
[e]. Gal. 3:13; Phil. 2:8
[f]. Matt. 12:40; I Cor. 15:3-4

Q. 28. Wherein consisteth Christ's exaltation?
A. Christ's exaltation consisteth in his rising again from the dead on the third day [a], in ascending up into heaven [b], in sitting at the right hand [c] of God the Father, and in coming to judge the world at the last day [d].
[a]. I Cor. 15:4
[b]. Ps. 68:18; Acts 1:11; Eph. 4:8
[c]. Ps. 110:1; Acts 2:33-34; Heb. 1:3
[d]. Matt. 16:27; Acts 17:31

Q. 29. How are we made partakers of the redemption purchased by Christ?
A. We are made partakers of the redemption purchased by Christ, by the effectual application of it to us by his Holy Spirit [a].
[a]. Titus 3:4-7

Q. 30. How doth the Spirit apply to us the redemption purchased by Christ?
A. The Spirit applieth to us the redemption purchased by Christ, by working faith in us [a], and thereby uniting us to Christ in our effectual calling [b].
[a]. Rom. 10:17; I Cor. 2:12-16; Eph. 2:8; Phil. 1:29
[b]. John 15:5; I Cor. 1:9; Eph. 3:17

Q. 31. What is effectual calling?
A. Effectual calling is the work of God's Spirit, whereby, convincing us of our sin and misery, enlightening our minds in the knowledge of Christ [a], and renewing our wills [b], he doth persuade and enable us to embrace Jesus Christ [c], freely offered to us in the gospel [d].
[a]. Acts 26:18; I Cor. 2:10, 12; II Cor. 4:6; Eph. 1:17-18
[b]. Deut. 30:6; Ezk. 36:26-27; John 3:5; Titus 3:5
[c]. John 6:44-45; Acts 16:14
[d]. Isa. 45:22; Matt. 11:28-30; Rev. 22:17

Q. 32. What benefits do they that are effectually called partake of in this life?
A. They that are effectually called do in this life partake of justification, adoption,

and sanctification, and the several benefits which in this life do either accompany or flow from them [a].
[a]. Rom. 8:30; I Cor. 1:30; 6:11; Eph. 1:5

Q. 33. What is justification?
A. Justification is an act of God's free grace [a], wherein he pardoneth all our sins [b], and accepteth us as righteous in his sight [c], only for the righteousness of Christ imputed to us [d], and received by faith alone [e].
[a]. Rom. 3:24
[b]. Rom. 4:6-8; II Cor. 5:19
[c]. II Cor. 5:21
[d]. Rom. 4:6, 11; 5:19
[e]. Gal. 2:16; Phil. 3:9

Q. 34. What is adoption?
A. Adoption is an act of God's free grace [a], whereby we are received into the number, and have a right to all the privileges, of the sons of God [b].
[a]. I John 3:1
[b]. John 1:12; Rom. 8:17

Q. 35. What is sanctification?
A. Sanctification is the work of God's free grace [a], whereby we are renewed in the whole man after the image of God [b], and are enabled more and more to die unto sin, and live unto righteousness [c].
[a]. Ezk. 36:27; Phil. 2:13; II Thess. 2:13
[b]. II Cor. 5:17; Eph. 4:23-24; I Thess. 5:23
[c]. Ezk. 36:25-27; Rom. 6:4, 6, 12-14; II Cor. 7:1; I Pet. 2:24

Q. 36. What are the benefits which in this life do accompany or flow from justification, adoption, and sanctification?
A. The benefits which in this life do accompany or flow from justification, adoption, and sanctification, are, assurance of God's love [a], peace of conscience [b], joy in the Holy Ghost [c], increase of grace [d], and perseverance therein to the end [e].
[a]. Rom. 5:5
[b]. Rom. 5:1
[c]. Rom. 14:17

[d]. II Pet. 3:18
[e]. Phil. 1:6; I Pet. 1:5

Q. 37. What benefits do believers receive
from Christ at death?
A. The souls of believers are at their death
made perfect in holiness [a], and do
immediately pass into glory [b]; and their
bodies, being still united to Christ [c], do
rest in their graves till the resurrection [d].
[a]. Heb. 12:23
[b]. Luke 23:43; II Cor. 5:6, 8; Phil. 1:23
[c]. I Thess. 4:14
[d]. Dan. 12:2; John 5:28-29; Acts 24:15

Q. 38. What benefits do believers receive
from Christ at the resurrection?
A. At the resurrection, believers being
raised up in glory [a], shall be openly
acknowledged and acquitted in the day of
judgment [b], and made perfectly blessed
in the full enjoying of God [c] to all
eternity [d].
[a]. I Cor. 15:42-43
[b]. Matt. 25:33-34, 46
[c]. Rom. 8:29; I John 3:2
[d]. Ps. 16:11; I Thess. 4:17

Q. 39. What is the duty which God
requireth of man?
A. The duty which God requireth of man,
is obedience to his revealed will [a].
[a]. Deut. 29:29; Mic. 6:8; I John 5:2-3

Q. 40. What did God at first reveal to man
for the rule of his obedience?
A. The rule which God at first revealed to
man for his obedience, was the moral law
[a].
[a]. Rom. 2:14-15; 10:5

Q. 41. Wherein is the moral law
summarily comprehended?
A. The moral law is summarily
comprehended in the ten commandments
[a].
[a]. Deut. 4:13; Matt. 19:17-19

Q. 42. What is the sum of the ten
commandments?
A. The sum of the ten commandments is,

To love the Lord our God with all our
heart, with all our soul, with all our
strength, and with all our mind; and our
neighbor as ourselves [a].
[a]. Matt. 22:37-40

Q. 43. What is the preface to the ten
commandments?
A. The preface to the ten commandments
is in these words, I am the Lord thy God,
which have brought thee out of the land of
Egypt, out of the house of bondage [a].
[a]. Ex. 20:2; Deut. 5:6

Q. 44. What doth the preface to the ten
commandments teach us?
A. The preface to the ten commandments
teacheth us, That because God is the Lord,
and our God, and Redeemer, therefore we
are bound to keep all his commandments
[a].
[a]. Luke 1:74-75; I Pet. 1:14-19

Q. 45. Which is the first commandment?
A. The first commandment is, Thou shalt
have no other gods before me [a].
[a]. Ex. 20:3; Deut. 5:7

Q. 46. What is required in the first
commandment?
A. The first commandment requireth us to
know and acknowledge God to be the only
true God, and our God; and to worship
and glorify him accordingly [a].
[a]. I Chron. 28:9; Isa. 45:20-25; Matt.
4:10

Q. 47. What is forbidden in the first
commandment?
A. The first commandment forbiddeth the
denying [a], or not worshiping and
glorifying the true God as God [b], and
our God [c]; and the giving of that
worship and glory to any other, which is
due to him alone [d].
[a]. Ps. 14:1
[b]. Rom. 1:20-21
[c]. Ps. 81:10-11
[d]. Ezek. 8:16-18; Rom. 1:25

Q. 48. What are we specially taught by

these words, "before me," in the first commandment?

A. These words, before me, in the first commandment teach us, that God, who seeth all things, taketh notice of, and is much displeased with, the sin of having any other God [a].

[a]. Deut. 30:17-18; Ps. 44:20-21; Ezek. 8:12

Q. 49. Which is the second commandment?

A. The second commandment is, Thou shalt not make unto thee any graven image, or any likeness of anything that is in heaven above, or that is in the earth beneath, or that is in the water under the earth: thou shalt not bow down thy self to them, nor serve them: for I the Lord thy God am a jealous God, visiting the iniquity of the fathers upon the children unto the third and fourth generation of them that hate me; and showing mercy unto thousands of them that love me, and keep my commandments [a].

[a]. Ex. 20:4-6; Deut. 5:8-10

Q. 50. What is required in the second commandment?

A. The second commandment requireth the receiving, observing, and keeping pure and entire, all such religious worship and ordinances as God hath appointed in his Word [a].

[a]. Deut. 12:32; Matt. 28:20

Q. 51. What is forbidden in the second commandment?

A. The second commandment forbiddeth the worshiping of God by images [a], or any other way not appointed in his Word [b].

[a]. Deut. 4:15-19; Rom. 1:22-23
[b]. Lev. 10:1-2; Jer. 19:4-5; Col. 2:18-23

Q. 52. What are the reasons annexed to the second commandment?

A. The reasons annexed to the second commandment are, God's sovereignty over us [a], his propriety in us [b], and the zeal he hath to his own worship [c].

[a]. Ps. 95:2-3, 6-7; 96:9-10
[b]. Ex. 19:5; Ps. 45:11; Isa. 54:5
[c]. Ex. 34:14; I Cor. 10:22

Q. 53. Which is the third commandment?

A. The third commandment is, Thou shalt not take the name of the Lord thy God in vain; for the Lord will not hold him guiltless that taketh his name in vain [a].

[a]. Ex. 20:7; Deut. 5:11

Q. 54. What is required in the third commandment?

A. The third commandment requireth the holy and reverend use of God's names, titles [a], attributes [b], ordinances [c], Word [d], and works [e].

[a]. Deut. 10:20; Ps. 29:2; Matt. 6:9
[b]. I Chron. 29:10-13; Rev. 15:3-4
[c]. Acts 2:42; I Cor. 11:27-28
[d]. Ps. 138:2; Rev. 22:18-19
[e]. Ps. 107:21-22; Rev. 4:11

Q. 55. What is forbidden in the third commandment?

A. The third commandment forbiddeth all profaning or abusing of anything whereby God maketh himself known [a].

[a]. Lev. 19:12; Matt. 5:33-37; Jas. 5:12

Q. 56. What is the reason annexed to the third commandment?

A. The reason annexed to the third commandment is, that however the breakers of this commandment may escape punishment from men, yet the Lord our God will not suffer them to escape his righteous judgment [a].

[a]. Deut. 28:58-59; I Sam. 3:13; 4:11

Q. 57. Which is the fourth commandment?

A. The fourth commandment is, Remember the sabbath day, to keep it holy. Six days shalt thou labor, and do all thy work; but the seventh day is the sabbath of the Lord thy God: in it thou shalt not do any work, thou, nor thy son, nor thy daughter, thy manservant, nor thy maidservant, nor thy cattle, nor thy stranger that is within thy gates. For in six

days the Lord made heaven and earth, the sea, and all that in them is, and rested the seventh day: wherefore the Lord blessed the sabbath day, and hallowed it [a].
[a]. Ex. 20:8-11; Deut. 5:12-15

Q. 58. What is required in the fourth commandment?
A. The fourth commandment requireth the keeping holy to God such set times as he hath appointed in his Word; expressly one whole day in seven, to be a holy sabbath to himself [a].
[a]. Ex. 31:13, 16-17

Q. 59. Which day of the seven hath God appointed to be the weekly sabbath?
A. From the beginning of the world to the resurrection of Christ, God appointed the seventh day of the week to be the weekly sabbath [a]; and the first day of the week ever since, to continue to the end of the world, which is the Christian sabbath [b].
[a]. Gen. 2:2-3; Ex. 20:11
[b]. Mark 2:27-28; Acts 20:7; I Cor. 16:2; Rev. 1:10

Q. 60. How is the sabbath to be sanctified?
A. The sabbath is to be sanctified by a holy resting all that day, even from such worldly employments and recreations as are lawful on other days [a]; and spending the whole time in the public and private exercises of God's worship [b], except so much as is to be taken up in the works of necessity and mercy [c].
[a]. Ex. 20:10; Nch. 13:15-22; Isa. 58:13-14
[b]. Ex. 20:8; Lev. 23:3; Luke 4:16; Acts 20:7
[c]. Matt. 12:1-13

Q. 61. What is forbidden in the fourth commandment?
A. The fourth commandment forbiddeth the omission or careless performance of the duties required, and the profaning the day by idleness, or doing that which is in itself sinful, or by unnecessary thoughts, words, or works, about our worldly employments or recreations [a].

[a]. Neh. 13:15-22; Isa. 58:13-14; Amos 8:4-6

Q. 62. What are the reasons annexed to the fourth commandment?
A. The reasons annexed to the fourth commandment are, God's allowing us six days of the week for our own employments [a], his challenging a special propriety in the seventh, his own example, and his blessing the sabbath day [b].
[a]. Ex. 20:9; 31:15; Lev. 23:3
[b]. Gen. 2:2-3; Ex. 20:11; 31:17

Q. 63. Which is the fifth commandment?
A. The fifth commandment is, Honor thy father and thy mother; that thy days may be long upon the land which the Lord thy God giveth thee [a].
[a]. Ex. 20:12; Deut. 5:16

Q. 64. What is required in the fifth commandment?
A. The fifth commandment requireth the preserving the honor, and performing the duties, belonging to everyone in their several places and relations, as superiors, inferiors, or equals [a].
[a]. Rom. 13:1, 7; Eph. 5:21-22, 24; 6:1, 4-5, 9; I Pet. 2:17

Q. 65. What is forbidden in the fifth commandment?
A. The fifth commandment forbiddeth the neglecting of, or doing anything against, the honor and duty which belongeth to everyone in their several places and relations [a].
[a]. Matt. 15:4-6; Rom. 13:8

Q. 66. What is the reason annexed to the fifth commandment?
A. The reason annexed to the fifth commandment is, a promise of long life and prosperity (as far as it shall serve for God's glory and their own good) to all such as keep this commandment [a].
[a]. Ex. 20:12; Deut. 5:16; Eph. 6:2-3

Q. 67. Which is the sixth commandment?
A. The sixth commandment is, Thou shalt

not kill [a].
[a]. Ex. 20:13; Deut. 5:17

Q. 68. What is required in the sixth commandment?
A. The sixth commandment requireth all lawful endeavors to preserve our own life, and the life of others [a].
[a]. Eph. 5:28-29

Q. 69. What is forbidden in the sixth commandment?
A. The sixth commandment forbiddeth the taking away of our own life, or the life of our neighbor, unjustly, or whatsoever tendeth thereunto [a].
[a]. Gen. 9:6; Matt. 5:22; I John 3:15

Q. 70. Which is the seventh commandment?
A. The seventh commandment is, Thou shalt not commit adultery [a].
[a]. Ex. 20:14; Deut. 5:18

Q. 71. What is required in the seventh commandment?
A. The seventh commandment requireth the preservation of our own and our neighbor's chastity, in heart, speech, and behavior [a].
[a]. I Cor. 7:2-3, 5; I Thess. 4:3-5

Q. 72. What is forbidden in the seventh commandment?
A. The seventh commandment forbiddeth all unchaste thoughts, words, and actions [a].
[a]. Matt. 5:28; Eph. 5:3-4

Q. 73. Which is the eighth commandment?
A. The eighth commandment is, Thou shalt not steal [a].
[a]. Ex. 20:15; Deut. 5:19

Q. 74. What is required in the eighth commandment?
A. The eighth commandment requireth the lawful procuring and furthering the wealth and outward estate of ourselves and others [a].

[a]. Lev. 25:35; Eph. 4:28b; Phil. 2:4

Q. 75. What is forbidden in the eighth commandment?
A. The eighth commandment forbiddeth whatsoever doth, or may, unjustly hinder our own, or our neighbor's, wealth or outward estate [a].
[a]. Prov. 28:19ff; Eph. 4:28a; II Thess. 3:10; I Tim. 5:8

Q. 76. Which is the ninth commandment?
A. The ninth commandment is, Thou shalt not bear false witness against thy neighbor [a].
[a]. Ex. 20:16; Deut. 5:20

Q. 77. What is required in the ninth commandment?
A. The ninth commandment requireth the maintaining and promoting of truth between man and man, and of our own and our neighbor's good name [a], especially in witness bearing [b].
[a]. Zech. 8:16; Acts 25:10; III John 12
[b]. Prov. 14:5, 25

Q. 78. What is forbidden in the ninth commandment?
A. The ninth commandment forbiddeth whatsoever is prejudicial to truth, or injurious to our own, or our neighbor's, good name [a].
[a]. Lev. 19:16; Ps. 15:3; Prov. 6:16-19; Luke 3:14

Q. 79. Which is the tenth commandment?
A. The tenth commandment is, Thou shalt not covet thy neighbor's house, thou shalt not covet thy neighbor's wife, nor his manservant, nor his maidservant, nor his ox, nor his ass, nor anything that is thy neighbor's [a].
[a]. Ex. 20:17; Deut. 5:21

Q. 80. What is required in the tenth commandment?
A. The tenth commandment requireth full contentment with our own condition [a], with a right and charitable frame of spirit toward our neighbor, and all that is his [b].

[a]. Ps. 34:1; Phil. 4:11; I Tim. 6:6; Heb. 13:5
[b]. Luke 15:6, 9, 11-32; Rom. 12:15; Phil. 2:4

Q. 81. What is forbidden in the tenth commandment?
A. The tenth commandment forbiddeth all discontentment with our own estate [a], envying or grieving at the good of our neighbor, and all inordinate motions and affections to anything that is his [b].
[a]. I Cor. 10:10; Jas. 3:14-16
[b]. Gal. 5:26; Col. 3:5

Q. 82. Is any man able perfectly to keep the commandments of God?
A. No mere man, since the fall, is able in this life perfectly to keep the commandments of God, but doth daily break them in thought, word, and deed [a].
[a]. Gen. 8:21; Rom. 3:9ff, 23

Q. 83. Are all transgressions of the law equally heinous?
A. Some sins in themselves, and by reason of several aggravations, are more heinous in the sight of God than others [a].
[a]. Ezek. 8:6, 13, 15; Matt. 11:20-24; John 19:11

Q. 84. What doth every sin deserve?
A. Every sin deserveth God's wrath and curse, both in this life, and that which is to come [a].
[a]. Matt. 25:41; Gal. 3:10; Eph. 5:6; Jas. 2:10

Q. 85. What doth God require of us, that we may escape his wrath and curse, due to us for sin?
A. To escape the wrath and curse of God, due to us for sin, God requireth of us faith in Jesus Christ, repentance unto life [a, with the diligent use of all the outward means whereby Christ communicateth to us the benefits of redemption [b].
[a]. Mark 1:15; Acts 20:21
[b]: Acts 2:38; I Cor. 11:24-25; Col. 3:16

Q. 86. What is faith in Jesus Christ?
A. Faith in Jesus Christ is a saving grace [a], whereby we receive and rest upon him alone for salvation, as he is offered to us in the gospel [b].
[a]. Eph. 2:8-9; cf. Rom. 4:16
[b]. John 20:30-31; Gal. 2:15-16; Phil. 3:3-11

Q. 87. What is repentance unto life?
A. Repentance unto life is a saving grace [a], whereby a sinner, out of a true sense of his sin, and apprehension of the mercy of God in Christ [b], doth, with grief and hatred of his sin, turn from it unto God [c], with full purpose of, and endeavor after, new obedience [d].
[a]. Acts 11:18; II Tim. 2:25
[b]. Ps. 51:1-4; Joel 2:13; Luke 15:7, 10; Acts 2:37
[c]. Jer. 31:18-19; Luke 1:16-17; I Thess. 1:9
[d]. II Chron. 7:14; Ps. 119:57-64; Matt. 3:8; II Cor. 7:10

Q. 88. What are the outward and ordinary means whereby Christ communicateth to us the benefits of redemption?
A. The outward and ordinary means whereby Christ communicateth to us the benefits of redemption are, his ordinances, especially the Word, sacraments, and prayer; all which are made effectual to the elect for salvation [a].
[a]. Matt. 28:18-20; Acts 21:41, 42

Q. 89. How is the Word made effectual to salvation?
A. The Spirit of God maketh the reading, but especially the preaching of the Word, an effectual means of convincing and converting sinners, and of building them up in holiness and comfort, through faith, unto salvation [a].
[a]. Neh. 8:8-9; Acts 20:32; Rom. 10:14-17; II Tim. 3:15-17

Q. 90. How is the Word to be read and heard, that it may become effectual to salvation?
A. That the Word may become effectual to

salvation, we must attend thereunto with diligence, preparation, and prayer [a]; receive it with faith and love, lay it up in our hearts, and practice it in our lives [b].
[a]. Deut. 6:6ff; Ps. 119:18; I Pet. 2:1-2
[b]. Ps. 119:11; II Thess. 2:10; Heb. 4:2; Jas. 1:22-25

Q. 91. How do the sacraments become effectual means of salvation?
A. The sacraments become effectual means of salvation, not from any virtue in them, or in him that doth administer them; but only by the blessing of Christ, and the working of his Spirit in them that by faith receive them [a].
[a]. I Cor. 3:7; cf. I Cor. 1:12-17

Q. 92. What is a sacrament?
A. A sacrament is an holy ordinance instituted by Christ [a]; wherein, by sensible signs, Christ, and the benefits of the new covenant, are represented, sealed, and applied to believers [b].
[a]. Matt. 28:19; 26:26-28; Mark 14:22-25; Luke 22:19-20; I Cor. 1:22-26
[b]. Gal. 3:27; I Cor. 10:16-17

Q. 93. Which are the sacraments of the New Testament?
A. The sacraments of the New Testament are, Baptism [a], and the Lord's Supper [b].
[a]. Matt. 28:19
[b]. I Cor 11:23-26

Q. 94. What is Baptism?
A. Baptism is a sacrament, wherein the washing with water in the name of the Father, and of the Son, and of the Holy Ghost [a], doth signify and seal our ingrafting into Christ, and partaking of the benefits of the covenant of grace, and our engagement to be the Lord's [b].
[a]. Matt. 28:19
[b]. Acts 2:38-42; 22:16; Rom. 6:3-4; Gal. 3:26-27; I Pet. 3:21

Q. 95. To whom is Baptism to be administered?
A. Baptism is not to be administered to any that are out of the visible church, till they profess their faith in Christ, and obedience to him [a]; but the infants of such as are members of the visible church are to be baptized [b].
[a]. Acts. 2:41; 8:12, 36, 38; 18:8
[b]. Gen. 17:7, 9-11; Acts 2:38-39; 16:32-33; Col. 2:11-12

Q. 96. What is the Lord's Supper?
A. The Lord's Supper is a sacrament, wherein, by giving and receiving bread and wine, according to Christ's appointment, his death is showed forth [a]; and the worthy receivers are, not after a corporal and carnal manner, but by faith, made partakers of his body and blood, with all his benefits, to their spiritual nourishment, and growth in grace [b].
[a]. Luke 22:19-20; I Cor. 11:23-26
[b]. I Cor. 10:16-17

Q. 97. What is required for the worthy receiving of the Lord's Supper?
A. It is required of them that would worthily partake of the Lord's Supper, that they examine themselves of their knowledge to discern the Lord's body, of their faith to feed upon him, of their repentance, love, and new obedience; lest, coming unworthily, they eat and drink judgment to themselves [a].
[a]. I Cor. 11:27-32

Q. 98. What is prayer?
A. Prayer is an offering up of our desires unto God [a], for things agreeable to his will [b], in the name of Christ [c], with confession of our sins [d], and thankful acknowledgment of his mercies [e].
[a]. Ps. 10:17; 62:8; Matt. 7:7-8
[b]. I John 5:14
[c]. John 16:23-24
[d]. Ps. 32:5-6; Dan. 9:4-19; I John 1:9
[e]. Ps. 103:1-5; 136; Phil. 4:6

Q. 99. What rule hath God given for our direction in prayer?
A. The whole Word of God is of use to direct us in prayer [a]; but the special rule of direction is that form of prayer which

Christ taught his disciples, commonly called The Lord's Prayer [b].
[a]. I John 5:14
[b]. Matt. 6:9-13

Q. 100. What doth the preface of the Lord's Prayer teach us?
A. The preface of the Lord's Prayer, which is, Our Father which art in heaven, teacheth us to draw near to God with all holy reverence [a] and confidence [b], as children to a father [c], able and ready to help us [d]; and that we should pray with and for others [e].
[a]. Ps. 95:6
[b]. Eph. 3:12
[c]. Matt. 7:9-11, cf. Luke 11:11-13; Rom. 8:15
[d]. Eph. 3:20
[e]. Eph. 6:18; I Tim. 2:1-2

Q. 101. What do we pray for in the first petition?
A. In the first petition, which is, Hallowed be thy name, we pray, that God would enable us, and others, to glorify him in all that whereby he maketh himself known [a]; and that he would dispose all things to his own glory [b].
[a]. Ps. 67:1-3; 99:3; 100:3-4
[b]. Rom. 11:33-36; Rev. 4:11

Q. 102. What do we pray for in the second petition?
A. In the second petition, which is, Thy kingdom come, we pray, that Satan's kingdom may be destroyed [a]; and that the kingdom of grace may be advanced [b], ourselves and others brought into it, and kept in it [c]; and that the kingdom of glory may be hastened [d].
[a]. Matt. 12:25-28; Rom. 16:20; I John 3:8
[b]. Ps. 72:8-11; Matt. 24:14; I Cor. 15:24-25
[c]. Ps. 119:5; Luke 22:32; II Thess. 3:1-5
[d]. Rev. 22:20

Q. 103. What do we pray for in the third petition?
A. In the third petition, which is, Thy will

be done in earth, as it is in heaven, we pray, that God, by his grace, would make us able and willing to know, obey, and submit to his will in all things [a], as the angels do in heaven [b].
[a]. Ps. 19:14; 119; I Thess. 5:23; Heb. 13:20-21
[b]. Ps. 103:20-21; Heb. 1:14

Q. 104. What do we pray for in the fourth petition?
A. In the fourth petition, which is, Give us this day our daily bread, we pray that of God's free gift we may receive a competent portion of the good things of this life, and enjoy his blessing with them [a].
[a]. Prov. 30:8-9; Matt. 6:31-34; Phil. 4:11, 19; I Tim. 6:6-8

Q. 105. What do we pray for in the fifth petition?
A. In the fifth petition, which is, And forgive us our debts, as we forgive our debtors, we pray that God, for Christ's sake, would freely pardon all our sins [a]; which we are the rather encouraged to ask, because by his grace we are enabled from the heart to forgive others [b].
[a]. Ps. 51:1-2, 7, 9; Dan. 9:17-19; I John 1:7
[b]. Matt. 18:21-35; Eph. 4:32; Col. 3:13

Q. 106. What do we pray for in the sixth petition?
A. In the sixth petition, which is, And lead us not into temptation, but deliver us from evil, we pray, that God would either keep us from being tempted to sin [a], or support and deliver us when we are tempted [b].
[a]. Ps. 19:13; Matt. 26:41; John 17:15
[b]. Luke 22:31-32; I Cor. 10:13; II Cor. 12:7-9; Heb. 2:18

Q. 107. What doth the conclusion of the Lord's Prayer teach us?
A. The conclusion of the Lord's Prayer, which is, For thine is the kingdom, and the power, and the glory, for ever, Amen. teacheth us to take our encouragement in prayer from God only [a], and in our

prayers to praise him, ascribing kingdom, power, and glory to him [b]; and, in testimony of our desire, and assurance to be heard, we say, Amen [c].

[a]. Dan. 9:4, 7-9, 16-19; Luke 18:1, 7-8
[b]. I Chron. 29:10-13; I Tim. 1:17; Rev. 5:11-13
[c]. I Cor. 14:16; Rev. 22:20

Teaching, Christian
Keep reminding them of these things.
The Bible, 2 Timothy 2:14

Teaching, Unscriptural
To regularly hear unscriptural teaching is a serious thing. It is a continual dropping of slow poison into the mind.
J.C. Ryle

Teaching of apostles
The specific points which are clearly handed down through the apostolic preaching are these: First, that there is one God who created and arranged all things, and who, when nothing existed, called all things into existence, and that in the final period this God, just as he had promised beforehand through the prophets, sent the Lord Jesus Christ. Secondly, that Jesus Christ himself, who came, was born of the father before all creatures; and after he had ministered to the father in the creation of all things, for through him all things were made.
Origen

Teaching of Christ
The teaching of Christ is more excellent than all the advice of the saints, and he who has his spirit will find in it a hidden manna.
Thomas à Kempis

Teamwork
If everyone is moving forward together, then the success takes care of itself.
Author unknown

Teamwork divides the task and doubles the success.
Author unknown

You must undertake something so great that you cannot accomplish it unaided.
Phillips Brooks

The great cannot exist without the less, nor the less without the great.
Clement of Rome

When you hire people that are smarter than you are, you prove you are smarter than they are.
R.H. Grant

The great fault, I think, in our missions is that no one likes to be second.
Robert Morrison

It needs more skill than I can tell
To play the second fiddle well.
C.H. Spurgeon

Tears
See also: Patience; Revival and repentance
The soul would have no rainbow had the eye no tears.
John Vance Cheney

When the soul grows tearful, weeps, and is filled with tenderness, and all this without having striven for it, then let us run, for the Lord has arrived uninvited and is holding out to us the sponge of loving sorrow, the cool waters of blessed sadness with which to wipe away the record of our sins. Guard these tears like the apple of your eye until they go away, for they have a power greater than anything that comes from our own efforts and our own meditation.
John Climacus

The fruits of the inner man begin only with the shedding of tears. When you reach the place of tears, then know that your spirit has come out from the prison of this world and has set its foot upon the path that leads towards the new age.
John Climacus

I wept not, so to stone I grew within.
Dante

"It [weeping] opens the lungs, washes the countenance, exercises the eyes, and softens down the temper," said Mr Bumble. "So cry away."
Charles Dickens

Heaven knows we need never be ashamed of our tears, for they are rain upon the blinding dust of earth, overlying our hard hearts.
Charles Dickens

Tearless hearts can never be the heralds of the Passion.
J.H. Jowett

There is a kind of pleasure in weeping, for grief is assuaged and removed by tears.
Ovid

Sometimes tears have the weight of words.
Ovid

The good are always prone to tears.
Greek proverb

What soap is to the body, tears are for the soul.
Jewish proverb

Tears have a tongue, and grammar, and language, that our Father knoweth.
Samuel Rutherford

Above all, pray for the gift of tears.
Nilus Sorsky

The tearful praying Christian, whose distress prevent his words, will be clearly understood by the Most High.
C.H. Spurgeon

Tears and prayer
The prayers and supplications that Christ offered up were, joined with strong cries and tears, herein setting us example not only to pray, but to be fervent and importunate in prayer. How many dry prayers, how few wet ones, do we offer up to God!
Matthew Henry

Technology
A culture obsessed with technology will come to value personal convenience above almost all else, and ours does.
Robert H. Bork

It has become appallingly obvious that our technology has exceeded our humanity.
Albert Einstein

Technological progress has merely provided us with more efficient means for going backwards.
Aldous Huxley

Technology was made for man, not man for technology.
Thomas Merton

Television
Television has proved that people will look at anything rather than each other.
Ann Landers

Temperance
Temperate temperance is best; intemperate temperance injures the cause of temperance.
Martin Luther

We regard intemperance in any area of living as being inconsistent with the Christian life.
Moravian Covenant for Christian living

To go beyond the bounds of moderation is to outrage humanity.
Blaise Pascal

Temptation
See also: Bible, Reliance upon
My son, if sinners entice you, do not give in to them.
The Bible, Proverbs 1:10

No temptation has seized you except what is common to man. And God is faithful; he will not let you be tempted beyond what you can bear. But when you are tempted, he will also provide a way out so that you can stand up under it.
The Bible, 1 Corinthians 10:13 KJV

Blessed is the man that endureth temptation; for when he is tried, he shall receive the crown of life.
The Bible, James 1:12 KJV

When tempted, no one should say, "God is tempting me." For God cannot be tempted by evil, nor does he tempt anyone.
The Bible, James 1:13

If you have been tempted into evil, fly from it. It is not falling into the water, but lying in it, that drowns
Author unknown

Temptation usually comes in through a door that has deliberately been left open.
Author unknown

The best way to overcome temptation is to avoid the tempting situation.
Author unknown

If you have been tempted into evil, fly from it. It is not falling into the water, but lying in it, that drowns.
Author unknown

Whatever good is to be attained, struggle is necessary. So do not fear temptations, but rejoice in them, for they lead to achievement. God helps and protects you.
St Barsanuphius

Be thoroughly acquainted with your temptations and the things that may corrupt you – and watch against them all day long. You should watch especially the most dangerous of the things that corrupt, and those temptations that either your company or business will unavoidably lay before you.
Richard Baxter

We are ground between the millstones of temptation as grain that is ground into flour.
Ignatii Brianchaninov

Don't excuse yourself by your accusing Satan.
Thomas Brooks

He that will play with Satan's bait, will quickly be taken with Satan's hook.
Thomas Brooks

A humble heart will rather lie in the dust than rise by wickedness, and sooner part with all than the peace of a good conscience.
Thomas Brooks

Believe that as sure as you are in the way of God you must meet with temptations.
John Bunyan

Temptations, when we meet them at first, are as the lion that reared upon Samson; but if we overcome them, the next time we see them we shall find a nest of honey within them.
John Bunyan

The man who decides to struggle against his flesh and to overcome it by his own efforts is fighting in vain. The truth is that unless the Lord overturns the house of the flesh and builds the house of the soul, the man wishing to overcome it has watched and fasted for nothing.
John Climacus

Unwillingness to accept God's "way of escape" from temptation frightens me – what a rebel yet resides within.
Jim Elliot

Therefore it should be our care, if we would not yield to the sin, not to walk by, or sit at the door of the occasion.
William Gurnall

When Satan finds the good man asleep, then he finds our good God awake; therefore thou art not consumed, because God changeth not.
William Gurnall

Many a dangerous temptation comes to us in fine gay colors that are but skin-deep.
Matthew Henry

It is not possible without temptations for a man to grow wise in spiritual warfare, to

know his Provider and perceive his God, and to be secretly confirmed in his faith, save by virtue of the experience which he has gained.
Isaac from Syria

How often when I was living in the desert, parched by a burning sun, did I fancy myself among the pleasures of Rome! Sackcloth disfigured my unshapely limbs, and my skin from long neglect had become as black as an Ethiopian's. And although in my fear of hell I had consigned myself to this prison, where I had no companions but scorpions and wild beasts, I often thought myself in the company of many girls. My face grew pale, and my frame chilled with fasting; yet my mind was burning with desire, and the fires of lust kept bubbling up before me when my flesh was as good as dead. Helpless, I cast myself at the feet of Jesus.
Jerome, in a letter to Eustochium

He said not:
"Thou shalt not be tempted:
Thou shalt not be travailed:
Thou shalt not be afflicted."
But he said:
"Thou shalt not be overcome."
Julian of Norwich

The best way to drive out the devil, if he will not yield to texts of scripture, is to jeer and flout him, for he cannot stand scorn.
Martin Luther

I am tempted to think that I am now an established Christian,--that I have overcome this or that lust so long,--that I have got into the habit of the opposite grace,--so that there is no fear; I may venture very near the temptation--nearer than other men. This is a lie of Satan. One might as well speak of gunpowder getting by habit of resisting fire, so as not to catch spark. As long as powder is wet, it resists the spark; but when it becomes dry, it is ready to explode at the first touch. As long as the Spirit dwells in my heart, He deadens me to sin, so that, if lawfully

called through temptation, I may reckon upon God carrying me through. But when the Spirit leaves me, I am like dry gunpowder. Oh for a sense of this!
Robert M'Cheyene

I know well that when Christ is nearest, Satan also is busiest.
Robert Murray M'Cheyne

Temptation is a woman's weapon and man's excuse.
H.L. Mencken

Subtle he needs must be, who could seduce Angels.
John Milton

He that can apprehend and consider vice with all her baits and seeming pleasures, and yet abstain and yet distinguish, and yet prefer that which is truly better, he is the true wayfaring Christian.
John Milton

The devil, the prowde spirit, cannot endure to be mocked.
Thomas More

Never think we have a due knowledge of ourselves till we have been exposed to various kinds of temptations, and tried on every side. Integrity on one side of our character is no voucher for integrity on another. We cannot tell how we should act if brought under temptations different from those we have hitherto experienced. This thought should keep us humble. We are sinners, but we do not know how great. He alone knows who died for our sins.
John Henry Newman

Those who flee temptation generally leave a forwarding address.
Lane Olinghouse

We need then to examine some of the inadequate measures we often use in our attempts to safeguard the heart in the hour of temptation.
1. The love of honor in the world.

2. The fear of shame and reproach.
3. The desire not to disturb one's peace of mind,
4. The thought of the vileness of sinning against God.
John Owen

Let us keep our spirits unentangled by avoiding all appearance of evil, and all the ways that lead there. Guard yourself especially in your social contacts and your occupations, which all contain pitfalls to entrap us.
John Owen

There is no duty we perform for God that sin does not oppose. And the more spirituality or holiness there is in what we do, the greater is its enmity to it. Thus those who seek most for God, experience the strongest opposition.
John Owen

Let us learn more about the power of temptation in order to avoid it.
John Owen

Watch and pray. This injunction from our Lord implies that we should maintain a clear, abiding apprehension of the great danger we face if we enter into temptation. If one is always aware of the great danger, one will always stand guard.
John Owen

Do not flatter yourself that you can hold out against temptation's power. Secret lusts lie lurking in your own heart which will never give up until they are either destroyed or satisfied. In theory we abhor lustful thoughts, but once temptation enters our heart, all contrary reason is overcome and silenced.
John Owen

Forbidden things have a secret charm.
Tacitus

We find more than a thousand testimonies in Scripture to the great usefulness of temptation; for it is a special sign of God's love for a person to be tempted and yet kept from falling.
John Tauler

In temptation we are made aware of the ground of our own soul. When temptation exposes the stain and the roots of sin, then these are torn out, humility is born by the fear of God, and we are urged to flee to God, to seek His help and to hand our battle against sin over to him.
John Tauler

The devil does not tempt unbelievers and sinners who are already his own.
Thomas a Kempis

Do not be harsh with others who are tempted, but console them as you yourself would wish to be consoled.
Thomas à Kempis

Often take counsel when tempted.
Thomas à Kempis

We usually know what we can do, but temptation shows us who we are.
Thomas à Kempis

The voice of Christ: Write My words in your heart and meditate on them earnestly, for in time of temptation they will be very necessary.
Thomas à Kempis

So long as we live in this world we cannot escape suffering and temptation.
Thomas à Kempis

Little by little, with patience and fortitude, and with the help of God, you will sooner overcome temptations than with your own strength and persistence.
Thomas à Kempis

Some suffer great temptations in the beginning of their conversion, others toward the end, while some are troubled almost constantly throughout their life.
Thomas à Kempis

Temptation commonly comes through that for which we are naturally fitted.
B.F. Westcott

I can resist everything except temptation.
Oscar Wilde

Let no man think himself to be holy because he is not tempted, for the holiest and highest in life have the most temptations. How much higher the hill is, so much is the wind there greater; so, how much higher the life is, so much the stronger is the temptation of the enemy.
John Wycliffe

Temptation

John Newton
Letter to Mrs G.
June, 1777.
My Dear Madam,
Temptations may be compared to the wind, which, when it has ceased raging from one point, after a short calm, frequently renews its violence from another quarter. The Lord silenced Satan's former assaults against you, but he is permitted to try you again in another way. Be of good courage, Madam: wait upon the Lord, and the present storm shall likewise subside in good time. You have an infallible Pilot, and are embarked in a bottom against which the winds and waves cannot prevail; you may be tossed about, and think yourself in apparent jeopardy, but sink you shall not, except the promises and faithfulness of God can fail. Upon an attentive consideration of your complaint, it seems to me to amount only to this, that though the Lord has done great things for you, He has not yet brought you to a state of dependence on Himself, nor released you from that impossibility, which all His people feel, of doing anything without Him. And is this indeed a matter of complaint? Is it not every way better, more for His glory, and more suited to keep us mindful of our obligations to Him, and in the event more

for our safety, that we should be reduced to a happy necessity of receiving daily out of His fulness (as the Israelites received the manna) than to be set up with something of a stock of wisdom, power, and goodness of our own? Adam was thus furnished at the beginning with strength to stand; yet, mutability being essential to a creature, he quickly fell and lost all. We, who are by nature sinners, are not left to so hazardous an experiment. He has Himself engaged to keep us, and treasured up all fulness of grace for our support, in a Head who cannot fail. Our gracious Savior will communicate all needful supplies to His members, yet in such a manner that they shall feel their need and weakness, and have nothing to boast of from first to last, but His wisdom, compassion, and care. We are in no worse circumstances than the apostle Paul, who, though eminent and exemplary in the Christian life, found, and freely confessed, that he had no sufficiency in himself to think a good thought. Nor did he wish it otherwise; he even gloried in his infirmities, that the power of Christ might rest upon him.

Unbelief, and a thousand evils, are still in our hearts: though their reign and dominion is at an end, they are not slain or eradicated; their effects will be felt more or less sensibly, as the Lord is pleased more or less to afford or abate His gracious influence. When they are kept down, we are no better in ourselves, for they are not kept down by us; but we are very prone to think better of ourselves at such a time, and therefore He is pleased to permit us at seasons to feel a difference, that we may never forget how weak and how vile we are. We cannot absolutely conquer these evils, but it becomes us to be humbled for them; and we are to fight, and strive, and pray against them. Our great duty is to be at His footstool, and to cry to Him who has promised to perform all things for us. Why are we called soldiers, but because we are called to a warfare? And how could we fight, if there were no enemies to resist? The Lord's soldiers are not merely for show, to make an empty parade in a uniform, and to brandish their arms when none but friends and spectators are around them. No, we must stand upon the field of battle; we must face the fiery darts; we must wrestle (which is the closest and most arduous kind of fighting) with our foes; nor can we well expect wholly to escape wounds: but the leaves of the tree of life are provided for their healing. The Captain of our salvation is at hand, and leads us on with an assurance, which might make even a coward bold-that in the end we shall be more than conquerors through Him who has loved us.

I am ready to think that some of the sentiments in your letters are not properly yours, such as you yourself have derived from the Scriptures, but rather borrowed from authors or preachers, whose judgments your humility has led you to prefer to your own. At least I am sure the Scripture does not authorize the conclusion which distresses you, that if you were a child of God you should not feel such changes and oppositions. Were I to define a Christian, or rather to describe him at large, I know no text I would choose sooner as a ground for the subject than Gal. v. 17. A Christian has noble aims, which distinguish him from the bulk of mankind. His leading principles, motives, and desires, are all supernatural and divine. Could he do as he would, there is not a spirit before the throne should excel him in holiness, love, and obedience. He would tread in the very footsteps of his Savior, fill up every moment in His service, and employ every breath in His praise. This he would do, but alas! he cannot. Against this desire of the spirit, there is a contrary desire and working of a corrupt nature, which meets him at every turn. He has a beautiful copy set before him: he is enamored with it, and though he does not expect to equal it, he writes carefully after it, and longs to attain to the nearest possible imitation. But indwelling sin and Satan continually jog his hand and spoil his strokes. You cannot, Madam, form a right judgment of yourself, except you make due allowance for those things which are not peculiar to yourself,

but common to all who have spiritual perception and are indeed the inseparable appendages of this mortal state. If it were not so, why should the most spiritual and gracious people be so ready to confess themselves vile and worthless? One eminent branch of our holiness is a sense of shame and humiliation for those evils which are only known to ourselves, and to Him who searches our hearts, joined with an acquiescence in Jesus who is appointed of God-wisdom, righteousness, sanctification, and redemption. I will venture to assure you, that though you will possess a more stable peace, in proportion as the Lord enables you to live more simply upon the blood, righteousness, and grace of the Mediator, you will never grow into a better opinion of yourself than you have at present. The nearer you are brought to Him, the quicker sense you will have of your continual need of Him, and thereby your admiration of His power, love, and compassion will increase likewise from year to year.

I would observe farther, that our spiritual exercises are not a little influenced by our constitutional temperament. As you are only an ideal correspondent, I can but conjecture about you upon this head. If your frame is delicate, and your nervous system very sensible and tender, I should probably ascribe some of your apprehensions to this cause. It is an abstruse subject, and I will not enter into it; but according to the observations I have made, persons of this habit seem to live more upon the confines of the invisible world, if I may so speak, and to be more susceptive of impressions from it, than others. That complaint which, for want of a better name, we call lowness of spirits, may probably afford the enemy some peculiar advantages and occasions of distressing you. The mind then perceives objects as through a tinctured medium, which gives them a dark and discouraging appearance; and I believe Satan has more influence and address than we are aware of in managing the glass. And when this is not the case at all times, it may be so occasionally, from sickness, or other circumstances. You tell me that you have lately been ill, which, together with your present situation, and the prospect of your approaching hour, may probably have such an effect as I have hinted. You may be charging yourself with guilt for what springs from indisposition, in which you are merely passive, and which may be no more properly sinful than the headache or any of the thousand natural shocks the flesh is heir to. The enemy can take no advantage but what the Lord permits him; and He will permit him none but what He designs to overrule for your greater advantage in the end. He delights in your prosperity; and you should not be in heaviness for an hour, were there not a need-be for it. Notwithstanding your fears, I have a good hope, that He who you say has helped you in six troubles, will appear for you in the seventh; that you will not die, but live and declare the works of the Lord, and come forth to testify to His praise, that He has turned your mourning into joy.

I am, &c.

John Newton

Temptation

John Owen
THE ENTICEMENT OF INDWELLING SIN

Sin not only deceives, it also entices. People are drawn away "and enticed" (James 1:14). Sin draws the *mind* away from a duty, but it entices the *emotions*. We will consider three things:

Sin's enticement of the emotions, how sin accomplishes this, and our need to guard our affections because of this danger.

The affections are snared when they are aroused by sin. For when sin prevails, it captures the affections completely within it. Sin continually obsesses the imaginations with possessive images. The wicked "devise iniquity, and work evil upon their beds," which they also practice when they are given the chance (Micah 2:1). Peter says they have "eyes full of adultery, and they cannot cease from sin" (2 Peter 2:14). Their imagination continually fills their soul with the objects of their lusts.

The apostle describes the things in the world as "the lust of the flesh, the lust of the eyes, and the pride of life" (1 John 2:16). The lust of the eyes enters the soul, forcing the imagination to portray its intentions. John speaks of this as the lust of the "eyes" because it constantly represents these images to the mind and to the soul, just as our natural eyes present images of outward objects to the brain.

Indeed, the actual sight of the eyes often occasions these imaginations. Achan declared how sin had prevailed over him in Joshua 7:21. First, he *saw* the gold and the Babylonian garments, then he *coveted* them. Seeing them, he imagined their value to him, and then he fixed them in his desiring heart.

The enticement of sin is heightened when the imagination dominates over the mind. It implants vain thoughts within the mind, and delights secretly in its complacency. When we indulge with delight in thoughts of forbidden things, we commit sin, even though our will has not yet consented to perform the deed. The prophet asks, "How long will your vain thoughts lodge within you?" (Jer 4:14). All these thoughts come and go as messengers, carrying sin with them. Such thoughts inflame the imagination and entangle the affections more and more.

As we have already seen, sin always seeks to extenuate and lessen the seriousness of sin to the mind. "It is only a small offense," it says. "It will be given up shortly." With such excuses it speaks the language of a deceived heart. When there is a readiness on the part of the soul to listen to these silent voices – secret insinuations that arise from deceit – it is evident that the affections are already enticed.

When the soul willingly listens to these seductions, it has already lost its affections for Christ, and has become seduced. Sin entices like "wine when it is red, when it gives its color in the cup, when it moves itself attractively" (Prov 23:31). But in the end, sin "bites like a serpent, and stings like an adder" (Prov 23:32).

How, then, does sin deceive to entice and to entangle the affections?

First, it *makes use of the tendency of the mind*. If the mind is like a sly bird, sin will not capture it. "Surely in vain the net is spread in the sight of any bird" (Prov 1:17). But if a bird is distracted, its wings are of little use to escape from the trap. Thus does sin entice. It diverts the mind away from the danger by false reasonings and pretenses, then casts its net upon the affections to entangle them.

Second, sin takes advantage of the phases of life, and *proposes sin to be desirable*. It gilds over an object with a thousand pretenses which the imagination promotes as "the *pleasures* of sin" (Heb 11:25). Unless one despises these pleasures, as Moses did, one cannot escape from them. Those who live in sin, the apostle says, "live in pleasure" (James 5:5). It is pleasure because it suits the flesh to lust after them. Hence the caution, given, "Make no provision for the flesh, to fulfill the lusts thereof" (Rom 13:14). That is to say, do not nourish yourself with the lusts of the flesh, which sin gives to you through your thoughts or affections. He also warns us, "Fulfill not the lusts of the flesh" (Gal 5:16). When men live under the power of sin, they fulfill "the desires of the flesh and of the mind" (Ephesians 2:3). When sin would entangle the soul, it prevails with the imagination to solicit the heart by painting sin as something beautiful and satisfying.

Third, it *hides the danger* associated with sin. Sin covers the hook with bait, and spreads the food over the net. It is, of course, impossible for sin to completely remove the knowledge of danger from the soul. It cannot remove the reality that "the wages of sin is death" (Rom 6:23), or hide "the judgment of God, that they who commit sin are worthy of death" (Rom 1:32). But it so takes up and possesses the mind and affections with the attraction and desirability of sin, that it diverts the soul from realizing its danger.

In the account of the fall of man, Eve properly told the serpent, "If we eat or touch the fruit of that tree, we shall die" (Genesis 3:3). But Satan immediately filled her mind with the beauty and usefulness of the fruit, and she quickly forgot her practical concern for the consequences of eating. Likewise, David became so caught up in his lusts that he ignored the consequences of his great sin. It is said he "despised the Lord" (2 Samuel 12:9).

When sin tempts with such pressure, it uses a thousand wiles to hide the soul from the terror of the Lord. Hopes of pardon will be used to hide it. Future repentance also covers it, as well as the present insistence of lust and the particular occasion or opportunity. Sin uses many other excuses: extenuating circumstances, surprise, the balance of duties, the obsession of the imagination, and desperate resolutions. It uses a thousand such excuses.

Sin then proceeds to present arguments to the mind in order to conceive the desired sin.

Let us look now at the remedies for avoiding such deception of sin. Clearly, we need to watch our affections. The Scriptures say: "Keep your heart with all diligence" (Proverbs 4:23). We keep our heart in two ways.

First, we guard our affections by mortifying our members (Colossians 3:5). The apostle is saying, "You are to prevent the working and deceit of sin, which is in your members." He also says, "Set your affection on things above, not on things on the earth" (3:2). Fixing and filling your affections with heavenly things will mortify sin.

What are the objects of such affections? They include God Himself, in His beauty and glory; the Lord Jesus Christ, who is "altogether lovely... the chiefest of ten thousand" (Song of Solomon 5:10,16); grace and glory; the mysteries of the gospel; and the blessings promised by the gospel. If these were the preoccupation of our affections, what scope would sin have to tempt and enter into our hearts? (See 2 Corinthians 4:17-18.)

Second, let us fix our affections on the cross of Christ. Paul says, "God forbid that I should glory, save in the cross of our Lord Jesus Christ, whereby the world is crucified unto me, and I unto the world" (Gal 6:14). When someone sets his affections upon the cross and the love of Christ, he crucifies the world as a dead and undesirable thing. The baits of sin lose their attraction and disappear. Fill your affections with the cross of Christ and you will find no room for sin. The world put Him out of a house and into a stable, when He came to save us. Let Him now turn the world out-of-doors, when He comes to sanctify us.

Remember also that the vigor of our affections toward heavenly things is apt to decline unless it is constantly looked after, exercised, directed, and warned. God speaks often in Scripture of those who lost their first love, allowing their affections to decay. Let us be jealous over our hearts to prevent such backsliding.

THE POWER OF TEMPTATION (1)

It is the great duty of all believers not to enter into temptation. God indeed is able to "deliver the godly out of temptations" (2 Peter 2:9). Yet it is our great task to use all diligence so that we do not fall into temptation. Our Savior expresses His concern for His disciples by teaching them to pray, "Lead us not into temptation" (Matthew 6:13). Since our Lord knows the power of temptation, having experienced it, He knows how vulnerable we are to it (Heb 2:18). He rewards our obedience by keeping us "in the hour of temptation" (Revelation 3:10).

Let us learn more about the power of temptation in order to avoid it. Since temptation brings out many basic issues, Scripture has much to say about it. In the parable of the sower, Christ compares the seed sown on the rocky, thin soil to those who, "when they hear, receive the word with joy, but have no root, for they only

believe for a while" (Luke 8:13). The preaching of the Word affects them. They believe. They make a profession. They bring forth some fruit. But how long do they continue? Christ Says, "In time of temptation they fall away" (Luke 8:13). Once tempted, they are gone forever.

Likewise, in Matthew 7:26, Jesus speaks of the parable of the "foolish man, who built his house upon the sand." But what happens to this house of professed faith? It shelters its occupant, it keeps him warm, and it stands for awhile. But when the rain descends (that is to say, when temptation comes), it falls utterly, and its fall is great. This foolish man is like Judas, who followed our Savior three years. All went well for a time. But he no sooner entered into temptation—when Satan winnowed him—than he was lost. Demas preached the gospel until the love of the world entered into his soul, and then he turned utterly aside as well.

Among the saints of God, we see the solemn power of temptation. Take Adam, "the son of God," created in the image of God, full of integrity, righteousness, and holiness (Luke 3:38). He possessed a far greater inherent stock of ability than we have, since he had never been enticed or seduced. Yet no sooner did Adam enter into temptation but he was undone, lost, and ruined, and all his posterity with him. What should we expect then, when in our temptations we must deal not only with a cunning devil, but also with a cursed world and a corrupt heart?

Abraham is called the father of the faithful for it is his faith that is recommended as the pattern to all who believe (Rom 4:11-17). Yet twice he entered into the same temptation (namely, his fear about his wife). Twice he committed sin. He dishonored God, and no doubt his soul lost its peace (See Genesis 12 and 20).

David is called "a man after [God's] own heart" (1 Samuel 13:14). Yet what a dreadful story we read of his immorality! No sooner did temptation entangle him than he plunged into adultery. Seeking deliverance by his own devices, he became all the more entangled until he lay as one dead under the power of sin and folly.

We should also mention Noah, Lot, Hezekiah, and Peter, whose temptations and falls God recorded for our own instruction. Like the inhabitants of Samaria who received the letter of Jehu, we should ask, "If two kings were not able to stand before him, how then shall we stand?" (2 Kings 10:4). For this reason the apostle urges us to exercise tenderness toward those who fall into sin. Paul writes, "Consider yourselves, lest you also be tempted" (Gal 6:1). Seeing the power of temptation in others, let us beware, for we do not know when or how we also may be tempted. What folly it is that many should be so blind and bold, after all these and other warnings, to put themselves before temptation.

We need to examine ourselves to see our own weaknesses, and to note the power and efficacy of temptation. In ourselves, we are weakness itself. We have no strength, no power to withstand. Self-confidence produces a large part of our weakness, as it did with Peter. He who boasts that he can do anything, can in fact do nothing as he should. This is the worst form of weakness, similar to treachery. However strong a castle may be, if a treacherous party resides inside (ready to betray at the first opportunity possible), the castle cannot be kept safe from the enemy. Traitors occupy our own hearts, ready to side with every temptation and to surrender to them all.

Do not flatter yourself that you can hold out against temptation's power. Secret lusts lie lurking in your own heart which will never give up until they are either destroyed or satisfied. "Am I a dog, that I should do this thing?" asks Hazael (2 Kings 8:13). Yes, you will be such a dog, if you are like the king of Syria. Temptation and self-interest will dehumanize you. In theory we abhor lustful thoughts, but once temptation enters our heart, all contrary reasonings are overcome and silenced.

INADEQUATE SAFEGUARDS AGAINST THE POWER OF TEMPTATION

To be safe from such danger, we need to examine our own hearts. A man's heart is his true self. If a man is not a believer, but only a professor of the gospel, what will his heart do? Proverbs 10:20 says, "The heart of the wicked is of little worth." While outwardly it appears to have value, inwardly it is worthless. Because the sphere of temptation lies in the heart, an unbeliever cannot resist it when it comes like a flood.

No one, indeed, should trust his own heart. Proverbs 28:26 says, "He that trusteth in his own heart is a fool." Peter did this when he boasted, "Although all shall forsake thee, I will not" (Mark 14:29). This was his folly, his self-confidence. The heart of a man makes such wonderful promises before temptation comes. But "the heart is deceitful" (Jeremiah 17:9). Indeed, it is "deceitful above all things." It has a thousand shifts and treacheries, and when trial comes, temptation steals it away just as "wine and new wine take away understanding" (Hosea 4:11).

We need then to examine some of the inadequate measures we often use in our attempts to safeguard the heart in the hour of temptation.

1. The love of honor in the world

By one's walk and profession one obtains reputation and esteem in the church. So some argue, "Can I afford to lose such a reputation in the church of God by giving way to this lust, or to that temptation, or in dealing in this or that public evil?" This seems so strong an argument that many use it as a shield against any assaults that come. They would rather die a thousand deaths than lose their reputation in the church.

But what about "the third part of the stars of heaven"? (Revelation 12:4). Did they not shine in the firmament? Were they not fully aware of their honor, stature, usefulness, and reputation? Yet when the dragon comes with his temptations, he casts them down to the earth. Those who have no better defenses than the love of honor are inadequately equipped to deal with temptation. Sadly, it is possible for those with great reputations to suffer destruction when their only defense lies in their own good name. If this does not keep the stars of heaven, how do you think it will keep you?

2. The fear of shame and reproach

Not for all the world would some people bring upon themselves the shame and reproach associated with certain temptations. Their concern, however, tends to focus only upon open sins, such as the world notices and abhors. This motive proves useless when dealing with sins of conscience, or with sins of the heart. Innumerable excuses are offered to the heart when one relies on this as the predominant defense against temptation.

3. The desire not to disturb one's peace of mind, wound one's conscience, or risk the danger of hell fire

One might think that this would act as a major safeguard to preserve people in the hour of temptation. Indeed, we should use this as a major defense, for nothing is more important than striving to maintain our peace with God. Yet several reasons indicate this motive alone is not effective.

The peace of some only provides a false sense of security made up of presumptions and false hopes. Even believers cling to this. David enjoyed this false peace until Nathan came to see him. Laodicea rested in it while on the verge of destruction. The church of Sardis also claimed this peace while she lay dying. It is only true peace in Christ that keeps us, and nothing else. Nothing that God will not preserve in the last day keeps us now. False peace acts as a broken reed, piercing the hand that leans upon it.

Even the true peace we desire to safeguard our soul may prove useless as a defense in the hour of temptation. Why? Because we are so vulnerable to excuses. "This evil is so trivial," we say. Or we argue that it is so questionable. Or we argue that it does not openly and flagrantly offend the conscience. We rationalize with such excuses while maintaining our own peace of mind. We even rationalize that others of God's people have fallen, yet kept their peace and recovered from it. Facing a thousand such arguments—set up like batteries of guns against a fort—the soul finally surrenders.

If we only focus on the one safeguard of peace, the enemy will assault us elsewhere. True, it is one piece of armor for our protection, but we are commanded to "put on the *whole* armor of God" (Ephesians 6:11). If we depend upon this one element of defense, temptation will enter and prevail in twenty other ways.

A man, for example, may be tempted to worldliness, unjust gain, revenge, vanity, and many other things. If he focuses his attention on this one safeguard of peace and considers himself safe, he will neglect other needs. He may neglect his private communion with God, or overlook his tendency to be sensual. In the end he may not be one whit better than if he had succumbed to the temptation that most obviously harassed him. Experience shows that this peace of mind fails, therefore, as a safeguard. There is no saint of God who does not value the peace he enjoys. Yet how many fail in the day of temptation!

4. The thought of the vileness of sinning against God

How could we do this thing, when to sin against God is to do so against His mercies, and to wound Jesus Christ who died for us? Unfortunately, we see every day that even this is not a sure and infallible defense. No such defense exists.

Why do these motives fail us in the hour of temptation? Their sources betray their inadequacy. For they arise either from the universal and habitual disposition of our heart, or from the temptation itself. We should remain wary of such counselors.

THE POWER OF TEMPTATION (2)

It is helpful to consider the power of temptation in the light of what we have just said. The power of temptation is to darken the mind, so that a person becomes unable to make right judgments about things as he did before entering into temptation. The god of this world blinds men's minds so that they do not see the glory of Christ in the gospel (2 Corinthians 4:4). Likewise, the very nature of every temptation darkens the heart of the person who becomes tempted. This occurs in various ways.

First, the imagination and thought can be so obsessed with some object that the mind is distracted from those things that could relieve and help it. Someone might be tempted to believe that God has forsaken him, or God hates him, so that he expresses no interest in Christ. He becomes so depressed that he feels none of the remedies suggested to him will help. Meanwhile, he becomes obsessed with the temptation that fixates him.

Temptation also darkens the mind by the tragic confusion of the inclinations of the heart. Look around you and see how readily temptation entangles people's feelings. Show me someone not occupied with hope, love, and fear (of what he should not do), and I will quickly point out his blindness. His present judgment of things will be obscured and his will weakened. Madness immediately ensues. The hatred of sin, the fear of the Lord, and the sense of Christ's love and presence depart and leave the heart a prey to the enemy.

Finally, temptation gives fuel to our lusts by inciting and provoking them, so that they are embroiled in endless turmoil. One temptation—whether it is a lust, or a warped attitude, or anything else—becomes one's whole obsession. We might cite the carnal fear of Peter, the pride of Hezekiah, the covetousness of Achan, the uncleanness of David, the worldliness of Demas, or the ambition of Diotrephes. We do not know the pride, fury, and madness of a wrong deed until we face a suitable temptation. How tragic is the life of someone whose mind is darkened, whose affections are entangled, and whose lusts are inflamed, so that his defenses break down. What hope remains for him?

We observe this power of temptation both socially and personally. Public temptations, such as those mentioned in Revelation 3:10, "try them that dwell upon the earth." They also come in a combination of persecution and seduction to test a careless generation of believers. Such public temptations take varied forms.

First, public temptations come as the result of God's judgment on those who neglect or disdain the gospel, or who, as false believers, act as traitors. God permitted Satan to seduce Ahab as a punishment (1 Kings 22:22). When the world yields to folly and false worship in their neglect of the truth, and in the barrenness of their lives, God sends "a strong delusion, that they should believe a lie" (2 Thessalonians 2:11). This delusion comes with a judicial purpose to those who are selfish, spiritually slothful, careless, and worldly. As well, those who do not retain God in their hearts, God gives up to a reprobate mind (Rom 1:28).

Second, some public temptations spread infectiously from those who should be godly, but who are mere professors. Christ warns, "Because iniquity shall abound, the love of many shall wax cold" (Matthew 24:12). When some become negligent, careless, worldly, and wanton, they corrupt others. "A little leaven leaveneth the whole lump" (1 Corinthians 5:6, Galatians 5:9). The root of bitterness that troubles a man also defiles many (Heb 12:15). Little by little some mere professors of the truth influence others for evil.

Third, public temptations, when accompanied by strong reasons and influence, are too hard to overcome. This often takes place gradually. When a colony of people move from one country to another, they soon adjust to the customs of the local inhabitants. Likewise, prosperity often makes people morally careless, and it slays the foolish and wounds the wise.

We also see the power of temptation personally. These personal temptations enter the soul by their union with lust. John speaks of "the lust of the flesh, the lust of the eyes, and the pride of life" (1 John 2:16). They reside principally in the heart and not in the world. Yet they are "in the world" because the world enters into them, mixes with them, and unites with them. By such means, temptation penetrates so deep into the heart that no antidote reaches it. It is like gangrene that mixes poison with the blood stream.

Moreover, it is important to see that in whatever part of the soul lust resides, it affects the whole person. A lust of the mind (such as ambition, or vanity, or something similar) affects everything else. Temptation draws the whole person into it. But some will argue: "Why be so concerned about temptation? Are we not commanded to 'count it all joy when we fall into diverse temptations'?" (James 1:2). Yes, we should accept these trials. The same apostle admonishes the wealthy to "rejoice in that he is made low" (1:10). But James adds, "Blessed is the man that endureth temptation: for when he is tried, he shall receive the crown of life" (1:12). While God may try us, He never entices us. Everyone is tempted by his own lusts. Let us make sure that our own weaknesses do not entice us and thus seduce us.

As well, the objection may be raised that our Savior Himself faced temptation. Is it evil to find ourselves in a similar state? Hebrews 2:17-18 makes it clear that it is advantageous to us that Christ was tempted. He uses, as the ground of great promise to His disciples, the fact that they had been with Him in His temptations (Luke 22:28). Yes, it is true that our Savior experienced temptation. But Scripture reckons His temptations among the *evils* that befell Him in the days of His flesh, coming to Him through the malice of the world and its prince. He did not deliberately cast Himself into temptation. Instead He said, "Thou shalt not tempt the Lord thy God" (Matthew 4:7). Moreover, while Christ only had the *suffering* part of temptation, we also have the *sinning* part of it. He remained undefiled, but we become defiled.

Finally, some may argue, why should we be so careful about temptation when we have God's assurances? "God is faithful, who will not suffer us to be tempted above what we are able, but will with the temptation also make a way of escape" (1 Corinthians 10:13). "The Lord knoweth how to deliver the godly out of temptations" (2 Peter 2:9). Yes, God has given us these assurances, but it is questionable whether God will deliver us if we willingly enter into temptation. "Shall we continue in sin, that grace may abound?" (Rom 6:1).

It is wrong for us to enter deliberately into temptation and to think only of the near escape of our souls. We need to regard the comfort, joy, and peace of our spirits, and to realize that we sojourn here for the honor of the gospel and the glory of God.

THE DANGERS OF TEMPTATION

Having surveyed the power of temptation, we now want to consider the dangers of temptation's inception. Often we wonder if we have committed a specific sin. Rather, we should ask, "Have I entered into temptation?" We enter into temptation whenever we are drawn into sin, for all sin is from temptation (see James 1:14-15). Sin is the fruit that comes only from that root. Even to be surprised or overtaken in a fault is to be tempted. The apostle says, "Consider yourself, lest you also be tempted" (Gal 6:1). Often we repent of the sins that overtake us, without realizing how temptation starts in the first place. This makes us vulnerable to fall once more into sin.

Entering into temptation occurs in various ways. It often begins in a concealed and subtle way. For example, a man begins by having a reputation for piety, or wisdom, or learning. People speak well of him. His vanity is tickled to hear it, and then his reputation affects his pride and ambition. If this continues, he begins to seek it actively, using all his energies to build up his own esteem, reputation, and self-glory. Having this secret eye to its expansion, he enters into temptation. If he does not deal with this quickly and ruthlessly, he will become a slave to lust.

This happens to many scholars. They find themselves esteemed and favored for their learning. This secretly appeals to their pride and ambition, and they begin to major on promoting their learning. While they do good things it is always with an eye on the approval of others. In the end it is all carnal, making "provision for the flesh, to fulfill the lusts thereof" (Rom 13:14).

It is true that God in His mercy sometimes overrules such false motives. In spite of the ambition, pride, and vanity of the servant, God comes in grace to turn him to Himself and to rob him of his Egyptian lusts. Then once more, God consecrates the tabernacle which once housed idols.

But it is not only learning which temptation subtly corrupts. Temptation makes every profession and vocation a potential snare. Some find themselves the darlings, the celebrities, the popular ones in their own circle of friends and associates. Once these thoughts enter into their hearts, temptation entangles them. Instead of seeking to gain more glory, they need to lie in the dust, out of a sense of the vileness in themselves.

Likewise, when a man knows that he likes preaching the gospel or some other work of the ministry, many things begin to work in his favor. His ability, his simple presentation of the message, his constant exposure before the public, and his success in it all, expose him to temptation. These things become fuel for temptation. Whatever we like to do tends to feed our lusts and tends to cause us to enter into temptation, whether it is initially good or bad.

A man enters into temptation whenever his lusts find an opportunity for temptation. As I have already stated, to enter into temptation is not merely to face temptation, but to become entangled by its power. It is almost impossible to escape from temptation if it appropriately meets one's lusts. If ambassadors come from the king of Babylon, Hezekiah's pride will cast him into temptation. If Hazael is made king of Syria, his cruelty and ambition will make him rage savagely against Israel. If the priests come with their pieces of silver, Judas's covetousness will immediately operate to sell his Master.

We see many examples of this situation in our own day. How mistaken people are who think they can play over the hole of an asp and not be stung, or touch tar without being defiled, or set their clothes on fire and not be burnt. So if something in your business, your lifestyle, or your culture suits your lusts, you have already entered into temptation. If we have a propensity for unclean thoughts, ambition in high places, sexual passion, perusal of bad literature, or anything else, temptation will use various things in our society to entrap us.

Furthermore, when someone acts weak, negligent, or casual in a duty—performing it carelessly or lifelessly, without any genuine satisfaction, joy, or interest—he has already entered into the spirit that will lead him into trouble. How many we see today who have departed from warmhearted service and have become negligent, careless, and indifferent in their prayer life or in the reading of the Scriptures. For each one who escapes this peril, a hundred others will be ensnared. Then it may be too late to acknowledge, "I neglected private prayer," or "I did not meditate on God's Word," or "I did not hear what I should have listened to." Like Sardis, we maintain dead performances and duties in our spiritual life (Revelation 3:1).

In the Song of Solomon, the bride acknowledges, "I sleep" (Song of Solomon 5:2). Then she says, "I have put off my coat, and cannot put it on," which speaks of her reluctance to commune with her Lord (5:3). When she finally answers the door, her "beloved had withdrawn himself" (5:6). Christ had gone. Although she looks for Him, she does not find Him. This illustrates the intrinsic relationship of the new nature of the Christian and the worship of Christ. The new nature is fed, strengthened, increased, and sweetened by Christ. Our desire focuses on God, as the psalmist describes throughout Psalm 119. Yet temptation attempts to intervene and disrupt this relationship and desire.

VIGILANCE AGAINST THE DANGERS OF TEMPTATION

How then can we be vigilant, so that we "watch and pray"? (Matthew 26:41). This injunction from our Lord implies that we should maintain a clear, abiding apprehension of the great danger we face if we enter into temptation. If one is always aware of the great danger, one will always stand guard.

1. Always remember the great danger it is for anyone to enter into temptation

It is sad to find most people so careless about this. Most people think about how to avoid open sin, but they never think about the dynamics of temptation within their hearts. How readily young people mix with all sorts of company. Before they realize it, they enjoy evil company. Then it is too late to warn them about the dangers of wrong companions. Unless God snatches them in a mighty way from the jaws of destruction, they will be lost.

How many plead for their "freedom," as they call it. They argue that they can do what they like and try what they want, so they run here and there to every seducer and salesman of false opinions. And what is the result? Few go unhurt, and the majority lose their faith. Let no one fear sin without also fearing temptation. They are too closely allied to be separated. Satan has put them so close together that it is very hard to separate them. He hates not the fruit, who delights in the root.

We need a moral sensitivity to the weakness and corruption within us. We need to guard against the reality and guile of Satan. We need to recognize the evil of sin and the power of temptation to work against us. If we remain careless and cold, we shall never escape its entanglements. We need to constantly remind ourselves of the danger of the entry of temptation.

2. Realize we cannot keep ourselves from falling into temptation

But for the grace of God, we will fall into it. We have no power or wisdom to keep ourselves from entering into temptation, other than the power and wisdom of God. In all things we "are kept by the power of God" (1 Peter 1:5). "I pray," our Savior says to the Father, "not that thou shouldest take them out of the world, but that thou shouldest keep them from the evil" (John 17:15). In other words, Christ prays that the Father would guard us against the temptation of the world to enter into evil and sin.

Let our hearts admit, "I am poor and weak. Satan is too subtle, too cunning, too powerful; he watches constantly for advantages over my soul. The world presses in upon me with all sorts of pressures, pleas, and pretenses. My own corruption is violent, tumultuous, enticing, and entangling. As it conceives sin, it wars within me and against me. Occasions and opportunities for temptation are innumerable. No wonder I do not know how deeply involved I have been with sin. Therefore, on God alone will I rely for my keeping. I will continually look to Him."

If we commit ourselves to God in this way, three things will follow.

First, we will experience the reality of the grace and compassion of God. He calls the fatherless and the helpless to rest upon Him. No soul has ever lacked God's supply when he depended upon God's invitation to trust in Him absolutely.

Second, we will be conscious of our danger, and of our need for God's protection.

Third, we will act in faith on the promises of God to keep us. To believe that He will preserve us is, indeed, a means of preservation. God will certainly preserve us, and make a way of escape for us out of the temptation, should we fall. We are to pray for what God has already promised. Our requests are to be regulated by His promises and commands. Faith embraces the promises and so finds relief. This is what James 1:5-7 teaches us. What we need, we must "ask of God." But we must "ask in faith," for otherwise we will not "receive any thing of the Lord."

God has promised to keep us in all our ways. We shall be guided in such a way that we "shall not err therein" (Isaiah 35:8). He will lead us, guide us, and deliver us from the evil one. Base your life upon faith in such promises and expect a good and assuring life. We cannot conceive of the blessings that will ensue from this attitude of trust in the promises of Christ.

3. Resist temptation by making prayer of first importance

Praying that we enter not into temptation is a means to preserve us from it. People often talk about their wonderful experiences in maintaining this attitude of prayer, yet less than half its excellence, power, and efficacy is ever known. Whoever wishes to avoid temptation must pray. "Let us therefore come boldly unto the throne of grace, that we may obtain mercy, and find grace to help in time of need" (Heb 4:16). By doing this, our souls are set against every form of temptation.

After Paul instructs us to "put on the whole armor of God" (that we may stand and resist in the time of temptation), he adds: "Praying always with all prayer and supplication in the Spirit, and watching thereunto with all perseverance and supplication" (Ephesians 6:11,18). Without this attitude, we lack any real help.

Consider Paul's exhortation. "Praying always" means at all times and seasons (compare 1 Thessalonians 5:17). "With all prayer and supplication in the Spirit" implies expressing desires to God that are suited to our needs according to His will, by the assistance of the Holy Spirit. "Watching thereunto" means we are never distracted from this essential stance. "With all perseverance" means this is more than a passing whim, but a permanent inclination. By doing this we will stand.

If we do not abide in prayer, we will abide in temptation. Let this be one aspect of our daily intercession: "God, preserve my soul, and keep my heart and all its ways so that I will not be entangled." When this is true in our lives, a passing temptation will not overcome us. We will remain free while others lie in bondage.

4. Christ's word of patience includes God's pledge to keep us

Christ solemnly gave this promise to the church at Philadelphia. In Revelation 3:10 He promises to keep those who keep His word from the great trial and temptation which was to come upon all the world. The fulfillment of this promise involves all three Persons of the Trinity.

The faithfulness of the Father accompanies the promise. We shall be kept in temptation because "God is faithful, who will not suffer you to be tempted" (1 Corinthians 10:13). "He is faithful who promised" (Heb 10:23). "He will remain faithful; he cannot deny himself" (2 Timothy 2:13). When we stand under this promise, the faithfulness of God works on our behalf for our protection.

Every promise of God also contains the covenant grace of the Son. He promises, "I will keep you" (Revelation 3:10). How? "By my grace that is with you" (see 1 Corinthians 15:10). Paul suffered intensely from temptation. He "besought the Lord" for help and God answered, "My grace is sufficient for you" (2 Corinthians 12:9). Paul could add, "I will glory in my infirmities, that the power of Christ may rest upon me." The efficacy of the grace of Christ becomes evident in our preservation (see Hebrews 2:18; 4:16).

The efficacy of the Holy Spirit accompanies God's promises, as well. He is called "the Holy Spirit of promise" (Ephesians 1:13). This is not only because He promised the advent of Christ, but because He effectively makes good the promise within us. He preserves the soul of the one who follows these promises (see Isaiah 59:21).

5. God preserves us as we keep the word of Christ's patience

When we keep Christ's word, we guard our

heart against temptable tendencies. David prayed, "Let integrity and uprightness preserve me" (Psalm 25:21). God gave him a disposition that left no entry points for temptation to penetrate. In contrast, we read: "There is no peace for the wicked" (Isaiah 57:21). The wicked face temptation as a troubled sea, full of restlessness and storms. They have no peace. God delivers us from such troubles as we guard our heart to keep Christ's word.

Negatively, we guard our heart by mortification. The apostle James indicates that temptations arise from our own lusts (James 1:14). By eliminating them, we destroy the entry points for temptation. Paul says, "I am crucified with Christ" (Gal 2:20). To keep close to Christ is to be crucified with Him and to be dead to all the carnal desires of the world. Achan failed to mortify the lusts of his heart. When he saw "a goodly Babylonish garment, and two hundred shekels of silver, and a wedge of gold," he "coveted them" first, then he "took them" (Joshua 7:21). Sin seduced him. But a mortified heart and a crucified life will preserve us from these things.

Positively, we guard our heart by filling it with better concerns and values. The apostle Paul reckoned the things of the world mere loss and dung (Philippians 3:8). The new is so much better. As we daily taste the gracious goodness of the Lord, all else becomes worthless in comparison. One fills his heart with these better things by maintaining three concerns.

His first concern is *Christ Himself.* The love and presence of Christ always stay with him. He knows Christ is concerned about his honor, and that His plan is to "present him holy, and unblameable, and unreproveable in his sight" (Colossians 1:22). His Spirit is grieved when this work is interrupted (Ephesians 4:30). Because he knows Christ's intention, he avoids resisting His purposes, expressing contempt for His honor, despising His love, or trampling His gospel into the mud. Dwelling in his heart is the constraining love of Christ (2 Corinthians 5:14).

His second concern is *Christ's own victories over temptations.* Christ's life on earth included His triumphs over the frequent assaults of the Evil One. He resisted all, He conquered all, and He has become the Captain of salvation to those who obey Him (Heb 2:10). How can any follower of Christ deny the reality of His victory by living as a defeated Christian because of temptation in his life?

His third concern is *approval.* He has learned to enjoy the favor of Christ, to sense His love, to appreciate His acceptance, and to converse with Him. He cannot bear to become separated from Christ, as the spouse declared in Song of Solomon 3:4. Once she recognized Him, in no way would she let Him out of her sight. Never again would she lose His presence.

When a believer keeps the word of Christ's patience, it does not merely influence his concerns. It also affects the governing principles of his life.

First, he lives by faith in God (Gal 2:20). Faith works in all areas of his heart, emptying his soul of its own wisdom, understanding, and self-sufficiency, so that it may act now in the wisdom and fullness of Christ. Proverbs 3:5 gives us sound advice to guard against temptation: "Trust in the Lord with all thine heart; and lean not upon thine own understanding." This is the work of faith: To trust God, and to live in such trust of Him. When a man trusts himself, "his own counsel shall cast him down" (Job 18:7). Only faith empties us of our own self-sufficiency. We should not live to ourselves and by ourselves, but only for Christ, by Christ, and in Christ.

Second, he lives with concern for others. He shows love for God's people by not causing them to stumble over his temptations. David prays in Psalm 69:6, "Let not them that wait on thee, O LORD God of hosts, be ashamed for my sake: let not those that seek thee be confounded for my sake, O God of Israel." In other words, "Do not let me so misbehave that others, for whom I would lay down my life, should be ill spoken of, dishonored, reviled, and condemned because of my own failings." When someone preoccupies himself with the well-being of others, God saves him. In contrast, a self-centered man falls.

If God has promised that He will keep us, why do so many professors of Christianity fall into temptation? Is it not simply because they do not keep the word of Christ's patience? Because of disobedience, Paul says, "many are weak and sickly among you, and many sleep" (1 Corinthians 11:30). God chastens all those who fail to keep Christ's Word and neglect to walk closely with Him.

It would take too long to cite all the ways professors of Christianity fail to keep Christ's Word. We can simply summarize four ways they often fail. First, they conform to the world when Christ would redeem us from its delights and promiscuous compliances. Second, they neglect the duties which Christ has enjoined upon us to fulfill, from personal meditation on the one hand to public duties on the other. Third, they strive and disagree among themselves, despising each other and acting indifferent to the bond of communion between saints. Fourth, they make selfishness the end of life. When these traits characterize people, then the word of Christ's patience is fruitless among them, and God will not keep them from temptation.

FINAL EXHORTATIONS

If we want God to preserve us in the hour of temptation, we will take heed against anything that would distract us from keeping the word of Christ's patience. The following cautions will help us.

First, do not trust your own advice, understanding, and reasoning. Second, even if you discipline yourself earnestly (by prayer, fasting, and other such measures) to safeguard against a particular lust, you will still fail if you neglect such other matters as worldliness, compliance, looseness of living, or moral negligence. Third, while it is God's purpose to give the saints security, perseverance, and preservation from general apostasy, yet we must never use this as an excuse to abuse some other aspect of our walk with God. Many relieve their consciences with "cheap grace," only to find their perplexities intensified in other areas of life.

In addition, seek to determine the relevance of God's word to the particular context of your temptations. First, when you encounter the cult of celebrities, observe from His word how God overturns the values of human popularity. Second, consider the ways God sees things differently from the world. If you do so, you will be content to remain unnoticed by the world. Third, notice how God emphasizes faith and prayer. Esteem them better than all the strength and councils of men. Fourth, seek to recover God's ordinances and institutions from the carnal administrations that are under the bondage of men's lusts. Bring them forth in the beauty and power of the Holy Spirit.

The nature of worldliness is to neglect the word of Christ's patience. It slights God's people and judges them by the standards of the world. It relies on human counsel and understanding. It allows unsanctified people to walk in God's temple and to trample His ordinances. In all these ways let us remain watchful. Let us keep the word of Christ's patience if we cherish our safety. In this frame of mind, plead with the Lord Jesus Christ, in the light of His promises, to help you in your need. Approach Him as your merciful High Priest.

If you visited a hospital and asked how each patient fell ill, no doubt each would reply, "It was by this or that circumstance that I contracted the disease." After hearing them, would it not make you much more careful not to fall into their circumstances?

Or if you went to a prison, you might ask different criminals how they received their sentence. Would you not be warned that sin leads to certain judgment? "Can a man take fire into his bosom, and his clothes not be burnt?

Can one go upon hot coals, and his feet not be burned?" (Proverbs 6:27-28). Do we only realize the invincible power of temptation once it captures us? We conclude with three warnings.

First, if you ignore temptation, even though our Savior commands us to be vigilant as the only safeguard against it, then remember Peter. Perhaps you have been fortunate so far to escape trouble in spite of your carelessness. But wake up, and thank God for His gentleness and patience with you.

Second, remember that you are always under the scrutiny of Christ, the great Captain of our salvation (Heb 2:10). He has enjoined us to watch and pray that we enter not into temptation (Matthew 26:41). As He saw the gathering storm, He alerted His disciples with this warning. Does not His reproof grieve you? Or are you unafraid to hear His thunder against you for your neglect? (Revelation 3:2).

Third, realize that if you neglect this duty and then fall into temptation—which assuredly you will do—God may also bring heavy affliction upon you. He may even bring judgment, as evidence of His anger. You will not consider this warning mere empty words when it actually happens to you. Then what woe will betide you if you are not found full of godly sorrow.

Let us keep our spirits unentangled by avoiding all appearance of evil, and all the ways that lead there. Guard yourself especially in your social contacts and your occupations, which all contain pitfalls to entrap us.
John Owen

Temptation, Alertness to
Always remember the great danger it is for anyone to enter into temptation. We need a moral sensitivity to the weakness and corruption within us. We need to guard against the reality and guile of Satan. We need to recognize the evil of sin and the power of temptation to work against us. If we remain careless and cold, we shall never escape its entanglements.
John Owen

Temptation, Purpose of
The devil tempts that he may ruin; God tests that he may crown.
Ambrose

Temptation, Resisting
Resist temptation by making prayer of first importance.
John Owen

I cannot keep birds from flying over my head, but I can keep them from building under my hat.
Martin Luther

Temptation, Ways of escape
In the greatest temptations, a single look to Christ, and the bare pronouncing of his name, suffices to overcome the wicked one, so it be done with confidence and calmness of spirit.
John Wesley

Temptation and service
Whenever you wish to make a beginning in some good work, first prepare yourself for the temptations that will come upon you, and do not doubt the truth.
Isaac from Syria

Temptation and the Holy Spirit
It is the Spirit of God that is best able to discover Satan's plots against us; it is only He that can point out all his snares.
Thomas Brooks

Ten Commandments
Then God spoke all these words, saying, (1) "I am the LORD your God, who brought you out of the land of Egypt, out of the house of slavery. You shall have no other gods before me.
(2) You shall not make for yourself an idol [or "graven image"], or likeness of what is in the heaven above or on the earth beneath or in the water under the earth. You shall not worship them or serve them; I the LORD your God, am a jealous God, vesting the iniquity of the fathers on the children, on the third and the fourth generations of those who hate Me, but showing loving-kindness to thousands who love Me and keep My commandments.
(3) You shall not take the name of the LORD your God in vain, for the LORD will not leave him unpunished [or "hold him

guiltless"] who takes His name in vain.
(4) Remember the sabbath day, to keep it holy. Six days you shall labor and do all your work, but the seventh day is a sabbath of the LORD your God; in it you shall not do any work, you or your son or your daughter, your male or your female servant, or your cattle or your sojourner who stays with you [or "is in your gates"]. For in six days the LORD made the heavens and the earth, the sea and all that is in them, and rested on the seventh day; therefore the LORD blessed the sabbath day and made it holy.
(5) Honor your father and your mother, that your days may be prolonged in the land which the LORD your God gives you.
(6) You shall not murder.
(7) You shall not commit adultery.
(8) You shall not steal.
(9) You shall not bear false witness against your neighbor.
(10) You shall not covet your neighbor's house; you shall not covet your neighbor's wife or his male servant or his female servant or his ox or his donkey or anything that belongs to your neighbor."
The Bible, Exodus 20:1-16; Deuteronomy 5:6-21 NASB

The Ten Commandments are not multiple choice.
Author unknown

Man is an able creature, but he has made 32,600,000 laws and hasn't yet improved on the Ten Commandments.
Author unknown

If men will not be governed by the Ten Commandments, they shall be governed by the ten thousand commandments.
G. K. Chesterton

The Law of the Ten Commandments is the strength of sin because it creates self-knowledge.
Martin Luther

We have staked the whole of all our political institutions upon the capacity of mankind for self-government, upon the capacity of each and all of us to govern ourselves, to control ourselves, to sustain ourselves according to the Ten Commandments of God.
President James Madison

Testimonies to Christ

He [Christ] is my reason for waking up!
Eugenia Price

What Jesus means to me is this: in Him we are able to see God and to understand His feelings toward us.
Charles Schulz

Christ helped me win over myself. It's so clear to me now why in all things I must be a mirror of his teachings.
Stan Smith

It will be an ill day when our brethren take to bragging and boasting and call it "testimony to the victorious Christian life." We trust that holiness will be more than ever the aim of believers, but not the boastful holiness which has deluded some of the excellent of the earth into vainglory, and under which their firmest friends shudder for them.
C.H. Spurgeon

The greatest discovery I ever made was that I was a lost, guilty sinner, and that Jesus Christ, the savior of sinners, is my savior.
James Simpson
Discoverer of chloroform, on being asked what his greatest discovery was

Testimonies

Testimony to conversion
PATRICK, MISSIONARY TO IRELAND
"I was sixteen years old and knew not the true God and was carried away captive; but in that strange land (Ireland) the Lord opened my unbelieving eyes, and although late I called my sins to mind, and was

converted with my whole heart to the Lord my God, who regarded my low estate, had pity on my youth and ignorance, and consoled me as a father consoles his children…Well every day I used to look after sheep and I used to pray often during the day, the love of God and fear of him increased more and more in me and my faith began to grow and my spirit stirred up, so that in one day I would pray as many as a hundred times and nearly as many at night. Even when I was staying out in the woods or on the mountain, I used to rise before dawn for prayer, in snow and frost and rain, and I felt no ill effect and there was no slackness in me. As I now realize, it was because the Spirit was glowing in me."
Patrick's Confession

MISSIONARY TO INDIA
Amy Carmichael, the Irish missionary to India, was converted after hearing Anna Bartlett Warner's hymn *Jesus loves me* at a children's mission in Yorkshire, England.

WOMAN PRISON REFORMER
"I think my feelings that night…were the most exalted I remember…suddenly my mind felt clothed with light, as with a garment and I felt silenced before God; I cried with the heavenly feeling of humility and repentance."
Memoir of Elizabeth Fry

REFORMER
"Night and day I pondered until I saw the connection between the justice of God and the statement that 'the just shall live by his faith' (Romans 1:17). Then I grasped that the justice of God is that righteousness by which, through grace and sheer mercy, God justifies us through faith. Thereupon I felt myself to be reborn and to have gone through open doors into paradise. The whole of Scripture took on a new meaning, and whereas before the 'justice of God' had filled me with hate, now it became to me inexpressibly sweet in greater love. This passage of Paul became to me a gate to heaven."
Martin Luther

APOLOGIST OF THE 2ND AND 3RD CENTURIES
After meeting an old man by the sea who explained the weakness of Plato's philosophy and spoke about prophets more ancient than Greek philosophers who spoke about the truth about God and prophesied about Christ's coming, Justin Martyr wrote: "straightway a flame was kindled in my soul; and a love of the prophets, and of those men who are friends of Christ, possessed me; and whilst revolving his words in my mind, I found this philosophy alone to be safe and profitable."

4TH CENTURY THEOLOGIAN
Then I ran back to where Alypius was sitting; for, when I left him, I had left the apostle's book lying there. I picked it up, opened it, and silently read the passage [Romans 13:13-14] I first set eyes on: "Let us behave decently, as in the daytime, not in orgies and drunkenness, nor in sexual immorality and debauchery, not in dissension and jealousy. Rather clothe yourselves with the Lord Jesus Christ, and do not think about how to gratify the desires of the sinful nature." I didn't want to read any further, and it wasn't necessary. As I reached the end of the sentence, the light of peace seemed to shine on my heart, and every shadow of doubt disappeared.
Confessions, Augustine, Book 8, Section 12

MATTER-OF-FACT CONVERSION
William Booth's name became synonymous with some of the most amazing conversion stories in the pages of the history of Christianity. However, Booth's own conversion was straightforward and unemotional. He was wandering home at about 11 pm one night in 1844, when quite suddenly his soul was filled with God's Spirit. It was like Saul's Damascus Road experience. He experienced the light of God's forgiveness in his heart as he confessed his sins. He knew that he was now a follower of the Lord Jesus Christ.

A VERY "STRANGE" INCIDENT
Bristol, 1788: About the middle of the

discourse, when there was on every side attention still as night, a vehement noise arose, none could tell whence, and shot like lightning through the whole congregation. The terror and confusion was inexpressible. You might have imagined it was a city taken by storm. The people rushed upon each other with the utmost violence, the benches were broken in pieces, and nine tenths of the congregation appeared to be struck with the same panic. In about six minutes the storm ceases.

It is the strangest incident of the kind I ever remember, and I believe none can account for it without supposing some supernatural influence. Satan fought, lest his kingdom should be delivered up.

The Journal of John Wesley, 3rd March 1788, recording an incident during one of his evangelistic meetings.

WATERGATE POLITICIAN

After Charles Colson had served a prison sentence for his part in the Watergate break-in and cover up, he was racked with doubts about Christianity. He could not get the phrase "Jesus Christ is God" out of his head. In the best way he knew he had surrendered to God and asked him to take over his life. However, he had no certainty about his faith and he spent the next week studying the Bible. During this time he felt as if he made massive spiritual progress in his understanding about Christianity. Then he was able to articulate a prayer which he thought would never pass his lips. He told Jesus that he believed in him, and accepted him. He asked Jesus to come into his life, and he committed his life to his Lord.

Colson immediately had a sense of God's comfort and the knowledge that he could now face life with Christ in a totally new and reformed way. Colson now knew what it was to be born again in Christ.

BIBLE TRANSLATOR

In 1779 a National Day of Prayer was called, as England was at war with Spain and France. William Carey went to a prayer meeting in the small meeting-room of the local Dissenting congregation. One of the members read Hebrews 13:13: "Let us go forth therefore unto him without the camp, bearing his reproach." The words were familiar to William, but now they found a deep resonance in his heart. The world was still rejecting Christ, but William knew that he had to commit himself, not intellectually but with his heart. It came as the climax of several weeks of searching, and he realized that at last Christ had found him and given him peace.

PROFESSOR OF ENGLISH

C.S. Lewis was alone in his room at Magdalen College, Oxford, when he found that his thoughts kept returning to the subject of God, whom, he says, he did not want to meet. He gave in to God in 1929 when he knelt down and acknowledged that God was indeed God. He felt as if he was "dejected and reluctant convert in all England".

At this stage Lewis thought of God as being other than human, and he did not think about Jesus Christ being God incarnate.

As he saw the truth of Jesus being man as well as God, he again put up resistance, just as he had before he was prepared to admit that God was God.

This final step in Lewis' Christian conversion took place while he traveled on a bus to visit Whipsnade Zoo. It was a lovely sunny morning. When he left Oxford he did not believe that Jesus Christ was the Son of God. By the time that he arrived at Whipsnade he did believe that Jesus Christ was the Son of God. Yet Lewis recalls that he had not spent the journey deep in thought. He did not have any great emotional feelings linked to this change of heart. Lewis says that some people are very unemotional about some of the most important events in their lives. He likened his conversion experience to being like a man who, after a long sleep, still lies motion

BAPTIST PREACHER

I sometimes think I might have been in

darkness and despair until now had it not been for the goodness of God in sending a snowstorm, one Sunday morning, while I was going to a certain place to worship. When I could go no further, I turned down a side street, and came to a little Primitive Methodist Chapel. In that chapel there may have been a dozen or fifteen people. I had heard of the Primitive Methodists, how they sang so loudly that they made people's heads ache; but that did not matter to me. I wanted to know how I might be saved, and if they could tell me that, I did not care how much they made my head ache. The minister did not come that morning; he was snowed up, I suppose. At last, a very thin-looking man, a shoemaker, or tailor, or something of that sort, went up into the pulpit to preach. Now, it is well that preachers should be instructed, but this man was really stupid. He was obliged to stick to his text, for the simple reason that he had little else to say. The text was, "Look unto me, and be ye saved, all the ends of the earth."

Then the good man followed up his text in this way: "Look unto Me; I am sweatin' great drops of blood. Look unto Me; I am hangin' on the cross. Look unto Me, I am dead and buried. Look unto Me, I am sitting at the Father's right hand. O poor sinner, look unto Me! Look unto Me!"

Then he looked at me under the gallery, and I dare-say, with so few present, he knew me to be a stranger. Just fixing his eyes on em, as if he knew all my heart, he said, "Young man, you look very miserable." Well, I did, but I had not been accustomed to have remarks made from the pulpit on my personal appearance before. However, it was a good blow, and it struck right home. He continued, "and you always will be miserable — miserable in life and miserable in death — if you don't obey my text; but if you obey now, this moment you will be saved." Then lifting up his hands, he shouted, as only a Primitive Methodists could do, "Young man, look to Jesus Christ. Look! Look! Look! You have nothing to do but to look and live."

I saw at once the way of salvation. I knew not what else he said — I did not take much notice of it — I was so possessed with that one thought. There and then the cloud was gone, the darkness had rolled away, and that moment I saw the sun. Oh, that somebody had told me this before, "Trust Christ, and you shall be saved."

Testimony of non-Christian writers

About this time lived Jesus, a wise man, if indeed one ought to call him a man. For he was the achiever of extraordinary deeds and was a teacher of those who accept the truth gladly. He won over many Jews and many of the Greeks. He was the Messiah. When he was indicted by the principal men among us and Pilate condemned him to be crucified, those who had come to love him originally did not cease to do so; for he appeared to them on the third day restored to life, as the prophets of the Deity had foretold these and countless other marvelous things about him. And the tribe of Christians, so named after him, has not disappeared to this day."
Flavius Josephus, Jewish historian, AD 37-95

Tests

We turn to God for help when our foundations are shaking, only to learn that it is God who is shaking them.
Charles C. West

Thanksgiving
See also: Gratitude

Give thanks in all circumstances
The Bible, 1 Thessalonians 5:18

Today is a gift. That's why it's called the present!
Author unknown

Thanksgiving is a good thing: thanksliving is better.
Author unknown

We have short memories in magnifying God's grace. Every blessing that God confers upon us perished through our

carelessness, if we are not prompt and active in giving thanks.
John Calvin

What shall I give you, Lord, in return for all Your kindness?
Glory to You for Your love.
Glory to You for Your mercy.
Glory to You for Your patience.
Glory to You for forgiving us all our sins.
Glory to You for coming to save our souls.
Glory to You for Your incarnation in the virgin's womb.
Glory to You for Your bonds.
Glory to You for receiving the cut of the lash.
Glory to You for accepting mockery.
Glory to You for Your crucifixion.
Glory to You for Your burial.
Glory to You for Your resurrection.
Glory to You who were preached to men and women.
Glory to You in whom they believed.
Glory to You who were taken up into heaven.
Glory to You who sit in great glory at the Father's right hand.
Glory to You whose will it is that the sinner should be saved through Your great mercy and compassion.
Ephraem of Syria

One act of thanksgiving when things go wrong with us is worth a thousand thanks when things are agreeable to our inclination.
John Jewell

Thanksgiving is the end of all human conduct, whether observed in words or works.
J.B. Lightfoot

Theologian
Theologians are the servants of the Church.
George K.A. Bell

To be a theologian is to pray truly and to pray truly is to be a theologian.
Evagrius

Everything a theologian does in the church contributes to the spread of the knowledge of God and the salvation of men.
Martin Luther

That person deserves to be called a theologian who comprehends the visible and manifest things of God through suffering and the cross.
Martin Luther

For centuries, theologians have been explaining the unknowable in terms of the-not-worth-knowing.
Henry Louis Mencken

Theology
... different classes of objects separately treated by the diverse philosophical sciences can be combined by sacra doctrina (holy teaching, theology) which keeps its unity when all of them are brought into the same focus and pictured in the divine field of revelation: thus, in effect, it is like an imprint on us of God's knowledge, which is the single and simple vision of everything.
Thomas Aquinas

Theology is a dream of reason.
P. Aris

Theology: The human reason ... reaching out ... towards fulfillment of its deepest longings in a reality greater than itself, whose significance eludes our grasp but whose manifest presence draws us on.
P. Aris

Jesus loves me, this I know,
for the Bible tells me so.
Karl Barth's summary of his theology

In the Church of Jesus Christ there can and should be no non-theologians.
Karl Barth

Wherefore all theology, when separated from Christ, is not only vain and confused, but is also mad, deceitful, and spurious; for, though the philosophers sometimes utter excellent sayings, yet they have nothing but

what is short-lived, and even mixed up with wicked and erroneous sentiments.
John Calvin

Theology, not morality, is the first business on the church's agenda of reform, and the church, not society, is the first target of divine criticism.
Michael Scott Horton

Theology is but an appendix to love, and an unreliable appendix!
Toyohiko Kagawa

Everywhere, except in theology, there has been a vigorous growth of skepticism about skepticism itself.
C.S. Lewis

A theology without spirituality would be a sterile academic exercise.
John Macquarrie

The foundation of true holiness and true Christian worship is the doctrine of the gospel, what we are to believe. So when Christian doctrine is neglected, forsaken, or corrupted, true holiness and worship will also be neglected, forsaken, and corrupted.
John Owen

It is the heart that makes the theologian.
Quintilian

As wheels in a complicated machine may move in opposite directions and yet subserve a common end, so may truths apparently opposite be perfectly reconcilable with each other, and equally subserve the purposes of God in the accomplishment of man's salvation.
Charles Simeon

From time immemorial men have quenched their thirst with water without knowing anything about its chemical constituents. In like manner we do not need to be instructed in all the mysteries of doctrine, but we do need to receive the Living Water which Jesus Christ will give

us and which alone can satisfy our souls.
Sadhu Sundar Singh

Be well instructed in theology, and do not regard the sneers of those who rail at it because they are ignorant of it. Many preachers are not theologians, and hence the mistakes which they make. It cannot do any hurt to the most lively evangelist to be also a sound theologian, and it may often be the means of saving him from gross blunders. Nowadays we hear men tear a single sentence of Scripture from its connection, and cry "Eureka! Eureka!" as if they had found a new truth; and yet they have not discovered a diamond but a piece of broken glass.
C.H. Spurgeon

No subject of contemplation will tend more to humble the mind, than thoughts of God.
C.H. Spurgeon

There is something exceedingly improving to the mind in a study of the Divinity. It is a subject so vast, that all our thoughts are lost in its immensity; so deep, that our pride is drowned in its infinity.
C.H. Spurgeon

A theologian is a man who spends his time answering questions that nobody is asking.
William Temple

Important as it is that we recognize God working in us, I would yet warn against an over preoccupation with the thought. It is a sure road to sterile passivity. God will not hold us responsible to understand the mysteries of election, predestination and the divine sovereignty. The best and safest way to deal with these truths is to raise our eyes to God and in deepest reverence say, "Oh Lord Thou knowest." Those things belong to the deep and mysterious Profound of God's omniscience. Prying into them may make theologians, but it will never make saints.
A. W. Tozer

Theology is a form of reflection deriving from a kind of active participation in God's self-knowledge.
A.N. Williams

Theology, Systematic
There are some, no doubt, to whom it may seem presumptuous to attempt to systematize our knowledge of God. If we possess any knowledge of God at all, however, the attempt to systematize it is a necessity of the human spirit. If we know as much as two facts concerning God, the human mind is incapable of holding these facts apart. Systematization is an effort which the intelligence can escape only by ceasing to be intelligence.
B.B. Warfield

Thief on the cross
One thief on the cross was saved, that none should despair, and only one, that none should presume.
J.C. Ryle

Thinkers
Many highly intelligent people are poor thinkers. Many people of average intelligence are skilled thinkers. The power of a car is separate from the way the car is driven.
Edward de Bono

Thinking
See also: Reason
Every thought is a seed. If you plant Crab apples don't count on harvesting Golden Delicious.
Author unknown

Minds are like parachutes, they only work when open.
Author unknown

Watch your thoughts; they become words.
Watch your words; they become actions.
Watch your actions; they become habits.
Watch your habits; they become character.
Watch your character; for it becomes your destiny!
Author unknown

You are not what you think you are. What you think, you are.
Author unknown

Great minds discuss ideas;
average minds, events and happenings;
small minds, people and things.
Author unknown

It's not what you think, it's what the Bible says.
Author unknown

To be free from evil thoughts is God's best gift.
Aeschylus

A Christian is a person who thinks in believing and believes in thinking.
Augustine

Our life is what our thoughts make it.
Marcus Aurelius

All that we are is the result of what we have thought.
Buddha

The human mind is, so to speak, a perpetual forge of idols.
John Calvin

Holy Spirit, think through me till your ideas are my ideas.
Amy Carmichael

Our life is what our thoughts make it.
Catherine of Siena

In thinking, keep to the simple.
Tao Te Ching

The diseases of the mind are more destructive than those of the body.
Cicero

Not only are you what you think you are, more so; what you think, you are.
Anthony J. D'Angelo

I think; therefore I am.
Rene Descartes

Our greatest need is to teach people who think – not what, but how.
Thomas Edison

The release of atom power has changed everything except our way of thinking ... the solution to this problem lies in the heart of mankind. If only I had known, I should have become a watchmaker.
Albert Einstein

It is the sign of a dull mind to dwell upon the cares of the body, to prolong exercise, eating and drinking, and other bodily functions. These things are best done by the way; all your attention must be given to the mind.
Epictetus

Among mortals second thoughts are the wisest.
Euripides

Thinking is the hardest work there is, which is probably the reason why so few engage in it.
Henry Ford

The conventional view serves to protect us from the painful job of thinking.
J.K. Galbraith

All truly wise thoughts have been thought already thousands of times; but to make them truly ours, we must think them over again honestly, till they take root in our personal experience.
Goethe

Rationality is opposed to absurdity, not to mystery.
Os Guinness

What luck for rulers, that men do not think.
Adolph Hitler

The soul is dyed the color of its leisure thoughts.
W.R. Inge

People demand freedom of speech as a compensation for the freedom of thought which they never use.
S. Kierkegaard

A nation or civilization that continues to produce soft-minded men purchases its own spiritual death on an installment plan.
Martin Luther King, Jr.

Nature gave men two ends – one to sit on and one to think with. Ever since then man's success or failure has been dependent on the one he used most.
George R. Kirkpatrick

There are two ways to slide easily through life: to believe everything or to doubt everything. Both ways save us from thinking.
Alfred Korzybski

An open mind, in questions that are not ultimate, is useful. But an open mind about ultimate foundations either of Theoretical or Practical Reason is idiocy. If a man's mind is open on these things, let his mouth at least be shut.
C.S. Lewis

It is never enough for us simply to know. We must also weigh.
John MacCunn

Readers are plentiful: thinkers are rare.
Harriet Martineau

The surest way to corrupt a young man is to teach him to esteem more highly those who think alike than those who think differently.
Nietzsche

Change your thoughts and you change your world.
Norman Vincent Peale

As a man thinketh in his heart so is he.
Proverb

Most people would sooner die than think; in fact, they do so.
Bertrand Russell

As soon as man does not take his existence for granted, but beholds it as something unfathomably mysterious, thought begins.
Albert Schweitzer

You never think a right thought, never do a right act, you never make any advance heavenward except by grace.
C.H. Spurgeon

The greatest battles are fought in the mind.
Casey Treat

Thinking, Avoiding
There is no expedient to which man will not resort to avoid the real labor of thinking.
Joshua Reynolds

Thinking, Maturity in
We are to be children in heart, not in understanding.
Thomas Aquinas

Thinking and action
To think evil is very much the same as doing it.
Aristophanes

Nothing is more terrible than activity without thought.
Thomas Carlyle

Brains first and then Hard Work.
Eeyore, A.A. Milne

Thinking and character
We can't choose our relatives, but we can choose our thoughts, which influence us much more.
Author unknown

Thinking and speech
They never taste who always drink;
They always talk, who never think.
Matthew Prior

Thinking systematically
It is plain that we are required to know the revelation that God has given us. Yet we would not adequately know that revelation if we knew it only in its several parts without bringing these parts into relation to each other. It is only as a part of the whole of the revelation of God to us that each part of that revelation appears as it is really meant to appear. Our minds must think systematically.
Cornelius Van Til

Thirst
I was dying of thirst. When my spiritual eyes were opened I saw the rivers of living water flowing from his pierced side. I drank of it and was satisfied. Thirst was no more. Ever since I have always drunk of that water of life, and have never been athirst in the sandy desert of this world.
Sadhu Sundar Singh

Thirst, Spiritual
As the hart panteth after the water-brooks.
The Bible, Psalm 42:1

Thought
Give careful thought to your ways.
The Bible, Haggai 1:7

Time
A thousand years in thy sight are but as yesterday when it is past, and as a watch in the night.
The Bible, Psalm 90:4 KJV

Time is given us to use in view of eternity.
Author unknown

Don't waste time, its all we have.
Author unknown

Dost thou love life? Then do not squander time, for that is the stuff life is made of.
Benjamin Franklin

When thou dost look upon my face,
To learn the time of day:
Think how my shadow keeps its pace,
As thy life flies away.
Take, mortal this advice from me
And so resolve to spend
They life on earth, that heaven shall be
Thy home when time shall end.
Inscription on sundial

I am a shadow, so art thou,
I mark the time, dost thou?
Inscription on sundial

Yesterday is history. Tomorrow is a
mystery. And today? Today is a gift. That's
why we call it the present.
Babatunde Olatunji

Time is what we want most, but what,
alas, we use worst, and for which God will
surely most strictly reckon with us when
time shall be no more.
William Penn

In God, time and eternity are one and the
same thing.
Henry Suso

Time, Redeeming the
Place a high value upon your time, be
more careful of not losing it than you
would of losing your money. Do not let
worthless recreations, idle talk,
unprofitable company, or sleep rob you of
your precious time. Be more careful to
escape that person, action or course of life
that would rob you of your time than you
would be to escape thieves and robbers.
Richard Baxter

Time, Use of
Little drops of water, little grains of sand,
Make the mighty ocean and the pleasant
land. So the little minutes, humble
though they be, Make the mighty ages of
eternity.
Julia A. Fletcher

Tiredness
Life is one long process of getting tired.
Samuel Butler

Today
Look to this day…for yesterday is but a
dream, and tomorrow is only a
vision…but today well-lived makes every
yesterday a dream of happiness and every
tomorrow a vision of hope.
Author unknown

Today is tomorrow's yesterday.
Make it count!
Author unknown

Today is the only time we can possibly live.
Dale Carnegie

The man is happiest who lives from day to
day and asks no more, garnering the
simple goodness of a life.
Euripides

Tolerance
Generation X is not tolerant of an
intolerant God.
Tom Beaudoin

We are reaping the bitter fruit of decades
of pathetic tolerance for all that is wrong in
ourselves and others.
Linda Bowles

There is a limit at which forbearance ceases
to be a virtue.
Edmund Burke

We ought to be much more tolerant about
faulty behavior. We can all fall into one of
Satan's traps here: it is so easy to give a false
impression of super holiness, as if we were
already angels, and ignore the company of
all who seem human in their shortcomings!
John Calvin

Tolerance is the virtue of the man without
convictions.
G.K. Chesterton

The equal toleration of all religions is the
same thing as atheism.
Pope Leo XIII

Tolerance is only another name for
indifference.
W. Somerset Maugham

In the world it is called tolerance, but in
hell it is called despair … the sin that
believes in nothing, cares for nothing,
enjoys nothing, hates nothing, finds
purpose in nothing, lives for nothing, and

remains alive because there is nothing for which it will die.
Dorothy L. Sayers

It is a hard case that we should think of all Papists and Anabaptists and Sacramentaries to be fools and wicked persons.
Jeremy Taylor

I may disapprove of what you say but I will defend to the death your right to say it.
Voltaire

Tongue
See also: Speaking
"He sighed," Mark 7:34. This sigh was not drawn from Christ on account of the single tongue and ear of this poor man, but it is a common sigh over all tongues and ears. Our beloved Lord saw full well what an amount of suffering and sorrow would be occasioned by tongues and ears. For the greatest mischief which has been inflicted on Christianity has not arisen from tyrants (with persecution, murder, and pride against the Word), but from that little bit of flesh which abides between the jaws. This it is which inflicts the greatest injury upon the kingdom of God.
Martin Luther

God has given us two ears, but one tongue, to show that we should be swift to hear, but slow to speak. God has set a double fence before the tongue, the teeth and the lips, to teach us to be wary that we offend not with our tongue.
Thomas Watson

Torture
Torture kills the human in the torturer and crushes the personality of the one tortured.
Dr Emilio Castro

Towns
God made the country, and man made the town.
William Cowper

Tradition
See also; Change; Customs; Habit

Remove not the ancient landmark.
The Bible, Proverbs 22:28 KJV

We Baptists don't believe in tradition; it's contrary to our historic position.
Author unknown

Tradition is an important help to history, but its statements should be carefully examined before we rely on them.
Joseph Addison

Montaigne is wrong in declaring that custom ought to be followed simply because it is custom, and not because it is reasonable or just.
Blaise Pascal

Be not the first by whom the new are tried, Nor the last to lay the old aside.
Alexander Pope

Tragedy
Rachel weeping for her children, and would not be comforted, because they are not.
The Bible, Matthew 2:18 KJV

Tranquillity
When we are unable to find tranquillity within ourselves, it is useless to seek it elsewhere.
Francois La Rochefoucauld

Great tranquility of heart is his who cares for neither praise nor blame.
Thomas a Kempis

Transformation
The desert shall rejoice, and blossom as the rose.
The Bible, Isaiah 35:1 KJV

Give unto them beauty for ashes, the oil of joy for mourning, the garment of praise for the spirit of heaviness.
The Bible, Isaiah 61:3

Nature forms us, sin deforms us, school informs us, Christ transforms us.
Author unknown

Fire transforms all things it touches into its own nature. The wood does not change the fire into itself, but the fire changes the wood into itself. In the same way we are transformed into God.
Meister Eckhart

All love in general hath an assimilating efficacy; it casts the mind into the mold of the thing beloved. Every approach unto God by ardent love and delight is transfiguring.
John Owen

When we see the humility and obedience of Christ, when we look on Christ as God's chosen servant in all this, and as our surety and head, it transforms us to the like humility and obedience.
Richard Sibbes

Travel
We travel to learn; an I have never been in any country where they did not do something better than we do it, think some thoughts better than we think, catch some inspiration from heights above our own.
Maria Mitchell

Treason
Truth to Christ cannot be treason to Caesar.
Samuel Rutherford

Treasure
Where your treasure is, there will your heart be also.
The Bible, Matthew 6:21

The man who has God for his treasure has all things in one.
A. W. Tozer

Trials
See also: Adversity; Affliction; Burdens; Difficulties; Hardships; Suffering
God will not look you over for medals, degrees, or diplomas, but for scars.
Author unknown

There can be no rainbow without a cloud and storm.
Author unknown

If you cry because the sun has gone out of your life, your tears will prevent you from seeing the stars.
Author unknown

God tries our faith so that we may try his faithfulness.
Author unknown

Great faith must have great trials.
Author unknown

So long as man has encouragement elsewhere, he does not encourage himself in the Lord his God. Now when God sees that his children fall in love more with the nurse than himself, then he removes the nurse, and causes their peace to be suspended and interrupted.
William Bridge

Though our private desires are ever so confused, though our private requests are ever so broken, and though our private groanings are ever so hidden from men, yet God eyes them, records them, and puts them upon the file of heaven, and will one day crown them with glorious answers and returns.
Thomas Brooks

Whatever sort of tribulation we suffer, we should always remember that its purpose is to make us spurn the present and reach out to the future.
John Calvin

No pressure, no diamonds.
Mary Case

The saint never knows the joy of the Lord in spite of tribulation, but because of it.
Oswald Chambers

One sees great things from the valley; only small things from the peak.
G.K. Chesterton

True virtue never appears so lovely, as when it is most oppressed; and the divine excellency of real Christianity, is never

exhibited with such advantage, as when under the greatest trials: then it is that true faith appears much more precious than gold!
Jonathan Edwards

God wishes to test you like gold in the furnace. The dross is consumed by the fire, but the pure gold remains and its value increases.
Jerome Emiliani

There is not an experienced saint, but will find, that by all the good things and bad things he hath been trysted with, by all the various vicissitudes and changes of providence, he hath come to see more of God than he saw before.
Ralph Erskine

Man's extremity is God's opportunity.
John Flavel

What does not kill me makes me stronger.
Goethe

God's wounds cure, sin's kisses kill.
William Gurnall

Those that go gold into the furnace will come out no worse.
Matthew Henry

In truth, without afflictions there is no life.
Isaac from Syria

As for trials, the more the better.
John of the Cross

In tribulation, immediately draw near to God with trust, and you will receive strength, enlightenment, and instruction.
John of the Cross

There is a deep peace that grows out of illness and loneliness and a sense of failure. God cannot get close when everything is delightful. He seems to need these darker hours, these empty-hearted hours, to mean the most to people.
Frank C. Laubach

God, who foresaw your tribulation, has specially armed you to go through it, not without pain but without stain.
C.S. Lewis

I did not learn my divinity at once, but was constrained by my temptations to search deeper and deeper; for no man, without trials and temptations, can attain a true understanding of the Holy Scriptures.
Martin Luther

No man ought to lay a cross upon himself, or to adopt tribulation, as is done in popedom; but if a cross or tribulation come upon him, then let him suffer it patiently, and know that it is good and profitable for him.
Martin Luther

Afflictions are but the shadow of God's wings.
George MacDonald

He that can apprehend and consider vice with all her baits and seeming pleasures, and yet abstain and yet distinguish, and yet prefer that which is truly better, he is the true wayfaring Christian. I cannot praise a fugitive and cloistered virtue, unexercised and unbreathed, that never sallies out and sees her adversary, but slinks out of the race, where that immortal garland is to be run for, not without dust and heat. Assuredly we bring not innocence into the world, we bring impurity much rather; that which purifies us is trial, and trial is by what is contrary.
Milton

Be not afraid of those trials which God may see fit to send upon thee. It is with the wind and the storm of tribulation that God, in the garner of the soul, separates the true wheat from the chaff. Always remember, therefore, that God comes to thee in thy sorrows as really as in thy joys. He lays low and He builds up. Thou wilt find thyself far from perfection if thou dost not find God in everything.
Miguel de Molinos

To learn strong faith is to endure great trials.
George Müller

In the storm the tree strikes deeper roots in the soil; in the hurricane the inhabitants of the house abide within, and rejoice in its shelter. So by suffering the Father would lead us to enter more deeply into the love of Christ.
Andrew Murray

Trials are medicines which our gracious and wise Physician prescribes because we need them; and he proportions the frequency and weight of them to what the case requires. Let us trust his skill and thank him for his prescription.
Isaac Newton

I ask'd the Lord, that I might grow
In faith, and love, and ev'ry grace,
Might more of his salvation know,
And seek more earnestly his face.
'Twas he who taught me thus to pray,
And he, I trust has answer'd pray'r;
But it has been in such a way,
As almost drove me to despair.
I hop'd that in some favor'd hour,
At once he'd answer my request:
And by his love's constraining pow'r,
Subdue my sins, and give me rest.
Instead of this. he made me feel
The hidden evils of my heart;
And let the angry pow'rs of hell
Assault my soul in ev'ry part.
Yea more, with his own hand he seem'd
Intent to aggravate my woe;
Cross'd all the fair designs I schem'd,
Blasted my gourds, and laid me low.
Lord, why is this, I trembling cry'd,
Wilt thou pursue thy worm to death?
"'Tis in this way," the Lord reply'd,
I answer pray'r for grace and faith.
These inward trials I employ,
From self and pride to set thee free;
And break thy schemes of earthly joy,
That thou mayst seek thy all in me."
John Newton

Our trials are as certainly mercies, as our comforts.
John Newton

The Lords appointments, to those who fear him, are not only sovereign, but wise and gracious. He has connected their good with his own glory, and is engaged by promise, to make all things work together for their advantage. He chooses for his people better than they could choose for themselves – if they are in heaviness, there is a need-be for it, and he withholds nothing from them but what upon the whole it is better they should be without. Our trials are as certainly mercies, as our comforts. Unless we are endued with fresh strength from on high, we are as liable to complain and despond as if we thought our afflictions sprang out of the ground, and the Lord had forgotten to be gracious to us.
John Newton

The way I see it, if you want the rainbow, you gotta put up with the rain.
Dolly Parton

Who is unhappy at not being a king, except a deposed king? All of these miseries of man prove man's greatness. They are the miseries of a deposed king.
Blaise Pascal

The diamond can not be polished without friction, nor the man perfected without trials.
Chinese Proverb

If God sends you a cross, take it up and follow him.
Use it wisely, lest it be unprofitable.
Bear it patiently, lest it be intolerable.
If it be light, slight it not.
If it be heavy, murmur not.
Quarles

There are times when God asks nothing of His children except silence, patience, and tears.
Charles Seymour Robinson

When the storms of life strike, it's what happens in you that will determine what happens to you.
Jerry Savelle

God examineth with trials, the devil examineth with temptations, the world examineth with persecutions.
Henry Smith

Trials are the winds which root the tree of our faith.
C.H. Spurgeon

The trials of the saint are a "divine pruning", by which he grows and brings forth abundant fruit.
C.H. Spurgeon

The hotter the fire, the purer the gold.
Charles Stanley

All our difficulties are only platforms for the manifestation of His grace, power and love.
Hudson Taylor

When a man of good will is afflicted, tempted, and tormented by evil thoughts, he realizes clearly that his greatest need is God, without Whom he can do no good.
Thomas à Kempis

It is good for us to have trials and troubles at times, for they often remind us that we are on probation and ought not to hope in any worldly thing.
Thomas à Kempis

Botanists say that trees need the powerful March winds to flex their trunks and main branches, so that the sap is drawn up to nourish the budding leaves. Perhaps we need the gales of life in the same way, though we dislike enduring them. A blustery period in our fortunes is often the prelude to a new spring of life and health, success and happiness, when we keep steadfast in faith and look to the good in spite of appearances.
Jane Truax

Trials

Letter from John Newton

At length, and without farther apology for my silence, I sit down to ask you how you fare. Afflictions I hear have been your lot; and if I had not heard so, I should have taken it for granted: for I believe the Lord loves you, and as many as He loves He chastens. I think you can say, afflictions have been good for you, and I doubt not but you have found strength according to your day; so that, though you may have been sharply tried, you have not been overpowered. For the Lord has engaged His faithfulness for this to all His children, that He will support them in all their trials: so that the fire shall not consume them, nor the floods drown them (I Cor. x. 13; Isa. xliii. 2).

If you can say thus much, cannot you go a little further, and add, in the apostle's words, "None of these things move me, neither count I my life dear. I rather glory in my infirmities, that the power of Christ may rest upon me: yea, doubtless, I count all things loss and of no regard, for the excellency of the knowledge of Christ Jesus my Lord; for when I am weak, then am I strong"? Methinks I hear you say, "God, who comforteth those who are cast down, has comforted my soul; and as my troubles have abounded, my consolations in Christ have abounded also. He has delivered, He does deliver, and in Him I trust that He will yet deliver me." Surely you can set your seal to these words. The Lord help you then to live more and more a life of faith, to feed upon the promises, and to rejoice in the assurance that all things are yours, and shall surely work for your good.

If I guess right at what passes in your heart, the name of Jesus is precious to you, and this is a sure token of salvation and that of God. You could not have loved Him, if He had not loved you first. He spoke to you, and said, "Seek My face," before your heart cried to Him, "Thy face, O Lord, will I seek." But you complain, "Alas! I love Him so little." That very complaint proves that you love Him a great deal; for if you loved Him but a little, you would think you loved Him enough. A mother loves her child a great deal, yet does not complain for not loving it more; nay, perhaps she hardly thinks it possible. But such an infinite object is Jesus, that they who love Him better than parents or child, or any earthly relation or comfort, will still think they hardly love Him at all; because they see such a vast disproportion between the utmost they can give Him, and what in Himself He deserves from them. But I can give you good advice and good news: love Him as well as you can now, and ere long you shall love Him better. O when you see Him as He is, then I am sure you will love Him indeed! If you want to love Him better now while you are here, I believe I can tell you the secret how this is to be attained: Trust Him. The more you trust Him, the better you will love Him. If you ask, farther, How shall I do to trust Him? I answer, Try Him: the more you make trial of Him, the more your trust in Him will be strengthened. Venture upon His promises; carry them to Him, and see if He will not be as good as His word. But, alas! Satan and unbelief work the contrary way. We are unwilling to try Him, and therefore unable to trust Him; and what wonder, then, that our love is faint, for who can love at uncertainties?

If you are in some measure thankful for what you have received, and hungering and thirsting for more, you are in the frame I would wish for myself, and I desire to praise the Lord on your behalf. Pray for us. We join in love to you.

I am. &c.

John Newton

Trials

Letter from Samuel Rutherford
Greetings – Disdain temporary glory
To Jean Brown,
Mistress,

Grace, mercy, and peace be to you. I am glad that you follow closely after Christ in this dark and cloudy time. It is a good thing to sell the things of this world in order to buy Him, for when all these days are over we will find that it was a good investment to have a part in Christ. I confidently believe that His enemies will be His footstool, and what are now growing flowers will be dead, withered grass. The honor and the glory will fall off many things that for a time appear beautiful.

Leave worldly comforts behind
It would be foolish to think that Christ and the Gospel would come and sit down at our fireside. No, we must leave our comfortable warm houses and seek after Christ and His Gospel. It is not the sunny side of Christ that we must expect, and we must not forsake him if we lack it. Let us set our faces against whatever we find in life, until He and we are though the briers and prickly bushes and on dry ground. Our soft nature would prefer to be carried through the troubles of this life in Christ's arms. But it is His wisdom, who knows what we're made of, that His bairns go with wet and cold feet to heaven. Oh, how sweet a thing it would be for us, if we would learn how to make our burdens light, by preparing our hearts for the burden, which requires us to make our Lord's will the law of our hearts.

Christ's light will shine
I find Christ and His cross not unpleasant or troublesome guests, as men would call them. No, I think patience makes the water Christ gives us good wine, and His dross silver and gold. We have a good reason for continuing to wait: before long our Master will be back for us and shine His light into the whole world, making visible the blacks and whites. Happy are those who will be found ready. Our hour-glass doesn't have long enough to run for us to become weary. In fact, time itself will dissolve our cares and sorrow. Our heaven is in the bud and growing up until the harvest. Why shouldn't we persevere, seeing that our

whole life time is a few grains of sand? Therefore I commend Christ to you, as your last-living and longest-living Husband, the staff of your old age. Let Him now have the rest of your days. Don't worry about the storm when you're sailing in Christ's ship: no passenger will ever fall overboard. Even the most sea-sick passenger is sure to come to land safely.

His great love – our little faith

I myself am in as sweet communion with Christ as a poor sinner can be. I am only pained that He has much beauty and loveliness, and I little love. He has great power and mercy, and I little faith. He has much light, and I poor eyesight. O that I would see Him in the sweetness of His love, and in His marriage-clothes, and were over head and ears in love with that princely one, Christ Jesus my Lord! Alas, my broken dish, my leaky bottle, can hold so little of Christ Jesus!

Christ on the auction block

I have joy in this, that I would gladly die before I put Christ's property at the disposal of men who choose to follow their own wills. Alas, this land has put Christ up for bid in a public auction. Blessed are they who would hold the crown on His head and buy Christ's honor with their own losses.

Family advice – farewell

I rejoice to hear that your son John is coming to visit Christ and taste of His love. I hope that he will not become careless or regret his choice. I have always (as I often told you in person) a great love to Mr. John Brown because I thought I saw more of Christ in him than in his brothers. I wish I could write to him, to encourage him to stand by my sweet Master. Please have him read this letter, and tell him of the joy I will have if he will stand for my Lord Jesus.

Grace be with you, yours, in his sweet Jesus,

Samuel Rutherford

Trials and prayer

Prayer and pains, through faith in Jesus Christ will do anything.

John Elliot

Trials and the Holy Spirit

The sign that the Holy Spirit is in us is that we realize that we are empty, not that we are full. We have a sense of absolute need. We come across people who try us, circumstances that are difficult, conditions that are perplexing, and all these things awaken a dumb sense of need, which is a sign that the Holy Spirit is there. If we are ever free from the sense of need, it is not because the Holy Spirit has satisfied us, but because we have been satisfied with as much as we have.

Oswald Chambers

Tribulations

See: Adversity; Affliction; Burdens; Difficulties; Hardships; Suffering; Trials

Trinity

Once grace had been revealed all were bound to explicit faith in the mystery of the Trinity.

Thomas Aquinas

The Trinity is a Trinity not merely in name or in a figurative manner of speaking; rather, it is a Trinity in truth and in actual existence. Just as the Father is he that is, so also his Word is one that is and is God over all. And neither is the Holy Spirit nonexistent but actually exists and has true being. Less than these the Catholic Church does not hold, lest she sink to the level of the Jews of the present time, imitators of Caiaphas, or to the level of Sabellius.

Athanasius

Every divine action begins from the Father, proceeds through the Son and is completed in the Holy Spirit.

Basil the Great

God is revealed to us as Father, Son, and Holy Spirit each with distinct personal

attributes, but without division of nature, essence or being.
James Boyce

Let us not be misled by the foolish argument that because the term "Trinity" does not occur in the scriptures, the doctrine of the Trinity is therefore unscriptural.
F.F. Bruce [The word "Trinity" does not appear in the Bible.]

Have we not one God and one Christ and one Spirit of grace shed upon us?
Clement of Rome

In the unity of the Godhead there be three persons, of one substance, power, and eternity; God the Father, God the Son, and God the Holy Ghost. The Father is of none, neither begotten, nor proceeding: the Son is eternally begotten of the Father: the Holy Ghost eternally proceeding from the Father and the Son.
The Confession of Faith of the Westminster Assembly of Divines, 1646

Though the word "Trinity", first used in its Greek form *trias* by Theophilus of Antioch [c. AD 180], is not found in Scripture, but the conception is there both implicitly and explicitly.
F.L. Cross

God the Father is fully God. God the Son is fully God. God the Holy Spirit is fully God. The Bible presents this as fact. It does not explain it.
Billy Graham

We therefore acknowledge one true God, the one First Cause, and one Son, very God of very God, possessing of nature the Father's divinity,--that is to say, being the same in substance with the Father; and one Holy Spirit, who by nature and in truth sanctifies all, and makes divine, as being of the substance of God. Those who speak either of the Son or of the Holy Spirit as a creature we anathematize.
Gregory the Wonderworker

In Christ Jesus our Lord, by whom and with whom be glory and power to the Father with the Holy Spirit for ever.
Ignatius

Without the Spirit it is not possible to hold the Word of God nor without the Son can any draw near to the Father, for the knowledge of the Father is the Son and the knowledge of the Son of God is through the Holy Spirit.
Irenaeus

The Church, though dispersed throughout the whole world, even to the ends of the earth, has received from the apostles and their disciples this faith: ...one God, the Father Almighty, Maker of heaven, and earth, and the sea, and all things that are in them; and in one Christ Jesus, the Son of God, who became incarnate for our salvation; and in the Holy Spirit, who proclaimed through the prophets the dispensations of God, and the advents, and the birth from a virgin, and the passion, and the resurrection from the dead, and the ascension into heaven.
Irenaeus

Think of the Father as a spring of life begetting the Son like a river and the Holy Spirit is like a sea, for the spring and the river and the sea are all one nature.
Think of the Father as a root, of the Son as a branch, and of the Spirit as a fruit, for the substance in these three is one.
The Father is a sun with the Son as rays and the Holy Spirit its heat.
John of Damascus

With the one and with the other
There was equality,
So Three Persons, one Beloved,
Loved all, and they were three.
John of the Cross

We are enclosed in the Father, and we are enclosed in the Son, and we are enclosed in the Holy Ghost. And the Father is enclosed in us, and the Son is enclosed in us, and the Holy Ghost is enclosed in us;

Almightiness, All Wisdom, All Goodness:
one God, one Lord.
Julian of Norwich

The monotheistic faith taken over from
Israel and held in common with Islam
must never be abandoned in any doctrine
of the Trinity. There is no God but God.
Hans Küng

Our salvation is free in the Father, sure in
the Son, ours in the Spirit.
Thomas Manton

For, in the name of God, the Father and
Lord of the universe, and of our Savior
Jesus Christ, and of the Holy Spirit, they
then receive the washing with water.
Justin Martyr

If the Holy Spirit were not eternally as He
is, and had received knowledge at some
time and then became the Holy Spirit
then the Holy Spirit would never be
reckoned in the unity of the Trinity, i.e.,
along with the unchangeable Father and
His Son, unless He had always been the
Holy Spirit
Origen

O Lord God almighty...I bless you and
glorify you through the eternal and
heavenly high priest Jesus Christ, your
beloved Son, through whom be glory to
you, with Him and the Holy Spirit, both
now and forever.
Polycarp

In the Divine economy of man's salvation
election is the special work of God the
Father--atonement, mediation, and
intercession, the special work of God the
Son--and sanctification, the special work of
God the Holy Ghost.
J.C. Ryle

Without the high order of personal unity
and diversity as given in the Trinity, there
are no answers.
Francis A. Schaeffer

The Three are thought of as one Essence
and Nature and Kingship. If a name is
attributed to One, it is by nature applied to
the others, with the exception of the terms
Father, Son, and Holy Ghost, or the terms
beget, begotten, and proceeding. These
terms characterize the three Persons. The
Son is begotten and the Spirit proceeds
simultaneously with the Father's existence.
Symeon the New Theologian

If you speak of "light", then both each Person
is light and the Three are one light; if you
speak of "eternal life," so each of Them is
likewise, the Son, the Spirit, and the Father,
and the Three are one life. So God the Father
is Spirit (cf. Jn. 4:24), and the Spirit is the
Lord (2 Cor. 3:17), and the Holy Spirit is
God. Each Person is God by Himself, and
together the Three are one God. Each One is
Lord and the Three are Lord.
Symeon the New Theologian

They are three, not in dignity, but in
degree, not in substance but in form, not
in power but in kind. They are of one
substance and power, because there is one
God from whom these degrees, forms and
kinds devolve in the name of Father, Son
and Holy Spirit.
Tertullian

We define that there are two, the Father and
the Son, and three with the Holy Spirit, and
this number is made by the pattern of
salvation ... [which] brings about unity in
trinity, interrelating the three, the Father,
the Son, and the Holy Spirit.
Tertullian

What doth it profit thee to enter into deep
discussions concerning the Holy Trinity, if
thou lack humility, and be thus displeasing
to the Trinity?
Thomas à Kempis

Triumph
God always causes me to triumph in
Christ Jesus.
The Bible, 2 Corinthians 2:14 KJV

As conquerors of old in their solemn triumphs used to lead their captives fettered with iron chains, so Christ having spoiled principalities and powers, made a shew of them openly, triumphing over them.... It is certain that Christ fought and overcame all his enemies: he gave them the last blow upon the cross, he seized on the spoil at his resurrection, and led them in triumph at his ascension into heaven, and by his peaceable possession of this throne His subjects enjoy the benefit of all.
Thomas Boston

Trouble
See also: Adversity; Difficulties; Trials
Man is born unto trouble, as the sparks fly upward.
The Bible, Job 5:7 KJV

Man that is born of a woman is of few days, and full of trouble.
The Bible, Job 14:1 KJV

God is our refuge and strength, a very present help in trouble.
The Bible, Psalm 46:1 KJV

In times of trouble, remember that God is:
Too kind to be cruel,
Too wise to make a mistake, and
Too deep to explain himself.
Author unknown

Troubles
See also: Worry
Be not dismayed at the troubles of the earth. Tremble not at the convulsions of empires. Only, fear God; only believe in his promises; only love and serve him; and all things shall work together for thy good, as they assuredly will for his glory.
Spiritual Exercises of the Heart, published in 1837 by an unknown author

Some folks treat God like a lawyer. They go to him, only when they are in trouble.
Author unknown

If you see ten troubles coming down the road, you can be sure that nine will run into the ditch before they reach you.
Calvin Coolidge

In trouble to be troubled
Is to have your trouble doubled.
Daniel Defoe

We should never attempt to bear more than one kind of trouble at once. Some people bear three kinds—all they have had, all they have now, and all they expect to have.
Edward Everett Hale

It is only under the shadow of the cross that we can appreciate the true weight of our own cross, and accept it each day from His hand, to carry it with love, with gratitude, and with joy.
Theodore Monod

I bless the Lord that all our troubles come through Christ's fingers, and that He casteth sugar among them; and casteth the spirit of glory in our cup.
Samuel Rutherford

We should judge by contraries. Therefore, if we be in misery, hope and wait for glory, in death look for life, in sense of sin assure thyself of pardon, for God's nature and promises are unchangeable; and when God will forgive, he lets us see our troubles.
Richard Sibbes

Griefs exalt us, and troubles lift us.
C.H. Spurgeon

Why are you so easily troubled? Because things do not happen to you as you desire. Who is the man who has all things as he would have them? Neither you nor I nor any man living, for no one lives in this world without some trouble or anguish, be he king or pope.
Thomas à Kempis

Trust
Psalm 23
A Psalm of David.
The Lord is my shepherd; I shall not want.
He maketh me to lie down in green

pastures: he leadeth me beside the still
waters.
He restoreth my soul: he leadeth me in the
paths of righteousness for his name's sake.
Yea, though I walk through the valley of
the shadow of death,
I will fear no evil: for thou art with me; thy
rod and thy staff they comfort me.
Thou preparest a table before me in the
presence of mine enemies:
Thou anointest my head with oil; my cup
runneth over.
Surely goodness and mercy shall follow me
all the days of my life:
and I will dwell in the house of the Lord
for ever.
The Bible, Psalm 23:1-6 kjv

I will say of the LORD, He is my refuge
and my fortress: my God; in him will I
trust.
The Bible, Psalm 91:2 KJV

Put not your trust in princes.
The Bible, Psalm 146:3

There are moments when whatever be the
attitude of the body, the soul is on its knees.
Author unknown

Some folks won't look up until they are flat
on their backs.
Author unknown

Trust the past to God's mercy, the present
to God's love and the future to God's
providence.
Augustine of Hippo

Trust the past to God's mercy,
the present to his love,
and the future to his providence.
Augustine of Hippo

In God alone there is faithfulness and
faith in the trust that we may hold to him,
to his promise and to his guidance. To
hold to God is to rely on the fact that God
is there for me, and to live in this
certainty.
Karl Barth

Every thing that a man leans upon but
God, will be a dart that will certainly
pierce his heart through and through. He,
who leans only upon Christ, lives the
highest, choicest, safest, and sweetest life.
Thomas Brooks

We often don't always know why things
happen to us and others in a given
situation or circumstance but we know
why we trust God who does know why.
Dave Brown

There is no other method of living piously
and justly, than that of depending upon
God.
John Calvin

Obedience is the Child of Trust.
John Climacus

God moves in a mysterious way,
  His wonders to perform;
He plants his footsteps in the sea,
  And rides upon the storm.

His purposes will ripen fast,
  Unfolding ev'ry hour;
The bud may have a bitter taste,
  But sweet will be the flow'r.

Judge not the LORD by feeble sense,
  But trust him for his grace;
Behind a frowning providence,
  He hides a smiling face.

Deep in unfathomable mines
  Of never failing skill,
He treasures up his bright designs,
  And works his sovereign will.

Blind unbelief is sure to err,
  And scan his work in vain;
GOD is his own interpreter,
  And he will make it plain.
William Cowper

This is what I found out about religion: it
gives you courage to make the decisions
you must make in a crisis and the
confidence to leave the results to a higher

Power. Only by trust in God can a man carrying responsibility find repose.
Dwight D. Eisenhower

All I have seen teaches me to trust the Creator for all I have not seen.
Ralph Waldo Emerson

Do not look forward to the changes and chances of this life in fear; rather look to them with full hope that, as they arise, God, whose you are, will deliver you out of them. He is your keeper. He has kept you hitherto. Do you but hold fast to his dear hand, and he will lead you safely through all things; and, when you cannot stand, he will bear you in his arms. Do not look forward to what may happen tomorrow. Our Father will either shield you from suffering, or he will give you strength to bear it.
Francis of Sales

Those who trust in love with all their being shall be given all they need.
For she brings comfort to the sad and guidance to those who cannot read.
Hadewijch

Have courage for the great sorrows of life and patience for the small ones; and when you have laboriously accomplished your daily task, go to sleep in peace. God is awake.
Victor Hugo

All will be well
All will be well, and all will be well, and all manner of things will be well.
Julian of Norwich

Set all your trust in God and fear not the language of the world; for the more despite, shame, and reproof that you receive in the world, the more is your merit in the sight of God.
Julian of Norwich

Quit sweating, quit wrestling. It is not TRY but TRUST.
John G. Lake

He who trusts in himself is lost. He who trusts in God can do all things.
Alphonsus Liguori

He will keep His word – the gracious One, full of grace and truth; no doubt of it. He said, "Him that cometh unto Me, I will in no wise cast out"; and "Whatsoever ye shall ask in My name, I will give it.' He will keep his word; then I can come and humbly present my petition and it will be all right. Doubt is here inadmissible, surely.'
David Livingstone's Journal, May 13th, 1872

Dear Lord, although I am sure of my position, I am unable to sustain it without you. Help me or I am lost.
Martin Luther

Let us keep to Christ,
And cling to Him,
And hang on him,
So that no power can remove us.
Martin Luther

Even if I knew that tomorrow the world would go to pieces, I would still plant my apple tree.
Martin Luther

Trust in yourself and you are doomed to disappointment.
Trust in your friends and they will die and leave you.
Trust in money and you may have it taken away from you.
Trust in reputation and some slanderous tongues will blast it.
But trust in God and you are never to be confounded in time or in eternity.
Dwight Moody

The very vastness of the work raises one's thoughts to God, as the only one by whom it can be done. That is the solid comfort – he knows.
Florence Nightingale

Trust Jesus, and you are saved.
Trust self, and you are lost.
C.H. Spurgeon

Quiet minds that rest in God cannot be perplexed or frightened, but go on in fortune or misfortune at their private pace, like a clock during a thunderstorm.
Robert Louis Stevenson

All God's giants have been weak men, who did great things for God because they believed that God would be with them.
Hudson Taylor

Teresa's Bookmark
Let nothing disturb you,
nothing frighten you;
All things are passing;
God never changes;
Patient endurance
Attains all things;
Whoever possesses God
Lacks nothing;
God alone suffices.
Teresa of Avila

I know God won't give me anything I can't handle. I just wish He didn't trust me so much.
Mother Teresa

I have held many things in my hands, and I have lost them all; but whatever I have placed in God's hands, that I still possess.
Corrie Ten Boom

Oh, how great peace and quietness would he possess who should cut off all vain anxiety and place all his confidence in God.
Thomas a Kempis

He rides at ease whom the grace of God carries.
Thomas à Kempis

Nothing in my hand I bring,
Simply to thy cross I cling;
Naked, come to thee for dress;
Helpless, look to thee for grace;
Foul, I to the fountain fly;
Wash me, Savior, or I die.
Augustus Toplady

To do thy will is more than praise,
As words are less than deeds;
And simple trust can find thy ways
We miss with chart of creeds.
Whittier, J.G.

Moment by moment I'm kept in his love,
Moment by moment I've life from above;
Looking to Jesus till glory doth shine,
Moment by moment, O Lord, I am thine.
Major Daniel Webster Whittle

O Lord, forgive what I have been, sanctify what I am, and order what I shall be.
Thomas Wilson

Trust and action
Trust in God, and do something.
Mary Lyon

The truly religious man does everything as if everything depends on himself, and then leaves everything as if everything depended on God.
Joseph Parker

Pray in the storm but keep rowing.
Danish proverb

Trust and work
A man's readiness and commitment are not enough if he does not enjoy help from above as well; equally help from above is no benefit to us unless there is also commitment and readiness on our part. Thus I entreat you neither to entrust everything to God and then fall asleep, nor to think, when you are striving diligently, that you will achieve everything by your own efforts.
John Chrysostom

Trust in people
Vain is the man who puts his trust in men, in created things.
Thomas à Kempis

Trust in self
Those who trust in themselves are worse than the devil.
John of the Cross

Truth

See also: Preaching

You will know the truth, and the truth shall set you free.
The Bible, John 8:32

But when he, the Spirit of truth, comes, he will guide you into all truth.
The Bible, John 16:13

Speak every man truth with his neighbor.
Ephesians 4:25

Those who would find truth must:
1. Desire it.
2. Pray for it.
3. Study it.
4. Practice it.
Author Unknown

Truth is the greatest gift of life and love is the exercise of that truth.
Author unknown

Truth is truth where e're it is found;
on Christian or on heathen ground.
Author unknown

Nothing ruins the truth like stretching it.
Author unknown

If you don't learn and know your truths, you cannot speak them. If you don't speak them, you will know a prison within. Tell your truths to yourself, and then to the others. The truth really will set you free!
Author Unknown

The things in the Bible aren't true because they're in the Bible—they're in the Bible because they're true.
Author unknown

If we hold on to God's truth, we won't be trapped by Satan's lies.
Author unknown

Pilate asked, *Quid est Veritas?* ("What is truth?" In Latin the answer is an anagram,

Est Vir qui Adest ("It is the Man who is before you.").
Author unknown

Truth is not always popular, but it is always right.
Author unknown

If any man can convince me and bring home to me that I do not think or act aright, gladly will I change; for I search after truth, by which man never yet was harmed. But he is harmed who abideth on still in his deception and ignorance.
Marcus Aurelius Antoninus

Men could not live with one another if there were not mutual confidence that they were being truthful to one another.
Thomas Aquinas

As a matter of honor, one man owes it to another to manifest the truth.
Thomas Aquinas

Truth sits upon the lips of dying men.
Matthew Arnold

A thing is not necessarily true because badly uttered, nor false because spoken magnificently.
Augustine of Canterbury

The truth is neither mine nor his nor another's; but belongs to us all whom Thou callest to partake of it, warning us terribly, not to account it private to ourselves, lest we be deprived of it.
Augustine of Hippo

Where I found truth, there found I my God, who is the truth itself. And thus since the time I learned thee, thou abidest in my memory; and there do I find thee whensoever I call thee to remembrance, and delight in thee.
Augustine of Hippo

Be so true to thyself, as thou be not false to others.
Francis Bacon

No pleasure is comparable to the standing upon the vantage-ground of truth.
Francis Bacon

The best theology would need no advocates; it would prove itself.
Karl Barth

The ascent to truth is by three steps, humility, compassion, and in the ecstasy of contemplation.
Bernard of Clairvaux

A Truth that's told with bad intent Beats all the Lies you can invent.
William Blake

The opposite of a correct statement is a false statement. But the opposite of a profound truth may well be another profound truth.
Niels Bohr

Where truth goes I will go, and where truth is I will be, and nothing but death shall divide me and the truth.
Thomas Brooks

Whoever lives true life, will love true love.
Elizabeth Barrett Browning

Truth never hurts the teller.
Robert Browning

Truth does not change because it is, or is not, believed by a majority of the people.
Giordano Bruno

There is no fit search after Truth which does not, first of all, begin to live the Truth which it knows.
Horace Bushnell

All truth is from God; and consequently, if wicked men have said anything that is true and just, we ought not to reject it; for it has come from God. Besides, all things are of God; and, therefore, why should it not be lawful to dedicate to his glory everything that can properly be employed for such a purpose?
John Calvin

Too often do we call the truths which offend us by the name of slander.
J.P. Camus

To kill a man is not to defend a doctrine, but to kill a man.
Sebastien Castello

Where truth is, there is God.
Miguel de Cervantes

Truth is the highest thing that man may keep.
Geoffrey Chaucer

The truth is incontrovertible. Malice may attack it. Ignorance may deride it. But in the end, there it is.
Winston Churchill

Man will occasionally stumble over the truth, but most times he will pick himself up and carry on.
Winston Churchill

A lie gets halfway around the world before the truth has a chance to get its pants on.
Winston Churchill

Nearly everyone will lie to you given the right circumstances.
Bill Clinton

The road to tyranny, we must never forget, begins with the destruction of the truth.
Bill Clinton

He who begins by loving Christianity better than truth will proceed by loving his own sect or church better than Christianity, and end in loving himself better than all.
Samual Taylor Coleridge

The greatest friend of truth is Time, her greatest enemy is Prejudice, and her constant companion is Humility.
Charles C. Colton

Falsehood is never so successful as when she baits her hook with truth, and no opinions so fatally mislead us, as those that

are not wholly wrong; as no watches so effectually deceive the wearer as those that are sometimes right.
C.C. Colton

Mr Lely, I desire you would use all your skill to paint my picture truly like me, and not flatter me at all; but remark all these roughnesses, pimples, warts, and everything as you see me, otherwise I will never pay a farthing for it.
Oliver Cromwell

Wherever truth may be, were it in a Turk or Tarter, it must be cherished. Let us seek the honeycomb even within the lion's mouth.
Johan de Brune

The truth will make you free, but first it will make you miserable.
Tom DeMarco

On a huge hill, Craggy and steep, Truth stands and he that will Reach her, about must, and about must go.
John Donne

Truth is the foundation of all knowledge and the cement of all societies.
John Dryden

Errors, like straws, upon the surface flow; He who would search for pearls must dive down below.
John Dryden

Whoever is careless with the truth in small matters cannot be trusted with important matters.
Albert Einstein

We need to recognize God's truth, no matter who's mouth it comes out of.
Elizabeth Elliott

All I have seen teaches me to trust the Creator for all I have not seen.
Ralph Waldo Emerson

God offers to every mind its choice

between truth and repose. Take which you please, you can never have both.
Ralph Waldo Emerson

If a million people believe a foolish thing, it is still a foolish thing.
Anatole France

Truth is the daughter of God.
Thomas Fuller

It is easier to perceive error than to find truth, for the former lies on the surface and is easily seen, while the latter lies in the depth, where few are willing to search for it.
Johann Wolfgang von Goethe

Nothing is more harmful to a new truth than an old error.
Johann Wolfgang von Goethe

Devotion to truth is the first and last thing we demand of genius.
Johann Wolfgang von Goethe

It is better that scandal arise than that truth be concealed.
St. Gregory the Great

Everyone may be entitled to his own opinion but everyone is not entitled to his own truth. Truth is but one.
Doug Groothius

Truth is not determined by majority vote.
Doug Gwyn

We seek no conquest over our adversaries; but only that truth may overcome falsehood.
St Hierom

There is no such thing as truth either in the moral or the scientific sense.
Adolf Hitler

To most of us nothing is so invisible as an unpleasant truth. Though it is held before our eyes, pushed under our noses, rammed down our throats- we know it not.
Eric Hoffer

Truth is not limited to the Scriptures, but it is limited by the Scriptures.
J. Grant Howard

It is the customary fate of new truths to begin as heresies and to end as superstitions.
T.H. Huxley

Truth is the first chapter in the book of wisdom.
Thomas Jefferson

There is no truth existing which I fear, or would wish unknown to the whole world.
Thomas Jefferson

The truth has set bounds. But evil and falsehood multiplies without end; and the more these (evils) are pursued, the more errors they produce.
Jerome

Our society finds truth too strong a medicine to digest undiluted. In its purest form, truth is not a polite tap on the shoulder; it is a howling reproach. What Moses brought down from Mt. Sinai were not suggestions but ten commandments.
Ted Koppel

I believe that truths are truths, however questionable the voice which utters them.
Warren Kramer

A Church which abandons the truth abandons itself.
Hans Küng

You don't always have to chop with the sword of truth. You can point with it, too.
Anne Lamott

Our enemies come nearer the truth in the opinions they form of us than we do in our opinion of ourselves.
La Rochefoucauld

Say the truth and shame the devil.
Hugh Latimer

If you look for truth, you may find comfort in the end; if you look for comfort you will not get either comfort or truth – only soft soap and wishful thinking to begin, and in the end, despair.
C.S. Lewis

A man can't be always defending the truth; there must be a time to feed on it.
C.S. Lewis

We believe that the truth is more than a system; but we also believe that the truth is one, even as God is one. And we believe, therefore, that the truth is systematic, and that the different truths are related.
C.S. Lewis

Truth is often eclipsed but never extinguished.
Livy

The truth of a proposition has nothing to do with its credibility. And vice versa.
Lazarus Long

If I profess with the loudest voice and clearest exposition every portion of the truth of God except precisely that little point which the world and the devil are at that moment attacking, I am not confessing Christ, however boldly I may be professing Christ. Where the battle rages, there the loyalty of the soldier is proved; and to be steady on all the battlefield besides, is mere flight and disgrace if he flinches at that point.
Martin Luther

A love which violates or even merely neutralizes truth is an "accursed love".
Martin Luther

Peace if possible, but truth at any rate.
Martin Luther

The desire for truth is the desire for God.
John Macquarrie

All truth, wherever it is found, belongs to us as Christian.
Justin Martyr

Man has always sacrificed truth to his vanity, comfort and advantage. He lives by make believe.
W. Somerset Maugham

The gulf between knowledge and truth is infinite.
Henry Miller

Servant of God, well done! well hast thou fought. The better fight, who single hast maintain'd. Against revolted multitudes the cause of truth.
John Milton

Truth is as impossible to be soiled by any outward touch as the sunbeam.
John Milton

But truth is so great a thing that we ought not to despise any medium that will conduct us to it.
Michel de Montaigne

[Truth] must be loved for its own sake.
Michel de Montaigne

The truth is a reality which we can hardly bear.
Hugh Montefiore

There are no eternal facts, as there are no absolute truths.
Friederich Nietzsche

Let us begin by committing ourselves to the truth -- to see it like it is, and tell it like it is -- to find the truth, to speak the truth, and to live the truth.
Richard M. Nixon

It is truth alone that capacitates any soul to glorify God.
John Owen

The Evangelical is not afraid of facts, for he knows that all facts are God's facts; nor is he afraid of thinking, for he knows that all truth is God's truth, and right reason cannot endanger sound faith. He is called to love God with all his mind.
J.I. Packer

Truth never envelops itself in mystery, and the mystery in which it is at any time enveloped is the work of its antagonist, and never of itself.
Thomas Paine

The history of the church ought properly to be called the history of truth.
Blaise Pascal

We know the truth, not only by the reason, but also by the heart.
Blaise Pascal

We do not run after the new; we do not run after the unknown; we do not run after the extraordinary; we seek what is right and fitting, and much that is right and fitting was said before us much better than we know how to say it ourselves.
Charles Péguy

Christ is the key which unlocks the golden doors into the temple of Divine truth.
A. W. Pink

Renouncing the honors at which the world aims, I desire only to know the truth... and to the maximum of power, I exhort all other men to do the same.
Plato

Plato is my friend, Socrates is my friend, but truth is greater.
Latin proverb

Truth fears nothing but concealment.
Latin proverb

Speak the truth, but leave immediately after.
Slovenian Proverb

Never let us be guilty of sacrificing any portion of truth on the altar of peace.
J.C. Ryle

Truth demands confrontation; loving confrontation, but confrontation nevertheless.
Francis A. Schaeffer

Let us rejoice in the truth, wherever we find its lamp burning.
Albert Schweitzer

All truth passes through three stages. First, it is ridiculed. Second, it is violently opposed. Third, it is accepted as being self-evident.
Arthur Schopenhauer

The most natural beauty in the world is honesty and moral truth. For all beauty is truth. True features make the beauty of the face; true proportions, the beauty of architecture; true measures, the beauty of harmony and music.
The Earl of Shaftsbury

The simple step of a courageous individual is not to take part in the lie. One word of truth outweighs the world.
Alexander Solzhenitsyn

We do not err because truth is difficult to see. It is visible at a glance. We err because this is more comfortable.
Alexander Solzhenitsyn

We are more likely to catch glimpses of truth when we allow what we think and believe to be tested.
Choan-Seng Song

Truth is always the strongest argument.
Sophocles

A sacred regard to the authority of God ought to lead us to reject an error, however old, sanctioned by whatever authority, or however generally practiced.
C.H. Spurgeon

We must never throw away a bushel of truth because it happens to contain a few grains of chaff.
Dean Stanley

Search not who spoke this or that, but mark what is spoken. Men pass away, but the truth of the Lord remaineth forever.
Thomas à Kempis

Rather than love, than money, than fame, give me truth.
Henry David Thoreau

Truth is the most valuable thing we have -- so let us economize it.
Mark Twain

I am very fond of truth, but not at all of martyrdom.
Voltaire

I believe that in the end the truth will conquer.
John Wycliffe

Truth, Defense of

Not to oppose error, is to approve of it, and not to defend truth is to suppress it, and indeed to neglect to confound evil men, when we can do it, is no less a sin than to encourage them.
Pope Felix III

Truth, Economic with

I didn't accept it. I received it.
Richard Allen
National Security Advisor to President Reagan, explaining the $1000 in cash and two watches he was given by two Japanese journalists after he helped arrange a private interview for them with First Lady Nancy Reagan

We are not retreating – we are advancing in another Direction.
General Douglas MacArthur

I was a pilot flying an airplane and it just so happened that where I was flying made what I was doing spying.
Francis Gary Power
U-2 reconnaissance pilot held by the Soviets for spying, in a interview after he was returned to the US

You don't tell deliberate lies, but sometimes you have to be evasive.
Margaret Thatcher

Truth, *Gospel*

Thomas Boston

1. It is the duty of all that hear the gospel, upon the revelation of Christ therein, without looking for any previous qualification in themselves, instantly to believe in him for salvation, both from sin and wrath, that only by so doing, will person be enabled in a gospel manner to forsake sin – that it is inconsistent with the method of gospel grace, and absolutely impossible, for a man to forsake his sins, in a way of gospel repentance, (which kind of forsaking can only please God), till the Spirit determine him to come to Christ as a Prince and Savior exalted to give repentance and remission of sins.

2. That though there is no universal atonement, yet in the word there is warrant given to offer Christ to all mankind, whether elect or reprobate, and a warrant to all freely to receive him, however great sinners they are, or have been.

3. That in justifying faith, there is a real persuasion in the heart of the sinner, that Christ is his; and that he shall have life and salvation by him, and that whatever Christ did for the redemption of mankind, he did it for him in particular; which persuasion is founded (not upon the uptaking of one's real regeneration, as the reflex assurance is, but) upon the promise of Christ in the gospel, made to sinners of Adam's family as such; and so there is resting upon him alone, for the whole of salvation.

4. That the gospel strictly taken, is only a declaration and promise, containing glad tidings of a Savior, and all of grace, mercy and salvation in him to sinners – that all precepts, particularly those enjoining faith and repentance, belong to the law – that as believers, holiness has no casual influence upon his everlasting happiness as a federal and conditional means thereof; but the perfect righteousness of Christ as a surety, is the believer's plea both with respect to law and justice, and that whether as to purchase, or actual obtaining the possession of everlasting happiness.

5. That believers being heirs of heaven, though they ought to be powerfully minded to obedience to the law as a rule, by a view of the excellency of their inheritance of God in Christ, by their having the begun possession of this inheritance, and by the sure hope of the perfect possession thereof, being secured by free grace, through the blood of Christ; yet they ought not to be influenced to obedience, by hopes of obtaining the possession of that inheritance, by any good works done by them; and that though believers are to entertain an holy dread of the majesty of God, and his power to cast into hell, and of the awfulness of his threatenings and judgements against sin and sinners, and to consider from these, the due desert of their sins; and though they ought to be influenced by the feeling or fear of afflictions in this life, temporal and spiritual, considered as the discipline of the covenant, sent by a kind Father on a kind design, to the study of habitual improvement of the blood and Spirit of Christ, for the fortifying of remaining corruption, and exercising gospel holiness; yet they ought not to be excited to obedience by any fear, that God shall for their sins actually cast them into hell; but ought always to believe their full security against falling into the pit, in order to influence them to a more cheerful obedience.

6. That believers are, through Christ, altogether delivered from the law as a covenant of works; the asserting of which, doth no way infer their being loosed from the law as a rule of life, and that though all unbelievers are under the law as a covenant of works, yet it doth not follow that they are obliged to seek justification by their own righteousness; nay, all of them are obliged to seek justification by the blood of Christ alone, without the works of the law.

7. That there is a wide difference between the law as a rule of life, and as a covenant of works – that believers are not under the law as a covenant of works, but are under it, as it is the law of Christ, or a rule in the hand of a mediator; that therefore a believer cannot sin against the law as a

covenant of works, but only against it as a rule of life – that God cannot see sin in a believer, as committed against the law as a covenant, but only as committed against the law as a rule of life; that therefore God can have no vindictive or legal anger at them for their sins, but only a Fatherly anger and displeasure; that therefore, believers ought not to mourn over, or confess their iniquities, in a legal manner, viewing them as committed by persons under the covenant of works; but ought to confess and mourn over them, as sins done against a reconciled Father, and breaches of his law as a rule of life.

8. That the grace of the gospel is so far from loosing men from the obligation of the law as a rule of life, that it superadds more weighty and powerful incitements to obedience.

Thomas Boston

Truth and action

God offers to every mind its choice between truth and repose. Take which you please, you can never have both.

Ralph Waldo Emerson

Truth and freedom

The spirit of truth and the spirit of freedom--they are the pillars of society.

Henrik Ibsen

Truth and love

I believe that unarmed truth and unconditional love will have the final word in reality. That is why right, temporarily defeated, is stronger than evil triumphant.

Martin Luther King Jr.

Truthfulness

The commandment of absolute truthfulness is really only another name for the fullness of discipleship.

Dietrich Bonhoeffer

Tyrant

If view of the success of my economic revolution in Uganda, I offer myself to be appointed Head of the Commonwealth.

Idi Amin

We're the most democratic country in Latin America.

Fidel Castro

I shall be an autocrat: that's my trade. And the good Lord will forgive me: that's his.

Attributed to Catherine II (the Great)

U

Unbelief
See also: Agnosticism; Belief; God, belief in

Unbelief is not the cause of sin; sin is the cause of unbelief.
Author unknown

Unbelief, and a thousand evils, are still in our hearts: though their reign and dominion is at an end, they are not slain or eradicated; their effects will be felt more or less sensibly, as the Lord is pleased more or less to afford or abate His gracious influence.
John Newton

None but the Lord himself can afford us any help from the awful workings of unbelief, doubtings, carnal fears, murmurings. Thank God one day we will be done forever with "unbelief."
Arthur W. Pink

Uncertainty
It is not certain that everything is uncertain.
Blaise Pascal

Unconverted
The besetting sin of the unconverted is to deny their guiltiness, to plead that they are as good as others, and to indulge still the vain and foolish hope that they shall enter into heaven from some doings, sufferings, or weepings of their own.
C.H. Spurgeon

Understanding
I have more understanding than all my teachers: for thy testimonies are my meditations.
The Bible, Psalm 119:99 KJV

He that knows not what the world is, knows not where he is himself. He that knows not for what he was made, knows not what he is nor what the world is.
Marcus Aurelius Antoninus

Man with all his shrewdness is as stupid about understanding by himself the mysteries of God, as an ass is incapable of understanding musical harmony.
John Calvin

A comprehended god is no god.
John Chrysostom

He that will believe only what he can fully comprehend must have a very long head or a very short creed.
Charles Caleb Colton

Seek first to understand, then to be understood.
Stephen R. Covey

What we don't understand we don't possess.
Johann Wolfgang von Goethe

I am the master of everything I can explain.
Theodor Haecker

If we could first know where we are and whither we are tending, we could then better judge what to do and how to do it.
Abraham Lincoln

It has pleased God that divine verities should not enter the heart through the understanding, but the understanding through the heart.
Blaise Pascal

Seek not so much to have thy ear tickled as thy understanding enlightened.
Nehemiah Rogers

From time immemorial men have quenched their thirst with water without knowing anything about its chemical constituents. In like manner we do not need to be instructed in all the mysteries of doctrine, but we do need to receive the Living Water which Jesus Christ will give us and which alone can satisfy our souls.
Sadhu Sundar Singh

All, everything that I understand, I understand only because I love.
Leo Tolstoy

Understanding spiritual truth
At that time Jesus said, "I praise you, Father, Lord of heaven and earth, because you have hidden these things from the wise and learned, and revealed them to little children."
The Bible, Matthew 11:25

Unfaithfulness
The lukewarmness of our prayers is the source of all our other infidelities.
François Fénelon

Unhappiness
The chief cause of failure and unhappiness is trading what we want most for what we want at the moment.
Author unknown

Uniformity
See also: Body of Christ; Unity
It is not necessary that traditions and ceremonies be in all places one, or utterly alike; for at all times they have been divers, and may be changed according to the diversities of countries, times and men's manners, so that nothing be ordained against God's Word.
Book of Common Prayer, Thirty Nine Articles, Article 34

Union with Christ
The heart of Paul's religion is union with Christ. This is the key which unlocks the secrets of his soul.
James Steward

The soul that would find me in the inner closet of a consecrated and self-detached life, and would partake of my sweetness, must first be purified from evil and adorned with virtues, be decked with the red roses of passionate love, with the beautiful violets of meek submission, and must be strewn with the white lilies of purity. It shall embrace me with its arms, excluding all other loves, for these I shun and flee as the bird does the cage. This soul shall sing to me the song of Zion, which means passionate love combined with boundless praise. Then I will embrace it and it shall lean upon my heart.
Henry Suso (God pictured speaking to a soul)

Union with God
Every soul no matter how burdened in sin, no matter how far away from God it has gone, no matter how close it is to damnation and despair, can find hope for pardon, mercy, and even perfect union in the mystical marriage with God. The soul created in the image of God was made for this union. Mystical union in this life is only transient and foretastes of the glory to come in the next. True mysticism is a gift granted to those who are extremely poor in themselves and who have learned to live for others, not themselves. This love is taught only supernaturally through the Holy Spirit. Every man should then aspire to perfect union with God. Nothing can give God greater honor than our love. Love alone makes the creature created by God capable of union with God.
Bernard of Clairvaux

Disciple. But being as I am in Nature, and thus bound, as with my own Chains, and by my own natural Will; pray be so kind, Sir, as to tell me, how I may come through Nature into the supersensual and supernatural Ground, without the destroying of Nature ?
Master. Three Things are requisite in order to this.
The First is, Thou must resign up thy Will to God; and must sink thyself down to the Dust in His Mercy.

The Second is, Thou must hate thy own Will, and forbear from doing that to which thy own Will doth drive thee.
The Third is, Thou must bow thy soul under the Cross, heartily submitting thyself to it, that thou mayest be able to bear the Temptations of Nature and Creature.
Jacob Boehme

The soul which is reduced to the Nothing, ought to dwell therein; without wishing, since she is now but dust, to issue from this state, nor, as before, desiring to live again. She must remain as something which no longer exists: and this, in order that the Torrent may drown itself and lose itself in the Sea, never to find itself in its selfhood again: that it may become one and the same thing with the Sea.
Madame Guyon

As soon as the two houses of the soul [the sensual and the spiritual] are tranquil and confirmed and merged in one by this peace, and their servants the powers, appetites and passions are sunk in deep tranquillity, neither troubled by things above nor things below, the Divine Wisdom immediately unites itself to the soul in a new bond of loving possession.
John of the Cross

True religion is a union of God with the soul, a real participation of the divine nature, the very image of God drawn upon the soul, or in the apostle's phrase, it is Christ formed in us.
Henry Scougal

Unity
See also: Body of Christ
Behold how good and how pleasant it is for brethren to dwell together in unity.
The Bible, Psalm 133:1 KJV

A threefold cord is not quickly broken.
The Bible, Ecclesiastes 4:12 KJV

Be ye all of one mind.
The Bible, 1 Peter 3:8 KJV

If we focus on our differences, our focus is on each other. If we focus with unity, our focus is on God.
Author unknown

In essentials, unity;
in non-essentials, liberty;
in all things, charity.
Richard Baxter, after Augustine of Hippo

Life together under the Word will remain sound and healthy only where it does not form itself into a movement, an order, a society, but rather where it understands itself as being a part of the one, holy, catholic, Christian Church, where it shares actively and passively in the sufferings and struggles of the whole Church.
Dietrich Bonhoeffer

Matters non-essential should not be the basis of argument among Christians.
John Calvin

Separation from evil is the necessary first principle of communion with Him ... Separation from evil is His principle of unity.
J.N. Darby

I may worship in a different building from you, I may worship in a different style, but all we hold dear is God's gift in Christ Jesus, who is our Unity. In Him we have all and lack nothing.
Michael J. Davis

Thou shalt not make a schism, but thou shalt pacify them that contend.
Didache

We must all hang together, or assuredly we shall all hang separately.
Benjamin Franklin

We have all come here in different ships, but we're in the same boat now.
Martin Luther King

Pope John Paul II, in calling for unified prayer by men of all faiths, shows he

believes there is a common foundation for all religions.
Hans Küng

Putting all the ecclesiastical corpses into one graveyard will not bring about a resurrection.
Martyn Lloyd-Jones

Again, men tell us that our preaching should be positive and not negative, that we can preach the truth without attacking error. But if we follow that advice we shall have to close our Bible and desert its teachings. The New Testament is a polemic book almost from beginning to end ... It is when men have felt compelled to take a stand against error that they have risen to the really great heights in the celebration of the truth.
J. Gresham Machen

As we draw nearer to Christ, we shall be drawn nearer to His people; and in our search for unity with the members we shall be drawn closer to the Head.
G. T. Manley

If ever we intend to take one step towards any agreement or unity, it must be by fixing this principle in the minds of all men -- that it is of no advantage to any man whatever church or way in Christian religion he be of, unless he personally believe the promises, and live in obedience unto all the precepts of Christ.
John Owen

For the truth's sake, Paul withstood and blamed Peter, though a brother. Where was the use of unity when pure doctrine was gone? And who shall dare to say he was wrong?
J.C. Ryle

Unity without the gospel is a worthless unity; it is the very unity of hell.
J.C. Ryle

To part with truth to show charity is to betray our Lord with a kiss. Between those who believe in the eternal verities and those who constantly cast doubt on them there can be no union.
C.H. Spurgeon

How can the Church call men to worship of the one God if it is calling to rival shrines.
William Temple

The constantly recurring question must be: What shall we unite with and from what shall we separate? The question of coexistence does not enter here, but the question of union and fellowship does. The wheat grows in the same field as the tares, but shall the two cross-pollinate? The sheep graze near the goats, but shall they seek to interbreed? The unjust and the just enjoy the same rain and sunshine, but shall they forget their deep moral differences and intermarry? ... The Spirit-illuminated church will have none of this.
A. W. Tozer

All Christians are called to unity in love and unity in truth.
The gospel of Jesus Christ: An evangelical celebration

Unity without verity [truth] is no better than conspiracy.
John Trapp

Diversity and division is infinitely more precious than a satanic unity.
John Whitcomb Jr.

Unity, Christian

The Churches belong together in the Church. What that may mean for our ecclesiastical groupings we do not know. We have not discovered the kind or outward manifestation which God wills that we shall give to that inner unity. But we must seek it.
Hugh Martin

1. How slow are we all to imitate our great Examplar, who in the most trying moments cried out, "Father, forgive them, for they know not what they do!"

2. How dangerous is a spirit of contention, of opposition, of vengeance! And how often were it in our power should we be disposed to call down fire from heaven, as Elias did!

3. How watchful over the growth of bad tempers ought we to be in the very beginnings of all religious controversies!

4. Then in the progress of them, how does it become us to pause often and examine ourselves, lest we should suppose we are doing God service, when in reality we are impelled only by heat, animosity and a desire of victory.

5. Lastly, when there really happens to exist in our motives some little good, are we not extremely apt to magnify it, till the fancied picture completely veils from our eyes that large admixture of evil, which on the whole miserably predominates. And is not this a fruitful source of deception?
Joseph Milner

Universe
See also: Nature

Philosophy is written in this grand book -- I mean the universe -- which stands continually open to our gaze, but it cannot be understood unless one first learns to comprehend the language and interpret the characters in which it is written. It is written in the language of mathematics, and its characters are triangles, circles, and other geometrical figures, without which it is humanly impossible to understand a single word of it; without these, one is wandering about in a dark labyrinth.
Galileo

Kepler said he was: "Thinking God's thoughts after him."
Kepler

The universe is one great kindergarten for man. Everything that exists has brought with it its own peculiar lesson. The mountain teaches stability and grandeur; the ocean immensity and change. Forests, lakes, and rivers, clouds and winds, stars and flowers, stupendous glaciers and crystal snowflakes — every form of animate or inanimate existence, leaves its impress upon the soul of man. Even the bee and ant have brought their little lessons of industry and economy.
Orison Swett Marden

Unseen

We must shift our interest from the seen to the unseen. For the great unseen Reality is God.
A. W. Tozer

Unstable

Carried about with every wind of doctrine.
The Bible, Ephesians 4:14 KJV

Usefulness

We may easily be too big for God to use, but never too small.
D.L. Moody

Utopia

We reject as a proud, self-confident dream the notion that man can ever build a utopia on earth.
The Lausanne Covenant

[Christianity's] assertion of original sin should make the Church intensely realistic and conspicuously free from utopianism.
William Temple

V

Vaccination
Vaccination is a direct violation of the everlasting covenant that God made with Noah after the flood. Vaccination never saved human life. It does not prevent smallpox.
Jehovah's Witnesses, The Golden Age, (predecessor to Awake!), Feb. 4, 1931

Values
There are so many men who can figure costs, and so few who can measure values.
California Tribune

Today, classic theological liberalism is no longer the church's main threat. As we enter a post-Christian world, one driven by consumer culture and the entertainment industry, we face more basic challenges, such as the radical devaluation of human life.
David Neff

Vanity
All is vanity and vexation of spirit.
The Bible, Ecclesiastes 1:14 KJV

An ounce of vanity can ruin a ton of merit.
Author unknown

We are so presumptuous that we should like to be known all over the world, even by people who will only come when we are no more. Such is our vanity that the good opinion of half a dozen of the people around us gives us pleasure and satisfaction.
Blaise Pascal

All is vanity but to love God and serve him.
Thomas à Kempis

Vernacular
I thank God that I have heard and find my God in the German tongue as neither I

nor they [the adherents of the old way] have found him in the Latin and Hebrew tongues.
Martin Luther

Vices
We make ourselves a ladder out of our vices if we trample the vices themselves underfoot.
Augustine of Hippo

The leader should understand how often vices pass themselves off as virtues. Stinginess often excuses itself under the name of frugality while, on the other hand, extravagance hides itself under the name of generosity. Often inordinate laxity is mistaken for loving kindness, while unbridled wrath is seen as the virtue of spiritual zeal.
Gregory the Great

Victory
Spiritual victory comes only to those who are prepared for battle.
Author unknown

It often happens that our passions lie dormant. If, during that time, we do not lay up provision of strength with which to combat them when they wake up, we shall be vanquished.
Francis de Sales

He conquers who overcomes himself.
Latin proverb

He who fears being conquered is sure of defeat.
Napoleon Bonaparte

Victory goes to the player who makes the next-to-last mistake.
Chessmaster Savielly Grigorievitch Tartakower

Viewpoint

"But it is always interesting when one doesn't see," she added. "If you don't see what a thing means, you must be looking at it wrong way around."
Agatha Christie

Vigilance

Eternal vigilance is the price of liberty.
Wendell Phillips

Vigilance and prayer are the safeguards of chastity.
Jean Baptiste de la Salle

Violence

We should do unto others as we would want them to do unto us. If I were an unborn fetus I would want others to use force to protect me, therefore using force against abortionists is justifiable homicide.
Paul Hill Pro-Life doctor killer

The modern choice is between non-violence and non-existence.
Martin Luther King

If you succumb to the temptation of using violence in the struggle, unborn generations will be the recipients of a long and dissolute night of bitterness, and your chief legacy to the future will be an endless reign of meaningless chaos.
Martin Luther King Jr.

Violence is an involuntary quest for identity.
Marshall McLuhan

In 1559 a more sinister turn was taken in the evangelical affairs. The persecuted church began to think in terms of armed resistance, even of armed revolt. The ranks of evangelicals now contained a large number of nobles, unused to suffering wrongs as patiently as the middle classes who had hitherto predominated.... Calvin was sounded as to his opinions on active revolt. He had already, in a letter to the church in Paris, made it clear that he was aware of the new situation brought about by the change in the composition of the church, and had spoken out strongly against the use of force: "Let it be your care to attempt nothing that is not warranted by his Word... It would be better for us all to be ruined than that the gospel of God should be exposed to the reproach that it has armed men for sedition and tumult."
T.H.L. Parker

Let us not forget that violence does not exist by itself and cannot do so; it is necessarily interwoven with lies. Violence finds its only refuge in falsehood, falsehood its only support in violence. Any man who has once acclaimed violence as his method must inexorably choose falsehood as his principle.
Alexander Solzhenitsyn

Virgin birth
See also: Bible, Inspiration of

Gabriel's statement: "You will be with child and give birth to a son."
Luke 1:31
Mary's response: "How will this be, since I am a virgin?"
Luke 1:34
Gabriel's answer: "The Holy Spirit will come upon you, and the power of the Most High will overshadow you."
Luke 1:35
Matthew's comment: "All this took place to fulfil what the Lord had said through the prophet [Isaiah 7:14]: 'The virgin will be with child.'"
Matthew 1:22-23

I have put no emphasis on the virgin birth in the course of this chapter. This is not because I do not believe in it, for I do; but because, as I understand it, the account of Christ's miraculous birth was given in the Gospels for the sake of those who had already come to believe in him and who wished to know the facts, but was never used as a means of evoking faith in those who were not yet convinced on other grounds as to who he was. After all, a virgin birth would be possible without any implications of deity.
J. N. D. Anderson

I believe in … Jesus Christ, his only son, our Lord, who was conceived by the Holy Spirit, born of the virgin Mary …
Apostles' creed

We believe and confess that our Lord Jesus Christ, the Son of God, is God and man; God of the substance of the father, begotten before the worlds; and man of the substance of his mother, born in the world.
Athanasian Creed

It would be improper in the light of our knowledge of genetics and embryology to say virgin births can never happen.
Professor R.J. Berry

We all with one accord teach men to acknowledge one and the same Son, our Lord Jesus Christ…begotten, for us men and for our salvation, of Mary the Virgin, the God-bearer…
Chalcedonian Definition

The entire Gospel stands or falls on the virgin birth.
David Cloud

He came from God, all the apostles believed, in a sense in which no other came; does it not follow that he came in a way in which no other came?
James Denney

While I most certainly believe that Jesus Christ was born of a virgin, I do not find anywhere in the New Testament that this particular belief is necessary for personal salvation.
Billy Graham

The Virgin Mary, being obedient to his word, received from an angel the glad tidings that she would bear God.
Irenaeus of Lyons

The virginal conception was understood from the very beginning as a statement about God and about Jesus, and only secondarily about Mary.
Graham Leonard

Also they teach that the Word, that is, the Son of God, did assume the human nature in the womb of the blessed Virgin Mary.
Philip Melanchthon

God could have become incarnate without being born of a virgin … So it is possible to believe that Jesus is the Son of God without accepting the Virgin Birth.
Keith Ward, Oxford University theologian

Virgin birth affirmed

As regards the Virginal Conception of Our Lord, [the "Virgin Birth" should, more accurately, be called "the Virgin Conception"] we acknowledge and uphold belief in it as expressing the faith of the Church of England.
Anglican House of Bishops in England

All of us accept that the belief that Our Lord was conceived in the womb of Mary by the creative power of God the Holy Spirit without the intervention of a human father can be held with full intellectual integrity.
Anglican House of Bishops in England

Virgin birth doubted

I would not put it past God to arrange a Virgin Birth if he wanted to, but I very much doubt if he did.
Bishop David Jenkins

In time, the virgin birth account will join Adam and Eve and the story of the cosmic ascension as clearly recognized mythological elements in our faith tradition whose purpose was not to describe a literal event but to capture the transcendent dimensions of God in the earthbound words and concepts of first-century human beings.
J.S. Spong

Virtue

Public virtue cannot exist in a nation without private, and public virtue is the only foundation of republics.
John Adams

The greatest virtues are those which are most useful to other persons.
Aristotle

Virtue is not left to stand alone. He who practices it will have neighbors.
Confucius

When was public virtue to be found when private was not?
William Cowper

I pronounce it as certain that there was never a truly great man that was not at the same time truly virtuous.
Benjamin Franklin

Virtue dwells not in the tongue but in the heart.
Thomas Fuller

Be not ashamed of thy virtues; honor's a good brooch to wear in a man's hat at all times.
Ben Jonson

Our virtues are most frequently but vices disguised.
Francis, Duc de La Rochefoucauld

I cannot praise a fugitive and cloistered virtue, unexercised and unbreathed, that never sallies out and sees her adversary, but slinks out of the race, where that immortal garland is to be run for, not without dust and heat.
John Milton

To be better than the worst, is not goodness.
Seneca

Vision
See also: Leadership; Revelations; Service
Where there is no vision, the people perish.
The Bible, Proverbs 29:18 kjv

Vision that looks inward becomes duty.
Vision that looks outward becomes aspiration.
Vision that looks upward becomes faith.
Author unknown

Dream the impossible dream. Dreaming it may make it possible. It often has.
Author unknown

The only limits are, as always, those of vision.
James Broughton

He who has no vision of eternity has no hold on time.
Thomas Carlyle

Out of the depths of my prison experience came the vision for Prison Fellowship's ministry, which not involves thousands of volunteers and brings the hope of Christ to prisoners throughout the US and abroad.
Charles Colson

I did think I did see all Heaven before me, and the great God Himself.
George Frederic Handel
[Handel wrote his oratorio, The Messiah in just 24 days. He worked on his masterpiece night and day and hardly slept or ate. One day his servant opened the door to find Handel at his work, with tears streaming down his face. Handel looked up and cried out the above words.]

Cherish your visions and your dreams as they are the children of your soul; the blue prints of your ultimate achievements.
Napoleon Hill

The most pathetic person in the world is someone who has sight but has no vision.
Helen Keller

Men will not live without vision; that moral we do well to carry away with us from contemplating, in so many strange forms, the record of visionaries. If we are content with the humdrum, the second-best, the hand-over-hand, it will not be forgiven us.
Monsignor Ronald Knox

An age is called Dark, not because the light fails to shine, but because people refuse to see it.
James A. Michener

If I have seen further, it is by standing on the shoulders of giants.
Isaac Newton

The real voyage of discovery consists not in seeking new landscapes but in having new eyes.
Marcel Proust

There is no gain except by loss; There is no life except by death; There is no vision but by faith.
Walter Chalmers Smith

Vision is the art of seeing things invisible.
Jonathan Swift

Vision, Beatific
To see God is the promised goal of all our actions and the promised height of all our joys.
Augustine of Hippo

Visions
I have multiplied visions, and used similitudes.
The Bible, Hosea 12:10 KJV

Your old men shall dream dreams, your young men shall see visions.
The Bible, Joel 2:28

Vidi arcana Dei.
I have seen the hidden things of God.
Catherine of Siena

Once as I rode out into the woods for my health, in 1737, having alighted from my horse in a retired place, as my manner commonly had been to walk for divine contemplation and prayer, I had a view that for me was extraordinary, of the glory of the Son of God. As near as I can judge, this continued about an hour; and kept me the greater part of the time in a flood of tears and weeping aloud. I felt an ardency of soul to be what I know not otherwise how to express, emptied and annihilated; to love Him with a pure and holy love; to serve and follow Him; to be perfectly

sanctified and made pure with a divine and heavenly purity.
Jonathan Edwards

Vocation
See also: Call; Calling; Calling of God
It's not listed in the Bible, but my spiritual gift, my specific calling from God, is to be a television talk-show host.
James Baker

When I have learned to do the Father's will, I shall have fully realized my vocation on earth.
Carlo Corretto

Many people mistake our work for our vocation. Our vocation is the love of Jesus.
Mother Teresa

The vocation of every man and woman is to serve other people.
Leo Tolstoy

The "layman" need never think of his humbler task as being inferior to that of his minister. Let every man abide in the calling wherein he is called and his work will be as sacred as the work of the ministry.
A. W. Tozer

Unless God has raised you up for this very thing [abolishing slave trade trading] you will be worn out by the opposition of men and devils. But if God be with you who can be against you.
John Wesley, letter to William Wilberforce ten days before Wesley's death

Votes for women
There are certain ladies of very great intellect, no doubt they are women by accident and they want to assume the position of men. Now I object to legislating for what, with all respect to the ladies, I may call freaks of nature.
Henry Labouchere, 1891

Women can gain nothing but they will be likely to lose a great deal. Fancy a Member (of Parliament) returning home and

finding there a politician in petticoats
ready to continue the debate!
Henry Raikes, 1879

Vows

Better is it that thou shouldest not vow,
than that thou shouldest vow and not pay.
The Bible, Ecclesiastes 5:5 KJV

Waiting for God
See also: Abiding
God aims to exalt himself by working for those who wait for him.
John Piper

Wandering
Not all who wander are lost
J.R.R. Tolkien

War
See also: Non-violence; Remembrance; Violence
In order for a war to be just, three things are necessary. First, the authority of the sovereign…. Secondly, a just cause…. Thirdly … a rightful intention.
Thomas Aquinas

We make war that we may live in peace.
Aristotle

To bomb cities as cities, deliberately to attack civilians, quite irrespective of whether or not they are actively contributing to the war effort, is a wrong deed, whether done by the Nazis or by ourselves.
George Bell

Never in the field of human conflict was so much owed by so many to so few.
Winston Churchill, speech in the House of Commons, 20 August 1940 on the RAF in the Battle of Britain

In War: Resolution.
In Defeat: Defiance.
In Victory: Magnanimity.
In Peace: Goodwill.
Winston Churchill

I know not with what weapons World War III will be fought, but World War IV will be fought with sticks and stones.
Albert Einstein

Every gun that is made, every warship launched, every rocket fired signifies in the final sense, a theft from those who hunger and are not fed, those who are cold and are not clothed. This world in arms is not spending money alone. It is spending the sweat of its laborers, the genius of its scientists, the hopes of its children. This is not a way of life at all in any true sense. Under the clouds of war, it is humanity hanging on a cross of iron.
Dwight Eisenhower, April 16, 1953

There never was a good war or a bad peace.
Benjamin Franklin

Since World War II there have been more than 140 wars.
Senator Mark Hatfield

For the Christian who believes in Jesus and his gospel, war in an iniquity and a contradiction.
Pope John XXIII

Mankind must put an end to war, or war will put an end to mankind.
John F. Kennedy

The past is prophetic in that it asserts loudly that wars are poor chisels for carving out peaceful tomorrows.
Martin Luther King Jr.

The atomic bomb is the biggest fool thing we have ever done. The bomb will never go off. I speak as an expert in explosives.
Admiral William Leahy, US chief of staff

War is evil, but it is often the lesser evil.
George Orwell

War is one of the scourges with which it has pleased God to afflict men.
Cardinal Richelieu

Warfare, Spiritual
We're in spiritual combat – cosmic combat for the heart and soul of humankind.
Chuck Colson

It must be remembered that there is spiritual wickedness at the back of all confusion and discord in the work of God. The servant of Christ must, therefore, practically recognize that his warfare is with these satanic beings and must be waged on his knees.
D. E. Hoste

When principles that run against your deepest convictions begin to win the day, then battle is your calling, and peace has become sin; you must, at the price of dearest peace, lay your convictions bare before friend and enemy, with all the fire of your faith.
Abraham Kuyper

A Christian's peace is peculiar; it flows from Christ, it is heavenly, it is holy peace. His warfare is as peculiar: it is deep-seated, agonizing, and ceases not till death.
Robert Murray M'Cheyne

A believer is to be known not only by his peace and joy, but by his warfare in distress.
Robert Murray M'Cheyne

Servant of God, well done; well hast thou fought The better fight.
John Milton

Christ tells us plainly, and without any qualifications, that we are involved in a war in which there is no room for neutrals.
Hugh Redwood

Am I a Soldier of the Cross?
 Am I a soldier of the cross,

A follower of the Lamb,
And shall I fear to own His cause,
Or blush to speak His Name?
Must I be carried to the skies
On flowery beds of ease,
While others fought to win the prize,
And sailed through bloody seas?
Are there no foes for me to face?
Must I not stem the flood?
Is this vile world a friend to grace,
To help me on to God?
Sure I must fight, if I would reign;
Increase my courage, Lord.
I'll bear the toil, endure the pain,
Supported by Thy Word.
Thy saints in all this glorious war
Shall conquer, though they die;
They see the triumph from afar,
By faith's discerning eye
When that illustrious day shall rise,
And all Thy armies shine
In robes of victory through skies,
The glory shall be Thine.
Isaac Watts

Warning
You have been once more warned today, while the door of the ark yet stands open. You have, as it were, once again heard the knocks of the hammer and axe in the building of the ark, to put you in mind that a flood is approaching. Take heed therefore that you do not still stop your ears, treat these warnings with a regardless heart, and still neglect the great work which you have to do, lest the flood of wrath suddenly come upon you, sweep you away, and there be no remedy.
Jonathan Edwards

Warnings to the Church

John Owen
"This know also, that in the last days perilous times shall come." II Timothy 3:1
The words contain a warning of imminent

dangers. And there are four things in them:
First, the manner of the warning: "This know also,"
Secondly, the evil itself that they are warned of: "Perilous times."
Thirdly, the way of their introduction: "They shall come."
Fourthly, the time and season of it: "They shall come in the last days."

First. The manner of the warning

"This know also" – "Thou Timothy, unto the other instructions which I have given thee how to behave thyself in the house of God, whereby thou mayest be set forth as a pattern unto all gospel ministers in future ages, I must also add this, 'This know also.' It belongs to thy duty and office to know and consider the impending judgments that are coming upon churches." And so, as a justification of my present design, if God enable me unto it, I shall here premise that it is the duty of the ministers of the gospel to foresee and take notice of the dangers which the churches are falling into. And the Lord help us, and all other ministers, to be awakened unto this part of our duty! You know how God sets it forth (Ezekiel 33) in the parable of the watchman, to warn men of approaching dangers. And truly God hath given us this law: If we warn the churches of their approaching dangers, we discharge our duty; if we do not, their blood will be required at our hands. The Spirit of God foresaw negligence apt to grow upon us in this matter; and therefore the Scripture only proposeth duty on the one hand and on the other requires the people's blood at the hands of the watchmen, if they perform not their duty. So speaks the prophet Isaiah, chap. 21, vs. 8, "He cried, A lion: My lord, I stand continually upon the watch-tower." A lion is an emblem of approaching judgment. "The lion hath roared; who can but tremble?" saith the prophet Amos. It is the duty of ministers of the gospel to give warning of impending dangers.

Again: the apostle, in speaking unto Timothy, speaks unto us also, to us all, "This know ye also." It is the great concern of all Christian professors and believers, of all churches, to have their hearts very much fixed upon present and approaching dangers. We have inquired so long about signs, tokens, and evidences of deliverance, and I know not what, that we have almost lost the benefit of all our trials, afflictions, and persecutions. The duty of all believers is, to be intent upon present and imminent dangers. "O Lord," say the disciples, Matt. 24, "what shall be the sign of thy coming?" They were fixed upon His coming. Our Savior answers, "I will tell you:

1. There shall be an abounding of errors and false teachers: many shall say, "Lo here is Christ," and, "Lo, there is Christ."
2. There shall be an apostasy from holiness: "iniquity shall abound, and the love of many shall wax cold."
3. There shall be great distress of nations: "Nation shall rise against nation, and kingdom against kingdom."
4. There shall be great persecutions: "And they shall persecute you, and bring you before rulers; and you shall be hated of all men for my name's sake."
5. There shall be great tokens of God's wrath from heaven: 'Signs in the heavens, the sun, moon, and stars.'"

The Lord Christ would acquaint believers how they should look for His coming; He tells them of all the dangers. Be intent upon these things. I know you are apt to overlook them; but these are the things that you are to be intent upon.

Not to be sensible of a present perilous season, is that security which the Scripture so condemns; and I will leave it with you, in short, under these three things:

1. It is that frame of heart which, of all others, God doth most detest and abhor. Nothing is more hateful to God than a secure frame in perilous days.
2. I will not fear to say this, and go with it, as to my sense, to the day of judgment: A secure person, in perilous seasons, is assuredly under the power of some predominant lust, whether it appears or not.
3. This secure, senseless frame is the certain pressage of approaching ruin. This know, brethren, pray know this, I beg of you, for

yours and my own soul, that you will be sensible of, and affected with, the perils of the season whereinto we are cast. What they are, if God help me, and give me a little strength, I shall show you by-and-by.

Secondly. The evil itself

There is the evil and danger itself thus forewarned of, and that is hard times, perilous times, times of great difficulty, like those of public plagues, when death lies at every door; times that I am sure we shall not all escape, let it fall where it will.

Thirdly. The manner of their introduction, "shall come."

We have no word in our language that will express the force of the original. The Latins express it by *immineno, incido*, – the coming down of a fowl unto his prey. Now, our translators have given it the greatest force they could. They do not say, "Perilous times will come," as though they prognosticated future events; but, "Perilous times shall come." Here is a hand of God in this business; they shall so come, be so instant in their coming, that nothing shall keep them out; they shall instantly press themselves in, and prevail. Our great wisdom, then, will be to eye the displeasure of God in perilous seasons; since there is a judicial hand of God in them, and we see in ourselves reason enough why they should come. But when shall they come?

Fourthly. The time and the season. They "shall come in the last days."

The words "latter" or "last days" are taken three ways in Scripture: sometimes for the times of the gospel, in opposition to the Judaical church-state; as in Heb. 1:2, "Hath in these last days spoken unto us by his Son"; and elsewhere it may be taken (though I remember not the place) for days towards the consummation of all things and the end of the world; and it is taken often for the latter days of churches; I Tim. 4:1, "The Spirit of vile lusts, and the practice of horrible sins." This rendered the seasons perilous. Whether this be such a season or not, do you judge. And I must

say, by the way, we may and ought to witness against it, and mourn for the public sins of the days wherein we live. It is as glorious a thing to be a martyr for bearing testimony against the public sins of an age, as in bearing testimony unto any truth of the gospel whatsoever.

Now, where these things are, a season is perilous:

1. Because of the infection. Churches and professors are apt to be infected with it. The historians tell us of a plague at Athens, in the second and third years of the Peloponnesian war, whereof multitudes died; and of those that lived, few escaped but they lost a limb, or part of a limb – some an eye, others an arm, and others a finger – the infection was so great and terrible. And truly, brethren, where this plague comes – of the visible practice of unclean lusts under an outward profession – though men do not die, yet one loses an arm, another an eye, another a leg by it: the infection diffuses itself to the best of professors, more or less. This makes it a dangerous and perilous time.

2. It is dangerous, because of the effects; for when predominant lusts have broken all bounds of divine light and rule, how long do you think that human rules will keep them in order? They break through all in such a season as the apostle describes. And if they come to break through all human restraints as they have broken through divine, they will fill all things with ruin and confusion.

3. They are perilous in the consequence: which is, the judgments of God. When men do not receive the truth in the love of it, but have pleasure in unrighteousness, God will send them strong delusion, to believe a he. So II Thess. 2:10-11 is a description how the Papacy came upon the world. Men professed the truth of religion, but did not love it they loved unrighteousness and ungodliness; and God sent them Popery. That is the interpretation of the place, according to the best divines. Will you profess the truth, and at the same time love unrighteousness? The consequence is, security under

superstition and ungodliness. This is the end of such a perilous season; and the like may be said as to temporal judgments, which I need not mention.

Our duty

Let us now consider what is our duty in such a perilous season:

1. We ought greatly to mourn for the public abominations of the world, and of the land of our nativity wherein we live. I would only observe that place in Ezekiel 9, God sends out His judgments, and destroys the city; but before, He sets a mark upon the foreheads of the men that sigh for all the abominations that are done in the midst thereof. You will find this passage referred in your books to Revelation 7:3, "Hurt not the earth, neither the sea, nor the trees, till we have sealed the servants of our God in their foreheads." I would only observe this, that such only are the servants of God, let men profess what they will, "who mourn for the abominations that are done in the land." The mourners in the one place are the servants of God in the other. And truly, brethren, we are certainly to blame in this matter. We have been almost well contented that men should be as wicked as they would themselves, and we sit still and see what would come of it. Christ hath been dishonored, the Spirit of God blasphemed, and God provoked against the land of our nativity; and yet we have not been affected with these things. I can truly say in sincerity, I bless God, I have sometimes labored with my own heart about it. But I am afraid we, all of us, come exceedingly short of our duty in this matter. "Rivers of waters," saith the Psalmist, "run down mine eyes, because men keep not thy law." Horrible profanation of the name of God, horrible abominations, which our eyes have seen, and our ears heard, and yet our hearts been unaffected with them! Do you think this is a frame of heart God requireth of us in such a season – to be regardless of all, and not to mourn for the public abominations of the land? The servants of God will

mourn. I could speak, but am not free to speak, to those prejudices which keep us from mourning for public abominations; but they may be easily suggested unto all your thoughts, and particularly what they are that have kept us from attending more unto this duty of mourning for public abominations. And give me leave to say, that, according to the Scripture rule, there is no one of us can have any evidence that we shall escape outward judgments that God will bring for these abominations, if we have not been mourners for them; but that as smart a revenge, as to outward dispensations, may fall upon us as upon those that are most guilty of them, no Scripture evidence have we to the contrary. How God may deal with us, I know not. This, then, is one part of the duty of this day – that we should humble our souls for all the abominations that are committed in the land of our nativity; and, in particular, that we have no more mourned under them.

2. Our second duty, in reference to this perilous season is, to take care that we be not infected with the evils and sins of it. A man would think it were quite contrary; but really, to the best of my observation, this is, and hath been, the frame of things, unless upon some extraordinary dispensation of God's Spirit: as some men's sins grow very high, other men's graces grow very low. Our Savior hath told us, Matthew 24:12, "Because iniquity shall abound, the love of many shall wax cold." A man would think the abounding of iniquity in the world should give great provocation to love one another. "No," saith our Savior, "the contrary will be found true: as some men's sins grow high, other men's graces will grow low."

And there are these reasons for it:

(a) In such a season, we are apt to have light thoughts of great sins. The prophet looked upon it as a dreadful thing, that upon Jehoiakin's throwing the roll of Jeremiah's prophecy into the fire, till it was consumed, yet they were not afraid, nor rent their garments, neither the king, nor any of his servants that heard all these words," Jer.36:24. They were grown senseless, both of sin and judgment. And where men (be they in other respects ever so wise) can grow sense less of sin, they will quickly grow senseless of judgment too. And I am afraid the great reason why many of us have no impression upon our spirits of danger and perils in the days wherein we live, is because we are not sensible of sin.

(b) Men are apt to countenance themselves in lesser evils, having their eyes fixed upon greater abominations of other men, that they behold every day; there are those who pay their tribute to the devil – walk in such and such abominations, and so countenance themselves in lesser evils. This is part of the public infection, that they "do not run out into the same excess of riot that others do," though they live in the omission of duty, conformity to the world, and in many foolish, hurtful, and noisome lusts. They countenance themselves with this, that others are guilty of greater abominations.

(c) Pray let such remember this, who have occasion for it (you may know it better than I, but yet I know it by rule, as much as you do by practice), that general converse in the world, in such a season, is full of danger and peril. Most professors are grown of the color and complexion of those with whom they converse.

This is the first thing that makes a season perilous. I know not whether these things may be of concern and use unto you; they seem so to me, and I cannot but acquaint you with them.

II. A second perilous season, and that we shall hardly come off in, is when men are prone to forsake the truth, and seducers abound to gather them up that are so; and you will have always these things go together. Do you see seducers abound? You may be sure there is a proneness in the minds of men to forsake the truth; and when there is such a proneness, they will never want seducers – those that will lead off the minds of men from the truth; for there is both the hand of God and Satan in this business. God judicially leaves men, when He sees them grow weary of the truth, and prone to leave it; and Satan

strikes in with the occasion, and stirs up seducers. This makes a season perilous. The apostle describes it, I Tim. 4: 1, "Now the Spirit speaketh expressly, that in the latter times" (these perilous days) "some shall depart from the faith, giving heed to seducing spirits, and doctrines of devils." And so Peter warns them to whom he writes, II Peter 2:1, 2, that "there shall come false teachers among them, who privily shall bring in damnable heresies, even denying the Lord that bought them, and bring upon themselves swift destruction; and many shall follow their pernicious ways." There shall come times full of peril, which shall draw men from the truth into destruction.

Three signs to note

If it be asked, how may we know whether there be a proneness in the minds of men in any season to depart from the truth? There are three ways whereby we may judge it:

1. The first is that mentioned, 11 Tim. 4:3, "The time will come when they will not endure sound doctrine; but after their own lusts shall they heap to themselves teachers, having itching ears." When men grow weary of sound doctrine – when it is too plain, too heavy, too dull, too common, too high, too mysterious, one thing or other that displeases them, and they would hear something new, something that may please – it is a sign that there are in such an age many who are prone to forsake sound doctrine: and many such we know.

2. When men have lost the power of truth in their conversation, and are as prone and ready to part with the profession of it in their minds. Do you see a man retaining the profession of the truth under a worldly conversation? He wants but baits from temptation, or a seducer, to take away his faith from him. An inclination to hearken after novelties, and loss of the power of truth in the conversation, is a sign of proneness unto this declension from the truth. Such a season, you see, is perilous. And why is it perilous? Because the souls of many are destroyed in it. The apostle tells

us directly, II Peter 2:1, of "false prophets among the people, who privily bring in damnable heresies, even denying the Lord that bought them, and bring upon themselves swift destructions." Will it abide there? No: "And many shall follow their pernicious ways, by reason of whom the way of truth shall be evil spoken of." Brethren, while it is well with us, through the grace of God, and our own houses are not inflames, pray do not let use think the times are not perilous, when so many turn into pernicious errors, and fall into swift destruction. Will you say the time of the public plague was not perilous, because you were alive? No. Was the fire not dreadful, because your houses were not burned? No; you will, notwithstanding, say it was a dreadful plague, and a dreadful fire. And pray consider, is not this a perilous season, when multitudes have an inclination to depart from the truth, and God, in just judgment, hath permitted Satan to stir up seducers to draw them into pernicious ways, and their poor souls perish forever?

Besides, there is a great aptness in such a season to work indifference in the minds of those who do not intend utterly to forsake the truth. Little did I think I should ever have lived in this world to find the minds of professors grown altogether indifferent as to the doctrines of God's eternal election, the sovereign efficacy of grace in the conversion of sinners, justification by the imputation of the righteousness of Christ; but many are, as to all these things, grown to an indifferency; they know not whether they are so or not. I bless God I know something of the former generation, when professors would not hear of these things without the highest detestation; and now high professors begin to be leaders in it: and it is too much among the best of us. We are not so much concerned for the truth as our forefathers; I wish 1 could say we were as holy.

3. This proneness to depart from the truth is a perilous season, because it is the greatest evidence of the withdrawing of the Spirit of God from His church: for the Spirit of God is promised to this end, "to lead us into all truth"; and when the efficacy of truth begins to decay, it is the greatest evidence of the departing and withdrawing of the Spirit of God. And I think that this is a dangerous thing; for if the Spirit of God departs, then our glory and our life depart.

What, now, is our duty in reference to this perilous season? Forewarnings of perils are given us to instruct us in our duty.

1. The first, is, not to be content with what you judge a sincere profession of truth; but to labor to be found in the exercise of all those graces which peculiarly respect the truth. There are graces that peculiarly respect the truth that we are to exercise; and if these are not found in our hearts, all our profession will issue in nothing.

And these are:

(a) Love: "Because they loved not the truth." They made profession of the gospel; but they received not the truth in the love of it. There was want of love of the truth. Truth will do no man good where there is not the love of it. "Speaking the truth in love," is the substance of our Christian profession. Pray, brethren, let us labor to love the truth; and to take off all prejudices from our minds, that we may do so.

(b) It is the great and only rule to preserve us in perilous times, to labor to have the experience of the power of every truth in our hearts. If so be ye have learned the Lord Jesus. How? So as to "put off the old man, which is corrupt according to the deceitful lusts"; and to "put on the new man, which after God is created in righteousness and true holiness," Eph. 4: 22-24. This is to learn the truth. The great grace that is to be exercised with reference to truth in such a season as this, is to exemplify it in our hearts in the power of it. Labor for the experience of the power of every truth in your own hearts and lives.

(c) Zeal for the truth. Truth is the most proper object for zeal. We ought to "contend earnestly for the truth once delivered to the saints"; to be willing, as God shall help us, to part with name and reputation, and to undergo scorn and contempt, all that this world can cast upon us, in giving testimony unto the truth. Everything that this world counts dear and valuable is to be forsaken, rather than the truth. This was the great end for which Christ came into the world.

2. Cleave unto the means that God hath appointed and ordained for your preservation in the truth. I see some are ready to go to sleep, and think themselves not concerned in these things: the Lord awaken their hearts! keep to the means of preservation in the truth – the present ministry. Bless God for the remainder of a ministry valuing the truth, knowing the truth, sound in the faith – cleave unto them. There is little influence upon the minds of men from this ordinance and institution of God, in the great business of the ministry. But know there is something more in it than that they seem to have better abilities to dispute than you: more knowledge, more light, better understandings than you. If you know no more in the ministry than this, you will never have benefit by it. They are God's ordinance; the name of God is upon them God will be sanctified in them. They are God's ordinance for the preservation of the truth.

3. Let us carefully remember the faith of them who went before us in the profession of the last age. I am apt to think there was not a more glorious profession for a thousand years upon the face of the earth, than was among the professors of the last age. And pray, what faith were they of? Were they half Armenian and half Socinian; half Papist and half I know not what? Remember how zealous they were for the truth how little their holy souls would have borne with those public defections from the doctrine of truth which we see, and do not mourn over, but make nothing of, in the days wherein we live. God was with them; and they lived to His glory, and died in peace: "whose faith follow," and example pursue. And remember the faith they lived and died in: look round about, and see whether any of the new creeds have produced a new holiness to exceed theirs.

III. A third thing that makes a perilous season is, professors mixing themselves with the world, and learning their manners. And if the other perilous seasons are come upon us, this is come upon us also. This was the foundation and spring of the first perilous season that was in the world, that first brought in a deluge of sin and then a deluge of misery. It was the beginning of the first public apostasy of the church, which issued in the severest mark of God's displeasure. Gen. 6:2, "The sons of God saw the daughters of men that they were fair; and they took them wives of all which they chose." This is but one instance of the church of God, the sons of God, professors, mixing themselves with the world. This was not all, that they took to themselves wives; but this was an instance the Holy Ghost gives that the church in those days did degenerate, and mix itself with the world. What is the end of mixing themselves in this manner with the world? Ps. 106:35, "They mingled themselves with the nations." And what then: "And learned their manners." If anything under heaven will make a season perilous, this will do it – when we mingle with the world and learn their manners.

There are two things I shall speak of on this head: 1. Wherein professors do mingle themselves with the world. 2. The danger of it.

1. Professors mingle themselves with the world in that wherein it is the world, which is proper to the world. That which is more eminently and visibly of the devil, professors do not so soon mingle themselves withal; but in that wherein it is the world, in its own colors – as in corrupt communication, which is the spirit of the world, the extract and fruit of vanity of mind – that wherewith the world is corrupted, and doth corrupt. An evil, rotten kind of communication, whereby the manners of the world are corrupted – this comes from the spirit of the world. The devil hath his hand in all these things; but it is the world and the spirit of the world that is in corrupt communication.

And how hath this spread itself among professors! Light, vain, foolish communication!-to spend a man's whole life therein; not upon this or that occasion, but almost always, and upon all occasions everywhere Vain habits and attire of the world is an other instance. The habits and attire of the world are the things wherein the world doth design to show itself what it is. Men may read what the world is by evident characters, in the habits and attire that it wears. They are blind that cannot read vanity, folly, uncleanness, luxury, in the attire the world putteth upon itself. The declension of professors in imitating the ways of the world in their habits and garb, makes a season perilous; it is a mixture wherein we learn their manners; and the judgments of God will ensue upon it. In this, likewise, we are grown like the world, that upon all occasions we are as regardless of the sins of the world, and as little troubled with them, as others are. Lot lived in Sodom, but "his righteous soul was vexed with their ungodly deeds and speeches." Live we where we will, when are our souls vexed, (so) that we do not pass through the things of the world, the greatest abominations, with the frame of spirit that the world itself doth? Not to speak of voluptuousness of living, and other things that attend this woeful mixture with the world that professors have made in the days wherein we live – corrupt communication, gaiety of attire, senselessness of the sins and abominations of the world round about us, are almost as much upon professors as upon the world. We have mixed ourselves with the people, and have learned their manners. But -

2. Such a season is dangerous, because the sins of professors in it he directly contrary to the whole design the mediation of Christ in this world. Christ gave Himself for us, that He might purge us from dead works, and purify us unto Himself a peculiar people (Titus 2:14). "Ye are a royal nation, a peculiar people." Christ hath brought the hatred of the devil and all the world upon Him and against Him, for taking a people out of the world, and making them a peculiar people to Himself; and their throwing themselves upon the world again is the greatest contempt that can be put upon Jesus Christ. He gave His life and shed His blood to recover us from the world, and we throw ourselves in again. How easy were it to show that this is an inlet to all other sins and abominations, and that for which I verily think the indignation and displeasure of God will soonest discover itself against professors and churches in this day! If we will not be differenced from the world in our ways, we shall not long be differenced from them in our privileges. If we are the same in our walkings, we shall be so in our worship, or have none at all.

As to our duty in such a perilous season, let me leave three cautions with you, and the Lord fix them upon your hearts:

1. The profession of religion, and the performance of duties, under a world-like conversation, are nothing but a sophistical means to lead men blindfold into hell. We must not speak little things in such a great cause.

2. If you will be like the world, you must take the world's lot. It will go with you as it goes with the world. Inquire and see, in the whole book of God, how it will go with the world, what God's thoughts are of the world, whether it saith not, "If it lies in wickedness, it shall come to judgment," and that "the curse of God is upon it." If, therefore, you will be like the world, you must have the world's lot; God will not separate.

3. Lastly, consider we have by this means lost the most glorious cause of truth that ever was in the world. We do not know that there hath been a more glorious cause of truth since the apostles' days, than what God hath committed to his church and people in this nation, for the purity of the doctrine of the truth and ordinances; but we have lost all the beauty and glory of it by this mixture in the world. I verily think it is high time that the congregations in this city, by their elders and messengers, should consult together how to stop this evil, that hath lost all the glory of our profession. It is

a perilous time, when professors mix themselves so with the world.

There are other perilous seasons that I thought to have insisted on, but I will but name them.

IV. When there is great attendance on outward duties, but inward, spiritual decays. Now herein, my brethren, you know how long I have been treating of the causes and reasons of inward decays, and the means to be used for our recovery; I shall not, therefore, again insist upon them.

V. Times of persecution are also times of peril.

Now, I need not tell you whether these seasons are upon us or not; it is your duty to inquire into that. Whether there be not an outward retaining of the truth under a visible prevalency of abominable lusts in the world; whether there be not a proneness to forsake the truth, and seducers at work to draw men off, whether there be not a mingling ourselves with the world, and therein learning their manners; whether there be not inward decays, under the outward performance of duties; and whether many are not suffering under persecution and trouble, judge ye, and act accordingly.

One word of use, and I have done.

Use 1. Let us all be exhorted to endeavor to get our hearts affected with the perils of the day wherein we live. You have heard a poor, weak discourse concerning it, and perhaps it will be quickly forgotten. Oh, that God would be pleased to give us this grace – that we may find it our duty to endeavor to have our hearts affected with the perils of these seasons! It is not time to be asleep upon the top of a mast in a rough sea, when there are so many devouring dangers round about us. And the better to effect this . -

(a) Consider the present things, and bring them to rule, and see what God's word says of them. We hear this and that story of horrible, prodigious wickedness; and bring it in the next opportunity of talk, and there slightly pass it over. We hear of the judgments of God abroad in the world; and bring them to the same standard of our own imaginations, and there is an end.

But, brethren, when you observe any of these things, how it is with the world, if you would have your hearts affected, bring it to the word, and see what God saith of it: speak with God about it; ask and inquire at the mouth of God what God saith unto these prodigious wickednesses and judgments – this coldness that is upon professors, and there mixtures with, and learning the manners of the world. You will never have your hearts affected with it, till you come and spear: with God about it; and then you will find them represented in a glass that will make your hearts ache and tremble. And then, -

(b) If you would be sensible of present perilous times, take heed of cantering in self. While your greatest concern is self, or the world, all the angels in heaven cannot make you sensible of the peril of the days wherein you live. Whether you pursue riches or honors, while you center there, nothing can make you sensible of the perils of the day. Therefore do not center in self.

(c) Pray that God would give us grace to be sensible of the perils of the day wherein we live. It may be we have had confidence, that though thousands fall at our right hand and at our left, yet we shall be able to carry it through. Believe me, it is great grace. Point your private, closet prayers, and your family prayers this way; and the Lord help us to point our public prayers to this thing, that God would make our hearts sensible of the perils of the time whereinto we are fallen in these last days!

Use 2. The next thing is this, that there are two things in a perilous season,-the sin of it, and the misery of it. Labor to be sensible of the former, or you will never be sensible of the latter. Though judgments lie at the door, – though the heavens be dark over us, and the earth shake under us at this day, and no wise man can see where he can build himself an abiding habitation – we can talk of these things; and hear of other nations soaking in blood; and have tokens of God's displeasure, – warnings from heaven above and the earth beneath; and no man sensible of them! Why? Because they are not sensible of sin; nor ever will be, unless God make them so.

I shall range the sins that we should be sensible of under three heads: – the sins of the poor, wretched, perishing world, in the first place; the sins of professors in general, in the second place; and our own particular sins and decays, in the third place. And let us labor to have our hearts affected with these. It is to no purpose to tell you this and that judgment is approaching; – for your leaders, and those that are upon the watch-tower, to cry, "A lion; my lord' we see a lion." Unless God make our hearts sensible of sin, we shall not be sensible of judgments.

Use 3. Remember there is a special frame of spirit required in us all in such perilous seasons as these are. And what is that? It is a mourning frame of spirit. 0 that frame, that jolly frame of spirit that is upon us! The Lord forgive it, the Lord pardon it unto us; and keep us in a humble, broken, mournful frame of spirit; for it is a peculiar grace God looks for at such a time as this is. When He will pour out His Spirit, there will be great mourning, together and apart; but now we may say there is no mourning. The Lord help us, we have hard hearts and dry eyes under the consideration of all these perils that he before us.

Use 4. Keep up church watch with diligence, and by the rule. When I say rule, I mean the life of it. I have no greater jealousy upon my heart, than that God should withdraw himself from his own institutions because of the sins of the people, and leave us only the carcase of outward rule and order. What doth God give them for? for their own sakes? No; but that they may be clothing for faith and love, meekness of spirit and bowels of compassion, watchfulness and diligence. Take away these, and farewell to all outward rule and order, whatever they are. Keep up a spirit that may live affected with it: get a spirit of church watch; which is not to lie at catch for faults, but diligently, out of pure love and compassion to the souls of men, to watch over them, – to wait to do them good, all we can. As it was with a poor man, who took a dead body and set

it up, and it fell; and he set it up again, and it fell; upon which he cried out, "There wants something within," to enliven and quicken it; – so is it with church order and rule; set them up as often as you will, they will all fall, if there be not a love to one another, a delighting in the good of one another, "exhorting one another while it is called today, lest any be hardened through the deceitfulness of sin."

Use 5. Reckon upon it, that in such times as these are, all of us will not go free. You find no mention of a perilous season in Scripture, but it follows some shall have their faith overthrown, others shall follow pernicious ways, and others shall turn aside. Brethren and sisters, how do you know but you or I may fall? Let us double our watch, every one; for the season is come upon us wherein some of us may fall, and fall so as to smart for it. I do not say we shall perish eternally; – God deliver us from going into the pit! but some of us may so fall as to lose a limb, some member or other; and our works will be committed to the fire that shall burn them all. God hath kindled a fire in Zion that will try all our works; and we shall see in a short time what will become of us.

Use 6. Lastly, take that great rule which the apostle gives in such times as those wherewith we are concerned, "Nevertheless the foundation of God stands sure," – 0 blessed be God for it! – "God knows who are his."

What, then, is required on our part? "Let him that nameth the name of Christ depart from evil." Your profession, your privileges, your light, will not secure you; you are gone, unless every one that nameth the name of Christ departs from all iniquity. What multitudes perish under a profession every day! Oh, that our hearts could bleed to see poor souls in danger of perishing under the greatest profession!

Will you hear the sum of all? Perilous times and seasons are come upon us; many are wounded already; many have failed. The Lord help us! the crown is fallen from our head,-the glory of our profession is gone, the time is short, – the Judge stands before

the door. Take but this one word of counsel, my brethren: "Watch, therefore, that none of these things may come upon you, but that you may escape, and be accounted worthy to stand before the Son of God."
Amen.
John Owen

Watchfulness, Need for
When we have God's Word pure and clear, then we think ourselves all right; we become negligent, and repose in a vain security; we no longer pay due heed, thinking it will always so remain; we do not watch and pray against the devil, who is ready to tear the divine Word out of our hearts.
Martin Luther

Weakness
But God chose the foolish things of the world to shame the wise; God chose the weak things of the world to shame the strong.
The Bible, 1 Corinthians 1:27

I have two planks for a bed, two stools, two cups and a basin. On my broken wall is a small card which says, "God hath chosen the weak things – I can do all things through Christ who strengthens me." It is true I have passed through fire.
Gladys Aylward

It will do us good to be very empty, to be very weak, to be very distrustful of self, and so to go about out Master's work.
C.H. Spurgeon

The acknowledgment of our weakness is the first step in repairing our loss.
Thomas à Kempis

We live in a world full of people struggling to be, or at least to appear strong, in order not to be weak; and we follow a gospel which says that when I am weak, then I am strong. And this gospel is the only thing that brings healing.
N.T. Wright

Wealth
See also: Affluence; Money; Poverty
Wealth maketh many friends.
The Bible, Proverbs 19:4 KJV

He that maketh haste to be rich shall not be innocent.
The Bible, Proverbs 28:20 KJV

It is easier for a camel to go through the eye of a needle, than for a rich man to enter into the kingdom of God.
The Bible, Matthew 19:24

What good is it, my brothers, if a man claims to have faith but has no deeds? Can such faith save him? Suppose a brother or sister is without clothes and daily food. If one of you says to him, "Go, I wish you well, keep warm and well fed," but does nothing about his physical needs, what good is it? In the same way, faith by itself, if it is not accompanied by action, is dead. But someone will say, "You have faith; I have deeds." Show me your faith without deeds, and I will show you my faith by what I do.
The Bible, James 2:14-18

If you want to feel rich, just count all the things you have that money can't buy.
Author unknown

To renounce wealth is the beginning and sustaining of virtues.
Ambrose of Milan

We all bow down before wealth. Wealth is that which the multitude of men pay an instinctive homage. They measure happiness by wealth; and by wealth they measure respectability. It is a homage resulting from a profound faith that with wealth he may do all things.
Augustine of Hippo

Gold can no more fill the spirit of a man, than grace his purse. A man may as well fill a bag with wisdom, as the soul with the world.
Robert Bolton

There are three things that earthly riches can never do: they can never satisfy divine justice, they can never pacify divine wrath, nor can they every quiet a guilty conscience. And until these things are done, man is undone.
Thomas Brooks

It is not the fact that a person has riches that keeps them from heaven, but the fact that riches have them.
Dr. Caird

Golden shackles are far worse than iron ones.
Mahatma Gandhi

There is nothing wrong with people possessing riches. The wrong comes when riches possess people.
Billy Graham

The disease of wealth knows no limit to its desire of more.
Gregory of Nazianzus

Those who are rich in this world cannot be made useful for the Lord unless their riches have been cut out of them.
Hermas

Few rich men own their own property. The property owns them.
Robert G. Ingersoll

God only, and not wealth, maintains the world; riches merely make people proud and lazy.
Martin Luther

A man that depends on the riches and honors of this world, forgetting God and the welfare of his soul, is like a little child that holds a fair apple in the hand, of agreeable exterior, promising goodness, but within 'tis rotten and full of worms.
Martin Luther

The mind grows wanton in prosperity, for it is hard to endure good fortune with calmness.
Ovid

I have made many millions, but they have brought me no happiness. I would barter them all for the days I sat on an office stood in Cleveland and counted myself rich on three dollars a week.
John D. Rockefeller

Lately in a wreck of a Californian ship, one of the passengers fastened by a belt about him with two hundred pounds of gold in it, with which he was found afterward at the bottom. Now, as he was sinking – had he the gold? or had the gold him?
John Ruskin

Gold is like sea water – the more one drinks of it, the thirstier one becomes.
Schopenhauer

Temporal prosperity is very unfavorable for spiritual development.
Charles Simeon

Wealth and riches, that is, an estate above what sufficeth our real occasions and necessities, is in no other sense a blessing than as it is an opportunity put into our hands, by the providence of God, of doing more good.
John Tillotson

If you have wealth, do not glory in it
Thomas à Kempis

Wherever riches have increased, the essence of religion has decreased in the same proportion.
John Wesley

The most terrifying effect of Christian corporate riches is that faith in God is substituted by business know-how and dependence on technical methodology.
John White

Prosperity and luxury gradually extinguish sympathy, and by inflating with pride, harden and debase the soul.
William Wilberforce

Wealth has corrupted the peasants of this and other lands in Germany. I have met peasant families who spend as much on the weddings of their sons and daughters, or christenings for that matter, as others on their homes, even with a plot and a vineyard.

Jakob Wimpfeling

Weeping
See: Mourning; Tears

Whitefield's funeral

John Wesley

ON THE DEATH OF THE REV. MR. GEORGE WHITEFIELD, JOHN WESLEY PREACHED AT THE CHAPEL IN TOTTENHAM-COURT ROAD AND AT THE TABERNACLE, NEAR MOORFIELDS, ON SUNDAY, NOVEMBER 18, 1770. GEORGE WHITEFIELD HAD ASKED THAT JOHN WESLEY SHOULD PREACH AT HIS FUNERAL.

"Let me die the death of the righteous, and let my last end be like his!" Num. 23:10.

"Let my last end be like his!" How many of you join in this wish? Perhaps there are few of you who do not, even in this numerous congregation! And O that this wish may rest upon your minds! – that it may not die away till your souls also are lodged "where the wicked cease from troubling, and where the weary are at rest!"

An elaborate exposition of the text will not be expected on this occasion. It would detain you too long from the sadly-pleasing thought of your beloved brother, friend, and pastor; yea, and father too: for how many are here whom he hath "begotten in the Lord!" Will it not, then, be more suitable to your inclinations, as well as to this solemnity, directly to speak of this man of God, whom you have so often heard speaking in this place? – the end of whose conversation ye know, "Jesus Christ, the same yesterday, and to-day, and for ever." And may we not,

I. Observe a few particulars of his life and death?

II. Take some view of his character? and,
III. Inquire how we may improve this awful providence, his sudden removal from us?

1. We may, in the first place, observe a few particulars of his life and death. He was born at Gloucester, in December, 1714, and put to a grammar-school there, when about twelve years old. When he was seventeen, he began to be seriously religious, and served God to the best of his knowledge. About eighteen he removed to the University, and was admitted at Pembroke College in Oxford; and about a year after he became acquainted with the Methodists (so called), whom from that time he loved as his own soul.

2. By them he was convinced that we "must be born again," or outward religion will profit us nothing. He joined with them in fasting on Wednesdays and Fridays; in visiting the sick and the prisoners; and in gathering up the very fragments of time, that no moment might be lost: and he changed the course of his studies; reading chiefly such books as entered into the heart of religion, and led directly to an experimental knowledge of Jesus Christ, and Him crucified.

3. He was soon tried as with fire. Not only his reputation was lost, and some of his dearest friends forsook him; but he was exercised with inward trials, and those of the severest kind. Many nights he lay sleepless upon his bed; many days, prostrate on the ground. But after he had groaned several months under "the spirit of bondage," God was pleased to remove the heavy load, by giving him "the Spirit of adoption;" enabling him through a living faith, to lay hold on "the Son of His Love."

4. However, it was thought needful, for the recovery of his health, which was much impaired, that he should go into the country. He accordingly went to Gloucester, where God enabled him to awaken several young persons. These soon formed themselves into a little society, and were some of the first-fruits of his labor. Shortly after, he began to read, twice or thrice a week, to some poor people in the

town; and every day to read to and pray with the prisoners in the county jail.

5. Being now about twenty-one years of age, he was solicited to enter into holy orders. Of this he was greatly afraid, being deeply sensible of his own insufficiency. But the Bishop himself sending for him, and telling him, "Though I had purposed to ordain none under three-and-twenty, yet I will ordain you whenever you come" -- and several other providential circumstances concurring -- he submitted, and was ordained on Trinity Sunday, 1736. The next Sunday he preached to a crowded auditory, in the church wherein he was baptized. The week following he returned to Oxford, and took his Bachelor's degree: and he was now fully employed; the care of the prisoners and the poor lying chiefly on him.

6. But it was not long before he was invited to London, to serve the cure of a friend going into the country. He continued there two months, lodging in the Tower, reading prayers in the chapel twice a week, catechizing and preaching once, beside visiting the soldiers in the barracks and the infirmary. He also read prayers every evening at Wapping chapel, and preached at Ludgate prison every Tuesday. While he was here, letters came from his friends in Georgia, which made him long to go and help them: but not seeing his call clear, at the appointed time he returned to his little charge at Oxford, where several youths met daily at his room, to build up each other in their most holy faith.

7. But he was quickly called from hence again, to supply the cure of Dummer, in Hampshire. Here he read prayers twice a day; early in the morning, and in the evening after the people came from work. He also daily catechized the children, and visited from house to house. He now divided the day into three parts, allotting eight hours for sleep and meals, eight for study and retirement, and eight for reading prayers, catechizing, and visiting the people. Is there a more excellent way for a servant of Christ and His Church? If not, who will "go and do likewise?"

8. Yet his mind still ran on going abroad; and being now fully convinced he was called of God thereto, he set all things in order, and, in January, 1737, went down to take leave of his friends in Gloucester. It was in this journey that God began to bless his ministry in an uncommon manner. Wherever he preached, amazing multitudes of hearers flocked together, in Gloucester, in Stonehouse, in Bath, in Bristol; so that the heat of the churches was scarce supportable: and the impressions made on the minds of many were no less extraordinary. After his return to London, while he was detained by General Oglethorpe, from week to week, and from month to month, it pleased God to bless his word still more. And he was indefatigable in his labor: generally on Sunday he preached four times, to exceeding large auditories; beside reading prayers twice or thrice, and walking to and fro often ten or twelve miles.

9. On December 28 he left London. It was on the 29th that he first preached without notes. December 30, he went on board; but it was above a month before they cleared the land. One happy effect of their very slow passage he mentions in April following: "Blessed be God, we now live very comfortably in the great cabin. We talk of little else but God and Christ; and scarce a word is heard among us when together, but what has reference to our fall in the first, and our new birth in the Second, Adam." It seems, likewise, to have been a peculiar providence, that he should spend a little time at Gibraltar; where both citizens and soldiers, high and low, young and old, acknowledged the day of their visitation.

10. From Sunday, May 7, 1738, till the latter end of August following, he "made full proof of his ministry" in Georgia, particularly at Savannah: he read prayers and expounded twice a day, and visited the sick daily. On Sunday he expounded at five in the morning; at ten read prayers and preached, and at three in the afternoon; and at seven in the evening expounded the Church Catechism. How much easier is it for our brethren in the ministry, either in

England, Scotland, or Ireland, to find fault: with such a laborer in our Lord's vineyard, than to tread in his steps!

11. It was now that he observed the deplorable condition of many children here; and that God put into his heart the first thought of founding an Orphan-house, for which he determined to raise contributions in England, if God should give him a safe return thither. In December following, he did return to London; and on Sunday, January 14, 1739, he was ordained priest at Christ Church, Oxford. The next day he came to London again; and on Sunday, the 21st, preached twice. But though the churches were large, and crowded exceedingly, yet many hundreds stood in the churchyard, and hundreds more returned home. This put him upon the first thought of preaching in the open air. But when he mentioned it to some of his friends, they judged it to be mere madness: so he did not carry it into execution till after he, had left London. It was on Wednesday, February 21, that, finding all the church doors to be shut in Bristol (beside, that no church was able to contain one half of the congregation), at three in the afternoon he went to Kingswood, and preached abroad to near two thousand people. On Friday he preached there to four or five thousand; and on Sunday to, it was supposed, ten thousand! The number continually increased all the time he stayed at Bristol; and a flame of holy love was kindled, which will not easily be put out. The same was afterwards kindled in various parts of Wales, of Gloucestershire, and Worcestershire. Indeed, wherever he went, God abundantly confirmed the word of his messenger.

12. On Sunday, April 29, he preached the first time in Moorfields, and on Kennington Common; and the thousands of hearers were as quiet as they could have been in a church. Being again detained in England from month to month, he made little excursions into several counties, and received the contributions of willing multitudes for an Orphan-house in Georgia. The embargo which was now laid on the shipping gave him leisure for more journeys through various parts of England, for which many will have reason to bless God to all eternity. At length, on August 14, he embarked: but he did not land in Pennsylvania till October 30. Afterwards he went through Pennsylvania, the Jerseys, New York, Maryland, Virginia, North and South Carolina; preaching all along to immense congregations, with full as great effect as in England. On January 10, 1740, he arrived at Savannah.

13. January 29, he added three desolate orphans to near twenty which he had in his house before. The next day he laid out the ground for the house, about ten miles from Savannah. February 11, he took in four orphans more; and set out for Frederica, in order to fetch the orphans that were in the southern parts of the colony. In his return he fixed a school, both for children and grown persons, at Darien, and took four orphans thence. March 25, he laid the first stone of the Orphan-house; to which, with great propriety, he gave the name of Bethesda; a work for which the children yet unborn shall praise the Lord. He had now about forty orphans, so that there was near a hundred mouths to be fed daily. But he was "careful for nothing," casting his care on Him who feed the young ravens that call upon Him.

14. In April he made another tour through Pennsylvania, the Jerseys, and New York. Incredible multitudes flocked to hear, among whom were abundance of Negroes. In all places the greater part of the hearers were affected to an amazing degree. Many were deeply convinced of their lost state, many truly converted to God. In some places, thousands cried out aloud; many as in the agonies of death; most were drowned in tears; some turned pale as death; others were wringing their hands; others lying on the ground; others sinking into the arms of their friends; almost all lifting up their eyes, and calling for mercy.

15. He returned to Savannah, June 5. The next evening, during the public service, the whole congregation, young and old, were

dissolved in tears: after service, several of the parishioners, and all his family, particularly the little children, returned home crying along the street, and some could not help praying aloud. The groans and cries of the children continued all night, and great part of the next day.

16. In August he set out again, and through various provinces came to Boston. While he was here, and in the neighboring places, he was extremely weak in body: yet the multitudes of hearers were so great, and the effects wrought on them so astonishing, as the oldest men then alive in the town had never seen before. The same power attended his preaching at New York, particularly on Sunday, November 2: almost as soon as he began, crying, weeping, and wailing were to be heard on every side. Many sunk down to the ground, cut to the heart; and many were filled with divine consolation. Toward the close of his journey he made this reflection: "It is the seventy-fifth day since I arrived at Rhode Island, exceeding weak in body; yet God has enabled me to preach an hundred and seventy-five times in public, besides exhorting frequently in private! Never did God vouchsafe me greater comforts: never did I perform my journeys with less fatigue, or see such a continuance of the divine presence in the congregations to whom I preached." In December he returned to Savannah, and in the March following arrived in England.

17. You may easily observe, that the preceding account is chiefly extracted from his own journals, which, for their artless and unaffected simplicity, may vie with any writings of the kind. And how exact a specimen is this of his labors both in Europe and America, for the honor of his beloved Master, during the thirty years that followed, as well as of the uninterrupted shower of blessings wherewith God was pleased to succeed his labors! Is it not much to be lamented, that anything should have prevented his continuing this account, till at least near the time when he was called by his Lord to enjoy the fruit of his labor? If he has left any papers of this kind, and his friends account me worthy of the honor, it would be my glory and joy to methodize, transcribe, and prepare them for the public view.

18. A particular account of the last scene of his life is thus given by a gentleman of Boston:

"After being about a month with us in Boston and its vicinity, and preaching every day, he went to Old York; preached on Thursday, September 27, there; proceeded to Portsmouth, and preached there on Friday. On Saturday morning he set out for Boston; but before he came to Newbury, where he had engaged to preach the next morning, he was importuned to preach by the way. The house not being large enough to contain the people, he preached in an open field. But having been infirm for several weeks, this so exhausted his strength, that when he came to Newbury he could not get out of the ferry-boat without the help of two men. In the evening, however, he recovered his spirits, and appeared with his usual cheerfulness. He went to his chamber at nine, his fixed time, which no company could divert him from, and slept better than he had done for some weeks before. He rose at four in the morning, September 30, and went into his closet; and his companion observed he was unusually long in private. He left his closet, returned to his companion, threw himself on the bed, and lay about ten minutes. Then he fell upon his knees, and prayed most fervently to God that if it was consistent with His will, he might that day finish his Master's work. He then desired his man to call Mr. Parsons, the clergyman, at whose house he was; but, in a minute, before Mr. Parsons could reach him, died, without a sigh or groan. On the news of his death, six gentlemen set out for Newbury, in order to bring his remains hither: but he could not be moved; so that his precious ashes must remain at Newbury. Hundreds would have gone from this town to attend his funeral, had they not expected he would have been interred here.... May this stroke be sanctified to the Church of God in general, and to this province in particular!"

II. We are, in the second place, to take some view of his character.

1. A little sketch of this was soon after published in the Boston Gazette; an extract of which is subjoined: – ["Little can be said of him but what every friend to vital Christianity who has sat under his ministry will attest."]

"In his public labors he has, for many years, astonished the world with his eloquence and devotion. With what divine pathos did he persuade the impenitent sinner to embrace the practice of piety and virtue! [Filled with the spirit of grace, he] spoke from the heart, and, with a fervency of zeal perhaps unequaled since the day of the Apostles, [adorned the truths he delivered with the most graceful charms of rhetoric and oratory.] From the pulpit he was unrivaled in the command of an ever-crowded auditory. Nor was he less agreeable and instructive in his private conversation; happy in a remarkable ease of address, willing to communicate, studious to edify. May the rising generation catch a spark of that flame which shone, with such distinguished luster, in the spirit and practice of this faithful servant of the most high God!"

2. A more particular, and equally just, character of him has appeared in one of the English papers. It may not be disagreeable to you to add the substance of this likewise: "The character of this truly pious person must be [deeply] impressed on the heart of every friend to vital religion. In spite of a tender [and delicate] constitution, he continued to the last day of his life, preaching with a frequency and fervor that seemed to exceed the natural strength of the most robust. Being called to the exercise of his function at an age when most young men are only beginning to qualify themselves for it, he had not time to make a very considerable progress in the learned languages. But this defect was amply supplied by a lively and fertile genius, by fervent zeal, and by a forcible and most persuasive delivery. And though in the pulpit he often found it needful by "the terrors of the Lord" to "persuade men," he had nothing gloomy in his nature; being singularly cheerful, as well as charitable and tender-hearted. He was as ready to relieve the bodily as the spiritual necessities of those that applied to him. It ought also to be observed, that he constantly enforced upon his audience every moral duty; particularly industry in their several callings, and obedience to their superiors. He endeavored, by the most extraordinary efforts of preaching, in different places, and even in the open fields, to rouse the lower class of people from the last degree of inattention and ignorance to a sense of religion. For this, and his other labors, the name of George Whitefield will long be remembered with esteem and veneration."

3. That both these accounts are just and impartial, will readily be allowed; that is, as far as they go. But they go little farther than the outside of his character. They show you the preacher, but not the man, the Christian, the saint of God. May I be permitted to add a little on this head, from a personal knowledge of near forty years? Indeed, I am thoroughly sensible how difficult it is to speak on so delicate a subject; what prudence is required to avoid both extremes, to say neither too little nor too much! Nay, I know it is impossible to speak at all, to say either less or more, without incurring from some the former, from others the latter censure. Some will seriously think that too little is said; and others, that it is too much. But without attending to this, I will speak just what I know, before Him to whom we are all to give an account.

4. Mention has already been made of his unparalleled zeal, his indefatigable activity, his tender-heartedness to the afflicted, and charitableness toward the poor. But should we not likewise mention his deep gratitude to all whom God had used as instruments of good to him? -- of whom he did not cease to speak in the most respectful manner, even to his dying day. Should we not mention, that he had a heart susceptible of the most generous and the most tender friendship? I have frequently

thought that this, of all others, was the distinguishing part of his character. How few have we known of so kind a temper, of such large and flowing affections! Was it not principally by this, that the hearts of others were so strangely drawn and knit to him? Can anything but love beget love? This shone in his very countenance, and continually breathed in all his words, whether in public or private. Was it not this, which, quick and penetrating as lightning, flew from heart to heart? which gave that life to his sermons, his conversations, his letters? Ye are witnesses!

5. But away with the vile misconstruction of men of corrupt minds, who know of no love but what is earthly and sensual! Be it remembered, at the same time, that he was endued with the most nice and unblemished modesty. His office called him to converse very frequently and largely with women as well as men; and those of every age and condition. But his whole behavior towards them was a practical comment on that advice of St. Paul to Timothy: "Entreat the elder women as mothers, the younger as sisters, with all purity."

6. Meantime, how suitable to the friendliness of his spirit was the frankness and openness of his conversation! -- although it was as far removed from rudeness on the one hand, as from guile [and disguise] on the other. Was not this frankness at once a fruit and a proof of his courage and intrepidity? Armed with these, he feared not the faces of men, but "used great plainness of speech" to persons of every rank and condition, high and low, rich and poor; endeavoring only "by manifestation of the truth to commend himself to every man's conscience in the sight of God."

7. Neither was he afraid of labor or pain, any more than of "what man [could] do unto him;" being equally patient in bearing ill and doing well.

And this appeared in the steadiness wherewith he pursued whatever he undertook for his Master's sake. Witness one instance for all, -- the Orphan-house in Georgia; which he began and perfected, in

spite of all discouragements. Indeed, in whatever concerned himself he was pliant and flexible. In this case he was "easy to be entreated;" easy to be either convinced or persuaded. But he was immovable in the things of God, or wherever his conscience was concerned. None could persuade, any more than affright, him to vary, in the least point, from that integrity which was inseparable from his whole character, and regulated all his words and actions. Herein he did: Stand as an iron pillar strong, And steadfast as a wall of brass.

8. If it be inquired what was the foundation of this integrity, or of his sincerity, courage, patience, and every other valuable and amiable quality; it is easy to give the answer. It was not the excellence of his natural temper, not the strength of his understanding; it was not the force of education; no, nor the advice of his friends: it was no other than faith in a bleeding Lord; "faith of the operation of God." It was "a lively hope of an inheritance incorruptible, undefiled, and that fadeth not away." It was "the love of God shed abroad in his heart by the Holy Ghost which was given unto him," filling his soul with tender, disinterested love to every child of man. From this source arose that torrent of eloquence which frequently bore down all before it; from this, that astonishing force of persuasion which the most hardened sinners could not resist. This it was which often made his "head as waters, and his eyes a fountain of tears." This it was which enabled him to pour out his soul in prayer, in a manner peculiar to himself, with such fullness and ease united together, with such strength and variety both of sentiment and expression.

9. I may close this head with observing what an honor it pleased God to put upon His faithful servant, by allowing him to declare His everlasting gospel in so many various countries, to such numbers of people, and with so great an effect on so many of their precious souls! Have we read or heard of any person since the Apostles, who testified the gospel of the grace of God through so widely extended a space,

through so large a part of the habitable world? Have we read or heard of any person who called so many thousands, so many myriads, of sinners to repentance? Above all, have we read or heard of any who has been a blessed instrument in His hand of bringing so many sinners from "darkness to light, and from the power of Satan unto God?" It is true, were we to talk thus to the gay world, we should be judged to speak as barbarians. But you understand the language of the country to which you are going, and whither our dear friend is gone a little before us.

III. But how shall we improve this awful providence?

This is the third thing which we have to consider. And the answer to this important question is easy (may God write it in all our hearts!). By keeping close to the grand doctrines which he delivered; and by drinking into his spirit.

1. And, first, let us keep close to the grand scriptural doctrines which he everywhere delivered. There are many doctrines of a less essential nature, with regard to which even the sincere children of God (such is the present weakness of human understanding) are and have been divided for many ages. In these we may think and let think; we may "agree to disagree." But, meantime, let us hold fast the essentials of "the faith which was once delivered to the saints;" and which this champion of God so strongly insisted on, at all times, and in all places!

2. His fundamental point was, "Give God all the glory of whatever is good in man;" and, "In the business of salvation, set Christ as high and man as low as possible." With this point, he and his friends at Oxford, the original Methodists, so called, set out. Their grand principle was, there is no power (by nature) and no merit in man. They insisted, all power to think, speak, or act aright, is in and from the Spirit of Christ; and all merit is (not in man, how high soever in grace, but merely) in the blood of Christ. So he and they taught: there is no power in man, till it is given

him from above, to do one good work, to speak one good word, or to form one good desire. For it is not enough to say, all men are sick of sin: no, we are all "dead in trespasses and sins." It follows, that all the children of men are, "by nature, children of wrath." We are all "guilty before God," liable to death temporal and eternal.

3. And we are all helpless, both with regard to the power and to the guilt of sin. "For who can bring a clean thing out of an unclean?" None less than the Almighty. Who can raise those that are dead, spiritually dead in sin? None but He who raised us from the dust of the earth. But on what consideration will He do this? "Not for works of righteousness that we have done." "The dead cannot praise Thee, O Lord;" nor do anything for the sake of which they should be raised to life. Whatever, therefore, God does, He does it merely for the sake of His well-beloved Son: "He was wounded for our transgressions, He was bruised for our iniquities." He Himself "bore" all "our sins in His own body upon the tree." He "was delivered for our offences, and was raised again for our justification." Here then is the sole meritorious cause of every blessing we do or can enjoy; in particular of our pardon and acceptance with God, of our full and free justification. But by what means do we become interested in what Christ has done and suffered? "Not by works, lest any man should boast;" but by faith alone. "We conclude," says the Apostle, "that a man is justified by faith, without the works of the law." And "to as many as" thus "receive Him, giveth He power to become the sons of God, even to those that believe in His name; who are born, not of the will of man, but of God."

4. And "except a man be" thus "born again, he cannot see the kingdom of God." But all who are thus "born of the Spirit" have "the kingdom of God within them." Christ sets up His kingdom in their hearts; "righteousness, peace, and joy in the Holy Ghost." That "mind is in them, which was in Christ Jesus," enabling them to "walk as Christ also walked." His indwelling Spirit

makes them both holy in heart, and "holy in all manner of conversation." But still, seeing all this is a free gift, through the righteousness and blood of Christ, there is eternally the same reason to remember, "He that glorieth, let him glory in the Lord."

5. You are not ignorant that these are the fundamental doctrines which he everywhere insisted on. And may they not be summed up, as it were, in two words, -- the new birth, and justification by faith? These let us insist upon with all boldness, at all times, and in all places; -- in public (those of us who are called thereto), and at all opportunities in private. Keep close to these good, old, unfashionable doctrines, how many soever contradict and blaspheme. Go on, my brethren, in the "name of the Lord, and in the power of His might." With all care and diligence, "keep that safe which is committed to your trust;" knowing that "heaven and earth shall pass away, but this truth shall not pass away."

6. But will it be sufficient to keep close to his doctrines, how pure soever they are? Is there not a point of still greater importance than this, namely, to drink into his spirit? -- herein to be a follower of him, even as he was of Christ? Without this, the purity of our doctrines would only increase our condemnation. This, therefore, is the principal thing -- to copy after his spirit. And allowing that in some points we must be content to admire what we cannot imitate; yet in many others we may, through the same free grace, be partakers of the same blessing. Conscious then of your own wants and of His bounteous love, who "giveth liberally and upbraids not," cry to Him that works all in all for a measure of the same precious faith; of the same zeal and activity; the same tender-heartedness, charitableness, bowels of mercies. Wrestle with God for some degree of the same grateful, friendly, affectionate temper; of the same openness, simplicity, and godly sincerity; "love without dissimulation." Wrestle on, till the power from on high works in you the same steady courage and patience; and above all, because it is the crown of all, the same invariable integrity!

7. Is there any other fruit of the grace of God with which he was eminently endowed, and the want of which among the children of God he frequently and passionately lamented? There is one, that is, catholic love; that sincere and tender affection which is due to all those who, we have reason to believe, are children of God by faith; in other words, all those, in every persuasion, who "fear God and work righteousness." He longed to see all who had "tasted of the good word," of a true catholic spirit; a word little understood, and still less experienced, by many who have it frequently in their mouth. Who is he that answers this character? Who is the man of a catholic spirit? One who loves as friends, as brethren in the Lord, as joint partakers of the present kingdom of heaven, and fellow heirs of His eternal kingdom, all, of whatever opinion, mode of worship, or congregation, who believe in the Lord Jesus; who love God and man; who, rejoicing to please and fearing to offend God, are careful to abstain from evil, and zealous of good works. He is a man of a truly catholic spirit, who bears all these continually upon his heart; who, having an unspeakable tenderness for their persons, and an earnest desire of their welfare, does not cease to commend them to God in prayer, as well as to plead their cause before men; who speaks comfortably to them, and labors, by all his words, to strengthen their hands in God. He assists them to the uttermost of his power, in all things, spiritual and temporal; he is ready to "spend and be spent" for them; yea, "to lay down his life for his brethren."

8. How amiable a character is this! How desirable to every child of God! But why is it then so rarely found? How is it that there are so few instances of it? Indeed, supposing we have tasted of the love of God, how can any of us rest till it is our own? Why, there is a delicate device, whereby Satan persuades thousands that they may stop short of it and yet be guiltless. It is well if many here present are

not in this "snare of the devil, taken captive at his will." "O yes," says one, "I have all this love for those I believe to be children of God; but I will never believe he is a child of God, who belongs to that vile congregation! Can he, do you think, be a child of God, who holds such detestable opinions? or he that joins in such senseless and superstitious, if not idolatrous, worship?" So we may justify ourselves in one sin by adding a second to it! We excuse the want of love in ourselves by laying the blame on others! To color our own devilish temper, we pronounce our brethren children of the devil! O beware of this! -- and if you are already taken in the snare, escape out of it as soon as possible! Go and learn that truly catholic love which "is not rash," or hasty in judging; that love which "thinks no evil;" which "believes and hopes all things;" which makes all the allowances for others that we desire others should make for us! Then we shall take knowledge of the grace of God which is in every man, whatever be his opinion or mode of worship: then will all that fear God be near and dear unto us "in the bowels of Jesus Christ."

9. Was not this the spirit of our dear friend? And why should it not be ours? O Thou God of love, how long shall Thy people be a by-word among the Heathen? How long shall they laugh us to scorn, and say, "See how these Christians love one another!" When wilt Thou roll away our reproach? Shall the sword devour for ever? How long will it be ere Thou bid Thy people return from "following each other?" Now, at least, "let all the people stand still, and pursue after their brethren no more!" But what ever others do, let all of us, my brethren, hear the voice of him that, being dead, yet speaks! Suppose ye hear him say, "Now, at least, be ye followers of me as I was of Christ! Let brother "no more lift up sword against brother, neither know ye war any more!" Rather put ye on, as the elect of God, bowels of mercies, humbleness of mild, brotherly kindness, gentleness, long-suffering, forbearing one another in love. Let the time past suffice for strife, envy,

contention; for biting and devouring one another. Blessed be God, that ye have not long ago been consumed one of another! From henceforth hold ye the unity of the Spirit in the bond of peace."

10. O God, with Thee no word is impossible! Thou does whatsoever please Thee! O that Thou would cause the mantle of Thy prophet, whom Thou hast taken up, now to fall upon us that remain! "Where is the Lord God of Elijah?" Let his spirit rest upon these Thy servants! Show Thou art the God that answers by fire! Let the fire of Thy love fall on every heart! And because we love Thee, let us love one another with a "love stronger than death!" Take away from us "all anger, and wrath, and bitterness; all clamor and evil speaking!" Let Thy Spirit so rest upon us, that from this hour we may be "kind to each other, tender-hearted, forgiving one another, even as God, for Christ's sake hath forgiven us!"

John Wesley

Wholeheartedness

Jesus gave his all for me. How can I give him less?

Author unknown

Christ is not valued at all unless he is valued above all.

Augustine of Hippo

What God asks is a will which will no longer be divided between him and any creature, a will pliant in his hands, which neither desires anything nor refuses anything, which wants without reservation everything which he wants, and which never, under any pretext, wants anything which he does not want.

F. Fenelon

Those who long to be one with love achieve great things, and shirk no effort.

Hadewijch

God will put up with a great many things in the human heart, but there is one thing

he will not put up with – a second place.
John Ruskin

Wicked, The

There is no peace, saith the LORD, unto
the wicked.
The Bible, Isaiah 48:22 KJV

Let the wicked forsake his way, and the
unrighteous man his thoughts.
The Bible, Isaiah 55:7 KJV

Wife

Whoso findeth a wife findeth a good thing.
The Bible, Proverbs 18:22 KJV

Will

Obedience is the burial of the will and the
resurrection of humility.
John Climacus

The education of the will is the object of
our existence.
Ralph Waldo Emerson

Strength does not come from physical
capacity. It comes from an indomitable will.
Mahatma Gandhi

Christian love, either towards God or
towards man, is an affair of the will.
C.S. Lewis

The will is a beast of burden. If God
mounts it, it wishes and goes as God wills;
if Satan mounts it, it wishes and goes as
Satan wills; nor can it choose its rider. The
riders contend for its possession.
Martin Luther

Will is character in action.
William McDougall

You have need of patience; and if you ask,
the Lord will give it: but there can be no
settled peace until our will is in a measure
subdued.
John Newton

Where there's a will, there's a way.
English Proverb

Great souls have wills; feeble ones have
only wishes.
Chinese Proverb

Will, Our
See: Obedience

Will-power
See also: Discipline; Free will

The line between good and evil passes not
between principalities and powers, but
oscillates within the human heart. And
even the most rational approach to ethics is
defenseless if there isn't the will to do what
is right.
Author unknown

You give God your will and He gives you
his power!
Author unknown

Will is to grace as the horse is to the rider.
Augustine of Hippo

Too many develop every talent except the
most vital one of all, the talent to use their
talents ... will-power.
Francis Bacon

An ounce of will-power is worth a pound
of learning.
Nicholas Murry Butler

Wills
See also: Death

I testify and declare that I trust to no other
security for my salvation than this alone,
that as God is the Father of mercy, so he
will show himself such a Father to me, who
acknowledge myself to be a miserable
sinner.
From John Calvin's will

Wine

Wine that maketh glad the heart of man.
The Bible, Psalm 104:15 KJV

Drink no longer water, but use a little wine
for thy stomach's sake.
The Bible, 1 Timothy 5:23 KJV

Winning

Winning is not everything. It's the only thing.
Vince Lombardi

Wisdom

See also: Knowledge; Learning; Proverbs
Wisdom shall die with you.
The Bible, Job 12:2

The price of wisdom is above rubies.
The Bible, Job 28:18

The testimony of the Lord is sure making
wise the simple.
The Bible, Psalms 19:7 KJV

So teach us to number our days, that we
may apply our hearts unto wisdom.
The Bible, Psalm 90:12 KJV

Wisdom crieth without; she uttereth her
voice in the street.
The Bible, Proverbs 1:20 KJV

Length of days is in her right hand; and in
her left hand riches and honor.
The Bible, Proverbs 3:16 KJV

Her ways are ways of pleasantness, and all
her paths are peace.
The Bible, Proverbs 3:17 KJV

Wisdom is the principal thing; therefore
get wisdom; and with all thy getting get
understanding.
The Bible, Proverbs 4:7 KJV

Wisdom is better than rubies.
The Bible, Proverbs 8:11 KJV

It is better, much better, to have wisdom
and knowledge than gold and silver.
The Bible, Proverbs 16:16 NLT

A wise man is strong; yea, a man of
knowledge increaseth strength.
The Bible, Proverbs 24:5 KJV

Be ye therefore wise as serpents, and
harmless as doves.
The Bible, Matthew 10:16 KJV

Wisdom is justified of her children.
The Bible, Matthew 11:19 KJV

For the wisdom of this world is foolishness
with God. For it is written, He taketh the
wise in their own craftiness. And again,
The lord knoweth the thoughts of the
wise, that they are vain.
The Bible, 1 Corinthians 3:19-20 KJV

Wisdom is the application of knowledge.
Obedience is the application of wisdom.
Author unknown

Without wisdom, knowledge is more
stupid than ignorance.
Author unknown

If you realize that you aren't as wise today
as you thought you were yesterday, you're
wiser today.
Author unknown

A wise man is one who has finally
discovered that there are some questions to
which nobody has the answer.
Author unknown

Wisdom is knowledge, rightly applied.
Author unknown

Wise men are not always silent, but they
know when to be.
Author unknown

The truly wise are those whose souls are in
Christ.
St Ambrose

A man may learn wisdom even from a
foe.
Aristophanes

We are ensnared by the wisdom of the
serpent; we are set free by the foolishness
of God.
Augustine of Hippo

The wisest man is generally he who thinks
himself the least so.
Nicolas Boileau-Despréaux

What the wise do in the beginning, fools do in the end.
Warren Buffett

The more accurately we search into the human mind, the stronger traces we everywhere find of the wisdom of him who made it.
Edmund Burke

See here, Psalm 119:24, a sentence worthy to be weighed of us, when David calleth the commandments of God his "counselors." For, in the first place, he meaneth that he might scorn all the wisdom of the most able and most expert men in the world, since he was conducted by the word of God, and governed thereby. In the second place, he meaneth that when he shall be so governed by the word of God, he would not only be truly wise, but that it would be as if he had all the wisdom of all the men in the world, yea, and a great deal more.
John Calvin

Where there is a feast of words there is often a famine of wisdom.
Catherine of Siena

Wisdom is often found under a shabby cloak.
Cicero

Should it be said that the Greeks discovered philosophy by human wisdom, I reply that I find the Scriptures declare all wisdom to be a divine gift.
Clement of Rome

You can't access wisdom by the megabyte. Wisdom is concerned with how we relate to people, to the world, and to God.
Edmund P. Clowney

By three methods we may learn wisdom: First, by reflection, which is noblest; Second, by imitation, which is easiest; and third by experience, which is the bitterest.
Confucius

Wisdom is humble that he knows no more.
William Cowper

He that never changes his opinions, never corrects his mistakes, will never be wiser on the morrow than he is today.
Tryon Edwards

Let us be poised, and wise, and our own, today.
Ralph Waldo Emerson

Common sense is genius dressed in working clothes.
Waldo Emerson.

He is a wise man who does not grieve for the things which he has not, but rejoices for those which he has.
Epictetus

Among mortals second thoughts are wisest.
Euripides

Where there is charity and wisdom, there is neither fear nor ignorance.
Francis of Assisi

Wisdom too often never comes, and so one ought not to reject it merely because it comes late.
Felix Frankfurter

One of the greatest pieces of economic wisdom is to know what you do not know.
John Kenneth Galbraith

It is unwise to be too sure of one's own wisdom. It is healthy to be reminded that the strongest might weaken and the wisest might err.
Mahatma Gandhi

Wisdom ceases to be wisdom when it becomes too proud to weep, too grave to laugh, and too full of self to seek other than itself.
Kahlil Gibran

Who is the wise man? He who learns from
all men.
William Gladstone

Those who have the largest hearts have the
soundest understandings; and he is the
truest philosopher who can forget himself.
William Hazlitt

Abundance of knowledge does not teach a
man to be wise.
Heraclitus

It is the province of knowledge to speak
and it is the privilege of wisdom to listen.
Oliver Wendell Holmes

Dare to be wise: begin! He who postpones
the hour of living rightly is like the rustic
who waits for the river to run out before he
crosses, yet on it glides, and will glide forever.
Horace

Little minds are interested in the
extraordinary; great minds in the
commonplace.
Elbert Hubbard

True wisdom is gazing at God. Gazing at
God is silence of the thoughts.
Isaac the Syrian

The art of being wise is the art of knowing
what to overlook.
William James

It is far easier to be wise for others than to
be so for oneself.
La Rochefoucauld

He who lives without folly isn't so wise as
he thinks.
La Rochefoucauld

The next best thing to being wise oneself is
to live in a circle of those who are.
C.S. Lewis

I don't think much of a man who is not
wiser today than he was yesterday.
Abraham Lincoln

Man is wise ... when he recognizes no
greater enemy than himself.
Marguerite of Navarre

All discoveries in art and science result
from an accumulation of errors.
Marshall McLuhan

The older I grow the more I distrust the
familiar doctrine that age brings wisdom.
H. L. Mencken

That which seems the height of absurdity
in one generation often becomes the
height of wisdom in the next.
John Stuart Mill

Wisdom's best nurse is contemplation.
John Milton

Wisdom is knowledge applied. Head
knowledge is useless on the battlefield.
Knowledge stamped on the heart makes
one wise.
Beth Moore

If we fail to anticipate the unforeseen, or
expect the unexpected in a universe of
infinite possibilities, then we may fall
victim to anyone or anything that cannot
be programmed, categorized, or easily
referenced.
Mulder, the X-Files

The only one who is wiser than anyone is
everyone.
Napoleon Bonaparte

Wisdom sends us back to our childhood.
Blaise Pascal

Pain makes man think. Thought makes
man wise. Wisdom makes life endurable.
John Patrick

A little learning is a dangerous thing.
Alexander Pope

A wise man makes his own decisions, an
ignorant man follows the public opinion.
Chinese proverb

It is better to weep with wise men than to laugh with fools.
Spanish Proverb

Even though you know a thousand things, ask the man who knows one.
Turkish Proverb

Those who wish to appear wise among fools, among the wise seem foolish.
Quintilian

A wise old owl sat on an oak,
The more he saw the less he spoke;
The less he spoke the more he heard;
Why aren't we like that wise old bird?
Edward Hersey Richards

Nine-tenths of wisdom consists in being wise in time.
Theodore Roosevelt

Knowledge is the power of the mind, wisdom is the power of the soul.
Julie Shannahan

Wisdom begins with wonder.
Socrates

One can have knowledge without having wisdom, but one cannot have wisdom without having knowledge.
R.C. Sproul

A man should never be ashamed to own he has been in the wrong, which is but saying in other words, that he is wiser today than he was yesterday.
Jonathan Swift

Wisdom is not studied in Paris, but in the sufferings of the Lord.
John Tauler

Knowledge comes, but wisdom lingers.
Alfred Tennyson

He is truly wise who looks upon all earthly things as folly that he may gain Christ.
Thomas à Kempis

Great wisdom is generous; petty wisdom is contentious. Great speech is impassioned, small speech cantankerous.
Chuang Tzu

Seek the wisdom of the ages, but look at the world through the eyes of a child.
Ron Wild

Wisdom is ofttimes nearer when we stoop than when we soar.
William Wordsworth

Wisdom and humility
The wisest word man reaches is the humblest he can speak.
Elizabeth Barrett Browning

Wise sayings
See also: Mottoes; Proverbs; Quotations
Wise sayings are like great men talking to us. It's the closest most of us can get to greatness. They are the cheapest teachers, consultants, advisers, guidelines, pilots, signposts, guardians and counselors. They make us wise in one hundredth of the time of any other sources of knowledge or wisdom. Get closely acquainted with them. They're short cuts to wisdom.
Author unknown

Wit
Wit is educated insolence.
Aristotle

Wit without discretion is a fool with a sword.
Spanish proverb

Witchcraft
Let no one be found among you who sacrifices his son or daughter in the fire, who practices divination or sorcery, interprets omens, engages in witchcraft, or casts spells, or who is a medium or spiritist or who consults the dead. Anyone who does these things is detestable to the LORD.
The Bible, Deuteronomy 18:10-12

Witness
See also: Example; Testimonies to Christ

Ye are the salt of the earth: but if the salt have lost his savor, wherewith shall it be salted?
The Bible, Matthew 5:13 KJV

Ye are the light of the world. A city that is set on an hill cannot be hid.
The Bible, Matthew 5:14 KJV

Let your light shine before men, that they may see your good deeds and praise your Father in heaven.
The Bible, Matthew 5:16

Neither cast ye your pearls before swine.
The Bible, Matthew 7:6 KJV

A Christian's life is the world's Bible.
Author unknown

Do you attract attention toward or away from God?
Author unknown

The world doesn't need a definition of religion as much as it needs a demonstration.
Author unknown

Ask yourself, If building God's church depended on me, would it ever get done?
Author unknown

It is better to live for God than to be perpetually talking about him.
Author unknown

People may doubt what you say, but they will believe what you do.
Author unknown

If you were arrested for being a Christian, would there be enough evidence to convict you?
Author unknown

Christianity is not just Christ in you, but Christ living his life through you.
Author unknown

Know him. Let him be known!
Author unknown

A good life is the best sermon.
Author unknown

The smallest light still shines in the darkest night.
Author unknown

Enthusiasm for God is contagious; has anyone caught it from you?
Author unknown

To make a difference in the world, let Jesus make a difference in you.
Author unknown

Be careful how you lead your life; you may be the only Bible someone gets to read.
Author unknown

I believe God is primarily calling me to be a witness where I am ... rather than a celebrity Christian speaking at a different church each Sunday.
Kriss Akabusi

One loving soul sets another on fire.
Augustine of Hippo

No fragrance can be more pleasing to God than that of his own Son. May all the faithful breathe out the same perfume.
Augustine of Hippo

You are ever active, yet always at rest.
You gather all things to yourself, though you suffer no need.
You grieve for wrong, but suffer no pain.
You can be angry and yet serene.
Your works are varied, but your purpose is one and the same.
You welcome those who come to you, though you never lost them.
You are never in need yet are glad to gain, never covetous yet you exact a return for your gifts.
You release us from our debts, but you lose nothing thereby.
You are my God, my Life, my holy Delight, but is this enough to say of you?
Can any man say enough when he speaks of you?

Yet woe betide those who are silent about you!
Augustine of Hippo

When the people see that you truly love them, they will hear anything from you.
Richard Baxter

Jesus Christ didn't commit the Bible to an advertising agency; he commissioned disciples. And he didn't commit them to pass out tracts; he said they would be his witnesses.
Joe Bayly

If a man cannot be a Christian in the place where he is, he cannot be a Christian anywhere.
Henry Ward Beecher

Our power in drawing others after the Lord mainly rests in our joy and communion with him ourselves.
J.G. Bellett

All great soul-winners have been men of much and mighty prayer, and all great revivals have been preceded and carried out by persevering, prevailing knee-work in the closet.
Samuel Logan Brengle

If I am afraid to speak the truth lest I lose affection, or lest the one concerned should say, "You do not understand", or because I fear to lose my reputation for kindness; if I put my own good name before the other's highest good, then I know nothing of Calvary love. If I am content to heal a hurt slightly, saying peace, peace, where there is no peace; if I forget the poignant words, "Let love be without dissimulation" and blunt the edge of truth, speaking not right things but smooth things, then I know nothing of Calvary love.
Amy Carmichael

Speak the Word and your miracle is in motion.
James Carnaghi

So many Christians interpret Christ's words to witness rather than to be a witness. And they see it as an activity instead of what it really is; the state of our being – what you do emerges from who you are.
Chuck Colson

For truth has such a face and such a mien, As to be lov'd needs only to be seen.
John Dryden

I once read in a Bible commentary that the word "Christian" means "little Christs." What an honor to share Christ's name! We can be bold to call ourselves Christians and bear the stamp of his character and reputation. When people find out the you are a Christian, they should already have an idea of who you are and what you are like simply because you bear such a precious name.
Joni Eareckson Tada

What you are shouts so loud in my ears I cannot hear what you say.
Ralph Waldo Emerson

He is the true Gospel-bearer that carries it in his hands, in his mouth, and in his heart… A man does not carry it in his heart that does not love it with all his soul; and nobody loves it as he ought, that does not conform to it in his life.
Desiderius Erasmus

Little self-denials, little honesties, little passing words of sympathy, little nameless acts of kindness, little silent victories over favorite temptations – these are the silent threads of gold which, when woven together, gleam out so brightly in the pattern of life that God approves.
Frederic William Farrar

If God can work through me, he can work through anyone.
Francis of Assisi

Preach the gospel everyday; if necessary, use words.
Francis of Assisi

He does not believe that does not live according to his belief.
Thomas Fuller

Our purpose is to be Christ in the world and display God in his fullness through our witness as individuals and communities. As we do that we join God's unrelenting quest to be known in all of his fullness, in the glory of his complete revelation.
William R.L. Haley

If a person is filled with the Holy Spirit, his witness will not be optional or mandatory – it will be inevitable.
Richard Halverson

We share our faith because of the love of God is shed abroad in our hearts and not out of self-interest.
David Havard

Don't try to give what you don't have.
Rodney Howard-Browne

If lips and life do not agree, the testimony will not amount to much.
H.A. Ironside

A religion confined to the closet, the cell, or the church, therefore, Calvin abhors. With the Psalmist, he calls upon heaven and earth, he calls upon all peoples and nations to give glory to God…Wherever man may stand, whatever he may do, to whatever he may apply his hand, in agriculture, in commerce, and in industry, or his mind, in the world of art, and science, he is, in whatsoever it may be, constantly standing before the face of his God, he has strictly to obey his God, and above all, he has to aim at the glory of his God.
Abraham Kuyper

Religion is not ours till we live by it, till it is the religion of our thoughts, words, and actions, till it goes with us into every place, sits uppermost on every occasion, and forms and governs our hopes and fears, our cares and pleasures.
William Law

If you read history, you will find that the Christians who did the most for the present world were just those who thought most of the next.
C.S. Lewis

It is the duty of every Christian to be Christ to his neighbor.
Martin Luther

We are called to be witnesses, not lawyers.
Donna Maddux

The greatest single cause of atheism in the world today are Christians – those who acknowledge Jesus with their lips and walk out the door and deny him by their live style. That is what an unbelieving world simply finds unbelievable.
Brennan Manning

Let me burn out for God.
Henry Martyn

God has called us to shine. Let no one say that he cannot shine because he has not so much influence as some others may have. What God wants you to do is to use the influence you have.
Dwight L. Moody

It is a great deal better to live a holy life than to talk about it. Lighthouses do not ring bells and fire cannons to call attention to their shining – they just shine.
Dwight L. Moody

Remember, a small light will do a great deal when it is in a very dark place. Put one little tallow candle in the middle of a large hall, and it will give a good deal of light.
D. L. Moody

You have not converted a man because you have silenced him.
John Morley

According to Gallup surveys, confirmed by other polls taken over the past fifteen years, 33 percent of all Americans over age 18 indicate they are evangelical or "born again" Christians. That translates into 59 million Christians, or one in every three adults, who experienced a turning point in their lives as they made a personal commitment to Jesus Christ.

This information should grip us with terror. It means that the greatest revival in history has so far been impotent to change society. It's revival without reformation. It's a revival which left the country floundering in spiritual ignorance. It's a change in belief without a corresponding change in behavior... .

The American Gospel has evolved into a gospel of addition without subtraction. It is the belief that we can add Christ to our lives, but not subtract sin. It is a change in belief without a change in behavior. It is a spiritual experience without any cultural impact. It is revival without reformation, without repentance... .

The proof of religious conversion is to demonstrate that we have both added a relationship with Christ and that we have subtracted sin (repentance). And we multiply proof to a weary world by what we do – our deeds, our obedience. What we do must confirm what we say. Our deeds are the proof of our repentance.
Patrick Morley

Show me that you are redeemed and then I will believe in your redeemer.
Friedrich Nietzsche

When confronted by those who, on professedly rational grounds, take exception to historic Christianity, he must set himself not merely to deplore or denounce them, but to out-think them.
J.I. Packer

A candle lights others and consumes itself.
Jewish proverb

The world is not waiting for a new definition of the gospel, but for a new demonstration of the power of the gospel.
Leonard Ravenhill

This is the age of the conference and study group – people talking about what they know they should be doing. In a subtle way, talking about something becomes an excuse for not doing it.
Gavin Reid

Worldly people sometimes complain with reason that "religious" persons, so-called, are not so amiable and unselfish and good-natured as others who make no profession of religion.
J.C. Ryle

It is always right that a man should be able to render a reason for the faith that is within him.
Sydney Smith

Never, for fear of feeble man, restrain your witness.
C.H. Spurgeon

When I saw the unwearied patience, that unflagging zeal, those enlightened sons of Africa, I became a Christian at his side, though he never spoke to me about it.
Stanley, on observing David Livingstone

We are not only to renounce evil, but to manifest the truth. We tell people the world is vain; let our lives manifest that it is so. We tell them that our home is above and that all these things are transitory. Does our dwelling look like it? O to live consistent lives!
James Hudson Taylor

Live your beliefs and you can turn the world around.
Henry David Thoreau

Gentlemen, I am nothing; you are nothing; Beethoven is everything.
Arturo Toscanini to the orchestra when rehearsing a Beethoven symphony

Witness and the Holy Spirit

If you have not the Spirit of God, Christian worker, remember that you stand in somebody else's way; you are a fruitless

tree standing where a fruitful tree might grow.
C.H. Spurgeon

Wives
See also: Husband
Giving honor unto the wife as unto the weaker vessel.
The Bible, 1 Peter 3:7 KJV

A perfect wife is one who doesn't expect a perfect husband.
Author unknown

In Jewish law a wife had no legal rights whatsoever; she was absolutely in her husband's possession to do with as he willed.
William Barclay

When Paul commands wives to obey their husbands, they are required to obey them as husbands, not as masters, nor as kings.
Charles Hodge

A gracious wife satisfieth a good husband, and silenceth a bad one.
George Swinnock

Women
See also: Suffragettes; Women's ministry; Women's rights
As regards the individual nature, woman is defective and misbegotten, for the active power of the male seed tends to the production of a perfect likeness in the masculine sex; while the production of a woman comes from defect in the active power.
Thomas Aquinas

A female is a kind of mutilated male.
Aristotle

Females are imperfect males, accidently produced by the father's inadequacy or by the malign influence of a moist south wind.
Aristotle

I know I have a body of a weak and feeble woman, but I have the heart and stomach of a king, and of a king of England too.
Queen Elizabeth I of England

Nothing could be more anti-Biblical than letting women vote.
Editorial, Harper's Magazine, November 1853

A woman is inferior to man in every way.
Josephus

To promote a Woman to beare rule, superioritie, dominion, or empire above any Realm, nation or Citie, is repugnant to Nature.
John Knox

Because I am a woman, I must make unusual efforts to succeed. If I fail, no one will say, "She doesn't have what it takes." They will say, "Women don't have what it takes."
Clare Boothe Luce

Men have broad and large chests, and small narrow hips, and more understanding than women, who have but small and narrow breasts, and broad hips, to the end they should remain at home, sit still, keep house, and bear and bring up children.
Martin Luther

Woman was God's second mistake.
Friedrich Nietzsche

Each time that a man prolongs converse with a woman he causes evil to himself, and desists from the law, and in the end inherits Gehinnom.
Rabbinic saying

Women are the real architects of society.
Harriet Beecher Stowe

I asked them why one reads in the synagogue service every week the words "I thank thee, O Lord, that I was not born a woman."
"It is not meant in an unfriendly spirit, and it is not intended to degrade or humiliate women."
"But it does, nevertheless. Suppose the service read, 'I thank thee, O Lord, that I

was not born a jackass.' Could that be twisted in any way into a compliment to the jackass?"
Elizabeth Cady Stanton

You are the devil's gateway; you are the unsealer of the [forbidden] tree; you are the first deserter of the divine law; you are she who persuaded him whom the devil was not valiant enough to attack. You destroyed so easily God's image, man. On account of your desert – that is, death – even the Son of God had to die.
Tertullian

The best compliment men can give a woman is that she thinks like a man. I say she does not; she thinks like a woman.
Margaret Thatcher

Women, we need you to give us back our faith in humanity.
Desmond Tutu

Women, Exploitation of
Trained to do all manner of mean tasks the Eskimo woman is used to enduring the weaknesses and appetites of men. But I still could not get used to what appeared to be a master-and-slave relationship between the hunter and his wife.
Raymond de Coccola, missionary in the Canadian Arctic

Women: Men have authority over women because Allah has made the one superior to the other. As for those whom you fear disobedience, admonish them and send them to beds apart and beat them.
Koran

Women and quotations
Of the 2,000 contributors in the fourteenth edition of Bartlett's *Familiar Quotations*, only 7.5% of the contributors were women, and only 0.5% of all the quotations cited were penned by women. The *Oxford Book of Quotations* bettered those percentages – barely: 8.5% women, 1% quotations by women.
Elaine Partnow

Women's liberation
Women who seek to be equal with men lack ambition.
Timothy Leary

Women's ministry
A fresh wind is blowing across this church of ours.
Barbara C. Harris, first Anglican woman bishop

If the Bible teaches the equality of women, why does the church refuse to ordain women to preach the gospel, to fill the offices of deacons and elders, and to administer the sacraments?
Elizabeth Cady Stanton, 1895

I believe that there are situations in which it is entirely appropriate for women to teach, and to teach men, provided that in so doing they are not usurping an improper authority over them.
John Stott

I still do not think it biblically appropriate for a woman to become a Rector or a Bishop.
John Stott

Women's rights
See also: *Suffragettes; Votes for women*
Learning, while at school, that the charge for the education of girls was the same as that for boys, and that, when they became teachers, women received only half as much as men for their services, the injustice of this distinction was so apparent, that I resolved to claim for my sex all that an impartial Creator had bestowed, which by custom and a perverted application of the Scriptures, had been wrestled from woman.
Lucretia Mott

What we suffragettes aspire to be when we are enfranchised is ambassadors of freedom to women in other parts of the world, who are not so free as we are.
Christabel Pankhurst

We are not ashamed of what we have done, because, when you have a great cause to

fight for, the moment of greatest humiliation is the moment when the spirit is proudest. The women we do pity, the women we think unwomanly, the women for whom we have almost contempt, if our hearts could let us have that feeling, are the women who can stand aside, who take no part in this battle – and perhaps even more, the women who know what the right path is and will not tread it, who are selling the liberty of other women in order to win the smiles and favor of the dominant sex.
Christabel Pankhurst

Better to die than to live in slavery.
Emmeline Pankhurst

Our trouble is not our womanhood, but the artificial trammels of custom under false conditions. We are, as a sex, infinitely superior to men, and if we were free and developed, healthy in body and mind, as we should be under natural conditions, our motherhood would be our glory. That function gives women such wisdom and power as no male ever can possess. When women can support themselves, have their entry to all the trades and professions, with a house of their own over their heads and a bank account, they will own their bodies and be dictators in the social realm
Elizabeth Cady Stanton

The prolonged slavery of women is the darkest page in human history.
Elizabeth Cady Stanton

But when at last woman stands on an even platform with man, his acknowledged equal everywhere, with the same freedom to express herself in the religion and government of the country, then, and not until then will he be able to legislate as wisely and generously for her as for himself.
Elizabeth Cady Stanton

By standing alone we learned our power; we repudiated man's counsels forevermore; and solemnly vowed that there should never be another season of silence until we

had the same rights everywhere on this green earth, as man.
Elizabeth Cady Stanton

Wonder
See also: *Mystery*
It was through the feeling of wonder that men now and at first began to philosophize.
Aristotle

Wonder is the basis of worship.
Thomas Carlyle

The world will never starve for want of wonders, but for want of wonder.
Gilbert K. Chesterton

He who can no longer pause to wonder and stand rapt in awe, is as good as dead; his eyes are closed.
Albert Einstein

Men love to wonder and that is the seed of our science.
Ralph Waldo Emerson

Two things fill the mind with ever-increasing wonder and awe, the more often and the more intensely the mind is drawn to them: the starry heavens above me and the moral law within me.
Immanel Kant

Whatever it be that keeps the finer faculties of the mind awake, wonder alive, and the interest above mere eating and drinking, money-making and money-saving; whatever it be that gives gladness, or sorrow, or hope, be it violin, pencil, pen ... is simply a divine gift of holy influence for the salvation of that being to whom it comes, for the lifting of him out of the mire and up on the rock.
George MacDonald

As knowledge increases, wonder deepens.
Charles Morgan

We have not the reverent feeling for the rainbow that the Indian has, because we know how it is made. We have lost as much

as we have gained by prying into the matter.
Mark Twain

A man who has lost his sense of wonder is
a mad dead.
William of St Thierry

Word of God
See also: Bible
The Word of God is not a sounding but a
piercing word, not pronounceable by the
tongue but efficacious in the mind, not
sensible to the ear but fascinating to the
affection.
Bernard of Clairvaux

The Word is the face, the countenance, the
representation of God, in whom he is
brought to light and made known.
Clement of Alexandria

Word of knowledge
We've had numerous occasions where God
has revealed sins of people, either through
a word of knowledge or a combination of
that and a word of wisdom or prophecy.
John Wimber

Words
How forcible are right words! ·
The Bible, Job 6:25 KJV

He multiplieth words without knowledge.
The Bible, Job 35:16 KJV

A word spoken in due season, how good is it!
The Bible, Proverbs 15:23 KJV

A word fitly spoken is like apples of gold in
pictures of silver.
The Bible, Proverbs 25:11 KJV

Let thy words be few.
The Bible, Ecclesiastes 5:2 KJV

Words, those precious cups of meaning ...
Augustine

Without knowing the force of words, it is
impossible to know men.
Confucius

Words must be weighed, not counted.
Polish Proverb

Handle them carefully, for words have
more power than atom bombs.
Pearl Strachan

Words which do not give the light of
Christ increase the darkness.
Mother Teresa

Words and action
Words without actions are the assassins of
idealism.
Herbert Hoover

Suit the action to the word, the word to
the action.
William Shakespeare

Work
In the sweat of thy face shalt thou eat bread.
The Bible, Genesis 3:19 KJV

Man goeth forth unto his work and to his
labor until the evening.
The Bible, Psalm 104:23 KJV

She looketh well to the ways of her
household, and eateth not the bread of
idleness.
The Bible, Proverbs 31:17 KJV

Whatsoever thy hand findeth to do, do it
with thy might.
The Bible, Ecclesiastes 9:10 KJV

The laborer is worthy of his hire.
The Bible, Luke 10:7

Whatever you do, work at it with all your
heart, as working for the Lord, not for
men.
The Bible, Colossians 3:23

Ideas won't work unless you do.
Author unknown

Hard work is the yeast that raises the
dough.
Author unknown

The only place where success comes before work is in the dictionary.
Author unknown

Genius is 1% inspiration and 99% perspiration.
Author unknown

If you want your dreams to come true, don't over sleep.
Author unknown

If it is to be, it is up to me!
Author unknown

Two things rob people of their peace of mind: work unfinished and work not yet begun.
Author unknown

I cannot work my soul to save,
For that my Lord hath done;
But I will work like any slave,
For the love of God's dear Son.
Author unknown

You draw nothing out of the bank of life except what you deposit in it.
Author unknown

God gives every bird its food, but he doesn't throw it into the nest!
Author unknown

Work becomes worship when done for the Lord.
Author unknown

The beginning is the most important part of the work.
Author unknown

Two thirds of promotion is motion.
Author unknown

Pleasure in the job puts perfection in the work.
Aristotle

I don't know anything about luck. I've never banked on it, and I'm afraid of people who do. Luck to me is something else; hard work and realizing what is opportunity and what isn't.
Lucille Ball

(a) You will show that you are not sluggish and servants to your flesh (as those that cannot deny it ease), and you will further the putting to death of all the fleshly lusts and desires that are fed by ease and idleness.
(b) You will keep out idle thoughts from your mind, that swarm in the minds of idle persons.
(c) You will not lose precious time, something that idle persons are daily guilty of.
(d) You will be in a way of obedience to God when the slothful are in constant sins of omission.
(e) You may have more time to spend in holy duties if you follow your occupation diligently. Idle persons have no time for praying and reading because they lose time by loitering at their work.
(f) You may expect God's blessing and comfortable provision for both yourself and your families.
(g) It may also encourage the health of your body which will increase its competence for the service of your soul.
Richard Baxter

Having once decided to achieve a certain task, achieve it at all costs of tedium and distaste. The gain in self-confidence of having accomplished a tiresome labor is immense.
Thomas Arnold Bennett

The first sign of a nervous breakdown is when you start thinking your work is terribly important.
Milo Bloom

Nobody made a greater mistake than he who did nothing because he could only do a little.
Edmund Burke

For anything worth having one must pay the price; and the price is always work, patience, love, self-sacrifice.
John Burroughs

Let us not cease to do the utmost, that we may incessantly go forward in the way of the Lord; and let us not despair of the smallness of our accomplishments.
John Calvin

The average person puts only 25% of his energy and ability into his work. The world takes off its hat to those who put in more than 50% of their capacity, and stands on its head for those few and far between souls who devote 100%.
Andrew Carnegie

In work, do what you enjoy.
Tao Te Ching

Honor lies in honest toil.
Grover Cleveland

Work to become, not to acquire.
Confucius

A man is a worker. If he is not that he is nothing.
Joseph Conrad

All growth depends upon activity. There is no development physically or intellectually without effort, and effort means work. Work is not a curse; it is the prerogative of intelligence, the only means to adulthood, and the measure of civilization.
Calvin Coolidge

I never notice what has been done. I only see what remains to be done.
Madam Curie

Plans are only good intentions unless they immediately degenerate into hard work.
Peter F. Drucker

If we all did the things we are capable of doing, we would literally astound ourselves.
Thomas Edison

Work is the meat of life, pleasure the dessert.
Bertie Charles Forbes

Nothing is particularly hard if you divide it into small jobs.
Henry Ford

You can't build a reputation on what you are going to do.
Henry Ford

God helps them that help themselves.
Benjamin Franklin

The world is filled with willing people; some willing to work, the rest willing to let them.
Robert Frost

The difference between what we do and what we are capable of doing would suffice to solve most of the world's problems.
Mahatma Gandhi

Work is love made visible.
Kahlil Gibran

Whatever you can do or dream you can, begin it. Boldness has genius, power, and magic in it.
Johann Wolfgang von Goethe

When work is a pleasure, life is a joy. When work is a duty, life is slavery.
Maxim Gorky

Labor disgraces no man, but occasionally men disgrace labor.
Ulysses S. Grant

All good work is done the way ants do things, Little by little.
Lafcadio Hearn

Help thyself, and God will help thee.
George Herbert

A servant with this clause
Makes drudgery divine;
Who sweeps a room as for Thy laws
Makes that and th' action fine.
George Herbert

Work is the greatest thing in the world, so we should always save some of it for tomorrow.
Don Herold

Our greatest weariness comes from work not done.
Eric Hoffer

I find that the harder I work, the more luck I seem to have.
Thomas Jefferson

I like work; it fascinates me. I can sit and look at it for hours.
Jerome K. Jerome

Genius begins great works; labor alone finishes them.
Joseph Joubert

The trivial round, the common task
Will furnish all we ought to ask;
Room to deny ourselves – a road
To bring us daily nearer God.
John Keble

I long to accomplish a great and noble task; but it is my chief duty to accomplish small tasks as if they were great and noble.
Helen Keller

All labor that uplifts humanity has dignity and importance and should be undertaken with painstaking excellence.
Martin Luther King, Jr.

Thank God – every morning when you get up – that you have something to do which must be done, whether you like it or not. Being forced to work, and forced to do your best, will breed in you a hundred virtues which the idle never know.
Charles Kingsley

There can be intemperance in work just as in drink.
C.S. Lewis

Never undertake anything for which you would not have the courage to ask the blessing of heaven.
Georg Christoph Lichtenberg

The harder you work, the harder it is to surrender.
Vince Lombardi

Do you think the work God gives us to do is never easy? Jesus says His yoke is easy, His burden is light. People sometimes refuse to do God's work just because it is easy. This is sometimes because they cannot believe that easy work is His work
George McDonald

God's greatest gifts to man come through travail. Whether we look into the spiritual or temporal sphere, can we discover anything, any great reform, any beneficial discovery, any soul-awakening revival, which did not come through the tolls and tears, the vigils and blood-shedding of men and woman whose sufferings were the pangs of its birth?
F.B. Meyer

We can't all, and some of us don't. That's all there is to it.
Eeyore (A.A. Milne)

Work will win when wishy washy wishing won't.
Thomas S. Monson

God hath work to do in this world; and to desert it because of its difficulties and entanglements, is to cast off His authority. It is not enough that we be just, that we be righteous, and walk with God in holiness; but we must also serve our generation, as David did before he fell asleep. God hath a work to do; and not to help Him is to oppose Him.
John Owen

Work expands to fill the time available.
Parkinson's law

If a man is called a street-sweeper, he should sweep streets even as Michelangelo painted, or Beethoven composed music, or Shakespeare wrote poetry. He should sweep streets so well that all the hosts of heaven

and earth will pause to say, Here lived a great street-sweeper who did his job well.
George Smith Patton

God is a busy worker, but he loves help.
Basque proverb

Everyone must row with the oars he has.
English Proverb

Who begins too much accomplished little.
German Proverb

No gain is certain as that which proceeds from the economical use of what you already have.
Latin Proverb

An ant on the move does more than a dozing ox.
Mexican proverb

If you want your dreams to come true, don't sleep.
Yiddish proverb

They say hard work never killed anyone, but I figure: why take the chance?
Ronald Reagan

Far and away the best prize that life offers is the chance to work hard at work worth doing.
Theodore Roosevelt

If you do not wish God's kingdom, don't pray for it. But if you do, you must do more than pray for it; you must work for it.
John Ruskin

It is a rough road that leads to the heights of greatness.
Seneca

Don't let Satan make you overwork and then put you out of action for a long time.
Charles Simeon

Thank God, I was born poor. I learned how to work.
Del Smith, the millionaire founder and

chairman of Evergreen International Aviation.

Diamonds are only chunks of coal that stuck to their jobs, you see.
Minnie Richard Smith

We have worked, we have even worked hard; but the question comes to us – "What have we worked for? Who has been our master? With what object have we toiled?"
C.H. Spurgeon

If we want a love message to be heard, it has to be sent out. To keep a lamp burning, we have to keep putting oil in it.
Mother Teresa

A scholar who cherishes the love of comfort is not fit to be deemed a scholar.
Lao Tzu

If you can't excel with talent, triumph with effort.
Dave Weinbaum

Always do more than is required of you.
John Wooden

The artist is nothing without the gift, but the gift is nothing without work.
Emile Zola

Work, Dignity of
One can spin, another can make shoes, and these are the gifts of the Holy Ghost; and I tell you that, if I were not a priest, I should esteem it a great gift to be able to make shoes, and would try to make them so well as to become a pattern to all.
John Tauler

Work and dreams
Ideas must work through the brains and the arms of good and brave men, or they are no better than dreams.
Ralph Waldo Emerson

Work and prayer
Work with all your might, but never trust

in your work. Pray with all your might for the blessing in God, but work at the same time with all diligence, with all patience, with all perseverance. Pray, then, and work. Work and pray. And still again pray, and then work.
George Müller

Pray to God, but hammer away.
Spanish Proverb

World
See also: Society
For the Christian, this world is an arena, not an armchair.
Author unknown

The early Christians did not say in dismay, Look what the world has come to; but rather in delight, Look Who has come into the world!
Author unknown

Christ in the heart, and the world under the feet!
Alleine

Remember him who gives death and life. Hate the world and all that is in it. Hate all peace that comes from the flesh. Renounce this life, so that you may be alive to God.
Abba Anthony the Great

If the things of the world delight you, praise God for them but turn your love away from them and give it to their Maker, so that in the things that please you may not displease Him.
Augustine of Hippo

All of the exterior, visible world, with all its creatures are a corollary of the spiritual world.
Jacob Boehme

We must look on all things of this world as none of ours, and not desire them. This world and that to come are enemies. We cannot therefore be friends of both, but must resolve which to forsake and which to enjoy.
Clement of Rome

In this world nothing is sure but death and taxes.
Benjamin Franklin

The "world" means the organization and the mind and the outlook of mankind as it ignores God.
M. Lloyd-Jones

The only fence against the world is a thorough knowledge of it.
John Locke

The world has become a global village.
Marshall McLuhan

Christianity believes that God has created an external world that is really there; and because He is a reasonable God, one can expect to be able to find the order of the universe by reason.
Francis A. Schaeffer

Hold everything earthly with a loose hand.
C.H. Spurgeon

The world passes away with all its concupiscence and deceitful pleasure.
Thomas a Kempis

The world rings changes, it is never constant but in its disappointments. The world is but a great inn, where we are to stay a night or two, and be gone; what madness is it so to set our heart upon our inn, as to forget our home.
Thomas Watson

We can only change the world by changing men.
Charles Wells

My brothers and sisters, the evangelical tradition is free salvation, scriptural holiness and social righteousness.
John Wesley
In the last letter he wrote, encouraging Wilberforce to continue the fight against slavery

Worldliness
See also: Covetousness

His wife looked back from behind him, and she became a pillar of salt.
The Bible, Genesis 19:26 KJV

Remember Lot's wife.
The Bible, Luke 17:32 KJV

Don't be squeezed into the mold of this world.
The Bible, Romans 12:2, JBP

The fashion of this world passeth away.
The Bible, 1 Corinthians 7:31 KJV

A child of the King shouldn't live like a slave of the world.
Author unknown

The ship's place is in the sea, but God pity the ship when the sea gets into it. The Christian's place is in the world, but God pity the Christian if the world gets the best of him.
Author unknown

If you keep in step with God, you'll be out of step with the world.
Author unknown

There is no surer evidence of an unconverted state than to have the things of the world uppermost in our aim, love and estimation.
Alleine

Whoever has Christ in his heart, so that no earthly or temporal things – not even those that are legitimate and allowed – are preferred to Him, has Christ as a foundation. But if these things be preferred, then even though a man seem to have faith in Christ, yet Christ is not the foundation to that man.
Augustine of Hippo

We can love the world, or love God. If we love the world, there will be no room in our heart for the love of God. We cannot love both God, who is eternal, and the world, which is transitory.
Augustine of Hippo

We must try to keep the mind in tranquility. For just as the eye which constantly shifts its gaze, now turning to the right or to the left, now incessantly peering up or down, cannot see distinctly what lies before it, but the sight must be fixed firmly on the object in view if one would make his vision of it clear; so too man's mind when distracted by his countless worldly cares cannot focus itself distinctly on the truth.
Basil the Great

Go to the grave, and see there the end of fleshly pleasure, and what is all that it will do for you at the last. One would think it should cure the mad desire of plenty and pleasure, to see where all our wealth, and mirth, and sport, and pleasure must be buried at last.
Richard Baxter

Watch against the master sins of unbelief: hypocrisy, selfishness, pride, flesh pleasing and the excessive love of earthly things. Take care against being drawn into earthly mindedness and excessive cares, or covetous designs for rising in the world, under the pretense of diligence in your calling.
Richard Baxter

Love not the world, for it is a moth in a Christian's life.
John Bunyan

Whosoever, then, makes himself thus a slave to earthly lusts, cannot be of God.
John Calvin

When secular interests, wealth, houses, lands and possessions are endangered, then many fall away from Christ.
John Calvin

The Devil binds men with the pleasures and conditions of the world, he catches them with the hook of pleasure.
Catherine of Siena

Our work here is brief but its reward is eternal. Do not be disturbed by the clamor of

the world, which passes away like a shadow.
Clare of Assisi

Unless there is within us that which is above us, we shall soon yield to that which is about us.
Peter Taylor Forsyth

Take heed of this squint eye to our profit, pleasure, honor, or anything beneath Christ and heaven; for they will take away your heart ... that is, our love, and if our love be taken away, there will be little courage left for Christ.
William Gurnall

Nothing is more contrary to a heavenly hope than an earthly heart.
William Gurnall

Whatever we have of this world in our hands, our care must be to keep it out of our hearts, lest it come between us and Christ.
Matthew Henry

Whoever marries the spirit of this age will find himself a widower in the next.
W.R. Inge

The soul that carries within itself the least appetite for worldly things bears more unseemliness and impurity in its journey to God than if it were troubled by all the hideous and annoying temptations and darknesses.
John of the Cross

I was never attached to power or valuables. I have not attachment to worldly things.
Imelda Marcos
On being accused, with her late husband, of misappropriating $2 billion from the state treasury.

Whilst the world is enthroned in men's hearts, honors and favors have more attraction than to suffer with the people of God.
John Owen

Build your nest on no tree here for, you see, God has sold the forest to death.
Samuel Rutherford

The ways, and fashions, and amusements, and recreations of the world have a continually decreasing place in the heart of a growing Christian. He does not condemn them as downright sinful, nor say that those who have anything to do with them are going to hell. He only feels that they have a constantly diminishing hold on his own affections and gradually seem smaller and more trifling in his eyes.
J.C. Ryle

You can in no manner be satisfied with temporal goods, for you were not created to find your rest in them.
Thomas à Kempis

Often recall the proverb: "The eye is not satisfied with seeing nor the ear filled with hearing." Try, moreover, to turn your heart from the love of things visible and bring yourself to things invisible. For they who follow their own evil passions stain their consciences and lose the grace of God.
Thomas à Kempis

Worldliness is an accepted part of our way of life. Our religious mood is social instead of spiritual. We have lost the art of worship. We are not producing saints. Our models are successful businessmen, celebrated athletes and theatrical personalities. We carry on our religious activities after the methods of the modern advertiser.
A.W. Tozer

Christianity commands us not to set our hearts on earthly treasures.
William Wilberforce

Love to God will expel love to the world; love to the world will deaden the soul's love to God.
Octavius Winslow

Worry
See also: Anxiety; Dying; Grace; Providence

… do not worry about your life, what you will eat or drink; or about your body, what you will wear.
The Bible, Matthew 6:25

Who of you by worrying can add a single hour to his life?
The Bible, Matthew 6:27

Consider the lilies of the field, how they grow; they toil not, neither do they spin.
The Bible, Matthew 6:28

Take therefore no thought for the morrow; for the morrow shall take thought for the things of itself. Sufficient unto the day is the evil thereof.
The Bible, Matthew 6:34 KJV

Do not let your hearts be troubled.
The Bible, John 14:1 KJV

If you believe that feeling bad or worrying long enough will change a past or future event, then you are residing on another planet with a different reality system.
Author unknown

Never try to carry tomorrow's burdens with today's grace.
Author unknown

Worry does not empty tomorrow of its sorrow; it empties today of its strength.
Author unknown

Worry is carrying a burden God never intended us to bear.
Author unknown

Today is the tomorrow we worried about yesterday.
Author unknown

You can't change the past, but you can ruin the present by worrying about the future.
Author unknown

Worry is a thin stream of fear trickling through the mind. If encouraged, it cuts a channel into which all other thoughts are drained.
Author unknown

If you worry about your problems you pay double what they are worth.
Author unknown

Worry is like a rocking chair, it'll give you something to do, but it won't get you anywhere.
Author unknown

I am free from worry … I am to "cast all my cares upon Him" 1 Peter 5:7.
Author unknown

Blessed is the man who is too busy to worry in the daytime and too sleepy to worry at night.
Author unknown

Fear and worry are interest paid in advance on something you may never own.
Author unknown

Worry kills more people than work.
Author unknown

Tomorrow has two handles: the handle of fear and the handle of faith. You can take hold of it by either handle.
Author unknown.

The freedom now desired by many is not freedom to do and dare but freedom from care and worry.
James Truslow Adams

In all trouble you should seek God. You should not set him over against your troubles, but within them. God can only relieve your troubles if you in your anxiety cling to him. Trouble should not really be thought of as this thing or that in particular, for our whole life on earth involves trouble; and through the troubles of our earthly pilgrimage we find God.
Augustine of Hippo

Never let the future disturb you. You will meet it, if you have to, with the same weapons of reason which today arm you against the present.
Marcus Aurelius

Much that worries us beforehand can afterwards, quite unexpectedly, have a happy and simple solution. Worries just don't matter. Things really are in a better hand than ours.
Dietrich Bonhoeffer

If only the people who worry about their liabilities would think about the riches they do possess, they would stop worrying.
Dale Carnegie

There was a man from Sung who pulled at his rice plants because he was worried about their failure to grow.
Confucius

Happy the man, and happy he alone,
He who can call to-day his own;
He who, secure within, can say,
To-morrow, do thy worst, for I have liv'd to-day.
John Dryden

As a cure for worrying, work is better than whiskey.
Ralph Waldo Emerson

I believe God is managing affairs and that He doesn't need any advice from me. With God in charge, I believe everything will work out for the best in the end. So what is there to worry about.
Henry Ford

Stop thinking about your difficulties, whatever they are, and start thinking about God instead.
Emmet Fox

Anxiety is the greatest evil that can befall us except sin; for just as revolt and sedition in a country cause havoc and sap its resistance to a foreign invasion, so we, when troubled and worried, are unable to preserve the virtues we have already acquired, or resist the temptations of the devil, who then diligently fishes, as they say, in troubled waters.
Francis de Sales

The reason why worry kills more people than work is that more people worry than work.
Robert Frost

He that fears not the future may enjoy the present.
Thomas Fuller

There is nothing that wastes the body like worry, and one who has any faith in God should be ashamed to worry about anything whatsoever.
Mahatma Gandhi

Don't worry about anything. Worrying never solved anything. All it does is distort your mind.
Milton Garland
Spoken at 103, when she was the oldest worker in the U.S.

I walked slowly out on the beach. A few yards below high-water mark I stopped and read the words again: WRITE YOUR WORRIES ON THE SAND.
I let the paper blow away, reached down and picked up a fragment of shell. Kneeling there under the vault of the sky, I wrote several words, one above the other. Then I walked away, and I did not look back. I had written my troubles on the sand. The tide was coming in.
Arthur Gordon

I worry until midnight and from then on I let God worry.
Louis Guanella

I have lost everything, and I am so poor now that I really cannot afford to let anything worry me.
Joseph Jefferson

Feed not your spirit on anything but God. Cast off concern about things, and bear peace and recollection in your heart.
John of the Cross

A man ninety years old was asked to what he attributed his longevity. "I reckon," he said, with a twinkle in his eye, "It's because most nights I went to bed and slept when I should have sat up and worried."
Dorothea Kent

The next moment is as much beyond our grasp, and as much in God's care, as that a hundred years away. Care for the next minute is just as foolish as care for a day in the next thousand years. In neither can we do anything, in both God is doing everything.
C.S. Lewis

Good morning, theologians! You wake and sing. But I, old fool, know less than you and worry over everything, instead of simply trusting in the heavenly Father's care.
Martin Luther, talking to the birds as he walked through the woods

He sat upon the spray of the tree, and he sang:
"Mortal, cease from toil and sorrow;
God provideth for the morrow."
Martin Luther
What Luther said the little bird said to him.

It has been well said that no man ever sank under the burden of the day. It is when tomorrow's burden is added to the burden of today that the weight is more than a man can bear. Never load yourselves so, my friends. If you find yourselves so loaded, at least remember this: it is your own doing, not God's. He begs you to leave the future to Him and mind the present.
George MacDonald

Worriers spend a lot of time shoveling smoke.
Claude McDonald

Happy is the man who has broken the chains which hurt the mind, and has given up worrying once and for all.
Ovid

Don't take tomorrow to bed with you.
Norman Vincent Peale

He who foresees calamities, suffers them twice over.
Beilby Porteus

Worry gives a small thing a big shadow.
Swedish Proverb

It ain't no use putting up your umbrella till it rains.
Alice Caldwell Rice

All worry is atheism, because it is want of trust of God.
Bishop Fulton Sheen

There is no need for two to care, for God to care and the creature too.
C.H. Spurgeon

"Each day has troubles enough of its own." So why anticipate them? If we do, we double them. For if our fear does not materialize, we have worried once for nothing; if it does materialize, we have worried twice instead of once. In both cases; it is foolish: worry doubles trouble.
John R. W. Stott

Oh, how great peace and quietness would he possess who should cut off all vain anxiety and place all his confidence in God.
Thomas A. Kempis

I am an old man and have known a great many troubles, but most of them have never happened.
Mark Twain

Worship
See also: Adoration; Praise
I have heard of thee by the hearing of the ear; but now mine eye seeth thee.
The Bible, Job 42:5 KJV

Let all things be done decently and in order.
The Bible, 1 Corinthians 14:40 KJV

Worship reminds us of values the world makes us forget.
Author unknown

They that worship God merely from fear,
Would worship the devil too, if he appear.
Author unknown

Worship that pleases God comes from an obedient heart.
Author unknown

The more a man bows his knee before God, the straighter he stands before men.
Author unknown

Of what significance is it to us that, on this particular occasion, at this particular time, there are but half a dozen of us, or thirty of us, or a hundred of us, gathered together for the breaking of bread and for prayers, when these acts themselves unite us with millions who have repeated them daily throughout the centuries and now gather unseen at our side?
Harry Blamires

Let us remember therefore this lesson: That to worship our God sincerely we must evermore begin by hearkening to His voice, and by giving ear to what He commands us. For if every man goes after his own way, we shall wander. We may well run, but we shall never be a whit nearer to the right way, but rather farther away from it.
John Calvin

So let us hold to this rule, that all human inventions which are set up to corrupt the simple purity of the word of God, and to undo the worship which he demands and approves, are true sacrileges, in which the Christian man cannot participate without blaspheming God, and trampling his honor underfoot.
John Calvin

Worship is transcendent wonder.
Thomas Carlyle

We may be truly said to worship God, though we lack perfection; but we cannot be said to worship Him if we lack sincerity.
Stephen Charnock

All worship is shot wrong that is not directed to, and conducted by, the thoughts of the power of God, whose assistance we need.
Stephen Charnock

Here might I stay and sing,
No story so divine;
Never was love, dear King,
Never was grief like thine!
This is my Friend,
In whose sweet praise
I all my days
Would gladly spend.
Samuel Crossman

Glory befits God because of His majesty, while lowliness befits man because it unites us with God. If we realize this, rejoicing in the glory of the Lord, we too, like St. John the Baptist, will begin to say unceasingly, "He must increase, but we must decrease." (cf John 3:30).
Diadochos of Photiki

And what greater calamity can fall upon a nation than the loss of worship.
Ralph Waldo Emerson

I don't know whether I've ever met an evangelical who does not lament the desperate, barren, parched nature of evangelical worship.
Thomas Howard

The glory of God is a living man; and the life of man consists in beholding God.
Irenaeus

Now, if you will prove that your ceremonies proceed from faith, and do please God, you must prove that God in

expressed words has commanded them; or else you shall never prove that they proceed from faith, nor yet that they please God; but they are sin, and do displease him, according to the words of the apostle, "Whatsoever is not of faith is sin."
John Knox

We should dedicate ourselves to becoming in this life the most perfect worshipers of God we can possibly be, as we hope to be through all eternity.
Brother Lawrence

Nothing should be done or sung or said in church which does not aim directly or indirectly either at glorifying God or edifying the people or both.
C. S. Lewis

The perfect church service would be one we were almost unaware of; our attention would have been on God.
C.S. Lewis

A man can no more diminish God's glory by refusing to worship him than a lunatic can put out the sun by scribbling "darkness" on the walls of his cell.
C.S. Lewis

To believe God is to worship God.
Martin Luther

Worship services in many churches today are like a merry-go-round. You drop a token in the collection box; it's good for a ride. There's music and lots of motion up and down. The ride is carefully timed and seldom varies in length. Lots of good feelings are generated, and it is the one ride you can be sure will never be the least bit threatening or challenging. But though you spend the whole time feeling as if you're moving forward, you get off exactly where you got on.
John MacArthur,

The great thing, and the only thing, is to adore and praise God.
Thomas Merton

Worship is the mind's humble acquiescence to the fact of God.
Peter C. Moore

Unless men see a beauty and delight in the worship of God, they will not do it willingly.
John Owen

This is the manner of their worship [Quaker]. They are to wait upon the Lord, to meet in the silence of flesh, and to watch for the stirrings of his life, and the breakings forth of his power among them.
Isaac Penington

Charismatic worship needs to have room for the Spirit as humble intercessor, as well as for the Spirit of triumphant power.
Tom Smail

God is not moved or impressed with our worship until our hearts are moved and impressed by Him.
Kelly Sparks

Whenever we fail to take public worship seriously, we are less than the fully biblical Christians we claim to be. We go to church for the preaching, some of us say, not for the praise. Evangelism is our speciality, not worship. In consequence either our worship services are slovenly, perfunctory, mechanical and dull or, in an attempt to remedy this, we go to the opposite extreme and become repetitive, unreflective and even flippant.
John Stott

Worship is the highest and noblest activity of which man, by the grace of God, is capable.
John Stott

Nothing else so soils the work of God and makes unclean what is clean as the deification of creation and the worshiping of it as equal to God the Creator and Maker.
Symeon the New Theologian

To worship is to quicken the conscience by the holiness of God, to feed the mind with the truth, to purge the imagination by the

beauty of God, to open the heart to the love of God, to devote the will to the purpose of God.
William Temple

Worship is the submission of all our nature to God. It is the most selfless emotion of which our nature is capable and therefore the chief remedy of that self-centeredness which is our original sin and the source of all actual sin.
William Temple

We are saved to worship God. All that Christ has done for us in the past and all that He is doing now leads to this one end.
A. W. Tozer

We have lost the art of worship.
A. W. Tozer

Till you can sing and rejoice and delight in God as misers do in gold, and kings in scepters, you can never enjoy the world.
Thomas Traherne

A holy reverence checks our speech,
And praise sits silent on our tongues.
Isaac Watts

The reading of the Scriptures with godly fear; the sound preaching, and conscionable hearing of the word, in obedience unto God, with understanding, faith, and reverence; singing of psalms with grace in the heart; as also the due administration and worthy receiving of the sacraments instituted by Christ; are all parts of the ordinary worship of God.
Westminster Confession of Faith

The acceptable way of worshiping the true God is instituted by himself, and so limited by his own revealed will, that he may not be worshiped according to the imaginations and devices of men, or the suggestions of Satan, under any visible representation, or any other way not prescribed in the holy Scripture.
Westminster Confession of Faith

Worship and witness
The Glory of God, and, as our only means to glorifying Him, the salvation of human souls, is the real business of life.
C.S. Lewis

Many a professing Christian is a stumbling-block because his worship is divided. On Sunday he worships God; on week days God has little or no place in his thoughts.
D.L. Moody

Worth
Worth begets in base minds, envy; in great souls, emulation.
Henry Fielding

The tiniest hair casts a shadow.
Goethe

Wounds of Christ
The wounds of Christ were the greatest outlets of his glory that ever were. The divine glory shone more out of his wounds that out of all his life before.
Robert Murray M'Cheyne

Wrath of God
See: God's wrath

Writing
Reading maketh a full man, conference a ready man, and writing an exact man.
Francis Bacon

Only the hand that erases can write the true thing.
Meister Eckhart

The most original authors are not so because they advance what is new, but because they put what they have to say as if it had never been said before.
Johann Wolfgang von Goethe

The two most engaging powers of an author are to make new things familiar and familiar things new.
William Makepeace Thackeray

Writing, Christian
The author would wish his work to be
brought to this test – does it uniformly
tend:
To humble the sinner?
To exalt the savior?
To promote holiness?
If in any one instance it loses sight of any
of these points, let it be condemned
without mercy.
Charles Simeon

Y, Z

Youth

Rejoice, O young man, in thy youth.
The Bible, Ecclesiastes 11:9 KJV

Remember now thy Creator in the days of thy youth.
The Bible, Ecclesiastes 12:1 KJV

The arrogance of age must submit to be taught by youth.
Edmund Burke

There is a feeling of eternity in youth.
William Hazlitt

There is a fountain of youth: it is your mind, your talents, the creativity you bring your life and the lives of the people you love. When you learn to tap this source, you will truly have defeated age.
Sophia Loren

The young people of today think of nothing but themselves. They have not reverence for parents or old age. They are impatient of all restraint. They talk as if they know everything, and what passes for wisdom with us is foolishness to them.
Peter the monk, 1274

Zeal

A zeal of God, but not according to knowledge.
Romans 10:2 KJV

There are few catastrophes so great and irremediable as those that follow an excess of zeal.
Edward White Benson

A certain nervous disorder afflicting the young and inexperienced.
Ambrose Bierce

Where zeal for integrity and holiness is not vigor, there neither is the Spirit of Christ nor Christ Himself; and wherever Christ is not, there is no righteousness, nay, there is no faith; for faith cannot apprehend Christ for righteousness without the Spirit of sanctification.
John Calvin

Zeal without knowledge is fire without light.
Thomas Fuller

Zeal is fit only for wise men, but is found mostly in fools.
Thomas Fuller

O if once our hearts were but filled with zeal for God, and compassion to our people's souls, we would up and be doing, though we could but lay a brick a day, and God would be with us.
William Gurnall

Blind zeal is soon put to a shameful retreat, while holy resolution, built on fast principles, lifts up its head like a rock in the midst of the waves.
William Gurnall

The danger of mistaking our merely natural, though perhaps legitimate, enthusiasms for holy zeal, is always great.
C.S. Lewis

By the time the average Christian gets his temperature up to normal, everybody thinks he has a fever!
Watchman Nee

That words be observed, wandering and idle thoughts be avoided, sudden anger and desire of revenge, even of such as

persecute the truth, be guarded against; for
we often mix our zeal with our wild-fire.
Samuel Rutherford

A zealous man feels that like a lamp he is
made to burn; and if consumed in
burning, he has but done the work for
which God appointed him. Such a one will
always find a sphere for his zeal. If he
cannot preach and work and give money,
he will cry and sigh and pray.
J.C. Ryle

Dear Crito, your zeal is invaluable, if a
right one; but if wrong, the greater the zeal
the greater the danger.
Socrates

Sometimes we are filled with passion and
we think it is zeal.
Thomas à Kempis

If thou shalt remain faithful and zealous in
labor, doubt not that God shall be faithful
and bountiful in rewarding thee. It is thy
duty to have a good hope that thou wilt
attain the victory: but thou must not fall
into security lest thou become slothful or
lifted up.
Thomas à Kempis

Zionism
Eventually it [the establishment of the new
state of Israel] will lead to the inauguration
of the true union of the nations, through
which will be fulfilled the eternal message
to mankind of our immortal prophets.
Dr. Herzog, Chief Rabbi of Palestine, 1948

Index of Sources